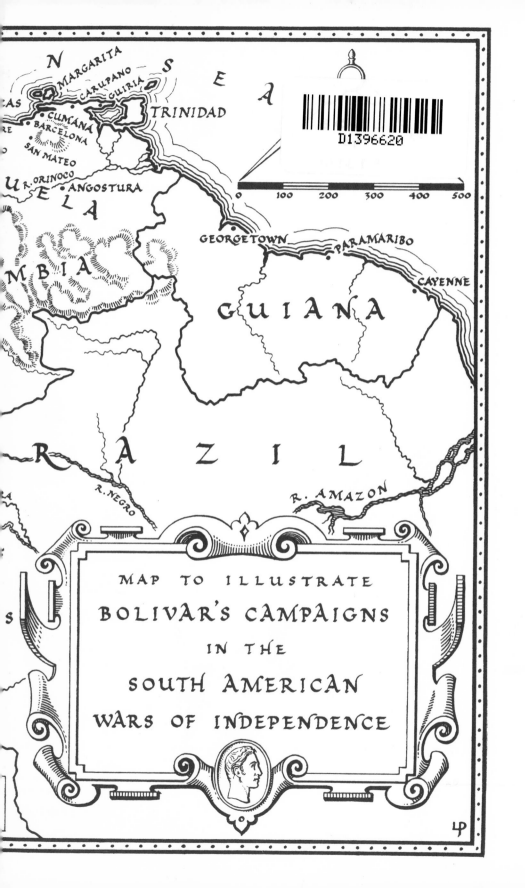

MAP TO ILLUSTRATE
BOLIVAR'S CAMPAIGNS
IN THE
SOUTH AMERICAN
WARS OF INDEPENDENCE

BOLÍVAR

SIMÓN BOLÍVAR

BOLÍVAR

BY

SALVADOR DE MADARIAGA
Hon. Fellow of Exeter College, Oxford

UNIVERSITY OF MIAMI PRESS
Coral Gables, Florida

Spaniards, men cannot take possession of a land without that land taking possession of them.

S. DE M., *The Three Caravels.*

My element is war.
SIMÓN BOLÍVAR.

TABLE OF CONTENTS

FOREWORD

BOOK I

FAILURE AND HOPE

PART I

PART II

PART III

BOOK II

VICTORY AND FRUSTRATION

PART I

FROM CHAOS TO VICTORY

PART II

THE SUN OF EMPIRE SETS

LIST OF ILLUSTRATIONS

FOREWORD

WITH this Life of Bolívar, a New World trilogy undertaken about ten years ago will be completed. A Life of Colón (Columbus) appeared in 1940; one of Cortés in 1941. The much longer gap between the publication of the second and that of the third Life is in part due to the pressure of other calls, particularly in the international field; but mostly to the fact that the difficulties which a life of Bolívar present to the student far exceed those which had to be met in dealing with Colón or with Cortés.

The first of these difficulties comes from the glut of material. Much of it lay more or less unexplored in the public and private archives; visits were necessary to Buenos Aires, Santiago, Lima, Quito, Bogotá, Popayán, Bucaramanga, Cartagena, Santa Marta, Caracas, Puerto Cabello, Habana and Mexico, as well as to the archives of the Quai d'Orsay and to the Public Record Office. Well seconded though he may be—and none more fortunate than I in this respect—the student of history soon finds that the first and most important part of research—that is the *search*—cannot be delegated. The crucial fact, the revealing word, has a way of turning up at the least expected moment and in odd ways of its own, impossible to foresee. A number of such " finds ", recorded in these pages, contribute to the new approach here made to the subject.

* * * * *

This approach was indeed inevitable for a number of other reasons. Bolívar has, so far, stood in history in a perspective conditioned by an erroneous view of the Spanish Empire and by a doctrinaire and somewhat naïve political philosophy fast becoming obsolete. As I attempted a few years ago to begin his Life with a general picture of its historical background, I soon realized that the frame of reference for such a background was inadequate and that, as a preliminary to the Life of Bolívar, I should have to write a critical history of the Spanish Empire.*

Many of the crude ideas entertained on this subject were due to mere ignorance, often indeed, to that " learned ignorance ", which is its most virulent form. Many were deliberately fostered by Spain's adversaries in those days; and in particular, by Spanish American separatists and by British businessmen and adventurers who were their natural allies. These Britons who then turn up in " the Spanish Main " were fiercely anti-Spanish

---

* *The Rise,* and *The Fall, of the Spanish American Empire,* published in 1947. I am glad to be able to record that much progress has been made in recent years in this respect.

but not particularly intelligent.* An Englishman who served in Bolívar's navy and published anonymously a book of Memoirs,† is gullible enough to write in his first chapter: " In one of the letters from Morillo to King Ferdinand, which was intercepted by Captain Chitty of the Colombian Navy, that unrelenting chieftain thus describes the measures which he adopted on entering the city of Santa-Fe-de-Bogotá: ' Every person, of either sex, who was capable of reading and writing, was put to death. By thus cutting off all who were in any way educated, I hoped to effectually arrest the spirit of revolution.' That such an extraordinary official document should be authentic might be fairly doubted, if the savage deeds, therein described, had not in reality been perpetrated." These grotesque accusations against the Spanish Commander-in-Chief were being spread all over Europe and America, and widely believed.‡ The campaign was so relentless and forceful in its effects that—as often happens in our day—it held its own even against personal experience to the contrary. Another British soldier of fortune who had gone to fight in Venezuela against Spain and there had become " Captain " Chesterton, was caught by the Spaniards. His head being filled with atrocity-stories, he was terrified. By then, Ferdinand had decreed the death penalty for all Englishmen caught waging war against Spain. Chesterton was, nevertheless, so kindly received by the Spanish Commander in Cumaná that he writes: " I began to surmise that the Spaniards were not the fiends their enemies had represented them to be." He was actually sent to Morillo under the escort of a Spanish soldier " a man of gentle and humane disposition ". In Caracas, General Correa assured him that his life was not in danger. Suffering from ague, he travelled on; and in Maracay, the Spanish Commandant and his family, moved to pity, housed him for a week. " I heard nothing but gentle accents; words of kindness and encouragement . . . and for a whole week, experienced the tenderest nursing. All this, be it remembered, was from the hands of an enemy reputed cruel and relentless." On a litter prepared by his " humane host ", Chesterton travelled on and at last arrived at Morillo's headquarters in El Pao. " As I approached the locality that harboured that dreaded man,

* Colonel Hamilton, for instance, sent by Canning as first commissioner to Bogotá, can write: " The ridiculous Spanish custom prevails still in Columbia, of offering a visitor any thing he may admire in the house; as the Columbians have assumed a new character, they should leave off these unmeaning compliments, and offer that only which they wish should be accepted. Mr. Cade and myself were much amused one morning at receiving a printed card from the Under Secretary for Foreign Affairs, with the following notice: ' La Señora de—tiene el honor de ofrecer a la disposición de vm. una niña que ha dado a luz. Señora de—has the honour of offering for your disposal, a little girl which she has brought into the world.' Having half-a-dozen children of my own in England, I declined the polite offer of receiving the new-born babe." (Vol. I, pp. 263-4.) Imagine a Colombian visitor in England believing that every London lady who signed herself " yours truly " meant " country matters ".

† Recollections of a Service of Three Years during the War-of-Extermination in the Republics of Venezuela and Columbia, London, 1828.

‡ Hamilton (Vol. II, p. 33): " Education was a serious crime in the estimation of Morillo, who was endeavouring to extirpate in Venezuela and New Granada, all men whose minds had been cultivated, knowing that ignorance and superstition were the firmest supporters of Spanish tyranny."

whose reputed deeds of rapine and bloodshed had filled civilized Europe with dismay, I experienced an acceleration of the solicitude that had so long consumed my peace." Would he be shot? " Shall I ever rise again? I was in the hands of despotic and revengeful enemies." Chesterton entered the room of the dreaded chief in a state of agitation. " While the Patriots denounced him as a sanguinary fiend, the Royalists, and the natives subject to his rule, panegyrized his forbearance and humanity. . . . He rose at my entrance, bowed politely, and handed me a chair. I breathed more freely and began to augur favourably. I saw before me a man, tall, and of large proportions, with dark hair and eyes, a full face, and features betokening some benevolence. He wore his morning costume, consisting of white pantaloons, jacket and waistcoat, decked with silver braiding, and his Hessian boots were edged at the top with silver, and had silver tassels. He always dressed studiously. His first address to me was one of apology, that I should have been compelled to travel so far in ill health. He proceeded to inform me that many of his friends had written to him on my behalf, and had begged, as a personal satisfaction to themselves, that I should be treated with consideration. He told me he had carefully perused my papers and evidence, that he had formed a favourable opinion of me, and ' desired the pleasure of some conversation with me '. With the utmost complacency he proceeded, ' You have suffered much in this wild country; stay, however, at my headquarters and rest yourself. I shall be happy to see you with the officers of my staff at my table; but in order to relieve your mind from all further anxiety, I announce to you that you are from this moment free, and after a time you may return to the coast by whatever route you prefer '."

Chesterton was Morillo's guest, moved as freely as he wished and was finally granted a passport to return home, with " the allowances of a Spanish Captain ". And yet, he was so steeped in the propaganda of his day that, as his later writings show, not even his repeated personal experiences enabled him to shake off the prejudice thus absorbed.

Much of this propaganda came, of course, from the headquarters of the patriots. Bolívar himself, as this Life will show, was an adept at forging papers. He was also so dyed-in-the-wool a propagandist that hardly any assertion of his can be taken at its face value and all have to be closely scrutinized in the context of his intention at the time. This applies in particular to " atrocities " of which he never hesitated to accuse any Spanish commander he thought fit; cases will be given in the Life; one, however, will be quoted here, in which Bolívar's indifference to the facts worked the other way, so to speak, *in reverse*. Few more cruel commanders will be found in the Spanish armies of those days than Colonel Don Basilio García. And yet, when, after a capitulation, García left for Spain, Bolívar wrote to Morillo recommending his ex-adversary not only for his valour and skill, but for his respect for the laws of war and for his humanity!*

*   *   *   *   *

The history of Bolívar is therefore bound to bristle with difficulties for the straightforward historian. Everything has to be studied through a haze of

* C.L., Vol. XI, p. 204.

a-historical notions. In what concerns Bolívar in particular, the documents are not always available, or are apt to fail at the most interesting point.* A moving, yet naïve, watch seems to be kept on the reputation of the hero, so that, more often than not, the narrative of events has to be redressed even at the cost of slowing up its flow.† A regular net of defensive works surrounds the fortress which defends the glory of the *Libertador*. The unfortunate historian who approaches harmless and defenceless is confronted with a labyrinth of deviating passages behind which, should he cross it successfully, he will have to meet a stout battalion of valiant pens.

At every stage in the life of Bolívar, from his birth (was he a pure white ?) to his death (did he die a Christian death ?) there will be debates and more debates around the facts; and the glory of the *Libertador* will be defended with a heroism worthy of Bolívar himself, not always with a due regard for the value of the ammunition handled or, indeed, of the position defended.

A case in point is the handing over of Miranda to the Spanish authorities after the Capitulation of La Victoria in 1812. If Bolívar has remained enshrined in the history of Venezuela as " the *Libertador* ", Miranda, his countryman, is also revered as " the Precursor ". It happens, however, that Bolívar was among those who delivered Miranda to Spain. An awkward moment in the story of the hero. " I shall beg of you "—a Venezuelan reader wrote to me while I was in Caracas in 1946—" to deal with the arrest of Miranda by Bolívar, Soublette and Lino de Clemente looking at the problem straight in the face and not sideways and as if walking on hot coals, as all others have done." To this unknown friend I answer as The First Player to Hamlet: " I hope we have reformed that indifferently with us."

*   *   *   *   *

All this knot of circumstances lends a peculiar sensibility to the historiography of Bolívar. One of the forms this sensibility is apt to take is a tendency to reject sources on grounds of prejudice. Contemporary authors who left books of Memoirs are brushed aside wholesale on the ground that they were disgruntled or had an axe to grind or were " slanderers ". The Frenchman Ducoudray-Holstein, the Englishman Hippisley, are two cases in point. Both authors contain invaluable data which no historian in his senses would throw away. True, Ducoudray left the service disgruntled, but far from rushing into print and indulging in propaganda, he retired to Haiti and earned his living by giving piano lessons.‡ And it is true that Hippisley, when Bolívar became powerful, wrote him an undignified letter of apologies in the hope of getting back some of the money he claimed to have lost; but this does not make his revelations less revealing.

*   *   *   *   *

* The *Diario de Bucaramanga* is a case in point. Kept secret until a relatively recent date, it was found mutilated precisely when Bolívar begins to speak on the war to the death.

† Since the Spanish edition of the present work will be available for the specialized student, I have limited myself in English to stating the facts; leaving the polemical pages for the Spanish edition to which I refer the specialist desirous to dispute my conclusions.

‡ It so happens that the only criticism Ducoudray called forth on grounds of inaccuracy accused him of a bias *in favour* of Bolívar. See Ch. XXVI.

The requirements of an historical perspective determined either by the Jacobin spirit of the French Revolution or by the three-hundred-years-old duel between Britain and Spain, dictated a number of features which Bolívar, San Martín, Iturbide and the rest had to possess. It so happened, however, that they didn't. A tension developed between what these men were and what they had to be. For generations, what they had to be prevailed over what they were.

There may be deeper reasons for this than the mere influence of ephemeral causes. " Collective memory is non-historical "—writes Mircea Eliade.* " This is due to the fact that the popular memory holds with difficulty ' individual ' events and ' authentic ' figures. It works by means of other structures: *categories*, instead of *events; archetypes*, instead of *historical* personages. The historical personage is assimilated to his mythical model (hero, etc.) while the event is integrated into the category of mythical actions (fight against a monster, enemy brothers, etc.)." And this author aptly quotes from Chadwick: " Myth is the last—not the first—stage in the development of a hero."†

Heroes, archetypes of a popularly simplified transfiguration of what actually was the secession of Spanish America, San Martín and Bolívar cut before the world a-historical figures protected from the historian by a kind of taboo. Both have entered during the nineteenth century into their mythical phase through a " resurrection " which frees them from the clay of facts or documents and from the impiety of research.

That this popular process was, and is, assisted by historians matters little, since historians may also side with collective memory against History itself. Not for lack of competence, for Spanish-American historians are excellent, nor for lack of intellectual honesty, for they state the facts; but for a superabundance of that collective spirit which in new nations gives forth the epic mood. Indeed, even in old nations, as shown by the epic of Napoleon, mythically and a-historically built by French historians.

Nor is Napoleon brought into the argument at random. It so happens that neither Bolívar nor San Martín can be understood until they are both recognized as replicas of the Napoleonic archetype. This idea runs like a connecting thread through many episodes of the present Life of Bolívar; but here and now one episode may well be singled out which in both lives outshines the others: the crossing of the Andes. In both cases, there were topical reasons sufficient to explain the operation. But deep down, the original impulse was the passing of the Alps by the secret archetype of both.

The depth and secrecy of this root which unites San Martín and Bolívar to Napoleon corresponds to the depth and secrecy of the root of their respective myths in Spanish America. Both San Martín and Bolívar are known on the Continent as *The Liberator*. On the surface, both their myths are built on the hero-monster idea; both are St. Georges slaying the dragon of Spanish tyranny. But all that is the surface. Deep down, San Martín

* *Le Mythe de l'Eternel Retour*, Paris, 1945–7, pp. 76, 74, 75.

† N. K. and H. M. Chadwick, *The Growth of Literature*, Cambridge, 1932–40.

and Bolívar rise above the other men in the memory and more so in the
imagination of Spanish America because they are the two Napoleons of the
New World; the two heroes who lead the banners of their respective countries
across the continent, just as Napoleon had done in Europe liberating nations
and dethroning kings.

*   *   *   *   *

Three strains may be discerned in these Spanish-American myths and
archetypes. The first is the come-back of the Continent, which, after three
centuries, *conquers its conquerors*. " Men cannot take possession of a land
without that land taking possession of them." Grafted into the land
through the natives, the Conquering Whites are conquered by the sap of the
New World rising to the White tops through the half-caste stem. This
process has been subconscious through three centuries. On becoming
conscious at the end of the eighteenth century, it could only express itself as
a protest against Spain. Thus the Spanish Crown, until then the protector
of the native against the rich Creole, became " the tyrant "; the Creole, till
then proud to call himself " a Spaniard " (i.e. a White), became " an
American "; and the European Spaniard, till then closely allied to the
Creole by ties of interests and family, became " the intruder ".

The second element was the " philosophic " and the " philanthropic " (or,
in the language of our day, the " radical " and " democratic ") trend of the
French eighteenth century, brought over to America by the Spaniards themselves, and more often than not, by the civil servants, army officers, Viceroys and even at least one archbishop. It was republican, equalitarian, and,
though, after 1812, it liked to call itself "liberal", was in fact Roussellian and
absolutist, if with an absolutism transferred from the King to " the people ".
This element dovetailed into the first in that it aimed at ousting the Spanish
Crown from the New World; but conflicted with it in that this eighteenth
century equalitarianism tended also to oust from power the rich Creoles
whose hope had been, on the contrary, to become more powerful on getting
rid of the control from Madrid.

Finally, there was Napoleon. This was one of those brilliant improvisa-
tions wherewith History instils an ever-renewed interest to its otherwise dull
pages. Napoleon was both the negation and the crowning achievement of
the French Revolution. He was in fact the archetype and the hero of
republicanism. No one dethroned more kings than he did. His coins bore
the inscription: REPUBLIQUE FRANÇAISE, NAPOLEON EMPEREUR. He was the
Emperor, i.e. the Chief, of a Republic. True he crowned himself, but with
a crown that sprang from the enthusiasm of his people, and broke the tradition
of Divine Right.

Thus, the relation between the Napoleon-myth and the Liberty-myth is
by no means what a superficial and relatively modern view would lead us to
believe. In his day Napoleon was not always seen as the tyrant against
whose misdeeds all freedom-loving peoples had to struggle*; he was, on the

---

* Too much, by the way, was made of this assumption in the popular view recently adopted
by many politicians in Great Britain, whereby England had fought the same fight against
Philip II—Louis XIV—Napoleon—the Kaiser and Hitler.

contrary, the heir of the French Revolution, the monarch risen from the ranks, the incarnation of the absolute sovereignty of " the people ", the dethroner of Kings and the " enthroner " of " the people ", the St. George slaying the monster of the old régime.

There was, therefore, ample room for harmony among the three elements—incongruous though they were—that composed the myths and archetypes of the Spanish-American emancipation. Out of a soil claiming the population as its own, rose two Creole Napoleons incarnating the revolutionary, anti-king, popular-absolutist drive of the new régime. The two Napoleons lent the driving force of their personal ambition to the movements for New-World emancipation and for New-Era régimes. This ambition did arouse against them the opposition of the liberal, intellectual classes; and, as they were men of their time, as well as archetypes, both Bolívar and San Martín felt the break with which this opposition hindered their imperial careers; but their popularity remained almost unimpaired. This circumstance gives rise to a maladjustment between the two historical and the two mythical figures, which, as will be shown anon, renders singularly delicate and complex the study of the two great heroes of Spanish America.

There is yet another reason for this. The two South American Napoleons remained true to type even to the end, for each had his St. Helena. Buenos Aires had no use for San Martín; Venezuela had no use for Bolívar. Death spared the northern Napoleon a long exile such as San Martín endured for years—more painful than those imposed by tyranny, for it was imposed by indifference. This neglect of the two Spanish-American Napoleons by their respective fatherlands determined their posthumous glory. Buenos Aires and Caracas had to atone for their crimes against their respective heroes by a century of hero-worship.

This explains the heat generated by the dispute over the monarchy. Was Bolívar a monarchist? Did he aim at a Crown? No issue raises a more irate levy of pens. But why should Bolívar's glory be diminished because he was a monarchist and dreamt of a crown? What is wrong with monarchies anyhow? And where do they go astray that they may not find themselves in the company of republics? The reason for all this heat is the friction between the second and the third element in the contribution of the Spanish-American archetypes. The Republican, " philosophic " and " philan-thropic" tradition, partly incarnated in, partly antagonized by, the Napoleonic element, and for this reason both attracted and repelled by the Napoleonic types, creates this ardent desire to guard the hero against any contamination from the Monster he is to slay. This conflict inhibited San Martín and Bolívar in their ascent towards the throne of Lima; it was not strong enough to arrest Iturbide in his ascent to the throne of Mexico.* The energy still deployed in guarding Bolívar, and even San Martín, against any " accusation " of monarchism or of monarchical ambition is but the reaction of the repub-lican sensibility of the days past, against the neomonarchist tendencies

---

* This is one of the reasons why Iturbide did not " resurrect " as a hero and archetype. The other reason was that he did not ride beyond the frontiers of his fatherland, freeing nations and defeating viceroys, as did San Martín and Bolívar.

inherent in the Napoleonic type. It works in complete independence of historical objectivity.

* * * * *

One final word. The upshot of this life and of that of San Martín turns out to be a paradox: the greatest single influence in the emancipation of Spanish America was Napoleon: for it was his example that put the steel of ambition into Bolívar and San Martín; and it was his attack on Spain that, by destroying the Spanish Crown, broke the legal and traditional links between the kingdoms overseas and the European Kingdoms; and by invading Spain prevented her from strengthening with her arms the majority which until 1819 was still in favour of the hispanic union.

This paradox, however, resolves itself into a lesson: The emancipation of Spanish America was one of the most significant achievements of Napoleon; perhaps the most significant. But it never entered into his plans.

Our thoughts are ours, their ends none of our own.

NOTE ON SPANISH NAMES

BOLÍVAR is stressed on the middle syllable, and actually sounds almost like the English word *believer*; identical as to stress, it only differs from the English word in that, of course, the first e of believer must be closed to sound like the o in *Bob* and the last e, opened, to sound like the a in *bar*.

Other names may appear under double spelling, due to a South American tendency to alter the original Spanish, thus *Valdez* for *Valdés*, *Arismendi* for *Arizmendi*. The South American variety will be printed in quotations where it occurs.

BOOK I
FAILURE AND HOPE

PART I
THE MAN AND HIS EARTH

CHAPTER I

THE EARTH

I

SIMÓN BOLÍVAR was born in Caracas on July 24th, 1783, the scion of one of the most illustrious families of the country. This country, Venezuela or Little Venice, sometimes known as Caracas, after its chief city, ruled then by a Captain General, was one of the kingdoms beyond the seas which, together with the European kingdoms under the Crown of Spain, made up the Spanish Empire.

The Captain-Generalship of Caracas comprised the province of Venezuela in the centre, the government of Maracaibo to the west, Guayana to the south, the government of Cumaná to the east and the Island of Margarita to the north-west. The sea bounded it to the north and to the east; Dutch and Portuguese Guiana to the south, and the Kingdom of New Granada to the west. When Bolívar was born, the Island of Trinidad, still Spanish, was governed by an autonomous governor.

The country was then simultaneously living three stages of civilization. The coast, on which lay most of the cities, was a seafaring, commercial and agricultural community; the *llanos* or plains were in the pastoral age; the inner lands of forest and river were still in their pre-Conquest state, though being gradually absorbed by a process of christianization and civilization, led by the Missions. Statistics of population can hardly be expected about this latter zone. The two first regions might be the home of anything between 720,000 and a million men. Of these, 12,000 were European Spaniards, 200,000 American Spaniards (i.e. Creole Whites) and the rest, men of Indian, Negro or, more generally, mixed blood, either black and white (mulatto), or Indian and white (*mestizo*), or black and Indian with or without white (*zambo*).

Slaves numbered at most 60,000, two-thirds of them in the central provinces, known as " Venezuela " *stricto sensu*, or Caracas. African free men were therefore much more numerous than slaves. There were many slaves in domestic service; but many more on the land; and these often owned plots (*conucos*) on which they worked on Saturday afternoon and on the numerous festivities of the Spanish Catholic calendar. Slaves in charge of cattle often had herds of their own, amounting in some cases to hundreds of heads. Slaves from the Antilles were automatically set free when they happened to land in Venezuela.

The *llanos* or plains were the abode of a cowboy race, the *llaneros* or *gauchos* of the north, nearly all *zambos*, with not a few mulattos and a few whites—who lived on horseback and ruled over immense herds of bulls and cows,

3

mules and horses, animals which, like the *llaneros* themselves, were on their
way back to nature from the civilization of their progenitors.

2

Caracas was then a city *grande, propre, élégante et bien bâtie*, of between
35,000 and 45,000 inhabitants, including 12,000 whites and 27,000 coloured
freemen.   In 1723, about the time Bolívar's father was born, its chronicler,
Oviedo y Baños, described it as follows: " Its streets are wide, long, and
straight, and as they slant and are slabbed, they neither make dust nor
tolerate mud; most of its buildings are low, for fear of earthquakes; some
made of brick, generally of adobe, but well conceived and planned; the
houses are so generously laid out that nearly all possess spacious courtyards,
gardens and kitchen gardens, that, watered by many canals which cross the
city fed through pipes from the river Cotuche, give forth a variety of flowers
with admirable abundance all the year round: it is embellished by four
plazas, three of them middle-sized and the main one large and square.   Over
and above the innumerable crowd of negros and mulattos which serve it,
it is inhabited by one thousand Spanish citizens, including two titles of
Castillian nobility which make it illustrious, and many more gentlemen of
well-known pedigrees, which ennoble it; its Creoles are sharp and quick-
witted, lovable and polite; they speak the Castillian language perfectly, without
any of those defects which vitiate it in most harbours of the Indies, and, owing
to the mild climate, are well made and handsome, and none will be found
either ill-shaped or suffering from any ugly deformity; generally stout-
hearted and bold-minded, and so much bent on polity that even the blacks
(when Creoles) hold it in contempt to be unable to read and write. . . .
The women are beautiful with reserve and amiable with distinction, and they
behave with so much modesty and reserve that it is hard to see among the
common sort a white living a scandalous life, and if so she pays for it with the
contempt in which she is held."

Though within 10·5 degrees from the Equator, Caracas enjoys a perennial
spring, owing to its altitude and to the east-west orientation of the smiling
valley in which it had been built.   " What more delightful "—writes
Humboldt—" than a temperature which remains by day within 20 and 26
degrees and by night within 16 and 18, and which favours the cultivation of
the banana, orange, coffee, apple, apricot and wheat ? "   Yet, the Caraqueños
complained of their climate and found the west wind so trying for their
nerves that many shut themselves up at home when it blew into the city
loading it with damp warmth; until the dry eastern wind which came from
the mountains restored the transparency of their native air and soothed their
aching heads.   This, of course, implied leisure, a blessing in those days
within everybody's reach.   The good families deemed it a social necessity
to own about twice as many slaves as their domestic service warranted—
so, they were idle and their servants worked half time; and as for the crafts-
men—all coloured freemen—they seem to have thought that work was only
to be undertaken when it was absolutely unavoidable.

3

The Church entered into this open conspiracy against work by holding as many religious festivals as possible in honour of one or other of the saints of the innumerable host of Heaven, each preceded by the *novena*, or nine days of prayer, and followed by the *octava*, or eight days of enjoyment, fireworks, concerts and other diversions; so that the life of the city rolled on in waves, the rising surge of the prayers for the next saint to be celebrated overlapping the riotous backwash of fireworks and music in honour of his predecessor. The chief event in these festivals was the procession, a slow river of colour, rhythm, music and aromatic incense, flowing between the steep banks of rows of houses hung with rich tapestries and alive with gorgeous flowers and gaily dressed women.

The Saint, of course, was not taken in, being as shrewd as holy people are apt to be. He knew perfectly well that his image which, swaying right and left in step with the four bearers, presided over the spectacle in a blaze of candles, a cloud of incense, and a polyphony of bells, trumpets and drums, was but a pious pretext to focus and organize the pleasure-loving trends of the people; and so, he lent himself good humouredly to the part he was expected to play; since, after all, the festival was not without true religious significance, for the Lord was praised by turning the senses of his creatures to the enjoyment of the beautiful; and moreover, while the procession lasted, all forgot their differences of rank and fortune and became equal in the presence of a higher life.

This religious core of the Spanish societies in the Indies was the chief force which endowed them with a cohesion and a unity all their own, working far below the surface, beyond reach of shallow observers and critics. It was like the air everyone breathed. The storms of later days, the excesses of the French and Negro revolutions and the reactionary policy which they called forth in Spain, have obscured the fact by distracting attention from the hard crust of the Church to its warm and irradiating core. Yet the fact is capital. The Church with its festivals, its standards of family life, its stress on spiritual equality, its tendency to improve the lot of the slaves and to free as many of them as possible, was a permanent source of the moral and social tendencies which gave Spanish life in the Indies its peculiar colour and charm.

" This nation is sedate even in the delirium of pleasure ", wrote Depons of the Caracas he knew well. " Three or four thousand persons go out of church without making any more noise than a tortoise walking on sand." But he was wrong in attributing the fact to the national character. " The Spaniards are, of all people known, those who do the least to establish a police for public tranquillity. The sobriety which is natural to them, and still more their phlegmatic character, render quarrels and tumults very rare." Depons was proved wrong by subsequent events among " Spaniards " of both sides of the Atlantic. That tranquillity he saw did not come naturally to the Spaniards. It was the result of social peace. Another Frenchman, after a scholarly study of a great bishop of Caracas (1756–70), gives a better and deeper picture: " It cannot be denied that, in spite of his childish exaggerations, the episcopate of Madroñero had a happy influence on the development of the Caraqueño society, for it gave the inhabitants of the city a taste for intimate gatherings, the pleasures of the spirit, the calm enjoyment of family life, and it awoke in them the artistic sense. Visitors to Caracas towards the end of the eighteenth century, such as the Comte de Ségur, Humboldt, the American Daune were struck by the concord and the patriarchal spirit which prevailed in the Caraqueño families, and at the same time, by the intellectual culture which they found."

4

On this last point, all authors are agreed. Depons, speaking of the rivalries between the officers who came from Spain and the Creoles, writes: " The Creoles have excellent natural abilities. They are capable of great application. We see among them profound theologians and eminent counsel." Humboldt, comparing the several kingdoms of the Indies in point of culture finds " a marked tendency to deep study of sciences in Mexico and Santa Fe de Bogotá; more taste for letters . . . in Quito and in Lima; more enlightenment on the political relations between nations . . . in Havana and Caracas." And he adds on Cuba and Venezuela: " In no other part of Spanish America does civilization look more European . . . despite the higher proportion of black population, one feels in Havana and Caracas closer to Cádiz or to the United States than in any other part of the New World."

This culture of the pleasant capital had three roots. The first was, as we know, the Church. The second, the University. As in all other kingdoms of the New World, Spain's educational activities in Venezuela began at an early date. The *Seminario Tridentino*, kernel of university life in Caracas, was founded in 1592 by Philip II, at the suggestion of Simón de Bolívar, the first ancestor of the *Libertador* to settle in Venezuela. He was at the time *Procurador* of Caracas in Madrid. Owing to the as yet small size of the city, the *Seminario* began as a simple Grammar School. The actual college was not set up till 1641; and it soon acquired the size and importance of a true University. But, in spite of repeated requests, the coveted honour of the name, and its attendant business of granting degrees, were slow in coming, owing to the opposition of the University of Santo Domingo, to which the students from Caracas had to apply—and bring their fees—in order to obtain a degree. In the end, Caracas had a University, as well as a *Seminario*, or University College. It was inaugurated on August 11th, 1725.

At the time of Bolívar's birth, the University of Caracas was an active centre of learning, jealous of its privileges, one of which was to have pre-cedence over every other institution in the capital. Two years after Bolívar's birth, in 1785, the list of Chairs included: Theology (Prime); Theology (Vespers); Canon Law; Institution of Laws; Moral Theology; Scholastic Philosophy; Grammar; Music (three Chairs for each); Holy Writ; Medicine. But these names mean but little without actual reference to the matters taught. " Theology ", for instance, was often in the academic language of the day applied to any branch of knowledge, since all is God and God is all. An examination of the actual theses presented by students for their degrees in the days of Bolívar's infancy shows that the University of Caracas cultivated physical, chemical and biological studies, and followed apace the development of English, French and German philosophy; so that Descartes, Leibniz, Bacon, Spinoza, Locke, Condillac, Lamarck figure among the authors discussed along with Kepler, Newton, Huyghens, Volta, Franklin, Lavoisier, Humboldt and Davy.

5

Still we need not imagine Caracas as a hive of men poring over books of philosophy and mathematics. It was above all a city of shrewd and alert men and of graceful and sprightly women whose chief aim in life was to live—as good a philosophy as any that ever blackened white paper. And there is little doubt that they lived their own lives in the way they pleased, and that a considerable part of their pleasure came from the arts and letters of the day. Caracas had a theatre. We need not take at their face value Depons' severe strictures on it: " All the pieces, in themselves most wretched, are, moreover, miserably performed." We have heard that before. In those days every Frenchman was a Boileau for whom Lope de Vega, Tirso de Molina and Calderón were nearly as barbarous as Shakespeare. The chief points to be gathered in his pages are that the theatre was cheap (all too cheap he finds), costing one real or sixty cents, and that it was frequented by high and low alike: " Rich and poor, old and young, nobles and plebeians, the governing and governed all most assiduously attend." We know from Humboldt that in the courtyard below men and women were separated, and there was no roof, so that " one could see at a time the actors and the stars ". And he adds this delightful touch: " As I had to waste much time in my observation of satellites owing to the foggy weather, I could from my box in the theatre make sure that Jupiter would be visible during the night."

Humboldt confirms Depons: " I found in many families of Caracas a zest for education, a knowledge of the masterpieces of French and Italian literature, a pronounced fondness for music, which is successfully cultivated and as is always the case with the fine arts, brings together all the several classes of society." Love of music was also noted by Ségur who was in Caracas at about the time of Bolívar's birth. " This Governor "—he writes—" introduced me to the most distinguished houses of the city; where we saw men perhaps too grave and taciturn, but on the other hand, a great quantity of ladies as notable for their beauty as for the wealth of their attire, the elegance of their manners and their talents for dancing and for music, as well as for a vivacious coquetry which knew full well how to ally gaiety with modesty." Cayetano Carreño, elder brother of Bolívar's tutor, was a composer of considerable talent; and a maternal relative of Bolívar, Father Sojo, as well as the French family of Blandin, organized private concerts in which as early as 1789 music of Mozart, Pleyel and Haydn used to be played.

Music is an art best enjoyed in passivity. A passive state, so fertile for the artist, is typical of the Spanish character in its most spontaneous form; nor would any Indian blood that might have strayed into the blue veins of the Caraqueños work against this tendency. Humboldt frowns at this indifference and lack of curiosity: " Used to a uniform and stay-at-home life, every one fears fatigue and the brusque changes of climate; it seems as if people lived here not to enjoy life but only to prolong it." But there was in this neither physical nor mental sloth. " There is widespread luxury and much gilt in the furniture of the wealthy houses "—writes Dauxion Lavaisse in 1807—" and everywhere more cleanliness and abundance than in Spain. One finds in Caracas as much luxury as in European capitals, and a refinement and an exaggerated courtesy which flow both from Spanish gravity and from the pleasure-loving ways of the Creoles."

6

Three were the chief sources of the incomes thus spent in pleasantly " prolonging life ": the land; trade; and State or City offices. Trade was usually either left to " Europeans ", i.e. Spaniards from Spain, or carried on on the sly, for " whatever may be done by the laws [which endeavoured to honour trade] the national opinion still refuses the consideration to commerce which it enjoys everywhere else ". Bolívar's father owned a clothier's shop, but in another man's name. Warehouses were tucked away inside private houses with no outward sign to reveal their existence to the passer-by. Yet, trade was a considerable item in the national wealth, particularly since Charles III had opened Spanish and Spanish-American ports to trans-atlantic traffic with the *Free Commerce Regulations* of October 12th, 1778. The chief profits were made in the New World. The Spanish merchants made but little. Depons puts it at three and a half per cent if at all. He means, of course, at the Spanish end of the chain of trade. The Catalans managed to do better business at both ends by keeping transactions almost entirely within their own people. The Basques had been the undisputed lords of Venezuela in the heyday of the *Compañía Guipuzcoana* which had enjoyed the monopoly of trade from 1728 till the Free Commerce policy was adopted in 1778.

Basques, Catalans, Canarians, and in general, non-American Spaniards, made up the bulk of the business community. The Creoles of the upper, white classes, were almost to a man landed gentry who, either for the sake of honour or for profit, sought government service when they did not find it in their cradles by privilege. For these men their own country seldom stretched beyond the narrow strip of coast line, two hundred leagues long and about twelve across, in which the amenities of civilization were concentrated. This civilization was rooted in a prosperous land-economy, itself based on slavery. Humboldt estimated the whites at two hundred thousand, of whom ten to fifteen thousand were Europeans (not including troops). Trade was mostly in the hands of the fifteen thousand " Europeans " while the two hundred thousand " Spaniards ", i.e. Spanish Americans,

had to leave Potosí. His last words to his followers were: " See that all the Basques leave Potosí, unless they leave it for the other world "; and " let all the nations [i.e. of Spain] be at one with the Creoles, for so the destruction of the Basques will be easier"; finally, his followers were to " resist in Potosí and never surrender their arms ".

It is illuminating to find this ancestor of Bolívar leading a civil war with a spirit so defiant and so close to separatism. These civil wars of Potosí which were known as the wars of the *Vicuñas*, because of the Vicuña hats one of the sides had adopted, are as much ancestors of the wars of secession as Xedler is of Bolívar; and (as was the case with the pure separatism of Aguirre the Tyrant) should be seen as psychological roots of that vigorous tree that was Simón Bolívar. Aguirre and Xedler are thus not merely two names in the family tree of the Bolívars; they are two symbols of the trends we are going to observe in the vast and rich landscape of Bolívar's spirit— trends which spring from the past of their own accord and in their own right, allowing us to observe them in their natural state, before the *ideas* of a later age have shaped, fed and adorned them in foreign garb.

5

The chaos in which Venezuela grew in the sixteenth century was both cause and effect of the lack of Church institutions and clergy. When Father Pedro de Agreda, second bishop of Venezuela, arrived in Coro (1560), he had to work as the parish priest of nearly every parish, for there was practically no clergy; and, to satisfy the desire of some local settlers to become priests, he had to set up schools and teach Latin himself. This neglect of the religious side of the conquest, due mostly to the prevalence of German influences, was one of the chief causes of the long chaotic period Venezuela had to endure, in sharp contrast with the organic growth of Mexico and of Peru. But another reason of the difference may well have been that Mexico and Peru had already a pre-Spanish tradition as organized States.

In the absence of such a tradition, and also for lack of an outstanding man such as Hernán Cortés, the coming together of an unorganized congeries of Indian States with a series of spirited adventurers styled governors, and of governors in search of adventures, had to be for generations richer in chaos than in peace and plenty. Not that the Spaniards were lacking in civic order. But this civic sense itself was apt to be local and municipal. Though municipal institutions in the metropolis were already feeling the weight of the royal authority, the tradition was still robust that made of them little kingdoms sovereign in the administration of their business and justice, and went so far as to endow the municipal council or *cabildo* of the chief city of a province with almost parliamentary powers.

Before his death in office, Villasinda, a Governor General, had decided that, pending the arrival of his successor, every province should be governed by its chief *alcalde*. This pleased the *alcaldes* very much indeed, and they sent a settler named Sancho Briceño to Madrid to negotiate that the concession should be given a permanent sanction by the Crown. This was granted by Royal *Cédula* (8.xii.1560), along with the rights: to receive from Spain one ship a year loaded with goods to pay only half the usual duty; and to import two hundred African slaves a year for the mines. There was another grant, which reads strangely after this: that a number of missionaries should come from Santo Domingo to preach the Gospels.

It is typical of Venezuelan history that this negotiation, the first in which a municipal, parliamentary or republican consciousness of a constructive character seems to dawn, should occur simultaneously with the chaotic separatism of Aguirre the Tyrant. Meanwhile, the " reduction " of the province, i.e. the war against the Indians, went on. The most successful campaign was that led by Diego de Losada under the governorship of Don Pedro Ponce de León (1565–9) against the Indians known as the Caracas. The chief resistance came from a spirited *cacique*, Guaicaipuro, headman of the Teques. Losada decided to destroy him and entrusted the expedition to a direct ancestor of Bolívar, Francisco Infante, *alcalde* of Caracas. In the course of this campaign, Losada turned his general headquarters into the city of Santiago de León de Caracas, a name to honour himself (Santiago, i.e. Diego), the Governor General, Ponce de León, and his adversaries the Caracas, whom he had repeatedly tried to win over by gifts and blandishments. By the wear and tear of time, both St. James and the lion were rubbed out of the name of the city and the Indians won. The city is plain Caracas to-day. It grew quickly at the expense of the less healthy Burburata, and became the capital of the province under Don Juan Pimentel (1576–82).

6

From 1587 to 1597 the province was governed by the General of the galleys of Santo Domingo, Don Diego de Ossorio, who has won a high reputation in Spanish-American history on the strength of the praise bestowed on him by the chronicler of Venezuela, Oviedo y Baños. The province was in turmoil owing to the mismanagement of public affairs by his predecessor Rojas. Ossorio had ideas, courage and diplomatic gifts. But having formed his plans, he thought it wiser to have them first approved in Madrid. So he sent to Spain his kinsman Simón de Bolívar, whom he had brought over with him from Santo Domingo. But the shrewd governor managed to have his emissary invested with the dignity of *Procurador*, or representative of the *cabildo* of Caracas.

Simón de Bolívar hailed from Marquina, in Biscay, and had been for fourteen years Secretary of one of the Chambers of the *Audiencia* in Santo Domingo when he went over to Caracas as accountant and magistrate in the Treasury. The family thus enters the stage from on high, in the upper ranks of the royal civil service. The *cabildo* appointed him representative not merely of the city, but of the province of which Caracas was the chief city, thus assuming the duties and privileges of a national parliament in a way traditional in Spain.

The point is not without interest, for Simón de Bolívar, the *procurador* is one of the roots of Simón Bolívar, the *Libertador*. The ancestor was a Spanish administrator and civil servant, born and bred in the public service, whose first action in his new fatherland was to represent the people, but also the Governor, i.e. to bring before the king the plans of an intelligent and active governor clothed as the desires of a community of Spanish citizens.

The settlers requested that the " personal service " of Indians prohibited by Royal *Cédula* (27.iv.1588) be restored; that the Miria Indians, who resisted the Spaniards and ate human flesh, should, when caught, be liable to " captivity " from the age of ten on; and that three thousand licences to procure black slaves should be granted; that pearls should circulate as currency at the rate of sixteen silver reales per peso of pearls; that two ships with goods be sent yearly to Venezuela, " for no ships come from Spain loaded straight for this governorship which is out of the general navigation of the fleets "; that the Governor be empowered to appoint officials direct " without meddling from the *Audiencia* of Santo Domingo or its President "; and that the *Audiencia* should not send special enquiring magistrates (*jueces de comisión*) except on very grave matters; that visits of inspection as to the treatment of the Indians should be made by the Governor and not by out-siders coming as *jueces de comisión;* that a local magistrate (*teniente general letrado de ciencia y conciencia*) be appointed by the governor to handle all the considerable number of law cases both civil and criminal awaiting study; and that cases on which there was an appeal to the *Audiencia* should be settled by the Governor. There were a number of other fiscal privileges and a grant for the hospital founded by Ossorio, for which freedom from Church interference was asked.

This list of reforms shows Ossorio to have been a convinced " separatist " from Santo Domingo, and a no less convinced protector of the interests of the white settlers. Bolívar was not equally successful all along the line, but he brought back a number of grants for the colony and some advance-ment for himself. The yearly ship had already been granted to Briceño, but the privilege seems to have lapsed. Bolívar brought it back as a con-cession to the *cabildo* to appoint a person every year who would bring over a ship to La Guaira on his own account. Grants of service were limited to the right to import one hundred tons of African slaves free from dues; and the *alcabala* tax was held up for ten years in exchange for a small tribute to be paid by the cities.

As for Bolívar himself, he was given the prerogatives of *regidor* or alderman of the city of Caracas with voice and vote. This was a curious departure from the republican traditions of the *cabildos* of Venezuela. One of Ossorio's first duties on arrival had been to right the wrong inflicted on the city of Caravalleda by his predecessor Rojas. Cities elected every year *regidores* who in their turn elected the two *alcaldes*. Rojas claimed the right to appoint the *alcaldes* of Caravalleda for the year 1586, and imprisoned the *regidores* who refused to recognize his nominees. The citizens abandoned the city altogether. Ossorio set the *regidores* free. And yet this very Governor Ossorio received Bolívar back from Spain as a *regidor* appointed for life by the king, and, in 1594, on his own initiative, obtained from Madrid an order declaring venal and permanent all the *regimientos* or aldermanships of his government.

This was then the trend which from Simón de Bolívar, the *procurador*, went down the centuries to animate in the heart of Simón Bolívar, the *Libertador:* a public spirited interest in the affairs of the community, but of the community of the white settlers, owners of the land, the mines, the cattle and the slaves; owners, in fact, of the Indians also; men of leisure, courage, pride and privilege, who esteemed highly the good opinion of their peers, but higher still the title of honour or the wand of office granted by the distant monarch in the kingdoms of old Spain.

7

The lineage of Bolívar and others like those of Villegas, Infante, Martínez de Madrid, Ladrón de Guevara, brought to the *Libertador* the sap of old Spanish oak and laurel. But Simón Bolívar would have been less representative as an historical figure, less complex as a human soul, and less rooted in the soil of the New World, had he been a pure white. Though the ambient forces and spirits might have influenced him, he would have been unable to gain access—as he did—to the deeper layers of the soul of the Indies if his family had not at one time or another—probably more than once—taken in both Negro and Indian blood. " What will the European nations say on hearing that Bolívar is a *zambo* ? " asked Simón Rodríguez or Carreño in his spirited defence of the *Libertador*. " What will the fair-headed men of England say, and of Scotland, and of France and above all of . . . Andalucía . . . a *zambo* ruling over Indians in Peru ! How shocking ! And what would wise people say if the author of this defence took upon himself to prove by means of documents or authorities, that Bolívar is a white of the first, second or thirtieth extraction ? a nobleman of the first or of the hundredth class ? Bolívar and his defender are both *zambos*, but neither of them is a fool."

This is as shrewd a page as ever was written by that crank whom the caprice of Fate made the companion of young Bolívar. The crafty schoolmaster, basking in the glory of his now famous " pupil ", was not going either to admit or to deny that in Bolívar's veins ran the three bloods which made the Indies; for, if he denied it, the *Libertador* would lose precious support in the masses; and if he admitted it, the *Libertador* would lose the prestige which still went with pure white blood. And the fact that the two attitudes mutually excluded each other by no means prevented them from living happily together in everybody's blood, whether white, black, Indian or mixed, including that of both Simóns, Rodríguez and Bolívar.

It may be safely assumed that the branches of Bolívar's family tree which have remained unexplored have strong chances of being rooted in the soil through Indian or black blood; for the universal colour prejudice would naturally work that way. One case is almost certain: that of one of Bolívar's great grandmothers who brought into the family the mines of Aroa, and the house in which he was born. Josefa Marín de Narváez was the illegitimate daughter of Francisco Marín de Narváez and of a woman of whom little is known. Marín says himself: " I have a natural daughter and I recognize her as such, whose name is Josefa; whom I had by a maid of good family whose name I do not mention out of respect, whom I might have married without licence when the child was born ". The chances that this " maid of good family " was dusky are overwhelming.

How could the illegitimate daughter of a lady either dark or left in the dark by all concerned gain access to a family as illustrious as that of Bolívar ? The answer is: wealth. Francisco Marín de Narváez was born in Cójar, in the kingdom of Granada. By a Royal *Cédula* of 1663 he bought from the Crown for forty thousand pesos the mines of Cocorote and the Lordship of Aroa, including the right to appoint and dismiss the local judges. In 1668, his daughter was born. No mention is made of the mother till, at his death in Madrid in 1673, he describes her as a *doncella principal*. The girl was brought up by her aunt, Doña María Marín de Narváez, founder of the Charity Hospital for Women, of Caracas; and both the aunt and the niece lived in the house of an uncle, Gonzalo Marín de Granizo. But on her father's death, Josefa, then five, became a wealthy heiress, and therefore attracted much attention. The Proveedor, Pedro Jaspe de Montenegro, Alguacil Mayor or Chief Constable of the Inquisition and *alcalde* of Caracas, mentioned in Marín's will as guardian when his sister came to die, grew terribly worried, having " come to understand that it is forbidden by law that women, except the mother and the grandmothers, should be guardians, for this office does not admit their sex "; and, in spite of Doña María's protestations, the *alcalde ordinario* of the day, overriding the will, handed the little girl (and the big fortune) over to his past or future colleague. Josefa was then seven. Within six years, the Proveedor married her to his nephew Pedro Ponte, who in his will, dated 1716, is candid enough to declare that " at the time I married, I had no capital nor any property, and the said my wife brought me some houses in this city in the square of the convent of San Jacinto, and an estate with cocoa plantations in the valley of St. Nicholas, within the jurisdiction of the city of Barquisimeto, and another estate also with cocoa plantations in the valley of Niaren, within the jurisdiction of the city of Nirgua, with a number of slaves in both, as well as the ownership of the lands depending from both estates, which were put into my hands by the said my uncle, as the guardian of the said my wife ".

There can be no doubt about the business acumen of the Ponte-Jaspe de Montenegro family which in this elegant manner absorbed the wealth of the gallant Marín de Narváez. Nor will anyone be surprised to hear that they all hailed from La Coruña, the capital of Galicia, where both uncle and nephew, as well as the nephew's father, mother and maternal grandparents, were born. The point should be reserved for later reference, along with this coloured strain which the hard working Gallegans brought to the family of the *Libertador;* for the nephew of the tutor and the wealthy ward, illegitimate and therefore almost certainly dusky, were the parents of María Petronila de Ponte y Marín de Narváez, paternal grandmother of Simón Bolívar.

CHAPTER III

THE HOME

I

BOTH the paternal and the maternal strains, the Bolívars and the Palacios, brought with them a tradition of wealth, comfort and power. At no time since the arrival of Simón de Bolívar in 1587 had the family been absent from the ruling circles of the country. On September 17th, 1593, Simón II, the son of Simón I, was granted the *encomienda* (or trust) of Quiriquire Indians of the valley of San Mateo, an estate which was to become the favourite country residence of the family.

The Bolívars were therefore firmly rooted in the Spanish traditions of the rich, aristocratic and powerful whites, resting on their religious faith, their monarchist loyalty, their titles and privileges, their Indians and their black slaves. Don Juan Vicente de Bolívar y Ponte, the *Libertador's* father, was the heir of all these strains. He lived in Caracas in the house of Josefa Marín de Narváez, in San Mateo in the *encomienda* of his ancestor the Royal Accountant. He was a Colonel of the Company of Adventurous Noblemen organized in 1786, and a leading personality in the country. His elegant figure is prominent in one or two sensational incidents of the turbulent period in which he lived. On February 24th, 1782, seventeen months to a day before the birth of his younger son who was to make his name famous, the Colonel, with two other aristocrats of Caracas, signed a letter appealing to Miranda as the " first born son of whom the mother country expects this important service ", and declaring themselves " ready to follow him as our leader to the end and to shed the last drop of our blood in noble and great things ".

What was it that these aristocrats were so resolved to achieve ? Who was the first born son to whom they appealed ? Miranda was not yet a rebel. He was a Lieutenant Colonel in the Spanish Army, whose reputation in his native Venezuela was due to his brilliant military career and to his share in the Spanish campaigns against the English in Florida, notably in the siege and surrender of the English garrison of Pensácola. Within weeks of receiving the letter from the three aristocrats of Caracas, he was to accept another English surrender—that of the garrison of Bahamas. He must have read the letter with mixed feelings, coming as it did from that set which had nagged and persecuted his father for having sported the uniform and stick of Captain of a regiment, being a shopkeeper *sine nobilitate*. Both Mirandas, father and son, were snobs, and deeply resented this persecution that not even the persistent protection of the Crown had been able to curb; a persecution led by a Captain Tovar and a Captain Ponte, as Miranda would certainly remember, reading at the foot of the letter the names of Don Martín de Tovar and Don Juan Vicente Bolívar y Ponte.

At the time, all these men were living in a kind of twilight of loyalties, rich in subtleties. Miranda was jeopardizing a brilliant future as a Spanish officer both by shady commercial enterprises and by ambiguous transactions with the English. He did not realize how far he went nor even how far he wanted to go in his wanderings between loyalty and disloyalty. As for Don Juan Vicente de Bolívar and his friends, they were voicing one of those " separatist " resentments which in the History of Spain are often observed alongside a complete loyalty to the Crown. The letter to Miranda is rich in revelations. The noblemen of Caracas are incensed at the " insults " they receive from the *Intendente* or chief local civil authority, and therefore from " every good-for-nothing Goth " (Goth being the nickname given to the European Spaniards in Spanish America); and the worst, they add, is that the Spanish proconsul " goes on treating all Americans, no matter their class, rank or circumstances, as if they were vile slaves ". These words define the position clearly enough. But the letter makes it even clearer: " We know full well what has happened and is still happening in communities such as those of Santa Fe or Cuzco, but we do not like the outcome of it, and, fearing similar consequences (with, moreover, the experience here at home of the León affair) we want to take no steps, nor shall we take any without your advice, for in your prudence we have set all our hopes."

So, these reformers put their hope in prudence, not in audacity. Their appeal was not the first, for in the same letter they write: " We have already fully informed you in letters we sent you in July of 1781, on the deplorable state of all this province." But they were certainly anxious to avoid events such as those they mentioned: The rising of Cuzco; that of Santa Fe; and the León episode in Venezuela. León was a Canarian, like Miranda's father, who in 1749 led a rebellion not so much against the government as against the Basques. This episode was but another offshoot of the latent civil war amongst Spaniards of the eleven nations in which a Xedler had taken such a prominent part. Another Xedler, a close relation of the Bolívars, acting as *regidor* of Caracas, took a hand in the negotiations when León entered Caracas at the head of an armed force. The topical cause was provided by both the qualities and the defects of the Basques who led the *Compañía Guipuzcoana;* too successful for the easy-going Creoles, the Basques were too domineering. León was a leader belonging to the " species " Cortés-Pizarro-Bolívar, though a minor member of it; with the same mixture of personal motives and public feelings, of legal forms and anarchical instincts. He was defeated, sent to Spain and finally pardoned by the King. Typical detail in the dramatic encounter between the governor Castellanos and the rebel León, two men stood by the governor in the public square. One was Miranda's father; the other one was Bolívar's.

The second episode mentioned by the aristocrats of Caracas was that of Santa Fe. It had originated in the little town of Socorro, in New Granada (to-day, Colombia), where the crowd had risen in protest against new taxes (16.iii.1780). Though seemingly popular, it was backed by the rich Creoles, one of whom, Don José Antonio Galán, was later sentenced to death. Don Juan Vicente Bolívar and his friends were entitled to dislike this death of one of their class in ignominious circumstances; as well as the tendency of a movement their class had inspired and hoped to control to get out of hand

and take on a truly revolutionary impetus. Here again, a telling detail: the movement became known as that of the *comuneros*, the name the Castillian rebels against Charles V had taken in the sixteenth century.

Finally, the Cuzco episode mentioned in the letter to Miranda is no other than the rebellion of Condorcanqui, which took place at the same time as that of the *comuneros* of Socorro. This Condorcanqui, who claimed to be a descendant of the Incas but seems in fact to owe his birth to a Spanish friar and an Indian married woman, led a picturesque sanguinary and widespread revolt in Peru; now in the name of the Inca Emperors, his " ancestors ", now in the name of Charles III, who, he asserted, had granted him vice-regal powers. Though confused, incoherent and disorderly, this rising revealed the strength of the inter-colour and inter-class tensions which lay dormant in the apparently quiet Peru; and in particular the possibility of provoking a wholesale rebellion of the Indian masses if care was taken at first to show respect for the King of Spain, whom the Indians held in great veneration. The white Creoles sided with the Spanish author-ities, though Condorcanqui did his best to win them over. Humboldt explains why: many, he says, were beginning to find it irksome to depend on a far-off power which they felt every year more foreign; " but they held back from the idea of supporting a movement which, headed by a half-caste and leaning on the Indian masses, might, if victorious, have deprived them of their privileges ". Hence the mention of this episode in the letter to Miranda among those " the outcome of which " Don Juan Vicente de Bolívar and his friends " did not like ".

2

Bolívar's father was thus a disgruntled Spanish-American aristocrat born and bred in Caracas but steeped in Spanish traditions, the chief works of whose library were the thirteen volumes of the *Ordenanzas Militares*, the *Comedias* of Calderón de la Barca, and eighteen volumes of the complete works of Feijóo, the enlightened critic and thinker of eighteenth-century Spain. He was proud of his titles and honours, which flowed from the Court of Spain. This was compatible with business; though sheltering behind a common man, Carrasco by name, Don Juan Vicente de Bolívar was the owner of a shop where he sold clothes imported from Spain in exchange for the cocoa he shipped to Spain from his estates. Don Juan Vicente's father, Don Juan de Bolívar Villegas, Lieutenant General of the Spanish armies, had deposited twenty-two thousand ducats in the Monastery of Monserrat, in Spain, to purchase one of the two titles of Castille which the King had granted the Monastery " so that it could meet the expenses of repairing and rebuilding ". The claim to the title remained alive throughout the century, and, while no papers have come to light to show that either Don Martín (Don Juan's heir), or Don Juan Vicente, who became the heir at Don Martín's death, took any step to further this business, the fact that the money—a considerable sum—was not claimed back does show that they meant to keep intact the claim to the title they had purchased.

Doña Concepción Palacios, mother of the *Libertador*, made her brother Esteban take up the matter in Spain in 1792; and the correspondence between Esteban and his father constantly refers to this theme, as well as to their own ancestry; for the Palacios were no less infatuated with their blue blood than the Bolívars. He did see, Esteban writes to his father, one of his ancestors, registered as a peasant farmer; but the other names he mentions are noble, and he is leaving an expert behind to look up the registers " and see whether some good thing can be found ". On October 27th, 1792, Esteban writes: " After this business [of the marquisate of San Luis for Juan Vicente, Simón's elder brother] is through, I intend to apply for a new grace with the title of Count of Casa Palacios for Simón, on the strength of the merit and services of his father." Little Simón (*Simoncito*) was nine when this letter was written. He just escaped being decorated with a futile title of Spanish nobility.

The family lived in the city of Caracas, in the house which it had inherited from the dusky heiress; and at times in the estate of San Mateo. They were *mantuanos puros*, i.e. a family whose women were entitled to wear the *manto*, a sign of the highest rank. On the Bolívar side, the family held in perpetuity one of the offices of *regidor* or alderman of the *cabildo* of Caracas; on the Palacios side, the office of *Alférez real* or royal standard bearer. Both would be among the most prominent officials who, clad in gold, silver, lace and silk, would ceremoniously call on the Captain General on days of *besamanos* or levees, and would then follow his Excellency to the Cathedral for solemn mass and *Te Deum*.

Social life in the Indies was held by a code of etiquette and ceremony stricter even than in Spain. Modes of address were formal; attire, visits, manners were not trifled with. No impromptu calls, no brusque ways were tolerated. A lady would not call on a friend in the afternoon without warning her in the morning. Children, though in law early emancipated from their parents to an extent which scandalized Depons, were in point of manners humble and deferent to them, and addressed them all their lives with the distant and ceremonious title of *Vuestra Merced*. The four children of Don Juan Vicente Bolívar, María Antonia, Juana, Juan Vicente and Simón, certainly felt the utmost respect for these forms of a vigorous tradition. " Every morning "—writes Depons—" before they rise from their bed, and every evening before they lie down, the children of the Spaniards, whether rich or poor, whether white or black, whether free or slaves, crave and receive upon their knees the benediction of father and of mother, and kiss, before they stand up, the hand that dispenses it. The same ceremony is repeated during the day, every time that the father, the mother, the uncle, the aunt, or the children return from abroad and enter the house." Depons adds that " these homages are, in general, merely external ". The value of forms and the discipline of certain gestures was beyond him as it is unfortunately to-day beyond most westerners.

When Simón was three, María Antonia was nine, Juana seven and Juan Vicente five; their parents sixty and twenty-seven. The first and the last of the children were dark-haired and pale; Juana and Juan Vicente were

rosy and fair. Simón's full names were: Simón José Antonio de la Santísima Trinidad. This last advocation was traditional in the family since the
days when Pedro Ponte Andrade Jaspe de Montenegro, with more names
than money, had married Josefa Marín de Narváez, with more money than
name. Pedro Ponte was a devout worshipper of the Holy Trinity, and had
endowed a chapel in the Cathedral to worship this divine mystery. He had
also built a special church for the same purpose. The chapel became a
kind of home beyond the bourne for the Bolívar family, whose scions were
usually interred in it. As for the church, it was begun in 1742 by the
architect Juan Domingo Infante, and finished in the very year—1783—in
which Simón Bolívar was born. The fact suddenly acquired a dramatic
historical importance when Simón Bolívar was twenty-nine.

3

Don Juan Vicente de Bolívar y Ponte died on January 19th, 1786. His
will is rich in historical data on the character, outlook and atmosphere of
this typical Creole of the eighteenth century. It consists of two parts: a
power of attorney granted by the dying man to his wife and to his father-
in-law to draft the will on notes supplied by him; and the will itself. The
first feature which strikes the mind on reading this document is the strong
religious, social and aristocratic traditions on which it rests. The dying
man begins: " In the name of God our Lord Amen ". And then he
describes himself with all his titles of military honour, including that of
" Commander on behalf of His Majesty of the Company of *Volantes* of the
river Yaracuy "; gives his native city its long traditional name, Santiago de
León de Caracas, and twice stresses his legitimacy: " legitimate son by a
legitimate marriage "; describing his father as *capitán poblador*, i.e. a
reminder of his ancestry as a conqueror. Then comes a long page on his
faith, moving despite its verbosity: " believing as I truly believe in the
Divine Mystery of the incomprehensible and most holy Trinity "; and,
placing himself under the protection of the Holy Virgin, he at last declares
that he delegates his powers to make a will to his wife and father-in-law.

There is in this page a detail which suddenly lights up the Spanish roots
of this tradition across three centuries: the testator gives to his wife and
father-in-law power, he says, " to draft and declare my testament within the
term laid down in law 33 of Toro ". The laws of Toro were a code prepared
by a Committee of jurists on the instructions of Ferdinand and Isabel and
passed by the Cortes at Toro in 1505. This American Spaniard, who but
four years earlier was ready to rebel under Miranda, goes on to dispose that
he is to " be shrowded with my military insignia and buried with the privileges
which I enjoy under military law in the chapel and vault of the Holy Trinity
of which I am the patron ". After which he gives instructions as to the
number of priests and friars who must accompany his body, and the lavish
amount of well-paid masses that are to be said for his soul.

This soul, who in his own estimation needed no less than two thousand
masses to steal into Heaven, was that of a man who had lived as fast as he

could before marrying at forty-six a girl of fourteen. He could pick and choose, for while his girlish wife brought to the joint estate " two slaves, Tomasa and Encarnación, about sixteen years of age ", he brought 258,500 pesos not counting the value of several landed estates. The description of his sugar, cocoa and indigo estates, " with the slaves to be found therein ", of his houses in Caracas and La Guaira, and of his furniture and silver, covers a whole page. He owes money to no one. He distributes his property between his four children and the fifth his wife is expecting at the time of his death. There is a veiled clause. Doña Concepción is to take four hundred pesos from his property " to carry out what I have imparted to her in order to relieve my conscience ". This kind of clause in a testa-ment was then usually connected with some liaison from the days before wedlock. It may have referred to Agustin Bolívar, who is left two hundred pesos " for one time " and without explanation; a person who, shortly after Don Juan Vicente's death, claimed to be his illegitimate son, and probably was. Not in vain had the Colonel of the white militia of Caracas invoked the mediation of " the Queen of the Angels, Most Holy Mary, our Queen and Lady ".

No less powerful an intercession than that of the gracious Mediatrix for all sinners would be needed; for the dying man would be certainly over-whelmed by bad memories. How had he understood his duties as leader of a Christian community, and trustee for his wealth, and above all the many souls Providence had put in his care? In 1765, Don Juan Vicente was thirty-nine. The bishop of Caracas was Don Diego Antonio Diez Madroñero, an upright prelate, illustrious in the Annals of the Spanish Church. During his pastoral visit, the bishop received many complaints about the behaviour of Don Juan Vicente Bolívar and his " loose ways with women " and how " in order to procure them he relies on his authority and power, calling them to his house and also through go-betweens ". The bishop " warned the witness that she must be sure about all she had said before on living in an evil way with her master; but she confirmed she had been his mistress these three years, and that even before that he lived intimately with another girl María Bernarda, and later with another one Josefa Rosalía, the *Chicota*, all of whom he used as he chose at the same time, calling the one he thought best with whom he locked himself in his bedroom or in a small room by the gallery ". One, Margarita, had told the witness how " he seized her hand and tried to force her into the bedroom; whereupon she told him she would shout if he did not let go; when, perhaps hearing how a daughter of the said Juana Bautista was coming, he left in a temper ". Margarita, however, dared not close her door to him later, " fearing his power and violent temper ".

Margarita's sister, María Jacinta, in a petition to the bishop, writes: " The trouble in which I find myself forces me to appeal to your protection as my father and shepherd, for I am beset by an infernal wolf who is bent on the Devil taking us both. This wolf is Don Juan Vicente Bolívar, who has been importuning me for days to make me sin with him, though I am a married woman, making use of every trick Lucifer has taught him, for he

sent my husband to Los Llanos, to his herds to fetch cattle, so as to remain
the freer to carry out his evil plans . . . he told me that wherever I went,
even though I hid under the earth, he would pursue me, which I doubt not
for he is most frightening and rancorous; for other days, he put in the stocks
my uncle Antonio Fernández, only because Juana Requena, his wife, distilled
some brandy . . . and this he did against my uncle, who is a holy man,
only because his wife made a statement to Your Lordship against Don Juan
Vicente . . . I warn Your Lordship my husband must know nothing about
this, for he is terribly afraid of Don Juan Vicente, and were he to know I
have written this letter he would take my life, for the Lieutenant-Justice
[Don Juan Vicente] would persecute him as he has my uncle. P.S.—After
writing this letter [I learn] that yesterday Don Juan Vicente imprisoned
in the Victoria jail my brother-in-law, the husband of my sister Margarita,
the one who fought with him to defend her honour; and this is for no
unlawful act. He is taken to La Victoria and not to our own prison here to
starve him and make him lose his tobacco plantation for it is now it needs the
most care. As I was going to close this, the Lieutenant had a cousin of my
husband's sent to prison, just for having written the letter in which my
brother-in-law asked for the tobacco to be sent. To-morrow they will come
and arrest yet another one to carry out their threats and see whether I
surrender. Do help me for God's sake, for I am on the brink of falling."

The bishop had this paper filed in the " Reserved file " he had opened on
the amorous adventures of the dissolute aristocrat. He was taking the matter
in dead earnest, and did not hide the strong censure, tinged with contempt,
which the abuse of power of the Lieutenant of Justice awoke in him. But he
took measures to avoid scandal; and to all the victims of Don Juan Vicente
he enjoined a religious life, avoidance of any dealings with Don Juan Vicente
Bolívar, and silence. As for the culprit, the bishop advised him " not to
believe in any of these stories, and, holding them in contempt, to avoid all
commerce with women, especially married, not to call to his house church-
school girls nor enter in theirs, and should he wish to show charity to them
to do so through the priest, all means whereby he would prove his innocence
and spare his Lordship the regret his Lordship would certainly feel in being
bound to believe what he now refused to believe and to have to correct him
by force of law."

4

The priest who had christened Simón was an uncle of his: Don Juan
Felix Jerez Aristeguieta y Bolívar. It goes without saying that he was
wealthy. On December 8th, 1784, when Simón was eighteen months, this
priest made his will, leaving the child he had christened at the head of a long
list of possible beneficiaries of an entail which comprised all his wealth, to wit:
his house in Caracas, between the Cathedral and the bishop's palace, with
all its furniture; and several estates with their slaves. The gift carried
with it a number of obligations flowing from the testator's character, about
which he leaves us in no doubt whatever. " I, the doctor Don Juan Felix

Jerez Aristeguieta, a priest . . . a nobleman, and of the first rank in this republic, which rank I enjoy without contradiction from the days of my ancient ancestors, conquerors of this province, say that, insofar as one of my chief wishes has been to ensure the perpetuation, lustre and prosperity of my family, to the greater glory of God our Lord . . . and that it may not fall from the station He granted us, and which my ancestors gloriously upheld together with the Holy Catholic religion we profess, and which we handed down from generation to generation in the service of both Majesties. . . ."

Both Majesties, that is, God and the King of Spain. These two loyalties are paramount in Doctor Aristeguieta's mind. The entail will be known as La Concepción, owing to his special devotion for this mystery. The beneficiary will see that the entail grows and does not decay; he will christen his first born Juan Felix and give him as his second name Aristeguieta, instead of the maternal name as was the custom; no cleric is to be entitled to the entail, and no person but legitimate sons by legitimate marriages; none either who happened to enjoy another entail; no women either. " Since one of the chief motives of the foundation is the permanency of my family in its highest lustre and splendour, the heir must be perforce married to a noble and equal person, with the acquiescence of my relatives " —a point Dr. Aristeguieta develops at length. The heir must live in Caracas, no excuse being admitted there-against except that of His Majesty's service. The testator declares twice in his will that he acts under the laws of Castille.

But the crown of this will is a clause which reads like a prophecy: " That in the same form must be excluded from the enjoyment and possession of this entail anyone unfortunate enough to fall into the ugly and outrageous crime of lese-majesty, divine or human, or into a similar one; and were it to happen (which God forbid) that, while in possession of this entail, he committed these crimes, it is my will that he be severed, and I do sever him, from the enjoyment and possession of it . . . as from twenty-four hours before he commits it." This could not be clearer: the priest who christened Simón Bolívar left his fortune to the child on condition that that child remained loyal to God and to the King of Spain, a condition which like every other one he laid down was " to be infallibly observed ".

5

This was the atmosphere of the home in which Simón Bolívar grew. His father died when he was three. The priest who baptized him and left him a rich man had died before. The chief persons left in the home were his mother and his maternal grandfather. Of his mother we have a letter and her will, both revealing her personality. Doña Concepción was a woman of a positive and practical turn of mind, capable of carrying multifarious affairs and the accounts of a rich household with an even head. There is no sentiment, there is even a certain masculine hardness in the letter, the more personal of the two documents. She deplores the flight of a slave, hopes he

will be caught and insists that her brother—to whom she writes—must
see to it; she then discusses the purchase of some negroes with a cool eye
on age, capacity and other conditions of the " pieces " to be bought, for, she
says, " one must not rush into this business of slave-purchasing, for they
have to be very good if one is to give for them the money one is asked. . . .
It makes one grieve to pay three hundred pesos for slaves which you cannot
use for more than eight years, and the black woman could hardly bring forth
many young ". Then, with no transition: " My father asks me how many
mules I have, and their ages, for he has heard about some. I told him that
when you came I should give him an individual account of each."

The style is harder, more direct, more businesslike than that of her high-
falutin' husband. She counts the value of the negress as a mother of future
slaves, and she knows every individual mule. Even on matters of religion
one feels that what she says in her will about her beliefs and the mysteries
is copied from that of her husband, and in fact cut down and simplified. In
her letter to her brother, her references to religion have a curious touch of
accountancy: " Juancho left because María de Jesús is expecting her confinement very soon, and I am well, I believe altogether recovered, thank God;
all the same, I have to pay for it by wearing religious dress, to prevent evil
effects; but I shall put it on willingly."

It is hazardous to attempt to build up a character on two documents.
Moods vary, and the most spontaneous document may not catch the mood
of the moment in which it is written. Yet, the one letter of Doña Concepción
which has come down to us is so full of life, that a number of the features it
suggests remain impressed on our imagination. Bolívar's mother lived in
her day, saw to her task, stood no nonsense and had no use for abstractions.
She was positive, practical and took her family, her wealth, her slaves and
her religion as a matter of course. She must have been a good mother,
neither too hard nor too tender, and an excellent housekeeper and manager
of her estates.

All this suggests a certain matter-of-factness about slaves, though not
necessarily ill-treatment. We know from Humboldt that, in general, the
treatment of slaves was better in Spanish than in other lands; and by his
will, Colonel Bolívar declared free three of his personal slaves and left his
clothes to one of them. Therefore the tradition of both the country and
the family seems to have been favourable to a good, homely atmosphere
with regard to the slaves. All this must be borne in mind when discussing
a point which bears directly on Bolívar's upbringing and character—but
the point must be discussed. In his *Defence of Bolívar*, Simón Rodríguez
writes " The Populace says . . . that when he was a child, he amused
himself killing little negroes with his penknife; that his mother pleased him
in this; and that when her son cried, she came out on the balcony and
shouted to her slaves: ' This child has nothing to play with; he has no more
little negroes: go to the estate and fetch him some! ' " Our first reaction is
to dismiss the subject as ridiculous. But brushing aside the caricature,
could there be something in it ? When Simón Rodríguez wrote his *Defence*,
both sides were exaggerating: Bolívar's enemies, particularly in Peru, were

piling accusations against him, some fairly well grounded, others wild; and Simón Rodríguez himself, in his pamphlet, took pleasure in repeating the wildest in even wilder terms the better to refute them. This particular one, he does not refute at all. He is content to state it in his inimitable, comic style as a parody.

But a parody of what? We do not know. Slave children may or may not have been given to little Simón to play with. Terrible as it sounds, we have no right, in view of Simón Rodríguez' indirect revelation, to dismiss the subject as an impossibility. For, as a matter of fact, we know that the habit existed in the English colonies of the New World. Charles Wesley noted it in Charlestown in his entry for Monday, August 2nd, 1736. " I had observed much, and heard more, of the cruelty of masters towards their negroes; but now I received an authentic account of some horrid instances thereof. The giving a child a slave of his own age to tyrannize over, to beat and abuse out of sport, was, I myself saw, a common practice."

It is a far cry from Charlestown to Caracas; but the fact that human nature cannot be trusted with absolute power does not depend on latitudes. The little we know of Doña Concepción does not suggest a faith alive enough, sensitive enough to react against such tendencies, if they existed in her son. The possibility of a certain amount of inconsiderate and despotic treatment of small slaves by their little master and their future *Libertador* cannot be altogether excluded. " Less than eight days ago "—wrote María Antonia Bolívar to her illustrious brother (29.i.25)—" I had to thrash one of the carpenters who came to repair the sugar engine for he said to me a number of insolent things which his foolishness suggested to him, but as I have sworn to allow insults from no one I seized hold of a yardstick and split his head open, and then had him beaten by my servants."

Doña Concepción had agreed to send her brother Esteban to Madrid to negotiate the grant of the marquisate to her elder son Juan Vicente. This decision may not have been wholly spontaneous. There are a number of clues to the growing intrusion of her family into the affairs of her children. Some of these clues can be found in her will. Her good father takes great care to see that his word is accepted as final in his accounts between him and his daughter and grandchildren; and her brothers are described as managers of one or other of the estates of either young Juan Vicente or Simón, and seem to be doing very well out of it. Doña Concepción evidently had a soft spot in her heart for her father and brothers who, in their turn, saw to it that her tenderness yielded them as much profit as possible. Esteban's journey to Spain and his long residence there should be seen in this light. The claim to the marquisate afforded an excellent reason-pretext for financing the young man at the expense of Juan Vicente; and Esteban's eagerness to decorate Simón with the title of Count of Casa Palacios may well have been an elegant device for carrying on his costly life at Court at the expense of his younger nephew, when the elder had already become a marquess.

All this evidently implied a certain amount of tacit complicity on the part of Doña Concepción, who possibly thought her sons' estates rich enough to carry her brothers on their backs without undue strain. It also implied a

certain common ground as to tastes, views and prejudices.   We know from a
letter of Esteban to his sister that she had advised him to seek a commission
in the King's Bodyguard.   It was the first letter he wrote on landing in
Spain and it contains a " reserved " paragraph that gives an excellent
summary of both family and national tensions: " *Reserved.*—I believe that,
if I am not mistaken, no one would benefit more than you by settling in
Spain, for the sake of both your health and the welfare of your children;
this is a most pleasant land, which I had forgotten, and as soon as I landed
I felt as if I had been born here, and forgetting love of country (though
not of home) I felt the most vivid desire to stay, but in some honourable
occupation . . . and the one I should select is that of Guard of the Body,
following your advice which I remember you gave me to that effect before
my departure, and also because I should thus be one of the members of the
Palace household which would enable me more easily to transact the business
which brought me here.   I have practically made up my mind to ask for
the Bandoleer as soon as I arrive in Madrid, assuming, of course, that you
help.   The Guards are to-day the most brilliant corps.   The mere fact of
joining entails a commission as sublieutenant and their salary has been
increased to half a peso a day; well, I wonder whether I shall get it.   I have
no idea whether my father may frown at it, and as for your coming to Spain,
should you ever do so, do not give me away as the author of the idea, for I
am aware of my country's way of thinking."

6

Doña Concepción died at the age of thirty-three on July 6th, 1792.   Her
father, Don Feliciano Palacios y Sojo remained at the head of the household.   He seems to have been a shrewd and active man, who knew where his
interests lay and had a keen family sense, though Esteban, his own son, was
inclined to criticize his lack of knowledge of the world.   He began by getting
rid of his two granddaughters.   Within the same year of their mother's
death he married them: María Antonia, who was fifteen, to Don Pablo
Clemente Palacios, and Juana, not yet fourteen, to Don Dionisio de Palacios
Blanco.   He writes to his son Esteban declaring himself delighted to be
rid of their money affairs, for on October 13th the young ladies were each
in her own new home.   The household was left practically womanless.
Simón Bolívar was nine.

BOLÍVAR—at the time of his marriage

BOLÍVAR'S FATHER—
Don Juan Vicente de Bolívar y Ponte

BOLÍVAR'S SISTER—
Juana

BOLÍVAR'S THIRD TUTOR—
Simon Rodriguez

CHARLES IV AND FAMILY (detail), by Goya (Prado, Madrid)

CHAPTER IV

THE MENTAL SKIES

I

THIS fact, that the home in which Bolívar grew up was motherless and sisterless from 1792, when he was nine, may not have received all the attention it deserves. Juan Vicente was eleven and *Simoncito* was nine when they were left in the care of their grandfather Don Feliciano Palacios. The two sisters were married the same year; the three young aunts soon after. Something must have ceased to grow in them at this time—a fact full of destiny for one of them and for the world. The underworld of common memories which they had brought to life from their father and mother was thus gradually closed to the light of the sun, and sank below their mental view, to be buried under new forms, habits and ideas.

Between their deeper selves and the daily world around nothing remained but the old man. He also was imbued with traditional principles and ways; but he was more distant, unable to fathom the two tender natures two generations away from him. In March, 1792, he writes to his son Esteban on privileges and the search Esteban is to make about the blue blood of both Bolívars and Palacios. Esteban imparts to him that his title as Alférez Real had been extended; " with the same privileges contained in the *Cédula* when it was first granted; I am infinitely glad "—his son adds—" because it will greatly please Your Worship, and all those who are envious will be disappointed ". Don Feliciano writes that he is working on his papers and on those of his grandson Juan Vicente, which will take more time, " because they have to be prepared by the *Audiencia*, and I do not know how we are going to put right the knot of the Marín woman ". On this Marín woman, more hereafter.

He was very pleased when his son had " the felicity " of becoming a Royal Guard in the special American company which was being organized at the request of " some rich Americans who reside at Court ". He wants a military order, and is sending an application, on the basis of " the modest deserts of my house and person and of yours ", and owns to some misgivings as to the difficulties which might arise in proving the purity of his blood, " which would be very painful to me ". But this and his other troubles all came suddenly to an end with his life (5.xii.93). The two boys were left isolated in their orphanhood.

2

Clause 57 of Don Feliciano's will reveals that he had consulted both boys as to who should be their guardian, and that neither had chosen Carlos, their elder uncle. When it came to " my grandson Don Simón de Bolívar " then eleven, " having asked him whom of his relations would he like for a tutor he answered as if he had already well thought it over that he wanted his uncle Don Esteban Palacios y Blanco ". Now Esteban was already in Spain. This shows that *Simoncito* did not hold his uncle Carlos in high esteem. Carlos was not the kind of man to impress his young nephew. Lazy, ungenerous and inefficient, he did not administer his nephews' fortune with a true sense of responsibility, and looked upon his wards partly as ewe lambs to fleece, partly as a nuisance to be put down. Esteban, who seems to have inherited more of his father's earnestness than any of his brothers, though not quite his upright ways, sends advice from Madrid—some of it straight, some merely worldly. Maria Antonia's husband, egged on by his father Don Manuel Francia, set eyes on the boys' estates as soon as their grand-father died, and tried to have a finger in that succulent pie. Esteban wrote to Carlos (31.x.95) that this revealed in the house of Francia " very humble beginnings, little shame, no honour, an unrestrained ambition ". His advice was drastic: " Rather destroy the income of the ward in proving your rights than allow those rascals to laugh at you ". He had perhaps forgotten that on May 23rd of the same year he had written to his brother Carlos this " confidential paragraph ". " I believe, my dear brother, that you will not waste time in taking advantage of the opportunity to foster the interests of your estates in every possible way now that you have money in hand; bear in mind that that is what suits you, and you should feel neither doubt nor fear in starting any enterprise which, given your skill and capacity in land cultivation, would no doubt get you the money back and the account would be correct "; after which encouragement to speculate with the capital of his wards he urges his brother to extend a similar protection to his own estates.

Esteban does not trust his brother's sense. " I keep thinking with much anxiety about the education of the boys and particularly about that of Simón " —a preference due to his being Simón's godfather, but possibly also to the early signs of outstanding intelligence the younger boy had evinced. And he objects to Carlos' plan to move to the house left to Simón by Father Aristeguieta, pointing out that the house had better earn its five hundred pesos a year; this will prevent " public criticism against you for taking advantage of the boy's trusteeship to live in his house; let alone that these boys are still growing and without any social duties, and therefore should live in modest houses during their minor years, while, if they get used from now to luxury and ostentation, it might be their ruin."

The two brothers are equally solicitous to get from their brother-in-law, Juan Felix Palacios, tutor of Juan Vicente, the expenses incurred by Esteban in relation to the marquisate, which both think should be paid out of the estate of their young nephew. In a letter on that point where Carlos complains of the " temerities of our brother-in-law and tutor of Juan Vicente ", he informs Esteban that he has been able to come to an agree-ment with their sister's husband. The whole tone of this correspondence shows a coldness towards the youngsters which they must have felt.

The two brothers Palacios were then living in the twilight of loyalties typical of their times. As soon as their father died, Carlos asked Esteban to

obtain for him the title of Royal Ensign which his father had displayed; and
Esteban was able to announce success, though he now airs a certain scepticism
about these honours " which only bring about expenses and heavy obligations ".   Esteban is getting disgruntled and somewhat disheartened despite
the enthusiasm with which he had arrived in Spain.   " I am serving the
King as a Royal Guard with no other hope than that of fulfilling the obligation laid on me by my upbringing and my birth "; and he adds: " Such is
the constitution of the men who allow themselves to be carried away by vain
glory."   He repeats that his brother should not trouble to take on the
dignity of Royal Ensign and goes on to say: " How I realize now the lack
of knowledge of the world in which our parents lived! "   Yet, in the same
letter, he suggests that, were Carlos to be able to place in Madrid ten to
twelve thousand pesos, he might get a commission as colonel, and even he
himself might also try this.

It is significant of this " twilight " period in which he writes that he feels
doubts when putting forward his proposal, not only because he does not
know how his brother stands in the matter of money, but because he does
not know what his brother's " way of thinking at present " will be.   Carlos
may at times have found it unpleasant to kow-tow to the Spanish authorities
in Caracas, for Esteban writes: " though you may find it unbearable to
bow your head, one must do so in circumstances such as this, and far more
so among the intrigue-loving peoples of America "—a point he makes again
and again in other letters.   He assures Carlos he might have had an Order
had he asked for it, and announces that he himself has been appointed a
Minister of the Auditing Tribunal, a real mark of favour; but he protests
against the decision of Juan Vicente's tutor to give up the hunt for the
marquisate at the time when, he vouches, it was nearly granted.   Carlos,
meanwhile, asked for a commission as captain (1.viii.98), fully aware that
the sudden access of good luck on the part of Esteban came from the fact
that Manuel Mallo, a countryman of theirs, had suddenly risen in the Queen's
favour.   On February 10th, 1799, Esteban announced that in August of the
previous year he had already sent commissions as captain for Carlos, as
lieutenant for Juan Vicente and as sub-lieutenant for young Simón who was
then fourteen years of age.

3

Bolívar's first nurse had been a lady of Cuban extraction, a close friend of
his mother, Doña Inés Mancebo, wife of Don Fernando de Miyares, later a
Governor of Maracaibo and a Governor General of Venezuela.   Following
a Creole custom Bolívar's mother, unable to nurse her baby, asked her
friend, at the time nursing one of her own, to mother little Simón also while
a wet nurse was found for him.   In later years Bolívar kept intact his respect
and affection for this lady, although she remained invariably attached to the
cause of Spain.   When the estates of all European Spaniards were being
confiscated by the patriots, he wrote to Colonel Pulido, Governor of Barinas
(18.viii.13), to prevent the confiscation of the Bocomi estate belonging to

Doña Inés Mancebo: "All you will do in favour of this lady will fit the gratitude which a heart such as mine knows how to preserve towards the person who fed me like a mother. It was she who during the first months of my life took me to her bosom. What better recommendation than this for a man who knows how to love and be grateful?" But Bolívar seems to have had no more than an intermittent and distant acquaintance with Doña Inés. Not so with his permanent nurse, the black slave Hipólita from the San Mateo estate, who was twenty-eight and was valued at three hundred pesos in 1791. As late as 1825 he wrote to his elder sister: "I enclose a letter from my mother Hipólita so that you give her all she wants and deal with her as if she were my mother: her milk fed my life and I knew no other father than she."

Hipólita had therefore been both father and mother to him. How strong was the "pull" which she had on him would appear from an anecdote related by Rojas: When Bolívar entered Caracas in triumph on January 10th, 1827, he saw Hipólita in the crowd. At once, he left his exalted place in the procession and threw himself in the arms of the negress, who wept for joy. The maternal bond is evident. But the paternal? "I have known no other father than she." This is a twofold revelation: Simón Bolívar had kept no conscious memory of his father, whom he had lost at the age of three; and none of the men around him had won a masculine authority over him such as this black woman had achieved. This woman and his mother must therefore have been his strongest links with the past.

His roots were bound to be complex. His blood was mixed; and though it was so very slightly, matters of character and spirit can hardly be determined by quantitative laws. Though the drops of Indian and black blood in his veins may have been few, were indeed few, the tensions which these drops brought to his inner structure were probably high—for he was high-pitched by nature. Add to it this two-coloured feminine influence on the still tender, self-ignorant body-soul, hailing back to two different worlds of memory, Christian Spain and pagan Africa; and the early disappearance of both, owing to the death of his mother and to the almost certain return of his black nurse to other more productive work as soon as the boy grew out of the nursery age—the gradual sinking of all this warm, vague, unprofiled, unspoken world of sensations and memories into a past denied access to the sun of the new days.

4

Fact and fancy have been woven in the current notions about Bolívar's teachers. The best sources allow only three figures to stand out among them. "It is not true"—Bolívar wrote to Santander on May 20th, 1825—"that my education was neglected, for my mother and my tutors did all they could to instruct me: they procured me first-rate teachers in my country. Robinson, whom you know, was my teacher in reading and writing and grammar; geography and literature were taught by the famous Bello; a special academy of mathematics was set up by Father Andújar, so much esteemed by Humboldt, only for me." This text, however, must be read bearing in mind that Bolívar was seldom able to be accurate. He himself says so, and proves it, in this very letter. " I am accused of being diffuse: it would be better to say that I am not accurate, for I really am not, because I am rash, careless and impatient." And he proves it when he says that he " was taught foreign languages with select teachers in Madrid "; for we know he was taught no other language than French.

An academy was set up in order to teach him mathematics, if by " academy " we understand a purely private institution. Such an academy or rather class of mathematics had been opened in 1798 by the Aragonese friar Andújar; classes were given in young Simón's own house. Father Andújar does not seem to have made as deep an impression on his mind as the other two men he mentions. Andrés Bello was hardly two years his senior; yet must have been much more developed mentally, to judge by Bolívar's own words about him in later life: " I know the superiority of this Caraqueño my contemporary; he was my teacher when we were of the same age, and I loved him with respect." Born in Caracas, it was also in Caracas that Bello was educated. He learned Humanities under Father Cristóbal de Quesada, philosophy in the Seminary of Santa Rosa, under a priest, " the kind, affectionate, and scholarly Montenegro "; and mathematics and physics at the University. Bello was a first-rate mind and was to leave an outstanding name in South American letters. According to Bolívar, Bello taught him geography and *belles lettres*. Despite his youth, Andrés Bello was a mind more solid than brilliant. There must have come a moment when the pupil felt he had to choose between Bello and his other teacher, Rodríguez or Carreño; for no compromise was possible between the romantic Roussellian optimist and the classic Catholic pessimist. Simón Bolívar was to write in later years: " His asperity has kept us apart up to a point, and that is why I desire to reconcile myself with him, that is, to win him back for Colombia."

Simón Carreño Rodríguez, *alias* Robinson, the third teacher of Bolívar, and most important of the three, was the younger brother of Cayetano Carreño, the composer. Born in 1771, he can hardly have taught Bolívar his " first letters ", for by April, 1792, when Bolívar was nearly nine, the teacher was unknown to Esteban Palacios, Bolívar's uncle, then sailing for Spain; and surely by then little Simón could read and write. But the influence of Simón the Elder on Simón the Younger had little to do with what children are taught at school. His biographers make much of his ideas on education, embodied in a Memoir he presented to the Council of Caracas under the title of *Reflections on the Defects which vitiate the primary school of Caracas and a way to reform them by means of a new establishment;* some authors even surmise that he was chosen as tutor by *Simoncito's* trustees because of his " modern " views on education. In fact he did not enter the family as a teacher at all but as an amanuensis. He struck Simón's grandfather, Don Feliciano, as an honest man and a good administrator. Though only twenty-one, he had travelled in Europe and, back in Caracas, had married a María Ronco; she gave him two children whom he named

Maize and Tulip. This was one of his many eccentricities. " Bolívar's tutor "—writes the Mexican historian Carlos Pereyra—" opens in the History of America a series of imitation-men who, fascinated by some man of universal fame, are not content with following or imitating him, but endeavour to reproduce him altogether. There is the Napoleon I, the Napoleon III, the Victor Hugo, the Taine, the Renan and the Nietzsche of every village. Simón Rodríguez wandered about the two worlds, living on the trade of Rousseau without the *Contrat*."

This is shrewdly observed. It is said that, as a protest because his brother insisted on saying grace before meals, he decided to drop his father's name Carreño and take that of his mother, Rodríguez. But there is more to it than that. When in 1797 he left his country, having been denounced to the authorities as a conspirator, he took the name of Samuel Robinson. He delighted in these changes, and travelled through names as he travelled through countries; but though he was eccentric enough, there was again more to it than mere eccentricity. Bolívar himself provides the key in a letter to Cayetano Carreño. " Your brother is the best man in the world, but as he is a cosmopolitan philosopher, he has neither a country nor a home nor a family nor anything."

This feature was to exert a profound influence on the young soul of Bolívar. Rodríguez was to incarnate for him a world poles apart from that tradition in which he had grown and which, now, in his womanless, fatherless home, was rapidly sinking under his conscious self. To this highly intelligent boy, Simón Carreño or Rodríguez brought a new world: the world of ideas. It was like a sky of glorious and luminous clouds over a treeless and solitary landscape. Justice, liberty, equality, republic, education, posterity, fraternity, nature, goddesses of the mind, mistresses of the heart, raised by the omniscient youth of twenty-one before the fiery eyes and glowing imagination of the child of eleven. Of all these new deities, one must have appealed to the keen child more than any other, for he was Spanish, and he felt himself hemmed in by traditions. Liberty! Away with all chains! No family. No home. No religion. No saints. Not even in one's name, whereas he had a rosary of saints for a name ending in la *Santísima Trinidad*. Vegetables as Christian names. Cynicism instead of reverence, a cynicism even about the most sacred things, even when uncalled-for. This family, so steeped in their genealogy had a tutor-secretary who thought it witty to say that he had not known his father, but knew very well a friar who visited his mother. And yet he was a legitimate child.

It is unlikely that this cynical thought was ever uttered as early as when, between twenty-one and twenty-six, Simón Carreño was teaching Simón Bolívar, himself between nine and fourteen. But the tendency was there. It meant rebellion against authority, anarchy against order, rationalism against religion, abstract thought against organic tradition, freedom for the self against inner and outer bonds. Yet the Roussellian Simón had his faith also, his ideals, and his proud and straightforward soul. Bolívar never wrote a word about his old teacher which did not express an almost unbounded admiration. Carreño was a crank and possibly a man playing a stage-part; but there was in him a core of honesty and disinterestedness which Bolívar was bound to observe. In 1824 he wrote to Santander: " He is a genius, a marvel of grace; I love him to the point of distraction." At the summit of his glory, he wrote to his old teacher on learning that he had just returned to the fatherland. " You formed my heart for liberty, for justice, for the great, for the beautiful. . . . You cannot imagine how deeply your lessons impressed themselves into my heart. Always present before my intellectual eyes I have followed them as infallible guides."

Carreño's was the strongest of the influences which formed Simón Bolívar. " Always present before my intellectual eyes "—it is admirably said, for it conveys the abstract character of this influence. It is this somewhat super-imposed, man-made idealism which comes to light in a magnificent sentence, truly Bolivarian in its force. " Come to me," says Bolívar to his old master, and " you will be enraptured beholding the immense fatherland you will find carved in the rock of despotism by the victorious chisel of the liberators." This child of the old Spanish Indies, with a world of ancestry under him— a world of friars and conquerors, of slave owners and planters, of Indian serfs and black slaves, living in an order of power, tradition and faith, this child deeply rooted in that earth in which an old and stubborn tradition of incredible strength lay buried, owed to the ambulant philosopher his light, his sky, his meteors and his clouds—the whole intellectual world of ideas and ideals spread like a glorious canopy over his head. And between that heaven and that earth—men crawling.

CHAPTER V

THE TIMES

I

WHEN Colón set foot on Guanahani he solemnly took possession of the new continent he had discovered in the name of Ferdinand and Isabel. This ceremony was repeated by every Spanish discoverer or conqueror who followed in Colón's steps. But men cannot take possession of a land without that land taking possession of them. And this come-back of the continent, whereby the conquerors were conquered by their conquest, is the chief process that during three centuries controls the evolution of the Spanish Empire. During these three centuries, two antagonistic forces are at work in the Indies: one a yearning upwards of the white blood, endeavouring to remain white by drawing as close as possible to the source and origin of its whiteness—Spain; the other the attraction of the earth, dragging the whites downwards towards the Indian and the black roots that link them with the land they had conquered and wished to rule from above, but which was conquering them and seeking to rule them from below.

At the time of Simón Bolívar's birth the second of these two forces is winning fast over the first. The white yearning towards Spain—sun and sky of the mental-moral landscape of the Indies—has gradually been deflected to other skies and other suns, as the traditional force of the faith and of the royal prestige of the Crown waned. The Creoles became philosophers and philanthropists. What Carreño was to be for Bolívar, the four philosophers, Montesquieu, Voltaire, Rousseau and Raynal, had been for thousands of keen American Spanish intellects. The ferment thus stimulated, stirred for different reasons by Jews, Freemasons and Jesuits, was to rise to explosive point under the example of the three revolutions—American, French and Negro.

Bolívar was born the very year the powers signed the treaty of Versailles in which the independence of the British American colonies was recognized. In that war, Spanish troops had fought with the rebels against the King of England, thus affording a dangerous example to the future rebels against the King of Spain. *Simoncito* was six when the French Revolution began; and that mighty European event unfolded its dramatic episodes during the ten years he lived in Caracas—1789–99—mostly under the influence of the revolutionary Simón Carreño. Finally the sanguinary events of Haiti, which set up a black republic, the first independent American nation after the United States, took place during the same years at close range of the youth's observation. All these events were to raise waves of political commotion in Venezuela under his very eyes between his eleventh and his fourteenth year.

2

He was eleven when, in his own city of Caracas, a free *zambo*, José Leonardo Chirinos, was executed and his head exhibited in an iron cage on top of a twenty-foot mast on the road leading to Coro and the valleys of Aragua where his S. Mateo estates lay. Chirinos had been one of the two leaders of a negro rebellion which had shaken the peace of the valley of Curimagua, in the Sierra of Coro. The other leader was a negro born in Africa, brought as a slave to Curaçao, and let loose in Venezuela where, *ipso facto*, he became free. This man (possibly landed in Venezuela precisely so that he could act as he did) became a kind of legal adviser to the blacks, among whom he spread " the law of the French " whereby political power was supposed to pass to the negroes. In the confused state of loyalties typical of the period, the whites played both the part of involuntary instigators and of victims of the rising. It was a local rebellion, in an area which counted about three thousand slaves out of the sixty thousand registered in Venezuela; and the militant rebels were no more than one hundred and fifty, poorly armed; but for a time they held the field by sheer terror. The local Lieutenant-Justice with ninety-one citizens reduced them to obedience in the end, and the black danger blew over.

3

Hardly dry the blood shed by this incident, much ink was spilt in the *cabildo* of Caracas, and much oratory flowed in its debates as a protest against a Royal *Cédula* of January 10th, 1795, whereby coloured persons were admitted to public offices on payment of relatively light sums—seven hundred to fourteen hundred reales. The *mantuanos* were incensed. They argued that such people had against them " the infamous origin of slavery, and the low origin of illegitimacy ". Carlos de Palacios y Blanco, head of Bolívar's home, was, as one of the *regidores* or aldermen of Caracas, one of the leaders of this protest. Simón Bolívar must have heard the passionate arguments which the *cabildo* brandished and finally wrote down on its records (14.iv.96); while Carreño would listen in sullen silence and possibly comment on them with his pupil in their long free walks. The *cabildo* recalled the supplication it had submitted to the King (13.x.88) to the effect that the privilege of marrying white persons and of taking holy orders, solicited by some coloured persons, should be denied them; and that, once these people were admitted to public offices reserved for " the whites and principal persons of the highest distinction in the republic, there would be no one ready to accept service in such public offices "; the *cabildo* deprecated that such equality should be granted to " low people who make up the greater part of the cities, and are by their nature proud, ambitious of honours and seeking to be the equals of the whites, despite the lower class in which they were placed by the author of nature ". Shrewdly working on the fears of the Crown, the *regidores* went on to ask: " How is it possible that the Crown should entrust national security and the defence of its rights to men who, far from looking towards Spain as the centre of their happiness, must perforce look towards the dark inhabitants of Africa whence they come to protect them and to set them in rebellion against the Spaniards, from whom they say they have received much injury ? "

These and similar arguments were sure to resound in Simón Bolívar's home, for the leaders of the protest of the whites against the equalitarian tendencies of the Crown were all men of his class, family and circle of friendships—chief of them his uncle Carlos, and the Marqués de Toro, both signatories of the petition eventually sent to the King (28.xi.96). Fearful, not merely of the rise of the coloured classes to public offices, but even of their growing hold on the arts and crafts, the *mantuanos* asked the King to force the coloured people to work in the fields, to limit their access to the crafts, and to break up the coloured militia into small formations. The King's answer was unfavourable to the *mantuanos*, and admitted coloured persons to practically every craft or office on payment of small sums. But when this answer reached Caracas, Simón Bolívar had already left his native city.

4

While the noblemen of Caracas were thus busy defending their privileges, their country lost an invaluable territory. On February 16th, 1797, an English force took the Island of Trinidad. England was at war with Spain. The Island, happy and prosperous till 1727, had been ruined by a pest of the cocoa plant, and by 1773 counted no more than a thousand inhabitants. A Royal *Cédula* (c.ix.76) granting lands to all Catholic foreigners who would settle there, and annexing it to the *Intendencia* of Caracas, was widely circulated in the Islands in both French and English; and a Frenchman from Grenada, Roume de Saint Laurent, drew up a plan for colonizing the Island with Frenchmen and their slaves. Within a few years the population had risen to 10,422, mostly Frenchmen with a sprinkling of Englishmen and Irishmen. The creative mind behind this activity was the new Governor, a naval officer, José María Chacón; the technician, an officer of Royal Engineers, José del Pozo y Sucre, an American Spaniard, who was to be in later years one of Miranda's collaborators in the negotiation with Pitt.

All came to grief as a result of the French Revolution. Not the least of Chacón's merits had been to have preserved the Island in quiet and safety during the years when Spain was at war with France, for nearly all the inhabitants were French, and most of them in sympathy with the revolution. But in 1796 Godoy went over to the French side and declared war on England (5.x). The first move of the British was an attack on Trinidad, which they had been preparing for months. Despite Chacón's repeated and timely warnings, the Island was not fortified. Admiral Apodaca had arrived in Trinidad towards the beginning of September with four of the line, one frigate and a brigantine, and some troops. An outbreak of yellow fever caused havoc among the newcomers and killed more than a third of them. Against this nearly helpless garrison, Admiral Harvey sailed with 59 ships, 1,244 guns and 6,750 men, including 1,700 Germans, under the command of General Abercromby.

The first ships were sighted on February 16th, 1797. Soon after Apodaca's ships were sealed off at Chaguaramas harbour and separated from Chacón's land forces in Port of Spain. Apodaca decided to try to escape if the wind were favourable; but it was not, and in fulfilment of the navy's regulations, he burnt his ships and took his forces by land over to Port of Spain. The British landed on February 17th. The French inhabitants, though allies of Spain, did not fight. Chacón had 600 men in all, more than 200 of whom were convalescent from the recent scourge. Arming coloured men was out of the question, for they were for the most part slaves brought over from foreign islands by their owners who had come to settle in Trinidad, and the Governor feared excesses such as those of the negro revolution of Haiti. On February 18th Chacón capitulated.

Trinidad became the basis of operations for the British in their endeavours to undermine the hold of Spain over her kingdoms beyond the seas. This was often clothed under words such as " emancipation " and " independence ". There may have entered a certain modicum of genuine " philanthropic " emotions (as the phrase then ran) in some of the British endeavours to " free " Spanish America from Spain. But the first Governor that England appointed in Trinidad to succeed the liberal and intelligent Chacón was the notorious Picton, whom Wellington describes as " a rough, foulmouthed devil as ever lived ". This Picton introduced torture in the Island and executed several negroes for witchcraft—a practice unknown in the Spanish Indies. It is also relevant to bear in mind in this connection that Sir Ralph Woodford, the third Governor, on taking office in 1813, wrote to Earl Bathurst the following significant words referring to the *cabildo* of Trinidad: " As it became indispensible [*sic*] to ascertain the power claimed, and duties exercised, by that Board, I required a statement thereof, but as they take their origin from the Spanish Law, which authorizes a *Cabildo* wherever there is a town sufficiently Peopled, they do not act under any other Charter or Instructions other than the Laws in general, and in which I apprehend they are not very intimately acquainted. . . . Their powers however as a deliberative body are very considerable, and such as I apprehend will greatly exceed your Lordship's views—but as a municipality they would be very useful if they were inclined to exert themselves in their duties. They consider themselves as the representatives of the People, and the Spanish Law authorizes them to question any act involving their interests."

It is therefore unlikely that any one outside the Spanish-American separatists swallowed the abundant professions for the freedom of Spanish America which Dundas (later Lord Melville) circulated precisely through Picton, the Governor of Trinidad. The actual positive form the future Spanish America was to take was not then—if it ever was—defined in British policy. This policy, for the time being, was content with loosening the ties between American and European Spaniards. Such was the chief task entrusted to Picton, to whom Dundas wrote (8.iv.97) promising help to all Spanish Americans who would rebel against their King and assuring them that the intention of His Majesty's Government was " merely to enable them to maintain their commercial independence, without any desire on the part of the King of England to acquire any Right of Sovereignty over them, or to interfere in their Civil, Political or Religious Rights; unless they themselves should in any degree sollicit this Protection ". This last reservation was as broad a hint as could be heard by any ear but that of Miranda, who in those days was plotting in London through Picton and Pitt.

Why " commercial " independence ? Because it was mostly on commerce that disaffection could as yet be based. For this reason, Britain took great care that trade relations between the mainland and the Islands, British, French or of other nations, went on unmolested, though in most cases, illegally. This was done even when, to that effect, it became necessary to leave in abeyance the " emancipation " of the Spanish Americans. When Carlos Palacios wrote to Esteban (28.vi.97) about the " infinite calamities this province has undergone and is undergoing on account of the war with the English", he was official rather than sincere, for Venezuela did a roaring trade in contraband. Young Simón must have lived all this, for it was his cocoa and his indigo that brought in the money, through Port of Spain, Demerara and Kingston.

5

Before his departure for New Spain and Old Spain, Bolívar witnessed the most serious of the risings which took place in his country, before his own. It was engineered by European Spaniards, who had been transported from Spain after their conviction as republican conspirators. The Crown itself exported the true revolutionary spirit to its own kingdoms beyond the seas, after giving them the unwise example of backing the North American rebels against the Crown of England. On February 17th, 1796, a number of Spanish republicans had attempted a revolution, then, of course, premature. They were sentenced to death, reprieved, and three of them transported to a fortress in La Guaira. There was freemasonry under it all, and the three Spaniards, Picornell, Cortés and Andrés, the three guests of His Spanish Majesty, became with the connivance of the authorities the honoured hosts of many a young revolutionary Creole. On June 4th, 1796, the prisoners vanished, and Picornell turned up in Guadalupe, where he published a translation of the *Rights of Man and of the Citizen*, and a revolutionary song, *The American Carmagnole*. The three Spaniards had brought to Venezuela a new spirit foreign to the Creole way of life: the equalitarian and abstract spirit of the French Revolution, which few men outside Carreño could then conceive, let alone accept. The enquiry into the conspiracy made by the *Audiencia* brought to light other contributory causes of the same kind: the arrival in La Guaira of French prisoners previously held in Santo Domingo and of many French émigrés who had left Trinidad for Caracas on the English taking possession of the Island; as well as the flood of foreign papers with which Caracas was being inundated, mostly by Picton.

The first truly equalitarian rebellion to take place in Venezuela was that which these movements of European origin stimulated in conjunction with Picton and with the British Consul in Cádiz, Gough. Mulattoes were implicated in it from the outset; the three Spaniards had fled under the protection of a mulatto sergeant who was supposed to guard them. It was another mulatto, a barber named Juan José Chirinos, who passed the fact on to the authorities. By July the conspiracy had failed and Carbonell, the Captain General, reported that " a considerable number of persons of all classes, one cleric, officers, sergeants, corporals and veteran soldiers, lawyers, landed men and private citizens, had been arrested ". Eventually, over eighty persons were implicated. Ten were transported to Spain, thirteen to Puerto Rico and over sixty were left unpunished. The two chiefs, as yet uncaught, were Don Manuel Gual and Don Joseph María de España. Gual was the scion of a well-to-do family of La Guaira, the eldest son of Don Mateo Gual who had defended the city against Admiral Knowles in 1743. España was the local magistrate in Macuto, the city in which Picornell and Cortés had hidden for two weeks before sailing for Curaçao. Both Gual and España were well educated, and honourable men. Gual had been in touch with Miranda. He was not caught and remained in touch with Miranda until his death in exile. España was caught in 1799 and executed in the Plaza Mayor of Caracas, known to-day as Plaza Bolívar (8.v.99). Simón Bolívar was no longer in Venezuela.

The youth—he was fourteen when the conspiracy was discovered—must have followed the events with a keen interest. The papers found in Gual's house breathed the new, equalitarian spirit which animated the conspirators. Their proclamation began with the words " In the name of the Most Holy Trinity ", which tallied with Bolívar's own family's chief devotion and even with his own Christian name; but it was steeped in the spirit of Rousseau, by then familiar to him, thanks to his tutor Rodríguez. The insignia of the conspirators was white, blue, yellow and red, a symbol of the four colours, the white, the mulatto, the black and the Indian, as well as of the four provinces, Caracas, Maracaibo, Cumaná, Guayana, and of the four principles, Equality, Liberty, Property and Security. The tribute of the Indians and the slavery of the blacks were abolished. Equality of the four colours of men was proclaimed. Harbours were opened to all the nations of the world. Carreño's spirit throughout—young Simón must have thought. And to be sure, in the same July, 1797, in which the conspiracy was discovered, Carreño said farewell to him and fled in a North American ship.

6

This conspiracy that so well embodied the spirit of Simón Bolívar's tutor, was severely condemned by his uncles. Carlos wrote to Esteban the story of the conspiracy in terms which would have angered Simón Carreño and perhaps also Simón Bolívar. " A conspiracy has been found out which had been plotted in La Guaira; its origin: three prisoners of State sent from that Court [Madrid] who had very cleverly escaped to Guadalupe leaving their detestable scheme in charge of four insensate men, and at their head, among others, Don Manuel Gual; and what is worse, in league with that rabble of the mulattoes, and putting forward the detestable system of equality."

Carlos goes on to say that, owing to adequate measures taken by the authorities, the " revolution " seems to be extinguished; then adds a telling detail: " having had the glory that there was no other garrison than the provincial militia, for the few veterans available were mostly scattered about in Santo Domingo, Puerto Cabello, and even those in La Guaira seem to have been contaminated, so that there are some in jail. . . ." This means that the regular soldiers were either away or not trustworthy; and that the authorities had had to rely on the militia organized and led by the local gentry. Hence the " glory " Carlos felt. Nor is that all: " The class of the nobility has fulfilled its duty, hastening to report for service to the Captain General . . . but, in spite of the loyalty showed by the best and soundest part of this people, we fear the consequences for us . . . and I am telling you so that as a good patriot you do all you can to influence those gentlemen there so that we are not taxed afresh on top of our sacrifices, and . . . try to foster the measures likely to secure the ownership of these dominions for the Sovereign, the chief of which is to uphold the class of the nobility and preserve for it the enjoyment of its rights and privileges, a measure which many Spaniards consider as a misplaced quixotism, but which is indispensable in America, since we live sunk in the midst of all this rabble and we have to keep them where they belong, and everyone in his class."

The noblemen of Caracas were however ready to pay for these privileges over the rabble with an equivalent subservience to the King of Spain; and they presented to the Governor (1.viii.97) an official protest against the conspirators in the form of an address to His Majesty. " The nobility of the city of Caracas, united in a body and humbly prostrated at the Royal Feet of Your Majesty " informed the King that they had offered themselves and their fortunes to the Governor who had formed a Company of Noblemen; that as such they had stood sentinel over the conspirators . . . and over the other armed forces in charge of the prison; and that they would " willingly sacrifice all our being, not only in the present circumstances but in any other which might occur to the greater glory and favour of the Royal Name of Your Majesty ". This loyalty, they went on to say, had been strengthened and endowed with new firmness and breath from the events.

This remarkable paper was signed by twenty-eight noblemen of the city headed by Count Tovar, including the Marqués de Toro and Don Manuel Monserrate. Tovar later explained to the Captain General (Carbonell) that there were points in the document with which he disagreed. Toro and Monserrate had spent the night collecting signatures. The paper was not only a protest of loyalty to the King but also an episode in a local feud between the two leading families of Caracas, the Tovars and the Toros, struggling for leadership of the nobility and through it—as they thought— of the country. A similar paper had been signed by even more people, including Carlos Palacios.

All these men who signed papers to the King, but in reality against each other, were Simón Bolívar's relations. In his own house, young Bolívar, then humming with the equalitarian ideas of Rousseau, heard nothing but contempt for the mulatto rabble; yet, many of these local magnates were beginning to find it irksome to depend on an authority so far removed from the scene of their own life.

The situation was clearly seen by Humboldt: " As Caracas is on the mainland and as its population is less mobile than that of the Islands, national habits have been better preserved than in Havana. Society there does not offer very lively or varied pleasures; but one finds in the homes that feeling of well-being which is inspired by a frank gaiety and a cordiality allied with politeness in manners. There are in Caracas, as wherever great changes are being prepared in ideas, two races of men, one might say two generations quite different. One which has remained small in numbers, preserves a keen attachment to the habits of old, to simplicity in ways of living, to moderation in its desires. This kind of men live only in the images of the past. America seems to them the property of their ancestors, who conquered it. Hating what is known as the lights of the century, they preserve their hereditary prejudices with care, as a part of their patrimony. The other kind of men, less concerned with the present than with the future, evinces a fondness, often unreasonable, for new habits and new ideas. When this fondness for the new is combined with love of a solid education, when it is restrained and directed by a strong and enlightened reason, its effects become useful for the community. I have known in Caracas among this second generation, a number of men equally distinguished by their fondness for study, the kindness of their ways and the loftiness of their feelings; I have also known some who, disdaining all that the Spanish character, literature and arts shows of value and of beauty, have lost their national individuality without gaining from their commerce with foreigners, concrete notions on the true bases of happiness and social order."

Young Bolívar was growing out of the first of these two " generations " into the second. His father, mother, grandfather belonged to the first; his uncles also, though not altogether impervious to the ferment of the age. His teacher Carreño belonged to the second and, as time was to show, to that part of it which Humboldt criticized for its " unreasonable fondness for new ideas and ways ". As for Simón Bolívar, he was gradually forming his own system of ideas. When he left La Guaira for his first voyage abroad (19.i.99), Simón Bolívar, at fifteen and a half years of age, was a youth rooted in aristocratic privileges and traditions but dreaming of freedom and revolution; attached to Spain by his deeper self, yet already estranged from Spain by his ideas and purposes.

CHAPTER VI

TO OLD SPAIN THROUGH NEW SPAIN

1

SIMONCITO had expressed his wish to go to Spain when he was eleven. Carlos had considered the matter and requested Esteban to have the boy exempted from the obligation to live in Caracas laid upon him by his uncle's entail. Carlos evidently was thinking of how to get rid of his nephew and ward; Esteban, of the boy's education, as shown in his letters. Thus, in one of June 28th, 1797: " I keep worrying about the education of those two boys and in particular of Simón's." Esteban was especially attached to the younger boy, whose godfather he was. This attachment, reciprocated by the boy, may have been one of the motives of the boy's desire to sail for Spain and away from a house left loveless by the loss of its women. In later years, the *Libertador* at the apex of his glory, on hearing that Esteban had at last returned to Venezuela, was to write to him a letter full of impressions of his childhood. " How many remembrances have flocked to my mind! My mother, my kind mother, so like you, rose again from the tomb and stood before me. My tenderest childhood, my confirmation, and my godfather, came together to tell me you were my second father! My uncles, my brother and sisters, my grandfather, the games of my childhood, the presents you brought me in my innocent days . . . crowded together to excite my first emotions. . . ."

Two were the motives for youths that led the upper Creole classes to wish to go to Spain. One was to perfect their studies. That is precisely the reason Bolívar himself gives for his being sent to Spain. " Later [after his first studies in Caracas] I was sent to Europe to continue my mathematics in the *Academia de San Fernando*, and I learnt foreign languages with picked masters of Madrid."

The voyage to Spain was also a natural stage in the formation of a young Creole. Simón had begun early his ascent on the ladder of honours. On January 14th, 1797, when not yet fourteen, he had been appointed a cadet in the battalion of White Volunteers of the Valley of Aragua, which his father had commanded. On December 31st of the same year, his military record reported: " Courage: assumed. Application: proved. Capacity: good. Behaviour: ditto. Condition: unmarried." On November 26th, 1798, he was promoted sub-lieutenant. Young Bolívar was therefore a regular member of the Spanish nobility overseas. The centre and sun of that nobility was the King of Spain. The capital Madrid. Thither Simón de Bolívar left on January 9th, 1799.

2

The voyage to Spain had to be circuitous, for there was a war on and the English were roaming about in the once Spanish seas. Simón Bolívar left

QUEEN MARIA LUISE, by Goya (Old Pinakothek, Munich)

*DON MANUEL
GODOY, by Goya
(Prado, Madrid)*

La Guaira on board a man-of-war, the *San Ildefonso*, bound for Veracruz. His cabin companion was a youth, Esteban Escobar, sailing for Spain as a King's scholar to enter the artillery corps college at Segovia. Young Bolívar conceived a great friendship and admiration for Captain Uriarte y Borja who commanded the ship, and used to say that his kindness made him worthy of his heavenly relative St. Francis Borja (Borgia). On February 2nd they cast anchor in Veracruz. But their next port of call, Habana, was blockaded by the British, and after a fortnight of enforced idleness Bolívar decided to visit the great capital of New Spain, the then almost fabulous Mexico.

Mexico, the *Morning Post* said on October 15th, 1804, was " the richest and most splendid city in the world, the centre of all that is carried on between America and Europe on one hand, and between America and the East Indies on the other ". A few years earlier it had been visited by Humboldt, who wrote: " The population of Mexico is more unequally distributed even than that of the United States. Civilization is even more unequal. Mexico, the city, has more institutions than Calcutta. There is an Academy of Painting and Sculpture. One can see every day students there drawing from the nude. Its collection of antique modellings is one of the biggest in existence. There is a botanic garden under the direction of Cervantes; a chemical laboratory. Two translations of Lavoisier's Elements of Chemistry have been printed in Mexico, none in Madrid. The new building which the mine owners of Mexico have built for the School of Mines cost them 700,000 pesos, i.e. 3,500,000 francs. The city of Mexico recalls Berlin, but is more beautiful; its architecture is of a more restrained taste. The King of Spain draws from Mexico 6 million pesos only." The Mexican statesman and historian Alamán, writing in 1849, completes the picture of this period of the Mexico Simón Bolívar visited: " Justice was administered with impartiality, though as slowly as was required by the complicated forms then prescribed . . . ; service in the offices was intelligent and efficient, and civil servants paid as much attention to the convenience of the public as to the interests of the Treasury. . . . Even between the coloured peoples and the Spanish race a certain trend towards union had set in and time had obliterated the odious limitations which the laws had imposed on the mulattoes. All this, and the widespread abundance and prosperity, produced a general well-being, nowadays remembered in America as are in ancient Italy the golden age and the reign of Saturn; and people look upon it rather as the fabulous times of our history than as something which actually was or which could possibly have existed."

Schools for the people were fostered, even in the tobacco factories, for the children of the workers to be cared for while their mothers worked. Many cities in New Spain were worth seeing for their fine buildings; but Mexico towered above them all as a truly noble capital, one of the richest in the world, in religious, public and private architecture, as well as in avenues, parks, cleanliness, lighting, thousands of carriages and magnificent horses and horsemen. The gold and silver currency of New Spain was then in keen demand all over the world; and Charles III sent his best engraver to make it as valuable for beauty as it was for its fineness. Public and private libraries were numerous and good and even when, as a result of the French Revolution, a reaction set in, books nominally forbidden circulated hardly less than the others. Luxury was widespread and the rich classes lived in the midst of lavish service, comfort and beauty.

3

It was in this class that Simón Bolívar, aged fifteen and a half, naturally found himself when he visited Mexico in 1799. We know from a letter of his (the oldest extant) that he stayed in the house of the *Oidor* Aguirre, for whom he had a letter of introduction from the bishop of Caracas, Aguirre's uncle. An *oidor* in New Spain was second to none but a Viceroy. It is likely, though not certain, that the *oidor* lived in the house of the Marquesa de Uluapa, one of the palatial houses of the city. The Mexico Simón Bolívar frequented was the most aristocratic and opulent. This word— opulent—will come under his pen in later years whenever he speaks of Mexico: " Opulent Mexico ". When in one of his many flights of imagination, he dreams of a reconstruction (without Spain) of the Empire he first wishes to destroy, he writes: " The metropolis would be Mexico, the only city in a position to be so, owing to its power, without which there can be no metropolis."

Deeply struck though he was with the opulence and the power of Mexico, he took it for granted as if it had been created *ex nihilo* by magic or by miracle. He was too young to realize that all he saw was the flower of three hundred years of creative history. He did not yet possess the insight to realize the human import of what he saw—not merely the wealth, but the manners, the culture, the arts and crafts, all the powers and graces of an advanced civilization fostered in three hundred years of peace: the gold, the silver, the diamonds and the pearls, the fine houses, the china services, the statues, the avenues of trees, the fine buildings of Church, State and nobility, the carriages and the horses, all that for him was just as God-given as the earth, the sky, the rivers and the grass. It just was there, as were the slaves who brought him his iced orangeade or his horse. It need not be discussed. The clever, wealthy lads of his day took their culture as part of the nature in which they themselves flourished, and leant back on their wealth and culture to look at the world and discuss it in the light of the ideas of the century.

What was the talk of Mexico then? In foreign affairs, the war with England and the disconcerting fact that Spain, the metropolis of that splendid continent, proved powerless to keep open the sea lanes of her trade and intercourse with her kingdoms overseas. " Between 1796 and 1801 "— writes Humboldt—" the mother country was unable to introduce more than a yearly average of 2,604,000 pesos of national and foreign goods. And yet in Mexico the stores were full of muslins from India and of English-manufactured goods." This situation was bound to be the talk of the town while Bolívar was in Mexico. There he was, visiting the capital, merely because the British fleet would not let the *San Ildefonso* sail from Veracruz.

Power is power, and this hard fact was bound to sink deep into the mind of Creole and Spaniard alike.

As to home affairs, Mexico was still commenting on the conspiracy against the Crown which had shaken it in 1794; a typically Spanish affair, faithful to the models of indiscipline afforded by the Conquest, and similar to the recent cases of civil war in both Spain and Spanish America. It was the first conspiracy of modern days, and far from originating from the Creoles, it had been conceived and led by European Spaniards. Don Juan Guerrero, its leader, hailed from Estepona in the Kingdom of Granada, Spain, and had come to New Spain by way of the Philippine Islands, as chief accountant of a ship. He had left his ship in Acapulco owing to illness and gone to Mexico City to claim his salary. The viceroy referred him to Manila. Smitten with resentment, Guerrero conceived an ambitious plan: to kidnap the chief military officer of the city, put himself at the head of one hundred and fifty soldiers, force the prison, free and arm the inmates of two prisons, secure the persons of the viceroy and of the archbishop and *oidores*, seize all the cash from the Mint, the Treasury and the wealthiest citizens, hoist a flag above the palace of the viceroy calling on the people to free themselves (he did not know from whom or from what), exempt the Indians from their head taxes and take possession of Veracruz to prevent the news from reaching Spain. He unfolded his plan to a Gallegan priest, whom he promised to make archbishop; and to an Andalusian barber, whom he promised to send as Ambassador to the United States. There were three Mexican accomplices: a retired officer of dragoons, a tobacco guard and another barber. Another Gallegan, a prosperous silversmith, prevailed upon one of the conspirators to confess it all to the archbishop. The case, still *sub judice* when Bolívar was in Mexico, was eventually settled in 1800, on the whole, leniently.

This was the first outburst of separatism in a series which was to make of the kingdom of New Spain the Republic of Mexico. Its features must be noted. The leaders were all European Spaniards. The separatism of these men had no connection with any grievances the Creoles of New Spain might harbour against the Spanish rule. The call to liberty and the remission of the head taxes of the Indians were mere tools for an operation to seize power for personal ends. Finally, the frontier between rebels and royalists did not leave American Spaniards on the one side and European Spaniards on the other; it cut right across the human frontier. These features are constant in the history of the Spanish Indies from the days of Cristóbal Colón to the days of Simón Bolívar—and even to the present day. The wars of emancipation were in fact wars of secession, i.e. Spanish civil wars.

4

On March 20th, 1799, the *San Ildefonso* put to sea to join a convoy due to meet in Habana, which was to sail to Spain under the command of a famous Spanish Admiral, Don Dionisio Alcalá Galiano. The Admiral dodged the British sea-hounds by sailing as far north as Newfoundland, keeping his course to himself and making for the bay of Biscay instead of the Andalusian ports. Bolívar landed in Santoña, went straight to Bilbao and, towards the end of May, 1799, arrived in Madrid. His godfather Esteban Palacios took him to the house of a countryman whose guest he was. This Venezuelan, Don Manuel Mallo, was a young guardsman, one of the many gallants gossip has at one time or another attributed to the Queen. On June 24th, Pedro Palacios, the younger brother of Esteban, arrived from Caracas after an adventurous voyage during which he had been in Puerto Rico and in Lisbon, had been caught by British corsairs who took all he had, and later by a British frigate whose crew behaved correctly. Too numerous for their generous host, the two Palacios brothers and their young nephew took a house of their own, in the *calle de Jardines*.

" Simoncito arrived, ever so handsome, with no education whatever but with parts to acquire it; very much down at heel, for I had to equip him anew "; so wrote Esteban to Carlos (29.vi.99). Simón had travelled in great style. He had borrowed four hundred pesos in Mexico and three thousand reales from the captain of the *San Ildefonso*. Carlos complained bitterly to Esteban: " Simón has spent countless sums superfluously in his voyage and, as I have told you, you must hold him in check, for otherwise he will get used to spending without any rules or economy; and also because he is not as wealthy as he thinks." This way of travelling seems to have been then not merely an indulgence but a kind of obligation for wealthy Creoles.

The situation was bound to weigh on Esteban's mind. He was by nature more earnest and responsible than his brothers. Pedro was gay and reckless. Carlos, very fond of him, praises him above his nephew Simón. All the same, he complains of Pedro's debts.

Those debts were far away and Pedro cared but little for anything but the here and now. Just landed in Lisbon after his adventurous voyages, he writes to Carlos: " On the Spanish consul's desk, on which I am writing, I read a copy of the Madrid *Gazette* and see my promotion to full lieutenant. I need not tell you that I alter my epaulettes at once." He came to Madrid in search of gold braid, Court lustre and enjoyment; and at any rate enjoyment. He sends a good summary of his life in Madrid: " I am reduced to spending most of the time at home reading and about as much in getting acquainted with all that is good in this Court, for, though I fear I may well have to return to America to live my frugal life in the country, I realize that I can hardly induce our brother, whose character is as funereal, retiring and punctilious as it was before he came over, to adventures and pranks which might yield good results."

5

" Pranks ", says Pedro. What pranks ? The many attractions a great city might offer to three young men ? But Pedro is writing on the subject of his advancement; and on the chances of his reaching the giddy heights of favour or of having to recede for life into the obscurity of his cocoa and coffee estates. The same word, prank (*travesura*), turns up in another letter, in a context which might reveal its secret intention. Pedro is writing to Carlos about the retirement of the Minister, Saavedra, whose favours had been for the whole family a source of hope, if not of power. " For the present, I seek nothing more than some adventure that may be going for either of us . . . for though we do enjoy some favour, it is too complicated to be explained in writing; on the other hand, Esteban keeps within the moderate influences impressed on him from the first by our good father, and, faithful to them, rules his conduct without entering into the intrigues and pranks which present circumstances require."

Cryptic, but perhaps revealing. " We do enjoy some favour, but it is too complicated to be explained in writing." Was Pedro hinting at the amorous intrigue which the Queen, according to gossip, was carrying on with Mallo ? This explanation of the favour enjoyed by the three Venezuelans held the field until 1932, enriched with picturesque and entertaining details. The official swain of the Queen was Godoy; but Mallo, so runs the *chronique scandaleuse* of the day, had ousted him temporarily much to the annoyance of the favourite.

Sober and unromantic historians must be content with the view that, though the Queen's temperament was one of the forces which shaped politics, it was not predominant; that the King had a will of his own and was by no means, at any rate in public affairs, the blind and supine tool of his wife; and that the pressure of international politics, and especially of France, was much stronger than the Queen's caprice in determining the rise and fall of ministers. Mallo's favour may have been the outcome of Saavedra's appointment to succeed Godoy as Secretary of State; but Godoy's " fall ", due, not to the Queen's fancy, but to the insistence of France, had been a put-up show. The Queen's lover had remained as powerful as ever in the shade of his retirement. Mallo's favour, whatever it was, would then be the effect and not the cause of Godoy's fall.

As late as September, 1797, Esteban had written to Carlos that he was determined to leave Spain for Caracas, even while Spain was at war with England, for he was tired of " waiting for the Messiah " and was penniless. But on August 1st, 1798, Carlos extols the high hopes raised in Caracas by the news " of Don Manuel Mallo's affairs and the favour the King and Queen bestow upon him "; and reports a rumour whereby Esteban was to be appointed Chief Accountant of Caracas. On August 28th of that year, Don Francisco de Saavedra, who was Minister of Finance, took over the State Secretaryship. He was an Andalusian of more façade than depth—a façade which Goya has immortalized in a portrait now in London. He had fought in Florida under Gálvez, alongside of Miranda; and after the surrender of the English in Pensácola, had been appointed Intendente of Caracas, a post he had held during the first five years of Bolívar's life (1783–8). Saavedra must have known Bolívar as a child; it was then he met Mallo who, born in Popayán, lived in Caracas. Ten years later (24.viii.98) Esteban was appointed Minister of the Auditing Tribunal of Spain, a dignified if not highly paid office. In announcing the news to his brother, he suggested that the moment was favourable for the two youngsters as well as Pedro to be sent to him. Mallo, he reported, had written for one of his own brothers to come over and he added: " Mallo's good fortune and that of all his house must be known over there; I can assure you that he is a happy man." There is a hint here of favour from other than Saavedra's power. In June, 1800, long after Saavedra's fall, Pedro was appointed Chief Constable of the *Audiencia* of Caracas.

Mallo's official position was that of *mayordomo de semana*, or weekly steward. He evidently was chosen by the King and Queen. There is no need whatever to attribute a bedroom origin to this choice. " Favour " came from the mere fact that the majordomo had easy, daily access to the royal persons. That this favour was not much (as observed by Pedro) follows from the fact that Mallo's position did not go beyond that of a welcome young man about the Court. Hence Pedro's impatience. He sought to break the deadlock by means of some " prank ". What was in his mind ? Possibly a bold attempt at entering the path so brilliantly trodden by Godoy and successfully enough by Mallo; and on the strength of his youth, his looks and his power, to make himself loved, charm the Queen and conquer a position in the palace which need not necessarily have added pepper and salt to the *chronique scandaleuse* yet could have yielded much bread and butter to the family. He may also have had in mind some shady financial combination of the many Saavedra's weak character and gipsy disposition favoured, or at any rate allowed. In any case, Esteban frowned at his brother's plans and made him give them up.

CHAPTER VII

THE SPANISH MARRIAGE

I

SHORN of the melodramatic stories which fancy had clad it with, young Bolívar's life in Madrid can be imagined full and instructive enough, enlivened by the Micawber-like and pleasure-loving Pedro, if hemmed in by the disciplinarian Esteban. Simón was found to possess little instruction. Don Simón Rodríguez or Carreño had evidently devoted more time to spirited generalities on human happiness than to the three R's. The spelling of Simón's first letter—written when he was over fifteen—is below the average that would be exacted nowadays of a boy of ten. But he had a first-rate brain and, it would appear, a fairly good inclination to learn. By August, 1799, Pedro reported: " Esteban keeps him very studious, and he willingly and punctually works at Spanish; writing, in which he has made much progress, dancing, and history in good books, while French and mathematics are in store for him." To judge by the account of his expenses during the first year of his stay in Madrid, he must have worked hardest at mathematics, much less at dancing, and least of all at French; for his teacher of mathematics cost 1,400 reales, for a whole year, while his dancing master took 480 for four months, and his French expenses did not exceed eighty, twenty of which were invested in a grammar and sixty in lessons during a fortnight. This should dispose of the somewhat fanciful lines devoted to the subject in a short biographical note drafted in later years by Esteban: " In his own house, he was awakened by his fencing master, followed by his French teacher, and later his dancing teacher; part of the afternoon was devoted to mathematics; to all of which he leant himself readily."

There is in Pedro's letter a disarming slip of the pen which he was too lazy to withdraw by rewriting the whole of it. Still referring to Simón, he says: " He is held fairly tight and keeps a middling behaviour, or should I say, good. So from this point of view, do not worry." The phrase reveals that the younger uncle and the handsome nephew were on excellent terms, and the older uncle found it hard to keep them in order. Esteban complains about it to Carlos even though mildly and patiently, for he had for Simón " more love than I could say, and though it means for me a good deal of trouble, I do it with pleasure ". Carlos answers recommending strong measures, with that coldness towards young Simón he so often evinces: " You say he takes much of your time to attend to his education and I well believe it . . . you must not allow that to harm your interests, so that you must talk to him hard or else put him in a boarding school, should he not behave with the good sense and application he ought to; I am writing to him in that sense." Esteban did nothing of the kind, and Simón went on mixing his stern studies with the amusements of the big capital.

2

Madrid was then a city of 200,000 inhabitants. " Most streets are very beautiful "—writes Laborde—" and there are some which would pass for superb in any capital of Europe . . . particularly the calle de Alcalá which surpasses them all . . . wide enough for ten carriages to pass abreast." Bourgoing pronounces it " the widest in Europe". He writes that " Madrid is in general well laid out: the streets, although not in a direct line, are for the most part wide, and tolerably straight. The infrequency of rain, and the vigilance of the modern police, for which it is indebted to the count d'Aranda, made it one of the cleanest cities in Europe." True he adds that " except the Prado and its avenues, the city has no elegant quarters to boast ". But both Bourgoing and Laborde extol the works of art the Royal Palace and the mansions of the nobility offered to the visitor; and both do justice to the many establishments devoted to charity and education in which the city abounded, the academies, the public libraries, " which contain all the works of history and of science one can desire ", and the admirable Botanic Gardens organized by Charles III close to the Prado.

The beauty of the royal houses, not only of Madrid, but of Aranjuez, La Granja and El Escorial, must have been familiar to Simón Bolívar; for Esteban was keen to display the art treasures of Spain before his nephew, and when Pedro arrived in Madrid for the first time he found that both had gone to Aranjuez. Madrid was too much for Pedro's pen. " For the present, I can say nothing about this city, because its size, the variety of its aspects and everything else I omit mix up one's ideas." Madrid was not very large then, but it was extremely lively and colourful—more perhaps than at any period of its history before or after. The wave of prosperity prepared by the peaceful reign of Ferdinand VI and fostered by the creative reign of Charles III was breaking in a froth of colour, movement, enjoyment, in a motley society Spanish and foreign, popular and aristocratic, to the accompaniment of the Andalusian guitar and of the strains of Mozart and Boccherini. The beauty of it all has remained for ever alive in the canvasses and tapestries of Goya—an excellent background on which to imagine our youthful Creole moving about, opening his large eyes under his curly hair, a small figure but supremely elegant in his Kashmir breeches and turquoise blue dress coat with velvet collar and steel buttons and white leather waist-coat; or clad in his Spanish cloak with crimson velvet lining; or again in his blue uniform with lions and castles (for which he paid 24 reales) and his smart sword.

The people of Madrid, with an eye for beauty and smartness, would stare and smile, well pleased with the appearance of the youth. They were as always good-humoured and kindly. " The nature of the people "—writes one of Madrid's chroniclers—" is sweet, peaceable and mild, which makes them wise, temperate, subtle and eager for knowledge in the liberal and the mechanical arts as well as in the deeper sciences. The Catholic Queen [Isabel] used to say that the natives of Madrid were so good-natured that they could be compared with the best of her kingdoms." But there were all kinds of people, as in all big cities, including the scum which got churned together with the sedate middle classes and the handsome noblemen during the " turmoil of the fairs of St. John and St. Peter and the festivities of Holy Week and Corpus Christi ". In such places and occasions a young " American " was apt to be in keen demand. We might have guessed it; but we know it through the songs then popular in the theatres:

> From America I have come,
> Between the wind and the water,
> In a ship all made of wood . . .
> As soon as I was ashore
> I met a kindly young girl
> With her knob-dotted mantilla,
> Who stole my heart all at once.
> She asked me whether I wanted
> To go with her to her house.
> She would entertain me, singing
> A new song, of the most modern . . .
> The supper was not so light:
> It cost me one hundred pesos. . . .

We are at liberty to imagine Simoncito, under the giddy guidance of Pedro, running such risks. María Pulpillo, one of the most famous *tonadilleras* or singers of light songs, of the period, used to sing a few years earlier a *tonadilla* to this effect:

> To please serious-minded people
> I begged an Italian friend
> To sell for their weight in gold
> Three pounds of my warbling trills.
> Unless I find an American
> I shall have to give up singing.

3

These songs suggest the high expectations which Creoles were apt to raise in many an adventurous feminine breast. Simón was not always in a position to meet them, even though in the account of his expenses for his first year in Madrid, under a total of 36,775 reales, there is an " unexplained " item of 12,258. This was a not inconsiderable sum for a single youth in a city in which one could be served a pie of three pigeons and two pounds of mutton for twelve reales and a big turkey for thirteen and a half. But we need not charge it all to the light side of life. There was then much in Madrid to attract a keen young man. There was good music, both in private houses (such as that of the Duchess of Benavente, where Haydn sonatas, quartets and symphonies were played) and in public concert rooms. During Lent in 1797, the year before Bolívar's arrival, eighteen concerts were given in the theatre de la Cruz; the works were by Mozart, Pleyel and Haydn; and there were some complaints owing to " the neglect of national

musicians such as Boccherini, Gutiérrez, etc.". Madrid was very fond of
Italian opera, first introduced by Charles III the very year of Bolívar's birth.
There was the theatre, a national art which Aranda had considerably improved in its material aspects, and in which the struggle was keen between
the school of French classicism, backed by Aranda, and those who preferred
the Spanish tradition. This struggle went beyond the theatre and contributed—with its spice of civil war—to the vitality and zest of intellectual
life in Madrid.

It was an alert life, stimulated by the great French leaders, Montesquieu,
Voltaire and above all Rousseau. In this, as in every other walk of life, the
reign of Charles III had provided the main impulse; and though later,
under the impression of the French Terror, Floridablanca had tried to shut
doors and windows to foreign ideas, and Godoy had followed suit, the
pressure of events was too strong for a State whose very servants conspired
to bring into the country the air of the century. If young Bolívar mixed at
all with the intellectuals of the day, he must have found in Madrid many
disciples of Rousseau as ardent as his tutor Carreño. Clavijo, one of the
most prominent, had prevailed upon Aranda to prohibit the *Autos Sacra-
mentales*, or allegorical religious plays; Quintana, the poet, bestowed his
attentions on America, naïvely taking the attitude of wholesale condemnation
of Spain usually adopted abroad, which made him burst forth at the end of
one of his poems:

Virgin of the world, innocent America!

The Duke of Almodóvar had published in 1784 his translation of Raynal's
*Histoire Philosophique et Politique des Etablissements et du Commerce des
Européens dans les Indes;* an anonymous translator, probably a " philosophic "
priest known as Marchena, had published in London in 1799 a Spanish
translation of the *Contrat Social*.

We have no direct knowledge of the part Bolívar took in all this life,
intellectual and otherwise, of Madrid. He was perhaps too young to realize
the meaning of what he saw and experienced. And since no strong trace of
these days in Spain is found in his later correspondence, or in his confidences
to his Boswells, it is possible to surmise that he just let himself live, balanced
between his gay and his serious uncle, tasting life as it came and allowing
his deeper self unobserved to absorb ancestral influences.

4

After living in the *calle de Jardines*, Simón Bolívar settled in number 6,
calle del Príncipe, close by; and later, number 8, *calle de Atocha*, in the
house of an illustrious countryman of his, the Marqués de Ustáriz. This
Spanish-American magnate enjoyed great prestige in Spain. As early as
1778 Miranda had found him governing Extremadura as Intendente of
Badajoz; and in 1792 (July 25th) Esteban wrote to his father: " Last night
the Marqués de Uztaris arrived here and there is a rumour which keeps
recurring that he is going to become a minister, but as he is an American,
we had better wait to believe it till we see it."

Young Simón was staying at Ustáriz' house when he met and fell in love with the girl he was to marry; and the marqués acted as his guardian through the romance till the wedding day. María Teresa Josefa Antonia Joaquina Rodríguez de Toro y Alayza was a first cousin of the Marqués de Toro of Caracas, and of his brother Don Fernando, friends of the Bolívar family and leaders of the anti-Tovar faction in that city. Her father Don Bernardo Rodríguez de Toro, born in Caracas, lived in Madrid, where he had married Doña Benita Alayza, born in Valladolid, a sister of the Marqués de Inicio, Count of Rebolledo. María Teresa was born in Madrid twenty months before her husband, on October 15th, 1781. She was not beautiful; but she had grace and gentleness.

The Toro family lived on the other side of the Puerta del Sol, number 2, *calle de Fuencarral*, in a new and up-to-date house. On March 20th, 1801, Bolívar was granted a passport for Bilbao; and on the same day he wrote to Pedro that he had been granted permission to go to Bilbao (he was an officer in the army) by the King and by Mallo. Evidently Mallo kept some kind of supervision over his life. But where was Esteban? His eclipse at this moment is one of the mysteries of Bolívar's life. Esteban was put under arrest in the Monastery of Monserrat, the very place that had sold to Bolívar's family the title of Castille for which Esteban had striven in Madrid. Why, and exactly when, he was arrested, we do not know. That he had fallen as a friend of the fallen Mallo has been generally assumed, though it is not certain that Mallo's influence at Court and Esteban's imprisonment were throughout coincident. The situation afforded young Simón an opportunity to express genuine affection for his " kind godfather " in a letter to Pedro (23.viii.801). In this same letter he informs his uncle that the marriage will take place by proxy in Madrid. But there were delays, and Simón, still in Bilbao, on December 29th, 1801, was in Bayonne on January 13th, 1802.

5

Why he left for France is not known. He may have stayed till April, though the Ambassador, Azara, signed a passport for him in Amiens on February 16th. This city was then the centre of the diplomatic activity which led to the Peace of Amiens whereby France and Spain came to terms with Great Britain. By that Treaty, Spain lost to England the Island of Trinidad which nature had meant to be part of Bolívar's own country. It seems that he witnessed the festivities whereby Paris celebrated the peace. But he must also have watched with some curiosity the rise of that Bonaparte who was to be the chief star in his inner horizon. In that year, 1802, Victor Hugo was born in Besançon

vieille ville espagnole,
Jeté comme la graine au gré du vent qui vole,

and, as the poet was to write later evoking the time of his birth:

Ce siècle avait deux ans. Rome remplaçait Sparte.
Déjà Napoléon perçait sous Bonaparte.

How far Simón Bolívar was in a position to see this, we cannot say. Rather than the political events, as yet somewhat unshaped and recondite, he must have observed in France the general air of order, prosperity and urban beauty which in itself and by comparison with Spain must have struck his keen mind and vivid imagination. He was ever free from the francophobia which afflicted Miranda, and, while not a blind imitator or admirer, he could appreciate the genius of France.

If we were to believe O'Leary, one of Bolívar's Boswells, this visit fostered republican feelings in the youthful Creole, for he assumed that the more advanced state of France was due to the republican institutions which France enjoyed. O'Leary also says that " the possibility of separating South America from the metropolis was a subject often discussed between the two friends ", i.e. Ustáriz and Simoncito, an old, respected statesman and a stripling of seventeen; and he depicts Ustáriz putting forward objections " with arguments of such soundness as to have cooled the ardour of his young companion had he not held his convictions so deeply ". This is the second attempt at describing Bolívar as a kind of Jesus in the Temple confounding mature statesmen with his innate wisdom; for he is also supposed to have so frightened the viceroy of Mexico with his revolutionary convictions at fifteen that the viceroy had seen to it that he left for Spain at once in spite of the British blockade.

Oh mon Dieu, délivrez-moi de mes amis, car de mes ennemis je me charge. What Voltaire wrote Bolívar might well have repeated. These stories lend him an attitude and a state of mind wholly alien to his character and to his way of thinking at the time. True he was witnessing the persecution of his favourite uncle in circumstances which he could but resent; but no trace remains in any paper of his or of his family or friends of any political effects of this fact in his attitude towards the mother country; while there are many of Esteban's own staunch loyalty after his fall from favour. Esteban was no blind admirer of Spain, on which he had at times expressed critical and disillusioned views. As early as 1793 he wrote to his father: " now that I know this place I realize how ignorant we who live in those parts are and how those who go there from here seek to dazzle us." This man was no fool. Simón was bound therefore to take note of the fact that such a man with such an experience remained attached to Spain through thick and thin. " I do not wonder "—Esteban wrote in 1803 to Pedro (back in Caracas)—" that you are not at ease there, for I, even after my misfortune, and now that I enjoy a certain amount of liberty, I have not dreamt of returning home unless the King orders me to."

Bolívar's own letters show unmistakably that at this period, under the influence of Ustáriz, of his father-in-law and of his bride, of his uncle Esteban and of the general atmosphere of Spain, he returned temporarily to some spiritual communication with the ancestral traditions which since the death of his parents lay hidden in his being. For instance, whatever influence Simón Carreño may have had in drawing him away from the old faith to the abstract deism of the *Vicaire Savoyard*, Bolívar's own utterances in Spain have a fresh, candid aroma of belief. Writing to Pedro about Esteban's tribulations, he says: " My prayers are few and of little efficacy for the subject for which I pray; yet I shall not cease to apply them all to the happy end of the interest which you have in this affair." And again, on the death of Pedro's steward: " In the end, God is the author of all our happiness, and therefore they cannot but happen for our own good. This reflection comforts us when we are in tribulation; and so you ought not to forget it."

The wedding took place in the month of May, 1802. It is a singular fact that Bolívar, who was later to prove himself a keen voluptuary and a promiscuous lover, chose as a wife a woman of no particular beauty. The idea that he married her for money is unthinkable; for he was at least as wealthy, and his character was above such calculations. He married her he did not know why. But deep down in his soul his choice must have been determined by two facts: she was older by twenty months, i.e. definitely older in those ages, for he was eighteen; and she was both of Madrid and of Caracas, a living synthesis of his two fatherlands. In his older wife, he sought his dead mother and the roots of his Spanish and Creole being which he felt withering since the days he had lived, under the influence of Simón Carreño, wandering in mind and body. When in May, 1802, Simón Bolívar, not yet nineteen, left Spain with his young maternal wife, he felt more Spanish than he was to feel in all the rest of his tragic life—save perhaps on his deathbed.

CHAPTER VIII

THE WANDERING YEARS

I

IN the early summer of 1802 Simón and Teresa Bolívar settled into a life of private happiness. In January, 1803, a malignant fever cut short this dream. Teresa Bolívar died. This sudden end of the life of a young woman of twenty-one, a private, quiet life, may well have been one of the key events in the history of the continent. Had Teresa lived, Simón Bolívar might have regained contact with his deeper self, re-established the free flow of ancestral beliefs and traditions into the channels of his clear mind, achieved that synthesis of head and heart which he was to be denied for the rest of his days, and lived a prominent life—for prominent it would have been in any case—as one of the leaders of a Spanish America less rent by civil war than he was to make her. That all this need not be dismissed as arbitrary or conjectural is shown by no less an authority than Bolívar himself. " See how odd things can be "—he said once to Peru de Lacroix—" had I not become a widower, my life might have been quite different; I should not be now General Bolívar, nor the *Libertador*; though I own that my character is not one to be content with being Mayor of San Mateo."

Death had it otherwise. Not yet twenty, Simón Bolívar was a widower. For the third time, fate severed him from his past. Father, mother, wife— fate denied him all access to his deeper self and cut him loose in a world of principles and ideas, words and hopes. " I loved my wife much "— he said in later years—" and after her death I swore never to marry again. I have held my word." These words do not express marital fidelity; but rather that attitude of both challenge and resentment towards fate, often found in Spanish life and art. " I tried marriage "—he seems to have thought or felt—" I tried tradition, I tried peace with my own past buried in me under so many dead. I have failed. So, now, farewell to all that. I am free."

Simón Bolívar left his fatherland for the second time. What remained ashore was no part of his soul. His uncles were not connected with him by ties of particular affection, and one of them, Carlos, deserved the cold letters in which the young heir referred to the mismanagement of his property before his coming of age. " Had you "—Simón rightly argues in his letter to his uncle—" presented your accounts when I arrived, I should have had time to examine them." But Carlos evidently had waited till the last moment, and his nephew refused to pass them. This episode reveals a singular ripeness of will and character in the young man then twenty. He acted firmly though not discourteously, without undue hastiness towards a guardian who was certainly careless and probably worse.

Before leaving for Europe he borrowed money, possibly to finance an operation described anon. According to custom, he appealed to the Superintendent of the Royal Treasury in Caracas. His application, dated

August 9th, 1803, shows him living in the twilight of loyalties typical of the period. He begins his request describing himself as " Simón de Bolívar, a neighbour and landowner of this province "; using the particle *de* which he had a tendency to discard, as indeed he does in the signature of the document. This tendency was probably due to the influence of Carreño, who professed the same contempt for family tradition as for any other tradition, and took and shed names as a street dog takes and sheds collars. The idea that the particle is a sign of nobility, though not well founded, was and still is widespread in Spain and out of Spain. We can picture to ourselves the still fluctuating young Creole beginning his letter with a proud " Simón de Bolívar " under ancestral influences, and ending it " Simón Bolívar " under that of his tutor. But there was another oscillation in the letter. In the very first sentence, we can guess him subconsciously thinking: " Yes, a neighbour and a landowner, but I am d—d if I will say I am an officer in the King's army as well." Bolívar was then a lieutenant in the Spanish army; and at this moment he might have been expected to say so, since he was asking for a government loan. He offered, of course, excellent security, and his request was in strict accordance with custom. But it was not granted. The reasons adduced by the Treasury may have been sound and sincere: " the needs of the Royal Treasury ", and " the present circumstances "; but they may also have been the outcome of some official or private coldness towards the applicant.

2

In the summer of 1803, Simón Bolívar left Caracas for Cádiz. This choice of port adds weight to the detail supplied by Mosquera, one of his biographers: that he " sold some of his lands, gave others to his brother and sisters . . . and freighted a ship which he loaded, sailing for Cádiz with enough funds to live for many years and to travel in Europe ". Cádiz was still the chief commercial centre for the Indies, and there was no reason why Bolívar should have gone so far out of his way (for he really was going to Europe north of Spain) had he not decided to pay his way by a commercial transaction. Here again, the enterprise, the imagination and the executive ability should be noted in a youth of twenty.

He landed in Cádiz towards the close of 1803, after a stormy voyage. After a short stay, he left for Madrid to join his father-in-law to whom he brought some melancholy mementoes of Teresa. The meeting of the two men was sad in the extreme. " Bolívar spoke of this interview with tenderness "—writes Mosquera—" remembering the tears that father and son had mixed. ' I have never forgotten this scene of delightful torment, for the grief from love is a delight '—was the saying with which Bolívar used to conclude his narrative." His stay in Madrid was not long. An Order had been promulgated by the city requesting non-residents to leave, owing to a temporary shortage of food; but the real motive of Bolívar's prompt departure was that " his life in Madrid, amidst the friends who had known him loving, loved and happy, became as unbearable for him as that of

Caracas ". After his failure to regain his Spanish and Creole roots, he was fleeing from the two soils which had fed them. He sought the movement and the freedom of his mental skies. He left for France, where he knew he would find Carreño.

He has himself described this movement of his inner self from private to public affairs, i.e. from his Spanish soil to his universal Heaven, in a conversation noted by Peru de Lacroix. " I returned from Europe to Caracas in the year 1801 with my wife . . . my head then was full only of dreams of the most exalted love, not of political ideas, for these had not yet struck my imagination. My wife dead and I desolate . . . I returned to Spain, and from Madrid went on to France and later to Italy. I was beginning to take some interest in public affairs. Politics attracted me, and I followed their varied movements." The mood of the spirit and its change from fixity to motion and from concrete to abstract is admirably if unwittingly conveyed in these words. " Varied movements." The phrase is typical, not only of politics but of Bolívar as well, who at this time begins to share in that perpetual motion his tutor had borrowed from Rousseau. Carreño had been wandering ever since his dabbling in conspiracy had forced him to leave his native shores. He had been in Jamaica; then in Baltimore, then over to Europe, where, in Bayonne, he taught Spanish and translated Chateaubriand. It is at this moment that Bolívar turns up and, with his generous purse, redeems Carreño from his school and sets him again in motion.

3

Henceforth, two themes weave themselves in the wanderings of Bolívar: the road and Napoleon. He arrived in Paris early in May, 1804. On August 1st Humboldt landed in Bordeaux on his return from a voyage in the New World begun in 1799 in the company of a young French naturalist, Bonpland. A good part of his time had been spent in Venezuela. He had landed in Cumaná on July 16th, 1799, had stayed in Caracas from November 21st, 1799, until February 7th, 1800, and after his famous travels in the Orinoco valley had sailed from Nueva Barcelona for Cuba on November 24th, 1800.

Bolívar, who knew how liked and admired Humboldt had been in his country, must have endeavoured to see him. According to O'Leary, Humboldt, asked by Bolívar whether in his view the Spanish colonies would be able to govern themselves, delivered himself of the opinion that " they had already reached their political maturity, but that he knew no man calculated to lead their emancipation ". Humboldt was " extremely attentive and admired the warmth with which Bolívar maintained the necessity of separating Spanish America from the metropolis ". Thanks to Boussingault and to Mancini, this Paris acquaintanceship was to blossom out—on paper— into so close a friendship between the famous and mature German scientist and the young Creole of twenty-one, that Humboldt took Bolívar with Gay Lussac for his ascent of Vesuvius.

The facts are much less picturesque. Humboldt's opinions on the relations between Spain and Spanish America are well known from his works, some of which were written precisely at this period. " Throughout the world "—he says to his brother (7.x.1800)—" there is perhaps no land where one could live with more enjoyment and in greater peace and security than in the Spanish colonies where I have now been travelling for the last fifteen months." He records repeatedly the generosity with which the Spanish Government fostered scientific studies both in the European and in the American kingdoms. On landing at Bordeaux, he promptly corrected an article published in Baltimore and reproduced in the *Journal de Bordeaux*. " It is well known that I went to Madrid in 1799 merely to seek the Court's permission to carry out scientific research at my expense in the vast colonies of Spain. This permission was granted me with that liberalism which is typical of our century, and to which we owe our rapid progress in human knowledge. His Catholic Majesty, having taken much interest in the success of my expedition, deigned to honour me with his most magnanimous protection."

Humboldt's attitude towards the problem of Spanish America was far wiser than anything which either Bolívar (then far too young and immature) or O'Leary, foreign to Spain and biased all his life, could ever understand. Bonpland himself, says O'Leary, " lost no opportunity to encourage Bolívar in his enterprise and to assure him that the revolution would produce sons worthy of her "—this during the very days when

Déjà Napoléon perçait sous Bonaparte !

This may have been possible in a Frenchman who, despite his scientific training, might easily fall a prey to Jacobinism. But Humboldt was of a sterner fibre and knew the New World to be more complex. He writes pointedly: " There is some astonishment in Europe at the fact that the Spaniards of the metropolis, whose small numbers we have pointed out, have for so many centuries evinced so long and so strong a resistance; what people forget is that in all the colonies the European party increases of necessity by absorbing a considerable mass of Creoles. Family interests, the desire to live quietly without the fear of being thrown into an enterprise which may fail, prevent such people from espousing the cause of independence, or from seeking to establish a local and representative government, even though dependent on the mother country. Some, fearing all violent means, hope that slow reforms may make the colonial rule less oppressive; they see in revolutions nothing but the loss of their slaves, the spoliation of the clergy and the introduction of a religious tolerance they deem incompatible with the purity of the prevailing worship. Others belong to that little number of families who, in each commune, either through hereditary opulence, or owing to their age-long residence in the colonies, constitute a true municipal aristocracy. They prefer to be deprived of certain rights to sharing them with everybody; they would even prefer foreign rule to an authority handed over to Americans of a lower caste; they hate every constitution founded on equality of rights; they fear particularly the loss of their decorations and their titles which have cost them so much trouble to acquire and which are so essential a part of their happiness. Others again, and their number is very high, live in the country on the produce of their lands, enjoying that liberty which even under the most vexatious governments, prevails in all countries in which the population is so thinly distributed. As they do not seek offices for themselves, they see them with indifference filled by men whose very names are almost unknown to them, and whose power does not reach far enough to touch them. They would, no doubt, prefer to the old state of the colonies a national government and a full commercial liberty; but this desire does not exceed their love of peace and their indolent habits enough to induce them to undergo long and painful sacrifices."

4

There was a lady in Paris whose name looms larger in Bolívar's biographies than it did in his life. Madame Dervieu de Villars was before her marriage Fanny Trobriand Aristeguieta; and on the strength of this second name she claimed to be Bolívar's cousin. She also claimed—or confessed—twenty-eight years of age when her husband was fifty-six. Dervieu de Villars had been Commandant of the City of Lyon and commanding officer of its National Guard; on Charles X's accession (1825) he was made a Field Marshal. She seems to have been liberal with her favours to Bolívar, who, in his turn, appears to have idealized her into a reincarnation of his dead wife (possibly also of his dead mother) for he renamed her Teresa. The hint is clear. This episode was for him a posthumous attempt at gaining access to those subconscious layers of his self from which Simón Rodríguez Carreño was drawing him further away every day. The lady assured him she was a member of his family, and this, whether true or not, mattered little so long as he chose to believe it. Fanny Villars was a good hostess and now and then she may have succeeded in landing a big fish to let loose in her social pond. Humboldt may have gone there. She seems to have met him often enough to write to Bolívar (6.iv.26): " Baron Humboldt was here. . . . I do not know how the Baron manages to call himself your friend; in those days, when the success of your enterprise was doubtful, he and Monsieur Delpech were your keenest critics."

Bolívar is supposed to have seen Humboldt at the Prussian legation in Rome, where at the time Humboldt's brother, William, was the Minister. Illustrious names are bandied about freely, on the occasion of Bolívar's stay in Rome; and an excursion to Vesuvius is made up on the strength of Boussingault, who coolly asserts that Bolívar, Humboldt and Gay Lussac ascended together to the top of the volcano in 1804, a year in which none of them happened to be in Italy at all. Humboldt left Paris for Rome on March 12th, 1805, in the company of Gay Lussac; and the two scientists, with the geologist Leopold von Buch, left Rome for Naples on July 15th to climb Vesuvius, then giving signs of exceptional activity. On September 17th, 1805, Humboldt left for Germany. Bolívar had left Paris for

Rome in March; but travelling slowly and circuitously, *à la Rousseau*, with Carreño. He saw Humboldt in Rome, for he says so himself: " Accept the cordial feelings of one who had the honour of respecting your name before meeting you and of loving you when he saw you in Paris and in Rome." The silence of Bolívar on Vesuvius in this letter, O'Leary's silence, and the fact that no mention is made of Bolívar's presence during the Vesuvius expedition in the standard Life of Humboldt written when Bolívar was at the height of his glory prove that the story is a pure fabrication.

What remains of the Humboldt-Bolívar episode ? Bolívar must have been something of a separatist when he met Humboldt in Paris and he must have spoken freely about it to him as to everybody else. Fanny refers to the fact repeatedly. " I, to whom you entrusted your plans and schemes twenty-one years ago, place you above Washington, owing to the immense difficulties you had to conquer to set free a whole world." We need not take at its face value all that the grasping and ebullient lady wrote to her distant cavalier; but it is natural that in the effusions of his youthful passion, Bolívar should have spoken of the freedom of America. Humboldt would certainly listen with sympathy, because he held liberal views; but with reserve, because he knew the problem to be difficult; and because he could not possibly entertain a favourable opinion of a youth who was under the influence of Carreño. For Humboldt must have held in little esteem—probably less than he actually deserved—that extravagant " philanthropist ". Humboldt must therefore have been for Bolívar one of the unconvinced figures who, at the back of the young man's mind, tacitly counselled caution and emitted an unseen radiation of doubt.

5

It was at this period, that Bolívar received the strongest imprint of Carreño's mind and ideas. Under his guidance, the youth devoured Hobbes, Helvetius, Holbach, Hume, Spinoza, as well as Rousseau and Voltaire. These authors would make him feel more than ever severed from the roots of his past, and loose in the world. Helvetius and Holbach were preachers of pleasure, easily misunderstood as preachers of do-as-you-please. This doctrine is most attractive to the young, particularly when they are rich and free from family bonds. Bolívar spent months of profligacy in Paris, a well-known figure among the frequenters of the Palais Royal galleries, giving over to wine, women and song the liberty the philosophers taught him to cherish.

" I do not want to be like a tree, which grows roots in a spot "—said Carreño—" but like the wind, the water, the sun, all that which is ever in motion." In these words, Bolívar's mentor revealed the earthless, weightless nature of the realms into which he was leading his young friend. Other travellers take to the road to gain familiarity with the earth into the nooks and corners of which the road will lead them. Bolívar and Carreño took to the road led by a desire for motion as motion, but again not that motion in which Hobbes saw the origin of all mental life and even perhaps of consciousness;

but of motion as that state of permanent temporariness, of neither that-which-is-left-behind nor that-towards-which-we-are-moving so dear to the unrealist-idealist because it frees the will from all earthly problems and allows the mind unfettered scope.

Two Spaniards—whether of the old or of the new world—can hardly ever take to the road without falling into the Don Quixote-Sancho pattern. In their wanderings through France and Italy, Bolívar and Carreño call forth memories of the immortal pair. To be sure, they do not make up a servile parallel. Physically, the gaunt and wiry Bolívar and the thickset and some-what heavy Carreño remain faithful to the pattern. And there is also a certain parallelism between the saturnine tendencies of the Knight of the Doleful Countenance and the *Libertador* on the one hand, and on the other the jovial natures of Carreño and of Sancho. We may also discern a certain harmony between the exalted dreams of the two knights as between the more immediate concerns of the two squires. Mentally, there is a variation. Don Quixote was intellectual and abstract, and he feared nothing so much as just that knowledge of reality which would—he felt but dared not think—destroy his dreams; while Sancho knew no ideas, but only the direct impacts of facts on his mind, which he expressed in proverbs. In the case of our two Spanish-American friends, the intellectual relationship was subtle. The squire, not the knight, was now the abstract intellectualist and leader of the pair; while the knight, though apt to be led away by the generalizations of an older and better read mentor, had in his higher mental powers and keener intuition greater reserves of empirical wisdom than he himself even knew. And in this guise, Simón Bolívar and Simón Carreño set out on their travels on the road of history.

The knight needed a Dulcinea, and at least one other knight, an Amadis de Gaul as an example and inspiration. His Dulcinea was ready: " Virgin America " suffering atrociously under the tyranny of the Spanish giant through no fault of her own, for she was innocent as all maids are apt to be. His Amadis de Gaul rose suddenly with undreamt of splendour. His name: Napoleon. The year in which Bolívar arrived in Paris was that of Bonaparte's accession to the imperial Crown. Enghien had been executed a few weeks before, on March 21st, 1804; and a few days after, on May 18th, the imperial constitution had been adopted. The process whereby the Court of the First Consul became the Imperial Court took place under Bolívar's eyes; and both the knight and his squire were in Paris when Amadis de Gaul was crowned in Notre Dame (2.xii.1804). Was Bolívar present ? Carreño denies it: " and I must say that on that day, so notable and happy for the Frenchies, Bolívar and I stayed indoors in our hotel ". But Bolívar himself explicitly said to Peru Lacroix that he was there. We know from Boussingault that: " *C'était une manie du Général Bolívar de cherçher à imiter Napoléon I. Se trouvant à Paris en 1803 et 1804, il assista à une revue que le Premier Consul passait dans la cour des Tuileries. On le vit, les jours suivants, se promener avec le petit chapeau légendaire et la redingote grise. Humboldt et Gay Lussac, ses amis, le crurent atteint de folie. J'ai vu Bolívar, bien des années après, porter un uniforme bleu à revers, rappelant, par sa coupe, celui qu'affectionnait particulièrement l'Empereur.*" The point should therefore be noted that, on Napoleon, the negative attitude comes from Sancho-Carreño, but that Bolívar-Don Quixote was positive.

Bolívar's most scathing condemnation of Napoleon is quoted by his aide-de-camp O'Leary. " I worshipped him as the hero of the republic, as the bright star of glory, the genius of liberty. . . . He had himself made emperor, and from that day on, I looked upon him as a hypocritical tyrant, an insult to liberty and an obstacle to the progress of civilization. . . . How dreadful were the feelings of indignation which this melancholy sight [the coronation] produced in my soul, possessed as it was of a fanatical love of liberty and of glory! From then on I was unable to reconcile myself with Napoleon; his very glory seemed to me a glow from Hell."

The abstract, declamatory style of this page shows that it came from those mental skies of Bolívar over which Carreño was the chief influence. It cannot be taken therefore as a complete statement of Bolívar's attitude towards Napoleon. Bolívar himself entrusted to Peru de Lacroix a confidence (26.v.28) which at first sight appears to dispose of O'Leary's statement: " You may, no doubt, have noticed, that in my conversation with the persons of my household and others, I never praise Napoleon; on the contrary, when I speak of him or his deeds, I rather criticize than approve them; and more than once, I have called him a tyrant, a despot, and have condemned some of his great political measures and of his military operations. All this has been and still is necessary, though my opinion is different; but I must hide and disguise it to prevent the view gaining ground that my policy is an imitation of that of Napoleon, that my ambitions and plans are similar to his, that I also want to become emperor or king and dominate South America as he has done Europe; all this would have been said had I made known my admiration and my enthusiasm for that great man. My enemies would have gone further still: they would have accused me of wanting to set up a nobility and a military State similar to Napoleon's in power, prerogatives and honours. Do not doubt but that all this would have occurred had I shown myself, as I am, a keen admirer of the French hero; had I been heard praising his policy, speaking enthusiastically of his victories, commending him as the first captain of the world, as a statesman, as a philosopher and as a man of science. These are my opinions on Napoleon, but I have taken the utmost care to hide them. The St. Helena Diary, the campaigns of Napoleon and everything connected with him are for me the most agreeable reading and the most profitable; there it is that the arts of war, of politics and of government should be studied."

Peru de Lacroix may overstress the Bonapartist accent; but he can hardly have made it up. In any case, whatever Bolívar's views in 1828, his condemnation of Napoleon in 1805 was more sincere than this later page suggests. The youth of twenty-two, still powerfully influenced by his tutor, did condemn Napoleon " the tyrant " in his brain as much as he admired Napoleon the hero in his heart. The most faithful and complete account of the impression which Napoleon's coronation made on him is recorded in another page of Peru de Lacroix's diary (10.v.28): " I saw in

Paris "—said Bolívar—" the coronation of Napoleon in the last month of 1804. That magnificent scene aroused my enthusiasm; but less owing to its pomp than because of the feeling of love which an immense people evinced for their hero. That general effusion of all hearts, that free and spontaneous movement of the people, excited by the glories, the heroic exploits of Napoleon, whom in that moment more than a million persons acclaimed, seemed to me, for the recipient of so many ovations, the highest degree of human aspirations, the supreme desire and the supreme ambition of man. The Crown Napoleon laid on his head I looked upon as a miserable thing. What seemed great to me was the universal acclaim and the interest his person inspired. This I own, made me think of my country's slavery, and of the glory which would be achieved by the man who would free her. But how far was I from imagining that such a fortune was in store for me! "

6

Here we have at last the complete picture of Bolívar's mind as the rays of Napoleon's glory illumine it. The great thing for Bolívar in Napoleon's coronation was " the universal acclaim and the interest his person inspired "; and this, he confesses, made him think of his country's slavery and of the glory which would be achieved by the man who would free her. These are his very words; and they could not be truer to the dynasty of Don Quixote to which Simón Bolívar belongs by birthright. Don Quixote's worship and aim was Dulcinea; he himself was sincerely convinced that this was so. He was indeed more convinced of his devotion to Dulcinea than of Dulcinea's actual existence. But, for all that, Don Quixote's chief aim was the achievement of his own glory; and Dulcinea was but a creation of his fancy in search of a lady to serve, so that while serving this lady he should be able to earn for himself the glory of heroes and the fame of knights.

Virgin of the world, innocent America!

So Bolívar, when, beholding Napoleon's glory, he thought of the glory to be won by her Liberator. He thought only of the slavery which Dulcinea-South America suffered. A city acclaiming an emperor?—what was that to a continent acclaiming a Liberator? Glory was there, shining in the gold and damask of ceremonies, clamouring in the frenzy and enthusiasm of crowds; glory for a man to conquer. So, there must be a Dulcinea. Don Quixote-Bolívar thought then—and not before—of that unhappy maid kept in the dungeon of tyranny by the Spanish giant; of whose dreadful suffering he knew very little directly but very much indeed from what Sancho-Carreño often told him. And so, knight and squire left for Italy more than ever in the style of the Knight of the Doleful Countenance and his squire. Only this time it was the squire who had to remind the knight that glory was for Dulcinea and not Dulcinea for glory.

Bolívar and Carreño left Paris in March, 1805, mainly because the young Creole had wasted his strength in the pleasures of the capital, and his health needed to be restored. One of his companions, a cousin of his wife, Fernando de Toro, had led him to the hazards of the green cloth where he had lost more money than he possessed at the time. He had to swallow his pride and appeal for funds to Fanny de Villars. Carreño may have thought that a swift eclipse from Paris was needed for more reasons than one. They left for Lyon by public conveyance; and after a few days' rest there, sent their baggage forward and took to the road on foot *à la Rousseau*. They passed by Chambéry, to honour the *Vicaire Savoyard* and visited *Les Charmettes*, one of the sanctuaries of the prophet; but wherever they went, the glory of Napoleon followed them; for everywhere they saw triumphal arches and other preparations to receive the hero of France. When they arrived in Milan, the city was expecting the Emperor, who was there to crown himself King of Italy. Bolívar was present and saw Napoleon laying on his head the iron Crown of the Kings of Lombardy (26.v.1805). There was a military review in Montechiaro, which Bolívar and Carreño witnessed; and Bolívar's reminiscences, recorded by Peru de Lacroix, confirm all we know about his relation to the great Emperor. " The throne had been placed on a knoll in the midst of the plain, at the foot of which he and his friend had taken a vantage site so as to be able to observe the Emperor, who looked at them several times through a small telescope; and then his companion said: ' perhaps Napoleon, who is watching us, will think we are spies '; an observation that caused him [Bolívar] some concern and made him withdraw. I," H.E. continued, " centered my attention on Napoleon and saw no one but him out of that crowd of men: my curiosity could not be satiated, and I assure you I was very far from foreseeing that one day I also was to be the object of the attention and if you like of the curiosity of a whole continent, and one may say also, of the whole world. How numerous and brilliant was the suite which Napoleon had around him and how simple was his attire! All the men of his suite were covered with gold and rich embroideries, and he wore only his epaulettes, a hat without braid and a tunic without a single ornament; I liked this; and I should have adopted such a fashion in our countries had I not feared that people might have said I did it to imitate Napoleon." These words reveal the parallelism Bolívar felt between himself and Napoleon.

Don Quixote-Bolívar and Sancho-Carreño passed successively through Verona, Vicenza, Venice, Padua, Ferrara, Bologna, Florence, Rome and Naples. Venice, says O'Leary, defrauded Bolívar, possibly because, having given its name to Venezuela (Little Venice), he thought he would find something worthier of that honour. Dulcinea was evidently growing wonderful in his imagination, apace with his own ambition to save her. He stayed some time in Florence, where he studied Italian and read some of the classics of Italy—though not Macchiavelli, against whom he harboured what O'Leary calls " the common prejudice which makes of this great and calumniated patriot the equivalent of craftiness and crime ". And, through Perugia, he arrived in Rome where all was ready for the final scene in which he was to be armed a Knight Errant—the oath on Monte Sacro: " To tread the earth the Cincinnati and the Reguli had cultivated, to breathe the air the Scipiones had breathed; to remember the great minds and the heroes

who had been born and bred there, thanks to whose genius and valour
Rome had become the wonder and the mistress of the world—these reflections aroused lofty ideas in his youthful and ardent imagination and took
possession of his fancy, full of classic reminiscence and of modern philosophy."
So says the Irish Moor who wrote his life.   And the Spanish Moor who
wrote the life of the other Don Quixote: " His fancy became full of all he read
in the books . . . and the idea that the whole fabric of his dreamt inventions
was true became so settled in his imagination that there was for him in the
world no history more certain."

This, of course, led Don Quixote to imitate the Marquess of Mantua, and
to swear to

> Eat no bread at cloth-decked table
> Nor with wife in bed to lie

till he had fulfilled his knightly task.   And so, says O'Leary of Don Quixote
of Caracas: " The memory of the heroic epochs of Roman history called
forth at the sight of the Capitol, aroused in his being hopes for the future,
and, determined to bring them forth, or at least to attempt it, he ran to the
famous Sacred Mount to which Sicinius took the Plebeians of Rome, exasperated by the exactions, injustice, arrogance and violent deeds of their lords,
the patricians.   On the Sacred Mount the sufferings of his Mother-country
overpowered his mind, and feeling in all its intensity

> *La procelosa e trépida*
> *Gioia d'un gran disegno*
> *L'ansia d'un cor che indocile*
> *Ferve pensando* . . .

he fell on his knees and made a vow, of whose faithful fulfilment, the emancipation of South America is the glorious witness."

The road which led Don Quixote-Bolívar and Sancho-Carreño to Monte
Sacro had passed by Paris and Milan.   The youthful knight who on the
Sacred Mount made a solemn vow to liberate his Dulcinea-Mother-country
was still dazzled by the sight of what glory really was.   It was the ambition
to emulate the splendours of an imperial life, to be the sun of a solar system
of resplendent marshals and the star that drew to itself the ovations of a
whole continent that made Bolívar a knight errant in the service of the
freedom of South America.   The oath of Monte Sacro was the outcome of
the two coronations of Napoleon.   Twice Simón Bolívar had seen Napoleon
crown himself, the first time with the imperial Crown; the second, with the
iron Crown of the kings of Lombardy.   On Monte Sacro, Bolívar crowned
himself in the presence of an imaginary world he fancied at his feet: he
crowned himself a martyr or a hero, as his fate might decide.   Outwardly,
towards the vast crowds beyond the horizon, he vowed to liberate his mother-
country.   Inwardly, in the recesses of his soul beyond even his own gaze,
he vowed to make Simón Bolívar emperor of the New World.

CHAPTER IX

THE MAN

I

THIS is the moment to attempt a full length portrait. Bolívar was then twenty-two, and, according to the pictures of the period, still immature and somewhat pleased with himself. But we possess better descriptions of his looks and countenance at a later date. Here is one by a friendly hand: " General Simón Antonio Bolívar will be forty-five on July 24th of this year (1828); but represents fifty. He is of middle height; his body is thin and gaunt; his arms, thighs and legs, lean. His head is long, wide above and very sharp pointed below; his forehead large, clear, round and furrowed deeply whenever his face is not animated, or when he is angry or ill-humoured. His hair is crisp, bristling, abundant and greying. His eyes have lost the fire of youth but preserve the vivacity of his character, and are deep, neither small nor large; his eyebrows are thick, wide apart, rather straight and greyer than his hair. His nose is well proportioned. His cheekbones are prominent, and his cheeks fallen in, and his lower lip protruding; his teeth white and his laughter pleasant. His chin long and pointed. His complexion dark and sunburnt, further darkened when in a bad mood, for then the lines of his forehead and temples become deeper, his eyes turn smaller, his lower lip protrudes further and his mouth becomes ugly; in short, a different countenance comes out, evincing heavy, sad thoughts and sombre ideas. When he is in a good humour, all this vanishes and the spirit of the Lord shines over his face."

Here is another portrait, sketched nine years earlier by the unfriendly and disgruntled Colonel Hippisley: " General Bolívar is a mean looking person, seemingly (though but thirty-eight) about fifty years of age. He is about five feet six inches in height; thin, sallow complexion, lengthened visage, marked with every symptom of anxiety, care, and, I could almost add, despondency. He seemed also to have undergone great fatigue. His dark, and, according to report, brilliant eyes, were now dull and heavy, although I could give them credit for possessing more fire and animation when his frame was less harassed. Black hair, loosely tied behind with a piece of riband, large mustachios, black handkerchief round his neck, blue great coat, and blue trowsers, boots and spurs, completed his costume. In my eyes he might have passed for any thing but the thing he really was. Across the chamber was suspended one of the Spanish hammocks, on which he occasionally sat, lolled, and swung, whilst conversing, and seldom remained in the same posture for two minutes together."

Bolívar, then, was small. Napoleon was also small. But both possessed that personal aura which made them seem tall on great occasions. The President of the Colombian Congress in 1821 wrote of Bolívar that " he was thin, of middle size but of an extraordinary vivacity "; and that, despite his short stature, when, on the day of his inauguration as President, " he entered the hall of Congress, with his sabre dragging, in his brilliant uniform of Commander-in-Chief, wrapped in the aura of glory of his two last campaigns, he seemed extraordinarily tall, and as if the white feather on his hat could touch the ceiling ". This was similar to the " magical " effect Napoleon produced on outstanding occasions. But Bolívar's physique differed from Napoleon's in one important respect: success made Napoleon fat. Bolívar remained thin all his life. True, his success was never steady enough to allow him to settle down to a life of sedentary enjoyment of power; and this in itself would have justified the difference. But there were deeper causes which explain the gaunt appearance he preserved till his death.

The recurrence of " sad and heavy thoughts and sombre ideas " may be detected in all the portraits of Bolívar except those of his first youth. The background of his eyes is sad when the rest of his features may be defiant and assertive—merry he never seems to be, in his portraits at any rate. Some of his diarists have depicted him at times gay and talkative. Sadness in him evidently was the natural state into which he dropped when passive and unsolicited by company. Nor is this sadness of his eyes abstract and general, but a moroseness with roots in it. Any Galician knows it at first sight for that *morriña* which the natives of Galicia develop away from their fatherland. Whenever he is left in peace, he turns sad, but with the wistful sadness of a Gallego. And Peru de Lacroix supplies a physical feature which confirms it: his head, he says, was large above and narrow and pointed below—the typical Galician head.

This feature of his character must be connected with his love of movement. In a hammock, he was always rocking to and fro; walking, he outstripped all his staff; on horseback, he tired everybody out; in conversation, he moved constantly; he was an inveterate dancer. He told Peru de Lacroix that " in the time of his campaigns, when his headquarters were in a city, town or village, dances were arranged nearly every night, and that his pleasure was to dance and valse, then vanish from the room to dictate some orders and dispatches, and again dance and work again; that in this way, his ideas became clearer and stronger, and his style more eloquent; in one word, dancing inspired him and excited his imagination ". The same observer says that " spiritual and bodily activity keeps the *Libertador* in continuous agitation. Anyone who would observe him in certain moments without knowing him might think he was mad. In our afternoon walks his pleasure is sometimes to walk very fast and try to tire out those who go with him; on other occasions he runs and jumps leaving everybody else behind; then he waits for them and tells them they cannot run. He will do the same when riding. When the bad weather prevents our going out, H.E. gets his own back by lying on the hammock and rocking fast, or walking along the corridors of the house sometimes singing, sometimes reciting verse or conversing with others who walk with him. When discussing with his friends, he suddenly changes the conversation or the position of his body. It seems as if there were nothing stable in him." The two features, sadness when in repose, constant itch to move, are evidently related. Bolívar had to churn his inner self in order to rise to the requirements of life. In a quiescent state, he fell below the level of energy which life required of him, and his whole being seemed to withdraw into the black cave of his eyes, sombre and sad with *morriña*.

2

We have already observed this tendency to perpetual motion in both Bolívar and Carreño, and seen in it a form of the desire to get away from that too too solid earth which so awkwardly refuses to rise to the clouds of unreal idealism. Such a tendency could not cause much anxiety to Carreño's soul. His temperament was jovial and earthly, his whole being plebeian; his roots did not possess the tenacity and the vigour those of the aristocratic Bolívar owed to two centuries of domination. This aristocratic sense remained very much alive in Bolívar in spite of the influence of his intellectual and republican self. When his friend the Marqués de Toro was already a division general of the republic, Bolívar said of him " that he granted more merit to his title of marqués than to that of general " (a fairly illogical attitude for a marqués of the Spanish Court leading armies of rebels against it). Bolívar added, no less illogically, " the marqués is the prototype of frankness, amenity and joviality of our good ancestors; he is truly noble in his sentiments, in his behaviour, as he is by his birth ".

These glimpses into Bolívar's mind illustrate the cause of his sadness in repose and of his vivacity in motion. He was aware of a gap between his faiths and his ideas; and his being was ever taut in an endeavour to conciliate the two irreconcilable parts which composed it. That is why Bolívar's eye never gained either the steadiness or the serene brilliancy of Napoleon's glance. He never looked at his interlocutor. And as for the fire of his eyes, which all observers praise, it was for all a sign of energy, for none a sign of peace. In this, Napoleon was his superior. Napoleon had no doubts. He was of one piece. Bolívar's inward landscape was bleak and barren; his underlife flowed unseen, unable to rise to the light of the intellectual sun since all his accesses to it had been blocked by the death of his father, mother, wife. Above the barren land, there stretched a sky which Carreño had painted with the brightest colours borrowed from the European masters. There shone the perfect shapes of liberty, fraternity, philanthropy and democracy, angel-winged, ethereal clouds; and, in opposition to them, shedding a light too resplendent to be shut out because of its impure origin—the imperial sun of Napoleon.

Bolívar shared the three bloods of the New World. Though a white for practical purposes, small proportions of Indian and negro blood flowed in his veins; enough, even had they been ten times smaller, to gain him access to the collective memories and reactions of the two varieties of man on which in the New World fell the burden of labour and obedience. Without them, Bolívar would be neither representative of a continental awareness at a given moment in history nor even coherent; since many of his utterances which, under the assumption of his three-blood American nature, are explicable and natural, would, were he a pure white, become the ravings of an irresponsible demagogue.

3

As a white, Bolívar was heir to a tradition of power and government which took itself for granted to the point of ceasing to be aware of itself. That the white owned the land, the cattle, the slaves and whatever Indians were " reduced " or assimilated, was no more the subject of doubt and discussion than that day is day and night is night. This white tradition of power and government had two roots: the conqueror and the friar. The conqueror was himself the heir of the tradition of the reconquest of Spain from the Arabs; a struggle of eight hundred years during which the Spanish hidalgo acquired a notion that a spear furrowing a field of Moors yielded more wealth and honour than a plough furrowing the land. As if Providence had designed it deliberately, the end of this long struggle had come the very year in which America was discovered; and as if that hint from above had not been broad enough, the man who discovered the New World, as he himself took care to point out, bore a twice symbolical name: Cristo-ferens Colón-izer. This made of the whole New World in Spanish eyes a kind of afterthought of Providence, whereby the spears, now idle for lack of Moors, could go and earn honour and wealth against the new infidels. Such a tradition, deeper than any thought or theory, gave the whites of America, " conquerors' sons " to a man, their superb assurance about their right to rule and not to work.

The conquerors had more especially fulfilled the task symbolized in the second part of the Discoverer's name. They had colonized America. The friars took the task suggested by the first name: they christianized it. The creative work of the Church of Spain in the New World is one of the finest achievements in history—so fine that not even the corruption and the crimes which sullied its name in the seventeenth and eighteenth centuries can diminish it. The Spanish Church brought to the New World the principle of the freedom of the Indians, and that of the Christian equality of all men. For a century, it struggled hard to check the exploitation of the natives, which the conquerors tried to justify on grounds of expediency and lack of labour with arguments brandished nowadays by other conquerors in other fields. The Church set up most of the educational and charitable institutions which soon dotted the whole continent; and acted in general as the advocate of the weaker and defenceless part of the population, without bias of any kind as to colour.

The tradition of the churchman was intertwined with that of the lawyer, the border between civil and religious law being then undefined. The Church was the *alma mater* of the gown-men who, with the cape-and-sword-men, heirs to the conquerors, share throughout three centuries the government of America. For this reason, the trend of the gown-man was often found to be favourable to the underdog, whether Indian or negro. The cape-and-sword-man and the gown-man, carry on respectively the traditions of the conqueror and of the friar; as types of transition between the chivalrous and crusading times and the days of politics and democracy. They are to this day represented all over South America and Spain by the " generals " and the " doctors " or intellectuals, struggling each to incarnate a different mode of life and of government. The cape-and-sword-man stands for honour and glory. He wants to govern unfettered, subject only to a justification after the event—that of his own honour. If he has done wrong, he loses his honour. Therefore, trust him since he is even more concerned than you are in his own success. Glory thus becomes, despite its apparent egotism, a real social value.*

This principle, whereby his actions need not be justified till after they have borne fruit, allows the man of action wide freedom in the choice of means and methods. That is why it was so much in favour with the conquerors. Hence the frequent cases of indiscipline with which the path of the Conquest bristles at every step. The most famous of these cases, their symbol and often their model, was the neat legal fiction whereby Cortés broke loose from the allegiance he owed Velázquez, who, as Governor of Cuba, was his superior officer. By turning his army into a city, which he called Veracruz, and by securing from that city's municipal, i.e. parliamentary, institutions his own reinstatement as Captain General and Chief Justice, he became an authority depending only from the King through the people, thus evicting Velázquez. But Cortés knew full well that nothing but a victory would fill these empty forms with the substance of power; and, back in Spain, he justified his act of indiscipline with the empire he had conquered.

These conquerors saw glory as princely and stately life. When they broke discipline they knew that if they failed they would die on the scaffold, as did Gonzalo Pizarro; but that if they succeeded, they would be great lords. There was a good deal of Sancho in these Don Quixotes before whose eyes the devil was continually setting " here and there, and everywhere, a bag full of gold pistoles, so that methinks, at every step, I am laying my hand upon it, embracing it and carrying it home, buying lands, settling rents, and living like a prince ". Once they had undergone all their toils and secured not the bag full of pistoles but a whole kingdom of gold and silver, these men lived in dignity, refinement, greatness and culture, with chapels of singers, guests by the hundred, and servants galore.

Unlike them, the gown-man and his prototype the friar, did not stand for honour but for virtue; he did not want to act unfettered, but within the four corners of a written law. He did not act first and justify his deeds after the event by the glory which they might bring him; but waited to

---

* This principle was clearly stated by Cortés in one of his letters to Charles V in which he begs the Emperor (who had instructed him to appoint the municipal authorities out of lists of nominees presented by the towns themselves), to let him keep to his own system, which was to appoint them freely himself. For, he argues, the towns would present whosoever suited the personal interests of the local authorities and not " the good of the republic ", while " the Governor, since all order and harmony in the councils redounds to his honour, and the reverse to his infamy, obviously will pay more attention to what is fitting ".

act till he had defined the principles on which to found his action, so that, for him, justification came before and not after the event. These two types, conqueror and friar, cape-and-sword-man and gown-man, general and doctor, are like two trends which mix their actions and reactions throughout the three centuries of Spanish rule, and beyond. They are of course mixed in all men; there was hardly a conqueror in whom the friar-like element was altogether absent, hardly a friar who was not a bit of a conqueror as well; and the same applies to the cape-and-sword and the gown trends in the middle period, and to the generals and doctors of our days. But one feature of this tradition is well worth emphasizing: the conqueror-cape-and-sword-general trend is a monarchist, the friar-gown-doctor trend a republican tradition. This is of course implicit in their respective vocations, in their birth (friars being often of humble origin) and in their respective standards, honour for the first, and virtue for the second. The cape-and-sword-men sent to govern the Indies went as viceroys; the gown-men nearly always as presidents.

All these traditions were alive in Bolívar, who was above all, and whatever his mixtures, of the blood of the conquerors. Simón I was a gown-man. Other strains in the *Libertador* conveyed the impetus of the conqueror to the core of his being. When he stood on the Sacred Mount swearing to destroy the Spanish sway over America, he acted as a genuine scion of that very Spanish sway he wanted to destroy, without which neither he nor his fortune would have existed. He was essentially a cape-and-sword-man, while his squire and mentor belonged to the gown species. And later, when on his fancy-winged horse he ploughed with his sword the field of tyrants, he was, to be sure, as convinced that he galloped on a crusade as were the Spaniards who had ploughed with their spears the field of Moorish or Indian infidels; but he was also as eager as they were to carve for himself in History a princely estate. Undisciplined, of course. Glory for a Spanish conqueror nearly always began with indiscipline. "His Excellency"— notes Peru de Lacroix—"declared to us that the beginning of his career had been a disobedience to the express orders of Colonel Labatud, Commander in Chief of the forces of the State of Cartagena which towards the end of 1812 were active in the province of Santa Marta." But if glory began with indiscipline it might end in power and a princely state—unless it led to the scaffold . . . or to a Spanish dungeon, as did Miranda's.

Nor was this glory material, impersonal, economic, such as can be handed over to other persons. None of these men, neither Cortés nor Bolívar nor any between them, would have been content to turn his deeds into shares, as did Francis Drake. No shareholders need apply. Glory, for these men, is personal, not transferable; upwards not forwards; an end in itself, no means for anyone or anything; a spire, not a bridge. Bolívar was not thinking of becoming wealthier than he was; he was not even really thinking of becoming a crowned king or emperor of Venezuela or of the Great Colombia. He was not thinking at all. He was feeling, rising, tending, aspiring to his highest self. Both from his native idealism and from the influence of his philosophic friend, he had gained a Castillian contempt for the trappings of power. He was enchanted with the austerity of Napoleon's appearance—as he would have been with the austerity of Philip II—and felt how far more majestic it was than the jewel-shop-window chests of the imperial marshals and attendants. The crown Bolívar sought was not that of any kingdom on the map: he wanted to be king of History, which covers all the space of the earth and all the time of mankind.

4

So far, the white. But, even if in small porportions, Bolívar was also a *pardo* and a *mestizo*. The *pardo*, or mulatto, comes out not merely in a number of physical features—his crisp and bristling hair, his lower lip, his jet-black eyes, the elongated skull—but in that exuberance, that buoyancy, that turbulence which often bursts forth boisterously in him, his immoderate love of dancing, his sexual appetite, a tendency to gaudiness and to sensuous joys, in opposition to his Castillian austerity, his torrents of Eau de Cologne. . . . Through his black blood, Bolívar gained access to that African soul, rich in animistic forces, which the crime and cruelty of the whites transplanted to the New World. And the white in him took towards the black in him both the domineering and contemptuous attitude of the conqueror and the Christian and charitable attitude of the friar. As a cape-and-sword-man, Bolívar was apt to look down upon the blacks and mulattoes. As a gown-man, steeped in the doctrines of the friars which his friend Carreño had translated into the language of the French Revolution, Bolívar felt himself to be the champion of all men, including the blacks. The negro in him was indifferent to Spain, with which he was connected with nothing but ties of resentment for a liberty and a country lost. But this resentment of the negro towards Spain was much weaker and far less dangerous than the feelings harboured by the Indians and made vocal by the *mestizos* ; and for two reasons. There was no community, no mass behind the blacks; only loose individuals coming from different parts of Africa at different times. And the black knew that in Spanish lands his brethren were treated better than under any other flag in the New World and could gain their liberty more easily. Withal, the fact that Bolívar had black blood in his veins must have made it much easier for him to rise against that Spanish world which also lived in him and was the most forceful tradition in his soul.

Less apparent (though not altogether absent) in his features, the Indian was also an element in Bolívar's complex composition, and lent him traits both of the pure native and of the *mestizo* psychologies. That sadness we noted in him as the normal attitude of his quiescent moments, Spanish and particularly Galician though it is, has also a definite connection with the passive sufferings of the patient Indian overcome by a stronger people. There are in Bolívar's life stretches of passivity in which he seems incapable of action. They may well be due to temporary returns of the Indian hidden in his depth. The long patience with which he can wait for enemies or events is an Indian feature of his complex character. And there is a curious wistfulness in his references to the Indian days of the New World which would be inexplicable without his Indian blood.

But the Indian in the history of America, after the risings of the first epoch when the Conquest had not yet asserted itself, is hardly ever able to rebel without *mestizo* leadership. As a *mestizo*, Bolívar ranks with Condorcanqui of Peru and Villarreal of New Spain as a leader of the native men of America against the white usurpers. Unless we accept Bolívar in this capacity, many of his most forcible utterances against Spain make no sense— for he was a Spaniard himself. " A continent separated from Spain by immense seas, more populated and richer, submitted during three centuries to a degrading and tyrannical dependence. . . ." " Three centuries did America groan under this tyranny, the hardest that ever afflicted mankind. . . ." " The ferocious Spaniard, vomited on the coast of Colombia to convert the most beautiful part of the world into a vast and odious empire of cruelty and loot. . . . He signalled his arrival in the New World with death and desolation: he wiped out from its earth the original race; and when his fury found no more beings to destroy, he turned against his own son settled in the soil he had usurped." If Bolívar had no Indian blood, the fact that he wrote these lines would have sufficed to have him housed in a lunatic asylum. Simón Bolívar I and most of his ancestors were " Spaniards vomited in Colombia to spread death and desolation ". The original race " wiped out " by these ancestors of Bolívar was still swarming round him in excellent health while he wrote these frantic words. The feelings which drew his hand to write them confirm that Bolívar was a *mestizo* better than any genealogical enquiry. Now the *mestizo* is the shiftiest character in America. Within the soul of the *mestizo*, the conqueror and the conquered people live together. Unlike the negro, uprooted and transplanted, the Indian remained in the lands once his; and so, when locked up by mixed birth within the same skin with a white, he was at the same time in the Indian community and out of it; in the Spanish community and out of it. The tensions within the *mestizo* soul were the strongest in the Indies. They kept the *mestizo* in unstable equilibrium, ready to fall this way or that, to the white or to the Indian side of his being.

Owing to the prestige of the white strain, the soul of the Indies developed a yearning upwards towards the white blood. For three centuries, white blood in the Spanish New World meant Spanish blood. Hence the stubborn attachment of the Creoles to the name of " Spaniards ", leaving for the Spaniards from Spain that of " Europeans ". For them, to call themselves Spaniards was essential, for that meant that they were whites. This yearning upwards, towards the white, ruled all social life, in particular sexual relations, legitimate or illegitimate; everyone sought to improve his or her degree of whiteness in preference to his or her wealth. Any Spaniard from Spain, whatever his station or even his education, could thus make a good marriage by bartering his white blood for a cocoa estate or a silver mine in the shape of a more or less dusky lady. Inversely, the earth of the Indies pulled the white blood from the top downwards to the native and black stocks. The whites, conscious of this trend which worked through love affairs and weddings or through (to use a picturesque Spanish saying) unions behind the Church, sought the more to attach themselves to that Spanish heaven which would protect them against the earth of coloured blood. When the evolution of all things, the philosophic ideas of the century, the French Revolution, the weakness of the Spanish State, the expulsion of the Jesuits, loosened the links between Spain and her kingdoms overseas, many Creoles gradually veered in their attachment from white Spain to white Europe. They sought help in the culture of France and England. The heaven of ideas took for them the place of that light from above which radiated from the Spanish Court and had made them shine as the aristocracy of the New World. Till then, they had been the apex of society because they were the heirs to a glorious past, the bearers of Spanish honours, titles and decorations. Henceforth, they would be on the apex as the harbingers of a glorious future, the bearers of the new ideas. So Bolívar. As a philosopher and a man of his century he remained an aristocrat.

5

Despite the flourish of names of great thinkers in his letters and conversation, it is doubtful whether Bolívar was an assiduous student of the philosophers he mentions. He was too swift, too much of a man of action, to have pored over Locke or Hobbes, Rousseau or Helvetius. That he could quote Voltaire we can readily believe. Voltaire can be read at a draft, as one drinks clear, sparkling water. Bolívar, moreover, was very much of a Spaniard, and as such he shared in that tendency of all Spaniards to go straight to nature for their ideas, trusting no brain but their own to procure them. The Spanish peoples are like forests in which every tree stands on its own ground and feeds from the earth through its own roots; not, as is the case with other nations, like a river in which a tradition flows smoothly from generation to generation. The Spaniard therefore takes life from below rather than from the past, from his own self rather than from tradition; so that, in the matter of ideas and culture, every Spaniard begins all over again. So Bolívar. And therefore, without altogether excluding the influence of the ideas and tendencies which floated, so to speak, in the mental air of his day, we must bear in mind that the chief influence on Bolívar's thought was that of Bolívar himself.

We may then expect that his attitude towards the deeper things of life will be as complex as every other aspect of his composite being. The more so as, after all, Bolívar was not a thinker, but a man of action. His natural trend was not to build up a coherent image of the world as a system; it was to go out to life and impress on it the seal of his personality. He had a keen mind and wrote a concise, incisive style; but, again, he was not a writer, if by that is meant an artist whose medium is the word. Bolívar cannot therefore be expected to possess a solid and single structure of philosophy of life of his own. Thoughts he had many, sharp and clear. Thought he had none.

In his conscious moods he was a materialist and a rationalist. In conversation with Peru de Lacroix, he spoke superciliously about the old and modern philosophers who had " held forth " over the soul. " ' I dislike '—

he added—' dabbling in metaphysics on false bases. It is enough for me to know that the soul has the faculty of feeling, that is, of receiving the impressions transmitted by our senses, but not that of thinking, for I do not admit that there are innate ideas. Man has a material body, and an intellect also material, represented by the brain, and according to present-day science, the intellect is just a secretion of the brain; for me the brain dies with the body, and once the brain is dead, there is no more secretion of intellect. You may gather from all that what my ideas may be on the Elyseum, the Phanarus or Tartarus and on the sacred fictions with which mortals are still so much concerned.' That philosophy, Sir—I said to the *Libertador*—is very lofty, and I see but few men in this country capable of rising so high. ' Time, my friend '—His Excellency replied—' education and the freedom from prejudice which it breeds, and a certain inclination of the mind will gradually initiate my countrymen to natural things and free them from their fondness for supernatural things.' "

It is clear from this page that Bolívar had not examined teleological questions closely enough to rise above what his French aide-de-camp considered " a very lofty philosophy ". He could be shallow and limited, to the point of denying himself that elbow room of doubt which the mystery of life and our own inadequacy to grasp it require. But, again, he was not a philosopher in our modern sense of the word; though he constantly and rightly considers himself as one in the sense the word had in his time, i.e. a man emancipated from the dogmas and creeds of the Church. Within this field, he can be acute and penetrating, as in his remarks to Peru de Lacroix on forebodings. " I know Socrates and other wise men did not despise their forebodings, but I should rather call that wisdom weakness, cowardice, or if preferred, excessive prudence; Socrates called his forebodings his Daemon; I have no such Daemon, for I do not trouble about them. I am convinced that future events are hidden by an impenetrable veil, and hold for a fool or a madman the man who carries his fears beyond the bounds of reason, and thinks his life is in danger because he had such or such a dream; because a wanton impulse of the will, expressed in the absence of his reason, has put before him a future danger; because in his inner self, something has bidden him not to do something, not to go further but to retrace his steps, not to offer battle on a Friday or on a Sunday. . . . Out of millions of presentiments and dreams, hazard has confirmed but a few, and these are quoted and not the others." Here the two rationalistic arguments are put forward with clarity: statistics, and what we should now call the activity of the subconscious.

Should the need be felt to find a " source " for these views, it is at hand on the family shelves of the Bolívars. The Spanish Benedictine Feijóo held on dreams exactly the same opinions Bolívar was to put forward two generations later. The trend to turn to nature rather than to books, has always been more a feature of character than a philosophy with Spaniards. Introduced in European culture by the Spaniard Vives one generation before Bacon, it was more strongly represented in Spanish letters even in earlier days than is generally realized; and often by churchmen such as

Mariana in the seventeenth century and above all by Feijóo, Bacon's admirer, in the eighteenth. The complete works of Feijóo were one of the standard collections in the library of Don Juan Vicente de Bolívar. What is inherited is not stolen, says a Spanish proverb. Bolívar had inherited not only the books in which Feijóo had expressed in classic Spanish the tendency to read in nature rather than in books, but the tendency itself. He was a keen enquirer and his views on men and things were gathered at first source, from men or from persons well versed in the matter of the enquiry. Ultimately, the chief influence on Bolívar's thought was his own experience. He had a mind of his own, not easily hoodwinked by books or fooled by events. Early in life, some voice in him, possibly a warning from his religious family traditions, possibly a demand from his logical mind, made him realize that a society needs a collective faith, some centripetal force to balance the centrifugal trends of that liberty which was for him a second nature.

He was a pessimist. It is enough to look at his eyes. Rousseau, dreams of his youth, abstract principles of liberty for all, none of these could conquer the inner, fundamental pessimism of his black orbs which knew all that need be known about man from the world behind the eyes and the face, the world of the inner self. Unlike Rousseau, for whom all the trouble was in society, and all that was good came from man, Bolívar was sure that the individual could not be trusted; and, having, as he thought, discarded religion, sought in society the force that would counterbalance individual anarchy. " Too much time have I lost "—he wrote—" serving men, who, as Voltaire used to say, do not deserve even to be ruled." All his life he pursued the dream of some social force, which he tried to conjure up in his constitutions and charters. " Stand up for my *Moral Power*, dear friend "—he wrote to Arboleda (15.vi.23)—" I myself, its author, am waiting to behave well till a tribunal exists to condemn what the laws cannot prevent; I mean that my own weaknesses are only waiting to redress themselves for a tribunal to put them to shame. This motive, shame, is what acts as hell in the case of freethinking men, philosophers and men of the world. . . . Therefore we must seek a half-way between these two extremes and create an institute based on the authority of fundamental laws and of the irresistible force of public opinion."

6

Bolívar was then fully aware of the fact that " philosophy " does not provide a sufficient centripetal force to keep together a society of anarchists— and all men are potential anarchists. He wanted to call out from the depths of the collective " It " its own Spinozian " endeavour to persevere in its own being ", and to build on it that Moral Power which he had dreamt to add to the three powers of Montesquieu. But, as time went by and his experiences crumbled into frustrations, he evolved back to the beliefs of his childhood. How far did he become again a son of the Church he had abandoned in his youth? There are historians who claim him as a good

Catholic. Whatever the view that may be taken on this evolution, one fact is clear. Bolívar's thought was as composite and complex as the rest of his character. In fundamentals, he was not at one with himself.

We may now be able to attach a new meaning to his constant need of movement. It was most difficult for him to reach spiritual equilibrium. Between the many rival centres of force which ruled his inner horizon, wide spaces of indetermination stretched in fearful and solitary emptiness. Bolívar kept in constant motion in flight from that void. His diarists have left on record how unhappy he was till he had reached a decision. "H.E. is at times silent and taciturn: then it means that he has some worry or some scheme in the making, and until he has taken his decision, which usually is not long in coming, he remains ill-humoured and uneasy." It was this vast empty space, crossed and recrossed by tensions, which he feared most. And it was because of the horror of it in which he lived that he could not suffer quietness and physical repose. As with aircraft, he could only hold the air by dint of speed.

Two features of his character may be linked with this sense and craving for speed. One is his fondness for Voltaire. True, Voltaire was the author who best fitted the century; and a man of sharp intellect, abstract ideas and a universal scope for his thoughts, could not but enjoy the works of the Patriarch of Ferney—a name, by the way, which aptly conveys the hidden ecclesiastical tendencies of the "philanthropic" school. But, beneath this ideological attraction, Bolívar must have felt at home with Voltaire because no author in western culture has achieved such swiftness of thought and phrase. Bolívar, quick and always impatient, must have enjoyed as a kind of rest the company of this master mind as swift as his own.

The second feature of Bolívar's character related to his sense of speed is his fondness for feminine adventures. When his wife died, he made up his mind not to marry again, and lived through a series of affairs, often overlapping, and none strong enough to tie him to constancy. There is a connection between the first love, cut off by death, and the rest, successively dissolved by life. In his marriage, as we see it, Bolívar subconsciously sought to regain access to his own self, blocked since the death of his mother. This attempt having been broken when he was already hardening into manhood, the access had to remain blocked. The child in him was buried for good and all. He became a man. The sealing of his underself dried up the desire for progeny which would have carried on that tradition he now was severed from. He advised his friends not to marry. On becoming a widower, he became an individual loose in the world. Young and healthy, he would of course seek women; and in Paris, on the first outburst of his newly-won liberty, he gave himself over to them to the point of endangering his health. This merely physical appetite could find satisfaction in the humblest of women; a lively if unsavoury story from Bolívar's own lips, recorded by Peru de Lacroix, shows him taking safety in flight from the irate inmates of a brothel in London, covering his retreat with handfuls of banknotes. When excited, for instance at the end of a good meal, he indulged in obscene talk.

But there was in his thirst for women something more than animal desire.
In this, as in other features, he was Don Quixote to Simón Carreño's Sancho;
of whom it is said that, having been deprived of an Indian woman, with
whom he lived, by another man, he wrote to him: " Kindly return my
woman, for I need her also for the same aims for which you keep her."
With all his inconstancy and his sensuousness, Bolívar's need of women was
of a higher sort.   There was in it a yearning to escape from his inner void.
Man-and-woman-love is normally the mutual completion of two comple-
mentary incompletes; the mutual satisfaction of two unsatisfied lives which
find in each other the elements each lacked for its balance.   This is the
case when both parties are at peace with their own past, which, through
them, seeks to knot itself into a new future.   But in the case of Bolívar,
divorced from his past, love of woman could neither look to the future nor
be reciprocal.   He was careful to point out to Peru de Lacroix that he was
not sterile.   Having remarked that he was the only one of the family to be
without offspring, he explained that his wife had died soon after their
marriage, and he had not married again, " but people should not think me
sterile, for I have a proof of the contrary ".   In this he may be referring to
a natural son.   There is a hint to that effect in one of Fanny's later letters.
" Your godson, Simoncito Briffard (I hope he is the only one you have in
Europe), is worthy of your kindness, and has the keenest wish to go and
join you "—writes the cousin from Paris on April 28th, 1823.   The passage
seems to want to say more than it says, for if *filleul* was not meant for " natural
son ", why hope that Bolívar had no more in Europe ?   Little is known of
this youth.   All we know about the interest Bolívar took in him is the
" kindness " to which Fanny Villars refers; and the hint about going to
join him does not seem to have borne fruit.   Bolívar's love of women did
not point to the future.   Nor was it reciprocal.   For him there were no
women in the concrete; only woman in the abstract.   All women were for
him the feminine on legs.   In this feminine, he sought possession as a
male temperament, and rest from his inner void in an activity which absorbed
him absolutely and was in itself its own end and justification.   Swift in
love as in thought and in action, Bolívar never kept an attachment for long,
nor was he faithful while it lasted—another sign of the abstract nature of
his love.

This inner speed again was the outcome of the unstable equilibrium of
his soul.   Throughout his life he will pass swiftly from one to another of
his inner points of vantage, taking refuge now in one now in another of his
centres of force against the agony of conflicting tensions which they inflicted
on him in the intermediate spaces.   Hence the changes in his looks, amounting to the revelation of a different man, noted by Peru de Lacroix; and the
shiftiness of his eyes so often noticed, as for instance in this first-hand
description seldom quoted: " His eyes are full and dark, and when directed
straight [i.e. when Bolívar is steady in one of his centres of force] forward
piercing; but they are more frequently employed in sidelong glances at the
persons he is conversing with, or those he is surrounded by, and he seldom
looks directly at even inanimate objects, turning his head on one side like a

hare." Here is the contrast between a Bolívar set on one of his centres of force, knowing where he stands and radiating energy, and a Bolívar lost in the wilderness of indecision, haggard with doubt. Such is the cause of his contradictions, his sudden changes, his unexpected turns of will and behaviour. " I know "—he said to Peru de Lacroix—" how difficult it is to be always the same man, and that when one does not possess invariable principles one cannot keep a uniform behaviour." Now cruel, now kind, now grasping, now generous, now petty, now magnanimous, now passive and quiescent, now impatient at the smallest delay, now an autocrat, now a republican, now a white contemptuous of the castes, now the leader of the castes against the whites, now straightforward and plain, now shifty and crafty, now brave and indomitable, now depressed and even subject to incredible accesses of fear, Bolívar has always been a mystery soul, a problem for the psychologist, a puzzle without a key. The solution of the problem is in the problem itself. It is the very complexity of his character which makes his character clear. As with the atom, not understood till its name was found to be a misnomer and its structure a system of structures in constant motion, so with Bolívar: his character can only be reduced to a unity when it is analysed into its components—a system of centres of force moving about in his mental skies and in the underground caverns of his traditional self, and exerting on each other powerful tensions.

The disruptive forces of such a system must have been terrific. Bolívar must have lived under a constant threat of mental collapse. An Englishman who claims to have known him writes: " He is decidedly the best shot I ever saw. I have never seen him miss a single bird, although he has brought down at least two hundred in my presence." An outstanding testimonial to the concentration of which he was capable. But he was well aware of the danger there was for him in losing control. The same observer describes a scene in which Bolívar seems to have suffered from the effects of drink; and though this may be possible (it was at the end of the banquet to celebrate the armistice with Morillo) the unanimous opinion of those who write about him is that he was abstemious, in the sense that he partook of wine moderately and with discrimination, caring more for quality than for quantity. There was, however, one kind of nectar Bolívar was utterly unable to resist: glory. The exultation which the company of his enthusiastic followers was apt to arouse in him was similar to a kind of intoxication. There are a number of descriptions of end-of-banquet scenes in which Bolívar, drunk with excitement and " glory ", though not with drink, stood on the table and walked from end to end of it, crushing crockery and glasses with his victorious feet.

Such was the price Bolívar had to pay for the complexity and force of his inner system. Nothing could have saved him from that mental collapse which threatened him at every turn but another natural force in his character strong enough to counteract the dispersive effects of the several planets which pulled his being to and fro in the horizons of his soul. This force was an egotism which made his personal self, his ego, a sun capable of holding together all those planets. Egotism and its chief manifestation, ambition, become thus in Bolívar's life bare necessities without which there could be for him no sanity, perhaps no life at all. When on the top of the Sacred Mount Simón Bolívar swore to free his country from the tyranny of Spain, he was swearing to rescue Simón Bolívar from insanity and death. For Bolívar, a life of glory was the only alternative to a miserable life as a mental wreck such as his nephew (most like him) lived. But when, at twenty-two, he saw himself ascending the peak of glory, Bolívar did not yet possess the inner force which alone could hold together his many and discordant parts. His youthful petulance and vanity were not of the fibre which his unruly self needed. They had first to be crushed by the hammer of adversity.

PART II

BOLÍVAR DECLARES WAR ON SPAIN

CHAPTER X

MIRANDA'S FIRST FAILURE

I

WHILE the youthful knight swore on the Sacred Mount to free his country, an older and a more battered one was trying his hand at it. Miranda would indeed be admirable for his refusal to acknowledge failure had he been more capable of learning from it. Before the turn of the century he had had dealings with Pitt, both before and after his revolutionary adventure in France, as a general of the armies of the Republic. Twice he had had proof evident that Pitt had used him as a mere tool to force Spain to conform to the designs of Britain; while, in France, he had seen imperialist greed so clearly behind the screen of " liberation " with which the young Republic covered her ambitions over the New World, that he had declined an offer to go as commander and governor of St. Domingue and in fact as hardly more than a Spanish-American decoy for a purely French enterprise.

One of the men who took part in his attempt and failure, the American Biggs, has left a good portrait of the man at this time: " He is about five feet ten inches high. His limbs are well proportioned; his whole frame is stout and active. His complexion is dark, florid and healthy. His eyes are hazel coloured, but not of the darkest hue. They are piercing, quick and intelligent, expressing more of the severe than the mild feelings. He has good teeth, which he takes much care to keep clean. His nose is large and handsome, rather of the English than Roman cast. His chest is square and prominent. His hair is grey and he wears it tied long behind with powder. He has strong grey whiskers growing on the outer edges of his ears, as large as most Spaniards have on their cheeks. In the contour of his visage you plainly perceive an expression of pertinaciousness and suspicion. Upon the whole without saying he is an elegant, we may pronounce him a handsome man. He has a constant habit of picking his teeth. When sitting he is never perfectly still; his foot or hand must be moving to keep time with his mind which is always in exercise. He always sleeps a few moments after dinner, and then walks till bed time, which with him is about midnight. He is an eminent example of temperance. A scanty or bad meal is never regarded by him as a subject of complaint. He uses no ardent spirits; seldom any wine. Sweetened water is his common beverage. He is a courtier and gentleman in his manners. Dignity and grace preside in his movements. Unless when angry, he has a great command of his feelings; and can assume what looks and tones he pleases. In general his demeanour is marked by hauteur and distance. When he is angry he loses discretion. He is impatient of contradiction. In discourse he is logical in the management of his thoughts. He appears conversant on all subjects. His iron memory prevents his ever being at a loss for names, dates and authorities. . . . He appeared the master of languages, of science and literature. . . . Modern history and biography afforded him abundant topics. He impressed an opinion of his comprehensive views, his inexhaustible fund of learning; his probity, his generosity and patriotism. After all, this man of renown, I fear, must be considered as having more learning than wisdom; more theoretical knowledge than practical talent; too sanguine and too opinionated to distinguish between the vigour of enterprise and the hardiness of infatuation."

In the early summer of 1807, one year after Miranda's failure, and about the time Simón Bolívar returned to Caracas after his wandering days, the French naturalist Dauxion Lavaysse, touring the islands of the coast in the interest of his science, arrived in Cumaná. " Having entered a grocer's shop "—he writes—" I found him busy making paper bags with copies of the *Declaration of the Rights of Man*, of the *Contrat Social* and of bulls, genuine or forged, of Pius VI, excommunicating the French nation." The shopkeeper explained that he had brought all those papers from Trinidad after the Treaty of Amiens. They were the stock of propaganda which the British Government and Miranda were spreading over the Spanish coast. The chief English agent was Lieutenant-Colonel Picton, the notorious Governor of Trinidad. Miranda's collaboration with Picton had begun immediately after the British occupation of the Island in 1797. " Permitt me to Congratulate you "—an English friend of Miranda wrote then to another English friend of Miranda—" on the Event of Peace; & especially on our retaining Trinidad. I am afraid it is no matter of Congratulation to our friend Martin." Martin was a code name then used by Miranda. The Englishman, Turnbull, who had financed Miranda for years, assumed that his Venezuelan friend would deplore the loss of Trinidad. Miranda had already given away not only Trinidad but Margarita and Puerto Rico, in fact, every Spanish island in the New World but Cuba, when drafting his own instructions as chief South American representative in Great Britain (22.xii.97).

The situation was very much as if some English exiles in the seventeenth century, after seeing how the King of France seized and later permanently acquired the Isle of Wight, had gone on appealing to the French Government for help to liberate Britain from her oppressors, with the Isle of Wight as a base. When in 1799 Miranda presented to Pitt a petition from one Vargas, a *mestizo* from Bogotá, with the usual appeals for help to " shake off the yoke of so odious an oppression as that of the Court of Madrid ", the sentence which must have struck Pitt's mind—if he read the paper at all—may well have been this pathetic one: " Therefore, if Great Britain wishes to weaken her enemies and to acquire an eternal right to the gratitude of Spanish America (the inhabitants of which are the simplest in the world) this is the moment." " The inhabitants of which are the simplest in the world ",

Pitt would read again, and smile. By then, the British Government had been receiving from South America a regular hail of " Don Juliáns ".*

All these Don Juliáns came on separate errands; all brought a tale of outrageous oppression, on which the British Government had—as will appear anon—views of its own; and all asked for military and financial help for their nations to rebel, and for personal help to subsist while the manna of liberation fell on their native soil from the British skies. All were discreetly and politely received, scrutinized for any capacities they might evince to become the willing and knowing, or unwilling and unknowing, tools of British policy, and accordingly dismissed or kept on short strings of English banknotes, in their turn kept in a good state of repair by contraband trade with the countries to be eventually liberated or otherwise disposed of as might suit the interests of His Majesty.

2

These visitors were all kept studiously apart. Miranda, pensioned by Pitt to the tune of £1,000 a year, more or less regularly paid, knew nothing whatever about the Peruvian Jesuit Vizcardo, pensioned £300, till this eminent victim of Charles III and of Aranda died embittered against England (17.ii.98), leaving his papers to the American Minister in London, King. One of these papers was the famous *Letter to the American Spaniards*, in which the disgruntled Jesuit urged his countrymen to sever their ties with the mother country. Miranda had this Letter printed and sent to Trinidad to be distributed all over Venezuela by Picton, and he never ceased to make use of it—nor did the grocer in Cumaná, who found the paper on which it was printed as useful as Miranda did the text. Miranda was kept in England virtually a prisoner, for he was refused the papers to leave the country. He grew restive and resentful. It was a strange paradox that a would-be liberator should enjoy no liberty. In his hurry to leave for Trinidad he had his friend Pownall explain to Pitt (who would not receive him) that the revolution in Spanish America would take place anyhow, whether by the people, who would set up a Jacobin system, or by the wealthy landowners, who would organize a regular government under the protection of Britain. Pitt did not tremble and gave no passport. Miranda then bethought himself of the changes which had taken place in France. Bonaparte was no Jacobin. He wrote to the First Consul as a French citizen, which he considered himself to be when necessary, and asked leave to reside in France. There was no answer. He wrote again. He had friends in France, and between them and King, the American Minister, they succeeded in enabling him to leave London (September, 1800) for the Hague and later Paris. But Fouché, after a close interrogation, during which Miranda spoke bitterly of the British Government who " hated the principles of liberty they have seen established in France ", had him expelled from a France in which the

* Count Don Julián, to avenge a wrong done to his daughter by the King of the Spanish Goths, Don Rodrigo, went over to Morocco and brought in the Moors to rule Spain for eight centuries. Possibly legendary, but a useful symbol.

principles of liberty were no longer in fashion. The would-be liberator went back to England.

He left Paris (22.iii.01) and by way of Holland arrived in Gravesend on April 21st. He immediately wrote to Pitt. The tune had of course changed again. The Spanish territories were still to be saved, but whether from England or from France depended on whether Miranda happened to be in France or in England. This time, South America was to be saved again from the " French Jacobin system " by allowing Miranda the means to lead a revolution of the upper classes, to which he belonged, if not as the son of a Caracas shopkeeper, at least as a Count which everybody thought he was— including at times himself. Pitt's ministry had resigned, and Miranda had to begin all over again with the new men, mostly with Vansittart, who strongly objected to any share of the United States in the plan of emancipation. Miranda was of course ready with a constitution. It revealed that *mestizo* inspiration which was at the basis of nearly every plan of this kind. It was based on the *cabildos* and *alcaldes* of the Spanish régime, whose powers were to remain " as in the past ". The armed forces were to be placed under a *Hatunapa*; and the Assembly of the *cabildos* was to appoint two *Curacas*— a native name for local chiefs, familiar in Peru, but as foreign to the Indians of Mexico as that of *alderman*. A theoretically well-built system of assemblies based on the *cabildos* and topped by a legislative body under the name of *Concilio Colombiano*, would appoint the executive officers, two heads of the State with powers for ten years, under the title of *Incas*. One of the *Incas* was to reside permanently in the federal city, and the other was to be travelling about the provinces of the Empire. A city named Colombo, to be erected somewhere in the region of Panama, was to be the capital.

The horse is thinking one thing and the groom another one—says the Spanish proverb. Miranda's head was teeming with *Incas* and *Curacas*, St. Vincent and Vansittart were thinking of naval bases and trade; and the negotiations with Miranda were handy to frighten Spain into making whatever peace Britain wanted. Miranda suggested landing in Coro with three hundred men and equipment for twenty times as many, whom he would recruit on his stride inland. He soon realized that some of his friends, Vansittart in particular, were thinking of conquering Venezuela rather than of freeing her; and put it to them that there was to be " neither monopoly nor conquest ". Later in the month (August, 1801), he realized that he had been used as a tool in order to ensure the success of the peace of Amiens, the signature of the preliminaries of which was announced on October 2nd: " This is in substance the outcome of so many tortures in our affair "—he wrote in his diary (16.viii.01)—" and here we are at the mercy of England, who will deliver us to Spain or to France, whichever suits her interests, in spite of the definite stipulation we made when I arrived here that if England was not in a position to help us, we should go to our country to do what we could ourselves. . . . Heavens alive, what bad faith! Poor Americans, how your fate goes knocking about in the world! "

3

The peace of Amiens was little better than a truce. The ink was not yet dry on its documents when Miranda and his English friends were preparing fresh schemes to emancipate Spanish America from Spain or to conquer it for Britain, according to the side of the table on which the maps were spread. Miranda dreamt of Caracas; Admiral Popham, of Buenos Aires. Spain, offended by the high-handed way in which Bonaparte had sold Louisiana to the United States in 1803, remained neutral in the new phase of the endemic Franco-British war; but Bonaparte forced the Spanish Government to pay for its military neutrality at the rate of six million French pounds a year. This suited the party in Britain which wanted war with Spain; but Pitt was not in a hurry about that, and he kept the Creole adventurer waiting in London, dangling before the Spanish Ambassador as a bait.

War between France and England had begun again in May, 1804; not till December of that year was Godoy able to spur Charles IV to action despite the repeated attacks of the British Fleet against Spanish ships at sea. Miranda had no grounds whatsoever to plead ignorance of Britain's intentions. He knew the British had kept Trinidad for good—an island belonging by nature to his country; and he had cut out and filed an article published by the *Morning Post* (Wednesday, 15.x.04), a strange mixture of sense and nonsense, in which the intentions of his would-be allies were revealed.

" Spain is to be subdued in America, not in Europe "—wrote the *Morning Post*. " Her valuable settlements on the other side of the Atlantic, are vulnerable at two points. These points are, the rich and defenceless kingdom of Peru and the kingdom of Mexico. . . . By adopting proper measures, no ship will be able to pass from La Vera Cruz to Europe without our permission, nor any European vessel thither. Thus deprived of the articles of consumption, which they had been accustomed to receive from the mother country, and which are necessary to their accommodation, the inhabitants of New Spain will readily submit to that Power which alone can supply their wants; and which will guarantee to them the free exercise of their religion, with a more indulgent Government, and a more advantageous market for their produce. From La Vera Cruz to Mexico, the richest and most splendid city in the world, the centre of all that is carried on between America and Europe on one hand, and between America and the East Indies on the other, is a *mere walk* of not two hundred miles, on a well-known, frequented, and public high road."

After expatiating to its heart's content on the cruelty and tyranny of the Spanish Administration of the New World, the *Morning Post* went on to ask: " Is this a condition of society to be preferred to one which ensured the enjoyment of property ? On the contrary, does it not embolden and invite a spirited enterprise ? " The editor, of course, would not have written such questions had he not known the answers to them. Nor were they quite what Miranda would have wished. " The Spanish-American colonies no longer preserve the traces of that grandeur and that freedom which distinguished their Castilian progenitors. They have contracted an obsequiousness and submission of character, to which the rigour of their Government has unhappily reduced them. From a people so debased, what resistance is to be expected by the disciplined troops of Britain. It is problematical, whether they would not look upon an attack from this country as the rallying point of deliverance. If then, Spain should provoke such an attempt . . . the British Empire would find its interest best served, and its glory best upheld, not by ransacking the bowels of the earth to explore new mines of gold and silver; not by depopulating those countries by eternally working those old mines, but in raising out of these poisonous caverns, the victims of avarice, indolence and lordly pride; and in restoring to the Indian world the liberty and happiness of which they have been unjustly deprived for ages. . . . What *rational* prospect there is of a successful and permanent colonization in these empires "—the London paper goes on to say—" and of an hearty co-operation on the part of the mild and timid Indians, as well as the native colonists, may be easily supposed from the natural feelings of a race now bowed down with the sense of the common bondage of Prince and People. . . . We have transplanted our equal and enlightened laws to the remoter banks of the Ganges, and millions of men are refreshed and protected by it. . . . A vigorous Administration will render the British Empire as expansive as its name, bid its thunders roll on the shores of the Pacific and proclaim to future generations, that Britain, while contending for its own freedom and independence, was the restorer of the Indian world."

Impervious to these teachings, Miranda kept on trying to obtain British help for his plans. One of his chief supporters was Lord Melville, the man who had sheltered Picton from the accusations made against him for his cruel rule in Trinidad. Melville's fall (April, 1805) was a setback for Miranda. More trouble came from Pitt, whose policy towards Spain was a subtle blend of attraction and of repulsion. At this moment, Pitt appears to have been simultaneously preparing for a general attack on the Spanish New World and negotiating to detach Spain from France. This meant that while Miranda's activities might be useful, they had better be carried out from another base than London. Pitt secretly prepared Popham's expedition against Buenos Aires; and, at the same time, sent Miranda to the United States, well provided with funds: six thousand sterling and authority to draw up to another two thousand.

4

Miranda arrived in New York on November 4th, 1805. There was at the time much tension between the United States and Spain. The country was still in an adventurous and pioneering spirit, hardly recovered from the exhilaration caused by the sudden acquisition of Louisiana; casting ambitious eyes on Florida and dreaming of conquests even beyond—all of course at the expense of Spain. " In 1804, John Adair, a valiant soldier, who later served under Jackson, at the battle of New Orleans, wrote to James Wilkinson, the ambitious freebooter: ' The Kentuckyans are full of enterprise and although not poor, as greedy after plunder as ever the old Romans were; Mexico glitters in our eyes—the word is all we wait for '." Aaron Burr, somewhat beyond the pale since the duel in which he had shot Hamilton dead, had bought an estate in Louisiana, and formed the ambitious project of conquering Mexico and perhaps also of organizing a secession of the western States of his own country, for his benefit. Burr feared that the arrival of Miranda might reduce him to second fiddle in this scheme. He seems to have been unaware of the fact that the British Government was using him as a tool just as it was using Miranda.

Burr's megalomania saved the United States from a war of secession which in those early days might have proved fatal. " To all appearances "—wrote Casa-Irujo, the Spanish Minister in Washington, to his government (28.i.1807)—" Spain has rescued the United States from this threat to her integrity, for she would have been destroyed had Wilkenson entered fully into Burr's views, a fact which might have been expected, for Wilkenson detests the Government, and the separation of the Western States was ever a favourite plan of his. Burr's silly and stubborn insistence on his wild schemes against Mexico has undone him. Wilkenson is completely ours; he gets a substantial pension from the King, and his commonsense and military training made him certain that such an expedition would end in disaster. No doubt he foresaw that the uncertainty of success, should the adventure be attempted, might leave him like the dog in the fable, bereft of the honourable office he now fulfils and of the generous pension he gets from the King. These are reasons he could not reveal to Burr, owing to their secret character; and when the Colonel [Burr] insisted on carrying out a scheme so contrary to Wilkenson's interests, no other way out was left to the latter than the one he took. [He denounced Burr to the Government.] In this way, not only does he make his pension secure, but, on the strength of such a signal service, he will ask for an increase, or for a liberal lump sum in reward."

Thus was Miranda rid of a possible rival in the field of South American adventure by an American military Commander in the secret pay of the King of Spain. Now and then, Burr does turn up in the laborious negotiations of the veteran Creole with Jefferson and Madison. The two men looked askance at each other, and while Burr " declared that he had carefully refrained from giving him [Miranda] an opportunity to disclose his views about the emancipation of the Spanish Indies ", Miranda accused Burr of being a " detestable and infamous " man who had betrayed him to the Spanish Minister. Jefferson held aloof; but Madison gave Miranda to understand that, provided the laws of the Republic were not openly violated, there was no objection for private American citizens to enter the business and supply all that was needed. Madison asked Miranda to delay his departure from Washington (14.xii.1805) to dine with him on the 17th. Colonel William Smith, Miranda's friend and constant adviser in matters American, was Inspector of New York harbour. Miranda, who had dreamt of conquering Venezuela at the head of an army of Englishmen and Americans, found himself gently let down first by Britain then by the United States to the level of a freebooter. He began to dabble in small ships and in secondhand arms. He, who had seen himself as a modern reincarnation of the majestic Incas, was to steal out of New York harbour in an expedition to smuggle liberty into Venezuela as if liberty were a cargo of British goods.

5

The *Leander* was cleared by the customs on January 23rd, 1806, and sailed down the river on January 26th. She was the property of Samuel G. Ogden, a friend of William Smith. " I begin my epistolary journal "—writes James Biggs, the chronicler of the expedition—" by informing you that the *Leander* is a ship of about two hundred tons burden, commanded by Captain Thomas Lewis, who is reputed to be a man of intrepidity, and a thorough master of his profession." So much for the ship. Now for the men. First the officers. " A number of Americans, some of them gentlemen, and persons of good standing in society, though mostly, I believe, of crooked fortunes, have embarked." To this first contingent, " between twenty and thirty persons have been added to the service as officers ", Biggs writes in Trinidad, and he adds: " A few of them are respectable men; but the greater part are low and worthless characters." As for the rank and file, there is a page in the narrative which is full of information. The author is shocked at Miranda's passion in a quarrel with the skipper. " It is not a little important to ask "—he comments—" that he, who holds our fortune in his hands, and is to govern us, should be able to govern himself. We depend on the sailors, who are bound to us by nothing but the ship's articles, who are nearly one hundred and fifty, to join the army; but this cannot be effected without the co-operation and countenance of Lewis. All of them, except about twenty volunteers, collected from the butchers' stalls in Bear market, to be dragoons, and exchange the clever for the broad sword, have sailed with him before, and are very much attached to him."

What kind of armament had been supplied ? Here again, Miranda seems to have been caught talking, if not napping. " One side of the quarter deck is occupied by a printing press, at which several young men of that profession are busy in striking off the general's proclamations to the people of South America, and setting the types for printing our commissions. The other side is taken up with two groups of Mars' youngest sons, employed with military books; some studying, some reading, and others looking at the pictures. His excellency is at the head of one of these parties, philosophizing on various subjects, and passing from one to another with his peculiar volubility. At this moment he is painting the dangers of a military life. . . . I am sorry to find he loves dearly to talk of himself; I believe that vanity and egotism, which are qualities destitute of any recommendation whatever, are generally associated with other traits that have no claim to approbation. I must confess too, that he appears not a little tinctured with pedantry. . . . Next is seen the armourer's bench, with all his apparatus for repairing old muskets, pointless bayonets and rusty swords. This tinker has his hands full, as our arms are none of the best, and seem to have been already condemned in some other service. Whoever purchased them for the expedition, was either no judge of arms, or he has been kinder to himself than his employer. . . . A few feet from the place where I am now writing, is a noisy set of animals called volunteers, going through the manual exercise under the direction of a drill sergeant, who looks as bold as a lion, and roars nearly as loud."

While Miranda sailed towards Haiti, Casa-Irujo sent messages to the several Spanish governments overseas and asked for explanations at Washington, backed by his French colleague Turreau, who wrote to him (7.ii.06) reporting an interview with Madison: " I sought his eyes, and strange to say, I found them. I believe I saw in them the confirmation of our fears. He was most depressed while I asked for a definite explanation of the steps in question." Some show of action had to be put up in Washington, and a customs officer was dismissed. Meanwhile, Miranda wasted much time in Jacquemel, while Lewis went to Port-au-Prince; and after many vicissitudes and not a few quarrels between the three chief men on board, Miranda, Lewis and Armstrong, the *Leander* with two schooners, the *Bee* and the *Bacchus*, tried to land on the night of April 27th on the coast of Venezuela not far from Puerto Cabello. The attempt failed. The *Bee* and the *Bacchus* were captured with the loss of sixty officers and men, including William Smith's son. Ten of the captured men were shot and over forty sent to prison. The *cabildo* of Caracas protested vehemently against the " abominable monster " Miranda. Among the men who took up arms against Miranda was Juan Vicente Bolívar, brother of the future *Libertador*.

6

Miranda decided to withdraw to Trinidad. But the *Leander* was chased by the English sloop of war *Lily* (25.v.06), whose captain, Donald Campbell, found the crew " perfectly dissatisfied and nearly in a state of mutiny ". The *Lily* escorted the *Leander* to Grenada, where the Governor, Maitland, received Miranda well and, says Biggs, gave him " encouragement to expect important assistance from the British in a second attempt upon the Spanish Main. . . . These circumstances revived the spirit of our volunteers; who had grown rather sick of their undertaking and disposed to abandon Miranda." Maitland's optimism was perhaps justified. Campbell had imparted to Miranda the news of Pitt's death. The new Prime Minister, Lord Grenville, wrote to Lord Auckland on June 5th, 1806: " An immense question is opening by this attempt (successful hitherto) of Miranda's on the Caracas. The thing was launched by our predecessors, as a matter of connivance only, without any plan for acting in consequence of it. How far shall we now countenance it or engage in it ? " Grenville believed it successful because the wildest rumours had circulated in America on the adventure, which they depicted as a success, and some had found their way into official reports for the British Government, including those of Captain Campbell himself.

The day after Grenville wrote thus to Auckland the *Leander* arrived in

Bridgetown, Barbados. "Twenty-five or thirty volunteers have joined us here "—writes Biggs—" In this number may be half a dozen gentlemen; the rest, I fear, must pass for vagabonds." This was the outcome of an agreement which Admiral Sir Alexander Cochrane had signed with Miranda against the opinion of Lord Seaforth, the Governor, and of General Bowyer, Commander in Chief of the West Indies troops. The *Leander*, the *Lily*, the English brig *Empress* and the schooner *Trimmer* sailed for Trinidad (20.vi.06); and on the 24th they arrived in Port of Spain. The expedition, writes Biggs, " is to be assisted by English supplies and naval forces, though by no regular troops. The British authorities here have perhaps not sufficient confidence in the plan to give it this aid; and if they were disposed, could not do it without disobliging extremely the French and Spanish party here, which is numerous and influential. The inhabitants, being chiefly of these nations, it is not easy to get men to enlist." Nevertheless, Governor Hislop, Picton's successor, gave all the support in his power, and even permitted volunteers to be recruited from the militia. Miranda was very pleased and went so far as to overdraw on the British Treasury by as much as £688 : 2 : 0. Success seemed so certain that Turnbull and Co. printed commercial circulars expecting at last some return from their heavy outlay in financing Miranda.

On July 25th, 1806, the squadron sailed into the Gulf of Paria. It was composed of the *Leander*, sixteen guns; the *Lily*, twenty; the *Empress*, twelve; the *Attentive*, fourteen; the *Provost*, ten; the *Bulldog*, *Dispatch*, *Mastiff*, gunboats of two and three guns; the *Trimmer*, and the *Commodore Barry*, unarmed merchantmen. They had left Trinidad on the 24th. " The maledictions of many and the blessings of few attended us from Trinidad where we were far from being popular ", writes Biggs; and having pointed out that the total force did not exceed four hundred, he remarks: " It is evident he must have great dependence on the readiness and the ability of the inhabitants to join his standard ". But Miranda depended on nothing but his imagination. On the morning of August 3rd, 1806, the troops landed close to La Vela de Coro, on the open sea coast, threatening, across the narrow strip of land, the city of Coro on the shores of the lake of Maracaibo. The fort was taken and the Colombian flag hoisted on it. Miranda landed at 11.30 and at once ordered a march on Coro, " conducted with so much order and silence, that the footsteps of the troops were scarcely heard ". By early morning, they entered Coro. " A most solemn or rather dreadful stillness pervaded the whole place." The city had been wholly evacuated, yet the invaders in the main square managed to exchange a number of volleys which wounded Colonel Kirkland, Miranda's private secretary, and five men, killing a New York negro. Biggs blames Miranda who, he says, exhilarated at his easy victory, ordered a *feu de joie* which was misunderstood by one of his two " divisions ".

During the five days he stayed at Coro, Miranda endeavoured to attract his countrymen to enrol themselves under the banner of liberty. All in vain. He wrote to Cochrane (6.viii.06) asking for reinforcements and promising to take Caracas before the end of the month. He might have taken it without reinforcements. On the strength of the information supplied by the commander at Coro, Caracas believed that Miranda had fifteen hundred men; and a letter from the city said: " We have men, but we are disarmed. We can trust only the Queen's regiment, hardly one hundred and eighty men. The General hopes to receive ten thousand men, but they are all militia men who have scarcely heard a shot, and at the first encounter all will be in a turmoil. Not a single officer in the regiment of Caracas itself has ever been under fire. They are all sabre-rattlers who think of nothing but dressing and eating well." But the English reinforcements were not forthcoming and the officer in charge of the defence of the district, Salas, effectively blockaded Miranda, though with but poor troops far inferior in armament and training to the invaders. Miranda decided to withdraw. On the night of the 9th he told his troops they were to advance, but in the morning, having followed their officers, who were in the secret, they found themselves at La Vela de Coro again. On August 13th, 1806, Miranda and his men took to sea towards Aruba. " The Spaniards would have nothing to say to us ", wrote Biggs the next day on board the *Leander*. " They had no thoughts of accepting our proffer of liberty; and we could not oblige them to take it. Miranda, so long the idol of his foolish followers, is not known by them. They wondered who he was; and what brought him in such guise into their country. They viewed him as a marauder whom they were to fly from, or destroy, instead of a deliverer to be made welcome." In the personal record of the officer of white volunteers Juan Vicente Bolívar, the Marqués de Toro, commanding officer of the battalion wrote: " On March 5th, 1806, he took service in the barracks with the white battalion of these Valleys, and on August 10th, he marched towards Coro with the said battalion . . . against the traitor Miranda."

CHAPTER XI

THE WAITING YEARS

I

LITTLE is known of Bolívar's life between the oath scene on Monte Sacro and his arrival in Caracas in June, 1807. With or without Rodríguez, he returned from Italy to Paris, where he stayed till about the end of 1806. It was then that he had himself admitted as a freemason, though, it would seem, out of mere curiosity and without much faith in it. " That had been enough "—he said in later years to Peru de Lacroix—" to realize how ridiculous this old association is." It seems that his relations with Fanny Villars took then a particularly tender turn; for, even if the grasping lady, in her later years, raised the value of these old-time events in order to cash them in at a higher price, all cannot be pure invention in what she writes and suggests. She was in Italy, probably at the same time as Bolívar, but possibly in other company than his. She speaks of her letters, " and those of my old travelling companion in Milan "; and, referring to her son, adds " *dont j'étais grosse en Italie* ", which obviously means " while you were there ". In Paris, they must have seen each other pretty freely, for every member of the family, including General Dervieu de Villars himself, speaks of Fanny's affection for Bolívar, though none says a word about Bolívar's affection for Fanny. The lady herself, somewhat ambiguously, refers twice to the house in Paris " where you have seen me "; and to the " tender friendship which can never alter nor increase, for you had so deeply rooted it in my heart that it had become one with the life of your cousin ". And this touching detail: " I had added "—to a number of mementoes she had sent him—" a handful of plants of those we used to go to fetch together at the flower market, and which have thriven so astonishingly that they seem proud of the hand that planted them."

For Bolívar, all this can hardly have meant more than an episode. His heart was too masculine to be absorbed or even led away by it from that interest in public affairs he was already beginning to feel. His model, Napoleon, had won the battle of Ulm and Austerlitz while Bolívar was touring Italy and making a speech on Monte Sacro; he had won the battle of Jena and given the Crown of Naples to one of his brothers and that of Holland to another, become President of the Confederation of the Rhine, enslaved Austria and conquered Italy, while Bolívar was sorting flowers at the flower market with Fanny Villars. We may be certain that, in 1806, Bolívar's mind was busier with Napoleon's victories in Europe than with his own victories—if such there were—over Fanny Villars.

Nor was Napoleon the only figure then spurring him to action. In the very field he had marked out for his great deeds, another knight, already famous, was at that very time riding on his high horse. Dulcinea-Venezuela was in danger of being rescued by Don Francisco de Miranda ere Don

Simón de Bolívar had taken the field. " The news we are getting about Miranda's expedition "—Bolívar wrote to a friend (23.vi.06)—" is somewhat sad; for it is claimed that he plans to incite the country to rebel, which may do much harm to the inhabitants of the colony. But in spite of it all, I should like to be there already, for my presence in my own country might spare me much damage; yet, fate will keep me far from it, and without the slightest resources." The impatience of the unemployed knight can be felt in these lines in which Miranda's expedition is condemned perhaps less because of its aim than because of its leader. Unable to draw money from his country owing to the war, he borrowed two thousand four hundred francs from a French friend, Alexandre Dehollain, and sailed for the United States towards the end of the year (1806). His last words to the Villars family were: " *Vous entendrez parler de votre cousin Simón Bolívar* ".

2

He left Paris for Hamburg where he took ship for the United States; landed in Boston, visited New York and Philadelphia and sailed from Charleston to La Guaira, where he arrived in June, 1807. This voyage was significant. He did not go by way of France and Spain. He deliberately chose the way Hamburg-United States; that is, since Spain was then at war with Britain and France also, he deliberately crossed the line. True he may have chosen the northern route in order to sail under a neutral flag; but a lieutenant of the Spanish army, as he then was, might have preferred to sail via Spain in a Spanish man of war and face the music. The point is important, for it dates a phase in the evolution of his loyalties.

Indirectly, this fact, though generally taken for granted, sheds much light also on the real situation in Venezuela, which Miranda's failure might tend to oversimplify. We have seen the Marqués de Toro signing a certificate for good services to Juan Vicente Bolívar on the occasion of Miranda's attempt. But by then, despite appearances to the contrary, both Juan Vicente and the Marqués himself were already veering in their loyalty to the Crown.* The Creoles were then leaders of the events which were to culminate in secession. Yet they were no " traitors ". Toro, Juan Vicente Bolívar, Miranda, living in an era of transition, were men whose fate had been to be born " Spaniards " and to have to die " Venezuelans "; just like so many others of their contemporaries.

Simón Bolívar, home again after three years abroad, would eagerly listen to all these impressions conveyed to him by " goths ", as royalist Spaniards were then nicknamed, and " patriots ". Caracas had been consternated by the event. " The Captain General with a considerable attendance of officers, civil servants, surgeons, barbers, chemists and armed forces of all

---

* The British agent William D. Robinson wrote from Barbados to Admiral Sir Alexander Cochrane (10.x.06): " Miranda has the secret and warm support of every respectable Creole in the province, the Instant he presents himself with some force to inspire some Confidence— his friends have been disappointed that he has not made his appearance with two to three thousand troops, a force more than adequate to have placed him ere this *in possession of the Capital*."—*P.R.O., Adm.* 1/327.

kinds left on August 12th to take positions in Valencia or San Carlos, where-from he might send reinforcements anywhere. He took with him over two thousand mules laden with arms and ammunition "—wrote a Caraqueño to one of his friends. The whites, reported Salas, commanding officer at Coro, had behaved admirably and the coloured men also; but " he [Miranda] took La Vela, entered the city [of Coro], summoned the inhabitants: no one paid any attention to his proclamation and other tricks; he was for ten days in possession of the territory, and was shamefully expelled by the same people who, according to what he claimed, had appealed to him to come ".

Miranda had not been expelled from his country by the power of Spain, but by his own countrymen. Why? Because he was out of touch with the life of his country, as he himself, in moments of lucidity, seems to have realized. In religious affairs, for instance, he was at most a deist in the Voltairian sense. " The moment the service begins "—writes Biggs, describing life on board the *Leander*—" Miranda leaves the deck, and when it is ended, reappears. Does he mean to have us understand that he has no religious faith? If as a philosopher, he deems religion false, as a politician, he should allow it to be useful." That is precisely what an ancestral instinct —his mother's voice piercing in him through his " philosophy "—forced him to acknowledge, leading him to a number of contradictions. The " abominable system of administration " he came to destroy had not, he wrote in his Proclamation, " uprooted from our hearts those civil and moral virtues which a holy religion and a regular code had instilled in our way of living thus fostering an honest national character ". Hardly the language to arouse a nation to rebel. Biggs, who had gone to the rescue of the Venezuelan people from the yoke of Spain, concluded: " Whether human nature or the people of that country are so interested in the success of the project of emancipation as we republicans are apt to imagine seems to me to admit a question. I reflect that amidst all their alleged grievances, they have great wealth and prosperity; and whatever they suffer, they have in general no pain from the consciousness of oppression."

3

None of these considerations can have escaped Bolívar and his friends when, in Caracas, hardly ten months after the events which prompted them, the rich Creoles took stock of the situation. The revolution was their own; not that of the people. After all, the agents of the Government of Madrid, by the force of things, had tended to work for democratic equality against the Creole oligarchy. Possibly things were not as clear to those who lived then as they are to us. The rich Creoles sought to shake off the yoke of Madrid, bound to be more irksome for them than for the humble classes, not because it fell more heavily on their shoulders, but because they felt abler to assume power.

This feeling of self-sufficiency was much stimulated by the dramatic events of Buenos Aires. Sir Home Popham had been sent from England at the head of a fleet, with an expeditionary force to wrench the Cape from the

Dutch. Having done so, he thought it might be a good thing to nip off for England the tip of South America as he had done the tip of South Africa. Whether this had been prearranged with Pitt or not is a secret Pitt took meanwhile to the grave. But on June 24th, 1806, the Viceroy of Buenos Aires, Sobremonte, was most annoyed at having to leave the theatre because a British fleet was in sight. He put together all his belongings and fled to Córdoba, beyond reach of the British guns. The English landed in Los Quilones, and two days later were in Riachuelo, then about a league from Buenos Aires (now, within the city). Popham took the city with fifteen hundred men. But the citizens organized for resistance; and by August 12th Beresford, who was in command of the English army, was forced to capitulate. The two leaders of the city had been General Liniers, a Frenchman in the service of Spain, and a wealthy Spanish merchant, Don Martín Alzaga; many Spanish-born citizens had also taken part in the fight. Nevertheless, the effect of this episode was that the official world of Spain had fled to Córdoba while the spontaneous vigour of the local community had redressed the situation. Liniers' skill and Alzaga's activity and generosity raised a militia of nine thousand men; and when, in the following July, General Whitelocke came fresh from England with ten thousand men to reconquer the city, the British arms underwent a second defeat which raised high the self-confidence and self-consciousness of the new community.

This success shed a clear light on the failure of Miranda, and particularly on one feature of it which seemed of good omen for the Creole leaders. Miranda had been beaten, but not by Madrid. He had been beaten by Venezuela. That fact more than compensated for their defeat. For though it is true that the conscious aim of these Creoles was to conquer a fuller and a more direct political power over a community they already controlled socially, they were in so doing reaching out towards a deeper aim than they perhaps realized. " Our thoughts are ours, their ends none of our own ", they might have truly said. Whether they knew it or not, what they thought in their minds to be a movement for securing more power over the castes was in its depths a movement towards a greater intimacy and solidarity with the castes. It mattered little, therefore, that they and they alone were then feeling their way, albeit cautiously and surreptitiously, towards secession; and that " the castes " remained loyal to the Spanish system which for centuries had protected them against the whites; for the chief feature of the situation which Miranda's invasion had revealed was that it was the country itself, not the Spanish government, that had repelled the invader; and this fact was bound to release forces which could but lead to independence.

4

There were other features still hidden in the revolution which the Creoles were now doomed to lead if not altogether to shape—features which would have made most of them stand back with horror, and which later, when experience was to reveal them to their astonished eyes, would make some of those pleasure-loving, well-off, refined and generous men rue their rashness and their lack of foresight. Rich, many were to lose their wealth; young, many were to lose their lives; and the fair country of which they were the chief ornament was to be rent by a bloody civil war upon the release of savage energies which—had they but dared pierce inwards—they might have guessed in their secret selves.

As if to let us catch a glimpse of these hidden forces, Simón Bolívar became at this time entangled in an episode of sheer defiance and violence far beyond what the circumstances warranted. He was staying at his Yare estate, inherited from Dr. Aristeguieta, when, owing to a dispute over the boundaries of their respective lands he had a brawl with his neighbour Dr. Antonio Nicolás Briceño (24.ix.07). The versions given by the two adversaries differ widely. Each accuses the other of being the intruder and the aggressor, and depicts himself peacefully attending to his land with his slaves. Briceño asserts that he went that very afternoon to call on Bolívar; they embraced in the presence of their friends and it all ended in a dinner at Bolívar's house, where the slaves organized a dance. He probably keeps at least as far away from the facts as Bolívar. But there are one or two points in his case which deserve notice. First there is his remark to the effect that Bolívar " says he treated me with indulgence, in a tone I did not wonder at, for I knew his petulant style to be typical of him ". This is valuable as a contemporary judgment on young Bolívar which other documents of the period will confirm. Then he alleges that the reason why Bolívar revived this quarrel before the Courts after it had ended amiably, was because he wanted to force Briceño to agree to let him build some indigo tanks on Briceño's cocoa lands. Briceño proves his contention with two letters addressed to him by Bolívar; one (25.ix.07), the day after the incident, in which Bolívar calls him " friend " and asks him finally to answer yes or no to the request about a right of way and other concessions; and another (21.xi.07), truly petulant and even bullying: " Sir:—If the unheard-of leniency with which I tolerated your criminal attempt against me on September 24th should encourage you to insult me again, I regret to say that the Government will soon be informed of your strange behaviour; for I am determined not to tolerate the slightest offence from you. Please tell my steward whether you oppose or not the right of way I need through to St. Gertrude."

5

This otherwise trifling incident takes on an historical importance for a number of reasons. The two protagonists belong to the white wealthy class, which already at this very time is preparing to lead the country to secede from Spain. They are related through Briceño's wife. They are within a few years to take a prominent part, and one of them, Briceño, a sinister part, in the war of secession. Finally, the procedure followed on the occasion of the action instituted by Bolívar against his neighbour will reveal the relations between these leaders of Venezuelan society and the Spanish authorities. Bolívar's letter to Briceño is an ultimatum, meaning:

" Either you let me build the right of way, the tanks and the rest or——"
What was the threat ?—that the Government would soon know. Bolívar was
therefore confident of being able to use the Spanish Government in Caracas
as a weapon which any adversaries of his should fear.

Within nineteen days of his first appeal to the authorities, he had secured
a decision from the acting President, Governor and Captain General, Don
Juan de Casas, whereby Briceño was to be put under arrest and his goods
under embargo. Such was the exorbitant power the Bolívar family wielded
within official circles in Caracas. But, of course, Briceño was not altogether
powerless, and he had a good case. On July 5th, 1808, he argued that the
decision was a notorious insult and injury inflicted on him for, owing to his
birth and his profession, he could only be arrested for crimes punishable
with dishonourable penalties; and he objected to the Government's legal
adviser because he was a tenant of Bolívar. Another judge was appointed,
who suspended the decision of the first till further information had been
obtained. The matter dragged on. Briceño sold his land to get away from
his " petulant " neighbour, and Bolívar withdrew the power of attorney he
had granted his lawyers and kept away from Caracas. Briceño suspected
his adversary was hedging and dodging; but Bolívar's absence was due to
reasons of more import.

Before we come to that, however, a letter from Bolívar must be considered,
for it completes the picture of this young man of twenty-six, who is already
conspiring against the régime that had made him powerful. " August 1st,
1809. Mr. President, Governor and Captain General: Don Simón de
Bolívar, with the respect due to Your Lordship, puts before you: that having
been appointed by Your Lordship as Lieutenant Chief Justice of the Yare
Valley, and having taken the oath before the Court of the Royal *Audiencia*,
I presented myself yesterday in the *Cabildo* through my solicitor Don Miguel
Montero, being myself indisposed, to take possession of my office, having
first sent notice to the gentlemen of the *Cabildo* by means of a visiting card,
a courtesy which seemed to me sufficient to satisfy the rites of urbanity; but
having received a message from the *Regidor*, don José María Mora, informing
me that I was to go personally to call on him or bring my card, and the
Cabildo having refused to receive my solicitor until I have fulfilled the
customary ceremonies, I find myself bound to appeal to You for the rebuff
of which I am the victim, and to point out that there is no law nor order
requiring that the Lieutenants Chief Justice in order to be received by a
Cabildo should personally call on the *Regidores;* that this habit is abusive
and cumbersome, that it has no other origin than the caprice of the *Regidores*
and the servile acquiescence of the lieutenants, and should therefore be
abolished; in view of which I entreat Your Lordship to call an extraordinary
meeting of the *Cabildo* for it to give me possession of my office through my
solicitor, declaring that I have fulfilled the ceremonies of courtesy by sending
my visiting card, and that, henceforward a personal visit shall not be required,
for such is the way to deal with the justice which I represent. In Caracas
on August 1st, 1809. Simón de Bolívar."

This is the only letter that he signed " Simón de Bolívar ". It is swollen with patrician pride.   The future *Libertador* looks down on the *Regidores* who, in his day, were the representatives of the people, conscious of it, and punctilious as to the respect due to them by the authorities appointed by the Crown.   None of this for Bolívar.   He had been appointed Lieutenant Chief Justice from above and he was not going to trouble to take possession of his functions in person.   His steward was good enough for that.   An almost mediaeval sense breathes through this lordly and haughty letter.   Written in the midst of Bolívar's preparations for a rebellion against Spain, it throws a vivid light on the motives which at the time animated the class of rich whites in which that rebellion was being hatched.

CHAPTER XII

FREEDOM FROM WHAT?

I

WHILE Bolívar and Briceño were waging a civil war of their own over a right of way, Miranda tried to rescue from defeat the remnants of his expedition. He was stubborn in adversity; and, on August 22nd, 1806, in Aruba, where the force had settled after its retreat from the mainland, Biggs wrote: " He looks for a considerable reinforcement to be sent to this island by the British." This implied a radical change in his views, for one of the motives which had impelled him to attempt the " liberation " of Venezuela with a band of foreign adventurers was his desire to keep the British out of it for fear of their imperial ambitions. Even at Barbados and Trinidad, while he was hourly receiving the hospitality of British commanders, he insisted that he " must accept of the assistance of the British at that time, but he never intended they should obtain any power in his country ".

How far he thought he could keep out of his country a power to which he had constantly to turn for help is a mystery of his character. He sent pressing appeals to the British authorities in London and in the West Indies; but found the British commanders, even his staunch supporter Admiral Cochrane, far more cautious after his failure. Captain Dundas, R.N., came to Aruba and insisted on his evacuating the Island. He left, under British escort, for Trinidad (27.ix.06) where he arrived at the end of October. He was not well received. On the way out, " the Government house was given to Miranda for his residence; and took the name of headquarters. The Governor and officers, civil and military, paid him the respect which corresponded to the rank he claimed. . . . The tables are now changed. We are treated with infinite contempt as a body . . . we are laughed at and scoffed by the very populace in the streets." Squabbles about pay, law suits, complaints about Miranda's indifference to the fate of the prisoners left in the mainland, made the situation darker. Miranda sent to Britain Count Rouvray who returned empty-handed. In December, 1807, he sailed himself for London in the frigate *Alexandria*. " His enthusiasm, after all the dampers it has received, was not extinguished. He said that he expected to be in Caracas in the following summer."

He brought letters of recommendation from Cochrane to Castlereagh. By then, the British Government was brewing a more active policy towards Spanish America; and Sir Arthur Wellesley, the future Wellington, had been asked to prepare a plan for landing in Venezuela. The Buenos Aires setback had not cooled the ardour of the City, for which the Spanish Empire remained an Eldorado as glittering as in the days of Raleigh; and while a Court Martial severely reprimanded Popham for having abandoned the Cape garrison to go to conquer Buenos Aires, the City presented the reprimanded

Admiral with a sword of honour. Wellesley thought Venezuela the most fertile country in the world and a valuable colony for Britain; but deemed it wiser to let it remain politically independent. This suited Miranda well enough. The plans for an expeditionary force went ahead, and 13,000 troops were concentrated in Ireland due to sail in July, 1807, from Cork, under the command of Wellesley. In the view of Miranda, the landing was to take place in Puerto Cabello and the first objective was to be Caracas. Miranda was certain that if 10,000 British troops were landed 20,000 Venezuelans would soon join them. Under British officers, these Venezuelans would then take the rest of the coastal strip from Guayana to Panama. Nevertheless, the British Government kept an open mind as to the destination of Wellesley's army. Mexico? Buenos Aires? Venezuela? In the end, it went to Spain.

2

Napoleon had thrown off the mask and attacked his ally, Spain. By the Treaties of Fontainebleau, Portugal was dismembered between the King of Etruria and Godoy, reserving a territory to be exchanged for Gibraltar and Trinidad; Charles IV was to become Emperor of the two Americas. Portugal was to be invaded by French and Spanish troops upon her anticipated refusal to join in the continental blockade. Junot marched into Spain towards Portugal with a strong army nine days before the signature of the treaties (27.x.06). On November 30th the French entered Lisbon whence the royal family had sailed for Brazil in British vessels. While Charles IV and his son Ferdinand rendered public their dissensions and appealed to Napoleon, more French armies entered Spain under Dupont and Moncey, the best Spanish troops being kept idle in Hanover by the wily Emperor; and every military place of northern Spain was occupied by the French under all kinds of pretexts, in some cases even, as in Pamplona, by sheer treachery. The people, who hated Godoy and did not realize what Napoleon was after, were in favour of the French while they believed that Napoleon would oust Godoy and bring back Ferdinand. But Godoy was ousted by purely national means—a riot in Aranjuez (17.iii.08) which led to Charles' abdication on March 19th.

While the people rejoiced, Murat occupied Madrid (23.iii.08). Ferdinand VII entered his capital on the following day. But the French ambassador was the only head of a diplomatic mission who would not recognize him. Charles asked to negotiate a number of small private affairs, and Murat seized the opportunity to make him withdraw his abdication. Vying in baseness, father and son put themselves in the hands of Napoleon. On April 10th Ferdinand left Madrid leaving a Council of Government under the direction of his brother Antonio. Despite the opposition of the people (who, in Vitoria, went so far as to cut the harness of the horses of the King's carriage) Ferdinand crossed the frontier and arrived in Bayonne where he was told he must abdicate. Both father and son abdicated in favour of Napoleon (May 5th and 10th, 1808). These events were concealed from the people of Spain; but the Infante Don Antonio received a letter from Charles asking that his younger son the Infante Don Francisco de Paula should be sent to France. The crowd congregated to witness his departure on May 2nd, 1808, was moved by the boy's tears, became riotous and was mowed down by a volley from a French battalion suddenly arrived upon the scene. The people, first without leaders but soon led by three young officers, Daoiz, Velarde and Ruiz, fought the whole day against the French army. They were of course defeated; Daoiz and Velarde lost their lives; a sanguinary repression followed, in violation of the capitulation. But the War of Independence had begun.

Independence—from whom and from what? The men of Madrid, and soon of every other city of Spain, who rose in those days, had no doubts in their minds: independence from the Frenchman. Spain was then deeply monarchical, had idolized Ferdinand VII, and sought nothing more than the felicity of seeing him back on his throne. But how could a sudden impulse for independence stop at that—stop indeed anywhere while its original energy lasted? On the day the Spanish nation rose to demand the King back, she rose to demand, and she rose. And the rise in itself, and the rise to demand, were far deeper, far more important facts in the history of the country than the miserable King who happened to be the object and immediate motive of the impulse.

The first *Junta* formed to lead this popular rising against Napoleon was that of Asturias. Two points deserve notice: it was led by noblemen such as Santa Cruz de Marcenado and Toreno; and the two men chosen to lead the crowd were Don Ramón de Llano Ponte and Don Manuel de Miranda—a mere coincidence, as if an historical imp had sought to link together these men who rose for Spanish independence in Asturias and the Bolívar y Ponte and the Miranda who were planning the independence of Venezuela. The Junta decided to raise 18,000 men, and was soon able to count on troops sent by Murat to coerce it, but who, all but their five commanders, went over to the cause of the people. On May 25th, 1808, the Junta declared war on Napoleon. By May 30th, it had sent three messengers to London. On June 7th, early in the morning, the three emissaries had their first interview with Canning. On June 12th Canning wrote officially that His Majesty was ready to grant every kind of help to assist them in their endeavour as well as to extend the same aid to any other part of the Spanish kingdom which would eventually evince the same spirit and intentions.

On May 30th, Don Francisco Sangro sent by the Junta of Galicia arrived in London and announced that the whole of Spain had risen against Napoleon. The pattern of these risings was always the same: a mixture of popular and military elements; the trend also: *for* Ferdinand VII and *against* both the French and Godoy, whom the people suspected of being the instrument of Napoleon. The structure of the Juntas was also the same everywhere: representatives of all classes and institutions gathered round the municipal council of the chief city, under the chairmanship of the Captain General or of the bishop, unless the persons who happened to hold these offices were favourable to the French or to Godoy. Seville also organized its Junta;

but this time, partly because its chairman, Don Francisco Saavedra, was an ex-minister of the Crown, partly because the city was then rich, populous and well situated to act as the centre of resistance, partly for lack of concrete news of the other risings, the Junta of Seville chose to consider itself as a national and sovereign body, and took the name of *Junta Suprema de España e Indias*. This Junta was moreover able to count on the strongest military force available in the Peninsula: the army in San Roque, opposite Gibraltar, under Castaños, which came over to the national cause of its own accord; and the troops of Cádiz, under Solano, who hedged and was negative, but in the end was murdered by a crowd of patriots.

These events aroused the wildest enthusiasm in London. Everywhere, the Spanish envoys were acclaimed by the people; and the first night the Asturians appeared at the Opera, as the guests of the Duke of Queensbury, the acclamations were so prolonged that Toreno, one of them, says they held up the play for an hour. Spain, till then one of the chief objects of British ambition and animosity, became an ally, a real, not a merely political ally. Napoleon and Talleyrand had at last achieved for England what England had never brought off for more than short-lived periods—the break between France and Spain. King George declared in Parliament that Britain would preserve the independence and integrity of the Spanish monarchy (4.vii.08).

Wellesley saw the opportunity which his rash rival Bonaparte had given him. " This "—he wrote on hearing the news from Spain—" would appear to be a crisis in which a great effort might be made with advantage; and it is certain that any measures which can distress the French in Spain must oblige them to delay for a season the execution of their plans upon Turkey, or to withdraw their armies from the North." But of course he kept his mind open. " One month would probably be sufficient to ascertain the chances of advantage to be derived from the temper of the people of Spain." If the chances were good—good for Britain, of course, i.e. good to beat Napoleon in Spain—then the Cork expedition was to go to Spain; if not, to Venezuela. Like General Boulanger towards the end of the century who, on receiving a sword of honour in Paris, is said to have exclaimed: " With this sword I swear to defend the Republic and if need be to attack it ", Wellington with the troops waiting in Cork was equally ready to defend the integrity of the Spanish monarchy or to distintegrate it.

It so happened that " the temper of the people in Spain " was " good ". Wellesley had therefore to tell Miranda that Venezuela would have to wait. " I think I never had a more difficult business "—he later told Earl Stanhope —" I thought it best to walk out in the streets to prevent his bursting out. But even there he was so loud and angry, that I told him I would walk on first a little that we might not attract the notice of everybody passing. When I joined him again he was cooler." So says Wellesley. But he only seemed cooler. " You are going to Spain. You will be lost "—he went on saying— " Nothing can save you; that, however, is your affair; but what grieves me is there never was such an opportunity thrown away." Miranda did not see that, by attacking Spain, Napoleon had secured the independence of the

South American Kingdoms for good and all: for he kept England away from them, destroyed the prestige of the Spanish monarchy, and called from the depths in every one of the American Kingdoms national movements which, coming from below, were bound to achieve in the New World the fusion of the leading whites and the coloured masses.

3

The ignominious fall of the Spanish Crown at the feet of Napoleon in Bayonne, followed by the rise of the Spanish nation against the invader, produced effects of the utmost complexity in the Indies. A distinction must be made between the people and the upper classes; and within the upper classes, between the official and the unofficial worlds. The highest Spanish authorities were inclined to side with the winner, to accept the authority of Joseph Bonaparte and simply to carry on as if all that had happened in Spain had been a change of dynasty. This attitude should not be too rashly condemned as unpatriotic. For a century in Spain, French influence had been associated with progress, the lights of the century, down with the Inquisition, commonsense and no heroics, good-humoured latitude in matters of feminine fidelity instead of fierce Castillian " honour ", science instead of faith, in one word a number of features which cultivated men and women in Spain had learnt to like and appreciate. This association of " progress " with France did not suffer—as it might have done—from the rise of Napoleon. The progressive world of Europe was inclined to forgive much to the man who had delivered the world from the nightmare of the Terror. Furthermore the highhanded ways of the British Fleet with Spanish ships, and the hardly veiled support Britain constantly gave Miranda and a host of other American Spaniards in their " disloyal conspiracies " was bound to maintain in the conscious, politically minded governors of the Indies an inclination towards solidarity with France—by whomsoever France happened to be impersonated.

The leading classes of the Indies were closely connected by ties of friendship and even of family relationship with their rulers. Both the official and the unofficial sectors of the upper classes comprised European Spaniards and Creoles. The tendency to side with Bonaparte was therefore bound to radiate fairly far afield into the more influential circles of the Creole society. It did not openly clash with the stronger and more general trend towards separatism already prevailing in these Creole circles. By the time Napoleon attacked Spain, this trend had already been active for years in every centre of Spanish-American life and culture, spread by secret societies.

These societies were not necessarily masonic, though they may have been more or less directly inspired by the methods and rites of Freemasons. Miranda was perhaps a Freemason himself. He is said to have been a " Philadelphian ". This was a secret society organized in the French army against Napoleon. It had been preceded by that of the " Olympians ", constituted under masonic forms towards 1804, with no outward political aims beyond vague professions of equality and fraternity, and ostensibly seeking nothing but mutual promotion of its members up the military ladder. The true aim, a secret jealously guarded by the leaders, was the murder of Napoleon. It was symbolized in the seal of the society: an arm brandishing a dagger, coming out of the clouds, and under it a bust of Caesar falling to the ground. This society merged later into that of the Philadelphians, for fear of Fouché, who had discovered some of its plans and leaders in Boulogne, precisely in the vicinity of England where Miranda worked, and a city he used to cross in his travels. All this may well explain the coldness with which Napoleon and Fouché had received Miranda when, disgruntled at Pitt's dilatory ways, he had tried to work his plans from a French base. Whether Miranda was or was not the founder of the Lautaro Lodge, so prominent in those days, is again doubtful, though there seems to be no reason to doubt O'Higgins' good faith when he states it. On meeting Miranda, O'Higgins throws himself into the arms of the Precursor and cries out: " See, my Lord, the sad remains of my countryman Lautaro; in my bosom burns the same spirit which then freed my country Arauco from her oppressors." The very extravagance of these words vouches for their authenticity. How a Spaniard of Irish origin, son of a Viceroy, could consider himself the reincarnation of an Araucanian Indian who, after betraying his Spanish master, had led his native brothers against that Spanish Christendom and civilization to which O'Higgins owed his very language and thoughts, can only be explained by the fact which rules all this period: the conquered land had conquered the conquerors. O'Higgins was Lautaro and Miranda wanted to be an Inca.

The Lautaro Lodge or *Caballeros Racionales* or *Gran Reunión Americana* imparted some co-ordination to the movement for independence. The activities of Freemasons in the Indies were at times British at times French inspired. Miranda's chief correspondent in Buenos Aires, Saturnino Rodríguez Peña, belonged to the *Southern Star*, a Lodge set up by the English (in whose pay he was) during their brief occupation. The centre of these English-masonic activities was in Cádiz where the headquarters of English trade with the Indies, both licit and illicit, were also established.

<h1 style="text-align:center">4</h1>

While the upper classes were split by Napoleon's attack on Spain, some siding with the new French monarch, Joseph Bonaparte, others seeing in the European events but a fresh stimulus for their separatist tendencies, the people in the Indies reacted exactly like the people in Spain: they manifested their thrice secular attachment to the Crown by generously bestowing their loyalty on the infamous Ferdinand VII. In Spanish America as in Spain, Ferdinand VII became for the people a symbol. But of what ? In Spanish America the symbol was more complex than in Spain, for it included elements common to both the European and the American Spains. The young King represented the Spanish reaction against Godoy's French ways. Behind the soldiers of Bonaparte, who used the churches of Spain as stables for their horses, lurked the godless Jacobins. This anti-French feeling, partly political, partly national, stimulated the movement against Napoleon in both Spain and Spanish America.

Over and above these aspects common to the old and the new Spains, there was something specifically American in the attachment of the people of the Indies to Ferdinand VII: the Spanish Crown had traditionally stood for their rights against the excesses of the upper classes. This tradition could, up to a point, be traced back to the mediæval kings of Spain, often inclined to side with the common man against the nobleman—so that men who lived in royal lands were apt to be envied by those who lived in lands of lesser lords. But in the New World it had been refreshed, and given a different turn and flavour, by the Church, and in particular, by monks and friars. This circumstance strengthened the attachment of the lower classes of the Indies to what they thought Ferdinand VII stood for; particularly when they saw that the young " philosophers " who were so enthusiastic about emancipation were sometimes apt, as Humboldt shrewdly pointed out, to ill-treat their slaves with a copy of Raynal in their hands.

The picture, complex enough, was made more so by the intimacy between American Spaniards and European Spaniards, as well as by their common tendency to civil war. While many Creoles remained ardent Royalists throughout, not a few European Spaniards were to embrace the cause of the American separatists. This illustrates the element of " pure " civil war which the struggle contained on both sides. Indeed, the spirit of civil war came from Spain even in the presence of the enemy. " The news of the general insurrection in Spain "—writes the " patriot " agent Fajardo— " reached Mexico on July 29th, 1808. The enthusiasm which it had produced was still in full swing when the arrival of two deputies from the Junta of Seville was announced, who came to claim the sovereign command of Spanish America for that corporation. Such was the general disposition in favour of the peninsula, that it appears probable that the Mexicans would have acceded to the demands of the Junta if, during the debates in a meeting of the civil and military officers which the viceroy had convened, despatches had not arrived announcing the establishment of the Junta of Asturias, and expressly warning the Mexicans against acknowledging the Andalusian Junta. It may easily be conceived how this declared rivalry must have affected the opinions which the Mexicans had formed of the spirit of the Spanish revolution."

Thus, at the very moment when the peoples of Spanish America were feeling in the closest union with those of Spain, when they would have been ready to recognize not only the sovereignty of Ferdinand VII, King of all the Spanish kingdoms, but even that of the Spanish nation, which would have indeed lowered the status of the American kingdoms to that of mere colonies—at that moment, it was from Spain herself that the spirit of indiscipline, of rivalry and of separatism came to the Indies to stimulate whatever separatism was already afoot overseas. The nations of the New World, that of their own accord and by a kind of natural growth were beginning to feel of age, found themselves solicited by the several authorities which claimed to be the heirs of Charles V and Philip II as sovereigns of the Indies; and the very fact that these authorities—Joseph Bonaparte, Ferdinand VII, the Junta of Seville, the Junta of Asturias, later the Junta Central—were many and not one, invested every one of the Spanish-American nations with the *de facto* sovereignty of deciding which of these *de jure* sovereignties it would recognize. In the end they all answered the question by recognizing none but themselves.

5

In so doing, the Spanish nations overseas, and the chief cities which usually took upon themselves to speak for the whole nation, acted on a vigorous Spanish tradition. In a petition presented to the Viceroy Iturrigaray (5.viii.08), the *cabildo* of Mexico put forward such a doctrine in no uncertain terms: " Juntas of the Government, and respectable bodies of the cities and kingdoms, can meet in exact conformity to the law, which ordains that all arduous cases shall be considered in general assemblies. As at present, owing to the seizure of the King, the sovereignty is vested in the nation, in order that its interests may be consulted, the authorities, together with the municipalities, which are the heads of the people, do exactly the same as would the monarch himself for the general welfare. Mexico acts under the same principles as Seville, Valencia, and the other cities of Spain; and she is empowered in like manner as the above two faithful capitals, to do what she conceives is advisable in such an emergency."

The *cabildo* of Mexico did by no means jump from this to revolutionary conclusions. Why should it, since, far from innovating, it proclaimed that it acted in strict accordance with the law ? It suggested a Junta " composed of the Royal *Audiencia*, the archbishop, *cabildo* and deputies from the tribunals, ecclesiastical and secular bodies, the nobility, and principal citizens as well as the military ". Such a choice of membership would nowadays hardly be considered as *democratic;* for there is in it no trace of " the people ", in the narrow sense of the word. Nevertheless, for the *cabildo* and for the public opinion of the day, it was adequately representative. Thus, one of the reasons the *cabildo* gives why the Junta is necessary is " to satisfy the wishes of the people, by restoring to them those means they formerly had to appeal to the Council of the Indies, or to the person of the King ". And again, having pointed out that the Junta will be " the only means, in consequence of the absence of the monarch, by which the Kingdom, being thus united, may overcome all its difficulties ", the *cabildo* goes on to say: " This union of authorities is likewise necessary, as being the best means to produce unanimity in the minds of the people."

These texts show that the first impact of the events of Spain on the Kingdoms beyond the seas set going reasonable, statesmanlike, loyal and traditional reactions. What the Spanish Americans seem at the time to be groping for was a consolidation of the congeries of Kingdoms which the Spanish Empire had always been, by fostering in each of them institutions sprung from Spanish public law, through which the political sap of each of the New World nations should be able to circulate into the whole. In this first phase at any rate, the sincerity and fervour of their loyalty could not be doubted. Though some leaders and precursors might harbour far-reaching plans, public opinion was loyal to a surprising degree. " Spanish law "—writes Fajardo in 1817—" required the establishment of a regency, instead of a Junta central; but its sway was acknowledged, and so efficaciously supported by the Spanish Americans, that more than ninety million dollars had been sent to Spain from her American settlements previous to the beginning of 1810." He is speaking of gifts for the war.

True there were some disturbing factors. One was security. " What will become of us, should Spain be conquered ? was the universal question " —writes Fajardo. And there is hardly a Junta in the New World that does not put defence in the forefront both of its plans of action and of its reasons for coming together. Defence, of course, against the French. But the British, though helping Spain to shake off the yoke of Napoleon, were nonetheless intent on disintegrating the Spanish Empire. Despite this double danger from outside, the ties of common tradition would have kept together the peoples of the Spanish world but for a number of internal factors, the chief of which were: the selfishness of the European-Spanish commercial classes in both the new and the old world; the high-handed action of some Spanish authorities towards the representative aspirations of their peoples; the short-sighted and inexperienced policy of the provisional governments of Spain; and the separatist ferment which had been fostered in the American Juntas by an active and skilful minority.

6

It is a curious comment on human nature that the Junta Central of Spain, a leading body which owed its very existence to the mushroom growth of provincial Juntas all over Spain, instead of working through them, curtailed their powers and endeavoured to rule through the old-time authorities. Its regulations (1.i.09) aimed at the virtual elimination of the Provincial Juntas from the Government of Spain, when their spontaneous birth and patriotic vigour should have refreshed the springs of political life in the country. This policy of the Junta in Spain explains its policy in America. Instead of fostering the creation of local Juntas overseas, the Junta Central remained passive and cold towards those actually born there. It did, however, take two decisions with regard to the kingdoms beyond the seas: it declared them " an integral part of the nation "; and asked them to elect one deputy each to form part of the Junta Central on the same footing as the deputies elected from the Spanish provinces. This was open to criticism; for the Junta Central was composed of two deputies for each of the provinces of Spain; and there seemed to be no reason why the huge viceroyalties of the Indies should have a lesser representation.

This tendency to discriminate against the kingdoms overseas was a godsend for that minority of American leaders already working for separatism. Yet it was but natural. To begin with, there was distance. This is one of the many ways in which human nature is absurd, yet human and natural. The viceroyalties were vast, but so far away that it was beyond the power of the men in Spain to make the mental effort needed to equate Peru with Catalonia and New Spain with Aragon.   And then there was that " maternal " feeling: " Those people over there, they are ours ", so thought the men of the Junta Central in their depths, " ours not as chattels, slaves or even subjects, ours as children.   We are indeed fine and liberal parents to let them discuss with us on a footing of equality."   And this " generosity " having exhausted their stock of liberalism, the men of the Junta reduced the representation of the Kingdoms overseas to one deputy per Kingdom instead of two—or even instead of a good many more in proportion to population.   Absurd again, yet natural and human.

Then there was the mixed character of the population.   This came to the surface in the next crisis of the new representative institutions, when the Junta Central, yielding to popular pressure, convoked the Cortes.   This was done on the basis of the most liberal and equalitarian principles applied to that date anywhere in the world.   There was in London at the time an enlightened Spaniard, Don Alvaro Flórez Estrada, Procurator General of Asturias, who in 1811 commented on the decree of the Junta Central convoking the Cortes.   He was a stern critic of the Junta, but he praised the decree for its liberal and democratic spirit.   He pointed out, however, that " by one of those inconsequences which are so common in men, the Junta Central on this occasion did not grant America the quantitative representation it was entitled to on the basis of its whole population including Indians and Negroes but only with regard to the population of Creoles and Europeans ". This, however, he condones, owing to the backward state of the Indies. " What reason cannot approve is that the suffrage in the Indies should not have been popular as in the Peninsula, but on the contrary should have been entrusted to the *cabildos*, since no people can be called free in which all its citizens are not in a position to make use of such an inalienable right."

Both points were taken up by the New World malcontents.   Estrada remarks that, as to the first, the reproach was unfounded.   True the Indies were granted 24 deputies for 15 million people, but out of them, 8 million were Indians and 4 black; so that, leaving these 12 million out of account, the remaining 3 million were granted 24 representatives, which worked out at the same rate as in Spain.*   The decision to have the American deputies elected by the *cabildos* was one which could hardly be objected to by the Creole oligarchies whose class held firmly nearly every *cabildo* in Spanish America.

---

* A similar situation had developed in the Federal Convention of 1787 which framed the American Constitution, for the South and the North disagreed precisely on the same difficulty. The South claimed simultaneously the right to keep its slaves, of course voteless; but also that of counting them in the assessment of representatives to be granted to each district. " Mr. Gerry "—writes Madison in his diary—" thought property not the rule of representation.   Why then should the blacks, who were property in the South, be in the rule of representation more than the cattle and the horses of the North? "   In the end, the article was passed on January 11th, 1787, in the form of the strangest compromise: slaves were to be counted as three-fifths of their number.   It was moreover drafted so as to skirt round the word *slave*, which is not used at all in the text, yet is left in exclusive possession of the meaning of the sentence.

But the trouble came from the fact that between the Spanish authorities in the Peninsula and the leaders of the movements for secession in the Indies no compromise was possible. Grave mistakes were made by the Junta of Seville, by the Junta Central and, worst of all, later, by the Regency. But even if these provisional governments had been blameless, the leaders of secession would not have been able to act otherwise than they did. " Let justice be altogether on your side; but generosity cannot approve your behaviour "—wrote Flórez Estrada. " It would be lacking in generosity on your part to have suffered for three hundred years all the evils with which despotism chose to overwhelm you . . . and when we were going for the first time to enjoy the privilege of being all free, and to form the most powerful empire in the world, without having to make any conquests or usurpations, when in order to attain all these great aims nothing was needed but to work together in harmony—then you separate from us, so that, divided and without force, we may all become the prey of one or of several tyrants. The fact will have no weight for you that you owe your fatherland to those Spaniards whose descendants are now in the Peninsula shedding their blood to reconquer a freedom which they will not be able to obtain without your help! You will be so lacking in generosity as to forsake us in our plight, when, had it not been for our struggle, you would not have been able to escape the change wherewith the crafty Oppressor of the Continent would have shackled you before you had heard either of our situation or of his intentions! We do not want you to be slaves. We want you free; we want you equal with us." And the shrewd and generous Asturian summed up the situation in this significant phrase: " But above all, Americans, your brothers in Spain ask you: ' What are you after? Do you want to be free only? Or do you want to be free, but separated from us and without taking any interest in our own freedom? ' "

CHAPTER XIII

BOLÍVAR DECLARES WAR ON SPAIN

I

ON July 24th, 1808, the very day Bolívar was twenty-five, the *Fiscal* of the *Audiencia* of Caracas reported the arrival (on the 15th) of two French officers sent by their Government with news of Napoleon's cession of the Crown of Spain to his brother Joseph. " The news ran soon throughout the city . . . whereupon there were riots in streets and squares, execrations against the usurpers and repeated hurrahs in favour of the adored name of Ferdinand VII. That very afternoon the citizens of Caracas swore allegiance to Ferdinand and raised the Royal Standard, if not as sumptuously as on other occasions . . . with an enthusiasm which it was impossible to restrain."

In a letter to Sir Alexander Cochrane (La Guaira, 19.vii.08) the same events are told by Captain Beaver, R.N., who goes on to say: " The French were first publicly insulted in the coffee house, from whence they were obliged to withdraw; and the French Captain left Caracas privately, about eight o'clock that night, escorted by a detachment of soldiers, and so saved his life; for about ten o'clock his person was demanded of the governor by the populace, and when they learned that he was gone, three hundred men followed him, to put him to death. Though coldly received by the Governor, I was surrounded by all the respectable inhabitants of the city, and hailed as their deliverer. The news which I gave them from Cádiz was devoured with avidity, and produced enthusiastic shouts of gratitude to England. Returning to the Governor about five o'clock, the first thing I demanded was the delivery to me of the French corvette, or at least the permitting me to take possession of her in the roads, in consequence of the circumstances under which she had entered. Both these he positively refused, as well as to take possession of her himself; but, on the contrary, he told me he had given order for her immediate sailing. I made him acquainted with the orders I had given for her seizure if she sailed, to which he assented; and I at the same time told him, that if she were not in the possession of the Spaniards at my return, I should take her myself. He replied that he should send orders to the Commandant of La Guaira to fire upon me if I did; to which I replied, that the consequence would fall upon him: and I further told him, that I considered his reception of me at Caracas as that of an enemy rather than of a friend, while at the same time I had brought him information of hostilities having ceased between Great Britain and Spain; and that his conduct towards the French was that of a friend, while he knew that Spain was at war with France. He replied that Spain was not at war with France; to which I again replied, what could he consider as war, if the captivity of two of her kings, and taking possession of Madrid was not to be so considered ? He only replied, that he knew nothing of it from the

Spanish Government, and that what your despatches informed him of he did not consider as official."

2

This picture throws the features of the situation into sharp relief: the pathetic loyalty of the people to Ferdinand VII, symbol and incarnation of Spain; the no less pathetic attachment of the more respectable members of the city to the naval officer in whom they saw the symbol and incarnation of their deliverer England; and the sullen distrust of the Governor towards the traditional adversary of Spain in the New World.   But the people would not have it.   An uncle of Simón Bolívar, the City's standard-bearer, Don Feliciano Palacios, proclaimed the King amidst the most delirious enthusiasm of the people shouting: " Castille and Caracas for our Lord Don Fernando VII and all the descent of the House of Bourbon! "   Not daring to run counter to the enthusiasm of the people, the Captain General, Don Juan de las Casas, set up a Junta (16.vii.08), with delegates from the *Audiencia*, the *cabildo*, the Army, the clergy, the Royal Treasury, the Consulate and the nobility, and two legal experts.   At the meeting of the Junta " the papers of Bayonne were read, and it was decided to uphold the throne of Ferdinand, as the people demanded it alarmed at the French ".

But the ferment was operating at its most active precisely in these upper layers where the Captain General had chosen his Junta.   One of the deputies of the *cabildo*, Echezuria, protested against "the election of the members appointed by the President without consulting or asking for the consent of the citizens ".   The Governor accepted to suppress his first Junta and wrote to the *cabildo*: " I have decided that a Junta must be formed in this city on the model of that of Seville, and in my desire that it should be done in full agreement with those interested in it and for the common good of all, I hope that you will inform me of all that you might think advisable on this delicate matter with all possible speed."   Events in Caracas were taking a turn not unlike that in the cities of Spain, such as Cádiz, where the people, all out for Ferdinand, came into conflict with lukewarm authorities.   But while in Spain the established authority was challenged only insofar as it was not loyal enough, in Caracas it was challenged by the upper classes as an authority as such, its loyalty being brought into the picture and questioned only in order to enlist popular support.   This was revealed by the very text of the answer to Casas' request.   " No Spaniard has been able to acknowledge for his King and natural lord, nor shall ever acknowledge any other person than our beloved sovereign Ferdinand VII "; wrote the *cabildo*, undoubtedly protesting too much—" we all have sworn him, and after him his legitimate successors.   Our laws therefore and our Government are ever the same, and consequently the legitimately constituted authorities.   To cease to recognize them would be openly to contradict ourselves; to disobey them would be an evident attempt against the supreme law of good order and public peace."   The Junta which the *cabildo* proposed after this preamble was also to be presided over by the Captain General, and in the main did not differ much from that chosen by Casas; but it included one notable innovation: the " plebs " was to be represented. This shows to what an extent the magnates of Caracas were sure of being able to lead the people the way they wanted. At this juncture, an emissary of the Junta of Seville arrived in Caracas, and this fact may have influenced Casas in the decision he took not to proceed with the scheme.

3

On the day he wrote to the *cabildo* asking for its advice as to how to set up another Junta (27.vii.08), Casas sent his son to warn Simón Bolívar against the dangerous friends he received. A Captain Manuel de Matos, disgruntled owing to commercial losses which he attributed to the Government, went about advocating the extermination or expulsion of all European Spaniards, " to make ourselves rich out of their wealth ", and to come to an agreement with the English. He was imprisoned and later released; he seems to have been a fit guest for a mental hospital. Matos is the only person young Simón mentions by name, outside his own brother, in his letter from Veracruz (March, 1799) when sending messages to his friends. Two relatives of Simón Bolívar, José Felix Ribas and Juan Jerez Aristeguieta, were implicated in his plot. All this explains young Casas' visit to Simón Bolívar soon after the plot had been discovered. " You know I am your friend "—the Governor's son said to Bolívar—" and that I esteem you though I do not see you often; so that I should be very sorry to see you in trouble; I should take it as a favour if you did not hold gatherings or receive guests in your house, for they do you much harm." Bolívar answered: " I am desperately anxious to get rid of spongers who importune me; I asked no one to come, and I am innocent of all these slanderous accusations."

The scene is typical of the time. The young men of Caracas, to whom the Captain General's son went to counsel wisdom and caution, were leading the movement against Spain. They were the young bloods of the city. Ribas, eight years older than Simón, was fonder of gambling than of reading, as may be gathered from the spelling and low style of two of his letters. Bolívar's answer to Casas junior was of course a mere *ruse de guerre*. He was already one of the chief leaders in the permanent conspiracy against the rule of Spain, and his home in Las Gradillas, by the river Guayre (the very house he had inherited from Father Aristeguieta on the express condition that he should remain faithful to the King of Spain and to the King of Heaven), was rapidly becoming the headquarters of separatists and " philosophers ". " Sheaved together in the house of Simón Bolívar, close to the Guayre river ", writes Urquinaona, a Creole official in the service of the Spanish Regency, "and pretending to follow the ideas manifested by the Government in the hour of its tribulation, they tried to destroy it and to set up an independent rule, under the very plan of the Junta, which would dazzle the people with the pompous name of ' Junta for Upholding the Rights of Ferdinand VII '."

It was, of course, an open conspiracy. Bolívar knew full well that his denials would not be believed. He announced to Casas junior " that on the following day he was leaving for his estate, so that no one should use his name for anything "; and he did go—thereby arousing in Briceño a suspicion that he had left the city to escape the legal consequences of the dispute between them. But this period of his life was one of youthful petulance and arrogance, in which his aristocratic privileges from the past and his democratic dreams for the future combined to keep him buoyant and happy as a young cub. He was, thanks to his wealth, the centre of a society or group of young social and literary leaders who met in his house for rich meals and ardent talks. Most of them were wealthy landowners; some came from official circles, such as the two *Oidores*, Don Felipe Martínez and Don José Bernardo de Asteguieta. His own uncle Pedro, now *Alguacil Mayor* or Chief Constable, was also a regular guest. Pedro and the *Oidores*, however, soon realized that in this parliament of wits there was an inner, dangerous, circle, and cautiously withdrew. The spirit of this underground activity of Bolívar's gay company was not so gay. It aimed at " a Creole Junta or Congress ", independence and drastic action, not excluding getting rid of the Captain General and of the Regent of the *Audiencia* by murder.

4

In the small compass of the little city, these men, European and American Spaniards, official and unofficial, passed from one party to another and from revolution to repression under the influence of circumstances. The Marqués de Toro would, in the morning, as Colonel of the Militia, attend a meeting at the Captain General's, to devise measures against a conspiracy, and in the evening, in his capacity of young blood of Caracas, join a meeting of conspirators at Bolívar's house. Traitors ? by no means. Partly, in depth, the shiftiness inherent in their mixed blood; more on the surface, the changing lights of the times, the inconstancy of fortune in the events of Spain, the mobility of a state of affairs in which the Caraqueños could not tell whether they would end as Spanish subjects of a Bourbon, Spanish subjects of a Bonaparte, British subjects, or independent men. In this picture of changing colours and undefined outlines, few were the men who stood firm and knew what they wanted. One of them—Bolívar.

The end of the rule of Casas, practically the end of the year 1808, went by in a struggle between the patriotic, pro-Ferdinand tendency of the people; the pro-French conservative tendency of the authorities and of a number of well-to-do whites, both European and American; and the revolutionary and separatist drive of a number of rich whites, mostly pro-British. Casas' initiative inviting the *cabildo* to submit plans for a Junta provided an object on which the three forces were to converge. When Don José Meléndez Bruna, sent by the Supreme Junta from Spain, arrived in Caracas (5.viii.08) and announced the surrender of Dupont, in Bailén, to General Castaños (19.vii.08) and with it the failure (as it seemed then) of Napoleon's aggression on Spain, there was great rejoicing in Caracas. But the privileged classes held fast to their schemes of independence and tried to win popular support;

and Don Antonio Fernández de León, later Marqués de Casa-León, an opulent landowner living in almost oriental splendour amidst slaves and retainers, loudly protested that neither the Captain General nor the *Audiencia* had power to recognize the Junta of Seville, or to declare war on France and make peace with England, for such things were " exclusive rights of the people ".

On October 24th, 1808, the Marqués de Toro put in the hands of the Captain General a letter he had received from Miranda (London, 20.vii.08), urging him to put himself at the head of the *cabildo* and set up " a representative municipal body to take charge of the Government of that province " and to send representatives to London to discuss with the British Government " all that might be advisable for the security and future destiny of the New World ". The marqués considered that Miranda had inflicted " an outrageous insult " on him and threw him overboard as a traitor and a man who " brazenly ungrateful to the country which tolerates his presence seeks to distort the remarkable offer the whole world knows the King of Great Britain has made, and the ministry and the people have expressed, to help Spain against the common enemy with no other interest than that of upholding the integrity of this monarchy ". Despite these words, ably drafted to keep on the right side of Britain, the wealthy marqués had been plotting against the monarchy before that date. He was to plot again within a few days, following the lead of his fellow-potentate Fernández de León, who had come from his Maracay estate to Caracas to force Casas to constitute a Junta according to his views. No one but Toro and José Felix Ribas would sign his paper; but another petition very much on the same lines did win the signatures of many men of mark, including Ribas and Toro. Fernández de León demurred at first. It was not his paper. Ribas was angry and accused him of " wishing to hide his hand after he had exposed them all, being as he was the chief promoter of the scheme "; and drawing a weapon—pistol or dagger, it is not certain—forced him to sign. Some signed believing it was all done in agreement with Casas; others withdrew their signatures; others did not sign, one of them, Simón Bolívar, " because the paper had not been drafted as he wished ". Simón and his brother Juan Vicente Bolívar left Caracas for their estate in San Mateo.

The two young Bolívars were by then ardent republicans and separatists. The petition was, in form at any rate, monarchist and loyal. It aimed at " concurring with all available means in the preservation of our holy religion, the restoration of our beloved king, the perpetuation of the unalterable union of the Spanish peoples and of the integrity of the monarchy ". And the Junta was to be left " in full and free exercise of the authority, which it will have to wield in the name and on behalf of our august sovereign our lord Ferdinand VII whom God preserve ". Miguel Joseph Sanz, a lawyer of repute, who had been a trustee of Simón Bolívar's estate during the boy's minority, was put under strong pressure by the Ribas faction to make him sign; but finally declared to them that he thought the plan was " monstrous and insensate ". In an argument with Pedro Palacios, Sanz pointed out that " the people were already murmuring, for they believed that these

persons sought to usurp the Government and to tyrannize over them ".
Sanz advocated that " since it was asserted that the Captain General gave
his consent ", the plan should be brought to the knowledge of the people by
posters " so as to wipe out the idea the people had conceived that a usurpation
was meant and that the people should know more about what is being
planned and therefore feel more trust in it ".

The movement was not popular. " The darkies resisted it believing
they would lose their liberty." The people were hostile to the upper classes
and favourable to the rule of Spain—a genuine, spontaneous, traditional
feeling, on which the authorities played rather irresponsibly. The walls of
the city were covered with lampoons against the nobles who conspired to
destroy the peace of the humble classes; and Fernández de León went about
the city defacing them and deliberately posing as the leader of the conspiracy. The real leader was Ribas, in whose house the " upset " was
concocted which would " without fail . . . separate these provinces from
the metropolis". When, however, a number of signatories withdrew their
names, the ringleaders rushed the business through and presented the
document to the authorities (24.xi.08). The paper was read at a special
meeting of the *Audiencia;* whereupon a captain of the battalion of coloured
men and another one of Grenadiers declared themselves ready to withstand
the intrigues of the aristocrats. Within twenty-four hours, the *Audiencia*
decreed the arrest of all the signatories—a comfortable confinement in their
respective houses or in their country estates. Within three months (18.ii.09),
all but one were reprieved and restored in their dignities and offices, the
amnesty explicitly declaring that the incident would not debar them " from
public offices of the royal service or from any other advantage ". There
was one exception: Fernández de León was sent to Spain as " the original
author of everything ", and as " a person who in the present circumstances
would undoubtedly be most pernicious in his way of thinking ". Soon
after his arrival in Spain, the Junta Central resigned its powers and a Regency
of five members was appointed. One of them was to represent America.
The man chosen first was the very brother of this rebel sent back to Spain
by the Venezuelan authorities. But he could not hold the appointment for
long. He happened to have been born in Europe.

5

On May 17th, 1809, the new Captain General landed in La Guaira. Don
Vicente de Emparán, a naval officer, had been Governor of Cumaná, where
he had earned golden opinions. " This province "—writes Dauxion
Lavaysse—" its capital and its other towns are honourable monuments to
the prodigious influence of an enlightened, wise and distinguished
Governor . . . prosperity had become general in all classes, and a considerable number of new fortunes had been made . . . a new quarter or
suburb which vies with the old town, took the worshipped name of *Emparán."*

A few years later, the effects of this excellent leadership were observed by
a Captain in the Spanish Army just come from Spain to fight against Bolívar.

" This city "—writes Captain Sevilla—" is small but beautiful and abundant in food. Its straight streets, laid out at the foot of the hill on which the castle rises, are wide and spacious. A crystalline river divides the city into two parts, offering the majority of the inhabitants magnificent bathing in the very patios of their houses. There are families who bathe three times a day. Splendid kitchen gardens offer their round-the-year green on the banks of the river, from the main bridge of which can be enjoyed a gay and picturesque landscape. Fish, both sea and river, is delicious and abundant. The population is composed half of whites and half of Indians, very few of them are coloured [i.e. black or mulatto]. The women are numerous, as white as alabaster, their hair and eyes of ebony, and lovely in the extreme. Rightly are they known as the Andalusians of America. The Indians have always been distinguished for their constant fidelity to the Spanish cause."

Humboldt knew Emparán in Cumaná. " Don Vicente de Emparán showed us cotton dyed with native plants, and beautiful pieces of furniture made exclusively with wood from local trees; he took a keen interest in physics, and much to our astonishment, asked us whether we thought that under the beautiful sky of the Tropics the atmosphere contained less nitrogen than in Spain, or whether the rapidity with which iron rusts in these countries was merely due to a higher humidity as shown by the hair-hygrometer. Don Vicente de Emparán loved science too much to find it strange that we should come from so far to collect plants and to determine the position of a few places by astronomic means. . . . The marks of deference he gave us in public during our long stay in his Government have contributed in no small measure to secure for us a favourable reception everywhere in South America."

This Governor was not afraid of responsibilities. " Don Vicente de Emparán "—writes Dauxion Lavaysse—" when Governor of Cumaná, took upon himself to allow the ships of friendly and of neutral nations to trade without restriction in the ports of his Government. His sovereign, far from blaming him for having softened the strictness of prohibitive laws in view of the requirements of the situation, bestowed upon him praise and favour." This touch completes the portrait. Emparán was a fair example of enlightened despotism. He belonged to the school bred in the previous generation by Aranda and Roda; men of talent, clear in mind, efficient in administration, enlightened in policy, definitely aristocratic in outlook, but of an aristocracy founded on ability rather than on nobility—men used to govern from above, knowing what they wanted for the good of the people better than the people themselves, and therefore little disposed to argue with the people. This type of man had been fostered in Spain under French influence, and nothing but the excesses of the French Revolution could have cooled their enthusiasm for France. When the French Revolution gave forth an enlightened despot, who checked its excesses and canalized its progressive drive, they returned to their first love. Emparán came to Caracas at the express wish of Napoleon.

He was of course coldly received because of his pro-French tendencies; but the young separatists flocked round him, and Simón Bolívar became one of his closest companions. The political " climate " which had produced the new Captain General was nearly the same as that in which the separatists throve. All were *philosophers;* all wanted to achieve the good of the people without being disturbed by too much meddling from the people; all were enlightened despots. Emparán had arrived from Spain in the company of two notorious separatists: Don Fernando de Toro, a brother of the Marqués and Simón Bolívar's companion in gay Paris, who returned to his country decorated with the title of Inspector General of the Militia; and Don Agustin García, who came back as Colonel, having been sent to Spain by one of Emparán's predecessors because " his presence is not advisable ".

6

On July 30th, 1809, Miguel Joseph Sanz sent to the King a Representation protesting against the persecution which Emparán, as a tool of the two brothers Toro, was inflicting on him, for having witnessed against them at the enquiry on the formation of the Junta. Sanz and his son-in-law, a Captain Rodríguez, had shown a staunch pro-Spanish attitude at the enquiry, and taken steps to delay the conspiracy " and to restrain its leaders, who were openly running about in the streets, on foot and on horseback, in search of partisans ". Their statements were made public. Hatred between the two sides knew no bounds. " So public and shameless is their hatred, that they do not take off their hats to each other, and pass each other with a threatening mien and a challenging glance." Sanz, appalled when he saw Emparán land flanked by Fernando de Toro and García, wrote to the King that all loyal persons " feared the time had come to turn disloyal or to die of loyalty ".

Sanz goes on to say that, since the reason why Don Francisco de Toro persecuted him was his own " determined loyalty and manifest opposition to the independence of these provinces ", he " meditated on the circumstances, and finding that General Emparán was a notorious friend of the Toros and of Don Simón Bolívar, their cousin-in-law, resolved to sacrifice himself once for all with the noble and generous object of opening General Emparán's eyes ". Rodríguez' idea was to draft a representation explaining the true position to the Captain General; but Sanz prevailed upon him to call on Emparán and talk the matter over first. " As it told against the Toros "—Sanz goes on to say—" General Emparán heard it with the utmost indifference and coldness ", but agreed to receive a written statement. Rodríguez wrote it and delivered it the very evening (21.vii.09). " At 11.30 in the morning of the 22nd, Don Fernando Toro crosses the most public streets of the city, accompanied by his relative Don Simón Bolívar, both armed with sabres. They enter the house of Colonel Fierro, our friend, one of the keenest opponents of the attempted Junta, and challenge him. They walk on to my house, enter it with the utmost discourtesy; they do not find Rodríguez; they walk out in the street waiting for him; he arrives, unarmed; and in the very street, also challenge him."

The scene is full of life. The two young bloods were evidently behaving in a way familiar to all those who have witnessed similar incidents caused by young, overbearing officers, unable to control their hot passions before the " insolence " of mere civilians like Sanz and his son-in-law—for though Rodríguez displayed the title of Captain, he was in reality a civilian decorated with a uniform. To add insult to injury, the aggressors, two notorious separatists, counted on the friendship and indulgence of their close friend the Governor. On this, Sanz is definite, and expressly accuses Emparán of being aware that Don Fernando was going to challenge Fierro and Rodríguez precisely at the time he did, since he sent them an order to stay at home. As a consequence of this incident Sanz was ordered away from the city by the Governor, on the ground of " public peace and the security of my person [Sanz'] for it is but natural that the persons I have offended may try to avenge themselves ".

The incident shows how unexpected the relations between the characters and the story turn out to be. Owing to social and intellectual affinities, the Captain General was on far closer terms with the young revolutionary separatists than with the humbler fry whose loyalty to Spain had been the standby of his predecessor and should have been his own standby in days soon to come.

Throughout the year 1809 the situation in Spain went from bad to worse; and the news that reached the cities overseas made it seem more alarming. The more competent the authorities, the less they believed in the possibility of preventing Napoleon from conquering Spain outright. This scepticism of the Governors came to meet a growing sense of popular independence and of republican feeling in the governed, fostered in part by the situation, in part by the very doctrines of popular sovereignty which came from the Junta Central itself. The leaders of the revolutionary faction in Caracas realized all this; and a plot to upset the Government was ready for action on December 24th. Emparán, of course, knew about it, since the plotters were all his friends. He took prompt measures, and, for the time, weathered the storm. Bolívar was one of the conspirators; for, as he was in the following year to tell a prominent Spanish official in Caracas who advised moderation and good sense: " All that is very well painted; but my associates and I have declared war on Spain and we shall see how we come out of it." Note the word: WAR.

CHAPTER XIV

THE NINETEENTH OF APRIL

I

O N November 19th, 1809, the Spaniards lost the battle of Ocaña while Wellington, after his victory in Talavera, was playing Achilles with Portugal as his tent. This disaster opened the gates of Seville to the French. The Junta Central withdrew to Cádiz. It was by then so unpopular that those of its members who went by land took their lives in their hands. Towards the end of January, 1810, it dissolved itself, handing over its powers to a Regency of five members which would summon the Cortes for March 1st. The Regency showed no haste in fulfilling this part of the programme; the Provincial Juntas showed still less in recognizing the authority of the Regency; Cádiz set up a new Junta; and the French armies kept advancing southwards. Realizing the deplorable effect all these events would produce in America, the Cádiz Junta closed the port in the hope that things would soon look brighter. Later, when hope reborn began to cast a rosier colour on things in fact much the same, the Junta reopened the harbour but, as events were to prove, with little discrimination. The first ship to arrive in Venezuela was the private brig *Nuestra Señora del Carmen*, which entered Puerto Cabello bringing letters full of news of anarchy and failure in the Peninsula (15.iv.10). On April 16th, Emparán promulgated an edict declaring there was no news from Spain. " On the 17th he received the news of the invasion of Andalusia and the dispersion of the Junta Central . . . and the news was announced by an edict affixed in all public places on the morning of the 18th as if it had been of the most satisfactory kind." Urquinaona, the Creole civil servant of the Regency who reports this, does not realize that, for Emparán, who was an *afrancesado*, news of a French success in Spain was bound to be good news.

Meanwhile a conspiracy was afoot under the leadership of Emparán's closest friends, the two brothers Toro. The conspirators met at the *House of Mercy*, which was by then the barracks of the Aragua Grenadiers. The Marqués de Toro was Colonel of the Regiment and his brother Don Fernando was their Inspector General. Emparán kept at the head of his best troops these two men, one of whom, Don Fernando, in 1811 was to state the position as follows: " Everybody knows that in spite of my friendship with Don Vicente Emparán, dating from long before his appointment to the Captain Generalship of Caracas, I never lost interest in the cause of my country's liberty, and that I often spoke to this authority on the necessity of our emancipation should the Junta Central come to be dissolved or Spain to be subjugated. The first agents of our glorious revolution entrusted to me their just and honourable designs, and my house was one of the places where many of them used to meet to discuss the matter and to contrive the means to bring about the operation. It was in my house that, with the assent of my brother Don Francisco [i.e. the Marqués], the plan was prepared to attack despotism with the troops in the barracks of the House of Mercy; and as this plan failed for reasons known to all. . . ."

What reasons ? Emparán, a close friend of the conspirators, thought it better to check their ardour. He knew the *pronunciamiento* was to take place on April 1st. On March 20th he had some leaders arrested; then he did nothing for ten days, hesitating to strike against his own social kith and kin. During a feast, in his presence, Bolívar drank a toast to the independence of Spanish America. " This as well as his previous behaviour "—adds O'Leary—" aroused suspicion in the local Government, whose tolerance towards Bolívar and other young men of Caracas by no means revealed a tyrannical government."

" . . . and as this plan failed for reasons known to all "—goes on Don Fernando Toro—" my brother provided mules for many of the conspirators to escape from the persecution of the tyrants, as is well known to Don Mariano Montilla, one of the first co-operators of our liberty. While this was going on in Caracas, I had gone to Valencia to promote the revolution there with the help of the troops of that district and of that of Aragua; for which purpose my brother joined me, and . . . we had taken all the necessary measures to ensure the success of the task, when the caraqueños, by their action on April 19th, deprived our own efforts of their opportunity."

There were therefore two wings or poles to the movement: the Toro brothers on the one hand and the *cabildo* on the other. And while we should not overemphasize the distance between them, the Toros evidently stood for something very much like a *pronunciamiento*, while the *cabildo* were thinking rather in civic and republican terms. Once again we witness that interplay between the cape-and-sword-men and the gown-men that weaves Spanish public life. It might well provide the explanation for Bolívar's curious eclipse during these crucial days. That he took no part in the event of April 19th is certain. O'Leary says that " a feeling of delicacy which honours him very much—his friendship with Emparán—was the cause of his abstention from any active part in the events of April 19th ". This explanation cannot be accepted even if it comes from Bolívar himself, which is possible. But the fact that a military coup was ready should the civic coup fail sheds a flood of light on Bolívar's attitude. He was a military young blood who stalked sabre-rattling the streets of Caracas to " punish " or " teach a lesson " to any civilian who dared to be right against Don Fernando de Toro, his boon companion. These plans of the gown-men of Caracas were all very well but the true way was that of the barracks, and his cousins-in-law, the Colonel-Marqués and the dashing Inspector of Militia, were seeing to that. So, why trouble about that small fry of the *cabildo*? He held aloof and in readiness—in barracks—at Tuy, waiting for the Day.

Nor is this all. A few years later, in Curaçao, one of the leaders of the Caracas Junta, Martín Tovar Ponte, explained to Level de Goda that Bolívar had refused to join in the *cabildo* conspiracy because Tovar could give him no guarantees that upon the downfall of the Spanish authorities an aristocratic Government would be formed; a refusal which Tovar justified on the ground that the Venezuelan nobility was neither numerous nor wealthy enough to govern the country. It was then that Bolívar decided to leave Caracas. José Domingo Díaz, a Caracas royalist, wrote a few years later in his Memoirs: " The royal income in Caracas used to leave a surplus of six hundred to eight hundred thousand pesos per year, generally forwarded to Spain. The Intendentes . . . had this surplus distributed equally between the European and the American businessmen and landowners, taking drafts in favour of the Ministry of Finance payable within four months on the security of the corresponding signatures. In this way the money did not leave the country and the persons concerned drew a considerable profit. On the 10th, 11th, 12th and 13th of that month, part of this surplus had been distributed. The Marqués de Casa León had received forty thousand pesos; Don Simón Bolívar thirty thousand."

2

While the cape-and-sword-men, the Toros and Bolívar, were laying their plans on the classic Spanish military *pronunciamiento*, the gown-men were scheming in the *cabildo* on the lines of a Palace revolution. Their leader was of course a priest. Don José Joaquín Cortés Madariaga was born in Santiago de Chile on July 8th, 1766, in a social class similar to that of Bolívar. The founder of the New World branch of his family on the male line was Don Alonso Cortés Mancha, who had come to Peru as a soldier in 1654. Don Alonso hailed from Medellín, the birthplace of Hernán Cortés, Conqueror of Mexico, and was of the same stock, as was proved in 1777, when the future Canon was eleven, at the request of his parents, and by no less an authority than Charles III's King at Arms.

In the century between the arrival of Don Alonso Cortés in Peru and the birth of Don José Cortés Madariaga in Chile, the family took in growing affluents of New World blood which, for reasons often stated in these pages, was bound to be mixed with Indian strains. This was no bar to aristocratic claims. Don Francisco Cortés, father of our hero, strove to be decorated by the Crown with a marquisate. Baulked in this, he left Peru for Santiago de Chile, where he married the daughter of Don Francisco Madariaga, a Biscayan who, being Royal Treasurer, was the most powerful man in Chile. Don Francisco Cortés had ten children, one of whom, Don José, was to be the rival of Bolívar in the liberation of America.

He was not yet twenty-two when he was proposed by the Church chapter of Santiago for the benefice of San Lázaro. For over ten years, his career is chequered and noisy, owing to the conflict of the forces which rule his early life: the lustre and power of his family; his ambition; and his cantankerous, quarrelsome and violent character. In 1794 he left for Spain, with letters recommending that certain Church benefices should be granted to him. The University made him its representative to negotiate that the King should approve its new Charter and that the Pope should issue a bull recognizing it.

Little is known about his stay in Madrid and less still about his travels in

Europe. While in Rome he seems to have obtained the title of Papal Protonotary. It is said that in 1799 he lived in Cádiz in the house of La Cruz, a banker and a man of letters; that this house was the abode of the chief cell of Miranda's secret society, *Reunión Americana;* and that, on Miranda's instruction, he left for Chile. All this may have happened. Cortés left Cádiz (12.iv.02) with the benefice he had come to fetch in his pocket—a canonry of the Cathedral of Santiago. Eleven months later no news of him had reached Santiago and he was thought to have perished at sea. But, thrown on the Costa Firme by contrary winds, he turned up in Caracas and seized the opportunity of a vacancy in the Cathedral there to ask and obtain a transfer from Chile to Venezuela. On July 23rd, 1803, he was appointed Canon of the Cathedral of Caracas and on July 28th the bishop and Chapter formally received him as such.

During the seven years between his inauguration as a canon and his début as a public orator and revolutionist, Cortés seems to have been possessed by the desire to leave Caracas. He is constantly asking permission to leave his post, which the *cabildo* repeatedly refuses him. The turbulent canon therefore can hardly have been working in Venezuela for Miranda. His name is often mentioned in legal quarrels with his colleagues in the Church Chapter, who declare that " for six years he has kept away from the service of his canonry and from the Church "; and at the time of his sudden appearance on the political stage in 1810 he seems to have been under some legal prosecution. Emparán granted him leave to sail for Spain (12.ii.10), on the strength of his resignation as a canon, much to the displeasure of the local Church authorities; and when (revealing the material core of the quarrel) Emparán wrote again on March 7th that the monthly fees of the (resigned) canon be deposited in the Royal Treasury, Cortés protested, and was strong enough to obtain from Emparán a cancellation of this order and a confirmation of his passport to leave for Spain. This proof of strong favour on the part of the Governor General, against the wishes of the local Church authorities, is dated March 17th, one month and two days before the canon is to play a leading part in deposing the Governor General. Why Cortés did not leave for Spain is not known. We gather from all this an unromantic impression of a man whose chief motive was personal ambition and whose character was turbulent, violent and most difficult to integrate into a well ordered society.

3

The uneasy situation created by news received from Spain made the path of the Caracas separatists easier. Two *regidores*, Tovar and José de Anzola, prevailed upon the first Mayor, José de Llamosas, to call a meeting of the *cabildo*, since its own edicts had confirmed the extinction of the Spanish government and it was therefore necessary to set up one in Caracas. It seems that a kind of popular chorus was secured for the events of the coming day by some distribution of bounty in the suburbs of the city; though the detail would appear to strain somewhat the foresight of the patricians of

Caracas—Montilla, Ribas and Tovar—to whom it is attributed. At eight o'clock the *Ayuntamiento* or *cabildo* was sitting. Its first decision was to summon the President of the *Audiencia*, i.e. the Captain General, to " resolve on the affairs which may occur ". At this moment Emparán began to tread the path of concessions which led him to his fall and to that of the régime he represented. He might have pointed out that the only authority empowered to call an extraordinary sitting of the *cabildo* was the Captain General; but he meekly obeyed the summons, and merely observed that, since the emissaries sent by the Regency had arrived in La Guaira, their arrival in Caracas should be awaited. Both these emissaries, Don Carlos de Montúfar, son of the Marqués de Selva Alegre (a magnate of Quito), and Don Antonio Villavicencio, a naval officer, were Creoles of Quito and separatists. The majority of the *cabildo* of Caracas, unaware of what the active minority were after, accepted the suggestion of Emparán. The plan missed fire, and as it was Holy Thursday, everybody moved to the Cathedral. It seems that the public, though scanty, was mainly composed of persons in the know; they crowded at the gate of the Cathedral; and as Emparán, followed by the *regidores*, walked towards the porch, the young conspirators from the ranks of the crowd shouted the old Spanish cry: " *A cabildo, a cabildo!* " This was quickly taken up by their slaves and by the crowd. One of these young men, Francisco Salías, seized the Governor by the arm and challenged him: " The people summon you to the *cabildo*, Sir! " Emparán was nonplussed. A mere gesture of his gloved hand, the lifting of his gold-tipped stick would have made the company of grenadiers within a few yards of him disperse the crowd without bloodshed. The gesture was not made, and as if to forestall it, the Captain in command, Don Luis Ponte, a nobleman of Caracas, withdrew with his men—an act for which he was a few days later promoted to the command of the battalion. The *regidores* and Emparán returned to the City House.

Two lawyers, Don Felix Sosa and Don Germán Roscio, had been added to the *cabildo* as " representatives of the people "—through the quiet wire-pulling of Cortés, who had also arranged that the Church authorities should appoint two other representatives. But when the two priests delegated by the archbishop arrived at the City House, they found the door closed on them. Cortés, disliking the archbishop's choice, had arranged for the *cabildo* to replace the two representatives by two other priests, a brother of José Felix Ribas and Cortés himself. He, however, preferred to keep away from the City House and to wait for his moment roaming about the Cathedral. Timid at first, the two representatives of the people, Roscio and Sosa, proposed to the enlarged *cabildo* to constitute a Junta under the Captain General; but, when Roscio was at work drafting the papers accordingly, some of the conspirators sent for Cortés. The Canon entered the hall where the *cabildo* sat and took a seat opposite Emparán, whom he harangued, demanding a Government with power of its own and the deposition of the Captain General. Disconcerted at first, Emparán declared that he would appeal to the people and walked to the window. The crowd shouted: " *Viva, viva nuestro Capitán General!* " Cortés stepped out on to the balcony, addressed the crowd, and asked them whether they wanted to be governed by Emparán. Behind both the Captain General and the Canon, the *Regidor* Dionisio Palacios (the husband of Juana Bolívar, Simón's sister) signalled in the negative. A Dr. Villarreal, a relative and friend of some of the conspirators, began the shouts of No! The crowd followed. A rule which had lasted three hundred years was over and a devastating civil war had begun.

The leaders of separatism trod cautiously on their uncharted path. Outside, the Grenadiers, both white and coloured, and a growing crowd shouted: *Death to the French !* and *Long live the Fatherland, Religion, Ferdinand VII !* A middle-class public of " military men and civilians, lawyers, doctors, surgeons, chemists and students " encircled them, followed and watched over their discussions. A number of lawyers, priests and friars, more or less self-appointed or chosen by the small cell of leaders grouped round Martín Tovar Ponte and Cortés Madariaga, had enlarged the old *cabildo* giving it the air of a Convention, under the name of *Junta Suprema Conservadora de los Derechos de Fernando VII*; and in view of " the impossibility in which that very Government [the Regency] finds itself of attending to the security and prosperity of these territories and of administering full justice in all affairs which fall under the supreme authority ", the *cabildo* declared itself justified by natural law " to set up within the very bosom of these countries a system of government calculated to make good these deficiencies, through the exercise of the rights of sovereignty which owing to this very fact has been vested again in the people ". It was in virtue of this decision, which he there and then accepted, that Emparán gave over his stick, the insignia of his authority, to the first Mayor of Caracas, in the old Spanish tradition which assumed national representative powers to be vested in the *cabildo* of the chief city of the Kingdom. Once again, as when under Philip II it had sent Simón de Bolívar to Spain as Procurator of the whole Province of Venezuela, the *cabildo* of Caracas, without even noticing it, took for granted that its first Mayor was entitled to represent the whole nation in accepting the surrender of his vice-regal power from the hands of a Captain General and Governor appointed by the King.

The impulse behind the Junta came however from men outside the *cabildo*: Roscio, Cortés Madariaga, José Felix Ribas. Roscio, a man of mixed blood and of Italian origin on his white side, became Secretary for Foreign Relations. There were three other Secretaries: for Finance, for War and Navy and for Justice. A Court of Appeal, following the model of the old *Audiencia*, was set up under the Marqués de Casa León, returned from Spain with a much sobered revolutionary ardour. The command of the armed forces was of course given to Don Fernando de Toro; but there were many European Spaniards not only in the new civil administration but in the military commands, the majority of which were given to them. A telling detail: the Junta took the title of Highness.

A new set of ideas held the field, though the words used in official documents were those of yesterday. In the name of Ferdinand VII measures were taken which implied complete sovereignty. Count Tovar, the aged father of one of the *cabildo* leaders, was made a Field Marshal; freedom of trade was granted to friendly and neutral nations; export duties were abolished; Indians were relieved of their taxes, and, later, slave traffic was prohibited. An Academy was founded for the study of mathematics and a patriotic society for fostering agriculture and industry. The " philosophic " trend of the new masters revealed itself in their attitude towards the Church. The archbishop was officially informed that churches would be closed and street processions forbidden " until things are organized ".

It would be, however, wholly unhistorical to blame the leaders on the score of " disloyalty " and to praise the crowd on the score of their " loyalty " to Ferdinand VII. In the historical circumstances, the leaders were right and the crowd were wrong. Once the Crown had fallen to the gutter in a French city the sovereignty had devolved on the people. But the people over whom the King of Spain had ruled for three centuries was essentially plural. The plurality and dispersion of sovereignty was therefore a logical and inescapable consequence of the fall of the Spanish Crown. The crowd was not aware of this; the leaders were, and it was their right as leaders to draw the political consequences of their conviction. Nor was there any need, in this respect at any rate, to split the movement because some of them aimed at an independent republic and others at a kingdom under Ferdinand VII in a purely personal union with Spain. For the time being, the ultimate constitution of the country was far less important than the fact that there was to be a constitution, to be evolved by the nation itself and not to come as a charter from Spain.

The ground on which the revolutionists of Caracas stood was solid and in complete accord with the traditions of Spain. They were wrong in disputing whether the Regency was or was not the legitimate power *in* and *for* Spain. In fact, by venturing on this ground, they gave themselves away as lawmongers rationalizing their preconceived separatism. But when arguing that Alexander VI had granted the New World to Ferdinand and Isabel and their legitimate successors, but not " to the Peninsulars, nor to the Peninsula, nor to the men of the Island of León, nor to the French "; and when they asserted that, failing a King, the territories belonged " to the discoverers and settlers now represented by us ", the leaders of Caracas might perhaps lay themselves open to attack from their own Indians, but certainly not from the Spaniards of and in Spain. As for the European Spaniards living in the Indies, the leaders of Caracas held open the hand of friendship to them, declaring that " they are our brothers and are cordially and sincerely united to our cause ". This was so—for whichever the cause a Venezuelan espoused, independence, home rule or old rule, he was sure to find a European Spaniard by his side. There was but one people and the line which divided it was not drawn by birth but by ways of thinking and by friendship, interest and family ties.

4

There was hardly a city in the Spanish Kingdoms overseas where the Spanish crisis was not producing similar effects. At the start, a reaction identical to that of the Spanish cities against the French invader and for

Ferdinand VII; later, a more self-assertive movement towards home defence, home rule, independence. All these cities had behind them three centuries of humanities, of peace, of wealth; they all therefore had a group of leaders alert to the historical realities of their days. Though seemingly directed against Spain, and often handling words and driven by passions fiercely anti-Spanish, the movements of secession and emancipation were therefore the logical outcome of an historical evolution grounded on the Spanish humanistic culture of the kingdoms beyond the seas.

In this autumn of the Spanish rule, governors and viceroys began to fall like dead leaves. But the first of them to do so was blown away by no revolutionary wind. The Governor of Upper Peru was deposed by the *Audiencia* of La Plata after a long wrangle over competence and powers—and regularly, if somewhat drastically. La Plata (or Chuquisaca or Charcas) was an old University city; and students took a prominent part in the movement. The sight of a Spanish Governor dismissed from office, however regularly, was in those days exhilarating. In La Paz, a *Junta Tuitiva* was set up, double-edged, of course, " conservative of the rights of Ferdinand VII " and irresistibly drawn towards independence. A knot of civil wars split the reformers. The viceroy sent a Creole Commander, José Manuel Goyeneche, to restore order, which he did without much difficulty, in a straight fight against the only revolutionary leader who took the field on behalf of South American independence: Don Juan Antonio Figueroa, a European Spaniard. This incident dramatized the fact that the ferment then working in Spanish America was by no means dividing its populations on the line New World versus Old World. When La Paz was overcome (25.x.09) Goyeneche had the leaders executed.

Peru however had remained and was to remain to the last the most faithful to the rule of Spain among the Spanish Kingdoms of the Indies; and its troops were to play a prominent part in the repression of the rising of Quito. Here again, it was in the University that the trouble began. The President, Count Ruiz de Castilla, an octogenarian, was deposed by a *Junta Conservadora de los Derechos de Fernando VII*, in the now classic style, under the leadership of the usual Creole slave-owner and aristocrat, the Marqués de Selva Alegre (whose son had arrived in Caracas as an emissary of the Regency just in time to stimulate the events of April 19th). The movement of Quito was of the type Bolívar and the Toros had prepared for Caracas when they were fore-stalled by the gown-men. It was a *pronunciamiento*. The names of the *Junta Suprema* were chosen at a private meeting in the house of an opulent lady of the city, Doña Manuela Cañizares; and on August 10th, 1809, " Salinas, who commanded the only two companies of regular troops available in Quito "—for such was the force with which Spain held a whole continent in peace—" went to the barracks, read the charter constituting the new government to the soldiers and having secured their approval, seized the person of the President, Ruiz de Castilla, whose guards yielded with much ease."

The Junta, which gave itself the title of Majesty, set up a *Senate*, and a *Falange*. On August 16th, 1809, an open *cabildo* announced in Quito that the Constitution was approved (thus again assuming parliamentary powers over the whole Kingdom) and all notables took, in the Cathedral, the oath of " obedience and fidelity to Ferdinand VII as our King and natural lord; loyalty to the principles of the Junta Central [of Spain of course]; and faithfulness to the unity and purity of the Catholic, Apostolic, Roman religion ". But the Junta failed to win over public opinion; and thought wiser to reinstate Ruiz de Castilla as President upon a solemn promise that he would intercede with the viceroy and the Crown to prevent reprisals. Troops, mostly half-caste, arrived from Lima, and Castilla put all the leaders in prison. An attempt at freeing the prisoners by force led to the murder of twenty-eight of the men awaiting trial, in circumstances which, though still obscure, do not allow us to exonerate the Spanish authorities, at any rate, from crass incompetence, if not worse. In the course of later riots the octogenarian President Ruiz de Castilla was dragged out of a convent where he had taken refuge and murdered. Many other leaders on both sides lost their lives.

These events created a powerful impression all over Spanish America. The viceroy of New Granada had ordered all local authorities to recognize the Regency. In Santa Fe the usual conspiracy was brewing. Riots broke out prematurely and, on the same day fixed for the military coup (20.vii.10), the viceroy was forced to accept a Junta which proclaimed him its President. Its members swore to " shed the last drop of their blood to defend our sacred Catholic Apostolic Roman religion, our most beloved Monarch Ferdinand VII and the liberty of the fatherland ". The viceroy behaved loyally; but, on a rumour that he was arming his guard against the people, he was imprisoned; mob rule prevailed for days, but peace had been luckily restored when news came of the Quito events. Most of the provinces of New Granada followed the lead of Santa Fe; some remained loyal to Spain; others claimed their right to set up governments of their own.

All these movements were taking place ostensibly to maintain the independence of the Spanish Kingdoms overseas against any eventual invader—at the time, Napoleon. But there was one of the American Kingdoms which had had actual experience of invasion and signal success in repelling it. Buenos Aires had recently beaten off a British invasion, so that when the French invasion overpowered Spain, the patriots of the Plata may have been tempted to smile superciliously. Their victory had been due to a sacred union between the Frenchman Liniers, who became viceroy, the Creoles, and the European Spaniards. But, as danger vanished, union vanished with it; the viceroy was after all a Frenchman just like the new would-be invader; and the European-Spanish element, grown uneasy, organized military formations—not, of course of Spaniards, but of Galicians, Catalans, Biscayans—the three predominant Spanish nationalities. This did not please Don Cornelio Saavedra, Colonel of Patricians, and in the spirit of the Potosí civil wars rather than in that of republican Argentine patriotism, which it would be pure anachronism to attribute to him, he dissolved these Peninsular formations. Colonel Saavedra did not want to have so many Colonels in the city. Alzaga, the Spanish-European whose wealth and skill had been at the core of the resistance against the British, had later tried to have Liniers removed, but was himself removed to Patagonia; and on the way thither, rescued from exile by General Elio who ruled Montevideo with a firm hand. Meanwhile the Junta Central sent a new viceroy, Don Baltasar Hidalgo de Cisneros, who was met by the patriots with a demand for an open *cabildo*. This led of course to a *Junta Gubernativa Provincial del Río de la Plata*, set up on May 25th, 1810.

5

The Council of Regency set up to govern Spain for the exiled King was composed of five members: the bishop of Orense, chosen for his spirited reply to an imperial invitation to go to Bayonne; Don Francisco Javier Castaños, the victor of Bailén; Don Francisco de Saavedra, the ex-minister; Don Antonio Escaño, an intelligent and good-natured naval officer; and the Mexican, Don Miguel de Lardizábal.

This Council of Regency issued a proclamation to the peoples overseas (14.ii.10) announcing to them the convocation of the Cortes for March 1st. It had been drafted by Quintana, the poet, in the naïve vein of his own poem on " the virgin of the world, innocent America! " The Regency of Spain officially informed its overseas " subjects " that they were " raised to the dignity of free men; you are no longer the same men as before, bowed under a yoke the harder the more distant you were from the central power, looked upon with indifference, oppressed by greed and destroyed by ignorance. Bear in mind that . . . your destinies no longer depend on ministers, viceroys or governors; they are in your hands."

This Proclamation was one of the forms taken by the promise to call a meeting of the Cortes inherited by the Regency from the Junta Central. How was it kept? Weeks went by and the Regency did nothing. The deputies of the provincial Juntas were getting restive; two of them, a priest and a nobleman, called on the Regents and put before them the national clamour. Within twenty-four hours a decree was issued fixing no date, but definite enough. Meanwhile the Regency had to face growing difficulties from the New World while nominally governing a country for the most part under enemy occupation. A letter addressed by the Regents to Emparán (14.i.10) had been answered by something calling itself *Junta Suprema* (3.v.10). The Junta pointed out to the Regency that, in Spain, " various institutions have succeeded each other with no other common feature than a self-defined claim to wield a delegation of sovereignty which, since it has not been made by the monarch nor by the community of the Spaniards of both hemispheres, can only be void, illegitimate and contrary to the principles sanctioned by our very laws ". " Our laws ", that is the laws of the community of Spaniards of both hemispheres.

6

The Regency was confronted with documents of a more uncompromising nature. On May 20th, 1810, the Junta, reporting on abuses committed in

America by agents of the Crown, pointed out that under the existing laws nothing could be done, since the central power, too distant, " believed itself engaged by all the decisions and behaviour of its representatives ", and that anything short of a fundamental reform was " vain, precarious and chimerical " and " insufficient to make [Americans] tolerate the deprivation of so many advantages, so many blessings which only await the beneficent influence of independence to develop ".

Three days before these words were written, on May 17th, 1810, a decree was issued in Spain under the authority of the Regency opening all the harbours of the Indies for direct trade with the European nations and their colonies. The news burst as a bombshell in Cádiz, where the old trade monopoly, though considerably reduced by the reforms of 1778, was still the chief source of wealth. At the noise, even the Regency woke up, to discover that a measure of such importance had been passed and published with almost frivolous neglect by its Finance Minister, at the instigation of an official and of Don Estéban Fernández de León. The order was withdrawn when printed copies of it had already left for America; and the incident did much to embitter the struggle. The attitude of the commercial community of Cadiz was represented as odious; but the worst was that decisions of as much importance to Habana and Buenos Aires as to Cádiz were taken far away from the New World cities and close to the dominant city of the Old World.

The news of the events of Caracas reached the Regency on July 4th, 1810; soon followed by news of similar events in Buenos Aires, which arrived in Spain towards the end of August. For a time, nothing was done; for the Regents thought that, once the Americans heard that Spain, though overrun by the French, was not overcome by them, all disturbances would cease. The Council of the Indies was consulted and on its advice it was decided to send overseas a magistrate with full powers, a few warships and troops. The choice fell on Don Antonio Cortabarría, " a magistrate respected for his integrity, but old and without the slightest knowledge of America "; his zone of action was to comprise Venezuela, the Islands, New Granada and New Spain. In a similar capacity, Don Francisco Javier de Elio was sent to Buenos Aires with five hundred men and a frigate. Both had been instructed to use no force till all means of persuasion had proved useless.

CHAPTER XV

INDEPENDENCE UNDECLARED

I

TOWARDS the beginning of June, 1810, news of the events of Caracas reached the Marqués de Someruelos, who, as Captain General of Habana, wielded considerable military and naval power. He was a wise man; he thought he would negotiate with the leaders of Caracas, to spare the country a civil war. The negotiator was at hand. Don Francisco José Heredia, appointed *Oidor* of the *Audiencia* of Caracas in October, 1809, happened to be then in Habana awaiting the ship that was to take him over. Heredia was born in Santo Domingo in 1776, of a well-to-do Creole family. At twenty he was a doctor of canon and civil law; in 1809, at thirty-three, he had reached the high rank of *Oidor*. He enjoyed a great reputation in the Indies, and had married a lady of Coro, in Venezuela. Someruelos sent him on his mission in a warship. But, as the ship called at Santo Domingo, Heredia heard that Caracas was preparing an armed expedition against Coro, a city faithful to the Spanish cause; and that the Governor of Maracaibo, Don Fernando Miyares, had been appointed President, Governor and Captain General of Venezuela. This forced Heredia to divert his ship towards Coro.

Miyares—whose wife was that intimate friend of Simón Bolívar's mother who had fed him at the breast—was a Creole with good friends at Court. Layard, Governor of Curaçao, informed the Earl of Liverpool that it was " reported " that the new Captain General had paid forty thousand dollars for his appointment. He did pay for it, but not so much. He was a strong-handed, rather than strong-willed, and a narrow-minded man. From the outset, therefore, the gown-man Heredia found his mission of peace thwarted by the " cape-and-swords ". The Junta of Caracas had sent three messengers to Coro to win over the one time capital to the new ways; but Coro had a grudge against Caracas, the upstart city which had deprived her of her primacy; and so chose to remain on the Spanish side rather than play second fiddle to Caracas again. The emissaries, realizing that Maracaibo would follow Coro, resolved to retrace their steps and report their failure; but the *cabildo* of Coro forced them to proceed on their mission, and had them escorted thereto. Miyares arrested them and sent them to Puerto Rico. Heredia realized how useless it was to try to make the Captain General understand that " such an imprudent step might have been and should have been avoided ".

The civil war was beginning. Its complexity was baffling. The provinces and cities that sided with Caracas did so for local reasons of a complex and unexpected character. Cumaná, where the Junta was largely made up of European Spaniards, appointed as Commander in Chief Don Juan Manuel de Cajigal, a European Brigadier of the Spanish Army who had remained in

Cumaná after his term of office as Governor.* In Barcelona the Junta declared for the Regency, though it recognized Caracas; but it seceded from . . . Cumaná, which was the authority closest by. In Barinas, on hearing of the events of April 19th, an open *cabildo* laid down two principles: provincial home rule and respect for the King's rights. In Valencia, Fernando de Toro was organizing a regular *pronunciamiento*, and that was that. In Puerto Cabello, the success of the Junta was due to a personal quarrel between a naval officer and a Catalan tradesman. As for Calabozo, the European Spaniards were no less enthusiastic than the American for the change of allegiance; and it is said that one of the most enthusiastic of these European Spaniards was an uncouth Asturian, later to become a chief actor in the civil war on the Royalist side: José Tomás Boves.

All this explains the situation in the cities which remained " loyal ". For even in Coro and in Maracaibo, local governments were also formed. " In Coro "—writes Heredia—" the *Ayuntamiento*, enlarged with a number of private persons, took over the government. The same happened in Maracaibo, though somewhat more moderately out of respect for General Miyares; so that, in its own way, a revolution took place also in the territory which recognized the Regency. As for Guayana, they always did there what they wished without consulting anybody." The difference between the " loyal " and the " disloyal " parts of the country was therefore merely formal. In substance the whole country *became* independent, whether their first independent words were for or against independence; and the opposition between the two parties—merely verbal though it was—led to a civil war because it sharpened and provided with a banner and a cause latent and old roots of strife such as the rivalry between Coro and Caracas and the distrust with which the coloured classes looked upon the white leaders.

2

Canarians, Catalans and Biscayans, owners of most of the public houses of Caracas, had been among the most enthusiastic " patriots " of the new fatherland. Numerous vexations inflicted on them by the officials of the new régime rapidly cooled their ardour. The trends of public opinion began to veer early, and in ways so disquieting that, on June 22nd, when the revolution was hardly two months old, a Court of Public Safety had to be set up. Sparks of rebellion against the rebels burst first in Caracas, later in the Valleys of Aragua, then in Caracas again. Three European Spanish brothers and a few Creoles plotted to upset the Junta and to put the country under a Committee of Churchmen under the archbishop Coll y Prat. Two European Spanish captains denounced the conspiracy to the authorities, but it seems that actual failure was due to the reluctance of the Church leaders to sacrifice a sentry. Most of the culprits were absolved and some sentenced to the vaults of La Guaira. The incident, however, was exploited by José

* He was a cousin of the Cajigal who, as an intimate friend of Miranda, had been involved in long legal proceedings for contraband.

Felix Ribas, restive with demagogic ambitions; when the news of the Quito events reached Caracas, he led a crowd through the city demanding the expulsion of all European Spaniards. Under his leadership, the walls of the city were covered with printed notices asking for vengeance. " Let the knife, let death be our motto ", was said in these posters in which the Spaniards were described as cannibals. The Junta had to counter with an edict promising that adequate revenge should be taken; but, meanwhile, wisely expelled Ribas, his brother and a surgeon named Gallegos.

In order to meet the danger of the " loyal " provinces, the Junta of Caracas concentrated 3,000 men in Carora, under the command of the Marqués de Toro. Mérida and Trujillo seized the opportunity to pass over from the Cádiz to the Caracas persuasion. Heredia tried to negotiate. Toro was willing; Miyares, though reluctantly, authorized Heredia to negotiate, on hearing that Lord Liverpool had written to the governor of Curacao throwing over the Junta of Caracas. But when everything was ready, Cortabarría, the agent of the Regency, arrived in Puerto Rico; and Miyares, sheltered behind the new authority, withdrew his consent.

This gave the Marqués de Toro an opportunity to prove his generalship. His first encounters were successful. Elated by them, he appeared with his 3,000 men and some artillery, before Coro (28.xi.10), " an open city "—says Heredia, where—" there were only 600 fusiliers, 200 men on horses and mules and about 1,000 men with spears and arrows who were of no use whatever; but we had some artillery . . . though with little ammunition." Why did Toro give up the fight and withdraw to Carora ? Strategic explanations have been put forward. None can vie with that of Heredia, who was a witness of the events he relates: " On the 29th, after a comedy which they styled ' attack ' and which really was a refusal to attack the adversary owing to the horror everyone felt at the first act of civil war, the Marqués withdrew in complete disorder, losing even his trunks." And he adds: " No one thought in Maracaibo of celebrating this victory with a *Te Deum* or any other acts of public rejoicing, for hearts were not hardened yet to the point of rejoicing and thanking the Lord for the destruction of our brothers. Someone suggested that an example should be made on the officers caught, but General Miyares turned a deaf ear and succeeded in having the matter dropped till the author of the suggestion was ashamed of himself."

3

On September 24th, 1810, the Spanish Cortes met at the Island of León, off Cádiz. For electing members for the constituencies occupied by the French, which in fact were the majority, makeshifts were adopted, such as the designation of substitutes pending the election and arrival of the regularly elected representatives. This was also done with regard to the Indies. The temporary representatives for " Caracas " or Venezuela were Esteban Palacios, Simón Bolívar's uncle and godfather, and Fermín Clemente, related by marriage to one of his sisters. The Regency, in the hope of discrediting the Cortes, had arranged that the sittings should be public—which was exactly what the Cortes wished, though for the opposite reason. The first act of the Cortes was to adopt a proposal of one of its members, Muñoz Terrero, a priest who had been Rector of Salamanca University, whereby national sovereignty was declared to be vested in the Cortes. True, there sat in the Cortes a number of American members provisionally admitted as substitutes; but it was evident that, on the day sovereignty was taken from the King, it could only pass, not to the nation, but to the nations, in plural, over which the King had ruled.

It was this circumstance which made an agreement difficult between the European and the American deputies. During the debate on Muñoz Terrero's proposal the American deputies suggested that, when sending the decree of the Cortes to America, it was necessary to " speak to its inhabitants about the equality of rights between them and the Europeans, and the extension of their national representation considering they were an integral part of the Monarchy, as well as to grant an amnesty or complete oblivion of the excesses which had taken place during the disputes in some of those countries ". As these suggestions from the American members fell on minds which had not reflected on the situation, the debate began to get heated; and Don José Mejía, member for Santa Fe, thought it wiser to ask for a private sitting. Finally, the Cortes passed a decree (15.x.10) proclaiming equality between the Spanish citizens of the Kingdoms of both sides of the Ocean, and an amnesty.

December, 1810, and January, 1811, were spent in debating the ways and means to grant in fact that equality which the decree of October 15th had laid down as a principle. The Cortes finally declared (9.ii.11) " that American representation in future Cortes must be absolutely equal in its mode and form to that of the Peninsula . . . in accordance with the decree of October 15th ". It was also decided to abrogate all laws which prohibited or restricted the cultivation in the Indies of certain plants such as the vine and the olive tree; though such prohibitions had been often disregarded and never enforced as rigidly as was that of the tobacco plant in Spain which, in a spirit of reciprocity, had been proscribed in favour of the tobacco planters of the Indies.

" So "—concludes Toreno—" the Cortes decreed successively everything needed to achieve a perfect equality between America and Europe; but, since they did not decree America's independence, it availed little." What neither Toreno nor most Spaniards of his time seemed able to realize was that the American Spaniards, in seeking their independence, were acting exactly on the same impulses and for the same reason as the European Spaniards in fighting against Napoleon. Nor were many American Spaniards more enlightened. While European Spaniards like Someruelos and even, at first, Cortabarría, sided with American Spaniards such as Heredia, Urquinaona or Villavicencio, in their desire for peace and a friendly agreement, American Spaniards like Aréchaga, the prosecutor of Quito, Miyares, the Governor of Maracaibo and José Domingo Díaz, the ardent royalist of Caracas, were for stern measures and no compromise with the rebels.

4

Cortabarría was at sea while the Cortes voted their equalitarian decree of October 15th. He arrived in San Juan de Puerto Rico on October 24th, 1810. His first decision was to set free the three delegates of the Caracas Junta sent under arrest by Miyares. His instructions sufficed for this. But it seems that Admiral Cochrane had also intervened; while the three prisoners themselves had presented a supplication to His Majesty (6.vii.10) which, whether sincere or simulated, added nothing to their dignity. Meanwhile, Toro had been defeated and the situation in Spain was on the whole less desperate. Cortabarría wrote to Heredia that " since the restoration of the . . . Cortes was to be expected, and the two representatives for Venezuela, Palacios and Clemente, had been designated, and the decree of October 15th promulgated, and our arms and those of our allies were victorious, all difficulties should be easily conquered ".

He thought the moment had come to approach the men of Caracas direct. But he had never fully understood the position. For him, negotiation was practically synonymous with paper-war. From the moment of his arrival he had carried on a kind of guerrilla-warfare by means of " proclamations and dissertations which he tried to spread throughout the country, with which he achieved nothing ". Towards the end of November, he sent to Caracas an official emissary, Don Martín Espino, a naval officer, " the man least fit in the world for such a task ", says Heredia, who may be excused for adding that he would have been a better man himself, as he certainly was. Cortabarría demanded recognition of the authority of the Cortes, and of Miyares as Captain General; restoration of the *Audiencia*, and disbanding of the troops raised since April 19th. And he brandished a threat of blockade.

" In these civil dissensions "—writes Heredia at this point—" two ways only are possible: either to use force vigorously or to negotiate frankly. The first course was not possible, for there was no force; the second was adopted but by such tortuous ways." Curiously enough, the Junta of Caracas was no less tortuous. Had it contended that, precisely because the Regency and the Cortes were a perfectly legitimate authority in Spain, the Junta of Caracas and the Congress they were electing were also a perfectly legitimate authority in Venezuela, they would have stood on unshakable ground. But the leaders of Caracas gave away the irrational origin of their attitude by arguing that none of the authorities set up in Spain was in their view legitimate as a Spanish authority—whereby they reasserted in words of their own the formal unity between Venezuela and Spain at the time when in fact and in intention they were breaking away from Spain; and they went so far as to declare themselves the " true vassals " of Ferdinand VII.

This muddle-headed argument was re-stated about a month later when another answer had to be drafted (1.ii.11) to yet another emissary sent to Caracas directly by the Cortes on the initiative of the two deputy members for Venezuela, Palacios and Clemente. He was a Venezuelan himself, Don Feliciano Montenegro Colón, and he arrived in a corvette of the Spanish Royal Navy, the *Sebastián*, with letters for the old *cabildo*, now superseded by the Junta. The two deputies reported on their work at the Cortes and requested the designation of two regular members. The Junta again answered that the Cortes were as illegal as the Regency; that Palacios and Clemente had no mandate to represent Venezuela, and that whatever they did as deputies was null and void. Finally, the Junta defined a true and solid doctrine in conformity with pre-Bourbon Spanish theory and practice: " America had no more right to rule Spain than Spain to demand of America a homage due only to the royal person of Ferdinand VII." Yet, even this doctrine became obsolete on the day both the Cortes of Cádiz and the Junta of Caracas declared the national sovereignty vested in the people. The paper-war was at an end; Cortabarría had begun hostilities by declaring the blockade of Venezuela (21.i.11) in virtue of the powers conferred on him by the Regency, should persuasion fail.

5

Every step in this rise of the Venezuelan nation had revealed the vigour of the Spanish political traditions implanted in the soil of the New World. On this Spanish tradition of localism came to be grafted and to blossom, at least for a time, an exotic idea: that federalism which, for quite different causes, had emerged as the compromise between unity and anarchy in the United States. The phrase *Confederation of Venezuela* was already current in Caracas by the autumn of 1810. This was natural in a country in which the Caracas Junta, though self-styled *Suprema* and *Highness*, and though enlarged with a few provincial representatives, was bound to allow provincial Juntas as much free power as they cared to take, since after all it was no more than a provincial Junta itself. As relations with Spain deteriorated, the situation became too lax for a country in danger of war; and the Supreme Junta decided to proceed to a general election for a *Congreso Nacional Conservador de los Derechos de Fernando VII.*

Here again, the Junta of Caracas remained faithful to the Spanish tradition, which it actually invoked to assert the right of the citizen " to contribute with his vote to delegate those personal and real rights which existed originally in the common people and have been restored to it by the interregnum of the monarchy ". The Junta based all its actions on this interregnum, in particular the need to call the Congress in view of the right of the peoples of America to organize their life until " the complete solution of the present crisis "; a right which was implicit in that other right, never denied to the *cabildos*, to meet and confer whenever they thought fit. But it went further and declared that the provinces of Venezuela would remain " faithful to their august sovereign, ready to recognize him in a legitimate government, and resolved to seal with the blood of the last of their inhabitants the oath they took on the altars of loyalty and patriotism ". One of the items on the programme of the Congress was to be " to come to an agreement eventually with the legitimate government which may be set up in the metropolis, should she save herself from the barbarians who occupy it ".

For the election, the Junta followed closely the rules laid down by the

Spanish Junta Central. There were to be two degrees: in the parishes, every five hundred men would choose an elector by signed ballots; the count to be made by a parish-commissioner in the presence of the priest and of five respectable citizens; these " principal electors " would meet at the chief city with a *cabildo*, where they elected one deputy for every thirty thousand inhabitants. The Junta officially prescribed for the polling morning " a solemn mass to the Holy Ghost in the main church of the parish, recommending to the piety of the faithful that they should implore divine help to choose aright "; and " that during the vote, the bells of all the churches should ring in the usual way as when there are public rogations ".

Few better titles to historical distinction can be exhibited by the Juntas which then governed Venezuela than that of having presided over these elections; " one of the few "—writes Dr. Parra Pérez, their historian— " ever held in Venezuela with no governmental pressure of any kind." There were a few European Spaniards in the Congress, including Francisco Iznardi, born in Cádiz, who became its secretary; and at least two Creoles from outside Venezuela: Yanes, a Cuban, and Sata, a Peruvian. But of course most of the deputies were Venezuelans, with a strong proportion of *mantuanos*, including the three brothers Francisco (the Marqués), Fernando and Juan Toro. But where was Bolívar ?

6

Bolívar was at sea, was in London, was in Caracas again, but was not at the Congress. And it is curious that this fact should be taken for granted— for, to be sure, it is significant. The Junta took its decision to call a Congress on June 11th, 1810. On June 9th Bolívar sailed in an English frigate for London. The young officer who had turned his back on the gown-men of Caracas on April 19th turned his back on them again on June 11th. He was a cape-and-sword man. What had he to do with all those talkers ? " We have declared war on Spain ", he had said in 1809. He was not interested in *cabildos*, in parliaments, or in words. He was interested in war. He sailed for London because it was in London that he could find the two chief factors he needed for his war: British help and Miranda.

British help would—he knew—be forthcoming. How or even why, he did not quite know. He had but little experience of foreign nations, and none of Britain. He just felt that, since he had declared war on Spain, Britain would take kindly to him. But at twenty-seven he was unable to fathom the deeper waters of British policy that had baffled the much older Miranda. Britain was Spain's ally against Napoleon, and it would be unseemly for her to foster in the New World the cause of those whom Spain herself considered as her rebel subjects. From the outset, the Junta of Caracas had endeavoured to enlist British sympathy; and the British authorities on the spot had grown so much used to helping " the cause of Spanish-American freedom " (often hardly distinguishable from that of British trade and even of British contraband) that they felt rather awkward in their new rôle of friends of Spain. They wrote to London for instructions; and the London ministers sent them decorous answers urging respect for the interests of Britain's ally in Europe, tempered by consideration for the interests of British trade, present and future, in the New World. On September 22nd, Brigadier General Layard, Governor of Curaçao, wrote to Lord Liverpool acknowledging receipt of his instructions on how to deal with the Spanish question . . . and of his secret instructions on the same theme. But his correspondence gives abundant proof both of his strong backing of the Junta against Coro and Maracaibo and of the fact that this bias was general in the British colonies and approved in London.

On July 14th, 1810, Layard wrote to Roscio, then Foreign Secretary of the Supreme Junta of Caracas: " Most illustrious Sir!—I have the honour to enclose, for the information of their Highnesses the Supreme Junta, a copy of the letter which I thought advisable to address, to Vice-Admiral the Honourable Sir Alexander Cochrane, K.B. and I sincerely hope that the Admiral will demand the restitution of the Deputies of their Highnesses, confined in prison at Porto Rico. . . . I cannot express in adequate terms, the satisfaction I experienced the 11th instant, on the return of the Deputies of Your Highnesses from Jamaica, particularly as they are so much gratified at the reception they met with and the complete success which has attended their Mission. As the Missionaries from Maracaybo have been treated in a very different manner at Jamaica, and their immediate departure in consequence after the arrival of Lieut. Colonel Montilla, the marked and pointed difference of conduct which has been observed by the Commander of the Forces, Admiral and Governor in that quarter cannot fail producing the most beneficial effects and fully prove the sincerity and confidence of those high authorities in the administration of your Highnesses. I have observed with the most singular satisfaction the very handsome and liberal offers tendered to your Highnesses by Lieut. General Sir George Beckwith, K.B., Commander of the Forces in the Windward and Leeward Islands and Colonies. Such unanimous occurrences as your Highnesses have now received must convince the Governor of Maracaybo and the Commandant of Coro that throughout the British Colonies your Highnesses must and will experience that support to which your meritorious services are so justly entitled."

Hardly a neutral attitude for a British authority to take as between Spain and Spain, for officially the Junta of Caracas was of course Spain even in its own eyes. Layard returns to the theme in a dispatch to Lord Liverpool dated July 31st, 1810. " I am convinced that the favourable sentiments, which are now felt, towards the British nation, and which (if fully cultivated and cherished) may lead to almost any arrangements whether of a political or commercial nature, which His Majesty's Government may judge proper to direct. . . . Should His Majesty's Government view, in a favourable light, the Conduct of the Supreme Junta of Venezuela—Coro and Maracaybo must and will cease all further opposition to the existing government—In which case, I humbly conceive, that no military assistance, in Troops, will be required in this quarter, but that an increase of our naval Establishment will be necessary.   All communication having ceased between the Government of Jamaica and the Deputies from Maracaybo, after the arrival, in that Island, of those from Caracas—in short, all the Governors, Generals, and Admirals throughout the British colonies, in this quarter, having adopted a similar uniform conduct, will, it is supposed, produce a strong sensation in Maracaybo and Coro."

Layard informed Lord Liverpool (2.x.10) that, as a result of the visit of his secretary Robertson to Caracas, he had obtained an " abatement *exclusively* of the fourth part of the duties both on importations and exportations, whether by British or Spanish colonial vessels trading between the Province of Venezuela and the British Colonies.   Our merchants have uniformly complained that unless some exclusive advantage could be obtained in our favour over the Americans, we could never cope with them, as they are unable to carry on their trade at much less expence—the object now attained is therefore a very material one."   And in the same dispatch, after expressing his expectation that " the whole of Venezuela will be united in the course of a month ", of course under the Junta of Caracas, he added: " Captain Rider [whom he was sending to London] can also state Your Lordship the superior advantages which this colony possesses over every other in this part of the world as a Naval Station and how very desirable it is that the adjoining coast, containing the four ports of La Guayra, Puerto Cavello, Coro and Maracaybo should be attached to whatever naval establishment may be determined on for this colony.   The Province of Venezuela seems to depend entirely on Great Britain for naval protection—having done away their own naval Department."

These are the facts and trends Bolívar could not fathom when he sailed for London in search of British help to feed his war on Spain, and in search of Miranda to lead it.   The Junta was by no means keen on Miranda; but there is nothing to warrant the view that, in seeking the veteran General, Bolívar broke his instructions.   Lukewarm and cautious though it was, the instruction on this point means definitely: " by all means, see him if you think it wise and useful ".   " We "—wrote the Junta—" consistent in our behaviour, must look upon him as a rebel against Ferdinand VII "; and should the emissaries sent to London come across him, " they would know how to treat him as befitted these principles and according to the degree of immunity enjoyed in the territory where he might happen to be "; the hint is broad enough, but the Junta made it still broader: " and if his present position could in any way that were decent contribute to the aims of the Mission, let him not be rebuffed ".

Bolívar went straight ahead with his plans for war.   His decision to go to London bore but little relation to the motives of the Junta, a number of the members of which felt no sympathy for him.   He had to ask to go to London; met evidently with a rebuff; and had to purchase his appointment by offering to pay the expenses of the mission.   The Junta agreed, but reluctantly, and gave him as a chaperon Don Luis López Méndez " on whose experience and capacity more confidence was felt ".   The' embassy was completed with Bolívar's early companion and tutor, Andrés Bello, as secretary.   The

Venezuelan historian Baralt describes López Méndez as " a turbulent man with a backshop to his mind ". Their credentials were drafted in the name of " Don Fernando VII, King of Spain and of the Indies, and in his royal name, the Supreme Junta for maintaining his rights in Venezuela "; and the delegates are described in accordance with the old respect for classes: " in the first place, the Knight Colonel Don Simón Bolívar; in the second, the Commissioner Inspector Don Luis López Méndez; and in an auxiliary capacity, the Royal Army Service Corps Major and first officer of my State Secretaryship, Don Andrés Bello ". Their mission was to inform the King of England of " the installation of the Supreme Junta " in which the sovereignty of the country was vested owing to " my [i.e. Ferdinand VII's] incapacitation and the dissolution of the Government which provisionally represents me in the Peninsula ". Nothing was to be contrary to " the fundamental laws of the Spanish monarchy ". The instructions include this phrase: " Sight should not be lost of what we write to the Regency and to the Junta of Cádiz as to our scanty means, due to despotism and bad administration, all of which it would be easy to belie or to make equivocal, were superfluous expenses to be noted." Considering that the money came from Bolívar, and in view of his ostentatious and luxurious taste, there is little doubt that this hint was meant for him.

CHAPTER XVI

INDEPENDENCE DECLARED

I

AFTER thirty-one days on board H.M.S. *General Wellington* Bolívar, López Méndez and Bello landed in Portsmouth (10.vii.10) and were granted official facilities to travel on to London. The British capital was used to such visits of Spanish-American " beggars of independence ". But these three newcomers arrived as representatives of a *Junta*, a word which the struggle of the people of Spain against Napoleon had endeared to the English nation. Their reception was bound to be somewhat complex. While the keen City stretched a hand as eager as ever towards the fabulous trade of Spanish America, the people of England felt at one with the Juntas of Spain, and were naturally led to admit the Junta of Caracas to the same friendship, readily assuming that it came in the same spirit.

But did it ? That must have been the question the Marquess of Wellesley asked himself when the two ambassadors entered his private room at Apsley House on June 16th, 1810. The fact that the meeting took place there, in his London family mansion, and not at the Foreign Office, shows that Wellesley was aware that Bolívar and his companion were not coming as faithful servants of Ferdinand VII, despite the impeccable credentials they put before him. The British statesman knew also that Bolívar had lost no time in seeking Miranda, nor Miranda in putting his countrymen in touch with prominent Londoners, including the Duke of Gloucester. Now, Miranda was by then a " traitor " in Spanish eyes, since he had openly taken arms against his King and country in 1806; while Bolívar and his two companions, as well as the Junta which sent them—whatever their ultimate designs—claimed officially to represent Ferdinand VII. This explains Wellesley's attitude. Fully informed by the British authorities on the spot, he could harbour no illusions as to the loyalty of the three emissaries ; if he interrogated them as he did it was less to hear answers which he could anticipate, than to put on record his official loyalty to the Spanish ally.

The situation does not seem to have escaped the emissaries, who steered through its dangerous shallows skilfully and successfully. Wellesley began by making clear his position as Spain's ally. " The first words of the Minister "—write the emissaries to Caracas—" were that the Revolution of Caracas had been made on an erroneous principle, entirely inconsistent with the present state of Spain, and that in case we had taken the resolution to separate ourselves from the central Authority, considering that the cause of the Metropolis was in a desperate situation, he could assure us from the most authentic facts, that the Military operations of Spain, its Government, and the public Spirit offered more than ever every foundation to expect a favourable issue." Wellesley, add Bolívar and López Méndez, " made repeated and strong reflections respecting the intimacy and confidence actually subsisting between the Government of Cádiz and the Court of London, which not only required the refusal of an official reception, of the Commissioners of Caracas—but even to cut off all kind of communication between them and His Britannic Majesty's Government. He represented, as an important point to the interests of the Spanish Nation and its Allies, the firm Union of the free parts of the Monarchy, in order to join their efforts against France—and therefore, in the most friendly manner advised us to come to an arrangement with the Regency promising at the same time that satisfaction would be given us, for all offences, and a reform made in all such local, or temporal, abuses practised against us; for which purpose, he offered that Great Britain should intercede, in a serious manner."

The emissaries brought instructions to accuse the Spanish authorities in Caracas of pro-French leanings. In these instructions, the *Junta* pointed out that the emissaries were " on no account to omit the circumstance that the two main leaders in command of the troops of this Province [Venezuela] were the Captain General, Don Vicente Empáran, and the Major Artillery Inspector, Don Agustin García: both lived in Madrid under Murat's Lieutenancy, were included in the capitulation of December 4th, 1808, and are sworn friends of the French government: the former was granted his rank of division general by Murat and his appointment as Captain General of Caracas from Napoleon ".

Bolívar, who led the visitors, threw over his friend Emparán without wincing, describing him as *afrancesado*. He represented to Wellesley as an " oppressive, illegal and ignominious procedure " the measures Casas had taken towards the initiators of the Caracas Junta, and proceeded: " The people of Caracas had hoped that these illicit and violent measures would be at least disapproved by the Spanish Government, an opinion strengthened by the appointment of a new Captain General. But the newcomer was unfortunately committed to the French party . . . and had sworn allegiance to Joseph Bonaparte."

To round up the picturesque disorder of ideas and attitudes in this tragicomedy of history, Wellesley, in the course of an argument on the right of the peoples overseas to break away from the mother-country, gave it as his opinion that " every action aiming at separating any of the parts from the Central power is an essential and radical attack against the Constitution, whichever it may be; such an action could only be based on the principles which, under the name of *rights of man*, had produced the French Revolution, and are already altogether discredited ".

The emissaries insisted on " the sincere determination of the people of Caracas to accept the decision of the majority of the Spanish Empire, fully and legally represented, and to remain united with the mother-country for as long as she keeps free or resists our common enemies; and that one of the chief objects of the Caracas revolution was to preserve for the monarch his dominions in Venezuela in all their integrity, sheltering them from French intrigue and seduction ". Wellesley argued that " such a dependency from the metropolis, while refusing to recognize its government, was purely nominal; and as his visitors alleged that even in Spain several provinces had done as much, Wellesley countered with the testimony of his son Richard, who was present. With youthful vehemence, Bolívar replied that Venezuela was ' too small a fraction of the Spanish Empire for its behaviour to exert any but a negligible influence on the success of the (Peninsular) war '. Wellesley smiled and congratulated the emissary on the ardour with which he defended his country's cause; whereupon Don Simón de Bolívar retorted that His Lordship showed a much greater ardour in upholding the interests of Spain "—an answer, it must be owned, fit rather for a colonel of the Militia than for a diplomat. This very petulance of the colonel-ambassador may have led Wellesley, " doffing his ministerial character and speaking just as a sincere friend ", to warn his visitors that " many intriguers were anxious to approach them; that some may have done so already; and that their mission demands much circumspection." The allusion to Miranda is obvious. The conversation had begun at 8 p.m. It was 10. The emissaries took leave.

On Thursday, July 19th, at 6 o'clock, Wellesley received them again. The two commissioners report a beginning of success at this stage. " The Minister appeared to become gradually more accessible to our demonstrations, and told us that the wishes of the People of Caracas . . . were most cordially received, with every sentiment of kindness and gratitude by His Majesty, and that . . . England never would look upon us as Enemies." This was as broad a hint as a British Foreign Secretary could allow himself in the circumstances. But Wellesley went further still: " He then promised us that we should have the most powerful protection against France, and that Great Britain would employ her mediation to prevent all Hostilities against us on the part of the Spanish Government, provided we would also promise not to withdraw our assistance from the Mother-Country, during the Contest against the Common Enemy; and he finally required that we would frame a Note (not official) of the object of our Commission, in order to answer separately upon it, and to terminate the Negotiation in as favourable a manner as the Treaty of His Britannic Majesty with the Government of Spain could allow."

The Commissioners reduced the Note to four points: " Protection against France; Mediation of the British Government with Spain; His Britannic Majesty's Guarantee to the Agreements we may make with the Regency in that respect; and suitable orders to all British commanders, especially with respect to our Commerce ". And they add that " to all these, very favourable answers were given by the Minister, always refusing however to give an official appearance to our Mission . . . the Basis of our Negotiations has been the continuation of our Fidelity to Ferdinand the 7th, and the sending succour to the Peninsula, as further will be agreed upon, between this Government and the Regency ".

Not unnaturally, Bolívar and López Méndez conclude that " the conduct of the Minister could not be more favourable " considering the influence of the " agents of the Regency ", which, they wrote, " is certainly very great in this Capital ". They go on to describe Wellesley's situation and in particular to point out that: " The Union between England and the Central

Government of the Peninsula has never been so intimate as since the establishment of the Regency, almost erected by the influence of Great Britain—the said Marquis Wellesley during his Embassy in Spain, has been the most active person in soliciting the Installation of that new form of Government by disapproving the proceedings of the Central Junta and intimating in the strongest manner, the necessity of constituting a better organized Supreme Power. The results of the operation of the Allies ought therefore to be decisive, not only for the political or Ministerial Credit of the Marquis, but also for the Military Opinion of his Brother Sir Arthur Wellesley who, under the title of Lord Wellington, commands the British Armies in Spain and Portugal, and in reality, has the direction of all the operations of the present Campaign." Therefore, they conclude, " those important circumstances were enough to oblige the Minister to observe such conduct with us as would not hurt in the least manner, the confidence subsisting between Great Britain and our Mother-Country ".

Bolívar and his companion record two details of interest: " the first was that the Minister asked us, if we had any objection, that true copies of the Dispatches received from Curaçao and also of our Credentials, should be given to the Spanish Ambassador, saying that he considered it to be a measure necessary for preserving every appearance of good harmony with the Government of Spain—to which we manifested no objection. . . . The second point was that he informed us, that one of the Public Papers contained the News of the Regency having issued orders for a Blockade of our Ports . . . a measure . . . particularly contrary to the interests of the Allies themselves . . . and he promised us to employ his best services for the suspension of it, as well as to prevent all other Hostile-like Acts."

2

Wellesley tried to clear himself and the British Government in the eyes of the Regency in a Note which he sent both to the emissaries from Caracas and to the Spanish Ambassador (8.viii.10). It is skilfully drafted, and leans on the fact that the Venezuelans had insisted on their fidelity to the King. Wellesley had to feign ignorance of a number of facts he knew, even if not officially. Miranda, against whose " intrigues " he had warned his visitors, was on the best terms with his own son Richard, whose initials, R.W., can be seen at the foot of some *Notes on Caracas*, to be found in the Foreign Office files, which the Secretary of State must have studied; and in these notes, his son wrote: " I think it will be found a chimerical attempt to preserve them to the Parent State excepting as Allies and subjects of the same sovereign . . . their objects are: the alliance and friendship of England *even against the Parent State*—the freedom of their country from every Government in Spain but that of Ferdinand the 7th. On the second they are most resolute and vehement." Why? What was there in Ferdinand VII? The answer is in the Spanish tradition. Haggling over " whom it is exactly I am to obey " was ever in Spain the favourite way of escape from obedience. As Ferdinand VII, exiled and dethroned, could send no orders anywhere, to obey a King who could not command was an admirable posture for rebels to take—particularly when they were sure that France would win and that Ferdinand would never reign again. The loyal majority in America was pleased; and the Separatist leaders also.

Wellesley found this formal loyalty to Ferdinand VII a convenient cover for his own behaviour. His son wrote in his *Notes on Caracas*: " Of the four Powers who can contend for this vast prize, the United States and France have an interest in promoting insurrection against the Parent State; the former, to enjoy the trade without restriction, the latter to acquire by tumult the Colonies. . . . The Agents of both have for many years . . . filled the country. . . . But the United States are feared and hated as neighbours. France is an enemy since the Usurpation of Spain, and is besides excluded from the American Commerce. England has the advantage of the popularity which her generous assistance of Spain has secured in America; and of the great commercial benefits which, already felt in the increase of the contraband trade, would be incalculable if the intercourse were free. It cannot be doubted that by making a skilful use of the bond of allegiance to Ferdinand England may prevent a total or sudden separation from Old-Spain, may compel the latter to alter her colonial system and may preserve the colonies from the influence of France." So, when the Foreign Secretary based his note to the Spanish Ambassador on the loyalty of the Venezuelans to Ferdinand VII, he could entertain no illusions as to such loyalty—a fact which by the way explains the calm with which Bolívar accepted the note.

Bolívar's position in London was somewhat ambiguous. He was an officer of the Spanish Army, promoted from captain to lieutenant colonel by a Junta calling itself *Conservative of the Rights of Ferdinand VII*; and he was being received by the British Foreign Secretary in his private house in order not to cause umbrage to the Spanish Ambassador—on whom, of course, Bolívar would not dream of calling. Even so, the youthful negotiator had succeeded as to the first aim that had brought him to London: British help. He now devoted his energies to securing the second: Miranda. In order to appraise Bolívar's attitude towards Miranda at that time due note should be taken of the fact that he was an amateur in military affairs; for he had acquired his gold braid by birth and privilege, and had never devoted any study to the profession of arms. And as he had a first-rate mind, he must have been painfully aware of his military shortcomings. Miranda, on the other hand, enjoyed a high reputation as a professional. There was another reason why Bolívar insisted on winning Miranda. He distrusted the faction—perhaps the majority—which, in the Junta, still remained favourable to the Spanish connection, however modernized. He was for independence, and even for " war ". For those who thought as he did, the arrival of Miranda in Caracas was bound to be invaluable, for it compromised the Junta and publicly committed it to an open anti-Spanish policy.

Miranda was living in London on a pension paid him by the British Government. He received Bolívar and López Méndez with joy as the harbingers of a new hope. On August 3rd he wrote to the Junta congratulating it on the events of April 19th and praising Bolívar and López Méndez. A few days later he asked in writing to be received by Wellesley to negotiate his return to Venezuela; he wanted his pension to be continued and a free passage in a British warship. Meanwhile, he acted as host to his countrymen and introduced them to some British celebrities and oddities, such as Wilberforce and the educational reformer Thomas Lancaster. Bolívar was then able to enter into the social life of London, in which he may have cut a somewhat exotic figure, with his fine clothes, his attractive looks and his two black servants. O'Leary says that he devoted much time to the study of British institutions; and since he remained all his life a keen admirer of Britain—rather than of England or the English—there is no reason to doubt this testimony. Miranda taught him also the art of engineering press campaigns and propaganda; a letter published in the *Morning Chronicle* (5.ix.10) and supposed to have come from Cádiz had in fact—it is believed—been concocted by Miranda and Bolívar in Grafton Street. The British Government had to explain the matter as best they could to the Spanish Ambassador—not an easy task, since the letter advocated independence for Venezuela and war on Spain. In spite of which, the British Government put a corvette of the Royal Navy, the *Sapphire*, at Bolívar's disposal for his return to La Guaira. He sailed on September 21st. Bello and López Méndez remained in London, actually in Miranda's house. Miranda entrusted his luggage to Bolívar, but the British Government thought it more discreet that so declared an enemy of their Spanish ally should not leave on a British warship; and the old revolutionary leader sailed on October 10th in a merchantman.

3

Miranda and Bolívar were for a time together in Curaçao towards the end of November; and were probably still there when the Marqués de Toro gave up his half-hearted attack on Coro. Bolívar landed on December 5th, 1810; but it took him a week to break the resistance to admit Miranda, and not till December 12th was Roscio able to write to Miranda granting him " permission to come to this city ", of Caracas. Miranda had landed in La Guaira on the 10th, from an English brig, H.M.S. *Avon*. But the British Government, less aware than Bolívar of the significance of Miranda's arrival in Caracas at that time, assured Hodgson, the new Governor of Curaçao (through Liverpool), that Miranda had left Britain without informing the Government of his intentions; though Wellesley had received several written statements from Miranda on his plans, which the Foreign Secretary had neither answered nor left unnoticed, since he had sent Miranda a verbal message to the effect that he had nothing to say. Since, moreover, H.M.S. *Sapphire* had conveyed to Venezuela, not only Bolívar, but the baggage and papers of Miranda, Lord Liverpool's protestations to Hodgson were a sham.

The Junta, however, was left in no doubt. Layard wrote to Lord Liverpool on December 17th, 1810: " The *Avon* returned here on the 13th instant

from la Guayra, where General Miranda was received with every demonstration of applause; on the departure of the *Avon* he had not yet proceeded
to Caracas—but their Highnesses, the Supreme Junta, immediately on his
arrival at la Guayra being notified, deputed Colonel de Bolívar and Mr.
Tovar, the President's brother, to wait on the General, and to signify their
extreme satisfaction on his safe arrival." Layard informs his chief on the
displeasure with which Miyares watched this event from Maracaibo. To
Roscio, Layard had already written on October 29th: "You will have by
those prudent measures avoided to imbrue with blood a territory which
under a paternal administration and the powerful protection of Great Britain
will inevitably become the seat of Arts and Industries, and must ultimately
acquire benefits incalculable." While Miranda was waiting in La Guaira,
Layard wrote to Roscio (11.xii.10): "Most sincerely do I congratulate
their Highnesses, on the safe arrival of their respectable first Deputy (Colonel
de Bolívar) from London, and that his Colleague remains. The previous
arrival of the Deputies of their Highnesses from Porto-Rico—together with
that of General Miranda and Colonel de Bolívar—will I hope prove fortunate
events for Venezuela." It is therefore obvious that the Junta could only
conclude that Great Britain looked with favour on that very arrival of Miranda
in Caracas before which even the Junta hesitated.

4

Miranda had inherited his father's fondness for military dress. He landed
wearing the uniform of 1793, i.e. of a French revolutionary general: cocked
hat, blue gold-embroidered tail coat, a curved sabre, short white trousers
and golden-spurred boots. Why? This man who had so often spoken
against the French revolution, why did he land from a British man-of-war,
displaying the uniform of a French revolutionary general? There are two
answers: one, that Miranda was soon to prove in Caracas that he was not
really as averse to French revolutionary ideas as he had often said, and at
times sincerely thought; the second, that a uniform is a uniform and a man
may look very handsome in it.

How enthusiastically did La Guaira and Caracas receive him? On the
whole not very. He had a *succès de curiosité* with the crowd, while the
leaders were divided: some, mostly the younger Creoles, took him to their
hearts as the true leader of the true revolution both against Spain and for a
new equalitarian and free world; while the more reflective men felt uneasy
about the Jacobin, foreign tendencies of a man who did not in fact know his
country. The men in one or other of these factions were not always what
might have been expected. The white aristocrat Bolívar was for Miranda;
the dark-skinned and plebeian Roscio was one of the wise men who frowned
and doubted. Bolívar offered Miranda the hospitality of his house in
Caracas. One of the men who had strenuously opposed his return, Cortés
Madariaga, went also to La Guaira to greet him, and became one of his
keenest followers.

Miranda was outwardly well received by the Junta, yet not as well as he expected, and as, on the whole, he deserved. The Junta made him a Lieutenant General but he " was not pleased, for he expected the rank of full general and the salary which lieutenant generals ought to have in America in accordance with the Regulations of Spain ". It was noticed that he remained cold and unresponsive when greeted or when his health was drunk. Congress met on March 11th in the house of the Count of San Javier (that very nobleman who at the head of the nobility of Caracas had refused to present him for a commission in the Battalion of Whites which his snobbish father had dreamt for him). Its two secretaries were Antonio Nicolás Briceño (who had waged a private civil war against Bolívar), and Miguel Joseph Sanz (who had complained to the King against the vexations of Emparán and the ill-treatment inflicted on him and on his son-in-law by the young bloods Fernando de Toro and Bolívar). The serpent of Venezuelan independence coiled itself upon itself in strange ways. This Sanz had ended his " representation " to the King with a fine flourish, attributing the hatred of the Toros to the fact that " my heart is Spanish, my behaviour is Spanish and I shall die a vassal of your Majesty "; and in 1809 had signed himself: " One of your most faithful vassals kisses your royal Majesty's feet ". In 1811, he was one of the two secretaries of the Congress that voted the independence of Venezuela.

On March 28th, the Junta Suprema ceased to exist and handed its powers to a Triumvirate. Miranda, by far the biggest man in Caracas at the time, had every right to expect the chief executive post in the nation. His was the longest history of endeavour and sacrifice, the finest record of military and political experience. And yet he was passed over for three obscure men. Why did all this happen? There were objective reasons: fear of Miranda's Jacobinism was one of them. It took a double form: the aristocracy were all for independence, but not in favour of shopkeepers' sons. The clergy were afraid of Miranda's indifference and atheism—or deism. An Irishman, William Burke, turned up in Caracas. He had written a good deal in England on behalf of Miranda about South America and her rights. He began to write in the Gaceta de Caracas articles on religious tolerance which shocked the religious-minded and further alienated public opinion from the Jacobin General. Miranda called on the archbishop and expressed his indignation at Burke's behaviour; but this visit was a purely formal manoeuvre. Over and above these objective reasons, the chief cause of the trouble was personal. Miranda was a big man surrounded by little men, and the little men wanted for themselves the power that should have gone to him. " Eight votes out of thirty-one, that is what he got in Congress. He received the news at home, and expressed his grief saying: ' I am glad that there are in my country persons apter than I am to assume supreme power '."

5

Miranda was a stranger in his fatherland, because he had lived abroad far too long, and because he came from another age. He was a man from the era of enlightened despotism, a Voltairian, no adept of Rousseau. Soon after his arrival, a Commission was set up to draft a constitution. Miranda, who sat on it, submitted to his colleagues the same chimera with an Inca head, an English body and Spanish feet, which he had put before Pitt. He became suspect on both flanks: a Jacobin revolutionary for the aristocrats, he was a reactionary monarchist for the revolutionists. He found himself in a dilemma: a leader without a country to lead, he had either to betray his ideas or to go out of business.

A new phase began in his life. Miranda was essentially an *ambitious opportunist*. To the very last, he had kept open an avenue of reconciliation with the Spanish Government, and after years of secret (though not unknown) activities against Spain, still wrote to Floridablanca, the Spanish Prime Minister, that the two could settle everything in half an hour's talk " chair to chair ". He was anti-French with Pitt, anti-English with Bonaparte. All this must be borne in mind when, after years of anti-Jacobin propaganda in Great Britain, we see him in Caracas from 1810 to 1812 at the head of a Jacobin demagogic revolution. The instrument was at hand. On a decision of the Supreme Junta (14.viii.10), a number of *mantuanos* and intellectuals of Caracas had founded the *Sociedad Patriótica*, an imitation of the Spanish " Economic Societies of the Friends of the Country ". This institution might have been useful, had it remained faithful to its model, and devoted itself to economic studies. But it soon degenerated into a Jacobin club.

This was the instrument Miranda chose in order to further his ambition, obviously no longer his policy. When, in April, 1811, the exiled demagogues José Felix Ribas, his brother, and Gallegos, returned to Caracas, he sought their alliance. He still had the valuable support of Bolívar and, strangest of all, probably through Bolívar, that of the brothers Toro. His first tactics aimed at conquering the street and the coloured crowds. On April 19th, 1811, he led a procession of enthusiasts who celebrated the first anniversary of the Supreme Junta with fiery speeches for independence. Miranda carried a yellow standard, a symbol of independence, and was followed by a spectacular troop of Indians decorated with tricolour ribbons who were acclaimed by the crowd. With his " indefatigable loquacity " Miranda courted the crowd and " showed himself ever ready to support their claims ". He then tried to conquer the *Sociedad Patriótica*, by making it more popular and open to all; but when in May he offered himself for election as its President, he did not even gather enough votes to be Vice-President.

His mind was always full of constitutional ideas, and, in this at any rate, he was in tune with his time and country. Both in New Granada and in Venezuela the events of 1810 had led to an outburst of localism and anarchy, every province deeming itself a State and every city a province. Cartagena felt towards Santa Fe as independent as Santa Fe towards Cádiz, and the mood which led the patriots of Santa Fe to secede from the Spanish Regency led those of Cartagena to link up with the Regency in a spirit not so much of union with Spain as of separatism from their own chief city. " Anarchy tore the provinces asunder "—writes the Colombian historian Restrepo— " and made rapid strides." This was the spirit. The form it took was an imitation of the constitution of the United States. But, while in the north the constitution expressed the union of one time separates, in the south, the charters written in imitation of it expressed the disintegration of what had been united for three centuries.

Independence and Confederation, the two ideas of the day, are thus two forms of the same impulse. And so was also the third trend to be observed then—the return to the Indian roots—a logical reaction from separatism with regard to Spain. The grafted civilization of the Indies, withdrawing itself from the Spanish foliage, was bound to seek the Indian root. Miranda had dreamt of a constitution crowned with two Incas. On March 30th, 1811, the *Serenísimo Colegio Constituyente Electoral* of Santa Fe promulgated the Constitution of the State of Cundinamarca. What was Cundinamarca ? A *mestizo* name, a Spanish corruption of the pre-Spanish name of New Granada; as *mestizo* as that " Serenísimo " the college gave itself with as much solemnity as the Indian alcaldes used to wear their wands of office in their villages.

In March, 1811, Cortés Madariaga arrived in Santa Fe to negotiate a treaty between Cundinamarca and Venezuela. His reception in Santa Fe points again to the strong *mestizo* spirit of these South American risings. The Junta of Santa Fe, in a speech of welcome, said to this descendant of Hernán Cortés: " Providence, who raised a Cortés in the sixteenth century to be the scourge of millions of men in our continent and the model of so many famous wicked men who, on the ruins of the Empire of Atahualpa, raised the throne of despotism to oppress the simple inhabitants of South America, was pleased to create another Cortés in the nineteenth century, to vindicate the rights of mankind scandalously outraged by those semi-barbarians who, in the shadow of a holy religion they betrayed, spread nothing on this soil but desolation, death, torture and chains."

Miranda had written to the Supreme Junta of New Granada (11.i.11) saying that the Canon who went " with a most important mission, will tell your Highness all I could suggest from here about a political union between the kingdom of Santa Fe de Bogotá and the province of Venezuela, so that forming together one social body, we should now enjoy more security and respect, and in the future more glory and happiness ". New Granada and Venezuela split themselves asunder and endeavoured to join the bits together. The treaty was acclaimed as a great step forward, pleased no one and was never applied. But the journey of the Canon by land, back to Caracas, hazardous and picturesque, was useful to the cause of independence, for he spoke everywhere with ardour and eloquence. His return strengthened Miranda, to whose party he was known to belong, and whose federative ideas he had carried in triumph to Santa Fe. This success and his assiduous work with the coloured castes, secured at last for Miranda the Chair of the *Sociedad Patriótica* ; which, under his leadership, became more than ever a Jacobin club. Its sittings were often tumultuous and always lively. About two hundred members took part, some of them members of Congress, who, disgruntled because their views had not prevailed in the official parliament, came to air them again in the unofficial one. Bolívar was one of the moving spirits of this revolutionary house.

6

The growing influence of Miranda, precisely on the demagogic sector of Caracas, seems to have induced the leaders of the Government to reverse their unwise attitude and to provide the veteran agitator with a seat in Congress. On June 28th, 1811, he was admitted as a member for El Pao. Roscio, his sworn enemy, wrote soon after to Bello: " After my long letter [June 9th, 1811] Miranda was admitted in Congress as member of one of the constituencies of Barcelona, and his behaviour as such has won for him a better reputation. He has borne himself well and has argued wisely." He nursed his party for all that—a curious mixture of men, not all well knit together by friendship and confidence. Bolívar was one of them, but his two enemies, Cortés Madariaga and Sanz, belonged also to the party, as well as José Felix Ribas, Salías, Tejera, Espejo and the brothers Carabaño; all men who in the Patriotic Society stood for independence and inflamed the crowd with speeches of more emotion than erudition and more enthusiasm than judgment. Congress met in the chapel of the University, and endeavoured to hold its debates in the calm which its own dignity and the place it met in required. This was not always easy, for the sittings were public, and the crowd did not always respect or even understand the demeanour of their deputies. The press contributed to the general excitement to such an extent that on June 18th, 1811, Congress delegated Roscio to the Executive to request that the press should be restrained by censors.

Such was the political apparatus under which Caracas led the country to the Declaration of Independence. Orea, the Venezuelan agent in Washington, had anticipated it, presenting on May 17th a Note to the American Government in which he announced that " the United States had taught Venezuela the road of freedom and of social virtues. . . . The Venezuelans have realized their rights and sworn in their hearts to uphold them or to die . . . they have tarried in declaring their absolute independence, . . . under the compelling force of political motives ". Orea's Note was well received in Washington, and his optimistic report did much to stimulate the debates which the Congress of Venezuela had at last to engage in under strong pressure from the Patriotic Society.

Montenegro, the Creole who had been sent by the Regency the previous year, and had accepted office as Permanent Secretary of the War Office of the Republic, escaped from Miranda's house, where he had been imprisoned as a suspect, and went over to Cortabarría (29.vi.11). This event strengthened the revolutionaries against the moderates. But the revolutionaries themselves were divided. Cumaná claimed the right to live as free from Caracas as Caracas from Cádiz and protested when Miranda argued in Congress that Caracas, i.e. the Central Government, had the right to compel Cumaná by force of arms to obey the Government—which was exactly Cortabarría's position towards Miranda. The issue was seized upon by those in Congress who objected to the pressure from the *Sociedad Patriótica*, and who urged that Congress should move to another city inland, away from its demagogic pressure. The leader of this group was Briceño—which was but natural, since Bolívar was one of the leaders of the *Sociedad Patriótica*. In this heated atmosphere, Congress passed a *Declaration of the Rights of the People* (1.vii.11), in which the people were assured of their sovereignty " imprescriptible, inalienable and indivisible; liberty, security, property, equality before the law, temporariness of public office and, last but not least, happiness as the aim of society ". However, only landowners were to vote.

On July 3rd, during a debate on Orea's reports, Miranda, " whose speech was not taken down verbatim owing to an unforeseen accident, maintained that a declaration of independence was necessary ". So says the official record of the sitting. But Father Maya, a respected cleric, reminded his colleagues that they had been elected to constitute a body " to preserve the rights of Ferdinand VII ", and courageously protested against the violent and tumultuous attitude of some members of the Patriotic Society, including Bolívar, who came armed to the bar, to intimidate the wavering deputies. Many hesitated on the threshold of independence, fearing the effect on England and the consequences in the provinces still loyal to Spain—Coro, Maracaibo and Guayana. This last argument was ably put to the Congress by Roscio. But Miranda spoke again and advocated " to run the risks and enjoy the advantages " of decision, whereby he drew the loud applause of the public at the bar; while a royalist priest, Méndez, was so roused by the speech that he rushed at the General to slap him in the face. This incident seems to have put an end to the debate.

It was of course revived that very night in the hotter atmosphere of the Patriotic Society, and this time the speaker was not Miranda, but Bolívar. His address (as handed down by tradition, for no verbatim record seems to have been preserved) was both a defence of the Patriotic Society and a vehement plea for boldness and swiftness. " It is not that there are two Congresses. How could a schism be fostered by those who are best aware of the need of union ? What we want is that our union be effective and such as to carry us forward to the glorious undertaking of our liberty. To be united in order to rest, to sleep in the arms of apathy, that, yesterday, was error: to-day it is treason. Congress is discussing what should have been decided already. And what do they say ? That we must begin by a Confederation, as if we were not already confederated against a foreign tyranny. That we must wait upon the results of the policy of Spain: what is it to us that Spain sells her slaves to Bonaparte or keeps them, since we are resolved to be free ? Such doubts are the sad consequences of the chains of old. That great designs must be prepared with calm: are three hundred years of calm not enough ? The Patriotic Society respects Congress as it must, but Congress must hear the Patriotic Society, a centre of lights and of all the revolutionary interests. Let us fearlessly lay the foundation stone of South American liberty. To hesitate is to be lost. Let a commission from this body convey our feelings to our sovereign Congress." The Patriotic Society approved Bolívar's motion and decided to send Dr. Miguel Peña to present it to Congress the next day. The moving spirit was Miranda; the orator Bolívar; the messenger Peña. The two last were to deliver the first to the power of Spain within just over a year.

On July 4th, the day after Bolívar's address, Peña appeared before Congress to present the motion adopted by the Patriotic Society and delivered a speech in which he declared: "We detest Ferdinand VII." He argued that fear of England should stop no one since "the English had never been able to conquer one single foot of the Spanish continent". Under a tumult from a rowdy bar, Congress voted a motion to consult the Executive. But the Executive answered that very day giving its blessing to the idea. That night Caracas gaily celebrated the anniversary of the independence of the United States. The next day, the hall of Congress was crowded with an eager public which uproariously applauded the republicans and hooted and booed the moderates. The President reported the affirmative answer of the Government and Miranda rose at once asking for an immediate declaration. Before the morning was over, Congress, with the one exception of Father Maya, voted in favour of independence amidst the wildest enthusiasm. Roscio and the Cádiz-born Isnardi, Secretary of Congress, were entrusted with the drafting of the document which, voted on July 7th, was formally presented to the Executive on the 8th by a delegation composed of Roscio, Isnardi and Fernando de Toro, under the name of *Declaration of Independence of the American Confederation of Venezuela*. The oath to be administered to all Venezuelans of over fifteen, included recognition of the sovereignty and of the absolute independence of Venezuela and of the duty to "uphold in its pure and intact state the Holy Catholic Apostolic Roman religion, one and exclusive in these lands, and to defend the mystery of the Immaculate Conception". "What"—asked a Caracas paper—"has the mystery of the Immaculate Conception to do with our independence?"

What indeed? Neither Miranda nor Bolívar nor Paúl, who drafted the oath, were known as adepts of the mystery of the Immaculate Conception. But the clue is suggested by the same newspaper, which goes on to ask: "If mysteries are so useful in the founding of republics, what was wrong with the mystery of Ferdinand VII?" This was shrewdly asked, but has so far remained unanswered by historians. The leaders of the revolution knew that the people did not fall in with their views. The people felt attacked in their own faiths and ways. The leaders therefore—though separatists to a man—covered their movement at first by raising the standard of "the rights of Ferdinand VII". When the time came to shed this pretence and declare the independence of the country, the "mystery of Ferdinand VII" had to go; and therefore, another mystery became necessary to mystify the crowds. Hence the Immaculate Conception. The cryptic query of the newspaper of Caracas thus becomes transparent; and Miranda's visit to the archbishop, sanctimoniously to protest against the articles of William Burke he himself was inspiring, also. But the fact that the movement was born so to speak "illegitimate", and with an original lie, was to be one of the causes of the civil war which that fateful July 7th, 1811, let loose on the erewhile happy country.

PART III
WAR TO THE DEATH

CHAPTER XVII
THE EARTHQUAKE

I

" IN the city of Santiago de León de Caracas "—wrote Cortabarría to the Regency—" a lion-cub is born which will give much food for thought to the European nations and a good deal to do to Spain." The cub began by spreading strife and dissension at home. " The new Republic "—writes Heredia—" took the name of United States of Venezuela, giving this status [of States] to the provinces of Caracas, Barinas, Cumaná, Nueva Barcelona, Margarita, Trujillo and Mérida. The need of humouring those whose vanity led them to desire a place on the stage, forced Congress to grant them this status which they were unable to maintain. . . . Thus the Confederation became a weak and monstrous congeries of many bodies full of heads but short of feet and hands."

The first effects were good; there were more persons pleased with the power and dignity of office. But the system was top heavy and too aristocratic to please a people aroused by speeches in praise of " holy demagogy ". It " was lavish in military promotions and salaries as if the nation were solidly constituted and ten times richer and more populated. It set up armies for the east and for the west . . . the officers of which displayed a luxury and a love of soft comfort fit for sybarites rather than for republics." Of course, the day came only too soon, as soon as the two million and a half pesos found in the Royal Government Chest had been " gaily squandered ", when " it was felt that the income of the province was not equal to the expenses of a State struggling to make by war its first attempts at existence ".

The Creole civil servant Urquinaona describes Venezuela: " In 1809 the province had grown so rich that far from needing the subsidy of 200,000 pesos wherewith it used to be helped from the Mexican Royal Chest, it exported 140,000 cwts of cocoa, 40,000 of coffee, 20,000 of cotton, 50,000 of salted meat, 7,000 sacks of indigo, 80,000 skins, 12,000 mules, young bulls and other land produce, the value of which rose to 8,000,000 pesos, leaving one and a half million net for the customs and very nearly two, counting the increase in other taxes. The farmers, who make up the common mass of the inhabitants, were used to receiving in their houses 20, 25, 30 and even as much as 52 pesos per cwt of cocoa. The current price for coffee before the revolution had been 18–20 pesos per cwt. Their indigo used to be even better than that of Guatemala, particularly as it was cheaper to convey to the European market; and so more and more land was constantly being sown. Merchants, on top of their own business, could count on the useful and safe trade with Cádiz, Veracruz, etc., wherefrom they drew advantages so well known that it might be said without exaggeration that the merchants of the Peninsula, of New Spain, and of foreign countries, were dependent on the agriculture and industry of Venezuela. The goods for home consumption could be found in abundance at fair prices. Public expenses, limited to the upkeep of a small number of military and civil servants, were met by the customs and monopolies. No one was molested as to the way he wished to handle his property. Civil liberty was respected and individual security protected, in spite of the usual vices which go with all human governments."

The men who led the revolution against such a state of things were keen " philanthropists ", " philosophers ", readers of Rousseau and Montesquieu, lawyers and general thinkers; but there was hardly one among them who knew or had any interest in economic and financial affairs. Miranda's personal finances bore no examination. None of these men stopped for a moment to think of the economic consequences of what they were planning beyond, perhaps, imagining that English help could be bought with commercial concessions; and if they did, none possessed the economic, i.e. the statistical-psychological, knowledge required to think aright. They were not aware of the fact that, once disintegrated, the several parts of the Spanish Empire would become the prey of the economic and financial apparatus developed by the two Anglo-Saxon Powers. Foreign houses, admirably prepared to dictate terms, came to their harbours and took away the fruit of their labours at prices no longer remunerative. The golden days of the Spanish Empire were over.

Taxation, never heavy in the Indies, could hardly be a solution for the new régime, with trade reduced to such an extremity. Congress appointed a committee of three, Miranda one of them, to advise on the question of a new currency; but Miranda left for the Valencia campaign, and paper money was put in circulation on the security of the national income from customs and the tobacco monopoly. As, however, there was no such income, the notes fell disastrously. Copper coins, till then unknown in the country, were minted and made compulsory. Draconian measures were adopted to force people to accept the new unpopular coinage and notes. " The police had to meddle in the minutest transactions, for, according to the law, the notes had to be accepted and change had to be given in silver for half a real; whereon more than fifty disputes arose every day in every public house where many people flocked to buy just anything merely in order to receive silver change for their bills." Good money vanished, and " as tradesmen and farmers no longer received the advances granted by the Royal Treasury, trade and farming were paralysed. Business between Caracas and the country ceased almost completely, because provincial people preferred to withhold their produce rather than exchange it for discredited paper." Prices rose rapidly. An *arroba* (about 25 lb) of meat worth four silver reales, was quoted forty-eight paper reales. Civil servants were but intermittently paid, and soldiers had to live on the generosity of private citizens.

Discontent grew. The Government realized the danger, and as an amendment to the Rights of the Press, a set of Rules on the Freedom of the Press was issued (l.vii.11) by the legislative section of Caracas, article 8 of which declares that " All writings subversive of the system adopted and established in Venezuela, consisting mainly in her liberty and independence of any other power or sovereignty outside her territory, are forbidden "; and that " authors, publishers and printers who publish writings contrary to the system of Venezuela as shown in article 8 shall be punished with death ".

2

The only hope for the revolutionists lay in the stupidity of the Spanish authorities. It was justified. Official Spain remained as uncompromising as Caracas, and hardened in 1811, as the British Government grew colder towards " the rebels ". Bolívar's promissory notes remained unpaid in London. The rough ways of Hidalgo and of Morelos, leaders of the Independent Party in Mexico, were driving the British public away from the cause of American independence. Hodgson, who had succeeded Layard as Governor of Curaçao, was neutral with a slight pro-royalist bias. Tucker, his second (who took over when Hodgson fell ill with yellow fever), was actually against independence, fearing the roaring contraband trade England made would come to an end. The three Wellesleys were for caution. The Cortes voted equality between Americans and Spaniards but felt no sympathy for separatism. Cortabarría and his agents carried on an uninterrupted activity. Their hand was probably at work in the unsuccessful attempt of a few friars at Maturin to upset the Republic, at the beginning of 1811. A more serious rising took place in Cumaná on March 5th, when a number of Catalans and Creoles seized the castle with the intention of re-establishing Spanish authority. This movement was easily put down and the conspirators expelled and deprived of their fortunes. Some tried to return, working from Trinidad as a base. The Government of Caracas sent an emissary to Trinidad to request the British authorities to remain neutral. He was a young man soon to rise to fame: Santiago Mariño.

Valencia was disgruntled because it had not been given the status of a separate State; but the Whites were averse to any conspiracy against the Republic. The coloured classes raised the royalist banner (11.vii.11). " Valencia, the most faithful Valencia "—said their Manifesto—" has recovered the freedom she lost on April 19th." The Government sent against the rebels, first the Marqués de Toro, who was defeated, then Miranda. After a first setback, Miranda forced the city to surrender (13.viii.11) for lack of water, food and hope of support. He was later accused by his enemies of having taken it with unnecessary bloodshed.

On July 11th also a number of Canary Islanders, riding mules and covered with tin-plate corselets, gathered at Los Teques, in the neighbourhood of Caracas, and, shouting *Long live the King! Down with all traitors!* rode towards the arsenal. The storekeeper, whom they had tried to win over, had warned the Government. They were easily beaten and most of them caught. " The prisons "—write Poudenx and Mayer, usually reliable— " were crammed with partisans of Ferdinand VII. On Miranda's advice, twelve or fourteen of these unhappy prisoners were sentenced to death. They were shot and later beheaded; their bodies were hung and their heads exhibited in cages on poles on the roads leading to the city. This dreadful sight struck terror in the hearts of all peaceable citizens, staining with blood that first page of the history of the emancipation of the Spanish colonies."

It is at this point that war to the death may be said to begin. Juan Escalona, " that blackguard " as Bolívar was to say of him later, was put by the republicans in charge of the royalist prisoners. His instructions to his agents were that, should the prisoners attempt to escape, " the officer in charge will attend first to them, beheading or shooting them, as their existence is of no importance while it is important to get rid of traitors to the last one ". Escalona also ordered windows to be walled up " leaving only one small hole on each ", and instructed that " at any hour of the night the officer on duty may think fit, he may call on the prisoners, and, without using words or talk, make them understand they are accused and deserve to pay for it ".

Something had changed in the atmosphere of the Indies. The people of Venezuela had been noted for their mild and amiable ways by visitor after visitor. Thus Depons: " This nation is sedate even in the delirium of pleasure "; and Humboldt: " Nature has endowed them with a certain amenity and mildness of habits which may fall into softness and sloth just as the energy of some European peoples may degenerate into dourness." This mildness of the Venezuelans was due to inner peace, to the stability of a quiet and, on the whole, happy life within the channels of an old civilization guided by the Church and Crown. Throughout three centuries, the Crown had maintained a tradition of moderation and mildness in matters of punishment. The first Bishop of Mexico was severely rebuked for having executed the *cacique* of Tetzcuco, Don Carlos Mendoza; Philip II rebuked his great Viceroy Don Pedro de Toledo for having beheaded Tupac Amaru; and Depons, after describing the aims of the 1797 conspiracy as " the destruction of the existing Government and, upon its ruins, the erection of a republican form of government, the total abjuration of the Spanish Government and a proclamation of independence ", goes on to say: " I relate a trait of clemency which does honour to the reign of Charles IV. He dispatched a secret order to the *Audiencia* to . . . refrain from sanguinary measures . . . and not to punish as a crime, what might be only the effect of seduction and ignorance. This order threw the *Audiencia* into perplexity. It obliged them to depart from the system of rigour; consequently, there were fewer victims, but the intention of the King was that there should be none."

This was a different spirit from that which the civil war had let loose in the once happy country. Spaniards and Americans fought on both sides; and the only clear issue was—hatred. The London *Morning Chronicle*, a paper favourable to the cause of American independence, published a letter dated La Guaira, 3.viii.11, in which the situation was described in its true and sad colours. "Everything is in turmoil in South America: every day people are imprisoned on suspicion of plots against the Government, and visitors from outside the city dread to come together; in one word, not only trade but even society are held up: the order of the day is: *Liberty and Equality*. Yesterday I left Caracas at five in the afternoon, and by then no one knew anything about the army sent against Valencia. . . . Every day dispatches are received from General Miranda but not made public; daily also volunteers are equipped for the Government; traitors are beheaded and their heads exhibited on poles, with a notice underneath which reads: 'This man was killed as a traitor to his fatherland.' Two were hanged yesterday, sentenced by the Patriotic Society; but their crimes are not made public. The time for imprisoning is at midnight: a platoon enters the house, forces the man out of his bed, and the next day he loses his life. . . . We deem it dangerous to be seen talking together in the street; and more so to criticize the Government. Although we only meet privately we cannot tell whether our own servants are our spies."

3

At this stage, Bolívar, already a rich man, became twice as rich. His brother, Juan Vicente, died at sea. In May, 1811, he had been sent to the United States in a similar capacity to that in which Simón Bolívar had gone to London. But he had not been successful, and Roscio complained that in spite of the sums sent to him to buy arms, Juan Vicente sent weaving, paper and minting machines. The fact was that Juan Vicente Bolívar had adopted more moderate views than the crude separatism dear to Miranda and to his brother Simón. Roscio accused him of allowing himself to be influenced by the Spanish Minister, Don Luis de Onis. But the merit is entirely due to Juan Vicente.

The emissaries, Juan Vicente Bolívar and Telesforo de Orea, arrived in Baltimore on June 5th, 1810. They were received first by Dr. Thornton, a close friend of President Madison, and later by the Secretary of State, Robert Smith, and by the President. Smith did not accept Juan Vicente's credentials, but gave vent in no uncertain terms to his sympathy for the independence of Venezuela and, on Juan Vicente suggesting a memoir to develop the mutual interest of the two countries, gave him an appointment for seven o'clock that very evening. Juan Vicente did not honour the appointment, and sent a farewell note instead; whereupon Smith called on him (a courtesy the Secretary of State had not yet extended to the Spanish Minister, as Onis acidly remarks), but found the young Caraqueño had already left.

He had gone to see the Spanish Minister in Philadelphia, to whom he declared himself ready to negotiate an agreement. His plan was moderate; complete equality was to be granted between Creoles and Spaniards as to offices, and a share in the economic administration of the country and in the repression of abuses; but he was ready, indeed eager, to accept that the constitutional status of Venezuela should remain unaltered.

A fresh delegation of Caraqueños arrived in New York with Orea, who had gone to Caracas and returned with powers to oust and supersede Juan Vicente (25.iv.11). Onis reports to the Spanish Government that Juan Vicente had informed him of the fact: " that instead of an agreeable answer, he had received letters from his brother and friends to the effect that he was being superseded by Don Telesforo de Orea, born in Tenerife, one of those knaves without good blood or property, who are leading the revolution, and that the people shout for his head and the confiscation of his property, which is the largest in the country, only because he had negotiated with me: I saw his brother's original letters in which he advises him to leave for Europe and on no account to return to Caracas ". On May 3rd, Onis reported that he had ascertained through a friend of Orea that " Miranda has lost much esteem in his country, and has failed in his attempt to win over the clergy; that Orea, though an unreliable man, holds pessimistic views on Venezuela, for, on coming here as an emissary, he brought over most of his property for safety, as do most Europeans who leave Caracas ".

On August 10th, 1811, Onis reported that Juan Vicente had succeeded (through Simón and other friends) in freeing his property and in being allowed to return to report on his mission. Juan Vicente had visited him and shown him a letter from Simón in which he advised him to return without fear, for, on reflection, it was now thought in Caracas that his attitude, far from being treason, proved his true patriotism. Juan Vicente told Onis that on his return he would endeavour to work for a reconciliation with Spain, " without which not only he but his brother and all sensible persons foresaw that they could not survive "; Juan Vicente thought this time more favourable " because Miranda is again on top and is trying to build up a party with the coloured people, to the utmost consternation of the Whites ".

4

Juan Vicente sailed, towards the end of July, on board the brig *Neri*, and, during a storm off the Bermudas, perished at sea. Bolívar took possession of his brother's fortune, 25,000 pesos fuertes a year, which more than doubled his own. There is no question that he did so, though in later years various magistrates of the Republic he presided over spent much ink trying to prove that he was only an administrator and not the owner of his brother's estate. But there is no question that he had no right to do so. One of the conditions of his uncle's entail—the basis of his own fortune—was that the beneficiary could not be at the same time the owner of another entail. Since, *de facto*, at any rate, Simón had accepted Juan Vicente's fortune, he had lost thereby all right to his own. Since, moreover, he was by then openly waging war against Spain, he had also forfeited his right to his uncle's entail, which explicitly deprived of such a right all persons guilty of *lèse majesté*. This double fact is worth mentioning, for it brings out a feature constantly recurring in Bolívar's life and one that must be duly emphasized, for otherwise his portrait loses truth and accuracy: *Bolívar had no respect for the law when it stood in his way.*

No reflection is meant on his generosity. Bolívar was generous to a fault. For him, what mattered was power, and therefore, money as power, and freedom from the fetters of all law as power, were equally attractive. His brother had left three illegitimate children. It is said that he adopted them. He helped them, but did not hand over to them, or to their mother, their father's fortune. Both his individual temper and his class sense demanded power. The tradition of privilege in which he was born and bred found a way to survive the levelling earthquake of the revolution he himself led. As late as August 7th, 1823, the Supreme Law Court of the Northern District of the Republic he himself had founded invoked the "privileges of the absent while on public duty" to find excuses for the fact that, thirteen years after his brother's death, Bolívar had not yet chosen which of the entails he was to call his own, though (in so far as the war allowed it) he had all along been enjoying them both as their owner; and the Court went as far back as the oldest laws of Castille to recall the right of military men to be protected while waging war; taking care to point out that "this was no privilege of the Liberator of Colombia nor of the high office he fulfils, but applies to the last soldier at war".

But Bolívar felt also a personal need of freedom from all law. This was part of his cape-and-sword psychology. An authoritarian and fond of power and command, he was a bad subordinate, and obedience did not come natural to him. This element in his character, rather than any external or political circumstance, accounts for his stand-offish attitude on arriving in Caracas after his diplomatic sortie. He stared at the Junta and liked it not. "Bolívar was not in agreement with the way the affairs of Venezuela were handled, and he withdrew to his house"—writes Mosquera, who knew him well. This is the second in a long series of similar attitudes, of silent, contemptuous withdrawals, which he will often adopt—the result partly of pride, partly of a certain sense of his own inability to co-operate with other men on any basis other than that of command on his part and obedience on the part of the others. That is why he did not belong to the first Venezuelan Congress. True, he was away during the election; but so was Miranda, a stranger to his own country for a lifetime; and yet Miranda managed to be elected for El Pao in the province of Barcelona, while Bolívar remained unseated.

Much has been written about an estrangement between Miranda and Bolívar at this stage. Direct evidence proves that Miranda continued to distinguish Bolívar and Bolívar to love and respect Miranda. Bolívar fought well in Valencia, and was by no means shoved aside by his chief, whose report to the Ministry of War mentions Bolívar in a list of officers worthy of the gratitude of the nation. True Bolívar was apt to spend much time in the solitude of one or other of his estates. But what else could a great man do? And Bolívar, whatever else he was not, was a great man. How could such a man be content to share in the small quarrels which made of Congress a cockfight or a village market? Miranda had to waste much time defending himself as commander-in-chief against accusations, some weighty, some trivial. He was prone to consider that in wartime private fortunes should be at the disposal of the commander-in-chief. He was haughty and short, particularly with his countrymen, of whose military talents he had a poor opinion. The upshot of it all was an atmosphere of petty arguments which must have bored a man made for big things and for few men, such as Bolívar was. It is fair to surmise that, if he kept away from Miranda, it was to keep away from all that. Whenever Miranda needed him, Bolívar responded readily.

5

While Caracas argued, the provinces fought local, civil wars of their own. East and west were constantly on the alert during the autumn and winter of 1811–12. Comings and goings of all kinds between Puerto Rico and Coro or Maracaibo, campaigns with no apparent or definite purpose, kept the royalists busy. An aide-de-camp of Ceballos, Commander-in-Chief in Coro, reports about the summer of 1811 that, on hearing of the arrival of two warships from Puerto Rico, " Ceballos came in person to combine his expedition with the naval commander. . . . This commander gave him some funds and landed at his orders Don Domingo de Monteverde with three officers and one hundred and twenty marines. With this reinforcement, Ceballos doubted not of the success of his expedition ". Little did he know that the young naval officer just landed would oust him and his chief Miyares from their commands, destroy the first Venezuelan Republic, drive Miranda to exile and death, and make a reconciliation impossible between Spain and Venezuela.

In December, 1811, the province of Caracas elected its Legislature or Provincial Chamber. On January 29th, the Congress of Venezuela resolved to go into recess on February 15th and to meet again on March 1st in the new federal capital—Valencia. Much time was lost in wranglings over the status and rights of the several governments and over the persons to be put at the head of affairs. Miranda grew sulkier finding himself excluded from the government. In the west two men started a pro-Spanish movement which was to swamp the first republic: Torrellas, and the Indian Reyes Vargas. Torrellas was parish priest at Siquisique and San Miguel. He sent word to Coro that, if helped, he was ready to lead his parishioners to secede from Caracas; " while the famous Reyes Vargas offered one hundred fusiliers under him as well as the whole Indian population, which obeyed him with enthusiasm ". Ceballos received confidential letters from Venezuelan republican officers saying: " Caracas is full of Frenchmen . . . we shall die for our King and put an end to that vile nation. We are on the brink of starting war against Caracas to defend our Christian religion. Here they want to put the French over us and we shall die to defend the law of God and our own King."

On March 10th Ceballos sent Monteverde with 264 men to back the priest and the Indian. Torrellas was in fact of the expedition. On the

17th Siquisique raised the royal standard and received Monteverde with shouts of joy and peals of bells. The soldiers of the republic wept and embraced him. Monteverde found himself overnight the idol of the people, a true liberator indeed. He lost his head, but as the war was being fought in fact between chaos and chaos, this did not prevent him from winning victory after victory. He took Carora, despite the gallant defence put up by a European-Spanish major at the head of 300 men. " Here "—he wrote to Cortabarría—" the troops were allowed a general plundering, of which they profited passing well." The meaning of this will become apparent later. Ceballos was beginning to feel uneasy about Monteverde, who wrote of " conquering " Barquisimeto, where the people begged for arms to fight for Ferdinand VII. At this stage nature intervened dramatically.

6

" The earthquake "—writes Heredia—" took place on Holy Thursday, March 26th, 1812, at seven minutes past four in the afternoon, and was one of the biggest and most terrifying ever seen on the earth. It was felt from the Gulf of Paria to Santa Fe, on the whole coast to Cartagena, and many leagues out at sea. . . . In Caracas the churches of La Pastora, San Mauricio, La Merced, Santo Domingo and La Trinidad collapsed, and this last one was actually reduced to dust, so that it was thought for a long time that it had sunk underground. All these churches were at the time crowded with persons who found their graves there when they least thought of it. The canon Don José Cortés y Madariaga, one of the leaders of the revolution, later told with much animation the impression of horror he received when, after the noise and bustle of people in La Merced, a profound silence set in as everybody there was buried under the ruins. In Caracas and La Guaira there perished close upon ten thousand people, and about four thousand in other cities. Those who survived withdrew to the open country, where they lived exposed to the weather for days until they were able to build themselves some huts."

The church of the Trinity, precisely the one the earthquake destroyed most thoroughly, had been built by one of Bolívar's ancestors and finished the very year Bolívar was born and christened with, among other names, that of " the Holy Trinity ". Dr. José Domingo Díaz, born in Caracas and an eyewitness of these events, wrote later: " The temple of the Holy Trinity, which, on very robust pillars, supported an enormous dome, rose on the northern and higher side of the main square. At the opposite end could be seen the gallows on which eight months earlier the bodies of the men shot in July had been hanged. This temple, close to the large Veteran Barracks, was the military church, and on the pillar of one of its chapels, set aside for military services, were painted the royal arms of Spain. The church collapsed on its own foundations; not one single stone fell outside its area, and only one big stone, broken off from a pillar, leapt out, rolled across the square and knocked down the gallows. Nothing remained standing but the pillar with the arms of Spain, which could be seen from everywhere in that heap of ruins."

" The fact "—writes Heredia—" that this disaster took place on the same day the venerable solemnity of which had been interrupted and profaned two years earlier with the first act of the revolution, filled the common people with terror, and even many who took pride in being *esprits forts*, for they looked upon it as a punishment for that twofold crime. One of the most enthusiastic patriots assured me that in the most anguishing moments people clamoured for mercy and forgiveness from the King as much as from God." This is confirmed by Dr. Díaz: " While the Prior of the Dominicans, standing on a table in the midst of a stunned and weeping crowd, was uttering a vehement sermon, while Dr. Don Nicolás Anzola, one of the *regidores* who had figured in the events of April 19th, screamed, on his knees, to be forgiven by Don Fernando VII, while we all looked on our graves open at our feet, the steward of the hospitals came upon the scene with the happiest smiling face I ever saw, congratulating all and sundry for the fact that God had made His will so patent by destroying even the houses built by the Spaniards."

Much has been made of the influence of the priests on the people to explain these events. But the clergy were by no means royalists to a man. Indeed, the majority were for independence, and there is abundant proof— including a report from Captain Forrest of H.M.S. *Cyane* to Admiral Sterling —that the reaction was general and spontaneous. The Government, on the other hand, took the power of the clergy in earnest. Díaz reports that " towards the evening, the Government had news of the spirited sermons preached that afternoon in the square of the Dominicans and in the atrium of San Felipe . . . as well as of the general commotion caused by these events of the pillar of Trinity church. . . . The Government, led by Miranda, ordered the two churchmen to be shot and the pillar to be demolished; but the first order was not carried out for fear of the people, and no one was found to dare to carry out the second."

The Government tried to coerce the archbishop into giving a rationalistic explanation of the event. Don Narciso Coll y Prat was a learned Catalan prelate, pious and courageous. He had landed in Venezuela in July, 1810, despite some opposition from the recently created Junta; but he accepted the situation, swore fidelity to the Junta and kept his head above the turmoil. Heredia writes: " The Government of Caracas fulfilled its duties and the archbishop went about the streets administering spiritual and bodily help to those who still breathed, and, forgetting his own person, went everywhere." The Government wrote from Valencia on April 4th requesting the arch-bishop to publish a pastoral letter explaining that these natural phenomena could at most punish moral vices, but not political views. The archbishop, after some resistance, did so, very much on the lines requested, though not quite in the spirit expected. The Executive drily answered: " The pastoral letter is not the paper wished and asked for by the Government. You are ordered to have it filed as anti-politic, and to prohibit its circulation."

We owe to Dr. Díaz one of the most vivid scenes of this historic day, on which Bolívar, in the lurid light of the disaster, appears for the first time in his true greatness. " It was four o'clock: the sky of Caracas was extremely clear and bright: an immense calm heightened the force of an unbearable heat: a few drops of rain were falling without the slightest cloud to be seen, when I left my house towards the Cathedral. About one hundred paces before the square of San Jacinto, the earth began to move with a frightful noise: I ran towards the square: some balconies of the General Post Office fell at my feet as I entered the square; I placed myself beyond reach of the ruins of the buildings, and there I saw fall on its own foundations most of the church; there also, in the midst of dust and death, I witnessed the destruction of a city which had been the enchantment of natives and foreigners. The strange roar was followed by the silence of the grave. I was alone in the midst of the square and of its ruins; I heard the laments of those who were dying inside the church; I climbed over the ruins and entered. I saw about forty persons dead or dying under the rubble. I climbed out again, and I shall never forget this moment. On the top of the heap I found Don Simón de Bolívar in his shirt sleeves, who was also climbing to see what I had seen. On his face could be read either the utmost terror or the utmost despair. He saw me and addressed me these impious and extravagant words: ' If nature opposes us, we will fight against her and force her to obey us.' By then, the square was full of people screaming."

Bolívar on that heap of ruins is the only man who speaks the language of the future. He does not waste time in arguing with the archbishop over the exact limits of Divine Justice and of public policy and private morals. He does not, like a fool or a madman, dash about sword in hand, forcing out of improvised pulpits superstitious priests who sermoned the crowd for their betrayal of Ferdinand VII—as some of his biographers will have us believe. He utters words which, in their " extravagance " express his will power, that diabolic tension of a Promethean will which is the root-cause of his greatness.

7

" Some Congress deputies assured me at the time the Government was removed to Valencia that they and many others were convinced that the new republic could not last and would end like children's play." So wrote Heredia, long before the earthquake. On April 3rd, 1812, the Executive Council of Three was granted dictatorial powers. But Monteverde took city after city, and the situation became graver every hour. The dictatorship first offered to the Marqués de Toro, who declined it, was accepted by Miranda with the title of Generalissimo (23.iv.12). The appointment displeased the Toro faction but Bolívar remained faithful to the cause of independence and to Miranda. He went to Maracay, where, says the War Secretary, he " raised these populations from the depression in which they were ", and promised to go to La Cabrera in order to " do the same among the troops ". Finally, he wrote to Miranda (2.v.12) that he, Miranda, " would do an incalculable amount of good if he came in person to visit that part of the country ".

The advance of Monteverde was swift. The chief reason of his success was the general enthusiasm for the King's cause, the desertion of the republican troops and his own carefree disregard for both military prudence and discipline. Easy victories brought him to the gates of Valencia, which he entered unopposed on May 4th, " amidst thousands of acclamations ". When Ceballos came to take over the command, Monteverde resisted him. What was his strength? It is here that his policy of allowing every town he took to be sacked by his troops becomes clear. Ceballos " gave Monteverde the strictest orders not to allow on any account the terrible looting of the cities ". Ceballos forbade looting; Monteverde allowed it. That is why, when Ceballos claimed his command, Monteverde was able to retain it—for he was not at the head of regular soldiers, but of a motley crowd of improvised fighters, including many Venezuelans.

Though a curse to the cause he ostensibly defended, Monteverde had good points. His personal honesty is vouched for by no less a witness than his adversary Heredia, who says: " far from drawing any personal profit from the reconquest, he spent his limited savings on it ". This confirms the concrete nature of Monteverde's aim in allowing looting. He was not out for loot but for power.

Nevertheless, Monteverde's situation was " very critical ". One hundred leagues from his base, no reserves, no ammunition. He should have been lost. But the Republic could not man its units. " Recruiting became a true man-hunt which left the countryside empty of farm hands and filled the barracks with humiliated and abashed recruits." One of Miranda's officials speaks of recruits manacled. Desertions were endemic. Miranda's policy does not seem to have gone further than to induce his adversary to waste ammunition while waiting for better days. But the days that came were always worse. On the night of June 11th–12th Monteverde took a height which outflanked Miranda's right. Miranda withdrew to La Victoria, about sixty leagues from Caracas, but he had to sacrifice " the considerable and well-provided stores of the army commissariat ". On the 20th, Monteverde attacked La Victoria but was repulsed. Miranda did not pursue him, as he would certainly have done had he trusted his own forces. The situation of Monteverde was precarious and he thought of a regular retreat. He had 4,000 cartridges and no hope of help. Behind his back, the only port available, Puerto Cabello, was in the hands of a republican garrison under Colonel Bolívar.

He was saved by Miranda. At this juncture, the Generalissimo shows signs of a Fabian attitude now and then punctuated with spurts of energy. He proclaims martial law and promises the emancipation of all the slaves who come to serve under his banner. Financial affairs distract him, and Casa León, appointed by the republic and Government to administer the Treasury, reports no funds and no way to procure them. Intrigues weave themselves round him at home; and he weaves intrigues abroad. José Felix Ribas, whom he had appointed Governor of Caracas, ruthlessly persecutes European Spaniards and even *mantuanos*, confiscates their goods and reduces them to prison and chains. Last but not least a rebellion of the negroes of Capaya and Curiepe threatens the capital and calls forth in his imagination the horrors of the Haitian revolution. Strangely enough it was about this time that he wrote to his agent Martin (2.vii.12) requesting him to go to the Aux Cayes " and bring up to 500 negroes for the army ". Miranda must have been thinking of the possibility of coming to an agreement with Spain, impressed by the fact that Spain had voted the most liberal and idealistic constitution Europe had ever known. This was perhaps the reason of his strange inaction. On July 5th, 1812, the Generalissimo and his headquarters celebrated the anniversary of the independence of Venezuela, and in the afternoon Miranda gathered his officers at dinner. He was sipping his coffee and talking away as was his wont when a courier was announced. Miranda disappeared into his office and did not return. The courier had brought him a letter: " July 1st, 1812. General: An officer, unworthy of the name of Venezuelan, with the help of the prisoners, has seized the castle of San Felipe and is now submitting the city to a fearful fire. If Your Excellency does not attack immediately on the rearguard, this place is lost. Meanwhile, I shall hold it as long as I can.—Simón Bolívar." The letter was four days old. Puerto Cabello had fallen.

CHAPTER XVIII

THE HAMMER OF ADVERSITY

I

THE loss of Puerto Cabello is the key event in Bolívar's life. The facts have been told by Bolívar himself in a report submitted to Miranda on July 12th, 1812. The port was then of the utmost importance to the republic. It was a base, the biggest depot for food and ammunition, and one of the two chief ports for foreign supply ships. At the time, it was also a formidable position in the rear of Monteverde, who had rashly manoeuvred himself into a hopeless situation between Miranda in La Victoria and Bolívar in Puerto Cabello. The Generalissimo, who had a predilection for Bolívar, gave a signal proof of it by entrusting him with one of the most important commands. Indeed, that was to be one of the causes of the catastrophe; for Bolívar's notions of the art of war did not go beyond those of the cavalry amateur; and to hold a place like Puerto Cabello in the tragic conditions in which he had to do it was then still beyond his knowledge and experience.

The city and port were controlled by the Castle of San Felipe, the vaults of which housed a number of Spaniards sentenced to prison in 1810 as accomplices in the Linares plot. The Castle, commanded by Colonel Aymerich, contained supplies for three hundred men for three months, as well as most of the gunpowder available. Aymerich went to his future father-in-law's house to be married, leaving the fortress under the command of his second, Vinoni. This fact is known from other sources than Bolívar. Let us now see how Bolívar puts the matter to his chief: " It is believed that the motives which led sublieutenant Vinoni to sell the fortress were that he had defaulted on the funds of his company, on the one hand, and on the other the lure of command or wealth this traitor expected as a reward for his felony. . . . This unworthy officer is a man of a detestable behaviour, without honour or talent. I was aware of none of these facts. The commandant of the Castle, Ramón Aymerich, who lived in it, is not guilty; beyond being an officer of honour and intelligence, he is so punctilious in the fulfilment of his duties, that it is doubtful whether any fitter man can be found to govern the Castle of San Felipe with as much zeal and vigilance." Now, this does not make sense. A traitor of detestable behaviour is second in command of the key post in a key city; and his two immediate chiefs know nothing about his lack of honour and talent, and one of the chiefs praises the other highly when this other, leaving the detestable traitor in charge, goes to enjoy himself at his wedding. The Bolívar this report reveals is not ripe yet for great things.

He is moreover upset. At three o'clock before dawn on July 1st, he wrote his first letter to Miranda, in which he spoke of the " dreadful fire " the Castle was pouring over the city; and the words recur in his report:

" The enemy continued his artillery and rifle fire on the city in the most dreadful and mortiferous way." From this report, it would appear that Bolívar did his best in the hopeless circumstances in which he was, particularly as, every day, single soldiers or even entire units went over to the enemy. He tried to keep up the spirit of the city, going as far as to invent some victories which he celebrated with fife and drums in the streets; but the heart of Puerto Cabello was not with the republic; and after a four days' struggle he left the city with his staff, eight men in all, in a ship commanded, by the way, by a European Spaniard.

He was safe. But he was unhappy. In his inner self he felt humiliated. His report reveals it in every line. " In the morning of the 5th my situation was so desperate that . . . I was urged to try to arrange a retreat, even if only for my person and my staff. Nevertheless, my resolve to fight while there was a soldier never wavered." Then, he sails away with his fellow officers; but a *post scriptum* shows that his resolve, as defined above, had broken down and that his taking to sea had been premature: " After we had embarked, about forty soldiers of Aragua who had been wandering about gathered together and embarked in transport craft and launches, with two hundred rifles, food and a few civilians." No wonder that the frustrated commander winds up his report to his chief with the depressed words: " As for me, I have done my duty, and though the stronghold of Puerto Cabello is lost, I am innocent and I have saved my honour: I wish I had not saved my life and had left it under the ruins of a city which should have been the last refuge of the liberty and glory of Venezuela! "

2

This is the utterance of a man of honour who feels that he has not lived up to his own standards. It is not we who are judging him: it is he who thinks so. It matters little for our purpose whether, in the circumstances, Bolívar did well or badly according to standards of military science and honour valid for all. The point is not what we think of Bolívar; but what Bolívar thought and felt about Bolívar. And, on that point, the documents are clear. Over and above the report just quoted, written in Caracas on July 14th, a week after his flight from Puerto Cabello, there are two pathetic letters to Miranda. In that of July 12th, Bolívar says: " How shall I dare take pen in hand to write to you when Puerto Cabello has been lost in my hands ? My heart is broken . . . my spirit is so depressed that I do not feel courage enough to command a single soldier; my conceit had made me believe that my wish to do well and my ardent zeal for the fatherland would do office for the gifts of leadership which I do not possess. I therefore beg you either to put me under the most subordinate of your officers or to grant me a few days to recover. . . . I find myself in a kind of deadly distraction." Then he announces he is preparing a detailed report of the events in order, mark the words: " to save in public opinion your selection and my honour " —a striking confirmation that Bolívar realized the importance of the post for which Miranda had selected him.

This picture of a man in ruins is moving because of its sincerity. The reasons for his state of mind turn up time and again in the form of excuses. " I did my duty, General "—he writes at the end of the same letter—" and had one single soldier remained, I should have fought with him against the enemy; if they abandoned me, it was not my fault. I left nothing undone to retain them and to engage them to save the fatherland; but oh! it has been lost in my hands." This is the thought which tortured the proud and unhappy officer. Two days later, on July 14th, he wrote again an even more anguished letter: " Filled with a kind of shame I take the liberty to send you the enclosed report, hardly a shadow of what really happened. My head, my heart, are good for nothing at present: I therefore entreat you to grant me a very few days to see whether I succeed in recovering the usual mettle of my spirit. Having lost the last remaining and the best military base of the State, how could I fail to be beside myself, General ? For Heaven's sake, do not force me to see your face! I am not guilty, but I am unhappy, and that is enough." This utterance, straight from the heart, confirms the fact that Bolívar's inner being, his self respect, his confidence, his " conceit ", his pride, his hope, were all in ruins; and that the vigorous young *conquistador* who, on the heap of ruins of Caracas, had challenged outer nature, was now bleeding and broken under the heap of ruins of his inner nature.

What did the Commander-in-Chief write to his subordinate officer ? " My dear Bolívar: From your letter of the 1st instant I learn the extraordinary event of the Castle San Felipe. It makes us realize what men are. I anxiously await further news from you and shall write more fully tomorrow." Could this be more friendly and even more affectionate ? Let us then dismiss all the stories of dissensions between Miranda and Bolívar. The fact is that Bolívar did not preserve enough inner unity to face Miranda. He was disintegrated—more so than another man would have been, because he was made up of mutually distant and powerful centres of force in conflicting tensions; because he was great, and because he was diabolically proud and egotistic. At this time, Bolívar was too tortured to be anywhere but in a very hell of depression, in the centre of a tornado of violent passions which was to make him sink into abjuration and infamy.

3

The loss of Puerto Cabello, though fatal in actual fact to the strategic situation, to the morale and to the prestige of the new republic, did not fundamentally change the situation *as reflected in Miranda's mind*. Nothing but his secret, possibly subconscious, decision to come to terms with Monteverde can explain his inaction at this moment. Like many other republicans, he had ceased to believe in the republic. Puerto Cabello did not alter his inner trend; but it gave his intention a better air in which to breathe openly. Caracas was dismayed on hearing that Puerto Cabello had fallen; and in La Victoria the feeling that there was nothing for it but to capitulate became general. No one however dared open the subject for fear of Miranda's indignation and of his despotic authority, till he himself dropped a hint in conversation with Casa León. Miranda called a meeting attended by two members of the Executive, Roscio and Espejo, by Casa León and others (12.vii.12), and there explained that " in spite of the enthusiasm with which he had always desired and worked for the emancipation of his country, he realized it had become impossible to obtain it or to keep on fighting without exposing the provinces to utter ruin; and therefore, he proposed as the only remedy, the restoration of the late Government, by means of a capitulation with the royal army in the favourable conditions to be hoped of the liberal principles then prevailing in the metropolis ".

These are the words of Heredia, who knew Casa León well. They confirm our surmise that what misled Miranda at this juncture was the liberal and generous spirit of the new Spanish Constitution. The meeting unanimously approved his words. But the party Miranda was going to capitulate to was not the Cortes of Cádiz, that had voted the Constitution: it was Monteverde. On that very day Miranda sent the Spanish Commander a request for an armistice. Monteverde, " whose situation was no less critical, held himself happy at being offered what he could hardly have dared imagine ". Yet he coolly answered that he agreed to hold a conference, but not until he returned to San Mateo, and that meanwhile all military operations should cease, except that " the troops on the march to take their positions by sea and land opposite Caracas would continue as arranged ". As it is not usual for a Commander to announce his movements to the adversary beforehand, this must have been a piece of bluff. Miranda bluffed back. If that were so, he would consider himself free " to act from now on against our enemies ". Monteverde was not ready to risk this. He agreed, though insolently, dropping the respectful " Don " before his adversary's name, and fixing a time limit of forty-eight hours (15.vii.12). The negroes of Curiepe were closing on Caracas; and Soublette, Miranda's secretary, wrote to Casas, commander at La Guaira, to enquire into the loyalty of the ships' commanders and to chain and put in irons all suspected citizens, secure them on board pontoons and, if need be, sink them.

Miranda sent Monteverde proposals which showed quite a different man from the one who had dictated such cold-blooded orders. The struggle was " to be referred to the mediators appointed by England, and awaited any day "; meanwhile both sides were to " consider each other as brothers and members of a political association which they will probably form ". Monteverde found this unsuitable, considering " the nature of the matter and the advantageous state in which the royal arms had been put by a succession of uninterrupted triumphs ", and he granted two hours to Miranda's plenipotentiaries to come to brass tacks. The two envoys refused, yet asked to have Monteverde's views. That very night (19.vii.12), they had a conversation with him. The next day, they offered what practically amounted to complete surrender to the army of the Regency, within the laws of the Spanish Cortes and an amnesty for all. Monteverde granted forty-eight hours to agree to his conditions. Miranda sent Fernández de León to negotiate.

The " agreement " which León referred to Miranda included: amnesty to apply only to territories not yet occupied by the royal arms; paper money not to circulate at all while the Government, i.e. Monteverde, decided what to do with it; the capitulation to be no obstacle for the inhabitants of Venezuela to enjoy the benefit of the laws of the Cortes. In his covering letter León wrote to Miranda: " In this state of affairs, and considering all the circumstances, I believe I must remain here, to ensure my peace." This may have been meant as a warning to Miranda; if so, Miranda did not heed it. Within the peremptory twelve hours demanded by Monteverde, he ratified this capitulation which was almost an ultimatum (25.vii.12).

The republic had lost, but the King had not won. The true winner was Monteverde. He availed himself of this opportunity to secure for himself official sway over his " conquest ". Miranda had appointed Sata y Bussy, his War Secretary, as delegate to execute the capitulation. With the complicity of this worthy (who took the opportunity to change sides) Monteverde drafted a wholly unnecessary document on the way the capitulation was to be carried out, the first article of which naïvely reveals its true purpose: " The delegate of the army of Caracas lays down as a condition of this pact that the carrying out and fulfilment of all that has been previously stipulated, as well as the occupation and possession of the province of Caracas, must belong exclusively to Don Domingo Monteverde, with whom this agreement was begun; nor will the peoples of Caracas agree to any change on this point." When Miyares, on his way back from Puerto Rico, landed in Puerto Cabello, he received a letter from his subordinate officer, Monteverde, requesting him to withdraw to Coro for the sake of the public good, since the rebels he had reduced to obedience refused to obey anybody but him. The country continued in fact divided: Coro, Maracaibo and Guayana remained faithful to Miyares; but the central region, including Caracas and Barinas, as well as Cumaná in the east, were held by Monteverde. The flags and colours had changed; anarchy remained.

4

It was in utter anarchy that Miranda found Caracas. The Whites, especially the European Spaniards, had been hounded out of their houses and confined in dungeons laden with chains, without any legal formality, whatever their opinions or record. José Felix Ribas, the Governor appointed by Miranda, who bought and sold human lives to enrich himself, explained to his chief that the European Spaniards " are our natural enemies " and he added in a letter to Miranda: " Do not forgive those wicked Spaniards, General, whom we have reduced to prison; they own the few millions of pesos in currency which exist in the country, and this is the golden key of Philippus." Meanwhile the republic drew but little profit out of this persecution, for the goods of the " accused " went to swell the pockets of one or other of the sharks the revolutionary storm had brought to the surface. Miranda removed Ribas and appointed one Quero, whose reputation would soon be as bad if not worse. This happened on Miranda's return from La

Victoria on July 26th. Caracas was then threatened by mulatto troops in the west and by the negroes of Capaya in the east. Quero, under cover of defending the city against the negroes, sent a column of Spaniards to take positions in Dos Caminos, with Spanish royalist flags hidden in their luggage " to unfurl them if and when necessary ". He was not the only one preparing to work his passage home.

There were many reasons for this. Monteverde was the winning side; and after all, it was but a civil war, with Spaniards and Creoles mixed on both sides. Moreover, the winning side was by now exploiting the good name which the new principles of the Cortes of Cádiz had won for Spain. Finally, for reasons of his own, Monteverde had discovered the virtues of democracy on the day democracy had delegated its sovereignty on him, and he, like another Cortés, had found it convenient to receive his authority from the city of Caracas in order to shake off that of Miyares its chief. Though a Creole, Miyares spoke of nothing but " rebels " and " punishment "; so, Monteverde urged his chief to withdraw to Coro and await His Majesty's pleasure, since the Cortes had ordered that the rebels be treated with mildness and moderation. He declared that he owed his command to " a proposal made by the Caraqueños " and that Venezuela had returned to obedience " impelled less by force than by reason ".

Miranda, dogged by the suspicion and protest of many of his officers, who did not understand his policy and still less his secretive and mysterious ways, prepared to leave the country. He had begun to think of evasion as early as July 15th, ten days before the signature of the capitulation, when Leleux, his French aide-de-camp, had conveyed most of his papers to La Guaira. He himself went to La Guaira the following day. On the 18th, ten thousand gold pesos were delivered by León to the English merchant, Gage Robertson, on Miranda's account; and orders were given to get ready the brig *Celoso* and three gunboats. Finally, Miranda had taken great care to include no sea craft in the capitulation, and Monteverde, though a naval officer, exhilarated with his land victories, had not noticed it.

In Caracas, Miranda thought of little else than his own safety and that of the many officers who had come from abroad to Venezuela to fight by his side. He informed the municipal Council of Caracas of the signing of the capitulation, but did not make it public, leaving it to the many deserters who flocked into the city to broadcast the news. He also ordered the demobilization of some units on the 28th. Soublette sent Leleux detailed instructions on how to pack Miranda's books and maps and put them on board the brig *Watson*, which was to sail for Curaçao. The rump of the republican army arrived in Caracas closely followed by the army of Monteverde; and when the republican officers called on Miranda for orders, he advised them to go home and rest, but said nothing of his intention to leave for La Guaira, which he did that very day (30.vii.12), at 3 o'clock p.m. That same day, Monteverde entered Caracas, which he was anxious to save from the negro rebels. The road between Caracas and La Guaira was crowded with fugitives,

5

The *Sapphire*, the very corvette of the British navy which had brought to
La Guaira the person of Bolívar and the luggage of Miranda in December,
1810, had entered La Guaira the day the capitulation had been signed
(25.vii.12). His Majesty's navy is always punctual. She was due to sail
soon, this time with the person of Miranda and the luggage of Bolívar.
But Bolívar wished it otherwise and Miranda did not sail.

Miranda arrived in La Guaira towards nightfall on July 30th with Soublette
and two servants. The city was still covered with rubble and ruins caused
by the earthquake, in the midst of which could be seen the human ruins
and rubble of the republic. There was a feeling of the-devil-take-the-
hindmost in the air and no one thought of anything but flight. Miranda
could have embarked that very day. His baggage had been transferred
from the *Watson* to the *Sapphire*, and Robertson, with his 22,000 pesos,
was already on board; but he preferred to stay the night in the Customs
House, then also the Governor's residence, as the guest of Casas. Captain
Haynes of the *Sapphire* writes: " As soon as I could disengage him from
the crowd who encircled him, I informed him of my Officer and Crew being
on board the *Zeloso*, and that as matters were so well arranged I should
withdraw them. He entreated me not to do so and informed me that he
had every reason to fear that I should have full exercise for my Humanity;
that he did not expect the incidental arrival of a British ship of War, and
had consequently kept that Brig as the mainstay of the unfortunate adventurers who had embarked in the cause of Independence under him." This
shows that Miranda was popular and need not have feared the crowd; and
that he was not confident of the capitulation being faithfully observed by
Monteverde. Haynes dined at Casas' that evening with Miranda and Dr.
Peña, the civil Governor of La Guaira; and in the general conversation, it
was suggested that Miranda should remain on shore that night. Miranda
consented, much to Haynes' displeasure, who feared that something might
happen to him, and urged him to go on board, though speaking less plainly
than he would have done had he trusted the other persons present. It seems
that Casas had seen to it that Miranda's bedroom could not be locked.
Towards three in the morning, he was rudely shaken out of his sleep.
Bolívar and two other men were in his room. They bade him dress. He
realized he was in unfriendly hands, dressed, came out of the room, and
seizing a lantern from Soublette's hand, raised it to the faces of the conspirators: " Cabals, cabals . . . these people are good at nothing but
cabals." In the dark, still night, Bolívar, Casas and Peña forced Miranda
to walk all the way to the Castle of San Carlos where they locked him in
a dungeon. That very night, Peña left for Caracas to inform Monteverde
of the fact. On the way he crossed a courier Monteverde sent to Casas, to
order the closing of the harbour pending the arrival of the royal authorities,
or else he, Monteverde, would " consider all covenants so far agreed to as
null and void ".

Such are the facts. Now, the documents. Monteverde wrote to Hodgson

(19.viii.12) claiming the money taken by Miranda from the Government chest. " Very happily "—he added—" the military commander Don Manuel María de las Casas, who was appointed by Miranda to the command of La Guayra (but already corresponded with me knowing that I came to take possession of said city from the town of Victoria) had the wise and prudent precaution to demand two bonds from Mr. Robertson for said amount." So that by July 20th (the date of the first of these bonds) Casas was already squinting towards the Royalist camp, and acting accordingly. On August 26th, Monteverde wrote from Caracas to the Spanish Government: " . . . those who had been contaminated, but in some way or other have acted contrary to the malignant intention of the rebels, must be forgiven for having gone astray, and we must even bear in mind their acts, according to the fruits thereof in the service of H.M. In this category, Sir, are found Manuel María de las Casas, Miguel Peña and Simón Bolívar. Casas and Peña were in charge of the government of La Guaira; the former in military, the latter in political affairs, when the rebels of this province tried to escape through that port with their dictator Miranda, taking away what remained of the Royal Treasury. . . . As soon as I set foot in this city I gave the strictest order to have them arrested in La Guaira; but, luckily, when my orders arrived, though sent with the utmost speed, Casas, by Peña's advice, and by means of Bolívar, had put Miranda in prison and made sure of all his colleagues there. An operation in which Casas exposed his life, which he would have lost had his orders been disregarded, just as Peña and Bolívar also ran the same risk. Casas completed his work most satisfactorily [more praise of Casas]. I cannot forget the interesting service of Casas, Bolívar and Peña, owing to which the persons of all three have been respected, and passports for foreign countries given only to the second, since his influence and connections might be dangerous in the circumstances."

This document is crucial and final. Miranda was delivered to the Spanish authorities by Casas, Peña and Bolívar, and in conditions which made Monteverde think that the three men deserved a reward. As proved by Monteverde's report, it was done spontaneously and not at the request of the Spanish authorities. In the case of Casas and Peña the reward was immunity. In the case of Bolívar, a passport. Why did Bolívar hand over Miranda? The matter is ruled by a paragraph in Heredia's Memoirs. Heredia was there. He moved among these men whom he knew personally. He was the soul of honour. He may err; he cannot lie. He has no axe to grind. Here is the text: " While in La Guaira, when Miranda went there to embark, he [Bolívar] was one of those who plotted and carried out the arrest of this unfortunate man, his intimate friend, whom he had previously taken pride in having brought to Venezuela; an infamous act, from the black stain of which he will never be able to wash his reputation. Through Don Francisco Iturbe, Tithe Treasurer, he obtained a passport from Monteverde, and he left for Curaçao towards the beginning of August, 1812, showing himself converted from his revolutionary ideas, and resolved to take service as a volunteer in Lord Wellington's English army, to regain the favour of the Spanish Government. This disposition of his mind, which his most intimate friends assured me to be sincere, was altogether altered when he learnt in Curaçao that, soon after his departure, Monteverde had sequestered his lands and the income he had counted on to keep himself decorously in his new career."

This, again, is unanswerable. Bolívar delivered Miranda in order to ingratiate himself with the Spanish Government and cross the line—just as Casas and Peña and Juan Toro and dozens of the most prominent men of the republican party did at the time. Heredia asserts the fact without the slightest reservation. Bolívar left converted and resolved to join not the British army, but Wellington's British army, i.e. the army fighting for Spanish liberty. And he then adds that the sincerity of this intention was vouched for by Bolívar's most intimate friends. This puts it beyond doubt that Bolívar expressed this intention in conversation—whether he was sincere or not; a fact it is important to bear in mind for later use.

Two contemporary documents in Bolívar's own hand fully bear out Heredia. In a letter he wrote to Iturbe from Curaçao (10.ix.12), there is a significant postscript: " Were any rumours to arrive there reflecting on my political behaviour or my ways, you may deny them with the certainty that they are untrue. I warn you, not because I think that it might happen, but because I understand there are here many ill-meaning persons from Caracas desirous to win favour with the Government by acting as informers." Since Don Francisco Iturbe was a high official of the Spanish Government and a European Spaniard, thanks to whose protection Bolívar had left La Guaira in freedom, this proves that Bolívar was determined to behave as a good Spaniard and afraid of being accused by informers of not doing so. On September 19th, he wrote again to Iturbe to ask him to see that another man was appointed instead of Ascanio (who had left for the Canary Islands) to administer his fortune, that his houses in the City were rented, and other details to that effect; witness to his confidence that his interests were safe in spite of his past political activities. This must be noted for further reference. Then he added: " What I most instantly press on you is my claim that the authorities lift the embargo on my brother's estate, which, owing to his death, I must inherit, and do not forget that in order to come into the ownership of this property I am ready for every possible sacrifice." What could an exiled Bolívar sacrifice to the Spanish Government but his political position ?

6

There are few cases in History better proved by first-hand documentary evidence than this. Three contemporary witnesses, two of them, Monteverde and Bolívar, directly concerned, and the third, Heredia, a close observer, have left accounts which, independent though they are, dovetail perfectly. Monteverde says that Bolívar asked for passports for foreign countries, and Heredia says that Bolívar wanted to join Wellington's army; Monteverde says that Bolívar spontaneously delivered Miranda and deserves a reward for it; and Heredia says that he did it to be rewarded; to which Bolívar adds that he is anxious to be believed when he says he will behave in a manner satisfactory to the Spanish Government; Heredia says that Bolívar changed his mind when his estate was confiscated, and Bolívar writes that in order to gain possession of his brother's estate (let alone his own, which he assumes safe) he will consent to any sacrifice. The whole story is summed up and confirmed by the Cuban Yanes, who knew Bolívar well and served under him: " Bolívar, through an honourable Spaniard, Don Francisco Iturbe, obtained a passport from Monteverde and with a few of his friends arrived in Curaçao, meaning to sail for Europe to serve in Wellington's army; but as he learnt that his property had been sequestered and Monteverde's violent and despotic deeds, and that were he to return to Caracas he would have the same fate, he decided to go to Cartagena for help to free his country from that perfidious tyrant."

CHAPTER XIX

BOLÍVAR'S FIRST EXILE

I

WE know nothing about Bolívar's doings between July 30th–31st, when he delivered Miranda to the Spanish authorities, and August 26th, when, with Iturbe, he called on Monteverde to obtain his passport for " foreign countries ". He must have spent most of the time on the complicated arrangements a fortune such as his would require. That much may be gathered from his letters to Iturbe. The day after his visit to Monteverde, Bolívar sailed from La Guaira (27.viii.12). It seems that he tried first to sail in the vessel of an English merchant, Mr. F. L., to whom Monteverde had written a letter of recommendation, but who refused to take him on board owing to his conduct towards Miranda.

He left, however, soon afterwards in the Spanish sloop *Jesús, María y José*, for Curaçao. Apart from Bolívar, the passengers were José Felix Ribas, Vicente Tejera, Manuel Díaz Casado and a nephew of Ribas, Francisco. José Felix and Francisco Ribas travelled on the same passport, which Monteverde had granted them because they were relatives of his. We do not know why Díaz Casado and Tejera were allowed out of the country; but since Díaz Casado, " the worst scoundrel which Venezuela ever produced ", as one of his countrymen has written, was notorious for having diverted to his private purse wealth confiscated on political grounds from European Spaniards of Caracas, it may be assumed that he used some of it to get away with the rest. Tejera is stigmatized by the Venezuelan biographer of Ribas as a " perfidious and insidious man "; and both figure in a warning sent by Miranda to Ribas, through Soublette, while Ribas was Governor of Caracas: " A number of persons have written to the General that you keep by your side persons who scandalize public opinion, such as Díaz Casado, Sosa, Ramírez, Tejera, etc." Bolívar therefore left the shores of his native country in the company of men of poor reputation.

Meanwhile Miranda wrote paper after paper to the *Audiencia* of Caracas from his gaol. That was a tense moment in the History of the emancipation of the Spanish Kingdoms of the New World: the Precursor and the future Liberator both fall heavily on the battlefield of life. But the Precursor's fall is the last: for him, liberty is over, and life itself is almost at an end; while for the Liberator, the fall is but the crisis of heart and character which is to make him what till then he had only striven to be: the leader of a continent in travail. Both were at the time turning their thoughts towards reconciliation with Spain; but in a different spirit. Miranda was at the end of a career of disappointments and frustrations. He had delved below words and facts, to the region of impulses and character; and had come to realize the fundamental unity of all Spaniards, whether born in the New or in the Old World. As late as May 8th, 1813, he wrote to the

Audiencia explaining that his aim in capitulating had been " to reconcile Americans and Europeans so that henceforth they should form one community, one family and one interest, so that Caracas should give to the rest of the Continent an example of her political views and a proof that she preferred an honourable reconciliation to the hazardous movements of a devastating civil war ".

This attitude was condemned by the patriots in his day and is often condemned in our own. But Heredia was right in concluding: " Spain and mankind are indebted to Miranda for this good deed." Far from being due to decadence, fatigue or cowardice, the capitulation was the outcome of a wisdom capable of learning from experience.

The Miranda who capitulated was far in advance of his time. He saw a united, yet free, federation of Spanish States living together in mutual freedom under the aegis of the constitution of Cádiz on which he writes: "A monument that sheds glory and honour on the representatives who framed it. . . . The Venezuelans believed that it would be the rainbow of peace, the anchor of liberty, and the first and most important step taken by the mother country in favour of the American continent." So wrote Miranda from the vaults of Puerto Cabello in March, 1813. When Level de Goda visited him in Puerto Rico, his dream still lingered: " His person and head were a library on legs. I was enchanted. The Captain General (Don Salvador Meléndez) in whose house I lived, held him in high esteem. The proceedings of the Cortes and the Cádiz newspapers were eagerly sought by the learned old man and I gave him abundantly of both; Meléndez was generous enough to have the papers sent him through me even before reading them."

Miranda's arrest was a monstrous abuse of power on the part of Monteverde. From the day he and Bolívar share the infamy of arresting him, Miranda passes from prison to prison, from the vaults of La Guaira to Puerto Rico, and from Puerto Rico to Cádiz where he died (14.vii.16). Considering the standards of those days, his jailers were not harsh; but the mere fact that he lived in prison at all was a legal and a moral crime. The main responsibility for it falls on Ferdinand VII; but the Regency can by no means be exonerated, since its régime lasted long enough to have saved Miranda from the clutches of the King. " Sometimes "—writes one of his prison companions—" as he paced a small enclosure in Cádiz, he would stop, lift in his hand the heavy chain that ran from pillar to pillar, and say: ' To think that the first link in this chain was forged by my countrymen! ' "

2

While Miranda had come round to believe in a Spanish federation based on true reconciliation, through an age-long experience, and for good and all, Bolívar was thinking of getting himself accepted in the Spanish camp by way of Wellington's army, merely in a passing excess of depression, due to his failure at Puerto Cabello. Within a few months, on December 15th, 1812, he would write in his Memoir to the citizens of New Granada these significant words: " The raw recruit thinks everything is lost when he is defeated once; for experience has not shown him yet that courage, skill and constancy redress ill-fortune." On board a Spanish sloop, sailing towards Curaçao, Bolívar was still in the mood of that raw recruit. He had not reached yet the self-denying attitude of Miranda turning towards Spain for the sake of peace and sense, i.e. for the sake of everything but his own self. He was turning to Spain (through Wellington) for the sake of Bolívar, who having failed on one side thought it better to try his luck on the other.

The small group of fugitives had a bad crossing, and on September 2nd arrived in Curaçao. " I was detestably received "—Bolívar writes to Iturbe—" for hardly had I landed when my baggage was embargoed for two very odd reasons: because my belongings were in the same house as Miranda's and because the brig *Celoso* had contracted debts in Puerto Cabello which I was now to pay because I was commandant of the harbour when the debts had been contracted. . . . I am therefore without means to feed my life, which I am beginning to look upon with too much loathing and horror." He did find in the Island a few friends who offered him hospitality; but he knew then the hardest time of his life. He begged Iturbe to " combine with Juan José Toro so as to send me something to live on; for I have hardly any means left wherewith to subsist while the answer to this letter comes ". He borrowed one thousand pesos in Curaçao to be paid in Caracas, swallowing the humiliation of a demand from the lender to be guaranteed by Juan Nepomuceno Ribas; and when he claimed his two trunks of silver and clothes arrived in Caracas on board the *Sapphire*, we may gather the attitude of the authorities from the fact that Hodgson in his report to Liverpool says the trunks had been claimed by " a D. Simón Bolívar ".

These months in exile must have been useful to him. Till then, he had been a spoiled child of nature and of society. After the inner humiliation of his failure as leader in Puerto Cabello, and the inner infamy of his conduct towards Miranda, these outward and visible humiliations of the penniless and despised, or at least not respected, exile in Curaçao must have increased the intensity of his searchings of heart. There is an echo of all this in the letter he wrote to Iturbe on September 19th of that fateful 1812 in which he was reborn. " As the straight and courageous man must be indifferent to the onslaughts of ill-fortune, I am armed with constancy, and look with disdain on the shots of fate. On my heart no one has sway but my own conscience; it is at peace and nothing disturbs it." The conscience that spoke thus of itself was hard at work.

Bolívar could not afford to remain for long in a state of suspended animation. His resolve to join Wellington's army as a means to re-enter the Spanish commonwealth was but part of the storm caused by his failure as a commanding officer. A reaction of his vigorous spirit was bound to set in sooner or later. This reaction would not be free to take any course he might wish to impress on it. Bolívar had to justify himself in his own eyes and in the eyes of the world for having delivered his chief and friend to his enemies. This act, an asset while he remained at the gates of the Spanish camp, would become a heavy liability were he to return to the revolutionary wilderness, unless he endeavoured to brand Miranda as a traitor to the revolution. Thus to condemn Miranda became for him a psychological necessity; and while it is unlikely that Bolívar came to such a conclusion by a logical process, it is certain that it emerged in his thought after a sub-conscious elaboration of identical import.

Outwardly, a field had to be found in which Miranda's " treason " could be displayed. There was, of course, the capitulation; but the question whether a leader should have capitulated or not can seldom be a live issue; for it is retrospective and complicated. Bolívar succeeded in convincing himself that Miranda had acted through cowardice, which is extravagant enough. But a clearer issue had to be found. This was Miranda's attitude towards the European Spaniards. There are reasons for thinking that it was suggested to Bolívar by Ribas and Díaz Casado. These two men were keenly interested in the issue: Casado because he had to justify his loot of Spanish property; Ribas because he had been the chief instigator, if not the actual creator, of the policy of persecuting Spaniards to the death.

3

This policy consisted in persecuting European Spaniards as such, whether they were favourable to the Republic or not. It altered the very basis of the civil war which, till then, had cut across the whites on lines of personal opinion, not of origin. Many, possibly the majority, of the Creoles were faithful to the Spanish connection, or " royalists "; many European Spaniards were in favour of independence, or " republicans ". In his report to Miranda on the loss of Puerto Cabello, Bolívar deplored the death in action of Colonel Jalón, of whom he said, " he alone was worth a whole army ". Jalón was a European Spaniard. The bullets that killed him were from Coro, i.e. Creole. Ribas acted in complete disregard of all this. León complained to Miranda (20.vii.12) that widespread arrests were taking place: " From these arrests there have not been excluded either the most ' patriotic ' Europeans, or those who have fought on our side, or those who, owing to their connections in the country, or having their sons in the service of the government, or being otherwise deeply committed to our cause, should, it would appear, have been protected and esteemed and not persecuted." To this, Ribas retorted, also in a letter to Miranda: " They are our natural enemies, awaiting the moment to destroy us. See what those Catalans have just done in Curiepe and what has just happened in Puerto Cabello."

This last argument must have been prominent in the conversations between the two exiles, the uncle and the nephew. Ribas had been deprived of his governorship of Caracas by Miranda precisely because of his persecu-tion of the Spaniards; and Bolívar found the Spanish prisoners handy scapegoats to pay for the loss of the Castle of San Felipe under his command. Moreover, just as Bolívar had his La Guaira episode to redress, so Ribas had in his past an episode to avenge on Miranda; for, during the Valencia campaign, he had lost a position in conditions which had drawn from the General the sternest rebuke. " Listen to your own honour and judgment. Do not let yourself be cowed by information from pusillanimous men. Retake your position, for what has happened is a shame." So wrote Miranda to Ribas on May 28th, 1812; and Ribas could not have forgotten it in September, talking to Bolívar in Curaçao.

There was, therefore, a pure white, Spanish civil war element in the attitude of Ribas and Bolívar. But there was in it an Indian element as well; the voice of the depressed and dispossessed men in revolt against the conquerors and usurpers. Heredia, commenting on the rivalry between whites and mulattoes which set in after the counter-revolutionary attempt in Valencia, says that " the *guerrilleros* who later tried to form a party under the King's colours, excited this rivalry till it became proverbial with the hot-headed Europeans that the mulattoes were loyal and the white Creoles revolutionary, whom it was necessary to make an end of ". The seeds of what was later known as war to the death were equally alive on both sides. As for Bolívar's own seed, it was probably planted—on favourable soil—in Puerto Cabello; was nursed by Ribas and grew to gruesome proportions during his exile in Curaçao.

4

All the authorities, civil and military, who witnessed the end of the first Venezuelan republic are agreed that Monteverde's triumph was due to public opinion. The country being with Spain, Monteverde, with no military talents whatsoever, was able to beat the republicans who had the military and economic resources of the province at their disposal, with just his personal bravery and two hundred and thirty men. Aware of the fact that his position was irregular, he sought a basis for his power in partisanship. His party was twofold: he was a naval officer born in the Canary Islands. He endeavoured to found his military power on sailors and his administration and political power on " Islanders ", i.e. Canarians.

As early as April, 1812, when he took San Carlos, an Islander whose name happened to be Vicente Gómez, called on him, and Monteverde, " informed of his loyalty, appointed him his secretary ". This man and his brother Antonio bear most of the responsibility for Monteverde's chief crime and folly: the violation of the convention of San Mateo. Vicente Gómez had been an enthusiastic patriot or republican. Many Islanders had figured prominently as members of Congress, secretaries, envoys, magistrates, and had gained a reputation of staunch patriots by lending themselves to " arrest and lead to the gaol of La Guaira and Puerto Cabello " royalists accused of conspiring against the republic. Nevertheless they succeeded in winning favour with Monteverde, possibly because Monteverde realized that they were in his hands owing to their past. Under their influence, Monteverde appointed to military posts a number of men who, though European born, and professional officers, had taken a prominent part in the revolution. Then, while good officers remained unemployed, and Monteverde wrote to Spain complaining of lack of officers, he placed his naval colleagues in civilian and military posts.

The Islanders Antonio and Vicente Gómez and the Caraqueño lawyer José Manuel Oropesa succeeded in bamboozling Monteverde into believing in the absurdest conspiracies, " to such an extent that he dared not go out, nor take any food but that prepared for him by one lady, and always brought to him under the escort of the priest Rojas, to prevent any poisoning on the way ". As soon as he arrived in Caracas, he ordered the arrest of eight " patriots ", evenly divided, four Creoles (Cortés Madariaga, Juan Pablo Ayala, Roscio, Paz Castillo) and four European Spaniards (Isnardi, Manuel Ruíz, José Mires and Antonio Barona), whom he sent to La Guaira in chains. This caused so much alarm in the city, that, under pressure from Casa León, whom he had appointed Intendente, Monteverde published a proclamation (3.viii.12) solemnly promising that he would " keep his promises ", though carefully pointing out that the general amnesty provided for in the capitulation did not cover actions of later date. Nevertheless, under the pretext of a trifling incident, he sent a circular to local authorities (13.viii.12) ordering them to arrest and send all suspects to La Guaira or Puerto Cabello. This document put the liberty of every man in Venezuela into the hands of newly appointed " Spanish ", but in reality " Monteverdian " authorities, most of whom were eager to avenge the wrongs done to them or to their kith and kin during the republican period. Lists of persons to be arrested were established in conditions of utter irresponsibility in most cities, notably in Caracas.

Such a breach of the capitulation could not be justified at all. Monteverde argued that the republicans had broken it first; but he was never able to substantiate this claim when challenged by men of integrity, such as the Regent of the *Audiencia*, Heredia. The best contemporary authorities, men as loyal to Spain throughout as the Creoles Heredia and Urquinaona, agree that Miranda and—insofar as they could—his republican friends respected their obligations. As to the argument that a capitulation concluded with rebels need not be respected, Heredia rightly spurns it, showing by many examples from Spanish history that treaties with rebels were always respected by Spain. Moreover, when Monteverde sent his first eight prisoners to Spain, in October of that year, he was so sure that his argument would not be accepted in the mother country, that he excused his action alleging that the eight men were guilty of treason committed after the capitulation; and the Regency repeatedly wrote asking for proof of this, insisting that actions previous to the capitulation could not be accepted against the prisoners.

Nevertheless, insofar as the prisoners were not released, and considering the still worse case of Miranda, the Regency itself was guilty of at least hypocrisy; since all the men should have been released, and the many more later imprisoned by Monteverde also. Towards the end of November, 1812, Heredia reckoned at seven hundred and twenty-three the prisoners made in violation of the capitulation. Monteverde therefore stands condemned. One point, however, must be emphasized. Monteverde jailed

over seven hundred persons: he killed none. Heredia, than whom no
sterner critic of Monteverde's folly could be found, nor better informed
either, writes of this period that " during all this unwise persecution, no
blood was spilt, nor were there in the whole district during the year of
Monteverde's command more deaths than those of two or three men guilty
of the Barinas conspiracy against the army, who were, there and then,
courtmartialled in the military style, and those of Briceño and a French
officer caught with him, also executed at headquarters . . . it never occurred
to Monteverde that a man could be killed in cold blood without being
legally sentenced, and whatever he did during his term of office, it was in
the sincere belief that the action was just ".   Heredia also points out that
" despite the deadly climate, and in over six months that such overcrowding
of prisoners lasted, only one died who was already sick when he was arrested ".
This refers to Puerto Cabello.   " In La Guaira only three or four died out
of six hundred who were there at different times within the narrow precincts
of the vaults."   This is a fact which sets the episode in its true place and
proportions, as seen from our vantage point; but in the days of Monteverde,
and before the arrival of Bolívar, it was not Monteverde's correct attitude
towards human life which was observed, but his arbitrary despotism towards
human property and freedom.   And this was to become Monteverde's debt
out of which Bolívar made much capital.

5

Though Heredia says that Bolívar changed his mind and gave up his
idea of joining Wellington's army on hearing that Monteverde had confiscated his property, the news of this spoliation may just have been the
last push which determined the move.   As late as September 19th Bolívar
was declaring himself ready for any sacrifice in favour of Spain in order to
inherit his brother's estate.   On the other hand, his own estates were not
actually confiscated, and the tacit or express agreement with Monteverde
under which he left La Guaira for Curaçao was scrupulously respected,
though not by Bolívar, who had given his word of honour never to meddle
again in public affairs.   In spite of this promise there is little doubt that,
from the very first, the tendency to carry on the fight lived in his inner
being, even when he sincerely thought it dead.   Turning over in his head
schemes of personal vengeance and justification, afterthoughts on the failure
of the republic, and forethoughts on its chances of rebirth, Bolívar, from
Curaçao, could observe to the West the gradual loss of popularity Monteverde
was undergoing, and to the East the political moves in the neighbouring
country.

New Granada had lived years of change and of chaos since some of her
leaders had entered the path of independence—of course under the banners
of Ferdinand VII.   Don Antonio Nariño, a wealthy aristocrat of Santa Fe,
had ousted President Lozano and done away with the federal constitution
which the new republic of New Granada had given herself in naïve imitation
of the United States.   Nariño was an authoritarian and a centralist *à la*

Bolívar. Nevertheless New Granada had not yet made it officially clear that she meant to break with Spain. This cautious policy was determined by the fierce opposition to independence which revealed itself in some of the provinces. Pasto, for instance, was already beginning that long-drawn fight against independence which in years to come was to exasperate Bolívar; and Cartagena still recognized the Regency and the Cortes, to which in the summer of 1811 she had nominated a deputy.

Despite this fact, Cartagena carried on a civil war against the neighbouring province of Santa Marta; because Cartagena was less royalist than Santa Marta, the most royalist of all the provinces, where a strong group of European and Creole Spaniards had fortified and organized themselves. The real cause of the trouble between the two cities was, however, both deeper and less significant. Cartagena and Santa Marta were rival cities, on either side of the mouth of the Magdalena river, and they both sought in an apparently political feud an outlet for their local feelings, and a means to paralyse the trade of a rival. Hence the persistence of the civil war even after Cartagena, passing from one extreme to the other, declared herself independent, not only of Spain but of New Granada herself, proudly becoming the *State of Cartagena*. New Granada was then living days which were to be admirably described by Wellington to Stanhope, three years after Bolívar's death, with reference to Spain herself: " You may depend upon it that the real government of the Spanish provinces was in the *Cabildo*—and a fair good government it was; and the royal power by the captain-general was the only thing that kept them together. Remove or weaken that power, and the provinces will all fall asunder and set up for themselves."

What with her war against Santa Marta, her constitutional growing pains and her economic and financial troubles, Cartagena decided to trust her destinies to a dictator. *Separatism, dictatorship:* the leitmotiv of all Spanish history. The dictator of Cartagena was a young lawyer of twenty-four, Manuel Rodríguez Torices, who took office in the spring of 1812 and organized the defence of his little republic against the royalists of Santa Marta, who were being reinforced from the Antilles. The position seemed dangerous because the royalists in Santa Marta were in strategic command of the approaches to western Venezuela, i.e. that part of Venezuela which had remained attached to Spain, and whence, during that summer, Monteverde was to win all too easily his way eastwards into Caracas. Meanwhile, the rest of New Granada was rent by another civil war between the centralists, led by Nariño, President of the State of Cundinamarca (old style: province of Santa Fe) and the federalists, who had organized a union of a number of other provinces. This civil war had ended—for a time—in an agreement signed in Santa Rosa the very day Miranda lost his liberty in La Guaira (30.vii.12). On the 11th and 12th, Cartagena elected as President the same Torices, till then her dictator. But the young republic was faced with growing difficulties both from outside and from her internal economy; and the once proud city, queen of the commerce of the Indies, knew poverty, paper money and financial panic for the first time in three centuries.

The sight before Bolívar, waiting in Curaçao, could not be more disconsolate. From Quito to Cumaná, the cause dear to his heart was either defeated by the arms of the Regency or forsaken by the people, or disintegrating into anarchy. The Santa Marta royalists, elated by Monteverde's success, and well informed as to the chaotic situation in Cartagena, crossed the river and blockaded the city. Had they sent one thousand men to attack it, they might have taken it. Torices sent two messengers to the viceroy designate of New Granada, who resided in Panama, ostensibly to seek a compromise; but the royalist troops before Cartagena intercepted a letter in which the envoys revealed their true mission to be to gain time and to spy. The viceroy had them arrested, but set them at liberty again at the request of Admiral Stirling, who had guaranteed them a safe passage. It was then that Bolívar decided to cross over from Curaçao to Cartagena and to join in the struggle. In the company of the two Venezuelan brothers Carabaño, Miguel and Fernando, of Antonio Nicolás Briceño, José Felix Ribas, the two *mantuano* brothers Montilla and the European Spaniard Colonel Manuel Cortés Campomanes, who had sided with the republic, Bolívar arrived in Cartagena in the course of October. They were most welcome, for the little republic had no officers. But Bolívar was by no means the most welcome of all. The most important command, that of the column being organized to reconquer the Sabanas, west of the city, was entrusted to the Spaniard. Bolívar was sent to an obscure post on the banks of the Magdalena.

6

Brave and generous, Bolívar was not humble. This command was certainly below what he wished or expected. He had come to Cartagena in her hour of danger and need; but he was not ready to give up the rank which he felt was his. Before leaving the city for his distant post, he turned to public opinion and drafted two papers, his two first political manifestoes. The first (27.xi.12) is addressed to the Sovereign Congress of New Granada, and signed by " Simón Bolívar, army Colonel and Commandant of Puerto Cabello "; and " Vicente Tejera, a Minister of the Supreme Court of Caracas ". The second, dated " Cartagena de Indias, December 15th, 1812 ", is entitled: " *A Memoir addressed to the Citizens of New Granada by a Caraqueño* "; and is signed Simón Bolívar. Both are outstanding for a lucidity of expression, a felicity of style and a political maturity which mark their author as a first-rate mind. Bolívar was then twenty-nine.

His ideas and judgments were not all sound. For instance, what he says about Miranda; since he attributes to " unheard-of cowardice " the capitulation of La Victoria, which, he says, " covering us with shame, delivered us back again to the yoke of our tyrants ". Nor was his attitude about European Spaniards consistent in a man who had seen some of them fighting by his side and dying for the independence of Venezuela; who had, or so he claimed, been able to leave Venezuela thanks to a Spaniard; and who landed in Cartagena to carry on the fight in the company of a European

Spaniard. We know that he was voicing the feelings of Ribas and giving vent to his own resentment as the defeated commander of Puerto Cabello. But there was more to it than that. In these two utterances, the true and authentic Bolívar reveals himself to the world as he was by nature and as he had become by adversity: a man determined to be carried away from political realism by no abstraction, from ruthlessness by no pity; a shrewd and penetrating intellect indeed, but no gown-man at all: a cape-and-sword-man, definitely.

In both documents, Bolívar analyses the causes of the disaster which had befallen the republic. He does mention the earthquake but rightly dismisses it as of " a second order ", putting first " errors committed by the Government ". One was not having attacked Coro by sea as soon as it became evident that this city would not follow the lead of Caracas. Then he mentions the failure to raise regular armies; " an insensate dissipation of capital and public income on frivolous objects, when they should have been devoted to the war, setting aside a fund for the needs of the State; a stupid leniency towards the ungrateful and perfidious Spaniards . . . and finally religious fanaticism ". Bolívar reveals himself here, in his thirtieth year, long before he ever experienced the responsibilities and frustrations of office, a scathing critic of political idealism. " The codes our magistrates consulted were not such as could teach them the practical science of government, but those formed by some well-meaning visionaries who, imagining aerial republics, endeavoured to reach political perfection assuming the perfectibility of the human lineage. So that we had philosophers instead of leaders, philanthropy instead of legislation, dialectics instead of tactics, and sophists instead of soldiers."

Who could pen a pithier formulation of political pessimism, and how is it possible to attribute to disenchantment *in later years* that authoritarian tendency, that disdain for debate and discussion, that cape-and-sword contempt for the gown, which breathe in Bolívar's words and live in his thought from the very first ? True his criticism of the federal government the doctrinaires of Caracas had given to their country could not be more justified. But his attacking pen delves deeper than mere federalism, to the very citadel of liberal democracy, the suffrage, in terms which leave no doubt as to what he thought of parliaments and congresses, again, from the very first. " Popular elections made by the rustics of the country and by the scheming inhabitants of the cities, add yet an obstacle to the practice of federal government with us; for the former are so ignorant that they vote like machines; and the latter so ambitious that they turn everything into party strife."

This young man who, but five months earlier, with his head in his hands, sunk in shame, thought himself unworthy of commanding the meanest private, had so far recovered that he found strength of thought and style to castigate the republic for having wished to be republican. What did he want ? What would he have done ? He evidently saw a country free from Spain; but governed by a firm and aristocratic hand, led by a pure and patriotic, but a ruthless, heart. No words of his are sterner than those in which he condemns the "tolerant system". He writes, for instance: "From this was born the impurity of the crimes against the State, brazenly committed by the discontented, and particularly by our born and implacable enemies the European Spaniards, who had remained in our country maliciously to keep it ever in turmoil. . . . The doctrine on which this conduct rested had its origin in the philanthropic maxims of some authors who maintain that no one has the faculty to deprive a man of his life even when that man has committed a crime against his country. . . . A criminal clemency!" In these words lies hidden the seed of the war to the death.

CHAPTER XX

WAR TO THE DEATH

I

BOLÍVAR may well have given the most striking measure of his spirit when he decided to reconquer his lost country from the banks of the Magdalena. Assets he had none but himself and a few friends such as Ribas. The territory he was taking as a base was the western end of a country split into four warring parts: to the west, Santa Marta, royalist and backed by the neighbouring Venezuelan provinces of Coro and Maracaibo, centres of royalist resistance; to the east, Cartagena, independent under young Torices; to the south, the central part of New Granada, Cundina-marca, a centralist republic under the dictator Nariño; and round Tunja, a cluster of other provinces loosely united under a federal constitution whose president was a supporter of Bolívar, Dr. Camilo Torres. The military force of Tunja was but small; Cartagena might dispose of three thousand men; Nariño had hardly more.

When Bolívar was sent to command his one hundred men at Barrancas, the hero of the Cartagena troops was Labatut or Labatud, a French adventurer who had already tried his hand in Venezuela and, on the fall of Caracas, had offered his services to the neighbouring State. With two to three hundred men, he had gained two or three local victories and so won the rank of Commander-in-Chief of the Magdalena front. As he was preparing an attack on Santa Marta, the Spanish commander, despairing of being able to defend it, had left the city by sea; and Labatud entered it (6.i.13) and granted an amnesty, pending further depredations—for after all, war was his business.

The Spaniard Campomanes and the Venezuelan brothers Carabaño were no less successful up country; so that the royalist troops on the left banks of the Magdalena seemed to be thoroughly beaten and disorganized. On the mouth of the river Sinu, Miguel Carabaño won a victory and, writes the Colombian Restrepo, " gave no quarter to a single prisoner, ' to placate ', as they said, ' the shades of so many victims sacrificed by the Spaniards out of hate for liberty ' ". This was the kind of warfare prevailing on November 26th, 1812, to the west.

Bolívar took the small river port of Tenerife (23.xii.12), then sailed on towards Mompox which he entered amidst scenes of popular enthusiasm (27.xii.12). Labatud complained to Cartagena about his junior's insub-ordination; but who was " Cartagena " but the insubordinate junior of Santa Fe? Labatud's claim to have Bolívar court-martialled did not prosper, and there and then, in Mompox, the scene of his first victory, the young leader was declared Commander of the military district and granted some reinforcements, which, though including fifteen armed river craft, did not raise his force beyond the five hundred figure. In the circumstances, however, this was not negligible. Bolívar took it up river without delay, occupied Banco, which the royalists had evacuated, and branching off into the river César, fought and won an encounter in Chiriguaná (1.i.13), thus auspiciously beginning the year of his first triumph. On January 8th, he wrote to the Tunja Congress: " Soon I shall take Ocaña. All these operations have taken fifteen days." He did take Ocaña, and was again enthusiastically received by the population. In less than a month, Campomanes, Bolívar, Labatud and the Carabaños had cleared the province of Santa Marta, all but the valley of Dupar. Bolívar had seized artillery and ammunition in useful quantities, and opened the Magdalena again when the regions inland were beginning to feel the lack of essential goods.

These first campaigns had thrown up a number of facts: the first was that the Spanish hold of the country was precarious. The second was that allegiance was just as precarious either way, for everybody wanted peace rather than the victory of this or that side. For instance, after the first campaign was over, and when Bolívar, with his usual drive, was turning his laurels into fuel for the next campaign, that which was to take him to Caracas, " there was "—writes Restrepo—" in the Mompox troops so widespread a desertion that he felt bound to have a few soldiers shot; a decision which, though necessary to uphold military discipline, raised bitter complaints from the authorities and population of Mompox ". Finally, the campaigns had revealed a commander of decision, rapidity and outstanding executive ability; a man, moreover,. who realized that the shifting loyalties of the masses and the vacillating attitude of the adversary were excellent materials for victory.

2

It was imperative to take Venezuela so as to save New Granada. The cause was one. Bolívar suggested to his Granadino friends an advance on Maracaibo from Santa Marta and on Barinas from Cúcuta, before reinforcements for the royalists came from Spain and destroyed that unique opportunity. But though the plan was sound and clear, the answer from Tunja was not forthcoming. Bolívar, a guest commander in a brotherly land, had no authority to invade his own country with the forces entrusted to him by his host. Here again, Monteverde came to his help. He ordered an offensive into New Granada from Venezuela. The commander of the advanced Spanish forces, Colonel Ramón Correa, began to move forward towards Pamplona, a district protected by the Granadino commander Colonel Manuel Castillo. The Governor of Pamplona and Castillo wrote to Bolívar for help. But Bolívar pointed out that he was still awaiting an answer to his proposal.

The authority he craved arrived at last (8.ii.13). It was not all he wanted, but it was something. He left Ocaña with 400 men and spare rifles to arm Castillo's troops; but a difference of opinion arose between the two men. Castillo, more interested in keeping his country safe—possibly also, in remaining within striking distance of his own country's civil wars—advocated a plan limited to a district relatively close to Pamplona; Bolívar, who considered the matter as a mere first step on his march towards Caracas, disregarded his colleague's advice, took Salazar de las Palmas, where Castillo meant him to remain entrenched, advanced on San José de Cúcuta and expelled the Spanish troops from the city and district (28.ii.13).

Cúcuta was looted. The merchants, mostly Catalans, fled, leaving their homes and stores unprotected. In answer to complaints from Tunja, Bolívar pointed out that his troops were " the most disobedient and disorderly of New Granada "; but also that if they had not taken the booty themselves they would never have seen any, since, during the Magdalena campaign, though the booty had been substantial, it had not reached the soldiers " owing to those who had remained in charge of it ". On the other hand, he argues, " the looted shops belonged to our enemies; if any patriots have suffered damages, I have not heard of it, and on hearing of it, I have indemnified them ". He evidently authorized implicitly the looting of all those who did not think like him. But there was more to it than that. In answer to the charges made against him by Castillo, Bolívar wrote from Cúcuta to the President of the Union (7.v.13): " Colonel Castillo, who disapproves my behaviour so much, promised his troops that he would let them sack La Grita, if it were necessary to take it by force; while I have never uttered such words to my troops, though I should have done it, to encourage them, for they came most discontented, and they deserted by the hundred ". This reveals a certain rivalry between the two commanders, both anxious to keep troops under their command and to court them and keep them happy—a pretorian attitude inevitable in the circumstances, identical with that of Monteverde, and, as we shall see later, with that of Boves.

Withal the taking of Cúcuta was a brilliant success which strengthened Bolívar, both materially and morally. Arms, ammunition, money enough to pay two months' arrears and some gratuities to his officers and men, clothes to give each soldier a set of underclothing, " for many came naked, especially those of Cartagena ", were substantial advantages for such a poverty-stricken army. But, above all, he justified his bold step on the edge of indiscipline, and he acquired the moral authority needed to lay his plan of reconquest again, and with more assurance, before the now " United Provinces of New Granada ". He sent his relative Ribas to Santa Fe, to enter into any treaties he might think advisable; speaking with a voice in which, despite his youth (he was just short of thirty), the assurance of a statesman could already be perceived. By March 21st, 1813, he had received his commission of brigadier of the Union, granted him with every expression of praise and encouragement. José Manuel Castillo, who had arrived in Cúcuta after him, gladly concurred in these honours and praises, and though a senior man, proposed that Bolívar should take command of the united forces—about one thousand men—who were to go forward. The invasion of Venezuela was at last to begin.

3

Bolívar's operation might have been indefinitely thwarted through the inertia of his friends and the intrigue of his enemies, had it not been for Monteverde's insensate policy. Towards the end of 1812, Monteverde decided to prepare in Barinas an expedition to reconquer New Granada. He recruited an army " with the utmost violence, the recruits being kept locked up till the moment of marching, so that most of them deserted, and remained wandering in the hills and deserts for fear of punishment, forsaking their families and occupations ". With this army, he was to launch a hazardous conquest, while he was not in a position to hold Caracas without reinforcements from Spain. Finally, though there were trained military leaders available, he gave the chief commands of his force to naval officers, such as Antonio Tiscar. The outcome of it all was that " the Governments of New Granada, in order to create a diversion, aided Bolívar's plans, which they would in all likelihood have looked down upon in other circumstances ".

Monteverde had more military training and a better military history than he is generally credited with. As a naval officer he had fought in Toulon, St. Vincent and Trafalgar, where he had been wounded and taken prisoner; as a land officer he had fought in Talavera and in Ocaña, where he had also been wounded. He was as brave as Bolívar and had a far longer and better experience of war. Both were men of drive and temerity, ambitious, and prone to indiscipline. But Bolívar had a mind and Monteverde had none; so that action in Bolívar was directed and persistent, while in Monteverde it was the toy of his changing moods and passions or of the influences he happened to be undergoing.

At the time, he was under the influence of the two brothers Gómez, who made him launch forth into a policy of absolutism and irresponsible tyranny wholly at variance with Spanish tradition. The *Audiencia*, under Heredia's leadership, stood courageously by the prerogatives of civil power, and of the laws protecting the citizens against the Executive; but Monteverde, though at times conscious of his responsibilities and willing to compromise, was too often stampeded into illegal persecutions through vanity, fear and ignorance of the law. On November 27th, 1812, on the pretext of some plot which failed to materialize, many good people of Caracas were the victims of the coarsest Islanders and *zambos;* and Cervériz, who commanded in Caracas, won for himself the nickname of Cerberus. The seeds of still worse events were sown during those days, and Heredia records that " many a man who boasted of having dragged Mr. So-and-so on foot tied to the tail of his mule, perished later at the hands of Bolívar ".

The *Oidores* wrote to the Regency (9.ii.13) pointing out that the Venezuelans, far from rebelling, had been most patient, when, having " given themselves up under the faith of a capitulation, this capitulation had been scandalously broken by the very man who had granted it "; and drew a vivid picture of the state of the country: " the cities startled, all families discontented, thousands of persons in flight and wandering from town to town, from hill to hill, fleeing from ferocious persecution, all parties ablaze with a factious spirit, and this Supreme Court offended and slighted. . . ." In January, 1814, Monteverde set all prisoners at liberty. He was even preparing some popular rejoicings to celebrate the event, and the poetical compositions to be sung at the ceremony were already written; but his Islanders were on the watch, and a new conspiracy was " discovered " and announced to the public in an official proclamation (11.ii.13) whereby its inventors achieved the aim they had in view—the continuation of strife and repression—but also aims beyond their power to see, for it afforded much encouragement to the true conspirators: Bolívar to the West and Mariño to the East.

4

The East had submitted spontaneously to the Spanish authorities. The situation was so easy that Monteverde's emissaries left the Province in charge of the very Junta which had led the rebellion, with Colonel Vicente Sucre at its head. The new Governor, Colonel Ureña, had no difficulty in keeping the vast province in peace, with but one hundred men from Coro. His success was due to commonsense and strict respect for the capitulation. This policy was resented by the dominant European colony, composed of prosperous but narrow-minded Catalans, who complained to Monteverde. On October 30th Ureña received an order from Monteverde to arrest a number of persons implicated in the rebellion and to send them to Caracas. Ureña refused, for the measure was contrary to the capitulation; and appealed to the *Audiencia*. By the time the *Audiencia* heard of it, Cervériz had already been sent to Cumaná with secret instructions from Monteverde which in fact put in his hands the liberty and property of every citizen, in utter disregard of the Governor. Cervériz had arrived in Venezuela in 1811 as a lieutenant in a company of convicts. He was a cruel and unintelligent man, a common thief, who made no scruple of turning to his personal use the baggage of any prisoner that came his way.

He arrived in the city on December 15th, 1812, and, says Urquinaona, " in combination with the Catalans, he began to put into operation his tumultuous arrests at one o'clock in the night, coolly informing the Governor the next morning, with a request for twenty pairs of shackles and a ship big enough to convey the prisoners to La Guaira ". The Governor protested against the violation of the constitution, which, in accordance with his instructions from Spain, he had promulgated (13.x.12)—the first Spanish authority to do so in Venezuela. This increased the fury of the Catalans and the resentment of Monteverde, who disliked the constitution. The Catalans appealed to Monteverde and Ureña to the *Audiencia*. The *Audiencia* was firm and officially approved Ureña's action (25.i.13); but Monteverde, on the advice of his Venezuelan legal adviser, Oropesa, finally delivered Cumaná to the arbitrary rule of despotism.

A group of dissidents fled in the brig *Botón de Rosa*, and took refuge in the tiny island of Chaca-Chacare, off Trinidad. They were soon reinforced by a new wave of fugitives from Cervériz' rule. It was from this base that the first re-invasion of Venezuela by the patriots was to take place; and its leader was not to be Bolívar, but Santiago Mariño. Mariño was " of Irish extraction, and allied to the Leinster family ". The English seaman who records this fact held him in high esteem, and praised his " great military skill and undoubted bravery ". He paints him " tall and athletic, and has a very open countenance which is a perfect index to his mind "—a notable contrast with Bolívar, who was often sombre or at least dark and unrevealing —" his manners are elegant and his education extensive ".

Mariño had to rely mainly on foreign help. Don Matías Farreras, Governor of Guayana, had warned the Spanish authorities that an expedition from Trinidad had left for Chaca-Chacare. General Monro, then Governor of Trinidad, wrote to Bathurst (29.i.13): " A new revolution has recently broke out on the adjacent continent, which though of very contemptable origin and confined to a few vagabonds, may . . . soon extend itself and subvert the Royal Government of the Province. . . . The first notice I received of this projected movement was from the [Spanish] Commandant of Guiria, stating that he had reason to believe an Expedition was preparing at the small Island of Chacachacaré, in which many of the free people of colour embodied in our Militia were intended to be employed, for the purpose of attacking him in his government." Monro ordered an official enquiry. One witness declared that he had heard of " ten dollars having been offered by Mr. Valdez and Santiago Mariño [to] any person who would go on the expedition "; and another that " Valdez said their intention was to cut off the heads of all the European Spaniards on the Main ". A third witness said that " at the conclusion of the last revolution he received a letter from Santiago [Mariño] requesting him, this deponent, to furnish ten negroes to assist in another revolution which he refused and he told Santiago that being sixty-five years of age, he would have nothing to do with the revolution ".

" On the 13th of January of 1813 "—writes Urquinaona—" they appeared on the coasts of Huiria in loose groups; the troops of Cumaná went out with the intention of dissolving them ", but on February 3rd, Monteverde had to report that these " loose groups " " had forced him to withdraw with grave danger for his life ". Mariño wrote to Trinidad: " On the 13th at three in the morning we entered Guiria, on the 14th Punta de Piedra and on the 15th Irapo, with general rejoicing." But Mariño was still hard pressed for men, and wrote to Trinidad asking for " one hundred Frenchmen more and some arms, the only thing we stand in need of, to make the province of Cumaná, Margarita, Barcelona, independent ". This request for more Frenchmen turns up again in other letters of his, for, despite the tyrannous ways of Cervériz, the rising was not popular yet. Mariño had written to the Marqués de Toro from Guiria (16.i.13), urging the aristocrat of Caracas to help in the cause. Toro, then residing in Port of Spain, forwarded the letter to Monro the very day it reached him.

The attitude of the English authorities towards this invasion of Spanish territory by an expedition armed and organized from British territory was shifty, being ruled by the necessities of trade, the general trend prevailing in London to elbow Spain out of the New World, local fears as to the effects of a revolution in Spanish territory, the ups and downs of the events in Venezuela, and finally the needs of general decorum and respect for an ally. Monro wrote to Liverpool (6.viii.12) that privateering was making trade difficult in the smooth water of the Golfo Triste (between Trinidad

and the mainland), " and therefore both supplies and doubloons are scarce ".
He proposed that the Gulf should be neutralized, backed with a petition to
the same effect from a " large body of merchants " (25.viii.12).   The
Ayuntamiento of Trinidad wrote to the Prince Regent (10.ix.12) that " it is
to be feared that a conspiracy of the slaves may occur owing to the dangerous
information they receive from the Spanish Mainland nearby ".   When,
after Bolívar's successes, there came Bolívar's failures, the British Government grew nervous, and Bathurst wrote to Sir Ralph Woodford, Governor
of Trinidad (28.xi.13), expressing his surprise that the attack on Guiria
could have been prepared in Trinidad " by the common enemy ", insisting
that neutrality must be respected and that Guiria must be returned to the
Spaniards, a measure to be explained to Monteverde on the ground of the
conviction of the British Government that the expedition against Guiria
was composed principally of Frenchmen acting under the French revolutionary flag.   On October 16th, 1813, Bathurst says: " I trust the
measure . . . will have the effect of proving to the royalist party (what I
am concerned to state that they may hitherto have had occasion to doubt)
that H.M.G. are determined to adhere to the neutrality which they have
uniformly professed ".   But events moved quicker than did the attitude of
the British Government in their endeavour to catch up with them; and on
February 10th, 1814, Bathurst wrote again to the Governor of Trinidad
approving his hesitation to act in the matter of returning Guiria to the
Spaniards, in view of the progress of the insurgents.

Mariño was fortunate: his enemy helped him better than his friends.
Cervériz, on hearing the insurgents had taken Maturin, sent against them
an officer, Don Antonio Zuazola, who behaved even worse than his chief.
" From the day he left Cumaná, he began to burn houses and grain lofts
belonging to the peaceful inhabitants, to mutilate and murder persons, till
desperation made them all flock to Maturin, where without distinction of
age or sex, they shut themselves up swearing to die rather than surrender."
Thus these upstart chiefs appointed by Monteverde were fostering the spirit
of independence which the separatist leaders had been unable to arouse.
Cervériz had promised a *peso fuerte* for every ear of an insurgent.   During
the enquiry made in 1813 on this campaign, a witness said " that they brought
out many persons who were hidden in the estates and they mutilated and
killed them ".   Another one, " that he himself was busy in ferreting out
hidden persons, who were beheaded, and that, on a wounded man being
found, they informed Zuazola, who ordered him to be killed there and then ".
Another one, that " in the hills and within the city those who surrendered
were murdered; a wounded man was found in a ranch and murdered; and
in Cumaná the peso offered was not paid to them in spite of the many ears
they had sent ".   The Catalans displayed the ears on their hats.

But these cruel Spaniards had their allies among the Venezuelans themselves.   Monteverde's adviser and instigator was a Caracas barrister,
Oropesa.   Cumaná under a Cumanese Governor was driven to despair.
The *Alcalde* of Cumaná wrote to the Governor: " The political chief
continues openly to spread the spirit of discord in order to set up a

party with arbitrariness and terrorism." The same opinions were aired by the military Governor in his letter to the Regency: "Seven hundred and more men compose the army sent against the eastern insurgents. More than eight hundred go to the south, and every other military post is garrisoned. All these forces are Cumanese, with hardly a hundred Europeans to help them. And how could the paltry one hundred and fifty Catalans who make up the Ferdinand VII Corps, taking no more trouble than to cover the main square, sleeping at home within sight of their shops, run counter to, and crush with their resentments, the loyalty of those who forsake their properties and families in order to expose their lives in the army ? "

Such were the methods whereby Monteverde was preparing the loss of the province. Mariño was no longer in need of foreign help; the persecuted and the thirsty for vengeance increased daily. Maturin was to be the first outstanding triumph in his campaign. Monteverde was heavily defeated (27.v.13), losing fifteen officers and nearly all his European troops; he himself was able to escape alive thanks to his *zambo* orderly Palomo, for " the insurgents would not shoot at coloured men ". His sinister adviser, the Canarian physician Antonio Gómez, fled to Trinidad and never returned to the country he had done so much to ruin.

5

During April and May, a series of dissensions with Castillo held up Bolívar's plans. In the end Castillo resigned; and his resignation was accepted by Congress. Bolívar received the order to advance on Mérida and Trujillo (7.v.13); but Congress enjoined him to swear fidelity to the Government of New Granada and to restore the provincial authorities displaced by Monteverde; a committee of three, appointed by Congress, was to take all necessary measures to that effect in the liberated territories.

Monteverde had no clear idea of the best way to use troops in Venezuela. No one had. The peculiar strategy which the geo-political circumstances of the country required was actually being evolved during these civil wars. He had a good frontier—the Andes; a good base—the rich province of Caracas; but few men and poor communications. Colonel Correa with seven hundred men held the chief gate into Venezuela in La Grita, where he controlled the passes from the Magdalena valley, and the approaches to the Maracaibo lake and to the Apure river. Farther north, Captain Cañas barred the way to Trujillo with five hundred men. Captain Oberto, with one thousand men, was entrenched in the high ground of Barquisimeto, with the port of La Vela de Coro behind. These positions built up a kind of vanguard line behind which Tiscar commanded fifteen hundred men in Barinas, Izquierdo twelve hundred in San Carlos and Yáñez nine hundred in Guasdualito, on the Apure. Finally Monteverde had in Caracas about seven hundred men.

Bolívar was determined to break through all these forces with about six hundred and fifty men. What was his secret ? Speed and terror. First speed. On May 7th he wrote to the Executive of the Union stating his plan and his requirements. His plan is clear: Mérida and Trujillo first, then straight on to Caracas. He feels confident of "being able to appear before Caracas with no more munitions than we have, if we act rapidly ", but should time be given for the enemy to reorganize, the ammunition would be wasted in vain. He begs for freedom of action, even beyond Mérida and Trujillo; and, in exchange, he offers that a committee of two or three army officers should be appointed with whom he would consult on all operations. This paper evinces the executive clear-cut mind and the no less clear will of a great leader.

Next to speed, terror. In March, 1813, when Bolívar and Castillo, still on fairly good terms, were preparing their joint expedition to Venezuela, Dr. Antonio Nicolás Briceño, Bolívar's one-time neighbour, came to submit to them a sinister document he had published in Cartagena (16.i.13). This was the famous War to the Death plan. This document, drafted by Briceño and signed mostly by French adventurers, is far more mercenary than sanguinary. Out of its fifteen articles no less than six bear on how to squeeze money out of well-to-do Spaniards for the private benefit of the officers and men of the expedition; and such is the haste of the would-be liberators to liberate themselves from poverty that article 6 stipulates that, " in order to fulfil these conditions the more punctually, the said property shall be distributed in every city entered by the republican troops without delay, except when prevented by the need of leaving at once in pursuit of the enemy ". Article 2 said: " As this war has for its first and chief aim to destroy in Venezuela the accursed race of European Spaniards, including the Islanders, they must be debarred from joining the expeditionary force, however patriotic and sound they may seem, since not a single one must remain alive." Article 9 ran: " The fact of presenting a number of heads of European Spaniards, including Islanders, shall be deemed sufficient to deserve reward and a commission in the army; so that any private, on presenting twenty heads of the said Spaniards, shall be promoted effective ensign; if thirty, lieutenant; if fifty, captain; and so forth." This paper was endorsed, curiously enough, in French, and signed by eight comrades in arms of Briceño, two of whom were Venezuelans and six French.*

Bolívar and Castillo did not reject the plan outright. They adopted it, though with unimportant amendments; all but Article 2 " insofar as it aims at killing all European Spaniards, for, *for the time being*, this will only be done with regard to those found armed, while the others, who may appear blameless, shall be made to follow the army so that they can be watched, pending the approval or disapproval of the general Congress of New Granada, to which the war-to-the-death document shall be sent ". Article 9 was therefore also held up. Even so limited, however, the decision was a serious breach of the laws of war and of the law of nations, which put the two leaders on a level with the infamous Cervériz and the murderous Zuazola.

Arguments as to who began are irrelevant, for in fact there are no two separate parties, but only two sides of one and the same people: Spaniards

* " French ", however, in those parts and days was apt to mean " French-speaking Negroes ".

and Creoles on both sides. The theme of " death to the enemy " recurs time and again throughout the centuries. Xedler—to begin somewhere— giving as his parting instructions to the Creoles of Potosí to exterminate the Biscayans; D. Francisco de León, defining his task as " the expulsion of the Basques till not one man of this race remains in the province "; Condor-canqui claiming to have received from Charles III a commission to " hang, behead and destroy the lot " of those who would not join him; Matos, a close friend of Bolívar, advocating in 1808 the extermination or expulsion of all European Spaniards. We read in Heredia that it became proverbial towards 1808 among European extremists that the darkies were loyal and the white Creoles revolutionary, and that therefore it was necessary to make an end of the whites. In 1810 José Felix Ribas tried to induce the blacks to rebel " in order to exterminate the whole European caste and to seize absolute control over Caracas ". All this happened before Cervériz and Zuazola committed their atrocities on the eastern front—but it might equally well have been the other way about.

What about Bolívar himself ? The tendency was as strong in him as in any man of his blood, upbringing and political attitude. The *mestizo* in him was bound to feel the complex emotions which often led to anti-Spanish hatred. But the Spaniard in him was enough to arouse such fierce wars against his brethren, without the help of his Indian blood. At about the same time, Espoz y Mina, the Navarrese hero of the wars against Napoleon, issued a proclamation to the effect that " in Navarra, a war of Extermination, without quarter, is declared against the French Army, without distinction of soldiers or chiefs not excepting the Emperor of the French ". Bolívar's tendency to a war of extermination must therefore not be explained away or rationalized, since it was but too natural in him. Cultivated and heightened by Ribas during their campaigns and in Curaçao, it had become for him a real obsession since the loss of Puerto Cabello, caused by the rebellion of a handful of Spanish prisoners. Being natural, this tendency knew neither cause nor reason. Bolívar had to rationalize it and give it currency by attributing it to some cause or other: now reprisals, now policy. But the critic and student should not believe that if Bolívar killed Spaniards in August it was just because Monteverde or Cervériz or Zuazola or Boves had killed Creoles in July. Such a view of the facts of History is puerile. It robs the history of great men of its greatness, which is its tragic sense. The fact is that Bolívar found Briceño's plan to his taste. Death to the Spaniard ? Good!

But Bolívar was no Zuazola, no Boves. He was a man with a mind. He saw that the plan should be tempered till he was free to act as he pleased in his own country. Hence his " for the time being ". He saw that the offering of military promotion to the highest price in Spanish heads was as foolish as it was odious; but that, once purged of its absurdities, the plan would expedite his campaign by driving terror into many Spaniards and inducing them to abandon the fight. Urdaneta, so often his companion in arms, formulated it with the utmost clarity: " From this two necessary consequences flowed: the Spaniards, knowing they would find certain death, would be cowed, as actually happened; and the Creoles would flock to Bolívar's arms, as it was necessary they should. The result, the occupation of Caracas, fully justified the measure." Bolívar himself declared it so in a letter to Santander (1.xi.19): " Remember the violent springs I had to set in motion to obtain the few means which keep us alive; to bind to us four guerrillas, which contributed to our liberation, it was necessary to declare war to the death." Such then was Bolívar's conscious aim in declaring war to the death. That is why he reduced it to Spaniards actually caught armed. He thus satisfied his two passions at the same time: terror was serving speed.

6

While Castillo was on his way towards the positions occupied by Correa in La Grita, he heard that Briceño, technically his subordinate officer, had issued a proclamation declaring war to the death on all Spaniards and offering freedom to all slaves who should murder their masters, if Spanish. " It was his object, as he himself said, to terrorize them into leaving the territory of Venezuela." To this effect he beheaded the only two Spaniards he found in San Cristóbal, two old men of over eighty. One of them had been his own host. Briceño sent the heads to Bolívar and to Castillo with letters, the first line of which was written with his victims' blood. Castillo answered on the very evening (9.iv.13) protesting indignantly and insisting that no punishment should befall an accused man without the forms of law. Bolívar raised two objections: forms of law had not been respected, and the authority of the commanding chief had been disregarded. There was no protest as to cruelty. Here are his own words. " Henceforth you shall on no account shoot or carry out any other major sentence without first putting before me the proceedings to be regularly established in accordance with the laws and orders of the government of the Union. I note your proclamation, which you must send me before issuing it, for these acts are of my exclusive jurisdiction; were every commander to assume the prerogatives of the commander-in-chief, the army would soon sink into total chaos." To judge, however, by a later answer from Briceño, the possibility of a later protest from Bolívar on grounds of cruelty should not be altogether excluded.

Castillo took La Grita without difficulty (13.v.13), for Correa was in full retreat towards Mérida where he hoped to establish a fairly solid position in line with his colleagues of Trujillo and Barinas. It was at this moment that Castillo held his war council in Bolívar's absence to protest against an advance beyond Mérida, and later resigned. The command of the Granadine contingent fell to a young officer: Francisco de Paula Santander. Bolívar, realizing that the situation was dangerous, went to La Grita, where he was received in an ambiguous way by the young commander at the head of his troops. Bolívar ordered Santander to advance. Santander demurred. Whereupon Bolívar said harshly: " There is no alternative. Either you shoot me or I shoot you." Santander was dismissed and the army advanced under Urdaneta.

Bolívar moved on towards Mérida on Correa's heels; but the Spanish commander resolved to withdraw again. Heredia will tell us why. The population of the whole region of Mérida and Trujillo had been subjected to the vexations of the authorities on the slightest suspicions: " Colonel Correa, a just and moderate man, who had caused none of these evils, unable to avoid them, realized that he could not resist in a country where it was but natural that the very stones should rise against the Spaniards ". Hardly had Correa withdrawn from Mérida than the city proclaimed its independence from Spain mostly under the leadership of a European Spaniard, Don Vicente Campo Elías, who was the purest example of civil war to the death that can be found: " I should destroy all Spaniards "—he used to say— " and then shoot myself so that not a single man remain of this accursed race."

Bolívar entered Mérida on May 30th and put it under the civil governorship of Don Cristóbal de Mendoza, who had been President of the Caracas Executive. Declaring that " he had instructions from the Congress of New Granada to restore the Venezuelan constitution ", he organized the Executive Government of the Province (5.vi.13), but took care to lay down that " in all matters pertaining to the war, [Mendoza] would receive his orders direct from the Commander-in-Chief as if they emanated from this sovereign authority ". While in Mérida, Bolívar received the news that Briceño, who had broken loose from his command, had been defeated on his way to Guasdualito, and caught by the royalists. He issued a proclamation (8.vi.13) in which he painted Spaniards in the blackest colours, oddly enough, comparing them to the Jews: " Fugitive and wandering, as the enemies of the God-Saviour, they see themselves turned out of every place and persecuted by all men "—a parallel which, in the light of events closer to us, throws some light on the method under Bolívar's madness. He recalled how the Spaniards had " violated the sacred law of nations in Quito, La Paz, Mexico, Caracas, and lately in Popayán "—then went on to accuse them of having made " frightful carnage of our war prisoners and our peaceful countrymen " in Barinas. " But these victims shall be avenged. These executioners shall be exterminated. Our kindness is exhausted, and since our oppressors forced us to a deadly war, they shall disappear from America and our land shall be freed from the monsters which infest it. Our hatred shall be implacable and the war shall be to the death."

In referring to the " carnage of our prisoners in Barinas ", Bolívar was anticipating and assuming that Briceño and his accomplices would be summarily shot. But they were judged by a court-martial, " not devoid of equity for those days ", and, such death sentences as there were, were just. One man was set free, two sentenced to serve in the royalist army, two received ten years; and eight, including Briceño, were sentenced to death and died courageously. Bolívar received the news when he was already in Trujillo (14.vi.13). Leaving it to one of his lieutenants, Girardot, to pursue Cañas, who with a royalist force was hurrying westwards to Barquisimeto, Bolívar began at once to prepare his march forward to Caracas. But on the night of June 14th–15th, he drafted the most famous and infamous of his proclamations. Short of its rhetoric, and reduced to its principles, this proclamation sentenced to death all Spaniards who would not " actively and effectively " co-operate with the patriots against Spain; while offering to treat as Americans those who should pass to the republican cause; and promised a general pardon to all Americans whatever their actions against the patriotic cause. Its conclusion was: " Spaniards and Canarians, be sure of death even when neutral, unless you act effectively for America's liberty. Americans, be sure of life, even if guilty."

There is a copious literature to justify this utterance; many have endeavoured to explain it by exaltation, excitement, passionate desire to avenge events of far away and long ago. Nothing of the kind bears any relation to the facts. Those who would explain it by opposing to it similar utterances by Cervériz or other ferocious royalist leaders forget that anything these men said or did was local, personal, more or less unruly or tolerated or put up with by their chiefs, but with no official or general character. At no time were such deeds perpetrated without the constant protest of the *Audiencia*, never tired of proclaiming the law which condemned them. *For the first time in the Venezuelan civil war, Bolívar made a law of the war of extermination.* This legal and general character of the Trujillo decree was the new factor for which Bolívar was responsible. He had been travelling towards it in his mind ever since Cartagena, Curaçao, perhaps Puerto Cabello. We know all the stages. He is avenging nothing—for if he were, why except from it the guilty Americans? He is taking no reprisals. He is carrying out a policy which he proclaimed necessary in his letter to the Congress of New Granada (27.xi.12), and in his Memoir of December 15th. By his proclamation Bolívar opened a gulf between the Creoles and the Spaniards; he cut hard through the flesh and the spirit of that nation, till then formed of two kinds of Spaniards closely allied by ties of family, friendship and interests; and of the wound, poisoned by hatred, he made a political frontier. They belittle him who merely set him off against Cervériz, Zuazola and the others. Though he himself will use such arguments to suit his purpose, he acted of his own accord, led by an ancestral fire and by the unconquerable drive of a hard soul, cutting a merciless road through the hearts of men towards his historic goal.

CHAPTER XXI

BOLÍVAR'S FIRST TRIUMPH

I

BOLÍVAR'S proclamation of war to the death implied a double act of indiscipline. He was still the subordinate officer of the Government of the Union; he issued this proclamation without consulting the Government as to whether they approved this kind of war, or even knowing whether he would be authorized to carry on the war at all. New Granada was passing through another crisis. Santa Marta had been recovered by the royalists, who threatened Cartagena. The Union was loth to disperse its troops. But Bolívar's dilemma was clear: either stay in Trujillo, allowing Monteverde to regroup his forces and counter-attack, probably with a stronger army than his; or else rush forward and risk all for all. With his usual courage, he wrote to Congress: " My decision therefore is to act with the utmost speed and vigour; to fly on to Barinas and wipe out the forces defending it, thus leaving New Granada free from the enemies who might overcome it."

The military merits of these campaigns are a technical matter. The fighting units were small; the intelligence scrappy; the commissariat nearly non existent. The campaign was more in the style of guerrilla warfare on both sides. The outstanding merit of Bolívar at this time was his drive, his purpose, his tenacity, his speed, the clarity of his conception and the courage of his resolution. His situation seemed far from bright. Miyares was still in Maracaibo, and Ceballos in Coro, provinces that had never wavered from the Spanish cause; on his right, Tizcar, in Barinas, might still have, for all he knew, the 2,600 men Monteverde had put under his orders to recover New Granada. And there was Monteverde behind it all, with whatever troops he had—which Bolívar probably did not know.

In fact, the situation was more favourable than he thought. " Monteverde " —writes Heredia—" returned to Caracas towards the beginning of June [i.e. about the time Bolívar entered Mérida] leaving the remainder of the army of Barcelona under the command of General Cagigal. . . . He arrived unexpectedly on a dark and stormy night, despite which more than 400 persons, who had returned to their houses attracted by the confidence the persecuted felt in the behaviour of Tiscar [the temporary Governor], went to sleep in the open out of the city as soon as they heard of Monteverde's arrival, for fear he might inaugurate his return with a general imprisonment." In his suite, the defeated Captain General brought " as chaplain and steward a degenerate capuchin of the Apure Missions, Father Coronil, who by his manners and speech, seemed rather a brigand than a Franciscan ". Heredia goes on to say that once in San Carlos, Coronil " exhorted the soldiers to leave no one alive above seven years of age ", which brought an instant protest from two other friars, " to rub out that impression in the ignorant men, who, being brown-coloured needed but little encouragement to kill white people ".

Gay and irresponsible in the days of his success, Monteverde showed no mettle in adversity. He had few men, but Bolívar had fewer still. He had lost the heart and trust of many people, but the country was still, despite his criminal behaviour, overwhelmingly Spanish. He lost a month in Caracas apparently stunned by the successes of his rival. During this month of June, Bolívar took Trujillo, reorganized its government, regrouped and refreshed his armies, and left Trujillo (28.vi.13) towards Guanare, a bold move to prevent the enemy from cutting his communications with New Granada by outflanking him. By a brilliant combined operation with Ribas, he cleared the triangle Mérida–Trujillo–Barinas in less than five weeks, and took Barinas on July 6th.

2

This same day (6.vii.13), Monteverde left Caracas for Valencia to collect some troops and sent Colonel Izquierdo to San Carlos to the south and Captain Oberto to Barquisimeto to the south-west. These two men were competent officers and prepared themselves for defence; but Monteverde went on wasting his time in small intrigues, fear of conspiracies and petty persecutions. Heredia records that in Valencia, " believing it a measure of security, a number of persons were imprisoned without informing the judicial authorities, and were deposited in the Hospital . . . every Islander and Biscaian had the pleasure of leading to prison in person his particular enemy . . . so that, on being free again, as they soon were, with the wound of their insult yet fresh, they became the instigators of the cruel vengeance which sullied the American name in the subsequent phase ". To which words the aggrieved Creole adds: " The first victims were some of the keenest promoters of these arrests, who were unwise enough to remain in the city and appear before Bolívar with their tricolour cockade. Bolívar had them shot the very day, despite all entreaties, and the poor wretches paid with no less than their lives the silly satisfaction they had enjoyed four or five days earlier."

Such was, in fact, the speed of Bolívar's advance. Technically, his plan was not sound. He had divided his troops dangerously, sending Ribas through El Tocuyo towards Barquisimeto while he and Urdaneta went through Araure towards San Carlos, and Girardot was marching towards them from Nutrias on the Apure. Considerable mountains separated the two chief bodies of his troops. Had Monteverde preserved any generalship, he could have destroyed Bolívar. Speed was of course an asset as well as a risk. In this case, Bolívar's speed was not merely due to military strategy; there was political strategy in it as well. Bolívar's notions of Mariño's progress in Cumaná were vague; but all he heard filled him with impatience. On July 25th he wrote to the President of the Union: " I fear that our illustrious companions in arms, those of Cumaná and Barcelona, may free our capital before we are able to be there and share this glory; but we shall fly and I hope that no liberator will tread the ruins of Caracas before I do."

When Bolívar wrote these words, the last but one real battle of the campaign had been fought and won by Ribas against Oberto whom he defeated in Los Horcones, between Barquisimeto and El Tocuyo (22.vii.13). Bolívar occupied San Carlos without a shot; and within two days, at Tinaquillo, defeated Monteverde's second, Izquierdo, who lost his life (31.vii.13). Monteverde wrote to Colonel Fierro, whom he had left in command at Caracas, that "owing to Izquierdo's defeat, he was left without troops, so that he had to abandon Valencia and perhaps the whole province, and go to Puerto Cabello which was defenceless", and added: "You can, if you so think, put yourself in the best state of defence, for the enemy will go straight to that city." In Valencia, "August 1st dawned in the utmost confusion. Drums rolled everywhere and the Europeans and Canarians, so brave in peace time that they had formed themselves into a cavalry corps, thought of nothing but flight; while the *zambos*, belauded as most faithful, ran about everywhere so drunk that it was feared they might begin their exploits by murdering the whites and looting their homes".

So writes Heredia: "A contingent of five to six hundred men, in the time it takes to travel from Barquisimeto to Valencia, having shot barely 200 cartridges without a single township rising in their favour before their arrival, and without having to reach Caracas, nor even La Victoria, destroyed the national government." Bolívar's plan had succeeded. His rapid victory, so similar to that of Monteverde the previous year, had been due to the same cause: a fluctuating political situation, apt to follow the fate of the party that won in the field; a military situation no less shifty; and the gross error and incompetence of the authorities—republican in 1812, royalist in 1813.

3

In the case of Bolívar, however, his progress had been greatly accelerated by the terror he announced in his proclamations and by the ruthless way in which he applied it. This factor is vividly brought to light by Heredia. He recalls how, when Fierro, acting Captain General, received Monteverde's news, he called a Junta to inform the remaining civic and Church authorities of the situation. "The surprise caused by the news, when we did not even know that the insurgents had entered San Carlos, is difficult to describe. We all looked at each other, considering our own situation, seeing our own ruin as unavoidable; and while our imagination was thus busy it was not easy for reflection to deliberate with serenity." Fierro was asked what military forces he could count on. There were three hundred regulars and six hundred voluntary soldiers, but "among the former, many were Creoles who could not be trusted overmuch, while the latter, intent on saving their interests and family, were leaving the service". A Captain Bengoa declared himself ready to fight with the three hundred regulars against twice their number. But it was decided to negotiate.

Fierro left Caracas on August 4th at eight in the morning, a few hours before Bolívar entered La Victoria. The Fiscal of the *Audiencia*, in his report, condemns him as a coward, arguing that he should have stayed to represent one of the two parties to the capitulation. There is some force in this view, which has been generally followed since. But Heredia writes: " The Governor could have done nothing else. As soon as the Junta meeting was over, the brave volunteers of the Fernando VII battalion had endeavoured to escape to La Guaira feeling already in their throats the knife with which Bolívar had threatened them. Even those who were on duty left their posts that very afternoon, and forty or fifty arrived in Curaçao with guns and cartridge pouches. . . . A man is known to have arrived in this guise as far as Havanna. As soon as the bad characters realized this, they began to run about looting, some of them armed with the guns found in the guard rooms." The effect of Bolívar's policy of terror is plain.

The Junta had appointed as its delegates Casa León, Iturbe (to whom Bolívar owed his life), Dr. Felipe Fermín Paúl (a man who managed to pass from one camp to another with the utmost ease), and a brother of José Felix Ribas, Father Marcos Ribas. Bolívar received them well, was jovial, and offered them, says Bolívar himself, " their lives and property, with absolute oblivion of the past ". And he goes on to say: " But this mission was but a blind to give themselves time to embark in La Guaira·taking away arms and ammunition and to spike their artillery . . . and the wicked men left leaving the Canarians and Spaniards to our just vengeance." Whereupon Bolívar paints a picture of disorder, yet moderation, the key to which is this sentence. " Had it not been for the stock of kindness ever living in Americans, we should have found the capital flooded with blood."

We know from Heredia that what little " moderation " there was on that day was due to the Archbishop. But the pictures drawn by the Fiscal of Caracas and other citizens are terrible enough. " Sons leaving behind their parents, parents their children, husbands their wives, all their interests and fortunes, to flee from the death awaiting them had they remained in the city . . . innumerable families were left behind and sacrificed, in Caracas as in La Guaira and the cities inland, who, as we were told later, were ignominiously murdered, or shut up in prisons and vaults with the fiercest inhumanity."

This is not quite the picture painted by Bolívar. But Bolívar was a man of action, for whom statements were tools. He had so ably used false reports as to his strength that many royalists had come to believe he had a force of 17,000 men, about ten times what he actually had. From La Victoria he wrote to the Government and *Municipio* of Caracas that his motives in granting the capitulation of La Victoria were " to show the universe that in the midst of victory, the noble Americans forget the injuries received and give rare examples of moderation to the very enemies who have violated the law of nations and broken the most solemn treaties. This capitulation shall be religiously respected, to the shame of the perfidious Monteverde and to the glory of the American name ". Only four days before he wrote these words, on entering Valencia, he had ordered a great number of Spaniards to be done to death.

4

On August 6th, 1813, Simón Bolívar aged thirty years and thirteen days, entered Caracas in triumph. Twelve beautiful maidens in white, decked with the national colours, crowned him with laurel and flowers, while the young hero stood in full dress uniform, bareheaded, holding in his hand a baton of command. Through streets of houses in ruins, but gaily decorated, and echoing with enthusiastic acclamations, Simón Bolívar passed for thirty long minutes, drinking fast the heady wine of glory so dangerous for his physical and moral health. While living this unforgettable hour the young leader would perhaps cast a mental glance on that day, September 2nd, 1812, " just eleven months ago ", when he had landed, a fugitive, in Curaçao; or on that day, July 2nd, 1812, " just thirteen months ago ", when he had failed in Puerto Cabello and, with his head in his hands, thought himself unfit to command the humblest private; perhaps even on that day, now distant in a dusty past, when he had sworn on the Sacred Mount to liberate his country from the Spanish yoke. More recent, more pressing, he might think of that morning, " just a few days ago ", when on entering Barinas he had heard that there were also patriots and liberators in the Eastern provinces, and how he had feared that he might arrive late to share with them the glory he was now enjoying alone, as the one and only Liberator.

But when the acclamations died out and the festivities were over, the *Libertador* had to attend to a situation by no means bright. Venezuela was still split into three parts: Maracaibo, Coro and Puerto Cabello were Spanish; Barinas and Caracas were his; Cumaná and Barcelona were under the Liberator of the Eastern Provinces, Santiago Mariño. His writ was law, but only over one-third of the country. He decided that, at least over that third, it would rule unchallenged. This was not an easy task. There were at least three traditions in the country which worked against it: the first was the infatuation of the " federalists " bent on imitating the American Constitution because it invested with an honourable political cloak of foreign make an all too national tendency to localism and anarchy; the second was the " gown-man " tendency to organize the government under republican forms, leaving the military strictly confined to warfare purposes; and the third was the tendency of the upper classes to obey no one but themselves, and of the lower classes to remain attached to the rule of Spain. Finally, Bolívar had to watch over his worst enemy, his own unruly and arbitrary temperament, which at times deprived his words and deeds of all authority.

To counter the federalists, he wrote a long political letter to the Governor of Barinas, an advocate of the old federal constitution, wisely apportioning to him the supreme administration of civil and criminal Justice without appeal, while reserving for himself war, peace, negotiations with foreign powers and finance. On August 9th he issued a Manifesto to appease the gown-men fearful of his dictatorial intentions. " An Assembly of prominent persons, of virtuous and wise men, must be solemnly called together to discuss and sanction the nature of our Government and the magistrates who shall wield its powers in the exceptional and critical circumstances which surround the Republic." Note the " virtuous and wise men ", a Roussellian touch which at once betrays the rootless character of this promise. Bolívar was not necessarily insincere in making it; he probably meant it honestly; but it was a promise wandering in the clouds of his mental skies, which the next winds might and would drive away.

The next sentence ushers in what was to be a long series of dramatic gestures of renunciation and resignation. " The Liberator of Venezuela renounces for ever and formally protests that he will accept no authority but that which may lead our soldiers to the dangers implied in saving the country." The ungrammatical turn of the phrase from the pen of a man so able to express himself clearly, shows that it came from the un-logical levels of his mind. Bolívar was already the dissembling dictator, the Cæsar disguised as a democrat he was all his life to be. A few days earlier, in La Victoria, he had said to his close friend Iturbe: " Have no fears about the coloured people; I flatter them because I need them; democracy on my lips, and aristocracy here "—and he pointed to his heart. And Heredia notes that " meanwhile he assumed the whole military and civil power, publishing laws in his name and on his own authority ". It did not occur to him, nor possibly to anyone else, that he was in fact assuming dictatorial powers on the most important issue of all: that of the constitution of the new government. When he granted full judicial sovereignty to the Governor of Barinas, on whose behalf did he divest—and whom did he divest of such powers; and by whose authority did he hand them over? " A kind of Triumvirate was formed "—Heredia goes on to say—" with José Felix Ribas who came as second in command and took over the military government of Caracas, and Cristóbal Mendoza . . . but always the so-called Liberator retained absolute control as generalissimo, on account of the war. There was no law but his will, nor other principles of justice than massacre and loot."

Under his supreme authority, Bolívar organized three departments of State entrusting them to men well known in the country. As Secretary of State, he appointed Antonio Muñoz-Tebar, who had been second head of the first semi-independent Junta under Llamosas; as Secretary for War, his friend Tomás Montilla, one of the wealthiest of Caraqueños; Bolívar's choice for Justice was not so good; Rafael Diego Mérida " was in Spain at the beginning of the revolution "—writes Heredia—" and though he then returned to Caracas, far from taking a prominent part in it, was persecuted by Miranda, and was under a cloud [among the republicans] owing to the strict way in which he carried out his duties as clerk of the Court, in the trial of the 1798 conspirators ". Heredia reports that Mérida had been imprisoned as a suspect by Monteverde, though there were no grounds for it; and that when freed, " he came out of prison like a wild beast, so that out of vindictiveness he went over to the party of Bolívar whom he served with all the ferocity of his intrepid and sanguinary character ". Bolívar wrote later of him as " a perverse man "; and in 1828, he said: " His nature is accursed by Heaven; it seems as if poison ran in his veins, and the spirit of Satan resided in his mind."

Perhaps as the natural reaction of so strenuous and so successful an exertion, Bolívar at this time let himself go to the pleasures of power. He loved luxury, ease and pleasure as much as any man, and they were then in his reach. He was well surrounded by men all too eager to take upon themselves the task of governing; and, a young hero of thirty, he was the idol of women. One of the twelve maidens who had crowned him with laurel had become his mistress; and this girl, Josefina Madrid or Machado, soon became a power behind the throne. She is described by Ducoudray Holstein as extremely intriguing and vindictive, and, not particularly beautiful. Commenting on Bolívar's growing unpopularity because " he acted as a sovereign and absolute master, following no other law than his own will and caprice ", Ducoudray Holstein goes on to say: " The fair sex, and particularly his favourite mistress Segnorita Josephina Ma— commonly called Segnorita Pepa, had the greatest influence in many nominations."

5

With an adviser such as Mérida, Bolívar's justice could not but suffer. But Bolívar was not a sanguinary man. He was inhuman, indifferent to suffering, and even to human life when necessary in his view. At the time, when the need for terror had ceased, he would have been content to get rid of the Spaniards of Venezuela by emigration. That is perhaps why he promulgated a decree in which he invited foreigners to come and settle in Venezuela. This policy tallies with the generous conditions which he offered all Spaniards wishing to emigrate, in his Capitulation of La Victoria. Bolívar was in earnest about this. He was convinced of the danger which the presence of European Spaniards in the country meant for the Republic as an independent State; and he needed foreign immigration to replace the terrible losses inflicted on the white population of Venezuela by his war to the death. He himself wrote from Caracas to the Congress of New Granada (14.viii.13): " After the battle of Tinaquillo, I advanced without dallying though the cities and *pueblos* of Tocuyito, Valencia, Guayos, Guácara, San Joaquín, Maracay, Turmero, San Mateo y La Victoria, where all Europeans and Canarians, almost without exception, were shot."

Nor was this the worst. For, in the words of Restrepo, who later was Bolívar's Cabinet Minister, and wrote under his eye, " Bolívar was not the only one who ordered European Spaniards and Canarians to be sacrificed, for his subordinate officers went beyond his orders. Colonels Ribas and Arismendi were outstanding champions of War to the Death and believed they increased their glory granting no quarter to any Spaniard or Canarian who fell into their hands. The picture of these murders, if it were possible to draw it in all its horrible details, would make people tremble. But it would be to inflict martyrdom on the sensibility of our readers." José Domingo Díaz confirms what Restrepo says and does not say. " On August 18th, most of the Spaniards and Canarians of Caracas and other townships were imprisoned, and on the 20th the first blood was shed. . . . On that day the factious Ribas gave a banquet in his house to thirty-six guests. At five o'clock Dr. Vicente Tejera, one of them, begged leave to offer a toast, and . . . said they must solemnize the act by every one of the guests drinking the death of a prisoner of his choice. The idea was greeted with acclamation; the list was completed, and within half an hour thirty-six persons perished on the Cathedral Square—among them, Don José Gabriel García, one of the kindest men ever known." Bolívar cannot havé been present at this Banquet of Death; for, had he been present, Díaz, who hated him, would have trumpeted the fact.

In Bolívar's eyes, terror was a weapon, just like propaganda. We are to see him using terror as a catapult to force his way into a city. Monteverde was in Puerto Cabello. Had Bolívar thought in military, rather than in political, terms, had he feared less to lose the race against Mariño, he would have gone to Puerto Cabello before going to Caracas. For Caracas was his, anyhow; while Puerto Cabello could, if given time, be turned by the royalists into a base for reinforcements and supplies. Monteverde lost no time in preparing the city for defence. Bolívar tried to take the city without a fight by a threat of War to the Death. He was at the time receiving entreaties upon entreaties from prominent men of Caracas to refrain from putting to death the Spaniards and Canarians of the capital; he declared he would yield, but in a form which amounted in fact to buying Puerto Cabello with the blood of all these men, more than four thousand of them. His decision was to abide by the Capitulation of La Victoria if Monteverde approved it. Now the Capitulation stipulated that Bolívar was to receive the whole province of Caracas, including, of course, Puerto Cabello and its castle. Bolívar sent Monteverde a Commission composed of four Spaniards and one Venezuelan, Felipe Fermín Paúl. They were to negotiate the ratification of the Convention of La Victoria, which in practice meant the delivery of Puerto Cabello and a general exchange of prisoners; and, adds Restrepo, " lest the negotiation failed to secure Puerto Cabello Bolívar wrote to Monteverde demanding the surrender of the city with everything in it belonging to the State, the only means, he said, to save the innumerable Spanish and Canarian prisoners in his [Bolívar's] power "; and he gave Monteverde to understand " that at the slightest delay all would be exterminated ".

Bolívar sent his commissioners to Monteverde on August 9th, 1813. On the 10th he wrote to the commander in La Guaira: " In spite of previous orders for the deportation of prisoners of war, I order you confidentially to keep under arrest in their houses all Spanish officers; and sergeants and other ranks in the vaults, under the strictest watch. No ship must be supplied nor the exit of a single prisoner allowed." An objective estimate of the episode will be found in the History of Restrepo. " Had Monteverde, without firing a shot, delivered up this bulwark of the Spanish power in Venezuela, he would have added an indelible blot to his poor reputation. No one aware of the laws of the army and of military honour can hold a different opinion." Restrepo is confirmed by no less a witness than Simón Bolívar. In his report to the President of the Congress of Nueva Granada, Bolívar writes: " I have intimated to Monteverde to surrender at once the

City of Puertocabello, handing over everything in it belonging to the State, armament, artillery, munitions, ships, funds and archives. This is the only way left him to save the numberless Spanish and Islander prisoners in my power, and I have made him understand that on the slightest delay they shall all be exterminated." Monteverde was a fool; but he was a brave, indeed a foolhardy, man. He refused to treat on the terms suggested; which placed Bolívar in an awkward position, for he was loth to sacrifice four thousand men. Ortigosa and Linares assured Heredia that " he then still shrank from cold-blooded murder, and sincerely wished to find a way out of the awkward situation in which those wretches put him ". But the awkward situation was of Bolívar's own making. It was his famous proclamation that made him a prisoner of his own words.*

6

In all fairness to the Liberator, due notice must be paid to his youth and inexperience on the one hand—and to the difficulty of the situation on the other. One of his chief merits at this time is the care and skill he bestowed on the training of his army. He had arrived in Caracas a victorious general but with hardly any troops worth the name. This is aptly illustrated by Heredia. After copying a paragraph of Bolívar's proclamation showing his soldiers " like tutelar angels freeing you from the forests, and tearing you from the dungeons where you lay in terror, or laden with ignominious chains ", Heredia adds: " All this is false. The persecution was over when this ferocious army crossed the borders of Venezuela and advanced marking its progress with the death of numberless innocent people. . . . Sequestered property had been handed back, and the only persons in prison, though not in dungeons nor in chains, would have been so in any time under any Government." Then, again, he quotes an enumeration of battles (echoes of the Napoleonic style) " in which ", wrote Bolívar, " five armies totalling ten thousand men have been defeated," and adds: " All this bombastic description contains no more truth than the names of the cities and the speed of the progress which was impressive; but there were neither battles, but only skirmishes and dispersions or withdrawals; nor armies, but tumultuous gatherings of persons without discipline, who, all put together, would not add up to half the number boasted of, and among

---

* Bolívar was apt to land himself in such situations through his fiery character; as shown in his negotiations over Zuazola and Jalón. The murderous Basque chieftain had been caught on September 2nd after a defeat at the hands of the patriots. On Bolívar's orders, Urdaneta, his Chief of Staff, wrote to Monteverde offering an exchange for Jalón, the Spanish-born regular officer who had fought on the side of the patriots. Bolívar offered to exchange other officers; the offer to be accepted within three hours or Zuazola would die. Monteverde refused, though declaring himself ready for exchanges of " persons of equal character "; and threatened to take two American lives for every Spanish life taken by the other side. Bolívar's retort was characteristic: " If the intruding ex-Governor Monteverde is ready to sacrifice two Americans for every Spaniard or Canarian, the Liberator of Venezuela is ready to sacrifice 6,000 Spaniards and Canarians he holds in his power for the first American victim." He had Zuazola hanged. Monteverde respected Jalón's life but shot four other officers. Bolívar held his hand.

whom there never were over 500 trained men." Since Bolívar conquered Caracas with fewer troops than Monteverde had, it follows that he arrived in Caracas with no troops worth speaking of—and certainly with less than five hundred trained men. Yet, we know from the same witness that by December 5th, about four months later, two Spanish divisions were beaten by troops of which Heredia says: " They included the best troops Bolívar had put together in Caracas and the Aragua valleys, were very disciplined and came full of enthusiasm, or else their leaders felt it."

This was Bolívar's greatest achievement during the first weeks of his government. No easy matter, either. The country was devastated and disorganized in its body, split and, on the whole, hostile, in its soul. The negroes of a number of places, including San Francisco de Yare, where Bolívar had an estate, rose and proclaimed their allegiance to Ferdinand VII (26.viii.13). Bolívar decreed the confiscation of the property of all the Spanish émigrés; then a forced loan of 120,000 pesos, to be paid mostly by the lukewarm. He had also counted on voluntary donations, but in this he was so disappointed by Caracas that he wrote to José Felix Ribas (21.ix.13): " The Commander in Chief decides that in this capital forced donations shall be required in proportion to everybody's income; including from Americans whose opinions are contrary to the republican system of Venezuela. Nothing but utter impossibility will be deemed a valid excuse, and by shooting three or four of those who may refuse you will teach obedience to the others."

This was no vain threat. Under suspicion of conspiracy and with no form of trial, he had sixty-nine Spaniards and Canarians shot in a few days, beginning the day he wrote to Ribas (21.ix.13). A few days earlier, on the 17th, Mérida, his Minister of Justice, wrote to Mendoza, the civil Governor of Caracas: " The Commander in Chief of these States has resolved that all European Spaniards and Islanders, with no exception whatsoever, are to be sent to the La Guaira vaults and prisons under due custody and safety. I am directed so to inform you, so that you carry it out strictly." Ribas wrote to the acting Governor of Caracas (15.x.13): " At eight to-morrow you shall imprison all Spaniards who may be at liberty, even those to whom I myself or General Bolívar may have given safe conducts, who shall not merely be imprisoned but secured with iron-fetters." The day before, the Magistrates of Caracas had bestowed on Bolívar the title of *Libertador*. The military situation was none too bright and the ceremony may well have been one of the measures devised to stimulate the zeal of the not too patriotic patriots. Success was not forthcoming. On November 15th, Ribas, Military Governor of Caracas, had the following proclamation posted all over the city: " The Government have seen with utter amazement that the call to arms sounded this morning had no effect whatever. . . . The call to arms shall be repeated this afternoon, at four, and anyone not present on the Main Square or in the Capuchin Canton, or found at home or in the street, shall be shot with no more than three hours of chapel, and no other justification than that needed to prove his absence."

Such were the methods by which the liberty of Venezuela had to be fostered.*

The first impression of these facts on the mind is that the ideals for which the rich leaders fought had but little to do with the desires of the people. This, however, did not necessarily condemn the rich. If unwise in their separatist imperious haste, from the point of view of world structure, they were wise in their desire to raise the standard of self-government and of freedom. But the trouble was far deeper than the mere duel—Spanish rule versus separatism—to which it is usually confined. The trouble, as time was soon to show, came from the fact that Venezuela had entered a period of chaos as the outcome of the weakening or disappearance of the only force capable of balancing the anarchical tendencies of the individual—the monarchy. The tradition, the weight of the State, the depth of the religious and historical roots of the system, had kept the country in peace and placidity, and every man quiet and self-controlled; when the imposing edifice fell to the ground by the combined effects of Napoleon's aggression and of local disaffection in the leaders, the dispersive forces of all individuals gave themselves free play. *Venezuela fell the victim of chieftains who pulled this way and that, as ambition and opportunity allowed. That they fought for or against Spain was of secondary importance. The main point is that they all fought each for himself.* Bolívar, Briceño, Mariño, Monteverde, the Indian Reyes Vargas, the priest Torrellas, the Catalan Millet, Carlos Blanco were but the first in the field of a series of unruly, undisciplined captains of fortune, scaling the slopes of power which the fall of the monarch had left vacant for any man to seize. Some took a republican, some a royalist flag. Some passed from one flag to the other. The political chaos reflected itself in their individual souls, giving rise to lawlessness and untold cruelty. Soon one of the most vigorous of them was to take the field, to devastate the land and to oust Bolívar from Caracas.

* " During more than two hundred and fifty years "—writes the Frenchman Depons— " Spain has possessed the province of Venezuela and its dependencies, without sustaining its authority with troops of the line." And the Venezuelan José Domingo Díaz says that " from 1787, when the *Audiencia* was set up in our country [till the end of the Spanish rule] the death penalty was inflicted only on eleven persons, fully convicted of cruel murders ".

CHAPTER XXII

THE FIRST DICTATORSHIP

I

THE man known in Venezuelan history as Boves, whose real name was José Tomás Bobes y de la Iglesia, born in Oviedo, capital of the Principality of Asturias in Old Spain, on September 18th, 1782, was ten months older than Bolívar. His father was a modest clerk in the municipal offices of the city; his mother was a foundling, as her name, " of the Church ", reveals. He lost his father when he was five, and his mother was left with two daughters and a boy to bring up on no income whatever. She worked as washerwoman and domestic help, and later settled in Gijón, where young José Tomás, thanks to his mother's thrift and devotion, was able to enter the *Instituto Real Asturiano*, where he learnt mathematics and seamanship, and finally obtained his pilot's certificate for the merchant navy. Young Boves, however, aimed higher. He left Gijón for Ferrol, where, after further study, he successfully passed the examinations for the Royal Navy.

It is almost certain that he got into trouble, probably for protecting contraband instead of checking it; for he left the service in Coruña, to take command of a merchant brig, the *Ligero*, which plied between the Peninsula and Trinidad. At this time, Boves paid his mother a yearly pension. After two years in command of the *Ligero*, he went ashore and became correspondent of the shipping firm in Venezuela; later he settled on his own in Calabozo, where he developed a business in mules and horses with the Indians of the Plain. He soon acquired among the Indians a reputation for physical force, for he was tall and athletic, as well as for fair and honest dealing. He was generally known by the natives as *Taita*, meaning father and chief. Gradually, the pilot ashore fell in love with the horses he dealt in. He lived close to the emerald green plains where the *Llaneros* lived a free and natural life. Soon he overmastered those masters of horsemanship, and gave himself over to the more active part of his business, the getting and convoying of the horses and mules, leaving its sedentary side to an old, loyal Indian.

Fate then provided the provocation which was to transfigure this horse-dealer into a powerful cavalry chieftain and a monster of cruelty. Towards the end of 1812, Escalona (who, in 1809, had initiated the ill-treatment of prisoners in La Guaira) entered Calabozo with a recruiting party. Some of the men broke into Boves' store and summoned him to join up. He refused, whereupon they overpowered him and, bound hand and foot, conveyed him to prison in a cart. Presently, Escalona called on his prisoner, still in shackles, and struck him in the face repeatedly. Venezuela was to pay dearly for those inconsiderate slaps in the face of a spirited man. Meanwhile a number of houses of Spaniards were being broken into by the

republican soldiery, some of whom entered his, murdered the old Indian
storekeeper and looted and gutted the store. The royalist Indian chieftain
Reyes Vargas arrived on the scene and saved Boves' life. Boves offered his
services to Monteverde and was granted a commission as a cavalry captain
with the task of recruiting a squadron of lancers among his customers.

In a matter of days the new captain was in Calabozo at the head of eight
hundred lancers—and what lancers! Men of the soil, still in the pastoral
stage of civilization, true Spanish grafts onto the Indian stem and root,
forming with their horses a single being in perfect unison; men who fed on
meat hardly roasted and slightly salted, wild honey and draughts of sour
milk; who slept on the earth with their saddles for pillows, or, if trees were
available, on hammocks. The *Llaneros* were the finest raw material for
cavalry that could be found in the world. They should have been a godsend
to Monteverde in those early days of 1813, when Bolívar was preparing his
raid on Caracas. But he was not able to do anything with them. It is
generally reported that he was content with appointing Boves military
commander of Calabozo, and that Boves sent away most of his men, keeping
only a few for his garrison. The episode is obscure; but the most reasonable
explanation is that Monteverde, who had risen through indiscipline, felt
uneasy in the presence of a man at the head of so many accomplished
horsemen—and managed to get rid of the force.

As military commander in Calabozo Boves discovered in Espino, a *pueblo*
on the Orinoco, a plot in support of the Mariño rebellion. He began to
show signs of his cruel nature by submitting his victims to a torture of his
invention: he had them " executed " with blank shot. The population
grew tired of his arbitrary ways and obtained (we may be sure, without
difficulty) that Monteverde should send him to serve under Cagigal, then
operating against Mariño and Bideau. This was to be the beginning of a
rivalry due to qualities and defects on both sides; for Cagigal was a good
regular officer with European notions of generalship, an enlightened man,
contemptuous of loot and cruelty; while Boves was a wild rough rider,
generous enough personally but who delighted in loot and blood.

2

In point of cruelty, Boves had a rival in the other camp: Arizmendi.
In Arizmendi's case, it began also with undeserved and inhuman ill-
treatment undergone at the hands of his enemies. He had been leader of
the local movement that in the Island of Margarita had seconded the Junta
founded in Caracas on April 19th. When Margarita set up its own Junta
(4.v.09), Arizmendi became Commander of Arms. When, in 1811, the
Republican Government sent an expedition to Guayana, he became the
leader of the Margaritan contingent. All this weighed heavily against him
when the Island fell under the sway of Pascual Martínez. This man was
a Spanish sergeant who, soon after being promoted a lieutenant, had crossed
the line and become an insurgent or patriot, then turned coat again on
personal grounds. He had served under Monteverde during the raid from

Coro to Caracas and distinguished himself for his prowess against the defenceless when the battle was over. He was nevertheless promoted Governor of Caracas, where he behaved abominably. Possibly to send him away from the capital, Monteverde gave him the governorship of Margarita.

Arizmendi, Commander of the Militia of Whites or Spaniards, a " moderate man of peaceful ways ", having taken up arms for the Republic, feared for his life. He took refuge in one of his own estates inland. Martínez seized his young children and threatened to shoot them if their father did not come out of hiding. Arizmendi gave himself up. He was conveyed to the vaults of La Guaira and his wife and children were turned out of their home and reduced to utter poverty. The *Audiencia* took up the fight on behalf of all these persecuted Margaritans and succeeded in setting most of them free—including Arizmendi. The Margaritans had not till then taken sides in the civil war going on in the Mainland; but Arizmendi, while still in La Guaira, led a conspiracy against Martínez. He made the mistake of returning to the Island, where Martínez promptly put him in prison again, having perhaps had wind of the plot. But Martínez left at large far more of his ex-victims than was good for his health. After a phase of submission, during which the plotters procured themselves some weapons, the Island rose against the garrison with so much spirit that the garrison had to surrender on June 13th, 1813. Arizmendi had twenty-nine of them murdered on the spot.

This rebellion was a godsend for Mariño who, after a brilliant campaign, had forced the Spanish forces to shut themselves up in Cumaná. They were about eight hundred men with forty guns. To besiege them adequately Mariño needed a sea force. Margarita was an island of fishermen. They provided a few small ships and their crews; commanded by an Italian adventurer, Giuseppe Bianchi, who promoted himself *Admiral*. The Governor of Cumaná, Antoñanzas, and his second, the Venezuelan Quero (who had been Governor of Caracas under Miranda and turned coat), pretended to negotiate but managed to get away (2.viii.13). Antoñanzas was wounded and died of his wounds in Curaçao. Mariño took Cumaná and one hundred and twenty-two Spaniards were instantly shot. Cervériz, who commanded in Yaguaraparo, withdrew to Angostura, not without first executing one of Mariño's lieutenants, Bernardo Bermúdez de Castro, which again made of the victim's brother, Francisco, a bloodthirsty monster. Mariño sent his second, Piar, to Barcelona, where Cagigal had withdrawn after a skilful campaign with inferior troops. But, on hearing of the fall of Caracas, Cagigal had decided to withdraw towards the Orinoco and Guayana (19.viii.13). Two of his lieutenants, Boves and Morales, preferred to stay in the plains. They had discovered something new, for, as Restrepo says, " no one knew yet the importance of the Venezuelan plains ". Bolívar and Mariño knew nothing about it. It was Boves and Morales who discovered the plains. Thanks to these two rough, very rough, Spaniards, true fighting was to begin.

3

Mariño, who no less than Bolívar had adopted the style of *Libertador* and *Dictador*, sent two emissaries to Caracas to inform his colleague of the liberation of the eastern provinces and to negotiate a political agreement.

Bolívar was shrewd enough to realize that the emissaries were sent to inform him just as much of the rise of Mariño in the eastern part of the country as of the fall of the Spanish rule. Once again, the permanent law of Spanish political psychology—that separatism leads to dictatorship—was verified. Separatists from Spain, the two chiefs separated from each other in order to dictate each to his half of the land. The Liberator turned dictator as a matter of course. " For the moment "—writes Restrepo— " no progress could be made in so important a field, for neither of the two supreme chiefs would submit to the other." It seems, however, that they made each other mutual offers of military help, and that Bolívar asked Mariño to send a division urgently to beat the threatening forces being gathered in *Los Llanos*, and to lend him his naval forces to blockade Puerto Cabello.

The siege of this city and harbour was of course the chief military task before Bolívar; but, though he might easily have taken it while he drank the wine of glory in Caracas, by August 20th Monteverde had put it in a good state of defence. By then also Bolívar had to attend to other cares; the Blacks of the Tuy valley were dispersed but by no means defeated; and Boves had inflicted a first defeat on a republican unit in Santa María de Ipire; while the Indian Reyes Vargas, with the partisan priest Torrellas, was harrying his communications with the west. Against so many dangers Bolívar was left with about eight hundred men. Nevertheless, he besieged Puerto Cabello and even tried to take it by surprise on the night of August 31st; an operation not very wisely led, which ended in defeat and losses (particularly of officers) the struggling republicans could ill afford.

On September 13th the Spanish frigate *Venganza*, a naval schooner and six transports with the Regiment of Granada, were in sight off La Guaira. The patriots had had intelligence of their coming. Ribas went to La Guaira to catch the whole expedition by ruse. The Spanish flag was flown and the Spanish Colonel Mármol was brought out from the vaults and terrorized into acting as a decoy for his comrades. He was by then " nearly dying and so much beside himself that he did not know what he was doing ". The chief officer of the frigate, who had landed, noticed " his cadaverous looks and his broken speech ", conceived suspicions of the whole proceedings and hastened to convey them to his chief. The expedition was thereby saved. Received with enthusiasm at Puerto Cabello, these reinforcements nevertheless increased the food crisis. A sortie was deemed necessary; but it was defeated in Naguanagua, on the way to Valencia, an action which did much honour to the patriots since, for the first time, they beat well organized and trained European troops. The patriotic contingent was commanded by a young Granadino, Girardot, who was killed in battle. Bolívar chose to attach much pomp and glory to this event: he decreed one month of mourning for the whole nation, and the solemn burial of Girardot's heart in a special chapel to be built in the Cathedral of Caracas. With a true politician's eye for public opinion, the young dictator sought both to satisfy the feelings of New Granada and to stimulate the patriotism of his own fellow citizens by means of a ceremony in the grand style.

This decree was signed in " Valencia on September 30th, 1813, 3rd year of our independence and first of the war to the death ". Bolívar had adopted this style for all the documents he signed—which clearly showed his grim determination. Obviously he was inclined to the death penalty as the short-cut to securing obedience. He issued a proclamation (6.ix.13) threatening with death all Americans " who joined the Royalists to upset order and public peace ", or even those under vehement suspicion thereof. Also during the siege of Puerto Cabello, he signed a decree sentencing to be shot all those who would defraud the Tobacco Excise, as well as all magistrates " guilty " of having mitigated this penalty through connivance, bias or any other cause. About that time, José Domingo Díaz, anxious for the fate of the prisoners under threat of extermination in the dungeons of La Guaira, had presented a petition with many signatures of Spanish exiles to the Governor of Curaçao, General Hodgson. The Governor wrote to Bolívar who answered in a long document typical of his clear and forceful style and of his disregard of any facts which did not suit him. Thus the execution of Briceño and his companions, a strictly judicial affair, conducted on the whole irreproachably, is presented as one more atrocity on a level with the iniquities of Zuazola and Cervériz.

4

By then, two new Spanish leaders had been recruiting in the Plains: Boves to the east, Yáñez in Barinas. Boves and his lieutenant, Morales, had gathered together about two thousand lancers, whom they had armed with spears made with iron bars torn from windows. This was the force which defeated the patriots in Santa Catalina, between Calvario and Calabozo (20.ix.13). Boves was ruthless with the defeated and allowed his troops to loot the city of Villa del Cura. Bolívar sent against the two Spaniards another Spaniard, Campo Elías, who, after putting together one thousand infantry men and fifteen hundred horse in an incredibly short time, met and defeated Boves at Mosquiteros, close to Calabozo. Campo Elías ordered many executions in Calabozo as a punishment for the help the city had offered Boves, and shot many Creole soldiers caught prisoner in the ranks of the defeated royalists.

Meanwhile Bolívar kept writing optimistic reports to Mariño's commissioners; but the Dictator of the East was not forthcoming. Had the two Liberators acted in concert at this stage, Boves would have been deprived of his freedom of movement in the Plains, caught between Bolívar in the west and Mariño in the east; but, though defeated at Calabozo, Boves was able to gallop away, while Mariño remained passive and expectant, and Bolívar grew more and more careworn at the sight of the Spanish forces being prepared against him in the west. About mid-September, one of Bolívar's commanders, García de Sena, had defeated the royalist Indian, Reyes Vargas, at Cerritos Blancos, not far from Barquisimeto. Ceballos left Coro with three hundred and fifty foot (22.ix.13), but gathered several other contingents on his way to Barquisimeto, till he could count about two thousand men. Bolívar had sent Urdaneta to oppose him; but Urdaneta reported that he would need reinforcements, and Bolívar resolved to bring them in person. Of course, he took command. The battle was fought in the neighbourhood of Barquisimeto (20.x.13), and Bolívar was defeated, his troops fleeing in a panic, leaving on the battlefield four hundred dead and about as many prisoners who, being in the hands of a regular officer, were respected.

But Bolívar's reaction at the defeat was terrible. " After the setback in Barquisimeto "—writes his countryman Juan Vicente González—" Bolívar ordered Ribas from Caracamate *to shoot all Europeans and Canarians and to enlist all the men available in the city of Caracas, especially all young students.* Ribas eluded the death orders, but carried out those concerning the students with formidable impatience." Behind this impatience was the untiring haste and impatience of Bolívar himself. In a few days, another force had been put together. Meanwhile the royalist side was frittering away its strength through lack of one commanding personality. Ceballos' victory had remained fallow. Monteverde sent Salomon (the commanding officer of the Granada regiment come from Spain) to threaten Valencia; but Bolívar, instead of waiting for him, sought him while he was still on the way and ousted him from his positions in Vigirima (25.ix.13). While these events took place in the north, troops in the south and east were converging against Bolívar. Yáñez, with about two thousand five hundred men, had forced the republicans to abandon Barinas (2.xi.13); Ceballos moved from Barquisimeto towards Araure, where a force of over three thousand seven hundred, including eleven hundred horse, was being concentrated. Bolívar was also getting his men together to meet the emergency. His rallying point was San Carlos.

Neither of these " armies " would have passed muster in Europe at the time. Nevertheless, Bolívar's feat was remarkable. Fresh from a galling setback, he had put together the biggest force ever mustered by a republican general (Miranda's army at San Carlos excluded) through long marches in forbidding and often hostile lands. Araure was, for Ceballos, an excellent spot at the meeting of the valleys of the rivers Acarigua and Sarare; the first leading to the Tocuyo valley, faithful to Spain; the second to the Plains, still a boundless preserve of pro-Spanish cavalry; defeated, he could withdraw safely in either of these two directions; victorious, he could advance to San Carlos in Valencia or even Caracas. There were between San Carlos and Araure numerous *guerrillas*—or, to give them their local name, *montoneras*; and masses of pro-Spanish Indians behind Araure.

This general hostility of the population kept Bolívar blind to his adversary's dispositions. Between December 1st and 4th, 1813, his troops moved on from San Carlos to the Araure Plain; but they were tired after four days of forced marches and he camped to the east of the city. The battle began at five in the morning (5.xii.13), disastrously for the patriots, whose vanguard was all but destroyed. Bolívar was not put out, and by a skilful use of his cavalry succeeded in routing first Ceballos and later the more stubborn Yáñez. By one o'clock the royalists were in flight, some towards Barquisimeto, others towards Guanare. " The enemy "—writes Urdaneta, Bolívar's second in command—" left more than one thousand dead on the battlefield; and as all the Spaniards and Canarians who had so far escaped from the war [to the death, he means], or those who had been let off by some chiefs, were there, many of them, under the terror of defeat, thought that the best way to save themselves was to climb up the trees, wherefrom they were shot down dead. The patriot soldiers, embittered by the heroic death of the battalion of *Valiant Hunters*, gave quarter to not a single man." That evening, the prisoners were shot. Then, Bolívar took a few military dispositions and left for Caracas.

5

In the hour of his triumph, Bolívar was sobered by three orders of problems: the people were with Spain and against him; Mariño refused obedience and even reasonable co-operation; and the military force of the royalists was being rapidly reorganized. His attitude was characteristic of the man: he felt that, provided his power was well established and un-disputed, his victory over obstacles was assured. That faith was to be the secret of his success. Faith not in his cause but in himself; and not in himself as the tool of higher powers—which had been the faith in the eyes of Colón and of Hernán Cortés—but in his own personal self, whose fiery personality shone in his jet black eyes with a mineral, earthly light. Power, more power. And to get it Bolívar, again characteristically, found in his Spanish roots the Cortesian way, and in his European skies the French procedure. He resigned his powers.

He was too much of a realist to be unaware of the fact that, since the people of Venezuela were with Spain and not with the republicans, the young republic had to rest on the Army, a conclusion which suited his pretorian temperament. He therefore worked from the first to establish his hold upon the Army. He was ever careful to keep his chief lieutenants happy. He went as far as to grant one of them, Ribas, a rank in the Army higher than his own. The *Cabildo* (by the way, with no powers whatsoever for such a thing) made him Captain General and gave him the title of *Libertador* (14.x.13); but in his speech of thanks he took care to point out that the true liberators were his officers, of whom he named several, and his troops. Generous and noble, no doubt, and sincerely born of a heart which knew how to be grateful, this attitude was also shrewd and political; for Bolívar was resolved to be the undisputed head of the State, and he knew he could only found his authority on the armed forces. For the same reason he instituted the *Military Order of the Liberators*, which he granted to his army commanders and was later to offer to his rival Mariño.

His correspondence with Mariño shows him at his best; patient, skilful, clear, high-minded and ready to take the risks to which generosity exposes ambition. During November and December, 1813, he wrote often and always in this vein. He was willing to keep the two military establishments separate, but thought it indispensable to unite the nation politically, and advocated that the province should soon elect their representatives who would elect the President. He flatters Mariño and says that " as a reward for the sacrifices of your Excellency and for the victories which had crowned them, I should wish you to become President ". He failed to win Mariño over, because Mariño mistrusted him. Being ambitious himself, he guessed his rival's ambition; and he kept away, under cover of his own army.

After all, it was on his army that Bolívar also relied for his own political authority, now strengthened by his victory over Ceballos, a regular general. By the end of the year, and seeing that all his attempts at union with Mariño had failed, Bolívar thought the time had come to have his dictatorship confirmed by the civic authorities. He called a meeting of all the " civil servants and heads of families " of the city (2.i.14). It was a kind of informal and local parliament, in the style of a Spanish *Junta*. He took the chair and made one of his typical speeches: " I gave you laws, an administration, a government; but I am not the sovereign. I long to hand over my power to your representatives, and hope you will relieve me of an office which someone else among you may worthily hold." Then the Governor of Caracas, Mendoza, moved that Bolívar be confirmed as dictator. Whereupon Bolívar refused: " I have not come to oppress you with my victorious arms. . . . A lucky soldier does not acquire the right to rule over his country . . ." and much more to that effect. (Or, as Bernal Díaz makes Cortés say in similar circumstances: " I don't want that, I don't want that, but drop it into my hat.") Then one Alzuru let the cat out of the bag: " Let us grant supreme dictatorial authority to Simón Bolívar by acclamation, so that, being instituted as our First Magistrate, he, as well as the Republic, may be freed from the kind of dependency under which he has been acting as the commissioned officer of the Congress of New Granada." Just so had Cortés got rid of his subordination to Governor Velázquez by resigning his powers before the *cabildo* of Veracruz. Dictatorship as a way to separatism; separatism as a way to dictatorship.

Bolívar still resisted; and as Mendoza had spoken of the task of uniting East and West, he took the opportunity to get rid of Mariño. " For the Supreme Power, there are illustrious citizens who deserve your choice better than I do. There is General Mariño, Liberator of the East, a leader worthy of taking your destinies in hand." Needless to say, the *Cabildo* would not hear of this; and Bolívar had to bow to its decision and accept that dictatorship which he had never dreamt of letting go from his firm hands. He had what he had striven for; and he saw to it that the proceedings included a profuse note of thanks to New Granada, so as to make it clear that his subordination to the sister country was at an end. True he added that the Venezuelan people ardently desired total union with New Granada;

and he had himself invested with a mandate to endeavour to bring it about: but this time he would be able to treat as an equal with the Granadinos.

This scene has been presented as either a model of democratic behaviour or an unscrupulous comedy on the part of a political adventurer. It was one more of the thousand acts performed by Spanish cape-and-sword men to cover themselves in the eyes of the gown-men of the country. Steeped in law, but anarchists at heart, the Spanish conquerors usually behaved in this manner. Bolívar remained faithful to a tradition many centuries old. What therefore should be emphasized at this juncture is, not his thirst for power, but his respect for form. A Boves, a Monteverde, as thirsty for power as he was, would not have risen to his conception of the importance of form. A comedy, no doubt; but well played and with a good intention. The need of the day was that he should rule unfettered; the need of the morrow, that republican institutions should remain intact.

But the scene is too reminiscent of the way in which Bonaparte had had himself appointed First Consul for life not to have been an imitation of this illustrious precedent. We know how deeply Bolívar admired and imitated the Corsican. In Bolívar's speech of thanks on receiving the title of Liberator there is a phrase which deserves attention: " Your Lordships have acclaimed me Captain General of the Armies and the Liberator of Venezuela, a title more glorious and satisfactory for me than the sceptre of all the empires of the earth." Is it not strange that this republican should suddenly speak of sceptre and of empire when no one was thinking of such things—no one but him, who did not even know he was thinking of them ? In the un-explored recesses of his ambitious soul shone still the two coronations of Napoleon.

6

" Day of much, eve of nothing "—says a Spanish proverb. On January 2nd, 1814, Bolívar was confirmed in his dictatorship by an assembly of sorts; on January 3rd he had to write to Mariño imploring him not to withdraw the small fleet which was blockading Puerto Cabello. The rivalry between the two dictators was enabling the royalists to regroup for their counter-attack, and though union in their own ranks was by no means closer than was the case with the patriots, they were ultimately to succeed. There were two reasons for this: the first was that the country was still on the whole with Spain and against the liberators; and the second was that the Spanish leaders formed a ring round Bolívar which only Mariño could—but would not—try to break.

That the country was with Spain is the constant lament of all the republican writers of the period, beginning with O'Leary, Bolívar's confidant and aide-de-camp. The documents bring it out in sharp relief and at times in lurid colours. Bolívar issued a proclamation (7.xii.13) referring to those of his countrymen who " fled to the woods, preferring that desperate fate to returning to the bosom of their brethren and seeking the protection of a government which works for their good ". He offers them a last chance, but only for one month. He reiterated his amnesty and widened it to cover all deserters provided they reported back with their arms; forbade all authorities to shoot, or otherwise punish, anyone reporting of his own free will; but confirmed that they were to shoot all persons caught with arms or conspiring (28.i.14). This state of affairs explains why, after a victory as complete as that of Araure, when it is said that Ceballos had to gallop away with but twenty men, there should have been no pursuit, save the brilliant swift march of Bolívar in the vicinity of the battlefield.

Meanwhile Bolívar was in the centre of a ring of Spanish commanders and chieftains. The first to be ready was Boves. Bolívar had sent a thousand men to keep him in check; but they were wiped out by Boves at San Marcos on the Guárico (8.xii.13). The dreaded leader found the way open towards Calabozo, a disaster forecast by Bolívar in a letter to Mariño (27.ix.13) asking him to send troops to Calabozo. Further east, Yáñez had gathered enough troops to threaten Barinas, which he took (28.i.14); while Urdaneta, who was supposed to cover this front for Bolívar, came and went. In a brush with a detachment of Urdaneta's forces, close to Ostino, Yáñez was killed and his troops fled leaving his body, which the patriots quartered and distributed to several garrisons (2.ii.14).

After Boves' victory in San Marcos, Bolívar had rapidly organized a force under Campo Elías to prevent the victor from advancing farther north. Campo Elías took his position in La Puerta, about two and a half leagues from Villa de Cura, with twelve hundred foot and five hundred horse. The republicans were routed, but Boves was wounded and his lieutenant Morales was content to seize Campo Elías' park of arms and ammunition in Villa de Cura (3.ii.14). Bolívar was in the neighbourhood of Puerto Cabello which he still hoped to reduce by hunger and thirst. But on receiving the news he had to concentrate his efforts on Valencia and to ask Urdaneta to send him whatever forces he could spare. On February 8th Bolívar received a letter from Leandro Palacios, Commander in La Guaira, pointing out that his garrison was small and the number of prisoners he held was high. On that same day Bolívar wrote an order to shoot all Spanish prisoners without exception, whether in the vaults or in hospital. Over eight hundred victims were accordingly shot in La Guaira under Palacios, in Caracas under Arizmendi and many more by Bolívar himself in Valencia on February 14th, 15th and 16th.

An ocean of explanatory ink has been poured over all this blood. No explanations are necessary. But the first wave of ink came from Bolívar himself. Within a week of the deed, he issued his *Manifesto to the nations of the world on the War to the Death* (24.ii.14). It is useless to look for arguments, logic or even sense, in this paper. Bolívar never meant his propaganda to be anything but what such things usually are: acts, not thoughts.* This Manifesto is important not because of what it says but

---

* Compare his *thoughtful* letter to the Secretary of State of New Granada in which he says of Correa that he behaved with " the valour of a soldier and the honour of a noble chief ", with this proclamation to his soldiers, where the same " noble chief " has become " the despicable Correa ".

because of what it reveals. Bolívar had the thousand Spaniards executed for three motives: He wanted to get rid of European Spaniards altogether. He was afraid, in general; afraid of defeat, of failure. And he remembered Puerto Cabello. So he says in his Manifesto: " After the light of truth had allowed us to enter into the secret of their machinations, to give them shelter in our midst would have been tantamount to sheltering vipers blowing their poisonous breath into our own; to become the accomplices of their crimes; to allow their intrigues to develop; openly to jeopardize the fate of the republic, which had already been lost once by the rise of the Spanish prisoners in the castle of Puerto Cabello, who having gained control of it on July 1st, 1812, instantly brought about the ruin of all Venezuela." It is idle to imagine Bolívar sitting in judgment upon the Spaniards and, after carefully sifting the evidence (including many deeds which happened later), condemning the prisoners to death. It is irrelevant to argue that if he had not shot the prisoners he would have been in danger; for why were there so many prisoners if not because of Bolívar's decision to carry out a war to the death ? The outcome of it all was his order to have these hundreds of men shot. Bolívar was acting on his own will and impulses, along a line of thought and emotion which was his and his only—though, of course, rooted, through him, in his history, his land and his three bloods and memories.

And who can deny that on that dark day he gave vent to passions rising from a past unimaginable even for himself ? For the atrocious cruelty of the actual executions cannot be set aside on the ground that the Governors of La Guaira and Caracas, and not Bolívar, were responsible for it; since Bolívar knew full well who these two men were. Arizmendi, in particular, was a type of human being even worse than Boves, for Boves could get drunk with death in battle, but did not trade in human blood; while Arizmendi bought lives with hard dollars. It was this man, the lowest and most cruel and sadistic that even those days produced, whom Bolívar chose as Governor of Caracas; and it was Bolívar who chose as Minister of Justice the infamous Mérida, " a great counsellor of crimes ", whose half-brother Díaz Casado made money out of the victims sentenced to death by making them believe that he would save them. No portrait of Bolívar which shrinks from these facts can be said to be written in earnest. And no account of the slaughtering of the nine hundred Spaniards is true which forgets that, as Juan Vicente González says: " In Caracas executions had never ceased." The Venezuelan historian goes on to say: " but from the fatal 12th, morning and afternoon shootings went on in the Main Square, in St. Paul and Trinity Square and in the slaughterhouse. . . . To spare ammunition, sometimes the victims were murdered with *machetes* and daggers ". As for La Guaira, " the victims came out in twos, joined together with shackles, and so were led amidst shouts and insults, each carrying the wood which was to consume his body. Few succeeded in being shot; most of them were given away to voluntary murderers who tried a *machete* or a dagger on them, or at times their muscular strength, by throwing a huge stone at their victim's head." This Venezuelan author, justly indignant, provides the saddest detail of all: " Over such scenes could be seen running with delight, dressed in white

and adorned with yellow and blue ribbons, deadly nymphs who on the blood
and the muddy remains, danced the obscene dance known as the *Palito*."

Such was the orgy which had been released—by whom? That the
terrible passions which it let loose live a life of their own in the animal, nay,
in the diabolic depths of human nature, no one can doubt; and that glimpses
of them had come to the surface of American life we know, since we have
seen Spanish merchants beheading the poor Indian, chained to a convoy
when he got too tired to walk on; or Aguirre the tyrant murdering his
companions in the Amazon. But we also know that, under the old dispensa-
tion, Church and State had kept these passions under a reasonable restraint
which had given to foreign visitors the impression that the Venezuelans
were men of a quiet disposition. Who released these passions? The war
declared on Spain by the inexperienced and fiery Bolívar; and the war to
the death proclaimed later by the fiery and inexperienced Bolívar. Truth is
exacting and it demands that conclusion. And, since Bolívar saw it, and
saw it done by the men he had chosen and never repudiated for their deed,
and did it himself, the full responsibility rests on Bolívar: leader and chief
authority of the public life of his day.

CHAPTER XXIII

FLIGHT EASTWARDS

I

DESPITE his serious wound, Boves was preparing his next stroke under cover of constant attacks by his two lieutenants, Morales and Rosete. Rosete with a rabble of negro slaves and shouting *Long live Ferdinand VII!* took Ocumare, sacked and looted it and left three hundred bodies on the streets, many of them in the church (11.ii.14). Ribas came to the rescue and expelled him from the city, shooting every prisoner. Bolívar, who knew that Boves was getting ready to attack him, awaited the onslaught in broken country, where he would be able to neutralize his rival's cavalry. He fortified his estate of San Mateo between La Victoria and the Lake of Valencia, and tried to hold the line running through Valencia to Puerto Cabello, where it joined the troops he still kept covering the port and city. He had about twelve hundred infantry, six hundred horse and four pieces of artillery. After several unsuccessful attempts at taking San Mateo and a short siege (10–25.iii.14), Boves, impatient, again attacked Bolívar's stronghold both from the hilly flanks and down in the valley, frontways. He was repulsed (25.iii.14).

This battle is famous because of the Ricaurte episode. Left by Bolívar with fifty men to hold the estate house, where the ammunition had been stored, Ricaurte, surrounded by Boves' soldiers, ordered his men to withdraw towards headquarters, and blew up the fort, sacrificing his life but destroying most of the enemy column and saving the day. Such was the official version at the time. Bolívar, however, told Peru de Lacroix later: "I am the author of that tale; I made it up to raise the spirit of my troops, to frighten the enemy and to extol to the highest pitch the soldiers of New Granada. Ricaurte died on March 25th, 1814, marching downhill from San Mateo in retreat with his men, and I found him on the path face downwards, dead, with his back burnt by the sun." We are not concerned here with Ricaurte— who in either version gave his life like a brave soldier; but with Bolívar. Throughout his career as a leader he showed the utmost skill and imagination in setting up before the crowd scenes, myths and legends of a dramatic force such as the crowd needs to remain faithful to a cause.

At last Mariño was approaching, and as he brought more men than Bolívar had, Boves, with his usual decision and mobility, wheeled round to meet him. By March 31st the vanguards of Boves and Mariño came upon each other at Bocachica, between La Puerta and Cura. The two sides fought stubbornly and both had to give up the fight owing to lack of ammunition. Boves withdrew towards Valencia, to meet Ceballos, while Mariño crossed the most difficult passes through the hills of El Pao and Zarate, towards La Victoria.

He lost many deserters on the way; so did Bolívar, who had to order a general comb out of deserters with instructions to shoot all forthwith (7.iv.14).

Boves had hoped to enter Valencia with Ceballos who had set siege to it on March 29th; but Urdaneta defended it well, and when Boves appeared (25.iv.14), Ceballos had just made up his mind to raise the siege for lack of ammunition. As Boves had none either, his arrival meant no relief. Ceballos withdrew towards San Carlos. An episode occurred then which sheds much light on these wars. Ceballos ordered Boves to go back to the plains and collect more cavalry while he would keep by him the troops Boves had brought. Boves obeyed, probably with his tongue in his cheek; but no sooner had he gone than his soldiers began to desert, and so Ceballos, for fear of losing them all, sent them to Calabozo where they would be able again to fight under their favourite chief. This shows that the flag was of much less importance to the *Llaneros* than the chief; a forecast of the dramatic change which was to take place in the war when these wild men of the plains, Boves dead, found a chief to their liking, but who happened to fight on the other side.

2

After a brief visit to Valencia, which he found dreadfully devastated, Bolívar returned to La Victoria and set about to prepare an attack on San Carlos. He entrusted the expedition to Mariño, with Urdaneta, one of his own men, as chief of staff. The young leader, acting, it would seem, rashly and against the advice of Urdaneta, was heavily defeated at El Arao, near San Carlos (16.iv.14). Bolívar had to give up the assault on Puerto Cabello and returned hastily to Valencia. The war was laying the country waste. The once flourishing fields, bearing such rich harvests, were now barren and desolate. He had seen his own house at San Mateo shattered and his sugar canes fed to cavalry horses. Bolívar was, perhaps for the first time, impressed by the curse the war was visiting upon his country. He issued a proclamation (6.v.14) striking an unusual note of sincerity and pessimism. " The war is becoming more cruel and the hopes of a prompt victory I had aroused in you have vanished. Our own brothers, joined to our tyrants by centuries of slavery, delay, God knows for how long, the day of liberty. The Army has done what it could. . . . It could not perform the miracle of altering immemorial habits in a day. Soldiers, if God tries us with so many obstacles and setbacks, He forsakes us not; He wants us to deserve by our endeavours and virtues what for other peoples might be the task of years. One more effort and we shall destroy the enemies of the fatherland." Then comes this strange confession, suddenly bursting through the crust of his politics from the depths of his being: " We are living terrible days; blood flows in streams; three centuries of culture, of enlightenment and of industry have vanished."

Meanwhile Cagigal had cut his way through from Coro to San Carlos with ammunition for Ceballos. Bolívar sallied forth to meet Cagigal, a cautious general inclined to let trouble take the initiative. Cagigal sought the plain, for he was stronger in cavalry; Bolívar the broken and marshy country, for he was stronger in infantry. Their meeting which never actually reached the status of a pitched battle gave rise, however, to a number of singular fights in true mediaeval style between officers of both sides—a strange happening in the nineteenth century. Bolívar withdrew again to Valencia followed by Cagigal. He was short of food, in a country which had been, till four years earlier, one of the richest in land produce in the whole world. Fed on short rations of ass meat, the soldiers brought by Mariño began to desert; and Bolívar, having lost two hundred, shot all the leaders of the deserters and one in five of the rank and file. Ribas arrived then from Caracas with eight hundred men; thus reinforced, Bolívar attacked Cagigal who had chosen a strong position in Carabobo, with well protected flanks. The battle began at nine in the morning (29.v.14). The forces were about equal; the leaders as different as they could be. Bolívar was a guerrilla chief with no other training than that of his own improvised campaigns, while Cagigal was a professional, used to the European style of fighting. The guerrilla chief won over the general; decision over indecision; and genius over talent. Cagigal fled with most of his remaining cavalry towards El Pao, while Ceballos withdrew to San Carlos.

"This victory"—writes Heredia—"might have settled the fate of the province had the insurgents exploited it, pressing on Puerto Cabello and seeking Boves before he had time to gather strength. Bolívar lost one month in triumphant festivities to celebrate his victory; and by the beginning of July the two famous Liberators had to contend with a cloud of cavalry of *zambos* and negroes threatening Caracas, from the plain of Ocumare, and the valleys of Aragua and Valencia, from Villa de Cura." This was Boves' cavalry. Indifferent to the fate of Cagigal and Ceballos, Boves had remained in Calabozo till the very day Cagigal was defeated; and he began to operate when he alone was on the stage on the Spanish side. Bolívar, remembering the defeat of Campo Elías at La Puerta, sent Mariño to occupy that position. A curious reaction, almost a superstitious gesture on his part. It seems that the thing to do at the time would have been to concentrate all his strength on Boves; but Bolívar dispersed his forces, sending Urdaneta in pursuit of Ceballos and Jalón after Cagigal. This defective disposition may well have been due to his political prepossessions which led him to keep as many leaders as possible pleased with the feeling of holding more or less independent commands. But if tradition does not fail, Bolívar may well have sent his lieutenants to fight because, resting on his laurels, he was at the time enjoying with Josephine Madrid a kind of Capua he had set for himself in a villa close to Caracas. It was probably at this time, when he was enjoying the roses of power, that he proposed to Archbishop Coll y Prat that, in order to end the Boves war, Spain should make him, Bolívar, a viceroy, and he would disarm his lieutenants.

He was rudely shaken by the news that Boves was in the vicinity of La Puerta. It is a small plain about ten miles from Villa de Cura with a narrow pass at each end. Mariño had taken excellent positions on the pass closer to Villa de Cura. It was easy to defend and made Boves' cavalry useless. Boves realized this, and his plan consisted in forcing Mariño down to the plain. On June 15th Bolívar with his staff arrived on the scene and took command. Boves was soon able to write: " The rebels, enemies of mankind, have been totally defeated in La Puerta under the command of the so called generals Bolívar and Mariño." Heredia writes: " Bolívar, astounded at the carnage without quarter which ended the battle, fled with such speed that he was the first to bring the news to Caracas within a few hours."

3

With Bolívar, the republic had been defeated. But with Boves, what had triumphed ? Certainly not the rule of Spain. The rule of Spain, insofar as it had survived the fall of the monarchy at Bayonne, was then incarnated in a few men: Cagigal, Ceballos, Vázquez and Heredia, for none of whom did Boves care a brass farthing. Cagigal, so deeply impressed by the atrocities of the war that he declared himself unable to converse for five minutes on the subject, had more than once tried to take reprisals, though under legal forms. But Heredia on the legal, and Brigadier Vázquez on the military side, had prevented him from carrying out his plans. This resistance of two upright men, one an American Spaniard and the other a European Spaniard, was like an island of the old Spanish order left standing in that upheaval.

Boves, though a European Spaniard, was not working for Spain. He led his *llaneros* by two abject passions: loot and racial hatred. He, a white, carried on a ruthless war to the death against the whites. " ' In the plains ', he used to say, ' not a single white must remain ', for two reasons: the first, because he had set aside that territory for coloured people; the second, to ensure a retreat in case of a setback, for he did not trust the whites, whose company always displeased him while he ate and amused himself with coloured people." His chaplain, Llamosas, who wrote these words, asserts that he killed all white men wherever he went and distributed their property to the mulattoes. Llamosas vouches for the fact that Boves had given orders for all white patriots to be killed quietly without any formality, and that his best friend would be the man who had killed most. Indiscipline in his force was endemic and apparently not unwelcome to him. When his men ceased to obey a particular officer they asked Boves to dismiss him and appoint another—which Boves did. In substance, this attitude was identical with that of Monteverde, even if it went much beyond in point of crime. In both cases the leaders were endeavouring to build up a career for themselves by allowing their troops to do as they pleased.

Such an army under such a leader struck terror everywhere it went. Valencia capitulated (9.vii.14), but Boves broke an oath taken before the Holy Sacrament and allowed his troops to murder three hundred soldiers, sixty officers and ninety civilians. He had all the furniture and property of the citizens gathered in stores, to protect them, he said, from looting; but in fact to make it easier for his men to help themselves. And Heredia adds: " On the following night, he gathered all the women into a dancing party, while he rounded up all the men and had them led out of the city where they were speared to death like bulls. . . . The ladies in the ballroom swallowed their tears and trembled hearing the hooves of Boves' horses, for they guessed what was actually happening; while Boves, whip in hand, made them dance the *piquirico* and other dances of the country, of which he was very fond. The massacre went on for a few nights."

As for Caracas, which Bolívar had fortified before the battle of La Puerta, it was emptied by Bolívar on his flight to Barcelona. Heredia is scathing in his condemnation of Bolívar for this. " No one but an insensate man in his wanderings, an enemy of his country, lacking in all human kindness, could have conceived such a thought. Although it must be owned that the horror caused by the cruelties of Boves' army which advanced looting all and killing the whites, made it easier to carry out what seemed impossible. From the 6th to the 8th of July the city was left nearly deserted. . . . Out of the 40,000 souls of the beautiful city there remained only the nuns of the two convents, a few friars, the archbishop and, following his example, the canons, as well as between 4 and 5,000 persons who chose to await death at home rather than go to meet it in the hazards of flight." Here again Heredia tells of the courage and coolness with which the archbishop saved the lives of many persons from murderous brigands who had entered the city before Boves. One of those who remained was Casa León. One of those who wished to remain was María Antonia Bolívar. Her brother forced her to leave.

Boves paid no attention to Cagigal, who, in law, was his chief. After his success in La Puerta he wrote to Cagigal: " I have recovered the arms, the munitions and the honour of the Spanish flags lost in Carabobo "; in which he was right at any rate on the score of the arms and ammunition. Cagigal seems to have been paralysed by the power and drive of this man. In Valencia he witnessed Boves' worst atrocities, unable to assert his authority. He left for Puerto Cabello to complain to Madrid, while Boves took on the titles of " Governor of this province, President of the Royal *Audiencia*, Captain General and Political Chief of all the Provinces which constitute Venezuela, General Commanding officer of the Spanish Army ". This implied a complete disregard for the authority, not only of Cagigal, but of the Spanish Regency; since Cagigal held from the Regency his appointment to succeed Monteverde, who, wounded in the mouth, had retired to Spain. Boves handed over the political government of Caracas to the chameleonic Casa León, and the military Government to the Venezuelan Quero, who had betrayed Miranda; and he promptly left for the east where he had sent his lieutenant Morales in hot pursuit of Bolívar.

4

After his defeat at La Puerta, Bolívar fled to Caracas and, hastily collecting all the money and property he could, fled on eastwards. In his train he carried all the gold and silver of the churches of Caracas. Under his leadership a Concord between the *Priesthood* and the *State* had been concluded whereby authority was granted by the clergy to the State to lay hands on the jewels of the Cathedral (12.ii.14). Twenty-four boxes of wrought silver and jewels weighing 27,912 ounces had to be handed over. These were the boxes Bolívar took away. What became of them? Heredia says that "monstrances, ciboria, chalices and other jewels as precious for their materials as for their craftsmanship, were later used to endow the Order of the Liberators to whom they were allotted in Cumaná". Events, however, were more dramatic and complex.

No one seems to have wondered why Bolívar fled east instead of west. After all, he had a relatively strong force under Urdaneta in the region of San Carlos and he might have thought of seeking a retreat towards Cúcuta and New Granada whence he had started on his way to Caracas at the beginning of the year. But he went east, not west. Might this not be because he felt the eastern way less dangerous for a man so heavily laden with silver? The west was not merely apt to be fought over from the several bases in the hands of the royalists, it was also infested with bands of armed thieves. There is yet another indication that Bolívar's movements were apt to be hampered by the silver: the fugitives from Caracas and whatever aid Mariño was able to send them from the east met at Aragua, a city on the river of the same name; where Bolívar and Bermúdez (one of Mariño's lieutenants) organized a resistance against Morales. There were differences between Bolívar and Bermúdez as to how to dispose the troops; it seems that Bolívar gave way because he did not feel at home in those eastern districts. But Restrepo provides a curious detail: "Nothing could resist the number and the valour of the *llaneros*, and the patriots were broken to pieces. Realizing that all resistance was useless, Bolívar withdrew with many of the people from Caracas towards Barcelona. Bermúdez carried on the fight till 2 o'clock in the afternoon and then withdrew towards Maturin."

It is clear that Bolívar went his way when he might still have fought on and that the fact that he had in his charge 28,000 ounces of wrought silver had something to do with it. He was making for the coast. From Barcelona he went to Cumaná, where he found Mariño, with whom, as events were to show, he had some kind of agreement; but he also met Ribas and Piar, i.e. the vice-Bolívar and the vice-Mariño of those days. The very day of his arrival in Cumaná (25.viii.14), he learnt that Bianchi, the Italian adventurer who acted as Admiral for the Republic, was sailing away with the silver, hoping to repay himself for the prize money owed him by the Republic. Bianchi had bribed the garrison of the Castle of San Antonio which commanded the harbour. All the officers of the city were already on board. Bolívar and Mariño decided to follow the silver.

5

Here is Ribas' version, in his letter to Martín Tovar. "All you have been told about Bolívar and Mariño falls short of what they have done: they stole away by sea in the night of the 26th of last month, taking away the small fleet with all the silver of the churches of Caracas, gold and precious stones, all the powder, rifles and war material, leaving us extremely defenceless. At sea, they shared it all with Bianchi, who commanded the fleet, numbering nine ships. Bianchi went his way with the ships and articles allotted to him, and Bolívar and Mariño with theirs arrived in Carúpano, driven thither by hunger and thirst, for they had no provisions; there, I fell upon them, arrested them and took from them the silver, war material and rifles of their share, leaving them under parole; but as soon as I rode away, they broke their word and fled with the two ships they had brought, bribing the commanders.

A modern Venezuelan historian, Don Vicente Lecuna, has put forward another picture based on the memoirs of a republican officer, Trinidad Morán, who was on the spot at the time. Señor Lecuna lays stress on the fact that Bolívar did not embark on any ship belonging to Bianchi, but " on a ship of the State commanded by an honest and courageous officer ", Felipe Esteves. " Once on board "—writes Señor Lecuna—" the *Libertador* sent word to Bianchi to return all the wrought silver he had on board his ship, without delay. The pirate sent ten boxes ", and so forth. A good and kind pirate indeed. Mosquera will tell us how good. " The presence of Bolívar and Mariño on board the ships, the shame felt by some of the captains and the noble way in which the two chiefs of the republic treated that man, forced him to steer towards Margarita, and there he delivered the arms and ammunition, and part of the ships, keeping three of the best and the jewels in his possession, alleging that Cumaná owed him more than 40,000 pesos in prize money." Dr Lecuna writes: " though the *Libertador* had no means wherewith to force Bianchi to obey, he secured his obedience." How do we know it? Because, we are told, " Bolívar himself says so in a manifesto published on the occasion of Piar's revolt in 1817." But what does Bolívar say in that manifesto? " In the midst of the calamities of the war, the Italian Bianchi mutinies against the constituted authorities and steals the last relics of the Republic. We succeed in leading this infamous pirate to Margarita to do ourselves justice and make use of the last remainder of our expiring existence. Fate willed that General Piar should be then in Margarita. . . . General Mariño and I, leaders of the Republic, were unable to land because General Piar had seized hold of the Fort and bound us to put ourselves at the mercy of a pirate more generous and milder than he, though of equal rapacity." It is evident that either Bolívar and Mariño forced Bianchi to deliver them part of the silver and go to Margarita to be punished, or that they made a treaty with him on the basis of sharing the church silver. If the first, with what force did they coerce Bianchi, and why did Bianchi, a " rapacious and infamous pirate ", swallow his humiliation and save Bolívar and Mariño from Piar, and why did he not take back the silver he had been made to disgorge?

There is only one story that makes sense. Bolívar and Mariño embarked either to follow the silver with which Bianchi was sailing away or, more likely, because it always had been their intention to sail away with the sinews of war and of power in order to return to power through war. We should not forget Bolívar's hurry to quit the battlefield of Aragua and Mariño's hurry to put the silver on board ship. And then, was Ribas wrong in reproaching the two leaders for abandoning their armies and sailing away?

Why the two of them ?   Would not one have done ?   Why not leave Bianchi to Ribas and Piar or to Bermúdez, while the two leaders stayed on land and carried on the war ?   Why should the two symbolic men, the two Liberators, be the first to sail away?   Did they not realize that by thus embarking together they inflicted a deadlier blow to the cause than the loss of the church silver would have been ?   Is it not evident that the episode is moulded and dominated by dark distrust of everybody by everybody, not excluding Bolívar's distrust of Mariño and Mariño's of Bolívar ?

Subsequent events confirm this view.   Larrazábal makes much of the fact that Bolívar and Mariño did come back after all to Carúpano.   But they only did so for sheer lack of food and water, which they could not obtain in Curaçao for fear that their cargo of silver might be confiscated by the British authorities.   They had to come back.   Ribas put them both under arrest as deserters.   Ribas wanted the silver; and he got it by making Bolívar pay for his liberty.   Bolívar signed an order authorizing one Joaquín Marcano to receive the sixteen boxes of wrought silver aboard one of the ships.   This silver had to be paid over to Ribas.   " Before leaving, Bolívar put in the hands of General José Felix Ribas thirty-six cwts of wrought silver and jewels of gold and the money rescued from Bianchi, expressing the wish that they should be useful to the liberty of the fatherland "; so writes Morán.   And that he did pay it over to Ribas cannot be doubted. " There "—writes José Domingo Díaz of the final battle in which Ribas was defeated later—" perished many of the chief families from their heads to their slaves, and there also were caught thirty-six cwts of jewels of silver and gold stolen from the Seditious [Bolívar] in his flight from the churches of Caracas, which were punctually delivered to the archbishop and to the churches to which they belonged, an operation which I witnessed by order of the Government."   This tallies with the letter of recommendation to the Congress of New Granada which Ribas gave Bolívar, a strange document indeed unless the bargain between the two men is admitted; as well as with the fact that Bolívar and Mariño arrived rich in Cartagena as we know from Ducoudray-Holstein.

What are we to make of all this ?   First and foremost we must keep above suspicion the honour of the two young fallen dictators.   Neither Bolívar nor Mariño had any sordid side to their character.*   But this said it is plain that both kept an obsessed eye on the silver because for them it meant power, and that this obsession made them neglect other actions which might have altered the look of things and certainly improved the figure they cut in History.   The place of Bolívar at the time was with Urdaneta's troops; leading an orderly withdrawal towards New Granada.   In fleeing east with the cash instead of withdrawing west, Bolívar made a great mistake to the

* A man who disliked him, Ducoudray-Holstein, says of Bolívar: " I must, however, render justice to General Bolívar, in saying that he has never been an avaricious or money-making man, for he is generous, and cares little or nothing about money.   I have seen him often emptying his purse, and giving his last doubloon to an officer who asked him for some money on account of his salary; and when he was gone, he would turn to me and say, laugh-ingly, ' this poor devil is more in need than I, and this golden stuff is worthless to me.   I have given him all that I possessed '."

detriment of his good name as a leader; and the underlying cause of the mistake was the secret root of most of Bolívar's misfortunes and the chief weakness of his character as an historical hero: that he was thirstier for personal glory than for the achievement of the aims from which glory would shed its light on him.

6

No adequate estimate can be made of these events without bearing in mind that, while Mariño and Bolívar sailed away, fighting went on against the royalists both east and west. In the east, Ribas, Piar and Bermúdez carried on the struggle. Ribas and Piar had appointed themselves *Libertador* and Supreme Chief of the west and of the east respectively, but neither Bermúdez in Maturin, nor the French Negro Bideau in Güiria, had recognized Piar; while in the real west, the real leader was Urdaneta. Morales threatened Maturin with 6,500 men against Bermúdez' 1,250 (7.ix.14). Tired of being besieged, the patriots attacked on the 12th and won an unexpected success, rich particularly in war booty. Piar had taken Cumaná (29.ix.14), but refused to comply with Ribas' request that he should join him at Maturin. Boves heard of this, broke his march towards Urica, where he was to meet Morales, and destroyed Piar's force (as well as many of the peaceful fugitives of Caracas whom he overtook there and had murdered).

The news reached Bermúdez and Ribas while on their way to offer battle to Morales. The impetuous Bermúdez broke away from Ribas (who returned to Maturin) and with his eastern troops took the shortest but most difficult route to meet Boves, whom he awaited in the heights of Los Magueyes. Boves arrived, defeated him and put him to flight towards Maturin (9.xi.14). Ribas and Bermúdez quarrelled again over strategy and left Maturin together but asunder, towards Urica where they met Boves in battle on December 5th. The patriots were defeated; their cavalry fled and their infantry was wiped out by Morales. By Morales, because at the beginning of the cavalry encounter, Boves, who always fought like a private, was struck in the heart by a republican spear.

Much eloquence has been wasted on his death and much vain imagination on describing what might have happened had Boves not died at thirty-two and so early in the war. The hard fact is that, though born in Spain and fighting under the Spanish flag, he never fought for Spain. Boves fought only for Boves. His ways were so anarchical, so sanguinary, so destructive that the idea of his loss having been a loss for Spain is simply grotesque. On the day he died, the cause of Spain may not have won anything; it certainly lost nothing. On the other hand, the cause of an independent Venezuela lost a man who, wherever he went, recruited friends for the enemies of Spain if not precisely for the Republic. The Republic, moreover, owed to Boves two advantages: the first was a new, original school of war. Inept on the political field owing to his savage ways, Boves was in a way a genius at the particular warfare which the country needed. He created the specific, local way of using the native cavalry supplied by the Plains: lightning marches and rapid attacks in fields ready for easy manoeuvre; flexible and swift tactics which Bolívar would learn and digest. And he trained and gave a collective spirit and pride to the *llaneros*, men with no strong attachment to either side, apt to follow blindly a chief who knew and loved them no matter for whom this chief fought. When Boves died the *llaneros* lost their chief. By then, the next chief, this time a Creole and a patriot, was ready to come and lead their squadrons—but in the opposite camp.

Morales, with Boves' army or band, took Maturin (10.xii.14) after a stubborn defence by Ribas and Bermúdez. He behaved abominably to the conquered city while Bermúdez and Ribas disappeared with a handful of followers. After a few days of hiding with no other company than that of a slave, Ribas was betrayed and caught; he was beheaded by the *zambo* Royalist chieftain Barrajola; his head was sent to Caracas and exhibited in an iron cage on the road to La Guaira covered with the Phrygian cap he used to display " as a symbol of liberty ". This detail is typical of the *mantuano* turned demagogue. He had ever been a thoughtless, empty-headed imitator of the worst and shallowest sides of the French Revolution; though born with a sound military instinct which made him the most brilliant of Bolívar's lieutenants. He died pelted with insults by the very crowds he had courted and flattered.

While these events took place in the east, Urdaneta fought a losing battle in the west. He withdrew westwards, waited at El Tocuyo for news of Bolívar and, on learning that all was lost and that Bolívar was in flight eastwards, withdrew towards New Granada. His small army was the rearguard of an immense emigration. Urdaneta wrote to the Government of New Granada asking for protection and suggesting that a strong force of cavalry should be organized in Casanare to guard against Boves. The Government of New Granada answered granting him and his troops the protection he had asked for, and suggesting that he himself devote as many men as he could afford to organizing the Casanare cavalry. This Urdaneta did by sending thither a few of his officers; one of whom, José Antonio Páez, was to be the successor of Boves as the leader of the *llaneros*, and, though a republican and a patriot, more of a scourge for Bolívar than ever Boves had been.

CHAPTER XXIV

BOLÍVAR TAKES SANTA FE AND LOSES NEW GRANADA

I

SENT by New Granada to rescue Venezuela from thraldom, Bolívar had failed after an initial sensational success. As he himself put it later to Peru de Lacroix, " he had counted on a patriotism and an enthusiasm which he had not found in Venezuela; with a national spirit which did not exist and which he could not create ". His men " were refused every help while the Spaniards found spontaneous aid in all the *pueblos* ". A few months later, when news of his success with the Government reached Margarita, the exiles there, all republican friends and near relations of his, drafted an Indictment of his eleven months as ruler of Venezuela which no impartial student of the man and his time can disregard.

The " last remains of the unhappy inhabitants of Venezuela and the foreigners who feel as they do " declare in this document their astonishment at hearing Bolívar has again been entrusted with the command of troops, a fact they hold as " incredible ". They raise eleven accusations against his " criminal and hare-brained conduct ". The first, to have cut himself loose from New Granada in the hour of his triumph. The second, to have taken grave decisions against the advice of others, notably " those which flooded the provinces with blood in violation of his promises and against the principles of mildness and leniency which distinguish all Americans. Thus, he was seen oppressing innocence and preparing the extermination of the greater part of his brothers ". The third, " to have given no government to the peoples of Venezuela . . . keeping them under a military despotism ", and, " in order to put a good face on this degrading system, to have organized an assembly, or rather a comedy in San Francisco, where he was elected dictator by his friends and commensals, and by speakers he had prepared beforehand ". The fourth, " his most culpable leniency towards the dishonourable means wherewith Don José Felix Ribas and his immense family and base retainers endeavoured to enrich themselves . . . with a shameful sale of human blood ". The fifth, his bad choice of collaborators, " youths without experience or reputation " and in particular " of Don Rafael Diego Mérida, his Minister of Justice, the most active instrument of the sacrifice of the first victims of American freedom ". The sixth, that " if he did promptly take the field, with no less swiftness did he return to the capital to receive incense and puerile offerings ". Given over to pleasures, his accusers say, he discredited morality and forgot the public cause. The seventh, that " he was several times heard to say that *military tactics were useless, and that all writings on the art of war were puerilities and chimaeras.* With such luminous principles he has led to the grave thousands of his brothers." There is a notable eighth: " Nothing can be raised against Don Simón Bolívar as to venality or illicit use of State funds; but he bears the heavy responsibility for whatever all the Ribas people as well as the person he appointed to decree confiscations did ". The ninth accuses Bolívar of having sacrificed many troops with promises of help he could not honour. The tenth, to have forced Caracas to emigrate. The eleventh, to have said that the people of Venezuela " neither want nor deserve liberty ".

When the bitterness of defeat is discounted, what remains of this document collects the general judgment formed in his own time about the rash and inexperienced young man who had assumed sole command over the country. It tallies with everything that can be gathered directly from other sources. But how is it then that this man, with so heavy a score against his credit, could have reached so easily the apex of power and keep it even after defeat and start again ? The answer is that despite his many shortcomings, Bolívar was head and shoulders above his contemporaries in sheer power of will and mind.

His superiority shines in the Carúpano Manifesto, in which he answers in advance all these strictures. Dated September 7th, 1814, when he had lost everything, even most of the Church silver, this document is amazing for the serenity of its mood, the clarity of its thought, the terseness of its style. Nothing short of complete quotation could do it justice; for it is admirable in form and in substance from beginning to end. He boldly stands before his countrymen for judgment: " far from holding the senseless presumption of being guiltless of my country's catastrophe, I feel the deep grief of believing myself to be the instrument of your frightful misery ". But he asks his countrymen to be " just in their grief as the cause is just which determines it". " Your brothers, and not the Spaniards, have torn your breasts, spilt your blood, set fire to your homes and condemned you to exile." And so, his failure was due to the gigantic size of the task: " The destruction of a Government whose origin is lost in the darkness of time; the subversion of established principles; the mutation of customs; the upsetting of opinion and the establishment of liberty in a country of slaves." And he winds up this period with a characteristic sweep: " Though desolation and death be the reward of such a glorious endeavour, that is no reason to condemn it, for it is not that which is accessible that must be done, but that which our right entitles us to do."

The man who, in the hour of defeat, could write such words was pre-destined for greatness. His power to go to the heart of things evinces— under all his dross—a golden purity of heart and mind. " It is not for common men to estimate the eminent value of the kingdom of liberty, so as to choose it rather than blind ambition or vile greed. The decision on this important question has determined our fate: it was in the hands of our countrymen, who, perverted, decided against us: the rest was consequential on a decision more dishonourable than fatal, and to be deplored more for its essence than for its results." This is magnificent—and in the circum-stances, almost inhumanly so. Here, the intellect of this man of thirty-one, at grips with the chief themes of human destiny, attains the vision and the eloquence of an experienced genius. " It is malicious stupidity to attribute to public men the vicissitudes which the order of things brings about in

States . . . and even though grave errors or violent passions in the leaders cause frequent setbacks to the republic, these setbacks must be explained with equity, seeking their origin in the primitive causes of all our misfortunes: the fragility of our nature and the power of fate on all our affairs. . . . To hope that politics and war may march in step with our plans while we go forward blindly feeling our way with the sole strength of our intentions and the sole help of the limited means under our control, is to wish to achieve the effects of a divine power with springs which are but human."

Beneath this philosophical austerity, an alert political will was at work. Bolívar is preparing his return by way of New Granada. He must ingratiate himself with the *Granadinos* whom he had so cavalierly dismissed as soon as he had entered Caracas in triumph. While he declares that he will disdain answering the accusations levelled against him, he announces that he reserves " this act of justice for a tribunal of wise men who will judge with righteousness and knowledge my mission in Venezuela. I speak of the Supreme Congress of New Granada, the august body which sent me with its troops to your help ". But when, as he is certain he will, he has vindicated himself, then " I swear to you that, Liberator or dead, I shall always deserve the honour you bestowed upon me; and that no human power on earth can stay me in the course I have set for myself till for the second time I come to liberate you by that western path drenched with so much blood and decked with so many laurels. . . . Do not compare your physical forces with those of your enemies, for the spirit should not be compared with matter. You are men, they are beasts; you are free, they are slaves. Fight and you shall conquer. God grants victory to constancy." Such was the spirit in which Bolívar left his country.

2

He sailed from Carúpano (7.ix.14) and (as he dared not call at Margarita for fear Arizmendi might make short shrift of him) steered towards Cartagena where he arrived on September 25th, 1814. This once prosperous city was then the capital of one of the four authorities into which the revolution had broken up the Kingdom of New Granada. In Cundinamarca, i.e., the original province of Santa Fe de Bogotá, Nariño resisted all attempts at federation, partly because he was a centralist, partly because of personal ambition. In Tunja, a federal government and Congress gathered together most of the other provinces of New Granada under one political roof; Cartagena was a law unto itself; and finally, in Santa Marta, the Spanish party was still predominant.

Nariño, fallen into the hands of General Aymerich in May, 1813, while fighting in Pasto, a district strongly royalist, had been sent to Spain, " very much against the wishes of the cruel and ignorant *Pastusos* "—writes Restrepo —" who indignantly asked for, and wished to have the sight of his execution ". His successor in the dictatorship of Cundinamarca, his uncle, Manuel Bernardo Alvarez, was a man of strict religious views, who disguised his coolness towards independence as opposition to a confederation with the

Congress provinces. Cartagena also opposed this confederation, being in favour of a different one based, not on the old Kingdom of Granada, but on the coastal territories between the Orinoco and Cape Gracias a Dios. The capital of this federation would be in Maracaibo. The city-republic of Cartagena passed a law approving this Union, sent an emissary to Bolívar, declared him " a deserving son ", and wrote his name in golden letters on the National Archives, for he " had not seen with indifference the chains of Spanish barbarity ". By then Bolívar was too hard pressed to think of golden words and coastal federations; and, with an eye on realities, addressed himself, not to Cartagena but to Tunja, asking the Congress of New Granada to designate a delegate who, with one appointed by him, should go to Europe to put before the victors of Napoleon—whose defeat was already foreseeable— the rights of the South American republics. These delegates found no favour in London; but their failure by no means tells against Bolívar's foresight. In the midst of all the petty wars which made his path so difficult, he was the only man with a world-wide vision.

The defeat of Napoleon by Spain, Russia and England was endangering the cause of the Spanish-American separatists. This danger was graver than most people dreamt of at the time—including for Spain; for Ferdinand VII, on his return from exile, promulgated a decree (4.v.14) abolishing the constitution and, under the pretext of returning to an old régime which was in fact more liberal and enlightened than met the eye, established as base and stupid a despotism as Spain had ever known. By an irony of History the President of the Cortes at the time was an American, Don Antonio Joaquín Pérez, representative for Puebla de los Angeles, in New Spain, who calmly looked on when Ferdinand abolished the Cortes. Pérez was one of the sixty-nine members of the Cortes who had volunteered to send a letter to Ferdinand VII in praise and support of absolutism. One of the grievances Ferdinand VII brandished against the Cortes was that they had acted " without any news of those [provinces] which were supposed to be represented by the deputy-representatives of Spain and the Indies ".

These events in Spain were due to the same forces which determined those in Spanish America. The Cortes had been the work of gown-men— hence the brilliant part played in them by liberal priests, carrying on the republican tradition of the great days of the Spanish Church. The reaction against the Cortes came from cape-and-sword men, such as Elio, the general commanding officer in Valencia. The constitutional movement was led by well-to-do aristocrats and upper middle class men, such as Toreno and Argüelles; the people on the other hand were so enthusiastic in their blind devotion for Ferdinand VII that they encouraged him to tear the constitution to shreds. The King threw all reserve to the winds, and, as Monteverde, his overseas counterpart had done, engaged in a lawless persecution of the wisest leaders of reform as well as of demagogues and trouble-makers. The effects of this change in Spanish affairs were soon to be felt in the Indies. Ferdinand issued another decree (24.v.14) in which he announced to his American " vassals " that his presence had dispelled all strife in Spain and should do so among his American subjects; that he had sought information from American-born persons in order to meet their grievances, and that he would soon call new Cortes to establish a moderate monarchy. Lardizábal, the Mexican member of the one-time Regency, who now belonged to the " servile " party, also wrote to America asking his fellow Americans to hear the voice of the " beloved " King.

3

This alarming news made enough impression in New Granada to incite the Tunja Congress to fresh endeavours towards union with Cundinamarca. But though Alvarez, the dictator in Santa Fe, appointed a delegate, and though a treaty was actually signed bringing Cundinamarca under the rule of the Tunja federation (11.viii.1814) Alvarez hedged and finally refused to ratify this treaty. In Cartagena, Torices, another dictator, was steering a difficult course between the aristocratic party led by García Toledo and the demagogic party led by the brothers Piñeres.

Ducoudray-Holstein writes that " Bolívar and Mariño were received in Cartagena in a manner beyond their most sanguine hopes ". He goes on to say that " General Bolívar, on arriving at Cartagena, had taken up his quarters at the Palace of the Bishop (who had emigrated) where Mrs. Soublette and her two pretty daughters were established a fortnight before Bolívar's arrival. The two sisters, whom I visited various times, talked always with the greatest enthusiasm of General Bolívar, whom they designated even then by the name of *poor Simón* (in relating to me the events at Caracas, where they had formerly resided with their mother and their brother Charles) and to whom they appeared to be uncommonly and tenderly attached. The inhabitants of Caracas and Laguaira, those of St. Thomas de La Angostura, in Guayana, and every stranger who resided at the latter city in 1818-19, will confirm this fact, the source, as they say, of the high standing of Charles Soublette, the present secretary-general of the president-liberator." This house, the bishop's palace in Cartagena, soon became a busy political centre in which Bolívar, Mariño and the two Piñeres plotted against Torices and Toledo with a zest enhanced for Bolívar by the fact that Toledo's chief military adviser was his old rival Castillo. We see Bolívar " busily engaged with the Pineres in his private room ", and " going into and out of his cabinet a great many gentlemen ". And we read that " when the two Pineres had settled everything with General Bolívar, they had very frequent secret conferences with him and their partizans. Marinno, and a great many Caraqueño officers, were initiated; the former living in the house of Gabriel Pineres. The latter gained about twenty deputies of the most intriguing and noisy class; and the money which the dictators had brought with them served to gain more adherents. At that time more than 800 strangers were assembled at Cartagena, counting the owners and the crews of privateers. Among them Pineres had a strong party, because Torrices had laid heavy duties on the prize merchandise, and had limited the privateering business, by which Cartagena subsisted in a great measure at that time. Pineres, knowing the persons concerned in the privateers were not much satisfied with those restrictions, employed every means to foment this dissatisfaction."

What was Bolívar doing there? To begin with, the Indies were still subconsciously one big nation, even more so than Spanish America is nowadays. Then, Bolívar was no more a foreigner in Cartagena than a man from Santa Fe would have been. Then, the party of Toledo was the party of Castillo, his sworn enemy. Moreover, the brothers Piñeres in Cartagena stood for very much the same trend of policy and feeling which he incarnated in Venezuela: anti-Spanish, demagogic, " philosophic ", a mixture of what we should call to-day left and right, or, as he himself said, " democracy on our lips, aristocracy in our hearts ". Finally, for Bolívar, Cartagena was a stepping stone to higher command. All this is described, though with an unfriendly zest, by Ducoudray-Holstein. " Gabriel Pineres proposed confidently to General Bolívar the office of general-in-chief, if he would assist him to be chosen President. The latter accepted the proposal, with the secret intention, as well-informed persons say, of putting aside Pineres, and naming himself dictator of Cartagena, in order to employ all the means which the province had at that time to march against the Spaniards."

Bolívar, however, attained the high command he aimed at before the intrigues of Cartagena were ripe. There was a Venezuelan army in Cúcuta, commanded by Urdaneta. Bolívar moved southwards towards it. From Ocaña, he wrote Urdaneta a diplomatic letter (27.x.14) expressing his satisfaction at the fact that his countrymen had " saved the army of Caracas ", and adding a bitter-sweet compliment: " I esteem this service as the greatest victory, though there may be some who will criticize so wise and successful an operation." He announces to him that he sends him an aide-de-camp to explain the events which had brought him to New Granada, while he gets ready to come in person " to share your hardships, dangers and privations ". He hopes Urdaneta will do all he can " to conciliate the spirit of the Granadino troops with the Venezuelans; and to convince General Robira and Colonel Santander of the purity of my intentions, and of my high esteem for their talents and virtues ", for he was not thinking, he says, of depriving them of their authority, and his ambition was to serve as a simple soldier. This was his chief difficulty throughout. No one would believe him when he said solemnly: " I deem it my glory to serve well and not to command." The letter is curious because it shows how early Santander had begun to cross his path.

It is also curious because, set beside what he wrote the next day to the President of New Granada, it allows us to catch a glimpse of his mind at work. " On entering this city "—he writes to the President from Ocaña— " I have received disastrous news about General Urdaneta's army, informing me that my presence there is absolutely necessary, to check the grave evils which threaten the republic upon the imminent destruction of that army. As nothing is more important for me than the safety of the republic . . . I have resolved to go first to Cúcuta." No word about this in his letter to Urdaneta the previous day. Was he being discreet with Urdaneta, or was he trumping up a pretext in his letter to the government? Here again he promised to " fly to that capital" (his usual sense of speed) to justify himself and to prove " that my intentions have never been guided by aught than justice and public safety ". The President wrote on the margin of the letter: " Seen to-day, November 22nd. It has not been found necessary to send an answer."

The Tunja Congress had decided to coerce Cundinamarca into the Union and to that effect had secretly requested Urdaneta to come to Tunja from Cúcuta where he then was. Obviously the commander of the army who was to perform such an operation would be in an outstanding position to dictate political events. This explains Bolívar's manoeuvres to supersede Urdaneta as commander of the only Venezuelan army then in being. On his way to Tunja, Urdaneta passed through Pamplona, where his troops, hearing Bolívar was due there the next day, demanded to wait till he arrived. Urdaneta refused. The soldiers disobeyed him and took the road by which they knew Bolívar was coming. Cries of *Viva el Libertador!* resounded when they saw him. Urdaneta had to bow to the facts and call on Bolívar whom his soldiers had brought in triumph to the city. There was a parade, at Bolívar's request, and his address was typical: " You have filled my heart with pride. But at what cost ? At the cost of discipline and subordination. Your chief is the well deserving General Urdaneta, who deplores, just as I do, the excess to which your love has led you. Soldiers, let such acts of indiscipline never happen again. If you love me, prove it by remaining disciplined and obedient to your chief. I am but a soldier coming to offer my services to this sister nation. Our fatherland is America; our enemies the Spaniards; our ensign, independence; our cause, liberty."*

4

The Pamplona episode over, Urdaneta marched on towards Tunja. " On arriving with his troops in the city of Santa Rosa "—writes Restrepo— " Urdaneta learnt that in the close-by territories of Paipa and Sogamoso, there were five Spaniards in residence, one of them Don Juan Jover, well known for his fine qualities. The general and his Venezuelan troops, resentful at the great evils the Spaniards had caused the fatherland, hated them to death. . . . Urdaneta decided to have these five Spaniards arrested, to seize their property and to report later to the government. The Spaniards were arrested and the officer in charge took their lives alleging that they had tried to escape and that they would cause much harm to the cause of independence. Such was the excuse the general gave to the government of the Union. . . . This deed, the first of its kind the republicans committed in New Granada, caused a grave scandal and was considered by many as a real murder; while others believed that it was necessary to carry out such a

---

* Bolívar's biographer, Larrazábal, is moved almost to tears by this example of generosity and military duty. He is unable to see in Bolívar's action the shocking act of indiscipline it actually was in a man who was " but a soldier " and the humiliation of Urdaneta which it implied.

policy in order to exterminate the European Spaniards, for otherwise we should never be independent." Restrepo writes " some " and " others "; but he means " Neo-Granadinos " and " Venezuelans ".*

Bolívar, to whom as newly appointed commander-in-chief Congress wrote on the matter, answered (28.xi.14) that " he was filled with the greatest indignation at so scandalous a deed, and that such a thing would never occur again on the part of the officers of his army ". We shall soon see what became of this promise. Meanwhile, he went on to Tunja, where he was admirably received (22.xi.14). President Torres, his staunch friend, sent him a luxuriously harnessed horse, which he returned, saying " before accepting any present I must give an account of my behaviour during the mission I was given in Venezuela ". He did present himself before Congress and he pleaded his cause well. Congress exonerated him and gave him command over the troops—mostly Venezuelan—with which it hoped to reduce Alvarez, the dictator of Cundinamarca. Santa Fe was more Catholic, conservative and pro-Spanish than the Congress of Tunja; not because it was more " backward ", but, on the contrary, because the old culture had in Santa Fe deeper roots than in the remaining provinces, in which it had become easier for the thin layer of " philosophers " to claim to represent a mass which in fact did not follow them—which explains why they had to seek the help of Venezuelan soldiers to reduce the capital.

Bolívar besieged the city. During the siege, he sent a letter to a friend in the city (8.xii.14) to dispel " the lies and stories " about him. It is illuminating to find at the outset in this letter a hark-back to Puerto Cabello, rueing that he had not shot the prisoners " as I ought to have done "; and again, after recalling his offers to exchange four hundred Spaniards for two hundred patriots, and Boves' cruelties: " what was I to do with no garrison in La Guaira and nearly one thousand Spaniards in gaols and castles ? Was I to await the same misfortune as in Puerto Cabello, which destroyed my country and robbed me of my honour ? " This is a striking confirmation of our view as to the hidden springs of his war to the death. Then: " As for your present state, I affirm under my word of honour that the government has not declared a war to the death nor have I waged it, nor will I ever in this peaceful country where the Spaniards have behaved in a way quite different from Venezuela. The Jover affair was strongly condemned by the government and even more so by me. You must realize that since my object in coming to this country is to seek help, I am not going to be such a fool as to offend its government and public opinion which hate the war to the death." We are presently to see what became of these protestations. But, stranger still, he goes on to say almost with the same stroke of the pen: " My aim is to spare my brothers' blood, and that is why I want you to parley so as to shelter those inhabitants from the horrors of a siege and an

* O'Leary is more outspoken. " We should also bear in mind that in New Granada the troops of Venezuela were looked upon with much envy and not a little aversion . . . an act of rigour committed shortly before this time by General Urdaneta with a few Spaniards in the province of Tunja had so deeply offended the constituted authorities that the people began to feel justified motives of alarm, for it was not yet used to the excesses which typified the revolution later."

assault I shall have to order soon, when millions of innocent victims will die and not a Goth or Regentist will be left alive."

The letter is impressive for its self-assurance and its incoherence. " You know that I am more generous than any man with my friends . . . terrible with those who offend me." And much more to that effect. But who was he but a defeated chieftain ? Yet, his voice is sure, his threats are stern. There is no doubt in him as to his final victory. This core of self-certainty which, after his disintegration at Puerto Cabello, never falters in him, was not cool and serene; it was exasperated and feverish, bursting out of his volcanic soul in lava of exaggeration. " My troops, which are comparable to and even better than the best of Napoleon "; or these hallucinated words of his second letter to the same friend (who had rejected his advances): " Santa Fe shall be a terrifying sight of desolation and death. I shall bring two thousand firebrands alight to reduce to embers a city which would be the grave of its liberators." And around this centre of exasperated will, a circle of inconsistencies: a denial that he carries on a war to the death, and a threat that no Spaniard will be left alive; the assertion that " his troops are invincible and the same which have conquered in one thousand fights "— he, a fugitive from a defeated Republic.

Alvarez had prepared the city for the attack. He had five hundred soldiers of the line and nine hundred volunteers. The excommunication of Bolívar and his followers by the Church authorities of Santa Fe proved ineffective; and a distribution of daggers to the women of the city was of no avail. Bolívar addressed an appeal to the besieged (7.xii.14): " Heavens have destined me to be the Liberator of oppressed peoples, and so I shall never be the conqueror of a single village." He offered immunity of life, property and honour. The city refused to surrender and defended itself street by street with the utmost gallantry. " The lower classes "—writes Restrepo—" opposed the most stubborn resistance." Finally, with no water and nothing but the Main Square left to fight on, Alvarez capitulated (12.xii.14): Cundinamarca was to enter the Union, in exchange for " a complete guarantee of order and property to all the citizens of Cundinamarca without distinction of origin ".

Restrepo records that " as the soldiers of the Union were masters of nearly the whole city by force, it became impossible to avoid looting, particularly in the Santa Bárbara quarter. The Venezuelans, irritated, killed also some European Spaniards. For all lovers of science, the looting that the invading troops committed in the Observatory was most painful. The building suffered very much and the soldiers took away or destroyed the books, instruments and invaluable papers contained therein." Ducoudray Holstein provides another fact: " Notwithstanding this capitulation, signed and ratified by Bolívar, he permitted the pillage of a part of this beautiful and large city, during forty-eight hours; and when Alvarez and many other inhabitants of Bogotá made him the strongest representations against such behaviour, he replied in an angry tone, that he was authorized by the laws of war to act as he did, because the inhabitants of the city had resisted his troops, and deserved punishment. . . . The excesses and cruelties committed, particularly against females, were horrible, and his troops loaded themselves with gold, silver and jewels of every kind."

Bolívar himself confirms this in his note to the governors of the Archdiocese: "More humane to the people of Cundinamarca than its own government, I abstained from what was allowed me by the laws of war on the major part of the city, occupied by my troops"—a clear admission that he allowed the sacking and looting of the quarter of Santa Bárbara. At the time Bolívar was a general without an army and therefore without political power. He was bound to seek control of the first in order to win the second. He was letting his troops plunder Bogotá in order to secure their favour in case he had to struggle against Urdaneta, Castillo, or even the Congress of Tunja. His leniency towards his troops was therefore a calculated act in order to secure power by pretorian means—in the style of Monteverde, of Mariño, of Boves, and even of his secret model, Bonaparte.

5

On January 23rd, 1815, the Union Government inaugurated its labours in Santa Fe, where it had moved from Tunja. The chief event was to be an oration by Bolívar. It reveals Bolívar carried away (it would seem) by his anti-Spanish passion to the wildest assaults against historical truth and even against the every-day facts of his own time. He is in fact " justifying " the behaviour of his troops. Describing the past of the New World he says: " Tyranny and Inquisition had degraded to the level of brutes all Americans and sons of the conquerors who had brought them these ominous presents. . . . To yield to force was our only duty; the biggest crime was to seek justice and to be aware of the rights of nature and men. To speculate on sciences, to calculate the useful and to practise virtue were attempts against tyranny, more easily committed than forgiven. Dishonour, expatriation, death often followed talents, acquired to their ruin, by illustrious victims despite the obstacles opposed to the cultivation of the mind by the dominators of the hemisphere." This farrago of empty slogans must have sounded strangely out of place in the highly cultivated, rich city whose astronomical observatory had just been destroyed and looted by Bolívar's troops. And then, the scion of a family that had governed Venezuela for two hundred years and still owned herds of slaves in it, in his shrill, harsh voice, went on: " But we, have we led the destiny of our fatherland ? That very slavery, have we controlled it ? Not even the faculty of being the instruments of oppression have we been granted! "—a strange revelation both of blindness to the facts and of the secret impulses of the heart that spoke.

His speech, still full of the pride of his recent victory, abounds in military promises. " Santa Marta and Maracaibo shall be liberated by the superb army of Venezuelans and Granadinos you have entrusted to me." He then goes on to offer advice on justice, finance and public opinion; and winds up with a phrase which would have been fine had it been true: " Civil war is over; above it shall rise domestic peace; the citizens rest at ease under the auspices of a just and legal government, and our enemies tremble."

But was this so? Within a few weeks we are to see Bolívar forgo the liberation of Santa Marta and Maracaibo in order to indulge in civil war. The Union had rewarded him with the rank of Captain General. The capitulation of Santa Fe had yielded considerable quantities of arms and ammunition; and Bolívar was requested to prepare an expedition to take Santa Marta, where, it was feared, Morillo's expedition coming from Spain might land. He left for Santa Marta; but before his departure he endeavoured to apply his war to the death principles to the fallen city to which he had promised a complete guarantee of life and property without distinction of origin, i.e., including European Spaniards. He therefore proposed to Congress what O'Leary describes as " the most rigorous measures against the chief promoters [of the defence] and in order to terrorize the royalists, still a very powerful party in New Granada ". What this meant is clear enough, but it is made clearer by the following words: " Congress "— writes Madrid, one of its members—" believing that conciliation was to be preferred to rigour sent me to the Liberator to prevent the execution of the Spaniards linked up with the chief families of the country. Hardly had I suggested to him the wishes of Congress, when he answered: ' Tell them they shall be obeyed, but that some day they will have to repent. This country is unavoidably going to be occupied by the Spaniards, but never mind, I shall come again.' "

This scene throws a clear light on Bolívar's motives when he started his war to the death, and confirms the analysis of them we made at the time. Under his *idée fixe*, he had forgotten his letter to his friend in Santa Fe, his assurances that, since the Spaniards of New Granada had behaved quite differently from those of Venezuela, they would not be in danger, and his solemn and signed capitulation. It also explains things still to come precisely during his voyage down the Magdalena river towards Santa Marta. Bolívar's fame gained general acceptance for his appointment to command that expedition; but many also, writes Restrepo, " saw new dangers and discord brandishing its incendiary torches if Bolívar went down the river Magdalena ". Cartagena was in the throes of anarchy, between the Piñeres party and the Toledo faction, behind whom still stood respectively Bolívar and Castillo. The young Colonel Delhuyar, a favourite officer of Bolívar, who had commanded the troops besieging Puerto Cabello until the battle of La Puerta, was military commander in Cartagena, and had served Bolívar's interests with a *coup d'état* (5.i.15) whereby he imprisoned Toledo and Piñeres (the latter with his own connivance) and forced the Assembly to appoint as Governor a Caraqueño and a friend of Bolívar, Pedro Gual. Castillo had left the Magdalena line, which he was supposed to guard against the Spaniards, to join in the civil war, settling in Turbaco, close to the city. Gual, however, turned out to be a man of energy and of independent views, and after endeavouring, in vain, to effect a reconciliation between the parties, invited Castillo to enter the city and, with his backing, exiled the Piñeres.

In the course of these negotiations, Gual wrote to Bolívar asking whether he would be ready for a reconciliation. Bolívar answered with candour and generosity: " Not merely with General Castillo, who is on our side, but with

Ferdinand VII, who fights against us, should I reconcile myself for the liberty of the republic." And he declares himself ready to sign and make public a mutual discharge of insults received. The tone and style of this letter are frank and clear. But he was not trusted. His letters to Amador, who had become President of the State of Cartagena, remained unanswered. "Let us save the Republic, Mr. President. . . . For my part, you shall have every possible deference." Again, he was not believed. Cartagena knew that he meant to enter the city and reduce it to obedience by force.

The upshot of it all was that Castillo became Military Governor of Cartagena. On his way south therefore Bolívar had the choice between two civil wars: one against the Spaniards of Santa Marta; the other against the Creoles of Cartagena. He had left Santa Fe (24.i.15) to embark at Honda on the Magdalena river, and some of his troops were already afloat, taking down river a number of European Spaniards to be expelled from the republic. "The Venezuelan captain Francisco Alcántara, in charge of forty, had sixteen killed, on the excuse that they had become tired. The Governor of the province of Mariquita, León Armero, had also nine courtmartialled as bitter enemies of Independence, one of them the Capuchin Father Corella; he had them killed, as well as two other Spaniards accused of desertion. These executions caused much scandal in New Granada, whose peoples hated such bloody scenes." Restrepo, who writes all this, goes on to say: "The newspapers, and notably the *Antioquia Gazette*, declaimed loudly against them, and their authors were unable to justify themselves except by recalling the cruelties and immense evils the Spaniards had inflicted on the peoples of Venezuela. Bolívar, though he told the Union Government that he had ordered Alcántara to be prosecuted, tried to justify these murders in part by recapitulating the crimes and cruelties the Spaniards had committed on the Americans; wherefrom he inferred that the new governments of America were authorized by the law of nations to use retaliation, destroying enemies whom it was impossible to win over. Nevertheless the Union Government was never prepared to accept such principles; it condemned the facts and prohibited such executions for the future."

This page disposes of much that has been written since on the sufferings of Bolívar's tender heart when he had to append his signature to the war to the death decree. In all fairness to Bolívar, the deplorable quality of his officers and troops must be borne in mind. Mariano Montilla, speaking of these troops, after Bolívar had left them in charge of Palacios, reports in June, 1815, that while many officers were " brave soldiers and virtuous men, many are the acme of corruption, prone to robbery, murder, drunkenness, debauchery and indiscipline ". And Sata y Busi, referring to the army of Cartagena, wrote to his family in February, 1815, " my command is imaginary and theoretical; my troops have deserted, the officers are left alone, and are so bad that, leaving out a dozen, those who are not in prison should be there ". As for the troops, after the first days of enthusiasm, fruitful in volunteers, soldiers had to be pressed into the army; and " the troops looked like dishonourable chains of convicts ". All this must be borne in mind.

Still, the page of Restrepo quoted above shows that persecution and death of Spaniards came natural to Bolívar. He was not dragged, induced, deceived or perverted into such a policy by circumstances or by other men. In this as in every other aspect of his life, good or bad, he was a leader.

6

Voyaging down the Magdalena towards Santa Marta, Bolívar chose a civil war against Castillo in Cartagena rather than that civil war against the Spaniards in Santa Marta for which the Union Government had given him an army. Castillo, who was a vain and foolish man, had published a libellous pamphlet against Bolívar. Presently, Castillo received from Bolívar a request for arms and ammunition; but the Government of Cartagena grew suspicious at this request; for, writes Ducoudray, " those best informed, considering the character of general Bolívar, suspected that his real intention was to render himself master of Cartagena, to displace Castillo, and to punish him in revenge for the affront received in January, 1813 . . . to march a second time against Caracas, and with the troops of Cartagena united with his own, then re-establish his lost dictatorship ".

Bolívar's messenger to Cartagena had been Tomás Montilla. One of Castillo's chief advisers at the time was Mariano Montilla. These two rich *mantuano* brothers were thus divided by that truly fraternal civil war. Tomás Montilla, in danger of death from his infuriated adversaries, was only saved by his brother's intervention. On his advice, an officer was sent to Bolívar, then at Mompox, with letters from Amador and Castillo; this officer met with " a very harsh reception ", and was insulted as a spy; Castillo wrote circulars to all the *pueblos* ordering them to deny all help to Bolívar's troops, and withdrew his land and river forces into the city and port of Cartagena. Bolívar advanced on Cartagena under various pretexts, climate among them, and one reason which he himself gave to the Union Government: " in order to force the leaders of Cartagena to a respectful attitude and to see whether by fear it was possible to make them deliver the help so often asked of them ". This does not make sense. We are told Bolívar could not take Santa Marta because he lacked the means which Cartagena possessed; and that, therefore, he *had* to go to besiege and take Cartagena and wrench from the obdurate city the means to fight Santa Marta. How could he then force Cartagena without means ? As all this is sheer nonsense, the sense must be somewhere else. Bolívar wanted first to get rid of Castillo and then to liberate Santa Marta and Venezuela, but on condition that he would be the one and only *Libertador*. He tried to negotiate with Castillo and even invited him to an interview; but Castillo did not come, fearing a trap. The negotiations of the priest Marimón, sent by the Union to effect a compromise, failed; Marimón, on the whole, sided with Castillo against Bolívar, the chief reason for this being the massacre of the Spaniards at Honda.

After a month spent at Mompox, partly in these negotiations, partly in " the festivals, balls, dinners of which amusements Bolívar is a passionate friend ", he took his forces down the river and gave orders to seize the armed boats with which Castillo kept open his communications with Honda and Bogotá. This was a hostile action against Cartagena. Castillo prepared the city for defence, and went so far as to poison the well of a position outside the city which it was assumed Bolívar would occupy—the hill of La Popa. Bolívar was in a precarious position; unable to take the city, losing men to disease, thirst and the poisoned well, surrounded by a hostile population. He sought to parley, and the Provincial Government answered suggesting that he should retreat to Ocaña with his Venezuelan soldiers, leaving only the Granadinos. Meanwhile Morillo's expedition, ten thousand strong, coming from Spain, arrived in Santa Marta (25.iii.15). The next day, Bolívar sent the Union Government a letter asking to be relieved of his command, for " he was readier to go to the scaffold than to continue in command ".

Did he mean it? Earlier he had written to Marimón that " since the supplies set aside by the General Government to destroy the enemies of the fatherland were denied him, no doubt out of hatred for his person, the Commissioner should accept his resignation and provide a ship in Sabanilla for him to sail in safety to a foreign colony ". Marimón answered requesting him to resign his command into the hands of a senior officer, excluding Mariño and Miguel Carabaño, and informing him that a ship would be ready. Whereupon Bolívar, who had no intention whatsoever of resigning, called a Council of War to get himself " plebiscited " back into his command; from which War Council he got a decision to carry on the siege and " uphold the authority of the General Government ".

The General Government had repeatedly disapproved his actions during the siege, which thus became on his part an act of open indiscipline and of pretorian politics. The suspicions of Cartagena were justified. Bolívar did think of seizing power in Cartagena, and not for the Piñeres but for himself— an event which, had it come to pass, would have been beneficial for the cause he had at heart, the fight against the Spaniards, since it would have removed from the stage an inefficient and vain commander, and unified the forces of the two republics under his command. Nevertheless, the factions in Cartagena were against him, the Venezuelan troops were disliked for their cruelties against the Spaniards; Castillo was popular; and Bolívar himself did not succeed in hiding his pretorian ways. He attacked everybody; but in particular the Government of Cartagena. " There is here an evidently proved plot not only for independence but for insurrection; an aspiration to set up here the capital of New Granada, to monopolize trade and to come to terms in any event with the Spaniards." This was not so. In fact, as soon as the news of Morillo's landing in Santa Marta was known, Amador and Marimón called on Bolívar at La Popa " and made him the most urgent representations upon the dreadful consequences of a civil war in such circumstances, urging him to join his remaining forces with those of Cartagena, and march united against their common enemy. They offered him the command-in-chief, ammunition, provisions, and all necessary supplies, to enable him to keep the field; but all was in vain; he replied, he would consent under one condition, which was, that Cartagena should open the gates to him, and receive him with his troops into the fortress ".*

But Morillo landed troops in Santa Marta and the two rivals had to think hard. Towards the beginning of May Bolívar sent a flag of truce to Castillo. An interview took place (8.v.14) in a small house at the foot of La Popa; Bolívar passed the command of his army to his cousin Florencio Palacios, on the express condition that Palacios would be under the immediate order of the Government of Cartagena. On the very day the agreement was signed, May 9th, 1815, Bolívar sailed in the British war brig *Découverte* for Jamaica.

* Ducoudray, vol. I, p. 236.

PART IV

FROM EXILE TO DICTATORSHIP

Chapter XXV

MORILLO

I

ON the day on which Bolívar sailed towards Jamaica (9.v.15), Ferdinand VII signed a decree in which he announced his desire to " put an end to the calamities which afflict several provinces of my American dominions ", and " to receive as a true father those who, having realized the evils they were bringing on their fatherland with their rash and criminal behaviour, should wish to reconcile themselves cordially with him ". This style was deceptive. In point of fact, the decree gave official sanction to the failure of a long-drawn episode of mediation on the part of Britain. Castlereagh, as early as 1811, had begun to try to reconcile the Regency with the Spanish-American rebels. The chief aim of the British Government had been to prevent the diversion of Spanish blood and treasure from the war against Napoleon to what amounted to a civil war. The negotiations were laborious and ultimately failed, mainly for three reasons: the Cádiz merchants were loth to give up their privileged position in the trade of the Spanish-American continent; the Regency, consciously liberal, was subconsciously filled with a desire to coerce the Spanish Americans into obedience; and the Spanish Cortes and Regency never quite shook off their mistrust of British motives—a mistrust Castlereagh did not deserve, but which Pitt and Melville had earlier justified. The Cortes and the Government refused to give the kingdoms beyond the seas a position co-equal with Spain in matters of trade—although such a position had been traditionally taken for granted under the Austrian dynasty; the Regency, moreover, had tried to make it a condition for accepting British mediation that the British Government should co-operate with Spain in reducing the rebels by force should mediation fail—a suggestion which Castlereagh rightly refused to countenance; finally the suspicion of British motives, constantly fed by the odd habit the British Navy had acquired of conveying Spanish-American rebels to and fro, contributed not a little to the failure of Castlereagh. Sir Henry Wellesley wrote to him from Cádiz (5.vii.12): " I regret . . . to state that the last letter from the Minister for Foreign Affairs has compelled me to signify to him that I consider the Mediation as terminated."

If mediation had proved impossible while Spain was ruled by the Cortes and the Regency, how could it succeed under the infamous Ferdinand VII? The decree of May 9th, 1815, spoke of mediation merely as a figure of speech. Ferdinand understood no language but that of force, and it was by force that he meant to solve what, in essence, was the problem of the political coming of age of the Spanish kingdoms beyond the seas. To this effect, an expedition had been envisaged by the Committee of Generals set up in July, 1814, to reorganize the Spanish armies after the War of Independence. At the suggestion of General Castaños, the conqueror of Bailén, the expeditionary force was entrusted to the division general Don Pablo Morillo. The new commander Bolívar was going to meet in the field was, unlike Bolívar, a man of the people. Born in Fuentesecas, in the neighbourhood of Toro, in May, 1778, he was five years older than Bolívar; and, at the early age of thirty-seven, had risen from the ranks to the top of the Spanish army. A youthful prank when he was not yet thirteen had made him enlist in the Marines. He had served in many naval encounters of the period, including the battle of Toulon, where he had been wounded, and the battle of Trafalgar, where he had also been wounded and made prisoner. The War of Independence was his opportunity, for it gave him scope for his gifts as a leader of men. At the battle of Bailén, as an infantry lieutenant, he was noticed by the commander-in-chief, Castaños. From then on, he rose to fame and power owing to his boldness and resource. In April, 1809, a fortnight before Caracas set up its Junta, Morillo, then thirty-one, wrote his report on the surrender of the French garrison of Vigo into the hands of Captain Crawford, R.N., and of " Colonel " Don Pablo Morillo—for the youthful officer had had to promote himself a colonel in order to appease the French commander's qualms about surrendering to a lieutenant. His victory at Puente Sampayo over Marshal Ney (8.v.09) gave him at last a military status beyond dispute. He became colonel of a regiment he himself raised and organized, which was to make famous its name of *La Unión*.

Promoted a brigadier (14.iii.11), he served with the British division commanded by General Hill, and took part in the operations leading to Wellington's victory at Albuera. He was beginning to experience difficulties with the British soldiers, whom he found all too prone to grab by force what scarcity, disorder, misunderstandings natural in persons of different language, and other causes, denied or delayed. In one case, when a British officer had asked for hay, and Morillo had sent him with a Spanish officer to get it from the village Mayor, Morillo noticed that the British soldiers were helping themselves from the villagers' houses, looting them as well while taking the hay; he personally expostulated by gestures with some British soldiers, but they paid no attention, and when he raised his stick to threaten the worst offender, he was surrounded by the others and actually beaten. His own troops came upon the scene, and he sent three British soldiers under arrest to General Hill. His division campaigned northwards from Extremadura to Castille and the Basque country; and, with another Spanish division, took part under Wellington in the battle of Vitoria, which Morillo actually began, and, though wounded early in the day, fought through to the end. Wellington chose him as one of the generals to be portrayed in a group of the victors which he commissioned.

2

This victory opened the gates of France to Wellington. Morillo and his troops, camping in Roncesvalles, could look down upon that France whose armies had spread blood and tears all over Spain for so long. He knew the temper of his men, the memories of houses looted, of churches turned into stables, of *guerrilleros* shot for defending their homes. He issued a proclamation urging discipline, union and good behaviour. But he got into trouble very early. Complaints began to pour in about his troops. He repeatedly pointed out that the French could not tell one Spaniard from another, and that the disorders were committed by the Spanish volunteers of the British and Portuguese divisions. He owned, however, that the lack of food from which his division suffered, despite his constant complaints, was bound to produce evil effects. He had given away to Sir Rowland Hill some information which deprived his protestations of much of their force. " His officers and soldiers received by every mail letters from their friends congratulating them on their good fortune because they were in France and egging them on to profit by their situation in order to get rich." Hill told Wellington, who decided that strong measures were necessary. His division was punished: men and officers were to remain in formation from one hour before dawn till one hour after sunset, until further orders.

This decision deeply embittered Morillo, who wrote to General Wimpffen (19.xii.15): " I repeat that these troops have observed a stricter discipline than in their own country; and since they have so far been a model of good behaviour, I do not deem it possible to exact any more from officers and soldiers who, in their own billets, have to purchase everything, including light and salt, so that the French civilians feel prouder than the Spanish soldiers who not only have conquered, but carry in their memories the sad plight in which they have left their unhappy country, destroyed and ruined by the troops of the Tyrant."

This episode reveals the training and attitude of Morillo in matters of discipline and military behaviour. He was a soldier risen from the ranks, a man of the people. He was ready to make allowances for feelings and failings of human nature; but he " suffered more than he could say " at the idea that his soldiers might misbehave. All this accusing, defending and punishing, be it noticed, was about abuses that in no way touched on blood crimes or the taking of human life. This should be borne in mind in order to assess later events beyond the seas. For the present, the facts contribute to outline the figure of this self-made general, brave, straight, bent on discipline, self-taught and evidently able, as shown by his clear, straightforward style, with occasional dashes of real talent—and always sincere.

3

" At eight a.m. on February 17th, 1815, a moving sight, similar to that of Trafalgar, could be observed from the walls of Cádiz. Eighteen men-of-war and forty-two transports raised anchor, obeying the signal of the flagship

San Pedro, and sailed towards the Rota Bank, three leagues from the city. Thousands of handkerchiefs fluttered from the terraces as a farewell to beloved beings whom, with but few exceptions, they would never see again." Captain Sevilla, author of these lines, was on board with his regiment of La Unión, and so was his brother Manuel. Their uncle, Don Pascual Enrile, was naval commander of the expedition and chief of staff of the army he was conveying under the command of Morillo. Admiral Enrile could boast of leading " the most numerous fleet which had crossed the Atlantic since the discovery of America ". The flagship, *San Pedro*, was however the only ship of the line, imposing enough with her sixty-four guns. Two frigates of thirty-four, a corvette of twenty-two, a sloop of thirteen and thirteen gun boats made up the list of warships. They escorted the forty-two transports in which an army of 10,642 men was conveyed, composed of six infantry regiments of twelve hundred men apiece and a battalion of six hundred and fifty, two cavalry regiments without their horses, for there were many horses overseas; one mixed regiment of artillery and a battalion of engineers, plus a number of auxiliary services.

Formidable enough, considering the forces it was sent to meet, this expedition was not without its own weaknesses. The navy had not recovered from the deadly blows it had received from England while fighting as an unwilling ally of France; " Ferdinand's ministers neglected this part of defence to such an extent that it came to be wholly disorganized. Shipyards were deserted and stores empty; and the worst was that pay was apt to be casual . . . seventy years' salary being due." Nor was the army more reliable. Despite the leading part some generals had taken in the reaction led by Ferdinand VII, the corps of officers, honeycombed with freemasons, saw with displeasure the despotic ways of the King and his friends; Morillo, as a prominent leader of the resistance against Napoleon, had been approached by liberal conspirators, though without success. Great hopes were raised about a *pronunciamiento* that would rid the country of Ferdinand's despotism. These facts explain in part that from the middle of December, 1814, until February 17th, 1815, when it sailed, the expeditionary force was confined to barracks. There was no relish for overseas service in the army, and, had the soldiers been at large, desertions would have been numerous. This again had contributed to the hope liberals entertained that, in order to save themselves the voyage, the army might have been willing to be diverted to intervene in home politics.

And yet, the troops did not know the worst. They had been made to believe that they were sailing to Buenos Aires. On the 25th, after eight days' sailing, at dawn, the flagship sent around a boat with two officers on board (Sevilla goes on) " bringing us the unhappy news that we were not sailing towards the Río de la Plata but to Costa Firme. Such was the order carried by secret letters to be opened at that parallel. The news caused general consternation. We all knew that in Buenos Aires and Montevideo the rebels were divided, and that one of the parties was awaiting the king's troops to come over to us; while in Costa Firme there was no quarter and the war was waged with a savage ferocity." The ships were later paraded before Morillo and his general staff in order to raise the depressed spirit of the " poor soldiers "; and the fleet sailed on to its fate. On April 6th, 1815, it passed opposite Carúpano " looking like a golden cup from the sea ". The Spanish flag was flown from the fort, and presently Morales arrived to meet the general. They agreed to take Margarita first, according to Morillo's instructions. " Morales asked permission to embark a *zambo* regiment, the terror of the enemy." On their way to Margarita they found two British frigates sailing in the midst of the convoy. Morillo was no longer under Wellington. He called one of the captains on board and told him that, if they had not sailed away within three hours, he would sink them. They sailed away.

On his way to Margarita, Morillo may have pondered over his political instructions, drafted by the " Universal Minister for the Indies ", then the Mexican Lardizábal, who, once one of the constitutional Regents, had accepted a ministerial post under the despotic King. The instructions, nevertheless, with one important exception, are an honourable document. " Once Margarita has been occupied, mild methods shall be used to pacify it, and only persons caught with arms shall be arrested, and ships and other property belonging to other than vassals of the King seized. Thereafter, the government to be left in charge must be of good judgement, active and watchful." The importance of the island was defined " on account of its short distance from Cumaná and of its being to windward of the den of corsairs and the shelter of all the insurgents expelled from the continent ". As for the attitude he was to observe towards the rebels, the principles formulated under items 4 and 8 were shrewd and generous: general amnesty and a pardon within a time limit; but, and this was the one serious lapse from wisdom in the instructions, beyond this time limit, a price would be set on the heads of those who would not surrender. The blacks found armed were to remain free as citizens but enlisted as soldiers and their owners were to be indemnified; exiled leaders were to be sent to live in Spain, and persons of doubtful behaviour to be also sent to Spain " under some pretexts flattering for them "; finally, there is a paragraph obviously hinting at the Boves-Morales-Zuazola-type of chieftain: " In a country in which murder and looting is unfortunately organized, it is advisable to get rid of the troops and chiefs who have waged war there, and those who, as is the case with some of our own fighting parties, have exploited the name of the king and the country to promote their own personal ends committing horrible deeds, must be sent away with many flattering outward gestures, and given posts in the New Kingdom of Granada or in the blockade of Cartagena."

4

At dawn on April 7th, 1815, the Spanish fleet sighted Pampátar, the chief city and port of Margarita. Arizmendi and Bermúdez who commanded it, raised the Spanish flag; but Morillo was not taken in, not even when the fort was found to use the fleet's own code of signals; for one of the fleet's ships, the *Guatemala*, which had sailed out of sight during the storm and had arrived first at the island, was aground on the shore, having been enticed under the guns of the fort by similar wiles. After some negotiating, Morillo landed on the 9th, and the city and fort were occupied. The island offered to surrender if forgiven for its past deeds, and Morillo accepted at once. On the 10th he occupied it, finding it fairly well armed. On the 11th, Morillo left for Asunción, the capital, where he re-established the royal authority under Colonel Antonio Herraiz as Governor, to whom he gave instructions such as those he himself brought. Of the two chieftains, Bermúdez, with five hundred men and three hundred rifles, had fled to Chacachacare, where his mother had an estate; Arizmendi remained and reported to Morillo (11.iv.15) under cover of Morillo's proclamation granting an amnesty to all rebels. This scene is important because it shows at work three protagonists: Morillo, Arizmendi and Morales. It has been preserved for us by Captain Sevilla. Much that was to come has its seed in it.

Arizmendi fell on his knees weeping tears of repentance. Morillo bade him rise, saying that the King was more generous than his enemies, and that, in his royal name, he forgave him. Morales' eyes flashed. He pointed a vindictive finger at the prostrated chieftain, his rival both in war and in cruelty, and said: " General, do nothing of the kind. This man at your feet is not repentant; he is deceiving you miserably. . . . With that same tongue now asking for mercy he ordered five hundred peaceful Spaniards, merchants of Caracas and of La Guaira, to be burnt alive, and those who escaped were speared to death. They had taken no part in the war. In their name, general, I ask that justice be done, punishing him according to the law, not as an insurgent but as a common criminal." " Never mind "— retorted Morillo—" I forgive him. He will remain the more bound. Arizmendi, rise, recover, and be loyal to the noble nation to whom you owe a second life." Arizmendi rose to his feet and left the room and Morales said to Morillo: " General, I can now say that you will fail. In decreeing his pardon and that of other chieftains hidden in this island, you have decreed the death of thousands of Spaniards and of loyal Venezuelans who will be murdered by them." Morales went on to advocate the wiping out of the " poison " which still remained in the island, while the rest of the country was at peace, and concluded: " A mild and kind policy is all very well for peace time; in war time, it is mistaken for weakness. . . . General, Spain will lose these dominions and you will lose your fame as a shrewd statesman and a brave soldier if you follow the policy you have initiated in Margarita." " Brigadier "—Morillo drily retorted—" I have asked you for no advice."

Morillo amnestied everybody, save a European Spaniard, a renegade cavalry commander whom he sent " in irons on board the ship to be prosecuted for his sanguinary behaviour towards his own countrymen ". On April 20th, 1815, he sailed on board the *Ifigenia* for Cumaná, leaving but a small garrison in Margarita. Most of the fleet went to the island of Cocho for water; and there, probably owing to sabotage, the biggest ship, the *San Pedro*, crammed with ammunition, clothes, food and money, took fire and blew up (23.iv.15). Nearly the whole artillery and eight thousand rifles were lost, as well as invaluable stores of all kinds. It was a crippling blow to the expedition. Meantime, Morillo began to put into practice his plan of operations in Cumaná. He withdrew the flags under which the royalist chieftains had fought, giving them official colours and ordering that any person guilty of killing a man who had surrendered on the battlefield should be shot. He then sent a small expeditionary force to Peru; and having reorganized the civil and political authority of the eastern zone, sailed for La Guaira (3.v.15), where he arrived on the 6th. Two days later, a first contingent of his troops was sent to Caracas. As Captain Sevilla was among them we can see them enter the city—the first regular troops from Spain Caracas had ever seen. " In order to show off my Andalusian [i.e., small] feet, I had put on a pair of boots which hurt me badly; when I arrived, I could hardly walk. But I forgot all about it on entering the beautiful city of Caracas. Its streets, terraces and balconies were crammed with people who acclaimed us with *Vivas* to Spain, the King and the Army. Handsome young women, sumptuously dressed, shouted hurrahs, greeting us with their handkerchiefs as if we were the Messiah. The reception filled us with enthusiasm. I no longer felt my boots." On the 11th, Morillo entered the city followed by a brilliant staff. " He came on foot, frowning, and his lower lip hanging down—a sign of a very bad mood. Forthwith, he ordered the hussars to be mounted on the first horses available, and commanded that every afternoon we should go out for training and manoeuvres."

On the same day, Morillo addressed a proclamation to the inhabitants of Venezuela: "We are your brothers; the King is our common father; domestic dissensions undermine the opulence of nations and turn them into the toy of others. We do not come to shed your blood; we are not thirsty for your blood; we are not led by any spirit of faction. See the proof of it in Margarita. The arms of the King entered it unconditionally. Several of the leaders of the insurrection and all the general staff of the rebel units are there; they have sworn fidelity to Ferdinand VII; and there they are in peace. . . . My powers enable me to forgive, to reward and to punish: do not bind me to use any but the two first so that I may fulfil the wishes of the King. But if you force me to unsheath my sword, do not accuse the most clement of kings for the torrents of blood that will flow." On the 17th he issued a similar proclamation to the inhabitants of New Granada: " I shall soon be in your midst with an army that always was the terror of the enemies of our Sovereign; and then you will enjoy the quietness already general in these provinces." He again exhorted them to get rid of their leaders: " Let those wretched creatures get out of the sight of troops which do not come to shed the blood of their brothers, nor even that of the criminals if such a thing can be avoided, as you have seen it was avoided in Margarita."

5

On leaving New Granada for his second exile, Bolívar had handed over his troops to his relative Florencio Palacios. Desertion and disease had reduced them from 2,400 to 700. According to his agreement with Castillo, the troops were to receive food and ammunition but were to pass under

Castillo's command. This they resisted. A sharp trial of strength between the two commanders ended in the Caraqueños being " conducted with a guard to some vessels which were about to sail and banished to foreign countries, without any regard for their future welfare and comfort ".

All this took place on the eve of the siege which was to end the so-called independence of Cartagena. By then, another and graver peril had arisen. On May 12th, 1815, two emissaries sent with due credentials from the Governor, Amador, landed in Jamaica: Ignacio Cavero, Senator, and John Robertson, Brigadier General. Their mission was thus defined by Admiral Douglas: " to offer the city of Cartagena and the fortresses immediately dependent thereon in deposit until they should know the result of the mission sent to London for the purpose of obtaining an acknowledgement of their Independence; and in case it should not be favourable to their wishes, the possession of Cartagena to remain in the hands of the British forces, until they could obtain from the government of the Peninsula such conditions as might be necessary for the security of the persons and property of the inhabitants of New Granada ".

The dissensions between the leaders and the futile generalship of Florencio Palacios were disastrous for the cause of independence in Cartagena. " The favourable attitude of the people towards independence "—writes Restrepo— " disappeared when it saw itself oppressed by troops which claimed to be friendly and lived at its expense." Montalvo, the Spanish commander in Santa Marta, asked Morillo to send him a few ships and about four thousand men to blockade Cartagena. Morillo answered that he was coming himself with twice that number. The government of the Union had at most three thousand men scattered in Cúcuta, Casanare and Popayán. Anarchy was general. The return of Napoleon to Paris had aroused extravagant hopes of embarrassment for Spain in Europe—as extravagant as the fear it aroused in Bolívar lest Napoleon should carry on the war in South America after his defeat at Waterloo. In these circumstances the slightest success over the Spaniards was welcome for the patriots. A Spanish unarmed frigate, the *Neptuno*, conveying General Hore, Governor of Panamá with his family, eighteen officers, two hundred and seventy-four soldiers and two thousand rifles with other military provisions, fell into the hands of the rebels. The soldiers were pressed into the republican army; the officers locked up in the jails of the Inquisition. A number of citizens asked in writing that the officers should be shot. Amador and Castillo refused. During the night of July 6th, 1815, nine republican officers and two civilians forced their way into the prison and murdered fourteen Spanish officers, leaving seven others only wounded because their lantern gave out.

The city of Cartagena is built at the northern end of a bay ten miles long and about a mile wide, lying between the mainland and the island of Tierra Bomba, with two communications with the open sea: Boca Grande, north of the island, closed by special contrivances to all but light craft, and Boca Chica, to the south, the real entrance to the port, well defended by the forts San Fernando and San José. A chain of fortresses surrounded it, all well provided with artillery. It was a formidable bastion which Vernon, in

1741, had found too hard a nut to crack. This time, however, it was in the incompetent hands of Castillo and Amador. The population, enlarged by immigration from the countryside, had risen to 18,000; and though the authorities ransacked the country, the city was doomed to hunger from the outset of the siege. Emissaries were sent to the West Indies and to the United States, but the Spanish blockade was too effective. There was no money. The church silver was commandeered, and the city lost then some of the priceless heirlooms which were its pride, such as a wrought silver sepulchre which weighed eight thousand oz., a classic ornament of its Easter ceremonies, and a silver palm once looted by the French corsair Pointis and returned to the city by Louis XIV. A forced loan of 40,000 pesos failed, and the citizens were urged to give up their jewels, but did not. Morillo intercepted a letter (7.ix.15) in which Castillo estimated that, even counting horses, mules and dogs, he had food for at most forty days.

6

The Spanish main force sailed from Santa Marta (15.viii.15), landed without opposition at Arroyo Grande, and gradually took all the approaches to the city while forty ships closed the circle of the blockade by sea. Morillo settled his headquarters at Torrecilla, near Turbaco, about twelve miles from Cartagena. By September 1st, the encirclement of the city was complete, and the loss of Barú Island, from which it drew its only supplies, made its plight more severe. Two sorties ended in disaster and gloom.

Amador called a meeting of the Legislature (13.x.15) to propose to them the one measure he considered calculated to save the city after sixty days of siege. " We had not yet breathed from Bolívar's siege "—he said—" drawn out till May, when, in the middle of August, began a new siege from the Spaniards." The government did all it could, but what with the rainy season and the enemy, " the city had been reduced almost to the deplorable state in which it had been left by Bolívar's hostilities ". The day would come when there would be no supplies. A break through was out of the question. " Shall we treat with an enemy which has not deemed it right to make the slightest intimation thereto, and treats us as insurgents ? " (Morillo had endeavoured to obtain the surrender of the city by " mild and gentle means " on September 22nd, but it did not suit Amador to acknowledge the fact.) " To exist, to be happy, are the first wishes of man's heart." But how ? Here the President of the beleaguered city comes at last to brass tacks. " Can we doubt that in these circumstances we can no longer keep our independence ? . . . We must seek our existence and happiness in other ways. Let us save the State from the horrors we may expect from a resentful and blood-thirsty enemy; let us offer the Province to a wise and powerful Nation, capable of saving and governing us, let us put her under the shelter and protection of the monarch of Great Britain."

The unfortunate President of a State which thus sought to become a British colony had the documents read in which he had already offered to pawn his country for money and arms; and then he put his motion to a debate. The legislators " agreed unanimously that in the circumstances, the proposal was the only one which could save the State, and that . . . His Excellency may, in the time and manner he thinks fit, solemnly proclaim His Britannic Majesty and send out a mission to impart this decision to the authorities of Jamaica, so that, being considered as a part of His Majesty's dominions, His Majesty grant the city his powerful protection ". The military were, however, summoned first to be heard as to the likelihood of other ways of procuring food; but their answer was negative as to that, though they declared themselves ready " to uphold any decision taken by the government except that of capitulating to the Spaniards ". It was then finally decided to empower the government to proclaim " the August Monarch of Great Britain, and to inform our Legation in London so as to ensure under his August shade and protection the prosperity to which his new subjects of Cartagena aspire, and to swear fidelity in our name ". Among the signatories of this strange document are, Amador, of course, and a number of senators and representatives, as well as José Francisco Bermúdez, Manuel Cortés Campomanes (a European Spaniard) and Mariano Montilla. Castillo did not sign. As for Miramón, the agent of the Congress of New Granada, he gave " the approval of the General Government and I declare that not the slightest objection to the carrying out of what has been decided will be raised by either the Government or the United Provinces ".

Great Britain was not, of course, ready to take on such a heavy liability. The besieged city had to undergo the worst experiences of hunger and disease. The struggle for power continued within its walls; and four days after these lamentable papers had been drafted, Castillo was deposed (17.x.15), replaced by the Venezuelan Bermúdez, and imprisoned with much indignity. On November 11th–13th, the Spaniards took the island of Tierra Bomba, and the wretched inhabitants of Cartagena were reduced to the strict limits of their city. Their sufferings were so unbearable that the *Junta* decided on an exodus of women, children and old people (5.xii.15). Morillo sent a parliamentarian with a letter pointing out that he would have been within his rights had he forced the fugitives back into the city, but that he was too much moved at the sight of so much misery. He offered to keep them, but the city must be surrendered within three days. The garrison had already decided to evacuate it. Many did succeed in sailing away through the Spanish fleet, " which, either owing to neglect or to tolerance, did not attack them ". Morillo was humane. He had given orders—writes Sevilla—that " no harm was to be done and no ill-treatment inflicted on any citizen who did not resist ". In these conditions, it is strange that Morales, who entered Boca Chica on the 7th, should have massacred four hundred citizens there. The story is handed from one text to another; no source is given, and nothing is said on Morillo's reaction to this gross breach of discipline. O'Leary explains that the troops were Venezuelan. Torrente attributes the fury of the troops to the death of their Indian leader Pacheco, and says nothing of Morales.

CHAPTER XXVI

EXILE IN JAMAICA AND HAITI

I

BOLÍVAR arrived in Jamaica on May 14th, 1815, and left on December 18th. The seven months he spent there taxed his endurance to the full; for they submitted him to the worst form of slavery for a proud man—poverty. Fond of luxury and pleasure, he could be the most austere of men; born to silk and velvet, pearls and gold, he would eat off the bare boards of a Jamaican inn table and sleep in the hammock of a boarding house without even a sense of privation. The real hardship came from the shrinking of his field of action. A British merchant, Maxwell Hyslop, was his main financial standby in these years, the more trying for the generosity of the exiled leader, who felt responsible for the welfare of many of his companions. " I have not a dollar left "—he wrote to Hyslop (30.x.15)— " I have sold the little silver I brought over. No other hope remains but your favour. Were it not for that, despair would drive me to put an end to my days by violence, so as to spare myself the humiliation of imploring help from men more callous than gold itself. . . . Your generosity must be gratuitous, for I am not in a position to offer any reward, having lost everything; but my gratitude will be eternal." " Gave £100 as a loan "— wrote Hyslop in the margin.

Bolívar spent the loan in having his letter to the Government of Granada printed; and wrote again to Hyslop (8.xi.15): " With those siz onzas I meant to pay my month, and I shall be unable to do so if you are not kind enough to replace them." On December 2nd he wrote to Hyslop and to Ignacio Cavero, as emissaries of the Government of Cartagena, thanking them for their suggestion that he should go to the help of the besieged city, then hard pressed by Morillo. But two days later he had to come down to mean realities: " I have to trouble you again with my entreaties "—he wrote to Hyslop—" I had to leave the house in which I lived, because the crazy ways of the woman who served me put an end to my patience. This accursed woman makes me now pay more than one hundred pesos for extras; but as she is such a gossip, so perverse and talkative, I do not want her to drag me before a magistrate for so little and expose me to have to be violent with her because of her insolent ways. I have not got a cent, and so entreat you to send me one hundred pesos to pay this woman."

The fear of publicity evinced in this letter might well be due to his amatory activities, to judge by the elaborate efforts he himself, as well as others, made to explain away the fact that he was sleeping in someone else's hammock when the dagger meant for him struck and killed another man in his own. His story to Peru de Lacroix abounds in lame explanations of the fact that he happened to be sleeping in new quarters without any of the friends who had been living with him knowing about it—not even his black servant who had committed the crime. It appears that he was spending the night with a pretty young Dominican lady, Luisa Crober, when his negro boy, Pío, believing him to be asleep in his own hammock, stabbed one Amestoy, who was to leave for Aux Cayes the following morning with a message from Bolívar. " This infamous attempt "—writes O'Leary —" has been attributed to General Morillo's instigations, but from my knowledge of this personage, I incline to dissent from such a view, which has perhaps no other foundation than that of party spirit. I cannot believe that a Castilian officer could have had recourse to such a vile and cowardly way for ridding his country of an open and declared enemy."

Coming from the man who enjoyed Bolívar's intimacy and confidence for a longer period perhaps than any other, this declaration amounts to a definite statement that in Bolívar's eyes Morillo had had nothing to do with the crime. If it is not more categorical, the reason might well be that either Bolívar or his friends published in the Kingston papers an article asserting that " 2,000 pesos have been offered by some Spaniards to the black Pío for murdering his master, general Símon Bolívar. . . . The prisoner has not so far revealed the names of those who bribed him." Then, after a narrative of the murder, with the usual shamefaced explanations of Bolívar's absence: " This is the third time that an attempt is made against the life of general Bolívar by the lowest and most criminal Spaniards, and in every case he has escaped miraculously."

How are we to conciliate Bolívar's confidences to O'Leary, evidently exculpating Morillo, and this article written in Jamaica almost certainly under his direct inspiration ? The key is to be found in another of Bolívar's Boswells. Here is what Mosquera has to say on the subject. To begin with, he knew the names of the two men who had bribed the negro boy: " a European Spaniard and one born in America, whose obscure names we must withhold." He had therefore inside knowledge of the facts, and this is his story: " The case followed its legal course, and the magistrates, failing to obtain from the accused an accurate statement, allowed the Liberator to cross-examine him in the presence of Mr. Hyslop. The habit of obeying his master conquered his obstinacy, and he confessed the names of those who had induced him to commit the crime. Bolívar, Hyslop and an English lawyer met on the matter and agreed that a one-sided statement without proofs, from the accused, proved nothing fully, and that by thus making suspicions fall on two men the moral effect of accusing the Spaniards would be lost, for it was more advantageous to impute to them the origin of the crime in order to excite public opinion against the enemies of liberty. One of the two men had connections with Moxó [the Spanish Commander in Caracas] whence the common opinion spread among those who came to know the facts confidentially. Several of my friends who knew the facts told them to me, as I have related them, at Kingston, in 1818; and when I now and then spoke to Bolívar I found that the event afflicted him and I refrained from going into details."

This testimony seems final. Yet it is not possible to rule out the possibility that the attempt had emanated from Moxó. After all, Morillo had official instructions to put a price on the head of all the leaders who would not accept to be reconciled with Spain; and there does not seem to be much difference between putting a price on someone's head and paying for his assassination. Nevertheless Mosquera's report seems to point to Bolívar's own camp, for otherwise why should Bolívar be afflicted by the memory of the event? Bolívar deliberately concealed the names of the instigators in order to be able to accuse " the Spaniards ", and make political capital out of the crime. The official Jamaican authorities gave him every help in this and allowed him almost a free hand. The two previous cases mentioned, though without details, in Bolívar's article may well have been just so much fuel for propaganda.

2

Propaganda was in fact the chief activity of Bolívar while in Jamaica. Letters and pamphlets galore flow from his pen. The chief aim of all these writings is to enlist British protection and support. Bolívar was more conscious than most South American leaders of the humiliation which this attitude implied. " Had a glimmer of hope remained in me "—he wrote to Sir Richard Wellesley (27.v.15)—" that America might triumph unaided, no one would have been more eager than I to serve my country without degrading it to the humiliation of seeking foreign help." Yet he sought it—an inevitable result of his decision to " declare war on Spain "; and he even added: " such is the cause of my departure from the mainland ". This was of course by no means the case. Once on this slippery ground, Bolívar follows the example of Miranda and of some Mexican " patriots " of an older generation, offering Britain slices of Spanish America as a bait for help. " With this aid, we can shelter the rest of South America, and at the same time the provinces of Panamá and Nicaragua could be handed over to the British Government, which could make these countries the centre of world trade by opening canals that, shortening distances, would make the control of commerce by Britain permanent."

Bolívar was aware of the positive side of British foreign policy, and while adducing idealistic arguments such as liberty, justice, and even the " innocence " of America, he lays stress on the material advantages Britain expected from an emancipated New World. Commerce untold, industries to be developed, are made to glitter before the eyes of Great Britain. " What immense hopes this small part of the New World presents to British industry! "—he writes to Hyslop, referring to New Granada—" I shall not speak of the other regions which only await freedom to receive continental Europeans in their midst, and so form another European America, with which Britain, by increasing her weight in the political balance, will reduce the weight of her enemies." And to Richard Wellesley: " The balance of the world and the interest of Britain are in perfect harmony with the salvation of America. What a vast perspective my country offers to her friends and defenders! Sciences, arts, industry, culture. . . . England, almost exclusively, will benefit from the prosperity of a hemisphere which will, almost exclusively, count her as its benefactress."

The imaginative propagandist left a free rein to his fancy. Hyslop was told that " the mountains of New Granada are of gold and silver; a handful of mineralogists would exploit more mines there than those of Peru and New Spain ". This note of irresponsible exaggeration unfortunately prevails also in what we should describe to-day as his atrocity campaign. In his letter to the *Royal Gazette* (18.viii.15) he speaks of Las Casas as one who " saw with his own eyes this new and beautiful part of the Globe, populated by its native Indians, soaked later with the blood of twenty million victims; and he saw also the most opulent cities and the most fertile fields reduced to horrid solitudes and frightful deserts ". The events of Quito are told in a wholly capricious manner; in Mexico " more than a million inhabitants have perished in the peaceful cities, in the fields and on the gallows "; and he, the initiator of the War to the Death, adds, with a curious distinction in his mind, possibly an echo of his uneasy conscience: " It is not merely a war to the death which the Spaniards had declared on that opulent empire, but a war of extermination." He goes on to describe the worst atrocities committed in Venezuela by Antoñanzas, Zuazola and Rosete as well as Boves, never mentioning that these four men could hardly have perpetrated such crimes without the collaboration of their troops, Venezuelan almost to a man; and that the other side had at least an equally heavy score; finally, he crowns his irresponsible paper with a repulsive detail incriminating Cevallos, a Spanish general known for his decent and clean way of fighting.

Bolívar is writing as a pamphleteer. He knows Spain is going through a crisis and that she has not yet found a new political basis to replace the old. And yet, he writes: " The aim of Spain is to annihilate the New World and to wipe out its inhabitants, so that no vestige remains of civilization, or of the arts, and the rest of Europe may find here nothing but a desert, and may not find an outlet for her manufactures; and meanwhile Europe tolerates the destruction of this beautiful part of the world to satisfy the perverse aims of an inhuman and decrepit nation who, envious and jealous of the others, tries to destroy what her impotence prevents her from holding." Incoherence follows passion like a faithful dog. Bolívar, *mantuano*, Lieutenant Justice of his district, too haughty to call on the *cabildo*, favoured as a businessman with the fattest loan from the Royal Treasury, head of a family that had controlled the government of his country for two centuries, writes in his *Reply to a Gentleman of this Island* that the Americans were " deprived of their rights, left in a state of permanent infancy . . . absent from the universe in all that concerned the science of government and the administration of the State ". The tyranny and the oppression of Spain are described in black terms. Then, suddenly: " The South American lives in ease and plenty in his native land; he satisfies his needs and passions at small cost; hills of gold and silver put at his disposal easy wealth for him to purchase European objects. Fertile fields, plains populated with animals, and abundant rivers with rich fisheries feed him overflowingly; the climate exacts no clothes and hardly a habitation." And again: " The Spanish farmer [in America] does not oppress his servants with excessive work; he treats them as companions, educates them in the principles of morality and humanity prescribed by the religion of Christ. As his mildness is boundless, he exerts it with that kindness which a familiar intercourse inspires."

But it is not certain that Bolívar was aware of his incoherence. He may well have been the first victim of his own propaganda. Perhaps he did not see that the Spaniards could not be guilty of seeking to destroy " the opulent Empire of Mexico ", or of having turned America into " horrid solitudes and frightful deserts ", since Mexico was after all an opulent empire and Venezuela anything but a horrid solitude when the Spanish-American civil wars of secession began; or that the Creoles could not at the same time have been tyrannized over and excluded from power as well as happy, mild, civilized landowners in the quiet and undisturbed possession of their wealth, free from wars, hardly taxed at all, and at most subject perhaps now and then to the visit of a stern bishop come to demand in the name of Christian ethics that a dissolute landowner respect the womenfolk entrusted by providence to his social power. At any rate Bolívar does not see that when, with a fine sweep and perspective, he advocates union among Spanish Americans, he is yearning, into the future, for that which his country and the whole New World had received as a gift of History in the past from their common Spanish origin.

3

One day, at the beginning of November, 1815, a corvette of twenty-four guns arrived in Cartagena Bay, off Boca Chica, and her owner called on the Commander, the French adventurer in the service of Cartagena, Ducoudray-Holstein. The visitor was sick, and Ducoudray took him into the spacious Government House which he occupied in the city. The newcomer was a staunch friend of Bolívar, Louis Brion. A few years later he rose to high rank in the service of Venezuela, when he was thus described by Colonel Hippisley: " a native of the island Curaçao; in stature about five feet five inches; thin make; his limbs firm, and well put together; rather a round face, much sun-burnt, and pitted with a few marks of small-pox; short black hair, dark penetrating eyes, and good teeth; a Jewish cast of countenance, which, however, is rendered more expressive of his real situation by the full moustachio which he wears on his upper lip. In person and manner he displays a good deal of ease, and on a first appearance he is even rather prepossessing; he speaks English, and understands it well; he is as good a Frenchman as he is a Spaniard, and speaks the latter tongue with true Castillian pronunciation."

During his stay with Ducoudray-Holstein in Boca Chica, Brion spoke often about Bolívar. " He told me "—writes Ducoudray-Holstein—" that Dr. Rodriquez had just arrived from Cartagena, where Bermúdes, in consequence of his apathy and half measures, was generally despised." After some parleying, Brion, Ducoudray-Holstein and Rodríguez decided to bring Bolívar back and put him in command of the patriots besieged in Cartagena.

Bolívar had just declined an invitation to return to Cartagena brought him by Cavero and Hyslop. But this time he accepted with alacrity; for, while the first proposal meant being smuggled into a dying city, the second meant going to its rescue at the head of a relatively well appointed force. The privateer *La Popa* was well armed and fast and Brion's corvette *Dardo* had " fourteen thousand stand of arms and a great quantity of warlike stores ". Bolívar left Kingston on board *La Popa* on December 18th, 1815. On the 17th he had written his last request for funds to Hyslop: " You know I must leave tomorrow, and I need a number of things for me as well as for other Venezuelans I am taking over, my first purpose being to increase the forces of Cartagena." On the 19th in the afternoon, the *La Popa* met at sea the privateer *Republicano*, whose captain, Barbafán, told Bolívar that Cartagena had fallen and that Ducoudray-Holstein had left to join Brion at Aux Cayes, in Haiti. Bolívar then altered course and went to Haiti.

4

He arrived in Port-au-Prince on December 31st, 1815, in the evening, and was received by Pétion, President of the Negro Republic, on January 2nd, 1816. Haiti was the only free republic of the New World outside the United States. Pétion received Bolívar cordially, and made an excellent impression on him. " I hope much of his love of liberty and justice ", Bolívar wrote to Brion immediately after the interview. His decision to settle in Haiti as a base for his liberating expedition was momentous. Henceforth the republican cause was committed to a policy of equality of rights between whites and blacks on the Main Land, and therefore to the abolition of slavery. Both sides in the Venezuelan wars had, of course, wooed the blacks with promises of emancipation; but never had either of them committed itself to the cause of the negroes as openly and clearly as when Bolívar called on Pétion and sought his help against Spain. For the race of men brutally brought to the New World to toil in slavery for the whites, that day was a day of victory and, if not of revenge, of compensation. That white visitor whom Pétion received with an affable smile was Simón Bolívar, the direct descendant of that Simón de Bolívar, brought up on the same island two centuries earlier, who, settled in Caracas, had called on Philip II to seek permission to import several tons of black slaves yearly in Venezuela.

Pétion made the freedom of his brothers a condition for his aid. Bolívar wrote to him (8.ii.16) that he was *accablé du poids de vos bienfaits*, and added: *En tout vous êtes magnanime et indulgent. Nos affaires sont presque arrangées, et sans doute dans une quinzaine de jours nous serons en état de partir. Je n'attends que vos dernières faveurs; et s'il m'est possible j'irai moi-même vous exprimer l'étendue de ma reconnaissance. Dans ma proclamation aux habitants de Venezuela et dans les décrets que je dois expédier pour la liberté des esclaves je ne sais pas s'il me sera permis de témoigner les sentiments de mon coeur envers Votre Excellence, et de laisser à la postérité un monument irrécusable de votre philanthropie. Je ne sais, dis-je, si je devrais vous nommer comme l'auteur de*

GENERAL MORILLO

FERDINAND VII IN UNIFORM, by Goya (Prado, Madrid)

notre liberté. Could Simón de Bolívar have guessed that a descendant of one of those negroes he was importing under licence by the ton, and one of his own descendants, and a namesake of his to boot, would some day change places in the tragicomedy of life, and a Simón Bolívar write in court-like style that he owed his liberty to the son of a slave?

Bolívar devoted much time and attention to the political and military preparation of his new venture. He settled in Aux Cayes, a sheltered harbour on the southern coast of the island, and the residence of Robert Sutherland, one of those British businessmen who put their wealth at the disposal of the rebel Spanish kingdoms beyond the seas, whether out of sheer idealism, or in a spirit of speculation or again as secret agents of the British Government. Bolívar found many refugees from Cartagena in Aux Cayes, among them Ducoudray-Holstein whom he made his chief of staff. There were many prominent men about, far too many: Mariño, Piar, Bermúdez, the two Piñeres, Father Marimón, the ex-commissioner of New Granada in Cartagena, Zea, the Granadino botanist and politician, and a number of more or less influential foreigners such as Brion, Ducoudray-Holstein and the French corsair Aury. At lower levels, there were enough obscure *émigrés* for a chorus. Bolívar bethought himself of an Assembly.

We are able to attend it thanks to Ducoudray-Holstein. " General Bolívar was seated upon an elevated large armchair, and the military chieftains lower, and on common chairs, on the right and left of the general: opposite to him sat the secretary of the assembly, and on his left, his right, and behind him all the other members who had been invited to the assembly by written handbills signed by General Bolívar. I must confess that this armchair, elevated about two feet, gave offence to me and to many others; it had the air of a throne, and a monarchical distinction. . . . General Bolívar opened the session with a long prepared speech in which he attempted to show the necessity of having a central government, or a united power in one single person, and he therefore requested the assembly to name such a one before the expedition departed." Brion then put forward Bolívar's name, and flatly explained that he would give his credit and his ships ' to assist General Bolívar, but *nobody else* '. Whereupon, he proceeded to ask everyone present, thus: ' Do you consent, General Mariño, that General Bolívar, as captain-general of the armies of Venezuela and New Granada, shall be our only commander—yes or no? ' And he turned round, naming each of us by name; and so Bolívar was named our commander-in-chief, *uniting all the powers*, of which nothing was before mentioned in a positive and explicit manner, either by Bolívar or Brion. When the secretary had read the articles " (" I must mention here ", says Ducoudray-Holstein in the preceding page, " that these articles were already drawn up ") " Bolívar requested that no one should go out before they were reduced to form, and signed by each of us. Article 3 [on dictatorial powers] was put, to which Aury objected, and refused positively to sign the paper. This refusal was the cause of the first dissension among the chiefs of the expedition; and from that time Bolívar was very angry with Aury; and that resentment lasted until the death of the latter."

Aury, who had rendered substantial services to Cartagena during the siege and was owed a great deal of money, requested a schooner, the *Constitución*, to be handed over to him in payment of his service and in settlement of his debt. He offered, if so paid, " to bring three other armed vessels belonging to him and [to] engage four or five other owners of privateers to join in the expedition ". Marimón, who was the only representative of Cartagena on the spot, liked the idea. But Bolívar " annulled the just award made in favour of Aury and tore it in pieces, [and] he requested General Marion, the Haytien Governor of Aux Cayes, to put a guard of Haytien troops on board of the *Constitution*, in order to drive Aury's men from the vessel, and to take it for himself. . . . The consequence of this arbitrary act was that our expedition lost, with Commodore Aury, more than 400 good sailors, and about fifty foreign officers, with eight armed vessels . . . full one half of our forces were lost to us."

5

These quarrels between the leaders did much to compromise the prestige of the exiles and of their cause. No less than four challenges to duels had to be transacted: Mariano Montilla *v.* Bolívar; Mariño *v.* Brion; Colonel Hugo *v.* General Piar; and Ducoudray-Holstein *v.* Soublette. Ducoudray-Holstein was Bolívar's second in the first and Brion's second in his affair with Mariño. He relates how he cut short this affair by secretly warning the Governor, General Marion. The quarrel between Ducoudray-Holstein and Soublette does not seem to have been settled at all. Ducoudray and Soublette had come from Cartagena to Haiti in Aury's ship *Constitución*; and there, for the second time, it would appear, Ducoudray had occasion to humiliate Soublette in public on differences over rank and authority. While in Aux Cayes, Ducoudray had to accept the youth—for he was a very young man—as his chief assistant. He did not like it, and he writes: " Soublette, who had never commanded four men, was raised, by the favour of General Bolívar, to the grade of lieutenant-colonel in the staff, and was a great favourite of the latter." For the reasons for this favour, Ducoudray refers to Hippisley's description of the relations between Bolívar and Isabel, Soublette's sister. Hippisley, moreover, provides a portrait of Soublette which strengthens Ducoudray's narrative and case as well as his general authority and reliability. " Of this man, Colonel English and the British officers, who had been at the last actions at Villa del Cura and Ortiz, spoke most degradingly; the former officer, Colonel English, had seen him seeking shelter behind a tree, during the action at Ortiz, and had reproached him with his cowardice. This Soublett is, however, an exception to the general conduct of the patriot officers, who certainly are not destitute of courage, and is, I believe, the only instance of such weakness in the land service. General Soublett is a very handsome figure of a man; about twenty-five years of age; tall, thin, and well proportioned; remarkably neat in his dress and appearance: half-cast by birth and complexion: he is about five feet ten inches in height, rather a handsome and European style of countenance; black hair and large moustachios; a smile more than prepossessing, a general lover, amongst the female part of the province, by whom he is well received, and has no disappointment in affairs of gallantry to complain of: he has, however, been a martyr to his pleasures, and makes an infamous boast of retaliation in this respect."

One day, Bolívar spoke about Soublette's complaints to Ducoudray, who (he writes) " asked for pen, ink and paper, and immediately wrote to Soublette, in Bolívar's chamber, the following note in French, which Soublette understands passably well: ' I have just now heard from General Bolívar, that you speak and spread falsehoods against me, like a coward, in my absence. I give you notice that, if you continue to do so, I will treat you as you deserve, and mark your face with my whip wherever I can meet you '." Ducoudray handed the note to General Bolívar, who warned him against Soublette's vengeance; but the Frenchman laughed at this and dispatched the note to Soublette who, from that day on, avoided him.

There are two ways of getting rid of this narrative: one is to forget all about it; the other, to decide that Ducoudray made up the whole story. Neither of them makes good history. The narrative must be taken as on the whole correct. Bolívar should have settled the business without allowing it to reach such extremities. Why did he fail to intervene effectively ? There is only one answer: he felt the lack of moral authority which his illicit relations with Isabel Soublette inflicted on him. He knew he was responsible for the rise of the young man for reasons that had nothing to do with military prowess or competence. His amatory adventures were a constant source of embarrassment for him. At that time, he often went to the house of Lieutenant-Colonel Juan Valdés, " whom Bolívar appointed during his dictatorship, Governor of Laguaira, in recompense of certain connections with his handsome wife. . . . Valdés seldom received any company, and Bolívar did not like a great assembly when he was there."

Ducoudray discloses these facts in the course of a long and circumstantial narrative of Bolívar's affair with Mariano Montilla. The description of the several scenes, the details of space and time, the attitudes and motives of all concerned are so precise, so telling, and (but for one important detail) so concordant, that their very mass and cogency carry conviction. He relates that one day, when he was away from Aux Cayes, Mariano Montilla suddenly turned up to offer his services to Bolívar, who granted him an interview for that very evening at seven. Ducoudray came back to Aux Cayes at six, when Bolívar was at dinner, and found him nervy and worried. At ten minutes to seven, Bolívar rose, asking Ducoudray to follow him, and left the house hastily, as it turned out, for fear of meeting Montilla. They crossed the square to Valdés' house, where Bolívar spoke in whispers to one of his aides-de-camp, a Captain Chamberlain, a Jamaican-born British subject. Chamberlain left and returned with a Venezuelan, Captain Hernández. More whispers. Chamberlain and Hernández leave. Chamberlain returns alone and whispers in Bolívar's ear with visible satis- factory effects. " We retired, General Bolívar, intendant Zea, myself and the two aides-de-camp together. The General took us, Zea and myself, each by the arm, and said, in a jesting manner, that he was now well escorted in case Montilla should attempt anything against him."

The next morning, Ducoudray was hastily sent for. Bolívar showed him a challenge in French sent by one Charles La Veaux, on behalf of Montilla, who made Bolívar responsible for a pasquinade slandering him, that had been posted up in the town during the night. The pasquinade was signed Hernández. Ducoudray took the matter up and saw Montilla and La Veaux. Montilla told Ducoudray that he was sure the author was Bolívar. Ducoudray did not believe it, and finally settled the matter on two conditions: Bolívar would give Montilla " an honourable testimony enabling him to show it to whomsoever he pleased ", and Hernández would be brought to him that afternoon to apologize. Bolívar agreed to both conditions, and copied and signed the letter to La Veaux prepared by Ducoudray-Holstein to satisfy the first of them. Hernández was then prevailed upon to call on Montilla with Ducoudray. He was dejected all the way, and spoke mysteriously about it all. La Veaux accepted his confused mutterings as an apology, then told Ducoudray that the true author of the pasquinade was Bolívar. Two days after these events Montilla left Aux Cayes. A year later, after the failure of the expedition had brought back most of its members to Haiti, Captain Chamberlain met Ducoudray again at Aux Cayes, and after dinner, " when he had drunk pretty freely ", he revealed that the pasquinade had been the work of Bolívar who had it signed " Hernández " without Hernández' assent. Ducoudray contradicts himself badly here; for he shows us Hernández coming and going with Chamberlain during that evening at Valdés' house, while now he makes Chamberlain say that Hernández was out that day " and would not return that evening ". Yet, the details are too many and the story has too much body not to stand in the absence of concrete proof to the contrary.

The more so as it is possible to gather from other sources not only a confirmation of the features Ducoudray emphasizes in Bolívar but also proofs of his objectivity; for at times he tells events in a more favourable light to Bolívar than the actual facts would justify. Here is for instance what a first-hand authority has to say on Bermúdez at Aux Cayes: " *Quoique Bolívar se fût reconcilié avec Bermudes, depuis les remontrances de Pétion, et qu'ils parussent être dans les meilleurs termes, il est certain néanmoins que le commandant en chef conservait à son ancien lieutenant rancune de ses menées avec Aury, et qu'il était résolu à ne pas l'employer dans l'expédition. . . . De son côté Bermudes jalousait Bolívar. . . . Toutefois, les intérêts respectifs voulurent qu'ils jouassent encore de la dissimulation. Bolívar s'était efforcé par des manières cordiales d'inspirer une sorte de confiance à Bermudes. Ainsi il put facilement lui persuader que la Popa le recevrait à son bord avec ses gens et son bagage. Plein donc d'assurance dans la parole du commandant en chef, Bermudes avait fait tout naturellement ses préparatifs de départ, et attendait impatiemment l'ordre d'embarquement; mais quelle fût sa surprise et son indignation . . . lorsqu'un beau matin en se levant, il voit la Popa à la voile, et lui-même encore à terre. Le capitaine avait positivement reçu l'ordre de Bolívar de ne pas le prendre à son bord. Désespéré, Bermudes accourt aussitôt chez le commandant de l'arrondissement, à qui il racconte, les larmes aux yeux, ce qui lui est arrivé. Comment, s'écria le général Marion, la Popa est parti sans vous prendre! . . . Je ne me serais jamais douté qu'un homme du caractère du Général Bolívar fût capable d'une pareille action."*

The writer of this page is the Haitian Senator Marion, son of the general to whom Bermúdez went with tears in his eyes, on discovering that he had been left behind by Bolívar. Senator Marion adds: " *Ducoudray-Holstein raconte tout différemment cette affaire. Il prétend que ce fut de son propre mouvement que Bermudes resta Aux Cayes indigné qu'il fut de la conduite arbitraire de Bolívar à l'égard d'Aury. . . . Je suis fâché que l'intérêt de la vérité me force à contredire un homme pour lequel j'ai professé de l'estime, qui a été pendant plus d'un an mon maître de musique et avec lequel j'ai passé d'agréables moments Aux Cayes. Il paraitrait que le général Ducoudray aurait été mal renseigné, ou bien que sa mémoire lui aurait fait défaut en cette circonstance."* It is clear, therefore, that Ducoudray did not seek deliberately to expose Bolívar's weaknesses, but tried to report things as he honestly believed them to have occurred.

6

On April 10th, 1816, an expedition sailed from Aux Cayes to liberate Venezuela. It had been financed by the Haitian State and by the Curaçaoan mulatto Louis Brion. In Brion's case the motive can have been no other than adventure and a certain flamboyant taste for titles and uniforms: " Officers in the Colombian Navy are entitled to a comparative rank in the army, by which they may be addressed on all occasions, and to wear its uniform if they please. According to this regulation, Admiral Brion ranked as captain-general; and was usually seen on his quarter-deck, attired in an English hussar jacket and scarlet pantaloons, with a broad stripe of gold lace down each side, a field marshal's uniform hat, with a very large Prussian plume, and an enormous pair of dragoon boots, with heavy gold spurs of a most inconvenient length. He always signed himself captain-general and was so addressed by his officers and men; and if any of them neglected this title, or substituted that of Admiral, they seldom regained his favour." In the case of Haiti, the motive was a natural desire to liberate the negroes of Venezuela not merely from Spain but from serfdom as well; and this fact, coupled with the predominantly negro composition of the troops that Bolívar was taking over, led to the belief that Bolívar was sailing to found a negro republic in Venezuela.

All authors mention the army chiefs and officers on board; and Ducoudray waxed both eloquent and merry about the women also; but no one speaks of the " other ranks ". This gap is both filled and explained by Bolívar, who, in 1816, referring to his second expedition, told a friend that " his friend Pétion was helping him with four hundred men and the necessary transports ". Therefore Pétion had also supplied the rank and file for the first—and, as will be seen anon, about twice that figure.

All this family party was conveyed in a fleet composed of six schooners and an armed sloop. The expedition was detained for a long time owing to " the calm of spring ", says Mosquera. Restrepo is more involved: " It underwent a calm which forced it to delay longer than necessary." Why and how could the calm force Bolívar to delay " longer than necessary " ? Does this not reveal in Restrepo a secret disagreement with his own explanation ? A modern Venezuelan authority, Don Vicente Lecuna, throws that calm to the winds, and attributes the delay to some sailors Bolívar had secretly sent to recruit troops in St. Thomas. But, though he comes closer to the facts, since he speaks of St. Thomas, he does not come close enough. What Bolívar waited for all those days of " unnecessary delay " was coming from St. Thomas; but it was not sailors.

Let us now turn to Ducoudray-Holstein who was there. " Scarcely had we arrived at the Island of San Beata, when the whole squadron was detained by—a woman! it was no other than *Miss Pepa M*, the dear mistress of General Bolívar. She alone, by her secret virtues, had the power to detain the whole squadron, and about a thousand men, during more than forty-eight hours, at anchor! . . . When Bolívar was named commander-in-chief, by the assembly held at Aux Cayes, he wrote to Miss Pepa, who resided with her mother and sister at St. Thomas's, to come and join him without delay. He expected them daily with great anxiety, and deferred the departure of our expedition from one day to another, during more than six days. At last Commodore Brion, grown impatient, declared to him frankly that it was high time to embark, and that he would not and could not wait any longer. Bolívar, therefore, was obliged to sail without his mistress, and we departed."

Ducoudray writes on: " Before we arrived at the Island of La Beata, some leagues from Aux Cayes, a fast-sailing pilot-boat brought the lucky tidings to General Bolívar, that his dear Miss Pepa, with her mother and sister, had arrived at Aux Cayes, from Thomas's. This letter caused a bustle on board. . . . Brion was strongly opposed to waiting the arrival of Miss Pepa . . . but the entreaties of General Bolívar prevailed at last, and he consented to wait." Bolívar sent the *Constitution* to Aux Cayes with three officers, including Soublette, to fetch the lady, who made them wait a whole day. The foreign officers were incensed, and only consented to remain on strong objurgations from Brion. Palacios, Bolívar's cousin, and a number of other Caraqueños, resigned and were sent ashore close to Jacquemel. Brion, " who had been against the admittance of any female on board the squadron ", refused to let Miss Pepa on board the Commodore's vessel, and the lady had to remain on the *Constitution*. " Bolívar made his toilette in a superb style, and left our vessel to pay a visit on board the *Constitution*, where he remained the whole day and night, and came the next morning on board the Commodore, who was [sic], as well as myself, and the other officers, highly displeased at having lost about four days at anchor."

The fleet sailed round the arc of the lesser Antilles, and by May 2nd was within sight of the Three Monks, not far from Margarita. This island had been retaken from Morillo's men by Arizmendi. In the early hours of that morning, they sighted a large brig and a schooner with which the royalists were blockading the island. The Commodore's ship and three others, attacked one of them, the *Intrépido*, of fourteen guns; while the remaining three under Mariño attacked the schooner *Rita* of seven guns. Captain Ocampo, who commanded the Spanish ship *Rita*, was mortally wounded. As for the commander of the *Intrépido*, the brigadier Iglesias, he was, according to Ducoudray, " wounded and then killed by our men, who took the vessel by boarding. They entered the cabin with drawn swords while the surgeon was dressing his wound, and killed him; the surgeon attempted to appease them, and was murdered too ." Brion was wounded and on the spot raised by Bolívar to the rank of Admiral. As for Bolívar himself, he did not fight. Ducoudray describes him in a most unfavourable light. He thought boarding was a folly and feared that, were he to be wounded or killed, the expedition would be lost. Brion told him to help hand cartridges with Zea, the intellectual on board; but Bolívar took a post inside the longboat " which in armed vessels is generally fixed over the cabin windows ", and from there he watched the fight. " This position which Bolívar chose for himself, was surely the safest place in the vessel."

So writes Ducoudray-Holstein, who was there. No service is rendered to history by pretending that this page of a well authenticated witness does not exist. Can Ducoudray have invented the extremely detailed account he gives of the engagement, and the collapse of all sense of leadership it reveals in Bolívar ? " He sat down on the boat, and requested me to take command of the officers, whom I had provided with arms and ammunition; and Brion entrusted me with the command of the volunteers, so that I had to survey the whole infantry of about 160 men." The fight was hard and caused about fifty casualties to Ducoudray's men; " but when our number increased, and their brave commander felt himself mortally wounded, they . . . lost all hope; and about thirty of them stripped off their clothes and jumped overboard, in hopes to save their lives by swimming to the Three Rocks. At this moment General Bolívar, having all this time been sitting very safe in the longboat behind his beam, perceived these naked unfortunate men swimming at a very short distance from him; he took his pistol and killed one of them—took the second, and fired at another. When all was over, and the brigg was taken, he jumped out of his boat, came with a radiant face to me and said, ' My dear friend, you fought bravely, but I too have not been inactive; I killed my man; but unfortunately missed the second! ' I, who had passed several times from one side of the vessel to the other, always seeing my commander leaning his head close to the beam, was surprised, and asked how he could kill a man in his boat ? ' Ah ', said he laughing, ' with my pistol in the water! ' "

Could Ducoudray have made up this story from beginning to end ? " Such was Bolívar "—he writes on—" in the action of May 2nd, 1816. I was there; I saw him, he spoke to me, and I commanded, in his place, our corps of officers and volunteers, who will testify to the truth of my plain statement, if they are now living, and not interested, and out of his reach." In these circumstances, it does not seem possible to brush aside this episode as the heinous lucubration of an enemy. Ducoudray could not lie outright when there were still so many eyewitnesses of the scene about; and on the other hand, he could praise Bolívar handsomely when he thought that such a praise was due. We have to take in this episode in our estimate of Bolívar's character. Moreover, does it not fit into the general picture of the man? At sea, Bolívar was not in his element. The excitement of movement was denied him. No walking, no galloping. Just the narrow space of a small deck. His spirits could not rise. On such occasions, he felt helpless, tossed to and fro in the voids of his soul, unable to settle firmly on one or other of his cores of resistance. Bolívar could be both brave and even rash, and cowardly and even contemptible. And as for his shooting at the Spaniards swimming for life, it fits also with his passion for war to the death.

CHAPTER XXVII

BOLÍVAR FAILS IN VENEZUELA AND MORILLO CONQUERS NEW GRANADA

I

THE key event which gave a base to Bolívar's expedition on Venezuelan territory, Arizmendi's revolt in Margarita, is usually told as if it had been caused by a new wave of oppression on the part of the Spanish authorities. Arizmendi needed no such provocation. He broke his word and his oath of fidelity because he was athirst for ambition and power, and because, as Bolívar later said of him, he " always did as he pleased ". The English seaman often quoted in these pages, who knew him well and swore by him, left this portrait of the famous Margaritan: " He is by birth half Creole and half Indian; his features are those of the former, while his hair closely resembles that of the latter. His person is large, athletic, and muscular, though spare and thin; and he is capable of enduring almost incredible fatigue and privation. He is about fifty-four years of age, though in appearance older; continued anxiety, his hard mode of living, together with several wounds, having done more than time to increase the deep furrows which mark his weather-beaten countenance. Thus strongly indented, his aspect exhibits a peculiar ferocity of expression, which his smile only increases. His laugh never fails to create a momentary shudder, and the dreadful distortion of the muscles of the face which it produces, can only be compared with that of the hyena when under similar excitement. His displeasure is always signified by this demoniacal grin, accompanied by a low lengthened exclamation resembling the suppressed roar of a tiger, his eyes at the same time flashing vengeance; and should the object of his rage be at these moments within its compass, death inevitably ensues. His general appearance might impress a superficial observer with a belief that he is so accustomed to scenes of horror and bloodshed, they afford him gratification rather than uneasiness. I am, however, strongly of opinion, that the sanguinary measures which he has adopted against the enemies of Colombia have resulted more from the state of a mind goaded and tortured to revenge by the fiend-like barbarities to which so many of his kindred and countrymen fell a sacrifice, than to any original want of humanity; and that if he had lived in more peaceful times, he would have been an ornament to the society in which he moved."

This was the leader who led Margarita to rebel for the second time. His chief weapon to arouse the island was a spate of false news. He spread rumours that Morillo had been killed, Cartagena liberated and the army of Morillo exterminated; and he wrote to several Margaritans describing himself in Blanquilla island with ships and 2,500 men, and inviting them to meet him in a secret place on November 15th, 1816. Obviously, had the new governor's oppression been the motive force of the rebellion, Arizmendi would not have stood in need of deceiving his friends. The Spanish governor, Urreiztieta, learned of the plan in time to round up many of the conspirators, some of whom lost their lives there and then; but not Arizmendi, who fled unscathed, and attacked by surprise the garrison of the harbour of Juan Griego, killing all its members outright (16.xi.16). Thus reinforced with eighty rifles, he attacked Norte, defeated and put to death the garrison and set about to organize a rebel army. It was then that he confided to his partisans that there was no such a thing as the Blanquilla expeditionary force.

Moxó, whom Morillo had left in command at Caracas, was a harsh man; and he wrote to Urreiztieta: " Brush aside all humane considerations and shoot every man you catch, with or without arms, and those who have helped them, after a mere hearing." It seems that Urreiztieta did not even worry about that hearing. But when his successor, Pardo, wrote to Moxó that Arizmendi's wife had given birth to " a new monster " in jail and should be beheaded, since her husband had put all his Spanish prisoners to death, Moxó refused and sent the lady to Cádiz, whence she eventually fled from prison and returned to the fatherland. Fighting continued for weeks and Urreiztieta was seriously wounded by an explosion of ammunition in the castle. On May 2nd, the Spaniards heard shouts of joy in the enemy camp. Bolívar's expedition was in sight. They gave up their positions and withdrew to Pampátar.

Ducoudray relates how heavily the idea of meeting Arizmendi lay on Bolívar's chest. He rightly points out that " Arizmendi was well informed that Bolívar had treated him in his manifesto, published in Cartagena in September, 1814, as an intriguer and an ambitious man "; Bolívar, in his turn, had every reason to know what sort of a man the Margaritan tiger was. " One day I saw him walking with a quick step to and fro on deck, absorbed in thought, and melancholy. ' What is the matter with you, my dear General, are you unwell, or has something happened ? '—' Oh no ',—replied he—' but we are approaching the island of Margarita where Arizmendi commands, and I fear this man and his character; he is obstinate and cruel '." Bolívar went on: " Arizmendi is a very dangerous, ambitious man, who governs the island of Margarita with great despotism; he is an absolute brute, without any education or knowledge, and of low extraction." Ducoudray remarks here that " Bolívar thinks much of birth and good family ".

This little scene explains what happened when the squadron entered Juan Griego, the port of Margarita (3.v.16). Bolívar sent first Brion and the chief of the naval staff, a Frenchman named M. Villarette, to speak with General Arizmendi. " One hour afterwards, Arizmendi arrived on board to compliment the commander-in-chief. . . . Bolívar embraced Arizmendi, with that kind of frankness and cordiality which appeared so natural in him, took him by the arm, after having presented me and the Intendant, and invited him down into the cabin, where they remained alone more than an hour. They appeared, in mounting on deck, very well satisfied with each other, and Arizmendi invited us, Bolívar, Zea, Mariño, Piar and myself, to come on shore in the afternoon, where horses would be in readiness to convey us to the Villa del Norte, the headquarters of Arizmendi. After a splendid dinner, the ball began, which lasted the whole night. But not a single word passed which had any connection with business; Bolívar was so totally engaged in dancing, of which he was pasionately fond, that he thought of nothing else."*

2

Business, however, was being transacted. Bolívar had his authority ratified by an Assembly of the new forces. Arizmendi, says Ducoudray, "was four times as strong as Bolívar" and "much better instructed in military matters than Bolívar himself". Bolívar, however, had genius. Both had one feature in common: a passionate hatred of the Spaniards. "On our landing at the port of Juan Griego"—writes Ducoudray—"Arizmendi, Bolívar and I were talking, when I heard suddenly the discharge of musketry. I turned round to see what caused this firing. Bolívar told me, smiling, ' it is nothing, my dear friend (speaking with me always in French), General Arizmendi has ordered some Spanish prisoners, landed from our squadron, to be shot.' These unfortunate men were, on landing, tied together, while others dug a large hole, before which they kneeled down, and were shot in the back, so that they fell into their grave, which was immediately filled with earth."

This was the true link between the two men. In the words of Vicente Tejera, in his Ode to that very expedition:

> For, while in our nation,
> Indian blood will flow,
> We swear detestation
> And extermination
> To the Spanish foe.

Bolívar sent a message to Colonel Pardo, the Spanish commander in Margarita, requesting him to surrender the posts he still held, and informing him that action had been taken to end the war to the death by sparing the prisoners caught at sea; Pardo answered refusing to surrender and pointing out that the Spanish government had never declared a war to the death, and that the practice thereof would stop if the insurgents ceased to apply it.

* "During about a month of our being in the same vessel, and very intimate, he never asked me a single question on military tactics or anything concerning our art. His great employment was to play at backgammon with me, or with Brion, or Zea, to walk up and down the deck and talk on very common topics with one or another of his officers, or to sleep. I saw him three times reading in a book in about a month's time; and when he did, it was the first one he had found in our cabin; and this not half an hour at a time. His favourite topics were, when with me and Brion, to speak of his stay in Paris, and to give us detailed particulars of his good fortune in this capital; and sometimes he asked me many questions about Napoleon, the dresses of the ladies and gentlemen at Court, and what kind of ceremonies were necessary in order to be presented, etc.; another time his talk was about his moustachios, and those of the officers, the modes of dress and uniforms in the French and English armies; but never could I speak a single word about military tactics, drills, etc."—Ducoudray, p. 319.

Bolívar left it at that and turned his attention to the mainland. He began in his usual way by a proclamation (8.v.16) announcing Arizmendi's revolt and the reorganization of his forces " with the help of our magnanimous Admiral Brion. Venezuelans "—he added—" your brothers and your foreign friends do not come to conquer you; but to fight for liberty."

On May 25th, 1816, Bolívar put to sea towards the mainland. He had chosen for landing the small harbour of Carúpano, opposite Margarita, where, if successful, he would cut off the Spanish garrisons of Maturin and Güiria from Cumaná. At dawn on June 1st, the landing took place under protection of the artillery of the ships, and the two wings of the army, under the command of Piar and Soublette, found no difficulty in gaining possession of the heights and the port. Mariño and Piar asked then to be given weapons to go and recruit in the east; and, though Bolívar realized that what they had in mind was to secede and set up their own separate establishments, he let them go against his best judgment and the opinion of his advisers. Neither returned, of course, though they sent some troops. Meanwhile, Bolívar found no response in his countrymen. Carúpano was deserted and the Liberator found that his countrymen did not want to be liberated. He grew angry: " Considering that instead of contributing to the restoration of liberty "—he thundered at the inhabitants of Upper Carúpano on June 21st—" they enlist of their own free will under the flag of the Spanish tyrants and most actively co-operate to our destruction, so that not one of them has so far taken arms under our own, despite the many calls made to them these twenty-one days. . . ." Bolívar then gave his countrymen an ultimatum to return within twenty-four hours, after which " the place would be burnt out and no rebuilding of it would be allowed ". So much for the whites. As for the slaves, whom Bolívar had declared free (2.vi.16), under the reasonable condition that every able-bodied man between the ages of fourteen and sixty was to enlist within twenty-four hours, he wrote on June 27th to General Marion words which are no less revealing on this question of the slaves than on Bolívar's own use of fact and fancy to suit his purpose. " *Je m'empresse de vous informer que nous venons de recevoir de nombreux renforts de patriotes venant de Güiria. Leur courage et leur jévouement m'assurent la prise très prochaine de Cumaná. Les habitants des ulaines nous sont également dévoués. Nous en attendons quelques détachements que nous esperons recevoir dans quelques jours. J'ai proclamé la liberté absolue des esclaves. La tyrannie des espagnols les a tellement rendus stupides, et a imprimé dans leur âme un tel sentiment de terreur et de crainte, qu'ils ont perdu jusqu'au désir d'être libres! Beaucoup d'entre eux ont suivi les Espagnols, ou se sont embarqués à bord de bâtiments anglais qui les ont vendus dans les colonies voisines. Il s'en est présenté à peine une centaine, tandis que le nombre des hommes libres qui ont pris volontairement les armes, est considérable. Les espagnols font tous leurs efforts pour entraver nos opérations en ramassant leurs troupes, mais notre petite armée, animée du sentiment de la liberté, suffira pour les anéantir.*"

The royalists, few and sparsely garrisoned, stood away. In fact, each side seems to have exaggerated the strength of its adversary. The chieftains

Monagas, Rojas, Zaraza and Sedeño, who led guerrillas south of Aragua, tried but failed to come to the coast in the hope of obtaining arms and ammunition. Mariño and Piar stood away; in fact Mariño was organizing in Güiria his own dictatorship and " libertadorship ", with his own general staff, and recruiting soldiers for his own political aims, thanks to the arms and ammunition he had wrung from Bolívar. In Carúpano, discontent was rampant. Ducoudray tried to organize a foreign legion in order to gather together the activities of the many foreign officers that hung about; but only succeeded in arousing suspicions in Bolívar's heart already embittered by Mariño's desertion. Ducoudray tells the story with a wealth of lively details that carry conviction, and describes Bolívar in the " family circle " of Miss Pepa, her mother and sister, commenting on all these events. He resigned and left, suspected—much to his indignation—of having attempted to depose Bolívar and to raise Brion to the command of the army. Brion himself grew restive. He had supplied three thousand seven hundred guns on condition that once landed he would be repaid at the rate of a *fanegada* (rather more than a bushel and a half) of cocoa apiece. There was no cocoa in Carúpano, and Brion pointed out that " his crew are very much disgruntled for they have not had any salary for three months, and therefore it is imperative to go to a spot where there is some land produce, for expenses are high and he has to recover those he had incurred ". Bolívar had intelligence that the royalists were planning a combined attack on Carúpano by land and sea. He made up his mind to sail towards the west —fearing perhaps that the east was too much in the hands of Mariño—and to land nearer his native Caracas. What was he landing for at the head of a foreign army in a land that did not want him? He was landing as a " Caudillo " to found a kingdom for himself (a republican kingdom of course) just like Mariño, Brion, Arizmendi, Boves, Monteverde and the rest.

He put to sea (1.vii.16), and wrote to Arizmendi with superb assurance (2.vii.16): " The news you have sent me about the movements of the Spanish fleet have led me to leave Carúpano and march swiftly to the heart of Venezuela, to end the war, depriving the enemy of all its resources. Events will justify the enterprise. Should I be unlucky, I shall lose naught but my life, for it is always great to attempt heroic things. I shall land on the coast of Ocumare, at the head of one thousand men, and within eight days I shall take the capital, from where I shall march towards the Orient to help our brothers who are there fighting for the same cause." This, of course, meant that, as soon as he had taken Caracas, he would settle with his rival Mariño and show him that there was only one *Libertador*.

3

At dawn, on July 6th, 1816, the little fleet of fourteen ships was seen off Puerto Cabello; by seven o'clock they had sailed back towards Ocumare, where they landed at midday. Soublette, with nearly the whole force, advanced inland during the night to seize the pass of La Cabrera, which controlled communications between Ocumare and the lagoon of Valencia, beyond the coastal sierra. He found little opposition. He marched farther and took Maracay after a brush with some Spanish cavalry. It seems that this very success reacted unfavourably on the fortunes of the patriots, for their fleet—all made up of foreign corsairs—assuming that the wealthy Caraqueños would be frightened and flee towards Curaçao, decided to unload the stores, dump them on the shore and hurry away to blockade La Guaira, lured by the booty. But Soublette, frightened by the approach of Morales, retreated to Las Piedras, below La Cabrera on the coast side (9.vii.16). Bolívar sent him reinforcements as well as a stiff note of rebuke: " Audacity must save us. What you may think rash is certainly the best, for today prudence is in temerity." Bolívar was right, for Morales arrived in San Joaquín with no more than four hundred men, while Soublette was hiding behind the sierra with at least five hundred and seventy. Morales had to advance and seek him. The encounter (10.vii.16) induced Soublette to a further retreat towards the coast. Morales, reinforced by his second, Bausá, attacked and defeated Soublette and also Bolívar, who had at last come to the front (14.vii.16).

But these " battles ", mere affrays between guerrillas of a few hundreds of men on both sides, and in broken country well known to both sides, were never final. Bolívar's plan was to pass through and around his victors to Aragua and the plain of Caracas. The parks were to be re-embarked by Villaret, the only sailor available. There were difficulties: indiscipline, distrust, greed, and eagerness to get away. The Venezuelan colonel (as he was then) Salom, who was present, provides a revealing sidelight on Villaret: " He was a coward, who chose to keep the boats busy from sunset until he sailed off, transporting a number of French negresses with their children and baggage and other French subordinate officers, rather than saving a quantity of armaments and munitions which remained derelict on the shore." As for Bolívar, his doings had better be told in the words of the official bulletin of his own army (20.vii.16): " The Supreme Chief of the Republic, observing that the enemy had won some ascendancy over our troops in the fight of July 14th . . . ordered a retreat [took several other decisions] and left for the harbour at five p.m., letting it be known that he would return at eleven or twelve at night. His purpose as he gave to understand to several officers, was to have the park, armament and ammunition, put on board and have it forwarded to Admiral Brion's fleet [which was at sea] so as to carry out a landing at another part of the coast, without saying whether he meant to lead this important operation in person. Very powerful reasons must have induced the Supreme Chief to embark without dictating his last orders to his army, and, what is more, leaving behind war material on the shore."

No more scathing condemnation of dereliction of duty on the part of a commander-in-chief was ever penned by his subordinates. We are told that one of Soublette's aides-de-camp, Alzuru, was sent to tell Bolívar that all was well; and, whether through confusion or malice, he reported that the enemy had cut his way through between the city and the harbour. But, if Alzuru had come from the army front and did later return to it, Bolívar could have gone with him to lend his moral support to his troops. This Alzuru episode is but a story to cover the fact, so often observed before, so often to be observed again, that Bolívar was a bad loser, and when things went awry, thought of little else but flight. In this case, however, the story does not end there. We have seen how Bolívar lost two days on his way to Carúpano waiting for his mistress; and how this tallies with the scenes Ducoudray-Holstein tells so well, of Bolívar lolling among his friends in his mistress' house. All this is confirmed by Bolívar's closest friend, Soublette, the brother of his former mistress. Asked by O'Leary to explain what had happened in Ocumare, Soublette wrote: " The *Libertador's* departure from Ocumare in 1816 is one of the most obscure events; I dare not tell it, for my memory is very much weakened. . . . This event was mixed up with love, and you know that Antony, despite the danger in which he was, wasted precious moments by the side of Cleopatra. What is certain is that we all in Ocumare defended and justified the *Libertador's* behaviour, and that all the blame was shed on his aide-de-camp Alzuru. I never had the opportunity to inquire into all the circumstances, nor did we think about it; in Curaçao, it was ill spoken of; in the army, well; and so it was left. But I am positive that, in Ocumare, we waited for H.E. till very late, and then we learnt through Alzuru that he had sailed off leaving no orders and that Salom was on the shore where the utmost confusion prevailed. . . . It must be borne in mind that we were against the *Libertador* coming with us on our perilous march inland, but we swore to him we would not embark, and expressed our wish to him that he should embark, for even if we were lost, were he saved, the hope of freeing our country would not be at an end; there was a fine struggle in H.E.'s house, as he would not promise to embark and on the contrary prepared a small valise [to accompany the expedition by land] and sent his luggage aboard, and at nightfall he left for the shore to expedite the loading of the war material on the only ship left." Soublette then tells how he sent Alzuru to inform Bolívar that the enemy had halted for the night, and how then " Alzuru returned with the news that the *Libertador* had embarked, the shore was in chaos, the ship had cut its cables, people had thrown themselves into the water so that many had been drowned, all the armament, munitions, printing press, etc., were on the shore, and Salom did not know what to do ".

While his army, derelict and leaderless, tried to save itself from Morales and did in fact reach Choroní, Bolívar went to Bonaire where he was joined by Brion, who forced the two French captains to return the war material in dispute. This may have softened Bolívar's reproaches to Brion for having left the shore in search of loot; but Brion made vehement reproaches to Bolívar for having sailed away leaving his companions helpless. Bolívar gave him a diplomatic mission to the Mexican patriots and to the United States to find money for the cause; and the Admiral-Ambassador left for New Orleans (26.vii.16) with the sloops *Bolívar*, *Constitución* and *Arizmendi*, the first of which was wrecked off the isle of Pines (26.viii.16), so that Brion, Villaret, Forsyth and other foreign friends of Bolívar ended their voyage in Jamaica. Meanwhile Bolívar (after a brief sea-reconnaissance to Choroní) sailed to Cumaná, but by way of Puerto Rico in search—he says to Arizmendi —of food and water, which he hoped to procure, if need be by force, in one of the smaller Spanish islands; but possibly out of respect for the Spanish naval forces cruising at the time on the Venezuelan coast. While on the coast of Puerto Rico, he came across a sloop whose skipper was prevailed upon to take on board the three ladies in whom he was personally interested and land them safely in St. Thomas, which he did. The *Indio Libre* in which Bolívar was sailing had run aground and had to be raised with the help of the sloop; and the voyage of Antony, rid of his Cleopatra and family, continued uneventfully till he landed in Güiria (16.viii.16).

4

Bolívar was by no means at the end of his trouble. He brought in fact some of it on board. We left Bermúdez in Aux Cayes, appealing to General Marion with tears in his eyes against Bolívar's defection. " *Eh bien* "— General Marion advised—" *je vous conseille d'aller trouver le Président Pétion, il a le coeur bon, compatissant, et je suis persuadé qu'il fera quelque chose pour vous.*" Bermúdez followed the advice and Pétion gave him facilities to return home. After declining an offer to serve in Mexico, Bermúdez was thus able, through Pétion's help, to board an American ship for Margarita where Arizmendi, on Bolívar's orders, did not allow him to land; he then sailed on and arrived in Ocumare at nearly the same time as Bolívar's own expedition. On July 8th he received a stiff letter from Bolívar. Reminding Bermúdez of his cabals to secure the command of the expedition, as well as of " the definite and express decisions you and your companions publicly took against my life ", Bolívar concluded denying Bermúdez and his friends permission to land and enjoining on them to prepare to move to another ship that would convey them to " a friendly colony ".

Bermúdez went to Bonaire. And so, eventually, did Bolívar—after his defeat and flight from Ocumare. The two men kept away from each other, yet could not separate, and when Bolívar left for Güiria on the *Indio Libre*, Bermúdez also sailed thither on another ship; for hate is a tie as strong as love. He arrived in Güiria two hours before Bolívar. There he met Mariño, to whose ambition he was bringing as an ally the urge of a vindictive hatred. At the time, the quarrel was even. There were three ambitious men, of varying degrees of merit, each seeking to carve for himself a province to rule. There is nothing whatever to justify the view—yet—that Bolívar's cause, i.e. Bolívar's own glory and power as the aim and the independence of Venezuela as the means, was in any way superior to Mariño's or even to Bermúdez'. The only difference—Bolívar's inherent greatness, his magnificent imagination, his sense of unity, his historical perspective—was, in the nature of things, invisible to his rivals, indeed not altogether clear to Bolívar himself. For Bermúdez and for Mariño, Bolívar was just one like themselves; a man with a sword, ready to use it for his own advantage. Each for himself was the law. The two local leaders received the westerner

GENERAL J. A. PÁEZ,
from an engraving

VIEW OF A CABULLA ON THE RIVER SUARES,
COLUMBIA, from an engraving

VIEW OF THE PASS FROM HONDA TO BOGOTÁ,
from an engraving

with cold enmity. Presently, a riot, possibly prepared, broke out against Bolívar (22.viii.16). *Down with Bolívar! Long live Mariño and Bermúdez!* shouted the crowd. Bolívar's life seems to have been in danger, not merely from the crowd but from Bermúdez who drew his sabre to strike him dead there and then. Two of their countrymen, Colonel Isaba and the lawyer Marcano, stepped in and prevented a crime which might have had untold historical consequences. Bolívar took refuge in a *flechera* (a long canoe in use in American waters) eventually to board again the *Indio Libre*, to sail for the third time away from his country.

5

The expedition had failed since it had not allowed Bolívar to set foot on the continent for good; but it had nevertheless achieved at least two substantial results for the patriots: it had started a military march headed by the Scot, McGregor, which, through a number of victories, led the little band to Barcelona; and it had forced the Spanish Captain General Moxó to move towards the coast many forces then usefully occupied in the Plains. Left leaderless in Ocumare, the small band of patriots moved on towards Choroní along the coast, at 2 a.m. (14.vii.16), and finding that Bolívar was not there either, decided to put McGregor at their head. McGregor beat the Spanish troop under the command of the Venezuelan Quero at Quebradahonda (10.viii.16), and later at San Diego. Reinforced by the chieftains Zaraza and Monagas, McGregor beat López at El Alacrán, in a fight in which both sides had as auxiliary troops Caribbean Indians armed with arrows, and occupied Barcelona (13.viii.16). Then Morales, sent by Moxó with just over a thousand men, advanced on Barcelona, and McGregor wrote to several chieftains for help. Mariño was besieging Cumaná, which was his " Caracas ", for he was the *Libertador* and *Dictador* of the east; but Piar, who was not too pleased with his subordinate position, seized his opportunity for advancement and sent McGregor four hundred men by land, while he himself took to sea to be there in time. As he had a higher rank than McGregor he knew he would command. The two armies met at El Juncal, close to the sea (27.ix.16). The patriots won a battle in which McGregor distinguished himself by his personal courage. But, after some quarrels and intrigues, he left the service of the republic, and so Piar conquered an army for his own use.

The obvious thing for him to do, had he had in mind Venezuela's independence first and Piar's power second, would have been to reinforce Mariño who, with Bermúdez as his second, was still hammering away at his Cumaná. But he bethought himself of another chieftain, Cedeño, who was holding sway in the rich province of Guayana. He would join him, become his chief and have his own province to rule. This he did with some success, while Moxó, in Caracas, held a Council of War to decide whether he would sacrifice Margarita or Cumaná. He decided to sacrifice Margarita. Pampátar was quietly evacuated by night (13.xi.16) and Moxó was able to reinforce the Spanish commander Cires in Cumaná, while Mariño had to raise the siege so that Piar could conquer Guayana, just as Bolívar before him had to leave Ocumare and Carúpano so that Mariño could conquer Cumaná. Páez, meanwhile, the republican counterpart of Boves, the idol of the *llaneros*, was galloping about his south-west carving for himself also a career which would lead him eventually to oust Bolívar not only from Venezuela but from life itself; and here and there, all over the country, chieftains rode at the head of troops more or less disciplined, on their way, as they thought, to glory and power. McGregor had gone to try his hand at Panamá and even a Spaniard from Spain, Mina, finding Spain disappointingly pacified, crossed the seas in search of adventures and eventually landed in Haiti in search of funds, arms and Negro cannon-fodder to " liberate " Mexico from his own kith and kin.

Bolívar arrived in Haiti early in September. Pétion wrote to him (7.ix.16) in a generous and magnanimous way: " you have failed; such things happen; you will succeed ". Bolívar paid him back with no ungenerous hand, if in the only wealth then at his disposal: words. On October 9th, 1816, he wrote to Pétion, who had just been made Permanent President: " *Votre Excellence vient d'être élevée à la dignité perpetuelle de Chef de la République, aux acclamations libres de ses concitoyens, seule source légitime de toutes puissances humaines! Elle est donc destinée à faire oublier la mémoire du grand Washington, en se frayant une carrière d'autant plus illustre, que les obstacles sont supérieurs à tous les moyens* ". Mina, the nephew of the legendary *guerrillero* Espoz y Mina, had written to him from Baltimore. Bolívar was then, it would appear, solicited to share in Mina's expedition, in the success of which he did not believe. He lost a number of European officers to Mina, but won over some from him; and he set about to negotiate through Gual with American businessmen for arms and ammunition as well as for general commerce.

He was busy with all these plans when no less than three messages reached him from the mainland requesting him to return and lead the struggle. Those who appealed to him recognized that, despite his faults, there was something in him that raised him above all his rivals. Grit, faith, intellectual power and that strange magnetic force the born leader emanates, were his four gifts; and how fascinating and compelling they must have been to force back to him those who, but weeks earlier, had been calling him a coward and a traitor to his face, owing to his flight from Ocumare. Such are the contrasts which make his life unlike any other. Bolívar, now scared into flight, now returning at the behest of those he had forsaken in danger, is a more human and real being than the solemn general we are bidden to contemplate, always in marmorean self-mastery. The men who had seen him leave Ocumare knew that, in spite of temperamental defections, Bolívar was head and shoulders above the others, the only leader with the mental powers needed to stand up to Morillo, then getting ready to return to Venezuela.

First Arizmendi, then Zea on behalf of a number of military leaders, finally Brion appealed to him to return. It seems that the leaders who appealed to Bolívar, fearing Morillo's return, thought it best to serry their ranks. On the other hand, they would not have him back as a dictator, and if we are to believe Ducoudray-Holstein they demanded two conditions: that he should assemble a Congress; " that he should direct the military operations only, and should not meddle with the administration of the Republic ". Ducoudray adds that " he consented to comply exactly with their wishes ". Two facts come to strengthen this version. One is the choice of the emissary: Zea, the Granadino scientist, a frequent, if not energetic, advocate of civilian versus military government; the other one is Bolívar's own outburst of civilian feelings precisely at this time. Thus, in a letter to Cortés Madariaga—but the reappearance of the fiery canon must first be explained.

Sent to Spain by Monteverde along with Roscio and Paz Castillo, Cortés Madariaga and his two companions escaped from Ceuta to Gibraltar in February, 1814. General Campbell who commanded in Gibraltar delivered them into the hands of the Spanish Government; but the British Government held the action improper and claimed back the prisoners. Everybody seems to have been wrong in this episode. The Spanish Government should never have held in prison men protected by a general amnesty; Campbell should never have handed back political refugees, for in those days, though not always in ours, such a deed was held to be dishonourable; and the British Government, having insisted on getting the prisoners back, should have seen to it that they remained in Gibraltar or in England, instead of which it allowed them to return to Jamaica, " considering that the Spanish Government might entertain some jealousy at their remaining at Gibraltar "; and to these words, written from Downing Street (15.vi.16), Henry Goulburn, Under Secretary for War and the Colonies, added that H.M. Government " being altogether unaware of the place to which these persons may have proceeded [they had been in Jamaica from the beginning of the year] they cannot undertake to prevent their return to Venezuela, further than by instructing the Governor of Jamaica to prevent such proceeding on their part ". These three patriots travelled freely all over the Antilles on British naval vessels.

Bolívar wrote to Cortés Madariaga on the eve of his departure for Venezuela (26.xi.16): " It is in vain that arms destroy tyrants if they do not establish a political order capable of repairing the devastations of the revolution. The military system stands for force, and force is no government; so that we need our civil leaders, who, escaped on planks from the shipwreck of the revolution, may guide us back through the sands into a harbour of salvation." And he asked him to convey to his two companions an invitation to " contribute to the liberty of our country ". To Arizmendi, however, he wrote more to the point : " The ships are ready which must load our arms, ammunition, clothing and helmets and a few friends and volunteers who follow me to Venezuela." He sailed on December 21st from Jacquemel and landed in Juan Griego, Margarita Island, on December 28th, 1816.

6

After a siege of one hundred and sixteen days Morillo had taken Cartagena (6.xii.15). " The most painful sight of all my life "—he writes, and even his severest critics acknowledge that he and his troops behaved with humane and generous feelings. Bermúdez and the other leaders had fled with two shiploads of booty, including church jewels, which the Spanish cruising fleet recovered for the most part, including a valuable monstrance, a present from the city of Santa Fe to the cathedral of Cartagena. Sevilla writes that " Morillo had sent orders to the general staff officers to warn all heads of units that no harm was to be done. . . . The besieged had not eaten for twenty-two days, save leather soaked in tanning tanks. Women once beautiful and rich, men of the cream of this once opulent trading centre, all who could move, tumbled over each other to finger in our men's haversacks for a bite of bread. Before such a sight, our men, forgetting that those people had murdered our companions [he refers to the murder of the fourteen officers of General Hore's force] gave them all the food they were carrying "; and the officers subscribed from their private funds to distribute a ration of soup to every one in the city. After the dead bodies had been disposed of, the city had to be carefully disinfected. Through a stratagem, Morillo soon received thirteen ships loaded with flour and meat which were being sent to Cartagena by sympathizers of the patriots. He imposed a war contribution of one hundred thousand pesos on the community.

Morillo prepared at once to move on to Santa Fe. His plans were based as much on political as on military considerations. He decided to attack or threaten all the provinces simultaneously. " In the Insurgent Secretariat " —he writes—" can be seen the plans and orders based on a reunion of their forces; but not a single province obeyed, and on feeling themselves threatened, each assumed supreme command, seceded from the government of Santa Fe and appointed its own dictator." Separatism and dictatorship, the law of all Spanish public life. This consideration emboldened him to divide his troops and he successfully brought about in this way the reconquest of the whole of New Granada after a relatively brief campaign. Exactly five months after the fall of Cartagena, two of his lieutenants, La Torre and Calzada, entered Santa Fe (16.v.16). He himself, with his general headquarters, left Cartagena (16.ii.16) on a journey designed to acquaint himself with the country. The expedition took the left bank of the Magdalena and crossed the Cauca at Magangué, arriving in Mompox towards the beginning of March. It was there that Morillo heard of Arizmendi's rebellion in Margarita, an event which bit deeply into his mind and may well have been the cause of the gruesome decision he took then of having the body of Carabaño, a " rebel " leader, who had just been court-martialled and executed, quartered and exhibited on the approaches to the city. He hurried on to Santa Fe through Ocaña, Bucaramanga, Socorro, Vélez and Puerto Real, and arrived in the capital on March 26th, 1816.

It was an original arrival, better told in the words of an eyewitness:

" On the 26th we marched seven leagues, to the beautiful city of Zipaquirá, where they offered H.E. a ball, during which, every now and then, the ladies silenced the band to recite poems in honour of Morillo and of his army. He was not unaware of the fact that many of those nymphs had acted exactly in the same way towards the rebel generals; so that he drew in somewhat, and still more so when told that in Santa Fe, where other Spanish generals with more titles to be esteemed, had suffered so much scorn and mockery, an ovation without precedent in the annals of the viceroyalty was being prepared in his honour. . . . The general ordered the army to follow him at about a league's distance, donned a long coat which covered his whole body and part of his head, and a wide straw hat with no insignia whatever, which hid his face, and with General Enrile, his steward and his groom, rode on towards Santa Fe. He had not gone a league when he saw a brilliant squadron of luxuriously dressed ladies and gentlemen on horseback, and some in carriages. At sight of the four men, the amazons and their escort silenced the music and stopped the newcomers. One of the ladies who rode ahead of the others on a magnificent white horse, was the first to speak, while forcing her steed—a pure Andalusian—to prance gracefully: ' Sir '—she said with a sweet harmonious voice, while fixing Morillo with her wide black eyes—' we greet the glorious army come to purify the main-land. This delegation of ladies of the Bogotan nobility, which I have the honour to preside, as well as that of the gentlemen present, wish to meet and congratulate the unconquered General Morillo. Can you tell us where we could find him ? ' He glanced at the brilliant gathering of beautiful women, riding so gracefully on their rich palfries, and after a brief pause, answered: ' Thanks, ladies and gentlemen, for the flattering words you have uttered through such a pretty mouth in honour of the army to which we belong. But the commander-in-chief . . . comes further back.' And with a courteous but cold gesture of the hand he rode on. As he entered the city, he saw along the way to his abode countless triumphant arches and decorated chariots, Spanish flags, flowers, damask hangings on all the buildings and signs of the greatest enthusiasm and of the purest Spanish patriotism. He asked for Morillo's house, entered and locked himself in. . . . Presently the rumour went about that the General was at home and that he had rejected the reception prepared for him. . . . A commission was formed to find out the truth of the matter. The General received it courteously in his uniform. ' Gentlemen '—he said—' you must not wonder at my attitude. A Spanish general cannot associate himself with the joy, feigned or sincere, of a capital in which his horse might slip treading on the blood still fresh of H.M.'s soldiers, killed by the treacherous lead of the rebels shooting from your houses '."

This Morillo was not the same man who had taken Margarita with forgiveness in his heart and entered Cartagena with so much grief at what he saw. The key to the change is supplied by the same eyewitness, Sevilla. In the narrative just quoted he tells how Morillo remained impassive before the enthusiasm he saw in the streets, and comments: " Morales would have embraced him, had he been there." It all went back to that scene in

Margarita, when Arizmendi had knelt in tears before Morillo, and Morales had advised his chief not to trust "the treacherous Margaritan", only to be rebuked by Morillo and ordered to be silent. Morillo felt humiliated; he was, after all, a soldier, and a tough one; he had tried his best to apply the conciliatory way and from the day of his arrival in Caracas to the day he had entered Santa Fe he had marked every step of his progress by a decree of amnesty. But the thought of Arizmendi worked on him and hardened him daily. In Santa Fe he spread wide the nets of his military police; many patriots who had remained behind trusting to an amnesty decreed by La Torre, were arrested. He set up a court martial to judge the prisoners who had to answer for some crime other than mere war (such as desertion from the Spanish army) and a Committee of purification, " so necessary in countries in turmoil in which resentment and vengeance cry so loud ". He reversed his previous policy and showed himself a stern governor: from June 5th to December 12th one hundred and two men were executed.

One hundred and two too many. True, some of them, at any rate under the laws and ideas of the time, had fully deserved it; for instance, those who had murdered the fourteen officers in their jails; true also that men such as Villavicencio, who was a Spanish officer on the active list, was technically a traitor and had to be shot; but the generals who, like La Torre, Correa, Montalvo and a number of others in the Spanish army, including Morillo himself until Arizmendi disappointed him, stood for leniency, were right, since even a " traitor " such as Villavicencio, Spanish though he was by his uniform and oath, was born in Quito, and therefore was bound to feel a " patriot " in his heart; and the times required imagination and magnanimity. Morillo, however, had tried the magnanimous way, but—there was Arizmendi, weeping at his feet and murdering the Spanish garrison in Margarita as soon as Morillo turned his back on the island. Let us read Sevilla: " On May 30th, the King's birthday, the municipality of Santa Fe gave a splendid banquet to General Morillo and his staff. . . . At the end of the ceremony, over fifty ladies, most of them weeping, came before the general, asking forgiveness for their husbands, sons, brothers, all of whom were in jail as rebels. . . . The tears, sobs and entreaties of those ladies could have softened a rock. . . . Morillo made noticeable efforts not to be moved; he remained silent with just a ' please, rise, Madam ' now and then to the ladies who knelt before him. For a while, he let them speak; then, with a faltering voice, he spoke: ' Ladies, my king, who, as a Spanish gentleman, has generous and humanitarian sentiments [all this was unfortunately far from true], has invested me with his sovereign faculty, the most beautiful a monarch possesses: that of pardon. He has instructed me to forgive whenever the safety of the fatherland permits it. So that on treading American soil for the first time, in Margarita, I forgave all those who begged to be forgiven as you are begging now. Do you know how I was repaid by the ungrateful person who with tears appealed to H.M.'s clemency ? As soon as I turned my back, the rebel flag was raised again, and, more sanguinary than ever, they murdered the officers and men I had left there. Those who have been murdered also had mothers, wives, daughters who today will curse a thousand times the improvident general who was candid enough to believe the faithless protestations of those wretched men. Had I, instead of granting a pardon, shot twenty leaders, my conscience would not be heavy as it now is with the remorse that haunts it. I share the grief I see in your faces, but I cannot forgive when the safety of the country does not allow me to do so."

Morillo's sincerity is proved by the detail Sevilla goes on to relate; how one of the ladies asked that at least the prisoners be transferred to better quarters, a request which he granted at once and saw that it was carried out without delay. Morillo is moreover right in emphasizing as he does in his *Manifesto to the Spanish Nation* that the prisoners were " never sentenced without being heard nor without the competent defence which our military law provides for: all were judged according to the laws; their files are extant: let them speak ". Sevilla goes on to say that after the banquet the general and his officers went for a ride. " As we were passing by the convent at the end of the Real street, then occupied by officers and men of the enemy who had been taken prisoners, we heard shouts, above which one voice, saying: ' Forgive us, general, for we are not guilty, but were led astray: forgive in the name of the King and we shall henceforward be faithful servants of His Majesty '. ' Poor men '—we heard Morillo mutter—' They are the sons of the people, exploited by those ambitious men whom I was resolved not to reprieve in spite of so many entreaties. Not the arm that wounds, but the head that commands is the guilty party.' The supplications of the prisoners, waving their arms through the railings, went on. The general stopped and with thunderous voice he shouted: ' Do you swear to be faithful to His Majesty's Government ? ' Hundreds of voices answered yes. ' Very well, I forgive you in the name of the King.' And on the spot he ordered us to open the gates of the prison. The wretched prisoners, in a frenzy of happiness, embraced us like madmen. They all ran to throw themselves at the feet of the general. Most of them were country people, Indians and negroes."

This attitude, that the masses had been misled, was ingrained in Morillo and it led him to strong anti-clerical measures. " Where the priest has been of the right kind "—he wrote to the King (31.v.16)—" the people have imitated him. Many or most of the priests have been the instigators of the new ideas." And again: " Over there [in Venezuela] the clergy and all the classes [he means: all but the people] aim at the same object, independence, with the blind belief that they are working for the coloured man." He also points out that, with the single exception of the Capuchins, religious orders are all " perverse ", i.e. anti-Spanish, notably the Augustinians whom he recommends the King to have recalled to Spain. This belief led him to exile priests to Spain and to ask for Spanish-born clergy instead. Withal Morillo must bear the responsibility of a cruel and unwise repression, whether psychologically justified or not by the behaviour of Arizmendi. The Spanish Bishop of Popayán in a letter to Pope Leo XII accuses Morillo and his colleagues of having spread disaffection like lightning *propter nimiam crudelitatem modosque impoliticos ducum hispanorum.* Morillo was a competent governor. He set in motion a vast plan of road building; restored the law courts, political and civil order and military discipline; he turned his attention to administrative and economic problems; distributed vaccines and in general attended to the health of the countryside; and organized arts and crafts schools, and schools for orphans and for beggars' sons. He evidently looked forward to an era of general peace and prosperity; and though uneasy about Bolívar since Arizmendi's revolt, did not seem to consider the danger as very serious, at any rate at first. The year 1816 thus drew to its close as, with New Granada conquered and, in the odd phrase of the day, " pacified ", Venezuela was again threatening the Spanish power. On December 9th, 1816, Restrepo, who was to be Bolívar's Secretary of State and historiographer, wrote from Kingston, Jamaica, to Sánchez Lima, the Spanish Governor of Antioquia: " Here I shall remain until I am able to obtain a reprieve from our august sovereign the lord Don Fernando VII. Meanwhile my behaviour shall be the most faithful to His Majesty, as I shall be able to prove if need be, for I have for a long time detested all revolutionary ideas and my only wish is to live quietly in the bosom of my family." On January 1st, 1817, Bolívar wrote from Barcelona to Briceño Méndez, acting Universal Minister to Piar, acting Supreme Chief of the Republic: " You will satisfy the wishes of all our citizens if you succeed in subjecting the country [Guayana] which has done us so much harm and can be so useful to us. But, this done, will you not rush to break the fetters of your other brothers who suffer the tyranny of our enemy? Yes, yes, you will run with me all the way to the wealthy Peru. Our destinies call us to the ends of the American world." Morillo decided to lead his army in person against Bolívar.

Chapter XXVIII

MORILLO LOSES MARGARITA AND GUAYANA; AND BOLÍVAR IS DEFEATED AT EL SEMEN

I

WHEN Bolívar landed in Juan Griego, Margarita (28.xii.16), Arizmendi had sailed to Barcelona with four hundred men. Bolívar issued a proclamation calling on all Venezuelans to meet in Margarita, then free, and " to open your sessions and organize yourselves according to your own will. The first of your decisions will be celebrated by the acceptance of my resignation." This will be his leitmotiv throughout his life. In tune with it, he wrote an admirable letter to his rival Mariño (29.xii.16). On the past, he is tactful: " At the head of forty friends you entered the Orient at the same time as I entered the Occident. We helped each other mutually and by our own endeavours rose to an equal dignity." He reminds his rival how they both had ridden together the storms of Carúpano, Cartagena, Güiria. On the present he writes frankly: " I am your best friend. Unfortunately, your friends are not mine. . . . Your behaviour may have changed, but I am certain that your heart never does "; and then writes these astounding words which could so evidently be turned against the writer: " You feel the passion for glory: try to preserve it as pure as you acquired it: ambition is a stain on true glory and the greatest splendour of such a brilliant adornment comes to it rather from moderation than from power. Power without virtue is an excess and not a legitimate faculty: you have as much as suits the happiness of the country and your own honour: do not, in search of more power, lose that which has cost you so many sacrifices." The man who wrote these words was still in Margarita, barely on the threshold of the country to be " saved " and ruled—by whom ? That was the question Mariño would be asking on reading such excellent advice. Bolívar guessed as much, and wrote on: " Dear friend, do not believe that it is my wish to command you; on the contrary, you must persuade yourself that I crave to submit myself to a centre of authority which will lead us all with equal stern uprightness. I cordially wish our common leader to be a man of an inflexible and impartial character; were it not so, we shall have to suffer much from factions which always increase in times of ill fortune and also with the passing of the days."

How sincere was he ? The answer is clear but not simple. He was sincere in yearning for a " centre of authority " incarnated in an upright, inflexible and impartial man, strong enough to hold in check the chieftains and would-be liberator-dictators the country was swarming with; he was not sincere in hiding his conviction that there was no such " centre of authority " outside his own heart, a conviction in which, after all, he happened to be right. This fact, the superiority of Bolívar over all other chieftains, and his own consciousness of it, are to rule his actions and always to explain, if not always to justify, his policy and his movements.   On the other hand, the very limits of his superiority are also to account for this or that failure, defeat, error of judgment, or even crime, in his dramatic life; as well as for his ultimate political defeat, exile and solitary death.   For Bolívar was incomparably the finest of the leaders the wars of Spanish-American emancipation threw up, by general, human standards; but it happened that, in specific gifts of a more limited scope yet more directly required for such wars, he fell below the standard set by popular leaders of guerrillas like Piar or Páez; so that the pattern of his life would be dictated by the fact that the greatest patriot and the most accomplished statesman by far in all the country had to struggle for power against inferior rivals on a plane of partisan prowess which was precisely that in which he was their inferior.

For the time being, there were at least three men who acted as Supreme Chief of the Republic, at any rate over as much territory as they could control with their troops: Mariño in Güiria;   Piar in Barcelona and the region towards Guayana;   and Páez in the Apure.

Born on June 13th, 1790, of a humble family in the neighbourhood of Acarigua, in the Province of Barinas, Antonio Páez, after an affray at seventeen, in which he killed his man, fled to the Apure and took service on a cattle farm.   This meant lassoing wild cattle for sale, by day, and sleeping in a cabin furnished with horses' skulls and heads of alligators, by night. When Venezuelan patriots, undaunted by Miranda's failure, rose against Monteverde in the Plains, Páez followed his master, Don Manuel Pulido, who had been given a commission as Lieutenant Colonel by the Republicans. His dash soon made him so famous among the *llaneros* that, when Boves died, it was on him, though he was on the other side, that fell the poncho of the dead Spaniard.   Fighting on his own ground with his own men, with no weapons but spears which they made for themselves, no clothing but their own skins, no food but meat without salt, Páez paid but little heed to State or General Staff, to victories or defeats, and waged a war of his own in his own way and on his own land.   With four hundred men, he had inflicted a dramatic defeat on the Spanish colonel López, who commanded fifteen hundred (16.ii.16).   This action, known as the battle of Mata de la Miel, enhanced his popularity.   A few months later, he was called to a small assembly or junta by the heads of the forces which, pursued by Morillo's troops, had passed from New Granada to Venezuela, and who, in order to restrain their own anarchy, had decided to set up a " government ".   This small group, a mixed array of lawyers and chieftains, appointed Colonel Serrano as Supreme Chief and Francisco Yanes, a " doctor " of Cuban origin, as Minister of State, while Colonel Santander was given command of the troops.   Páez acquiesced in all these appointments, probably with his tongue in his cheek.   Santander sent him away on a horse-catching expedition, and when Páez returned, his army " mutinied " and insisted on their chief dissolving the government and taking in his hands both the civil and the military command.   Páez obliged his troops (September, 1816).

2

Morillo was in Mompox when he heard that suspicious sails at sea might be the expedition which Bolívar was preparing in Aux Cayes. He was worried about the situation in Venezuela and in particular about Margarita and Guayana, the strategic importance of which he fully realized. " I considered that province [Guayana] of so much importance that I made bold to tell H.M. in Madrid that, if it were to be lost and occupied by force, Caracas and Santa Fe would be in danger "—he wrote. And as for Margarita: " If Margarita were to be lost, it would be fortified by the insurgents, and a whole expedition would be necessary to recover it." He decided to send Morales whose name, he said, " in that country is worth several battalions ". He insistently asked for a reinforcement of four thousand men " to land in Margarita ". He was persuaded that the core of the rebellion was Venezuela; and yet had appointed as Commander there a man unworthy of his trust. Don Salvador Moxó, " a Catalan, a cavalry officer, was small and round, with eyes somewhat bulging, well educated, polite in his intercourse and at table, cruel and very simulating, and in the smallness of his body there was not enough room for the fire of his temperament ". As late as August 31, 1816, Morillo was still asking the Minister of War to confirm Moxó as actual Captain General of Venezuela, owing to his " much prudence, military talents, firmness and indefatigable activity ". But, as he soon noticed when bad news began to pour in from Venezuela, Moxó had lost the country for good and all. Margarita had been evacuated because, despite repeated messages from its local governor Pardo, Moxó had sent only small detachments of ill-clad and poorly armed local troops, which were destroyed piecemeal by the rebels, while he kept a strong Spanish regular garrison round his person at Caracas; and by a similar policy he had allowed Mariño and Piar to win victory after victory in the east. This bad commander was an even worse governor. He was amassing a comfortable fortune by means fair and foul, such as granting permits to stay in Caracas to a dangerous rebel for a payment of 20,000 pesos; or letting an English corsair buy a ship caught by the Spanish navy in Puerto Cabello, soon armed against Spain by her new master; or allowing anyone to be armed no matter against whom, so long as he paid him for a permit.

Sending La Torre before him, Morillo left for Venezuela towards the middle of November. La Torre, with a newly recruited battalion trained in thirty days, a few veteran companies and eighty hussars, crossed the Andes between December, 1816, and January, 1817. They performed a feat which, though never commented upon, is no less outstanding than the famous passing of the Andes Bolívar was to achieve later in the opposite direction; indeed, more remarkable, at least for the European members of the expedition not hardened to the ways of the land.

On January 28th, 1817, La Torre came across thirteen hundred *llaneros* under Páez. His troops, many of them raw, in square formation, stubbornly withstood the terrific onslaught of that wild cavalry. Páez set fire to the dry grass and soon the solid square of men, unable to manoeuvre without courting defeat and massacre, were also threatened by flames whipped into a fury by a strong wind. " Our ears could already perceive the sinister bursts of laughter of our enemies gloating over their diabolic victory "—writes Sevilla who was present. " In that situation, without budging from our positions, we all turned our eyes to our general, who, on horseback, in the centre of the square, scrutinized the horizon." The General ordered a retreat through the flames; some soldiers were burned and wounded by the explosion of their own cartridges, but the army was saved by a marsh which La Torre's eye had guessed behind the flames. A few days later, Morillo, after joining forces with La Torre in Paso del Frío, wrote to Moxó (2.ii.17) complaining of the state of things he had found in Venezuela. No food, not even a small hospital. All he got for an answer was a letter enclosing a report from Lorenzo Fitzgerald, the Governor of Guayana, in which this Irishman in the service of Spain painted in sombre colours the situation of the Province, once opulent, but by then stripped of its wealth by the war, and warned that if the Missions were occupied, all hope of food would vanish. Morillo's two chief ideas were Margarita and Guayana. Margarita was lost and Guayana was going.

3

Bolívar landed in Barcelona (31.xii.16) with valuable support: at least eight armed ships, and four other vessels, each armed with one gun, and with seventy men on board. Pétion had been generous in arms and ammunition. Bolívar had also brought from Haiti many French and British officers. And, above all, Bolívar had brought back Bolívar. Many officers then serving under Piar or under Páez (Urdaneta and Santander among them) asked their chiefs for their passports and flocked back to the chief of chiefs.

But Bolívar was not yet worthy of himself. Instead of waiting to consider the general situation—his barely seven hundred men, the two thousand Piar and Mariño could put together in Guayana, the twelve hundred of Mariño in Cumaná, the two thousand of Páez in the Apure—and integrating them all in a co-ordinated effort to meet Morillo who was descending the Andes towards him, Bolívar chose to come down from the height of leadership to which his colleagues in the field had raised him, and descending to the level of a mere Mariño, Piar or Páez, to dash his ill-prepared seven hundred men against the Spaniards in a futile attempt to conquer—what ? Caracas, his political estate. He led his seven hundred men against a competent Spanish officer, Captain Jiménez, who had a well prepared and entrenched body of nine hundred Indians at Clarines. Bolívar and Arizmendi were so utterly defeated that they returned in headlong flight to Barcelona with but a handful of officers.

Nothing daunted, Bolívar set about to put Barcelona in a state of defence. He sent Soublette to Mariño with a letter pointing out that it was useless and even impossible to take Cumaná if Barcelona were lost, and urging him to come to his help. Mariño demurred. Bolívar fortified the Convent of

St. Francis with six heavy guns from Brion's vessels and shut in the inhabitants in the improvised citadel. The inept Spanish commander del Real withdrew towards Clarines, allowing Mariño, at last brought to reason, to enter Barcelona with his twelve hundred men (11.i.17). According to O'Leary and Mosquera, Bolívar's plan was to evacuate the city altogether, for he did not think he could defend it against the new commander Aldama, come to supersede del Real. This, however, does not tally with Bolívar's letter to Mariño. It is more likely that, feeling Mariño hostile and Barcelona rather a trap, he preferred to try his fortune near Piar, just as Piar before him had tried his fortune near Cedeño, and by the same process, the authority of a higher rank, to acquire the command of an army in being. Once again, however, we see Bolívar galloping away from a garrison in danger without leaving adequate instructions and guarantees for its defence. He had locked up in the *Casa Fuerte* (the *Casa Débil*, as a witty local lady called it) " thousands of rifles, a large quantity of cartridges and other war material he had brought from abroad ". He gave orders that Mariño was to cart all that away, and be ready at any moment to come to the rescue of Freites, left in command in Barcelona, should he need it. But Mariño and his companions, as Bolívar was bound to suspect, had no intention of following these instructions. They quarrelled with each other, followed each a different direction— Mariño, of course, to Cumaná, others to Aragua and beyond—and Freites was left to his fate. Bolívar left on March 21st or 25th, 1817 (the actual day is in doubt). On April 5th, Aldama was in Barcelona, and on the 7th he forced his way into the Casa Fuerte, where his troops behaved with unbelievable cruelty.

Barcelona fell the victim of the diverging ambitions of Mariño and Bolívar. Mariño took his army back to Cumaná, on the northern coast. Bolívar went in search of an army towards Angostura, on the banks of the Orinoco. The army he was after happened to be commanded by Piar, the bold mulatto who, more than once, had stood in his way and reproached him for his sudden flights. Piar and Cedeño had threatened Angostura towards the middle of January, 1817. On January 17th they tried to storm it by a frontal attack, but failed. This failure gave an opportunity to some officers to leave and join Bolívar's headquarters. Possibly in order to retain them with the prospect of a brilliant and profitable operation, Piar bethought himself of raiding the Missions of Caroní, where twenty-two Capuchin friars had managed to keep a numerous Indian population in peace and prosperity. There were no arms there. The friars were dispossessed and arrested in the Monastery of Caruache, and Piar handed over to the republican priest-colonel, José Felix Blanco, the administration of that vast centre rich in grain, cattle and horses. At this point, Bolívar turned up. Let now his own aide-de-camp, Mosquera, carry on the story: " On hearing that twenty-two Capuchin friars were held prisoner, it was but natural that, bearing in mind their tenacity in upholding the Spanish cause, he should give vent to his bitter feelings against them, and so he did. Lieutenant Colonel Jacinto Lara and his aide-de-camp Monzón found in Bolívar's vehement utterances a sufficient stimulus to consider the massacre of the friars a good and patriotic action, whereupon, a few days later, on their own authority, they carried out such a crime." No punishment was inflicted on the criminal officers and, as will be seen anon, Lara remained one of Bolívar's right-hand men.

Bolívar did not stay long with Piar, though long enough to acquire from him the conviction that Guayana was the most important base of operations for the republican cause. General La Torre was coming to reinforce Angostura. One night, a spy brought the news that La Torre and his lieutenant Ceruti had left the city by river at the head of their troops. Piar thought it likely that the movement aimed at the Caroní Missions. He moved so as to prevent this attack on his rich preserves. The two forces met at San Felix, and Piar won a brilliant victory, literally destroying the Spanish force. He is generally credited with the shooting of one hundred and sixty prisoners. But a republican soldier of the period recorded that Piar massacred eight hundred Spanish prisoners " who, tied two by two, back to back, were speared and thrown into the Orinoco ". La Torre spent a sleepless night in a forest nearby and was able to gallop away at dawn.*

The situation was on the surface not very favourable for Bolívar. Of his three rivals in the field, one, Mariño, turned his back on him; the other two, Páez and Piar, won battles without consulting him. At the time, Bolívar seems to have counted on nothing but the prestige he still enjoyed among the majority of the Venezuelan chieftains, owing to his magnetic power and to the sheer superiority of his intellect. He began with Páez, offering him the rank of Brigadier General if he would recognize his authority. Páez accepted. Bolívar also succeeded in drawing to his side his inveterate enemy Bermúdez. But he had forgotten the promises of civilian government and of respect for the republican ideas in the name of which he was supposed to be fighting. The man who was to refresh his memory was then busy writing constitutions in Margarita. " General "—wrote the Canon Cortés Madariaga from Pampátar (25.iv.17)—" here I am in this island since the 18th having come from Kingston and Barbada, in both of which I merited from their respected admirals the offer of two warships for my crossings. . . . They desired Captain Stirling, commander of H.M.S. *Brazen*, who brought me here, to confer with you and the Admiral [Brion] on how best to co-ordinate our mutual relations, already afoot, and entrusted me with a few confidential items not to be ventured to the risks of the pen." Cortés goes on to explain that London demands certain written assurances in order to include Venezuela in the recognition of the independence of South America " to be sanctioned in a few months "; but only for " such provinces and kingdoms as possess organized governments with forces and resources capable of enforcing respect for their liberties ". This leads him to insist on " the need to re-establish the government in recess with its legitimate division of powers . . . without which we shall be held in contempt by the

---

* A curious document might explain how the patriots were informed of the secret march of their adversaries. The Governor of Guayana was Don Lorenzo Fitzgerald, an Irishman in the service of Spain. On July 29th, 1817, Brion, acting as Bolívar's admiral, issued an order declaring that, in the light of the information conveyed to him by deserters, Fitzgerald was not an enemy of the independent cause, and that he was to be treated with as much consideration as if he were a republican chief.— *Yanes*, vol. II, p. 224.

world and fall a prey to anarchy ".   He reminds Bolívar of the words Bolívar
had written to him from Haiti: " Force is not government."   Two days
before writing this letter, he had drafted a long-winded and bombastic
Manifesto brushing a picture of the whole continent in its fight against
" decrepit Spain ", recalling his past services and offering himself for future
ones.   But there was a touch of uneasiness in his letter to Bolívar about the
" apathy " of the Island, and he went as far as to say that, if Arizmendi did
not come back soon, " I wonder whether it will not in the end succumb
to the enemy ".   Morillo was approaching.

Mariño was in Cariaco, on the mainland; and Cortés Madariaga crossed
over with his political papers in his trunks.   On May 8th, 1817, Mariño, as
the " Second Chief of the Republic " (whatever that meant), called together
a kind of Congress of eleven persons, including Brion, Cortés Madariaga and
Zea, and gave the floor to the Canon who explained that " having come to
understand through a reliable channel that South America is on the brink of
appearing before the world in all the dignity due to her ", he brought news
that " made him hope that Venezuela would be included in the common
prosperity of the South of America within the current year and through its
foreign relations ", on condition that a regular government were established.
The Admiral seconded him.   All those present agreed, and felt sure that
the Supreme Chief would also agree.   Whereupon, Mariño formally withdrew so that his countrymen could be the freer to appoint him Commander
in Chief.   The Congress then appointed an Executive Committee composed
of Francisco Javier Mayz, Bolívar and Fernando Toro, the last by no means
with his acquiescence, for he had obstinately remained in exile from the
early day in which he realized that the Revolution he had led was threatening
his social power as a landowner.   Bolívar and Toro were to be represented
by Zea and Cortés until they arrived; and Mariño was to be Commander
in Chief of the Republic.   The seat of government for the time being was
to be in Margarita (Pampátar, 12.v.17).   The new government decreed that
the Congress would be addressed as *Honourable*, the Executive Committee
as *Respectable*, the Judiciary as *Upright* and the Captain General and Admiral
as *Honourable* only by courtesy.   Everything was now ready for action—
everything but Bolívar's blessing.

Pending its arrival, the new government took itself in dead earnest.   Its
constitution as a federal government enabled Mariño to hold an election in
the territory of Cumaná.   Some kind of an assembly emerged therefrom,
and met in Cariaco (28.v.17).   This Cumanese assembly decided to appoint
Mariño President of the State of Cumaná, and bestowed on him all the
powers, military and civil.   As such, he offered himself to the Admiral of
the Republic as " particular chief of this province, who will understand his
chief glory as a total sacrifice in favour of the common weal ".   Meanwhile,
Morillo's lieutenant Jiménez reoccupied Cariaco and Carúpano.   On
May 29th, the government decided to transfer its residence and that of the
Upright Judicial Power to Maturin, whereupon they wrote to the Honourable
Admiral ordering him to provide shipping for themselves, their officers and
their families.   The Honourable Admiral, however, had decided to trim his

sails and to navigate closer to Bolívar's than to Mariño's coasts; and so he answered that, on orders from the Supreme Chief (a power unknown to the new constitution) he could only provide transport to Guayana (i.e. to a territory under Bolívar's military control) where he himself was to report with the forces under his command. " And with this "—concludes Yanes— " the general government stood dissolved."

4

This firm stand against civilian meddling was fully justified in the circumstances. After all, the true basis for normal republican institutions was at the time illusory, and Cortés Madariaga's lucubrations could not have been less timely. On the other hand, this time, as many other times before and many more still to come, Bolívar's contemptuous dismissal of the " so-called government " expressed *both* his statesmanlike sense of the requirements of the hour and the dictatorial temperament which, far from having evolved through a long, disenchanting experience, had been from his early youth an essential feature of his character.

The issue, moreover, was not as cut and dried as might be thought; and, even among the military, loyalty to Bolívar was by no means incompatible with a desire to check his omnipotence. Bolívar wrote to his friend and collaborator, Colonel Briceño Méndez (13.vi.17), that he had heard that Arizmendi was trying to organize a government " in opposition to that which resides in Margarita "—a step which " might lead to fighting and even bloodshed during election time, since elections can only be held by soldiers, officers and army chiefs, for there are no free men but the military ". Briceño answered from Upata (16.vi.17) as a man who thinks there ought to be a civil government but knows Bolívar will have none of it. " All that is wanted is to give you a Senate or Council, so that there is something democratic and representative in our form of government, and that there is somebody who works on civil and political matters while you are busy with war . . . to prevent the jealousy, fear and mistrust, sown among the generals and especially against you. They say that General Mariño, no longer in fear of your absolute power, would return in good faith to his duty, a thing not to be hoped for by any other means; that the other chiefs, the soldiers and the people, will be appeased, and will conceive hopes of being free." Finally Briceño writes he would like to be spared the sacrifice of having to speak again on the subject.

Bolívar's answer could not have been more characteristic. " I did not know you to be so timid "—he chafes. " It is not me that you fear, for you speak your mind freely enough. . . . You seem to imagine that we are in such a situation as we were in, in Cartagena, Güiria or Carúpano, where circumstances were against me and when the party spirit triumphed over justice and the fatherland. If I have been moderate so far, it has not been out of weakness; do not believe that plots can be strong enough to destroy us. I never was in a happier position, though any man may say what he wishes. At my voice, three thousand men will obey, who will defend blameless people and brook no factions. Believe me, Briceño, you must fear nothing. You are not in Constantinople or in Haiti; there are no tyrants here, and no anarchy, while I breathe sword in hand. If I have so far tolerated some disorders, fear no more; for I am going to correct them, and to breathe with more freedom." So that was clear. Briceño could not possibly have written in favour of a Senate and of civil government unless he were afraid; we were not in Haiti—alas for Bolívar's sincerity in praising Pétion above Washington!—and there were to be neither tyrants nor anarchy while Bolívar had three thousand men who obeyed his voice. He was going to stop all disorders, i.e. to silence every other voice likely to be obeyed by another three thousand men.

The dreaded voice was Piar's, a chieftain as powerful as Mariño but more determined and dangerous because of his dash and of his gifts of leadership, as well as of his hold over the castes owing to his being a mulatto. Piar had acquired considerable prestige with his victory at San Felix over La Torre, whom he had forced to seek refuge in Angostura; and was at the time besieging the unfortunate city. When La Torre with his fifteen hundred men arrived in Angostura towards the beginning of April, the city had been besieged for two months by about eight hundred patriots under Piar. The disastrous defeat of San Felix deprived it of any hope of food; and hunger became the most dreaded enemy. The Spaniards had no naval forces there while the patriots could always count on those of the foreign corsairs who swarmed in the mouth of the Orinoco hoping to acquire good cargoes of cocoa or coffee. An amphibious sortie was attempted with gunboats on the river and two hundred men, to prevent a battery being erected by the republicans four leagues away. At dawn (18.v.17), the soldiers landed and massacred several groups of patriots caught in their sleep, but, from a nearby wood, a vigorous fire greeted them. The Spanish commander, Echevarría, went forward and nearly caught Bolívar in person, who had to flee precipitately, leaving behind his magnificent mule with a luxurious harness. Captain Sevilla bought the bit from a private. The sergeant presented the saddle to Echevarría and the pistols to La Torre.

But this brilliant episode brought no relief to the city. Towards the middle of July the situation was desperate. The military, led by Echevarría, were all for breaking through the besiegers and saving, at any rate, the fighting force; but an old man, a wealthy Creole, spoke then: " I had six sons; one died of hunger, another was killed by the enemy; the other four are fighting for their king; my four daughters, two married, two unmarried, are gathering grass in the streets to keep alive; their father is rich in gold but has not one crust of bread to offer them for his thirty grandchildren. In my case are all the families of Guayana, white, black or Indian, levelled by misery. You cannot forsake us. If we must leave the city, let us leave it all together." Many more days passed by. In the end, the old man's advice prevailed. The whole city—what remained of it—left by river; many were lost to Brion's attacks on the water; some arrived with La Torre in Grenada (9.viii.17)—yellow skeletons who could not even eat, for they died when they took food. This disaster for the troops of Spain gave Bolívar as good a hold over Guayana as in the circumstances he could wish. Henceforth, the patriots would have a solid base for their operations.

5

More than half of Morillo's army was American, for he had lost many soldiers to disease and was short of officers and of non-commissioned officers. He was disillusioned and pessimistic, now that he had measured the full import of Moxó's incapacity and dishonesty. Just as Bolívar had allowed his better generalship to be clouded by his desire to take Caracas, so Morillo, at this juncture, instead of concentrating his troops against Piar and Bolívar in Guayana, was deflected from this right course by his obsession with Margarita and Arizmendi—" the hypocritical and despicable Arizmendi ", as he says in the second sentence of the proclamation he addressed to the Margaritans (17.vii.17), three days after landing for the second time on the Island. Leaving La Torre to defend Guayana, he, the commander in chief, had not marched where his military brain would have decided, but where his bruised heart had dictated.

With reinforcements just arrived from Spain under General Canterac, he landed in Punta de Mangles (15.vii.17). The landing was not easy, and he himself had to take personal command of a battalion in difficulties. In his report he emphasizes the natural defences of the Island but pays a handsome tribute to the bravery of the defenders. On the 17th, he issued a proclamation offering complete forgiveness " if you submit at once ". But the alternative reflected the temper of the general once bitten twice shy: " If in spite of this offer which I make in the service of humanity and as a consequence of the principles which have always ruled my behaviour, you insist in your rebellion, I shall march against you with all my considerable forces; desolation and terror shall march in front of them, and if the traitors of Barcelona have finished now their miserable existence, in this disloyal Island there shall remain not even the ashes or the memory of the rebels who rejected the compassion of our sovereign and who sought stubbornly their own extermination." On July 20th, Aldama's division landed. The Spanish troops advanced steadily but with difficulty; and, though Pampátar was taken (24.vii.17) and Juan Griego also (1.viii.17) news came of the loss of Guayana and the threat to Caracas, and Morillo decided to evacuate Margarita; that is, he decided, too late, to do what he should have done at first, to concentrate on the Main Land. On August 19th, 1817, he arrived in Cumaná. In September he was back in Caracas with over seven hundred men wounded and sick. Moxó had abandoned his post and left the country, well provided with ill acquired funds.

Bolívar, now master of the river Orinoco, felt in a position to tackle his rival Piar. He had not lost sight of the activities of the bold and ambitious mulatto, and had been watching in particular Piar's bickerings with the Priest-Colonel José Felix Blanco, who commanded and administered the rich estate of the murdered Capuchins of Caroní. Several letters of Bolívar to Blanco written at this time advise patience. Piar was not happy. Bolívar wrote amiable letters to him and refused to accept his resignation in the friendliest and most patient of terms. He did his best, and it would appear sincerely, to retain this man in his service, if, of course, under his orders. However, Piar insisted on leaving and asked for his passport to go abroad. It was granted him on June 30th, but on July 23rd Bolívar instructed Bermúdez to summon Piar to general headquarters and, should he refuse to come, to arrest him. Piar did not come, for he did not trust Bolívar's intentions, and eventually Cedeño, Piar's own lieutenant, caught him in Aragua, and brought him, a disarmed prisoner, to Angostura. Bolívar called a meeting of officers to make sure of his ground, and the fallen leader was abandoned by all his one-time friends. A court martial presided over by Brion sentenced Piar to death, and he was executed on the main square of Angostura on October 16th, 1817. He was thirty-five.

Bolívar's tears and regrets are insincere. The court martial was a plain denial of justice, since one of the accusations, that of desertion, makes nonsense of the rest, which are hardly more substantial. The execution was, on the other hand, fruitful as an act of force in a country in which nothing but force seemed to be of any avail. It was a pretorian act in a pretorian society. Nothing illustrates it better than the decree promulgated by Bolívar ten days before Piar's execution, whereby the property of all Spaniards and of all Royalist Creoles was distributed to the army to the tune of twenty-five thousand pesos to the commander in chief, twenty thousand to division generals, fifteen thousand to lieutenant colonels and so on to the privates, who were to receive five hundred each. " Have it broadcast among the army under your command "—he wrote to Páez—" with all the solemnity of a national decree." And after explaining in another proclamation (30.x.17) that " it is impossible for the present to set up a good representative government, an eminently liberal constitution, which is the aim of all my endeavours and the most ardent wish of my heart ", he organized a Council of State in Angostura, this time composed exclusively of his yes-men.

6

Towards the end of 1817, the situation in Venezuela had assumed a certain symmetry. The west was loyal or servile, the east was rebel or patriotic. Morillo had his rearguard protected by the viceroyalty of New Granada, by now reduced to obedience; Bolívar held the incomparable base of Guayana and the Lower Orinoco, and (thanks to Brion on the one hand and to the secret or overt sympathy of the British Navy) the sea to windward. The actual forces of both sides were poor. The march through the Andes had weakened Morillo's army; the troops of Aldama's division were the only seasoned soldiers left him; and he drew the attention of the war minister to the fact that all he had left to hold New Granada was a Creole garrison with a sprinkling of officers and sergeants from Spain. His own army in Venezuela was short of leaders; La Torre was seriously wounded; Aldama and Warleta were ill with scurvy; Calzada was little more than a guerrilla chieftain; his two professional colonels were wounded. There were among his officers too many incompetent upstarts promoted by " every commander who cares to act as a miniature king "; there was no food; stores were dwindling; and the viceroy of New Granada was hostile and would send no help. Towards the middle of November, Morillo's troops were disposed as follows: the column of Jiménez was raiding the coast of Cumaná, while local battalions with some artillery and cavalry garrisoned Cumaná and Barcelona; small infantry garrisons defended Caracas and La Guaira; a small force of artillery and the fugitives from Guayana garrisoned Puerto Cabello; local militias held the valleys of Aragua and the city of Valencia. As for the fighting " divisions " (a word by no means to be given its modern technical sense), the first, under La Torre, covered the line El Sombrero to Calvario; the second was spread between Caracas and Valencia; the fourth, under Aldama, was in Nutrias; and the fifth, under Calzada, in Camaguán.

Bolívar seems at this stage to have entertained a hope of inflicting a final blow on Morillo. His idea was to hold Guayana with Bermúdez' forces, i.e. with the men previously commanded by Mariño, mainly liberated and enlisted slaves from the big estates; to gather all the forces at his disposal, meet Páez, who was campaigning on his own in the Apure valley, in the south-west, bring him over for good and all (hence his show of force to impress his rival) and fall on the Spaniards with all the Venezuelan might at last united. He had promulgated a so-called martial law, in fact a compulsory service law, for all men between fourteen and seventy. But what was his strength? That depends on his correspondent. He writes to his agent in London, López Méndez, that he leaves for the Apure with six thousand men " perfectly equipped ". " The force led by Bolívar "— writes O'Leary who ought to know—" amounted to nearly three thousand men, two thousand of them infantry; the cavalry was armed with spears, and of the infantry. fourteen hundred only had rifles and the rest arrows." But he was well armed for all that, since Páez' division consisted of one thousand horsemen and two hundred and fifty infantry men.

On January 30th, 1818, Bolívar and Páez met for the first time. O'Leary describes Páez thus: " He was of middle height, robust and well shaped, though the lower part of his body was not proportioned to his bust; his chest and shoulders, very wide, his neck short and thick, a big head, covered with dark auburn hair, short and wavy; dark, quick eyes, straight nose with wide nostrils, thick lips and a round chin. His clear complexion told his good health, and would have been very white but for the sun. Caution and mistrust were the chief features of his physiognomy. The son of humble parents, he owed nothing to education. Wholly illiterate, he knew nothing about the theory of the profession which he had practised so much, and was unaware of even the simplest words of the craft; the slightest emotion or contradiction gave him strong convulsions which for a time deprived him of his senses. . . . As a guerrilla chief, he was without rival. Rash, active, brave, fertile in stratagems, quick in conception, resolute in execution, swift in movement, he was the more formidable the smaller the force under his command. Lacking in method, knowledge, moral courage, he was valueless in politics. Without being cruel, he did not spare blood, and he has been known to have it shed when humanity, patriotism and policy would have counselled sparing it. His ambition was boundless. It and his cupidity were his dominant passions. He was able to acquire an exceptional hold over the *Llaneros* by allowing looting and by relaxing discipline."

As soon as he knew that Bolívar was four leagues away, in the cattle farm of Cañafistola, Páez rode to meet him. The two men alighted and embraced each other, and set about immediately to devise plans for the campaign. The first difficulty was the crossing of the Apure. There was no river craft. " I shall provide them ", said Páez. " Where from ? " asked Bolívar. " I shall seize those we shall find in the river opposite."—" But how ? "— " With my cavalry," answered Páez. Bolívar rode on towards the river, still incredulous. Páez selected fifty men who rode to the river edge after loosening the girths of the horses so as to be able to drop the saddles on the ground without dismounting. At the edge of the water, he turned to them and said: " We must take those *flecheras** or die. Let those who wish follow their Uncle." (That was Páez' nickname with his men.) Holding their spears with their teeth, they dashed into the river, infested with alligators, and captured fourteen boats under the fire of the Spaniards on the other side. Bolívar could hardly believe his eyes. Bolívar was for Páez the bookish general, as opposed to the partisan leader which he knew himself to be. But Bolívar, who knew only too well his own shortcomings as a strategist, was bound to look upon these feats of his rival with the wary eye of the connoisseur. Here was a man who knew how to lead, hold and reward his men; a man who might eventually beat him at his own game of seeking political power by pretorian ways.

As soon as he heard of the conjunction of Páez and Bolívar, Morillo, who was in San Carlos, moved to Calabozo, where, on the day after his arrival (12.ii.18) he was attacked by Bolívar at the head of 4,100 men, 2,500 of whom were mounted. Morillo had just over 2,000 men. He won the first battle and forced Bolívar to give up his attempt at taking Calabozo; but Bolívar was—or seemed to be—sure of his victory. He sent Morillo a note typical of his style: " Our humane feelings have many times, contrary to all justice, held up the sanguinary war to the death the Spaniards wage against us. For the last time I offer the cessation of such a dreadful calamity, and I begin my offer by returning all the prisoners taken on the battlefield. Let this example of generosity be the greatest insult for our enemies. You and all the wretched garrison of Calabozo will soon fall into the hands of the victors, so that its unfortunate defenders can flatter themselves with no hope whatever. I reprieve them in the name of the Republic of Venezuela, and I should forgive even Ferdinand VII, were he, as you are, locked up in Calabozo. Profit by our clemency or resolve to share the lot of your destroyed army." Morillo did not answer; but in his report to the War Minister (Villa de Cura, 26.ii.18), he completed the story: " He gave back just three prisoners, and they were the batmen who happened to be foraging; for the whole company of Navarra which was surrounded in the Mission

---

* River craft in general use in the Orinoco basin.

was put to the sword by his orders." Morillo succeeded in evacuating Calabozo despite his rival's watchfulness (apparently because the officers told off to watch him were led astray by the prospect of looting). He left the city during the night of the 14th, with a long trail of " wounded, sick, ambulances and baggages and an emigration of the faithful inhabitants who sought the protection of H.M.'s troops ". He was following the river Guárico towards El Sombrero, where he defeated the patriots (17.ii.18), and was able to continue his undisturbed march to Villa del Cura, where he arrived on the 23rd. Bolívar occupied El Sombrero on the 17th in the evening and gave orders which both exculpate and inculpate him. " Policy as well as humanity " had led him to suspend the War to the Death. " You must therefore "—he writes to Colonel Rangel—" respect this decision and see that it is respected by the troops under your command who must be prevented from putting to death any person, whether Creole or Spanish."

Had Bolívar been in fact what he was on paper, the Supreme Chief of the Venezuelan Republic, he would have established his headquarters in the city of Ortiz " on the edge of the enemy territory, threatening at the same time San Carlos to the west and Valencia and Caracas through the valleys of Aragua ". His heart felt always the magnet of the capital, his native city, while his military instinct pointed always towards the chief adversary. On hearing of the evacuation of Calabozo by Morillo, Caracas, then very anti-patriot, fled in a body to La Guaira, La Torre having informed the authorities of the city that it might be lost. For once his heart's wishes and his brain's decisions might have been in harmony. He sent Soublette, his chief of staff, to explain his plan to his seconds, Cedeño and Páez. But Páez was not an urban and aristocratic Caraqueño; he was a rough rider of the plains. To Bolívar's arguments he opposed a stubborn negative. He was to remain in the vicinity of his native river, close by the banks of the Apure; and he justified this primal preference with so-called military arguments in favour of Calabozo as a base, centring round the advantages of undertaking an operation to take San Fernando, a besieged city which was in any case bound to fall. This obsession with San Fernando, as later events go to show, was due to the lure of booty to be won there. On February 21st, 1818, Páez, Cedeño and Rangel rode to meet Bolívar with their cavalry (brought from Calabozo without his knowledge). At four o'clock, Bolívar and his three generals began their backward movement towards Calabozo. The Supreme Commander had been commanded to move where he did not want to go. Páez, Cedeño and Rangel were chieftains, each intent on his own power and fortune. Bolívar, who had challenged the power of Spain, had now to contend with scores of little Spains, dust of conquerors. What was he moreover but a more intelligent, refined and high-minded version of Páez ? He had to bow to the inevitable. He never forgave Páez for it; and on May 15th, 1818, he wrote to Brion from San Fernando that " the action of February 12th delivered us Venezuela and the Spanish army, but we have not known how to profit by the fortune which came to us ". He exaggerated wildly as to the actual chances lost but there was no doubt as to where the responsibility lay in his mind: " What has contributed most to prolonging this campaign has been the rash resistance of San Fernando and the obstinacy of General Páez in taking this city, which would in any case have had to surrender owing to our blockade since I arrived here." The army was in a parlous condition; there were no rifles; desertions were numerous. " The army has almost melted away "—he wrote to Páez; " the whole brigade of Colonel Vázquez deserted last night, so that hardly one hundred men remained with him. General Cedeño's division is also beginning to desert, and last night, some soldiers left from General Monagas'. I cannot send troops after them, for I do not trust those who remain, who probably would follow their example; nor do I see any remedy but to arrest and punish the deserters. They can go nowhere but towards San Fernando and they are sure to present themselves to you or to go home. In any case, you can arrest them and send them to the army to be court-martialled." This was a clear confession that the soldiers preferred Páez to Bolívar (being *llaneros* like Páez). And Bolívar went on: " News from Ortiz and the Guadarrama show that circumstances favour us. I am resolved to march [i.e. towards Aragua]; but as I can do nothing without cavalry, you must, with the utmost speed, send me the squadrons you promised me as well as those of Guayabal and Camaguán . . . I can do nothing without you."

On March 3rd, 1818, unable to resist the lure of Caracas, Bolívar moved on towards San Pablo with whatever forces he could muster, without waiting for Páez' squadrons. By March 11th, the army, reinforced with Monagas' cavalry, entered Villa de Cura. Morillo was in Valencia; La Torre, in the position of Las Cocuizas, barred the way to Caracas. Bolívar left Monagas in Maracay and went forward to dislodge Monagas. The mere approach and threat of Bolívar raised a panic everywhere and particularly in the capital. Feliciano Palacios, his kinsman and successor in the command of his troops in Cartagena in 1815, wrote: " In a few hours and as by an electrical move-ment, the population of the whole city in a body rushed to the shores of La Guaira; nearly every man or woman of every age left his or her fatherland, wealth, comfort, to run away from the hated Republic and seek the govern-ment of the King. In every village that heard the news, all fled to the mountains." Meanwhile the Spaniards were advancing on both sides of the lagoon. The two armies met at last (16.iii.18), on the undulating plain watered by the rivulet Semen, close to the defile of La Puerta where so many battles had been, and were to be, fought. It might have been a victory for Bolívar, for Morales' troops were not strong enough to resist the onslaught of the patriots; but fresh troops brought by Morillo caused some disorder among the republicans, and Morillo himself, thinking the occasion demanded his own example, led a charge which routed Bolívar's troops though it cost him a serious wound and nearly his life. Bolívar lost eight hundred dead, four hundred prisoners and all his papers.

Towards the end of the month, Bolívar moved on to Calabozo. In the cattle farm of Rincón de los Toros, not far from San José, he was nearly caught and killed as he slept under the foliage of a grove of trees at some distance from the camp, when a party of eight Spanish soldiers, under

Captain Renovales, sent in the still of night by Colonel López, stealthily approached to within a few yards of his retreat. Renovales and his troop came upon Santander, acting chief of staff to Bolívar in Soublette's absence. The Spaniard had been told the password by a deserter. They asked to see the Supreme Chief. Santander called: " General! " Bolívar leapt from his hammock and instinctively ran to his horse. A volley rent the still air. The chaplain and two colonels fell dead. Bolívar tried to mount his mule, which shied at the report of the shots. In the confusion, he called one of his captains to let him ride on his horse, but the captain retorted the horse would not stand two riders. A sergeant let him have a horse, but it stumbled and fell. To save himself, Bolívar threw off his red gold-embroidered jacket and his showy hat and fled until Colonels Rondon and Infante offered him a good horse, so good indeed that Bolívar suspected his two colonels meant to trap him and deliver him to the enemy; but, as it turned out, the mount was that of Colonel López, and on it Bolívar did at last reach Calabozo (18.iv.18), and after vain attempts at joining Páez, he withdrew to San Fernando on May 3rd. The day before, Páez had been defeated at Cojedes.

Chapter XXIX

THE BRITISH AUXILIARIES

I

IN his report on the battle of Semen, Morillo says that " among the insurgent dead there are more than forty officers, of which ten are Englishmen in their service ". Where did these Englishmen come from ? The war was depopulating Venezuela since it was mostly with Venezuelan manpower that it was being waged. Bolívar wrote to Brion (15.v.18) that the patriots had " destroyed five or six thousand men of Spanish troops most of them European ". He reckoned the royalist army at 10,000 to 12,000 (half of them Spanish): " they have neither horses nor cavalry, but their infantry is most excellent, and on the high ground above Caracas they are invincible owing to their *resistance* to our cavalry, because we have just five hundred infantry men. The Spaniards cannot enter the plains without risking to have to return very much chastened and with less than half their troops. But neither can we enter Caracas unless we considerably increase our infantry." Though both before and after the defeat of Semen Bolívar had endeavoured to recruit men by blandishments, amnesties and force, the crop had been but meagre. The Guárico region was royalist to the core; the majority of the chieftains remained faithful to Spain. " Their fidelity was justified by the general opinion of the population. When the patriots entered any township, many families, when not all, fled to the woods." Bolívar gave orders to respect the population and to induce it to remain at home; and to " forbid all robbery, violence, vexation or any excess calculated to arouse the hatred of the populations against us ". But the populations did not trust their would-be liberators.

Morillo also was short of soldiers, of officers, of generals. But, in the long run, the country would probably have favoured the Spanish forces had not a new element come to upset the balance of power in favour of the patriots.

Castlereagh maintained his official policy of opposition to any intervention in the affairs of Spanish America on the part of any nation outside Spain; and on November 27th, 1817, the Regent had issued an order forbidding British subjects to take any part in the war between Spain and the rebels beyond the seas. But this official policy was lined with a tacit tolerance even to the actual aiding and abetting of the Spanish-American agents who were busy in England recruiting British volunteers. We know from the Memoirs of Hippisley, one of the British recruiting " colonels ", that the original stimulus, so far as he was concerned, came from " a friend, to whom several gentlemen in the mercantile world had expressed their full conviction of the ultimate success of the Independents in South America, if aided and assisted by officers and men from Great Britain "; and having set down how he decided to help in this cause, he adds: " With this resolution, and the approbation of my friend (whose high rank in the army of Great Britain, and whose experience in military matters, was as distinguished as his name was honoured, loved and respected),* I presented myself to the Venezuelan agent, López Méndez." Hippisley was soon immersed in the multifarious activities of equipping and organizing his regiment, competing for saddlery and uniforms with other rivals in the field; and in the course of his narrative, he writes: " During the publicity which the formation of the several corps, and the open exposure of the clothing, caps, accoutrements, and horse appointments, for the officers and non-commissioned officers, daily and hourly displayed in the windows of the shops of the various tradesmen employed, no interference of, or notice from the British government obtruded itself; and all concerned felt convinced that the Ministry did not disapprove of, but tacitly consented to the exertions that we were making in the cause of Spanish South American Independence! Even when the question was put to some gentlemen, who held places of trust and confidence in the higher departments of the state, it was answered, ' be speedy in the preparations and arrangements. Avoid, as far as possible, too great notoriety. Speak little on the subject in public. Make no unnecessary bustle in completing the whole of the equipments and in embarking the officers and men. And, above all, hasten your departure from England with all the celerity in your power.' Thus spake ——, ——, and ——."

Nothing could be more entertaining than the pages in which, with a delightful insularity, Hippisley endeavours to set up an English military unit, with its collective spirit, manners, mess-comradeship and traditions, to serve in conditions so different from those he and his friends dreamt of. Their dress and undress uniforms, their magnificent saddlery and harnesses, their weapons and field-luggage to go to serve alongside of men who fought naked and barefoot, on horses without saddles and with a spear for all their weapon, who ate roast meat without salt and slept on the ground, would be comic had they not from the first been doomed to be tragic and heroic as well. The convivial trend alive in English regiments bore fruit from the first. " Colonel Campbell's corps of riflemen, at least the officers composing the regiment, had rendered themselves very conspicuous: go where you would, the Venezuelan riflemen were the subject of observation, and, notwithstanding their colonel's efforts, extreme publicity was given to all their movements. The frequency of their mess-dinners, and other parties, in and near the metropolis; the appearance of some of the gentlemen at the public places of amusement in uniform; and last but not least, the excellence of the regimental band, which attended the officers wherever they dined together, were the themes of general conversation." As for Hippisley's own regiment, they had decided to offer a cold collation to López Méndez himself, whom the officers, by the way, had not yet met. " Mr. Mackintosh, the saddler, had very obligingly offered the use of his drawing-room and eating-parlour for his reception and that of the officers of the first Venezuelan hussars. . . . The officers had been directed to meet in the drawing-room,

* Wellington ? He was by then a Spanish grandee, and Spain had granted him a handsome estate near Granada.

a quarter of an hour before Don Méndez's expected attendance, in order that they might be disposed in the circle according to rank and seniority. . . . Whilst waiting in full expectation of the arrival of the general (as many of the officers had heard M. Méndez denominated, and actually believed him to be), the door was thrown open, and, with apparent state, in walked an elderly black man, with head well powdered, decorated in a rich looking uniform of drab with scarlet facings, collar and cuff. The whole of the line of officers, with regularity and precision, rose spontaneously, and formed the circle; and, after a graceful bow from all, in which motion and time combined, the whole remained steady to receive the personage in uniform; who, all astonished at the reception given him, advanced no further, yet with two or three very genteel bows in return, complimented the entire circle. How much longer the equivoque had been kept up I know not, had not I, who at the first was all wonder at the general movement, and afterwards so completely convulsed by laughter as not to be able to speak, relieved the suspense of the whole, by informing the officers that the personage whom they had mistaken for the general, or Don Méndez, was only the black man George, a faithful servant of a gentleman who had obligingly lent him and his services for that day's attendance."

2

The chief cause of López Méndez' success in recruiting these British units was twofold: on the one hand, the old standing tradition which in Britain identified Spanish America with Eldorado, an Eldorado till then closed and inaccessible like a continental Tibet, but now, thanks to the patriots, within reach of any hand bold enough to fight its way into it; and on the other, the widespread unemployment the British officer class was undergoing at the end of the Napoleonic wars. Men and material were then abundant on the market, and adventurers of all kinds were quick to seize their opportunity. Some enlisted or offered their services: Sir Gregor MacGregor for instance, or that MacDonald who, according to Morillo, had perished in the battle of Semen; others tried to organize themselves in units, lured by contracts under which López Méndez offered them higher rank and salary than they had enjoyed on active service in Europe. By the close of 1817, an expedition of five ships, *Britannia, Emerald, Dawson, Prince* and *Indian*, was ready to sail with the officers and men of five regiments in command of five self-styled colonels, Gilmore, Hippisley, Wilson, Campbell and Skeene. Their total complement did not rise beyond 800 men; but their equipment was excellent and they took over a substantial load of arms and ammunition sent as a speculation by London merchants. Skeene and his regiment perished in a storm which destroyed S.S. *Indian*. The remaining regiments ran a number of adventures first in the Swedish Antille San Bartholomé, then in Georgetown, Grenada and later in other more or less hospitable ports of the Antilles. News of the war as it actually was being waged in Venezuela had somewhat cooled the naïve enthusiasm of the volunteers; hardships, war to the death, no pay, no uniforms, no Eldorado. Many deserted; others fought duels and brawls and met with financial troubles of all kinds. In the end, about one hundred and fifty men under Hippisley, Wilson, Campbell and Gilmore succeeded in reaching Guayana at one time or another during the second quarter of 1818.

Hippisley, who arrived in San Fernando on May 22nd, 1818, issued stern orders to his men which call to mind the famous saying attributed to Wellington on inspecting reinforcements sent him to Spain from England: " I don't know how they will impress the enemy but they terrify *me!* " He knew only too well the poor quality of the recruits he had brought over and, in his orders, let it be known that " any man seen drunk, either on or off duty, shall be punished as severely as the military cause of the Venezuelan service permits ". He was rash enough to add: " Bolívar has an abhorrence of, and an antipathy to, a drunken soldier "—which hardly tallies with his own observation : Tomás Montilla, he writes, is " a great favourite with the general in chief, Bolívar, and is about 27 years of age, excessively neat in his person and appearance, but unfortunately so addicted to drinking, that he is scarcely known to go to his hammock sober at night ". Hippisley, who had already seen poverty, anarchy and intrigue dogging the steps of the patriotic cause in Angostura, was impressed by the air of defeat and disaster he found in San Fernando. He describes dramatically how Cedeño was saved from instant death by Páez after a drunken brawl: " Having followed the stream of idlers to the upper part of the town, we came to the prison, where some of his friends met the fugitive, and enabled him for the present to escape the fury of the soldiery, though an immense crowd had surrounded the house, and report said that they were cutting off the general's spurs previous to his being executed. In a few minutes after, he was led out by an officer holding him by the left hand, as a gentleman would hand a lady, and I perceived that the highest respect was paid to this personage, who frequently placed his own left hand on his breast, and uttered some words vehemently in Spanish: the spectators and soldiery bowed their attention and forbearance. Sedeno is a tall thin man, and looked at that moment nothing like a general, but a thief, or some other rascal, just taken in the act. His companion and guardian was a man of about five feet seven inches high, rather fleshy; plump, round face, fair complexion, and most prepossessing countenance. He appeared in a dark blue jacket, sabre, cocked hat, with a large silver cockade in front, as he wore his hat, as the sailors say, fore and aft."

3

Páez was in fact the master of the place, since, in San Fernando, he, and not Bolívar, was the actual commander of the actual troops. Páez had courted the favours of all the British commanders. " I had the opportunity " —" Colonel " English told Hippisley—" of becoming intimately known to that gallant chief, and receiving several marks of his friendship and approbation. Among other presents, he gave me four horses from his own stud." Hippisley himself, while in Angostura, had received a letter from Páez, dated March 28th, 1818, which shows how keen the chieftain of the Apure was to make friends among the British newcomers. Hippisley sent him " a handsome cap and feather, a full regimental bridle, a pair of strong brass spurs, etc."; and had received " the most kind and friendly assurances in return ". On arriving in San Fernando, he called on Páez. The *llanero* chieftain received the Englishman cordially and begged him to write every three weeks. " I asked him if he wished me to stay ? to which he answered that the chief [Bolívar] would not permit it, as he wanted the English for a reinforcement to the army before Cumaná."

The design is plain. Bolívar, without an army in the Apure, was seeking to secure an army in the Lower Orinoco, with Soublette in Angostura to receive the shipments of arms which Brion was trying to obtain in the Antilles from the City speculators, and to recruit more Englishmen, since there were few Venezuelans left, and most of them " belonged " to Páez. English, so-called colonel, out of clerk in the British commissariat, had been sent to England by Bolívar (14.v.18) on a secret mission which Hippisley soon discovered was that of recruiting more volunteers to the tune of £50 to be paid him per head, plus the rank of brigadier general and the command of one of the regiments on his return; another person with no military past at all had also been entrusted with a similar mission; whereupon Hippisley decided " to seek by similar means to reimburse the expenses I had already incurred ". This was plain to Páez, who was no fool. He managed to win over to his party the so-called Colonel Henry Wilson; who won over the so-called Major Trewren, second to Hippisley. The quality of this first batch of volunteers had better be described by Colonel Hippisley: " Colonel Wilson was at the head of only a hundred men, and half of them deserters and mutineers from another corps; a drunken, debauched lieutenant colonel, who could not dismiss a common parade; a still more drunken major, but yet, when sober, a good soldier; a set of captains and subalterns, who, with the exception of two, had never served in any regiment before, the whole of whom, in point of horsemanship, had been laughed at by all Páez's cavalry, either as horsemen or swordsmen ".

On May 23rd, liquor began to flow freely among the British rank and file. Hippisley noticed that Wilson and his officers were particularly generous with their bottles. He expostulated to Wilson who pointed out: " Your men and mine are mad to remain in hopes of plunder under Páez's command." From that moment on, Hippisley's affairs went from bad to worse; Bolívar gave him successively contradictory orders, first to return to Angostura, then to land and consider himself at liberty to join General Páez, then verbal orders to embark for Angostura. " In the meanwhile, Major Trewren and several of the officers, with the second major whom I had recently appointed (Major Ferrier), had paraded the whole of the detachment and by the light of a large fire on the beach were haranguing the men. I found the greater part drunk, to which offence they now added open and daring mutiny. I insisted upon silence, and an explanation from Major Trewren for presuming to order a parade without my leave and for such a purpose. Quietness was restored, and Major Trewren publicly informed me that it was to take the sense of the officers and men for joining General Páez; that himself and

Major Ferrier, and most of the officers, had determined to do so; upon which some of the men shouted and cried, ' Colonel Trewren and General Páez for ever! ' I drew a pistol from my belt and threatened to shoot the first man who dared to name any officer to their command but myself. I then addressed the whole of them, stated or rather re-capitulated what I had done for them. . . . Some of the drunken officers then called to the men to join them, whilst Major Ferrier recalled their attention by telling them, if they joined General Páez they would soon have rank and money at command. ' The most of the men ', said he, ' have served under Wellington in the Peninsula, who hung or shot any of them for plundering; here the brave Páez will give you leave to plunder, and to do everything to obtain riches from the enemies of the Republic.' At this moment, I perceived Colonel Wilson; he was amongst my people: as I was advancing towards him, he called out, ' Follow me, my boys; bring your arms with you '; and having led the way, the greater part of the officers and men followed, shouting out, as soon as they gained the bank, ' General Páez for ever!—General Wilson for ever!—Colonel Trewren for ever! ' "

4

In the midst of scenes of the utmost anarchy, stores pilfered, boats ransacked and confiscated, Hippisley succeeded in leaving for Angostura that night, to present his grievances to Bolívar. But where was Bolívar ? " The fire not having been renewed, had nearly gone out, and the night was dark; yet by the shouts which for a few moments filled the air, I learnt that the chief Bolívar had embarked, and that his flechera had dropt down below the town. He must, however, have heard the uproar, and learnt the state of affairs with me, though he chose not to notice them. Whether he was too anxious for his own safety I know not, but the manner of his stealing off from San Fernando was extraordinary. At this time the town and environs were crowded with troops; Páez's cavalry, Sedeno's cavalry, and a few of the infantry, amounting together to nearly two thousand men. The remainder were occupying the out-posts, and forming a cordon round the land-side of San Fernando."

On the following day, Páez had all his troops formed on parade in Achaguas; and he gave the British volunteers the place of honour, on the right of the line, " no doubt as a tribute and homage to our handsome uniforms, which contrasted so sharply with the rags and almost the nakedness of the rough and brave *llaneros* ". So says O'Leary, who was there as an officer in Wilson's corps; but Páez' views were more far-sighted. Wilson gave a dinner for Páez and flattered him heavily. It was agreed there and then that Wilson and the chiefs of the Apure armies who were present would proclaim Páez captain-general of the army on a day of the ensuing week. On that day, every chieftain bringing along as many *llaneros* as he could muster, a regular exhibition of cavalry prowess was held, after which Páez rode in surrounded by a brilliant staff of thirty to forty chiefs and officers and was acclaimed commander in chief. An " act " was read declaring him captain-general; whereupon Wilson promised him to recruit a corps of some thousands of men in England; and Páez gave Wilson leave to go to Angostura with letters for Bolívar. Páez was evidently sure that Bolívar was powerless against him. But Bolívar was not powerless. He had himself and he had the sea. Wilson was arrested, and later expelled from the territory of Venezuela; and Bolívar wrote Páez a stiff letter demanding the documents for " the government " to prosecute the guilty. No one, of course, was guiltier than Páez; but Bolívar did not mean to take any action against the dangerous *llanero*, who on the other hand thought wiser not to resist openly. Páez tore up the " act " and let Wilson be expelled.

5

When he arrived in Angostura (5.vi.18), Bolívar found the usual chaos among his generals. Bermúdez and Mariño were at loggerheads in the region of Cumaná, and Mariño had threatened Bermúdez with force if he advanced towards Cumanacoa (end of April). Bermúdez had sent young Sucre to negotiate with his rival; and Sucre, though skilful and wise for his years, did not succeed beyond avoiding bloodshed. Bolívar had to send Urdaneta who, in the end, brought Mariño to his senses. Mariño issued a proclamation (26.vi.18) recognizing Bolívar's authority—events would show how little and for how long. Bolívar was induced to rely more and more on foreign help. He decreed that foreigners would be exempt from taxes and from military service; a necessary precaution when two months earlier Montilla had got into trouble with the English merchants of Angostura for resorting to peremptory ways to pay Hippisley's hussars: " This was done by the governor and council issuing their mandate to all the civilians in Angostura of every description and of every country (even to the English merchants, who had already advanced large loans to the Republic), to bring to the government house, on the succeeding day, a certain sum, in hard cash, agreeable to a rating on each, as previously fixed upon by the council, under the penalty of imprisonment and the seizure of their stores, goods, articles of every kind, household furniture, etc." The soldiers were in " hope and expectation ". " When the Great Table in the hall at the government house . . . groaned under the extorted weight of heavy metal, extracted, without the aid of chemistry, from the iron chests where it had been concealed," a counter order returned the goods to their owners and freed an English merchant who had preferred to be arrested rather than disgorge. Hippisley was first informed that the governor and council had reconsidered the orders. " Montilla probably was drunk when he issued them." But while other means were found to meet the just claims of the British volunteers, Hippisley was able to learn the true reason of the change of front. A British ship had been reported on the Orinoco with clothing and equipment for 10,000 men, and another British ship, the *Hunter*, arrived in Angostura with supplies for Colonel Wilson's corps. It was indispensable to create a good impression and to soothe the incensed British colony.

The loss of Angostura by the royalists had *ipso facto* meant its loss by the

Venezuelans, i.e. by its owners. Hippisley describes the city as " one line of houses (all built of stone) extending for nearly a mile, and about one hundred paces from the highest water mark, when the Orinoco is full. . . . In this line, are some very excellent mansions of large dimensions, and in general, with stuccoed fronts; some with verandahs or balconies to the first floor windows. . . . Here are the dwellings of the principal merchants, English and American, several of whom have been residents since Angostura was taken from the royalists." The two best mansions were that of Brion and that of Soublette's sister, Bolívar's one-time mistress. Several other streets forming a chess board of stone-built houses, about two English acres, completed the city. The chief advantage of the city was that it controlled the mouths of the Orinoco and the sea. Brion, the Admiral of the Republic, was then scouring the Antilles for arms. He had met Hippisley in Old Guayana and learnt from him of the intrigues and dark dealings between the military adventurers, the corsairs and the speculators, who were squeezing their way through towards Angostura and Margarita between the meshes of the inefficient Spanish Navy, with the hardly hidden connivance of the British Navy. Chacón, the Spanish naval commander, was in Georgetown, repairing his ships. Brion rescued from the Spaniards the *Britannia* which had sailed to Haiti to sell a cargo of arms there; purchased the services of two French corsairs, Joly and Bernard, with good vessels, acquired the *Emerald*, and, under cover, now of Swedish, now of Dutch harbours, dodged the Spanish Navy. On July 12th, 1818, he entered Angostura among loud acclamations. He brought a valuable cargo of arms. He could not be paid in cash; but he obtained full ownership of the three best houses in Angostura and the privilege to run steamships on the Orinoco.

It is no reflection on Bolívar's dash as a *guerrillero* to say that he is more impressive behind a desk than on horseback. His letters and papers dated from Angostura show a firmer grasp of things, persons and ideas than his adventures over the plains of his fatherland. His dispute with Hippisley shows him dignified and energetic. Hippisley's own story pictures a shifty, mean and deceitful Bolívar. The British Colonel did not tune in with the Venezuelan; and he had disliked Bolívar from the outset. His narrative shows an insular inability to take in even the most elementary facts of a foreign environment. He mauls the language badly and hardly ever gets a vowel right, calling Calabozo Calaboza, Montilla Montillo, Angostura Angustura; and most comic of all, having heard the patriots refer to the Spaniards as *godos*, i.e., Goths, he solemnly dubs them *Godoys*, mistaking the nickname for an allusion to the once powerful Minister of Charles IV. As the *British Monitor* (which published his book in instalments) explained, " his object in joining the Patriots was with a view of providing very handsomely for his family ". He was as prickly with grievances as a hedgehog and wanted to have them cleared up in argument with a harassed Bolívar as if both were sitting comfortably somewhere in Threadneedle Street. In point of £ s. d. he may have had a case. But he was a braggart—though very likely a brave and even a foolhardy man. " Two thousand Britons could have marched without impediment from one corner of the province to the other, even unattended "—he writes, and it is in this spirit of national, rather than personal, defiance that he approached Bolívar. " I produced my accounts "—he writes. " His reply was worthy of himself—full of subtility, evasion, deceit, dishonour and base ingratitude. The account might be perfectly correct—he did not doubt its accuracy on any point; but where was Mr. Méndez' signature ? Could I produce his order for the payment ? Why did not Mr. Méndez advance the money in England, or obtain credit for it amongst the regular merchants there ? Having then twirled up his mustachios, and looking fierce, he repeated these questions. I turned up and twisted my mustachios (which were as large as his own, though not so black), and having desired the interpreter to inform the General, I expressed my astonishment at the refusal to settle my account." Hippisley was rash enough to threaten Bolívar with exposing him in London. " The chief rose up in a passion, and explained, I was at liberty to act as I pleased; neither himself nor the government of Venezuela were to be intimidated by my threats." Their correspondence shows a cool, courteous, firm and intelligent Bolívar, standing his ground with dignity and exacting from Hippisley every ounce of what was due to his country. When Hippisley left, Bolívar sent him a kind, friendly and, in the circumstances, magnanimous message. He bought from the Englishman his cocked hat and feather and would have bought also his aiguillette had he been able to curb his pride to ask Hippisley how much he wanted for it.

Just after the Hippisley incident had been closed (mid-June, 1818), Bolívar had to face another with the agent of the United States, J. B. Irvine. The correspondence (July–October, 1818) shows Bolívar at his best. Irvine had been sent by the government of the United States with a twofold mission: as an unofficial but definite mark of sympathy from the Northern Republic and as a protest against the seizure of two American ships, *Tiger* and *Liberty*, which were bringing food and arms for the Spaniards besieged in Angostura the previous winter. There was another motive of friction between the patriots and the United States. The Island of Amelia, off the coast of Florida, had been taken from Spain by McGregor and later again by Aury, on behalf of the secret agents of the rebel South American governments. The United States stepped in and occupied the Island (22.xii.17). Thereupon the same agents, including Lino de Clemente, who represented Bolívar's government in the United States, protested officially and unofficially, but neither wisely nor moderately. Irvine brought this incident in his portfolio also. Bolívar wrote to Clemente (24.vii.18) explaining that, as he knew nothing about the Amelia Island incident, he recognized neither McGregor nor Aury as legitimate parties in the fight against Spain unless they held an authority from some independent government, and that Mr. Irvine had expressed the utmost satisfaction at this answer. But Clemente had not been able even to present his credentials, the Secretary of State having refused to see him owing to his outspoken comments on the occupation of Amelia. Irvine was not so successful on the matter of the two ships. The correspondence shows Bolívar as a masterful diplomat and a first-rate debater. He offered to submit the matter to arbitration, which Irvine brushed tacitly aside—and then Irvine threatened the independent government with the power of his nation. This brought out Bolívar at his best. " It would appear that your intention is to drive me to reciprocate your insults. I will not do it; but I do protest that I will not allow my government to be held in contempt nor to be insulted—nor the rights of Venezuela either. In defending them against Spain, a considerable proportion of our population has been wiped out, and what remains is ready to deserve an equal fate. It is indifferent for Venezuela whether she fights against Spain or against the whole world when she is out to repel an offence."

6

All these discussions with Englishmen and Americans seem to have mollified Bolívar's hispanophobia. He had received from a Spanish exiled general, Renovales, an offer of service. He answered (20.v.18) praising Renovales for his record in the war against Napoleon and for his integrity in sacrificing his brilliant situation and refusing to live as a slave under Ferdinand. " I feel an immense satisfaction in my heart when I consider that not all Spaniards are our enemies. . . . Your Excellency renders us a true service in offering us your active co-operation to re-establish the independence of America; and it will be greater if Your Excellency succeeds in drawing to our cause the greatest possible number of Spanish officers who may wish to adopt a free fatherland in the American hemisphere." This was a different Bolívar from the one who, in 1813, had decreed the War to the Death. The need of Spanish blood to restock his country, bled white by his older, passionate policy, is writ large in a letter to López Méndez (12.vi.18), where the effect of his experiences with Hippisley, Wilson and other is also to be felt. He insists on arms and ammunition, which he rightly considers as the first claim on their limited financial means; then goes on to say: " Next to arms, munitions and equipment, we should do very well with good officers, corporals and sergeants from Spain, of the many sympathetic to our cause who are residing in England and France because they prefer exile to slavery. These are far more useful than foreigners that do not know our language and need a long time to learn it, during which time they are useless." This drawback of the foreigners would be avoided " should they come in complete organized units able thus to operate as such from the day of their arrival ". He then returns to the Spaniards and opens a new vista with a fine sweep of political imagination: " Much could be done to obtain Spanish officers and other resources from Spain herself if we were openly to proclaim the principle which ought to be the foundation of our policy: ' Peace to the Spanish nation and war of extermination to its present government.' . . . Nothing should be omitted to separate the interests of the Spanish nation from those of her government and to make her see that her true advantages are in a close alliance with an independent America."

These political flights were his only compensation for the sordid quarrels for power amongst his lieutenants and for the daily miseries and worries of

a precarious, poverty-stricken and as yet inchoate nation and State.   In the
letter he wrote (12.vi.18) to Juan Martín de Puyrredón, the Director of the
United Provinces of Río de La Plata, in answer to his dispatch of November
18th, 1816, Bolívar rejoiced in the fact that relations had been established,
despite the delays due to distance and clandestinity, and went on to say that
the citizens of the United Provinces would be treated in Venezuela not only
as friends but as " members of our Venezuelan society ", for, he added, " one
only must be the fatherland of all Americans, since in everything we have
maintained a perfect unity ".   How far did he realize that the unity he thus
emphasized had been a creation of those three centuries of Spanish culture
which he now cursed, now wistfully beheld being destroyed under his eyes
and by his hands ?*   He is already building up in his mind a vast edifice of
continental dimensions, possibly a transfigured image of the Spanish Empire
he was at the time destroying in its obsolete form: " When time and the
arms of Venezuela complete the work of its independence or when more
favourable circumstances allow us to communicate more frequently and to
maintain closer relations, we shall draw nearer with the utmost interest and
ready for our part to conclude an American covenant which, forming with
all our republics one body politic, may present America to the world as an
example of majesty and greatness without match in the nations of antiquity."

* In his letter to López Méndez quoted above he opposes Spanish officers, whom he asks
for, as useful, to " foreigners " whom he believes costly and useless.

Chapter XXX

FROM ANGOSTURA, BOLÍVAR SEES THE STAR OF
SAN MARTÍN RISING OVER THE ANDES

I

A T this time, Bolívar was concerned over what he describes as " the Hispano-Russian expedition ". It was believed that the expedition would first land in Margarita. Bolívar ordered Arizmendi (13.vii.18) to evacuate the island with all its inhabitants should he find himself too weak to resist; arguing that, instead of exposing the island to an unequal struggle, it was best to organize the reconquest of Margarita from the mainland. But the evacuation of the inhabitants may have come under a different heading in his mind. One of the painful subjects of his meditation was what he described as the desertion of the civilian population towards the territories still under the sway of Spain. Even his family, even his mistress, seemed to prefer the Spanish flag to the flag of independence. His sister Antonia was in Havana. As for *la Señorita Pepa*, Bolívar was worried both as a man and as a leader, and wrote to his kinsman Leandro Palacios (11.vii.18): " Here they say that the Machado ladies [i.e. Pepita, her sister and her mother] have gone to Caracas; should this be the case, there is nothing more to be said; but if not, I should like to ask you a favour. Señor José Méndez Monsanto has orders to give Pepita 400 pesos so that those ladies can come here and I shall pay also their expenses on board ship on their way hither. I do this because I am assured that dire need drives the émigrés to go to Caracas [i.e. to Spanish controlled territory] while they can live here better than in the colonies [i.e. the Antilles under foreign control]. Do impress on that family that they must come, and tell Pepita that if she wants me not to forget her, she must come. On top of all this, a million things are being said which seem incredible, and in the doubt I feel most uneasy. [This might refer to Pepita's fidelity either to Bolívar or to Bolívar's cause.] In short tell me all there is to know about those ladies so that I may decide what to think and what to do."

But Leandro Palacios himself was not as sound as Bolívar desired on the public issue. He was an émigré himself and Bolívar can hardly veil the irritation this fact caused him. Thus (7.viii.18): " I assume that you still feel an interest in the cause of the Fatherland . . . that is why I am sending you news which may help you to deny the stories of the Spaniards and of the infamous Creoles who take pleasure in discrediting their country and in serving the King of Spain. Fortunately only the rascals have gone over to that party, and so have done us the service to purge the Republic of their vices." This was not so, as the end of the same letter shows: " If only the bad ones such as Mérida had left us, I should not regret it: but I am sorry for the unhappy ones who, out of weakness, have compromised themselves. You must endeavour to put an end to this scandalous and ignominious desertion and induce them all to come to Margarita or to this city [Angostura] led by you, who should show them the way, and put yourself at the head of their expedition." On the following day (8.viii.18), he wrote to Palacios: " This is only to enclose the letter herewith to be delivered into the hands of the person concerned, unless *the ladies who used to call themselves my friends*, as you say, have already left for Caracas. I should be sorry had they committed such a base action for it is a victory for our enemies, and it will give food for much comment. Do all you can to send them here, if they have not left yet."

2

In those days, the only leading, inspiring mind and will was Bolívar's. Though one of the many chieftains seeking to force their way up to the heights of power by pretorian means, he differed from the others in that his vision was truly national, indeed continental in its scope. Hence his constancy, his faith, his will ever taut in the struggle. Hence also his unscrupulous juggling with the facts. The letters to his generals, to his agents abroad, to his friends and relations, bear no more relation to the facts than suits his purpose. One example among many: Bolívar was thoroughly defeated at the battles of Semen and Ortiz. Here is his narrative to Arizmendi on the first encounter: " It was bloody and stubbornly fought on both sides; but victory remained on our side and the enemy lost one thousand men, counting dead and wounded, as they themselves confess. As I had infinitely fewer infantry than the enemy and we had fought frequent encounters and I had lost many rifles, I returned to the Plains to restore my losses and above all to ask for more arms and ammunition, which I lacked. I organized the army efficiently and I again defeated the Spaniards at Ortiz which I forced them to evacuate, and they had to withdraw to Villa de Cura, without being pursued because the forests protected them from our cavalry."

But what had become of the Russian expedition ? Ferdinand VII was surrounded by the dregs of Madrid. His favourite companions were barbers and valets. One of these, Antonio de Ugarte, private secretary to the King, had intrigued with the unscrupulous Tatischeff, the Russian Ambassador, to purchase a worthless Russian fleet for good Spanish doubloons. Ferdinand VII suffered from the chronic disease of all Spanish monarchs—bad finances. The only idea that came into his head was to restore the periodical arrivals of fleets laden with gold and silver from the overseas kingdoms of the Crown. This meant first to reduce such kingdoms to their old obedience, which in turn meant—as Morillo never tired of warning—many thousands of well-trained Spanish soldiers and, of course, a fleet to convey them. It was at this point that Ugarte and Tatischeff came in. The Russians would deliver in Cádiz five ships of the line and three frigates, ready to sail. The negotiations were so secret that even the Spanish admiralty was elbowed out of them. All the documents were afterwards destroyed; but this did not prevent the *London Morning Chronicle* from securing a copy of the two chief treaties (11.viii.17 and 27.ix.19), and from publishing them in December, 1823. The ships were paid for mostly out of the £400,000 owed by Britain to Spain to indemnify her for the abolition of the black slave traffic, the money being adroitly intercepted by the Ugarte-Tatischeff gang between Whitehall and Madrid; but they were useless and, with one exception, all had to be dismantled and broken up before 1823. The Minister who had the ships inspected on delivery was dismissed by Ferdinand, and the commanders appointed to navigate them were put on the retired list when they asked to inspect the ships before sailing. Beyond worrying Bolívar for a few weeks, the " Hispano-Russian " expedition achieved nothing else.

As for military plans, Bolívar had been thinking of Caracas the whole spring of 1818. In April, Soublette had explained to Bermúdez that Bolívar wanted an operation on the coast of Caracas. When Brion arrived with plenty of ammunition, and the confidence in a steady supply of men and raw material from Britain improved the situation, Bolívar's plans were matured. Events, however, induced him to alter his strategy. Captain Uribe, an emissary of the republicans of New Granada, brought him important news. San Martín had won a victory at Maypo (5.iv.18). " There are no longer any enemies in Chile ", he wrote in his dispatch to Buenos Aires. The situation in Peru had changed radically and Lima and Callao had fallen to the republicans; the south of New Granada was invaded by their troops; guerrilla warfare had developed in the north, so that, for the royalists, communications between Cartagena and Santa Fe had become precarious. Bolívar decided to organize the liberation of New Granada and to that effect he selected as commander in chief Francisco de Paula Santander, a young colonel of twenty-seven, a Granadino, ousted from his command the previous year by an intrigue of the audacious Páez. Santander had come over to Bolívar's leadership. Bolívar, however, always cautious, put close under him one of his henchmen, Justo Briceño. " Keep close to him "—he writes significantly to Briceño. But for the time being he does not evince more than a mere hankering to lead in person that expedition which was to be one of his chief claims to military glory. " I should go back to have the glory of leading that army, if the interest of both republics did not demand my presence here [Angostura], this place being the starting point of all operations, arms and munitions for all the divisions operating in diverse places, and above all, until we know the outcome of the relations between Europe and America. This will soon be known. The day of America has come."

3

As a continental leader, Bolívar was bound to look upon San Martín as his chief rival in the liberation of Spanish America. The Spanish Empire could be described as a pair of pincers open round the territory of Brazil, with the hinge on Lima, and the ends on the estuaries of the Plata and the Orinoco rivers. From the strategic point of view, Angostura was to Bolívar what Buenos Aires was to San Martín. On hearing of San Martín's triumph in Chile, Bolívar knew he must not waste time: he had to take New Granada as soon as possible or he would be late for the appointment which Fate (otherwise known as the nature of things) had pre-arranged between him and San Martín in Lima. (That physically this meeting actually took place in Guayaquil matters little. Politically, it all happened in Lima.)

José de San Martín, born in Yapegú, in the province of Misiones, in the viceroyalty of Buenos Aires, on February 25th, 1778, was five years Bolívar's senior. His father was a Spanish officer, and his mother a Creole. Sent to Madrid at eight, he studied at the *Seminario de Nobles*, and was granted a commission at eleven. He served in the Spanish army for over twenty years, in Africa, France, Portugal and Spain, where he took part in the battle of Bailén as a brother in arms of Morillo. In 1812 he returned to Buenos Aires, a lieutenant colonel of the Spanish army, displaying on his uniform the gold medal of Bailén. He was already in his heart a separatist, his mother's blood having proved stronger than his father's. San Martín was a silent and even secretive type of man, addicted to conspiracies and secret societies. He was a freemason, and soon became one of the underground leaders of the revolution who, from the dark recesses of the lodges, controlled public events. Entrusted by the revolutionary government with the task of organizing and instructing the army, he created a battalion of horse grenadiers whom he endowed with an iron discipline; and when this force, of which he was both the official and the natural chief, was hardly in being, he used it to expel the government and set up another one more to his taste (7.x.12). The victory of San Lorenzo on the shores of the river Paraná over the Spanish General Zavala (3.ii.13) confirmed his reputation, and he was offered the command of the army of Upper Peru. San Martín, however, had other views. He thought it useless to continue the struggle by way of Upper Peru, for the republican armies were always stronger on the low lands and the Spanish armies on the high plateau. His idea was to cross the Andes into Chile, to take Santiago and advance on to Peru, with Lima as his objective. Unlike Bolívar, who was swift and talkative, San Martín was silent and slow. An illness, some suppose feigned, but apparently genuine, served his purpose well. He resigned the command of the United Provinces and obtained the post of governor and intendant of the Province of Cuyo, at the eastern foot of the Andes. There, in the rich city of Mendoza, he set quietly to work, preparing for his self-appointed task. A rivalry with a brilliant soldier-politician, Alvear, threatened to shatter his well-meditated plans, for he was removed from his post on Alvear taking office as Supreme Director of the State in Buenos Aires; but San Martín proved too foxy for his rival, and under his quiet leadership the city and *cabildo* of Mendoza " spontaneously " staged such a protest that Alvear relented and reinstated him. San Martín would not be hurried. He spread wide the basis of his moral authority by an efficient, wise and disinterested, if exacting and ruthless, civil administration of his Province; but, throughout the years, he concentrated the best of his attention on his military establishment. His eye saw to everything; and, not trusting the politicians in Buenos Aires, he set up his own cloth mills, provender manufacture and even foundry and armament manufacture, which he entrusted to a friar fond of war. Two events came to favour his star: civil strife in Chile between two rival groups of republicans; and the changing political scenario in Buenos Aires. The first put into his hands both a pretext to enter Chile and a number of auxiliary troops; the second brought to office a man who sympathized with him and with his views: Juan Martín de Puyrredon.

At last everything was ready. San Martín had foreseen everything, made experimental expeditions, flooded the enemy with false news and expectations, pestered the government with requests for supplies of the most minute and specialized requirements, when he did not himself find an ingenious and usually popular and local solution, which was generally the case. Nor did he neglect spiritual things. On January 5th, 1817, he paraded his troops and made them take a twofold oath: to their Holy Patron the Virgin of the Carmen, and to the new white and blue flag of the United Provinces, whose independence had been declared on July 9th, 1816. Let those who simplify History solve as they wish the riddle of this dyed in the wool freemason and revolutionist who was a devotee of a typically Spanish title of the Holy Virgin as well as a monarchist.

He had selected two passes: that of Uspellata, opposite Mendoza, and that of Los Patos, near San Juan, both rising to between 10,000 and 12,000 feet, and only practicable in summer. The army consisted of three thousand infantry, seven hundred cavalry and two hundred artillery, with upwards of 1,200 men for auxiliary services; and it was to march in three divisions; the vanguard, under Soler, and the reserve under the Chilean leader O'Higgins were to go by the longer road of Los Patos; the rest, including all the artillery, under Las Heras, by Uspellata, but, to disperse the defence, he also sent minor forces towards Copiapó, Coquimbo and Talca. On February 8th, 1817, the Chilean end of the Los Patos pass, San Antonio de Putaendo, fell to the army of Soler; and on the same day, Las Heras took Santa Rosa de los Andes, at the Chilean end of the Uspellata pass. On the 10th, the two wings met at Chacabuco with almost mathematical precision. Six thousand out of the ten thousand mules had perished, as well as most of the horses; the casualties among the troops were very high; but a masterpiece of general staff work had been achieved.

4

The inept Spanish President of Chile, Marcó, had not even provided a commander in chief. Brigadier Maroto, appointed the day before, arrived on the spot in the evening (11.ii.17) and took command of about two thousand men, in a site utterly unknown to him. San Martín, aware of his advantage, resolved to give battle without even waiting for his artillery. The victory of Chacabuco (12.ii.17), opened to his army the gates of Santiago which he entered in triumph (14.ii.17). He was, however, of a modest and almost misanthropic disposition, and so avoided all formal ceremonies and devoted himself at once to the political organization of the country he had liberated—or thought he had. He called an assembly which unanimously voted him into supreme power; this, however, he refused, and, through a wider assembly, he had the Chilean O'Higgins raised to the dignity and office of

Supreme Director of the Chilean State. Meanwhile the pursuit of what remained of the royalist army seemed to have been forgotten, and the Spaniards were able to embark 1,600 good soldiers in Valparaiso for Peru and even to return to the help of their countryman, Colonel José Ordóñez, who had reorganized resistance to the republicans in Talcahuano. Ordóñez and San Martín, when both serving in the Spanish army, had on the same day (29.v.08), the one in Cádiz, the other in Valencia, played a similar part, defending in command of troops a prominent man threatened by the populace for his real or supposed pro-French view. Fate was to pit them against each other nine years later in Chile. For the moment, however, whether because he underestimated Ordóñez or for other reasons, San Martín returned to Buenos Aires leaving Las Heras in command of the army of the south. Las Heras had left Santiago on February 10th, 1817. His progress was so slow that, towards the middle of April, O'Higgins rebuked him for his " criminal indolence "; and finally left Santiago himself announcing that all would be over in twenty days. Las Heras defeated Ordóñez in a skirmish and entered Concepción (4.iv.17). The battle of Gavilán, which he won (5.v.17), with the help of O'Higgins' vanguard, strengthened the republicans but by no means destroyed Ordóñez, who took positions in the peninsula of Talcahuano, " Chile's Gibraltar ", as O'Higgins called it. With the technical advice of the French general Brayer (newly arrived with all the prestige of having been defeated at Waterloo), O'Higgins attacked Talcahuano at the head of a strong force of 4,000 Argentines and Chileans, but failed (6.xii.17).

Meanwhile San Martín was in Buenos Aires trying to organize a fleet. He realized that the control of the sea was an indispensable factor for victory. He returned and was enthusiastically received in Santiago (11.v.17). He had come back still faithful to his idea of liberating Peru. As commander in chief of the united army of Argentine and Chile, he began by sending to the viceroy of Peru a proposal for regularizing the war and exchanging prisoners. His biographer, Mitre, comments that under his humane feelings he hid military and political aims, to wit: " To make use of the good will of Commodore Bowlers, then chief of the British station in the Pacific, an admirer of his and very partial to the revolution; this was the most apparent aim, as the negotiations would begin under the auspices of England; the second was to present himself before America as a belligerent at the head of a powerful army, and to give publicity to the continental war; the innermost aim was to send over a shrewd agent who, under the guise of a parliamentarian, should initiate an underground war, preparing the way for his future expedition to Peru." His choice was an Argentine major, Domingo Torres, who sailed from Valparaiso on board H.M.S. *Amphion* (1.xi.17) and arrived in Callao as the viceroy Pezuela was preparing his expedition against the Chilean separatists. Torres failed in his public but not in his secret mission; and, within the viceroy's own secretariat, obtained all the data he desired on the Spanish plan, with which he returned to Valparaiso on board H.M.S. *Amphion* at the same time as the expedition itself was in sight of the Chilean shores (4-5.i.18).

Pezuela had made two mistakes: he had sent a smaller expedition than the situation required, not realizing that Peru had to be defended in Chile rather than in the highlands; and had appointed in command his relative Ossorio, when Ordóñez had so excellent a record in Talcahuano. The expedition landed in Talcahuano towards the middle of January. Seeing the patriot army in full retreat, Ossorio realized that his plan was no longer secret. He wasted much time in Concepción till at last, driven by Ordóñez, he decided to move northwards. San Martín, for fear that Ossorio would land in Valparaiso to take Santiago, had sent 4,000 men to defend the approaches, while instructing the southern army to take positions in Camarico, north of Talca. Ossorio crossed the river Maule (4.iii.18). After much coming and going, the two armies met at Cambarrayada (19.iii.18), a position where the royalists, with their backs on the Maule, had no possible retreat. At eight p.m., San Martín, warned by a spy that the royalists were going to attack during the night, decided to alter his position; but things went awry, and both he and O'Higgins had fled by eleven o'clock, while Las Heras organized a cool and skilful retreat. The Spanish generals had both collaborated to victory, each in his own way: Ordóñez had insisted on the battle being fought, had fought it and won it; Ossorio had retired to a convent near by and prayed to the Virgin of the Rosary.

No one slept in Santiago on the night when the news of the defeat spread like wildfire (21.iii.18), and the royalists dared shout *Long live the King!* while one of them prepared silver horseshoes for Ordóñez' mount. The Napoleonic Brayer gave it as his considered opinion that " there was no hope of reacting against such a defeat ". Within two days a report from San Martín announced that he was still in command of 4,000 men. On the 24th, O'Higgins arrived after a continuous ride despite a serious wound. On the 25th, San Martín himself, sombre and wan for lack of sleep, rode silently into the city. He was received with enthusiasm and, at the request of the people, delivered a brief address ending with the words: " I engage my word of honour soon to give a day of glory to South America." He withstood all attempts at evacuating the city and organized a camp on the plain of Maypo, six miles south of Santiago, though, in secret, he had prepared for a retreat towards Coquimbo and the Andes. The victory had been costly and not very fruitful for the royalists, so that they did not reach the river Maypo until April 2nd. The republicans had re-formed and were ready for a fight. Ossorio proposed a retreat towards Valparaiso; but Ordóñez insisted on offering battle at once. It began at 10 a.m. and, when O'Higgins galloped into the battlefield from Santiago at 5 p.m., it was still being stubbornly fought. It ended in one of the most decisive and fateful victories for the independents in the whole History of Spanish America. Ordóñez was taken prisoner with nearly every other officer.

5

The impact of these events on Bolívar must have been deep. He could not fail to realize that Maypo opened the gates of Lima to San Martín—

particularly if the control of the seas passed to the hands of the patriots. This, in Bolívar's eyes, could not be difficult since, in much more favourable circumstances, with Cuba and Puerto Rico in their hands, Spain was unable to ensure her sea communications in the Atlantic. The decision he took to send Santander to Casanare was a first recognition of the situation, the movement of a pawn on the continental chessboard as an answer to Chacabuco and Maypo. But his mind was not yet able to tear itself from the east. There were two motives playing in him: one, his obsession with Caracas; the other his correct estimate of the strategic importance of Guayana, the mouth of the Orinoco and the coast of Cumaná. He wrote to Bermúdez that eleven big Spanish ships had arrived in Cumaná, which together with those already there, made up a respectable force, and he feared they might be intended for an operation on the Orinoco and Guayana. He was not alarmed, however, for, thanks to British supplies, his park had grown prodigiously, and he had gunpowder for many years. He took swift counter measures. His idea was to liberate the coast, i.e. to remove the danger to Angostura. He explained it to Páez (29.ix.18) in a letter which began with a confession showing to what an extent the struggle was still a matter of chieftains and generals in the midst of the cold indifference of the people. " Dear General, we are to begin the campaign. I had desired to lead our infantry to the Low Apure, but it was impossible, because the troops having to go by land would all have deserted on the way; so, it was necessary to take Barcelona and Cumaná before passing on to Caracas. But this operation will be carried out without fail in October, and at the beginning of November without the slightest doubt, we shall be in Caracas." He then asks Páez to follow Morillo's steps moving at once towards San Carlos. He repeats he cannot tell how many troops he will have owing to probable desertions, but at the time of writing, he says, he has 3,000 infantry " though I have had many losses from desertion and disease ". He plans the invasion by sea, landing in Curiape, close to La Guaira, then again in Maqueitia, or at worst in Coro. He seems to have laid great store on an expedition of English volunteers to be commanded by Renovales. The expedition did start and Renovales was on board, but this time he had gone over to Ferdinand's authorities. This was not Bolívar's only setback. He was unlucky also in his lieutenants. Bermúdez, defeated in Río Caribe (13.x.18), had to seek a refuge in Margarita, and Mariño, though at the head of a strong army, was defeated in Cariaco (3.xi.18), leaving 300 dead on the battlefield. Bolívar, who had crossed the Orinoco (24.x.18) to meet Mariño and push on to Cumaná, withdrew to his base.

Yielding to the pressure of his civilian friends and even of some of his military commanders, who wanted his power limited by an authority based at least on " a shadow of a popular representation ", Bolívar convened a Congress to meet at Angostura on January 1st, 1819. The Council of State, in the words of his own confidant and aide-de-camp O'Leary, was but " a meeting of civil servants and military officers appointed by the chief with no other power than that of discussing some of the affairs which he had already settled ". Opposition was growing harder and louder. Bolívar feared that another leader, imitating Piar, might arouse the army against him on this truly republican issue. Peñalver, a staunch patriot and one of his most loyal friends, had strongly advised him to yield. Four years later, he wrote to Peñalver words which reveal the spirit in which he took this step. " You were the man who urged me most instantly to set up the Congress of Angostura, which gave me a greater reputation than all my past services, for men want to be served in a way that pleases everybody, and the way to please them is to invite them to share in the power and glory of command. I know full well that you contributed to the burial of all my enemies, whom I buried alive in the Congress of Angostura, for from that day they lost their jealousy and virulence; and to be sure, you were the only one who advised me to take such a step." He had, of course, seen to it that the Congress was amenable to his wishes, by a decree (18.vii.18) entrusting to local military commanders all political, municipal, judicial and electoral affairs. As a further measure of control of public opinion, Bolívar founded *The Orinoco Post* (*Correo del Orinoco*), a weekly which began to appear on Saturday, June 27th, 1818, with disarming modesty: " We are free, we write in a free country, and we seek to deceive no one. We do not thereby assume responsibility for official news, but by giving it as such, the question of deciding how much credit it deserves is left to the reader's judgement."

Having taken these precautions against any possible surprise on the part of the electorate, Bolívar called a meeting of the Council of State (1.x.18). In his opening speech he began by submitting his decrees as head of the Executive, then drew a flattering picture of the general situation referring to the " valiant Englishmen who, thirsty for a beneficent glory had come to our ranks " and announcing his intention to attack the enemy from every quarter with his well armed forces. " Strengthened by such flattering hopes I hasten to propose to the Council of State the calling together of a Congress of Venezuela." Let no obstacles detain them. " While our warriors fight, let our peaceful citizens carry out the august functions of sovereignty. . . . It is not enough that our armies be victorious, that our enemies vanish from our territory, nor that the whole world recognizes our independence; we need something more: to be free under the auspices of liberal laws emanating from the most sacred spring, which is the will of the people." He then proposed that a special Committee be set up to study how to carry out popular elections. This was done under Roscio as chairman, with five other members, including Peñalver. The Committee set to work at once, since " the Supreme Chief declared to the Council of State his vehement desire to see the government of the Republic restored as soon as possible to its representative forms, and recording how impossible it was for a general to be at the same time the magistrate and the creator of a new government, and that nothing was more incompatible with his personal character, his duty and his fate than the exercise of government functions ".

6

Bolívar repeated these sentiments in more solemn terms in a Proclamation to the peoples of Venezuela (22.x.18). He began with a rapid and tactful survey of the history of his activities, then dropped a heavy hint: " The battles of Mosquitero and Araure regained for us the West and the Plains. Then I flew from the battlefield to the capital, resigned my supreme powers, and, on January 2nd, 1814, reported to the People on the events of the campaign and on my civil and military administration. The People, as one man, answered with a unanimous voice of approval, conferring again on me the dictatorial powers I already held." How revealing this sentence is both of what had been going on in his mind in 1814 and of what he was brewing in 1818! His Committee, an emanation of his will, worked rapidly, and on October 24th, 1818, the Rules for the general election were ready. Given the circumstances, they were not unreasonable. Voting was to be limited to free men of twenty-one or over, or younger if married, owning property, or belonging to a profession or a liberal or mechanical craft, to land or cattle farmers, merchants with not less than three hundred pesos in capital, civil servants or military officers with not less than three hundred pesos salary, and to foreigners in the service of the Republic. There were some exceptions, on grounds such as desertion, infamy or living away from one's wife. The Rules recognized that in the nature of things the election would be a camp affair, since " almost all voters would be under military law "; officers, sergeants and corporals would all vote notwithstanding their lack of other qualifications; and the voting machinery was to be almost exclusively in the hands of the military commanders. The assembly would. be composed of thirty representatives.

While he thus prepared the meeting of representatives of the people who, following the classic pattern of Cortés in Veracruz, were to re-invest him with a municipal authority, Bolívar had to face another attempt at mediation on the part of Spain. López Méndez had presented to Castlereagh a note forestalling any such move (10.iv.18). Bolívar does not seem to have been sure of his own people's reaction should this step materialize, to judge by a series of articles which he had published in The Orinoco Post. In the end he published also an official statement in his own name, a magnificent witness to his fortitude, whatever may be thought of some of its premises; for at the time, though his armies bade fair to improve in armament and in foreign contingents, his military successes were still to come. In this statement, he began by pointing out that " the idea of a cordial reconciliation has never entered into the views of the Spanish Government "; then he added some arguments of a dubious force and one or two completely at variance with the facts; but he raised the level of the discussion by two points of undoubted value: " Venezuela had only desired the mediation of foreign powers on behalf of humanity, to invite Spain to discuss and conclude with her a treaty of peace and friendship, recognizing and treating her as a free, independent and sovereign nation "; and " from April 19th, 1810, Venezuela had been fighting for her rights; she has shed the blood of most of her sons, sacrificed all her wealth, all her enjoyments, and whatever men hold dear and sacred to recover her sovereign rights, and in order to keep them untouched, as Divine Providence had granted them to her, her people are resolved to be buried one and all under her ruins should Spain, Europe, and the whole world insist on curbing her under the Spanish yoke."

BOOK II
VICTORY AND FRUSTRATION

PART I

FROM CHAOS TO VICTORY

CHAPTER I

THE ANGOSTURA ADDRESS

I

ON the eve of February 15th, 1819, the city of Angostura, temporary capital of the Republic of Venezuela, spick and span under the lights of a general illumination, heard a boisterous salvo of artillery, for once, with general rejoicing. The Congress was meeting. " On the 15th, as the sun rose, there was another salvo. The representatives met at 10.30 in the hall of Government House which had been set aside for their sittings and the General Staff, the Governor of the City, and the General Commandant of the Province, and military officers met at the house of the Supreme Chief to accompany him to the ceremony. Three gunshots announced the departure of the procession, and the Representatives came out to the gates of the Palace to receive His Excellency. A numerous force which covered the street rendered him military honours." Thus began the Congress of Angostura, amid ceremonies every detail of which was meant to convey to all and sundry where was the substance and where the mere shadow of power. But Páez? . . . Mariño? . . . and the rest? They seemed to have more substance even than Bolívar. They had, however, less. For only Bolívar knew the secret of political wisdom: that appearance is as necessary a part of reality as the skin is of the body.

The *Orinoco Post* of February 20th, 1819, goes on: " The Supreme Chief opened the sitting reading a speech so full of interest and pathos that neither citizens nor foreigners could withhold their tears. His gestures, his accents, the expression of his face, everything witnessed to the truth of his sentiments and to his intimate adherence to the philanthropical liberal principles of which he made at that moment so passionate and solemn a profession. . . ˙ The phrases in which he concluded declaring the Congress constituted, and acknowledging in it the Sovereignty of the Nation, called forth the utmost enthusiasm, particularly when, his hand on his sword, he affirmed with energy: ' My sword and those of my renowned comrades are ever ready to uphold your August Authority. Long live the Congress of Venezuela! ' This cry oft repeated by all those present was followed by a salvo of artillery."

By acclamation, Congress elected Francisco Antonio Zea Provisional President. Bolívar then " took his oath on the Gospels, and received afterwards the oath of every other Member. The swearing ceremony over, His Excellency placed the President in the chair that he himself had occupied under the dais, and turning to the military corps, said: ' Gentlemen, generals and officers, my comrades in arms, we are but simple citizens, until our Sovereign Congress deigns employ us in the class and rank it thinks fit. Counting on your acquiescence I shall, in my name and in yours, give it the clearest proof of our obedience, by surrendering to its President the command I hold.' As he said these words, he drew closer to the President and, presenting his baton, proceeded: ' I return to the Republic the baton of general it had entrusted to me. To serve her, any class or rank that Congress may confer on me will be for me an honour; in it I shall give the example of subordination and of the blind obedience that must distinguish every soldier of the Republic '."

Then Zea spoke. He was a distinguished botanist praised by Humboldt and appreciated in Spain. Born in Bogotá, he had conspired with Nariño, and, sent to Spain, found, instead of punishment, a chair of botany and eventually the directorship of the botanic gardens of Madrid. He was one of the small band of Spaniards who had gone to Bayonne to pay his respects to Napoleon. This was not his first Congress. He had also belonged to the Congress of Bayonne which, under the imperious eyes of Bolívar's model, had approved and signed the constitution that Napoleon had tried in vain to dictate to Spain. This was the Zea who, under the imperious eyes of Bolívar, was now to pilot through the Congress of Angostura the Constitution which Napoleon's imitator was dictating for Venezuela. He spoke nobly and simply of the greatness of Bolívar's attitude which he naïvely declared " stamps this solemn ceremony with an antique character "; and he assured his audience that Bolívar was worthy of standing alongside of " the great beneficent Emperors Vespasian, Titus, Trajan and Marcus Aurelius ". More praise of Bolívar for having resigned, not when the fortunes of war were adverse, but when " authority was beginning to present a certain appeal to the eyes of ambition ". Whereupon he sprang on the Congress and on Bolívar the very surprise they all were waiting for: " But what, shall we allow General Bolívar to rise so high above his countrymen as to oppress them with his glory, and are we not at least to compete with him in noble and patriotic fields, by refusing to let him leave these August precincts without investing him with that same authority he has divested himself of so as to leave liberty unscathed, while in fact this is the only way to save liberty ? "—" No, no "—General Bolívar replied with firmness and vivacity—" Never, never shall I accept again an authority I have given up for ever on grounds of principle and sentiment." He then asked leave to retire and the President designated ten members to accompany him to the Palace gates. Congress decided to request Bolívar to carry on for forty-eight hours, then (16.ii.19) to appoint him permanently. Bolívar wrote a formal letter of resignation. " When this document was read to Congress "— writes the *Orinoco Post*—" various opinions were expressed on which there were long arguments, on which and on their result, the public will be informed in a supplement." No supplement was necessary. On the 17th Bolívar was informed that Congress had refused to accept his resignation, and that he had been confirmed as President of the Republic. Bolívar bowed before the sovereignty of the nation.

2

In his report to the Minister of War on the battle of Semen, Morillo wrote that he had caught " many staff officers whose papers, maps and books remained in my power, along with the secretariat of Bolívar, who, it is asserted, on entering Caracas intended to be proclaimed King under the title of Simón I, King of the Americas ". In a later report to the Minister, he again says: " The rebel Simón Bolívar, who styles himself Supreme Chief of the Republic of Venezuela, and was scheming to be proclaimed King in the capital of Caracas. . . ." Similar words occur in Hippisley: " Bolívar would willingly ape the great man. He aspires to be a second Bonaparte in South America, without possessing a single talent for the duties of the field or cabinet. He would be king of New Grenada and Venezuela, without genius to command, consequence to secure or abilities to support the elevated station to which his ambition most assuredly aspires." Of course, Morillo was his adversary in the field, and Hippisley wrote in bitter resentment. But it is not reasonable to dismiss as mere calumnies these statements from two contemporaries unknown to each other who write in the same vein at the same time. Why should Morillo slander Bolívar in a confidential document? And was, after all, an " accusation " of seeking a Crown likely to damage Bolívar in England, where the only objection to recognition of the Spanish-American countries was their republican trend?

It so happens that Bolívar has left a first-hand document on his own political ideas at the time. The speech he delivered before the Congress of Angostura on February 18th, 1819, is a statement carefully thought out, even though he himself was to write later that he had " put it together in the utmost disorder ". Whatever one may think of the ideas it contains, they certainly do not spring from a mind caught unawares; they are the expression of a meditated opinion matured by experience. He begins by assuring Congress that " nothing but a compelling necessity, together with the imperious will of the people, would have induced me to submit to the terrible and dangerous responsibility of a Dictator and Supreme Chief of the Republic ". At this, smiles and grins must have twitched the faces of the honourable congressmen. He then modestly disclaimed any merit or responsibility, in either the good or the evil of the past years, and asserted that the title of " good citizen " would be even more precious for him than that of Liberator, granted him by Venezuela, or that of Pacifier, granted him by Cundinamarca. He gave up his powers " cordially and sincerely ". " Continued authority in the same person has frequently caused the end of democratic governments."

Then, he presented his own Constitution, which he ushered in with a remarkable preamble: " We are not Europeans, we are not Indians; but an intermediate species between the Aborigines and the Spaniards. American by birth, European by right, we find ourselves in this conflict, that we must dispute our titles of ownership while we have to remain in the country of our birth against the opposition of the invaders." A hint on his part that, while he spoke against the Spaniards, he did not speak for the Indians. He is in fact standing for the rights of the Creoles against both Spain and the pre-Spanish owners of the land. Lest any doubt remained on this score, Bolívar went on to formulate a thought he himself found paradoxical: " Not only had we been robbed of our liberty, but also of the exercise of domestic and active tyranny." He meant that tyranny over the people was freely enjoyed by the European Spaniards who wielded the official wand, while they, the Creoles, were deprived of such a privilege. This was not the complaint his father's son should have raised, for the good bishop of Caracas, who was a Spaniard appointed by Spain, had been the only refuge from the tyranny of Don Juan Vicente de Bolívar over the womenfolk of his unfortunate farmers and slaves. Nor could the heir to municipal honours and offices in Caracas and a lieutenant justice of San Mateo say truly that the Creoles " were not permitted any share in their domestic affairs and internal administration " He said it, and even added these revealing words: " This had made it impossible for us to follow the course of public affairs; nor did we enjoy the personal regard which the splendour of power raises in the eyes of the crowd and which is so important in great revolutions."

The lack of knowledge, power and virtue in the people of Venezuela is then described as the inevitable outcome of the Spanish régime; and then Bolívar comes to the next step in his difficult ascent. " Liberty "—says Rousseau—" is a succulent food but of difficult digestion." Will the people be strong enough for it ? Let the Legislators meditate; let them study the past. To be sure, " Democracy is the only system calculated to ensure liberty, but where is the democratic government that has united power, prosperity and permanence ? " Let them look at China, at the Roman Empire, at France and Britain—all aristocracies, all monarchies. Yes, the first Congress of Venezuela was magnificent in its republicanism; but " how shall I dare say it ? Shall I venture to profane with my criticism the sacred tables of our laws ? . . . I feel certain that the Government of Venezuela must be reformed, and though many citizens think as I do, not all have the courage to own in public their adoption of new principles." He then devotes a passage to his admiration for the Constitution of the United States, but wisely adding . . . for the United States; and recalls how Montesquieu had insisted that laws should conform to the requirements of climate and people. Hence, his analysis of the people of Venezuela: " Born all of the same mother, our fathers differ by origin and blood, are foreign to each other and differ visibly in their skin." Therefore, on the basis of political equality, let the laws recognize the natural differences of genius, temperament, force and character between men.

Therefore, Bolívar goes on to say, let us bear in mind History. Having laid down in a phrase that sounds as if it had been written today, that " the most perfect system of government is that which yields the maximum of happiness, the maximum of social security, the maximum of political stability ", he recommends his countrymen to study the British Constitution. He does not suggest a servile imitation of it. " When I speak of the British Government I refer only to whatever it has of republicanism ", he asserts, and adds at once: " And, indeed, can one describe as a pure Monarchy a system which acknowledges the sovereignty of the people, the division and balance of powers, civil liberty, freedom of commerce and printing, and all that is sublime in politics ? " Therefore, let them adopt a legislative power similar to that of the British Parliament. Their Chamber is already a true image of the will of the people. " If the Senate, instead of elective were hereditary, it would in my opinion, be the basis, the bond, the soul of our Republic." He develops this idea with eloquence and shrewdness; then explains that the first Senators would be elected by the Chamber of Congress, while their successors would have first claim on the State, which would educate them carefully, " for from their infancy they would know the career Providence had in store for them, and from their tenderest years they would raise their souls to the dignity which awaited them ". Nor would they constitute a nobility, since the senatorship would not be a privilege but a duty and a profession. Nevertheless, the names of the founders of the Republic should be perpetuated by entering the class of Senators.

This difficult hurdle being disposed of, he again seeks strength for the next in the British Constitution. Accurately and neatly he describes the barriers that limit the King of England as head of the Executive, and concludes that the Executive Power in England " is the most perfect model, whether for a Kingdom, for an Aristocracy or for a Democracy ". By " Executive Power " here he means the King of England. Then he says: " Let this Executive Power be applied to Venezuela in the person of a President appointed by the People or by its Representatives, and we shall have taken a long step towards national happiness." What Bolívar wanted was therefore a President for life, an uncrowned King. But with a difference: " Exorbitant as the authority of the Executive Power may seem in England, it might not be in Venezuela. In all republics, the Executive must be the strongest of the powers, since all conspires against it; in monarchies, the strongest must be the Legislative since in them everything favours the monarch." What Bolívar wanted then was a President for life but with stronger powers than those of the King of England. It is childish to argue whether he was a monarchist or a republican, whether he wanted to be crowned as King or not. The issue must be removed from the field of words to that of meaning. If the words *monarch* and *monarchist* are in the way because they call forth the idea of kingship, let us coin another set of words to correspond to what he had in mind. Bolívar was a *monocrat* and what he wanted was, well, if the word monarchy will not do, let us call it a *monocracy*.* A republic with a hereditary Senate and a President for life is not really a republic.

The issue is obscured by two sets of prejudices: one, naïvely held nearly everywhere in the American Continent, south of the Canadian border, which holds the republican form more " advanced " than the monarchical;

* When I wrote this page I thought I was coining the words *monocrat* and *monocracy*. Several months later, I discovered that Bolívar had coined them before me, to express what he was after. (Letter 13.ii.30, to Fernández Madrid and others.)

and the other, which refuses to see to what an extent the Spanish character is refractory and inimical to true republican institutions. When these two prejudices are brushed aside, what stands out is this; *Bolívar did want a monocracy; and Bolívar was right*. True, his opinions were the intellectual flowers of a dictatorial and imperial temperament; but they happened to be right for all that. Indeed, what strikes the mind at this period is the wisdom of Bolívar's political ideas, the maturity of his criticism, the depth of his observation, the originality of his views. Far from yielding to those demogogic notions which have led to compulsory suffrage and to the granting of the vote to the illiterate in his own native land, Bolívar would divide citizens into active and passive, so as, he says, " to stimulate national prosperity by the two strongest levers there are, that of industry, and that of knowledge ". He would lay down " just and wise restrictions on primary and electoral assemblies so as to dam popular licence and avoid the blind tumultuous flooding which in all times had led elections astray "; he would finally set up a Moral Power, independent of the Executive, in charge of the political education and the moral guidance of the people. We may question the efficacy of some of his ideas, the practical value of others; but one thing is certain: his was a positive mind, free from the shallow rhetoric of most of the politicians who surrounded him; and had Congress listened to him and granted him his uncrowned kingship and even his hereditary senate, the new State would have begun its independent life under better auspices.

Chapter II

FROM ANGOSTURA TO BOYACÁ

I

THE first quarter of the year 1819 was spent in an endeavour to resist Morillo's invasion of the region of the rivers Apure and Arauca, Páez' own kingdom. After a brief visit to Páez' army at the beginning of the year, Bolívar had left his powerful lieutenant in charge of the defence of the Apure, while he returned to Angostura to open the session of Congress. Páez had then his headquarters in San Fernando. From his base in Calabozo, Morillo decided to take the offensive. His plan was to get rid of Páez' army and then reconquer Guayana. Morillo crossed the Apure (24.i.19) by San Fernando, which Páez had left scorched; then the Arauca, a more formidable obstacle (14.ii.19). Páez was somewhat taken aback. He thought wiser not to risk his four thousand men, despite his far better cavalry, in an open battle against seven thousand good soldiers, and withdrew, herding away all the cattle he could muster and setting fire to the tall grass, sheltering his own infantry on an island of the Orinoco well-stocked with food. Morillo resolved to give up this vain pursuit, which confirmed the wisdom of Bolívar's dictum, that the Spaniards could do nothing in the Plains nor the patriots in the heights.

By then Bolívar, having left his Congressmen debating the Constitution, was sailing up the Orinoco to meet Páez' army again. In Araguaquen, at the confluence of the Orinoco and the Arauca, Anzoátegui brought him about three hundred Englishmen, mostly men of Hippisley's expedition (11.iii.19). Anzoátegui had lost most of his infantry, owing to " the most scandalous desertion "; so that the English came to liberate Venezuelans who would not liberate themselves. The *llanero* held the infantryman in contempt, and gave him the worst meat available. Páez and Bolívar were hardly ever in agreement; and as soon as Bolívar arrived, discord broke out again. Bolívar was all for attacking Morillo; Páez objected. He estimated at six thousand the men under Morillo, a figure Bolívar had some hesitation in believing; and he again advocated keeping Morillo busy away from Caracas, thus enabling Urdaneta to take the city with the fifteen hundred men Bolívar had put at his disposal. This sounds businesslike enough; but there is a delicious human undertone to it all. Páez was as happy as a king warring about in the Plains. He was, of course, as good a patriot as any; but his chief interest was less to save the Republic than to live the life of a warring chieftain in the Apure. For him, Bolívar was just a fly in his ointment, a meddler. His dearest wish was to get rid of him. Bolívar, on the other hand, for similar human reasons, was as much the man of Caracas as Páez was the man of the Plains; and, being a bigger man and a statesman as well, saw in Caracas the symbol and the key of the liberation of the country. Hence, for Bolívar, Caracas was an obsession. When Páez blandly objected to Bolívar's eager arguments for giving battle to Morillo and breaking through to Caracas, that it was best to keep him busy away from Caracas while Urdaneta took it, the sly *llanero* was touching Bolívar on the raw and he knew full well that Bolívar would either leave post haste to take command over Urdaneta, a consummation devoutly to be wished, or be driven to a rash and impatient action against Morillo. The latter was the course Bolívar took.

He crossed the river Arauca at San Juan de Payara, and once there, unable to resist the temptation, went forward and fought his battle. He was repulsed with the loss of four hundred men, about half his contingent (27.iii.19). O'Leary attributes this setback to three causes: Colonel Pigott, who commanded the battalion of Rifles, organized as an English unit, was left in the lurch by his native guides; the Indians fled at the sound of fire (they nearly always did—though brave enough facing arrows); and Páez fell into an epileptic fit. This last detail is telling. There was a tension between the two leaders. " This setback "—says O'Leary—" cooled somewhat the enthusiasm of the army and dissipated Bolívar's hopes of surprising Morillo in his general headquarters." Bolívar withdrew towards the Arauca; and, on hearing that Morillo was approaching, called a Council of generals and, in the end, following Páez' advice, recrossed the Arauca. A brilliant skirmish at the Queseras del Medio, allowed Páez to inflict heavy losses on Morillo by typical guerrilla methods (3.iv.19). Bolívar issued a proclamation praising the battle, distributed stars with a liberal hand and had the names of the one hundred and fifty heroes published in the *Orinoco Post*. He had witnessed Páez' brilliant victory from the opposite side of the Arauca, and there he remained, while Morillo, with his strong army, controlled the left bank, unable to cross over owing to lack of canoes. Each side devoted its time to gathering cattle for lack of a more warlike employment. Morillo returned to the island of Achaguas (11.iv.19); and, as the rainy season was approaching, he decided to leave, not wishing to keep his army exposed to the seasonal floods. He crossed the Apure (14.v.19), and returned to Calabozo.

This was not a brilliant campaign, for either Bolívar or Morillo. Bolívar suffered mostly from impatience, the torment of quick beings slowed down by the sluggish march of events. " Patience, general "—said Páez to him— " behind the hill there is a plain." And Bolívar retorted: " Patience! Patience! There is often as much laziness as weakness in letting oneself be led by patience. How much virtue must one have to withstand so many hardships; the burning sun, wind, dust, meat from lean bulls, with no bread and no salt, and dirty water. If I do not desert, it is because I don't know where to go! " He lived just like any of his soldiers, as indeed he had to, in those parts. " He rose at dawn, rode to visit the several units and to encourage them with some friendly word or flattering memories. Followed by his General Staff, he drove behind his army; at midday he alighted to bathe when there was any water; he lunched like everybody else on meat, and rested on his hammock; then dictated his orders and his letters, which he did constantly swinging on his hammock. As soon as the troops had eaten their short rations, the march continued till a clump of trees or a small wood was seen wherein to camp, failing which, camp was struck in the open." This kind of life, day after day, became intolerable for that impatient man. He was moreover out of his element; he was in Páez' element. He realized that he had been defeated in his art, while Páez had been victorious in his. This increased his impatience. One day he had just given some orders for an immediate operation; " as his impetuous and impelling temperament "—writes O'Leary, who was present—" never brooked the slightest delay, seeing that Colonel Alcántara, instead of galloping off to carry out his orders, remained calm with a wallet in his hand, as if noting down something, he shouted in a temper: ' Have you not understood my orders ? '—' Yes, General '—answered Alcántara, who was a good observer—' but let me note down the date when your fortune has changed. Henceforth, good luck will be on your side ' ". Time proved him right.

2

Bolívar was still undecided. He had been defeated by Morillo but he was still thinking of Caracas. He first had had in mind to pursue Morillo across the Apure; then thought it better to collect cattle for wintering in Barinas; for such, says O'Leary, was his intention at the time, so as " to get possession during the winter of the territory west of Caracas, a hilly country free from the floods of the Plains ", says Restrepo. The problem of what to do with one's infantry in a flooded land was common to Bolívar and Morillo, though it left Páez indifferent. Restrepo says that the decision to march to Barinas was agreed to between Páez and Bolívar. This refers, no doubt, to the meeting in Cañafistola, close to the ford of Setenta, where both meant to pass the Apure on their way to that city. But Páez was against it, and says so himself, " for in that city we should not find means for our needy army, and instead of going to Barinas (where Bolívar said we should at least find some tobacco to sell in Guayana and procure funds) I believed it would be better for Bolívar to march on to New Granada through Casanare ". Now this may be an after-the-event attempt of Páez to deprive others of the glory of having thought first of the Andes expedition; but it sounds true to life. Páez always thought of operations that would send Bolívar as far away as possible. It was then, when Páez, on orders from Bolívar, had already left for Guasdualito, that Colonel Jacinto Lara arrived with news from Santander. He was welcome because of the news, but even more so because he brought some salt, which drew to his billets all the gourmets of the army.

In half a year, General Santander had pacified the two warring republican factions which held sway in Casanare, had set up an army of twelve hundred infantry and six hundred horse; and had inspired enough respect in an expeditionary force sent against him by the Viceroy of Santa Fe, the cruel and stupid Sámano, to induce its leader to withdraw. This leader, a young artillery captain, Barreiro, had been sent by Morillo to Sámano, then lacking in officers as well as in men. Sámano belonged to the hard school. He had brushed aside the prudent advice of the *Audiencia* and ruthlessly applied martial law. The shooting of a young woman, Policarpa Salavarreta, for republican activities of a spirited character had stimulated the independent cause. The country lived in a shifty state of allegiances, natural in those days. Power *in being*, combined with intelligence, might have performed wonders and even achieved some form of union with Spain on the basis of home rule; but the Spanish commanders chose the way of oppression, though lacking both the means to hold the country by force and a legal ground appealing, at any rate, to the liberal part of public opinion, local, universal and even Spanish. To garrison such an immense country, with communications of incredible difficulty, Sámano had at most 9,880 men (according to Santander), about a thousand at least of them scattered between Cartagena and Quito. No wonder Santander was able to report to Bolívar that a liberating expedition would find a nation ready to acclaim it.

It is claimed by many Colombian authors that the idea of crossing the Andes and taking Bogotá was brought from Santander to Bolívar by Jacinto Lara. This is very likely, for the idea was obvious. It is contended by Venezuelan authors that Bolívar was in no need of such inspiration. This is certain, for the same reason. On the plane of conscious military thinking, a number of factors induced Bolívar to operate in the Andes; in particular the fevers, " hunger, exposure and other hundreds of ills that would destroy most of his army were he to remain during the winter in that torrid country ". But, since he was bound to know that the crossing of the Andes would be much deadlier for his armies, another motive must have been at work in his mind. This motive was twofold: Bolívar crossed the Andes to move *away from* Páez and *towards* San Martín.

3

On May 23rd, 1819, Bolívar called a meeting of his army commanders in a dilapidated hut of the village of Setenta on the banks of the Apure. There was no table; the seats were the skulls, whitened by the rain and the sun, of some cattle killed recently for rations by a royalist guerrilla. He put forward as his plan: to take the enemy by surprise, invading New Granada by way of Cúcuta with the division of Páez, while Santander would try a diversion in Casanare. This, however, was not his true plan, but merely the first of the two screens of secrecy he was laying round it. He wrote to the Government at Angostura (26.v.19) restating this plan and adding a typically Bolivarian touch: " Speed shall be the motto of this campaign. We shall not allow Morillo any time to threaten our rear, for when he can do something against us, we shall be coming back on him with twice or thrice as much force as we are taking away." He sent Zea instructions for ensuring the safety of Venezuela; and Páez orders to be in Cúcuta on June 25th, 1819, with as many cattle as he could possibly gather together. Should he be threatened, he might return to Apure. Páez, however, did nothing of the kind, being resolved to remain in the Apure; he did not even send the three hundred horses he had promised Bolívar out of the sixteen hundred he had in reserve.

Bolívar's plan implied three stages: the Upper Apure; Casanare; the valley of Sogamoso, on the high plateau leading to Bogotá. A glance at a map will show the formidable obstacles the army had to conquer. In its first stretch, from Guasdualito to Tame, it had to cross a net of rivers falling from the Andes, all swollen by the rains. Though leather boats were available for those who could not swim, and to protect the ammunition, in most cases this meant wading across with the water up to the waist. From June 5th, when the Arauca was crossed, to June 13th, when, on arriving in Betoyes, they burst into cheers on receiving a ration of bananas and some salt sent by Santander, the soldiers had to cross river after river, often exposing their bodies to the voracious *caribes*, small fishes so fond of human blood that they crowd on the slightest wound or scratch and have been known to be deadly if too many of them feed on an unfortunate swimmer. After one hundred and twenty miles of this painful march, the army arrived in Tame " in a lamentable state ".

4

Bolívar had ridden on to Tame to meet Santander. He found there two infantry battalions and two squadrons of cavalry which raised his force to three thousand four hundred men. A momentous decision had to be taken: which way was the army to choose ? The crossing of the Andes would be a formidable enterprise by any; but after pronouncing first for the Pass of La Salina de Chita, to the north, as shorter and more convenient for the troops, Bolívar in the end decided to take that of the Pisba Moor. Why? It is not certain; probably because, being the most inhospitable and difficult passage of all, the enemy would be the more surprised. It meant, however, a march of over one hundred miles at the foot of the chain, still having to cross river after river in the height of the rainy season. From Tame to Pore, the capital of Casanare, " all the way was flooded; the territory was rather a small sea than a solid land ", writes Santander. On June 22nd they began the ascent. We have to imagine this powerful spirit, in his small, lithe body, standing at the foot of the most forbidding obstacle on earth after the Himalaya, leaving behind (under the threat of a relatively strong Spanish army) a number of rival chieftains of doubtful loyalty, and a weak and not very capable government; a leader who but a few days earlier had had to quell rebellion and treachery in the ranks of his own companions, some of whom had conspired to depose him and raise Páez in his stead; a man of thirty-five, who, then in perfect health, was capable of an untiring physical and moral activity; who never complained; for whom no hardship was unbearable, no march too long, no task too menial; who would cheerfully load mules and canoes, or swim his horse back and forth to help across the rivers weak soldiers or women. Fully conscious of the gigantic risks he was running, this man was endeavouring to conquer nature at her most powerful only to meet an army better equipped, more numerous and of course fresher than his own; staking his all with the scantiest means, no guns, no machinery, no organization, no commissariat, hardly any clothes, just the skin and the bones, the muscles and the hearts of those Venezuelan soldiers most of whom were men of the hot Plains awed by the icy heights, and the rest, Englishmen, as foreign to the heat of the low lands as to the rarefied and chilly air of the Andean Moors. And as we imagine him there at the foot of the Andes, with the bow of his will taut ready to shoot his arrow over the mighty chain and hit Santa Fe and victory, we must marvel at the miracle of strength he was about to perform.

The *llaneros* beheld such stupendous heights with awe and wonder, and marvelled at the very existence of lands so different from theirs. " Men used in their Plains to cross torrential rivers, to tame wild horses and to win in straight fights over bulls, tigers and crocodiles, felt chastened by such strange nature. . . . Many deserted." Rain fell day and night; and the earth underfoot, nearly always steep, became treacherous like polished glass. The *soroche*, a disease of the extreme heights, attacked many of them with nausea, a sleepy powerlessness and, unless some kind comrade by beating, lashing, pushing and slapping, prevented the sick man from yielding to his sickness, death foaming at the mouth. On they went, through the mournful cold moors, under low grey skies, among " hooded friars ", the only plants that dare bloom in those lofty solitudes. And every spirit might have yielded and every body might have fallen but for the great spirit in the small body of their leader who went silently on among them dreaming of future days.

5

He must often have longed for a brush with the enemy. It did not occur until Paya (27.vi.19), where the vanguard, under Santander, had to dislodge a force of a hundred royalists from a fort commanding the road on which Bolívar's army was advancing, but commanded by hills to the north and east. The garrison retreated towards the main force with which Barreiro guarded Sogamoso. Bolívar issued a proclamation: " An army of Venezuela, together with the valiant soldiers of Casanare, under the command of Santander, comes to free you. From more remote climates, a British legion has left the motherland of glory to win the fame of being the saviours of America." And he crowned his eloquence with his usual touch of propaganda unfettered by truth or fact: " You had succumbed in years past to the power of the veteran tyrants sent you by Ferdinand VII under the ferocious Morillo. This same formidable army, destroyed by our triumphs, now lies in Venezuela." He took care, however, to add that the liberating army should not be feared, for he remembered the evil effects of the first Venezuelan expedition on the public opinion of New Granada.*

* How far this promise was to be kept may be gathered from a letter written after his victory about a year later and from about the same place. On March 29th, 1820, Bolívar wrote from Sogamoso declaring himself convinced that the population was trying to poison his soldiers, and giving it as the outcome of a careful enquiry that no more than four households in the city, which he mentioned by name, were favourable to the cause. He then goes on: " I am resolved to have all delinquents shot. This event has determined me to order all provincial governors to seize hold of all the priests and citizens of their respective

Bolívar resumed his march (2.vii.19). The army was entering more pleasant lands on " the north-east side of the beautiful green valley of the Paya river, skirting steep inclines, winding slowly over rocky ridges, and fording mountain torrents ". The best way for that time of the year was that which the royalist detachment had taken towards Labranza Grande. Bolívar, however, stuck to his first decision to penetrate by the moor of Pisba, then considered as practically impassable in the summer, or rainy season. The march was so terrible that the men sacrificed their rations to climb more lightly without throwing away their rifles. Even so, the wife of one of the soldiers managed to bring forth a child; " next morning "— writes O'Leary—" I saw her with her new-born baby in her arms, marching in the rear guard of her battalion. After childbirth, she had marched two leagues through one of the worst roads on a slippery, broken soil." As the main body of the troops arrived in Socha, the first village of the Province of Tunja (6.vii.19), and glanced back at the white crests they had crossed, they swore they would die fighting rather than repass them. Socha is in the valley of the Sogamoso river which, from the neighbourhood of Tunja, flows towards the Magdalena on a plateau about nine thousand feet above the sea, of equable climate and relatively rich soil. The population were friendly, indeed, Bolívar wrote to Soublette, enthusiastic. Many soldiers had died. The cavalry arrived without horses, saddles or even weapons. " The army "—wrote Santander—" was a moribund body." Bolívar had to display his unbounded energy. Four days were enough for him to endow that dying body with enough life to give battle. Though taken by surprise, Barreiro reacted promptly, and opposed to the patriots two outposts of about eight hundred men each on either side of the river, in Corrales and in Gámeza. Repulsed in Corrales, the royalists gathered all their forces in Gámeza on the right bank of the Sogamoso, where it receives the Gámeza river. Bolívar was in an awkward position, for part of his cavalry and the British legion were still in the rearguard. Barreiro had crossed the Gámeza. Prudence would have counselled a defensive passivity. Bolívar led his troops towards the adversary, and Barreiro, disconcerted, recrossed the Gámeza, to take up again his strong positions in Peña de Tópaga. Bolívar decided therefore that he could risk an offensive. The battle lasted eight hours and remained undecided. Bolívar withdrew to Tasco to await his cavalry and his Britons. It was of course indispensable that he should wait for his men to rest and his parks to be restocked; but the reasons why Barreiro did not seize his opportunity to destroy the tired and naked army are not so obvious. In this, as in the rest of his campaign, the trouble for

---

(Continued from foot of previous page)

provinces who may be known to be enemies of the cause and have them sent to my headquarters; to confiscate their property and pass on to the State all that may be useful for it and its army, leaving the rest for the families of those who are married; and so that this decision produces a general effect, I herewith extend it to the whole department, in which I beg you to have it carried out. My intention is to have all these persons sent to Venezuela, where they will remain as hostages to answer for the behaviour of their families, who will be made to understand that their father, brother or relative will pay with his life should the government of Cundinamarca suffer the slightest injury from them; and the prisoners themselves will be warned to inform their families of this fact."

Barreiro came from the unreliability of his troops. Time worked for Bolívar; but as he was temperamentally impatient he moved first. He tried to outflank Barreiro by Santa Rosa and Duitama, leaving the royalists in Sogamoso to the east; for after all he had no base, or rather his base was everywhere, and therefore he could never be said to be actually cut off, while by his movements, he threatened to cut Barreiro from Tunja and Bogotá.

On July 20th, 1819, Bolívar was in Corral de Bonza. This forced Barreiro to move from his strong position in Tópaga to the hills of Bonza, a strong position also, but more directly on Bolívar's way towards Tunja. During the night of the 22nd (July, 1819), Bolívar sent a battalion under Santander to attempt to outflank his foe by Paipa. Rain and darkness made them lose their way. He tried then another outflanking movement by the Vargas Swamp. At ten o'clock in the morning of July 25th, 1819, the army crossed the Sogamoso, then swollen by the rains, on hastily improvised rafts; and at twelve, as they were marching to the east of the swamp, Barreiro's men appeared on the heights. They were about two thousand. Barreiro placed his cavalry in the plain and with his infantry commanded the road. Bolívar's cavalry was composed of two hundred and fifty *llaneros*, armed with lances and riding without saddles. The Spanish cavalry numbered six hundred well armed and equipped men. This time, Bolívar's rashness had put his army in an almost hopeless tactical position. He was saved from destruction by the magnificent courage of the British legion followed by a charge of the *llaneros* which surprised and disorganized the royalist cavalry; but even so, at nightfall neither side had gained a victory and both had lost so heavily that both retreated from the battlefield, the royalists to Paipa and the patriots to Corrales de Bonza. Though technically indecisive, the battle of Vargas proved in the end for Bolívar the true key to final victory.

6

Despite " the enthusiasm " Bolívar reported in the population, the people were passive. In Duitama, three days after the battle of Vargas, he proclaimed martial law and enacted that all men between fourteen and forty, married or unmarried, were to present themselves for service with their horses and mules within twenty-four hours under pain of being shot, all civil or military authorities to undergo the same penalty should they evince any remissness in the application of the order. His army, reduced to eighteen hundred men by his losses in Vargas, as well as by desertion, began to swell again with new recruits, who were trained almost under enemy fire.

On August 3rd, 1819, Bolívar led his troops on the advanced posts of the Spanish army; Barreiro left Paipa and took up a prepared position on a height commanding the roads to Tunja and to Socorro. Bolívar then occupied Paipa and crossed the Sogamoso; but having first puzzled the royalists by recrossing the bridge in daylight, he crossed it back again at night and, skirting the swamp, outflanked the royalist army and succeeded in reaching Tunja, where he arrived at eleven o'clock on August 5th, 1819. This march in the night is one of his masterpieces. The garrison of six hundred, left in the city by the Governor, who had gone with a battalion to reinforce Barreiro, was taken prisoner. As Bolívar had come only with his cavalry, less than three hundred men, the reasonable view is that the garrison were Granadinos of doubtful loyalty. Barreiro, however, was not cut off. He had withdrawn to Motavita, a league and a half to the north-west of Tunja, a spot from which he had two ways to go back to Santa Fe: one by Samacá and a shorter one by Tunja and the bridge of Boyacá. He chose the first, and started at dawn (7.viii.19) but, changing his mind soon after, he turned to the left towards the road which made it indispensable for him to pass by Boyacá. Bolívar, who, with his troops ready in the main square of Tunja since dawn, was himself observing the movements of his adversary from the yellow hills that command the picturesque old Spanish city, gave at once the order to march on the main road. The bridge of Boyacá is at the lowest point of a ravine, between high, broken hills, covered with woods to the right and the left. Barreiro, unaware of the presence of the whole independent army, had leisurely halted his men for a meal, when his vanguard crossed the bridge and discovered Bolívar's infantry on the crest of the hill. The battle was brief and all turned on who was to hold the bridge. Details, and even a fact as important as whether the royalists were defeated north or south of the bridge, are still in dispute; but Barreiro, with his second, Jiménez, and sixteen hundred soldiers, surrendered. Among the officers, Bolívar found Vinoni, the man who, in 1812, had betrayed him to the royalists and had forced him to flee from Puerto Cabello. He had him executed on the spot. On that day, he slept at Venta Quemada and on the 8th he rode on towards Bogotá. On the 10th, on the bridge of El Común, he heard that the Viceroy Sámano had fled; he rode on the faster and entered the capital at five o'clock amidst the acclamations of the population.

The battle of Boyacá was essentially political both in itself and in its consequences. From the military point of view it was little more than a skirmish: it lasted about two hours and cost very few casualties—twenty is the figure generally accepted. The situation had been shrewdly estimated by Bolívar before he crossed the Andes. Owing partly to the inept policy of the Viceroy Sámano, but mainly to the confluence of many historical currents, New Granada was poised in unstable equilibrium between two loyalties, ready to fall one way or the other at the slightest sign or incident. He, therefore, rightly thought that any event likely to strike the imagination of the Granadinos as a dramatic defeat of Spain would determine a political landslide. Hence his decision to take Santa Fe. The reproach often made by strategists, that Spanish-American generals instead of destroying the enemy force would hurry to occupy the capital, though more than once deserved by Bolívar at the beginning of his campaigns, no longer applied in 1819; for by then Bolívar was fighting in a civil war: from which two consequences flow: one, that if you take the capital, you are likely to impress the enemy force into " surrender ", i.e. into coming over to your side; the other is that the soldiers whom the military critics would have Bolívar destroy were his own kith and kin, easily shiftable to his own side. There is abundant textual proof that this was what actually happened at Boyacá. Morillo had written from Calabozo to the Ministry of War (12.v.19) that New Granada " is garrisoned down to Quito by American troops, whose loyalty on these occasions is only too well known ". And writing after Boyacá he says: " The division of Barreiro was composed of three thousand Venezuelans very well seasoned "; and again: " As those troops are mostly American,* they must be by now increasing the forces of the rebel general." This is fully confirmed by O'Leary: " To increase his army quickly, he incorporated into it the American soldiers taken prisoner in Boyacá, because they could be trusted in the ranks of the independents; and he also incorporated the Spanish prisoners, who were comparatively few." This is the key to the events of that campaign. Bolívar knew that if he failed he risked being shot by his own kith and kin in Spanish uniform; but that he had very strong chances of being lucky enough to induce them to desert. He deserved to be the luckiest of men for his political insight, and for the truly heroic constancy and faith that he maintained in adversity and during the dreadful suffering of the ascent; he deserved defeat for his rash behaviour in the swamp of Vargas, where he was saved by the courage of his English allies; he again deserved his luck for his masterly manoeuvring of Barreiro; but as for Boyacá, it had already been won at Vargas and the fighting amounted to little more than a face-saving operation to justify the desertion of the Venezuelan troops to their right allegiance.

* I.e. Spanish-American.

CHAPTER III

MORE BRITISH HELP

I

SCATTERED over the huge territory of the New Kingdom of Granada, the few Spanish forces that remained were no major problem for Bolívar, who was therefore able to turn to the political aspect of his conquest. Technically, he had no authority for any but provisional measures taken on military grounds, pending an organization of their own fatherland by the Granadinos themselves; but Bolívar does not seem to have given a single thought to this—a feature in which we may discern the survival in him of that Spanish régime he was outwardly abolishing; for, that feeling of being at home which every Spanish American still has in every Spanish-American country is due to the common origin they all owe to Spain. He issued a decree (similar to that he had promulgated in March of the same year for Venezuela) putting the political life of the country under military commanders, while civilian authorities were confined to petty justice and police. He issued an order (11.ix.19) setting up a provincial government under his own presidency; but, as was his wont, delegating most of his humdrum powers to a vice-president who was to be Santander. By accepting the post, Santander recognized Bolívar as the *de facto* sovereign of New Granada. Bolívar also appointed a Court of Justice and a number of provincial Governors.

The weakest side of the new State was finance. Though he issued a bulletin announcing that half a million pounds had been found at the Mint, it seems that the sum was but modest. The private property of all citizens not distinguished by their active loyalty to the cause was confiscated, but, writes O'Leary, "the Intendant appointed turned out to be unworthy of the trust implied in his functions, and the product of the confiscations was shamefully dissipated". Further exactions were needed to feed the army and to pay its salaries. Bolívar resorted to them without hesitation, not without provoking a protest from Santander. He did not like to be crossed, and he answered his Vice-President in terms which reveal many things—including his character: " Great measures to support an enterprise without resources are indispensable, though terrible. Remember the violent springs I had to set in motion to obtain the few successes to which we owe our life. In order to bind to our cause four guerrillas, it was necessary to declare War to the Death; in order to gain a few faithful partisans, we had to free the slaves; in order to recruit the two armies for the last and for the present year, we had to decree the formidable Martial Law; and in order to obtain the 670,000 pesos which are on their way to Guayana, we have asked and taken all public and private funds within our reach." Here is as clear a text as could be wished to penetrate into the workings of the man. Necessity knows no law; great aims require great means. This Bolívar was not the man to allow lesser men to cross his path—and who in America was not a lesser man than he ? A few days later he received disquieting news from Angostura. What was happening in his own Venezuela, while he, Napoleon-like, conquered New Granada ?

Colonel English had been successful in his recruiting mission in England. He had arrived in London in December of 1818, and in a few weeks had raised a brigade of 2,000 men from the regiments disbanded by the British government; " and a finer body of troops for its number, was perhaps never seen ". So writes a seaman who came from England to serve Bolívar; and he goes on to say: " the clothing and appointments were exactly on the British style, and exceedingly well supplied; and twelve ships were fitted out and stored abundantly with provisions and all things necessary for the prosperous conveyance of the brigade to the Island of Margarita, which had been appointed the depot ". When these and other expeditions organized in Ireland arrived in Margarita, they found that Bolívar had appointed Urdaneta to command the British legions. The first contingent of Colonel English's brigade, under a Colonel Blossett, landed towards the end of 1818. The bulk of the expedition arrived in Trinidad three and a half months later, and there, if we are to believe the anonymous seaman, was threatened by the " Trinidadian " fleet, the Governor, Sir Ralph Woodford, being hostile to such an un-neutral action on the part of Britons. The expedition sailed on hastily for fear of Woodford, and arrived in Margarita on April 19th, 1819.

But the more men arrived in Margarita, the more difficulties they created, for there was in the island little food and no money. The only source of revenue, naval captures, precarious as it was, " could only enable them to exist for a short time, as General Urdaneta, with a degree of cupidity which signalized the whole of his conduct, had appropriated a considerable portion of it to himself, which he expended either in the inordinate gratification of his personal wants, or squandered away in gambling ". Fed on sugar cane rations three times a week, the stout Britons began to grumble, and finally mutinied. Brion " denied the famished troops a portion of the provisions with which his ships were literally crammed ". Eventually the brigade, paid and disciplined, marched from Pampátar to Juan Griego to embark for the mainland in July. A Margaritan contingent was also to embark; but here, Arizmendi stepped in. He had desired to lead the British contingent, and was jealous of Urdaneta; he harangued his fellow-islanders, who refused to embark and took position on the heights leading from Juan Griego to Pampátar. Urdaneta had Arizmendi's home surrounded during the night by an English detachment under Major Davy, and General Manuel Valdés, entering his bedroom, forced him to embark for Angostura without allowing him time to dress (28.v.1819).

2

This deprived Urdaneta of five hundred out of the eight hundred islanders who had volunteered to serve; the expedition sailed towards Barcelona (14.vii.19): twelve hundred men including three hundred Margaritans and some German volunteers. On the 17th, they landed at Pozuelos, two and a half leagues from the city. The cavalry, dismounted, was led by Colonel Stopford; the infantry, by Blossett; the artillery by Woodberry; and the mixed force of Margaritans and Germans by Uslar. Brion landed two columns, each under one of his two aides-de-camp, Colonel Jackson and Major Graham. All these names lend a particular flavour to Brion's remark on his victory in his letter to the Government: " There never was a chief better obeyed nor a better served fatherland." Whose fatherland ?

The occupation of Barcelona was a barren success for the cause of independence. An Englishman, George Chesterton, who was of that army has left us a portrait of Urdaneta which explains this failure. " General Urdaneta, the Commander of the land forces, selected be it remembered by Bolívar himself, was of diminutive stature, pale, effeminate, and a slave to indolence. He was a man so inert, and apparently mindless, that no cause could by possibility have been confided to a more incompetent leader. It was vain to look in him for one redeeming characteristic: not the remotest fitness for command could be discerned. A miserable sensualist, he took the field accompanied by two mistresses, and lounged from morning till night in a hammock, the slave to women and cigars." The Spanish garrison, two hundred men, had settled in Piritu, where it had been reinforced. Urdaneta might have attacked them there since, though his numbers were fewer, the foreign contingent was well seasoned and armed. But he preferred to wait for Bermúdez who preferred not to come; and he spent his days gambling in idleness, allowing his army to run out of food, of patience and of discipline. A surprise attack by a Spanish force awakened Urdaneta's energies for hardly longer than the time it lasted; and at last, tired of waiting for Bermúdez, he re-embarked his troops on August 1st, 1819, to convey them by sea to Cumaná. He attacked Cumaná most incompetently, and then decided to lead his troops all the way to Maturin across difficult country, while Bermúdez arrived in Cumaná too late and was severely defeated. Bermúdez had been left by Bolívar as Commander in Chief, while Urdaneta had been instructed to go to the Apure; and Bolívar had put it in writing that Urdaneta was, if need be, to co-operate with Bermúdez, " without it ever being understood that this division belongs to the army of the Orient ", i.e. that Urdaneta is under the orders of Bermúdez. The strange behaviour of Urdaneta at this time may well have been due to this personal pique; perhaps, however, also to the fact that he distrusted his Englishmen, many of whom deserted, in disgust at the killing of the prisoners, the indolence of the leader and the lack of pay. Bermúdez, on the other hand, had taken over the command of the Oriental army on orders from Bolívar, removing Mariño; and when, having wasted much time, he at last arrived in the neighbourhood of Barcelona, Urdaneta had left, the Spaniards had reoccupied the city and the campaign had been a futile waste of time, money and human life.

Meanwhile, Zea, the sharp-nosed botanist whom Bolívar had placed in Angostura at the head of Congress as an owl over a nest of hawks, was doing his best to govern like an eagle. This is not easy, least of all when a true eagle with actual claws is about. Now the United States might be very democratic and very republican; but they happened to have chosen an eagle as the symbol of their union and their coat of arms; and there was sure to be something in it. So Zea was made to understand in unmistakable terms when Irvine, the American agent, having returned to Washington with a negative report on the claims of the United States against the Independent fleet for the capture of the American sloops, the American Government sent Commodore Perry with a warship to carry on the conversation (26.vii.19). As Zea was not Bolívar, and as Perry behind his guns was not Irvine behind his inkstand, the claims were granted.

A secret negotiation, so far undisclosed, seems also to have been carried on then. Sir Ralph Woodford appears to have believed so in view of the two dispatches he wrote to Bathurst on July 27th and August 18th. In the first, he points out that " the country within the Gulph [of Paria] is nearly abandoned by both Parties and a more fortunate moment will not occur for H.M.'s Government to obtain the possession of it from the Court of Madrid ", that the coast of the main land opposite Trinidad, in view of its importance for the peace and the tranquillity of the Island, was " a desirable acquisition "; and that " the detachment of two companies from this garrison would be the extent of military force required ". He saw other advantages in it. That strip of main land, in British hands, " would be a shelter for those who fly from the indiscriminate slaughter which attends the successful party, and it would remove that temptation to the slaves to desert, and that very pernicious example to the free blacks and coloured people (who are daily increasing in numbers and wealth) which it otherwise will continue to afford to those classes in this Island ". Possibly in order to strengthen his plea, Woodford added that he had information " of a negotiation being on foot between the government of the United States and General Bolívar for the purpose of obtaining some port in this neighbourhood and there is none that would answer their purpose as a portion of the Coasts of this Gulph ". From an officer of the Perry mission whom he had interviewed, Woodford had learnt " that the mission is a secret one ", and that " on the success of Commodore Perry's negotiation depends the proceeding of the squadron to Buenos Aires ". Woodford wrote again (18.viii.19): " There is every reason for believing that an arrangement is 'ere this concluded for the cession of some portion of the adjoining country to the United States." He fears the aim of the United States might be to settle in Margarita, and says that " the possession of it by the Americans would be a source of eternal Annoyance to this Island ". He reiterates his plea for " keeping the Portion of Country which by reason of the Political changes on the Spanish Main is become indispensible [sic] to the safety of this colony ". On the fly leaf of his first dispatch, Bathurst set down his attitude to all this. " He cannot consider the temporary non occupation of any part of the Spanish Territory in S. America by either of the contending parties as affording just grounds for taking possession of it with a British Force: and . . . he must consider such a course even if adopted with the consent of one of the Parties as altogether at variance with those principles of strict neutrality which the Prince Regent has uniformly maintained ".*

3

Foreign affairs, however, though important, were not the most difficult of the tasks of the intellectual Vice-President. There was the Constitution. Congress was poor but it worked very hard. In the midst of so much uncertainty and destitution, the Congressmen of Angostura carried on the discussion of the draft constitution left them by Bolívar with the composure, the concentration and the intellectual distinction of an old-standing European parliament. Peñalver, the Army Intendant, the man who had advised Bolívar to call that Congress, gave his views on the proposals (24.vii.19). They were not unlike Bolívar's: republicans by all means, but let us have a genuinely national, and not an imitated constitution; one in harmony with our ways and land. His conclusions were: " An Executive Power for life, a Senate for life, and a Chamber of Representatives elected for seven years are, in my opinion, the institutions corresponding to the state of civilization and to the habits of Venezuela, for they are those which come nearest to the Monarchical Government to which they have been used without departing from the Republican Government which they intend to adopt." The Constitution, proclaimed on August 15th, 1819, decided for a Senate for life, though not hereditary, and for a President elected for four years only. It is typical of the situation that the Constitution thus voted was not published " until the ideas of the *Libertador* about it were known ". A special Council of Administration and War was set up by Congress. But while the parliamentarians worked hard, two disgruntled generals were joining forces under their feet: Arizmendi in jail and Mariño, deprived of his command by Bolívar's order.

Mariño had presented himself before Congress in his double capacity as a representative and as an ex-commander who came to ask why he had been deprived of his command just the day after he had defeated the enemy. Zea, who was under orders to bring Mariño back to Congress so as to allow free scope to Bermúdez in the field, would not listen to those who advised him to reappoint Mariño to his command; and, faithful to a fault to Bolívar, maintained his previous decision. A military *pronunciamiento* was for Mariño the only way out. Rumours were spread of disasters in New

---

* Whether Perry did or did not broach the subject in Angostura is not certain. The description of his mission in Roscio's instructions to Manual Torres does not mention the subject, but there is an ominous ring in the word *ostensible* in the opening sentence: " On the 26th last, Commodore Perry arrived here on a government mission. The ostensible one was to claim damages for two schooners, etc. . . ." No mention is made of the " unostensible " part of the mission. Moreover Woodford mentions one Dr. Salazar as the agent sent to Washington to negotiate the territorial cession; and this Salazar figures in Roscio's instructions in a sentence which, again, may cover a secret meaning. He goes, says Roscio, to attend " the opening of the sessions of Congress and will return when they end or else earlier if the main object of his mission came to be fulfilled ". No mention is made of this " main object ".

Granada, and on September 14th, 1819, Colonel Diego Morales arrived with the news that the royalists were advancing in strength on Angostura. A panic was avoided because Zea summoned the scaremonger and saw through his intrigue; but the Assembly met in a scene of some disorder, Mariño arriving insolently rattling his sabre. After a long and somewhat undignified wrangle, Zea resigned, and the conspirators went at once to fetch Arizmendi who, on the shoulders of rebel colonels, passed from his prison to the seat of Vice-President and head of the Government. Arizmendi dismissed Urdaneta and Bermúdez, put Mariño at the head of the troops and arrested Urdaneta; he then confiscated all cattle hides (then more valuable than the whole meat) and decreed that he alone would be able to dispose of them. He tried to raise " a brigade of 4,000 men consisting of Creoles, *zambos* and Indians, by a sort of conscription, and was succeeding as well as could be desired ", even if at times those who tried to desert had to be executed. Nor was he less efficient in his handling of strikes, for when, in need of *flecheras*, he found that the shipwrights had struck for higher wages, " he caused four or five gallows of a great length to be erected by his soldiers, and having assembled all the carpenters in the city he told them that unless six *flecheras* were ready for launching in fourteen days, he would hang every one of them ". These executive ways, curiously enough, seem to have endeared him to some of the leading English volunteers; and Arizmendi himself played up to them, for it was his policy, as much as that of anyone else, not excluding Bolívar, to build up a force on which he could personally rely. He thus issued a decree highly favourable to the foreign legions, granting them equal rights with the Venezuelan and an equal share in the eventual distribution of national property.

4

Everybody was then thinking of the English, including Morillo. On March 26th, 1819, from Achaguas, he had addressed to all English volunteers a proclamation offering them a free return home or admission into the service of the King of Spain; he held then an order from the War Minister (8.ii.19), declaring that the King of Spain had decided " in general " to sentence to death all foreign adversaries caught fighting or helping the insurgents. These decisions had not been altogether ineffective, " for such was the disgust of the men at the non-observance of any one stipulation in their favour, that scarcely an individual could be found to resist the lure, and the whole legion was prepared to desert ". So writes Chesterton, who mustered his company to appeal to them as Englishmen " to cling, for the honour of our country, to their motto ' morir o vencer ' ". It should be pointed out that Chesterton, during the crossing from England to Trinidad, had written the anthem of the British Legion (which had been forwarded to London and promptly inserted in the *Morning Chronicle*) in words suited to the air of " Ye gentlemen of England ", on the refrain of " vencer o morir "; a stanza of which deserves to be quoted here:

Behold with pride yon hallow'd Isle
    Where freedom's root has thriven,
Your march is sanction'd by her smile,
    And cheer'd by that of Heaven.
        To plant the tree
        Of Liberty
    Is ever hail'd on high:
        Then falter none,
        But sally on
    To conquer or to die.

Nevertheless, the gentlemen of England did not appear convinced by
Chesterton's eloquence. " Even my most trusted non-commissioned officer
looked unutterable incredulity, and seemed manifestly infected with the
general disquietude. That very evening nearly forty men deserted and it
was evident that the whole force was prepared to follow their example. A
sudden incident of the Morro opportunely occurred to arrest this overt
defection. At noon a band of half-naked blacks arrived at our head-quarters,
bringing with them, as prisoners, five British fugitives, who had sought to
join the enemy. A general court martial was forthwith convened." Five
men were sentenced to death but two only were shot. " But for this timely
example, it was more than conjectured that two hundred men would have
decamped that very evening." This, however, was not the only case of
desertion in the Legion. A number of English deserters were caught and
shot by the Independent chieftain Montes; and a fairly numerous group of
them fought a regular battle with a detachment of Venezuelan soldiers in
which nineteen Britons lost their lives. More lives, however, came sailing
from England lured by the Spanish Eldorado of Drake's days. " It looks as
if the English armies all wanted to come over to this continent "—wrote
Morillo to Madrid from Calabozo (12.v.19)—" Europe must look on with
wonder while, from a Power friendly to Spain, come the considerable means
our enemies possess to wage war on us . . . the army of Bolívar is mostly
composed of English soldiers, Guayana is garrisoned by Englishmen; more
than 1,500 men of the same nation have come to Margarita, and the warships,
the numerous parks of all arms, the munitions, the clothing, the food,
all the elements for making war and fighting for independence have sailed
from the harbours of the King of Great Britain."

These Englishmen were like manna for the Venezuelan generals. They
provided exactly what their armies needed: a military backbone, training,
discipline, and even that minimum of military order: uniforms. Arizmendi
must have received with alacrity the news of the arrival of more Englishmen
to his good island of Margarita. This was the famous " Irish Legion ", by
then already legendary even before it had arrived or possibly existed.

The commander of this Irish Legion was Devereux, the son of an Irishman
executed for his part in the rebellion of 1798. He had made some money
by introducing a cargo of coffee into France when blockaded by the British
Navy; and had arrived in Cartagena at the time Bolívar was besieging it.

It seems that he had already offered them to raise an Irish legion. When " Colonel " English began actually to recruit, Devereux obtained from Bolívar at Angostura a regular contract with a promise of a commission of divisional general if he brought the men.

This was the first instalment of the legendary Irish Legion that, sick and famished, landed in Margarita soon after Arizmendi had taken power in Angostura. " They found the yellow fever raging with extraordinary violence. Upwards of 750 thus perished, and among them many fine young men who had purchased commissions as before described. The whole of them to their astonishment and horror found that the Government had never given any authority to Devereux or any other individual to dispose of any rank in their service . . . and many of them having expended their last shilling to embark in the cause, were reduced to the necessity of selling their clothes for present subsistence . . . and with the proceeds many of them departed for the United States . . . no small number of whom died of starvation before the necessary relief arrived. Devereux had taken care not to go out with them to Margarita, but had remained in Ireland and England, living sumptuously on the money of which he had drained them. One or two spirited young men challenged him in Dublin. He escaped privately to Liverpool, where he chartered a coal brig to convey himself and his staff to Margarita."

CHAPTER IV

FROM BOYACÁ TO ANGOSTURA

I

BOLÍVAR, victorious in Boyacá, arrived in Santa Fe on August 10th, 1819; but he did not make his official and solemn entry into the city until September 18th, 1819. This delay would appear to confirm those who assert that, on his first arrival, he was by no means warmly received. To enter the city, he and his officers and men went out to San Diego, where the army had been paraded: Grenadiers of the Guard, Rifles and British Legion. With the civil authorities, the procession entered the city under a shower of flowers, a volley of hurrahs, and the joyful peal of church bells. Bolívar and his two lieutenants, Santander and Anzoátegui, were first taken to the Cathedral where they listened on their knees to a *Te Deum*; then, out again to the main square, where on a specially built platform, under a tricolour damask dais, decorated with six statues which symbolized the virtues of the hero, Bolívar was seated with Anzoátegui on his right and Santander on his left. The square was packed, the windows decorated and full of people, and the sky was blue. After a solemn silence, a choir sang a hymn in honour of Bolívar; and then, twenty maidens dressed in white, brought the crown and the decorations in a small silver basket. One of them laid a crown of laurel on Bolívar's brow. He rose, took it from his head and exclaiming, " Those soldiers are the men who deserve it ", he laid it first on Anzoátegui's head, then on Santander's, and finally threw it to the battalion of Rifles. The crowd cheered wildly. One of these maidens, Bernardina Ibañez, became the successor of " Miss Pepa ", who, also dressed in white, had received Bolívar in triumph in Caracas. Bernardina eventually married Ambrosio Plaza, who died fighting in Carabobo; she then became the wife of Florentino González, a Colombian who, on learning too much about her, conceived such bitter hatred of Bolívar as made him one of the chief conspirators against Bolívar's life in 1828.

Bolívar did not tarry in Bogotá. He left for Venezuela on September 20th. He had not the patience to live like a civil servant, and even the president of a republic is a civil servant. His life followed regularly the same pattern: he secured all powers, either on the battlefield or in a congress, or by a combination of both; he had one of his nominees appointed vice-president to do the donkey work and moved on. Having found in Santander a good vice-president for New Granada, he left Bogotá for Angostura (20.ix.19). He went through Tunja, Velez, Socorro, San Gil and Bucaramanga to Pamplona where he arrived on October 19th. This was quick enough, but he found it too slow. At every spot he had to remain longer than he wished, to satisfy the eagerness and the enthusiasm of the crowd. Nevertheless, he was not happy about the Church, and in an entertaining letter written in a light-hearted mood, he imparts to Santander that, in their " pretty, unctuous, contrite language ", the Church must explain that the government of the

Republic is legitimate and holy. The military situation occupied his mind even more. From Pamplona (1.xi.19) he complains: " Soublette has left me nothing but useless, useless, useless rifles. I fear very much that we may not be able to put together twelve hundred counting all we have in the three provinces, I mean, rifles in a position to fire at all." The same Soublette had fought against La Torre the indecisive battle of the Alto de los Corrales in the region of Cúcuta (23.ix.19); and after a temporary retreat, La Torre had returned to Grita. There was some alarm, which Bolívar tried to stem with a proclamation (2.xi.19). His state of mind was, however, less calm than his words. " I recommend to you "—he wrote to Santander from Soatá (14.xi.19)—" to behave towards General Anzoátegui and his men with the utmost consideration, for, as they are hopelessly eager to return to Venezuela, the least motive will increase their despair and that may lead to disorder and even to desertion. I recommend this to you in a friendly way and in the interest of New Granada, and because I am convinced that on the day this division leaves the country, it will be occupied by the enemy. It is impossible for them not to attack again within two months."

Five days later, Anzoátegui died suddenly at the age of thirty. But though the news deeply affected Bolívar, who was very fond of this general, he had then to turn to the situation which had developed in Angostura. On November 13th he had received a heavy bag from Guayana. The outcome of it all can be read in a number of telling phrases in his letter to Santander dated in Soatá the following day. " The force of La Torre is not worth my staying to beat it; but the fifteen hundred Englishmen of D'Evereux and the intrigues of Mariño and Arizmendi are very much worth my attention. Every moment is precious." " Now we need money over there, more than ever, to calm people, to satisfy the English and to buy arms." " Señor Zea, who is disgruntled, advises me to call a congress here. We cannot get on with that of Venezuela: what should we do with two ? I warn you never to listen to such suggestions. I am resolved to resign unless Congress goes into recess for the whole of the coming year. When one is not looking, it votes exactly the law most contrary to the aims I have in mind. A new Vice-President who is doing and always did just what he wanted. A body with two heads, what can it do ? " " I have just received a fresh courier from Angostura, slightly more satisfactory than the preceding one. All write full of joy over the battle of Boyacá and, according to Señor Zea, the news arrived just in time; but all my friends and even those who are not, urge me to fly thither to prevent the defeated members of both sides from returning. I fly to follow this advice and my own inspiration." The sense of his own greatness breathes through these words; and he was great: O'Leary notes how he left pensions out of his private fortune to the widows of patriots killed by the Spaniards wherever he passed. Some of these pensions amounted to as much as fifteen hundred pesos and none was less than five hundred. Meanwhile he paid little or no attention to his own comfort. " He carried no bed in his field luggage, and his attire was simpler and his table more frugal at this time than that of many generals of his army."

2

Santander remained in Santa Fe, with mixed feelings. To be left as a " Vice-President " (a translation of " Vice-roy " into the republican language), therefore as the republican viceroy of New Granada, at twenty-seven years of age must have flattered the brilliant young man; but to have to answer for the security and loyalty of a huge, well populated and still (despite the havoc of the civil war) prosperous country with a handful of soldiers was not a responsibility to be taken lightly. Boussingault, who knew him a few years later, wrote of him: " *J'en ai conservé un souvenir peu agréable. Un bel homme, figure intéressante, les yeux un peu obliques, dénotant du sang indien; poli, instruit, très laborieux. C'était dans toute l'acception du mot, un bon chef d'état major. On lui contestait la bravoure injustement peut être.*" He was a willing and elegant dancer and a gambler as inveterate as every other South American general of the period except Bolívar and Sucre. Impressed by his situation, Santander spoke to Bolívar about it, but in a somewhat unexpected manner. Since Bolívar was taking away all the military units, Santander argued that he would have to shoot the thirty-eight officers caught in Boyacá, for otherwise he would be in danger. Bolívar forbade him to do so. He probably knew that Calzada had taken many patriots who had been unmolested and remained throughout in Spanish hands. Bolívar had written to Sámano suggesting an exchange of prisoners " man for man, grade for grade, post for post ".

According to Mosquera, Bolívar explained to Santander that, if the Viceroy left them to their fate, Barreiro and his brother officers would be then free and willing to enter the service of the republic. This was to be expected in a civil war in which the issue independence versus dependence often meant very much what we today describe as left versus right; and a man like Barreiro would be loyally serving as an officer a State whose policy at the time was repugnant to him, while, once freed from his allegiance by the viceroy's action, he might follow his own political views and cross over to the republicans. Barreiro, moreover, was betrothed to a young Granadina whose brother was an independent officer. All this created a peculiar atmosphere. On the evening of Boyacá, Santander had invited Barreiro to dinner and drunk his health; he had called on him in person and even expressed his confidence that the exchange of prisoners suggested to Sámano would be successful.

During the night of October 10th, 1819, the prisoners, who till then had been living in comfortable quarters, were put in iions and transferred to a house in the Main Square, then used as barracks for a body of cavalry. During the night or at dawn, they were informed of Santander's decision to have them executed; and " shortly before midday, marching in lines of four, they were led to the opposite side of the square. Barreiro, Jiménez and two other officers bound to him by friendship and duty, despite the heavy irons they dragged, had to walk all the way across the square ". Barreiro was younger than Santander by one year, for " he was born in Cádiz on August 20th, 1791. He had graduated in the Artillery College of

Segovia, and fought in Bailén and Talavera; he had a cultivated mind and was so handsome that he was known in Bogotá as the Adonis of women ". Under the arch, at the gate of Government House, Santander, on horseback, presided over the scene. A silent crowd watched behind the soldiers. " As he arrived on the spot where his sufferings were to end, Barreiro who was accompanied by a priest, called Colonel Plaza who commanded the troops, spoke a few words to him and, taking from his chest the portrait of the young woman he had meant to marry, begged him to deliver it to her brother, who was serving under Plaza's orders. An instant later he was ordered to kneel and was shot in the back." The remaining thirty-seven officers, some of them Creoles, were shot after him. A looker-on who objected on the ground that Bolívar had reprieved the prisoners was shot on the spot. Santander then harangued the crowd, " and preceded by some musicians, he rode through the chief streets singing the refrain of a song referring to the event."

The view has been put forward by a Colombian historian that " some amorous rivalry may have influenced Santander "; while this is not impossible, it seems unlikely, since Santander would have been a subhuman monster had he sacrificed the other thirty-seven men as well for such a reason. The explanation would appear to be twofold: Santander was more prone to violence than is generally realized; and he lost his nerve. As for the first, the proof comes from him. " My fibre is ardent "—he wrote to Azuero (17.vi.21);—" my temper is diabolic, and I don't know whether I shall have virtue enough not to hang so many ungrateful men and impostors who keep attacking Bolívar and me." This was no vain utterance. On April 7th, 1820, he wrote to Bolívar: " I am unofficially informed that Lt. Colonel Patria and Adjutant Terneros have murdered Pedro Agustin Vargas who was in jail. I do not know on whose orders this has been done, but I know it is a monstrous deed which will involve us in a thousand murders. Every authority or officer will repeat these outrages in order to rob the victims, and will want to justify himself on the score of having acted against a Goth [a Spaniard]." Bolívar's officers, wherever he went, asked leave to courtmartial and shoot Spaniards, in order to bag their wealth. This follows from Bolívar's letter to Santander (22.iv.20), in answer to the above complaint: " On what you say about Patria and Tornero, I have asked the Governor of El Socorro for information. When I passed through El Socorro, I authorized the Governor to courtmartial and sentence upwards of six persons of the most perverse, following the laws, after hearing the opinion of the political Governor, and without violating the pardon granted at our coming. Colonel Fortoul was authorized by me to courtmartial and sentence the Goths of Pie de Cuesta and Girón; and he had nine shot and others sentenced to minor penalties. I believe Patria must have done the same, for I do not believe him capable of murdering anybody." This brought out the following characteristic comment from Santander: " The Vargas affair pleased me in substance but not in form. I only complained to you because I received complaints from El Socorro. I do not accuse Patria but Torneros, who is hot-headed and terrible. He himself related to me all the devilish tricks he played in El Socorro, and suddenly cried out: ' Oh if I only had here as much freedom as I had there! ' Withal this officer pleases me much; he is intelligent and brave. I hope you have not cashiered him. Fortoul had been authorized to punish publicly: that is the regular and the chastening way. I never said a word against that. I find an inner pleasure in having all Goths killed."

So much for Santander's character. As for the circumstances in which he had to act, it is plain that they made him lose his nerve. He himself says so in two letters, one official and one private, to Bolívar. The official letter is lamentable and woven with contradictions: the people are alarmed and protesting against the conspiracies of the prisoners, and yet they are not to be trusted should the conspiracies succeed; his other arguments are no less incoherent. His private letter is even worse. " At last I had to get rid of Barreiro and his thirty-eight companions. The sparks of danger made me mad and nothing good could come from keeping them in prison [i.e. alive]." Then he asks to be covered. This fear of collapse explains his callous attitude at the execution and the undignified scenes by which he tried to win over the populace. Bolívar was indignant and dictated a firm rebuke in which he said that " he would be put in the bitterest situation were Sámano to accept the exchange "; but, fearing Santander's resignation at a time when La Torre was threatening Cúcuta, he sent him instead a bitter-sweet letter showing his displeasure through an apparent approval: " I hear with regret the perfidious behaviour of our war prisoners which has forced Y.E. to have them executed when we were negotiating for an exchange so honourable for the Republic, owing to the approval foreign nations grant to all measures of culture and humanity on the part of belligerent peoples. Our enemies will not believe truly . . . that our severity is an act of justice and not a reprisal or a gratuitous vengeance. But be that as it may, I thank Y.E. for your zeal and activity in trying to save the Republic with that painful measure. Our reputation will certainly suffer; as a reward, the applause of our peoples and their new ardour in serving the Republic will be our comfort." This statement can by no means be interpreted as an approval of Santander's action; neither can it be invoked as a proof of Bolívar's humanitarian feelings. The atmosphere, the intentions and the text point to a mere desire to conquer foreign sympathies. Bolívar was above all a politician. In his offer of exchange to Sámano he had put first the British officers and men, to win over English opinion; then the officers caught in Santa Marta and Margarita, to win over New Granada. What worried him about the Barreiro episode was the reaction abroad. As for the thirty-eight human lives, they did not interest him at all.

3

On December 11th, 1819, Arizmendi, who had gone to Maturin, arrived in Soledad, opposite Angostura, on the Orinoco. The river is here about seven hundred and fifty yards wide. He heard the bells of Angostura pealing gaily, salvoes being fired, rockets and fireworks, all the signs of a people rejoicing: flags could also be seen waving and *flecheras* decked out. He was pleased, if surprised, at this reception of his capital to its Vice-President, and he sent an aide-de-camp across to ask for a *flechera* and officially to announce to the authorities that he had come back. Time went by but no *flechera* came. Though impatient, he thought that a more solemn reception was being prepared. He sent another man and yet another. None returned. At nightfall, he crossed over in a small canoe with his secretary. As he arrived ashore, another salvo was fired. He landed; but though he was wearing all his regalia, no one came to pay homage to him. " What can this be ? "—he asked his secretary; and suddenly both heard a crowd shouting: " *Long live Bolívar !* "—" Farewell, General "—said his secretary; and he hurried away.

Arizmendi walked dejectedly to Government House and " was nearly among the first persons of rank who received Bolívar in the grand hall ". So says the English seaman, who goes on to describe the meeting: " As soon as they met, all the fears I had entertained respecting the welfare of my staunch supporter Arizmendi were dissipated. Bolívar advanced to him with the strongest marks of esteem and cordiality and evinced the same apparent affectionate joy that he would have shown at meeting a brother from whom he had been long separated. He embraced the general, kissed his veteran cheek, encircled him in his arms, and pressed him to his bosom repeatedly, exclaiming as if with the warmest delight ' *Mi querido general* '." Arizmendi knew better than his English friend. But the day of joy was not yet over. A banquet was offered by the Vice-President to the victorious President, to which were invited upwards of five hundred military men and civilians. " The hall of the Government House which was immensely large, and the other lower apartments, were splendidly fitted up for the occasion, and bands were stationed to play republican tunes which continued till a late hour. His Excellency thanked the British officers en masse for their services, and bestowed on them the warmest eulogiums. After many flowery speeches had been made, the usual republican toasts given, and the custom of demolishing the glasses had been complied with, His Excellency, uninfluenced by wine, which he had used sparingly, retired with General Arizmendi leaving the party to enjoy itself as long as was agreeable."

Within twenty-four hours the lavish host was dismissed from his Vice-Presidency and given the command of the Eastern Region, " where he had not the slightest interest and was scarcely known, in the room of General Mariño, who was a host within himself in that quarter ". Precisely. Mariño was thus left without a command. The British Legion was put back under Urdaneta. Then Bolívar bethought himself of his Congress. He ordered it to meet, for which he gave " scarcely an hour's " notice to Arizmendi, who did not attend. The meeting was called for December 14th at two o'clock. " The President, who had been closeted from an early hour with the leading members of his own party, amongst whom was General Urdaneta, went superbly dressed in the uniform of a French Field Marshal in procession to the hall." Three salvoes announced that his Excellency had left his palace; and, writes the *Orinoco Post*, " as he entered the square of the Sovereign Congress, he was saluted with twenty-one, a battery having been placed to that effect in front of the building ". The crowd cheered wildly; Bolívar turned about " ere he went into the hall, to make his acknowledgements. He commenced a long oration, which was at every period interrupted by their acclamations and expressions of fidelity. H.E. at length exclaimed, ' these affectionate people quite overpower me ', and fell as if fainting, upon which the foremost of them eagerly ran to raise him and in their struggles for the honour of supporting the *Libertador*, the rich dress he wore was so mutilated that he was obliged to return to his chamber to equip himself anew." " The Congress in a body came out to receive H.E., and its President, by a singular gesture, yielded to him the chair and bid him speak."

He spoke with his wonted skill and grace, putting forward the merit of his companion in arms and praising the people of New Granada. This afforded him an easy transition to the scheme he had brought all the way from Santa Fe: the union of Venezuela, Colombia and Quito under one single constitution. O'Leary is the authority for the view that Bolívar's interest in this was not merely the political advantages of the operation but also his desire to " right the wrong done to a great man: by calling our Republic Colombia and our new capital Las Casas, we shall prove to the world that we can be free and capable of honouring our friends and benefactors of mankind, for Columbus and Las Casas belong to America ". The scheme was ready in his pocket, and Congress, since " the commission of representatives of both republics had prepared a report and a draft bill to that effect, decided to suspend every other business in order to devote its attention to this ". On the 17th the bill was passed, the Republic of Colombia was founded and the chief officers were elected. Bolívar had Zea elected as Vice-President of Colombia; and as Vice-Presidents of the component republics, Santander for New Granada, and for Venezuela, Dr. Roscio, " an old, superannuated man enfeebled by debauchery "—writes the English seaman. As for Quito, it was thought best to liberate it before giving it a Vice-President. Bolívar was, of course, elected unanimously as over-all President. The new law contained two changes, both symbolical of the times: the name of New Granada was abolished in favour of Cundinamarca and that of Santa Fe in favour of Bogotá.

What was Bolívar's inspiration in all this and how was it received? In Bolívar's mind the vision was Napoleonic. The very style of his utterances at the time, the subtle relation between the all-powerful military dictator and the subservient if decorative persons immediately below, suggested the Bonapartist model. Zea, whose spine had been trained to bow by Napoleon himself at Bayonne, had all along been Bolívar's instrument in Angostura; Roscio, as Zea himself writes to Bolívar, had kept an attitude " constantly the noblest and most liberal, contrary to what we had thought at first. If it had been left to him, not a syllable would have been altered in the draft constitution ". The constitution Bolívar had presented to the Congress of Angostura a few months earlier was already a Bonapartist construction, the first wing of the building he was now completing. The fusion of the three republics was taking place only on paper, and even that not quite regularly. The Congress of Angostura could no more represent New Granada than the four or five deputies for Casanare whom Santander had practically nominated; while the vote of even this shadow-Assembly, if we are to believe a British observer, had been carried " by a small majority, which he had taken care to ensure by his weight and party influence, and that never failing source of corruption, bribery ". The same observer asserts that " had it not been for such men as Páez, Montilla, Mariño and some few more, the Republic would have changed its appellation for that of kingdom, years since ". Mariano Montilla, who was one of the chief opponents of the fusion, " took advantage of his situation as member of the Senate to denounce it and its promoters, with the greatest severity, as persons endeavouring to enrich themselves at the expense of the community at large. Upon one occasion I heard him while pointedly and emphatically addressing Bolívar, directly tell the latter that the next thing he would aim at would be to form the Republic into a monarchy and raise himself to the head of it ". These notes from an English observer, independent of both Hippisley and Morillo, confirm that Bolívar's policy followed that which led Bonaparte from being a general of the Republic to become First Consul and then crown himself Emperor.

SIMÓN BOLÍVAR—THREE STUDIES

CAPTURE OF THE
SPANISH GUNBOATS
BY LLANERO
CAVALRY—
from an engraving

CHAPTER V

THE ANXIETIES OF POWER

I

" A CONSIDERABLE time was now taken up in balls and feasts given by, and in honour of, the President, and little was thought of besides the enjoyment of the moment." Thus writes the anonymous seaman about this period of the nascent Bonapartist Court of Angostura, confirming again that tendency to dancing and enjoying life which recurs at every hour of Bolívar's career. He errs, however, in thinking that little else was thought of. Far from this being the case, the indefatigable chief was thinking and acting in all directions at once. His two main ideas at the time were Caracas and London; the political capital and recognition. For the first, he chose Mariano Montilla; for the second, Zea. He sent Mariano Montilla to Margarita to take command of the Irish troops and, in co-operation with Brion's fleet, to operate on the coast, to take Caracas; if he could not put together more than a thousand men, he was to land in Río Hacha and take Santa Marta. Bolívar explained this plan to Brion on December 14th, 1819, adding the kind of argument he knew would appeal to his corsair-admiral: " I am most pleased to be able to assure you that within three months you will be able to dispose of 25,000 pesos, and in the whole coming year, of more than 100,000; for, out of the million pesos I have ordered to be sent from Santa Fe, I have earmarked a part to meet at any rate two-thirds of your credits, and if, as I hope, Caracas is taken, I shall have the pleasure to see that you are fully paid."

Writing to Santander, however (22.xii.19), Bolívar is more cautious about Caracas. This letter is one of those leaves of life that he shed now and then from his evergreen heart: " I came as lightning and all was done as I wished. Zea is Vice-President of Colombia and the father of this Republic, for he was her main begetter. Arizmendi's activity is being used in the east; Mariño is here, ill, and will later go west, wherever I say, and I still do not know what to do with this man." He is leaving the next day, despite the religious festivities, for the army is already on its way towards the Apure and he fears Páez. " The army will be immense ", but at present he lacks rifles, though he is expecting them in great numbers. " I shall send 10,000 to Cundinamarca or go mad. I shall send them against the whole world within a month." He then speaks of Margarita and of Devereux, informs Santander of Montilla's expedition, and ends with this disarming and charming confession of so many things: " Zea is leaving [for London] to have us recognized as he cannot fail to do in these favourable circumstances, . . . All this is true, most true, nothing that I say in this letter is in the least exaggerated, in which everything is what is called pure truth, and told with the frankness professed towards you by your friend from the heart—Bolívar."

Two days earlier, in a more official vein, Bolívar explains that one of his reasons for founding the Republic of Colombia was to impress foreign powers and so induce them to recognize the independence of the States that had rebelled against the Crown of Spain. " In ten years of struggle and of unspeakable hardships . . . we have experienced the indifference with which the whole of Europe and even our Northern brothers have looked on while we were exterminated. Among other reasons, may be quoted as the first, the multiplicity of sovereignties so far set up. . . . The Republic of Colombia presents all the means and resources needed to uphold the rank and the dignity to which it has been raised and to inspire in foreigners confidence and security as to its capacity for maintaining them." He informs Santander that his London agents Peñalver and Vergara report that the attitude of the British people is very good and that they have not lost hope of raising the three million peso loan for which they had been sent, although they have found Señor Real, the agent for New Granada, in jail for a debt of 150,000 pesos. Peñalver was one of Bolívar's trusted friends.

Having thus settled both military and diplomatic affairs, his indefatigable spirit set him again on the move. He had remained in Angostura only fourteen days. On December 24th, 1819, he left for the Apure and arrived in San Juan de Payara on January 10th, 1820. Had he a plan? It is not certain. He had an urge, an impatience. He had hoped to put himself at the head of Páez' fresh army and to advance straight at Morillo's main force; but he found Páez' cavalry in an unfit state for a campaign owing to an epidemic among the horses; while his infantry was weakened by desertion. Páez, moreover, feared that Morillo's apparent passivity hid an intention to draw Bolívar to the mountains where the Spaniard felt stronger than in the plains. Bolívar, on the other hand, feared that too much delay might allow Morillo to receive the reinforcements he had asked for from Spain. Under the argument, struggled the two temperaments, never reconcilable, of the two strongest men in Venezuela. Bolívar knew only too well that he could not master the indomitable *Llanero*. What was he to do? Exactly what he had done a year earlier in the same situation: seek another city, another army, another man he would be able to control. He decided to give up his Venezuelan campaign and to go to rule New Granada over the head of Santander.

2

Ruling, however, was irksome for Bolívar if it implied administration and detail. For most of the first half of 1820, he lived in one or other of the small cities on the borders between Venezuela and New Granada. He rose at six a.m., dressed quickly, and from his bedroom-study he went to the stables to keep on his horses that " master's eye " which, according to the Spanish proverb, makes them thrive. He returned to his room and read till nine (at this time, Voltaire and Montesquieu). He then took breakfast and received his War Minister, his private secretary and his Chief of Staff.

The first was Pedro Briceño Méndez, a well-to-do young man born in Barinas. His Chief of Staff was Salom, an indefatigable if somewhat ruthless officer. Much of their work seems to have consisted in handling personal petitions, upon which Bolívar pronounced speedily. Nor did he sin on the side of tenderness. At times he went so far as to dictate scathing remarks on the stupidity of his amanuensis. He was hard because he was impatient. He dictated his letters either swinging on his hammock or pacing the room and reading a book while the secretary wrote the phrase. This work took about two hours, after which he read till five. He then dined, frugally, with water for his only drink " as a matter of necessity rather than choice for when the market permitted, his table lacked neither rich foods nor vintage wines ". He rarely stayed a whole hour at table; and after his dinner he would ride. He spent the evening in conversation with his Staff and, at nine, took to his hammock where he read till eleven. His official work and his reading did not exhaust his mental energies: he writes political articles for the official papers of Bogotá and Angostura; a keen and alert journalist, he recommends to Santander that the *Gazette* must be made livelier, and is aware of all the tricks of publicity and propaganda. " I am sending you extracts from a note from our agent in the United States "—he writes to Santander—" so that you have them published in the *Gazette* as a letter received from the North: on no account to appear to come from us." He seems even to have courted the favours of the poetic Muse, with what success is unfortunately not known.

His executive trend is manifest in everything he wrote about the constitution. There is a hardly concealed merriment in his remarks on the civilians *qui croient que c'est arrivé*. The Congress of Angostura had closed its sittings on January 19th, 1820, and Zea had written an eloquent Manifesto for the occasion. Bolívar writes to Santander: " We have not spoken of trifles for days. Señor Zea's Manifesto seems to me very elegant, though it contains a few small and misplaced expressions." He never lost sight of the chief political realities: collective psychology and power. To one of his English friends, William White, he wrote from San Cristóbal (26.v.20), defending his Constitution against the criticisms of the Englishman in terms which do honour to his shrewdness. " Read my speech as a whole. It proves that I put no trust in the moral sense [we should say today *social* sense] of my countrymen, and without republican morality there can be no free government." And to Santander (1.vi.20): " Neither liberty, nor laws nor the most brilliant education will make of us moral men, let alone republicans and true patriots. Friend, it is not blood that runs in our veins but vice mixed up with fear and error." More pointedly still, he wrote from Pamplona to Santander (7.iv.20): " If we triumph, I am resolved to follow the example of Sulla and I have no doubt that the Colombians will be grateful to me for their liberty as the Romans were to Sulla for theirs. If we are beaten, there shall be neither Court nor fatherland; and if I die, I answer for all with my life."

He was a born dictator; and the tone of his letters, the mood and the humour are those of the man at the top, who takes that position as to the manner born and could take no other even if he wanted. He felt the strain, and even owned the fact to his, as yet, faithful adviser. After a dismal list of " I hope this " and " I hope that ", he concludes (10.iv.20): " From here I ask your advice in case it comes in time. This is the time to tell me all frankly, for my indecision is such that I lie awake every night without being able to settle my mind on a resolution." But in concrete matters, he just commands. Santander often reproached military chiefs for their exactions in spite of the solemn promises made to the Granadinos on the day of victory. He asks Santander to " squeeze " the provinces to procure the 30,000 pesos a month he needs to keep his army: " Let them be seized wherever they are and sent monthly to this army. . . . If we do not come to an agreement on the monthly 30,000 pesos I shall have to scrap my plan and throw myself at an unfavourable time on the enemy held country in order to feed my army, under right of conquest. These countries of Cúcuta and San Cristóbal would deserve to be treated as enemies, for they have towards us the ill-will and malice of enemies; but there is nothing on which to avenge ourselves, for they grow nothing but bananas, difficult to convey to the barracks." Two days earlier he had written: " This division will perish if not paid a competent salary, for the situation is that everybody is an enemy and no one wants to serve." Anxiety made him ill. " I was very ill at San Cristóbal and that is why I came here [Cúcuta]. No one knows yet what I suffered from; but I know I am worse, and very much inclined to sleep and rest, which for me is a very bad disease."

3

Personal matters worried him greatly, for few men around him, possibly no one but Sucre, were as disinterested as he. He soon had to record the sad fact with regard to Zea. " Zea is so good "—he writes with bitter humour to Santander (30.v.20)—" that he has done things you cannot imagine. He has had some new Welsers take possession of the Missions, and is putting pressure on Congress to have the Missions handed over to some foreign adventurers, an insult to justice, to reason and to the Liberators." This sentence carries a considerable load which had better be inspected. The Missions were, of course, the rich Missions of Caroní, which had been developed by the Aragonese Capuchins, the last community of whom had been murdered by Colonel Lara. The Welsers were the German bankers to whom Charles V had farmed Venezuela in payment of his debts. But who were those foreign adventurers, through whom now Zea was playing Welsers to the Republic? They were English businessmen, particularly one Hamilton who had turned up in Angostura in 1819 as purser of one of the arms-carrying ships and had remained there as a general factotum and agent both for the Republic and for London's interests, combining business with pleasure and opening factories along with Masonic lodges. The transaction commented on by Bolívar can hardly have been honest; for Bolívar wrote to Santander (22.vi.20) that Soublette (who had by then superseded Zea as Vice-President) had written to him " horrors on the state of Guayana because Señor Zea had delivered the Missions over to Hamilton as part payment of the interests of his debt. This means that over 30,000 heads of cattle have been given away while he [Soublette] had to buy meat in the United States to feed the government and the troops. He says that foreign observers think it is criminal for me to tolerate such diabolical absurdities ". That the transaction was an insult to justice and to reason is obvious. But Bolívar had added also ". . . to the Liberators ".

This third point will be explained anon. Bolívar went on about Zea: " He has given permission to Mariño to leave for Trinidad and has written to me that he is taking him away northwards as his agent. The first is terrible, for it leaves us a germ of a civil war; and the second absurd for it will discredit us even more than we already are. As the Financial Secretary would not dispose of the funds otherwise than under my instructions, Zea took the management of them from him, and as he was responsible before Congress he had this responsibility removed by Congress: everything, everything, everything to please all and sundry against my express orders that funds were to be spent on nothing but armaments. He gave Páez authority to buy all the goods of the Apure and to draw against the Treasury. Imagine the loss. Roscio put it to him, and so did Sucre, that they were authorized to send Mariño to me alive or dead; but he paid no heed. I forgive him his disobedience but not the damage done. He has had I don't know what prerogatives, as well as 50,000 pesos in full ownership, granted to his wife if he were to perish during his mission."

Zea had by no means neglected his personal interests. Few men round Bolívar did in those days, and he looked down on it all with that strange indifference he was able to retain even on the affairs closest to his heart— for he had that ultimate, almost playful disinterestedness without which no great cause is ever greatly served. Brion was one of the men whose greed he had constantly to satisfy. Too often presented as a benefactor of the Republic, Brion was out for profit and money as well as for honour and gold braid.* Bolívar had to write to Santander (20.vii.20): " The Admiral has contracted heavy debts which we must satisfy, at least in part, so as not to discourage those who lend us money and are willing to be enterprising. We must help him somehow or other. . . . We must squeeze the provinces of Antioquia and Chocó, so far deprived of nothing and put them on a level with the northern provinces which we have squeezed to the uttermost. Send orders to them to provide 100,000 pesos, 50,000 for Montilla's troops and 50,000 for the Admiral, for his fleets and his recent debts."

* O'Connor, an Irish adventurer who served with him at this time, confirms what other observers had already noted. During the expedition led by Montilla on Río Hacha, O'Connor relates, considerable quantities of Nicaragua wood were found in the yards of all the houses, for this was the chief produce of the country. " The Admiral grabbed it all and he must have made a big sum of money and quickly, for within very few days, merchantmen arrived in the port and bought the stuff to sell it in the Islands. As for the Army, not one real was found for its salaries."

4

But even Santander complained that he had no money. He had carefully prepared his step. He had received Bolívar in Bogotá on March 4th, when the reunion of the two Kingdoms into one Republic had been duly celebrated by a Proclamation (8.iii.20). A literary festival could not be lacking in Bogotá. This time, it was not entrusted to pretty ladies, but to the Franciscan friars whom Bolívar, who did not attend, thanked duly and modestly the following day. Santander put at Bolívar's disposal a handsome country house on the outskirts of Bogotá; then Santander wrote to Bolívar (21.v.20): " And now, a personal matter. You have powers to grant national estates; grant me one in this country, such as, for instance, the little house of Vicente Córdoba, which may be worth 3,000 pesos. Can you believe, general, that I have no money? The Treasury no longer pays me any salary, for I do not find it honourable to draw any money when there is none for the privates." All things considered this letter does honour to Santander. True, he was asking for a house confiscated from a royalist; but he could have grabbed it without explanations. And what he was asking for was modest: a house worth three thousand pesos for a Vice-President whose (unpaid) salary was 20,000 pesos. " I find nothing, nothing, nothing strange in the fact that you have no money "—answered Bolívar with that treble repetition which was in him a frequent expression of emphasis and passion. " Are you a . . .? "—he adds mysteriously, probably meaning: " You would be a thief if you had." And then: " What I do find strange is that you should send me as news that which never was news for me."

This letter, however, supplies the key to that sentence quoted above, and only two-thirds so far explained, on the giving away of the Caroní Missions: " This action of Zea's had been "—said Bolívar—" an insult to justice, to reason and to the Liberators." Why to the Liberators? Because a law on national estates (mostly estates confiscated from wealthy royalist settlers, whether Spanish or Spanish American) had been voted by Congress for the benefit of the Army, and in particular of the officers. The Missions would have been a magnificent asset to enable Bolívar to keep his hold over his generals and officers since in fact he would have had in his giving some of the richest estates in Venezuela. And he drives home the lesson to the impecunious Liberator in Bogotá with merciless *apropos*: " About your private affair I say that I have no power to give away national property, but that I can do something more valuable if you ask me something worth while; dates cost nothing, and serving one's friends still less, and even less rewarding merit with the property of the community. Along with the little house of Córdoba, one might ask for something worth ten times as much. You will remember that I was omnipotent in all that business of national property when there were no legislators—do you understand me? Then, if you do understand, tear up this letter and remember what I am writing to you." Santander did not tear up the letter.

The youthful republican viceroy of Bogotá was already evincing that formal regard for law which was eventually to earn him the surname of

" The Man of the Laws ", of Bolívar's own invention. This tendency sprang from a desire to bind and control Bolívar rather than from any genuine respect for law in itself; and as Bolívar saw through the legalistic appearance into the power-trend reality that inspired it, Santander's stand was apt the more fiercely to bring out Bolívar's dictatorial urge. Bolívar kept sending draconian orders against all and sundry except the most devoted friends of his régime. He signed in San Gil a decree (23.ii.20) in which, beyond assuring the Granadinos that not a single recruit would henceforth be sent to Venezuela, and that no married man would be forced to serve, he offered, *de mi parte*, the property of all brigands, thieves and deserters to those who would apprehend them, and threatened with the death penalty those who would fail to denounce them. This kind of autocracy prompted Santander to write (23.iv.20) that the Home Secretary of the Republic is issuing a decree of general amnesty, and that he wonders how he is to carry it out " since it is almost in direct opposition to the orders of Y.E. on all persons unfriendly to the régime ". To which Bolívar coolly answers: " The reprieves and other directives from Congress cannot be carried out to the letter, for those gentlemen are at peace, and we are at war. I have been granted unlimited powers and this is a case in which to use them." Now, if Santander had been the genuine man of the laws his admirers depict he would not have commented as follows: " You have relieved me altogether about amnesties and other decrees of Congress, which seem adapted for a Republic at peace. I feel the same as to the constitution, for if we apply it absolutely, we shall upset our military and financial affairs." In the circumstances, this was not unreasonable; but it suggests that the usual antithesis between Santander, the republican puritan, and Bolívar, the caesarian militarist, is, to say the least, exaggerated.

5

Bolívar had chosen for his residence the region of Cúcuta, roughly equidistant from Angostura and Bogotá, and from the coast and the south His military plans had to look to the four points of the compass. Morillo controlled the coastal highland with a force which he estimated at 11,000 men; while La Torre, hard by, threatened the republican troops. In the south, Calzada, the Spanish commander who had salvaged whatever he could from the loss of Bogotá, threatened Popayán. The coast, as always, was strongly royalist. Bolívar seems to have passed at this time through some explicable hesitations. Montilla, whom he had instructed to attack Caracas if he felt strong enough, and if not, to descend on Río Hacha, had taken the second course. In Bolívar's mind, the main objective was Maracaibo. Another army, under Salom or Lara, was to be sent south against Calzada. Sure, and even cocksure, at first, he writes in March, 1820: " I have two offensive armies: the first marches on to Quito; the second is simultaneously invading the provinces of Cartagena, Santa Marta and Maracaibo. During this winter we shall succeed in gaining possession of these provinces, and in the summer I shall surround Morillo. If he seeks me he will find me and I shall destroy him; and if he waits for me, his ruin is inevitable."

It is more than doubtful whether he believed what he was writing. He was worried about Páez' " abuses and disorders " and above all about shortages of mules and rifles. He was to be disappointed about Devereux's expedition.

Devereux arrived in Margarita on January 20th, 1820. After much eating, drinking and speech-making, he asked to go to Jamaica to ship vast supplies of arms and ammunition, and did not return. The Irish contingents left in Margarita had to devote themselves to fishing sprats in order to eat. Montilla meanwhile had gone to St. Thomas to purchase food and armament and, on his return, reported to the War Secretary of the Republic on the expedition to Río Hacha, led in October of the preceding year by McGregor at the head of the English volunteer corps. The report was not particularly cheerful. McGregor had occupied Río Hacha without difficulty; but the English soldiery, many of whom had served in the Peninsular war, repeated here the tragic error they had committed in Badajoz and in San Sebastián, mercilessly sacking a city they were supposed to be liberating. The citizens of Río Hacha, incensed at their behaviour, had armed themselves with the first kitchen knives they could get hold of and only forty-six out of three hundred Englishmen had remained alive. Montilla concluded: " This shows that foreign troops without a national force to hold them in check will expose the arms of the Republic to setbacks." He nevertheless paid no heed to his own warning, and, though he had no other soldiers but seven hundred undisciplined Irishmen, he decided to attempt the expedition. Before sailing, Montilla concluded a written agreement with Brion whereby the businesslike Admiral bound himself to provide four hundred naval ratings for the first attack and two hundred for land service, while Montilla organized Creole troops to keep the Irish from looting; and O'Connor, one of the Irish commanders in the expedition, tells how " the Admiral lost no time in seeking to draw profit from the opportunity offered to him and suggested to us that we should issue a Manifesto, showing our resolve to put ourselves at his orders. I realized that I was in a country of intrigue."

On March 7th, 1820, the fleet left Juan Griego, and on the 12th it arrived in Río Hacha. The garrison withdrew to Santa Marta and the dwellers followed them, fearing a repetition of the McGregor episode. Montilla took an empty city; but gradually the population returned and he was able to begin his recruiting operations. He penetrated inland by the Upar valley, down which he was expecting an expedition promised by Bolívar under Urdaneta; but this was an ardently royalist region, and any man who strayed out of the main force was killed outright by the Indians. The whole vanguard of German engineers of the expedition was lost in this summary way. As the Urdaneta column did not materialize, Montilla decided to withdraw to Río Hacha. O'Connor warned him that this decision would bring about a mutiny of the frustrated adventurers, and so it did. The more irate, when Montilla refused to countenance the sack of Río Hacha as a compensation for the salaries due to them, got out of hand and the episode

ended in utter disaster. " I am not surprised "—wrote Bolívar to Montilla:
" I feared everything from those executioners, who, unless they are paid, do
not kill, and who are like courtesans who do not surrender till they have
been bribed." This, however, was unfair to O'Connor's two hundred
Irishmen, who had gallantly fought an action won, mostly thanks to them,
by Montilla against the Spanish leader Sánchez Lima. The bulk of the
force, persuaded (not without some ground) that the Admiral had funds
and would not part with them, mutinied again, sacked and set fire to the
city and, when embarked to be sent to Jamaica (4.vi.20), had to be threatened
with being sunk before they gave up their arms. The Southern expedition
had also failed. Antonio Obando had been defeated and dispersed before
Popayán. The armies of La Torre threatened to cut him off from the
Orinoco. Bolívar saw the horizon growing darker and darker around him.
Then Fate intervened. Bolívar was saved by the people of Spain.

CHAPTER VI

THE SPANISH PEOPLE SAVE BOLÍVAR

I

ON January 1st, 1820, Rafael Riego, a kind of Spanish Bolívar, at the head of his battalion, had proclaimed the constitution of 1812 and, in the name of its principles, had started a *pronunciamiento*-cum-revolution which, for the time being, at any rate, had overwhelmed Ferdinand's despotism. The pattern of events in Spain bore a close resemblance to that of the events in Spanish America. There were in the main three trends. The reactionary, despotic trend was represented in America by such men as the Viceroy Sámano, Brigadier Morales and the Venezuelan pamphleteer, José Domingo Díaz, and in Spain by Ferdinand VII and a number of generals such as Eguía, his War Minister, who were for a return to the old system. The extreme left of republican reformers, honeycombed with secret societies, believed in " philanthropy " as they said, or democracy as we call it nowadays, dreamt of government for, by and of the people, and had drafted the constitution of 1812 with only one chamber, universal suffrage and every " modern " idea. This trend was strongly represented both in Spain and in Spanish America, though more on the surface and on paper than in deeds and temperaments, for, when it came to practical politics, words were forgotten and personal authority asserted itself. Riego in Spain and Bolívar in America nominally led this current, though, in Venezuela, it was more genuinely represented by those " legislators " who aroused Bolívar's merriment. Finally, there was a middle zone of empirical, liberal-minded evolutionists, to whom, as events were to show, belonged Morillo himself, for he was to disown both Ferdinand's despotism and the somewhat naïve idealism of the reformers in a hurry.

When Ferdinand arrived in Spain after his long exile in France, the country was in the hands of the constitutionalists, mostly men of the second of these three schools. By temperament, the King harboured no friendly feelings towards the Charter of 1812. Yet, he gave no signs of despotic intentions until he was affronted by the tactless restrictions put on his movements and authority by the constitutional sticklers. In his turn, he gave himself over to the blackest and basest form of despotism. Men of the highest standing as leaders of the resistance against Napoleon, and therefore as upholders of Ferdinand, were driven to revolt against the very King they had fought so hard to bring back. Porlier in Galicia, Lacy in Cataluña, Richard in Madrid, Beltrán de Lis and thirteen other conspirators in Valencia, were executed. The despotic King decided in these circumstances to organize an army to restore his waning powers over his American subjects. This army was garrisoned in the neighbourhood of Cádiz. The reluctance of the Spanish soldier to fight in America, infiltration from freemasonry and the revolutionary temper of the country transformed this would-be instrument for the subjection of Spanish America into one for the liberation of Spain. It had been put under a Spanish General of Irish origin, O'Donnell, also known as Count de la Bisbal, a somewhat irresponsible climber who dabbled in freemasonry and revolution. But O'Donnell chose to turn against the conspirators and imprisoned most of them, including Riego and Quiroga, two battalion commanders known for their constitutionalist views (8.vii.19). By then, however, plans were too far advanced; and on January 1st, 1820, at eight o'clock in the morning, Riego, free again, proclaimed the constitution and led his soldiers against the commander-in-chief Calderón (who had superseded O'Donnell), arrested all the generals and won over the rest of the army.

Neither Riego nor Quiroga, who had followed his example, had any idea of how to use the army they had brought over to their opinion and command; and the *pronunciamiento* would have collapsed had not the latent revolution suddenly come into the open in nearly every part of the country. The pattern was the same as that of 1808 in Spain, and of 1810 in Spanish America. In city after city, a combination of popular and military risings proclaimed the Constitution; and on March 6th, the King had to issue a decree calling the Cortes. The next day, on being told that even his own generals were for the Constitution, Ferdinand issued a decree accepting it and submitted to a Consultative Junta that put him under a kind of tutelage until the opening of the Cortes, due to take place on July 19th, 1820.

2

On May 1st, 1820, Bolívar wrote to his friend William White: "The affairs of Spain please me very much, for our cause has been decided by Quiroga. Ten thousand enemies were being sent to us . . . and are now our best friends." As for England, "she fears revolution in Europe, but wants it in America; the one gives her untold worry, the other yields inexhaustible resources". Then he casts an unfailing (if easy) prophecy: "North America, following her arithmetical business policy, will seize the opportunity to procure the Floridas, our friendship and a considerable control over trade." And, with a quixotic touch, he concludes: "It is a conspiracy of Spain, Europe and America against Ferdinand. He deserves it, but it is no longer glorious to belong to so formidable a league against an imbecile tyrant." To Santander, he writes (7.v.20): "Persuaded that she can send no more reinforcements against us, Spain will come to the conclusion that she cannot win, and will then try to make peace with us to spare herself useless suffering." And to Soublette: "Even the liberals will have to flatter the army with a peace offer, since what is at stake is how not to come to America. . . . As it is in the interest of the liberals to spread liberal principles, against which they will meet with many opponents in Spain and in all Europe, the Cortes must decide in our favour." He then points out that Ferdinand and the serviles will also have to think of peace with America, and concludes that negotiations are inevitable and can only be delayed by the immediate tasks and dangers of both sides in Spain. Therefore, "it is our duty to procure our enemies the means and the opportunity to treat with us ", and suggests direct or indirect approach in London and in the United States, " publicly or privately, by the printing press, through friends and even through enemies ". He lays down only one rule: that it must be on the basis of the independence of the Republic, which, he adds, " is to offer peace on the basis of victory, since such is the object of the struggle ". Then comes a typical Bolivarian touch: " If by accident something were known about a diplomatic negotiation, let wings be put on the post, exorbitant premiums offered, so that the news reaches me flying. I desire that nothing be done without my knowledge in this matter. . . . In matters of peace as in matters of war, it is very important to be a veteran."

" Good news, dear general "—he wrote to Santander on June 19th, 1820— " Ferdinand VII has recognized the Cortes and the Constitution. . . . Who knows but that we may have already in Angostura inklings of a negotiation. And without any ' who knows ' about it, I affirm that it is already decreed in Spain. Put this date down, so as to check it up later, and you will see whether I am a good prophet or not." He was. On July 6th he received in El Rosario de Cúcuta a letter from General La Torre, informing him that Morillo, not knowing his whereabouts, had written to him at several addresses, suggesting, under royal instructions, a discussion on peace; and that he, La Torre, was empowered to propose an armistice for a month. Colonel Herrera was sent by La Torre to San Cristóbal to that purpose. In his talk with Bolívar the Spaniard evinced " a fair amount of frankness and even of good faith ", and made it clear that everybody on the Spanish side, Morillo in particular, desired peace. Bolívar answered La Torre (7.vii.20) in the following terms: " I accept with the utmost satisfaction, for the army *stationed here*, the armistice Y.E. proposes to me on behalf of the Commander-in-Chief of the Spanish army, for a month from yesterday. I regret that the Spanish envoys should have taken such a roundabout route in search of my headquarters; but Y.E. will be in a position to show them the way they must follow should they wish to treat on peace and amity with the Government of Colombia, recognizing this Republic as an independent, free and sovereign State. If these gentlemen's aim is not the recognition of the Republic of Colombia, Y.E. will be good enough to signify to them, from me, that I do not intend to receive them or to listen to any proposal not based on such a principle. I hope Y.E. will give me a categorical answer on the continuation of the armistice, or otherwise, within eight days, beyond which hostilities will be reopened."

3

Morillo was in Valencia, towards the end of May, 1820, when two Caraqueños, sent by Brigadier Don Ramón Correa, Military Governor of Caracas, informed him that, in view of the events in Spain, the citizens of Caracas asked that the Constitution of 1812 should be promulgated and sworn. This was a strictly loyal move, since it assumed that Venezuela was to be governed, like any other Spanish kingdom, by the constitution of Spain;

and incidentally confirmed that the Indies were never considered as colonies, but were always assumed to be kingdoms of the Crown of Spain, exactly like the eleven or twelve European Spanish Kingdoms. Morillo's answer was that he would return to Caracas at once. He rode forty leagues of bad roads in twenty hours and surprised the city by his sudden arrival. On the same evening, still mud-stained, he received the municipal council. Two days later the two circulars arrived from Madrid (11.iv.20): one prescribing the promulgation of the constitution of 1812; the other enjoining all Spanish authorities overseas to seek armistices with the Spanish-American rebels. Morillo wrote to Bolívar, Páez, Bermúdez, Zaraza, Monagas, Cedeño, Rojas and Montilla (17.vi.20), informing them that he was sending instructions to all his commanders to suspend hostilities for a month from the day the rebel commanders would be ready to do so themselves. This procedure proves that Morillo was not remiss in accepting the new state of things. Personally, he had everything to gain by it. He had failed in his mission. He was still stronger than his adversaries. He still could count on 12,000 men (rather less than half Spaniards of his expeditionary force, the other half Creoles), and he occupied practically all Venezuela, since the patriots only controlled Margarita, Guayana and the Apure valley. But though a good soldier and leader of men, he was too mediocre and lacking in originality to evolve his own solution for a military problem as novel as that which confronted him; and his wound and other illnesses had sapped his robust vitality. He had repeatedly asked to be allowed to leave for Spain. The armistice would provide him with a presentable final chapter.

Bolívar also could gain much by an armistice. His military situation was bad. New Granada was at the mercy of a bold royalist attack. His resources were so far below his requirements that at this stage he hardly knew what to do. But Bolívar throve on war and he seldom considered an armistice otherwise than as an instrument of war. Only once or twice, in a fleeting mood, does he seem to have envisaged the negotiations as a real procedure towards a real peace: before they began, in his shrewd forecasts of their coming; and immediately after he met Morillo, when, impressed by Morillo's frankness and sincerity, he wrote to Santander: " The armistice is advantageous to us, for, with a clear line of communications and a good unbroken battle-line, we are in the best situation to re-start operations in due time, should it be necessary, which I believe will not be the case, for the biggest advantage of the armistice is the end of this war, as we are assured ". With these two exceptions, Bolívar viewed the armistice as a war stratagem and worked behind it in a way which, however reluctantly, must be described as perfidious. This will become patent anon. On July 20th, he describes to Santander the visit of Herrera, Morillo's first emissary. " He was three days with us, living and conversing familiarly and with the greatest frankness. . . . He seemed sincere to me." On July 21st he answered from El Rosario the official letter Morillo had sent him on June 22nd. He insists on Colombia's solemn resolution (20.xi.18) " to struggle for ever against outside domination and to reconcile herself with nothing but independence "; sends Morillo a copy of the fundamental law of the Republic to that effect and concludes that " the armistice asked for by Y.E. cannot be granted until the nature of the negotiations entrusted to the emissaries, Sres. Toro and Linares be known ". On the same day he writes to Montilla hinting quick action in Cartagena, in view of the possibility of an armistice. He wants Montilla to concentrate on securing the Magdalena river, seizing Santa Marta and blockading Cartagena. All this was within his rights, indeed within his duties, as a commander-in-chief.

On the following day (22.vii.20), Bolívar writes to Santander that, despite Roscio and Revenga, who advocated acceptance, he was for " an absolute refusal unless there is an offer of independence. To conquer the Spaniards one must be made of steel. . . . Since the enemy wishes for an armistice, we must adjourn it, for it is certain that our interests are opposed ". He writes on July 23rd to La Torre, expressing the hope that Morillo's emissaries arrive soon, and adds: " I bless this moment of calm in which we see each other as men and no longer as wild beasts engaged in this detestable arena in a task of mutual extermination." He expresses satisfaction to Santander on the fact that the Spanish Commander addresses him as *President*, though of the Congress of Colombia (which he was not) instead of President of the Republic which he was. He waxes humorous and flippant about it in a letter to Santander, saying that he has written to La Torre " a lot of tender things to show that I am amiable and grateful for the title of President they have given me ". He was to be thirty-seven the following day, and jocosely adds: " though the girl is so tender, she is already talking peace with foreign ambassadors, and knows as much about politics, does the girl, as Macchiavelli ".

He keeps an eye on war matters and insists on reinforcements to occupy the Province of Santa Marta, and on sending Lara to take Maracaibo. Both Santander and Bolívar attached the utmost importance to these two ports—a point to be noted carefully. Cartagena was being besieged by the patriots. This is what Bolívar wrote to Montilla, while waiting for Morillo's emissaries: (1.viii.20): " Offer in the subtlest and most sagacious way up to 100,000 pesos or some military rank up to colonel to any person who may procure for you the taking of Cartagena; if he be a colonel, offer him the rank of brigadier general as well as the 100,000 pesos. To that end you may very well use as a pretext the armistice asked by Morillo. You will say that you have received orders to suspend hostilities, and will ask for a parliamentarian, so as to try to win over one of them with such handsome awards. See whether you could not at least win over the officer commanding the guard in the castle of San Felipe, or that of the Half Moon, or of Santa Catalina Gate, or of any other point in the Bay, or at Boca Chica. Should any of them deliver the city, you yourself shall have the same reward. You may affirm that Morillo has written to me, calling me President, and that the parliamentarian Herrera has assured me that Morillo has orders to conclude a peace by any means, and to recognize the Republic. With this news, which is true, you may advance your negotiations with some pro-Spanish Creole or Spaniard, wishing to stay with us." This was hardly the spirit that Morillo was entitled to expect, but might perhaps still be thought within

Bolívar's rights as a belligerent. Then he added: " My intention is not to conclude a peace until we have taken Quito, for Valdés is on his way thither, and he is meeting with no obstacles." Later letters of his are to show that in his anxiety to secure Quito he overstepped the bounds of loyalty towards Morillo.

4

At this stage, Bolívar received from his faithful Briceño Méndez a letter informing him that the situation of the Spaniards besieged in Cartagena for over a year was desperate. He evidently conceived the plan to reap himself that ripening victory, and wrote from San Cristóbal to Santander (8.viii.20): " While our troops get together I am going to run a race like that of Achilles and try and win in one flight Cartagena, Santa Marta and Maracaibo, within September ". He left Urdaneta and Briceño in San Cristóbal to receive Morillo's emissaries, with instructions which he defines with his inimitable humour: " They are precise, clear and as diplomatic as if they had been dictated on the fields of San Cristóbal where everything breeds cowboy politics." His mind is so much on war that he adds this sinister sentence, precisely in a letter addressed to Santander: " I plan that Sucre with the cavalry of the guards and 2,000 rifles at least, covers Cundina-marca by Trujillo, where Lara will join him with a good division while I with 7 or 8,000 men go to fetch Morillo so that we may make peace in Caracas as you did with Barreiro in Bogotá." Buoyant and sure of himself and of his cause he was incensed when, in Turbaco, he received a letter from General Torres, commanding the Spanish garrison besieged in Cartagena, asking him to suspend hostilities on the basis of recognition of the Spanish Con-stitution. He lost his temper, and answered in terms extravagant in them-selves and out of place on the eve of a negotiation. " Do you believe, Sir, that old and corrupt Spain can still dominate the New World ? Do you believe that the government of that nation, which has given the most terrible example of whatever is absurd in the human spirit, can succeed in shaping the happiness of a single village in the world ? Tell your King and your nation, Sir, that in order not to bear the stain of being Spanish, the people of Colombia are resolved to fight for centuries and centuries against Penin-sulars, against men and even against immortals if they were to side with Spain. Colombians prefer to descend to the eternal abysses rather than be Spaniards."

By then, Bolívar was not a man whose language was under anybody's control. He was a dictator; no one dared suggest to him that he was not absolutely right, let alone that he raved. He evidently realized that Cartagena was not as ripe as he had expected; and, having returned to his senses, he wrote to Santander on the following day (30.viii.20) that he had hopes of seeing Colombia recognized within 1821, but " if we lose one single battle I promise myself nothing, for the Goths are terrible as you well know "; an idea he will often reiterate at this stage. Meanwhile, Linares and Herrera, sent by Morillo, had presented in writing to Urdaneta and Briceño the proposals they were empowered to make: the " dissident " territories to swear the Constitution; the republican commanders to remain in command, but under the Spanish Commander-in-Chief, or directly under the metropolitan government. Urdaneta and Briceño rejected the proposals in vigorous terms. The Spanish commissioner pointed out that neither they nor Morillo had the power to treat on the basis of independence, but that " H.M. keenly desires the peace and prosperity of these countries, and if, in the present circumstances, when the Parliament of the Nation happens to be in session, the Government you represent would send envoys to the Court with full powers to put your wishes before H.M. they would be provided with safeconducts, and H.M. would receive them kindly and hear their proposals ". Had Bolívar desired a peace then, it seems that this answer left the door wide open; but Urdaneta and Briceño replied in a tone of utter extravagance: " As your mission offers ignominy instead of peace, you must not wonder that Colombia refuses to hear you." This was sheer nonsense, and Urdaneta and Briceño knew it; for they reported the matter reasonably enough to Bolívar, who wrote to Montilla (30.viii.20) that the aim of Morillo's emissaries was an armistice pending the arrival of Spanish ambassadors to Venezuela, or of Colombian ambassadors to Madrid; for the recognition demanded by Bolívar could only be granted by the Cortes.

But of course his mind was on war. In the very letters in which he informed Montilla and Santander of his negotiations, he enjoins on the one to take Santa Marta, on the other to push Valdés to take Quito before peace is signed. From Mahates, on his way to Cúcuta (30.viii.20), he instructs his two plenipotentiaries to inform Morillo's men that before he could agree to an armistice not based on the recognition of Colombia, he would exact the handing over of Barcelona, Maracaibo, Santa Marta and Cartagena. " This suggestion "—he adds—" must be made by way of talk, as a personal, not a government opinion." This meant, of course, that no armistice was possible; and reveals two things: that Bolívar had receded from his first attitude, favourable to negotiating; and that he attached a particular importance to Maracaibo, which figures in all his plans at this time as a port either to be taken by arms, or to be acquired by treaty. Nevertheless, he wrote from San Cristóbal to Morillo (21.ix.20) asking to reopen negotiations. Why? Suspiciously enough, he begins extolling the " frankness and purity of his intentions ". The facts are now clear. This offer of an armistice was a feint in the war. He writes to Morillo: " To make our correspondence easier and swifter I shall set my quarters in San Fernando de Apure towards the end of October." He meant exactly the opposite. O'Leary explains that one of Bolívar's motives was to hide his movements. Bolívar himself explains to Santander (24.ix.20): " The aim I had in view was to draw his attention away to San Fernando while our troops operated to the west "; and he adds: " Tell Valdés to be ready to move on to Quito upon the first order he receives, for I intend to send him to Quito as soon as I conceive the idea of an armistice or of an actual peace, so as to gain territory before the order to suspend hostilities reaches him, which order will be conveyed by a Spanish officer who shall proceed very slowly owing to the measures

LANCERS OF THE PLAINS OF APURÉ ATTACKING SPANISH TROOPS, from an engraving

COTTAGES AND NATIVES AT THE HACIENDA OF MONDOMO, from an engraving

VIEW OF THE PASS FROM QUINDIO AND THE CARRIERS WHO USE IT, from an engraving

we shall take thereto." Meanwhile he moved on towards Mérida. On his way to Trujillo, he came across a number of friars who rode forward to congratulate him. Regardless of the heavy rain, they dismounted from the mules and listened with unctuous smiles while their leader addressed Bolívar, until Bolívar, whose ear was less on the speech than his eye on the well-fed and rested mules of the friars, cut short the flow of words to demand of them the sacrifice of their magnificent mounts for the good of the fatherland.

5

Morillo was by no means taken in by Bolívar's diplomacy. He realized that his adversary was trying to divert his attention precisely to advance on Trujillo; and later wrote (16.xii.20): " Since hostilities remained open, I did not stop till I had expelled their vanguard from the town of Carache in the neighbourhood of Trujillo, with the twofold aim of being ready for a decisive action, were we to disagree, and of drawing away from Maracaibo the troops that were attacking it ". Bolívar had written to him from Trujillo (26.x.20), excusing himself for his absence from San Fernando and going more closely into the conditions of a possible armistice. " Inacceptable proposals ", Morillo comments from Barquisimeto (21.x.30)—" the perfidy of these enemies of the nation and the fraud and bad faith with which they act ", are his comment. Was he too severe ? Not if we are to believe Urdaneta, who was then Bolívar's military and diplomatic second; for he explains in his Memoirs that, when Bolívar arrived in Trujillo, realizing that his military situation did not warrant his diplomatic assurance, he " decided on the armistice to give time for all operations to be favourably combined and prepared for when the time of action came ".

The concrete fact which altered Bolívar's mind was a message from Páez, to whom Bolívar had sent his aide-de-camp Ibarra to request him to take Barinas. Páez replied that he could not move because the Plains were flooded. " The refusal of Páez in these circumstances made Bolívar's position more dangerous and the armistice more necessary." Páez wrote a note to Bolívar to the effect that " by lengthening as much as possible the duration of the armistice we should have time to discipline our troops, to receive armaments for reserve armies to be organized in New Granada and to hold this territory [New Granada], the possession of which seems always to depend on one single battle ". So, armistice there was to be; but . . . with an eye on Maracaibo. " Before the truce "—says Urdaneta in his Memoirs—" a party of us was told off under Colonel Justo Briceño who, with the support of the inhabitants of La Ceiba and Ceibita, should occupy the shores of the Maracaibo lagoon and seize as many embarkations as possible; because Bolívar planned to send a division to occupy Maracaibo before the armistice; but Briceño found difficulties which delayed his operations and as the truce intervened " . . . What ? The Spanish of Urdaneta is far from clear: " . . . they should not be proceeded with ".

The proposals Bolívar had sent Morillo from San Cristóbal included broadly an armistice for four to six months, but Santa Marta, Río Hacha and Maracaibo to be handed over. Letters went back and forth, Bolívar bluffing as to his immediate (though not his ultimate) strength, and Morillo showing himself patient and moderate as a man who actually desired peace. Had Morillo advanced a few leagues beyond Carache, it is O'Leary's opinion that Bolívar could not have resisted him. But Bolívar was a magnificent gambler. In the course of these preliminary parleys, one of the Spanish emissaries, Pita, assured him that he was authorized by Morillo to say that a withdrawal to Cúcuta would considerably ease the negotiations. " Tell him that he will withdraw to Cádiz before I do to Cúcuta ", answered Bolívar, and he wrote in violent terms to Morillo (21.xi.20). Morillo wrote back a calm disavowal of Pita's suggestion and urged him to end the war between brothers. But Bolívar's irritation made him ill, as he wrote to one of Morillo's plenipotentiaries, Juan Toro, his wife's cousin, now constitutional *alcalde* of Caracas. To Santander, he wrote (22.xi.20) that he had appointed as negotiators " out of protocol and out of contempt, Sucre, Briceño and Pérez ", three relatively junior men. But after more letters and parleys, he finally accepted an invitation to meet Morillo in Santa Ana. On the morning of November 27th, Morillo arrived at the meeting place with about fifty officers, including La Torre, and a squadron of hussars. To O'Leary, sent by Bolívar to announce his coming, Morillo asked: " What escort does he bring ? " " About twelve officers," answered O'Leary. Morillo sent back his men. The small group of riders who came with Bolívar was then seen over the brow of the hill. When Bolívar was pointed out to Morillo, the Spaniard asked: " What! That little man in the blue cassock, riding a mule ? "

The two men alighted, embraced each other and entered the best house of the village where Morillo had prepared a banquet in honour of his guest. " From Morillo downwards "—wrote Bolívar to Santander—" all Spaniards vied in their desire to please us and show us friendship. . . . There were toasts of much courtesy and of the most beautiful invention, but the ones that pleased me most were those of Colonel Tello and of General La Torre. The first ' to the victories of Boyacá which gave liberty to Colombia '; the second ' to the Colombians and the Spaniards, and let them march together all the way to hell if need be against despots and tyrants '. Morillo drank among many other most enthusiastic and liberal toasts ' to the heroes who died fighting for their country and for liberty '." So far Bolívar. But Morillo himself reports that he also drank the following significant toast: " Let Heaven punish those who may not be moved by the same feelings of peace and friendship as we are." In short (Bolívar himself again reports), a volume would be needed to record all the toasts.

CHAPTER VII

THE ARMISTICE

I

WE left Morillo and Bolívar in a mutual embrace, crowned, if not by the laurels of Mars, by the vine leaves of Bacchus. " The chiefs being carried to a bedchamber "—the anonymous seaman goes on to relate—" they slept in the same room, and all retired till the next morning, when the second part of the consequences of this friendly compact were known." Bolívar had his way, if indirectly, on the chief point: the documents were so drafted as to imply the recognition of the government of Colombia. The first of the two agreements concluded was a standstill convention, to last six months from the day of ratification. The boundaries of the armies were determined in an article (the third), a paragraph of which (the second) referred to Maracaibo. " The troops of Colombia that may be operating on Maracaibo at the time the armistice is intimated to them shall be allowed to cross Spanish-held territory to join the other republican units, provided that, while on Spanish territory, they are led by a Spanish officer." Article twelve stipulated that forty days' notice was to be given by the party who first decided to put an end to the armistice. The convention was to be ratified within sixty hours.

In his preliminary correspondence with Morillo, Bolívar had suggested a treaty " truly holy which should regularize the war of horrors and crimes which had until now drenched Colombia in blood and tears ". This treaty was concluded and signed on November 26th, 1820. It provided for respect for the life and comfort of prisoners of war and stipulated that the sick and wounded would not be considered prisoners, but would be left free to rejoin their flags when restored to health, and that they were to be treated at least as well as the home sick and wounded. Prisoners were to be exchanged rank for rank. Article seven stipulated that: " Since this war is due to a difference of opinions, and the persons fighting on both sides are related by very close ties . . . military and civilian officers caught serving under the flag of one party after having deserted from the other shall not be punished by death. Conspirators and disaffected persons will also be exempted." Other less important clauses were conceived in the same spirit. " The treaty regularizing our war "—wrote Bolívar to Santander—" does us much honour, because it has been proposed by us." This treaty, comments O'Leary, was signed and ratified by Bolívar in the same house in Trujillo in which seven and a half years earlier he had signed the war to the death decree. In Bolívar's mind it was designed to raise the prestige of Colombia abroad, particularly in England.*

* At that very period Bolívar struck a good friendship with the ferocious friar Ignacio Mariño, whom he addresses as " My dear chaplain and friend ", and to whom he gave the rank of Colonel. Now this priest did not shoot prisoners: he tied them up inside a sack and threw the sack into the river.

Bolívar was favourably impressed by Morillo. On November 29th he writes to Santander: " I saw Morillo the day before yesterday, and honestly believe he is a moderate man and of good intentions. . . . I really liked him." He was also impressed by the other Spanish generals. Writing to Morillo (30.xi.20), Bolívar makes special mention of " our General La Torre " with a truly affectionate possessive; and to Santander (29.xi.20): " When the treaties are published, in particular that regulating war, you must see that some praise is bestowed on the Spanish negotiators, who are excellent people and very humane; but you will single out Brigadier Correa who is the kindest man that treads the earth." It is well known that, both as to the length of the armistice and to the treatment to be meted out to deserters, Morillo had made more liberal proposals than Bolívar was ready to accept; while he was also the author of the idea that a pyramid should be erected on the spot where he and Bolívar had met. There is a genuine sense of joy in Morillo's narrative written from Carache: " No one can realize how interesting the interview was nor the cordiality and love that prevailed in it. We all did mad things out of joy for it seemed to us a dream that we were all there meeting as Spaniards, brothers and friends. Do believe that frankness and sincerity presided over the meeting. Bolívar exulted with joy; we embraced each other a million times and decided to erect a monument of eternal remembrance for the beginning of our reconciliation on the spot where we embraced first." The Spanish generals were to some extent carried away by the liberal wave then sweeping over the Peninsula; and Bolívar had the generous and delicate precaution of writing to Santander to use his narrative, but confidentially, for some of the verbal excesses committed by La Torre and others might do them harm. " It seems "—he wrote to Morillo (30.xi.20)—" that a universal mutation has taken place in our feelings enabling us to see everything under a more pleasant aspect. For my part, I own that my heart has changed with regard to my new friends. . . . I congratulate myself on having met men so worthy of my just esteem and whom, through the prejudices of war, we could only see surrounded by the shadows of error."

2

How sincere was he ? In his conversation with Peru de Lacroix on this episode he answers in no uncertain terms: " Never throughout my public life have I displayed more policy, more diplomatic cunning than on that occasion. . . . I went to that interview armed from head to foot, with my policy and my diplomacy well concealed under an ample show of frankness, good faith, trust and friendship; for it is well known that I could feel none of this towards Morillo, and that he could inspire in me none of those feelings in an interview of a few hours." Bolívar, in Santa Ana in 1820, may have been less insincere than he himself realized in 1828. Some insincerity there certainly was; and the conclusion is confirmed by three concrete cases which do little honour to him: those of Quito, of Barinas, and of Maracaibo.

As for Quito, Bolívar, who had just written to Morillo the cordial letter of November 30th quoted above, writes to Santander on December 1st: " We shall take Quito in any case. . . . While peace is being negotiated here, I could take to the road in time, were Valdés foolish enough to let go the opportunity he has to acquire immortal fame. There are many ways of delaying the official news of the armistice; among others, the letter might go astray; the messenger might become ill; or Valdés might declare himself independent of you while in Quito territory. Develop these ideas, which I just throw out."

That was the spirit. On December 11th, 1820, Bolívar wrote to Morillo from Barinas that he was going to leave in that city a brigade of 2,000 men of the Guards under Colonel Plaza, instead of the officer and twenty-five civilian observers prescribed by article 6 of the Armistice " as a proof of the sincerity and good faith which inspire this treaty ". Bolívar's excuse was that " the breach of the armistice is insignificant ". The rest of the letter is devoted to urging Morillo to ask the government to send pleni-potentiaries to negotiate a peace; but we know that Bolívar was just buying time. His bad faith over Barinas comes out in his letter to Colonel Plaza (16.i.21): " I shall be in Barinas in April, when I hope that all, all, all will be ready to begin the campaign, for I am resolved to finish the war in Venezuela this year, risking everything to obtain that. I had your latest news with the utmost satisfaction; I approve everything and hope even much more from you for my return." Right at the beginning of the armistice, therefore, Bolívar was endeavouring to settle in Barinas an officer in command of 2,000 men, in violation of the armistice, with instructions to begin immediately to prepare the resumption of the war. This time, however, he failed, for La Torre turned down his proposals.

3

The case of Maracaibo was the worst. The importance attached to this place by Bolívar and Santander has been noted. Morillo was no less alive to it, as he shows repeatedly in his despatches. The Governor of Maracaibo, Montenegro, had lost the confidence and friendship of the rich Whites because, not trusting their military prowess, he had brought in a Militia of coloured men to defend the city. The military command fell to Lt.-Col. Francisco Delgado, a Maracaibo citizen. Bolívar discreetly removed himself from the neighbouring district of Trujillo, while leaving it under Urdaneta who was a native of Maracaibo. These Delgados were four brothers, three of whom, including Francisco, had received honours from the King, while the fourth, Juan Evangelista, was a republican officer then serving in Pamplona. Urdaneta had him brought over to win his royalist brothers to the republican cause, which he eventually did. José María Delgado came to see Urdaneta under cover of some tobacco purchases. Urdaneta gave him 4,000 pesos, ostensibly to pay for the rations of the better part of the royalist garrison which was sent away on a forged order from La Torre, the forgery being made by Juan Evangelista, i.e. by Urdaneta, who placed a battalion in Gibraltar on the Lagoon ready to enter the city as soon as it had " spontaneously " declared for the Republic. Francisco Delgado, the royalist commander, proclaimed the independence of Venezuela on January 28th, and on the 29th, Heras, the commander of the republican battalion in Gibraltar, occupied Maracaibo. Urdaneta writes in his Memoirs: " Some have said that the glory of this operation corresponds to Heras for having occupied the city on his own responsibility, though having orders from Urdaneta not to do so; but such an assertion can only rest on lack of knowledge of the facts. There was an armistice on, and it was necessary not to give the Spaniards grounds for complaint. . . . Heras, therefore, received orders in accordance with the plan agreed with the envoys from Maracaibo, which he was to carry out until the occupation of the city; and he was also given counter-orders which he could show but was not to carry out; which in any case would be useful to answer Spanish protests, putting all the blame on Heras, who had agreed to be court-martialled in such a case. . . . Urdaneta and Heras were in agreement on all this, which has never been published before because it was not suitable for the honour of the nation."

4

So far, Urdaneta. Was Bolívar aware of all this? According to the local historian, José Felix Blanco, that was precisely the reason why he had put Urdaneta there; and a violation so gross could hardly have been committed by Urdaneta without Bolívar's agreement. On January 21st, 1821, Bolívar had heard in Bogotá that Urdaneta had requested Montilla to send the battalion of Rifles and the squadron of Hussars of the Guard to back an insurrection of the patriots in Maracaibo; and in an official letter to Montilla (not to Urdaneta) he disapproves of the idea as being contrary to the armistice. This makes his correspondence with La Torre about the episode the more significant. On January 25th, 1821, from Bogotá, in a letter in which he was already preparing the break and the renewal of hostilities, he wrote to La Torre stating the only condition under which he would be able to " resist the universal clamour of my army companions and of my fellow citizens " for war. His conditions were the surrender to the republicans of the remainder of the provinces of Cumaná, Maracaibo and Río Hacha; and towards the end of the letter, he singled out Maracaibo, to say that " only its possession could make our new sacrifice more bearable ". Why should he write thus to La Torre four days before Urdaneta took Maracaibo by craft?

La Torre's protest was characteristically moderate. On February 15th he rightly described the sending of troops to Maracaibo as " a public violation of the armistice "; and on the 25th he suggested as a conciliatory solution: " The troops sent to garrison it to be withdrawn to their original positions, the city meanwhile to govern itself as it thinks fit." Meanwhile Bolívar had written to La Torre a letter full of grief (19.ii.21). " I am sure you will do me the justice of believing that I have had no share in the recent insurrection of that desired city. I should never have placed myself of my own accord in a situation which is in every way most trying. How can I drive a respected friend such as you are to take steps contrary to your feelings, and how can I forsake a city now sheltered by our arms and protected by the fundamental law of Colombia? For me, both are a cause of regret, not to mention the cruellest of all: the suspicion of our good faith." Owing to the general dislike of the armistice, it is impossible for him to give back Maracaibo. His official letter to La Torre is a tissue of sophisms which he was too intelligent to have written with sincerity. " I shall begin by frankly declaring that I have disapproved the advance of Major Heras to the city and that he will be court-martialled for having exceeded his powers in that he did not await a decision of his chief before receiving under the protection of the arms of the Republic a territory belonging to Spain when hostilities were suspended." He goes on to stress the " spontaneous " character of the city's decision, knowing full well that the change-over had been a purely military affair; and concludes that " no claim can be raised against the uprising itself, and that the only *prima facie* ground for alleging a violation of the armistice is the unpremeditated step of Major Heras ".

That word " unpremeditated " betrays him. He evidently knew all, as indeed, by now, he must, since it is unthinkable that Urdaneta should have concealed from him the scheme that had already succeeded, even if he had done so before (which is more than doubtful). His defence of Heras' action, including the cool assertion that " the armistice treaty in no way guarantees the integrity of our respective territories ", is admirably written but worthless. Yet there is a superb assurance in his proposal that, should his right to protect Maracaibo be unacceptable for La Torre, he is ready to submit the matter to an arbiter, and he suggests the Spanish Brigadier Correa. He then puts four questions: Will hostilities be broken again if Maracaibo is not returned? If so will forty days' notice be given? If so, will they run from the day the notice is sent out or received? And must the notice be sent to all commanders of arms and divisions in the same way and with the same delays? " My behaviour will be the same as that of Y.E. in Venezuela as well as in Cundinamarca and Quito." He was thinking of war. When La Torre insisted on an answer to his conciliatory proposal, all he got was a notice that hostilities would begin again within forty days if the Spanish commissioners who had arrived in La Guaira were not ready to negotiate on the basis of independence (10.iii.21). " His true motive " —says Baralt, not only a Venezuelan but a Maracaibean historian—" was to keep the city of Maracaibo, ill begotten and ill retained, whatever he might say; for, without going into the substance of his arguments, and assuming that he was unaware of Urdaneta's tricks, it was obvious that Heras could not have arrived in Maracaibo on January 29th without first violating Spanish territory by crossing the Lagoon before the city's revolution; and, in fact, he left Gibraltar on the night of January 27th, when Maracaibo was still in the hands of the royalists."

5

His bad faith in this case was fatal to the negotiations of the two emissaries he had sent to Spain. He had sent Rafael Revenga and Tiburcio Echeverría to treat with the Spanish government on the basis of the independence of Colombia (24.ii.21), with powers to cede the Isthmus and Province of Panamá (then in Spanish hands) with, or even without, the acquisition of Quito; and to " offer as a compensation for the sacrifice Spain makes of her so called rights, that which Colombia makes by recognizing and guaranteeing the sovereignty of Spain in Mexico and the other lands and territories of America, which might not have reached peace and independence by the same means as Colombia ". The two messengers carried a somewhat bombastic letter from Bolívar to Ferdinand VII, yet with a good paragraph in it: " It is our ambition to offer a second fatherland to all Spaniards, but proud, but not overwhelmed with chains. Let Spaniards come to gather the sweet fruits of virtue, of knowledge and of industry, they shall not come to wrench the fruits of force." Revenga and Echeverría sailed for Cádiz on board a Spanish frigate; but when they arrived, the Spanish government, aware of the Maracaibo incident, would not confer with them. The Secretary of State, Bardaxí, wrote to them (30.viii.21) that in view of the armistice the King and the Government " had found no difficulty in allowing them to land although H.M. was already aware of the fact that, in the face of all that had been agreed and of the most sacred tenets of the law of nations, your chief, Bolívar, had broken the armistice . . . as he entertained the hope that such a generous policy on his part might pave the way for a pacification of those provinces, and that Bolívar, realizing the outrage he had committed, in breaking his word of honour and so debasing the honourable profession of arms, would have made some proposals to the Spanish Generals and put you in a position to be heard by H.M.; but as this has not happened, and no explanation has been given, your presence in Spain is useless and even harmful ".

The two commissioners left Spain in September for Paris and London, where they found much to do, if only to clean up the financial disorder created by López Méndez and Zea. López Méndez had lived difficult years in London as the representative of a government with little or no credit, and had lost the little credit he had by opening offices for the sale by auction of commissions in the Venezuelan army. José María del Real, his colleague for New Granada, had to serve a sentence in a London prison. Zea sought to restore matters, but either through inexperience or for other reasons, left the situation worse than he had found it. Three London speculators, Herring, Grahame and Powles, had bought most of the bonds of former Colombian debts for a song, and by inducing Zea to contract with them a loan of £2,000,000, had succeeded in raising their bonds to par. " I ought not to hide from Y.E."—Echeverría wrote to the Colombian Foreign Secretary—" that in Paris and in London it is believed by impartial and wise persons that this business has been and is being transacted in bad faith." And he goes on to say that " the gentleman in question was poverty-stricken until that contract was made and to-day he is a man with open house in this Court and in Paris ".

The arrival of Zea in the European capitals handling millions with such elegant ease explains the two letters Bolívar then received from his off-and-on cousin Fanny de Villars, otherwise Madame Trobriand. She compares him to Washington, then comes to brass tacks: " *Il me faudrait pour être heureuse et bien tenir ma place un peu plus d'aisance et il me serait doublement agréable de vous la devoir.*" But she is ready to serve: " *Notre grand livre et notre sol sont encore de ce qu'il y a de plus solide au monde. Si vous avez quelques capitaux disponibles, pourquoi n'en mettriez vous une partie à ma disposition par le canal de Madame Zea ou par tout autre? Le fond resterait à vous, et les intérêts seraient à ma disposition pour le temps que vous indiqueriez.*" This seemed a fair arrangement, but the lady meant it to be fairer still: " *L'espèce de représentation que cet arrangement me permettrait tournerait même au profit de votre nom, puisque tout le monde sait ici que je vous apartiens et que je m'y fais gloire de mon dévoument pour vous. Il est même des moments où cette influence pourrait n'être pas pour les affaires de votre pays sans avantages politiques. Vous connaissez l'action des salons de Paris et des ouvrages français sur les réputations et sur les événements de l'univers.*" Bolívar did not answer. He never answered this grasping woman who was so distant from his mind. But silence would not put her off. She wrote again from Lyon (5.ii.21), reminding him of the days " *si agréables* " which they had spent together in the house she still occupied. She again brought in Washington and then her law suit, her " *gêne* ", and: " *Dans votre position, mon cousin, vous n'avez qu'à transmettre un ordre à Londres à vos représentants ou à Monsieur Zea à Paris sur la maison Lafitte ou toute autre, de cent cinquante ou deux cent mille francs. . . . Si mes calculs étaient exagérés sur votre fortune ou vos moyens, vous auriez toujours la resource de faire acheter par votre gouvernement pour trois cent mille francs comptant, la maison que vous-même connaissez à Paris, et qui servirait de logement à l'Ambassadeur que votre République aujourd'hui reconnue par l'Espagne même, ne peut plus tarder à avoir en France.*"

This confidence in a " peace " which was going to enable Bolívar to recover his fortune was of course a reflection of Zea's conversations and opinions. He was a sceptical intellectual who had already served three sovereigns—Charles IV, Joseph Bonaparte, Bolívar—and felt ready to serve a fourth. He entered into private dealings with the Duke of Frías, Spanish Ambassador in London. How far they were unauthorized and how far Zea's proposals went beyond Bolívar's explicit or secret instructions is not clear. On February 4th, 1821, Bolívar wrote to several Spanish-American Governments that " the conversations and private communications begun in London between the Minister Plenipotentiary of Spain and that of Colombia in that Court had already prepared the ground which the new envoys would but follow ". The talks culminated in a plan for the settlement of the wars overseas on the basis of a confederation of Spanish nations under the King of Spain. Zea had conceived a Spanish Commonwealth on the lines of the present British Commonwealth, turning the Spanish-American nations into " dominions ". This plan was then but an idea without an historical body to incarnate it. Nor should responsibility for his failure be laid on the Spanish-American leaders, even though most of them would have rejected it, as Bolívar did. The responsibility belonged entirely to the Spanish Government, whose official stand was that " the chief basis for such a proposal, and therefore its whole character, are absolutely inadmissible ".

Zea himself found his authority not a little undermined by the stubborn attitude of López Méndez who refused to divest himself of his powers as official agent for Venezuela; and in order to prove himself one, signed a contract with a saddle manufacturer, James Mackintosh, for a complete armament and equipment for 10,000 men at £15 per man, and issued debentures for that amount on his own signature in competition with Zea. Such were the difficulties Echeverría had to contend with in London and in Paris, not only in the financial but in the political field. Recognition was beginning to be in the air. Henry Clay had presented a motion favouring recognition by the United States of the independent governments set up in Spanish America; and though it had not passed, it had prepared the ground for later success. Echeverría reported from London (2.vii.21) that Zea had called on Lord Londonderry who had told him he was awaiting an answer from the Spanish government in order to decide what to do on recognition of Colombia; and asked for a report on the negotiations between Colombia and Spain. But the final move in the matter was to come from Bolívar.

Chapter VIII

VICTORY

I

THE armistice had been a moral victory for the patriots. " By treating with the Spaniards on a footing of equality "—comments Urdaneta—" the population of the territories they occupied would see that the patriots were no longer treated as brigands, but as enemies worth at least as much as their adversaries; while the intercourse bound to set in during the armistice would restore confidence between the sons of the country and deprive the Spanish army of much of its moral force." This had been foreseen by Bolívar; and it was part of his policy to stimulate the process. O'Leary reports that the republican officers entrusted with the mission of notifying the armistice to local authorities " received orders to profit by it to acquire data and information on the forces and positions of the enemy, and those Bolívar gathered in this way were not of little value. According to the treaty, members of both armies were allowed to visit their friends and relations in the territory of the adversary; which, of course, worked in favour of the patriots, but was of little value for the Spaniards ". Morillo had written from El Tocuyo to his own armistice commissioners (10.xi.20) about " the duplicity of General Bolívar whose bad faith has gone so far as personally to have attempted to seduce the Hussars who went under a parliamentary flag escorting Captain Real." This was the policy Bolívar maintained throughout the armistice; and on the eve of breaking it, he still wrote from Trujillo to Santander: " I have ordered 1,500 rifles to be sent to Maracaibo, just in case, and to raise an army there. The enemy does not move, and I believe that the Maracaibo affair has afflicted rather than irritated him. They do not threaten us and you will have seen by my note to La Torre that we have the right to protect all Colombians who espouse our cause. We shall do so successfully with all those who may wish to follow that example. You must instruct all heads of units of this right we have to help those who embrace our cause, so that they do not miss some good opportunity as spontaneous as that of Maracaibo." The cynicism of this last taunt was of the best Bolivarian vintage.

But there was more to it than Bolívar's Machiavellian ways. When the priest Torrellas, the Indian colonel Reyes Vargas and several other royalist chiefs crossed the line and accepted the opportunity offered them to serve with the same rank in the republican army after years of fidelity to the Crown, when the brothers Delgado, of the white nobility of Maracaibo, " betrayed " their King, something deeper and more significant was happening than a mere turning of coats. In fact, the offer of the armistice by the liberal government of Spain can only be compared in its effects with the expulsion of the Jesuits in the preceding century. Like the expulsion of the Jesuits, it delivered a heavy blow precisely on the part of Spanish

America which had remained faithful to the King. Now, *without fidelity to the King, fidelity to Spain in Spanish America had no sense.* The authority of the King of Spain over Spanish America was a pure matter of tradition, carried over from the days when the conquerors remained faithful to their Monarch and grafted Spanish kingdoms on American roots and soil. Therefore, while the heirs of those conquerors remained faithful to that tradition, the sway of Spain over the Spanish-American kingdoms went on unchallenged and unanalysed, and the viceroys and Captains General were obeyed as emanations of a King who was enthroned in the heart of the American peoples. This situation underwent a twofold threat towards the turn of the century. The French Revolution transferred sovereignty from the Monarch as the embodiment of the nation to the nation itself; and the Spanish Crown fell to the gutter at Bayonne. These two events fostered a republican drive in the Spains overseas which European Spain would not have had the power to control, even if she had remained as strong as she had been in the eighteenth century; but the vigour of the royalist tradition in America was so powerful that, mostly with its help, republican separatism was kept at bay for years. And now came the King himself (for so it seemed and so officially it was) and stretched a hand of friendship to those republicans. That was the end of royalist tradition in Spanish America; and therefore the end of Spanish rule.

2

Bolívar, a master in political intuition, was fully aware of this, though the Spanish liberals do not seem to have realized it. Many of these Spanish liberals, imbued with French doctrine, were in fact democratic absolutists *à la* Rousseau, and felt indignant against the American separatists; for they, unlike the old-fashioned royalists, considered the territories overseas either as colonies or else as integral parts of a one and indivisible sovereign people, a collective heir to the old absolute King. Morillo, who was a royalist, though, as he was to prove it that very year in Madrid, an enlightened one, opposed to absolutism, saw what the change implied. " It is a delusion in my view "—he wrote to Madrid (26.vii.20)—" to believe that this part of America may ever want to unite to that hemisphere [Europe] and adopt the political constitution of the Monarchy. The dissident Americans [note he avoids the word *rebels*] have not fought to improve the system of government, and it is a mistake to believe them capable of ever agreeing to unite with the metropolis." He could see under his own eyes how the revolution in Spain was confusing minds, ideas and symbols. In one of his official dispatches he objects to the yellow and green cockades which the new liberals were wearing and reports that he had to remind the army that the only official cockade was red. This detail shows to what an extent the Spanish army itself was infiltrated with vaguely republican feelings.

The belief that the war was bound to be lost unless overwhelming re-inforcements were sent over had been the true cause of his desire to return.

Morillo enjoyed an immense prestige both with the royalists and with the independents. " The *llaneros* "—writes O'Leary—" who are sparing in their praise of other people's courage, belauded with admiration the cool intrepidity of the Spanish commander-in-chief and said that it was a pity he should have been born in Spain and a shame he was not a patriot." He was a man of the people and can hardly have enjoyed waging a war against the independence of one nation when he had made his mark warring for the independence of another. There is an incident in his advance on Carache which paints the man. In the course of a rearguard action, a man left behind, leaning on the body of his dead horse, held a number of Spanish cavalry at bay and killed two of them. Surrounded, wounded, and with his spear broken in two, he was on the point of perishing when Morillo turned up and shouted: " Spare that brave man! " The prisoner was taken to hospital, and when Morillo met O'Leary on armistice business, he spoke with enthusiasm of that soldier, whom he sent back to Bolívar without requiring an exchange and with a present of money for himself. Bolívar repaid his soldier with eight Spanish prisoners. This story is apposite. Where Morillo, for what he was worth, was just himself, Bolívar, though a far bigger man, was himself plus the stage. There was nearly always in Bolívar a touch of acting which led to insincerity.

Morillo actually left Venezuela without a word of farewell to his new friend. Bolívar was hurt and wrote to him that " nothing but the idea of some unexpected delay comforts me for your silence ". Morillo had handed over to La Torre in Barquisimeto on December 3rd, 1820; on December 4th, Fermin Paúl (the very man to whom the first revolutionary Congress of Venezuela had entrusted the task of drafting the oath of allegiance to the Independent Government and to the Immaculate Conception), now a faithful collaborator of Morillo, wrote to him of the consternation caused by the news of his departure. But Morillo was resolved to leave and sailed for Spain on December 16th, 1820.

His departure was one of the many excellent results the armistice yielded Bolívar. " The armistice "—he said later to Peru de Lacroix—" deceived even Morillo and made him return to Spain, leaving his army under the command of General La Torre, less active, less capable and less military than he was; this in itself was an immense victory." And he wrote to Rocafuerte (10.i.21): " General La Torre, who remains, is married to a relative of mine, and is also my friend; so that it seems that the expeditionary army wishes to come over to the liberating army and prefers a young and beautiful to an old and tottering fatherland." He could now prepare for a resumption of hostilities in much happier circumstances than he could have dreamt of when he had suspended them; he had a better public opinion, more men, Maracaibo . . . and San Martín's victory in Lima. " Though this may be unpleasant to you "—he wrote to La Torre from Trujillo (5.iii.21)—" I take the liberty to inform you that San Martín has taken Lima and that General Pezuela [the Spanish commander in Peru] has been defeated, so that this event enlightens the Spanish government on the true state of affairs in America." The news, however, which he rightly doubted two days later in a letter to Santander, was sure to be unpleasant to La Torre, but it does not follow that it elated Bolívar overmuch. On January 10th, 1821, he wrote to San Martín a letter which, though graceful and modest, betrayed his anxiety lest the hero of the south should reach before he did the heights of glory: the final liberation of America. Hence his hurry to liberate Popayán, Quito and Guayaquil. " The conqueror of Chacabuco and Maipo, the first son of the fatherland, forgets his own glory when he praises me so lavishly. . . . When I heard Y.E. had set foot on the shores of Peru, I held them as free, and I hasten, in advance, to congratulate Y.E. on the third country that will owe you its existence. I am on my way to fulfil my promise to unite the Empire of the Incas to the Empire of Freedom; no doubt it is easier to enter Quito than to enter Lima; but Y.E. can more easily perform difficult things than I easy ones; and soon Divine Providence, which so far has protected the banners of Law and Liberty, will unite us in some angle of Peru." Angle of Peru! What a curious phrase! And how accurate it is in depth in spite of its odd formal inaccuracy. For Guayaquil—or for that matter, Lima—was the summit of that vast angle formed by the Plata and the Orinoco which was the Spanish Empire. And it was on that summit that the two great men had to meet.

3

Haste was the lesson from the south; though, paradoxically enough, it came from a slow and Fabian general to the swiftest and the most impatient leader that ever was. Bolívar felt the pressure; but was in no need of it, for the facts of his own situation imperatively commanded haste. Everywhere his troops were being decimated by disease and want, for the cattle of the Apure were being diverted from war-confiscation to peace-trade under the protection of the armistice. As the estates confiscated from the owners who sympathized with Spain had been distributed among the independent chieftains, the new owners, once in possession of the cattle, preferred to sell them at a good price, or if need be at any price, rather than see them commandeered to feed their own troops. This problem was endemic in the Venezuelan wars; by itself, it would not have determined Bolívar to begin the war again. O'Leary definitely states that the misery of the troops, though real enough, was but a pretext. The rape of Maracaibo had given his armies immense advantages. Nor had this been the only breach of the armistice the patriots had exploited.

This situation was, however, not without difficulties. Owing partly to the obstacles described above, partly to Páez' usual malingering, the concentration of horses and cattle required for the campaign did not proceed as it should and Bolívar himself had to throw his energy into the task. The brake which obstacles opposed to his speed always raised a fever of irritation in his impatient soul; this, in turn, gave rise to temperamental changes in his views and action. His plan of campaign was wise and even brilliant. La Torre had about five thousand men between Barquisimeto and Valencia and another two thousand, under Correa, covering Caracas to the east.

Bolívar had Páez on the Apure and Urdaneta in Maracaibo, while he himself was in Barinas. Giving Bermúdez orders to attack and take Caracas before the end of May, he had arranged for the western troops to concentrate in Mijagual, from where he could threaten Guanare or San Carlos. Nervy and worried, however, Bolívar countermanded this plan on April 24th, just a week before Urdaneta and Bermúdez were supposed to begin their respective operations and sent half of his own troops, about three thousand men, to reinforce (and perhaps to tie up) Páez. Three days later he returned to his original plan; and, so far as he was concerned, his guard occupied Guanare by May 22nd–25th, 1821. Meanwhile Bermúdez had advanced from Barcelona on April 28th, and had entered Caracas on May 14th, 1821, while the Spaniards took refuge in Puerto Cabello. On May 20th, having defeated Correa himself and taken prisoner Brigadier Cires, one of the best Spanish commanders, Bermúdez occupied La Victoria.

This victory of the eastern commander threatened La Torre in the rear. La Torre had hoped to defeat Bolívar in Guanare before dealing with Bermúdez, against whom he held Correa's force to be sufficient; but in the evening of May 19th, 1821, he heard in Araure of the fall of Caracas. He decided to alter his plan: to defeat Bermúdez, to keep Urdaneta at arm's length and to cover Puerto Cabello. Leaving 1,700 men in Araure to watch over Bolívar, La Torre withdrew towards San Carlos with 2,800, and ordered his other commanders to be ready for a retreat. Bolívar heard the news on May 24th and at once decided to transfer the meeting point forward to San Carlos, for he foresaw that La Torre would recede to Valencia. On June 2nd he entered San Carlos at one end while the 1st and 5th Spanish divisions were still leaving it at the other. But while he advanced, Bermúdez had lost Caracas to Morales (24.v.21). Nevertheless, since Bermúdez' force remained in being and the Spanish commander had to tell off strong contingents against him, the part assigned to the eastern armies in Bolívar's plan remained as fertile as he had foreseen it. On June 7th, 1821, Páez joined Bolívar in San Carlos. On May 11th, Urdaneta had liberated Coro very much against the wish of the Coreans, who rebelled and declared for Spain as soon as Urdaneta had marched on; and while his second, Escalona, dealt with the rebellion, he arrived in Barquisimeto on June 13th with the 2,000 soldiers he had put together in Maracaibo. He was unable to continue owing to illness, but his force, led by Rangel, arrived in San Carlos on June 16th, 1821.

While he waited, Bolívar wrote a screen of words to hide his movements. On April 12th he had written to La Torre: " I cannot but feel grateful for the generous actions with which you accompany your letters, not only with regard to our prisoners but also with your proclamation concerning those who are not prisoners. So liberal a behaviour is the most characteristic feature of the glorious change in our principles." (This " glorious " would certainly be alien to La Torre who was naturally humane and not, like Bolívar, inclined to do good for the sake of " glory ", i.e., good opinion.) Bolívar went on to propose a new armistice with conditions which, for the time, La Torre could not accept. Nor was it Bolívar's intention that he should. Now, in San Carlos, while both Urdaneta and Páez were drawing closer, he put forward proposals on which he himself wrote to his Home Secretary (5.vi.21): " If he accepts them, we shall gain a thousand advantages in public opinion and finally destroy the morale, every day smaller and weaker, of his troops in proportion to their loss in physical force owing to the frequency of desertions. If, on the contrary, our proposals are rejected, we shall have gained time to gather together all our columns here. In any case, our offer is a gesture of generosity calculated to puzzle the enemy, and possibly to make him conceive false operations based on false principles, for he may attribute to weakness what is only due to policy." Soon after this, he rode forward to Tinaco to meet Colonel Churruca, sent by La Torre to suggest an armistice, pending news from Revenga and Echeverría; for the Spanish general had information that the Madrid government was so desirous of peace that it would even go to the length of recognizing Colombian independence. It is thought by Venezuelan authorities that Bolívar rode forward because he did not want the Spanish colonel to observe his own strength, Bolívar's intention at the time being to goad La Torre into an offensive out of the position he occupied in Carabobo. But La Torre, for obscure reasons, did not move.

The first loss the royalists suffered was that of Tinaquillo, which Colonel Silva stormed on June 19th, 1821. As a result of this setback, the royalists withdrew from the hill of Buenavista, on the road from Tinaquillo to Carabobo, which enabled Bolívar to use the direct road instead of that through El Pao, far more broken and easy to defend. Illogically enough, that was the way La Torre expected him to take and he had strongly fortified and defended the narrow entrance from Tinaquillo. But though Bolívar did come from Tinaquillo, he naturally refused to dash his troops against such strong defences. On June 24th, 1821, at dawn, he arrived in Buenavista. The Spanish army occupied the plain of Carabobo, five miles away. The Spanish artillery commanded the valley which Bolívar had to take to reach the plain. But through the hills to the west, a roundabout unfrequented path would, he was told, allow his cavalry to debouch into the plain on the rear of the Spaniards. He sent Páez' cavalry round that way so that he should arrive on the right flank of the Spaniards while the main force was engaged in the centre. Páez did so and after a difficult march reached a hilltop from which they could see the Spanish army two miles away. He rode impetuously on only to find himself sunk one hundred and fifty feet below the plain where the battle was raging. The Spaniards took advantage of his rash action and defended stubbornly what was now, for Páez, a hill above his head. The *llaneros* endeavoured to climb the hill but, unable to resist the Spanish fire, had to turn back. The British Legion drew the Spanish fire on itself while Páez' men reformed behind their stubborn defence. The coolness and determination of the British at this critical hour saved the day, which Páez' rashness and inexperience had nearly lost. " Steady, boys! "—quietly warned Farrier, their colonel, when the Spaniards advanced on their line, and he was one of the first of the many who fell dead. So protected, the youthful Páez (he was about twenty-five then) realized his error and sent back his men farther north, where, under cover of brushwood and trees, they were able to reach the plain and thus to attack the Spaniards from the rear, at the moment when Bolívar's main force arrived by the direct road. La Torre, whose force of about five thousand was half Peninsular and half Venezuelan, lost control of his troops. Some units disobeyed orders, others feared being taken prisoner, others deserted, so that the royalist army was soon in a rout—all but the regiment of Valencey whose retreat towards Valencia impressed Bolívar's men. La Torre lost his army and the independents won the cities of Valencia and Caracas.

4

The battle of Carabobo opened to Bolívar the gates of Caracas where he arrived on June 29th, 1821, in the company of his general staff and at the head of Páez' division. The city was deserted, for, despite Bolívar's proclamations, the memory of past excesses drove many to emigration and many more to hiding in the woods. Those who remained came forward and received him with joy. They were few, however; and Bolívar seems to have employed the short time he allowed himself in Caracas to reconquering his popularity there. " In order to effectually secure the affections of the people of Caracas, which he knew were ever on the wane "—writes the anonymous seaman—" H.E. ordered a succession of entertainments to be prepared for their diversion, and for several days there was nothing to be seen or heard of but dancing, feasting, and bullfighting. The theatre was made use of and all the officers who possessed any dramatic taste were requested to form themselves into a company, and thus several pieces were respectably performed."

All was not, however, verses and roses. Bolívar had still a number of military problems to solve: that of the Spanish troops he had allowed to escape from Carabobo, the cavalry of Morales, which had hardly fought at all, and the two regiments of infantry which had effected a masterly retreat; the rebellion of Coro, whose population remained obdurately pro-Spanish; his long dreamt-of expedition to the south, the conquest of Quito and . . . San Martín. He dealt with the first by a mixture of force and diplomacy. From Caracas (1.vii.21) he wrote to Colonel Pereira, the Spanish military commander, offering a capitulation. Pereira had first decided to cross the mountain to Ocumare and carry on the war in the high *Llano*; but when, with his eight hundred men, a host of emigrants and six hundred prisoners of war, he was already in Valle ready to march, he received orders to go instead to Puerto Cabello. This was but another of the consequences of the split in the Spanish army. The majority of the Spanish officers did not want to carry on the war. Carabobo had been fought half-heartedly. Pereira wandered about the mountains till his food gave out, and returned to La Guaira, where Admiral Jurieu, in command of three French ships, acted as mediator. Bolívar's proposals were generous, and Pereira accepted a capitulation (4.vi.21). Bolívar also proposed an armistice to La Torre, who had succeeded in concentrating over 4,000 men in Puerto Cabello and had also a force in Cumaná, while a number of the regular units were still fighting for Spain around Coro and in the hilly country about Caracas. Bermúdez besieged Cumaná, which finally capitulated (16.ix.21)—thus clearing the eastern part of Venezuela from Spanish troops. Coro, by the end of the year, was still in Spanish hands. Not so Cartagena, where Montilla, who knew that on July 24th most of the Spanish officers were to attend a masonic festival, seized his opportunity and so weakened the defences that Torres, the Commander, accepted his generous terms and delivered over the city, after a siege of 14 months (11.x.21).

5

Bolívar organized Venezuela under republican forms but on a strictly military basis. He knew full well that the actual boss would be Páez; but this leader of cowboys was not yet presentable, nor reliable either. So Bolívar put at the head of the State as Vice-President his henchman Soublette, an urban and even urbane general; while Páez, promoted to the rank of general in chief, was given the military and civil command over the Province. Though the wisest and perhaps the only possible in the circumstances, this arrangement was to lead to many a military setback, for Páez, who held Soublette in contempt as a soldier, proved unco-operative. Meanwhile, Soublette's authority was to suffer much at the hands of Bolívar himself. The law whereby all property belonging to émigrés was to be expropriated began to be applied at once. Aware of its bad effect on public opinion, Soublette decreed that the estates were to be administered by the heirs or relatives of the émigré owners in conjunction with the State. Bolívar butted in. This was a matter he never overlooked, for it touched on the very basis of his power, the gratitude of the military class for favours received. The true originator of the system had been Páez, as Bolívar explains through his Secretary for War, Briceño Méndez, to the Minister of External Relations and Finance, on June 20th, 1821. "When General Páez occupied the Apure in 1816, finding himself isolated in the midst of enemy country, with neither backing nor hope of obtaining it anywhere, and unable even to count on the general opinion of the territory on which he operated, he found himself bound to offer to his troops that all the estates that should fall to the government in the Apure would be liberally handed round to them. This was, among others, the most effective way for compromising those soldiers and increasing their numbers, for they all ran to share in similar advantages. General Páez was so convinced of the importance of this matter that, when he submitted and recognized the authority of H.E. the President, then Supreme Chief, he demanded nothing but the ratification of that offer. H.E. was not able to refuse it, and deeming it very fair in its aims, if too wide and unlimited, he decided to alter it and to extend it to the whole army. H.E. had the satisfaction of being justified by events, since the other divisions felt inspired by the same incentive as that of the Apure."

That Bolívar was thinking of not leaving in Páez' exclusive hands such a powerful lever of pretorianism is obvious. In an official letter, dated Bogotá, January 18th, 1821, Briceño Méndez reminds Páez that the handing round of national estates is to be reserved exclusively for the President, who only delegates this power to him insofar as his own army is concerned and only to the extent that the value of the estates handed over is to cover salaries due by law. Any concession beyond such limits is to be reserved for the President. (It was picturesquely added that, in Bolívar's mind, such concessions were meant to enable the military to strike root in the land, and Páez was to see that they were not wasted away, as they generally were, in gambling.) All this explains the alarm with which Bolívar heard of Soublette's easy-going ways with the estates confiscated after the battle of Carabobo. By decree signed in his own estate of San Mateo (27.vii.21), he revoked Soublette's order, dismissed the *Fiscal* who had been appointed, and ordered that no change of ownership should be granted without consulting him while he resided on Venezuelan territory. The decree actually said: " If in this way the requirements of the army are not met, H.E. is at a loss to know how he is to keep an army, since the people refuse to lend any help."*

For the first time for many years, he was able to visit his house at San Mateo, in the neighbourhood of Caracas, where he stayed a few days. His private affairs were in utter chaos; but he was not the man to worry about that. In a note to the Congress of Cúcuta, he informed the government that, at the instigation of his family and friends he knew in need, he had drawn 14,000 pesos from the Treasury of the Republic, in 1819, in Bogotá; he reminded Congress that the law on the distribution of national estates assigned 25,000 pesos to him, and that as President he was entitled to 50,000 a year from 1819. He concludes that he gives up all those rights and declares himself satisfied with the 14,000 drawn in Bogotá. Congress accepted the gift. Meanwhile he requested Congress to return to Don Francisco Iturbe the property confiscated from him as a Spaniard, thus showing how he remembered the man who had allowed him to escape in 1812; and he offered his property in holocaust instead. At about the same time, he gave powers to his nephew, Anacleto Clemente, the eldest son of his elder sister, María Antonia, to act for him in his private affairs— a choice events were not to justify. Anacleto, who was a captain in his army, was given permission to marry Rosita Toro, of a family, Bolívar wrote to her mother, " I love more than mine ". Bolívar wrote to Anacleto about a sugar mill in which both were interested (18.ix.21): " I bought it from its owner, although he was an Islander who happened to be in the

---

*" To Colonel Aramendi "—writes the Venezuelan historian Gil Fortoul—" (and like him were Rondón, Leonardo Infante and many more) the estate of a Spaniard had to be given at once. How he would manage it may be judged by a few of his deeds. In 1817, he killed by a few strokes of his sword Major Calixto García in Achaguas; in 1818, he came to grips with General Cedeño in San Fernando; Bolívar sent him to Angostura under arrest, but he escaped and returned to Páez' army." The story proceeds apace but, for our purpose, is clear enough already. Bolívar wanted to buy men from Páez to be sure of his Venezuelans while he conquered the south.

Canaries [and therefore, he means, he need not have paid for it]. I paid nothing, not even the first instalment, because the time for paying had not come when the Spaniards returned and its owner occupied it again, and in his hands it was ruined. Should the State confiscate it, no one has a better claim than I to acquire it for its value, which must be next to nothing, since the slaves cannot be sold to me nor bought by me, and since there is no sugar cane on the estate. You, as my proxy, must take all necessary steps, should the State confiscate it, for I shall take it on account of my future salaries; but if the State does not confiscate it, I have no money to buy it with and therefore its owner must keep it." For a man who had just conquered his country and was omnipotent, this is an admirable certificate of disinterestedness.

This same letter goes on to say: " I hear that your mother must have returned already, and that Juanica [his other sister] must also have come back. I shall be glad that the two unfortunate women are back in their homes." Juana, the younger, had been living in Guayana since 1817, after a period of exile in the Antilles. María Antonia, the elder, had a history that can be read in the petition she sent to the King from Havana, on February 14th, 1819, at the time her brother was crossing the Andes. She begins by stating that " nothing is more contrary to my way of thinking than the principles brought in by those fanatical adepts of the illusory freedom which they proclaimed . . . and which have led to the absolute ruin of those beautiful and fertile provinces. The misfortune (for so, Sire, it may be called) of having my brother at the head of the revolutionary faction could not but excite against me the hatred and abomination of the opposite persuasion." She then describes herself " hated by both sides ". When Bolívar entered Caracas for the first time, she saved many royalists by hiding them in her house in Macarao, at the western end of the valley of Caracas. Then came the battle of La Puerta (15.vi.1814) and, she writes to the King: " An absolute decree of the insurgent government in its last hours determined this horrible situation, ordering the emigration of all the inhabitants, the only solution the government thought calculated to save their lives. But this general decree was particularly applied to this petitioner, to whom an order was imparted by the government, backed by military force, which made her leave Caracas with all her family and go to La Guaira under the escort of a corporal and five soldiers."

María Antonia goes on to relate how she had to settle abroad (in Curaçao) with her four small children and a half-witted, epileptic husband. On August 28th, 1816, she had requested the *Audiencia* of Caracas (then under the Spanish régime) to order the restoration of her property. The *Audiencia*, she writes to the King, " declared me a loyal servant and faithful vassal of Y.M. and invited me to return to that country at my convenience and resolved that my property should be set free and returned to me ". She had appointed proxies in Caracas, but nothing had been done, perhaps, she says, because they had not dared to act for a person with so hated a name. She asked for a royal pension pending the recovery of her estates. The King granted her one thousand pesos a year; and on a second petition to the King (27.ii.20), Ferdinand VII, on June 24th, 1820 (exactly one year to the day before the battle of Carabobo), doubled the pension to two thousand pesos. One year later she returned to Caracas now freed by the " fanatical adepts of an illusory liberty ".

The return of his most recalcitrant sister sealed for Bolívar his hour of triumph. He was now, without dispute, the hero of Venezuela. The hour had come for him to raise his ambition much higher, and, turning his eyes to the Andes, he prepared to meet San Martín " in some angle of Peru ".

PART II
THE SUN OF EMPIRE SETS

CHAPTER IX

SAN MARTÍN ENTERS LIMA

I

WITHIN a week of his victory at Maipo (2.iv.1818) San Martín had again taken to the road towards Buenos Aires to prepare the next stage: the march on Lima. In June he was busy enlisting the services of the secret societies to that end. He was promised 500,000 pesos in Buenos Aires in June and denied them in Mendoza in July. He resigned on September 1st. On September 16th, the sum was offered again. He confiscated all the private money come from Chile to Buenos Aires and paid it with drafts against the government. That was his way. Unable to cross the Andes till the spring, he spent the winter preparing his plan. On October 29th, 1818, he arrived in Santiago, having crossed the Andes for the fifth time. But the march on Lima was in fact, as he knew only too well, " the sailing on Lima "; for the deserts of the Chilean North were an even more effective barrier to an army than the Andes. The general was therefore in quest of a fleet.

The Chilean Republic had founded its navy by seizing the Spanish brig *Aguila*, 220 tons, which had entered Valparaiso after the battle of Chacabuco, trusting to the Spanish flag the patriots kept waving over the forts as a bait. Armed with sixteen guns she became the *Puyrredón* in honour of the Director of the United Provinces, and was put in command of an Irishman, Raymond Morris. Just before the battle of Maipo, the frigate *Windham*, 800 tons, of the East India Company, had been bought in Valparaiso and become the *Lautaro*, less in honour of the Araucanian chief than in that of the Lautaro Lodge which, writes Mitre, " secretly governed the political life of both countries ". She was put under the command of George O'Brien and J. A. Turner, and the marines on board under that of Captain William Miller. " The officers "—writes Mitre—" were all either English or Americans, who spoke not a word of Spanish, so that, with the exception of Miller, not one of them was able to give a command to the Chileans who composed the greater part of the soldiery." As was often the case in Colombia, these men were all fighting as patriots, but of what *patria* it was not quite clear. They, nevertheless, fought magnificently; and on April 27th, 1818, a daring attack on the two Spanish ships that were blockading Valparaiso cost O'Brien his life and the *Lautaro* heavy damage, but forced the Spanish ships to raise the blockade. It is significant that the Chilean ships disguised themselves as British men of war, not excluding the flag, until they were close to the Spaniards. A Captain John Higginson replaced O'Brien in command of the *Lautaro*. Then the brig *Columbus*, sixteen guns, commanded by the American

403

naval officer C. W. Wooster (or Worcester), turned up and was bought, captain and all, by the Chileans, who renamed her *Araucana* (very symbolical, this naming as Araucanians those who in fact were Yankees). Finally, in August, 1818, the biggest ship that had ever navigated those waters was sent from London by San Martín's agent, Alvarez Condarco, and became the *San Martín*, commanded by William Wilkinson.

This navy was put under the nominal command of an " Admiral " of twenty-eight, Manuel Blanco Encalada, who had served in the Spanish navy and fought with distinction in Maipo. The youthful admiral led a fleet to Talcahuano, and, as he sailed under the Spanish flag, he was able on the way to receive despatches meant for the Spaniards that enabled him to attack Talcahuano (which he entered flying the British flag), and after a truly brave action, take possession of the Spanish ship *María Isabel* and later of five other transport ships. The Chilean Navy was in being.

The man then turned up who was to use it brilliantly. Thomas, Lord Cochrane, Earl of Dundonald, was one of those super individuals whose stature and fire burst through human institutions. He out-nelsoned Nelson by all the Drake that was in him. His eye for gold was as keen as Drake's. He writes himself in his Memoirs that " despite romantic notions " about " disinterestedness and patriotism ", the first and all-important motive why seamen fight is prize money. Born in Scotland on December 14th, 1775, he entered the navy under his uncle, the then Captain Cochrane, and, in 1800, owing to his brilliant service in the Mediterranean, was given command of H.M.S. *Speedy*, " a burlesque on a vessel of war ", of 158 tons and 14 four-pounders; yet it soon became " the marked object of the Spanish authorities " and with unbelievable daring took a Spanish frigate, the *Gamo*, of much larger tonnage and crew. After one of his well-rewarded cruises, he stood for Parliament for Honiton and was defeated by a candidate who paid five pounds per vote; elected later, he became in the House a severe critic of the corrupt ways then prevailing at the Admiralty. In April, 1809, owing to a quarrel with his chief, Lord Gambier, he fell out with the Admiralty. Bored and unemployed, he speculated. But while speculating, disaster befell him. On February 20th, 1814, at midnight, a Colonel De Bourg arrived at the Ship Hotel at Dover, and, with discreet indiscretion, let it be known that he was a confidential messenger to inform the government that Napoleon had been killed by the Cossacks, that the allied armies were advancing on Paris and that peace was at hand. He hastened on to London and his first call there was at Lord Cochrane's house, where he procured a coat and hat and vanished. On March 7th the Committee of the Stock Exchange published an advertisement offering a reward of 250 guineas for the discovery of the person who had perpetrated a hoax whereby many hundreds of thousands of pounds were realized by Lord Cochrane's uncle, Mr. Cochrane Stone. Lord Cochrane lost his rank in the navy and his mandate in Parliament and was sentenced to prison. After several fines and escapes, he met Alvarez Condarco, San Martín's agent, who offered him the command of the Chilean Navy. He accepted in May, 1817, sold his property and left for Santiago—but not till August 15th, 1818.

He reached Valparaiso on November 28th, 1818. Wooster (or Worcester) and two English officers who enjoyed serving under a young and inexperienced chief like Blanco Encalada, engineered a cabal to elbow Cochrane out; but Blanco Encalada patriotically submitted to the new Admiral's authority, and the storm blew over. On December 28th, 1818, Cochrane hoisted his flag on the *O'Higgins* (née *María Isabel*). On January 16th, 1819, he sailed out of Valparaiso towards Callao with five ships, and disguising two of them as American ships then expected there, entered the port. Fog and calm deprived him of the success his boldness deserved. He settled in San Lorenzo Island to prepare firebrands to set fire to the Spanish fleet, which he tried, with no success, on March 22nd; but, on March 24th, 1819, he succeeded in seizing a sloop and several merchantmen and withdrew to Huacho, where he met Blanco Encalada. He left him blockading Callao and sailed away to reconnoitre the coast of Peru and spread the news of the coming of San Martín. He returned to Valparaiso on June 16th, 1819, and sailed again on September 12th for Callao, where he sent a flag of truce to the viceroy bidding him to send out his ships, nearly twice as strong, to fight at sea. He wasted many days in Callao attacking the Spanish fleet with an invention of his, a rocket, which was a failure; and sailed on to Guayaquil, where he captured two large Spanish vessels (28.xi.19). Then, with the flagship alone, he resolved to capture Valdivia, the strong port of the south of Chile, entered it under Spanish colours, signalled for a pilot, made prisoner his escort of an officer and four soldiers, got all the information he wanted, sailed to Talcahuano for reinforcements, returned, landed and took Valdivia, thus reducing the royalist hold of Chile to the Island of Chiloé in the extreme south (January 28th–February 6th, 1820).

2

The year 1819 was spent in Spanish America under the expectation of the expedition Spain was preparing to liquidate the rebellion. It was to consist of 40 transports conveying 18,000 to 20,000 men, escorted by 35 men-of-war and 29 gunboats. San Martín proposed to Chile to attack it in the Atlantic with the Chilean fleet under Cochrane. The Scot rejected the plan. This was the first encounter between two men born to misunderstand each other. San Martín spent months astride the Andes, so to speak, con-spiring, corresponding, intriguing in his obscure and spidery way, trying to save his great idea of the march on Lima from the dangers that threatened it. That Spanish expedition was soon to vanish, since on January 1st, 1820, Riego, one of its commanders, led his regiment to the revolution that forced Ferdinand VII to accept the constitution of 1820. But San Martín was ordered by the government of Buenos Aires to concentrate all its armies in the capital. He would not be moved. He decided to disobey. By November 9th he had appraised O'Higgins of his intentions to insist on the Lima expedition, happen what might in Buenos Aires. By December 7th, 1819, he committed it officially to Rondeau. He was very ill. At the beginning of January, 1820, as Riego in Spain was putting an end to the dreaded expedition, and as the government of the United Provinces sank into sheer anarchy, San Martín crossed the Andes on a stretcher carried by four men.

On March 26th, 1820, he delivered into Las Heras' hand a thrice sealed envelope, to be opened only in the presence of all the officers of the Expeditionary Force. On April 2nd, 1820, in Rancagua, Las Heras opened the envelope before a meeting of all his fellow officers: it contained San Martín's resignation and a request that the officers elect another chief. Again the classic style of Cortés in Veracruz. The officers re-elected him; and so this general of the United Provinces was able to negotiate with O'Higgins with a semblance of democratic authority. Nevertheless, San Martín's step was more pretorian in form (if not in substance) than Bolívar's many resignations and even than the act of Cortés at Veracruz; and Mitre rightly points out that it was " a revolutionary act which, by the vote of a military congress, sanctioned an act of open disobedience, tying up an army to the person and to the designs of its general ".

On April 19th, 1820, the general thus " plebiscited " by his officers threatened O'Higgins with his resignation if the funds for the expedition were not ready within a fortnight. This urgency seems to have been due, at least in part, to a desire to counteract Cochrane's own plans for a similar expedition under his own command. The fiery admiral had already asked for a landing force in July, 1819. In the end, San Martín won, and was appointed commander-in-chief (6.v.20). The Chilean government went so far as to think of dismissing Cochrane, which San Martín prevented; but was glad to see San Martín go north. Eight thousand men to keep were a heavy charge on the empty Chilean Treasury; and then, as a Chilean author put it: " San Martín was a land Cochrane, with this difference that, though he did not ask for money, he did ask for power. The ambition to wield power, this sin of great men, was paramount in the Liberator [San Martín] to whom we owe so much. . . . Had not Peru then been in the hands of the Spaniards in 1820, no one knows what would have become of Chile, for it is difficult to calculate the outcome of discontent and ambition."

From 1810 to 1816, Peru had been governed by a great viceroy, Don José de Abascal, an old man, but honest, firm and competent. Thanks to his gifts, Lima had become the centre of resistance to the two rebellions, that coming from the north-east and Venezuela and that from the south-east and Buenos Aires. When he left for Spain in 1816, Chile was again in Spanish hands, and the rebellions of Venezuela and of Buenos Aires had been stemmed and thrown back on their bases. His successor, General Pezuela, was an absolutist; but his chief commander in the field, General Laserna, was a liberal. There were in the Spanish army a number of Peruvian generals who fought on the Spanish side because they happened to be absolutist by political conviction; while most of the Spanish generals, who were liberal, fought against the Peruvians as Spaniards, but against their own political convictions.

The liberals of those days had an incurable liking for secret societies. Aware of this, San Martín, soon after Chacabuco, had begun to honeycomb Peru with secret agents. By the end of 1819, the country was thoroughly leavened by such people, thanks mostly to masonic lodges. The Viceroy knew it; his Spanish officers also, most of whom were liberals and many freemasons. The royalist army split into an absolutist group, predominantly Creole and garrisoning Upper Peru with about 7,000 men, and a liberal and predominantly European group of officers, mostly in Lower Peru with about 8,000 men. The news of Riego's *pronunciamiento* and of Spain's return to the constitutional régime reached Lima when San Martín's expedition was expected to land any day, and came further to complicate an already complex situation. On September 17th, 1820, the Viceroy Pezuela, on orders from Madrid, solemnly swore and proclaimed the constitution of 1812. Nine days earlier, San Martín had landed in Pisco with his liberating army of Chileans and Argentines conveyed by Englishmen and Americans.

3

On August 20th, 1820, Lord Cochrane, on board the *O'Higgins*, led the expedition out of Valparaiso in twelve transports conveying an army of 4,430 officers and men; and six transports laden with war material. San Martín, as Commander-in-Chief, sailed in the rearguard on board a ship bearing his name. The escort, of eight warships, was manned by 1,500 officers and men, 600 of whom were English. San Martín landed at Pisco, about 140 miles south of Callao (8.ix.20), and occupied it without opposition, as well as the rich valleys above it; he mounted his cavalry with local horses, enlisted into his infantry the negro slaves of the estates and sent inland a reconnoitring expedition of a thousand men under Arenales, a European Spaniard in the service of the Independents. San Martín issued a proclamation in which he praised the Spanish constitution for Spain but rejected it for America. He had forestalled the instructions received by the Viceroy to negotiate with the dissidents on the basis of the constitution, or at least to arrange for an armistice while their representatives went to Spain. The Viceroy wrote to San Martín (11.ix.20), who answered (16.ix.20), accepting the negotiations. The parley began at once at Miraflores, in the suburbs of Lima. By October 1st it had failed; and while Arenales carried out a daring raid through Ica, Huamanga and Huancavelica, San Martín re-embarked his troops (28.x.20) and, much to Cochrane's disgust, instead of attacking Lima, landed at Ancón, about 25 miles north of Callao (30.x.20).

It is typical of Cochrane's attitude that the time spent in negotiation for a peace between brother peoples appealed to him as lost " in idleness ". All these changes, landings and delays exasperated the fiery Scot. He decided to attempt a daring enterprise—to wrench the Spanish warships from under the 250 guns of Callao. On the night of November 5th, 1820, he led the attack on the *Esmeralda* whose crew, caught unawares, was overpowered and let the ship be lost after a stubborn fight. Cochrane and his second, Guise, being wounded, they had to be content with this victory, in itself a magnificent exploit which ultimately led to the control of the Pacific by the Chilean fleet. Cochrane saw Lima in his hands. But San Martín, unmoved and untempted, led his army, not to Lima, close by and stunned, but to Huacho, to the north, where he arrived on November 10th, 1820.

The proposals for an armistice and the triumph of the constitutionalists in Spain had caused a wave of desertion in Peru, as in Colombia. Arenales, after his successful raid, had joined San Martín at Supe, on the coast. Suddenly, the Marqués de Torre-Tagle, a *Limeño*, who governed Trujillo for the King and had been in secret correspondence with San Martín for some time, arrested the bishop, a royalist, and declared for independence (24.xii.20). The whole coast from Guayaquil to the neighbourhood of Chancay, almost at the gates of Lima, was thus in the hands of the Patriots. San Martín had taken a dangerous position in Retes, near Chancay, and the Spanish generals decided to attack him there; but the royalist army was honeycombed with spies and San Martín, warned in time, decamped and withdrew to Huanca. This Spanish setback, on top of so many others, added impetus to a move to get rid of the Viceroy, who was accused of nepotism, irresolution and blindness to the fact that he was surrounded by disloyal persons, such as the Intendant Arrieta, his own private secretary and Generals Llano and La Mar, members of his war committee. The episode was but a part of the struggle then going on in Spain. The liberal officers disliked a reactionary Viceroy. On December 16th, 1820, the Municipal Council of Lima had officially asked the Viceroy to reopen negotiations with San Martín; whereupon a group of officers sent him a request that all military officers who had signed the municipal petition should be removed from their commands. Rumour had it that the petition had been favoured by the Viceroy himself. On January 29th, 1821, the army officers met in Aznapuquio camp, near Lima, and demanded the resignation of the Viceroy and his replacement by General Laserna, who, with the utmost reluctance, had to accept the onerous succession on the same day. Among the many consequences of this dramatic event, one of the first was the failure of an expedition which had left Huacho on January 30th, 1821, to take possession of Callao, in secret agreement with some royalist generals who had promised to hand it over to them.

4

Laserna appointed as Commander-in-Chief Canterac, a Frenchman in the service of Spain. His chief idea was to try to negotiate a peace and, if this failed, to carry on the war in the heights of Upper Peru. In February, 1821, the new Viceroy wrote to San Martín suggesting negotiations. San Martín accepted and the delegates met in Retes. The meeting failed. Laserna, however, complied with his instructions and again invited San Martín to negotiate (9.iv.21). By then the two armies were being decimated by yellow fever; but San Martín, faithful to his plan of blockading the Viceroy in his capital, sailed from Huacho on April 27th, 1821, back to Ancón and, with his troops and the guerrillas he had organized up country, he gradually reduced the Spanish garrison to the triangle Lima-Callao-Aznapuquio. Meanwhile the parleys went on in Punchauca, about five leagues north of

Lima, where the Spanish representative began by recalling that San Martín's delegates during the Miraflores negotiations had assured the Spaniards that a solution might be found by crowning in America a Prince of the house of Spain. The discussion veered from peace to an armistice. San Martín's men, perhaps to make it fail (for they were just playing for time), demanded possession of the fortress of Callao, to be returned if and when the armistice ended. To their amazement, Laserna's men, who were also playing for time, agreed.

This led to the interview of Punchauca between Laserna and San Martín (2.vi.21), in which, after many embracings and a good dinner with toasts in no way comparable either in number or in eloquence with those of Santa Ana, between Bolívar and Morillo, San Martín proposed to the Viceroy that a council of Regency be appointed, composed of Laserna as President and two other men, one a nominee of Laserna, another of San Martín; that a Spanish Prince should be crowned constitutional King; and that San Martín should sail for Spain in quest of such a Prince, leaving his army under the authority of the Regency. Laserna was taken aback and asked for two days' reflection; meanwhile, he counter-proposed that an armistice be concluded while awaiting Madrid's answer to San Martín's plan; a line from east to west, on the Chancay river, to cut Peru into a northern part to be governed by San Martín and his army, and a southern part to be governed by the Spaniards under the Crown; Laserna to sail to inform the King and San Martín, if he still desired a Spanish Prince, to sail on the same ship. San Martín rejected this plan.

Was he sincere? It seems that he was. But, before discussing the point, a glance at New Spain, then re-becoming Mexico, might be useful. By 1820, the separatist rebellion in New Spain had been crushed by the royalists; mostly because it had taken from the first a proletarian anti-rich turn, which had made the wealthy Creoles more cautious than in South America. For this reason, the revolution of 1820 in Spain determined a wave of separatism in Mexico, led this time by the conservative and reactionary classes, for fear lest the revolution of Old Spain should bring about radical changes in the social structure of New Spain. When the order to promulgate the Spanish constitution arrived in Mexico, the European Spaniards split into Serviles and Liberals, and the Creoles into Monarchists and Republicans. It seems that Ferdinand VII wrote to the Viceroy, Apodaca, a letter announcing his intention to come to Mexico to free himself from the thraldom of his Liberals. But fear of a military Liberal *pronunciamiento* forced the Viceroy to swear the constitution (31.v.20), and he went so far as to cease calling himself Viceroy and to display the title of Supreme Political Chief and Captain General. The newly acquired freedom of the press and the elections of constitutional municipal councils set up a ferment throughout the country. A conspiracy was afoot to form a government to rule Mexico under the Spanish Laws of the Indies, but independent of Spain, so long as Spain was governed by the Liberal constitution. The conspirators in search of a leader thought of Don Agustin Iturbide.

Son of a Spaniard and a Mexican Creole (like San Martín of a Spaniard and an Argentine Creole) of a good and well-to-do though not very wealthy family, Iturbide was born on September 27th, 1783, and was therefore two months younger than Bolívar. He entered the army very young and espoused the royalist cause at the beginning of the revolution. He was a good fighter, though cruel and grasping. He had rapidly risen to the rank of Colonel. At this time, when he was convinced that without an army command it was impossible to lead a revolution, the Viceroy appointed him to the command of the southern army (9.xi.20). This implied authority over an area from Tasco and Iguala in the Province of Mexico to the sea; and enabled him soon to unmask his intentions, which he did in a proclamation to all Mexicans, proposing to them his famous *Plan de Iguala* (24.ii.21). With the utmost deference for Spain, Iturbide proclaimed as bases for his revolution: 1.—The Catholic religion and no tolerance of any other; 2.—Absolute independence of the kingdom; 3.—Ferdinand VII, or a Prince of his family, to be Emperor of Mexico. Why Emperor and not King? Possibly because Montezuma was then supposed to have been an emperor. This proclamation cut the ground from under the royalists. In July, 1821, Iturbide was acclaimed Liberator of the Fatherland. In August, the new Viceroy, O'Donojú accepted the *Iguala Plan*.

The pattern of these events reveals a certain analogy with that of the events of Colombia and of Peru. In the three cases, a leader has to react to the offer of a liberal constitution on the part of Spain. In the three cases the Spanish constitution is rejected; in Peru and in Colombia, because the claims of independence are stronger than those of liberalism; in Mexico, because liberalism is repudiated and independence is sought by the black party as a guarantee against it. But, while Bolívar will not hear of a Spanish King, San Martín, no convinced Republican, believes a Spanish King might be a good solution; and so does Iturbide. Seen in the general setting, therefore, San Martín's proposal appears as a sincere endeavour to stabilize a traditional, courtly and royalist Peru at a time when his own country, endeavouring to develop republican institutions, sinks into anarchy. The proposal failed because the local authorities could not carry with them the loyalty of the officers, who demanded that the matter of independence should be reserved for the Central Government of Madrid to solve—in which they were right. The negotiations hung on, for it suited San Martín that they should. Lima became hungrier and hungrier. The Viceroy decided to evacuate it. This was the best he could do, for two reasons: his army was running to waste owing to the epidemic then devastating the lowlands, and would recuperate in the Sierra; and Upper Peru was still the stronghold of royalism in America.

5

Captain Basil Hall, who met San Martín on board the *Montezuma*, off Callao, on June 25th, 1821, describes the South American leader in a page worth quoting: " There was little, at first sight, in his appearance to engage the attention; but when he rose up and began to speak, his superiority was apparent. He received us in very homely style, on the deck of his vessel, dressed in a large surtout coat, and a large fur cap, and seated at a table made of a few loose planks laid along the top of some empty casks. He is a tall, erect, well-proportioned, handsome man, with a large aquiline nose, thick, black hair, and immense bushy, dark whiskers, extending from ear to ear under the chin; his complexion is deep olive, and his eye, which is large, prominent, and piercing, is jet black; his whole appearance being highly military. He is thoroughly well bred, and unaffectedly simple in his manners; exceedingly cordial and engaging, and possessed evidently of great kindliness of disposition: in short, I have never seen any person, the enchantment of whose address was more irresistible. In conversation he went at once to the strong points of the topic, disdaining as it were, to trifle with its minor parts; he listened earnestly, and replied with distinctness and fairness, showing wonderful resources in argument and a most happy fertility of illustration. Yet there was nothing showy or ingenious in his discourse. At times, his animation rose to a high pitch; when the flash of his eye, and the whole turn of his expression, became so exceedingly energetic as to rivet the attention of his audience beyond the possibility of evading his arguments. This was most remarkable when the topic was politics. But his quiet manner was not less striking, and indicative of a mind of more than ordinary stamp: he could even be playful and familiar; and whatever effect the subsequent possession of great political power may have had on his mind, I feel confident that his natural disposition is kind and benevolent."

San Martín explained his position and Basil Hall noted it down: " The contest in Peru, he said, was not of an ordinary description—not a war of conquest and glory, but entirely of opinion; it was a war of new and liberal principles against prejudice, bigotry and tyranny. People ask why I don't march to Lima at once; so I might, were it suitable to my views. I do not want military renown; I want solely to liberate the country from oppression. Of what use would Lima be to me, if the inhabitants were hostile in political sentiment? I have been gaining, indeed, day by day fresh allies in the hearts of the people. I have been equally successful in augmenting and improving the liberating army; while that of the Spaniards has been wasted by want and desertion. The country has now become sensible of its own interest, and it is right the inhabitants should have the means of expressing what they think." So far, San Martín, on his own procrastination, as if it were he who controlled it and not it him. On July 5th, the Viceroy issued a proclamation announcing his intention to leave the city. At once a move to run away on the part of the population set in. Basil Hall landed and rode from Callao to Lima. " It was with no small difficulty that I could make head against the crowd of fugitives coming in the opposite direction: groups of people on foot, in carts, on horseback, hurried past; men, women, and children, with horses and mules, and numbers of slaves laden with baggage and other valuables, travelled indiscriminately along, and all was outcry and confusion. In the city itself the consternation was excessive." But in fact Laserna had taken adequate precautions and San Martín behaved with so much talent and tact that all went smoothly, and he entered the city on July 12th, 1821.

CHAPTER X

SOUTHWARD

I

" TAKE for the Congress "—Bolívar wrote in April, 1821, to Gual, his Finance Minister—" the money that comes for the army, for in a short time hence half of the soldiers will be dead; and the other half will need nothing whether victorious or defeated . . . and it is not fit that Congress should have to be dissolved for lack of funds." These words, in which the superior anarchy of the dictator mingles with the exasperation of a generous and high-minded man fettered by meaner persons, reveal that Bolívar was in earnest about the Congress which, according to the constitution of Angostura, had to meet in El Rosario de Cúcuta to organize the Republic of Colombia. His standby for that Congress, Roscio, was dangerously ill and died soon after. On March 8th, 1821, from Trujillo, Bolívar wrote to Azuola to take charge of the government as Vice-President and gave him instructions worth quoting: " Try to open Congress as soon as possible with a very *simple* but noble speech; with neither studied phrases nor old-fashioned words. Much less still any praise for me; and as for the order of subjects, you will try to follow the speech delivered by Ferdinand VII before the Cortes, or by the President of the United States before Congress." Then he flourishes no less than eight reasons why he must refuse the presidency of the new Republic; and, since the State is still mostly military, suggests as President, Nariño, Urdaneta or Santander. Before any of these ideas could be carried out, Azuola also died.

On April 21st, 1821, Bolívar wrote from Barinas to Nariño,* now his definite choice for Vice-President: " The swift end of your predecessors must be a little melancholy for you. Heaven forbid that you follow them to the fatherland of the dead." He again expresses his keen desire that the Congress meet at once, and with his admirable common sense and rapid style, describes the circumstances which make of Colombia " instead of a social body a military camp ", and explains why he has not been able to remedy this, one of his reasons being: " Because there are many considerations to bear in mind in this astounding chaos of *patriots, Goths, egoists, Whites, coloured men, Venezuelans, Cundinamarcans, republicans, aristocrats, good and bad people,* and all the gang of categories into which the several classes subdivide, so that I have had many times to be unjust out of policy and I could not be unjust without impunity." He again insists that he does not want to be President and adds that in his opinion " the President must be an army man and a Cundinamarcan, and the Vice-President a civilian and a Venezuelan ". He repeats the same ideas in a confidential letter to his friend Peñalver, adding details that lend much sincerity to his utterance. He hated

* Nariño, a Granadino of Bogotá, not to be mistaken for Mariño, a Venezuelan rival of Bolívar.

administration. " Know that I have never seen an account, nor ever wanted to know what is spent in my household; as for diplomacy I am not fit for it either, because I am excessively naïve, very often violent." What then ? Did he really suggest that he should not be elected ? The truth is more complex: he was sincere in his desire to be left alone and free from minor worries, but he would have been mortally offended if Congress had not done violence to his desire and elected him.

Nariño was then fifty-six. He had recently returned from a long stay in Europe, mostly in Paris. He belonged to an older generation, that of Miranda and of Zea; and though he had suffered harsh prison loaded with irons in Cartagena and in Cádiz for years, his long absence in Europe was looked upon askance by his enemies among the independents. Bolívar, however, who wanted a Granadino as Vice-President and could not afford to do without Santander at the time, overrode all opposition (possibly under-estimating it) and had him elected. Difficulties of all kinds delayed the meeting when Nariño arrived in Rosario de Cúcuta towards the end of April. Only thirty-seven members had arrived out of ninety-five; so that the quorum of two-thirds was not available. Nariño decided to overlook this provision and convened the inaugural meeting for May 6th. " Rosario de Cúcuta, though small, is well built and compact ", writes the anonymous seaman. " It has several good and wide streets, branching at right angles from a plaza in its centre, at one corner of which, passing under a large, heavy stone archway, is seen the Government House, which is a commodious edifice, forming three sides of a square, the principal chambers and the hall of audience being in the centre. The whole is but ill contrived, as the stables are in the body of the building, and only separated from the best room by a thin wall, and the passage leading to them is under the suite of apartments generally occupied by the Governor. It surrounds a large paved court, in which stands a fountain. A little way farther down the street which leads from the plaza next to the government house, is the hall of the Senate, as it was then termed, a low building with an arched roof, in which the Congress were to assemble."

From the first, the Congress of Cúcuta revealed a tension between lawyers and generals; and the feeling against the two " tyrants ", Bolívar and Santander, was keen. Possibly to impress the military with its might, the Congress gave itself the official title of Majesty, by which it had to be addressed. Wrongs were well balanced. Bolívar and Santander were executive officers, impatient of restraint by lawyers of no obvious patriotism. Bolívar wrote to Peñalver (one of his closest friends, a man to whom, finding him in destitution, he gave over all his own silver and jewels): " I know of no advantage the second Congress had over the third; what I do know is that in Cundinamarca every member was given two hundred pesos, and in Venezuela, the Vice-President says he has been ruined by congressmen. . . . One single member received one thousand pesos." He is even harsher on the thieving that went on in Mérida. To Gual, his Finance Minister, he wrote on the same day: " You [in plural, i.e. ' you, civilians '] cannot imagine exactly the spirit of our military men. [The word *military* shows what was in his mind. Otherwise, he would have written: *troops.*] These are not those you know; they are those you do not know: men who have fought for long, who believe themselves highly deserving and humiliated and miserable, and without hope of gathering the fruit of the *earnings of their spears*. They are resolute and ignorant *llaneros*. Be convinced, Gual, that we stand on an abyss, or rather on a volcano ready to explode. I am more afraid of peace than of war, and with this I give you an idea of all that I do not say and that cannot be said."

2

While this letter was being written in Guanare, the Congress of lawyers for which it was really meant had been sitting for eighteen days without making much headway. It had begun by considering an official letter from Bolívar (Barinas, 1.v.21), in which, unable to bear any longer the pressure of criticism, the Liberator-President refused to consider himself President of the Republic now regularly constituted and added: " because my craft as a soldier is incompatible with that of magistrate, because I am tired of hearing myself described as a tyrant by my enemies ". He swore " the blindest obedience ", and by a swift return of his will ended: " but if the Sovereign Congress, as I fear, persists in my continuing as President of the State, I here and now renounce for ever the glorious title of citizen of Colombia and leave, in fact, the shores of my fatherland ". Congress was too well aware of the fact that all Bolívar meant was that his critics should be quiet; and so a dignified answer was sent, of course refusing to admit his resignation. Congress, however, though willing to take overbearing ways from Bolívar, was not ready to accept them from Nariño. He began by suggesting a removal of Congress to Bogotá; which offended the Venezuelans; then, he presented to Congress a draft constitution of his own. He was so much in a hurry that, in his letter to Congress (19.v.21), he asked permission to submit his draft in a serial form " as he gave a final shape to his notes ". Congress sent it to the constitutional commission where it was shelved. Nariño felt somewhat disgruntled.

During the preliminary debates before the actual constitution of the Congress, when many of its members " in solemn taciturnity, for three or four days successively, sat without uttering a syllable ", other events of a lesser import enlivened the usually sleepy streets of Rosario de Cúcuta. The picturesque figure of General Devereux and the handsome figure of Mrs. English, General English's widow, turned up in the hope of obtaining a reward or a redress for their services or grievances. Devereux (writes the anonymous seaman, who was there), " having calculated upon being well received and entertained at the expense of the government, had brought a numerous staff "; but Nariño " refused at once to acknowledge him as an officer of the Republic, and with his characteristic brutality ordered his servants to expel him from the house ". Nariño prevailed upon Mrs. English to accept his hospitality, but " made overtures to her of the basest description, and finding that she persisted in refusing them, turned her into the street at midnight with brutal violence without the means of procuring a shelter. Devereux . . . made this an excuse, and called the Vice-President out. But the challenge was no sooner received than he was, by the orders of Nariño, placed under close arrest, till the pleasure of the latter was known concerning him. The next day he was conveyed to one of the cellars which had always been used as receptacles for charcoal, and here he was kept 47 days upon no other support than bread and water, and so scant was the allowance of the latter, by the express desire of the malignant Vice-President, that, in order to allay the excessive thirst created by the particles of dust flying about his dungeon, he was obliged to drink the water he washed in."

The incident was at once seized upon by Nariño's enemies, chief among them the Santander group. Devereux appealed to Congress, which, after long and heated discussions, decided that the Irishman be given better quarters and every opportunity to clear himself, including free communications with Congress. Nariño refused to acknowledge the right of Congress to interfere in executive matters and declared that " in such matters he would never obey ". A motion was presented asking for the removal of Nariño from office, while Nariño sent Devereux to Bolívar under escort. Opposition to him went from bad to worse. He was ill with intermittent fever and dropsy and in the end resigned and was replaced as Vice-President of the Republic by a congressman, José María del Castillo.

3

Congress was able to devote its time to legislation and to the study of the constitution. But here also, lawyers and warriors were at loggerheads. On June 13th, 1821, Bolívar wrote from San Carlos to Santander: " In the end those gentlemen, the lawyers, will succeed in getting themselves proscribed from the Republic of Colombia as poets were from Plato's. Those gentlemen believe that the will of the people is their own will, not realizing that in Colombia the people are in the army." Painting then with forcible realism the motley population of the country, he concludes: " Don't you think, my dear Santander, that those legislators, more ignorant than wicked and more presumptuous than ambitious, will lead us to anarchy and later to tyranny and always to ruin ? So that if it is not the *llaneros* who carry out our extermination it will be the suave philosophers of a legitimised Colombia." Experience was withering his Rousseau-Rodríguez dreams (" this policy "—he says in the same letter—" which is certainly not that of Rousseau, will in the end have to be carried out so that those gentlemen do not destroy us "). The letter shows also that he was beginning to be frightened of Páez, the leader of those *llaneros* from whom he expected " extermination ".

Congress debated the liberation of the sons of slaves, the constitution and the appointment of the chief officers of the State. The law on the slaves was partly a compromise, partly a confession by Bolívar that he was unable to carry out his promise to Petion. This promise had been sincere, and he had carried it out as soon as he landed in Carúpano in 1816—but, of course, only on paper. The Congress of Angostura had not dared sanction Bolívar's generous decrees, for fear of losing support among the powerful landlords. Bolívar returned to his idea after the victory of Boyacá, ordering that all slaves who would enlist in the army would *ipso facto* become free; but on this point he met with stubborn opposition in New Granada. Finally, after Carabobo, he asked the Congress of Cúcuta to agree to a proposal, this time more modest, that all sons of slaves born in the future should be free (14.vii.21). Congress complied with his wishes, and on July 19th voted the law freeing all sons of slaves to be born in the future and levying a tax on successions in order to purchase and free a number of adult slaves every year. One of the considerations Congress had in mind was that there were many Venezuelan slaves or ex-slaves (no one knew exactly their legal status) fighting in Bolívar's army.

On July 12th, 1821, the Congress of Cúcuta formally adopted the union of Venezuela and New Granada to constitute the Republic of Colombia. Quito was left out altogether, for, though very much in Bolívar's mind, its destinies were still in the balance. As for the constitution, it differed but little from that of Angostura. It provided for a Senate, elected for eight years, and a House of Representatives for four; the electors to possess at least five hundred pesos of income, or to be men of a liberal profession; a President and a Vice-President elected for four years; a council of government composed of five secretaries and a member of the Supreme Court; article 128 granted the President full powers in such parts of the country where he happened to be waging war. This article had been written to fit Bolívar's will. Against the wish of some Venezuelans, notably Miguel Peña, who desired the capital to be in Pamplona, Cúcuta, or Maracaibo, Congress voted it to be in Bogotá, with an eye on the future annexation of Quito. Freedom of the press, the final abolition of the Inquisition and a somewhat limited religious tolerance were also adopted. Religious houses of less than eight friars or nuns were abolished, a measure aiming at acquiring for the State the untold wealth of fine buildings left empty, for educational purposes; the head tax on Indians was also abolished with the well-meant intention of wiping out an inferiority laid on them since the conquest.

Bolívar kept away from all this, partly because he was busy with his war plans, partly out of policy. " I shall say nothing "—he wrote to Santander from Tocuyo (16.viii.21)—" for I have no time, I mean about Congress, constitution, vice-presidents and such other tricks of Cúcuta and vicinity. These titles might make me write a ream, did I know how to write and had I time. More still, not even with words could I say half of what comes to my mind on such miserable miseries on which our life and soul depend, not to speak of our honour and glory." Congress decided to elect a President and a Vice-President, and that the elected persons should be required to come to Cúcuta. Bolívar was elected President by fifty votes out of fifty-nine; and (after a struggle with Nariño) Santander was elected Vice-President by two-thirds of the votes cast. Couriers were sent to both, and the one sent to Bolívar brought him pressing letters from Castillo, the President of the Congress, and from Gual, urging him to come. He answered them in his usual way, refusing, pointing out the dangers of putting all the powers in the hands of one man and the pressing requirements of the military situation; but what he resented was that the lawyers had smuggled into the constitution a clause forbidding the President to carry out the duties of the Executive Power when in the field, and reducing him therefore, when on active service with the army, to the position of Commander in Chief. In the end he came to Rosario de Cúcuta, where he arrived on September 29th, 1821. Both he and Santander expressed dissatisfaction with some of the articles of the constitution, but both swore it on October 3rd.

4

Master now of Venezuela, Bolívar turned his attention to that south which had haunted his mind ever since the star of San Martín had rapidly risen on the firmament of Spanish-American history. Throughout the preceding year, 1820, he had been urging action, swift action, in the south. But there were difficulties. Quito was a centre of republican opinion and activity; but Popayán, the Oxford of Colombia, was wavering, and Pasto and Patia were two hotbeds of royalism blocking the way towards Quito. " To struggle with Patia and Pasto "—Santander wrote to Bolívar on February 21st, 1820—" I hardly know what policy to follow; they are terrible peoples, the wall against which all our efforts since 1811 have always, always come to grief. They know admirably how to wage a partisan war. I am going to give orders for the chief leaders, rich, noble or plebeian, to be hanged in Pasto, and the rest of the population to be transported away to Venezuela, so that no one is left but the women and children, who can do no harm to us for the present and may change their minds." This attitude of exasperation and fear will afflict all the republican leaders, not excepting Sucre himself usually so self-controlled; and will rise to an almost diabolical fury in the tense soul of Bolívar. Pasto and Patia, with their obstinate resistance, were the obstacle that dammed the flow of his impatient energy, eager to conquer the south. Pasto and Patia had to be destroyed.

Their territory was as difficult to master as any in the southern continent. From Popayán, the chief city in the upper valley of the Cauca, an affluent of the Magdalena, broken country had to be crossed to reach the upper valley of the Patia while it still flows east of the Andean ridge, before it turns it to flow into the Pacific. The city of Pasto lies in a formidable position south of the river Juanambú. The land had always been rich, notably in cattle, with which it used to feed Quito farther to the south, as well as Popayán to the north. Under the Spaniards, the region was partly dependent on the Kingdom of New Granada, partly on the presidency of Quito. When the Spanish General Calzada had to leave Santa Fe in haste after the battle of Boyacá, he withdrew to Popayán and later to Pasto, whence he wrote for help to the President of Quito, Aymerich. With these reinforcements he surprised in Popayán (24.i.1820) the patriot leader Antonio Obando who, in the midst of hostile populations, had been kept in the dark about his coming by forced marches. Popayán was taken, and, though Obando was saved by a lady who hid him in her house, despite her royalist convictions, most of his men were murdered in cold blood by the ferocious Don Basilio García, a Spanish colonel in Calzada's army. The eyewitness who tells the story—one of the few García left alive owing to his youth, provides two side-lights on the war to the death. " I shall be fair to Calzada; he was not a cruel man; these murders were committed without his knowledge. After we passed Quilichao, Don Basilio tried to camp as far as possible from Calzada's tent to indulge unopposed in his ferocious instincts." Speaking of a Spanish sergeant, Dávalos, who hunted victims for Don Basilio, the same witness writes: " This man was one of the eight hundred Spaniards whom Piar took prisoner in San Felix and who, tied together two by two, back to back, were speared and thrown into the Orinoco. Dávalos survived, his companion's body having kept him afloat, and the stream led him to the delta where an Indian cured him: he hated us to death."

Both Santander in Bogotá and Bolívar wherever he happened to be kept their minds busy with the south. Bolívar wrote to Santander (5.ii.20) to instruct Salom " to prepare everything necessary for a big expedition against Pasto and Quito ". Santander wrote to Bolívar (17.ii.20) somewhat optimistically: " I doubt not but that Quito may be taken more easily than any other spot. Opinion is very favourable to the Republic and the regular forces the enemy has do not go beyond twelve hundred men." But two days later he wrote: " There is no longer any doubt that the enemy has taken the valley of the Cauca. . . . This, my people of Bogotá, made up of terrified patriots, of egoists and of dissenters, keeps me uneasy. Everybody is afraid. I find even my secretaries discouraged and lacking in firmness as soon as there is a slight setback."

Santander, however, within a few weeks of the defeat of Popayán, had set on foot a force which he entrusted to General Manuel Valdés, with Colonel Mires as his second in command. Valdés took the field at once and defeated Calzada's troops under Colonel López at Pitayó, north-west of Popayán (6.vi.20), an action again in which two hundred Englishmen of the Albion regiment decided the issue. The eyewitness quoted above provides a personal touch illuminating as to the human relations in these campaigns. When appealed to by a Spanish officer to save the life of this young prisoner caught in an earlier battle, Don Basilio García had signified his consent by drafting him into a royalist regiment which happened to be composed mostly of Spaniards. The prisoner managed to get himself transferred to a Creole unit, where he was serving when the battle of Pitayó began. He crossed a ravine under fire and came upon a troop of red coats, English volunteers fighting under Valdés, who nearly shot him dead. But a republican officer recognized him and soon after he was attached to Valdés' general staff, providing valuable information on the Spanish force.

5

His victory enabled Valdés to recover Popayán (16.vii.20). But the city was empty, for its inhabitants had fled, having had a deplorable experience of his brutality. He moved on southward, but, recalled northward by

Santander, lost a good opportunity to destroy his opponents, weakened by desertion, disease and general anarchy, and fell himself a victim to the same ills. Meantime, Calzada was in trouble with his rival . . . the bishop. Don Salvador Ximénez was " small in person, but well made, with a good-natured open countenance and lively grey eyes ", and when Colonel Hamilton visited him in 1823, he looked about sixty, but walked " with as much activity as a man of twenty-five ", and " in conversation was very animated and full of fun ". Born in Málaga, he was in Spain when Napoleon invaded the Peninsula, and like many other priests of his day, he became a leader of soldiers, was given a commission as a colonel and fought against the French. Ferdinand VII rewarded him with the see of Popayán, then worth twenty thousand dollars per annum. When Bolívar threatened his diocese, he left Popayán for Pasto and led the resistance of the fierce Pastusian royalists, fighting as in his younger days in Spain, " carrying a cross in one hand and a sword in the other, and fulminating excommunications from the pulpit against all those who carried arms against him ".

The bishop, though, was no fanatic. When Hamilton visited him, he introduced to Hamilton " a Pastusian lady, whose name I forget, who had the management of his household: the lady was about forty, rather handsome, and a fine figure. There was a story current at Popayán at this time, that the lady's husband had paid a visit to the worthy bishop to demand his wife, but that Sir Illustrissimo became indignant at the request, and in his passion gave the poor man a violent kick, threatening, if he was again troublesome about his wife, he would excommunicate him." Hamilton enjoyed his stay with this somewhat unorthodox prelate. " The bishop's family dinner shewed that the lady, who sat next me at table, understood well the culinary art, according to the Spanish taste. We did justice to some old Málaga wine, which was excellent; but I was amused to observe, that the bottle always made a quick countermarch to the bishop. After dinner we walked through a charming little summer-house, a few hundred yards from the house, which the bishop had recently built, and fitted up with much taste; a fine clear stream of water was murmuring close by the side, and the surrounding scenery was pretty and gay; in short the whole was like anything but a monk's cell. The country house of the bishop was tolerably large, he had built a wing of some extent, which consisted of ground-floor apartments for young men who belonged to the College at Popayán. The bishop had purchased a considerable estate with the house, which he intended to leave at his death to the Public College of Popayán; he was a liberal public-spirited man."

This warlike bishop, after duly excommunicating all his enemies, turned his attention to his own side. He disliked Calzada. When Manuel Valdés won the battle of Pitayó, the bishop left for Pasto where he organized a Junta under his own control, to limit Calzada's authority, and succeeded in scaring Aymerich to the point of making him come all the way from Quito to Pasto, where he gave Don Basilio García the command of the troops and had Calzada arrested. " Urge Valdés to act speedily "—Bolívar wrote to Santander on May 7th, 1820—" and to send us many slaves to re-stock our northern army." And three days later he instructed Valdés, through Santander, to harass the enemy if he could not engage a battle, an idea he repeats again and again. Events, however, had proved too strong for what both Santander and Bolívar had in mind. As early as January 20th of that year (1820) Santander had written to Bolívar: " We await you in March. If you do not come south, Lima will never fall under the power of the Republic. I note a kind of slowness in San Martín's operations." And on May 10th, 1820, Bolívar wrote to Santander: " A propos of Quito, should we defeat Calzada in Neiva, let our troops not stop till they reach Guayaquil." He added these curious words: " In that city there must have occurred a revolution." What had put in Bolívar's mind that idea that a revolution had occurred in Guayaquil? Was he engineering it? The revolution did occur, but five months later.

On October 9th, 1820, Guayaquil declared its independence. From whom? From everybody. Owing to its peculiar situation, on the coast of the Kingdom or Presidency of Quito, yet separated from it by the height of Quito above the sea (9,000 feet) as well as by its distance, Guayaquil had always occupied an ambiguous position between the viceroyalties of New Granada and of Peru. Spanish legislation assigned it to Peru for military matters and to New Granada for civil affairs. As late as April 6th, 1820, a Royal *Cédula* of June 23rd, 1819, in that sense had been posted up in Guayaquil. The revolutionary Junta sent emissaries to Cochrane, San Martín and Bolívar; and San Martín lost no time in sending two ambassadors, who found that the Junta, elected by the city, was led by the poet José Joaquín Olmedo, a man educated in Lima and of strong Peruvian sympathies. Cautious, however, the Junta went no further than declaring Guayaquil free to join whatever " association " it pleased. The Colombian party, led by three Venezuelan officers who had served in the Spanish army, organized a force, marched on Quito and were defeated at Huachi (22.xi.20); under pressure from the Peruvian party the leaders were imprisoned. Negotiations were begun to put Guayaquil's independence under the protection of San Martín, then not yet master of Lima, though fairly strong on the coast owing to Cochrane's naval strategy; and agreements were concluded to that effect. But the defeat which the Argentine Colonel José García underwent in Tanizahua on January 3rd, 1821, led San Martín's com- missioners to leave the city; and Guayaquil, in order to protect itself from the royalist troops, had to flood the surrounding plains.

6

Arms and their fortunes being then the chief factors that moulded political situations, the power of Colombia might then have made some headway, but for another defeat which Manuel Valdés suffered at the time. The armistice of Santa Ana had been concluded on November 26th, 1820. On December 15th, Santander wrote to Bolívar: " If Valdés has forsaken his dreadful slowness, the news of the armistice may not reach him until he is at least in Pasto. How slow the man is! I have written to him again to advance anyhow, quickly, flying, to enter the territory of Quito, but I have told him nothing, nothing about the armistice." To which Bolívar added orders (5.i.21) to attack Pasto " even though he had no force but his aide-de-camp ". Valdés had sallied forth from Popayán (2.i.21), " short of every supply ", most of his officers barefoot. Before reaching the river Juanambú, he received the news of the armistice as well as instructions from Santander to make sure that he passed the river before the armistice boundary commissioners arrived. Valdés did so and even went on towards Pasto in the hope of taking it, but was heavily defeated and his troops dispersed by a strong body of Pastusians (2.ii.21). When the fugitives, having recrossed the river, arrived in Salto de Mayo on February 4th, they found a new commander there awaiting them.

Infuriated by the resistance of the Caucans, Bolívar had written to the governor that " to punish them and make them serve as an example for the selfish cowards who may want to follow them ", he decreed: " 1.—That every man between 15 and 35 present himself to take arms within three days; 2.—Those who fail to do so shall be shot wherever they are and in whatever state they are; those not caught shall be outlawed, their goods confiscated and their families arrested; and 3.—By the end of the present month [January, 1821] 4,000 men must be gathered in Popayán, armed and supplied to march on Pasto ". On January 11th, 1821, he appointed Sucre to succeed Valdés. Antonio José de Sucre was then thirty-one. He was born in Cumaná, of a wealthy Creole family, and in 1802 began mathematical studies with the intention of becoming a civil engineer. He served from the first in the revolutionary army under Miranda in 1811–12 and in the eastern armies in 1813. From 1816 to 1817 he was chief of staff of the eastern army. The most faithful to Bolívar among the Venezuelan leaders, he seems to have managed to keep intact both his freedom of opinion towards Bolívar and his friendship with other men; and to his intelligence, authority, competence and courage, he added a rare gift in those days, that of a general ability to manage human beings which made him a successful negotiator. After Boyacá he was appointed head of the general staff of the whole army and he was one of the three negotiators of the armistice with Morillo. " Who is that bad rider coming to us ? "—asked O'Leary as he was arriving with Bolívar in Cúcuta. And Bolívar answered: " He is one of the best officers in the army; he knows as much of the profession as Soublette, is as kind as Briceño, as clever as Santander, as active as Salom. I am resolved to bring him out convinced that some day he will vie with me."

Bolívar did not hear of the revolution of Guayaquil till the middle of December, 1820, in Barinas. On January 10th, 1821, he wrote to Rocafuerte from Bogotá: " I am on my way to Quito and Guayaquil. General Valdés precedes me with the vanguard of the southern army and General Sucre will follow him closely. I am sending General Mires with supplies for that patriotic province." He was in fact sending one thousand rifles and ammunition. Not for a moment does he seem to have worried about the armistice. Yet Mires' expedition was a flagrant violation of clause one, which bound the parties to engage in " no hostile action in the whole extent of the territory in their possession during the armistice ". True, Aymerich, the President of Quito, had refused to include the Province of Guayaquil in the armistice; but the Province in which the reinforcements were prepared was so included. Sucre did not feel happy about the situation, and he wrote to Bolívar (27.iii.21) suggesting that all help to the Guayaquil independent party should be withdrawn. Bolívar passed the matter on to Santander, who wrote to Sucre that the treaty of Trujillo contained no clause preventing the Colombian government from " lending help to foreign peoples ", an argument that could hardly be convincing to either the head or the heart of a man like Sucre, since Bolívar took precisely the view that Guayaquil was part of Colombia and had no right to secede. Santander went on to say: " For these reasons the Government of Colombia has been ready to help the city of Guayaquil with troops and other supplies. I have therefore the honour to declare to Y.E. on behalf of H.E. the Liberator President that, since this help is no infraction of the armistice of Trujillo, we cannot agree to withdraw it as you suggest." It had been Bolívar's intention to go to Popayán to organize the southern campaign while the north was quiet; but on hearing of the defeat of Huachi and of the factions in Guayaquil, he changed his mind, and, regardless of the armistice, he decided (21.i.21) to send Sucre with full powers to negotiate the incorporation of Guayaquil in the Republic of Colombia. Sucre's powers were to include one thousand infantry men from the Cauca army.

When Sucre had arrived in Salto de Mayo to take over from Valdés, his heart had ached for the sufferings of the fleeing remnants of the army beaten in Juanambú, and he had given away all his luggage to the destitute officers. He gave orders to retreat to El Trapiche, where he proposed to reorganize the army with a view to breaking through to Pasto towards Quito. But he wrote to Santander that the plan to force a way to Pasto should be given up altogether, for the Pastusians would always win; and that Quito should be taken from Guayaquil by an army conveyed there by sea. Santander had passed this plan on to Bolívar (25.ii.21); and while Bolívar did not actually adopt it, his own decision, taken one month earlier, of sending Sucre with one thousand men to Guayaquil, was bound to appeal to Sucre as a step in the right direction. This order reached him towards the beginning of March, 1821. On April 2nd he sailed from Buenaventura on the corvette *Alejandro* with five hundred and fifty men, and another one hundred in a sloop. The voyage was difficult and slow and Sucre and his men landed in Guayaquil on May 7th, 1821. On the 15th he signed with the Junta an Agreement which granted a *de facto* recognition of the authority and protection of the Republic of Colombia over Guayaquil, and, what was more to the point, conferred on Bolívar any powers he might need to defend the city against aggression and authorized him to include it in all treaties he might conclude.

The first claim of Guayaquil was for reinforcements. Aymerich had about three thousand six hundred men in the heights. Sucre could hardly count on more than fourteen hundred. Strangely enough, Sucre, who had come to reinforce a " rebel " Guayaquil during the armistice, destroyed his own moral basis for defending his action by sending his aide-de-camp Borrero to Quito to request that the armistice should in this case be prorogued till June 24th, arguing that Guayaquil was now under the protection of Colombia. His purpose was to gain time for more reinforcements to arrive. These had been promised as late as April 4th, 1821, by Santander, who still assured Sucre that he was trying to spare the army a campaign in Pasto. But within a month Santander had forgotten Sucre's advice and was reinforcing Torres, the commander in Popayán, for an attack on Pasto; and Sucre had to be content with about 280 men, one hundred of them British, whom he received in June. Nonplussed, and fearing Aymerich, Sucre asked San Martín for help (13.v.21), while writing to his government: " If the enemy do not take Guayaquil, we have under our eyes an army [San Martín's] which desires the possession of this province and which, under the pretext of sending six hundred to a thousand men to defend it, would make us lose it for Colombia."

Though defeated by Don Basilio García (15.vii.21), Torres tried to force his way through Pasto; but, beaten by the royalist guerrillas, disease and desertion, he had to abandon even Popayán which was occupied by the royalists (12.ix.21). At the same time, Sucre had been in danger in Guayaquil; for the royalist Venezuelan Colonel Nicolás López, recently converted to the independent cause and given a command in Sucre's force, engineered a royalist rebellion with the help of the ships in the harbour, which would have succeeded but for a leakage of liquor to the sailors which led to a leakage of the news. Sucre was firm enough to quell the rebellion and shrewd enough to draw from it more military authority. Aymerich, who, hoping to take the city in conjunction with López, was approaching from Guaranda, decided to march on despite the failure of the plot, while his lieutenant González advanced also from Cuenca. Sucre manoeuvred boldly, attacked and defeated González three leagues from Yaguachi (19.viii.21), and, turning against Aymerich, forced him to retreat without fighting. The victorious general returned to Guayaquil where enthusiasm ran so high that, had he so desired, he might have achieved the accession of Guayaquil to Colombia there and then; but he was a wise liberal and respected the weight and slowness of local opinion. Perhaps he thought also, as a good general, that while the royalist force was in being, his victory was not certain. And in fact, on September 12th, González defeated him so heavily at Ambato that nearly all his force was lost. He was, however, able to reorganize his forces behind the labyrinth of flooded lands in Babahoyo. Meanwhile, Don Juan de la Cruz Mourgeón, the new Viceroy of Santa Fe, arrived from Spain to take command over the Spanish troops. He had been a brother in arms to San Martín in the Spanish war of independence With eight hundred men, he landed in Atacamas and " after a prodigious march through a deserted wood of a hundred kilometres crossing over the Andes ", he arrived in Quito on December 24th, 1821.

CHAPTER XI

THE BATTLES FOR QUITO

I

THE policy and doings of San Martín in Peru are hard to explain under the generally accepted view that he was a disinterested liberator of countries in distress. His outstanding actions as soon as the independence of Peru had been declared were to assume, not merely military command, but complete sovereignty over the country, and to organize a fierce persecution of the Spanish population. Let his chief biographer describe both: " When independence was declared, a deputation from the *cabildo* called on San Martín to offer him the government of Peru and to request him to accept it in the name of the people. He answered with an enigmatic yet earnest and kind smile that, being in possession of supreme command under the power of necessity, he would retain it if he thought it in the public interest, avoiding all inopportune meetings of congresses and committees which could do nothing but embarrass the management of public affairs with vain arguments, so delaying the victory of independence which should come before everything else." This is a remarkable utterance. True, Peru was then still at war; true there were still important troops in the Sierra. But if the country could not be trusted to govern itself with its " congresses and committees ", what was the point of " liberating " it ?

There are two answers to this question. The first is personal ambition. It is surely too easy to dismiss personal ambition in San Martín on the ground that he said he had none; and that he gave up the game in Guayaquil. *San Martín was as deeply influenced by Napoleon as Bolívar.* That the results were so different argues nothing against the identity of the cause. When the sun rises, its light reveals a pine and an oak, which remain, of course, different, though the light that manifests them is the same. San Martín disobeying the government of Buenos Aires, keeping silent over his plans, dominating the Chileans, quarrelling with the irate Cochrane, and " enigmatically " taking absolute power over Peru without accepting it from the *cabildo*, is an image of Napoleon reflected in a secluded lake, just as Bolívar is an image of Napoleon reflected in a swift river. The liberation of Peru was a conquest. San Martín felt very much like a monarch; as can be seen in the sudden passivity into which he left fall what then should have mattered most: the prosecution of the war; while turning to the setting up of the Order of the Sun, or to decrees on titles of nobility, or to the organization of his political household. None of these activities mattered at all then. What mattered was the Spanish threat. The fact that San Martín, neglecting it, turned his mind to stars and marquisates, shows that when he assured his hearers or readers that he had no ambition and would withdraw when all danger was over, he was misleading them. But San

Martín was honest.   Unlike Bolívar, in order to deceive others, he had first to deceive himself.

The second answer to the question: " why liberate Peru if it is not to be trusted to govern itself " was " independence ".   Under the words on the " tyranny " of the Spaniards lived a reality, that of a continent that, having rooted the whites to its soil through the native Indians, demanded total allegiance from the population that lived on it.   That in its turn explains the persecution of the Spaniard.   Mitre honestly recognizes that it was " rigorous and violent ", that it broke the solemn promises made by San Martín to the Spanish population, and that " public safety did not justify so much rigour ".   But Mitre again accurately explains the roots of the measure in San Martín's " instincts as an American Creole and as an enemy of the race " of the Spaniards.   Now, San Martín's father was a Spaniard. He was, therefore, expressing his mother, who was a half-caste.   The Order of the Sun, invented and founded by San Martín, manifests both these two urges: an imitation of the *Légion d'Honneur*, it reveals San Martín as an imitator of Napoleon; and the choice of symbol, i.e. the throwback to the Inca mythology, reveals his *mestizo* resentment.   Miranda *redivivus*, save that Miranda, having no Napoleon to imitate, modelled himself on European monarchs, mostly the King of England, disguising him as an Inca at the impulse of his *mestizo* blood.

This completes the parallel between the southern and the northern hero of South American emancipation; for Bolívar also hated Spaniards and persecuted them with a passion that would have been insane had he not shared with all his countrymen of the time the blood of the native peoples. What gave both Bolívar and San Martín that strong anti-Spanish passion was the three centuries of Indian dispossession which circulated in their veins with their mothers' blood; and the fury of it, far more vehement than that of any pure Indian, came from the clash of the two bloods within; from the duel between oppressor and oppressed, dispossessor and dispossessed, inside the same skin.   These, then, were the two impulses which drove San Martín and Bolívar: Napoleonic ambition and *mestizo* vindictiveness.   The first spelt dictatorship; the second liberation from the Spanish yoke.   The second made them brothers in arms; the first made them adversaries.

2

In the race for Lima, so far, San Martín was the winner.   When he entered Lima (12.vii.21) Bolívar was still in Valencia celebrating his victory in Carabobo, and for him " the south " was still more a hankering than a reality.   Jockeying for positions had already begun, however, as the presence of Sucre in Guayaquil clearly showed.   The regiment of Numancia, whose defection from the Spanish flag to that of the independents had been such a powerful factor in the success of San Martín, was entirely composed of Colombians; and Sucre was never able to wrench it from San Martín's clutches on that account, though the regiment itself, disgruntled, asked to be sent to Guayaquil. San Martín was gradually settling down as the master of Lower Peru. On July 28th, 1821, he proclaimed its independence from Spain; and, though he looked on with his uncanny passivity while Canterac came down from the Sierra (1.ix.21) to bring food to the Spanish garrison in Callao, and let him go back practically unmolested, no sooner had Canterac turned his back, than General La Mar, a Creole soldier in the service of Spain, then in command at Callao, delivered to San Martín the port, the garrison and the parks.

We owe to this situation a vivid illustration penned by Unanúe, the Peruvian scientist who was then one of San Martín's Ministers: " In the midst of a tumult caused by a false alarm, we saw yesterday in this city at one call all the mulattoes form in one battle line and march towards the City Hall armed with knives, and the priests and friars stand on the steps of the cathedral sword in hand." This sketch should be studied by those who see in the secession of Spanish America an emancipation from " bigoted Spain ". Unanúe goes on to say: " All this foreshadows a speedy end which will be completed by the protection of our celestial Patron [St. Rose of Lima] on whose day the liberating army set foot on our shores. We celebrated it as we could, by going to the cathedral."

What the freemason San Martín thought about it we do not know; but his Fabian policy was at any rate justified by this unexpected success at Callao. The success, however, was somewhat offset by the sudden flaring up in public of the long-drawn enmity between Cochrane and San Martín. Cochrane complained that San Martín refused to pay the fleet; and San Martín demurred, arguing that he was no longer a Chilean general, but the Protector (i.e. the Chief of State) of Peru. Hearing that considerable sums of gold and silver had been deposited on board ship at Ancón for fear of the Spaniards, Cochrane seized this treasure by force and, refusing all compromises offered to him somewhat late by San Martín, paid his fleet and kept the rest—though he later returned all of it that belonged to private persons. This action did more harm to San Martín, who lost much prestige therefrom, than to Cochrane, who had much less to lose and who, after several more high-handed adventures, left the Pacific to take service under the Brazilian flag.

On October 29th, 1821, Sucre wrote a long letter to San Martín offering him Colombian reinforcements. The offer, he explained, had been made when San Martín's military situation in Lima was less " brilliant ", and the *Libertador* had been anxious about it. But when Ibarra, Bolívar's aide-de-camp, arrived in Guayaquil with the proposal, the situation had changed so dramatically that, Sucre went on to explain, " the message must be considerably altered ". Therefore, Sucre wisely limited his proposals to mere questions: 1.—Was the state of the war in Peru such that to end it for good and all the Colombian troops might co-operate ? 2.—Could San Martín undertake to send transports from Lima to fetch them out of that mortiferous climate ? 3.—Should the said troops not be needed, could San Martín favour the acquisition of transports to convey them elsewhere where they could fight for the cause ? Sucre went on to explain that it was

Bolívar's intention to " postpone the campaign of Quito to that of Peru ", and that the massed forces of the patriots should go to Peru " because the two States being free, the small intermediate sections are insignificant ".

San Martín accepted in words and rejected in deeds this gift from his adversary with a tacit *timeo Danaos*; the ships he offered never reached the Colombian ports; Bolívar was unable to send his troops in time to Panamá and the only concrete result of this negotiation was to enable San Martín to send some of his men to Guayaquil. On December 13th, 1821, the Peruvian General Salazar, in the company of General La Mar (a native of nearby Cuenca), arrived in Guayaquil, where La Mar became commander-in-chief of the troops of the city. Bolívar wrote to Sucre from Cali (3.i.22): " I put no trust in anyone over there but you, for Cochrane has discovered things which prove only too well the bad faith of some persons. This secret must be for you the starting rule of your behaviour." And the previous day: " I empower you to take all measures you may need [so that Guayaquil be not attacked]. You will come to an agreement with the government of Guayaquil. Were it however to refuse you anything you might need, you are authorized to act on your own as you may think fit. . . . You must inform the government of Guayaquil . . . that my intentions are to liberate Colombia from Tumbes to the mouth of the Orinoco; that the sacrifices Colombia has made to recover its integral independence shall be frustrated by no human power in America; and, finally, that I hope when I enter that city, the government of Colombia will have been recognized by it; for I cannot go outside the territory of the Republic without injury to my duty and to my self-respect."

3

As soon as Sucre (who, despite his insistent requests, had failed to wrench the Colombian regiment of Numancia from San Martín) received a Peruvian expedition instead under the command of Colonel Santa Cruz, he launched his campaign towards Quito. He crossed the Guayaquil (23.i.22) with about a thousand men, well armed and disciplined, and met at Saraguro (9.ii.22) the vanguard of Santa Cruz under the command of a Venezuelan officer, Luis Urdaneta, a cousin of the general of the same name. This was the first meeting of southern and northern republican soldiers. On February 14th Santa Cruz arrived with the rest of his force, just over 900 men. Sucre waited there a month, both to restore his fatigued army and to receive Bolívar's orders for the campaign. They turned out to advise caution; because Bolívar (writing on January 6th) did not yet know that Sucre had a Peruvian contingent, and because, still underestimating Pasto, he thought he would himself enter Quito province from the north in April when Sucre, attacking from the south, would make it easier for him to take the coveted capital. While in Cuenca, Sucre received an order from Monteagudo, San Martín's Minister, removing him from the command of the allied armies (25.ii.22).

The trouble came from Guayaquil. Somewhat uneasy at the look of things in that city, Bolívar had written a stiff letter (Cali, 2.ii.22) to the government of Guayaquil announcing that the Torres division of Colombian soldiers was leaving for Guayaquil, and that he himself would soon follow; and he added: " I flatter myself that the Republic of Colombia will have been proclaimed in that capital before I enter it. You must be aware of the fact that Guayaquil is a complement of Colombia's territory; that no province has the right to sever itself from an association to which it belongs, and that the laws of nature and of politics would be transgressed, were we to allow an intermediate country to become a battlefield between two strong States, and that I believe that Colombia will never consent that any American power encroaches on her territory." Salazar forwarded this note to San Martín (7.ii.22); but by then San Martín was on his way to Guayaquil and Salazar's news reached him at Huanchaco, a port in Trujillo province, on February 20th or 21st. Upset and angry, he returned to Lima where he obtained authority from his Council of State to declare war on Colombia. He was, however, content with ordering (3.iii.22) that La Mar should be sent to command the allied troops Sucre had been leading northwards against Quito, and that Santa Cruz should return to Lima. Santa Cruz informed Sucre of the fact on March 29th. Sucre refused to let him go and intimated that if necessary he would use force. Meanwhile, owing probably to Bolívar's decision not to proceed with his plans for sending Torres by sea from Buenaventura (a decision he took on January 7th but which did not reach San Martín till March) San Martín also changed his mind and sent orders to Santa Cruz (12.iii.22) to remain in Sucre's army.

What of Bolívar ? He had spent the first three months of 1822 in a squirrel-like mental and physical coming and going. He wrote from Cali to Santander (5.i.22) that the chief campaign would be by Guayaquil and that he would send the Guards by sea. " Of course, if General Sucre takes Quito, and if the Pastusians do not defeat us." And yet he reported Cauca as a land even worse than Venezuela for desertions. Two days later, he wrote that for fear of sea risks he decided to send the troops " through the infernal country of Patia . . . hostile, devastated and deadly ".* Having vividly described the obstacles of all kinds which his plan of campaign had to meet southwards by land Bolívar added: " I fear very much that after so many sacrifices and so much noise, I may not dare to expose the fate of the Republic in this region to an infallible catastrophe." His letter of January 29th is even gloomier. He does not hope to gather more than 2,000 men, and, believing the enemy will have 4,000, adds: " I am going to offer a more adventurous fight than that of Boyacá, and just out of rage and spite." Then he launches forth the most extravagant piece of military fiction. He sends his aide-de-camp, Medina, to Santander, with instructions to come back to him in Patia towards the end of February with papers he must bring " with the utmost care and with the utmost

* It seemed, however, that what made him change his mind was the arrival of Mourgeón, whose march had been so bold that Bolívar had at first refused to believe it, as he says in this letter; for on that same day (7.i.22), his secretary Pérez wrote to the Minister of War and Navy that " Mourgeón's landing with 800 (or three thousand) forced our Supreme Chief to give up the Guayaquil campaign and to fight instead through Patia and Pasto ".

noise ". These papers are all to be forgeries, to wit: A secret note on a treaty between Portugal, France and Great Britain to mediate in the Spanish-American wars on the basis of the recognition by Spain of the independence of the Spanish-American nations; a Memorandum from Zea to Bolívar reporting a talk with the French Minister of Foreign Affairs, " whose name you will have to fill in, for I do not know it ", on the same subject; a copy of a letter from La Torre to Páez asking for an armistice, in order to negotiate a treaty on orders from Madrid, and an answer from Páez accepting it; and fake copies of the *Gaceta*, especially printed with a spate of false news on alarming events in Spain, such as " Morillo's death and other trifles of this kind, and Riego at the head of an army opposing Ferdinand VII's coming to Mexico ". Having given these instructions with a schoolboy's zest, he concludes that their object is to bamboozle the Spanish commander into letting him occupy Quito while the armistice lasts. Not content with these stratagems, he sent to Quito Colonels Antonio Obando and Paz Castillo, ostensibly to exchange prisoners, but with secret instructions to find out the actual strength of the enemy and to win him over. Mourgeón, who had generously set all prisoners free without conditions, intimated to Paz Castillo (Obando having fallen ill on the way) to return, and refused to see him. Bolívar also wrote at this time to the bishop of Popayán endeavouring to disarm his dreaded opposition.

While in Popayán, Bolívar heard that the Spanish commander in Panamá had declared himself and his province for the Independents. He sent O'Leary at once with 600 men to reinforce the expedition he still wanted to send to Guayaquil. He gave O'Leary his instructions (13.ii.22) and a letter for Lord Cochrane asking for the Admiral's co-operation; and with his usual wealth of imagination, he instructed the governor of Chocó to study the possibility of opening a canal through Panamá and to order in Jamaica " the instruments he might need for such an operation "—an order the governor did not take the trouble to carry out. He solemnly communicated to Aymerich (18.ii.22) the fancies and forgeries he had received from Santander. He was more worried than ever. From Cali he issued a proclamation (17.i.22) to the Caucans, the Pastusians and the Quiteñans; to these last he devotes a paragraph which does little honour to his pen: " The Colombian Guard directs its steps towards the ancient temple of the Father of Light. Trust in hope. Soon you will see the footsteps of the rainbow following the angel of victory." A second proclamation (Popayán, 18.ii.22) was addressed to the Patians, Pastusians and Spaniards. It was crammed with promises. " No Pastusian need hold even a remote fear of punishment or vengeance." As for the Spaniards, he offered them freedom to go home in peace or to become Colombians.

4

On February 9th, 1822, a Major José María Obando, a native of Popayán, who commanded the Spanish vanguard, turned coat and reported to Bolívar. He had a deplorable reputation for cruelty and even for

brigandage.   When Bolívar set eyes on him, he could hardly have imagined
that he was meeting the man who would cast the blackest shadow on his
life and who would precipitate his death.   Obando told him that the
Spaniards had at least 3,000 riflemen and 1,000 good horsemen.   Bolívar says
so, and either he or Obando exaggerates wildly.   Bolívar discussed with the
new recruit the best way to advance so as not to fail as Nariño and Valdés
in turn had done before him; for he feared the shame of " going all the way
to Juanambú and having to return like all those who have done the same
march ".

That is exactly what befell him.   Two days earlier Santander wrote to
him: " We still have before us again the river Juanambú and Pasto, the
terror of the army, and we must believe it to be the churchyard of the
brave, for there it was that Nariño lost 36 officers and Valdés 38 whom we
shall not replace easily.   Therefore you ought to take into account Sucre's
ideas of giving up altogether the hope of conveying any army through Pasto,
for it will always be destroyed by those populations, stubborn, sufficiently
seasoned for war, and always, always victorious."   Bolívar, however, was set
on his purpose, and he marched towards Juanambú by the way Valdés had
taken, dividing his army into three columns which met in La Alpujarra
(22.iii.22).   The road he followed left the direct road to Pasto by Berruecos
on the left.   He crossed the river Juanambú on March 24th, at Burrero.

Don Basilio García, the Spanish commander, a cruel, irascible absolutist,
was disliked by his liberal officers.   When, through intrigue, he had
succeeded in ousting Calzada and taking command, the division plotted to
go over to the patriots, and would have done so but for the murders of
prominent royalists committed by Manuel Valdés when he took Popayán for
Bolívar.   García was a man of caustic, dry wit.   On March 28th, 1822, he returned to Bolívar without comment the forgeries Bolívar had sent him to
depress the morale of his officers.   Bolívar tried yet another of his stratagems:
an armistice for a week or a fortnight.   García answered suggesting that
Bolívar recross the Juanambú and wait there the answer Aymerich might
make from Quito.   But behind this diplomatic screen, Bolívar moved on
and occupied Consacá (6.iv.22).   García had to take up a position south
of the Cariaco ravine, with his left on the Guáitara river, so that Bolívar
had to fight or give up his plan of marching on towards Los Pastos, which
was his objective.

The battle began on Easter Sunday (22.iv.22) and was at first so disastrous
for the patriots that the royalists crossed the ravine, raided the camp of
two regiments (Vargas and Bogotá) and took their flags and ammunition,
with some prisoners.   The battlefield was covered with dead.   But at
sunset, Valdés with the battalion of Rifles took the height which commanded
García's right, and the royalist troops, astonished, took to flight.   Bolívar
knew nothing of this, for Valdés' aide-de-camp who arrived at 11 p.m. to
inform him of the event was not very clear, and Bolívar was so depressed
by the massacre that he hardly listened to the news, believing it to be of
another disaster.   Fighting went on under moonlight till eight o'clock,
when the moon vanished beyond the clouds, and then both sides remained

motionless till 2 a.m. when García's second withdrew from the battlefield. Bolívar had also directed a retreat. " Our camp "—writes Obando—" was like a workshop, but of destruction. Over 15,000 rifles were broken, munitions and loads of equipment were burnt and everything that might have burdened our withdrawal was destroyed. Dawn came on the 8th and we had been unable to withdraw and remained in the same confusion; for a thick fog prevented us from seeing either the enemy camp or the position occupied by the Rifles. The Liberator was most depressed." And Obando sums up the day in a neat phrase: " Both sides lost the battle: we, our force; the Spaniards, the battlefield." According to him, Bolívar lost 800 dead and more than 1,000 wounded.

There followed an exchange of bitter-sweet letters and negotiations, Bolívar asking for the right of way, for he was the victor; García refusing. At last Bolívar had to return by the way he had come, harassed by royalist troops. He recrossed the Juanambú, and later the Mayo, " with the most aggrieved repugnance and almost humiliated ", according to his own words, to take positions in the territory of Patia, in the parish of El Trapiche, more than twenty leagues to the north of the battlefield. He was so depressed by the events as well as by the climate and the fatigue that during this retreat he had to be conveyed on a stretcher. This encounter, known as the battle of Bomboná, generally written up as a victory for the patriots, was therefore (judged by the permanent standard of all war, i.e. whose will prevails ?) one of Bolívar's worst defeats.

5

Bolívar's name and cause, however, were saved by Sucre's victory at Pichincha. Mourgeón had died suddenly in Quito (3.iv.22), depriving the royalists of a leader both active and liberal, and leaving Aymerich again in command. Sucre, at the head of 2,000 infantrymen and 4,000 cavalry, rode forward (14.iv.22) to join his vanguard at Alausí. The Spaniards went on retreating. On May 2nd, in La Tacunga, Sucre received another 200 men under a youthful colonel, José María Córdova. On May 13th, 1822, Sucre's army began the ascent of the Cotopaxí on the frozen flanks of which they spent the night. On May 17th the allied army (in the language of our day we would call them Argentines, Peruvians, Colombians and Venezuelans) descended on the other side and entered the valley of Chillo facing the city of Quito. Nicolás López, the royalist commander, had retreated to Quito. On May 21st, Sucre offered battle on the plains of Tumbamba, but the royalists, entrenched in the heights, did not budge. Sucre marched during the night to take a position to the north of the city cutting it off from Pasto. In the early morning fog, the vanguard lost its way and the fight began unexpectedly. Here again the English contingent played an important part. Sucre reports that the Spanish commander was on the point of outflanking the patriots with three companies of the regiment of Aragón when " the three companies of Albion which had remained behind with the park arrived and entering the fight with their usual bravery put the Aragón companies to total defeat ". On May 25th the city and forts were occupied, 1,100 prisoners, 14 pieces of artillery and rich stores falling to the brilliant young general.

O'Leary, then Sucre's aide-de-camp, rightly emphasizes the contrast between the attitude of Pasto and that of Quito. " The men of Quito "— he writes—" hated the royalists as much as those of Pasto the Colombians "; and he adds that the Quitoans had been constantly in touch with Sucre, helping him in every way. This should be borne in mind in all fairness to Bolívar who, not for the first nor for the last time, had had (in the Spanish saying) to dance with the ugliest lady. On the very day Sucre had planned to march through the night round the flanks of the Pichincha (23.v.22), Bolívar, who had been reinforced and was at the head of 3,000 men, wrote to García asking him to capitulate. Apparently oblivious of the treaty of Trujillo, he wrote on: " We have the right to treat the whole people of Pasto as prisoners of war, for the whole of it without exception wages war against us; and to confiscate all its property as belonging to our enemy; finally we have the right to treat that garrison with the utmost rigour of war, and to confine the population in narrow war prisons, in our sea fortresses." He endeavoured to justify this threat by alleging Spanish infractions of the treaty of Trujillo. In the meantime, some royalist officers, escaped from Quito, brought to Pasto the news of Sucre's victory. García immediately sent two officers to Bolívar, whom they found in Berruecos (6.vi.22), and concluded the capitulation—a decision obviously determined by Sucre's past victory and not by Bolívar's, which was still in the future.

The day after he had crossed the line, Obando saw Bolívar in Popayán (8.ii.22). After the interview, Colonel José Gabriel Pérez, Bolívar's secretary-general, took him to his office and told him: " We are going to march in triumph to Peru and wipe out the Spaniards, then we shall crown the *Libertador* precisely." This story being told by Obando, might be dismissed as a calumny; but this same Bolívar, in this same Popayán, in this same February (on the 9th), had written to Santander: " If Iturbide declares himself Emperor that will be the best thing in the world." And this same Bolívar, in El Trapiche, three months after finding it excellent that Iturbide should crown himself an Emperor, had issued a decree (28.v.22) organizing the *Libertador's* Guard in a style obviously imitated from the guard of Napoleon: with General Rafael Urdaneta as commander-in-chief, General Manuel Valdés as second in command and chief of the infantry division, General Sucre as chief of staff and General Barreto as chief of the cavalry brigade. And this same Bolívar, who, according to Obando, was to be crowned in Lima, was so obviously in the habit of suggesting to his entourage hopes of Napoleonic imperial courts that, in a private letter from his close friend and confident Briceño Méndez to Santander (18.vii.21), may be read the following postscript: " So we now have a common niece ? I am very happy; but I regret that the godfather should have spent so much on the christening. If only our princedoms and dukedoms turned up, we could afford everything; but how far they are still ! " And this same Bolívar, when the Spaniards capitulated, and without even waiting for their formal signature, rode on to Pasto where he was received at the outskirts by the secretary of the bishop of Popayán (5.ii.22) and the aide-de-camp of Don Basilio García, who asked him what were the honours the *Libertador* President was usually granted in such cases; whereupon he answered that the President of Colombia, when entering as a victor in a city, was granted the honours of a Roman Emperor. And how alive in his mind the memory of Napoleon was can be guessed by his answer to Colonel García who had offered to his victor his sword and staff: " Keep them, colonel, for you are worthy of them; but on your return to Spain tell the King that the descendants of the conquerors of New Granada have humbled the lion of Castille, defended as it was by the victors of the victors of Austerlitz." He rode on towards Pasto. The Spanish troops were lining the streets. When he entered the church, he did so under a canopy, a privilege reserved by Spanish clergy to crowned heads.

6

This sudden access of monarchism was the reaction of his depressed spirit after the humiliation of Bomboná, twice as bitter after he heard the news of Sucre's victory. His letter to Santander from Pasto (9.vi.22) makes sad reading. He begins by emphasizing the importance of the capitulation, " an extraordinarily fortunate achievement for us ", on the basis of the fierce nature of the Pastusians; and goes on to refute the view (which no one had put forward) that " his capitulation " might be due to the victory of Pichincha, which it certainly was. " Be certain that it was my intimation which brought it about, for here no one knew nor could know anything about Sucre's battle, nor was it known until the 1st." This was not so and Bolívar was bound to know it was not so. The news of the capitulation of Quito was known in Pasto *before* García capitulated, and in fact it determined García's capitulation. " Therefore, I do not want the success of my [sic] capitulation to be attributed to Sucre: firstly because enough glory remains for him, and secondly because it is true and very true that they were resolved to capitulate without having heard about Sucre and it seems to me it would be advisable to write a preamble on our respective glories for the *Gazette*. Sucre had more troops than I, and fewer enemies; the country favoured him, owing to its inhabitants and configuration; while we on the contrary were in a hell struggling with devils. The victory of Bomboná is much more beautiful than that of Pichincha. Our loss in both cases was the same and the character of the enemy chiefs very unequal. General Sucre, on the day of the battle, won no more advantages than I did; and his capitulation has not won for him more advantages than I have won, for, to tell the truth, we have taken the bulwark of the south and he has taken the Capua of our conquests. I believe that with a little delicacy, the Guard may be much honoured without detriment to Sucre's division."

With becoming modesty, and with that touch of worldly wisdom which from his youthful days seems to have graced his actions, Sucre had refrained from drawing on the republican enthusiasm of Quito until Bolívar arrived to reap the laurels his young lieutenant had grown for him. While the city was still under his sole authority, the Municipal Council of Quito had decreed that a pyramid would be erected on the hill of Pichincha bearing the words: " The sons of Ecuador to Simón Bolívar, the angel of peace and of American liberty "; and that a bust of Bolívar would be placed in the Council hall.

Bolívar did not tarry in Pasto. García had urged him to enter and pass through, for the Pastusians were eager to fight again and disliked the capitulation; and by June 10th he was already in Tulcán, on his way to Quito, with a good escort of his Guard. He found better and heartier friends as he moved south. On June 13th, 1822, he arrived in Otavalo, where he met a squadron of Río de la Plata Grenadiers come to act as a guard of honour for him. Two days later he arrived in Quito and was met by the civil, military and church authorities and by many enthusiastic citizens. The windows were decorated with tapestries and the women, in their best attire, i.e. at their most Spanish, smiled and threw flowers at the Liberator. In the main square, a richly decorated stage had been raised on which six girls were waiting. Bolívar ascended the steps followed by Sucre, Salom and others. One of the young ladies, María Arboleda, crowned Bolívar with a crown of artificial laurel sparkling with a brooch of diamonds; but Bolívar, after thanking her, took it off and put it on Sucre's brow, saying: " Lady, this crown befits the victor of Pichincha "; the young ladies of Quito, however, had thought of everything and María Arboleda, taking from a tray another crown of natural laurel, put it on Bolívar's head saying: " If you have yielded to the victor of Pichincha the crown of artificial laurel, here is one of natural laurel that I beg leave to put on your head." Whereupon the other girls crowned every man on the stage. After this scene, Bolívar and the authorities went to the cathedral where a *Te Deum* was sung. On his triumphant progress, this man may have been thinking that he was at last the master of a continent; but he happened to look up at a balcony, and his eyes met the eyes of Manuela Sáenz. The master of the continent had met his mistress—in more ways than one.

Manuela Sáenz was born in Quito in 1797, the illegitimate daughter of Don Simón Sáenz, a fiercely royalist Spaniard, and of Doña María de Aizpuru, a lady of Quito. A legitimate daughter of her father, Eulalia, married an *Oidor* and eventually settled in Spain. There were three legitimate brothers one of whom gained distinction in the patriot army after serving for a time as a royalist. Manuelita was twelve when the dramatic events of the first rising against Spain shook the city of Quito, in 1809. Her mother took her away to the country, where she acquired that horsemanship which would one day enable her, riding like a man and spear in hand, to repel an attack during a political rising in the streets of Quito. After some comings and goings due to the vicissitudes of the civil war, Manuelita, at seventeen, was sent for her education to the Convent of St. Catherine in Quito. Convents in those days in Spanish America were by no means holy places. A young Spanish officer, Fausto d'Elhuyar (the son of the discoverer of tungsten), ran away with her.

There was a scandal, but not overwhelming. Doña María tried to patch up matters and found the girl an excellent husband, the English doctor of Quito, James Thorne, whom the girl married in 1817 without love and possibly with some mental reservations. She soon became again d'Elhuyar's mistress; and eventually Thorne decided to transfer his practice and troubles to Lima. He was prosperous and certain of success, at any rate in the professional field. He started his Peruvian life in a well appointed house in Lima in 1818. Manuela lost no time in becoming a social figure of the brilliant capital, and the bosom friend of Rosita Campuzano, a Guayaquilian beauty, believed to have been the only woman to have softened the heart of San Martín. Both Rosa and Manuela were decorated with the Order of the Sun by the Protector of Peru and of one of them. Meanwhile, Manuela seems to have lived such a life that even Dr. Thorne's patience came to an end; and the young woman was sent back to Quito alone. Alone she was when Bolívar entered the city, and her heart. She gave herself to him, and in such a process, as is the way with women, she took him for herself. But of this he was not yet aware.

CHAPTER XII

THE GUAYAQUIL MEETING

I

ALL was not Capua and love affairs in Quito. The political situation of the newly conquered lands had to be settled. Sucre had exploited the enthusiasm of the Quiteños to induce them to declare the union of the old Presidency with the Republic of Colombia; for, he explained, that declaration would be the most agreeable reward and welcome they could give to the *Libertador*. The Quiteños, perhaps, says O'Leary, " with more enthusiasm than reflection and prudence ", did so (29.v.22). The new " department " of the Republic, named Ecuador, included the old Spanish provinces of Quito, Cuenca and Loja, all of which had shown their willingness to join Colombia, though Bolívar doubted that Cuenca and Loja were at heart with the patriots. It seems that Bolívar was thinking at this juncture of a more general assembly of the peoples of the south, which would express a solemn wish to adhere to the Republic, as a means for exerting moral pressure on Guayaquil; but that Sucre dissuaded him from such a step. So far, force had been, when not the only, at least the main element in the adhesions to the Republic of Colombia, as indeed in the very birth of the Republic itself. Bolívar had received in El Trapiche a letter from San Martín which, for all its friendliness, intimated to him to keep off Guayaquil and to let the city choose its own allegiance in freedom. Bolívar came to Quito already convinced that force should be used, if need be, to ensure that San Martín respected in Guayaquil " the rights of Colombia ".

What were those rights? A modern Venezuelan historian defines them thus: " The unquestionable rights of Colombia, established by Royal *Cédulas* and exercised for a long time, as is well known, by the Presidency of Quito." That was precisely the stand Bolívar took. In his official letter to San Martín (Quito, 22.vi.22), he declares: " I do not think as you do that the vote of one Province should be consulted in order to establish a national sovereignty, for it is not the parts but the whole of the people that deliberates in general assemblies freely and legally called." Bolívar, however, did not believe in his own words nor had he ever believed in them. Thus he wrote to Santander (5.i.22): " The affairs of Guayaquil demand my presence there with the Guard: it is in a chaos of ingratitude and of bad faith. Sucre has authority to act openly should those gentlemen defy my orders." " Those gentlemen " were the government of free Guayaquil freely elected by the city; whose removal by force he had decided to carry out; and again (Quito, 21.vi.22): " I have promised to send troops to Peru if and when Guayaquil submits "; it is clear enough; and clearer still: " Guayaquil may well involve us in one or other of two struggles: with Peru if we force it to recognize Colombia, or with the south of Colombia if we allow it to remain independent." And again: " You know what a

capital recently taken is, to which we have to give Colombian laws. . . ."
A " capital recently taken ". Rights or no rights, Bolívar meant to take
Guayaquil. In his letter to the Colombian Government asking for instructions on how he was to act towards Guayaquil and Peru he wrote: " In
this matter, I am ready to follow no other advice than that the Executive
Power may impart to me . . . but I must point out that if in the last resort
we believe ourselves justified in using force to contain Peru within its bounds
and to make Guayaquil enter those of Colombia, it is also my opinion that
force should be used as soon as possible." He recommends, however,
beginning with negotiations and repeats that he will await the answer of the
executive power, meanwhile abstaining from using force " in this affair of
the utmost gravity ". The Government answered to the effect that he was
to get Guayaquil by negotiation and, if not, by force.

2

On June 17th, 1822, Bolívar wrote to San Martín thanking him for the
collaboration of the Peruvian-Argentine division in the Quito campaign, and
offering to carry on his armies to the help of the Southern Patriots still
threatened by La Serna. We know his motives, for he set them down in a
letter to Santander: " If Guayaquil submits I shall send a couple of battalions
to Peru, as pointed out by Mosquera: first, so that our neighbours are not
more generous than we are; then, to help Peru before disaster overtakes it;
thirdly, for reasons of economy, since here we lack the wherewithal to keep
so many men; fourthly, to begin to fulfil the offers of mutual aid; fifth,
sixth and seventh, because I believe it advisable that they send us three
battalions from Peru in lieu of them when the war is over."
Don Joaquin Mosquera, of one of the patrician families of Popayán, a
brother of Bolívar's chronicler, had been sent to Lima in May to negotiate
a treaty of perpetual alliance prepared by Gual, and to obtain the release of
the Colombian battalion. Monteagudo, San Martín's minister, granted the
treaty after some haggling, precisely on Guayaquil, but stuck to the battalion.
Bolívar had to be content with Santa Cruz' brigade. He made Santa Cruz
a brigadier general and, in his own words, " flattered him "; but he saw to
it that at least half of the brigade's new recruits were Colombian; and that
the Colombian troops were sent to the city, while the Peruvian division went
to La Puna island, on the mouth of the river, and later, in the Chilean fleet
commanded by Blanco Encalada, left for Peru. In so doing, Bolívar was
complying with San Martín's desire to have Santa Cruz back for his own
campaigns; but in timing the despatch of Santa Cruz' division before his
own troops, he made sure that the " free " elections to be held in Guayaquil
would be " protected " by Colombian troops. For Bolívar, Guayaquil was
not a mere harbour to be attached to the Colombian Republic; it was a
stepping stone in his Napoleonic ascent; a milestone on his way to Lima . . .
and beyond. During a banquet offered by the city of Quito to the victors
of Pichincha, Bolívar, rising after many toasts for yet one more, declared:
" The. day is not far off in which I shall march the triumphant banner of

Colombia on to Argentine lands." There were five Argentine superior officers present. One of them, Lavalle, rose to remind him that Argentina was an independent republic.

The Junta of Guayaquil, fearing Bolívar's enmity, had sent La Mar to negotiate. Bolívar met him on the way to Guayaquil, received him cordially, took the utmost interest in his health (for La Mar was ill) and granted nothing. He waited in Guaranda from July 3rd to the 6th (1822) for his troops; and leaving La Mar behind in San Miguel, he went forth with his army and embarked on the Guayaquil river on July 11th. On that day, at 4 p.m., he entered the city, landing in the upper part. The triumphal arches sang: " To THE LIGHTNING OF WAR. TO THE RAINBOW OF PEACE." The scene was colourful, but this time with a political intention, for the ladies who decorated the windows displayed the three colours of Colombia, the white and red of Peru or the white and blue of independent Guayaquil according to their political leanings. As the salvoes were fired, the gunboats on the river struck down the Guayaquil white and blue and raised the Colombian flag. " Why so soon ? "—Bolívar asked. But as the salvoes ended, the Colombian flag was lowered and the flag of Guayaquil flown, and the crowds shouted: " *Viva Guayaquil Independiente.*"

Within twenty-four hours, the Colombian party, knowing itself backed by Bolívar's force, demanded that the Junta declare Guayaquil's accession to Colombia. The Junta refused; whereupon a similar request was sent direct to Bolívar. On July 13th, Bolívar sent an aide-de-camp to the Junta declaring his decision to take over the civil and military government of the city. Salom issued a proclamation declaring that Bolívar had taken the city and province under his protection, that Guayaquil was to adopt the flag of Colombia " like the rest of the nation "; that Bolívar assumed all powers and that the authorities would cease, but would be respected as heretofore. " I hope "—wrote Bolívar to Santander—" that the electoral Junta to meet on July 28th will let us out of this ambiguity. It will doubtless be favourable to us but, were it not, . . . I am determined not to allow . . . etc." But when all was over and Bolívar had obtained his vote from his assembly, Santander summed it all up accurately to a friend: " He Napoleonically carried out a coup à la St. Cloud, kicked out the Junta, formed another one with persons he could trust, and you will see that the department decided to accede to Colombia."

Before completing his task, Bolívar had, however, to get rid of San Martín. The Protector was not tackling the problem of Guayaquil in a less pretorian spirit than the Liberator. Mitre, his admiring but judicious biographer, acknowledges that, at the time Bolívar took Guayaquil, " San Martín on his part was getting ready to carry out a similar manoeuvre ". " To that effect he had sent before him the Peruvian fleet, which at the time was in Guayaquil, under the command of its Admiral Blanco Encalada, on the pretext of receiving the auxiliary Peruvian-Argentine division "; and with the troops and the navy, he had hoped to decide the vote of Guayaquil in favour of Peru. San Martín's idea was to go to Quito via Guayaquil, and to interview Bolívar with Guayaquil in his pocket. " Before the 18th "—he wrote to Bolívar (13.vii.22)—" I shall sail from Callao, and no sooner landed in Guayaquil, I shall proceed to greet you in Quito. My soul fills with thoughts and joy when I contemplate that moment; we shall see each other, and I foresee that America will not forget the day we embrace each other." But his plans were doomed to fail for two reasons : he was slow in action and far from clear in thought; while Bolívar was as swift as lightning and as clear as a sword. What was it exactly that San Martín wanted in Guayaquil ? He may have had hopes of winning the sympathies of the electorate for an accession to Peru or alternatively for an independence that would have left Guayaquil actually dependent on Lima; but no one knew for certain. Bolívar, however, knew he wanted Guayaquil for Colombia and was determined to get it by hook or by crook; and as for speed, when San Martín was writing to Bolívar that he hoped to see him in Quito, Bolívar was actually taking Guayaquil.

3

On July 24th, 1822, Bolívar celebrated his thirty-ninth anniversary. That night, San Martín, a man of forty-four, much worn out by ill health and the too frequent use of morphia in sleeping drugs, was sailing towards the island of La Puná at the mouth of the Guayaquil river. On the 25th, on board *La Prueba*, an ex-Spanish, now Peruvian ship, he met his two emissaries, Generals Salazar and La Mar, and the three members of the Junta of Guayaquil dispossessed by Bolívar. San Martín, who had expected the Junta to hand him over Guayaquil for Peru, received them with hardly veiled disdain and heard from Salazar and La Mar the melancholy story of the events which had radically altered the situation of the city. So that Bolívar, whom he had hoped to meet in Quito with Guayaquil in his pocket, was himself in Guayaquil and master of it. Bolívar lost no time in signifying the fact to the newcomer. He sent him an aide-de-camp with a bitter-sweet letter expressing his satisfaction at the surprise visit, his regret at not having time to prepare an adequate reception and, finally, his displeasure: " I do not know, moreover, whether the news [of San Martín's coming] is true, for I have had no communication worthy of credit." Impressed by the news, San Martín sent Bolívar two of his aides-de-camp suggesting a meeting on board his own ship, the *Macedonia*, so as not to excite the population. Bolívar's reaction was typical. He sent him four aides-de-camp with a letter saying: " I shall feel it as keenly as if I had been conquered in many battles that you do not come to this city; but no, you will not frustrate my desire to embrace on the soil of Colombia the first friend of my heart and of my country." There it was. San Martín may have had to read it twice. Guayaquil was the soil of Colombia and Bolívar would be San Martín's host. In the morning of July 26th, 1822, Bolívar went on board San Martín's ship and won him over.

San Martín landed and, between rows of Colombian soldiers presenting arms, rode to the house that had been prepared for him. Bolívar came out to receive the visitor. In the hall, the authorities appointed by Bolívar and the never failing young ladies were awaiting. One of them, Carmen Garaycoa, offered San Martín a crown of laurels set in gold. But the Protector was not the Liberator. He blushed, took the crown off his brow and mumbled something about not deserving it. The two men withdrew together. When Bolívar left, San Martín had to appear at the balcony to acknowledge the cheers of the people. He then called on Bolívar, and returned to lunch. Nothing happened in the afternoon; and there was much dancing in the evening. The next day, San Martín gave orders for his schooner to be ready to sail; and at one o'clock went to call on Bolívar with whom he remained closeted for four hours. At five, there was a banquet with many toasts; then a dance again, much enjoyed by Bolívar but watched coldly by San Martín. At one o'clock he signalled one of his aides-de-camp, and, as previously agreed with Bolívar, slipped out unnoticed and returned to his ship. " The *Libertador* has stolen a march on us "—he said the next day to his aides-de-camp, and to O'Higgins he wrote: " The *Libertador* is not the man we had imagined."

We can reconstitute the famous Conference because we possess three narratives dictated by Bolívar and a letter written by San Martín, which dovetail fairly well. Two sets of subjects and factors were intertwined: one, objective: the circumstances of the continent in travail and the tensions between its several parts; the other subjective: the temperaments and intentions of the two men. The first set was merely external and instrumental; the second was essential and dynamic. *Fundamentally, the meeting of Guayaquil was a duel of wills between two replicas of Napoleon.* The order of events, of these *inner events* which were the ones that mattered, can be established documentarily. Thus, Bolívar on San Martín: " He insisted that he meant to retire to Mendoza; that he had left a sealed paper to be presented to Congress resigning as Protector . . . that before he retired he would leave the bases of the government well established; that this should not be democratic in Peru for it was not suitable, and lastly that a single prince should be brought over from Europe to govern that State. His Excellency* answered that it was not suitable for America, nor for Colombia either, that European princes should be brought over, for they were foreign elements to our mass; that H.E. would oppose such a thing if he could; but that he would not oppose any form of government that any State may wish to give itself. The Protector replied that the coming of the Prince would be for a later period, and his Excellency insisted that the coming of princes would never be advisable; that H.E. had preferred to suggest to General Iturbide that he crown himself provided no Bourbons, Austrias or any other European dynasty came over. The Protector said that there was in Peru a strong party of lawyers who wanted a Republic and he complained bitterly about the character of lawyers. It is to be presumed that the design aims at a monarchy on the principle of crowning a European prince, no doubt in the hope of passing the throne later to the most popular man or to the one with the strongest force at his disposal. If the speeches of the Protector are sincere, no one is further from the throne than he. He seems

---

* Bolívar, speaking of himself in the report he was dictating.

very much struck by the drawbacks of power." And again Bolívar on San Martín: " He says that he does not want to be king, but that he wants no democracy either; what he wants is a prince from Europe to reign in Peru. I believe this last is merely *pro forma*." And now San Martín on Bolívar: " Bolívar and I together are too big for Peru. I have penetrated his rash schemes; I have understood his coldness at the glory which I might obtain if I carried on my campaign. He will spare no means, however audacious, to enter this republic [of Peru] followed by his troops, and perhaps I should not be able then to avoid a conflict to which we should be led by fate, giving thus to the world a humiliating scandal."

These texts are clear. Bolívar did not believe San Martín was sincere when he advocated a European prince for Peru; even though, if we are to believe Mosquera, the first thing San Martín did was to put before Bolívar the Act of the Peruvian Council of State (21.xii.21) entrusting two ambassadors with the task of finding such a prince under the auspices of either Britain or Russia. For Bolívar this European prince was a device to keep the throne ready for San Martín himself. Bolívar, of course, who resigned and retired every year or so, and always irrevocably, paid no attention whatever to San Martín's assurances that he meant to resign and retire. It is almost certain that Bolívar was right; and that San Martín's ambition was to be the monarch of Peru, though not necessarily with the title of king. But those who, like Mosquera, try to picture Bolívar as a champion of republican ideas are wide of the mark. Bolívar's own words prove that his ambition was identical: to become the Emperor of Spanish America under the title of *Libertador*. He took care to point out to San Martín that he would oppose the coming over of a prince, but *not* the form of government any State would adopt. The transplantation of European princes to the New World was unwelcome to him, not because he objected to the noun—*princes*—but to the adjective— *European*. Hence his argument about Iturbide: let him crown himself provided no European dynasty comes from Mexico. What Bolívar feared was not the monarchy, as a republican, but a rival, as a would-be monarch.

This began early. He had feared that Napoleon might seek to take refuge in the New World after Waterloo. In his letter to the President of New Granada (Kingston, 22.viii.15) he depicts in sombre colours the disastrous consequences of such an event; and there is a word in his picture that gives his secret thoughts away: " His spirit of conquest is insatiable; he has mowed in its flower the youth of Europe on the fields of battle in order to fulfil his ambitious schemes; similar designs will lead him to the New World hoping perhaps to exploit the dissensions which divide America to enthrone himself in this great empire." *To enthrone himself:* such was the aim of them all. But Bolívar, being by far the most intelligent of all these American Napoleons, realized that the style of his own enthronement had to be different, because the taste of the day had changed. " How mad those gentlemen who will have crowns against the opinion of the day, without merit, talent or virtues! "

4

That this is the correct interpretation of the Guayaquil interview is proved by the sequel. Had San Martín and Bolívar been what they professed to be, two liberators, they would easily have come to terms on the common ground of their common task. The emancipation of Spanish America from the power of Spain was an enterprise that could easily have absorbed the energies of both acting in unison. But the rise of a Napoleon in the political firmament of the continent implied the decline of every other star with equal ambitions. It was a case of either or. San Martín saw it only too clearly. True he declared himself ready to serve under Bolívar; but this offer was not accepted by Bolívar, who did not believe it sincere. One month later, San Martín wrote to his rival: " Unfortunately I am intimately convinced of the fact that either you have not believed my offer to be sincere to serve under your orders with the force under my command, or else that my person was in your way." Bolívar was, however, right. Even if San Martín were sincere in offering to serve under him he would not have been able to live up to his offer; and as for Bolívar, he was bound to find San Martín's person encumbering.

On the other hand San Martín was convinced that Bolívar would push on to Lima no matter what happened, or who was there; so he wrote in this same letter: " My decision is final: for the 20th of the coming month I have called the first Congress of Peru, and on the following day I shall sail for Chile, convinced that my presence is the only obstacle that prevents you from entering Peru with your army. I should have felt at the very summit of my happiness had I been able to end the War of Independence under the orders of a general to whom America owes her liberty. Fate has willed it otherwise, and one has to bow to it." Meanwhile, Bolívar, hearing that San Martín had again taken in hand the reins of power, wrote to Santander : " I believe General San Martín has taken the bit in his teeth and is thinking of achieving his enterprise as Iturbide did, I mean, by force; and so we shall have a kingdom at each flank both of which will end badly, as they have begun."

Thus, the Guayaquil Conference threw up this paradoxical result which time alone was to unravel: each rival mistook the immediate intentions of the other while accurately guessing his innermost trend and impulse. For, in fact, as time will show, Bolívar was at first hesitant about entering Peru and thought even of abandoning it to the Spaniards; while San Martín, contrary to what Bolívar suspected, did not leave Guayaquil to hoist himself up to a Peruvian throne, but to give up a struggle in which he felt defeated in advance. How illuminating though, that the two men should have misjudged the immediate future of each other precisely because of an all too accurate reading of the deeper reality hidden in each other and identical in both!

On the day (25.vii.22) San Martín received Bolívar on board the *Macedonia* in Guayaquil Bay, his Minister of War and of Foreign Affairs, Bernardo Monteagudo, was deposed by a riot of the populace in Lima. Monteagudo was a foreigner in Peru. The son of a Spaniard and of a slave of a Chuquisaca canon, he was an ambitious mulatto of sybaritic tastes, cruel and unprincipled. Nothing but a common hatred of the Spaniards could draw together this man and San Martín; and to this day the name of the Protector is not altogether cleared from the splashes of criminal mud the Minister of his choice left on him. This common passion led San Martín and his Minister to deplorable excesses. A decree was issued in Lima (24.iv.22) sentencing all Spaniards to exile and confiscation of their property should they appear in public wearing a cloak or be seen talking in groups of more than two persons; to the death penalty if seen out of doors after sunset; and to death and confiscation if found in possession of any weapon other than table knives. On May 4th, 1822, while the authorities were enjoying a grand ball to celebrate the creation of the Order of the Sun, troops were sent to the houses of all Lima Spaniards, who were shaken out of their beds and sent aboard the frigate *Milagro* in Callao. Stevenson, Cochrane's secretary, has left a picture of the sufferings of the victims on that night. Many were old and infirm, many half-dressed or with just their night-clothes on were made to walk the ten miles from Lima to Callao without being allowed food or any communication with their families, who swarmed round the frigate in small boats. San Martín allowed those who could pay for their passports to move to neutral ships, but they had to pay as much as one thousand and even ten thousand pesos for the privilege. Those unable to pay were sent to Chile. That this operation was by no means dictated by considerations of safety is proved by the fact that many of the Spaniards who bought their passports dared not sail to Spain because they had openly espoused the independent cause.

This dastardly action did much to harm the reputation of Monteagudo. His fierce persecution of all Spaniards, especially the wealthy, his personal luxury and insolence and his despotic ways fanned the fires of Peruvian nationalism. There was, however, another cause. Monteagudo had made many enemies for himself and for San Martín by his manoeuvres for fostering a monarchist régime with San Martín on the throne. Such was the situation which the French agent, Rattier de Sauvignan, reported to his government: " *Sous l'apparence de démonstrations de reconnaissance publique, on élevait des obelisques sur les places où l'on avait soin d'exposer le portrait du général San Martín orné d'une couronne propre à laisser du doute entre l'emblème de la victoire et celui de la monarchie.*" The crowd, instigated by Riva Agüero, President of the department, demanded his removal and arrest. The government had to yield. The crowd was not appeased, and the riot grew almost into a revolution against San Martín's own régime, the Protectorate, because of both its foreign and its monarchial character. Under pressure from the municipal authorities, the government exiled Monteagudo (29.vii.22). When San Martín arrived in Lima from Guayaquil (20.viii.22) it was evident that he had lost public opinion and even the backing of his own army. The day the first Congress of Peru met in Lima (20.ix.22), he resigned all his offices, military and civil, and on that very night he sailed for Chile and the obscurity of private life. " I am bored "—he said in his last message to the Peruvians— " hearing it said everywhere that I want to become a sovereign."

5

There are signs in Bolívar's correspondence that suggest at this stage the usual feminine adventures after his taking of cities. The same Carmen Garaycoa who, at his suggestion, had crowned San Martín, became a friend of his, and her sisters as well; though how intimate is not clear. A light-hearted letter of his (Cuenca, 14.ix.22) reveals a more than usual affection; he advises Carmen not to be jealous of the girls of the hills (i.e. of Cuenca) " because there is no reason for it with regard to persons so modest that they hide away from any military man "; and he writes this delightful paragraph: " The Church has taken hold of me: I live in an oratory; the nuns send me my food; the canons refreshment; my song is the *Te Deum* and my sleep is mental prayer and meditation on the beauties Providence gifted Guayaquil with and of the modesty of the hill girls who will see no one for fear of sin. In one word, my friends, my life is entirely spiritual and when you see me again I shall be turned into an angel." But in his retreat of El Garzal, where he worked while staying in Guayaquil, Manuela Sáenz was his constant companion. At this time, when he felt himself the strongest man on the continent, he wrote two letters to his friends Francisco and Fernando Toro, who had at last returned from exile to Caracas and had asked him to come back north. " But listen "—he says to Fernando— " I now belong to the family of Colombia and not to the family of Bolívar. I am no longer of Caracas only but of the whole nation." He had kept a touching fidelity towards these two brothers who had remained away during the trouble and the danger and returned rather ingloriously to recover their property at the time of victory. Fernando was said to be worn out and ill but the marquess had kept his gaiety.

He himself was feeling the strain of too much tension. He wrote to Santander (29.ix.22) that he had been in bed for days with headaches, a cold and boils; and asked him (27.x.22) to prepare the Bogotá country house for the simple life of a sick man: " I shall come very much out of repair, for the trip is very long and I am already very much out of order and worn out by cares which do not let me sleep and with physical pains, being moreover old and lacking in robustness." His chief worry at the time was the unsatisfactory position in Venezuela, when he was not yet sure of his sudden conquests nor of the ultimate fate of Peru. He declared himself ready to go north with two hundred veterans by Panamá, should Morales not be defeated by Soublette and Páez, but not until the fate of Peru has been settled. He was afraid not only of a Spanish victory but of the unsteadiness of public opinion in the south. The war was in itself a disaster. " By means of the enclosed Memoir you will be able to realize what the Kingdom of Quito was before the sacrifices and desolations of this campaign "—he wrote to Santander (Cuenca, 13.ix.22). " To ruin Venezuela twelve years were necessary; Quito was ruined in four days." Ten days later: " We have met with the greatest disappointment you could imagine about the income of this country, for the Spanish constitution had abolished the tributes [Indian head tax] and Sucre had abolished the *alcabalas*, the tributes and the

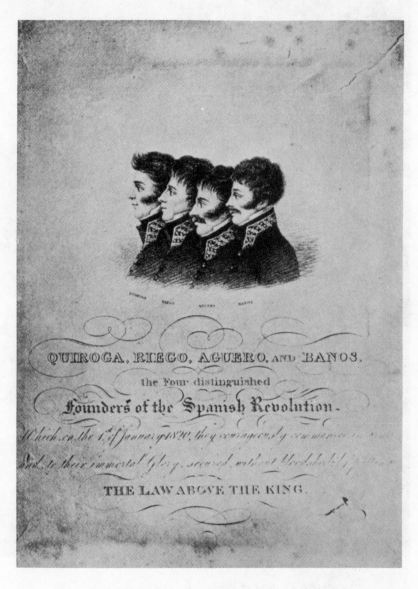

THE FOUR FOUNDERS OF THE SPANISH REVOLUTION

GENERAL JOSÉ DE SAN MARTÍN, by José Gil

brandy monopoly. I ordered everything to continue as before the promulgation of the Spanish constitution, as that was the only way to get some money
in." Again (Guayaquil, 3.viii.22): "This country is not very safe for us
and its garrison must be very loyal to us." And: "Be sure, my friend, that
this country is quiet because I am here with two thousand guardsmen and
even they would not suffice were I to go away without leaving the system
well established." The pretorian tone is clear. He had described the
situation of Guayaquil in a letter to Santander (29.vii.22) which reflects his
undisguised contempt for the forms of public opinion: "To-day the
members of the Electoral Committee of this Province are discussing its
adhesion to Colombia: I think it will be done, but claiming many graces
and privileges. I, as in charge of the Executive Power of this land, will
take over the Province, leaving the Sovereign Congress free in its sovereign
will to get out of the situation with its sovereign power." The Committee
argued over the matter somewhat too long for Bolívar's ways and on July 31st,
says O'Leary, "the Liberator intimated his wish that the discussion be
ended, the only reason for which was to declare the incorporation of the
Province in the territory of Colombia". This was at once done. A few
dissidents and a number of Guayaquil officers went into exile.

In a note from his secretary (9.ix.22), Bolívar offered Peru 4,000 men over
and above the first expedition he had already sent. He desired decisive
operations to be delayed till the arrival of the Colombian reinforcements;
and, should they be unsuccessful, the allied army was to withdraw northwards to join six to eight thousand men Bolívar would then provide. The
Peruvian Congress was not enthusiastic and answered that "in due time it
would make use of such an aid and that meanwhile all it needed was rifles
at a fair price". The Peruvian government was proud, distrustful and poor.
Paz Castillo, the Colombian colonel sent by Bolívar to Lima in command of
his first contingent, reported (8.x.22): "It is hard to realize the miserable
state of the opulent capital of Peru. In my opinion more than ten million
two hundred and fifty thousand pesos had been extracted from the safes,
taken away by San Martín." Bolívar was unhappy about the way Peru was
being governed after San Martín's departure. He liked La Mar, who had
been appointed the head of a triumvirate, "as good a military as a civil
man", but objected to the government on the ground that "it is Congress
that commands and the triumvirate only carries out". On October 14th,
he wrote to La Mar congratulating him on his appointment, but complaining
of the attacks against him, Bolívar, in the Lima press. Public opinion in
Peru was hardening in its nationalism. Alvarado, the Commander-in-Chief
left behind by San Martín, was an Argentinian; Paz Castillo was a Venezuelan: "Peru"—said a member of Congress—"must raise an armed
force able to destroy the enemy legions that occupy her soil without foreign
help; an army of her own to ensure her political independence." A law
was voted (17.xi.22) limiting to Peruvians all new vacancies in the army and
the navy; and the constitution (16.xii.22) explicitly forbade that the Executive
Power of the Republic should be vested either for life or on a hereditary
basis. Bolívar was across the border.

6

He had decided to go north (27.x.22) to help Santander fight political intriguers; then, two days later, changed his mind and turned his eyes on Peru; later he had to go north all the same, and he was in Quito on November 12th. The reason for this change was that a nephew of Boves, a colonel of the same name, who had surrendered in Quito after Pichincha, had fled to Pasto (28.x.22) and aroused the province for Ferdinand VII. Boves crossed the Guáitara river and defeated Colonel Antonio Obando. Bolívar got together two thousand men, " the most veteran corps of the southern armies "; but, as he put it himself to Santander, even " veterans have to be roped to be taken to the enemy ", for desertion was endemic. Boves defeated Sucre at Taindala (24.xi.22), Sucre withdrew to Túquerres, to await reinforcements. Mainly with the help of the British Colonel Wright, Taindala was retaken by the patriots (23.xii.22), and Boves was defeated on the 24th at Yacuanquer (24.xii.22). Pasto refused to surrender and fought on, but at last was stormed, and, writes O'Leary, " in the horrible massacre that ensued, soldiers and civilians, men and women, were sacrificed promiscuously ". A local historian adds that " the Republicans gave themselves over for three days to sacking and murdering defenceless persons, thefts and other excesses, going so far as barbarously to destroy the public archives and even the parish books ". Bolívar himself arrived in Pasto on January 2nd, 1823. He was inexorable and cruel. He confiscated all estates and gave them to his officers, drafted all the men into the army and sent them away, and left Salom in charge with orders to imprison and send to Quito and Guayaquil all who had not been militarized. Many committed suicide.

A sanguinary victory over Pasto, and a disquieting situation in Peru; a relatively quiet situation in New Granada, and a somewhat inglorious and sterile struggle in Venezuela against the Spaniards under La Torre first and later under Morales—such was the picture before the eyes of Bolívar towards the end of the year 1822. It was by no means rosy. Fortunately for him, however, there was a considerable improvement in the international situation of the country he had done so much to create. The United States had taken a more openly favourable attitude than ever before. Colombia had been represented in Washington since August 14th, 1819, by Manuel Torres, a European Spaniard. On February 20th, 1821, Torres presented a note, formally asking the American government for official recognition of Colombia. The American government made no answer. He repeated his request on November 30th, 1821, and on January 2nd and 18th, 1822, John Quincey Adams answered that the matter was under consideration, significantly adding that he would be grateful for early news of the surrender of Puerto Cabello or Panamá. On March 8th, 1822, President Monroe forwarded Torres' notes to Congress with a message foreshadowing recognition of the new Republics. On May 23rd Quincey Adams sent Torres a note informing him that President Monroe would receive him as Chargé d'Affaires of Colombia.

The step could hardly be considered by Spain as an unfriendly act since, at about the same time, Mourgeón, as Viceroy of New Granada, addressed Bolívar as " Señor Presidente de Colombia ". Spain was then drifting from left to extreme left (as we should now say); and France grew uneasy about it. The Congress of Verona had to discuss intervention in Spain, and, while England considered that recognition of the American Republics had by then become a matter of time, Wellington, on instructions from Canning, refused to collaborate in any attempt at checking the Spanish revolution against Ferdinand. Canning was right in pointing out that the Spanish left was not liberal enough in America; but, by refusing to intervene in Spain while allowing France to do so, Canning made reaction inevitable in Spain and therefore in her policy in America, and so made a break between Spain and Spanish America final and inevitable. But that is perhaps what he actually wanted. It certainly was what the London merchants wanted.

So, towards the close of 1822, Bolívar was like a man who, having successfully climbed a hill, scans the heights that still remain to be ascended with a body needing rest but a still eager mind demanding fresh exertion. Several of his utterances at this period suggest a sense of achievement and even of renunciation. " Nothing remains for me but to put away in safety the treasure of my success, hiding it in a deep retreat so that no one can steal it from me: I mean that nothing remains for me to do but to retire and to die. In truth, I wish for no more; for the first time, I have nothing to desire and am content with my fortune." He does not want to govern, he writes, because the constitution is not good: " but even if it were altered, I should not take power either, for I do not want my return to be attributed to ambition, and also because I want to rest after twelve years of storms. Two-thirds of my life have gone, and the third that remains I want to devote to taking care of my soul, for I must render to God an account of my life and I do not want to die without having cleared my accounts. I have come to the end of my career and must begin to decline, therefore must try to procure for myself an honourable and easy fall, for if I do not contrive it myself, I might be pushed down violently and lose all I have acquired."

It may be that these accesses of weariness were sincere for the brief time they lasted. But all that he did and wrote before and after suggests that even if such was the case, he used them as weapons in his crafty strategy towards the satisfaction of his chief passion, ambition. After emphasizing his longing for rest, he naïvely writes to his friends, the Toros: " Perhaps when I have returned to the Simón Bolívar class I shall want again to be President. If so I ought to be granted my whim as a reward for my services." And yet he felt overwhelmed by his task which he described magnificently in his letter to Santander (Ibarra, 23.xii.22): " We have two and a half million inhabitants scattered over a vast desert. One part of them is wild, another one in slavery, most of them are mutual enemies and all are vitiated by superstition and despotism. A fine contrast to oppose to all other nations on earth! Such is our situation; such is Colombia, and they will still want to divide her." Nor did he expect from Peru anything but disasters. " The question of Peru is, as De Pradt used to say speaking of the negroes of Haiti, so intricate and horrible that, no matter how considered, it offers nothing but horrors and disasters and no hope, whether in the hands of the Spaniards or of the Peruvians." But a curious paragraph in one of his letters to Briceño throws light on his mind towards the end of 1822: " This is worth something and can always be preserved ", he said, referring to the south; " I know not what Venezuela is worth nor how long it will last. I, in Venezuela, will not be able to do anything but to run the tempest on the seas and risk sinking with my ship; while here, sailing on the Pacific, I can anchor anywhere and fasten my ship to the best harbour and with the best safety. In one word, this might be for me a salvage plank." What was in his mind ? The rising star of Páez. Caracas had seen the rise of a party in protest against the constitution; a party against Bolívar and against union with New Granada. Soublette had reported the matter to Bolívar, who closed the year with a letter to Congress in which he signified that " The constitution of Colombia is sacred for ten years: it shall not be violated with impunity while blood runs in my veins and the liberators remain under my orders."

CHAPTER XIII

THE TEMPTATION OF PERU

I

BOLÍVAR spent the beginning of 1823 hesitating on the threshhold of Peru. Acting on his instructions, Paz Castillo, his commander there, had ingeniously warded off all attempts at involving Colombian troops in Peruvian operations. Faced with an intimation to put his conditions in writing, Paz Castillo set them so high that the Peruvian government preferred to let his contingent go; and the Colombians sailed from Callao to Guayaquil, " leaving remembrances not too pleasant " (8.i.23). In Bolívar's eyes this was but a *reculer pour mieux sauter*; and events would prove him right. But his mind was labouring under contrary forces. His Napoleonic and pretorian instinct struggled in him against a realistic common sense which enabled him to appraise the weight of the new democratic trends; and a fatigue, due to his declining physical forces, added a touch of scepticism and even of cynicism to his doubts. " There was a conspiracy in Buenos Aires in the month of August ", he writes to Santander (8.i.23) from Pasto. " That is what all these petty revolutionists want: little governments and more little governments to make revolutions and more revolutions. Not I. I do not want little governments: I am resolved to die under the ruins of Colombia fighting for its fundamental law and for absolute unity." On January 14th, after expressing the hope that Santander may successfully meet the challenges of 1823, he adds: " I then shall throw up the sponge and go to rest my bones wherever I can. It has long enough been said that I am ambitious, and I believe I am not; and to make sure in my own eyes that I am not, I am placing myself *hors de combat* so as to deprive myself of temptations." Then again, in the same letter, the theme of fatigue and age reappears: " Send me an order for me to draw my salaries as I may, so that I have enough to retire from the service: I am poor, old, tired, and I do not know how to live by begging; so that I hope you and Congress will do me this charity. The little I have left is not enough for my indigent family, ruined for having followed my opinions [this was by no means the fact, as we know from María Antonia's adventures]; were it not for me it would not have been ruined, and therefore I must feed it." Then, this prophetic sentence: " I foresee that in the end I shall have to leave Colombia and therefore I must have one loaf to eat."

This was the background of mood and feelings in which he reported the return of Paz Castillo's division, " safe and sound, but loaded with the curses of our Peruvian enemies ". He began to look on the Peruvian expedition with a pessimism born of his realistic observation of Spanish-American shortcomings. He saw the Spanish force in Peru, 12,000 strong as it was, raised to 20,000; and wrote to Santander: " We shall not be able to reconquer Peru, because Chile and Buenos Aires are torn asunder by civil war

and we shall be very happy if we do not fall into the same criminal madness."
He then goes on to reveal his new idea: peace with Spain. He sees in it
two advantages: that in the future a restored Colombia will have less to
fear from Spain than in her then weak state; and that by keeping a Spanish-
held territory between Colombia and the south, Colombia might escape
contagion from the southern anarchy. " Let us leave a lake of tyranny
between them and us." This implied his renunciation of the glory and
prestige of Lima.

But, as he really was in two minds about it, he again wrote to the Peruvian
government offering his services. On February 19th, he unfolds his military
plans to Santander: he wants 6,000 men at one stroke in Peru. He urges
him to do everything flying, flying, flying; to send even prisoners as recruits
and to tell the regiment of rifles that " they are being sent to garrison Cuenca,
so that they do not desert ". Money? It must be raised at all costs. He
had already written to him about his way to get it, in words which reveal his
ruthlessness and the incoherence which afflicted his mind whenever it
touched on Spain: " I shall meet every requirement, for we lack no resources
for years to come, though they will be soaked in tears and in blood, for these
people are very hard at giving, and they have not yet suffered the great
Spanish cruelties."

It is a curious comment on this somewhat incoherent utterance that, at
the time, Pasto was being ruthlessly " exterminated " for its loyalty to Spain.
One of Bolívar's subordinate officers and admirers, Colonel Manuel Antonio
López, writes in his Memoirs: " Of the prisoners made from Boves' force in
Pasto, 250 of the most dangerous and stubborn royalists were sent to Guayaquil, and so that they should not run away, they were tied in couples round
the upper arms; as they were skirting the Chimborazo, at a spot where a
rock juts out from the road, one of them broke the ranks dragging his companion and threw himself down crying out: ' I prefer to go to hell rather
than to serve Colombia.' Two broken bodies was all that could be seen at
the bottom of that abyss; but their companions carried their obstinacy
further. As they arrived in Guayaquil, the Liberator ordered that they
should be sent to Peru as recruits, and they were sent aboard the brig *Romeo*,
under the custody of five officers and eleven soldiers. After three days'
sailing, they mutinied, killed Lieutenant Durán and Sublieutenant Mejía,
cousins of the writer, and left half dead or useless Lieutenant Caicedo, the
remaining two officers, and six soldiers. As the ship had but twelve sailors
on board, the captain was not able to stem the mutiny and the mutineers
forced him to sail northwards, for they wanted to land somewhere whence
they should be able to go back to Pasto. The captain yielded to force and
sailed towards Tumaco . . . where luckily the whaler *Spring Grove* was at
anchor, to which the captain signalled for help, and at once the skipper sent
his boats with all his men armed, and succeeded in mastering the mutineers
all but well over forty that had already landed. The mutiny being now
under control and all the mutineers imprisoned in the hull, the ship sailed
to Guayaquil, where the *Libertador* had at once twenty-one of the leaders
shot. Those that had landed in Tumaco remained to be punished; and the

Liberator ordered that Colonel Carvajal with the squadron of Grenadiers and two companies of the Yaguachi battalion should follow the coast in pursuit, trusting me with the command of the column. We captured forty-three who were sentenced to death."

2

Quito and Guayaquil were complaining about " the destruction of industry, the upsetting of public income and the hateful taxes which have been imposed to restore it. An estate owner who, in the old days, paid thirty pesos tax on cattle, will now pay three hundred at least, in direct taxes "; they asked that " it should be declared that the present system of direct taxes is at an end and that the old system of finances of the Spanish government should be restored ". Sucre wrote to Santander: " I have had to order many strokes of the birch to soldiers, to arrest officers every day, to threaten at every moment to act arbitrarily; but in the end I have somewhat stemmed the evils which our troops were inflicting on the population. I am still unable to control the behaviour of most of the military who pass through from one province to another, for, with few exceptions, they imagine that this is a conquered country. . . . In Quito we maintained the monopoly on brandy, the tributes, the *alcabalas*, etc., and we have added to all these impositions of the Spanish government the salt monopoly which is harder than all the rest put together."

Bolívar was little interested in such matters. He would not be bothered with administrative affairs; as for military abuses, while he would always react with a sense of dramatic justice, as a good sultan, wherever a concrete case was brought before him, he quietly let his men do as they pleased, for he always preferred to keep his officers content, and he knew full well where power lay. While his lieutenants struggled with the day-to-day creaking of the machinery of government, he kept to his eagle heights. " I am awaiting at any time some mission from Peru calling me there "—he wrote (19.ii.23); but nothing came. Armero, his agent in Lima, had written to his secretary Pérez (9.x.22), that the Junta of Peru was meeting with difficulties about accepting Bolívar's offer of 4,000 men, because " a few unruly characters and more particularly some émigrés from Guayaquil will not cease raising rumours about H.E.'s ambitious aims over this State ". Bolívar, of course, would brush aside all these rumours as only too true, relying on sheer strength. In the letter previously quoted, he announced to Santander that he would send Valdés with 3,000 men: " These troops, unasked for by anyone, will enter as they can in order to hinder the delivery of Lima and Callao [to the Spaniards]." He warned Santander to reinforce the garrison of Pasto, " for otherwise it will rise again "—a safe enough prophecy—and as for Guayaquil, he says: " This city can no longer remain ungarrisoned by Colombian troops, for every day we are becoming more hateful there owing to the sacrifices we are exacting from that people, all of them, all commercial and miserly." But he wants Peru because of its resources and " the prestige of a capital such as Lima ". Then, having Peru, the Colombians can negotiate a better peace. " I cannot emphasize too much to you how anxious I am to go and take possession of Lima and of Callao, for in my hands all that will never be lost, while in those of that crowd it will at any time."

Bolívar wrote these words on March 12th, 1823. On January 19th and 20th of the same year, after a singularly inept campaign, General Alvarado, left in command by San Martín, had been defeated in Torata and Moquegua by Generals Canterac and Jerónimo Valdés. This defeat became known in Lima on February 4th and caused less dismay than might have been expected, owing to the prevailing ill-feeling " against all the commanders of Buenos Aires origin ". The Lima Congress was by no means blameless. It had wasted its time in futile discussions while things went from bad to worse; violent exactions were the rule rather than the exception, insecurity was so rampant that even when travelling in groups of twenty, honest citizens ran the risks of attacks from thieves from Lima to Callao; and the army had been clamouring in vain for equipment. The best general of Peru, the European Spaniard Arenales, repeatedly put the position to Congress, and when he realized that the military were growing restive, asked leave to retire; but on January 14th, 1823, a petition signed by him and all the heads of units under his command was presented to Congress demanding reforms. The news of the defeat of Moquegua came to increase the tension. The army, concentrated in Miraflores, in the neighbourhood of Lima, took an almost rebellious attitude. Arenales, urged to take the lead of the rebels, refused, resigned and left the command to his second, Santa Cruz. On February 26th, the army chiefs demanded that the Junta hand over the government to Riva Agüero, the instigator of the military rebellion. While Congress talked about it, the army advanced towards Lima. On the evening of February 27th, 1823, Riva Agüero was appointed by Congress President of the Republic.

3

Don José de la Riva Agüero belonged to one of the old, wealthy Spanish families of Peru. He was almost the same age as Bolívar, being born in Lima on May 3rd, 1783; and in his earliest days, when he forsook his studies in Madrid to wander about in Europe, had approached Canning with plans for Spanish-American independence. He returned to Lima by way of Buenos Aires, closely watched by the Spanish authorities as a separatist. He enjoyed great popularity with the coloured masses, who affectionately nicknamed him *Niño Pepito;* and, more ambitious than capable, endeavoured to exploit it in the same pretorian Napoleonic way for which there were already so many models about. As soon as he saw himself at the head of affairs, he had himself appointed Grand Marshal of the Armies of the Republic, theatrically refused the title, and finally bowed before the insistence of Congress. Actual military power, however, remained in the hands of Santa Cruz. Both men found themselves in a dangerous situation. Things had gone the way they had exacted from the point of view of power and office; but the two pressing problems of the new-born Republic—penury of men and of money—remained unsolved; while the Spaniards still threatened to attack from the south and Bolívar still threatened to help from the north. The priest Luna Pizarro, President of Congress, said: " If we let anarchy in, we shall give Bolívar a pretext to enter our country; a lucky warrior, he will be able to conquer our independence; but in exchange will try to become our despot and to dominate us like slaves. Events will confirm the exactness of my forecast."

Bolívar was no longer to knock at the closed door. He was bidden to enter. On March 1st, 1823, Riva Agüero appointed General Don Mariano Portocarrero as a Minister Plenipotentiary to negotiate with Bolívar on Colombian aid; and sent him to Guayaquil with a letter of fulsome praise for " the genius of America ", proposing an alliance. " The situation in which I have taken over power is the most calamitous; no money, no arms." He, nevertheless, expressed the certainty of expelling the Spaniards, " if you, as I hope, send three or four thousand brave men and as much material help as you can ". He promised that Peru would pay. Bolívar had already received a letter from him on February 3rd, and according to the reports he had at hand about the as yet future president of Peru, he considered Riva Agüero as " the personality most capable, patriotic, active and zealous for his fatherland ". Portocarrero presented his proposal to Bolívar in Guayaquil (18.iii.23); and on the same day Bolívar answered that the expedition was already on the way, that six thousand would be sent in all and that he himself was ready to go to Peru " when it requires my services ". What was in his mind can be gathered from a letter to Santander dated March 29th, 1823: " Nothing less than a magnificent army, with a very strong government and a Caesarian man can wrench Potosí and Cuzco from the Spaniards."

Who this Caesarian man could be, no one need entertain any doubt. The captain of the transports told him that unless he went to Peru himself it was no use to keep sending troops there; other persons, both military and civilian, concurred; but " Portocarrero has told me much more than that, for he assumes that I must go as far as Buenos Aires and Chile ". Bolívar knew then of the doings of Santa María, the Colombian Minister in Mexico, caught by Iturbide conspiring against the new-fangled " empire ". Iturbide wrote to him complaining; whereupon, writes Bolívar to Santander: " I have written to Iturbide, in answer to his magnificent letter, as it was decent and just that I should. No one detests Iturbide's behaviour more than I do; but I have no right to pass judgment on his behaviour. Few sovereigns of Europe are more legitimate than he. So that Santa María's behaviour is very reprehensible, if it has been as described." Behind the *pro forma* condemnation of Iturbide can be felt the secret sympathy for his act. Bolívar was thinking more and more as the Napoleon of America, both attracted and repelled by the imperial and Caesarian splendour of the vision, with Lima for its Paris. " Lima lives to-day like a dead body animated by vital spirits " —he writes—" the hope of my coming has revitalized that dead body. No one dreams, no one thinks, no one imagines that Peru can exist without me.

I fear that my coming to Lima may be looked upon with much suspicion by my enemies. There has been one Bonaparte, and our own America has had three Caesars. These pernicious examples harm my present reputation, for no one will be persuaded that, having, as they did, followed the military profession, I am not impelled by their hateful ambition. My three colleagues, San Martín, O'Higgins and Iturbide, have already met with their ill fate, which befell them because they did not love liberty; and that is why I do not want to suffer as they did owing to a slight suspicion. The desire to end war in America pushes me on towards Peru, but I am thrown back by love of my reputation, so that I hesitate and decide nothing."

4

He was sincere about his inner hesitations, but not as to his decision which, beneath them, had been taken much earlier. He would go to Peru. And he was daily taking measures to that effect. While he wrote these letters, a double negotiation was afoot for a treaty to define Colombian co-operation in the Peruvian wars. Without waiting for ratification of this treaty, Bolívar began to send on his six thousand men. They were commanded by Manuel Valdés, but Sucre, as head of the diplomatic mission, was to wield a higher authority. " I own frankly "—Bolívar wrote to Riva Agüero—" that Venezuela has not given forth an officer of finer quality or of greater merit." Meanwhile, following a policy constant and typical in him, he urges Riva Agüero to wait ahd risk nothing. " It would be folly for us to risk the fate of our arms even with vehement hopes of a victory "; when writing *even*, he meant *particularly*, for his secret idea was that there must be no Austerlitz but under the eyes of Napoleon himself, and one Pichincha was enough. He gave Sucre identical instructions.

The two chief points of these instructions are: no operations without me, and prepare the ground for my coming by an armistice with the Spaniards. The devoted Sucre carried out his mission faithfully. On May 14th, the Peruvian Congress decreed that " whereas despite repeated invitations from the President of Peru to the Liberator President of Colombia to come to our territory as soon as possible, he held out, pending the authority of the Colombian Congress, the President of Peru is to signify to the Colombian Congress that Peru ardently and unanimously wishes the invitation to take effect immediately ". Bolívar was, of course, shielding himself behind that permission of his Congress in order to come to Peru in his own time. But other statements of his, made to close friends, show that another factor was alive in his mind. What could it be? Let us remember that, after writing to Guayaquil that he hoped the Republic of Colombia would be recognized by the city before he arrived, for otherwise he would be transgressing Colombian law by going abroad, he did go to Guayaquil before Colombia had been recognized, and forced the recognition down the throats of the unwilling Guayaquilians, " Napoleonically ", as Santander commented. What then kept our Napoleon from crossing over to Peru? The answer is: Don Quixote. For Don Quixote was alive in Bolívar, as he is in every

Spaniard—indeed in every man. Like Don Quixote, Bolívar fought for his glory, and in order to serve his glory, he had projected it outwards into a Dulcinea which was Venezuela first, Colombia later. It was vital for Don Quixote that the world should believe in Dulcinea. It was vital for Bolívar that the world should believe in Colombia. Hence the somewhat inflated solemnity of his official style, his grand speeches to " assemblies " of thirty Congressmen, his " Your Excellency ", his " el señor General Cedeño ", " el señor Colonel Montilla "—hence also the solemnity with which he submits to and waits for " permission " from a " Congress " that, in his unguarded moments, makes him smile at his " respect for the law ". Bolívar waits before the borders of Peru for a word from Colombia in the mood of Don Quixote waiting before a fight with a windmill or a lion on the road to pray to Dulcinea—not caring to remember that the lady of their thought is of their own invention.

The Peruvian Congress which had been far from fervent on Bolívar's coming in 1822 was now the keener in that it hoped in this way to get rid of Riva Agüero, on the principle of the Spanish proverb that one nail drives out another nail. Riva Agüero, who, up to April, had sighed for Bolívar's coming, had now, for the same reason, cooled off. But public opinion in Lima was in favour of Bolívar's coming and by the end of May this point in Sucre's instructions was already met. The negotiations with Spain were more delicate. Sucre began by exploring the Peruvian government, on May 22nd; and finding that, though sceptical as to the outcome of the negotiations, it was not averse to opening them, he wrote to Laserna on May 27th, 1823, drawing his attention to the condition of affairs in Spain, threatened by an intervention from the European powers; and proposing an armistice and " the regularization of the war ". The proposal for a truce was merely dilatory; the proposal for regularizing war was mere propaganda. Within a few weeks Bolívar unleashed the utmost destructive fury on the Pastusians, as hereafter told. His idea was a truce of six years with Spain, after which he thought the independents would have gained enough strength to make victory certain. Laserna answered that he could treat on no other basis than that of the recognition of Spanish authority, " for I am not so far authorized to recognize any dissident government "; pointed out that order and peace prevailed only in the territories occupied by the Spanish army; and, as for the way of waging the war, he affirmed that he had never departed from the rules of " liberty and humanity ". Sucre did not succeed in signing a paper; and as for gaining time, the Spaniards did it all for him without his help.

5

On receiving the news of Iturbide's fall, Bolívar wrote to Santander: " The outcome in the cases of Iturbide, San Martín and O'Higgins proves what I have said a thousand times about the miserable mania of wanting power at any cost. For fear of a little more power, I am reluctant to go to Peru." This sounds well; but it precedes startling revelations: " I try to raise three battalions of men of this country [Guayaquil] but it will be of no avail, because when a unit is moved from one part to another, they all desert. Most of the recruits sent to Lima are married and with children. . . . I have exhausted the spring of my rigour to put together men and money for the expedition to Peru. Everything has been violence upon violence. The countryside, the cities have been laid waste to gather 3,000 men and two hundred thousand pesos. I know better than anyone how far violence can go, and all has been used. In Quito and Guayaquil we have taken every man, in the streets and in the churches, for recruits. Money has been extorted at the point of the bayonet." Then, in a later letter (29.iv.23): " The other day there was a terrible scandal in Quito, because we tried to take a few men for the Bogotá battalion; the result was that more than fifteen or sixteen persons were killed, Salom being in command. What a people! Another day, very much the same story, somewhat less grave with fewer dead, or none."

This is the background of facts on which his protestations of liberalism must be read. He was not altogether insincere in his liberalism. He was in fact almost a split personality about it. His liberal skies were apt to be reddened by the fiery, destructive volcanic explosions of his ambitious soul. He was bound to remember that he had chosen and accepted the name of Liberator when he inflicted on the wretched peoples he had liberated a violence, a blood-letting, a military oppression entirely unknown to them before their liberation. And for what? He will tell us in this very letter. He receives, he says, constant entreaties to go to Peru. " I don't know how I linger one more minute in this city. On the one hand the public interest, on the other my glory, everything calls me there. In fine, temptation is strong and I may be unable to resist it unless God holds me in his hand. The motive that calls me to Peru is so strong that I do not know how I am going to hold myself." These words are clear. Public interest was to be there to make things look respectable; but how could he really believe in that reason when he was plunging Quito and Guayaquil into misery to feed his glory? Then, there was that Iturbide, dethroned. " This is the case to say: ' He sinned against liberal principles, and so he succumbed,' as Bonaparte said of himself." Bolívar writes these words in the same letter in which he wrote about the fifteen victims of Salom in the streets of Quito, and about his temptation to go to Peru. He goes on: " I examine my conscience every day, and truly tremble at the sins I commit against my will, in favour of the cause, and by the fault of the Goths." And from this position, in which there is a genuine feeling of uneasiness and guilt, he glides on to a flippant and satirical attitude: " Friend, things are bad, one can no longer wield power, except for love of one's neighbour and with the deepest humility. To cover ourselves, ask His Holiness the Congress to give you a bull to allow us to sin against liberal formulas, with forgiveness of guilt and penance, for otherwise it shall have availed us nothing to have saved the fatherland as did Iturbide, O'Higgins and San Martín."

6

In Guayaquil, Bolívar had to scan the continent 800 leagues to the south and 800 to the north. The activities of Morales in Maracaibo kept him in constant alarm; and the power of the Spanish army in Peru (which he exaggerated) made him lie awake at night. He spent the spring discussing operations in Peru, and wrote to Sucre (Quito, 5.v.23): " I shall follow immediately to lead those operations and go to Arequipa or wherever the troops may be "; but he adds at the end of the letter: " unless God hinders it with some unforeseen event ".

The event did happen: Pasto rose again. But it should not have been unforeseen. Salom had been left in Pasto deliberately to oppress the Pastusians, as Sucre plainly hinted to Santander (Pasto, 27.xii.22): " General Salom remains there and will know how to get our own back considering the conditions the Republic had previously granted to Pasto . . . Salom knows full well how to manage these matters." He did. Confiscation, exile, forced recruitings, executions without trial and in repulsive circumstances, he stopped at nothing. On May 17th, 1823, many of the victims who were aboard the brig *Romeo* tried to escape back to their native city; but, caught by a force led by the patriot Carvajal and the Englishman Wright, they were shot. On June 6th, 1823, he authorized Colonel Aguirre, the commander in Quito, " to have shot without trial every man found with arms against the government, deserters or royalists, whatever their numbers, since the only way to quiet the country is to apply an inexorable rigour against factious persons ". On hearing of the mutiny in the *Romeo*, he ordered " to put in irons all the Tumaco persons [they were 106] and having taken down statements from the chief ones, to have them shot in order to prevent a flight that might have serious consequences ". On June 7th, he authorized the three officers in charge of the pursuit of the rebels from Guayaquil to Panamá " to shoot all rebels and deserters from the army of Colombia and of the enemy "; and on June 20th, in Garzal, he instructs Paz Castillo to send the Spanish officers prisoner to Peru and " as for the other prisoners, get rid of them in the way that may be the most convenient and expeditious for you ".

Little wonder the Pastusians tried for the third time to get rid of so much tyranny. A number of those who had " hidden in the woods and in the inaccessible crags of their hills "—writes O'Leary—" armed themselves with sticks, spears, and whatever weapons they could get hold of ", and advanced on the city (12.vi.23), under " a sagacious and brave " Indian, Agualongo, of whom O'Leary says " almost all the natives were his partisans ". Flores, a Venezuelan colonel, then in command at Pasto, was heavily defeated by the improvised army and leader at Catambuco; and later, Salom himself was defeated in El Puntal. Agualongo informed the *cabildo* of Otavalo that the rising was due to " the notorious, disastrous evils inflicted on this faithful population by Colombia, with its constant thefts, homicides and monstrous violences, destruction by fire of many houses, estates and three entire villages ". Bolívar put together troops against the rebels, collecting even the convalescent in the hospitals. He took the lead in person, in a state of mind which he betrayed in his Proclamation to the Quitoans on June 28th, 1823: " The infamous Pasto has again raised her hateful seditious head, but this head shall be cut off for ever. . . . This shall be the last time in the life of Pasto: she will pisappear from the catalogue of peoples, unless her vile inhabitants surrender their arms to Colombia without a shot. . . ."

He sallied forth from Quito with two thousand men, including some cavalry and four guns (5.vii.23). He wrote to Salom to withdraw slowly for " the intention of H.E. is to defeat the enemy in the open field and far from Pasto so that not a single one can return "; and to warn the villages that they were to kill or take prisoners any they might find defeated. In an unequal battle in numbers and armament, Bolívar defeated Agualongo at Ibarra (16.vii.23), and, writes Restrepo, " eight hundred bodies of Pastusians were left on the field, for no quarter was given ". This is a black page in the history of Bolívar. His behaviour after the battle was so sanguinary that even his most faithful historiographers stand back with horror at the indiscriminate and persistent bloodshed. His instructions to Salom amounted to an order to exterminate the population and replace it by outsiders. No metal whatever was to be allowed in the region. All men who presented themselves were to be sent to Guayaquil; those who would not come forward were to be shot; all families to be sent to Guayaquil. Salom carried out these instructions savagely; so savagely that he was again threatened by 1,500 Pastusians under Agualongo (19.viii.23). He defeated them near Catambuco; but soon a force about as strong was threatening him again. Salom wrote to Bolívar (25.ix.23): " I propose to Y.E. the only two methods calculated to end the Pasto war: a general and absolute pardon or the total destruction of the country; to-day I stand only by the second. . . . No idea can be conveyed of the obstinate tenacity and resentment of the Pastusians: if heretofore it is the majority of the population that has declared against us, now it is the total mass of them that wages war against us with a fury I cannot express. We have caught prisoner boys of nine and ten. This obduracy comes from their awareness of the way we dealt with them at Ibarra. They intercepted an answer from Major Aguirre on the sending of the handcuffs I asked for to despatch away in safety those who would report to me, in accordance with your instructions, and they fished out of the Guáitara river the bodies of two Pastusians who, with eight more others, I had delivered to Major Paredes with verbal orders to have them killed secretly." This policy was to keep Pasto in a state of rebellion for the rest of the year. Bolívar meanwhile had left the region and returned to Quito, where he arrived on July 31st, 1823. He was much impressed by the events of Pasto. He called a meeting or assembly of the notables of Quito and of its public bodies to select two committees: the first to designate all persons known for their pro-Spanish feelings, who were to be expelled from the territory of Colombia, though not deprived of their property; the second to designate the persons of Ecuador who would answer for the collection of 25,000 pesos monthly to pay for the garrisons. This done, he left for Guayaquil.

CHAPTER XIV

BOLÍVAR ENTERS LIMA

I

THE situation in Peru had changed dramatically while Bolívar was stamping down the rebellion of Pasto. Sucre's reports from Lima did not paint a satisfactory situation. Congress and the Executive now yielded to each other the honour of officially calling Bolívar in a way that suggested eagerness and sincerity in neither of them; now, on the contrary, endeavoured to wrench that honour from one another in the hope of each strengthening its own position. The army was moved by ambition rather than by patriotism; the Buenos Aires contingent suspected Santa Cruz of a plan to carve for himself a separate nation in Upper Peru at the expense of both Lima and Buenos Aires; and most military affairs, particularly the disastrous expedition to Intermedios and the second one to leave towards the middle of June, were in fact conceived and fostered by a commercial company " such as the India Company ", at which the Chileans felt disgruntled on business grounds; for this company was a Buenos Aires creation, owned mostly by Sarratea, General Martínez and other Argentine army men in partnership with the English Admiral Guise. The Chileans belonged to Bolívar's party and the Argentines were against him. This antagonism was in part at least a hangover from the opposition between Bolívar and San Martín. No one believed that Peru could be saved without Bolívar; but his coming was a risky business, as he might be driven to assume full authority or to hazard his reputation in a difficult campaign against still formidable Spanish forces. Santa Cruz' expedition had sailed southwards on May 15th and 16th. Sucre had turned down an invitation to take the command of a whole allied army (Colombia, Peru, Chile and Argentina), " in order ", as he wrote to Bolívar, " to force them to call you ".

On May 19th, Sucre asked Campino, the Chilean envoy, and it seems, many others as well, " whether it would be advisable that the *Libertador*, on arriving, should depose the present administration and take over the Executive power ". Everybody told him that " this step would considerably harm the popularity of the *Libertador* ". Sucre reported this to Bolívar, but went on working for Riva Agüero's fall, and even put his troops at the disposal of Congress in a note (23.v.23) which was " interpreted by the government, by Congress and by the people as an incitement to a change of government "..

At this stage, the Spaniards reappeared. After a serious rift between the Viceroy and Canterac over troops that La Serna wanted to stay in Huamanga and Canterac wanted to lead to Lima, Canterac had his way and came down to the coast with seven thousand men. There was a regular emigration to Callao and a war council decided to abandon Lima. Sucre was again offered supreme command and, this time, accepted it. On June 16th

Canterac settled in Lurin, close to Lima; and on the 18th he entered the
city amidst "open applause and silent complicities". The Spanish
commander (who happened to be a Frenchman) "found open arms and a
public opinion predisposed in his favour". It is the stranger therefore,
though it cannot be doubted, that Canterac demanded three million pesos
and three thousand rifles within three days under threat of setting fire to the
city; whereupon the *cabildo* retorted that in such a case three to four hundred
Spanish prisoners held by the Independents in Callao would be beheaded.

This is vouched for by Sucre who had locked himself up in Callao with
his 3,700 men and was in the thick of an intrigue against Riva Agüero.
Congress met in Callao and decided to send a fresh deputation to Bolívar
with a new invitation to come to Peru; and to grant dictatorial powers to
Sucre, while Congress and the President were transferred to Trujillo.
Sucre took his success with the utmost skill and moderation, and studiously
limited his own powers to the area of his military duties; but Congress
did not stop its attack on Riva Agüero and after increasing Sucre's dignities
and powers on June 21st, decreed, on the 22nd, that the President "ceased
in the exercise of his functions in all parts where war is being waged";
and finally, on the 23rd, deposed and exiled him. Sucre concluded an
agreement with Riva Agüero whereby the President would leave for Trujillo
and occupy Jauja with Peruvian troops; he would supply Callao by sea with
food, money and soldiers for replacements; while Sucre would remain
neutral in Peru's internal dissensions and would recognize him as President.

Canterac looked on from a peaceful and friendly Lima in which, writes a
Chilean historian, "persons of all classes were in sympathy with the enemy
[i.e. the Spaniards]. There were magistrates, civil servants and members
of Congress who went over to the royal standard, giving a deplorable example
later to be followed by many people." But the Spanish commander was
uneasy about the general situation. He had not heard of the existence of
Sucre's army until he was already in Huarachirá; and the news that Santa
Cruz was penetrating towards Upper Peru made him realize, somewhat
late, that the Viceroy had been right in opposing the departure of the troops
from Huamanga. Had Santa Cruz and his chief of staff Gamarra thought
less of carving military kingdoms for themselves and more about defeating
the Spaniards, the end of the Spanish way in the New World might indeed
have come about then. Alarmed at this possibility (which Santa Cruz was
to waste) Canterac sent Valdés on July 5th with a division of three battalions
of infantry, some cavalry and some artillery back to the Viceroy and left
Lima (16.vii.23) "accompanied by a numerous crowd that followed them
sharing their fate".

Sucre had lost no time. He had been preparing his troops to reinforce
Santa Cruz. He hesitated, for he mistrusted Santa Cruz and did not feel
the situation in Lima very satisfactory. Finally he sailed southward
(19.vii.23) only to find that his reinforcements were refused by Santa Cruz.
But Santa Cruz mismanaged his campaign. After landing in Ilo, he had
advanced straight towards Upper Peru and entered La Paz on August 8th.
Sucre was worried. He had come to help in good faith and now was left

A NATURAL BRIDGE OF ICONONZO,
from an engraving

*A ROPE BRIDGE
NEAR PENIPE,
from an engraving*

in danger. " If he has gone beyond Puno, our position will be bad; but if he holds Puno, we shall be safe "—he wrote to Bolívar (7.viii.23). By then, the Spaniard Jerónimo Valdés, marching with lightning speed, had taken Puno. Despite an undecided encounter in Zepita (25.viii.23), which he calmly put down as a victory, Santa Cruz had to order a hasty retreat that soon became a rout. His expedition had ended in complete disaster. Sucre had wasted his time, but had learnt much about the difficulty of commanding allied troops, and he reports to Bolívar how General Porto-carrero had refused horses for his cavalry on the ground that they were for Santa Cruz whom Sucre was on his way to help. His strictures are confirmed by the picture which Paz Soldán, the historian of the Peruvian campaigns, painted of the tensions of all kinds which divided the army. " The Argentines esteemed themselves better than the Chileans, whom they had freed; and as a reward, the Chileans detested them and denied them every merit, taking pleasure in denouncing their not very moral, in fact, if you will, scandalous conduct. Even in their physique there was a rivalry: the Argentines being, in general, handsome, tall, intelligent and very attractive in their ways and language. The Colombians, proud of their victories and of the fame of their hero, thought themselves above all Americans. . . . The haughtiness of northerners and southerners hurt the Peruvians in their self-esteem." These divisions, this licence, their exactions wherever they went and the traditions of three centuries explained why, in the south as well as in the north, the population by no means responded to the enthusiasm of the liberating armies. A Lima newspaper, the *Correo Mercantil* (18.ix.23), provided a lively scene as a comment to the entry in Arequipa of General Miller, an Englishman in the service of the patriots. " What a disappointment for those unnatural citizens who fled away with our enemies from this capital: what a dreadful lesson in repentance for so many unhappy women who, seduced by the King's troops, in the blind hope of a happy fate, disappeared with the Goths riding asses for lack of mules or horses."

Anarchy prevailed in Lima and in Trujillo. Riva Agüero, when deposed by Congress, had first acquiesced, then flouted Congress, and later sent an emissary to Santa Cruz to ask him to return to his troops. When this emissary, Orbegoso, arrived in Arica, he heard of Santa Cruz' disaster. The army chiefs decided to recall San Martín, and an " Act ", signed among others by Portocarrero and Admiral Guise, was sent to the Protector, then in Chile, on the eve of his departure from Buenos Aires, to call him back to save Peru. San Martín refused. He took care not to recommend Bolívar as a saviour, but advocated a sincere recognition of the authority of Congress. Meanwhile, in Trujillo, Riva Agüero had dissolved Congress (17.vii.23) and Congress had deposed Riva Agüero in Lima (23.vi.23). Sucre had left in Lima Torre-Tagle in nominal-political, and Manuel Valdés in real-military command; but, having " recognized " Riva Agüero, had made it a condition of Torre-Tagle's authority that he should cease as soon as Riva Agüero returned. Torre-Tagle had thrown the condition to the winds, bought Congress " with big sums of money drawn from the

Public Treasury ", and made himself President and Father of the Fatherland (8.viii.23). In far-off Mendoza, San Martín, on hearing that Torre-Tagle had been made President of Peru, had exclaimed: " I believe that all the power of the Supreme Being is not enough to liberate that unhappy country; only Bolívar, based on force, can do it." On Riva Agüero's protesting in strong language, Congress appointed Torre-Tagle President of the Republic (18.viii.23). Torre-Tagle declared Riva Agüero a traitor and decreed it a merit for any citizen to seize him dead or alive (19.viii.23). Sucre was away and Manuel Valdés was not Sucre. He sent a letter to Riva Agüero, well meant, but showing the force of Colombia and threatening the deposed President with the enmity of Bolívar in a manner that Sucre would never have demeaned himself to do. Riva Agüero was incensed. A *zambo* sergeant, Velarde, having arrived in Trujillo to spy on him, was arrested, accused, it seems, without foundation, of having come to murder him, sentenced and executed (30.viii.23). Two days later, in the morning of September 1st, 1823, Bolívar landed in Callao.

2

Sailing along the coast, on board the *Chimborazo*, towards the capital of the Spanish Empire he had done more than any man to destroy, Bolívar may have more than once turned inwards his fiery glance to scan his inner landscape. What was he really struggling for ? His glory. From Caracas, his Paris, through Bogotá and Quito, he was at last sailing towards Lima, his Rome. In Lima, the splendid capital of the viceroys, he would be crowned—oh not physically, or at any rate, not with a kingly crown—but in spirit and with a crown of laurels, though set in gold, as the Liberator of a continent. But . . . what lay on his path ? His fatherland, once prosperous, in ruins; while from Caracas to Pasto the loud acclamations of the cities reverberated hardly enough to cover the droning murmur of the suffering multitudes. Whom had he liberated ? The Indians ? They had crowded round Agualongo against him and for the King of Spain, and had held his lieutenants in check in the coastal regions from Coro and Maracaibo to Santa Marta and Cartagena. The poorer Creoles ? " All the lower classes in the Cauca as in Popayán "—he wrote to Santander (8.iii.22)—" are enemies of our service; but the rich are much to be recommended; particularly the families of Mosquera, Arboleda, Caicedo, etc." Was he then fighting for the rich, for his class ? Why then had his own sister María Antonia refused to follow him ? On May 29th, 1823, he wrote to his nephew Anacleto Clemente: " I had four letters of yours to-day in which you announce me the arrival of your mother in Caracas, which I have heard with much pleasure, for I did not want her to go about dishonouring my name by living amongst Spaniards, since she might have followed her sister's Juanica's example, who preferred everything rather than the shame of living among the enemies of her name."

But María Antonia was not alone in her choice. His closest friends and relatives, the Toro brothers, while not actually preferring the King of Spain (as María Antonia as well as their younger brother Juan had done), had also preferred exile to a life under that Republic they had so frivolously co-operated to bring forth. And as he sailed towards his glory in Lima, Bolívar would still be thinking of his Paris boon companion, his brother sabre-rattler in the streets of Caracas, that Fernando Toro who had exiled himself until after the battle of Carabobo and was now ingloriously dead. On May 30th, 1823, Bolívar had written to the Marqués de Toro: " You are left without your two brothers and I without a million friends, country-men and relatives. It seems that the fable of Saturn has come true: the Revolution is devouring its children; most of them destroyed by the sword, others by the scythe of misfortune, crueller than the cruellest war. I doubt not but that unhappy Fernando has been destroyed by sadness rather than by death." Did these melancholy thoughts well up in his heart while he sailed towards his glory? Did he realize that before rising in his imperial glory in Lima, a Lima shorn of its bygone splendours by the wars, he had scourged the Pastusians with the scorpions of conquest more ruthlessly than the hardest of the *conquistadores* he constantly castigated in his proclamation? As he sailed to liberate Peru from the heirs of the *conquistadores*, had he liberated himself from the *conquistador* in him? Was not the very name he had chosen for himself—*Libertador*—an echo of *conquistador*?

" On September 1st, the brig *Chimborazo* sailed closer to the coast, and from her deck, the Liberator was able to observe the fateful influence of metal on nature, that metal which, in the political and moral world, corrupts and vilifies everything." As soon as the *Chimborazo* was in sight, everything was set in motion to receive Bolívar in Callao. The whole army was paraded at the water front. As Bolívar set foot on Peruvian soil, he was carried in triumph to the house prepared for him in Lima. All available members of Congress, with Torre-Tagle at their head, had come out to the port to accompany the Liberator. A deputation from Congress officially came to his house to greet him. Bolívar thanked it for the honour and the trust and " assured them that Congress could rely on his endeavours provided abuses were put an end to and radical reforms were introduced in all the branches of the administration, which, so far, had been vicious and corrupted ". And O'Leary, who reports and even underlines these words, adds: " Torre-Tagle and his Ministers, who were present, heard his words attentively which they forthwith believed to be ominous."

3

Duly endowed with full powers by Congress (2.ix.23), Bolívar proceeded to get rid of Riva Agüero and sent him a letter (4.ix.23) amounting to an intimation to surrender. Congress, he explained, represents the nation, and is the very source of your authority. You cannot dissolve it and you must not disobey. Then, significantly: " Bonaparte in Europe and Iturbide in America are the two most prodigious men, each in his kind, which modern history presents." Neither of them, he goes on to say, was able to avoid his ruin, because both committed the political sacrilege of having " profaned the temple of the laws and the *sancta sanctorum* of all the social rights ". (How revealing, not only that he should mention Bonaparte, who was always in his mind—but that he should have added Iturbide to his list of " the two most prodigious men of modern History ", Iturbide, whose only claim to " glory " was that he had crowned himself an Emperor.) Bolívar then describes the events of Trujillo as " the blackest blot on the Revolution ", and plainly informs Riva Agüero that " on no account will you rule over Lima, nor your friends either, for we all shall arm in defence of Peru ". He nevertheless offered him his friendship and sent two emissaries to negotiate. One point should be noticed in this letter: Bolívar judges Riva Agüero not only on a Peruvian but on an American background; his last passage is typical: he speaks of " what America would suffer from your behaviour, though I cannot forget what you have done for America and in particular for Peru ".

The same day (4.ix.23), Congress consulted Bolívar as to the powers he required. For him the answer was clear: " All." But he was a far more cautious man than those two " prodigious " failures. His answer was eloquent and noble. He wrote a letter on September 5th declaring that he had come to fulfil " the unique aim of my life: the American war "; note again the continental note he strikes on setting foot in Lima, the true capital of Spanish America. He goes on to emphasize his dislike for administration, and declares his offer to Peru to be limited to " the use of my sword ". Congress granted him what he expected (10.ix.23): " Supreme military authority in all the territory of the Republic as the present situation demands ", and " a dictatorial political authority ". Congress voted him also a salary of 50,000 pesos, which he declined; and a Guard of Honour. It was an improvised affair, the motto of which *Die for Congress* can hardly have inspired Bolívar, who handed it on to Torre-Tagle with a recommendation to prepare seasoned troops for the campaigns ahead.

Lima, however, was a pleasure-loving city, eager for sights and shows; and on September 13th, 1823, at noon, through streets bedecked with flowers, tapestries and fine ladies, Bolívar with Torre-Tagle and every civilian, military and ecclesiastical authority who had a brilliant uniform to display, went to Congress " to recognize the sovereignty of the nation and to manifest his submission to it ". Amidst the wildest enthusiasm, Bolívar declared that " the soldier liberators will not return to their fatherland unless they do so covered with laurels and taking away as trophies the standards of Castille. They will conquer and leave Peru free, or they will all die." And when the President had answered with no less eloquence, and Bolívar had again promised " a free and sovereign Peru ", a member of Congress rose to speak: " The true day of our liberty has come. If the illustrious Liberator of Colombia, if the immortal Simón Bolívar deceives us, we shall have to give up for ever dealing at all with men." Then there was a banquet and toasts. As no one remembered the vanished Protector, Bolívar rose to drink in honour of his erstwhile rival—a typical gesture of his knightly ways—and then he rose again, glass in hand and drank " that the peoples of America may never allow a throne to be raised in the whole of their territory; that just as Napoleon sank in the immensity of the ocean and the new Emperor Iturbide was dethroned in Mexico, may all the usurpers of the American people fall and not a single one remain triumphant in the whole New World ". No one was there to say: Methinks Bolívar doth protest too much.

4

Meanwhile he was getting rid of Riva Agüero with the unwitting aid of his rival. Riva Agüero had tried for the second time to appeal to San Martín, who, this time, realizing what was afoot, waxed indignant: " How could you imagine that an offer of service from General San Martín "— he wrote himself to Riva Agüero—" could ever be made to a private person, let alone a despicable man such as you ? " He then sent another messenger to his henchmen, Santa Cruz, Gamarra and Guise; but by then Santa Cruz' and Gamarra's army had vanished, while Sucre's was in being; and so the two Upper Peruvians veered over to Torre-Tagle, followed by Admiral Guise. This left Riva Agüero no other way out than to treat with the Spaniards. In so doing he was sinning no more than every other independent leader who had tried such a way out at one time or another, for instance Iturbide, Bolívar, San Martín, Sucre, and at that very time, in Buenos Aires, Rivadavia. Riva Agüero sent Colonel Don Remigio Silva to the Viceroy with instructions to negotiate an armistice of eighteen months during which a permanent peace would be concluded with Spain. There was a reserved clause 5, whereby the Peruvian government agreed to " send away the auxiliary troops which were in Lima and Callao ", and should their chiefs resist " the Spanish and Peruvian armies together would oblige them by force to evacuate the country ". The Viceroy answered on October 12th, 1823, accepting to negotiate, in spite, he said, of his military preponderance. This answer was intercepted by some advanced forces of patriots and sent to Bolívar. So runs, at least, the official view. But according to Bedford Wilson, than whom no more faithful friend ever lived in Bolívar's intimate circle, these papers were forged by Bolívar for further use.

A close negotiation went on, until Congress angrily authorized Bolívar to use force against Riva Agüero (1.x.23). Bolívar sent him an ultimatum. Riva Agüero replied by sending Bolívar one of his army commanders, Don Antonio Gutiérrez de la Fuente. When La Fuente arrived in Bolívar's cabinet, Bolívar confronted him with the proofs of Riva Agüero's treachery which he had had prepared for the occasion; and La Fuente went over to him. The talks went on while Bolívar gathered his forces; and then he struck. On November 16th, from Supe, he issued a proclamation declaring that " the sovereignty of the people has been trampled under foot in Peru by one of her own sons, by a criminal of lèse majesté ". And he incited his soldiers to march to punish " the monster Riva Agüero ". On November 25th La Fuente seized Riva Agüero in Trujillo together with Herrera and four other " accomplices ". For this deed he was promoted to Brigadier

General. On December 1st, La Fuente received from Berindoaga, Torre-Tagle's (and therefore Bolívar's) War Minister, an order to shoot Riva Agüero and his six companions at once " in a secret place and without any formality ". La Fuente refused and sent Riva Agüero to Huanchaco on board an American ship, on which the deposed President thought he was sailing for California. To his dismay, he was landed in Guayaquil and jailed. The other five men were set free. Bolívar was wroth.

5

Bolívar, at last master in his own house, was able to take stock of the situation with a continental perspective. The year 1823 had brought about dramatic changes, not only in his own career but in the attitude towards South America of the three countries which concerned him most: the United States, Spain and Great Britain. The change was in part due to his own successes; but the chief asset of the Spanish-American separatists was the struggle going on in Spain between two extreme parties: the absolutists behind Ferdinand VII and the constitutionalists behind Riego, with the repercussions of this struggle among the European Powers. Goaded by that indefatigable advocate of the Spanish-American Republics, Henry Clay, the Government of the United States advanced, though cautiously, along the path of recognition while it still hoped to obtain Florida from Spain. On March 8th, 1822, Monroe had presented a message to Congress in which he proposed the recognition of the Spanish-American Republics. In June, 1822, Castlereagh had recognized their flags for sea trading. British foreign policy was now in the hands of Canning, whose generous eloquence draped a cold political intellect. The battle of Talavera had meant, for the Spaniards, deliverance from a foreign tyrant; for Canning, the opening of the harbours of Spanish America for British trade. The foreign policy of the United States was in the hands of the only man then available who could, and would, beat Canning at this kind of *Realpolitik*: John Quincy Adams. The movements of these two men with regard to Spanish America were determined by three factors: the political struggle within Spain; the interference of France in Spanish affairs, coupled with her designs on the Spanish Empire; and the encroachments of the Russian Emperor, owner of Alaska in the New World.

The extremism of Spanish liberals had frightened the monarchs of Europe; and, despite Wellington's efforts to browbeat them at Verona, they were determined to stop the Spanish danger. The Prussian, Austrian and Russian Ministers in Madrid had asked for their passports " in most violent and abusive language " (9-10.i.23). Chateaubriand instructed his Minister in Madrid, de la Garde, to ask for his (18.i.23). Louis XVIII, in a warlike speech from the throne, announced that 100,000 Frenchmen were ready to march into Spain to uphold legitimacy and the right of Ferdinand VII to grant or withhold institutions (28.i.23). Canning mobilized a new army of which he felt himself to be the Commander-in-Chief: public opinion. On February 11th, 1823, he delivered a threatening speech at Harwich.

He did not mean war, unless France tried to aid Spain to recover Spanish America or invaded Portugal. Moreover, his own king and even his colleagues, all but Liverpool, were against him; and George IV lived in hopes of a French descent into Spain to teach the constitutionalists a lesson. Nothing daunted, Canning sent a dispatch to France amounting to an ultimatum (31.iii.23) unless three conditions were respected: no permanent occupation of Spain; no annexation of Spanish colonies; no attempt on Portugal. The French did not answer. The army of the Duc d'Angoulême crossed the frontier into Spain (6.iv.23); Canning declared in the House of Commons (14.iv.23) that Britain would remain neutral, but concluded boldly: " Indifference we can never feel towards the affairs of Spain: and I earnestly hope that she may come triumphantly out of the struggle."

How far did all this suit the true interests of Spain ? Very little. Though the invasion of Spain by French troops was to be deplored, the aim of the French Prime Minister, Villèle, was excellent: to reform the Spanish constitution, making it bi-cameral and so to endeavour to find a middle way between the two wild schools that were threatening to destroy Spain. Had Canning joined the French in this endeavour, short of military intervention (which his collaboration would have rendered unnecessary), the history of Spain and that of Europe might have been happier. Canning preferred to follow that line of intervening by non-intervention which seems to appeal so much to British diplomacy. The campaign of the French was a walk-over. On May 24th, they were in Madrid. On September 30th, they took Cádiz. Ferdinand was set free from his constitutionalist subjects and entered Cádiz amidst general jubilation (1.x.23). On the same day, he issued a decree cancelling every " act of the government called constitutional that has dominated my peoples from March 7th, 1820, till to-day ". Disgusted with his Spanish relative, Angoulême left for France; and Ferdinand was able to fall back into his own subhuman self. " Canning," writes his biographer Temperley, " watched from afar, with silent contempt, the generous but ineffectual efforts of Angoulême to protect the hapless victims of Ferdinand." And again: " He had encouraged the constitutionalists as long as he could, because they were opposing France." The naïve Spaniards, however, had dreamt that Canning opposed France because he wanted to encourage the Spanish constitutionalists.

6

Canning, who had so far held his hand in Spanish-American affairs, felt free to act; and on the day he heard of the fall of Cádiz (10.x.23), accredited consuls to the chief towns of the Spanish New World; he also dispatched to Colombia and to Mexico commissions of enquiry with a view to later recognition. It was by then his opinion " that France meditates and has all along meditated a direct interference in Spanish America ". He instructed his commissioners to Mexico and to Colombia to favour—but not to propose—the setting up of monarchies there under Spanish princes, on condition that no foreign force be used thereto. He had all along felt that he had to bar the way to France, and had sought the backing of the United States for this. He had sent (20.viii.23) to the American Minister, Richard Rush, a memorandum suggesting a joint declaration on five points: 1.—The recovery of the colonies by Spain is hopeless. 2.—Their recognition as independent States is a matter of time and circumstance. 3.—Yet, no impediment to amicable arrangement with the mother country is envisaged. 4.—We aim not at the possession of any portion of them. 5.—Nor could we see any portion of them transferred to any other Power, with indifference. Canning follows this statement up with a note (23.viii.23) informing Rush that a Congress on Spanish-American affairs was being contemplated by the Powers. On the 28th, Rush offered him to sign without instructions if Canning recognized the independence of the Spanish-American States; to which Canning demurred for he preferred Spain to recognize them first. The matter was held in abeyance, in fact dropped to all appearances, because the United States did not agree to committing themselves openly to the view that they had no designs on Spanish territory; and because they had already recognized the Spanish-American Republics and would have no monarchies in the New World.

Determined to check France by all means, Canning summoned the French Ambassador, Polignac, to a parley which lasted six days, drafted a record of it, and made the unwilling Polignac sign it. The famous " Polignac Memorandum " showed: that Great Britain would recognize the Spanish colonies either in the case of any interference by force or by menace in the dispute, or of any attempt at restoring the commercial and coastal laws of Spain with regard to her colonies, which Britain considered as tacitly repealed; and that Great Britain declined to go into " a joint delibera- tion upon the subject of Spanish America upon an equal footing with other Powers ", and certainly not without the United States; finally that France remained definitely committed to abstain from armed interference in Spanish America. Canning hastened to circulate this document to the Powers. Chateaubriand was shocked at the suggestion that the United States should be considered at all in the matter; and Metternich, while emphasizing that the United States were opposed " to the fundamental principles, forms of government, manners doctrines, and civil and political régime of Europe " saw that Canning's suggestion went no further than blocking the proposed Congress by subordinating it to an unattainable condition, since the United States would decline any invitation to such a parley.

Adams would have seen to that. When he received from Rush the first overtures from Canning (9.x.23) the American Secretary of State passed them on to President Monroe who, impressed, communicated them to his two predecessors, Madison and Jefferson. The three statesmen were inclined to accept them. Adams had other views. For him, the news meant that Great Britain would fight a France which meddled in Spanish America. " My reliance upon the co-operation of Great Britain "—he was to write later—" rested not upon her principles, but her interest." He had seen through Canning. He would out-Canning Canning. He would " make up an American policy, and adhere inflexibly to that "—the more inflexibly as, in case of crisis, the British flag would have to do the fighting. Monroe, a Virginian, did not relish the idea; but Adams stood his ground and seized the opportunity afforded him by the absolutist doctrines then aired by the Russian Minister in Washington, Tuyll, on the occasion of an Ukase, forbidding all non-Russians to fish, trade or navigate within one hundred miles of the Alaskan coasts. " It would be "—Monroe declared—"more candid as well as more dignified to avow our principles explicitly to Russia and to France, than to come in as a cock-boat in the wake of the British man-of-war." On December 3rd, 1823, President Monroe delivered his famous message the text of which is now known as the Monroe Doctrine. It proclaimed: 1.—The principle of no entanglements in Europe, " meeting in all instances the just claims of every Power, submitting to injuries from none ". 2.—The U.S. would " consider any attempt on the part of the European Powers to extend their system to any portion of this hemisphere as dangerous to our peace and safety ". 3.—The U.S. could not interfere with existing colonies and dependencies, but would consider it an unfriendly act for any European Power to try to " oppress " or " control " those already recognized as independent by the United States. Canning was displeased. He thought the Doctrine " extravagant " and " not very intelligently stated "; and feared (apparently without foundation) that it would go so far as to prevent Spain herself from holding her kingdoms by force, which would " constitute as important a difference between his views of the subject and ours as perhaps it is possible to conceive ".

All this was happening while Bolívar the Colombian was struggling to become Bolívar the American. His envoy, Joaquín Mosquera, had signed in Lima with Monteagudo a treaty (6.vii.22) of perpetual union, in which the High Contracting Parties " bound themselves to induce the other States of the once Spanish America to enter into this covenant of perpetual union, league and confederation ". An assembly of all the States of Spanish America was contemplated in Panama. Mosquera had signed similar treaties in Santiago (21.x.22), and in Buenos Aires (8.iii.23). Santa María signed one in Mexico (3.x.23). Thus Bolívar endeavoured to restore the political unity of the Spanish-speaking world, which Adams was at the time sheltering behind the Monroe Doctrine and Canning behind the British Fleet. He was not successful everywhere. The Buenos Aires Treaty was not satisfactory, and, in a letter to Monteagudo (then already in exile) he complained of the objections of Buenos Aires: that the United States had not been invited; that a Colombian territory should not have been suggested for the Assembly. Bolívar is incensed at Rivadavia's remark that " we must not confirm Europe's opinion of our ineptitude "; but that we must " show her our capacity with well conceived and skilfully carried out plans". In this same letter, he mentions a scheme presented to Mosquera by the government of Buenos Aires for a Congress to meet in Washington to form an armed confederation against the Holy Alliance, composed of Spain, Portugal, Greece, United States of America, Mexico,

Colombia, Haiti, Buenos Aires, Chile and Peru. He rejects this scheme in a humorous but energetic vein as Britain's plan through Portugal as her instrument. On September 16th, 1823, from Lima, he wrote to Santander " a string of prophecies ": " the first, the occupation of Spain by the allies; the second, war between England and France, the third, the coming of the Bourbons to America; and the fourth, a general flare-up in the world; in Europe because the Liberals will be protected by the English, who will arm principles against princes; and in America because the Bourbons will bring principles opposed to ours though they be no other than the monarchist principles "; and he concludes with this shrewder sentence, where his inner disquiet as a would-be ruler of America can be guessed: " I believe that all Europeans in general have more or less of an interest in the independence of America, but governed by European princes. This matter, well pondered over, is of much importance and of the utmost gravity for us."

Chapter XV

THE BATTLE OF JUNIN

I

BOLÍVAR began the year 1824 in a precarious state of health. He did not spare himself. Over and above his relentless activity as the leader of a continental revolution, he consumed his slender frame in life's pleasures, most of all in his immoderate love of women. Lima's women were famous in the whole of America for their beauty and charm. They loved Bolívar and he let himself be loved by them. He wrote to Santander shortly after his arrival: " Lima is a pleasant city and it was once rich. . . . The ladies are very agreeable and handsome. We are having a ball to-night where I shall see them all." A few days later (20.ix.23) he wrote again: " I am more pleased every day with Lima. . . . The men value me and the women love me: this is most delightful; there are many pleasures about for those who can pay for them . . . I am enchanted; of course, I lack nothing. The table is excellent, the theatre passable, very much decorated with beautiful eyes and bewitching figures; carriages, horses, promenades, bullfights, *Te Deums*, nothing is missing, save money for those who lack it, for as for me, I have too much owing to my savings." He was drawing then a salary of 30,000 pesos, granted him for life by Colombia, and as much again, as equivalent to the salary of President of Peru. But he spent little on himself and was by then comfortably off, since his personal expenses were covered officially. On October 13th, 1823, Manuelita Sáenz arrived in Lima. This can hardly have improved Bolívar's health, for in point of sensuous eagerness, their meeting could be described in the Spanish saying as that of hunger with appetite. His hectic life as a universally admired Caesar galloped ahead. He had the satisfaction of using his prestige then to rescue from the dictator of Paraguay, Dr. Francia, his friend Bonpland, Humboldt's companion, whom Francia had imprisoned, and to offer Madame Bonpland and her family " an honourable situation in Colombia ".

On his way back from Trujillo where he had gone to settle a conflict of authority with Guise, Bolívar fell seriously ill in Pativilca (1.i.24). He described his illness to Santander as " a complication of internal irritation and of rheumatism with fever and bladder trouble, vomit and intestinal pains "; and attributed it to a long march in the Sierra. It was more likely due to his fast life in Lima, as he himself reveals: " If I go for my convalescence to Lima, both business and pleasure will make me ill again. . . . I am no longer able to strain myself without suffering infinitely "—he wrote to Santander; but the date of this long letter (7.i.24), six days after he had fallen ill, proves his indomitable energy. He adds, however, two significant details: " I am very much worn out and very old, and in the midst of a storm such as this, I represent old age "; and:

" now and then I am suddenly seized with attacks of madness, even though I may be in good health, when I completely lose reason without suffering the slightest illness or pain." The first emphasizes that mood of ageing and disillusion which Bolívar had begun to feel early in life and which had become almost predominant in the previous year. The sight of San Martín withdrawing from public life of his own accord fascinated him, as suicide does certain people in certain circumstances.

At bottom what was gnawing at his inner peace was the secret insincerity of his life. Had he fought for liberty or for glory? In a long letter to Santander (23.i.24), this theme comes to the surface, though in a peculiar way, to suit his disenchanted mood: " The Quitoans and Peruvians will do nothing for their country, and therefore it is not for me to tyrannize them into salvation. . . . Hitherto I have fought for liberty; henceforward I want to fight for my glory at the cost even of the whole world. My glory consists now in no longer wielding any power or having to do with anything but myself. My years [he was forty], my ailings and the frustration of all the illusion of my youth. . . . I am so mortally weary that I want to see no one, to dine with no one, and the presence of a man mortifies me." He then paints a vivid picture of the time, " a time of disasters, and since death will not take me under her protecting wing, I must hasten to hide my head amidst the darkness of oblivion and of silence, ere, from the hail of thunderbolts that Heaven is shaking over the earth, one may hit me and turn me into dust, ashes, nothing. It would be madness on my part to look on the storm and not to run for shelter. Bonaparte, Castlereagh, Naples, Piedmont, Portugal, Spain, Morillo, Ballesteros, Iturbide, San Martín, O'Higgins, Riva Agüero and Francia, everything falls, brought down by infamy or by misfortune—and I standing? It cannot be, and I must fall."

It is revealing that in this page, written in close touch with his inner self, Bolívar writes that word *demencia* which had come to his mind when describing his attacks of madness. The whole letter is written in a kind of twilight of reason. It confirms the guess made at the beginning of our study of this vast and tortured soul, whose inner tensions were too strong for sanity. Every time circumstances brought about a weakening of the chief force in his life, ambition, the inner tensions were bound to disintegrate his unity, bringing him to the edge of madness. This is a case in point. But by now we may carry our study one step further. Ambitious though he was, and strong enough to overpower any outside obstacle, Bolívar was beginning to realize that he would never reach the summit of power because his own character was in the way. There were three features of it which made him, time and again, stray from the path of his ascent: he was bored by administration; he was too pleasure-loving; and, above all, he was far too intelligent. He ran away from his official capitals and shoved the burden of government on his lieutenants as soon as he could. Of his pleasure-loving ways, volumes have been written. He loved women, banquets and balls. Of his supreme intelligence, his letters are a monument. And when a less acute mind would have been content with serving the hand that grasped the levers of power, Bolívar's wanders from the narrow path of action to look

around, observe, compare, forecast, enjoy ideas with that zest he brought
to everything in life. And so these three features of his character lead up
to but one result: he would not arrive *ad augusta* because he would not be
content with *per angosta*.

2

During this January of his *annus mirabilis*, however, Bolívar had enough
worries to feel justified in his pessimism. The military situation was not
good. The patriots were divided by a regular net of mistrusts and
contempts; while the Spaniards, in Bolívar's own words, were "tenacious
and pertinacious". The Spanish Commander in Chief, Canterac, with
his headquarters in Huancayo, and a column in Ica under Brigadier Rodil,
controlled all the country to Chincha. The northern army disposed of
8,000 men, not including 1,000 men who garrisoned Cuzco, where the
Viceroy, La Serna, resided. General Jerónimo Valdés, with his headquarters in Arequipa, commanded the army of the south, 3,000 men under
his immediate orders and 4,000 under Olañeta in Upper Peru, beyond the
Desaguadero, the stream that drains lake Titicaca. There were 2,000 more
men in mobile columns. The Spaniards planned to begin the campaign
towards April or May, at the close of the rainy season, occupy Lima and Callao,
and turn Bolívar out of Peru. To that end, Jerónimo Valdés and Olañeta
were to meet the northern army in Jauja. Bolívar meanwhile was struggling
with sheer anarchy. Torre-Tagle, without consulting him, had sent back a
Chilean contingent from Callao; Congress had sent back to their masters
all the recruits freed from slavery to be turned into soldiers; Peruvian
soldiers deserted "as soon as they are allowed to sleep in the open or in
long marches". He complained to Torre-Tagle and threatened his
resignation, which he announced as a fact to Santander on the same
date (7.i.24).

Santander, of course, would smile. Bolívar resigned as some people
cough, every hour or so, and for the same reason: a slight irritation in the
windpipe, which must be cleared before they speak out. And he did speak
out after every resignation. This time was no exception. On January 9th,
1824, while still weak from his illness, he dictated a long plan to counter
the danger he clearly saw. He could not face the Spanish army until he
had received a reinforcement of 6–8,000 Colombian soldiers (he asked for
12,000 in his letter to Santander). He estimated at six months the time
needed for their coming. If in this time the Spaniards attacked, the Patriot
army would be destroyed. He, therefore, saw no other way out than "to
treat with the Spaniards for an armistice, to gain time and see whether we
can meanwhile get together the whole Colombian army I am awaiting".
He went on to propose that Torre-Tagle should confidentially tell Congress
he knew for certain the Spaniards wanted to parley. The armistice must contain a clause enabling each side to break hostilities on sixty days' notice or
less, to impress the Spaniards and also "because it is the great secret that
we shall open hostilities as soon as we get the army from Colombia".

He would, however, not fight if the Spaniards accepted " to fall in with liberal and just ideas, as it is likely they would on realizing the superiority of our arms ". The officer to be sent must be " most sagacious ". He is to feed the Spaniards with all kinds of stories about " the misery of the country and the insolence of the allies "; and must, of course, be a Peruvian. He must, however, speak " about the forces under my command, my ability and my character in a tone of confidence and of boasting so as to succeed at least somewhat in impressing the Spaniards ". All this was to be conveyed to Torre-Tagle by one of Bolívar's own henchmen, Colonel Heres, who was to foster a favourable opinion among Congressmen, yet must present the scheme as Torre-Tagle's own " always feigning opposition on my part ". On January 15th, 1824, he writes to Heres that he withdraws to Trujillo and that he wants everything belonging to him in Lima to be sent to him there, " my horse, my saddle, my books, not excepting one straw ". He was sure Lima would be lost.

The idea of an armistice came from Sucre. But in Sucre's mind, it was to be a genuine negotiation for a genuine peace. Bolívar twisted it into a tricky truce. It so happened that towards the end of 1823, Torre-Tagle had sent a secret emissary to Canterac offering to hand over Callao. (Torre-Tagle was humiliated by Bolívar's short ways with him, and showed it, complaining, for instance, of the heavy taxes Bolívar levied to pay and dress smartly the Colombian troops.) The Spaniards answered that if Torre-Tagle fulfilled his promise he would regain the grace of the monarch and receive due rewards. It was then that Heres put before him Bolívar's proposal. Torre-Tagle asked to read it and copied it; then, with the approval of Congress, he sent his War Secretary, Brigadier General Don Juan de Berindoaga, to Jauja, to negotiate with the Spaniards. Berindoaga, Count of San Donás, was an ex-officer of the Spanish army. Whether with Berindoaga's own complicity or only with that of his aide-de-camp Herrán (a European Spaniard), Torre-Tagle, under cover of Bolívar's idea, tried to carry on his own negotiation with the Spaniards; Berindoaga was not received by Canterac but had talks with two Spanish subordinate Generals who advised him to join them in " sending Bolívar packing over to the other side of the Juanambú ". Whatever was then talked about or transacted, it was not what Bolívar meant; and may indeed have been the very opposite, for there is at least a suspicious sequence in time between the actual offer of Callao made to the Spanish authorities by Torre-Tagle in October, 1823, and its actual delivery by two mutinous sergeants during the first week of February, 1824.

Callao was then garrisoned by about 1,400 men of the Río de la Plata battalion composed of Buenos Aires and Peruvian soldiers under the command of two Buenos Aires generals, Alvarado and Martínez. The dungeons housed about thirty Spanish officers held prisoner. Two sergeants, one of them a negro from Córdoba (Argentina), Dámaso Moyano, and the other an Argentine, Oliva, organized a conspiracy of all the sergeants of Callao to demand their pay—which they accused General Martínez of pocketing and gambling in Lima. During the night of February 4th to 5th, the sergeants seized and locked up all their officers, including General Alvarado. There was much disorder for a day; but, fearing punishment, the leaders bethought themselves of the Spanish officers, and liberated one of them, Colonel Casariego, who persuaded them to deliver the place to the Spanish army. The sergeants first negotiated with their chiefs on the basis of a payment of 100,000 pesos and a passage home. Martínez, however, gave instructions to the ship's captain to send them back to be shot, and Moyano, who intercepted this order, decided to return and deliver Callao to the Spaniards, a solution which Torre-Tagle appears to have fostered by his remissness in finding the 100,000 pesos required. Casariego raised the Spanish flag over Callao, made Moyano a colonel and Oliva a lieutenant colonel, and wrote to Canterac to send a governor. Canterac was not surprised " in view of some news he had ". On February 29th, 1824, General Monet, with a strong Spanish force, entered the fortress.

But if Bolívar's affairs went from bad to worse because his allies went over to the adversary, they suddenly took a favourable turn because a powerful adversary crossed over to his side. This was the odd law of that truly civil war. Torre-Tagle, perhaps Berindoaga, and the two sergeants had left the Independent for the Royalist flag. Olañeta, with his 4,000 men, suddenly rebelled against the Spanish Viceroy. Whether he actually became a patriot is open to doubt. Olañeta was a Peruvian merchant who had attained the rank of Brigadier General in the Spanish forces as a bold guerrilla chief. He combined military and business activities in ways displeasing to his fellow generals, making his officers and men pay extortionate prices for food and drink whenever occasion allowed. He was, moreover, a dyed-in-the-wool absolutist, who hated the Spanish constitution. He had gradually built for himself a kind of military viceroyalty in Upper Peru. Hearing of the Decree signed by Ferdinand (1.x.23) foreshadowing the downfall of the constitutional régime, Olañeta issued a proclamation to the Peruvians (4.ii.24) declaring himself the Protector of religion and absolutism against " the Liberals, Jews and heretics " whom the Viceroy, Canterac and Valdés were supposed to defend. Olañeta refused to lend any help to the campaign against Bolívar. Valdés, called in by the Viceroy, had to strike. Two battles were fought with units of the Spanish army on both sides, but when, after the second, the battle of La Lava, everything pointed to the destruction of the rebel, Valdés was called away: Bolívar had won the battle of Junin.

3

When Joaquín Mosquera, his roving envoy in the south, came back to report, he found a miserable Bolívar convalescing in the modest white-washed house in Pativilca. " Thin, wasted out; I found him sitting on a leathern chair, leaning on the wall of the small garden, a white kerchief tied round his head, his linen trousers revealing his bony knees and fleshless legs, a hollow, weak voice, a cadaverous face." Such was the shaky abode of an indomitable spirit. No one could have guessed his physical state on reading the letters that poured out of that small house on the dusty main road in Pativilca during those feverish days. His black, fiery eyes followed every event relentlessly. To Heres, in charge of the bogus armistice with the Spaniards: " When Berindoaga returns or writes, make the utmost effort to learn everything from the first to the last word; from the simplest glances to the clearest actions. Copy, write, ask, even the servants who have gone with Berindoaga, on my behalf, what they have heard, learnt, seen. Tell Berindoaga to write a private letter to me saying everything, everything, everything, nor must you fail to do as much. The aide-de-camp who must have gone with him must come to see me to relate all details that might be illuminating. Of course, you must examine the effect of this mission on the public, and above all, on the government. Catch by surprise the secret of their hearts by a sudden and skilful enquiry. Above all, find out what the Goths say of me and of the Colombians."

On February 4th he wrote to Sucre, a lucid, vivid, long letter, sparkling with ideas and felicitous phrases; and again on the 6th, an outline of Berindoaga's news, just received. With his usual shrewdness, he grants no credit to Berindoaga's opinion that the Spaniards do not intend to attack northwards, but on the contrary, thinks " they would be fools if they did not do it now ". That was of course what the Spaniards were planning, and the fact that Berindoaga gave such an opinion should be counted as a strong hint of his complicity with the Spaniards. Then came the loss of Callao. It impressed him terribly, but brought out his energy, his lucidity and his terroristic tendency. To La Mar (8.ii.24): " War feeds on despotism and is not made for the love of God . . . you must show a terrible and inexorable firmness." To Salom (10.ii.24): " destroy the Pastusians ". His long letter to Santander (10.ii.24) is steeped in energetic and intelligent pessimism: " Friend: this world is crumbling down . . . all is lost . . . this country is sick with a moral pest. . . . Every rascal wants to be a sovereign, every rascal defends what he has by fire and blood, and will sacrifice nothing. I say these things of Peru and of Colombia and above all of Quito, the mirror of selfishness." He thinks of withdrawing all the way to Colombia, for he cannot remedy the weakness of his army, " being unable to smelt afresh our soldiers and officers who, being either frail or defective, lack the admirable qualities in which the Spanish army excels, that of marching and counter-marching without losing men. The soldiers of the Goths march fifteen or twenty leagues in one day, and they carry their food about in a small bag of coca and another one of barley or roast corn. On this they march for weeks and weeks; their chiefs and officers do not sleep in order to tend to them. I must tell you once for all, there is neither friend nor foe who does not come to tell me wonders of the Spanish army. The Quitoans are the only patriots and they are the most perverse, infamous rascals of the lot. Those of Cuenca have always been Goths; those of Guayaquil are Jews who think of nothing but their money, and though the more decent people are the most pro-Spanish, they are the more serviceable."

There was far more passion than judgment in all this; but due note must be taken again of the fact that, as late as 1824, Bolívar had to own that the bulk of the southern populations, i.e. what we describe as Ecuador as well as the Cauca valley in Colombia, were still pro-Spanish. This was another source of worry for him; for from the outset he had conceived his Peruvian enterprise as a reconquest from the north; implying a free passage to Ecuador (hence his *delenda Pasto*), and a sea base in Guayaquil. The loss of Callao, and by way of consequence of Lima, was not so dreadful a disaster provided his reinforcements came in time. But in the eyes of public opinion, it could not be more formidable. The loss of the two chief coastal cities gave the impression that the war was as good as over. On February 10th, 1824, Congress granted Bolívar dictatorial powers and went into a recess *sine die*. Bolívar was, of course, gratified; and he sent orders to General Martínez to save from Lima every possible thing that could be of use to the army. In itself, this order was no harsher than the circumstances warranted. Unfortunately, Bolívar's choice of the men to carry it out could not have been worse. As his own henchman, Heres, wrote to him from Lima on February 11th, 1819: " General Martínez has absolutely lost public opinion: he is generally hated." In those days, Lima observed how the general, told off by Bolívar to save her, was busy putting his own chattels in safety. True, Bolívar himself was not beyond that reproach (bearing in mind the peculiar nature of his own treasures), to judge by a letter from Heres to him, dated Chanquillo, 13.ii.24: " The little country-woman will leave Lima to-morrow. Martínez (the Major) was leaving Chancay to-day with the beasts of burden she needed, which I provided. I also gave him some armed servants of a friend of mine, so that the beasts should arrive safely, and then she might travel with a good escort. All this is safe."

4

Bolívar's ideas at the time are clear. About foreign affairs: he sees clearly what Santander does not. In answer to a confidential official letter in which Santander expresses his fears with regard to France, Bolívar writes from Trujillo (16.iii.24): " This fear does not seem to me well founded. . . . The English must side with us on the day the French side with the Spaniards; and the superiority of the English over the allies is such as to make us consider the event as a triumph." This was so; but the remarkable fact about it is the total silence about the United States and the brand new Monroe Doctrine. Bolívar goes on to argue that a French threat from the north would not make it less, but more, necessary to close the southern door, Peru. Here, he writes with even more than his usual energy: " For the same reason we should have to use our forces swiftly to destroy that Peruvian rabble, to return then against those French in the north with all the American forces I should know how to take with me, by consent or by force; for force feeds force as weakness feeds weakness." Towards Peru, his ideas were: " This is full of factions, and of traitors; some are for Torre-Tagle, others for Riva Agüero, others for the Spaniards, and very few for Independents. But all begin to fear me much; and they also say that everything will be cured with my recipe: an ounce of lead and

four drams of powder." About the war: pin as many Spaniards to the
south as possible, since a conjunction of Valdés with Canterac would spell
ruin for us. To that end, " let Salazar and the Chilean Minister frequently
write by ships that may be caught, pretending that the government is planning
to send such and such a force to southern Peru ". His situation in the
north preyed on his mind, for, he writes to Santander: " in May we must
triumph or perish. . . . The Spaniard Valdés is on the march with his
division, to unite with Canterac. The Goths will give us no time for
anything, for Torre-Tagle will tell them all our secrets about making them
waste time till our reinforcements arrive. Destiny may perhaps already
have fulfilled itself when you receive this letter! "

It is easy to imagine how relieved he must have been on hearing in
Trujillo (13.iv.24) that Olañeta had proclaimed the King absolute without
orders from the Viceroy. His tricks to keep the Spaniards in the south were
no longer necessary. He wrote at once to Olañeta from Huaráz (21.v.24)
with a cynical use of ideas as tools for his purpose; and offered his friendship
to the ultramontane and reactionary general on the ground that " La Serna
and his associate are very far from oppressing America for the benefit of
Spain; what they want is to keep Peru in order to deliver it to the defeated
constitutional faction, which was unable to defend its fatherland or to conciliate
the interests of Europe and of America." So, at the time when he wrote
to Sir Robert Wilson (28.i.24): " We have heard with a justified regret
that the good cause in Spain has been sold to the bad ", he wrote to Olañeta
slandering the good cause and the Spanish constitution, which he compared
to a monster and to the government of the Grand Turk.

This, however, was Bolívar the propagandist, an unscrupulous pamphleteer.
Bolívar, the leader of armies was another matter. His conclusions are as
lucid as usual: " All this shows that there is a division in the Spanish army
and that soon it will be torn asunder by factions and even fights. The final
outcome is: first, that Olañeta with his division is beyond Oruro, in retreat
towards Jujuy; second, that Valdés is beyond Oruro; third, that neither
can come to fight here in May; fourth, that the King will side with Olañeta;
and fifth, that La Serna, Valdés and Canterac will have to alter their political
opinions so as not to be persecuted by the government of Spain." An
accurate forecast in all counts. He then concluded that his best plan was
to take the offensive against Canterac in May; and bids Sucre take all
possible precautions, from the shoeing of the horses to the choice of the
roads the army must follow. His plan was to prepare, during what remained
of April, to march towards Jauja in May, to fight in June. It is a picturesque
detail that at this time his chief requirement is iron from Biscay for the
nails of the horseshoes. But the defection of Olañeta had so altered his
state of mind that, after writing to Heres on the news that England was
" blindly for us ", he adds: " Nothing can change the face of America when
God, London and we are determined."

5

Of the three, Bolívar relied mostly on the third, " we ", by which he meant the Colombians and above all himself. Chile, to which he had sent repeated appeals, had sent a battalion, half of which returned on seeing Callao in Spanish hands, while the other joined Bolívar's troops. The Government would send no more help, it would seem out of distrust for Bolívar's ultimate intentions. Nor was Buenos Aires more helpful, for, to a request for ships, it answered that Bolívar might find them in the United States or in Europe. " The Chileans have sent nothing nor will send anything "—he wrote to Santander on May 6th from Huamachuco. " Buenos Aires will do the same, for that little Republic is like Thersites, who knows nothing but intriguing, cursing and insulting. The Peruvian fleet is full of bad faith; I can count on it for nothing." Still, he was not depressed and commented: " I am myself astonished at my own coolness, but thanks to the lessons I learnt in Colombia, I now know my craft." As for this craft, he describes it magnificently: " I have become a potter of republics, a craft of considerable work, but glorious ".

This was his excuse for holding Peru with an iron hand. Himself in Trujillo, Sucre in the Sierra and Lara in Huamachuco exerted a military dictatorship, exacting inexorable contributions in men and money to man, feed, clothe and equip the army. Thus, Bolívar instructs his secretary, José Gabriel Pérez (Huamachuco, 6.v.24), to send: " Not only the money, silver and gold, but jewels and precious stones. Send me everything to headquarters, not only what there is at present in the Treasury at Trujillo, but also all sums specie and jewels coming from the Provinces. . . . Press for the gathering up of all taxes and the collecting of all Church jewels." Even so, he does not seem to have collected more than about 200,000 pesos, most of it in silver bars which were sold at seven pesos the mark. Meanwhile, Santander had obtained from his Congress authority to send reinforcements to Bolívar and to raise an army of 50,000 men. A first contingent of 900 under Colonel Córdoba had arrived in January and a second of 1,000 under Figueredo in May. Lara's division came when Bolívar was already in Trujillo, and was immediately sent on to the Sierra. Bolívar had taken personal command of the armies of the coast, leaving those of the Sierra under Sucre, who, with his usual efficiency, had drafted the long-suffering native, equally willing—or unwilling—to take on the Spanish or the Independent uniform. The English volunteer Miller commanded the guerrillas, a motley crowd, dressed, or undressed, in all kinds of accoutrements and armed with weapons from pistols to spears and bows. Under the all-seeing eyes of Bolívar and the tireless activity of Sucre, the army was trained during the month of May.

Bolívar was in the highest of spirits, as may be gathered from his letters, some of the most brilliant, witty, profound and human he wrote in his life. Despite the hopeless situation he had to deal with when Congress collapsed into anarchy and defeatism, he had built up his army of about 10,000 men almost miraculously; and the defection of Olañeta had raised his hopes of victory. He had at the time one of the feminine adventures that came to enliven his military life. Some time in May, 1824, in the midst of popular excitement, triumphal arches, church bells, flowers, bands, he entered Huailas on his way to the Sierra. The, by now, traditional young maiden in white presented him with a crown of flowers. He took the human flower within the next two days, and kept her for the campaign. Her name was Manuela Madroño. There is no mention of the whereabouts at the time, of the other Manuela. The company of his new mistress seems to have kept him in good cheer: " You will see that though I beg, I am not sad ", he wrote to Santander. And, somewhat hypocritically, urging Santander to send him at once his old friend and master Simón Rodriguez, who had turned up in Bogotá: " Instead of a mistress I wish to have by my side a philosopher."

There is a curious passage in this letter: " If you found yourself surrounded with traitors and enemies, jealousies and rages, dreadful conspiracies against the State and against your own person, you would not have the calm to wonder whether to send or not reinforcements to Peru." What is this conspiracy? While in Huamachuco (where this letter is dated on May 6th, 1824), Bolívar received a confidential warning that an officer had been sent to his army to murder him, a description of the man being enclosed. " The *Libertador* was alone in his room reading and re-reading the features of this description, when, with an infallible eye, he saw in his mind the very portrait of the Major he had two days earlier entrusted with the nail-and-horseshoe workshop; he instantly sends for him. When the Major entered, the *Libertador* had the paper still in his hand; he bid him sit down, and while he talked and paced the room, he gave himself time to compare more closely the Major's features and those of the description; till he was convinced that he was the man. The *Libertador* went on treating him with the utmost kindness, and after a long talk, while watching his movements, sent him away saying: ' I always place well officers that come to me and justify my hopes. You will be sent as military governor to a good city ' ".

Bolívar had reserved for himself a kind of military kingship and had appointed Sucre commander-in-chief of the allied army (13.ii.24). The youthful general had been much distressed by a motion presented to the Colombian Congress by the Colombian Minister of War, accusing him of the failure of Santa Cruz' expedition to the south; and his correspondence on the subject had driven Bolívar to write him a stiff though truly cordial letter (20.xi.23). Bolívar had a deservedly high opinion of Sucre, of whom he had written to Santander (10.x.23): " He is the best deserving Venezuelan I know, and should God give him a victory he will be my rival in military success, for from the Ecuador to the south down to Potosí he will have done everything." This was to become as good a prophecy as Bolívar ever uttered. It honours Bolívar that he wrote it in October, 1823, and that in February, 1824, he raised Sucre to the first post in his giving. Bolívar organized his own itinerant administration with the Peruvian José Sánchez Carrión as universal Minister and General Santa Cruz as Chief of Staff.

He put La Mar at the head of the Peruvian army of 3,000 men, who were well trained and fairly well equipped by the end of May. About the middle of June, Bolívar set his army in motion towards the Jauja valley, occupied by Canterac: Córdova took the road by Cajatambo; Lara by Chavin; La Mar by Huánuco, three ravines allowing the ascent of the Cerro de Pasco. A column of Indians carried supplies on their backs. The army had warm clothes for the heights and good French or English rifles for the infantry and pistols and carbines for the cavalry.

6

The march owed much to Sucre who had even set trumpeters at set distances to enable stragglers to find their way, prepared huts and stores of firewood by the roadside and even boxes of sweets for the officers. On the other hand the army lived on the country: " Horses and mules were taken from the fields and no questions asked as to whose they were, and all the cattle found on either side of the line was gathered and taken away in the rearguard." So writes O'Connor, the Irishman, appointed by Bolívar Chief of Staff of the allied army, who adds: " From the day Bolívar arrived in Huánuco, all the chiefs had to lunch and dine at his table, very well served by the way." He pays a fine compliment to Bolívar's universal mind with regard to men, no matter their nationality. Towards the end of July, the army was in the High Plain of Cerro de Pasco. Though fourteen leagues away by road, the Patriots, from the heights of Tarma, could see the Spanish army of Canterac, 9,000 infantry and 2,000 cavalry. They received a paper which circulated in Canterac's army in which the Spanish commander gave for certain a prompt victory. Bolívar, who also had his newspaper, wisely refrained from a battle of pens, and was content to remark to his officers " that for the first time he was going to have the opportunity of measuring his arms with both of such valiant leaders ".

On August 1st, 1824, the allied army paraded on the plain of Sacramento, under a warm morning sun that struck variegated colours from the snowclad Andean peaks. Bolívar arrived with Sucre, La Mar, Santa Cruz and Gamarra, and was enthusiastically received; skilfully playing on the string of luck in numbers, he promised his army a victory for August 7th, the anniversary of the victory of Boyacá. He mustered 7,000 men, the rest having remained behind in hospitals and rearguard establishments. That evening there was a banquet, followed by the usual interminable toasts. Urged by Bolívar, O'Connor rose, glass in hand, and said: " Since the Colombian army is here united to liberate Peru from the Spanish yoke, apparently against the will of the Peruvians, I drink to the hope that, should we be defeated, no one remains to convey mourning and grief to the fatherland." And he goes on to relate: " Hardly had I finished when the *Libertador* shouted: ' This is my toast.' He leapt on the table, emptied his glass and dashed it against the wall."

It was about this time that an episode occurred which reads like a page of Don Quixote. Miller and two colonels rode out to reconnoitre towards

Los Reyes, and galloped back with the news that the Spanish army was marching towards Cerro de Pasco. " The alarm caused by this news soon vanished, when it was found out that the said army was a herd of llamas. On August 3rd, the Patriot army began its march towards the Lagoon of Lauricocha, and on the 5th Sucre with his infantry on the heights and Bolívar with the cavalry on the plains moved towards Condocancha. At Rumichaca, as Bolívar was lunching in the open air, sitting on the parapet of a stone bridge, news came, true this time, that Canterac was on his way to Cerro de Pasco.

Leaving his camp near Jauja on August 1st, 1824, Canterac had camped on the 2nd in Tarma-Tambo. He had eight good infantry battalions, thirteen-hundred horse and eight good pieces of artillery—a better and stronger army than Bolívar's except perhaps in point of actual loyalty. On August 5th, he was surprised to hear that Bolívar was marching towards Jauja by way of Yauli, i.e. between the lagoon and the Sierra, in the opposite direction and on the opposite bank of the lagoon. For fear of being cut off from his base, he returned post-haste; which Bolívar knew early enough to decide to attack him on his way back. Canterac had placed himself in this unfavourable position because he had entered one side of the lagoon without reconnoitring the other. Bolívar's cavalry, with their right on the Junín hills and their left on a long swamp which prolonged the lagoon, were now on the plains. Disdaining the use of his artillery and ordering it to continue its retreat with the infantry, Canterac ordered a cavalry charge. This was coolly resisted by the Colombians, whose long spears disconcerted the Spaniards. Canterac had no force nearby to restore the position. Not a shot was fired, because the Spanish infantry did not take part in the fight and Bolívar's was paralysed by " soroche " (the sickness of the heights). It was a white arm battle. The struggle was long, and at nightfall no one knew how things had actually gone. Bolívar looked on, agitated first, impotent later, later even gloomy. " What is happening, general ? "— shouted Lara. " What ? That our cavalry has been defeated." " Is the enemy as good as all that ? " " Too good, since it has defeated ours." " Shall I go and charge with these men ? " asked Lara pointing to the cavalry-men who had been thrown back. " No, for we should remain with no cavalry left for the end of our campaign." At six-thirty, Colonel Carvajal came to announce that the enemy declared itself defeated. Bolívar sent several companies of sharpshooters after them, riding on the backs of squadrons of cavalry; but Canterac and his defeated horsemen rejoined their useless infantry and artillery during the night. Dejected, Canterac abandoned the province of Jauja and withdrew to Cuzco.

CHAPTER XVI

THE BATTLE OF AYACUCHO

I

BOLÍVAR was content to let Canterac go, not trusting his Peruvian infantry to pursue him without deserting, for, says O'Connor, "they were more royalist than the Spaniards themselves". On August 8th, 1824, Bolívar's army left Los Reyes, and on the 9th, at Tarma, he offered a banquet to his officers, during which he treated with a special distinction the German colonel Felipe Braun, who had led his cavalry to victory in Junin. Bolívar, probably brewing his return to Lima, offered the command of the troops to La Mar, the senior of his generals present; but La Mar declined and Bolívar was then free to appoint Sucre. Immediately after his appointment, Sucre received orders to leave for the rearguard, to collect the wounded, and mobilize the hospitals and the parks for the march. "Every one will justly observe that this was not a commission for a Commander-in-Chief", writes O'Connor. Sucre obeyed, carried out his mission, and on his return wrote a long letter to Bolívar, pointing out that "such a commission has been the cause of mockery and satire among those who are not my friends, and of wonder for those who esteem me". Unable to choose between his position and his desire to serve, Sucre concluded by asking Bolívar himself to advise him on the matter. From Huamanga, Bolívar answered (4.ix.24), assuring Sucre that his first idea had been to take that task for himself, considering that there was no danger in the vanguard and that the rearguard included what was most precious for the army; hence his choice of the best man. The episode ended happily, but, though Bolívar's letter is lofty and cordial, it does reveal his desire to make Sucre realize that though he was put at the head of the army, there was a master over him.

Canterac had no other salvation but a speedy retreat, because his army, more than three-fourths composed of Peruvian recruits, would have deserted. He marched 160 kilometres in two days and went forward again almost at once. He was retreating in the region between the two chains watered by rivers that could be crossed at all only with with great difficulty if bridges were destroyed; and studded by the three cities of Tarma, Huancayo and Huamanga. By August 28th he had crossed the river Pampas, and fifteen days later he was again on the march towards Cuzco. Bolívar followed in pursuit, benefiting by a regular crop of arms and parks which the royalist army left behind on its way. He acted as an itinerant legislator and administrator in the somewhat personal and oriental way that suited his style; paying special attention to the interests of religion, for he had realized the strong religious root of the pro-Spanish tendency of the Peruvian people. He ordered schools to be founded under the leadership of the clergy, exempted from taxes the townships scorched by the adversary, and took

great care to order an inventory to be made of the property of the exiles so
that his army should profit by the sale of it; on the other hand he applied
his somewhat summary jurisdiction with an energy that paralysed all
opposition. Whoever disobeyed was shot. Townships that refused help
were dealt with ruthlessly. Hearing from the Prefect of Huamanga that
some municipal councillors refused to attend sittings of the Council, Bolívar
threatened them with enlisting them as privates; and the head of a hospital
found remiss in attending to his duties was threatened with being shot.
These were no vain threats. In this province, a sergeant and two colonial
soldiers who sacked a peasant's house and raped his daughter, were shot
and quartered and their bodies exposed to the public view. He was in
his element in thus exercising absolute authority—a feature of his character
soon to create a serious conflict for him.

2

On October 6th, 1824, he wrote again to Olañeta, from Sañayca, offering
him an alliance which he thought in the nature of things; and having heard
that La Serna was moving from Cuzco to Limatambo, went in person to
reconnoitre the territory up to the Apurimac, with that minute care for
detail which he detested in civil affairs but never neglected in military
matters. He received then a number of important dispatches: the Peruvian
government had contracted a loan in London, which would leave about
three million pesos net to spend. Heres wrote that Bolívar's presence in
Lima was necessary or else the loan would be squandered away. So said
O'Leary, and he should know, for, in fact, Heres says, O'Leary was one of
the men who squandered it. Furthermore, three thousand of the twelve
thousand men Bolívar had asked from Colombia were on the way. Finally,
the Spanish fleet in the Pacific had been reinforced with a ship of the line,
Asia, and a brig, *Aquiles*. All this, wrote Heres, was worth a battle. Bolívar
resolved to leave for Lima at once, leaving Sucre in command. He left
Sañayca on October 7th, 1824, towards Andahuailas, where he arrived on
October 10th.

This move has been taken for granted by everybody. But is it not somewhat unusual for the head of an army facing an adversary, though locally
defeated, still formidable? True, technically, or rather nominally, the
Commander-in-Chief was Sucre; but we know from Sucre's letter to
Bolívar (Jauja, 28.viii.24) that it was a mere name " with a vague and informal
power "; nor could Bolívar have had any doubts about the value of his
presence and magnetism for his troops. That he felt guilty about it may be
gathered from O'Leary's lame excuses and mutually excluding explanations.
So that we may take for certain that Bolívar left the army knowing that he
was behaving shabbily. And so he was. The workings of his mind at
this moment are plain. *He was scared by Junin.* He saw defeat within
sight, a final and disastrous defeat for him, with a hostile pro-Spanish or
anti-Colombian population, Callao in Spanish hands, two good Spanish ships
on the coast, and practically no army to receive him there; with a near

certainty of being caught and sent to Spain to die in Miranda's cell. Two considerations became predominant in his mind: to remain near the coast for his own personal safety; and to organize a second army on the coast. The first was not due to cowardice. Bolívar was no coward, even though at times subject to panic. It was due to his awareness of the part he played in the destinies of the continent, in which he was right. This, in its turn, led to a third consideration: he must spare his glory; he must not risk defeat. The Spaniards were so strong that they could afford to pass by without engaging their infantry and their artillery, suffer a cavalry defeat, and march on, while his men remained petrified by the height disease. If defeat there must be, let it be Sucre's; if Sucre wins, all win, including and above all, the Supreme Chief. Time was soon to bear out that this thought —justified in the circumstances—had been in his mind when leaving Sucre inland. Bolívar left for the coast.

3

In Huancayo, on October 24th, he heard that the Colombian Congress had abrogated the law of October 9th, 1821, granting him full powers in all territories where war was actually being waged, full command in the south and the right to grant promotions in the army without consulting Congress. He was hurt. This setback was the natural outcome of a double set of forces: a genuine fear and dislike of his dictatorial ways; and that complex of jealousy, resentment, frustrated ambition and intrigue that dogs the steps of great men. The tension between him and Santander was already beginning to grow, and precisely in the form that became apparent later: the man of force versus the man of law. When Bolívar wrote for reinforcements and money at all costs, Santander answered: " You can do everything and get away with it, but I have a Congress on my back." Are we then again in the presence of the old Spanish opposition between the cape-and-sword man and the gown-man? In part, yes. But there is more to it than that. Santander was aggrieved at his position in the army; for other men younger and not always worthier were getting promotion over his head. O'Leary accuses him of having instigated the rebellion of Congress out of jealousy of Sucre's career. This may not be altogether untrue. Santander was not fully sincere when writing to Bolívar: " I believe that the more moderate we appear [towards Congress] the better we ensure our triumph "; as if he were in solidarity with Bolívar in the matter. He had passed on to Congress Bolívar's requests for reinforcements with a message (26.iv.24) in which he commented: " If, to fulfil the obligation to free Peru, which he took on of his own free will, the *Libertador* has thought it necessary for the government of Colombia to put at his disposal the scanty resources it can hardly spare to defend the Republic, the *Libertador* forgets that the Executive Power has to submit without fail to a Code of Laws." This was a broad hint to Congress to act against the Dictator.

Bolívar realized the attitude of Santander, and, for some time, broke off a correspondence in which he had always been open and frank with his lieutenant. He resigned and wrote to Sucre informing him of the situation and delegating on him the command of the Colombian army. This, however, was purely ostensible; for he remained Dictator of Peru, and after all the true Dictator is the man who shoots—which Bolívar still did freely wherever he went. Indeed, the tendency to punish with death any disobedience to his impatient will had become so ingrained in him that the two ideas came together to his mind even in jest. López tells how, after giving him some instructions for a mission, he added jokingly: " Don't you go and forget anything for I shall have you shot." This feature was not political; it was a matter of character and education. " From my earliest infancy I have been very badly educated in suffering nothing from anyone ", he wrote once to Santander.

Sucre knew Bolívar well and was not likely to take too seriously a threat of resignation from a man then so powerful. Nevertheless, he staged one of those pretorian moves the Colombians had learned, with many other vices and virtues, from the Spaniards. In Pichiagua headquarters, with all his Colombian and foreign—but not the other American—leaders of the army, he signed a letter to Bolívar (10.xi.24) speaking of the " dreadful insult inflicted on him by the Executive Power in consulting Congress as to whether the promotions Y.E. had granted in the army would be recognized in Colombia "; and urging Bolívar to remain at the head of his troops. Sucre sent this letter open to Bolívar, with a private letter assuring his chief that he would write direct to Bogotá until the collective petition of the chiefs of the army had been put before the government and acted upon.

Bolívar went on to Jauja, where he stayed till October 29th, 1824, pursuing his activities energetically, oblivious of his paper resignation. He then wrote to Sucre urging caution towards the Spaniards till considerable reinforcements had reached him. Bolívar was not likely to alter these instructions, irksome as they may have been to Sucre, for on arriving in Chancay (5.xi.24), twenty leagues north of Lima, he heard the news that Luis Urdaneta had been heavily defeated between Lima and Callao. He was indignant, and had several officers and men summarily shot for cowardice. During the night of November 7th, 1824, he entered Lima, dark, silent, closed upon itself in its own misery. Ramírez, a guerrilla chief displaying royalist colours, had been for months taking it and leaving it, as a pretext for all kinds of excesses. As soon as the Limenians knew that Bolívar was in the city, enthusiasm ran like wildfire. The crowd raised him on their shoulders and nearly suffocated him. Torre-Tagle, Berindoaga, the Peruvian Vice-President Aliaga and many more prominent citizens had gone over to the Spanish side and were in Callao. With his usual promptness and energy, he organized his own Peruvian government with Heres as his War Minister, and went on creating another army. He still kept writing for reinforcements. " General Sucre remains in command of the army with instructions to watch the enemy closely and profit by any advantages that may turn up. He has authority for everything, but a strong recommendation to be prudent until reinforcements have come from Colombia ", he wrote to Soublette, and he explained his reasons for this insistence on more troops:

" The Spaniards were equal in number and had no morale nor discipline; but they occupy admirable positions behind the river Apurimac, and to force them out we shall need many troops."

4

On October 22nd, 1824, La Serna, at the head of 9,310 men, with Canterac as Chief of Staff and Valdés, Monet and Villalobos as divisional commanders, left Cuzco; he crossed the Apurimac on the 25th at Agcha. La Serna's plan consisted in cutting Sucre's rear; but Sucre, with a freer and better military sense, did not care whether his " rear " were cut or not. He sent Bolívar a plan to leave the Peruvians with La Mar and, with the Colombians, forestall La Serna and give him battle. Bolívar roundly opposed it. The fact that Bolívar constantly insisted on keeping the army united and on not risking battle except if sure of victory was the basis of Ayacucho. Before victory, however, the allied army had to suffer defeat. From December 1st, for about a week, the two armies manoeuvred at so short a distance from each other that their outposts often had brushes without after-effects, for Sucre did not feel free enough from Bolívar's instructions and La Serna was in difficulties with his own generals and with Olañeta. On December 3rd, Sucre's army entered a narrow defile at Corpaguaico, close to Matará. Valdés had forestalled him, and taken strong positions. Letting the head of the column pass unmolested, he inflicted heavy losses on the rearguard artillery. Sucre lost some artillery, half of the battalion of Rifles and nearly all his park, including his personal baggage. From that day until Ayacucho, the Indians rebelled against their liberators and lay in wait to murder any straggler they could catch.

If we are to believe O'Connor, the position which the allied armies occupied in Ayacucho had been chosen by him. It was a small plain east-west, about a thousand yards long, at the foot of the Condorcanqui mountain chain, limited by two ravines, one deep and impassable; the other not so deep, a branch of which cut half the plain in two. This angle of the two branches to the right of the royalist troops was the knot of the battle. The Spaniards occupied the broken flanks of the Condorcanqui; Villalobos on the left, Monet in the centre, Valdés on the right. They now numbered short of 7,000 men. Sucre, with 5,700, had La Mar opposite Valdés, Córdova opposite Villalobos and Lara in reserve at the western end of the line. " The sun having risen on our front, over the majestic top of Cundurcunca, the landscape swam in light and seemed to have been retouched for the festival ", writes López, an eyewitness; and he describes how the military bands added to the excitement of that morning (9.xii.24) when the last of the suns that never set had risen. " At eight o'clock General Monet, a strong, smart, bearded man, walked down to our lines, called Córdova and told him that, as there were several Spanish officers who had brothers, relatives and friends in the republican camp, he came to ask whether they could not meet before the battle." Córdova consulted Sucre, who gave his consent. For about half an hour, about fifty men on each side, leaving their swords at the line, conversed in a neutral space between the two camps. " The Spanish Brigadier Tur, a young tall man of thirty-four, perhaps the one who had asked for the interview, ran to ask for his brother, a lieutenant colonel in the Peruvian army, about six years younger. ' Ah, my brother, how sorry I am to see you covered with ignominy '—he cried out; and his brother, turning his back on him, retorted: ' I did not come here to be insulted.' But the Spaniard ran after him, and throwing his arms round his neck both wept for a long time." Meanwhile, Córdova and Monet were engaged in a discreet conversation aside from the lively group. Monet suggested a peace; Córdova accepted on the basis of the independence of Peru. Monet drew his attention to the strength of the Spanish army; Córdova answered that the battle would decide that point. Monet withdrew and both armies breakfasted in peace; then, every man went to dress for battle as for a parade.

The Republicans were modestly dressed (with uniforms sent from Chile by O'Leary), covered with dark overcoats which in the distance must have seemed to the Spaniards as if they were to meet an army of monks; the Spaniards dressed in bright colours, of different hues to make it easier for the commander-in-chief to move them about; so that the Independent army could enjoy " on the yellowish green of the Cundurcunca the long moving lines of white, blue, green, grey, yellow, red and other shades, the gold braid, the rich banners ", the glitter of the metals and the starry decorations.

" Towards half-past ten our old friend General Monet turned up again at the line, in a resplendent uniform, and calling General Córdova, said: ' General, are we ready for our battle ? '—' Let us fight '—answered Córdova and he went to report the fact to Sucre." Following the plan that had been proposed, Valdés came down to attack, but the plan supposed that the Republican left would be thrown back on the centre and right, where, in its disorder, it would be attacked by the two other divisions. Valdés was successful and the patriots were beginning to yield. Two Spanish regiments under Rubin de Celis, without orders, ran then to share in the victory. Sucre sent reinforcements to La Mar and at the same time threw Miller's cavalry and Córdova's division, fully 2,800 men, half his army, against Rubin de Celis. Córdova gave his famous battle cry: " Soldiers, weapons at discretion. A victor's step! " With magnificent courage and discipline his soldiers advanced without shooting under the fire of the enemy. Monet was sent forward, backed by two units of the Gerona regiment under Canterac in person. This was precisely the sector of the Spanish army that gave way. Rubin de Celis was killed, confusion ensued and a wave of panic shook the whole royalist army and precipitated the defeat of the two divisions of Villalobos and Monet. The Independents were thus able to surround Valdés and defeat him also. Within two hours the final battle of Spanish America had been won by Sucre. It appears that the defeat was an after-effect of the War to the Death. The Spanish officers had depicted the Colombians as so ferocious that, at the slightest wavering in the fortune of battle, the army had fled. Sucre wrote to Bolívar: " The war is ended. The freedom of Peru is complete. As a reward for me I ask that you reserve your friendship for me."

5

This battle presents a number of odd features. First: it began with a fraternization tolerated by both commanders, though a sure way of demoralizing their armies. Second: this singular scene, which could have been negotiated by a junior officer, involved a divisional commander on either side. Third: these two commanders, under the eyes of their armies, held private converse for half an hour, while the official version of what they told each other could not have lasted five minutes. Fourth: the Spanish interlocutor came back two hours later to ask his opposite number whether he was ready for battle. Fifth: when the battle was at its height, the division that yielded and began the rout was precisely that of the fraternizing and parleying commander; and the two companies of *Gerona* which came to his rescue and gave way also, were under the personal command of Canterac, Chief of Staff and second to the Commander-in-Chief. Sixth: an army superior in numbers, training and discipline, with at least seven times more artillery, was defeated when it still had 2,000 soldiers who had to surrender after it was fought. Seventh: a man of Canterac's military talents submitted his cavalry to the handicap of having to come to the battlefield down gradients so steep that they made it a safe target for the enemy while the men had to walk down warily helping their horses. Eighth: the Viceroy threw himself into the scrimmage and was easily made prisoner. Ninth: the last battle, bound to be final for their country, was over, so far as the Spanish Generals were concerned, in two hours. Tenth: on this, his most splendid title to glory, the final battle of the war, Sucre's official report is most sparing of detail, and most hazy in outline; while the report of Canterac is strictly limited to justifying the capitulation, but gives no detail. Eleventh: Sucre's terms were extraordinarily generous.

All this admits of but one explanation. *Monet came to negotiate the capitulation of the royalist generals beforehand.* If this is accepted, everything becomes clear. The Spanish generals could hardly do anything else, unless they surrendered without fighting, which, as a matter of fact, Monet may also have proposed. Their position was untenable. On their left (politically speaking), the Independents; on their right, Olañeta. Ferdinand, absolute; and, sooner or later, sure to back Olañeta against them. Whom, what, were they fighting for? It is practically certain that Canterac and Monet headed this movement, and that La Serna and Valdés followed reluctantly. This would explain how La Serna deliberately threw himself into the thick of the battle, seeking a wound as an alibi. A last indication that the battle was for the Spaniards a face-saving manoeuvre comes from this other dialogue, reported by López, who was present: Valdés sat on a rock, dejected, while some fighting was still going on. A Major Mediavilla, who told the story to López, was with him. " ' Mediavilla,' said Valdés with a voice of bitter despair, ' tell the Viceroy that the devil has taken away this comedy '.—' What will you do ? ' asked the officer.—' I don't know ', answered Valdés.—' We can still conclude an honourable capitulation.'—' You are right ', answered Valdés." So, we have it from Valdés that the battle was *a comedy*.

6

The official capitulation after the battle was negotiated by Canterac with La Mar and it was as generous as could be. The army that surrendered comprised the Viceroy, fifteen generals, sixteen colonels, 552 other officers and 2,000 soldiers; nearly all these soldiers were taken over into the Independent army. The news of the victory arrived somewhat late on the coast because Colonel Medina, sent by Sucre with the report, was stoned to death by the Indians on the bridge of Isuchaca. Lima heard it on December 21st. That very night Bolívar issued a proclamation which does him honour. " The liberating Army under the intrepid and expert General Sucre, has ended the war in Peru and even on the American continent with the most glorious victory ever obtained by the arms of the New World." This time Bolívar was outspoken and unreserved in his praise of his young rival. The preamble to his decree of rewards begins: " Whereas this glorious battle is exclusively due to the ability, courage and heroism of General Sucre and of his generals, officers and army . . ." The rewards themselves were truly generous, if fully deserved. Sucre was made a Field Marshal and granted the title of *Libertador* of Peru. It was also decreed that a pyramid would be erected on the battlefield with his bust on it. There were two motives for all this in Bolívar's mind. The first was to put the battle of Ayacucho beyond and above the suspicions which its many odd features were bound to awaken, as they did soon enough, both in the New World and in Spain. The second was to set his own soul at rest. He must have felt the happier and more thankful for this victory for the release from his own sense of guilt towards Sucre, whom he had in the secret of his mind exposed and sacrificed to defeat.

There was, of course, as well a true gratitude grafted on a true friendship. Bolívar loved Sucre as a son and Sucre deserved it for his loyalty and for his independence and manly courage in telling Bolívar all his mind when he did not agree with him. There was perhaps also a certain mellowing of Bolívar's character, which is revealed by his correspondence. Not that the former man in him would die easily. It is worth noting how, one day before receiving the official news of the victory, when rumour was already alive with it, he wrote to Santander (20.xii.24) for the first time after a long lapse of silence, freed by Sucre's victory from the inferiority and humiliation Santander had inflicted on him. " Sucre has won the most brilliant victory of the American war. I deem him fully worthy of it "—he said to the man he believed to be jealous of Sucre's career. He then announced that within two months the Congress of Peru would have met, Callao would be taken, and so he would be free to leave for Europe; for he was tired of ruling. " Everybody is burning me with reproaches about my ambition and my wanting to be crowned; the French say it; in Chile, in Buenos Aires, they say it; here they say it, not to speak of the anonymous paper of Caracas. I want no more glories. I only have one-third of my life left, and I want to live." He wants 100,000 pesos to go to Europe, and if not as a grace, he will offer in exchange his Aroa mines, " the most beautiful property in Venezuela ". He says he is living on borrowed money as he refused the salary of Peru and as the salary of Colombia does not come. And of his situation in Colombia he acidly says it is due to Dr. Azuero, " an old enemy of mine, but a friend of yours ".

Of course he was not really thinking of leaving. On November 15th, 1824, he had written to the Abbé de Pradt inviting him to come to Venezuela and offering him a pension of 15,000 duros yearly on his own private fortune. The context of his correspondence shows him unabated in his determination and sense of command. And yet he was not simulating. Bolívar's texture, we know, was not of one piece: he had empty spaces, inner discontinuities in his being, which enabled him to be sincere in different directions at the same time. He did feel like leaving everything and going; but also like staying and firmly grasping the levers of power. At this time, however, after so many experiences, he seems to be labouring under some disenchant-ment. During his Junin campaign he had ridden daily beside O'Higgins, the one-time liberator of Chile, now exiled by his liberated country; and had not dared give him a command, for which O'Higgins was longing, fearing to offend the Chilean government whose help he needed. Then there was San Martín, whose star had set beyond the horizon; then, Iturbide: " Over here they say "—he wrote to Santander (10.xi.24)—" that Iturbide has been shot in Soto la Marina; I will be very glad if that is so, for he might have caused another revolution in Mexico." All this was working obscurely in his mind. He still speaks of " the great Napoleon ". But he was too penetrating to be content with appearances and he saw through his own Caesarism. His more intimate letters at this time reveal his anxiety: " I can frankly assure you that the past is a path of flowers and that my sorrow is still to come. The future is my torment, my torture; my sadness comes from my philosophy . . . I am more of a philosopher in prosperity than in misfortune. . . . If I am sad it is for you all, for my luck has raised me so high that it is not likely that I may be unfortunate. . . . In this unhappy revolution, victory is as unfortunate as defeat; we shall always have to shed tears on our destiny. The Spaniards will soon end, but we—when? Like the wounded doe, we carry in our flank the arrow which must, without fail, cause our death, for our own blood is our poison. Happy those who will die before witnessing the end of this sanguinary drama. They have at least the comfort of this ray of hope, that what is to happen may not happen. That is all I wish for after the war. Farewell, friend, take comfort in the thought that, however sad our death may be, it will always be gayer than our life." Such were Bolívar's thoughts on the revolution he had begun at the time it triumphed with Sucre in Ayacucho.

PART III

THE EMPIRE OF THE ANDES

CHAPTER XVII

THE TEMPTATION OF THE CROWN

I

THE year 1825 began for Bolívar under bright international auspices. On December 31st, 1824, Canning recognized Colombia. In January, 1824, he had offered to mediate between Spain and her overseas Kingdoms, and throughout the year had refused to countenance a Congress on Spanish-American affairs while secretly proposing to Spain to guarantee Cuba to her in exchange for a peaceful separation of the mainland countries. The Spanish government liked the guarantee but not the condition, and the offer fell through. A fortnight later (17.v.24), Canning wrote to À Court, his Minister in Madrid: " H.M. reserves to himself the right of taking, at his own time, such steps as H.M. may think proper in respect to the several States of Spanish America, without further reference to the Court of Madrid." " H.M." meant of course Canning. The King would have been horrified had he read the dispatch. On July 17th, Canning explained to the Austrian Minister that he had delayed recognition of Colombia and Buenos Aires because they were republican. Even so, the King and most of his ministers, including Wellington, thought Canning dangerous on this issue and tried to overthrow him, with the help of Metternich. The City came to the rescue of the Foreign Secretary. On June 15th, 1824, Sir James Mackintosh presented a petition bearing the greatest signatures in the City, asking for the immediate recognition of the Spanish-American States. Canning received it with sympathy, if with a decorous reserve; and in the teeth of Wellington's opposition forwarded to the King a Cabinet Minute (23.vii.24) urging that full powers to negotiate a treaty of commerce be granted to the British Consul General in Buenos Aires, and adding that this would amount to diplomatic recognition.

On the strength of reports from his commissioner to Colombia he then proposed to the Cabinet, through Lord Liverpool, at the end of November, the recognition of Colombia and Mexico, arguing that " sooner or later we shall probably have to contend with a combined maritime power of France and the United States ". On December 7th the Cabinet resolved that the question should be decided without reference to any continental power. Canning asked that France should promise to evacuate Spain, which she still occupied. The French government was elusive. Whereupon Canning put it to the Cabinet that " the great practical question for us seems to be how, in the event of an actual incorporation of the resources of Spain with those of France, such an accession to the power of France can best be counteracted. I have no hesitation in saying that this must be by a separation of the resources of Spanish America from those of Spain." Mexico, moreover, should be recognized because of the British capital invested in her mines, and because " an amicable connection with Mexico would oppose a powerful barrier " to the " ambition and ascendancy " of the United States. Colombia was added as an afterthought. Wellington threatened to resign; whereupon, on December 14th, Liverpool and Canning announced they would resign unless Buenos Aires, Mexico and Colombia were recognized. The Cabinet surrendered, but the King fought hard, until, frightened by Wellington's threat of a *coup d'état*, he gave way (30.i.25). Without waiting for his approval, " H.M." Canning had already acted on December 31st, 1824.

After the death of Manuel Torres in September, 1822, the Colombian government had sent to Washington, as Minister plenipotentiary, José María Salazar, who presented credentials to President Monroe in July, 1823. Richard C. Anderson, American Minister to Colombia, arrived in Bogotá on December 10th, 1823, and presented his credentials to Santander on the 17th. He brought instructions to negotiate a treaty of commerce, in which the Colombian government strove to include a compulsory arbitration clause, which the American government rejected. Colombia was no more successful in its endeavours to abolish the black slave traffic, for the treaty, proposed by Gual and signed by him and Anderson in Bogotá (10.xii.24), was rejected by the American Senate. During his stay in Bogotá, Anderson reported the arrival of Hamilton and Campbell, Canning's commissioners (1.iii.24); that of the Comte de Landos and Monsieur Raquier sent to Peru, and of Monsieur Mollien, sent to Bogotá, by the French government; and the general movement of European emissaries then flooding Spanish America, according to Gual (the Colombian Secretary of State), all averse to republican institutions. Anderson also reported the arrival of a Dutch gentleman from Curaçao to negotiate a treaty with Holland and to act as *chargé d'affaires*.

Anderson thought that the matter that interested the Colombian government most was the federation of American States. This had been a favourite idea of Bolívar from the very first; he had made an express reference to it in an article he had published in the London *Morning Chronicle* on September 5th, 1810; and throughout his copious political literature he will ever remain faithful to the unity of the (Spanish) American continent. An error of historical perspective is not always avoided with regard to this matter. It consists in crediting Bolívar with a kind of prophetic vision and of a synthetic power capable of uniting the twenty nations of Spanish America into a vast confederation. When Bolívar appeals to all " Americans " and addresses them as *Conciudadanos*, he is not so much calling out to the future as evoking the past. Bolívar did not advocate the unity of Spanish America; he took it for granted, lived, breathed it. His army was led by men coming from all Spanish-American lands, including Spain; his governments often included not merely Granadinos, such as Córdova and Zea, but Cubans such as Yanes; he appointed a Mexican, Santa María, as his envoy to Mexico; and a European Spaniard, Torres, as his first Minister in

Washington.   Much as he might devote his life to the destruction of unity created by Spain in the New World, his chief asset as a continental figure was precisely that unity.   Had New Granada been French and Peru British, Bolívar would have remained a mere Venezuelan and would almost certainly have died in a dungeon in Cádiz.   In his federating policy, moreover, Bolívar was not thinking in continental terms, not even in (as the modern phrase goes) Ibero-American terms; but in terms of " *la América antes española* ". He was, therefore, endeavouring to plaster together, with republican and federative cement, the old Spanish building he had all but demolished with his political explosives.

" Americans, count on life even though you be guilty "—he had written in his *War to the Death* decree of 1813; and in his Message to Puyrredón in 1818: " One only must be the fatherland of all Americans, since we have always had a perfect unity in everything."   His disastrous experience of disunity and distrust in Peru had not cooled his federating ardour.   Joaquín Mosquera was still entrusted with a roving mission to recruit countries for the Congress which was to reunite all Spanish Americans.   Bolívar had asked him to undertake this mission while the Colombian government was still in Cúcuta (10.x.21), and Santander as Vice President defined it (11.xii.21) as aiming at a Conference " of sister nations, so far separated and exercising full sovereignty owing to the course of human events, but united, strong and powerful to defend themselves against the aggressions of foreign power ". On January 8th, 1822, Bolívar had written on this point to San Martín, to O'Higgins, and to Martín Rodríguez, then at the head of the Buenos Aires government.   Having broken the chains of Spanish tyranny, he wrote, " we still have to lay the foundations of the social pact which must form in this world a Nation of Republics ".   The phrase, with its echoes of Rousseau, " dates ", and smacks of that period so naïvely credulous of the power of words.   As Bolívar's emissary, Mosquera negotiated in Lima with the then Foreign Secretary, Monteagudo, also a convinced advocate of a Spanish-American federation, with the approval of San Martín; so that on July 6th, 1822, a treaty was signed between Colombia and Peru in which, over and above a perpetual alliance between the two States, an agreement was recorded on a Congress or Assembly of American States to meet in Panamá.   Things were, however, slowed down by the reluctance of the southern States to follow Bolívar's lead.

Bolívar sent official invitations to meet in Panamá to the governments of Colombia, Mexico, Buenos Aires, Chile and Guatemala (7.xii.24).   He did so as Head of the Peruvian government and not as President of Colombia which he also then was; and he began his circular with the formal " Great and Good Friend " usual between heads of States.   It was meet that such a paper should have been signed in Lima and not in Bogotá, and, though by a man from Caracas, by the head of the Peruvian State; for its first object was to restore, under republican colours, the union of Spanish America which the Viceroy of Peru had incarnated, and which, for natural as well as for political reasons, had made of Lima the capital of the Spanish New World. Bolívar's second object was to widen the scene of his power and to become at one stroke the *monocrat* of the whole Spanish New World. This cannot be doubted when reading the circular, bearing in mind Bolívar's technique and his persistent use of assemblies to obtain dictatorships. He declares his aim to be " a system of guarantees which, in peace and war, may be the shield of our new destiny "; and " To lay the basis for such a system, and to consolidate the power of this great body politic [the ex-Spanish Empire] is the task of a sublime authority that must lead the policy of our governments, whose influence must preserve the uniformity of their principles, and whose mere name may calm our storm. Such a respectable authority can only exist in an assembly of plenipotentiaries . . . meeting under the auspices of the victory won by our arms over the power of Spain." On December 22nd, 1824, he resigned the presidency of Colombia.

2

Bolívar was governing Peru by means of three men: the Peruvians Unanúe and Sánchez Carrión, and the Colombian Heres. Unanúe, an old scientist, author of a monograph on the Climate of Lima, was Finance Minister. Sánchez Carrión, born in 1787 in Huamachuco, was a lawyer of eloquence, the arch-enemy of Monteagudo, and had been one of the leaders of the republican party as Secretary of the First Congress of Lima. Heres was an army man, subservient to Bolívar. He was hated in Lima; and so was Pérez, Bolívar's military Secretary; hence the quip: *Heres más malo que Pérez*, with a pun on Heres (*eres* " you are "), " you are worse than Pérez ". The quality of these men Bolívar would have round him is one of the most unpleasant features of his character. During the crisis which was soon to lead to his first dictatorship, the Marquess of Torre-Tagle received a number of influential Colombians and Peruvians in his house to discuss the situation. Pérez suggested a loan to soothe the troops. " How much will you contribute ? "—asked the Marchioness—" for, if one is to believe the public voice, you keep a mistress and a carriage "—an only too true accusation against the luxury in which some of these colonels lived while their troops starved. Pérez answered: " No one should believe in hearsay, for if we did, we should have to take it that you, Madam, share your favours between the Marquess and a young subaltern." Such was the level of Bolívar's most intimate collaborator.

In his peculiar personal way, he had also associated to his governing team Bernardo Monteagudo, San Martín's evil spirit, whom the Congress of Lima, under Carrión's leadership, had exiled. Monteagudo was the protagonist of South American monarchism. Bolívar had met him in the autumn of 1823 in Ibarra, between Quito and Pasto, where he had gone for a rest after his Pasto campaign. Monteagudo, in exile, called and was received " with hospitality and courtesy ". They had two interests in common: " Monocracy " and Spanish-American federation. Bolívar kept him about; and O'Connor tells how one day, almost exactly a year later, during the Ayacucho campaign, " in one of our marches, downhill, towards a village where we were to spend a night, Monteagudo who came silent and brooding close to me, struck his forehead and cried out: ' I have it.' ' What ? ' I asked. ' The cipher '—he answered." He referred to a letter from Canterac to Rodil (then in command at Callao), which had been intercepted. " The most difficult cipher I had come across in my life "—said the Spanish-American Fouché; but he had solved it. This man was the sworn enemy of Sánchez Carrión; so that, when he was found dead with a knife in his heart, in a street of Lima (28.i.24), public opinion pointed at Bolívar's Secretary of State. Bolívar found the actual murderer, a negro; had him brought to his presence and tortured on the spot, against all the laws of both Peru and Spain, and wrenched from him the confession that the instigator had been Sánchez Carrión. After consulting with Unanúe and Heres, the matter was silenced and the negro sent to Haiti. But Heres was an intimate friend of Monteagudo; and by May of the same year he had successfully contrived to poison Carrión with his own hand.

Bolívar was blamed for this and even accused by his enemies of having connived in the murder—a senseless accusation. He is to blame for having chosen as his confidential secretaries men among whom such things could happen; but that he could conspire to murder the man he had chosen as a confidential collaborator is out of the question. His keen interest in the crime was due to his belief that it was part of a royalist conspiracy to murder him. Bolívar was then beset by fierce enemies and his very success made him new ones every day. Peru was literally at his feet. Don Manuel Lorenzo Vidaurre, a Peruvian who had been *Oidor* of the *Audiencia* of El Cuzco, seeing once that Bolívar had some difficulty in mounting his horse, went on all fours, to have the honour of feeling on his back the great man's foot. Bolívar made him President of the Supreme Court. The women competed for the honour of being talked about as his mistresses; the men, of serving under him; and between the Epistle and the Gospel, hymns were sung in his praise more noteworthy for their adulation than for their elegance. It was in this atmosphere of personal rule that the Congress of Peru met. The country was less enthusiastic than the official world; and many members of Congress were adverse to Bolívar and more so to the prolonged Colombian occupation. The " liberators " soon found the people tired of them everywhere, for they behaved like troops of occupation. This happened even in Colombia. On February 8th, a curious scene had taken place in Bogotá. The Colombian Congress had met to consider Bolívar's resignation as President. " After the reading, the profoundest silence reigned over the hall." (This could hardly have been favourable for the outgoing President, for, as Santander wrote to Bolívar on May 6th, 1825, Congressmen " harbour a deadly hatred towards the Liberators of the fatherland ".) And Restrepo goes on: " When fifteen minutes had gone by without anyone breaking the silence, the President of the Senate called a division, and by the unanimous vote of twenty-one Senators and fifty-two deputies, the resignation was not accepted. Repeated hurrahs to Congress broke the majestic silence which till then had prevailed in the hall."

3

In the morning of February 10th, 1825, twenty-one salvoes announced to Lima that yet another of the colourful State ceremonies was about to begin whereby, throughout his career, Bolívar tied to his chariot nation after nation. A commission was sent by Congress to the Palace to inform Bolívar of its inauguration; and the President of Congress who headed it, anticipated Bolívar's intentions by declaring to him that " Congress shivers at the idea that Y.E. might utter one single word on resignation of that Supreme Authority by which a year ago our fate was saved ". In the company of the commission and following a solemn procession of all the authorities, Bolívar walked to Congress through streets lined by troops, and thronged with enthusiastic crowds who threw flowers and acclaimed their Liberator. After a brief survey of his military and political activities, Bolívar spoke words admirable for their cunning and boldness: " Let me congratulate the people on its liberation from the most dreadful things in the world: from war, by the victory of Ayacucho; from despotism, by my resignation." He then announced that, after finishing off the Spanish forces in Cuzco, he would return home. The President of Congress insisted on his remaining: " May Providence, having decreed to save Peru, grant her these new sacrifices from the genius of liberty! " Then Bolívar, bolder still and more cunning, reminded Congress that he was a foreigner and that Congress had no right to alienate the sovereignty of the people. But Congress was intent on delivering its sovereignty to Bolívar and a law was passed the same day granting him more powers even than he had wielded during the war. " I tried to hurt their national pride "—wrote Bolívar—" so that my voice could be heard and Peru would not be ruled by a Colombian "; but all in vain: " The voice of Peru spoke louder than that of my conscience." In fact, he had written to Santander (6.i.25) that he meant to remain for the time being, to finish up the Olañeta and Callao wars and to see the federation through. As for his state of mind, it can be gathered from the end of the letter, where, as usual, he handles together the three names uppermost in his mind: Iturbide's, Napoleon's and his.

" The utterances of some Congressmen "—writes the Peruvian historian Paz Soldán—" their gestures, their very enthusiasm, overstepped the bounds of the most abject servility." Congress passed a vote of thanks to Colombia, and resolved to strike a medal in token of gratitude and to erect a statue to Bolívar. Sucre was appointed Grand Marshal of Ayacucho and granted two hundred thousand pesos and a rich estate. Bolívar was given a million pesos for his army, which he took and distributed, and another one for himself, which he refused (though his heirs claimed it and cashed it in 1851). Not a single reward was voted for any Peruvian general or unit. Bolívar lost no time in getting rid of the details of government. He set up a Council of Government (24.ii.25) with La Mar as President and Unanúe and Carrión as Councillors, to which he passed on his powers by delegation, the Council being bound to carry out his instructions as transmitted by the War Minister (a Venezuelan) who would accompany him in his travels.

Time went by and La Mar was too busy besieging Callao, where the Spaniard Rodil refused to surrender despite Ayacucho. Carrión was ill. Bolívar replaced them respectively by Unanúe as President and Heres, his War Secretary, whom he decided to leave behind, adding as Finance Minister Don José María Pando, a Peruvian who had been Minister of State in Spain, a moderate liberal and a monarchist. Before leaving for the south, Bolívar, " fearing "—says a Peruvian historian—" that Congress, coming back to national dignity, might cancel its decisions ", decided to dissolve it; a proposal to that effect presented by two of his henchmen, Ortiz, a Colombian, and Pedemonte, was approved, " with a lucid though servile report ", and Congress committed suicide on March 10th, 1825.

How did Bolívar carry his success? With one exception, well. The exception was his sexual life. He gave himself to the pleasures of a city with an old tradition of beauty and elegance, where his political and military glory made him irresistible to the fair sex. His Lima days undermined his constitution and prepared his premature death. Otherwise Bolívar proved worthy of success. He remained as generous and courteous as usual, and towards Sucre and Santander a model of friendship and understanding. He constantly urged Sucre to be more ambitious. The youthful general had requested to be relieved of his command as soon as Upper Peru had been pacified, to attend to his family affairs, his father having died in the previous July. Bolívar writes: " My dear general, fulfil your destiny, yield to the good fortune that courts you, do not imitate San Martín and Iturbide who threw away the glory that sought them. You are capable of every thing and should not hesitate to let yourself be drawn by fortune . . . I am not ambitious, but I see that you ought to be a bit ambitious, to equal or excel me. Remember that you have in me a living father who will always rejoice in the glory of his son." These were no mere words. In a later letter, in which he has to differ somewhat sternly from his brilliant second, he rightly adds: " Believe me, no one loves your glory as much as I do. No chief ever paid a handsomer tribute to a subordinate. Even now, a narrative of your life is being printed, written by me, in which, to satisfy my conscience, I give you all you deserve." And so it was: a deed which honours Bolívar. There is a no less noble passage in a letter to Santander (9.ii.25), which must be quoted, for it gave rise to the famous surname Santander has had ever since: " The more I consider your government the more I see you as the hero of American Administration. . . . It is a glory that two of my friends and seconds should have turned out to be prodigies in my hands. Your glory and that of Sucre are immense. If I knew envy, I should be envious. I am the man of difficulties, you the man of laws; Sucre the man of battles." He was writing because he knew Santander to be green with envy; and in another letter: " My gratitude for Sucre has no limits: first, out of justice, then out of generosity, for he has wrenched from me the most beautiful laurel branch. He is the Liberator of the Empire of the Incas from the Juanambú to Charcas, therefore my rival in military glory, for which I am by no means disgruntled, for I want to deserve what remains, since, were I envious, I should not deserve one laurel leaf.

I say the same about you. No one loves and applauds you more than I, from the heart and from the brain; for I believe that the most beautiful crown is that of justice. Were I envious I should not deserve the name of man. Unfortunately it is a feeling that afflicts some notable persons, to the detriment of their qualities."

4

There is more than meets the eye in this generosity. That evinced to Santander evidently aims indirectly at Santander's envy. But Bolívar's generosity towards Sucre is no less calculated and purposeful. Not by chance nor by mere metaphor did he write such things as: " You have in me a living father who will always rejoice in the glory of his son." Bolívar had no sons. No sons, no dynasty. No dynasty, no monarchy. Now . . .

On March 7th, 1825, a few weeks only after that paternal letter to Sucre, Bolívar wrote to Restrepo these enigmatic words: " I have a secret idea that I cannot reveal while I am in power. It may save or damn Colombia; damn, I mean, should it not be carried out." What was the idea ? He is positive that it must remain secret while he is in power. The words immediately preceding are: " I wish really to be free from power in order to bestow upon my country a real blessing. This blessing will appear later." The mystery thickens verbally when the sentence immediately before is considered: " You flatter me much by saying that I shall be allowed to live in a well-deserved idleness, leaving me only nominally as president. This flatters but does not satisfy me." It seems, therefore, that what was in his way and prevented him from revealing his secret boon to the nation was not power, but his pre-eminent position as president, whether effective or nominal. Now, the day after he wrote to Restrepo on his secret idea, Bolívar wrote to Santander an important letter (8.iii.25). He is worried about the note of the French Minister published by the *Morning Chronicle* (1.ix.24) as a summary of the instructions given by the Duke of Ranzau to Monsieur Chasseriau, secret agent in Colombia. Bolívar had had it reproduced in the *Gaceta del Gobierno* (3.iii.25). He echoes the rumour that the French are sending 20,000 men to the Antilles and suggests that spies should be sent to find out the facts about it, and adds: " Moreover, I believe it most advisable to examine the ultimate aims of the French. You know that Polignac [French Ambassador in London] told the Peruvian envoys that France wants us to have monarchist, or at any rate aristocratic government. Polignac said also to the envoys of Peru that *it was almost indifferent to them that those to be crowned in America be European princes or revolutionary generals*. [It is Bolívar who underlines.] Therefore, all that would appear to be required by them is a system like the European, without any stress on tying us up to the Metropolis. In Spain, the French strove to have the constitution reformed in a way similar to their own. The Spaniards refused, much to their loss. Should we imitate them, I fail to see what we could gain. All Europe against us, and America devastated."

So, his secret idea was—a monarchy. The sequel of the letter makes it plain. " The English and the Americans are only occasional allies and very selfish. It seems therefore advisable to enter into friendly relations with the Allied Gentlemen [i.e. the Holy Alliance] speaking to them in an insinuating and sweet language to wring from them their final decision and gain time." And then: " If the [Spanish] Americans believed me I should present to them the means [i.e. the " secret idea "] to prevent war and preserve their full and absolute liberty. Meanwhile I insist on the Isthmus meeting." Note how his mind connects the Assembly to meet in Panamá and the idea of a monarchy, in confirmation of all that has been said above. And then, a clear revelation of his inner train of thought: " I ask nothing for me, nothing, absolutely nothing. You, who know me, and the others, who ought to know me, will do me that justice. So you ought to put all your trust in me and let me act with the allies. I shall say at once that I will never take on executive duties either here or in Colombia." This last statement may be discounted, since he repeated it all his life with perfect insincerity. But the rest is clear. At the time, the eve of the Congress of Panamá and the dawn of the official international life of the Spanish-American nations he had emancipated, Bolívar is definitely in favour of an understanding with the Holy Alliance on the basis of a monarchy or a confederation of monarchies; he will have no European princes, as he said many times before and after; he knows the French would accept the crowning of a revolutionary general; and he does not let go as to whether he, in person, would or would not take the Crown. But who else was there to take it while he lived ?

It so happens that Bolívar felt at this time a renewal of interest in the Incas, and particularly in Manco Capac. There were, of course, in any case, two motives to be discounted: his *mestizo* attitude, which, as usual all over America, finding no basis in the Chibcha, and shrinking from the sanguinary Aztec, took refuge in the Incas; and the fact that at this time Bolívar stood in Peru as the conqueror of the Spaniards, and that the political thing to do then was to leave in the shade his Spanish side and to appear as the avenger of the dynasty of Atahuallpa. His proclamations at this period are all in this strain. On February 10th, 1825, he says to Congress of his companions in arms: " They have fulfilled the heaven decreed mission entrusted to them by Congress: in Junin and in Ayacucho they have spread freedom over the whole Empire that once belonged to Manco Capac." All this was to be expected. But what was Manco Capac doing in his letter to the Bishop of Cuzco (28.i.25) in which every sentence begins Christian and ends Incaic ? " I shall always stand by the rights of the Sanctuary [whatever that may mean] and my heart will never part from the land of the Incas "; " I shall count it one of the favours granted me by Divine Providence in this Republic to have met your Eminence, and to receive your Apostolic blessing, when I have the honour to visit that land as dear to me as is commendable the memory of Manco Capac, who with so much wisdom and humanity knew how to found an Empire on the basis of a morality unknown to other peoples who held themselves to be more cultivated." What could all this hankering back mean in a man who was at the time explicitly founding his political institutions on Spanish public law ? For this Bolívar, who in his proclamations and letters to bishops, wiped out the three centuries of Spanish life as mere tyranny, rebuked Sucre (21.ii.25) for having called an Assembly of Upper Peru, on the ground that: " Neither you nor I, nor even the Peruvian, nor the Colombian Congress can break and violate the basis of public law we have recognized in America. This basis is that republican governments are set up within the boundaries of the old viceroyalties, captain-generalships and presidencies such as that of Chile." There is in all this an obvious contradiction. Whenever a man is at loggerheads with himself, one must suspect some hidden, unavowed intention, shaping that part of his thoughts which is out of tune with the rest.

5

On March 18th, 1825, Bolívar summoned a British secret agent Thomas J. Maling, who resided in Chorrillos, and had a long conversation with him. Maling sent a full report to Viscount Melville, then First Lord of the Admiralty. Bolívar began by referring to the instructions to Chasseriau, published in the *Morning Chronicle* (1.ix.24); but Maling goes on to refer to the subject " which seemed in fact to be his principal object in sending for me ": " France has declared she will not tolerate popular governments; that revolutions have distracted Europe for the last thirty years and that America can never see peace so long as she gave way to the popular cry of equality. And in truth "—Bolívar speaks on—" I am of the opinion of France, for although no man is a greater advocate of the rights and liberties of mankind . . . still I must confess this country is not in a state to be governed by the *people*, which one must allow after all is generally better in thought than in practice. No country is more free than England under a well regulated Monarchy; England is the envy of all countries in the world, and the pattern all would wish to follow in forming a new constitution and government. Of all countries, South America is perhaps the least fitted for republican governments. What does its population consist of but Indians and negroes who are more ignorant than the vile race of Spaniards we are just emancipated from. A country represented and governed by such people must go to ruin. *We must look to England for relief*. . . . And you have not only my leave but my request that you will communicate our conversation and bring the matter under the consideration of H.B.M.'s Government . . . officially or otherwise. You may say I never have been an enemy to monarchies upon general principles; on the contrary, I think it essential to the respectability and well-being of new nations, and if any proposal ever comes from the British Cabinet for the establishment of . . . a monarchy or monarchies in the New World, they will find in me a steady and firm promoter of their wishes, perfectly ready to uphold the Sovereign England may propose to place and support upon the throne. I know it has been said of me, I wish to be a king, but it is *not* [doubtful, notes Maling] so; I would not accept the Crown for myself, for when I see this country made happy under a good and firm government, I shall again retire into private life. . . . The title of King would perhaps not be popular at first in South America and therefore it may be as well to meet the prejudice by assuming that of ' Inca ' which the Indians are so much attached to." And very much more to that effect. Maling adds: " I have endeavoured to give you, my lord, the substance and, as nearly as I could, the words which were used by H.E." And on his explaining that all he could do was to convey them to the British Government privately, " H.E. was satisfied with my intention to write to your lordship and merely urged expedition, observing that the French were so busy in their intrigues that unless advantage were taken of this favourable moment when they might say they had no enemy in their country, more difficulty might attend the measure ". This report confirms what had become plain on reading Bolívar's letter to Santander: he was thinking of a monarchy, and of himself as a monarch, though he dared not yet show his hand.

Maling's report can still yield more facts of interest. We know from Bolívar himself that, as a result of Monteagudo's murder (in which he had seen the secret hand of the Holy Alliance aiming at his own person), Bolívar had expelled a French agent, Captain de Moges. Maling reports: " The Dictator having discovered some weeks ago that Captain de Moges, who was sent by Admiral Rosamel to reside at Lima, had been intriguing, sent him off at two hours' notice." The Admiral " arrived here on Thursday, and on Friday had his interview with the *Libertador* . . . both parties got very earnest and warm. . . . Rosamel tried to take up the business with a high hand. . . . Bolívar told him he had done no more to Captain de Moges than France had done by the South American Agents who had landed on her territory and who not only were sent away but had their papers seized. . . . The Admiral protested his instructions were most positive and unequivocal, to observe a most strictly neutral part, but that the *Libertador* had not only insulted his country by turning out a gentleman who held no public situation there, but also by certain paragraphs in his journals; alluding to one . . . in which the French are spoken of as the ' *invincibles* of Egypt, St. Domingo, and Waterloo '. Bolívar allowed he was aware . . . of a paragraph . . . but added ' that style of writing began with France; I have in the next room a collection of French papers, each containing personal insults to me ' . . . in short, after sparring for three hours, the Admiral, finding he could make nothing of him, in some degree cooled, and they parted friends. I visited the Admiral next morning, but he seemed mortified and full of spleen against Bolívar and his cause."

We know that Rosamel's mortification was also due to another cause. One of the officers present, a Dane in the service of France, has left another narrative of the interview. It took place in the Old Magdalen, a suburb of Lima where Bolívar preferred to reside for reasons of health. " Bolívar was in a blue gold-embroidered uniform; over his trousers he wore a pair of immense boots reaching above the knees. His mien and attitude were those of a perfect soldier. He was of middle size, very thin and of a lank constitution; a large, black moustache, beginning to grey, like his abundant hair, gave him a martial air, in sharp contrast with his feeble voice and wasted frame. His face was wan, dark and sunburnt, showing traces of the hardships he had undergone; while his lofty forehead and the earnestness of his manner called forth veneration, so that despite oneself one felt bound to bow before him, though he was free from any presumption or despotism. He impressed me as a great man. Admiral Rosamel was the very opposite of Don Simón. Handsome in the common sense of the word, tall and robust, his cheeks rosy, a smile on his lips, visibly anxious to show off; pleased with his looks, but of limited intellectual powers, he tried in vain to cover this shortcoming with formalities and pomp."

Admiral van Dockun, author of these Memoirs, writes that the conversation dealt at first with the French domiciled in Peru and with the neutrality of France in Spanish-American affairs (as related by Maling). But soon, too soon for the Admiral of the Bourbon Court, Bolívar brought in—Napoleon. " The English "—he said—" have suffered a great loss in the death of Napoleon; for the circumstances in which they held him were enough to keep the whole of Europe in check." Then: " Napoleon leaves great memories, and I am certain that all Frenchmen recall him in their hearts." On Rosamel murmuring something about the Bourbon dynasty, Bolívar, " with a mischievous smile on his stern face," retorted: " I feel certain that were the Duke of Reichstadt to turn up in France now, the whole nation, full of joy, would gather round the son of the great Emperor." Bolívar was almost certainly ragging the Admiral: " I never saw intellectual superiority so plainly manifest as in that famous interview "—comments van Dockun. But how significant that at that time the theme on which Bolívar's mind would play should be Napoleon.

6

On hearing the news that strong French naval forces were approaching, Bolívar wrote Santander (11.iii.25) a letter which brings out his many-sided personality: first, his generalship: he offers Santander ten to twelve thousand men and more to come; then, his genius for propaganda, always, so to speak, with his tongue in his cheek. " Do not forget to declare a crusade against the heretical and atheistic French, destroyers of their priests, temples and images, and of everything that is sacred in the world. The bishop of Mérida will come in handy for this, as well as all the fanatics available in churches, pulpits and streets." So writes the leader of the emancipation of America from bigoted Spain to Santander, in whose house the rosary was said every evening, about the French nation by then again under the authority of the Church and the Throne. Then, this news of the French danger arouses his political imagination: he sees a *universal* war to bring about " the triumph of the thrones over liberty ". He then sees England in alliance with the constitutional spirit of Portugal, Spain, Italy, Greece, Holland, Sweden and Turkey (to save herself from Russia's claws) taking sides with Spanish America against the Holy Alliance. Finally, to ward off this war, he proposes to Santander to come to an agreement with England in political and military matters, significantly adding: " I believe you must immediately enquire what is England's opinion on our American governments. These two lines deserve an immense explanation which I cannot provide owing to the distance and the insecurity of communications." The secret idea again. On March 23rd, convinced by Rosamel's assurances, he retracts all this. " The latest report from the War Office of Bogotá filled me with concern and induced me to contrive every means to stave off war; among which I gave great weight to a diplomatic expedient calculated to neutralize the anger of the Holy Alliance though it would have destroyed my popular reputation." As his fear of war is gone, he adds: " I cancel my proposal to offer France my influence towards a reform in part of our government. Since the evil shrinks, the extent of my sacrifices must also shrink. Make no use of my previous letter. You will understand that I am right in retracting."

The right view on all this is not simple. Bolívar was both attracted and repelled by the Crown. He saw himself as the Inca of a Great Colombia including all the Spanish lands round Brazil. His authoritarian and monocratic impulses reached out towards power; a move justified, and so to speak *natural*, owing to his superiority over all his contemporaries; but his Roussellian skies, the democratic clouds over his inner landscape, were not propitious. This inner hesitation was increased by his keen intellect, which illumined both the positive and the negative side of the balance of forces within him. When his heart drove him towards the Crown, his intellect objected that the slightest gesture thereto would destroy his popularity, i.e. the very basis on which he built his ambition. Hence his recantation to Santander. When his attitude beheld monarchy with the eyes of the century, not only his Roussellian clouds, but the cold light of his Voltairian wit, withered his willpower and made it evaporate into sceptical smiles. While in Cuzco, he wrote to Olmedo to thank him for a poem on the battle of Junin, two letters which are masterpieces of brilliant common sense, modesty, literary criticism and wisdom. No summary can do justice to them. One sentence must be quoted: remembering that the battle of Junin was exclusively fought with sabres, he writes to the poet: " All the heat of the torrid zone, all the fires of Junin and Ayacucho, all the rays of the Father of Manco Capac, have never caused a conflagration more intense in the mind of a mortal. You shoot . . . where not a shot was fired. You make of me a Jupiter; of Sucre, a Mars; of La Mar, an Agamemnon and a Menelaus; of Córdova, an Achilles; of Necochea, a Patroclus and an Ajax; of Miller, a Diomedes, and of Lara, a Ulysses. . . . You raise us as Jupiter's eagles raised the turtle to let it fall on a rock and break its hind limbs; you have so sublimated us that you have precipitated us into the abyss of nothingness, covering with an immensity of lights the pale glow of our opaque virtues. . . . Were I not so kind and were you not a poet, I should go as far as to believe that you had intended to write a parody of the Iliad with the heroes of our poor farce."

CHAPTER XVIII

THE BIRTH OF BOLIVIA

I

THE victor of Ayacucho had not slept over his laurels. He turned at once against Olañeta and Upper Peru. This meant a twofold problem: to get rid of Olañeta by treaty or by defeat, and to constitute Upper Peru. But how ? That high plateau had politically oscillated between Buenos Aires and Lima. On December 15th, 20th and 23rd, 1824, he asked for instructions on this point; and on January 3rd he was authorized to advance into Upper Peru and deal with Olañeta on the basis of independence and sovereignty of the people, actual allegiance having to be settled direct between the Congresses of Lima and Buenos Aires " provided the latter be freely, uniformly and legally constituted ". On December 19th, 1824, Sucre arrived in Cuzco where he had sent ahead, as Prefect, General Gamarra, an Upper Peruvian. He had to undergo the speeches and triumphal arches which so much delighted Bolívar but which, writes O'Connor, " were very much against the taste of his truly modest and really republican character ". He remained in Cuzco until January 19th, 1825, waiting for instructions. His army was mixed. He could only enter Upper Peru with Colombian troops, " for we are to work in a country that does not belong to Peru and seems to want to belong to no one but itself ". He had sent a Colonel Elizalde to negotiate with Olañeta; but the rebellious general wrote (22.xii.24) in a friendly way while issuing warlike absolutist proclamations (4-8.i.25). By January 19th, Sucre felt he had to use force. Ten days later, he was in Potosí, which he found " somewhat Goth, at least the chief people, and the populace patriot, but not very ". In Puno, at the beginning of February, he received Dr. Casimiro Olañeta, a lawyer of twenty-nine, a nephew of the general, who came over to the victorious side, hoping to build up an independent Upper Peru, free not only from Spain, but from Buenos Aires and Lima as well. He seems to have won over Sucre to his way of thinking.

Sucre wrote to Bolívar's War Secretary (1.ii.25) that, in accordance with his instructions, he would call an Assembly of Upper Peru to decide on their political organization, pending regularly constituted Congresses in Lima and in Buenos Aires. Bolívar's actual instructions spoke of an agreement between the Congresses of Peru and of Buenos Aires, " provided this latter be freely, uniformly and legally constituted ". Sucre speaks of " an agreement between the Congresses of Peru and Buenos Aires both uniformly, legally and freely constituted ". It would appear as if by extending to the Lima Congress the proviso Bolívar had laid down only with regard to Buenos Aires, Sucre was hinting at his chief's cavalier treatment of the Congress of Peru. Though his letters to Bolívar on the subject would not support such an interpretation, it seems likely that Bolívar read it so, and that this may have been the cause of the rebuke he sent him later. Sucre went ahead; and issued a decree (9.ii.25) calling a General Assembly of Upper Peru for April 5th, 1825; whereupon Bolívar wrote to him (21.ii.25): " You are under my orders in the army you command and can do nothing but what I order you to do." Then he went on to explain that according to the principles of public law, the States of Spanish America had to be founded on the limits of the Spanish vice-royalties; and: " Your moderation is odd: you will not use your authority as a Commander-in-Chief, the *de facto* head of the country your troops occupy, and yet you take upon yourself to decide a legislative operation." Fortunately for Sucre, his secret plan for getting Olañeta alive or dead by means of one of Olañeta's seconds, Medinaceli, ended in Olañeta's defeat and death in Tumula (1–2.iv.25). Two days later, Sucre wrote to Bolívar a humble letter on " his error ", reminding his chief that despite his repeated reports, he had been left without instructions and that Bolívar himself had told him that he meant to call an Assembly of these provinces. Meanwhile he would adjourn it until May 25th. Bolívar retorted from Nasca (26.iv.25) in a letter remarkable for its common sense, firmness and affection, insisting on correcting him, " for an evil that is not known cannot be cured "; and adds: " You are called to the highest destinies and I foresee that you are the rival of my glory having already robbed me of two magnificent campaigns; while you surpass me in affability and in activity as well as in your zeal for the common cause." This is one of Bolívar's finest letters; and it contains also surprising statements as to his intentions in Upper Peru, based on this principle: " You know that I have always professed worship for the people's will and veneration for laws and rights." So he says, and so he very likely felt at the time he wrote.

During his journey, the matter of the Assembly of Upper Peru had been radically altered by the arrival of an Argentine force under Arenales, with instructions to respect the autonomous wishes of the Province. Sucre lost no time in informing Bolívar (27.iv.25 from Chuquisaca). On receipt of the news, Bolívar dropped his objections and decided to have the Upper Peruvian Assembly meet, sending from Arequipa a decree to that effect (25.v.25). His motives he declares to be: " not to leave you in a bad light; to please Upper Peru; to comply with the wishes of Río de la Plata; to give a proof of the liberalism of the Peruvian Congress; and to shelter my reputation as a lover of popular sovereignty and of the freest institutions ". But he did not feel happy about it, probably owing to a subconscious desire to resist the separation of Upper Peru from Lima, as may be gathered from the decree itself, which breathes the sovereignty of Peru over the Upper Provinces, as indeed in the circumstances it was but natural that it should. With Bolívar, however, one must ever be on the alert, for his façades do not always correspond to the actual facts behind them. Everything in this correspondence with Sucre points to his refusal to recognize in Upper Peru a separate entity. Was this Bolívar's real way of thinking or only a frontage he turned towards Peru? He himself provides the answer in his letter to Sucre from Arequipa, May 30th, 1825: " Public opinion [of Upper Peru] favours the setting up of a State such as Chile or Guatemala, which are in every way like Upper Peru; I mean a wholly independent State subject only to the

American federation.   I believe this to be just and even necessary for the prosperity of these provinces."

2

On April 10th, 1825, Bolívar left Lima for a tour of Southern Peru.   This move is usually taken for granted; but it deserves some attention, for it was the first time that Bolívar, having secured dictatorial powers, *need not* have left the capital of the State over which he ruled, since there were no enemies worth his trouble, and if such there were, they were in Callao, at the gates of Lima.   And yet, no sooner had he been appointed a dictator than he left for a long journey, as in older days he used to leave to fight the enemy.   This shows that even in his military campaigns, he moved less perhaps towards the enemy than away from the political machine.   What he sought was freedom for his power, the enjoyment of an almost oriental omnipotence.   He was in his element, showering generous gifts on needy families; or pouring forth multifarious benefits as a debonair despot; or when, catching Vinoni among the Spanish officers taken in Boyacá, he had him hanged there and then without any form of law.   His tour of the southern provinces was conceived very much in the style of Harun al-Rashid. He took with him a considerable retinue, including his jester-philosopher Don Simón, who had returned to the fatherland with his pocket empty and his head full of ideas and fancies.   Bolívar would not have been a man of his time had his heart remained cold before the marvels to be expected from education.   It was a golden time for pedagogues.   One of them, Joseph Lancaster, after quarrelling with the Royal Lancastrian Institution he had set up in Chelsea, had emigrated to the New World and landed in Caracas to impart the benefits of his system to the Venezuelans.   Bolívar wrote to him (16.iii.25) very much pleased, and out of the million pesos voted, though not paid to him by Congress, and by him ceded to Caracas, he decided (without consulting Caracas) to send 20,000 to Lancaster: the sum to be paid in London by the agents of Peru.   This part of the transaction was, however, omitted, and if we are to believe O'Leary, Bolívar had to pay it out of his private purse.

The enlightened despot left on April 10th, 1825, with a parting Manifesto to the Limenians announcing that he went to better the fate of their brothers, whose government, so far, had been despotic (though, we gather, not enlightened) and wishing them, after so many alarms, a rest, but " in the smooth movement of liberty ".   In his retinue there was no room for Manuela Sáenz, to whom he wrote from Ica on April 20th a letter the ardour of which did not conceal his desire to get rid of her.   After years of a public and scandalous liaison under the nose of Manuela's husband (for he practised in Lima), Bolívar writes that they must separate so as to be no longer guilty.   " In future, you will be alone by your husband's side; I alone in the middle of the world."   He travelled towards Arequipa through the deserted coast, here and there cut across by narrow valleys green with tropical vegetation.   Everywhere he was received as a conqueror.   Many times, at nightfall, the hearts of the exhausted travellers were cheered by the constellations of lights announcing a cordial reception ahead. He went forth pouring blessings on his way. Everywhere the war had ravaged the one-time prosperous country. He reduced taxes, forbade the use of churches for burial, turned monasteries into schools, wielded in fact that immediate authority which was his chief delight—ignorant or oblivious of the fact that in most cases nothing came out of his decisions since there was no real State organization left to carry out his ukases.

3

On May 14th, 1825, he arrived in Arequipa. The city presented him with a horse harnessed in solid gold. Banquets and balls made him giddy for a month. The penniless *cabildo* endeavoured first to meet these extravagant expenses by " a voluntary subscription among the inhabitants ", but as this " plan was rather slow and offered no high hopes " the *cabildo* had to borrow by decree, i.e. more or less compulsorily, 12,000 pesos (then worth £2,500) from five British merchants, and, Bolívar being consulted, allowed them to recoup themselves out of the customs duties they owed. This is an interesting sidelight on Bolívar's indifference to the financial consequences of his acts. On June 10th, 1825, he left for Cuzco, where he arrived on the 25th and was received with unheard of magnificence. The streets were ablaze with brocade, silver and gold; crowns of roses and laurels fell from the windows and handfuls of coins were cast at the crowds that acclaimed him. He was presented with a gold harnessed horse and with golden city keys (which he gave over to O'Leary) and after a *Te Deum* in the Cathedral, he was crowned with a " civic Crown " of diamonds and pearls by the ladies of the city.

He stayed a month, gaily spent in festivities, but devoted also to the now usual shower of beneficent laws and decrees on all kinds of public affairs. He paid special attention to the welfare of the Indians and to restoring, says O'Leary, " their monuments which had been spared by time and by Spanish avarice ". In this he went so far that, says O'Leary also, " he declared in vigour the old Spanish laws which favoured them." Leaving Cuzco on July 26th, 1825, Bolívar arrived in Puno, on the shores of Lake Ticicaca, on August 6th. There again, says O'Leary, he bestowed " the blessings he had poured with a profuse hand over Arequipa and Cuzco; for reforms were not slow to come in all the branches of administration, such as cuts in expenses, foundings of schools and colleges of arts and sciences, rewards to patriotism in the sharing out of offices, protection to worship and to navigation ". Then he set out on the road again to meet General Sucre.

There was at this moment another difference between the two. On March 28th, 1825, Don Sebastián Ramos, the Spanish Governor of Chiquitos on the eastern edge of Upper Peru, had made a treaty with the Brazilian authorities over the border, ceding the territory to Brazil, and a Brazilian force from Matogrosso took possession of the Province. Its chief, Araujo, sent a threatening note to Sucre. This episode brought out some defects of Sucre's character usually under control: his impetuosity and a certain jacobinism. Not content with rejecting Araujo's insolent note, he answered (11.v.25) that the Colombian Governor had instructions not only to expel the invaders but " to penetrate into the territory which thus declares itself our enemy, spreading desolation, death and terror to avenge our fatherland ". He wrote to his representative on the frontier to send agents into Brazil " to revolutionize it, proclaiming republican and democratic principles, even licence, and every element of confusion and disorder, to make them repent of their unjust and perfidious aggression ". Sucre was ready to go as far as Rio de Janeiro. Bolívar cooled him down, and wrote to Santander (30.v.25) explaining that either the Brazilian coup was the first stroke of a war led by the Holy Alliance, in which case they would enter a world war with good friends on their side; or else it was an isolated act, merely " one of the many mad things the day will throw up ". He saw no signs of the first; but if it came, it was his opinion that " Peru and Buenos Aires should immediately occupy Brazil; Chile, Chiloe; while Colombia, Guatemala and Mexico would attend to their own defence and the whole America form one single cause." This incident, unimportant in itself, illustrates the feelings of both Sucre and Bolívar. Both reacted promptly, with a patriotism that was wider than their Venezuelan origin justified, but less wide than the American continent might have inspired. It was in fact a Spanish-American patriotism.

4

There was no one then in Spanish America endowed with that continental vision, that intellect, and, despite his ambition, that detachment which shone in Bolívar. He was moreover fortunate in having in Sucre an effective second. If now and then Santander grumbled, allowance should be made for the fact that he had accepted the duller and more effaced rôle in the partnership, while Bolívar and Sucre took the gold braid and the laurels. He worked hard in Bogotá while Bolívar and Sucre won battles and founded nations. The young Cumanese, raised to the apex of continental glory, second only to Bolívar, wrote to foreign Powers like a Potentate. On February 20th and on April 6th, 1825, he wrote to the Argentine government explaining his actions in Upper Peru, which he knew had raised suspicions in the then chaotic southern Republic. On May 9th, the Constitutional Congress of Buenos Aires resolved to send a special mission to congratulate Bolívar for his services to the New World, and declaring Upper Peru free to choose its destiny. Sucre invited Arenales, the Argentine delegate, to accompany him in an official visit to Chuquisaca, the old University city and cradle of the movement for independence; and, as usual in Spanish America, the cradle also of the new nationality. The two generals were received in triumph (25.iv.25). At the gates, Sucre was offered a Roman chariot, red and white, drawn by twelve young citizens. He refused to be conveyed in it and failed to convince Arenales to take that honour for himself; a compromise being struck by Sucre who suggested that the two generals would lay their swords on the seat of the chariot and walk behind it. So they passed through streets of noble buildings hidden by cardboard pyramids and obelisks, towards an " Ionic temple " where, under his own portrait, framed in silver, six children in white frocks harangued him in succession; and after a *Te Deum* in the Cathedral (in which he was received with a royal ceremonial) he was led to the Palace where, as he entered, a cloud emitted by a triumphant arch revealed a little girl inside who from mid-air greeted the victor of Ayacucho.

Bolívar had given Sucre instructions to keep the army away from the seat of the Assembly. There were to be no soldiers within twenty leagues and he himself was to remain " as far away as he could ". Sucre left for La Paz (2.vii.25). The Assembly met in Chuquisaca (10.vii.25), and its thirty-nine members took the oath. The first item was " to observe and protect the Roman Catholic Apostolic religion ". One of the first acts of this Assembly was to elect the man who was to wield true power; for Sucre had requested its President " to put at the disposal of the Assembly the baton of president of the Department, so that it should elect its own Governor ". The Assembly elected General Santa Cruz, a choice in accordance with the logic of facts, since in every nation the gown-men who crowded the assemblies realized the presence in their midst of a cape-and-sword man whom they could not afford to antagonize. Sucre was a Colombian, who would some day go home. Santa Cruz and Gamarra were Upper Peruvians who would remain about. They had to be reckoned with. For the time being Santa Cruz was in Bolívar's good books, in fact his candidate as Prefect of La Paz. The Assembly sent Bolívar a message of fulsome praise (19.vii.25) in which however no mention was made of his decree convoking the Assembly—a decree disliked in Chuquisaca for its implicit assertion of Peruvian sovereignty over the Province. Bolívar answered politely and modestly (3.viii.25). After protracted debates, the Assembly voted the independence of the new State (6.viii.25), " protesting to the face of the whole earth the irrevocable will to govern themselves and to be ruled by a constitution, laws and authorities they shall give themselves for their future happiness and the unalterable upholding of our Holy Catholic religion and of the sacred and holy rites of honour, life, liberty, equality, property and security ".

On August 11th the new State christened itself *República Bolívar*. It acknowledged in Bolívar its " good father and best aid against all dangers "; invested him with supreme executive powers while in its territory; decreed that his birthday should become for ever a civic day after his death, that a portrait of Bolívar would be exhibited in all public buildings and that a statue should be erected to him in all the chief cities. A number of similar honours were bestowed on Sucre including that of giving his name to Chuquisaca. A piece of gold was to be sculpted whereon (these men, named Serrano, Olañeta, Mendizábal, Landa and such genuine Spanish names, decreed) " a beautiful native, a symbol of America ", standing on the body of a lion, a symbol of Spain, would be embracing Bolívar with his right and Sucre with his left arm. A million pesos was voted for Bolívar to share out to the army; and as there was no such money in the land where

Potosí rose to Heaven on feet of silver, Bolívar was authorized to negotiate a loan. The Assembly appointed a delegation to present to Bolívar the act of independence, a request for a constitution, the withdrawal of his decree of May 16th or an explanation of it, and authority to leave Sucre at the head of the new State. With this errand, Drs. Olañeta and Mendizábal left for La Paz.

On August 16th, while the Assembly was sitting, Bolívar and Sucre met at Zepita, between Puno and La Paz. " As Sucre was alighting to embrace the *Libertador* "—writes O'Leary—" his sword came out of the sheath. Seeing it fall, I pointed out that it was a bad omen; the next day as Sucre was striking his batman with the flat of the same sword for some insolence, the sword broke: ' This is an even worse omen ', I said to him. ' I was just thinking the same ', answered Sucre." On August 18th Bolívar and Sucre entered La Paz; the by now customary horse richly caparisoned, and the golden keys, were offered Bolívar by the city; but when the customary delegation of ladies brought him the civic crown of gold and diamonds, Bolívar, who was proud as well as modest, passed it on to Sucre saying: " This reward belongs to the victor." After the usual round of banquets and balls he set to business. He gathered a committee of citizens to advise him on how to cure the ills of public life, but had to dissolve it for its anti-liberal and vindictive spirit. Thus was he constantly either begged to take on dictatorial powers as in Peru, or thrown back into dictatorial powers as in La Paz—an experience which, in a lesser man, might have corrupted his will, but in him led to ripeness, reflection and a melancholy scepticism. On October 5th he arrived in Potosí, where the idolatry his presence provoked took the form of asking him to sanction the change of the name of the city from *Potosí* to *Bolívar*. He had the good taste to refuse. He climbed the steep slopes of the Hill of Silver and on that height hoisted the flags of Colombia, Peru and La Plata. There he dreamt of federating all the Spanish lands of South America, and even of liberating the Philippines. He was already the idol of the people from Venezuela to Chile, and, as for Argentina, he himself had written from La Paz to Santander (19.viii.25): " the whole Argentine people, all the good patriots and even the government hope nothing good except from me ". On that day he must have felt like the monarch of Spanish America.

5

Brazil's independence had been recognized by Portugal under the good offices of Canning, on August 29th, 1825. The young Emperor, Don Pedro, had set his heart on swallowing the eastern bank of the La Plata river, what is now known as Uruguay. Realizing that Canning looked askance at his ambition, the government of the United Provinces of La Plata had decreed on October 25th the incorporation of the eastern bank. On October 7th a mission from this government to Bolívar, led by Alvear, arrived in Potosí. Its aim was to enlist Bolívar's sympathies in a war against Brazil. Bolívar put on an official mask and referred the delegates to the Ministry of Foreign

Affairs in Lima; but as he was in favour of the idea, he received the two plenipotentiaries, who made his mouth water by describing to him how glorious his return to Colombia would be by way of Río de Janeiro. He needed no outside prodding to see such visions of glory. He declared himself ready, provided the governments of Peru and Colombia agreed. He could dictate to Peru, but not to Colombia, where Santander, who had built himself a solid position, opposed the somewhat grandiose schemes of the Napoleon of South America, doomed in any case to fail owing to the opposition of Canning. Bolívar felt disappointed, for he was then dreaming continentally. " My right "—he wrote to Paez from Oruro on September 26th, 1825—" shall be on the mouth of the Orinoco and my left reach the margins of the La Plata river. One thousand leagues will be embraced by my arms, but my heart will always be in Caracas."

As the dictator of Peru Bolívar governed the country in a fatherly way. Roads, schools, law courts, liberation and protection of the Indians, every side of public life came under revision. He enacted that the Code of Laws drafted by the Cortes of Cádiz should become law in Upper Peru. His chief difficulty was finance; not because the country was lacking in resources, but because its resources were frittered away by an improvised administration unable to prevent leakage and corruption. This situation caused him some anxiety. In many ways, it was nevertheless of his own creation, as the outcome of the inevitable revolution he had unleashed. The Spanish-American Empire was at its best in organization, efficiency and wealth when the separatist revolution began in 1810. The continental civil war this revolution caused brought about the collapse of the State and the disintegration of nearly every source of wealth. Bolívar was no economist. The mines, for instance, which during the three centuries of the Spanish régime had yielded so much wealth, not merely to the Spanish Treasury, but mostly to Peru, were in a lamentable state for lack of labour, capital and skill. Bolívar decreed that the derelict, waterlogged, or collapsed mines were *ipso facto* to pass to the ownership of the State; and wrote to Santander that he should do the same in Colombia in order to sell them to an English company on account of the interests due on the national debt. In a long letter to him from Potosí (21.x.25) Bolívar says that he has sold the mines of Upper Peru for two and a half million pesos and has suggested to the Peruvian government to sell all its mines, land and property as well as other sources of revenue to England in exchange for the national debt, worth twenty million. Thus did Spanish America, opulent while Spanish, sell away its economic independence as soon as its political independence allowed it to do so.

Santander meanwhile organized State festivals in which champagne flowed generously, while his armies went unpaid; and Hamilton, the British agent, began to growl in tones which were to become familiar throughout the century. " John Bull has hitherto been a sincere friend and well-wisher to Colombia, but these sentiments will be changed, if he finds he has been assisting a country whose government in money transactions turns out to be on a par with that of the Beloved Ferdinand. The facility with which the new American government obtained money from England has caused extravagance; but the South Americans will now find the golden dream over, and that their precious metals must resume their old course across the Atlantic, in order to support the character of the new government." Was this deserved? Less than meets the eye; for Great Britain was sucking Spanish America dry of its good gold by the normal operation of commerce on a so-called equal footing, between a nation without exports or ships and the richest exporting and shipping nation on earth. Mollien, who visited Colombia in 1823, reporting that her rich metallic deposits could be developed, adds that this would be very much to be desired for " *ne traîtant qu'avec un peuple, les anglais, qui ne veulent presque pas recevoir de denrées, on ne peut payer ceci qu'avec les métaux précieux rétirés précédemment du sein de la terre par les espagnols. Ils passent donc á la Jamaique, et avec une telle rapidité, que bientôt dans la contrée de l'or on n'en trouvera plus un grain.*" There was little or no return trade. English ships, writes Mollien, "*l après avoir déposé les étoffes qu'ils apportent, s'en retournent sur leur lest mais en evant l'or et l'argent, dépouille de l'Amérique.*" He calculates English imports into America (presumably the whole continent) at £10,476,791. How thorough this gold pumping was can be judged by another observation of his: " *On ne doit pas être surpris de la quantité encore considérable d'or, malgré la diminution des produits des monnaies, que les anglais tirent du pays, en songeant qu'il provient en grande partie, de la fonte des bijoux et de la vaisselle dont chacun se dépouille* ". And he adds that there is much counterfeit money in Colombia and that it comes from Jamaica and Curaçao. Thus the de-golding of Eldorado began with political independence.

6

Bolívar gave the example for this public profligacy in his private life. After the return to Caracas of his only capable, perhaps too capable relative, his sister María Antonia, he had begun to recover his estates through her efficient activity. One of his richest possessions, which he himself described as " the most beautiful property in Venezuela ", the Aroa mines, was the object of laborious negotiations to have it farmed out to an English company. He approved the contract signed by María Antonia on October 12th, 1824, and insisted that payment was to take place in London. The contract was for nine years and the yearly royalty was to be ten thousand pesos during the first two years and thirteen thousand thereafter. Bolívar instructed his sister to sell the Aroa mines (24.x.25), " now that there is such a keen demand for mines in the foreign colonies. If we let this opportunity go by we may fail later, and when we want to ensure a fortune in England, we shall no longer be able to do so. We have enough estates and houses, which any earthquake may bring down. If we have one hundred thousand sterling safe in a bank in England, we can enjoy our three per cent, which is over 12,000 yearly "; and he adds that he will never be in need, but as he might die, his family might in any case want to go to Europe. Thus did Bolívar contribute unwittingly to impoverishing the nation by alienating its " richest property " to foreign capitalists, who would soon make a foreign establishment of it. " The contractors for your mines "—wrote María Antonia to him on July 30th, 1825—" want to settle a church and city of Englishmen there for the production of the copper: tell me what you decide." Two considerations must, however, be borne in mind: the scarcity, and even the utter lack of natural resources to work the mines for the time being; and the incomplete understanding of the economic aspects of independence still prevailing in those days.

The year had been for Bolívar one of pride in achievements and of much experience and learning. On June 8th, 1825, he wrote to Santander an official letter which began: " Yesterday I received with ineffable joy the glorious letter in which Y.E. informs me that Colombia has been recognized by the Lady of Nations, Great Britain." He had been acclaimed by the whole continent as its Liberator; and even in Buenos Aires, at the news of the battle of Ayacucho, his portrait was taken in a procession about the streets of the city with banners and torches and the elation lasted for a month. Lima had sent him and Sucre a sword of gold and diamonds and a uniform to match. He had become the idol of a continent. But, unlike most idols, he kept his head, and his ears and his eyes were ever awake and alive to the realities of time and place. There is a peculiar bitterness in his wholesale condemnation of his Venezuelan countrymen. " If I am not deceived "—he writes to Santander (8.v.25)—" I believe that rabble can only be kept at bay by the most inexorable rigour." He is referring to the politicians of Venezuela. He has seen that he has been proposed as candidate for a third term as President; and he refuses, though with rather mixed motives; for, after stating that his pride is in not being less liberal than Washington, he goes on: " I will have nothing to do with those abominable soldiers of Boves, with those infamous flatterers of Morillo, with those slaves of Morales and Calzada. Such were the leaders obeyed and liked by those fierce republicans whom we have liberated against their will, their arms, their tongues and their pens."

His anger had been aroused by news that the Venezuelans were restive under their union with New Granada and wanted to break away. At the time he was dreaming of a Spanish-speaking federation, his " dear countrymen " were trying to split the only union he had so far achieved. A dramatic recoil of fate: for this arch-separatist was to be defrauded in his loftiest ambition by the separatism of his own kith and kin. It is illuminating that, in this very letter to Santander, he writes: " The men of Buenos Aires and the men of Caracas, who live at the two ends of South America, are unfortunately the most turbulent and seditious of all the men of South America. Nothing but the American Congress [of Panama] can restrain them. That is why I am desperate for that Congress to meet, so that its mass may contain such diabolical extremities." This thought was bound to awaken in his secret self doubts about his own life work. Buenos Aires and Caracas had been the two cities that had initiated the revolution against " the mass " of the old régime, which had for years restrained them. Such first inklings, later to come to the surface of his mind, were then still probably hidden to his own observation; but they colour his moods and intentions. In the same letter, speaking of his money affairs, he says to Santander: " When I go to Europe I shall find there the royalties of my Venezuelan copper mine, which I have farmed out to some Englishmen for 12,000 a year. Providence, who guards my honour, has granted me this resource so that I need not receive money from any government in my old age."

Like all his professions of a desire to withdraw from public life, particularly if addressed to Santander, this one need not be taken too literally; it was not a definite intention; but it was a sincere mood. We can feel the workings of his heart in the letter he wrote to his uncle, Esteban Palacios (10.vii.25), as soon as he heard of his arrival in Caracas. It is an open-hearted and sincere letter; but after the more personal part has been disposed of, Bolívar enters, one feels, with a diffident and an almost pleading voice, into the sad subject of the changes his uncle will have observed: " You have come from the dead to see the devastations of inexorable time, of cruel war, of ferocious man . . . the fields watered by the sweat of three hundred years have been blasted by a fatal combination of meteors and crimes [the earthquake and the civil war]. Where is Caracas ? you will ask; Caracas no longer exists; but its ashes, its monuments, the land it stood on, have remained glowing with liberty and covered with the glory of martyrdom. This comfort compensates for all the losses; at least, it is my comfort; and I wish it to be yours." Bolívar was not sure that his uncle would agree with him. Was he sure himself ? The answer was no longer certain.

He still was, however, the Napoleonic leader of the continent. On hearing that Pasto had revolted again, he wrote to Santander from Potosí (21.x.25): " The Pastusians must be annihilated, their women and children taken away somewhere else and the country handed over to a military colony. For otherwise, Colombia will have to remember the Pastusians every time there is trouble or difficulty for a hundred years hence, since they will never forget our devastations, though all too well deserved." Yet, this downright oppression of a stubborn and proud people did not prevent him from seeing himself as the Liberator of the continent. He tells Santander (11.xi.25) that Alvear had confided to him in secret his plan to unite Bolivia and Argentina under the name of *Bolívar*, and requests Santander to " strive to the utmost so that the glory of Colombia does not remain incomplete, and that I am allowed to be the arbiter of all South America ". " Caesar in Gaul threatened Rome and I in Bolivia threaten all the conspirators of America and therefore save all the republics." Then, on rumours that Spain was preparing in Cuba an expedition against Mexico, he volunteers to go to Mexico or to Cuba and even to Spain. These dreams, the drafting of the constitution of Bolivia and his private affairs took the rest of the year. He had thought of staying in Bolivia to open the constituent Assembly; but in the end he resolved to return to Lima for the session of the Peruvian Congress to begin on February 26th, 1826. On December 29th, 1825, he delegated his Bolivian executive powers to Sucre. On January 6th, 1826, he left Chuquisaca for Lima.

CHAPTER XIX

THE "BOLIVIAN" CONSTITUTION

I

BOLÍVAR arrived in Arica on February 1st, 1826, and sailed on the *Chimborazo* on the 2nd. On February 7th he landed in Chorrillos, and on the same evening he arrived in his residence of La Magdalena, close to Lima. A fortnight earlier (23.i.26), the last Spanish garrison in South America had surrendered. Rodil, the stubborn commander in Callao, had held that city and port from December 10th, 1824, that is, for thirteen months. On receiving news of the capitulation of Ayacucho, he had refused to be included in it and had prepared to resist. He first believed that with Spanish warships holding the sea, and reinforcements from Spain, he would reconquer Peru; and he wrote to Admiral Rosamel for information as to possible European help. (Rosamel probably was giving him some help *sub rosa* by means of a so-called whaling ship off Callao.) When all his endeavours proved fruitless, Rodil held on all the same. Bolívar was wroth and had him declared outside the law of nations. When the Spanish ships, on orders from Madrid, left for Manila, Bolívar had an effective sea blockade organized by the Englishman Illingworth (known to Colombians as Illingrot) aided by a number of Spanish craft that changed sides under the leadership of a Spanish-born officer; while he made his trusted Salom come to lead the siege by land. Rodil held on, despite hunger, disease and conspiracies, which he repressed with a ruthless hand; and when thousands had perished (including Torre-Tagle) he at last parleyed, was granted generous conditions, and on January 23rd, 1826, left with his garrison and the honours of war (23.i.26).

Bolívar made his official entry into Lima on February 10th, 1826. The pleasure-loving city received with enthusiasm her hero, who had sought a fresh youth by shaving off his moustache and whiskers, at the request, it would appear, of the ladies of Potosí. La Mar, then President of the Government, with his General Staff, came to La Magdalena to fetch him: and Bolívar went again through one of those days of triumph he so much enjoyed, under arches of welcome, downpour of flowers, the music of church bells and bands and popular acclamations, a *Te Deum* in the Cathedral and a civic reception in which, for once, no white-dressed maidens came to crown his brow. The symbolic action, however, was not omitted. As one of the speakers who received him expressed the wish to see him again at the head of affairs, Bolívar burst forth: " That will be an insult to Peru, to the Council of Government, to good administration, to the flower of the citizens, to the conqueror of Ayacucho, to the first citizen, to the illustrious Field Marshal La Mar, that I should sit on this chair—I place him on it." And so he did physically, forcing La Mar to occupy the presidential chair, while, of course, in so doing, he morally sat on the whole nation and on her president as well. La Mar did not accept.

Lima became the centre of the continent and, as O'Leary puts it, Bolívar wielded " a power more absolute over a considerable part of South America and over the whole continent than the most exalted monarch of Europe over his dominions ". The liberating phase was over; the time had come to build up. How? Opinions varied; but in Lima, mostly within an orbit reminiscent of the city's splendid viceregal days. Some advocated a union of Peru and Bolivia, ruled by Sucre as President, presumably for life; others pointed out that no one but Bolívar could restore order in Buenos Aires and Santiago, and that a union of all the seven States under his authority was the only way out; a third party, led by Unanúe, openly advocated a monarchy, since the newly emancipated countries were not ripe for a republican system. There was of course one man only who could be considered for that throne. Bolívar let people talk.

Meanwhile he lived like a king. He had again retired to La Magdalena, the villa in the neighbourhood of Lima, where he could see the sun, denied to the city for six months of the year by a canvas of fog; and where, with more discretion than in his official residence, he could enjoy the pleasures to which he was so addicted: a good table, lively talk—and women. His feminine successes became legendary. They were tolerated or suffered by his official mistress, Manuela Sáenz, who knew her powers over him, and let him play, in exchange for a comfortable allowance, political power, and a freedom, perhaps not given but certainly taken, for amorous adventures of her own. " Les aides-de-camp m'ont raconté des choses incroyables "—writes Boussaingault of this phase of Manuela Sáenz, whom he knew well. " C'était généralement la nuit que Manuela allait chez le Général. Elle y arriva une fois qu'elle n'était pas attendue. Ne voilà-t-il pas qu'elle trouve dans le lit de Bolívar une magnifique boucle d'oreille en diamant. Il y eut alors une scène indescriptible. Manuela, furieuse, voulait absolument arracher les yeux au Libertador. C'était alors une vigoureuse femme: elle étreignit si bien son infidèle que le triste grand homme fut obligé de crier au secours. Deux aides-de-camp eurent toutes les peines du monde à le débarrasser de la tigresse. Les ongles avaient fait de telles égratignures sur la face du malheureux que pendant huit jours il dut garder la chambre."

All this cost money. According to the Peruvian Vidaurre, who, after having played stool for Bolívar to mount his horse, was to represent him at Panamá, the personal expenses of the Dictator during the four years he ruled Peru amounted to 300,000 pesos, not including the jewels and objets d'art presented to him, which would increase the sum by another 200,000. Riva Agüero asserts, on the faith of Peruvian State documents, that 8,000 pesos were spent on Eau de Cologne for Bolívar; while the Treasury of the Lima Consulate paid out to Manuela Sáenz 2,000 pesos a month, over and above the 1,000 monthly her patient husband Dr. Thorne paid her; and that Cayetano Freire, the head of the police, had orders to let her dispose of any amount she might require for jewels, furniture and small expenses. There is a homely letter of hers (April, 1826), excusing herself for having burst into his privacy when he would have preferred her not to be there: " I know you will be cross with me, but it was my fault. I came in through the dining-room and saw you had people in; I ordered fire to be brought to air some sheets in the next room, and as I was going there, I met everybody. I was so worried I could not sleep, so that it will be best if I do not come to your house unless you can see me or want to. Tell me whether you want to eat something before the bull-fight.—M. I am sending you some lunch which you will like."

2

It was but natural that in this atmosphere of success, adulation and unchecked power, his old urge towards " monocracy " should come to the fore again. His ideas, however, were not making much headway, and opposition to his aims and person had been growing steadily. Hardly a month after his departure for Arequipa, in 1825, two young officers, Cabero and Millán, were planning a conspiracy; caught by the police, they were shot. Towards the end of February, a conspiracy led by some Argentines and two of his own ministers was unearthed. It aimed at getting rid of him and of his troops. But Bolívar, " bewitched by Peru," needed his troops to stay on there. He noticed the undercurrent of resentment; but thought it could be put down by force, and, if need be, by terror. The Berindoaga case gave him an opportunity to " make an example ".

After the surrender of Callao, Berindoaga, caught at sea fleeing from the port, was sentenced by the Supreme Court; the sentence was ratified by the four Ministers of the Government; but the Municipal Council of Lima asked Bolívar to reprieve him. The war was over; and it had been, after all, a civil war. Bolívar was adamant. Berindoaga was executed. " This is the first time "—he writes to Santander (23.iv.26)—" Lima has witnessed stern justice enacted. The people have seen it with satisfaction and without the slightest regret, and even Berindoaga's relatives have preferred silence to supplication. Everybody has said that this example will produce a good effect; and I agree." What was in his mind? Why did he still think it necessary to hold Lima by examples? His aide-de-camp and biographer Mosquera provides the answer: " In our opinion, those who were then inducing Bolívar to dare to present a Constitution to Bolivia and to Peru, wanted the people to be intimidated by this inconsiderate severity." A glance at the letter in which Bolívar flattered himself on the " good effect " of the " example " bears out Mosquera's view. Bolívar revealed to Santander how he was getting rid of the Peruvian Congress.

In a letter to Santander (27.xii.25) Bolívar himself describes the Bolivian constitution he had prepared for Bolivia and in fact for all South America: " very strong, without violating any of the three unities and abolishing every privilege from slavery downwards ". An electorate would elect the Legislature and present three candidates for magistrates, prefects, governors, *corregidores* and priests. The Legislature was to be divided into censors, senators and tribunes. Citizens would be qualified by ability and not by fortune. " Those who cannot write, pay no taxes, or have no known business shall not be citizens." The Executive Power was to be vested in a President for life who would elect his own Vice-President, and as the Vice-President would be his successor, the scheme amounted to a kind of monarchy the line of which would be determined by the first President.

Congress was due to meet in February, and elections had to be held. " As I have just arrived "—wrote Bolívar to Santander (8.ii.26)—" I know but very few deputies and cannot therefore say what their views are, but I am sure that they will be mostly supporters of mine, i.e. of order and of America." Energetic measures had however to be taken to " direct " the electorate towards the channels the government, i.e. Bolívar, desired. Luna Pizarro, who had been the President of the first Congress, was elected for Arequipa and came to Lima in a militant, anti-Bolívar mood. Bolívar tried to win him over by offering him the presidency of Congress, but failed and veered from flattery to contempt. " One Luna Pizarro, a little priest, . . ." The Arequipans, " who are the Caraqueños of Peru," argued in a preparatory meeting that the Congress should be constituent and not merely constitutional. Bolívar opposed this through the Government; and as he made but little headway, he decided to dispute the credentials of all the deputies of the opposition; and, worse still, to have this matter settled, not by Congress itself but by the Supreme Court. The deputies protested and " some of them touched on a more delicate string: that the Colombian troops should no longer remain in Peru ".

This raised the pitch of Bolívar's irritation; and on March 1st he announced his own departure. There was a general outcry—how genuine ?—and he yielded to those who begged him to do what he had all along meant to do: he stayed. But he took the opportunity to deprive a score of deputies of their powers, " and though about 48 remain whose credentials are in order ", he writes to Santander, " I do not believe this Congress will meet until 1827, not only because 40 deputies are not enough, but because it will be necessary to have the credentials of the 20 altered or new elections held ". The intention to prevent Congress from working is evident. Nor does he hide it. " I feel no embarrassment in telling you that I have felt but little regret at all this; for meanwhile I can set the country in order, give it morale and find a person capable of serving in the Executive with that firmness and energy which are necessary here above all else."

3

This manoeuvre had two objects: to get rid of Congress and to disarm the opposition, already considerable, against his personal power. That is why, although the " Arequipans " had raised the constitutional question, and Bolívar was against the Arequipans, he was by no means against raising the constitutional question. Far from it. The 52 deputies who followed his dictates presented to " his " government, and " his " government accepted, a programme of three points: Congress to adjourn for a year; the provinces to be consulted on whether the constitution was to be reformed, and if so, whether wholly or in part; and who should be the head of the State. Bolívar wanted Peru to accept the constitution he had drafted for Bolivia, and, to that effect, to by-pass Congress and to consult the electoral colleges instead. This procedure was, of course, illegal. It savoured of the plebiscites whereby dictators, from Napoleon to Hitler, always tried to found their power on the misinformed masses, elbowing out the institutions evolved under a liberal way of life. Bolívar made his government proceed with the measure. His new Minister of State, Pando, issued a circular (1.vi.26) offering the Bolivian constitution to the electoral colleges, analysing it shortly and praising it highly. One of the objections which this Minister of Bolívar raised against the constitution of 1824 was that it " enhanced the municipal power ", i.e. the old Spanish institution which made dictatorship impossible and had made illustrious and prosperous the old family of Bolívar.

Pando's circular added impetus to the opposition. " For months "— writes Restrepo—" a rumbling rumour could be heard in the privacy of Peruvian families and gatherings. The promise made by Bolívar in his Proclamation of March 11th, 1824, was repeated and underlined, that he ' would after his triumph throw away the palm of dictatorship and return to Colombia with his brothers in arms without a single grain of sand from Peru and leaving it in liberty '." Resentment against the Colombian troops ran high. Two squadrons of hussars mutinied (6.vii.26), declaring they wanted to free themselves from the Colombians. A conspiracy was discovered aiming at expelling the Colombians and murdering Bolívar. It was due to break out on July 28th, 1826. Necochea was implicated, as well as several colonels and the Canon Requena. A special Court sentenced the conspirators to prison and expulsion. One of the conspirators, the Peruvian Lieutenant Aristizábal, sentenced to death, died declaring he gave his life for his country. The government expelled from Peru all the Chileans and Argentines, " a despotic decision, justly criticized ", said Restrepo; and he might have added, one which increased Bolívar's unpopularity. Nevertheless, the consultation of electoral colleges was proceeded with, and Bolívar's advisers persuaded him that the majority of Peruvians were favourable to the Bolivian constitution with him as president for life. In fact the electoral colleges elected him President. Restrepo points out that much of this subservience to Bolívar was due to " fear of Bolívar's absolute power. With the title of *Libertador* the Congress of 1825 had conferred on him a real dictatorship for an indefinite time. More than once, the weight of this authority fell on those who evinced an opposition to the actions or intentions of the man who wielded power in Peru ". The " example " of Berindoaga was having a " good effect ".

Bolívar's aim really was to clothe in legal authority his *de facto* and somewhat irregular power. At bottom, his monocratic, and even monarchical, hankering could not be nobler. He already enjoyed power *de facto*. He wanted it *de jure*. And he justified his secret policy in his own eyes, since he was sincerely convinced of the utter impossibility of governing South America under Republican institutions. Restrepo vouches for this and affirms that he often heard Bolívar express such views " of which he was profoundly convinced ".

That is why he drafted the " Bolivian " constitution, which he made

Peru adopt in August, 1826. In his mind this was to be the basis for a much wider plan than the mere establishment of the new Republic that bore his name. He describes it to Sucre in a letter from Magdalena (12.v.26). First he urges Sucre to have Bolivia adopt a constitution " that has achieved a perfection almost beyond any hope. Pando says it is divine, the work of genius, and as perfect as possible. Pando is a man incapable of flattery." He again says it is " the ark of alliance, the compromise between Europe and America, between the army and the people, democracy and autocracy, empire and republic; the great motive force of our social reform ". Peru, he says to Sucre, will offer Bolivia a Pact of union which must also do for Colombia " where I will have it adopted ". He wants " the most perfect union under federal forms ". The federal government to keep foreign affairs, war and federal finance, for each of which departments there will be a Chamber. There will be a President and a Vice-President. " The *Libertador* as Supreme Chief will visit every State every year." The Vice-President would govern (always his pattern: he moving about, someone else doing the work). He insists on unity: " Otherwise there would be so many disorders that people will clamour for an empire, for the army, the clergy and Europe demand it." Then, he adds this significant paragraph: " Friend, do not forsake us at this stage, when we need more than ever capable men, full of glory and popularity. For a brave man, danger is the true appetite and, as I am certain that you share my feelings, I have not doubted for an instant that, on knowing the great risk America is running, your desire to serve will have been quickened. Be sure that the greatest destinies await you. I have been offered a Crown which does not fit my head, and which I conceive, in the dark of future happenings, hovering over the brow of the victor of Ayacucho—and were it not that diadem, it would be that of laurel which rewards virtue."

Bolívar therefore wanted to found an empire of which he would be the first monarch under the title of Liberator, and Sucre the second, under that of Emperor. This can no longer be disputed. Nor is it clear why it should; for the idea was statesmanlike, generous, shrewd and truly great. His republican airs were but a pretence due less to hypocrisy than to tactical necessity. Alvear and O'Higgins wanted him to become the Protector of a Federation of Colombia, Chile and Buenos Aires. Pando and his government advocated an Empire from the mouth of the Orinoco to Potosí, for, they argued " they want peace with Europe at all costs ". His own preference for a Federation was purely tactical, for he feared the republican feelings of his countrymen.

Were they as republican as all that? Commenting on the penury of the Colombian Republic, Restrepo goes to the root of the matter. The trouble came, he says, less from the laws than from the civil servants, who would not apply them. " This vice which still subsists in New Granada, that of not respecting the laws, comes perhaps from the republican form of government, in which a large number of people concur in their making, and therefore feel no respect for them. How different was the respect we used to feel towards the obedience rendered to the laws emanating from the Cabinet of Madrid, sanctioned two thousand leagues away, and applied here with vigour and exactitude by the agents of the Spanish government." Does not this text of a close observer of those days suffice to justify Bolívar? The fact must be recorded again, and not for the last time, that what Bolívar was driving at was the reconstruction of the Spanish Empire without the Spanish King.

4

He knew that, as he wrote to Sucre, " A host of tyrants will rise from my grave and every one of them will be a Sulla or a Marius to drown in blood their civil wars." But even in this he was too optimistic. One had already risen: the very one who was to expel him from Venezuela and even from life. The set-up he had left in Venezuela after his victory in Carabobo had not lasted long. Soublette was left in charge as Vice-President, and the country had been divided into three military districts: Caracas-Barinas, under Páez; Barcelona-Margarita-Cumaná-Guayana, under Bermúdez; Coro-Mérida-Trujillo, under Mariño. The Spaniards were still in Coro and Puerto Cabello. Páez, disgruntled at being put under Soublette, a junior officer and without military prestige, took his appointed task half-heartedly, and more than once resisted or countered Soublette's instructions about the war against the Spaniards. Between Páez' ill-will and Soublette's incapacity the war dragged on in the region of Coro-Maracaibo-Puerto Cabello. When, under the Cúcuta Constitution, Venezuela became a part of the Colombian Republic, Soublette was appointed Intendant of Venezuela, a mere change of name, in fact a civilian and military boss over the three local bosses, Páez, Bermúdez and Mariño, Páez felt the more disgruntled. The *cabildo* of Caracas protested against the Constitution (1.i.22). Soublette forbade the official *Gazette* to publish the document, but the *cabildo* had it printed separately, and though Páez formally disapproved of the step, it fitted in so well with his state of mind that it is probable he inspired it. At a later stage in the campaign, after his long siege of Puerto Cabello which he had to give up (30.vii.22), Páez issued a Proclamation ordering a general enlistment, for which he alleged he had received powers from the Supreme Chief, and empowering local magistrates to commandeer persons of property for the war. Soublette revoked the order.

Morales kept moving here and there with new forces, but with the backing of the people. He took Maracaibo (6.ix.22). " War went out in some spots and the supporters of Spain made it flare up again elsewhere with added fury "—writes Restrepo. The Indians " yielded nothing of their royalist fanaticism. It became necessary to kill some of them and to transport others to Panamá and to Peru, a slow work of time and of much hardship ". " The province "—says Restrepo—" was thoroughly royalist."

Morales meanwhile penetrated inland as far as La Grita, but returned to Maracaibo after a somewhat fruitless campaign; and the Apure rose against the Whites. Páez was forced out of his apathy and met the danger by recruiting cavalry units. The defeat of the Spanish naval force by Padilla (with the efficient collaboration of the Englishman Walter Chitty) (24.vii.23) made the Spanish situation in Maracaibo perilous. Morales capitulated (4.viii.23). Calzada capitulated in Puerto Cabello (10.xi.23) and on November 15th, 1823, the last Spanish garrison in Venezuela sailed for Cuba.

This, however, did not put an end to the worries of the Independent Government. The structure which had held the country during three centuries had crashed, but a new structure had to be built. No trifle. Anarchy was rife. The *llaneros*, used to years of commandeering cattle, houses, land and goods, as if everything belonged to everybody, naturally carried on this way of life after being discharged; and bands of ex-soldiers turned thieves stole and killed cattle for the value of the skins and the fat, so that soon the plains of the Apure were covered with the whitened skeletons of its one-time wealth. Páez took a hand in repressing the evil; and the Government, with his collaboration, pursued the policy of sending the more dangerous hotheads to Peru. This, by the way, adds weight to the frequent complaints of the Peruvians against the Colombian army of occupation.

Even so, other outbursts of rebellion flared up: in Margarita, against recruiting; in Petare, where the slaves rebelled shouting: " Long live the King! Death to the Whites! " (9.xii.24). On July 24th, 1824, the body of a Lieutenant Perdomo was found in the river, at Bogotá; and a Colonel Infante was accused of having murdered him. He was sentenced to death. Infante was a ferocious and unruly negro who terrorized Bogotá with his adventures, but had fought bravely in the war. One of the judges, Dr. Miguel Peña, raised legal objections against the sentence; but he was in a minority of one and put himself in the wrong by refusing to sign the sentence. The cause of his stand (as events were to show) was his desire to appear as the champion of the coloured people against the Whites. He was a mulatto himself, who, as Civil Governor of La Guaira, had contrived with Bolívar to deliver Miranda to the Spaniards; inconstant in his allegiance during the early days of the Republic; and known to have made money to the detriment of the State by speculating with a sum of 500,000 pesos the Government had entrusted to him to convey from Bogotá to Caracas. For his defiance of the Supreme Court he was arraigned before the Senate, his refusal to sign being a breach of the law 107 of the " *Recopilación* of the Laws of the Indies ". Santander refused to reprieve Infante, who was executed on March 26th, 1825. Bolívar was worried, for Peña was the only Venezuelan of the Court, and too well known for his unruly character. He wrote to Peñalver from Cuzco, urging him to advise Peña " not to let himself go to wild extremes ". His description of Infante is worth quoting. " Everybody finds Infante was a criminal but him. Tell him no one loved and esteemed Infante more than I; but that no one was more ferocious; that many a time before he had said that his one and universal instinct was to kill everything that lived and to destroy everything that did not; that if he saw a dog or a sheep he struck it with his spear, and if a house, he burnt it. All this in my presence. He hated everything and could not bear anything standing." Peña was not convinced. He withdrew to Valencia in a black mood, brooding vengeance.

5

Two tensions kept Venezuela lively: a " federalism ", which strained at the leash of Bogotá; and a standing struggle between the military and the civilian authorities. The two were interlocked; for the military leader, Páez, was a localist. He had already more than once stood up to the Intendant, by then the ex-Marqués de Toro, and when, towards the close of 1824, Escalona was appointed, trouble went from bad to worse. Páez had brought some of the Petare conspirators before a military Court, to which Escalona objected, and the Central Government decreed that Escalona was right. As Páez had foreseen this, he had reprieved the prisoners. The local spirit was also vocal in the Municipality of Caracas in which, to quote a Venezuelan historian, " the tradition of the Spanish municipalities, always jealously watching over their powers, and often instruments of political progress in America, could be seen reborn under the Republic." This spirit inspired a protest by the city of Caracas against a Decree of the Executive (17.iii.25) sentencing to death all conspirators, confiscating their property and freeing all the slaves who would denounce those " who tried to arouse them against public peace "—an article, said the Municipal adviser, " which would cause more harm than the would-be conspiracies ". An article, let it be added, which proves that the decrees freeing all the slaves of the Republic had not been applied.

Such was the canvas on which Páez was to embroider. He called a meeting of the citizens of Caracas (9.xii.25) to enlist them in the army in virtue of his Decree of 1824, as General Commander of the Department. Incensed by their indifference, he summoned them again to the Monastery of St. Francis (6.i.26) " to make them feel all the weight of his authority "; and as few responded, he ordered his troops to arrest every man indiscriminately and send them to the barracks. The Municipality protested. Escalona forced Páez to withdraw the troops and set free all the arrested men in the evening. The troops, meanwhile, had committed such excesses that it looked as if the city had been looted by an enemy. Both Escalona and the Municipality complained to Congress. Santander reported to the Chamber, covering Páez and advising caution, yet leaving the door open for further action. A formal accusation against Páez was put before the Senate, which accepted it (27.iii.26). This entailed his supension as Military Commander of the Department. To make matters worse, Santander appointed Escalona to replace the man he had ousted.

Bolívar was displeased. Aware of Páez' position through Briceño Méndez, his niece's husband, whom he trusted, he knew from a letter of his (23.xii.25) that Páez was leading a military party ready for a *coup d'état*, ostensibly to declare Bolívar Emperor of Venezuela or even of Colombia. Páez himself had imparted the plan to Bolívar (1.x.25). " We must confess "—wrote Páez—" that Morillo spoke the truth to you in Santa Ana, when he said he had rendered a signal service to the Republic by killing off all the lawyers, but we must accuse ourselves of the sin of having left uncompleted Morillo's work, for we have not done as much with those we had still at hand."

Briceño had calmed Páez. Bolívar took the same line, and in a skilful and cautious way, showing his letters secretly to Santander and having them forwarded by him, he begged Páez to be patient and to wait till 1831, when the Constitution would have to be changed. Meanwhile he advised him to support the " Bolivian " Constitution in Venezuela.

6

But Páez was then breaking the Constitution in force. With the connivance of Dr. Miguel Peña and of a more or less spontaneous crowd, he secured his reappointment as Military Commander by the Municipality of Valencia on April 30th, 1826; and on May 3rd he issued a Proclamation officially assuming command; whereupon several other municipalities followed his lead, even Caracas, which had been the cause of his removal. The movement was veering from a personal to a party struggle, whereby the Páez party aimed at reforming the Constitution there and then instead of waiting until 1831. On May 14th, 1826, Páez took his oath before the Municipality of Valencia, " it being understood that he would not obey the orders of the Government of Bogotá "; and on May 29th he, the rebel, as the chief authority of Valencia, received the oath of the other authorities. Peña and Páez seem to have worked also on the caste and colour prejudice, airing their pro-mulatto views as leaders of what María Antonia Bolívar called the " pardocrats " (pardo, dusky). On Peña's advice, Páez visited the Apure to make sure of his llaneros.

Realizing the gravity of the incident, Bolívar dispatched O'Leary to Santander and to Páez. O'Leary discussed the matter with Santander, whom he found on the whole ready for almost any compromise; then went on to Páez, whom he found in his old wartime headquarters of Achaguas " sitting on a low stool, playing the violin, with a blind negro sitting on a chair in front of him ". O'Leary tried to solve the problem on Santander's lines; but Páez, who feared to perish like Piar and Infante, would not listen. By then he was governing Venezuela as a separate dictator. He had restored the Mint of Caracas (10.vi.26), abolished by the Central Government; and prohibited the circulation of letters and papers from neighbouring departments (25.vii.26), applying the measure with so much zest that the British Consul had to protest (26.ix.26) because he was not receiving his private correspondence. O'Leary reported all this to Bolívar, emphasizing the rebellious stand of Páez. Throughout his reports, the Irishman reveals his anxiety lest Bolívar condone the breach of the law Páez incarnates. He is, O'Leary writes to Bolívar, " an immoral, malicious, insidious man, unworthy of Y.E.'s protection ". He also insists on the danger to Bolívar's glory were he to accept the Crown or a dictatorship. Bolívar disliked all this advice and on his return received him coldly. " One of his aides-de-camp " —writes O'Leary in his Memoirs—" tried to comfort me, explaining that it all came about not through any fault of mine but owing to the Libertador's ill humour who, like Idomeneo, had vowed to sacrifice the first person he would come across. ' No ', I answered. ' Say rather that, like Agamemnon, he has killed his daughter: the Constitution.' "

The full impact of these events did not reach Bolívar until the summer. At the time when he was thinking of capitalizing his glory by rising to imperial power over a federation of three, perhaps five, perhaps all Spanish-American nations, a separatist movement was set on the march by the only man he feared—that Páez, who, shunning world glory, was content with his hold over the Apure. Was the continental Quixote to be defeated by the cowboy Sancho? He resolved to leave for Venezuela. The news spread like wildfire; and from August 13th to 15th, objurgations, shouts, harangues, prayers and petitions, were resorted to in order to keep him in Peru. He stood by his decision. Lima besieged him with her irresistible force. " A considerable number of beautiful and respectable Peruvian ladies "—assured Restrepo—" went to his house, surrounded him and demanded with the most instant entreaties that he remain in Peru." He gave in, wreathed in smiles.

The next day, August 16th, the electoral college of Lima province sanctioned the " Bolivian " Constitution. Bolívar was officially informed of it and was offered the presidency for life which he formally, but only formally, declined. Fifty-eight out of the fifty-nine electoral colleges of Peru confirmed Lima's vote. But how was this vote obtained? Captain Mamyneau wrote to the Comte de Chabrol, from Callao (9.xi.26): " *Le Collège Electoral fut convoqué; soixante députés sur trois-cents obéirent à la citation verbale qui leurs fut donnée; on leur fit lecture de la Constitution; l'Intendant de la Police leur distribua à chacun un billet portant les mots:* Bolívar Président à vie et autocrate, *que les electeurs répétèrent à haute voix lorsque la lecture du Pacte fondamental fur achevée. Ainsi se proclama Bolívar Président Perpétuel de la République, et pour que l'opinion publique ne pût pas argumenter de la brièveté de la session pour conclure que l'adoption avait eu lieu sans examen, on mit des sentinelles à la porte, et les électeurs ne purent sortir qu'à sept heures du soir quoiqu'avant deux heures tout fût déjà terminé.*" Sure now of Peru's opinion, but concerned about Venezuela, Bolívar, after one of the splendid parties he so much enjoyed, left Peru quietly at dawn on September 3rd. In Lima his faithful Lara remained in command of his Colombian troops—the same Lara who had murdered the Aragonese friars of Caroní.

CHAPTER XX

THE " SECRET IDEA "

I

HIS journey was to serve a double purpose: to settle Páez and to have himself acclaimed as a Dictator of all the lands that lay between Lima and Caracas. His weapon was pretorian. Like that of Napoleon, his Empire was to be founded on the barracks. He had sent before him an emissary whom he trusted: the youthful Antonio Leocadio Guzmán Blanco, the son of a Spaniard, an admirer of his deeds. Guzmán had left (8.viii.26) with letters from Bolívar to Generals Carreño, Páez, Urdaneta, Padilla, Flores, and to Cristóbal Mendoza (the only civilian on the list) advocating the immediate calling together of a Convention to reform the Constitution in order to secure dictatorial powers. The legal instrument for the new régime was to be the " Bolivian " Constitution, in which Bolívar saw " all the attractiveness of federation, all the solidity of central government, all the stability of monarchies ". Guzmán Blanco was successful in Guayaquil, Quito, Panamá, Santa Marta and Maracaibo. Everywhere with few exceptions (Pasto, under José María Obando, one of them) the " Bolivian " Constitution ousted that of Cúcuta in a truly revolutionary way. Letters from generals urging Bolívar to crown himself poured in. Páez and Mariño repeated the request they had made through Guzmán. Flores, Mosquera, Manuel Valdés, all wrote in the same sense, which Mosquera sums up thus: " The army in general is definitely for a constitutional monarchy and to this opinion have rallied the priests and a few men who hope to be counts and marquesses; and these ideas are making headway in the belief that the Holy Alliance will never recognize our independence owing to our institutions." This is borne out by the reports Canning was then receiving from his agents in Colombia. Urdaneta made it clear to Sutherland, British Consul in Maracaibo, that all the military chiefs were in favour of Bolívar's coronation. He complained that Great Britain had recognized Colombia while still a Republic, and assured him that this had been very much to the dislike of Bolívar, whose intention it was to found a monarchy under British protection. When Sutherland pointed out that such a plan required much secrecy, Urdaneta retorted: " Friend, much circumspection is necessary "; and as for the danger of civil war: " All will be done without a shot." Bolívar's plan, as revealed by Urdaneta to Sutherland, was to be crowned while enjoying a full dictatorship, so as to be able to ensure peace during the change over.

Santander was against. " With all the warmth of a loyal and sincere heart, I beg you not to approve such acts as those of Guayaquil and of Quito. . . . The scandalous acts of Guayaquil and Quito . . . that horrible dictatorship." Santander's letters are sound, wise, friendly and loyal. But the issue was not as simple as the Santanderists will have it. Urdaneta had written to Santander about having Bolívar crowned, and he had answered that, though he was the most monarchist man in the world, his duties prevented him from sharing in the plan. Urdaneta, however, thought that he would raise no obstacles, for he would benefit from the change. The fact is that, while a dictatorship was temperamentally the only form of government Bolívar could " live ", it so happened that at the time, it was probably the wisest course. Was Santander in a position to suggest a better way out ? After having painted the situation of the Republic in rosy colours, he was bound to confess to Bolívar great social evils which went far to justify some changes in the system. " We have no men to whom to entrust our Republic; some do not want to serve . . . others are good only for the battlefield, others are only after getting rich at the expense of the people . . . our laws are so exaggeratedly philanthropic that I wonder how we stand on our feet." And again: " Taxes are not paid, those who ought to get them do not, tradesmen defraud the customs, civil servants share in the fraud. The origin of our evils is in my opinion that, from the Constitution to the last by-law, all our laws have been too liberal." This was no new idea bred by experience in him. On August 28th, 1822, he had written to Lino de Clemente: " I believe that it might not be difficult to make the country accept a moderate constitutional monarchy. Particularly if, as a reward for his services, Congress were to offer it to the *Libertador*."

As for Bolívar's refusals, Santander had brushed them aside beforehand: " Everybody knows that the *Libertador* will turn down the proposal out of delicacy; he will publicly ask to be retired as a simple citizen; but in politics that will be given as much importance as such things get in such cases, and a unanimous decree of Congress will achieve our aim: he knows that it is the only form of government that can make our people prosperous." In 1822, therefore, both Santander and Bolívar aimed at a monarchy and Bolívar was to be its crowned head. Santander's opposition in 1826 was therefore an opportunistic mood due to personal ambition. He knew that Bolívar had chosen Sucre as his political heir. Had Bolívar chosen his heir on grounds of expediency rather than for objective reasons and in the public interest, as he had done, had he realized that Santander was more worth while winning over than Sucre, who was too loyal and disinterested ever to be a danger, Santander would have co-operated in the scheme and Bolívar would have been crowned in 1826. " And after your death, who is your successor ? Páez ? Montilla ? Padilla ? I want none of them as a crowned Supreme Chief for life." So wrote Santander to Bolívar on July 6th, 1826; and the sentence is the most revealing for its silence on Sucre, though Santander knew him to be the actual heir in Bolívar's mind. As early as December 25th, 1825, Bolívar had written to him: " General Sucre is necessary for this Constitution and without him there is nothing in it."

2

Bolívar took the opportunity of his journey back to Colombia to win over his army commanders to his " Bolivian " Constitution. He arrived in

Guayaquil at dawn (12.ix.26) on board the brig *Congreso* and at once issued a Proclamation in which, under the cloak of the noblest generosity, and mentioning no names, he put his own Vice-President Santander and the rebel Páez on an equal footing: " The cry of your discord reached my ears in Peru, and I have come to bring you an olive branch. Accept it as an Ark of Salvation. . . . I refuse to enquire who is at fault. . . . I bring you two arms to unite you in my bosom. Granadinos and Venezuelans, right and wrong, soldiers all of the liberating army and citizens of the great Republic . . . in your quarrel there is but one guilty man: I. For I did not come back in time. Two friendly republics kept me away, bewitched with immense gratitude and undying rewards. I offer myself as the victim for your sacrifice." This document in which the President deprived his own Vice-President of all authority, shows that Bolívar came ready to profit by Páez' self-seeking onslaught in order to bring down to earth Santander's construction which he also, and for different reasons, wanted to destroy. Exactly when and why he was to turn against Páez will be seen anon. The irregular system known as the " Actas " whereby groups of more or less qualified persons in every city declared him a dictator—a system he had himself initiated and advocated through Guzmán Blanco—received a purely formal disapproval and an actual recognition when Bolívar promoted to higher ranks in the army Mosquera and Flores and most of the officers who had instigated them. Wherever he went, he took official decisions of a dictatorial character without consulting the Government at Bogotá. (Among these dictatorial actions Restrepo records that, in Pasto, he had three royalist guerrilleros shot without waiting for their cases to be heard at law.) He arrived in Quito on September 8th, 1826, and left on October 5th, having appointed to the command of the city and province his henchman Briceño Méndez, pending whose arrival it was to be governed by his private secretary, an old unintelligent, drink-sodden man.

On entering Pasto Province, Bolívar received an intimation from José María Obando, who ruled it, to the effect that in that Province the constitutional order had not been altered. He answered it congratulating Obando on the fact. Then he arrived in the city (12.x.26), where he was well received. " The same day "—writes Obando—" as I was standing in the corridor with General Salom, Herrán and other officers, H.E. asked for a pocket knife . . . took my left epaulette and cutting the thread which kept the braid straps together, uttered these seditious words: ' An officer such as you deserves that I myself bestow on him the badge of colonel, the more so as I see others who, with less seniority and fewer services, have been promoted by Santander. Of course, it was enough for him to know that you were my friend.' " Obando, later, on receiving the commission, " knowing it to be unconstitutional, said courteously: ' Y.E. will have to confirm this on taking possession of the Government again.' Whereupon the *Libertador*, as if poking fun at my words, turned to the others and said: ' Do you see how imbued all these gentlemen are with this business of the Constitution ? ' "

The scene is alive with Bolivarism of the best brand; and it gains strength from another one also told by Obando about Bolívar's arrival in Bogotá. Two colonels were foremost in their republican ardour against the Napoleonic tendencies of Bolívar, Ortega and Vélez; and Vélez had even made his will " for he was resolved to act the part of Brutus as soon as Caesar came to the Capitol ". Ortega, who was Intendente-Gobernador, went out with a number of other officials and private citizens to receive Bolívar at Fontibon, and seized the opportunity to refer in his speech of welcome to the Constitution. Bolívar, whose countenance showed instant displeasure, stopped him short and burst forth: " Go away. You are an infamous man, a blackguard." The ceremony was at an end and while Bolívar rode ahead almost alone, there were many cries of " Long live the Constitution! ", and a few of " Long live Bolívar! " " But oh human frailty! "—Obando writes on; and he relates how, when " Brutus " Vélez went to call on him, " the *Libertador* scolded him for being his enemy, to which Vélez made answer that he was an enemy not of his person but of his opinion; Bolívar then, praising him for his firmness, put on his shoulder the two stars, the general's badge, and so everything was settled ". Soon after, an item for 4,000 pesos paid out to Vélez (farewell Brutus!) and another one of the same amount to Ortega, turned up in the Treasury books. With this and another promotion to general for Colonel Ortega, Bolívar cut off the arms of these two Bruti.

3

Santander had gone out to meet Bolívar much further afield, at Tocaima. The two men were already estranged. In Guayaquil a picture of financial corruption had been put before Bolívar by those who disliked Santander. The loan contracted in London by Francisco Montoya and Manuel Arrubla had, they said, been squandered away; and the two negotiators and Santander himself had lined their pockets with it. O'Leary, already in an attitude of " right or wrong my master Bolívar ", sets down these accusations without discussing them. The argument adduced by the Santanderists that Santander never was wealthy falls through, since he was a reckless gambler. He certainly allowed much agio and illicit profits to his political friends in order to ensure his re-election. A good observer, the French diplomatic agent Buchet-Martigny, is unfavourable to him in this respect. But Santander's friends were not the only exploiters of the British loan. Miguel Peña, whom for different reasons both Páez and Bolívar befriended, made 25,000 pesos by converting 500,000 from the loan he was supposed to convey from Bogotá to Caracas from good gold into *macuquina* currency; and Bolívar himself wrote on February 13th, 1827, to Urdaneta a letter revealing the game everybody was then playing, not excluding Bolívar's own friends. " Our good friend, Pepe Paris, has recommended to me a business of his which falls under your jurisdiction. I understand that he took 12 or 14,000 pesos out of the British loan to invest them and bring them over to America. The government orders him now to pay back this sum in Maracaibo; and I entreat you to grant him a delay of two or three months.

Paris tells me he cannot possibly pay it yet because he has not yet wound up the transaction."

This letter reveals the shameless exploitation of the British loan for speculating purposes in which the governing class was then indulging, and proves that Bolívar countenanced it. This adds credibility to the story quoted by many authors to the effect that while playing *tresillo* (a kind of bridge) with Santander at Hato Grande, Santander's estate, Bolívar, pocketing the money he had just won, said: " At last part of the loan has come my way." His indignant letters on the corruption of Santander's régime lose much of their value. The loan was frittered away in ill-prepared and worse-carried-out warlike preparations such as grandiose military purchases from American and British sharks. Posada Gutiérrez, a contemporary observer, paints an accurate and all too familiar picture of these stuffed crocodiles the armament merchants sold to the new and inexperienced Republic, " big iron kitchens, chains and enormous anchors for ships of the line, guns for ships, cannon balls of unknown calibre in enough quantities to stand three sieges such as that of Sebastopol ".

Bolívar had felt the lack of support for his ideas in Popayán, where he also received the news of a complete change of front in Lima. Admiral Guise and other enemies of his had been absolved by the Courts. This made him reflect and (as he writes to Santa Cruz) advocate that Santa Cruz and the other ministers put themselves at the head of the opposition and, giving up American plans, think only of Peru. How sincere was he? Not at all. Every act of his at this time contradicts these words. He writes in order to get the usual reaction of fidelity; just as he often resigned in order to remain the more powerful. He was surrounded by flatterers and in his circle it had become the fashion to blacken Santander and to side with Páez. The country was split into Santanderists or liberals, and Bolivarists or serviles; names taken over from Spain, where serviles were the followers of Ferdinand VII's absolute rule and liberals his adversaries. The two men, however, met in a friendly atmosphere and talked at length the whole night. Bolívar explained to Santander that he would stand by the Cúcuta Constitution, but that he would assume full powers under Article 128 to restore order; and after one or two years it was his wish to have the " Bolivian " Constitution adopted.

Santander returned to Bogotá in a good mood which calmed the agitated city. Presently, after the scene with Ortega, Bolívar entered Bogotá " almost alone and with but little public rejoicing, though all the streets he was passing through were profusely decorated. The day was very rainy " (14.xi.26). Santander in full dress uniform received him in the throne room of the Palace; for this rigid republican received " on a throne under a sort of canopy of rich crimson velvet, surrounded by the ministers, military and naval officers, public functionaries, etc., of the Republic ". He certainly did not sit on his throne on that day; but he stood in the midst of his brilliant suite with his secretaries of State, the President of the Senate, the judges of the Supreme Court, generals and a crowd of private citizens. He spoke, not without emotion; recalling the victories of Bolívar and adding that he " would be the slave of the Constitution and the laws, though always a constant admirer and a faithful friend of the *Libertador* ". Note the " though ". Posada Gutiérrez who describes the scene goes on to say: " No one breathed. Nothing could be heard but the beating of the hearts, while the *Libertador* drew within himself for a while. Then he stood up and, his face sparkling with animation, he answered." He approved the Government, declared himself respectful of the Constitution and called all Colombians to concord and peace. Relieved of its tension, the hall gave him an ovation. Eleven days later (23.xi.26) he issued a decree assuming unlimited powers.

4

In such a context must be considered the Congress of Panamá, which Bolívar fostered and at last succeeded in convening in the summer of 1826. Three were the purposes he had in mind: To widen the area of his authority and prestige to cover the whole of Spanish America; to impress the world with some show of diplomatic activity denoting stability and union among the new nations; and to settle the question of Cuba and Puerto Rico. The Congress was an idea of his, though no doubt Miranda and others had played with it. The representatives of the State he then directly controlled, Peru, arrived in Panamá a whole year before the rest and patiently waited for the others. Yet, it did not come off quite as he had dreamt it. As to membership, he was at bottom for a purely Spanish-American Congress, and therefore without either the United States, Haiti or Brazil (again his subconscious feeling as the heir of the Spanish Empire of America). Santander, however, on his own, had invited the United States, whose delegates did not reach Congress in time. Chile was not in a position to accept or refuse, being at the time so beset with anarchy that when Gual, the Colombian Foreign Secretary, was asked in Parliament which of the Chilean governments was being invited, he owned he could not say. Buenos Aires, then ruled by the lawyer Rivadavia, who suspected Bolívar's intentions, declined the invitation. The Congress thus became a modest Conference of Colombia, Peru, Mexico and Guatemala (then including all Central America). But—there was an Englishman.

Bolívar professed then to seek a federation of the whole of Spanish America, turning it into a kind of British dominion. The plan is put with admirable vigour and clarity in a letter he wrote to Santander (28.vi.25). He sees it in the form of a defensive-offensive alliance, for " our American federation cannot last if it is not taken under British protection ". He argues that " existence is the first blessing and the second is the mode of existence: if we tie ourselves up with England we shall exist, and if not we shall be infallibly lost ". Of course, a time might come when the Spanish-American nations would suffer from " England's superiority "; but " this very suffering will be a proof that we exist, and while we exist we shall have the hope of freeing ourselves from the suffering. While if we suffer in the pernicious unattachment in which we find ourselves, we shall disappear through our own endeavours to find an unlimited liberty ". Bolívar put these ideas before Canning through the British agent Ricketts. But Canning knew better than to adopt such a monster-foundling as the otherwise still-born Spanish-American Federation. He sent to Panamá a courteous, affable diplomat, Mr. Dawkins, with instructions to watch, speak unofficially but firmly and see mostly to four points: the principles of British maritime law to be respected; the United States to be kept from winning an excessive influence on Spanish America; the Spanish Americans to be induced to win over Spain to recognition through an indemnity; Colombia and Mexico to be put off from any designs they might have over Cuba and Puerto Rico. Dawkins acquitted himself admirably of his task. He won golden opinions from the Colombian delegates, whom he seems to have particularly distinguished, and succeeded, not without some luck, all along the line, except in what concerned a deal with Spain.

Bolívar had been thinking of Cuba and Puerto Rico for some time; but so had Mexico and so, of course, had the United States; nor were the two islands forgotten by either France or Spain. This brought in England. The two Spanish Antilles became the knot of an intrigue. On January 24th, 1821, in the instructions to the two emissaries he was then sending to Spain, Bolívar declared himself ready, in exchange for Spanish recognition, to recognize and guarantee the sovereignty and ownership of Spain over every American territory not yet independent—which included Cuba and Puerto Rico. On October 3rd, 1823, Santa María, the Colombian Minister in Mexico, signed a treaty of friendship and confederation with the Mexican Foreign Secretary Lucas Alamán, in which the two countries agreed to promote a general assembly of American States. In August, 1824, Santa Ana, the Mexican statesman, already adumbrated that Mexico should foster the independence of Cuba and Colombia that of Puerto Rico, meaning of course that Mexico should annex one of the islands and Colombia the other. The Spanish authorities in Cuba found out and dissolved a secret society of separatists under the name of *Suns and Rays of Bolívar*. But Bolívar had never wavered from his " realistic " policy towards the two islands; he put it squarely to Santander (20.xii.24): " I think it advisable that the Colombian government make Spain understand that if within so much time she does not recognize Colombia and make peace, these same troops will go straight to Havana and Puerto Rico. It is better for us to have peace than to liberate those islands. An independent Havana will give us much trouble. The threat is more valuable to us than an insurrection ". This business well carried out, may cause a great impression, should the Spaniards prove obstinate. Sucre can go to one island and Páez to the other." This was to be his policy throughout. At this stage, his sister's advice must have influenced him. Her opinion of the Cubans was not flattering. " They are of a treacherous spirit, and the Blacks and coloured men are without comparison worse than ours "—she wrote him (20.vii.25). He was already thinking of submitting the matter to the Congress of Panamá. But his stand remained the same: to threaten rather than to act.

Spain had sent six thousand men to Cuba under a French escort from

Martinique—which angered Canning and alarmed the United States. The American Government sought the help of Russia to ward off any annexation of Cuba on the part of France. In August, 1825, Canning suggested that the United States, Britain and France should make an agreement in respect to Cuba's status—but the United States were not interested, for though they objected to France taking Cuba, they had no such objection to taking it themselves. Canning had to be content with French assurances. However, point 3 of the five points the Colombian Government had suggested for discussion by the Congress of Panamá dealt with whether Cuba and Puerto Rico should be emancipated and if so, freed or annexed, and by whom. Colombia had contracted a loan mostly with the purpose of descending on the islands; for Santander's plan went beyond Bolívar's, and, not content with threatening, he had obtained from Congress authority to operate. He was expecting ships and armament from Europe. By the end of 1825, he had gathered a considerable expeditionary force in Cartagena. The United States intimated to Colombia (25.v.25) and to Mexico (25.xii.25) to abstain from interfering in Cuba and Puerto Rico, giving as their reason that they feared the effect on their own southern States of the emancipation of the Antillian slaves, which the Mexicans and Colombians would certainly proclaim. But Colombia and Mexico went on with their warlike plans and signed a treaty (17.iii.26) which implied in certain contingencies an attack on Havana. In the end, Canning settled the fate of the islands for the time being: he instructed Dawkins to point out that he was " far from denying the right of the new States of America to make a hostile attack upon Cuba "; and dropped the heavy hint that " neither England nor France could see the United States in possession of Cuba " but emphasized the danger implied in the attitude of the United States.

Bolívar, however, was less concerned with the islands than with the continent. For him the Congress was above all a way to enlarge his hold over the main land, a means to rebuild, without Spain, the Spanish Empire he had destroyed. Hence his insistence that the federation must be permanent. " At all costs the federal union must be preserved, if only in appearance. Its mere shadow saves us from the abyss, or at least prolongs our existence. I intend to go to the meeting, to put before it some of my ideas, which I keep in reserve." We know what such ideas were. " The Argentines want to restrict the powers of the Congress, and I believe that they must be widened infinitely and given a vigour and an authority truly sovereign." Note the word: sovereign. He is thinking of a constituent assembly for Spanish America: " I should like this Assembly to be permanent, so that, functioning as the arbiter of the differences which are bound to occur between new and neighbouring States, it should be the link that would unite them perpetually." The trend is clear. He saw himself as the head and arbiter of the dozen nations of Spanish America reunited after having fallen apart at the fall of the Spanish Crown. " Please note that it is I who submit this plan: that I am bound to be the head of this American federation, and that I am giving up the hope of so eminent an outlook in order to give its due priority to the stability of America.

England could never recognize me as head of this federation, since such a supremacy would belong to the British Government." This, of course, was tactical: to provoke a patriotic reaction and a call on him to lead the federation.

In this Napoleonic mood he writes to Santander on July 8th, 1826, from Magdalena that he sees the Congress of Panamá, then at last in session, " as a theatre show ". He was incensed by the " civilist " reaction against Páez and against his own dictatorial velleities. " Journalists are proclaiming that heroes are under the laws, and that principles are above them. There is ideology for you. This will be a celestial fatherland. Virgins and saints, angels and cherubs, shall be the citizens of this new Paradise. Bravo. Bravissimo. Let those Miltonian Legions trot down to check Páez' insurrection." He is beginning to feel defrauded by the Congress he had dreamt of on a continental scale. In a letter so windswept with inspiration that it reads like a storm, he says to General Páez (8.viii.26): " The Congress of Panamá is no more than was the mad Greek who thought that he could direct from a rock the ships that sailed by." The discussions had revealed mutual distrusts and jealousies. No one dared touch the word *boundaries*, an explosive for the delegates of those immense and empty lands. The Peruvian delegates had arrived on June 13th, 1825; those of Guatemala on March 18th, 1826; the Mexicans on June 4th. Finally the Congress opened its sittings on June 22nd, 1826, and closed them on July 15th. The four nations signed a treaty of perpetual confederation; an agreement to meet again in Congress every second year, in the Mexican city of Tacubaya; a Convention for common defence; and a military agreement to apply it. Bolívar opposed the ratification of these instruments by Peru and by Colombia. He disliked their military clauses, and found the transfer to Tacubaya put the Confederation too much under the sway of Mexico and of the United States. Briceño, in his report, points out to him that article 29 had to be amended by the Colombian delegates because, in its firm form, it stipulated that none of the allies would be able to change its form of government under pain of expulsion; but the Colombians secured a draft which enabled any of the confederates to choose the form of government it pleased. Coming from Briceño, Bolívar's confidant, this is clear enough. Nevertheless, Bolívar was not pleased, and wrote to him that the treaty of confederation " includes articles that might embarrass me in the execution of schemes I have conceived, which are in my opinion very useful and of great scope ".

5

What these schemes were may be gathered from the beginning of the same paragraph of the same letter: " The departments of Guayaquil, Ecuador and Azuay have proclaimed me a Dictator; Cauca and others may follow suit. This base will prop up my operations and provide means for me to organize everything." Written on September 14th, 1826, two months before his arrival in Bogotá, these words prove Bolívar's intention to upset the Republic. True, Páez' rebellion supplied him with a pretext; but it was no more than a pretext in his mind, which would provide him with the necessary full powers wherewith to upset the Republic of lawyers. It was essentially a feud identical to the old traditional duel between cape-and-sword men and gown-men, generals and doctors, which now pitted Páez against Santander; for Páez was a " general " and Santander, though at bottom also a " general ", had chosen to disguise himself as a " doctor ", in order the better to fight. This explains why, despite the advice of his best friend, and O'Leary's outspoken letters, Bolívar, who was a " general ", never wavered in his attitude: for Páez against Santander.

He had a good observer in Caracas, his sister María Antonia, who wrote him letters in which the vigour of will and motherwit burst through grammar and spelling. " Santander has put Páez on a precipice, and all of us, with his senseless measures trying to appoint Mendoza as Intendente, and as General Commander, Soublette, whom all here hate. It is believed here that Santa Ander wants to crown himself and they say that in such a case it must be you, not he." She complains then of the magistrates, all " vicious and thieves ", of the threat of civil war, and above all worries: " the freedom of the slaves, which she could not stomach ". He listened to her, but frowned at her politics. " I advise you not to meddle in politics. Let opinion and things flow, even though you believe them contrary to your way of thinking. A woman should be neutral in public affairs. Her family and domestic affairs are her first duties. A sister of mine must keep perfectly aloof in a country undergoing such a dangerous crisis, and where I am considered as the meeting point of all opinions." And again: " Do not meddle in politics. Sell our property for cash in England or the United States, and all will be well." But María Antonia had a will of her own.

In August, while Páez was in the Apure, the battalion also named Apure had mutinied in Caracas, as O'Leary put it, " forsaking the cause of Páez, the cause of dishonour ". Now, this counter-revolution of Caracas, as O'Leary calls it, was led by María Antonia, much to Bolívar's disgust. She wrote to him (16.xi.26) of her pleasure at receiving his portrait " after thirteen years that I had not seen you, not even a portrait "; and describing her house, full of those who came to see it, " some weep, some laugh ", and depicting the whole of Caracas eagerly awaiting him as a saviour, and " el Llanero " [Páez] having lost all the credit he had won and hated by everybody. She urges him to put his trust in the Holy Trinity " who has protected and will protect you, no doubt owing to the virtues of our ancestors who loved this great mystery "; and to bring over a bishop " to ordain and confirm " for there were no priests left. Possibly owing to the fidelity with which she respected the family obligations towards the great mystery, she had written on March 26th of the same year that, out of the entail of San Mateo, she had paid for the Holy Trinity festivals for the years 23–26, one hundred pesos each, including " music, wax, sermon, illumination and other expenses "; she wrote that the " Bolivian " Constitution was good and people liked it all " except the provisions on the freedom of slaves ".

Páez and Mariño, his second, parried the defection of the Apure battalion with reinforcements " whose lack of discipline and disorderly behaviour made the situation of the capital more critical ". On October 2nd Páez promised to withdraw the troops so that the people could express their opinion in freedom at the Assembly or *Cabildo* Abierto, which the Municipality of Caracas, under Páez' instigation, had induced Mendoza to convoke. The Assembly met (5.x.26) in a political setting due to Bolívar's own activities: the Bolivian Constitution, the " Actas " and his Proclamations. It met again on October 7th, 1826, under Páez, who assured all and sundry that Bolívar was not against the reforms the people wanted, and after a long debate, it was agreed that Páez should issue a decree calling electoral colleges to elect representatives to govern Venezuela. This was revolutionary, but no more than what Bolívar had been doing all along. The decree was issued on November 13th, the elections dated for December 10th and the new Congress was to meet in Valencia on January 10th, 1827.

6

Bolívar stayed in Bogotá eleven days and took two important decisions: to assume full powers and, during his absence in Venezuela, to delegate his powers, except for Venezuelan territory, to his Vice-President, Santander. This meant that Santander became a dictator in Cundinamarca, since Bolívar would be a dictator in Venezuela, and Briceño, in his name, in Ecuador. All this was done with the consent and, it would appear, the satisfaction of Santander. Furthermore, Santander, an expert on laws and on the ways of turning them, pointed out to Bolívar that, since they could not be legally President and Vice-President, unless they took their oath before Congress on January 2nd, 1827, and since Bolívar had no intention of calling Congress at all, Bolívar should grant Santander an authority to act as Vice-President after January 2nd by means of a letter which Santander wrote and Bolívar dated Rosario de Cúcuta, December 12th, 1826. This was done behind the back of the Government. Owing to a river being in flood, Bolívar did not go to Rosario de Cúcuta at all; but this did not prevent Santander from producing the letter on December 21st as if he had just received it, nor from answering it in fulsome terms worthy of " being described as servile ". Santander thus granted Bolívar of his own accord the widest dictatorship; and then endeavoured to transfer the responsibility of deciding whether the Vice-President should resign on January 2nd or accept Bolívar's authority (which he himself had asked for), to the President of the Senate. The President refused; and as soon as Santander saw himself again unopposed in the saddle and Bolívar away, he began a whispering campaign against Bolívar, criticizing every decision Bolívar had taken, even those adopted at meetings in which he himself had been present.

Bolívar meanwhile proceeded towards his native Venezuela, listening everywhere to complaints against General Santander—possibly because everybody knew that to be what he wanted to hear. Towards Páez he maintained a conciliatory, indeed a winning mood. Páez was in Valencia, where Ibarra brought him friendly, almost servile, letters from Bolívar. Though he had written to Santander: "Páez can do nothing unless he espouses the party of the rabble"; he writes to Páez in terms of fulsome praise, throwing over O'Leary, in an undignified manner, for his legalistic attitude against the rebel, "senseless, as if to deprive Venezuela of you were not to deprive it of its main pillar". He announces to Páez that he is bringing him presents: "A spear and a set of studs of gold I had made in Potosí for you . . . I wanted to remember you even though so far away." His correspondence at this time is all in this flattering vein. But, from San José de Cúcuta, on December 11th, he wrote a stern letter summoning Páez to come to terms and to spare Venezuela a civil war: "With me you have conquered; with me you have acquired glory and wealth; with me you may hope everything. But against me, General Castillo was lost; General Piar was lost; General Mariño was lost; General Riva Agüero was lost; General Torre-Tagle was lost. It would seem that Providence dooms to perdition my personal enemies, whether American or Spanish; and see how Generals Sucre, Santander and Santa Cruz have risen." Nevertheless, Páez was reserved. Memories of Piar and of Infante haunted him. He sent Dr. Miguel Peña and Colonel Cistiaga to Bolívar with instructions (26.xii.26) to negotiate. He was ready to fight if Bolívar insisted on obedience to Bogotá. That shows how little Páez understood Bolívar. So long as Páez had flouted no authority but that of Bogotá, Bolívar had remained only too friendly to him. If, now, he had veered to an unfriendly attitude, the reason was that Páez had revealed his personal ambition by standing up to Bolívar himself.

On boarding the *Estimbot* on his way to Maracaibo, Bolívar heard (25.xii.26) the news that Carabaño, on behalf of Páez, had attacked Briceño Méndez in Puerto Cabello. At once he aroused all his faithful commanders to send him troops for a struggle which he foresaw bloody and long; and eloquently raised the ghost of a colour-war. He was perhaps sincere, in part. A civil war was bound to loom in his eyes as a danger to be dreaded, for he knew the Republic was by no means consolidated. Coro, where he stood at the time, was still pro-Spanish; as he himself wrote to Urdaneta on the 24th of that month (xii.26): "I believe that if the Spaniards come near to these coasts, they will raise four or five thousand Indians in just this Province." Nevertheless, he exaggerates the danger of civil war in order to cover himself with enough troops to reduce Páez, of whom he is afraid. As he was to write to Páez on December 21st: "If I bring troops I have had a thousand motives for it." A week earlier, he felt strong enough to write from Coro about Páez' Proclamation, that he has read it with satisfaction "for in it I find my true feelings". But Páez had been rash enough to announce that Bolívar was coming as a mere citizen, and that was too much for the continental dictator: "Your Proclamation says that I come as citizen. What can I do as a citizen? How can I sever myself from my duties as a Magistrate? The nation has voted for *Reforms and Bolívar*. No one has disavowed me; no one has degraded me. Who is going to wrench the reins of command from me? Your friends and yourself? The indignity would be one thousand times bigger as an ingratitude than as a treason. I cannot believe it. . . . What have all Venezuelans that they do not owe to me? And you yourself, don't you owe me your existence? There is no legitimate authority in Venezuela but mine, supreme I mean. The Vice-President himself, as my decree prescribes, has no longer any authority here. I offer you with the utmost frankness all my friendship . . . but everything must go through the channels of order and true sovereignty, i.e. the national majority. What astounds me most is that you don't say a word about my supreme authority. . . . Believe me, General: in the shadow of mystery only crime will work. With me you will be everything, everything, everything. I leave to-morrow for Puerto Cabello where I await your answer."

Meanwhile Fergusson, his aide-de-camp, had sent Dr. Peña and Colonel Cistiaga to Trujillo as prisoners; and on December 16th Bolívar himself issued his own Proclamation in Maracaibo, addressed only to the Venezuelans. " Do not kill the fatherland." He pledges his word of honour to lead them to a Convention, a thoroughly unconstitutional act on his part; then, attacks Páez, without mentioning him: " No one but the majority is sovereign. He who supplants the people is a tyrant." Then, an ominous threat: " Woe to those who do not heed my word and fail in their duty." Páez' reaction was savage. " The veil is off. Bolívar comes knife in hand. He comes on behalf of the Government of Bogotá, forcing everybody to render homage and threatening all rebels. The time has come for action. Watch friends; don't let yourselves be hallucinated. Gallows and scaffolds he comes raising against us. Let us meet him with firmness, spears and swords." The year ended on this threatening attitude, both cape-and-sword-men with their swords high in the air.

CHAPTER XXI

A YEAR OF UNCERTAINTY
(1827)

I

THE year 1827 began with Bolívar and Páez glaring at each other in anger and fear. Both were brave, violent and ambitious; Bolívar was stronger, because he was more popular; but weaker, because he was more subtle and intelligent, less rash, and of the two, the less unscrupulous in his ambition. Páez had arrested Bolívar's emissary, Silva, as a reprisal for the arrest of Peña and Cistiaga; but on January 1st Silva arrived in Puerto Cabello with a message from Páez. This gesture was just what Bolívar was awaiting. At once, he issued a decree whereby Páez was confirmed as the chief civil and military authority of Venezuela, with Mariño as his *locum tenens* in Maturín; every action during the crisis being condoned and amnestied. This decree was immediately sent to Páez with a cordial letter, extolling the " ineffable joy " Bolívar had experienced in receiving his message, and imparting to him that Bolívar had " succeeded in convincing the government of the necessity of dividing Colombia into three States ". He went on to assuage Páez' fear of an interview, recalling how Morillo had come to see him with a squadron, while he was unescorted " for treason is too vile ever to enter the heart of a great man ". Then, more flattery: " You will be adored by all and as for me I shall see you as the god of peace. . . . You will be everything, everything in Venezuela through legal means." Bolívar need not have gone so far in his flattery nor in his official condonation; for Páez " was already powerless to resist him and would have submitted with a mere amnesty and some personal regard due to his military rank and services; but the *Libertador* had his eyes on Bogotá ".

Páez corresponded to Bolívar's decrees with another one acknowledging the authority of the *Libertador* and inviting his countrymen to receive him in triumph—which provoked such an outburst of enthusiasm in Bolívar that, in a Proclamation, he declared Páez the saviour of the fatherland. On January 4th, 1827, both left their headquarters to meet half-way. Páez was still distrustful and awaited Bolívar at the foot of the hill La Cumbre, in Naguanagua, well surrounded with partisans and troops. As they saw each other, both alighted and Bolívar opened his arms. Páez embraced him; their swords got entangled. While they endeavoured to disentangle them, Bolívar, smiling, said: " This is a good omen, General." He meant it. He had decided to win Páez for himself as an ally in his struggle against the Republic of lawyers which he saw incarnated in Santander; and he meant, arm in arm with Páez, to enter Caracas, where he was received in triumph on January 10th. In the company of delegates sent by the

Municipality as far as La Victoria, the two swordsmen entered the city under triumphal arches amidst the warmest enthusiasm, through streets bright with the flags of all the new republics and the stars and stripes. The carriage could hardly move; but, though Bolívar had insisted on having Páez sit by him, he was unable to wrench from the enthusiastic crowd a single *Viva* for his unpopular ally. Fifteen maidens, symbolizing military and civic virtues, presented Bolívar with two crowns of laurel; he laid one on Páez' brow and offered the other one to the people of Venezuela. Flags were displayed on which were written the names of several virtues: Bolívar handed on to General Toro the flag of Disinterestedness, to Don Cristóbal Mendoza that of Probity, to the British Representative that of Policy, to the City of Caracas that of Generosity, to Páez that of Valour—and kept for himself that of Constancy.

Festivals and banquets followed each other. On the 13th, the Municipality offered a banquet to 200 persons, a remarkable feat for a ruined city. Páez was given an opportunity to utter his gratitude. Bolívar had showered presents on him: over and above the spear and the studs, he had given him two Chilean horses, and no less a gift than the golden and gem-studded sword Lima had presented him after Ayacucho. The gift led Páez to a toast to the inviolability of his oath never to draw that sword except in defence of the liberties of the people. More girls in white, more palms, more music, and then, this: " From Caracas I went to the Apure to disarm 1,500 horsemen who refused to lay down their arms until they had ascertained Bolívar's attitude towards me." This was the reality under the rhetoric of the presents and the banquets. Before his departure, Páez had a confidential talk with Bolívar, who told him that he thought inevitable the separation of Venezuela and Colombia, and assumed that Páez would be the first President of Venezuela. Bolívar strongly advised Páez to oppose the federal system and to insist on the Bolivian Constitution. He also adumbrated that, should the Bolivian Constitution be adopted, he would settle in Venezuela. The sight of Bolívar living as a private citizen in a Venezuela ruled by Páez is too idyllic ever to have entered into the actual intentions of Providence. It was one of the many phrases Bolívar drew like curtains between his mind and others.

2

He was less insincere in his confidences to Páez about the Spanish Antilles. Bolívar's mind was at this time busy with plans for the liberation of Cuba and Puerto Rico. According to his talks with Páez, his motives were: that Cuba had become the refuge of all those Spanish Americans who had sided with Spain and desired a Spanish counter-offensive; that Havana and San Juan were excellent bases for such a counter-attack; and that Colombia had a strong army which it was dangerous to keep idle at home. According to Páez, Bolívar's plan was to send Páez with 10,000 infantry and 1,000 cavalry, take the two islands, free the slaves and with them organize an army and land in Spain to put the Spanish Liberals back into power. This last chapter of the fairy tale may well have been a flourish to fire the imagination of the *Llanero* chieftain. It is unlikely that Bolívar actually meant it, though he had spoken before, and would again speak, in the same vein. For the moment he was thinking of Cuba and Puerto Rico, and in his more sober moments only of Puerto Rico. In his letter to Sucre (6.ii.27) he speaks of 5–6,000 men under Páez, with Padilla in command of the Navy, to take Puerto Rico. " Then we shall see what we can do about Havana." He was aware of American opposition, but had allowed himself to dream of British help on the strength of rumours (which he mistook for official news) of a war between Britain and Spain on Ferdinand's refusal to countenance constitutional changes in Portugal. His letters of January, 1827, are full of it. From January 25th he begins to write about his plan to all his henchmen. He thinks that Britain would provide arms and money. On January 27th he writes to Canning congratulating him on his activities against " the treachery of the Spanish government " (which was far from Canning's mind) and discreetly expressing the hope that it may all end in the recognition of the Spanish-American Republics by Spain; he does not mention the Antilles. By February 6th, news came from Europe revealing that there was no such war between Spain and Britain; and Bolívar at once cancelled his plans, for, as he wrote to several friends, " without English co-operation we could do nothing ". The plan, nevertheless, remained alive in his mind.

He had at this time many a family business to transact. He was surrounded by women who harassed him with their quarrels and bickerings. María Antonia never tired of complaining about her sister Juanica and about the unmarried widow of his elder brother, Juan Vicente. Anacleto Clemente, María Antonia's elder son, was a good-for-nothing and a gambler, to whom Bolívar had to write stern letters threatening to disinherit him altogether. Hamilton describes how, during a wedding breakfast, Anacleto, drunk, wounded a German servant; and Santander complained to Bolívar about the sorry state in which his nephew had left the villa in the neighbourhood of Bogotá, from which (as María Antonia wrote to her brother) Santander had to expel him for he was living in it " with a lot of scoundrels including some Frenchmen who were found to be spies ". Despite her faults, María Antonia was the strongest character in the family, and Bolívar, though often led to scold her, held her in high esteem. " My sister, who has a good deal of talent . . ."—he wrote to Santander.

Bolívar mentions repeatedly that he wants to provide for his brother's children. But María Antonia warned him that any property given to them should be guaranteed against the extravagant tastes of their mother. In all this, Bolívar remains very much the master. He writes of leaving Juan Vicente's children this or that estate when he dies; but he keeps them on short strings while he lives; not for lack of generosity, but for lust of power. His niece Felicia was made to marry the mulatto General Silva, one of Bolívar's henchmen. The girl, though, according to María Antonia, interested in a Frenchman, complied out of love and respect for her uncle, but protested in a dignified letter against the threats Bolívar had used to wrench her acquiescence. We meet again that Bolívar, never able to bear contradiction and always ready to threaten and to dismiss, a tendency that was growing harder and harder as revealed even in his handwriting, which loses its round lines and becomes straight-jacketed. The capital B of his signature tends at this time to degenerate into a hasty M.

All this atmosphere of family quarrels was irksome to a man used to living and thinking in continental dimensions. He was, nevertheless, keenly interested in his affairs, and naturally relied on his family wealth for his independence in public life. He wrote to José Fernández Madrid, the Colombian agent in London (21.ii.27), informing him that he had sold the Aroa silver mine for 40,000 guineas of gold, and giving him power of attorney to invest the sum in British Government stock; the income to be added to the capital after paying the Abbé de Pradt the pension of 3,000 pesos a year Bolívar had promised him. The persistence with which he sought to ensure for himself a solid financial situation in London shows both his desire for independence of public salaries, and his foresight lest a political storm should drive him abroad. Still, this was but a mere precaution in his mind; for he - felt powerful and prosperous, and on hearing that his sister was contemplating the sale of the San Mateo estate, he jestingly wrote to her (9.iii.27): " If you will let me know how much you want for it, I know a rich man who has lots of money who would like to buy your San Mateo estate, which he prefers to others."

3

A political storm was at the time brewing against him both in Bogotá and in Lima. All the fault was by no means on the side of his enemies. His pretorianism was too open, almost too cynical, not to call forth an opposition which, even if rooted in personal resentments, did not lack objective grounds. His letters to Páez, who complained that the President did not go far enough in rewarding and protecting his own friends, prove that he granted promotion and commands to persons unworthy of them, merely because they were of Páez' faction (and therefore had rebelled against the constitutional authority which all, including Bolívar, had sworn to defend). Santander, whose fidelity to the Constitution was by no means above reproach, chose to stand for political puritanism and published unsigned articles against Bolívar in the unofficial pages attached to the official Gaceta de Colombia; other papers, such as El Conductor, published by another of Bolívar's enemies, Vicente Azuero, attacked him more violently. In these campaigns, two solutions to the political problem were advocated: either a federation or an actual separation of the three republics. Either would suit Santander, whose aim was to get rid of Bolívar and rise to the top in his own country. Driven by this ambition, he subscribed to 150 copies of El Conductor, paying for them with government money, and sending them along with the official newspaper. Bolívar resented Santander's attitude bitterly. His first impulse was to resign, and so he wrote to the President of the Senate, Luis Baralt (5.ii.27): " I resign, one, a thousand

and millions of times the presidency of the Republic." Of course, he did not mean it. No one believed him in Bogotá. The following day, he wrote Santander a letter which showed him determined to stay. He still thought that, with Páez in Caracas, Santa Cruz in Lima and Briceño in Quito, he was strong enough to oust Santander and to Napoleonize Spanish America. On December 9th, 1826, the anniversary of Ayacucho, the Peruvian authorities had sworn the Bolivian Constitution and declared him President for life with the titles of Father and Saviour of Peru.

At dawn, on January 26th, 1827, Pando, the acting head of the Peruvian Government, was refused access to the Palace by the guard at the gate. The President, Santa Cruz, was " ill " at Chorrillos. The bayonets on which the Government (regardless of Napoleon's dictum) sat, were Colombian, i.e. the third division of Bolívar's veteran army, left behind in Peru to keep the country wise and Bolivarian. But, though this division, of about 2,300 men, was commanded by one of Bolívar's closest friends, General Lara, it comprised a majority of Granadino captains and subalterns, who, led by Colonel Bustamante, the Chief of Staff, ousted the Venezuelan commanding officers and declared for the Constitution and against any attempts at dictatorship. Bustamante was acting at the instigation of Santa Cruz and possibly also of Santander. Manuela Sáenz, on hearing of the *pronunciamiento*, rode out dressed as an officer, entered one of the barracks and tried in vain to recover the regiment for Bolívar's allegiance. The *pronunciamiento* developed according to the best traditions: the *cabildo* met and, assuming parliamentary and even constitutional powers, declared the Bolivian Constitution abrogated, the previous one in force, and, therefore, Bolívar's powers at an end. Santa Cruz, suddenly restored to health, returned to Lima and was received enthusiastically. Two days later, on January 28th, 1827, he declared that " as the political constitution dictated by Bolívar had not been well received, the *pueblos* were called to elect representatives to a constituent assembly ". On the morrow (29.i.27), two Granadino junior officers sailed from Callao to Buenaventura in charge of Lara and other officers made prisoner by the mutineers, and with reports from Santa Cruz and Bustamante for Santander. The two emissaries arrived in Bogotá on March 9th, 1827. As soon as their message became known, some military commanders sent their bands out to enliven the streets; bells rang; rockets were fired; vivas were shouted and a personal witness adds: " Santander joined us in the street and went along with us for a while, showing in his face, in his harangues and his hurrahs for liberty, the intense pleasure which overpowered him, though at times he betrayed also an uneasiness he endeavoured to conceal."

The events of Lima were the outcome of a number of national and personal forces. The Peruvians felt aggrieved at the prolonged occupation of their country by the Colombian troops—quite apart from the behaviour of the troops themselves. This was a national feeling latent in all Peruvians, even in those, who, politically, benefited by the Colombian division. It was perhaps stimulated by a certain military swagger the Colombians took on, owing to their military laurels as conquerors of the conquerors of Napoleon, and to their undisguised contempt for the Peruvians as soldiers, more obvious in the Venezuelans than in the Granadinos, because they were the more military of the two. Lara, in particular, who was a ruthless and ill-tempered man, had made himself thoroughly unpopular not only with the Peruvians but with the Granadino contingent of his force. When, at one stage in his quarrel with the Government, he had suggested returning home with the whole army, the Peruvian Government had, nevertheless, begged him to remain; for the Government knew too well that its power rested on the presence of the Colombian division. At this stage, Santa Cruz bethought himself of splitting the division, getting rid of Lara and his Venezuelans, who stood for Bolívar, and retaining the Granadinos who would keep him in office. He knew he could count on the help, tacit or expressed, of Santander. Hence his tortuous attitude during the episode. Manuela Sáenz, who had been left behind in Lima by Bolívar, did her best to arouse the people against the Government and Bustamante. Vidaurre wrote to Santander on April 14th, 1827, that he dreaded a revolution because the Colombian Consul, Armero, and Manuela Sáenz " have continuously seduced, promised and even spent, the lady in particular, very high sums. With the accurate news I had of all that Armero and that woman were contriving, and after the scandal of her correspondence so offensive to public morals, I summoned him at four o'clock and told him: ' Manuela shall sail within twenty-four hours. If not I shall lock her up in Casas Matas.' I had her secure in a monastery, but she broke the rules and was constantly visited by officers." Fearing that the presence of the division would do more harm than good, the Government had them all shipped to Guayaquil; and on March 19th, 1827, Bustamante sailed from Callao with his 1,800 soldiers. The Government took this opportunity to get rid also of other inconvenient guests such as Luis López Méndez, once Bolívar's agent in London, now turned into his bitter enemy, and an accomplice of Bustamante; Córdoba, the handsome, brave but impetuous and unreliable hero of Ayacucho; and Manuela Sáenz, who tried to enliven the crossing by laying siege to Córdoba without succeeding in breaking his contemptuous indifference to her advances.

4

Santander wrote officially to Bustamante (15.iii.27), disapproving in principle, but excusing in fact, his insubordination. On March 16th Bolívar had written to Soublette: " Unable any longer to stand the perfidious ingratitude of Santander, I have written to him to-day that he is never to write to me again, for I do not want to answer him, nor ever call him a friend." This definite break had been due to Santander's persistent campaign of unsigned articles against Bolívar. Santander, however, kept his head and sent Bolívar a dignified and even friendly farewell. When news reached Bolívar of Santander's letter to Bustamante and of his share in the street rejoicings, his indignation knew no bounds. He felt betrayed by both Santander and Santa Cruz; while, in his own Venezuela, troops were mutinous in Valencia, Cumaná, everywhere. But he wrote to Urdaneta

(14.iv.27): " You know I like to call myself the man for tight corners. War is my element; danger my glory." And to Páez, obviously to attract him to his party: " The chief motive those gentlemen of Bogotá had to play such havoc with the Colombian Army was the union you and I had made, and the fact that I had not destroyed your friends. . . . See how important it is that we should remain united to preserve the peace of Venezuela and in due time to avenge this most iniquitous perfidy." Bolívar could be absolutely sure of one man only: Sucre; and Sucre was thousands of miles away and surrounded by enemies or false friends.

Nothing proves Santa Cruz' faithlessness better than his letters to La Fuente at this juncture. " Beware of Sucre, General. Mind, he is very astute " (19.ii.27); " The man I want to hear from is Sucre whose politics are terrible. Should he ask to sail, we must let him have all he needs; but he is not to enter our territory, where he has nothing to do " (3.iii.27). " Beware of Sucre, towards whom no mistrust and no caution are too much. Treat him well in your letters, but allow him no intrigues, and no setting foot on our territory save on his way to Arica [i.e. to sail away]. You must warn him that he is not to come this way, that the honour and security of the nation do not allow you to consent to it, or to fail to consider a single step of his this side of the Desaguadero as a hostile act. He would do it openly but will try to deceive you into giving your consent " (10.iii.27). Strangest of all these remarks on Sucre is this one from the sly Santa Cruz: " We must be on our guard about Sucre who in no way resembles the *Libertador*, always frank and always fair." And finally on April 19th: " I have also read the letter Sucre wrote to you with all the evil intent and the haughtiness that have taken root in his heart." Meanwhile the man to whom the two ambitious chieftains referred was struggling with his longing to retire to Quito and join the lady of his heart whom he meant to marry, but remained in Bolivia anxiously watching the situation and unaware that even among those who had implored him to accept, much against his will, the presidency of Bolivia, treason and disloyalty were already brewing and would soon bring about his downfall.

Anarchy spread over the five countries that Bolívar had dreamt of uniting. In connivance with the Peruvian Government, where Bolívar's erstwhile friends, Santa Cruz, Vidaurre and even Pando, had now turned against him, Bustamante sailed towards Guayaquil with his 1,800 men with the intention of detaching the departments of Guayaquil and Asuay and annexing them to Peru. This is at least what his enemies accused him of, particularly when Bolívar's emissaries privately offered him promotion in the Colombian army, which he refused. There seem, however, to be no documents available to confirm such an intention on the part of Bustamante, while reasons are not lacking for suspecting Bolívar of having made it up. Antonio Obando, sent by Santander and Soublette to take command of the division, was accepted by the troops. Nevertheless a struggle ensued complicated by a rebellion of the garrison of Guayaquil. Bustamante and López Méndez were taken prisoner (5.v.27), declared themselves ready to betray their Peruvian masters in exchange for freedom and doublecrossed both sides. This confusion grew out of the tangle of ambitions; for Santander backed everything that would weaken Bolívar's hold over the south, and Flórez, the most energetic of the commanders in that region, had, as time was to show, designs of his own. Meanwhile, in Peru, a new Congress met (4.vi.27), before which Santa Cruz, with a gesture learnt from Bolívar, surrendered his powers. Under the leadership of the shrewd Luna Pizarro, a priest, i.e. a gown-man, born enemy of all those cape-and-sword-men, Santa Cruz was however ousted, and La Mar elected President. Caught at his word when he expected to be compelled to save the fatherland à la Bolívar, Santa Cruz exclaimed that the election had been " a sudden surprise attack such as a traveller might suffer at the hands of professional brigands ".

5

The Congress of Colombia met in Bogotá and summoned Santander to take the oath (12.vi.27). He first argued that he had resigned but in the end complied. On June 16th both houses met together to discuss the resignation of the President and the Vice-President. In the end both were confirmed. Then the gown-men began to legislate with their usual disregard for the realities around them. They decreed that all subversive acts would be *forgotten* and, less wisely, that, public order being restored, the full powers granted to the Executive were abrogated and no Colombian would henceforward be bound to obey authorities not established by the Constitution and the laws. This was a direct blow at Páez, and at Bolívar who had invested him. Santander opposed the measure, how sincerely it is hard to say. News had meanwhile reached Bogotá of the general movement of troops Bolívar had ordered, all converging on New Granada. Ostensibly (as Bolívar took care to inform the Government on June 20th) this vast operation was directed at repelling the danger to the Southern departments implied in Bustamante's conspiracy and, so to speak, invasion of his own fatherland. In fact, it was one more of the pretorian measures Bolívar was taking to ensure for himself complete control of the whole of Colombia. Congress heatedly debated these movements of troops and the press allowed itself even more heat in its comments. Azuero in *El Conductor* advocated revolutionary means to protect liberty; and a conspiracy was afoot to confer full powers on Santander, who was not altogether alien to the move. Santander confided to Soublette that he had determined to resign, so as to lead the revolution to separate New Granada from Venezuela and Ecuador; but Soublette dissuaded him, and the conspiracy died out. The press campaign became more violent, now directed against the Convention which the Bolivarists wanted Congress to call, while the Santanderists opposed it, outwardly, and rightly, because the measure was unconstitutional, inwardly because they feared such a Convention might bring about a personal triumph for Bolívar and the final defeat of Santander. In the end the Bolivarists won, and Congress decreed, on July 25th, 1827, that a Convention would meet in Ocaña on March 2nd, 1828.

While Colombia was struggling with anarchy, the world was gradually recognizing it as an independent nation. The Netherlands and France sent Consuls-General to Bogotá, and the Colombian flag was officially admitted in French harbours. Sweden, Bavaria and the Hanseatic cities also recognized Colombia, as well as the Emperor of Brazil. But the greatest triumph for Bolívar in this field was the recognition of Colombia by the Pope, Leo XII. This enabled Bogotá and Caracas to receive back their archbishops, Santa Marta, Antioquia, Quito and Cuenca their bishops, and numberless cities and villages new priests. In a people still profoundly attached to its faith (a faith historically identified with Spain) this step from the Vatican meant the final consecration of independence. It was a great day for Bolívar who, by now far removed from his Jacobin youth, realized the importance of the issues involved. Sir Alexander Cockburn, appointed the previous year as British Minister Plenipotentiary, had come to Caracas to meet him. In April, 1827, Cockburn urged him to go to Bogotá and put himself at the head of the Government. Three days later, Cockburn insisted on behalf of his Government; and again on April 23rd, when he encouraged Bolívar to continue his public life. Bolívar took the opportunity to convey to Canning the importance of Spanish recognition; and when at last he thought the time had come to go to Bogotá, he left Páez in command in Venezuela, and sailed for Cartagena on board H.M.S. *Druid* in the company of his British friend (5.vii.27).

On July 9th, 1827, Bolívar landed in Cartagena and was well received by the population under the rule of his friend Montilla. When it was known in Bogotá that he had arrived and was coming to the capital by way of Ocaña, escorted by 800 well-seasoned Venezuelan soldiers under Salom, the excitement knew no bounds. Santander lost his head to the point of declaring that he would have preferred that the newcomer were Morillo rather than Bolívar and that Bolívar was coming in the mood of Bonaparte on his return from Egypt. This was only too true. Writing from La Carrera (24.viii.27) to José Rafael Arboleda, Bolívar insists that the army must be increased, that " I shall not separate myself from the army even half an hour ", and that " if Congress does not release me from the oath or is not willing to receive it through a commission, I shall give my oath to the people who are already beginning to release me from it ". Santander felt all this. Officially he sent a message to Congress declaring that he would not invest Bolívar with presidential authority until he had taken his constitutional oath. He proposed to his Government that a circular should be sent to the Diplomatic Corps protesting against Bolívar's illegal action; but the Secretaries of State, " who were friends of the *Libertador* ", turned down the proposal. Congress, no less excited, began to debate a bill forbidding Bolívar to bring the troops from Caracas to Bogotá. Santander was present.

Bolívar threw oil over these flames by behaving as was his wont with no respect for the laws of the country; assuming a dictatorial authority where he had none, granting appointments and promotions and ordering movements of troops in ways Santander, as the Vice-President of the Republic, was bound to resent. On his way to the capital he wrote to his friends there to encourage them. One of these letters, to Pepe Paris, evinces his pride in money matters. " Be good enough to call on Santander and ask him for my villa, where I wish to stay. I do not want the Government or any private person to spend anything. To feed me on the first day, borrow money and I shall pay." Then, in a post-scriptum: " I have not got a peso, but with God's help I hope to have some ", which was rather an understatement. Paris was one among a group of his friends who resolved to go out to meet him at Zipaquirá. Soublette, Colonel Herrán and Mosquera were of the party. They met Bolívar in El Socorro, where Mosquera had to put in a good word for Soublette, on whose loyalty Bolívar entertained some doubts. Bolívar sent Herrán back with letters for Santander and for Congress explaining that he had, through Panamá, less optimistic news on the situation in the south (that was the reason for making up or swelling the Bustamante conspiracy) than Santander claimed to have, hence the troops he was bringing; that he came to take his oath—and power. From Zipaquirá Bolívar sent Mosquera to the President of the Senate with letters to the same effect, requesting him to have the Assembly ready. So on September 10th, 1827, Bolívar rode into Bogotá through crowded streets, alighted at Santo Domingo Church where Congress was waiting, and took his oath without wasting a single minute of, at any rate, *his* time, if not the time of Congress. Then, there and then, writes Mosquera, " we were ordered to go to Government House to announce to the Vice-President that he had sworn his oath and that he was now the head of the Executive ".

6

On they all went to Government House where Santander awaited his Chief, now his adversary. The reception, though formal, was not lacking in outward friendliness on the part of Santander nor in the charm, tact and even cordiality that Bolívar could always master if he so wished. Santander offered his table which Bolívar accepted, and during luncheon was told that a number of leaders of the liberal party had left for fear of persecution. Bolívar begged Santander to recall them and to assure them that they would never have to suffer for their opinions. That evening, he left for his country house in the suburbs. The next morning, at eight, as Bolívar was still in bed, Santander in full uniform called at the house. Bolívar received him in his bedroom. Mosquera, who heard the conversation, reports that it began with Santander's apologies on the Bustamante imbroglio, that it ended with reminiscences of their past friendship and that Bolívar kept Santander for lunch. He adds, however, that in the afternoon, the Secretaries of State, who came on business, advised Bolívar not to trust Santander's sincerity. Bolívar requested Congress to continue in session and submitted to it the measures he had adopted in Venezuela, thus securing a formal approval of even his most high-handed actions. He also confirmed in their posts the Secretaries of State who had been serving under Santander: Restrepo for Home Affairs, Castillo for Finance, Soublette for War and Navy; while Revenga took over Foreign Affairs from Restrepo who had held the portfolio provisionally.

We can catch a glimpse of Bolívar at this period as he presides over a banquet in his villa: " The dining-room, between two gardens with wide bay windows, was an elegant room in the shape of an ellipse; and had the four seasons painted *al fresco* on its walls. At the head, a portrait of Bolívar crowned by two genii and this inscription: BOLIVAR IS THE GOD OF COLOMBIA. The *Libertador* sat alone, that is with no one right or left, at the head of the table which was set for thirty persons. Some of those present drank toasts to Colombia and to Bolívar without excessive flattery but fully expressing their feelings towards their hero. Bolívar heard them all with his usual indifference but with that mobility of eyes and body which was so typical of his character; and as champagne was served, he raised his glass and answered them all in short sparkling phrases which aroused general enthusiasm. As soon as he sat down, he was surrounded by his guests who, full of admiration, were eager to come close to him and touch his glass; they acclaimed him loudly and embraced him effusively. He, seeing himself mobbed, nearly smothered, stepped on to a chair and then on to a table and with long paces walked from one end to the other breaking plates and cups and upsetting bottles. The tumultuous crowd seized him at the other end and carried him in triumph to the reception hall." Such scenes recur often in Bolívar's life. One of them is recorded as early as 1818 by the Americans, Irvine and Anderson, and many other observers have reported almost identical episodes in later years. It is a revelation of Bolívar's almost insane will to power. Just as he paced the tables knocking down bottles and breaking china and glass, he paced the continent upsetting cities and breaking homes and human lives.

Bolívar did his best to govern and to pacify the land; while not forgetting that most important branch of political administration—patronage. Restrepo, who, as well as his historiographer was his Minister for Home Affairs, asserts that he took care " to reorganize all the branches of public administration and to appoint civil servants in his trust ". This was a wise precaution in pre-electoral days. He sent circulars to all authorities enjoining them to endeavour to restore comfort among citizens and parties, and, to that effect, to put a stop to the " paper-war ", and to induce all and sundry to give up writing against persons and institutions, so that the press could devote its attention to discussing means to cure the wounds of the fatherland. He also recommended that the election should take place in the best conditions of order and freedom and that the representatives selected should be honest and capable. The sight of " the tyrant " governing so wisely and so legally gradually cooled the atmosphere and restored calm. Congress voted Bolívar everything he asked for, notably full powers to grant army promotions, and authority to reform education. Bolívar made use of this last power in an unexpected yet typical way. He forbade the teachings of Bentham. This English reformer had written him (13.viii.25) a letter which Bolívar had received in Guayaquil many months later, though not the books which it announced. Bolívar answered (15.i.27) apologising for his delay, requesting the favour of a second remittance of books, and thanking Bentham for his offer to receive any young man Bolívar might wish to send to Hazelwood School.   He was soon to reverse his policy for reasons which will appear later.

Much as he endeavoured to preach order and peace, he does not seem to have fully mastered his passion against Santander.   Soon after his return to office, he had received a petition from the Vice-President requesting that an inquiry should be held as to " whether he [Santander] held any money in any foreign Bank, or whether during his term of office he had meddled in any business whatsoever ".*   The wise step might have been to declare that no such inquiry was called for and so to silence all gossip; or possibly, to carry on a swift and searching inquiry by some neutral Court if any could be found.   Bolívar took the worst possible course.   He declared that the matter did not concern him and passed the petition on to the Chamber where passions ran high and accusations of corruption were repeatedly made against Santander, while his friends defended him with equal heat.   Congress went into recess (5.x.27) without passing the budget; and as no decision was taken either on Santander's debate, the Vice-President remained thus under a cloud.   Whether that was what Bolívar sought with his tactics is not certain.   But on San Simón's day, October 28th, the civil servants (who had not been paid for four months when Bolívar arrived but, apparently, had been paid since) offered Bolívar a sumptuous ball.   Conforming to tradition, a maiden (Soublette's daughter) recited a sonnet, fortunately lost, and laid a crown of laurel on Bolívar's brow.   Bolívar rose and turning to Santander who sat on his right, laid it on his head, saying: " The Vice-President, as the first of the people, deserves this crown ".

The press does not seem to have followed Bolívar's advice.   In Bogotá the liberal campaign against him and his ideas went on with as much fire as before his coming.   Azuero was the leading pen.   Bolívar had among his most ardent friends two men more addicted to deeds than to words: Leandro Miranda, a son of the Precursor by an English mistress, and a *llanero* of huge size and physical strength, a descendant of one of his slaves, named Vicente Bolívar.   This Vicente had sworn " to break the fingers of those who write against Bolívar's dictatorship "; and on November 5th, 1827, in one of the central streets of the city he seized Dr. Azuero's hand and nearly broke his wrist, then threw him to the ground and would have taken his life there and then, but for the intervention of a passer-by who happened to be General Córdova, the hero of Ayacucho (himself at the time in Bogotá to answer before a Court for a similar case of violence in which he had killed his man).   This was the atmosphere of passion and excitement in which the general election took place.   Bolívar's orders severely forbidding all men in authority to meddle in the contest deprived his party of local leadership, as he had taken care to appoint his friends to such posts.   No doubt in his political pessimism he considered the fact of power a bigger

---

* Campbell, British Envoy in Bogotá, reported most scathingly on Santander's corruption, notably, at length, on 30.i.28.   On 13.ii.28 he concluded: " Should any unforeseen events cause the elevation of General Santander to power, I should dread the ruin of this country and its complete dissolution by a continuance of that venal and corrupt system which under his administration has involved Colombia in the disasters which now overwhelm her." P.R.O. F.O. 18/54.   Complete text published in the Spanish edition of the present work.

asset than the leadership of public opinion. His letters to his friends at this time reveal him driven by an urge to make all the representatives of his party hurry to Ocaña, where the Convention was to take place, before those of Santander. Other events occupied his mind. Fears, soon vanished, of a descent of Morales with a Spanish expedition; Canning's death, which he heard of on October 28th and which afflicted him deeply; the earthquake which shook Bogotá in the afternoon of November 16th, while he was in his villa; but on December 15th, 1827, in a letter to Arboleda who, in Popayán, had undergone considerable personal and material losses owing to the earthquake, he says that the evil from nature will soon be remedied but that " there is another one we cannot forget, and it is the one that the Great Convention may have in store for us ". He was certain that he would fail in the capital. He did. And not only in the capital. Santander was elected in Bogotá and in four of the Provinces. Soto and Azuero, also his adversaries, were elected in Bogotá. Bolívar ended the year in a mood of gloomy forebodings.

CHAPTER XXII

THE OCAÑA CONVENTION
(1828)

I

"**T**HIS election "—Bolívar wrote to Mariano Montilla (7.i.28)—
" has been carried out in the most infamous and iniquitous manner
imaginable." And after a passionate diatribe against Santander:
" I see no human way of keeping Colombia going; the Convention will do
nothing worth anything and partisanship and civil war will be the outcome
of it all." In his anxiety to secure a strong party he had expressed to Páez
the hope that " our friend Peña " should be elected—though he knew the
unreliable past of this shifty and corrupt politician. In order to keep a
close eye on the Convention he sent O'Leary to Ocaña under the cloak of
presenting a message. The Irishman left Bogotá on March 4th, 1828.
Determined this time not to incur Bolívar's displeasure by any deviation
towards Santander, he assumed from the outset an " anti " attitude. He
was a good observer for all that. When he arrived in Ocaña (15.iii.28), he
found there already forty-five deputies, making up " a fair of passions where
men have met to sell their whims ". The Santander faction was endeavouring to oust deputies friendly to Bolívar, and a Preparatory Junta, under
Santander's instigation, pending the arrival of the remaining members, was
already sitting and taking decisions. On March 16th he writes: " Three
o'clock. The Bogotá post of the 9th is just in. Soublette imparts to me
the unwelcome news about Bolivia."

The armies of Colombia in the south had been demoralized by idleness,
by money awards (which did not always materialize), and by the poor
example of their officers. When the Congress of Bolivia, following the
example of that of Peru, voted a million pesos to the victors of Ayacucho,
and asked Sucre to negotiate a loan of five million pesos in England to meet
that and other extraordinary expenses, Sucre retorted: " God forbid that I
should be so foolish as to leave Bolivia burdened with a foreign debt when
my mandate ceases." Bolívar had no such qualms. Eager to keep his
officers loyal to the hand that fed them, he saw to it that the million pesos
voted by the Peruvian Congress to the victors of Ayacucho came out of the
British loan. Nor was he content with what the Congress of Peru had given;
for we have it on the authority of his henchman Heres that he had " shared
out 1,500,000 pesos, half a million more than what the law had prescribed ".
And Heres adds: " The officers had received an equipment presented to
them by Y.E. in Arequipa without any charge on their salaries, and in Lima
Y.E. had granted sums to equip all the officers of the battalions of *Araure*
and *Caracas*." All this admits of but one interpretation: pretorian bribing.
The money thus spoken about, paid or not paid, was demoralizing the army.

In November, 1826, a squadron garrisoned in Cochabamba under the German colonel Braun, mutinied, suspecting that the colonel had gambled away the bounty voted for the unit by the Peruvian Congress. On this ground, other germs of unrest came to fructify. Santa Cruz, who, while he was President of Peru, had played the card of union with Bolívar (under himself of course), now ousted by La Mar from the Peruvian presidency, became a Bolivian separatist; and, with his countryman Gamarra, conspired to depose Sucre and establish himself as the uncrowned king of Bolivia. The two trends, ambition at the top, corruption at the bottom, met. The battalion of *Voltigeros*, stationed in La Paz, complained that, although among the victors of Ayacucho, they were locked up in barracks as mere recruits.* What angered them was that they should be kept indoors as mere recruits whom one locked up as a matter of course lest they deserted, while their officers spent their days and nights gambling away what they, rightly or wrongly, were convinced were their own arrears of salary or their bounty. So, shouting hurrahs to Gamarra and Santa Cruz, the battalion mutinied (24.xii.27), demanding 50,000 pesos, of which they got 40,000 from the Prefect. But as, well provided, they left towards Lima, a force sent after them caught them up at San Pedro de Ocomisto and exterminated them.

2

This was the news that reached O'Leary on March 16th. He thought it wiser to keep it to himself. On the following day, he had occasion to show an even greater discretion. A *chasqui* (courier) arrived with letters in which Admiral Padilla informed Soto, chairman of the Preparatory Junta, that General Montilla had rebelled and seized Cartagena. The incident was to give rise to far-reaching effects. Its root cause was a personal rivalry between the two protagonists. Padilla was a *zambo*, of whom Hippisley has left a picturesque portrait: " Commodore Paddillio would, if he wore a shade over his eye, be a more agreeable looking man; having received a cut down his cheek, extending to his eye on the right side, which seems as if starting from its socket, and gives to his countenance a horrid and terrific appearance; yet he is fond of dress, and cleanly in his habits. There is also a great deal of generosity and sociable conduct in this man, and he is as firm a friend as he is an implacable enemy. He never forgives an injury; but he has honour and courage sufficient to meet his adversary on a fair and equal footing; and although much used to scenes of bloodshed and murder, and ready to perform such tasks, too, when ordered by his superior, yet

* This may require an explanation. Colonel Hamilton, the first commissioner appointed to Colombia by the British Government, will supply it. It refers to Colombia but it applies just as well to Bolivia: " In passing by the gaol, I was surprised to see it full of young men; and on my remarking to the Commandant that I supposed there were many robberies in the neighbourhood, he replied ' Oh no,' the people were honest and quiet; that these prisoners were only young *volunteers*, from the Province of Neyva, going to join a newly raised regiment at Bogotá, and that these volunteers were confined for the night, to prevent their running away ". And Colonel Hamilton continues: " On the road we met with some more volunteers with their hands tied together, so that I suspect those who served in the Colombian armies are only volunteers by name."

there is no instance on record where he has suffered the victim to be tortured or butchered with any additional inhumanity."

These two men vied over the plums of power in Cartagena. Neither was at the time actually in command; but Montilla held a secret order from Bolívar authorizing him to take over civil and military command over the whole department in case of emergency—a detail not without a flavour of its own, bearing in mind that *the department had recently been enlarged to include the district and city of Ocaña, where the Convention was meeting.* Now, Montilla was a Venezuelan, a white, a Bolivarist; while Padilla was a Granadino, a *zambo*, a Santanderist. Montilla was, moreover, a refined and well-read aristocrat; while Padilla was an ignorant sailor transmogrified into an Admiral without ships to command. Both were ambitious. The occasion for an open quarrel arose about a statement or manifesto Montilla was hawking around among the military to overawe the Ocaña Convention. This manifesto was an intemperate document. It demanded a simple and vigorous government as well as a number of military privileges, and threatened an army rebellion should the Convention not comply. We know from a letter from General Córdoba to a friend that the manifesto was initiated in Bogotá and that the plan was to secure the signatures of all Colombian generals and officers; and from another letter to Bolívar, that, while Montilla was officially the collector of signatures, it was Bolívar who did the canvassing. It is not too much to say, therefore, that this typically pretorian intrigue had been initiated and was led by Bolívar in person. It so happened that, in Cartagena, the Venezuelan officers signed the statement while most of the Granadinos abstained, and were left in an invidious position. They gathered round Padilla, met in his house and stigmatized the signatories as *serviles;* a compliment which the Bolivarists returned by describing them as *factious.* Padilla, as a purely personal act, forced the General Commandant José Montes to resign; hearing which, Montilla, who was away in Turbaco, produced his secret order, assumed full powers and quietly drew to Turbaco the best units of the garrison during the night of March 5th, 1828. Padilla and his circle aroused the coloured populace and the Admiral had himself proclaimed civil and military chief. Realizing, however, that true power was in Montilla's hands, he left for Mompox, wrote his own version of the episode to Bolívar and sent a letter to the President of the Ocaña Convention " to offer his person, his small influence and whatever he had in defence of the Convention ".

There was as yet no real Convention and no President. Dr. Soto, a staunch Santanderist, presided over the Preparatory Junta. He accepted Padilla's message, called a meeting for that evening (17.iii.28) at seven and read Padilla's documents, praising him as a hero and a martyr for liberty; finally moved a resolution to the effect that Padilla be thanked for his zeal, and that his services be accepted to uphold the Convention. With the backing of Santander, the motion was carried. On the morrow, cooler opinions prevailed and the motion was considerably toned down. Then Padilla turned up and went to live in a house kept by Santander for himself and his colleagues. But he lost no time in calling on O'Leary to explain matters in his own way and to put himself right with Bolívar, blackening Montilla in the process. O'Leary advised him to return to Mompox, then, thinking better of it, to write to Bolívar. It seems that Bolívar intended to wind up the incident by sending Padilla to take command in Pasto. But Padilla, instead of following O'Leary's second advice, returned to Mompox. Montilla had forestalled this move and had sent to Mompox a strong contingent under Adelcreutz, a Swedish adventurer. Padilla decided to try his luck with the naval ratings and the people of Cartagena; but no sooner had he arrived secretly in his house than Montilla had him arrested (1.iv.28).

3

Bolívar was concerned at the result of the general election. " The Great Convention may well become the grave of the good cause and of the good citizens ", he wrote to a friend. His thoughts naturally wheeled back to full powers and dictatorship. A pretext was soon at hand: towards the beginning of February, royalist guerrillas began to stir in Venezuela (Zulia, Orinoco, Maturin). Instantly he had himself invested with extraordinary powers in those regions (19.ii.28), and he issued a decree (20.ii.28) providing that persons accused of treason and conspiracy would be summarily tried and, if guilty, executed forthwith. Páez dealt with the royalist trouble with promptness and energy; but Bolívar took the opportunity to move from Bogotá towards Cúcuta, drawn by a desire to be closer to Ocaña. On February 26th he decreed that, during his absence in Venezuela, four Ministers would remain in Bogotá to carry on daily business while he reserved for himself full powers in the territory of the whole Republic. All these measures added oil to the flames. The press campaign became more violent. On March 9th, a satirical paper, *El Zurriago* (the Whip), came out with an article which the militarists thought provocative; and one Luque, known for his drunkenness, in command of a regiment of the garrison, together with the Scot Fergusson, Bolívar's aide-de-camp, broke into the printer's office (it happened to be the State printer's) destroyed the material, whipped the workers and did as much harm as they could. Even O'Leary was indignant, and wrote to Bolívar, significantly adding: " I beg Y.E. to excuse me." For he guessed that Bolívar would side with Fergusson and Luque, and so he did, though putting on a mask of offended authority. The incident enabled him to issue another decree (13.iii.28) assuming full powers in the whole Republic except in the city of Ocaña where the Convention was to sit. This done, he left Bogotá (16.iii.28).

Ostensibly to meet the royalist threat in Venezuela, Bolívar left the capital impelled by two forces: the repulsion he always felt for the seat of office and administration; and a secret urge to be close to Ocaña. His enemies asserted that he wanted to coerce the Convention; and the fact is that he dotted with his faithful garrisons every city round Ocaña to the tune of fifteen thousand men; while he himself finally settled at Bucaramanga, a few leagues from Ocaña. His friends, however, retorted that between Bucaramanga and Ocaña lies the " deadly moor of Cachiri "; nevertheless, when Bolívar settled there (9.iv.28) he evidently was thinking of the Convention, obsessed by it and meaning to keep the Convention obsessed by him. Bucaramanga is one of the most elegant cities of South America, and, apart from the political tension in which he lived, Bolívar must have enjoyed his stay as a real holiday. The country is beautiful, undulating and open, rich in shapes and colour, well watered and wooded, with a rich ochre coloured earth that enhances the dark green of the vegetation and the pure blue of its skies. Low, one-floored houses, on whose gaily painted frontages iron railings or delicately carved wooden balconies cut patterns of an attractive symmetry, shelter simple, elegant and cool homes, breathing a Spanish tradition that makes one think of Cervantes. Bolívar settled in one of these houses; and in another one close by, his French aide-de-camp, Peru de Lacroix, wrote down every day the doings and sayings of the idle Dictator.

Peru the Frenchman was there with Fergusson the Scot, Wilson the Englishman, O'Leary the Irishman, who came and went from Ocaña. This military household, almost exclusively foreign, was yet another of the ways in which Bolívar subconsciously cut himself off from his kith and kin. It was again a pretorian feature of his, deliberately to choose foreigners for the posts of trust and command: the Irishmen Croftson and Whittle for the colonelcies of the two regiments in garrison at Bogotá; the Italian Chassebrune, the Englishman Chitty, the Irishman Egan, all commanding in Cartagena in important offices, the Swede Adelcreutz, the Irishman O'Connor and many others. This aspect of the matter is further illustrated by a detail Peru de Lacroix provides on Fergusson: " By order of H.E., he keeps a friendly correspondence with all the superior officers of the Colombian army who hold commands or posts: the letters he receives are read by the *Libertador* whenever they contain something of interest, and Fergusson answers or writes according to the suggestions, and on the points dictated to him by H.E. The correspondence is useful because it has the seal of friendship. . . . Those who correspond with Colonel Fergusson do not know that the *Libertador* is the soul and the motor of that epistolary commerce and that he sees their letters. They believe they are only corresponding with Fergusson." All this shows how Bolívar's partiality to foreigners worked as a means for holding the army.

But there was another side to it. Bolívar felt for Europe and everything European an admiration amounting to a sense of inferiority for everything American. So he wrote to Unanúe (25.xi.25): " I received to-day with astonishment the sword the good city of Lima has sent me. Truly it is in the best European taste. I should never have thought that such a precious jewel could be made in America." And to Santander (12.xii.25): " General Sucre and I have received two magnificent swords from the Municipality. They are very beautiful and such that they could not be made better in London." So much for things. As for persons, on the return of his uncle to Caracas, he wrote to Santander (10.vii.25): " He has frequented Courts and has sat in the Spanish Cortes as deputy representative for Venezuela; he has much sense and is fairly well-read; a man in every way like Peñalver but infinitely more of a man of the world for he has spent forty years in

Europe." And also to Santander (7.iv.26) on Pando, whom he had made Foreign Secretary of Peru: "He is very much like Revenga and in every way a better man, for he has lived all his life in Europe in the [Spanish] diplomatic service." Both the pretorian and the pro-European element in this favouritism towards foreign officers weighed heavily on his popularity, precisely among those closest to his heart and most necessary to his ambitions —the military. Even as subservient a man as Heres wrote to Briceño Méndez complaining of this foible (3.ix.27). At the time Bolívar had an Italian adventurer, Montebrune, as one of the leaders of the press of his party in Bogotá.

4

Bolívar thought of going to Ocaña himself and asked O'Leary's opinion about it in the first letter he wrote him from Bucaramanga (31.iii.28). On April 9th, 1828, the Convention officially began its work and elected as its President José María Castillo, whom Bolívar considered then as his trusted man. Before its sittings the Convention went to Mass on a motion of Santander. O'Leary was not very optimistic. He found that the two leaders of the Bolivarist party, Castillo and Joaquin Mosquera, were not "men capable of putting themselves at the head of a party. The extreme delicacy of Castillo and the aristocratic arrogance of Mosquera are powerless in an assembly composed mostly of men dull, foolish, ignorant and blinded by their passions; they can do nothing against the plebeian insolence of Santander, the shamelessness of Soto, the impudence of Gómez, the insanity of Vargas Tejada and the wickedness of Azuero ". Peña, whose presence had been so much desired by Bolívar, had been elected, but was excluded, for, writes O'Leary, " he was hated by friends and enemies and his presence was considered by some an insult to national decorum, by others a threat and by all with a kind of disgust ". The black sheep was of course Santander, on whom Bolívar wrote to O'Leary (13.iv.28) these ominous words: " General Santander asks me for guarantees and even for a passport, I shall not fail to seize this opportunity to make him realize his misery." Bolívar felt confident about his majority, which he considered sufficient (in a letter to Montilla) though he expected it to increase further by ten more members " who are on the way and have good principles ". He meant to keep the Convention on its toes and was preparing two messages, one on the vote of thanks to Padilla and another one on Peña's exclusion, both strongly worded. The pitch of his language on Santander was rising. On April 15th he wrote to Briceño Méndez: " It is strange that Peña's behaviour should be sat on by high criminals of State and by illustrious thieves who have ruined the Treasury of the Republic."

On April 17th, 1828, his first message was read. It began in his usual way, by now an empty formula: " I have the utmost happiness in returning to you the authority that had been deposited in my tired hands." He then paints a gloomy picture of the State and though declaring himself aware that he exposes himself to being suspected of " ambitious thoughts ", he goes on to analyse the reasons of the trouble that " our Government is in its essence badly constituted. . . . We have made of the legislative the only sovereign power instead of just a limb of it "; the Secretaries of State have been forbidden access to Parliament; popular representation has been made too general, and so, in some Provinces, " it has become indifferent and even not very honourable to represent the people "; the Executive is too weak; the law Courts are too powerful and, what he thinks even worse, possess " an absolute supremacy in military trials "; a fact in which he sees the cause of insubordination. He dares not propound positive plans, but ends begging the legislators to give " to the people, to the army, to the judge and to the magistrate, inexorable laws ". The chief impression left by this paper is that Bolívar is no longer the keen political debater and pamphleteer of his Angostura and Cúcuta days. His arguments have turned into complaints and hankerings. A disenchantment, a supplication, runs like a cold current under his still eloquent flow of words. O'Leary reported to him that it had caused " a great and favourable impression ".

5

The Convention carried on its work in an atmosphere of mounting political tension. O'Leary and Montilla put on hard the screws of despotic power. O'Leary had at his disposal the power of the official purse. He began early to report to Bolívar that many representatives would soon be bound to leave unless their expenses were paid. Thus, on March 20th: " The Venezuelans have been given five hundred pesos only. Within a few days they will have nothing to live on and, of course, will depart." On April 5th, he is more outspoken: " Be good enough to endeavour to send some money to help those who receive none for their daily expenses; the paymaster must be ordered to give priority to those I recommend." And on April 24th, Bolívar replies: " Spend the money as you think fit on those poor representatives, for we had rather give it all to them than hear them complain against the Government." As for Montilla, he sent Briceño and O'Leary, then in Ocaña, a letter from Santander to a friend, one Alejandro Vélez, *Chargé d'Affaires* in the United States, in which Santander gave his reasons for leading an opposition against Bolívar and for being converted to federalism. " I have thought advisable "—Montilla wrote to Bolívar—" to authorize those two gentlemen in Ocaña . . . to retain the original, to send you an exact copy through the same aide-de-camp, Montes, who conveys this." Bolívar wrote back on April 24th: " I am curious to know what means you have set in motion to get hold of that letter, about which you will be the butt of many a devilish comment." Montilla writes that he had obtained it through " a person favourable to order ", i.e. through a Bolivarist, and that " probably I shall be sent also all the letters posted in Ocaña for the United States and Jamaica, and, if interesting, I shall pass them on, for such is the intention of the person who hands them on to me and whom I shall name to you when we meet ". Not in vain had O'Leary to report his disgust that he " had heard the Spanish Government in America praised when compared with the present Government "; for, after all, Philip II had severely prohibited to his Viceroys any tampering with the correspondence of his subjects, since, he said, " there is oppression and violence in such an action, as well as a rudeness which cannot be allowed in a Christian polity ".

A curious tension developed soon between Bolívar in Bucaramanga and O'Leary and Briceño in Ocaña. Briceño and O'Leary kept writing in an optimistic mood; Bolívar kept rejecting their arguments and reproaching them for their blindness. The two observers were going by their common-sense and by what they saw. O'Leary, though now turned a violent and at times an undignified enemy of Santander, gave now and then a free opinion hardly to the liking of his chief. On Peña, his reports are objective. It is therefore probable that when both Briceño and O'Leary reported that things were not going too badly, they were right. The reason why Bolívar disliked their reports was precisely that he did not want things to go right. He wanted to sweep the Convention off the stage by a *coup de force*. Hence his aversion for all moderates. " If we have a majority "—he writes to O'Leary (24.iv.28)—" we must exploit it; and if we don't, we must not compromise; we must fight with our weapons in our hands, and rather be defeated, for defeat breeds reaction. . . . Absolute triumph or nothing." " I was very angry this morning, by no means with you, but with those who call themselves moderates, whom God deliver us from." There was nothing moderate about O'Leary, who found time to publish *The Harlequin*, an anonymous pamphlet against Santander, at which even Bolívar cried out: " How strong, this harlequinade against Santander! How furious Casandro [Santander] must have felt! O'Leary is terrible and his pen can distill the gall the writer feels in his heart against the person he dislikes! " Yet, this man, on receiving Bolívar's letter of April 23rd, was " sunk in melancholy after shedding a torrent of tears ", thinking (he wrote to Bolívar) of " the dreadful situation in which you were when you wrote it ". But Bolívar was not a man to weep over. He sent an emissary, Herrera, with a proposal to break up Colombia into its component republics while he would withdraw for good from public life (1.v.28).

This, of course, produced the effect he sought. Even Castillo, the head of the moderates, wrote: " You must bear for a time the reproach of being a usurper to hold Colombia and carry her to her happiness ", and much more to that effect. O'Leary was sent to Bucaramanga to appease the great man and to suggest to him that his friends, when sure of a majority, should present a motion calling him to Ocaña. He received the idea with an open mind. By May 14th he wrote to Urdaneta that his friends had thirty-five safe votes to pass the motion but were awaiting two more; then gave the news to which he attached the greatest importance, so great that he explicitly copied it from a letter Castillo had written to him: " We shall do nothing that is not useful; failing which, we shall go into recess and leave reforms in suspense; and if not even this can be obtained, we shall leave, denouncing the authors of the evil to public execration." That was music to Bolívar's ears. " Let our friends be united; let them order me to save the Republic and I shall save the whole of America; let them ask me to drive hence anarchy, and not even its memory shall remain."

But on the same day he wrote to Briceño Méndez: " I have thought much over my trip to Ocaña and come to the conclusion that it is not advisable. My coming will be ill interpreted and they will throw over me a net of moderation." Nevertheless, though he adds that such is his last word, he received with little moderation the news that the motion inviting him to come to Ocaña, presented by Castillo on May 13th on the assurance that he would have thirty-eight votes, had been lost, ten members having broken their promise. His letter to Briceño Méndez is quiet enough; but his private attitude was violent. At dinner, on the 22nd, he referred to the matter, accused O'Leary, Soublette, Castillo and Briceño Méndez of lack of sagacity; pointed out that everybody would believe the idea had come from him, and that the promoters were " idiotic fools "; then went on: " I say it frankly, had the motion been passed, I should have seen in it a trap by Santander to draw me to Ocaña in order to make me fall under daggers." Peru reports that he said this " with an extraordinary fire, a deep resentment and an oppressed heart ". And when riding out he repeated that O'Leary and his other friends " never thought that, had I gone to Ocaña, the Convention Hall might have been for me what the Capitol was for Caesar; not that I believe that Santander, Azuero and Soto would themselves have brandished the daggers; I know their cowardice, too well; but that they would have found one or more murderers to take on the affair ".

6

There are a number of documents of this period which reveal Bolívar's machiavellian duplicity and therefore his unabated ambition. On May 18th, 1828, he writes to Urdaneta about an article published by a new daily that saw the light in Cuenca, proposing a monarchy for the whole of America. " Of course everybody will say the plan is mine, and therefore I warn my friends to write against it, and since my enemies say it is mine we must say it is theirs." He instructs Urdaneta to obtain numbers 8, 9 and 10 of the paper, *Eco del Azuay*, to have the article reprinted in *El Amigo del Pais*, his own paper, with a preface he himself has written, but to come out anonymously or editorially, in which he at once points to Santander. His letters to Páez at this time are also significant. While he was reducing O'Leary to tears because of his pessimism, he writes to Páez full of confidence (30.v.28): " Everybody wants me to continue in power. . . . The Governments of France and England have declared themselves very favourable to me and have imparted these feelings to me through their ministers. From everywhere news comes to me that everyone is resolved to back me at all costs. . . ." On June 2nd he gave Páez instructions to send the Grenadiers to Cúcuta. He agrees with Páez that the country must be saved even if exceptional measures are to be taken; and adds: " The friends of the good cause in Ocaña write to me that their defeats have driven them to despair and that they are resolved to withdraw rather than sign a Convention which would ruin Colombia. I have answered that they must think it over carefully, for, should they rush to such a decisive step, we might run into a thousand dangers without a purpose. . . . I had proposed a solution that might conciliate all parties. . . ." We know that he insisted with the utmost energy on the withdrawal of his friends and would have no compromise. His letter to Páez is therefore one of the many curtains he drew round his true intentions.

His faithful Urdaneta, now Minister of War, echoes this attitude, and on May 21st writes to O'Leary: " I have feared half-baked rather than thoroughly bad results; for the former, while bringing no good to Colombia, would fetter us in our revolution." And on June 6th: " There is only one way out, and it is all agreed and ready "; while, on the 7th, he wrote to Montilla: " In agreement with all the authorities and a few important persons, the affair is organized and everything is so ready that it will not fail." To which he added on the 13th: " We must overrule all opposition, without looking at the means, even though they be bloody." We shall see this principle later echoed by Mosquera. By the end of May everything was ready for ending the Convention in the only way that suited Bolívar: by its desertion on the part of the Bolivarist group. This is clear from Briceño Méndez' letter to Bolívar (22.v.28): Should they fail to pass Castillo's draft for a constitution and should the commission's draft be preferred, he writes, " we are resolved to leave and dissolve the Convention. . . . The clamour of all the peoples for you to lead their destinies empowers us to have recourse to this way of salvation ". All is therefore clear as to the aims.

As for the means, Briceño Méndez is not less clear: " The 15,000 pesos which came from Barinas arrived to-day. . . . I shall leave here the 5,000 General Soublette tells me you reserved for the Convention, and on this I have spoken with Castillo and we have agreed that it is not advisable to hand them over, but that they must be shared out among the deputies of Venezuela who are the neediest. I am referring to the 4,000, and as for the remaining 1,000 they must go to the members from the south who are the ones who come next in point of need." Nothing, therefore, for the Granadinos. " This is the more necessary because these are the delegations on which we rely for a withdrawal, and they would not be able to do so if they lacked the means." Briceño Méndez' letter of the 27th is even more explicit; for he says that Santander is thinking of retaining them by force, " but we shall fight if need be ". This letter shows Briceño Méndez somewhat taken in by Bolívar's show of pessimistic inaction; but, on May 29th, Bolívar wrote him a significant and sibylline letter, stressing this pessimism, yet ending with these words: " Though this letter is so emphatic, it implies a thousand practical hints which I wonder whether you should consider for your action. I shall end saying that dangers point the way to safety." On June 1st he wrote to Arboleda: " The Grand Convention must be dissolved soon and badly." On June 9th, Bolívar's friends withdrew; but as fifty-five members remained the quorum was just sufficient. One more member was won over later, and the Convention was at an end.

On June 12th, 1828, the Bolivarist deserters published a *Manifesto to the Colombian people*, telling their story in their own way. On the same day

Bolívar left Bucaramanga for Bogotá, held for him by his henchman Herrán, who had written to him (12.ii.27): " I know no other constitution and no other law than the will of Y.E." On June 13th Herrán issued a Proclamation calling the citizens of Bogotá to a meeting at the Customs House, which he took good care to put under the shadow of 800 men with loaded guns. After reciting " a detestable harangue which his secretary had made him learn by heart " (writes Posada Gutiérrez), he proposed that an Act should be passed refusing to recognize any decision of the Convention and granting full powers to Bolívar. Córdoba, then Assistant Chief of General Staff, rode by, alighted from his horse, entered the hall whip in hand, sat on the arm of a chair and heard two speeches against Bolívar, but not three. As Dr. Juan N. Vargas was beginning to take the same line, Córdoba stood up and declared that he would not permit any attack on Bolívar in his presence and that no more talking was needed, but just to confer supreme power on him. Though bidden to speak on, Dr. Vargas withdrew. Herrán then produced his Act and it was voted and " signed by the servile and the timid ". It announced the intention not to obey the decisions of the Convention; to revoke the mandates of the representatives elected by Bogotá; and to confer unlimited powers on Bolívar. On receiving the document from Herrán, the Council of Ministers declared " most well founded and imperiously necessary the pronouncement of the capital "; and forwarded it to Bolívar in the hope that their own decision on it " will not be disapproved of by the Liberator and will at least deserve his indulgence ". Bolívar heard of the events of Bogotá on June 16th at El Socorro. On the same day Soublette wrote to him: " Y.E. must hasten on to the city in order to correspond to the longing with which the capital awaits you." And Restrepo wrote to Montilla on June 21st: " The *Libertador* is very pleased with the *pronunciamiento* of the capital and we received his answer within six days."

How carefully he watched his own game can be detected from two letters written in El Socorro on the day he heard the news. To Peru de Lacroix, speaking of the Act of Bogotá, he frowns at such *actos populares*, in the plural, for, he says, that of Bogotá will call forth others in the whole of Colombia, and explains that " it is not what I wanted ", for such things " spoil public morality ", etc. But, in a fragment to an unknown correspondent, he sends an injunction " that in their march they work on popular opinion, I mean that they stimulate it so that they follow the example of the capital ". And, of course, under the impulse of the garrisons, the example of the capital was followed by numerous cities; to which Restrepo, the Home Secretary, sent the " model " from Bogotá with a circular assuring local authorities that Bolívar would accept " such a difficult and delicate mission ". These " Acts " were far from spontaneous and a note of warning thereon can be heard in letters Bolívar received from his friends. Thus, in Popayán, opinion was so far from ready that Mosquera wrote to Bolívar on July 25th: " I thought best to keep the troops ready and armed in the barracks in case the coup went awry, so as to strike it myself by force, hanging four of the most insolent, launching the necessary proclamations and assuming an authority exclusively dependent on Y.E." No wonder Arboleda had written on the 7th: " I must not deceive you; everything is not due to conviction and enthusiasm . . . nevertheless, everybody has bowed down. . . ." And even Soublette wrote from Caracas, on August 14th: " It seems to me that the country in general, though adhering to the Bogotá *pronunciamiento*, has bowed rather to the influence of circumstances than to conviction. The coldness one perceives and the general isolation observed seem to me signs of discontent and of fear." This was the spirit and the attitude in which Bolívar found Bogotá when he entered it on June 14th, 1828.

CHAPTER XXIII

THE ATTEMPT ON BOLÍVAR'S LIFE
(1828)

I

BOLÍVAR arrived in Bogotá in a Napoleonic mood and assumed full powers which, indeed, he had been wielding all along and at times in wholly unexpected ways. His prohibition of the teachings of Bentham (12.iii.28) already mentioned has been explained because Bentham's views had been quoted against his ambition; others attributed it to the complaints he had received from fathers of families who considered Bentham's doctrines as " poisonous " for youth. The real cause is more likely to be his own reorientation towards the Church. At this time, the drama of power was played by Bolívar against Santander, and it so happened that while Bolívar, the ultraconservative, was a sceptical " philosopher ", Santander, the liberal, was a devout Catholic. Bolívar had to win over the Church. On August 22nd, he wrote to Cristóbal Mendoza from Bogotá: " As soon as I arrived in this capital I promulgated several important decrees which have been well received, particularly all those which aimed at supporting religion." The other pillar of his authority, and the stronger of the two, was the army. He increased its numbers to 40,000 men (7.viii.28), a ruinous measure which he tried to justify by exaggerating the danger of a European invasion and by increasing, with his own intemperate reactions, a political tension with Peru which was eventually to lead to a war. He issued a decree (27.viii.28) to act in lieu of a constitution until 1830, aiming at the official eviction of Santander by the abolition of the vice-presidency. This gave official sanction to a situation he had secured in February when, before leaving Bogotá for Bucaramanga, he had authorized the Ministers to meet and decide on State business without the presence of either the President or the Vice-President. This decree set up a Council of State packed with his friends, and declared " dominant the Roman Catholic Apostolic Religion ". He himself took the title of *Libertador-Presidente*.

This dictatorship rested mostly on a group of Venezuelan generals and Irish colonels. Bolívar wielded a power no Spanish Viceroy had ever known or dreamt of as possible. In fact, the life and treasure of every one of his subjects was in his hands. He was treated as a Viceroy. Bogotá witnessed the growth of a kind of Court which gave itself to an uninterrupted series of festivals and rejoicings. Adulation was the order of the day. Herrán, the parvenu Governor of Bogotá, led the van. In August, he planned a civic procession in which Bolívar in person would be carried shoulder-high through the streets of Bogotá; this was not to the taste of Bolívar (perhaps for security reasons) and Herrán had to be content with the portrait of the great man, which was promenaded on the shoulders of four *regidores*, while the remaining municipal councillors walked right and left bearing the free ends of ribbons attached to it; a crowd of youngsters followed. Herrán preceded the parade, flag in hand. There was no enthusiasm and Herrán thought better to guide the procession back home after one round of the Main Square. " How strange! No one acclaims the portrait! "—said Córdoba who looked on; and his interlocutor pointedly replied: " General, the people suffer from a bad cold. They can only cough." He was Florentino González, the husband of that Bernardina who had succumbed to Bolívar after his triumphant entry into Bogotá in 1819. He was conspiring against the too successful Caesar.

This military court might have taken on the charm and the polish of a city bred in the civilities of the viceregal period, but for Bolívar's foible for the irresponsible and irrepressible Manuela. " The ice of my years is requickened by your kindness and graces "—he wrote to her about this time. " Your love gives me back life, which is ebbing out. I cannot live without you. I cannot deprive myself of you, my Manuela. I have not as much strength as you to remain away. I see you though from afar. Come, come, come quick." She was then at the height of her beauty and of her power; and as Bolívar had taken up his residence in the official palace, she had taken a house in the Plazuela de San Carlos, at a short distance from it. Boussingault, who frequented her then, writes: " *Manuelita était toujours visible. Dans la matinée, elle portait un négligé qui n'était pas sans attraits. Ses bras étaient nus. Elle se gardait bien de les dissimuler; elle brodait en montrant les plus jolis doigts du monde, causait peu, fumait avec grâce; sa tenue était modeste. Elle donnait et accueillait les nouvelles. Dans la journée, elle sortait vêtue en officier. Le soir Manuelita se trouvait métamorphosée; elle éprouvait, je crois, l'influence de quelques verres de vin de Porto qu'elle affectionnait; elle mettait certainement du rouge. Ses cheveux étaient artistement arrangés. Elle avait beaucoup d'entrain, était gaie, sans esprit, se servant parfois d'expressions passablement risquées. Comme toutes les favorites des hauts personnages politiques, elle attirait les courtisans. Son obligeance, sa générosité étaient inépuisables.*" This woman who smoked, rode about the city dressed as a hussar and behaved like one, told fast stories and lived them even faster, could by no means lead the Court. The milieu in which Bolívar launched his dictatorship became more in tune with a camp or the barracks than with the ancient spirit of the courtly Bogotá. This circumstance contributed not a little to heighten the tension that was to lead to the tragedy of September 25th.

2

On March 28th, 1828, Manuela had written to Bolívar on the Padilla-Montilla episode: " Santander has done it again, as if all he had done before were not enough for us to shoot him. May God permit that all these wicked men die—Paula [Santander], Padilla, Páez . . . that would be a great day for Colombia." She was the protagonist of a scandalous episode which took place in Bolívar's country house close to Bogotá, where she was staying at the time towards the end of July, 1828, probably on Bolívar's birthday.

A fête was being given, and it may be assumed that it led to general drinking; for someone, apparently Manuela, suggested that Santander should be shot in effigy. A puppet imitating him was produced, seated on a bench and shot in the back by a detachment of Grenadiers in command of Crofton. This Crofton, one of the two garrison commanders chosen by Bolívar, was " formerly a corporal in the British service and an exceedingly illiterate person ". Bolívar was " particularly annoyed at " the episode, wrote Henderson privately to the Foreign Office; and he added: " General Córdoba, a young man who highly distinguished himself at the battle of Ayacucho, indeed the success of that day was mainly due to his bravery, is the person who has ventured to give his opinion to the Liberator on this transaction, and as he has confidentially entrusted his letter and the answer of General Bolívar to me *alone*, I beg leave to transmit them. . . ."

This letter had been lost and is full of interest. Here it is translated from a Spanish copy handed by Córdoba to Henderson in his own handwriting. " General: I know that Y.E. is informed of the event that took place a few days ago in the villa of Señora Sáenz, but perhaps not with complete accuracy. I know that Y.E. has been put to great inconvenience by this and has ordered an enquiry to be made on the authors of the deed, or rather of the crime, for so it was against the Government and against Y.E., against the laws, against society and discipline which should be observed by the army. But I am certain that this enquiry will lead to no results, and this will give your enemies grounds to back the opposition and adverse opinions. It will be said that Y.E. has tolerated or feigned not to see such a misdemeanour because it has been committed against Santander, your enemy, and this would imply a silly and ridiculous vindictiveness. It is said that the operation was carried out on a puppet figuring Santander, who was seated on a kind of bench and shot as a traitor in the back by soldiers of the Grenadiers who unfortunately were in the field on training; with the consent of the Commandant Croston [sic] no doubt since he was present at the party. It has been said that Señora Sáenz was the promoter of this scandal and led it. . . . There is general censure of the fact that the said lady meddles in government affairs and is heard. Y.E.'s friends regret such criticism and I more than any."

Bolívar's defence does not sound very convincing: " You know I know you and cannot resent what you say to me. I certainly am aware of the follies of my friends—more so than anyone else. This letter will show you that I do not spoil them. I shall suspend the commanding officer of the Grenadiers and send the men to serve elsewhere. He alone is guilty, since the rest are *legally* excusable; I mean that it is not a public crime, though it is eminently base and miserable. As for the amiable mad woman, what shall I say? You have known her for long, I have tried to get rid of her, but one can do nothing against a resistance such as hers; nevertheless, as soon as this episode is past, I intend to make the most determined effort to send her to her country or wherever she will go. But I will say that she never meddled except in begging [for people to be forgiven?]. I am not weak, nor do I fear to be told the truth. You are right one and a thousand times." Bolívar, however, did nothing of what he promised in this letter.

He kept Manuela by his side and as for Crofton, let Henderson speak: "Commandant Crofton, the principal actor in the affair . . . remained here at the head of the cavalry and was advanced in rank. He subsequently applied his whip to a young man whom he supposed to be of the liberal party and refused to accept a call of honour which was in consequence made upon him. The young gentleman and his friends made a representation to the *Libertador* on the subject, but as Crofton was allowed to remain in the service, the injured party, Señor Posada, asked for his passport and has proceeded to Jamaica."

Santander was no wiser. He was freer than he should have been with his opinions even though these opinions may not have been in themselves as black as his enemies would make out. A *Junta de Observación* had been set up before Bolívar's departure for Ocaña, to watch for a favourable moment to act; and the usual sprinkling of Frenchmen (Horment, Arganil) brought into the Spanish-American atmosphere imitations of Roman models of the Brutus and Cassius type. Under the benign title of *Philological Society*, ardent idealists met to talk Rubicon, Pharsalia and such dramatic topics; and a youth, Luis Vargas Tejada, wrote a monologue in verse on the suicide of Cato at Utica, soon memorized by all students and recited in public with cries of *Long live liberty! Death to the tyrant!* Both Bolívar and Santander looked on: Santander because he disliked the idea of political murder, preferring a change of government by a series of *pronunciamientos*, followed by the imprisonment of Bolívar and his death like Charles I or Louis XVI; Bolívar, because he was waiting for his opportunity to act. Everything was ready for August 20th, but for some reason which is not clear the blow was adjourned, apparently because Santander was still away and the conspirators refrained from action before hearing his opinion. He does not appear to have definitely rejected the idea of a conspiracy or even of a murder by others; rather does he seem to have countenanced it, if only tacitly. On being deprived of the presidency, he accepted Bolívar's offer to go to Washington as Colombian Minister (19.ix.28) and asked that Vargas Tejada should go with him as secretary of the Legation. It was in Vargas Tejada's house that the conspirators met.

3

The leaders of the conspiracy were a Frenchman aged twenty-nine, Augustin Horment, and a Venezuelan officer, Carujo. This Carujo was a man of some parts, a linguist and a mathematician. He was then Córdoba's teacher in French, English and military topography. He was an ardent republican and seems to have been the moving spirit behind the plot. The first attempt was to take place on August 10th, at the Coliseo (now the Teatro Colón), during a masked ball to celebrate the anniversary of Boyacá. Bolívar owed his escape to a prank of Manuela. What sort of a prank it is not clear. "She went there masked"—writes the British Consul James Henderson—"but soon took off her mask, which so much annoyed Gen'l Bolívar, that he left the Ball room very early, and thus frustrated the views of the conspirators." The most likely explanation is that Bolívar took this venial fault of his mistress as a pretext to go home, to prevent an attempt he had every reason to fear and of which he may have had a warning.　Santander was away and did not arrive till August 25th; a fact he later skilfully adduced in his defence.　When he arrived, he was consulted by the conspirators, who planned to murder Bolívar on September 20th, in Soata, where he was to stay with very few friends and no escort.　Santander strongly opposed any such move, at any rate while he was in Colombian territory.　In view of this attitude of the man whose name they needed, the conspirators decided to adjourn the blow again until October 28th, St. Simon's day.　But on September 25th a Captain Triana entered a room in the Artillery Barracks and told a Lieutenant Salazar: " I am coming from the Lodge, where all protect me, and we mean to do in that old man Bolívar who is a tyrant. Don't you know I am a mason ? "　This was the beginning of the last act of the conspiracy.　It suggests a masonic root to it.　Salazar reported Triana, and presently, Colonel Ramón Guerra, Chief of Staff of the Bogotá garrison, received an order to prosecute him.　Guerra, who was one of the conspirators, warned his accomplices, who resolved to strike that very evening.　Towards seven o'clock they began to gather at Vargas Tejada's house, and by ten o'clock over one hundred civilians and officers had been sent to the Artillery Barracks to arm and get ready; four or five did so, the others went into hiding. Guerra, who could have swung the balance from one side to the other, chose to remain the whole day at Castillo's house, a practical desertion.　At midnight, ten civilians under Horment and sixteen privates under Carujo entered the Palace after Horment had killed three sentinels.　Carujo sent his sixteen men to watch the building while Horment and his civilians went in, broke open two doors and disarmed Lieutenant Ibarra, who was in one of the rooms, to the shouts of *Long live liberty*!

Beyond the third door, a homely discussion was taking place.　" On the 25th, in the afternoon "—Manuela wrote later to O'Leary—" the *Libertador* sent for me; I answered I had a pain in my face; he sent a second message that I was less ill than he and that I was to come; as the streets were wet, I put a pair of shoes over my slippers; they came in handy for him to run away, as his boots were out for cleaning.*　When I entered, he was in his bath.　He told me a revolution was coming.　I said: ' There may be ten so far as you are concerned, to judge by the way you deal with warnings.' " (This was a reproach Bolívar well deserved, for a few days earlier a lady had come mysteriously to see Manuela to warn her of the conspiracy, and Bolívar had her sent away by Fergusson, on the ground that she implicated Córdoba, which had incensed him as a calumny on a friend; but he had all the same sent his friend Paris to interview her.)　Aware of what was in Manuela's mind, Bolívar retorted: " Don't worry, nothing will happen "; and then, she goes on to O'Leary: " He made me read to him while he was in his bath; then went to bed and slept deeply, with no other precautions than his sword and pistols handy; no other guard than the usual, no warning to the officer in charge, content with the assurances of the Chief of Staff that he would answer for everything.　Towards midnight two of his dogs barked,

* Note how small Bolívar's feet were.

and I heard some strange noises. I woke him up, and he seized the pistol and the sword and endeavoured to open the door: I held him back, made him dress, which he did with calm and speed, then said: ' Bravo. Now I am dressed. What do we do ? Barricade ourselves ? ' He tried to open the door again and I stopped him. Then I remembered what I had heard him say: ' Didn't you say to Pepe Paris that that window was handy for this kind of situation ? '—' You are right '—he said, and went to the window. I held him back while people were passing, but when no one was about, he leapt out, just when the door was being forced."

And so, as the door burst open, the conspirators saw a woman, sword in hand, quietly looking at them in the light of the lantern one of them was carrying. They came dagger in hand and their chests crossed by leather straps with pistols. " Where is Bolívar ? "—they asked. " At the sitting of the Council "—she answered. They saw the window open. " He has fled! " And one Lopote, a brute of a soldier, tried to avenge himself on her. " We kill no women "—said Horment coldly. She kept them wondering, looking for the Council room, until they became angry; and when she came across Lieutenant Ibarra, wounded, set about to tend his wound with her linen. " Has he been killed ? "—he asked. And she answered: " No, he lives." The conspirators then vented their frustration and fury on Manuela, who was so severely beaten with the flat of a sword that twelve days later, on October 7th, she was still confined to bed. She does not, however, seem to have felt the pain at the moment for she carried on her intelligent activities with admirable coolness. She heard Fergusson's heavy steps, and looked out. Fergusson saw her in the bright moonlight and asked about Bolívar. She begged him not to advance, to which the Scot made answer he would die as a soldier. And so he did, for Carujo shot him dead. Manuela called out Fernando (Bolívar's nephew) who was ill, and asked him to attend to Fergusson, whom she thought wounded, while she went upstairs to see the rest of the household. Urdaneta, Herrán and others rushed in asking for news. " And the funny thing was "—she concludes— " that they all asked: ' And where is he gone ? ' while not even the *Libertador* knew that ! "

4

Meanwhile, a party of artillery men had leapt over the wall between their barracks and the yard of the building where Padilla was imprisoned under the custody of Colonel José Bolívar. Suddenly Padilla heard Colonel Bolívar shout: " General, I am being killed." Colonel Bolívar, naked, was endeavouring to shelter himself behind Padilla while the soldiers and the officer threatened to kill Padilla if he stood in the way. Colonel Bolívar was seized, dragged down and shot dead. But by this time the Vargas battalion, faithful to the *Libertador*, was advancing in the square against the rebels. The artillerymen vanished and Padilla was left in the yard with the dead man and in a situation which led to the worst possible interpretation of his share in the episode, though he was as innocent of it as of the rest of the conspiracy. He seems to have escaped during the night, but " after the insurrection was put down he came up to General Bolívar in the Principal Square and embraced H.E. congratulating him on his escape ". As for Santander, he had spent the night in his sister's house, where a bed was always kept ready for him owing to " these political agitations "; and there he remained until late in the night when General Ortega passed on horseback with a party of soldiers, knocked at the window and told him there was trouble in the city. Santander had his horse saddled and left with Ortega for the Main Square.

When Bolívar fell on his feet, " a sentinel stationed not far from the window, it is said, mistook him for a servant of the Palace ". This mistake may well have been the easier for the fact that a man passing at the time, to join Bolívar and who left with him, was in fact Bolívar's pastrycook. They ran under the moonlight and hid under the bridge in the muddy bed of the river San Agustin, a few blocks away; there they stayed while shots were fired, soldiers fought and horses galloped about. At times they heard a shout for liberty or for Bolívar. Time went by, small troops on horseback passed now and then, pickets sent by Urdaneta to search for Bolívar. But, though they shouted *Viva el Libertador*, Bolívar, fearing a trap, lay low. After three anxious hours, Bolívar ordered his servant to go out carefully to find out who were those they could hear approaching; the servant recognized the officers, who recognized him and reassured him as to the situation. Bolívar came out of hiding and drenched, numb, covered with mud, he rode into the Main Square where he was received with enthusiasm. But, says his chronicler, Posada Gutiérrez, he, " with a sepulchral voice let fall: ' Do you want to kill me with joy when I am on the point of dying with grief ? ' " There is little doubt as to the cause of that grief. On that unhappy night, his precious glory had been tarnished for ever. We know how keenly he felt it; because, with that close watch he kept on his publicity, it is certain that he personally supervised the drafting of the report which appeared in a supplement to the *Gazette:* " H.E. came out to meet them "—says the *Gazette*, omitting of course all mention of Manuela Sáenz—" but being singlehanded against so many, he tried to barricade himself in his bedroom, and, as it became impossible to resist any longer, he flew to the street by the window and going round by a path of the city, succeeded in reaching the Vargas barracks. Finding the battalion out, he went to the Main Square, where he was received with indescribable joy." Details such as " flying " for " fleeing " reveal Bolívar's own hand in this text. The omission of his three hours of hiding is pathetic.

5

Still under this cloud, Bolívar summoned the Prime Minister Castillo and asked him to call a meeting of the Council so that he could resign his powers; to convene at once Congress, due to meet on January 2nd; to prepare a decree pardoning all the conspirators; and to arrange everything for his own departure abroad. Castillo, who had listened with crossed arms and downcast face, agreed to everything but the last, and advised him to withdraw to his villa as a private citizen, for his departure would strengthen the view that aversion to him was general and justified. Bolívar assented to this. All was, however, but a passing mood. Informed by Castillo, Urdaneta called on Bolívar with Córdoba, Whittle, Crofton, and many officers of the two regiments, who knew themselves as good as lost were Bolívar to leave. He listened to their entreaties and at last gave way. He cancelled his instructions to Castillo, declared himself an unrestricted Dictator, promised that very night 30,000 dollars to the Vargas battalion, and began a repression which adds nothing to his good fame. On Monday, September 29th, he appointed a Tribunal composed of Generals Paris, Córdoba and Ortega, Colonels Barriga and Arjona, and Drs. Pereira, Pareja and Alvarez, with his intimate friend Paris as President. This tribunal sentenced to death Horment, Zulaibar, Colonel Silva, and Lieutenants Galindo and López, who were executed. On Ramón Guerra, the Court split. Córdoba, Barriga, Arjona and Pareja voted for death, the others for thirty years' imprisonment. This was carried with Paris' casting vote. " The Liberator " —writes the British Consul to the Foreign Office—" on receiving notice of this latter sentence, dissolved the Tribunal, suspended Gral Paris from the Commandancy General, appointed Gral Córdoba Minister of War; and General Urdaneta, being a man of inflexible character in affairs of this nature, was named Commandant General, with authority—in conformity with the decree relative to conspirators—to proceed assisted by an Auditor of War (Auditor de Guerra) personated on this occasion by Col. Barriga to the sentence of all those in any way concerned with this conspiracy." Henderson also reports the shooting of the first five in the Main Square on September 29th (four days after the attempt) and adds: " General Urdaneta has proceeded with great activity in the solemn commission with which he is invested. He has revised the sentence of Guerra and this day has condemned him and General Padilla to be shot to-morrow."

Guerra's share in the conspiracy was so sly and odious that it somewhat attenuates this act of sheer despotism on the part of Bolívar. But nothing can excuse Padilla's judicial murder, on whom biased accusations began to be piled in the Supplement to the *Gazette* which came out on the 28th. Even the British Consul, whose feelings were strongly for Bolívar and who approves Guerra's execution, can go no further than this: " Independently of the charge hanging over General Padilla, relative to the insurrection at Cartagena, his participation in this conspiracy is proved by the declarations of a sergeant, that he, Padilla, could have saved the life of Colonel Bolívar, and that he took the sword of the latter and attempted to get over the walls into the barracks of the Vargas, with a view of placing himself at their head, this and some minor evidence, has been deemed sufficient for his condemnation." The British Consul reports that Colonel Torrens, Mexican *Chargé d'Affaires*, twice tried to put in a word of mercy for Guerra and finally called on Bolívar with a representation from Guerra's wife. Bolívar was angry and asked him not to meddle in the internal affairs of another country. Torrens insisted, and, rebuffed again, asked for his passport. " Take your passport and go "—retorted Bolívar, and when the Mexican left he typically observed aloud: " This person wishes to assume all the importance belonging to a Minister of England or of France." Padilla and Guerra were sentenced to be hanged; but they had to be shot first, because no one could be found to hang them. Fourteen persons paid with their lives, five of whom were artillery soldiers whose only crime had been to obey orders. The hounding of victims went on, and hills and forests were scoured for them. Bolívar led the operation in person with a relentless passion. Young Azuero (José Celestino) caught also and sentenced to death, died with a firmness which impressed the nation. " He approached the bench with apparent cheerfulness and wiping away the dust from the seat with his pocket handkerchief he sat down with perfect calmness . . . he declined the usual consolation offered by the clergy and crossing his legs, respectfully saluted the assembled people, almost at the moment of being launched into eternity."

How about Santander ? He turned up during the night and asked Urdaneta what he should do. Urdaneta managed to keep him about and actually arrested him the next day. He was accused of being an accomplice; but on October 21st Bolívar was still of opinion that the statements so far gathered " do not as yet make up a perfect enough proof to allow of his being judged and sentenced to death, for, according to my opinion and that of others, he must be judged with clemency rather than with rigour, since he is my enemy ". The British Consul reports: " There is a strong desire to lay hold of something to inculpate Santander, so far as to lead to his condemnation, but it is probable that he has acted with too much precaution to be implicated." Carujo was offered his life if he revealed all he knew; but even after he had spoken, the position of Santander remained at worst, ambiguous. It may be summed up thus: he must often have expressed private views favourable to the advantages Colombia would derive should Bolívar die; he shrank from murder; he would gladly have sentenced Bolívar possibly even to death, had he been able to sit in judgment on him; he knew there were plots about; he did not have the force to stop the process even though he knew, and also because he knew (for it cuts both ways), that the natural head of the State after Bolívar's death would be he; he could not denounce the conspirators decently; but the burden became too heavy for him and he actually sent Bolívar an anonymous letter of warning (21.ix.28) in the hope that, though he had disguised his writing, Bolívar would recognize it. Santander defended himself with the utmost coolness and intelligence. His sentence to death was one more iniquity committed by Urdaneta. The Council of Ministers objected, or, at any rate, declined to be associated with it at all. Bolívar was not a man to be checked by the opposition of a handful " of Doctors ". Yet, he bowed; and wrote to Páez: " My life remains in the air with this reprieve, and that of Colombia is lost for ever. I regret the death of Piar, Padilla and the rest who have perished for the same cause." Which cause ? Why did he bow ? The reason can be found in a dispatch from James Henderson to the Foreign Office. Reprieved and sent to Cartagena, Santander " was allowed two or three days to arrange his affairs . . . was visited by a great number of persons principally females, their husbands being afraid to call upon him. . . .

Six-sevenths of the respectable part of the inhabitants either called upon him or sent him some token of their esteem. The archbishop and the clergy generally have evinced a feeling decidedly in favour of Santander. . . . It was determined, I understand, had the sentence against Santander been confirmed, that a large body of the clergy and females, were to place themselves between the soldiers and that individual at the time of his execution ". Santander was conveyed to Cartagena by an escort under the Italian Montebrune who wrote a diary of the expedition and reported . . . to Manuela Sáenz.

6

By October 4th, " Bolívar had evinced his confidence in the public, as he was this day walking through the city attended only by two or three private friends ". He was broken, physically and morally; and his friends had been given much to think about. He had been on the brink of death by murder; and remained not far from death from exhaustion and sickness. What next ? By October 7th, James Henderson was reporting on the matter to the Earl of Aberdeen. His situation in Bogotá was considerable, not only as the British Consul and (in the absence of Campbell owing to illness) as the acting Minister, but also as the father of Fanny Henderson, who, at the precocious age of thirteen, had inspired an ardent love in young Córdoba, Bolívar's Minister of War. By this channel many a secret of State flowed from Bolívar's Council to H.M.'s in London. On October 7th Henderson was able to report to London: " The friends of General Bolívar conceive that a constitutional monarchy is their only hope after the death of that distinguished individual, but they believe, and I think justly so, that no European Prince would come here, that is, with the exception of a member of the Royal House of Spain, to any connection with which dynasty there is an insuperable, determined and general antipathy. Sr. Joaquin Mosquera, who is a member of the Council of State, of one of the first families of Colombia, and a man of the first talent and influence in the country, possessing much discrimination and sound understanding, is one of those entertaining the opinion, that the State would best prosper under free monarchical institutions. After manifesting, a few days since, his views very fully on this subject, he made many enquiries of me relative to H.R.H. Prince Leopold, from which I infer that the policy of inviting a European Prince at no very distant period, to assume the Royal Government of this country would soon be sustained by many proselytes.

This trend towards a monarchy gained ground under Bolívar's skilful leadership. Córdoba delivered into Henderson's hands (13.xi.28) a full report of a sitting of the Council in which a motion presented by Bolívar had been discussed. " That H.E. in view of the factions and conspiracies raised in the Republic against his government, wished to call together a National Assembly to report on his administration, give back his government and ask it to grant a Constitution to the nation. Restrepo and Vergara spoke against, since the nation had, by a unanimous and solemn decision, granted Bolívar unlimited powers. Revenga argued that there was a strong party of opposition, as shown by the September conspiracy; but his colleagues pointed out that this conspiracy was promoted by less than forty persons led by Santander, a personal enemy of the Liberator and an ambitious man." In the end the discussion was adjourned to the 15th and then Bolívar's motion was turned down—which is, of course, what he had presented it for. But over and above his written report, in his own handwriting, Córdoba gave Henderson a far more revealing interpretation of the meeting, which Henderson passed on to the Foreign Office. This report discloses why Bolívar presented his motion and why he wanted it rejected. "I have the honour of acquainting you, for the information of the Earl of Aberdeen that it is probable another change in the political régime of this State will speedily take place. The Liberator has requested the Council to discuss the expediency of his assembling the national representation, and through the private confidence of the Minister of War I am enabled to furnish you with a translation of a hasty sketch drawn out by him of that discussion. The proposition of the Liberator will be negatived, and the result will be that the army, and the principal towns of the Republic will be induced to petition H.E. to give the country a constitution himself, without convoking a Congress. If it is possible to accomplish the purpose, a constitutional monarchy will be arrived at, or some similar political arrangement. All the best informed people are decided against the republican codes." This is final. Bolívar it was who led the country towards a monarchy.

Age and the experience of men had brought about in him a compromise between his dictatorial tendencies and that Spanish pre-natal substratum which had so far remained buried and unexpressed in his life. Bolívar's monarchism emerges thus in later years, in its methods though not in its aim, as the negation of much of his political and military career. The Voltairian philosopher, the companion of that imitation-Rousseau, Simón Rodriguez, once in power, was leading the nation back to the Church. His henchman Herrán, in a proclamation to the Colombians (30.xi.28), gave them this password: "Religion. Fatherland. Bolívar." And in the correspondence of this period Bolívar will often appeal to bishops and priests for political help. He, the fanatical enemy of Spain, wrote to Páez (9.viii.28): "I also agree that justice should be established as it was in the time of the Spaniards." Sucre wrote to him constantly that they were building on sand. He had destroyed time-tried institutions which had worked with the weight and the prestige of centuries; but he had proved unable to build up anything instead. "He observed to me"—writes Henderson on December 4th, 1828—"that all his labours in the last eighteen years appeared to be bringing no other result than the opening Colombia [sic] to the commerce of the European nations." This was probably an echo of a letter from Sucre who had said to him (28.xi.28): "I must repeat that if the introduction of ordinary wool and cotton manufactured articles and even of wheat flour is not prohibited in the south, these provinces will be ruined." Yet another of the accusations against the Spaniards was thus going overboard. "It cannot be denied"—wrote Henderson on Bolívar—"that he is deficient of practical knowledge in matters of legislation, and I am besides fearful that he will not have the energy to maintain the position he has taken. . . . Not being surrounded by men of sufficient talent or experience, his views are thereby exposed to failure. The opinion that this country cannot prosper without a constitutional monarchy gains ground: it would not be surprising if . . . some proposition were made to the Liberator to look for a successor in a European Catholic Prince." Bolívar himself was so won over to the monarchical rule that, in a letter to Páez (9.viii.28), explaining the new organization of Venezuela and the office Páez would fulfil in it, he wrote: " In one word, it will be more or less a viceroyalty or vice-presidency." His mind saw the aim clearly; but his will was machiavellian and tortuous. And as he was swift and therefore devoured by impatience, he became easily despotic. At this time, even Henderson, so eager a partisan of his, writes scathingly about his indifference towards justice. " One complaint against the government of General Bolívar is that justice is not fairly administered, as the adherents of the Liberator are always allowed to escape." And he quotes several unsavoury examples.

PART IV

THE DECLINE

Chapter XXIV

THE WAR AGAINST PERU

I

SUCRE'S army remained in Bolivia as a Colombian detachment cut off from the main force. He held the country by sheer moral authority and elegance of behaviour. Surrounded by avid politicians and generals, he was disinterested in money matters and devoid of ambition. He was generous also.* But by 1828 his authority had been weakened by the insurrection of his soldiers on December 24th, 1827. The over-bearing attitude of some of his officers was a constant cause of friction; and the Argentine Minister in Chuquisaca, Francisco Ignacio Bustos, con-tributed to the trouble by intrigues backed by subsidies. The disappearance of Bolívar and the return of La Mar to Lima had left unemployed two ambitious generals, Gamarra and Santa Cruz, both Upper Peruvians or Bolivians; and the first, the more dangerous at the time, was a bitter enemy of Bolívar, who had apparently been too successful with his wife. A touch of racialism came to add its acid spice to this stew: the Indian-Spaniard of the Highlands expressed his dislike of the Venezuelan with the slogan: *Mulattoes, no.* Sucre, uneasy at Gamarra's doings, went to see him at the Desaguadero (11.iii.28) and returned convinced of his good faith. But Gamarra was incapable of such a thing; and, on April 18th, 1828, at dawn, a unit mutinied in Chuquisaca with shouts of *Long live Gamarra!* Sucre rose at once and rode to the barracks at the entrance to which lay the body of the captain of the guard. Sucre, in uniform, sword in hand, cocked hat and sash of office on, rode into the central court and was received by a volley of musketry which frightened his horse; he rode away hatless and swordless, his arm broken by a bullet. At the gates of the Palace he fell in a faint. He came to as he was being undressed on his bed: " Alas " —he cried out—" this had never happened during the war of independence."

At midday there was a meeting at the University and it was decided to call in Gamarra with his Peruvians. Sucre resigned and the Prime Minister, Urdinenca, took command. It was thought advisable to lodge Sucre in the seminary, but Olañeta's wife gave away the secret and he was brought back to the Palace, where Olañeta assured him of his loyalty and friendship in moving terms, and left at once to join his enemies. Urdinenca " betrayed his country ", says Sucre, meaning that he helped the Peruvians in. Gamarra

---

* Among other stories, one is told of a Captain Valentin Matos who made an attempt on his life, was sentenced to death by the Courts, reprieved by him and granted a passport to leave the country and who, on the day of his departure, found in his baggage an anonymous gift of 200 pesos—from Sucre.

invaded Bolivia under all kinds of specious pretexts. His campaign was easy and the treaty of Piquiza (6.vii.28) stipulated that the Colombian troops should leave for Arica by the route prescribed by Gamarra, and that the Peruvian army would occupy Potosí until an assembly had met to decide the future Government. Sucre was to resign at once. He did so on August 3rd, with a farewell message, if justifiably anti-Peruvian, noble and elegant. As he left with his small suite, he heard several voices shout: " Out with the mulattoes! "

The Peruvian Foreign Secretary, Mariátegui, was one of Bolívar's enemies. He sent to Bogotá as Minister Plenipotentiary Don José de Villa, who had been private secretary to General Berindoaga (whom Bolívar had executed). The hint could not be more direct; and Santander had assured Montebrune that the Peruvian Minister had come well provided with funds to contrive Bolívar's murder. López Méndez had assured Santander that the Peruvian Government " was resolved to spare no means to undo the *Libertador* ". Villa lost no time in getting in touch with the opposition; he passed on to Santander messages from La Mar, and was (so Santander thought) in touch with José María Obando. Ostensibly, he came to settle the outstanding questions between the two countries; but Bolívar refused to see him and he was told on March 3rd that, unless the Province of Jaén and the part of the Province of Mainas still retained by Peru had been returned within six months, the outstanding sum of $3,595,747 (the debt of Peru to Colombia as estimated by Colombia), had been repaid, apologies made for some insults and Armero re-admitted (after his expulsion) as *Chargé d'Affaires* of Colombia in Lima, " Colombia would conclude that Peru was leaving the decision to the arbitrament of war ". The press of Lima attacked Bolívar violently. It is, nevertheless, doubtful whether La Mar actually wished war or thought it necessary. He did not trust Gamarra; he wanted to draw his troops away, under the pretext of foreign war, and so had himself empowered by Congress to make war. As for Bolívar, he issued an intemperate Proclamation (3.vii.28) urging the Southern Colombians to arm, and ending with the ominous words: " My presence among you will be the signal for COMBAT."

La Mar's ambition was Peruvian; Bolívar's was continental and imperial. Hence his more warlike attitude and activity. He was determined to reconquer Peru. The Proclamation was followed by a Manifesto no less stiff and warlike. Meanwhile, he sent O'Leary to Lima to " negotiate ", in order to gain time. The Irishman left Bogotá (3.viii.28) just as Bolívar raised the army to forty thousand men on the combined threat of a Peruvian war and a Spanish invasion. " You will have seen in our press that we have declared war on Peru "—he wrote to Páez on August 9th, 1828—" but we shall, nevertheless, be unable to wage it soon, for we are waiting to hear about the Spanish expedition which threatens us daily and has forced me to issue a decree of alarm which you ought to cackle about as much as possible in order to frighten away the Spaniards and calm down the excited demagogues." The hint as to what was in his mind could not be clearer. Meanwhile, O'Leary wrote from Popayán (17.viii.28): " The Peruvians are very much opposed to the war." He complains about subaltern officers (Pasto, 25.viii): " The abuses they commit are incredible; the townships scream complaints. As for this province all is quiet. The Governor is a Spaniard named Gutiérrez, an excellent person and very popular here; it seems that he has been relieved of this command. This is regrettable, for he understands the Pastusians and can draw resources from the Province without displacing the inhabitants." From Quito he wrote again about Peru (1.ix.28): " All reject the war. La Mar fears it most." As for the departments he was crossing: " Men of all classes openly express their aversion to war. There is no enthusiasm here." From Babahoyo (28.ix) he reports cries of *Long live Peru!* and having had to fight against thieves; and on the 14th, from Guayaquil, that according to letters from Lima, " there is a strong party there in favour of the Spaniards, and the most zealous of its members include Pando, Luna Pizarro and La Mar. The news seems absurd but it is not." As for Guayaquil, O'Leary found it " in a sad state ". No income, no trade. " Public opinion, against us. In one word, Peru has much preponderance here." He saw Flores and Heres and advised Flores to win a victory, " It matters nothing that I may be in Lima." Flores, however, is even more explicit; for he writes to Bolívar (15.ix.28), he has agreed with O'Leary that the negotiations in Lima must last " all the time we need to organize the army and make it respected for its strength ". Meanwhile O'Leary reports that " the aversion for war shown here and in Ecuador is incalculable ".

Sucre left Chuquisaca on August 2nd, 1828, and arrived in Cobija on the 26th. In an English frigate he sailed for Guayaquil, via Callao, where he stayed from September 10th to 12th without landing, though invited to do so. He had thought of mediating between his country and Peru; but he read Bolívar's Proclamation and La Mar's answer of August 30th, and though he actually does not say so, felt critical, as well he might. He writes from his ship an objective and cool estimate of the military position and adds that his wound did not finally close till the day he arrived in Callao; that his arm, hand and fingers had lost movement; and that he expected to join his wife, the Marquesa de Solanda (whom he had married by proxy on the day he had resigned), in Quito. On September 19th, Sucre and O'Leary met in Guayaquil and talked the whole day. According to O'Leary, Sucre " says that he will do everything for Y.E. and for his country if a plan is adopted; but that he will not work without knowing why and for whom ". Perhaps he was thinking of some words he had written to Flores (3.ii.28) to the effect that Peru was very much divided, that a reaction favourable to Bolívar was always possible and that a Colombian invasion would destroy its possibility. Sucre was then thirty-five; he had considerable experience and an unrivalled prestige. He was shrewd, brave, straight and independent—by far the best man the Spanish-American revolution had thrown up. He was coming back to his country after an absence of many years, ready to serve, by no means eager for power, faithful to Bolívar, by no means ready to flatter him.

2

On October 4th, 1828, O'Leary wrote to Bolívar that Guayaquil was blockaded by Peruvian forces under Admiral Guise; while La Mar was moving northwards with four thousand men. O'Leary informs Bolívar that he has written to La Mar " in agreement with Messrs. Flores and Heres ". Sucre had left on September 23rd for Quito, where he had arrived on September 30th. He cannot have enjoyed the company of O'Leary. On October 20th, O'Leary wrote to Bolívar: " General Sucre *was* my friend, but I have or wish to have no friendship with any one who tries to recruit partisans for himself by unseemly means. I thought first of writing him a strong letter, but then preferred not to collide with him direct, so as to be able to mediate between him and Flores should dissensions occur between them. The behaviour of Sucre should hasten Y.E.'s coming." The most charitable interpretation of these lines is that O'Leary allowed himself to be bamboozled by Flores. This upstart, then a youth of twenty-eight, was a mulatto of Puerto Cabello, of obscure birth, who had begun life as a kind of barber-nurse in the army hospitals and, partly through valour, partly through intrigue, had risen relatively quickly to the rank of brigadier-general. He was ambitious and had made up his mind to carve a kingdom for himself, precisely in Quito. Sucre's arrival with his immense personal prestige, socially doubled now by his marriage into one of the first families of Quito, was a major disaster for him.

The calumny conveyed by O'Leary may have emerged in Flores' fertile brain. A letter from Sucre to Bolívar says: " I am told that you have been warned that I had written to General Santander on political matters. It would degrade me were I to endeavour to deny this calumny which is nevertheless worthy of the vile soul who tried to injure our good relations." And he goes on to write words suggesting the contempt of a man of good family for the upstart. " My behaviour is clear as light and my soul is formed by my principles and these by my education. No revolution was needed to pick me out from the mud." All this might apply to Flores, with whom Sucre was then on bad terms having complained of the upstart's scurvy treatment of his wife's estate, on which he had imposed outrageous exactions, although Sucre was owed many years' salary and was reduced to living on his wife's income. Sucre had just received the news that his brothers and sisters in Cumaná had been ruined by the rebels. Through all these ordeals he behaved with his usual moral elegance; and lived up to his spontaneous pledge to Bolívar that he would endeavour to remain friendly to Flores " because this union serves the public weal ". He even went so far as to make Flores his daughter's godfather, a fact of which Bolívar affectionately complained. The chief obstacle to this union was Flores' ambition. He had been acting Commander-in-Chief in the south for some time; while Sucre had been begging Bolívar to set him free to live with his family for the time being and thanked Bolívar profusely in his first letter from Guayaquil (21.xi.28) for having at last agreed to let him live " in retreat in Quito ".

But it was not to be. By October 8th, 1828, Bolívar was gently breaking the news to Flores: " Sucre must have already arrived. . . . I have therefore appointed him Commander-in-Chief of that army; and be sure I do not deprive you of the slightest glory. . . . I give you a successor to spare you a disaster." What disaster? One he dared not explain to Flores, though he did to O'Leary: " Something else threatens us: a disaster there. The Peruvians aim at dissolving us and will in fact succeed owing to the hatred the Southern populations profess to the leaders of the Republic, whom they accuse of all crimes and defects: they say that the subalterns behave like brigands and that the soldiers are thieves; that disorder is widespread; that no treasure is enough to satisfy the avarice of Generals and Intendants. Only against Illingrot [the Englishman Illingworth] and against González have I received no complaints of this kind. About Flores, Torres and Urdaneta [Luis] they write horrors. I can hardly believe it. . . ." No wonder that the distracted man " saw heavens open " (as the Spanish saying goes) when he heard of Sucre's arrival. " Blessed be the day on which you arrived in Guayaquil ", he wrote to his favourite lieutenants (28.x.28); " these papers contain your appointment as absolute chief of the south. All my powers, good and evil, I delegate them on you." He then announced that he meant to leave for the south in about a month; touched lightly on a number of other subjects and added: " I am answering now neither Flores nor O'Leary nor anyone else; that is why I want you to read this letter to them so that they know I have handed over Simón Bolívar's being to you. Yes, dear Sucre, you are one with me except in your kindness and my luck." Then this pathetic post scriptum, in which Bolívar reveals himself still the slave of ambition and of all its wiles and lies: " I shall never tire of recommending to you the worth of the Southern chiefs, as also my aide-de-camp, worthy of a special mention. But who is better than Flores and that incomparable Illingrot and the kind Torres and the shrewd Heres and the noble González and the brave and heroic Sandes, Urdaneta and other valiant men of that army, every one of whom I love in particular ? "

Sucre did not accept the appointment. He was sincere in his desire for a rest and he was against that war. With his usual frankness he had put his views before Bolívar more than once. Thus (6.xii.28): Guayaquil was too friendly to Peru and Quito and Azuay too poor. Military exactions were all very well when the country was in danger, but not for an offensive war. Finally: " I shall also say that I thought the declaration of war without control of the sea in the Pacific was premature." This was a direct condemnation of Bolívar's rashness from the point of view of a wise general. Sucre saw the chief danger for the south in the " relaxation of discipline and complete corruption which has set in in the army "; and he closed again insisting on sea power: " To achieve a durable peace it is necessary to destroy the Peruvian Navy." This was not easy, for Colombia lacked not only ships but sailors, and, as the few they had were foreign mercenaries, they were apt to bolt at the smell of better booty or better salaries. " The corvette *Pichincha*, sent to Panamá to fetch the *Girardot* battalion, mutinied at sea and sailed for Paita where she went over to the Peruvians; luckily she had on board only four guns and twenty sailors." James Henderson reported (15.x.28) that a secret order had been issued to arm one of the new frigates lying at anchor at Cartagena and to send it by Cape Horn to the Pacific. Meanwhile Guise attacked Guayaquil (22.xi.28), and was killed by a bullet on the 24th; he was most of the Peruvian fleet in himself, at least in O'Leary's estimate. Fulfilling one of Sucre's prophecies, the most the attack did was to cool the good opinion Peru enjoyed in Guayaquil. The Peruvian Navy, strong enough to make life impossible in the city, was not strong enough to take it; and Guayaquil was a desert. " No decent person is seen in the streets."

3

As a sequel to the attempt on Bolívar's life (25.ix.28), the conspirators had prepared rebellions in a number of provinces. The leadership of the conspiracy in the Cauca valley had been entrusted to Colonel José María Obando, who was " Arms Commandant " at Popayán under T. C. Mosquera. His chief assistant was Lieutenant-Colonel José Hilario López, one of the members of the majority in the Ocaña Convention (during which this plan had ripened). The plot was to break forth at Popayán on October 15th. Mosquera, forewarned, succeeded in putting together some force, neither well armed nor well instructed; but as he lacked the dash of Obando, he allowed the rebel to terrorize the countryside for a month, to rob the post, thus diverting a number of gold ingots on their way to the Popayán Mint, and to loot the estates of the rich citizens. Finally, at La Ladera, opposite the city, seven hundred of Mosquera's not very good troops, yet better than the raw and ill armed negroes and Indians of Obando, were defeated (11.xi.28). Mosquera himself, who had remained in Popayán with two hundred men in reserve, fled, leaving his men to be massacred by the ferocious Obando; " for "—adds Posada Gutiérrez—" in the Cauca wars no quarter is given as a rule, and the murder of defenceless adversaries who have surrendered is not thought criminal ". Obando won the prestige of victory as well as 1,600 rifles and war material he found in the city.

The citizens met in a kind of Assembly under the slogan: " Hatred and war to the tyrants, re-establishment of constitutional order "; all of which meant that Obando was to be Commandant General. His war chest was mostly composed of the six thousand pesos of gold he had grabbed from the post. Soon he took the field again towards Pasto, where he was able to raise 3,000 men by proclaiming to the Indians that he was fighting " for the King of Spain and for the Catholic religion ". He took Pasto without firing a shot (11.xii.28) and three days later wrote to La Mar offering his services and asking him to reciprocate the help Peru had received from Colombia by the mere fact that Colombia had been liberated from the *Libertador*. " The republicans of Colombia "—he writes grimly—" are resolved to compromise only with his ashes." Bolívar was at Chía, five leagues from Bogotá, where he had gone (8.xi.28) in the hope of spending

" two or three months in these fields resting and amusing myself ". When, on November 22nd, he received the news of Obando's rising (22.xi.28), he returned to Bogotá and decided to act with energy, fearing above all a conjunction between the Peruvians and the rebels. He appointed Córdova in command of a column of about 800 men of his best troops.

Nothing so illustrates the tragic irrelevance of all these turbulent wars as the fact that both Bolívar and Córdova should have had to turn to such futile purposes energies they were both devoting at the time to the study of the Panama Canal. Bolívar had been thinking of it for some time. On July 14th, 1827, Henderson reported to Bidwell: " I think it proper to mention to you that in a casual conversation which I had with General Bolívar, he took the opportunity to request if an occasion offered, that I would assure the British Capitalists of his desire to give the greatest facility for opening a communication, at the Isthmus between the two oceans. H.E., moreover stated, that, if required, he would even make the territory neutral." This was not a passing conversation, as shown by a letter from Córdova, as War Minister, to Bolívar (19.xi.28): " Following your suggestions I made the recommendations you ordered me to make that priority should be given to geographical engineers in the Isthmus, and so they have been stimulated and they have prepared some reports which they promised to have completed by next summer; we shall therefore know the difference in the levels of the two seas and whether it will be possible to open the Canal so often discussed." Within a week, the General was no longer speaking of the Canal; he had left for Popayán at the head of his troops to fight a civil war.

Córdova found no difficulty in taking possession of Popayán (27.xii.28). Mosquera was with him, but under his orders. Córdova was a brave, indeed a foolhardy man, petulant and irrepressible; Mosquera was not brave, was vain and touchy and belonged to one of the most powerful families of the Province. Córdova found out in Popayán how small Obando's force had been at La Ladera and told Mosquera somewhat impetuously how little he thought of him. This was the beginning of his tragic end; for Mosquera poisoned Bolívar's mind as to Córdova's fidelity. Bolívar was at the time more than ever inclined to suspect the heart of every man who did not surrender his brain to him; while Córdova was beginning to feel that all was not well with Bolívar's ideas either in home or in Peruvian affairs. López had left the city with the rebel troops and Córdova followed him up and beat him at La Horqueta (29.xii.28), but resolved not to pursue him and returned to Popayán the next day.

Bolívar was most of the time at Bojacá, in the neighbourhood of Bogotá; and on December 28th, he left southwards to put himself at the head of the army. Reporting this fact to London, Henderson added: " Although he gives out that he does not intend to enter Peru, I am still of the opinion . . . that it has long been a part of his policy to regain his influence in that Region and if he can effect his object, he will most assuredly take possession of Lima." Henderson adds that though Bolívar has sent to Castillo Rada, through Urdaneta, a message to the effect that he only leaves to " wrench a peace " from Peru, he has given the Government draconian orders to put every cent into the army, even the sums earmarked for the payment of the interest due to foreign bondholders. He knew that, at the time, England was claiming this payment " with threats ". This warlike, " Napoleonic " attitude was inner and confidential. Outwardly he was all moderation and peace. " You are right in saying that I must not go to Peru "—he writes to Briceño Méndez (18.xi.28), and similar professions are found at this time in his letters, particularly to civilians. But to Montilla: " For my part I have ordered the whole Republic to be set in motion, and I count on 10 to 12,000 men afield, and doubt not but that we shall conquer the Devil, for happily I am attacked on my strongest side, which is war." To almost everybody he writes then: " Without me, there shall be neither peace nor war." And his true intentions show through in these lines of a letter to O'Leary (19.xii.28): " I note the reluctance of the Peruvian Government to admit peace proposals from Colombia. Such behaviour at the very time Obando advocates action in agreement with the Peruvian army will the more justify our own in the eyes of the cultured world." Before his departure for the south, Henderson called on him. " H.E. appeared to entertain the fullest confidence of taking possession of Lima in the course of six months. He said there was only a faction opposed to him—much less formidable than that of Santander here—at the head of which was La Mar, and declared that the people of the Peru's were generally attached to him."

Still reluctant to take over command of the Southern army, Sucre was in Ríobamba when he received Bolívar's letter of October 28th ordering him to do so, and a report that Gamarra had come to reinforce La Mar with 3,200 men. " I did not hesitate and I started on my way at once." On January 27th, 1829, he joined the army at Cuenca; on the 28th he took command and on the 29th he began operations. The forward posts of the enemy were at Nabon, three days' march from Cuenca. Gamarra had joined La Mar. In a letter to that Flores he was superseding, Sucre wrote (18.xii.28): " I do not think it advisable to abandon Cuenca; I believe the enemy must be awaited at the gates of that city. The plain of Tarqui is a good battlefield; beyond it there is a strong position which I occupied on my way to the Pichincha campaign." As good a military prophecy as ever was made. He sent a message to Bolívar that he would write neither to him nor to the Government until after the victory. Traces of a split of opinion between O'Leary and Sucre as to the attitude towards Peru can be felt in the papers. Echoing Bolívar, O'Leary is warlike and uncompromising. At this time he received from the Peruvian Government a letter which he returned officially unopened, though he copied it before returning it; and he wrote to Bolívar (29.i.29): " If we win, I shall go with the army into Peruvian territory and offer new conditions to that government. Y.E. may be sure that, so far as I am concerned, I shall never sign any but the most honourable treaty with Peru." That " so far as I am concerned " is revealing. But Sucre, supplanting O'Leary as a negotiator, sent a note to La Mar (3.ii.29), reversing in fact O'Leary's refusal to answer the Peruvian request for conditions of peace. It is important to emphasize the motive Sucre puts forward: " That it is attributed to the Government of Colombia that, exploiting the military and enterprising spirit of its troops, it thinks of nothing but conquests." This was a direct allusion to Bolívar's secret intentions which Sucre could clearly read between the lines.

On February 11th and 12th Peruvian and Colombian commissioners met at Saraguro and Paquichapa; but the Peruvian demands were found exorbitant even by Sucre, and operations went on. After some manoeuvring, during which a Peruvian column occupied Cuenca (10.ii.29), Sucre resolved to occupy the plain of Tarqui. At 4.30 in the morning of February 27th a battle began between 1,500 Colombians and 5,000 Peruvians. A brilliant cavalry charge led by O'Leary decided the issue, and " at seven a.m. there were no more Peruvians on the battlefield ". Fifteen hundred soldiers lay dead. At least another 1,000 were wounded, prisoner or missing. La Mar with his cavalry and artillery was beyond a defile on a plain nearby. Sucre sent him an offer of capitulation on the same conditions as before the battle. La Mar first resisted, but in the end yielded; and Flores and O'Leary, with Gamarra and Orbegoso, concluded the Convention of Girón, laying down the bases for a treaty to be concluded when Colombian soil should have been evacuated. The Government of the United States was to act as a mediator and to guarantee the respect of the treaty by both sides.

4

" The *Libertador* arrived here on the 23rd and appears to me more robust and cheerful than ever "—wrote Córdova from Popayán (28.i.29). Bolívar had issued a Proclamation (26.i.29) urging the Pastusians to forsake Obando: " Leave him to that curse which pursues him and throw him to the torrents of the Guáitara or the Juanambú." He found Córdova's division " unable to move rapidly on the faction of Patia for lack of cattle and food "; and while he gave orders to remedy this state of affairs, he got ready to advance southwards, with the olive branch in one hand and the sword in the other. Córdova reports how he endeavoured to reduce factions through priests and other men of influence. Bolívar felt in a hurry to go south because he did not want either peace or war made without him; but Obando blocked his way towards the army commanded by Sucre; and in Popayán he heard Mosquera, Obando's deadly enemy, and Córdova, whose opinions after his stay in Popayán, were veering towards a more sympathetic view of the rebel cause, and who advocated a parley with Obando. Córdova took his opportunity to urge Bolívar either to withdraw from political life altogeher or to regularize his political situation by giving up his dictatorship. Bolívar listened to the first advice, about Obando, for it suited his purpose; but he resented the second, a fact Mosquera did not overlook. Two priests, Urrutia and Grueso, were sent to Obando. He was by no means easy-going. Impatient, Bolívar took the field (10.ii.29), sending Córdova ahead. This blend of force and attraction yielded its usual results, and Obando agreed to a deal whereby he was promoted to the rank of general, and the Pastusians were exempted from military service for a year. The " treaty " began: " The Government will protect the Roman Apostolic Catholic Religion in Pasto and in the whole Republic." It was concluded in Puente de Mayo (2.iii.29), close to Berruecos, a name to remember, where López, Obando's lieutenant, was the guest of Córdova for a night. " The result "—Córdova wrote to Henderson—" is not entirely contrary to my sentiments. This observation requires many explanations, but you, who know me, will probably anticipate them." As for Henderson himself, he reports to London the revealing fact that " the decree relative to the treaty with Obando has been kept quite secret and not published in any of the public prints here or in the south. In that treaty the Liberator found it necessary to accede to the terms of Obando and the Pastusians, for as that guerrilla chief had possession of three almost impregnable passes between the position of General Bolívar and Pasto, which would have required much time to have carried, and the uncertainty that prevailed as to the campaign with the Peruvians, induced H.E. to accept of the humiliating conditions offered."

Whatever his motives, Bolívar paid handsomely. On his way to Pasto, he met Obando at Chacapumba and both slept in the same room; and the next day he entrusted his life to his adversary, for he went forward with just four officers of his staff and entered Pasto at midday (8.iii.29), riding by the side of the man whom, but five weeks earlier, he wanted thrown to the torrents of the Guáitara, and through streets lined by troops but yesterday rebel. Suddenly his brow darkened. On the soldiers' hats he saw the name that Obando had given to the battalion: PADILLA. The reception must have been cold, since Bolívar himself describes it as " not bad "; and it should be set to his credit that he had the courage, indeed the foolhardiness, to remain for four hours (until Córdova's troops arrived at 4 p.m.) in the hands of Obando and his men. In his mind, these sacrifices were all indispensable to break the barrier of Pasto and to arrive in the south in time to prevent anyone from making war or peace without him.

But on March 9th he heard of Tarqui; Sucre had made war without him —and what for him was to be even worse, had made peace also. " When H.E. heard in Pasto of the preliminary peace entered into by General Sucre, he was much annoyed ", wrote Córdova later. We are in a position to watch his Machiavellian mind at work in his letters. We know from Henderson that as late as January 28th he was confident he would win Lima in six months; and from Sucre that he found it necessary to warn Bolívar against entering Peru. On February 5th, Bolívar assured Castillo that he was certain of peace with Peru before Congress met, and " believe that I shall on no account leave Colombia, knowing as you do that it is necessary to attend to Colombian needs, and above all wishing to put at the disposal of Congress the whole Republic in peace and quiet ". On March 9th (before the news of Tarqui) he writes in the same strain to Urdaneta, obviously for Castillo's consumption: " Tell all this to Señor Castillo and the other gentlemen of the Council so that they are informed of my views." And on the same day, to Páez, after the news: " We have finished the civil war with my decree and the foreign war with victories. We enter here as

reconciled brothers and we may do the same in Peru with equal ease."
Nevertheless, he wrote to Córdova from Rupibamba (1.iv.29): " I remain
in the firm purpose of making peace with Peru at all costs, thus bowing to
the national will of Colombia." The phrase betrays his desire for war
plainly. So he adds, with a wording no less revealing of his insincerity:
" I speak to you with ingenuousness. I cordially wish for peace." How
ingenuous he was may be gauged by his later letters to his friends, and in
particular by these words from one to Sucre (12.iii.29): " Should they not
deliver Guayaquil or should they break any of the articles of the Convention,
no matter the pretext, give notice that hostilities are broken and order the
advance of the army into Peru."

His inner decision to reconquer Peru must have increased Córdova's
estrangement; for Córdova, though far away from the spot, felt in the matter
as Sucre did. From Pasto he wrote to Henderson (14.iii.29): " The war
with Peru is finished in the most suitable manner to the interests of America,
the most conformable to my political opinion and the worthiest for Colombia
and her brave army." Córdova was this time objective. Sucre always was.
" He believes that in no case should we wage war but that we should limit
ourselves to work for Colombia "—wrote Mosquera to Bolívar. But there
were other motives for Córdova's displeasure. He had written Bolívar a
courageous letter on Crofton, who had been promoted, and on Manuela
who was still in every sense of the word Bolívar's mistress. " I was ill "—
wrote Bolívar to Urdaneta (9.iii.29)—" but I am well again. Tell M., to
whom I don't write for I fear lest curious people laugh at my foolishness,
that I am hers." No wonder the young general felt aggrieved. As early
as March 7th, 1829, Henderson reported rumours of dissensions between
Bolívar and Córdova, possibly premature and fostered by Mosquera. But
Córdova himself wrote from Pasto to the Hendersons (2.iv.29): " The
nation has no constitutional government, it is subject to the will of one man,
and of a man who already may be said to be in a declining state of health."
He feels he may have to serve his country in such a crisis but ends on a
pessimistic note about his disinclination to " treat with false and inconsequent
persons such as the greater part of my countrymen ". He remained,
however, in command at Pasto.

Bolívar had left Pasto on April 11th, 1829, and had arrived in Quito on
April 17th. There he met again his chief lieutenant Sucre, whom he had
not seen for years. Bolívar was forty-six; Sucre thirty-six. Sucre had
built up a home in Quito. After Tarqui, he had requested Bolívar to
relieve him from public duties. He was a free man, the only free man in
that crowd that surrounded Bolívar, in which everybody, including Bolívar,
was a slave of his ambition. Sucre loved Bolívar and would on no account
oppose him openly; but he was not the man to toy with truth. Mosquera
tells how one day in Quito, as he put before Bolívar a request from Santander
to be released from the castle of Bocachica, which Bolívar refused to read,
Sucre, who was present, insisted on the petition being considered, and
carried his point. Sucre was no less frank about Peru, and about personal
power, the two points on which he differed from Bolívar. The Convention

of Girón had seemed to Bolívar far too generous to the Peruvians; for he
did not desire peace with Peru but a war that would enable him to reconquer
Lima. His letters from Quito show him at this stage secretly desiring that
the Girón Convention might be broken by the Peruvians, ready to fight on
and more inclined to lean on Flores, whom he exalts and repeatedly describes
as a great man, than on his faithful Sucre. Córdova reported both facts
to Henderson. It is plain from many of Bolívar's letters of this period
that he had not given up the ambition to rule over Peru. " In July or
earlier there will be there a revolution in my favour ", he writes. This
was more than a mere prophecy, as revealed by Córdova in a letter to
Henderson (Pasto, 3.v.29): " There are a thousand probabilities that an
insurrection has taken place in Peru against La Mar and his government.
Gamarra had such intentions and was very confident of success." That this
letter betrays contacts between Bolívar and Gamarra cannot be doubted and
that Gamarra's secret intention was to betray La Mar and doublecross
Bolívar cannot be doubted either. Bolívar wrote again: " I have positive
assurances that the best part of Peru and of Bolivia are with me. . . . From
Piura an important friend writes to Loja asking for positive news of my
coming southwards for it is so demanded from Lima in order to carry out
a revolution." That this revolution was of his own concocting cannot be
doubted for he says nearly as much himself in a letter to Urdaneta: " The
news from Peru is excellent, no one doubts that next month we shall have
a revolution in Lima and in southern Peru. Gamarra has recently written
to Flores, with *infinite reserve*, that he will fulfil his promise as soon as La
Mar arrives in Guayaquil." " Here is good news for you "—he writes to
Urdaneta—" whereby we shall soon have peace or occupy Peru. I intend
to follow with 3,000 men to Piura to profit by the public spirit which is
very favourable to us and I am told that I should enter Lima without firing
a shot." To the same Urdaneta he had written on May 19th: " Within
three days I am leaving for the south to act in the military way according to
the circumstances. They write to me from Lima that if I come nearer to
Peru, my return there will be like that of Napoleon to France."

The Peruvians had played into his hands by backing out of the Girón
Convention. When the two Colombian commissioners arrived in Guayaquil
they were detained on board a warship and the Peruvian commandant of
the city suggested an armistice of forty days, while he received direct orders
from Lima as to whether he was to deliver Guayaquil to the Colombians
or not. La Mar had raised objections of a dubious value against the
Convention; one was that a number of Peruvian officers had been murdered
by Sucre's troops, which was only too true. When he returned to Piura
(covered by the Convention he now repudiated) he asked for men and money
to carry on the war at least to retain Guayaquil. This enabled Bolívar to
sound the trumpet call he had all along longed to hear. But his eagerness
to take Guayaquil in time for the changeover which he was expecting in
Peru made him launch a disastrous campaign in the flooded season. This
was sheer indifference to human suffering on his part. In his instructions
to Córdova, asking for more soldiers, he says coldly: " In Guayaquil many

deaths will occur before the city is taken, owing both to the climate and to the war." Both Sucre and Córdova were shocked. Mosquera had at last bitten into Bolívar's so far unshaken trust in Córdova. The young General was summoned to Quito where he arrived on April 16th, 1829, with his enemy and reporter Mosquera. Bolívar appointed Mosquera Chief of Staff, a post to which Córdova had every right. Disgruntled, he returned to Popayán, where he arrived on May 13th, 1829, and began negotiations with the Liberals, i.e. with Bolívar's enemies.

5

On June 1st, 1829, Bolívar was already in Ríobamba on his way to Guayaquil which he hoped to gain by parley or by force within the month. He then heard of the loss of the Peruvian frigate *Prueba*, destroyed by fire; which cheered him and encouraged him to go ahead with his military plans. But, as Sucre had warned, operations against Guayaquil in the rainy season were bound to be disastrous, for they made troop movements awkward and caused heavy casualties from sickness. The trends at work in Bolívar's mind are Peru, Empire, Dictatorship. Sucre's displeasure and Córdova's brewing revolt gain an impressive unity if they are considered in their mutual bearings. Bolívar's hurry to gain Guayaquil is due both to his desire to reconquer Peru and to his definite monarchist ambition. All this stands out in clear relief in the letters of Córdova to Henderson and in Henderson's reports to the Foreign Office. Córdova writes to Henderson (21.vi.29): " I have requested by the mail which departed yesterday my retirement from the service. I observe that the conduct of the Government is very contrary to public liberty. The whole is cunning, and intrigue, corruption and immorality. . . . H.E. thinks of marching on fortune,* and the anarchy and nullity into which Peru has fallen. He wishes to return there and to revenge himself well. But he runs much danger of being left without bread or a morsel." This letter, through the English of which can be read in Henderson's awkward translation Córdova's original Spanish, elicits from Henderson a comment which is important in that it shows how both men had till then remained partial to Bolívar. " I beg to draw your attention in particular to the latter, as from the great attachment of General Córdova to the Liberator, and his character of high principle, the course he has adopted is very surprising, and leads to the conclusion that all is not proceeding well, and that not only much corruption in general exists, but that the Liberator is prosecuting a dangerous game."

On June 27th, 1829, Córdova wrote again to Henderson: " I do not know what distrust I have of this war with Peru. I believe from a thousand anteceding circumstances that there is not frankness, and good faith on the part of General Bolívar. That he does not wish peace but to overturn that country, revenge himself on it, and govern it, if it were possible." Henderson forwarded this letter with a *private* despatch (14.vii.29) saying that Córdova's letter " shews that all the dispositions are making through

---

* Henderson translates literally from the Spanish *a la ventura*.

the proposed re-occupation of Guayaquil for carrying into effect the favourite object of General Bolívar, the invasion of Peru by Colombian troops. I have always apprised you that that was an unfortunate part of his policy—from it Colombia and Peru are at war—and although the general opinion and many circumstances opposed the immediate execution of his views, yet he never gave up the contemplation of that favourite purpose for one moment. It is a fair inference, even if the Peruvians had proceeded to the negotiation of a definitive treaty, that the unabated personal desire of General Bolívar to establish his ascendancy in the Perus, would have prevented any favourable result." Henderson insists again on his surprise at Córdova's new line, being " a most attached friend of General Bolívar ". He points out that Bolívar is determined to go to Lima which may cost him another attempt on his life; then reports that Caycedo has also asked to be retired and goes on to discuss the monarchy: " Many of the influential people are inclined to that system of government but they see danger in electing General Bolívar to the throne although that an attempt may be made by part of the Army to declare that individual Emperor. . . . General Sucre has suggested to the Liberator to resign, and that a British Prince should be invited to place himself on the throne. . . . When such generals as Sucre and Córdova begin to see that the policy of General Bolívar is inimical to the interests of the country . . . it is not to be wondered at that much concealed discontent prevails in other quarters. General Bolívar for the last twenty years has governed in South America according to his will, and the idea is current that it will be difficult or impossible for him to conform to any code of laws that does not invest him with a large share of power."

On August 5th, 1829, Henderson sent to the Foreign Office a *private* despatch particularly important. He enclosed a translation of the *Mirada a la América* (A Glance at America), " a pamphlet which has been printed at Cuenca and dictated by General Bolívar ". He explains: " It is calculated to put all South Americans in hostility with Colombia, but its main object is to pave the way for General Bolívar being either declared Emperor or President for life. The latter is the first point which he wishes to gain in the first instance. . . . The force that will be requisite to maintain such a political system, must eat up the scanty resources of the country. . . . Had the decree of the last Constitutional Congress—at which General Bolívar was so much incensed—to reduce the army to a moderate footing, been carried into effect and a peace maintained with Peru . . . there is no doubt that by this time a considerable remittance would have been made on account of the loan. As it is the country is totally impoverished by the marching and raising of troops. Agriculture is almost neglected, in consequence of the constant draining of its labourers for the army. And probably there is no country in the world where so many soldiers are lost by death, for as they have no tents on the march to protect them from the inclemency of the weather and as they are successively exposed to all the variety of climates peculiar to these regions . . . many sink under their sufferings. The armies of Colombia have always lost infinitely more men on these marches than in the combat. The last regiment which arrived here from the burning plains, 800 strong, has been reduced in a very short time to half of the number, ten and fifteen having died on a day. Thus it becomes necessary in order to sustain a campaign, like the present one, to drain the whole country of its peasantry." Henderson then quotes passages of a letter sent by Córdova to a friend in Bogotá, on July 5th, in which mention is already made of the *Glance at America* as " written in the office of H.E." It adds: " This will be printed in Cuenca, with the object of presenting the Government and State of the Republic in a picture of abomination the most horrible, that the Colombians may tremble at republican government and on their knees pray of H.E. to place the Crown on his head. H.E. wishes to conquer Peru for the purpose at least of revenging himself for personalities, if not to add it to Colombia and govern the whole with a military and despotic sceptre. . . . To comply with these orders, it is necessary to take by force in the Province of Neyva, in this department and the unfortunate south, mules, horses, cattle, and all without hope of any recompense to the proprietors."

Resuming his own views, Henderson goes on: " I am assured that much intrigue and government influence has been used where possible in the recent elections for the Congress, and the authorities began to circulate the notion of monarchy or presidency for life. At a public party, a few days since, the Prefect gave a toast and took the opportunity to declare that a vigorous Government must be stablized, and that General Bolívar must be at the head of it whether under the name of a kingdom, an Empire or Presidency for life. The toast was received very coolly and some of the New Granadine Generals, who were present, soon left the table. The President of the Council followed partially on the same subject, but being a timid man, he did not make any allusion to General Bolívar in the character of King, Emperor or President for Life. . . . One individual who was supposed to have made some observations inimical to the present Government was arrested and sent to Cuenca for trial, where he was acquitted. General Bolívar, nevertheless, fined him 10,000 dollars, for which his estate and cattle were seized and sold. . . . Luis Armero, brother to the Colombian agent expelled from Lima, arrived here yesterday, and I understand that he represents the whole country as being ripe for a revolt against the Liberator. General Sucre and General Córdova, he says, entertain the same sentiments. . . . Their popularity is unbounded from the Equator to Antioquia. . . . The people of New Granada say they may as well be under the King of Spain as be degraded and commanded by a Venezuelan faction."

6

Save in what concerned Sucre's stand, which is somewhat overdrawn, these reports of Henderson to his Government are borne out by Sucre's and by Bolívar's letters and even more so by Bolívar's actions. If another opinion, or a controversy, has been so far possible on those matters the fact is due to the many-sided character of Bolívar's letters, which permit many interpretations if they are not carefully read and collated. This character of his writings is in its turn due to at least three motives: as regards both Peru and monocracy he was at the same time determined in his will, but hesitating in his mind; he was by nature shifty and much addicted to concealing his game even from his closest friends; and the strategy he played all his life was that of accepting by force from others that which he was longing to grasp by himself. When these features of his character are borne in mind, his correspondence confirms Henderson's opinion. Bolívar was intent on wielding power over Great Colombia, Peru if possible, the whole South America if possible and even Mexico if possible, under an imperial authority of a monocratic form, with or without a Crown; and to that effect he was as ready to sacrifice the manhood and the wealth of his country and of the other countries as his model Napoleon had been in Europe. His shifty tactics, his denying that he wanted to be crowned and even that he wanted office, while working through all his friends for absolute personal power; and his constant assurances that he would never, never, never go to Peru . . . unless forced by a war, elicit nothing but attacks and accusations that he wants to be crowned as well as advice from his staunchest friends not to go to Peru. Is this not a sufficient proof that no one believed in his protestations any more?

On June 5th, 1829, La Fuente, on his way to the north in command of the third Peruvian division, expelled La Mar's government and temporarily took the title of Supreme Chief. He was acting for the triumvirate Gamarra-Santa Cruz-La Fuente, which was supposed to be friendly to Bolívar. La Mar and Gamarra were in Piura. On June 6th, a commission of officers brought La Mar a letter demanding his resignation. On June 9th, La Mar sailed for exile and death. On July 10th, Gamarra signed with the Colombians an armistice providing for the return of Guayaquil to Colombia. On July 21st, 1829, Bolívar occupied Guayaquil and received the visit of General Cerdeña, the Peruvian General who had commanded the garrison; on which he wrote to Páez these revealing words: " Cerdeña doubts that Peru will settle in the hands in which it is and is going to be; for it is believed that Gamarra will assume the presidency and also that he will last very little; so that in the end the Peruvians will have to call me. I told him I was resolved never to go to Peru, for I had too much to do in Colombia and I have had enough of power." Now, if that was so, he had said enough. Why then did he go on to add: " I beg this general to convey these ideas to my friends and enemies, and my absolute determination not to go for any reason unless the war forced me to it . . ." etc. Is he not proving his keen desire to influence public opinion in Peru, and therefore his secret design to go?

His deeds as usual belying his words, his good friends had to warn him. " Cerdeña tells you that La Fuente, Santa Cruz and Gamarra are your friends, and I am certain he is somewhat mistaken "—wrote Sucre to him (28.vii.29). " Of the first, I know nothing for or against; the second is a friend of naught but his own interests; the third is treacherous by nature and a worse enemy of yours than the bitterest Spaniard, but as he is low and vile, he will show himself your friend while he needs you." And Sucre repeats his " don't go to Peru ". In this as in everything, however, he was a wise empiricist rather than a dogmatic " liberal ". On July 14th, 1829, he had written to Bolívar these notable words: " From Bogotá they repeat to me that if you go to Peru Colombia is lost. I believe it also, and though I was opposed to the war, I think that if go you must, you had better go as a conqueror rather than be caught in the nets of perfidy. I believe it better to preserve an influence very much like a domination than to carry out any act of domination in that country." So Bolívar remained for months in Guayaquil, at the gates of Peru. On August 21st, 1829, he wrote to Soublette: " There will be a peace with Peru, where nowadays, the best opinion prevails in my favour. The government and our friends have written to me most satisfactorily through my aide-de-camp Demarquet, and we are awaiting their commissioners for the treaties; but there is by no means any the lesser need for the fleet to be sent to the Pacific, for these Peruvian gentlemen will keep their word while they are frightened, and we cannot maintain a big army in this country because it is ruined."

When he wrote these words, Bolívar was convalescent from a serious illness—an attack of black bile he calls it—which laid him prostrate for nearly a fortnight from August 3rd, 1829. These crises were but protests of his spare body torn asunder by the almost inhuman tensions which his fierce spirit forced it to bear. The two storms, the Peruvian and the monarchical, were then at their highest. On August 26th, 1829, he wrote to Páez: " We need nothing but a frigate now, for the Peruvians must give us back the small craft on signing the peace; let therefore the biggest be sent, but well equipped and soon." At last Peru appointed as its plenipotentiary Don José Larrea, a friend of Bolívar; and Colombia appointed Don Pedro Gual. They met on September 15th, 1829; and on September 22nd the treaty was signed. Sucre did not like it. He thought it was not clear, for in his *Bases* of Tarqui he had adopted for the frontiers those of 1809; while the new treaty took those of the year of independence which was 1810 for New Granada and 1820 for Peru. The treaty was certainly not as favourable to Colombia as the victorious party had the right to expect; but Bolívar himself provided the reason for this in a letter to Páez (13.ix.29): " We cannot stretch the thing out . . . for this country is in ruins and our troops are too numerous." Then, soon after the conclusion of the treaty, he left for Quito. Grave news from New Granada forced him to give up for the time being his ambitious designs on Peru.

CHAPTER XXV

A KING WITHOUT A CROWN

I

ON no subject was Bolívar more tortuous in word and deed than on that of the monarchy. We know why. Since his plan was to be offered the Crown and not to seize it, his attitude was not unlike that of Franklin Roosevelt during his second term, while public opinion half expected him to break with the tradition set by Washington and run for a third term. In a letter to Santa Cruz Bolívar wrote: " The Congress I have called will meet and will give us a strong government, according to the public spirit that prevails. . . . The form of Executive that will be adopted will be more vigorous than yours "; and then, these words which he wrote and later struck out: " Many are thinking of a hereditary government, but I oppose it with all my strength, because I do not want to bear all my life such an enormous weight to hand over afterwards to a descendant of mine." That he struck it out is no less significant than that he wrote it at all. His assurances, private and official, of his longing to leave public life for good, denied by his keen watch over his power, belong to the same tortuous tactics. They drew a frank reproach from Sucre (21.vii.29): " I do not know how to present to these gentlemen your idea of uniting all your friends in the south and in New Granada to fight against the demagogic faction, since in the same article you instruct me to announce to them that they are not to count on you for anything." Sucre, in fact, was not taken in by Bolívar's wiles. No one was. But he had a genuine respect and affection for Bolívar and he wrote to him straight enough, yet with tact. Answering one more of Bolívar's constant warnings that he meant to retire for good and all, he wrote (14.viii.29): " A time may come to silence your slanderers; but the best action now . . . is to constitute the country and to set its affairs on a stable and solid basis. Nothing else is worthy of you. To retire when the Republic is threatened by so many risks, merely in order to prove your disinterestedness, is a measure foreign to your character; and, to be candid, will be looked upon by the world as a mere trick, so that in the fray of parties, and when a thousand daggers may quarter the fatherland, you might be called back as the saviour and the conciliator." This was as straight a hint as could be expected from so faithful a man. By then, Bolívar had issued his pamphlet, *A Glance at America*, painting the continent in the gloomiest colours. " There is no good faith in America, neither between men nor between nations. Treaties are papers; constitutions, books; elections, fights; liberty, anarchy; and life a torment." And in his bitterness he practically condemns his own life work in words which mean nothing if they do not express a nostalgic regret for the Spanish days: " We lost our individual guarantees when, in order to obtain them perfect, we sacrificed our blood and our most precious pre-war possessions; and if we turn back our eyes to that time, who can deny that our rights were more respected ? " His conclusion was: " A Government strong enough to oppress ambition and protect liberty."

With his usual journalistic zest, Bolívar broadcast copies of his lucubration to his friends; and, imitating his favourite Voltaire, attributed it to " a friar who has a good deal of talent ". Sucre wrote to him (7.vi.29) that he had received three copies, " and I have had them circulated among all our friends here for very few copies have come ". This shows that Sucre was not averse to strong government, though he disliked Bolivar's arbitrary ways. Offered the command of the army in Bogotá, he refused (7.x.29): " If the outcome of Congress offered a normal working of public affairs and if you bind yourself to achieve a stable and definite régime, I shall serve you in any other capacity. I do not refuse to serve. What I try to do is to serve knowing the system and the purpose; for there has been neither a purpose nor a system for a long time, and I am a little tired and ill to work in a haphazard way." That was his stand. In this, however, as in the matter of Peru, Sucre is remarkably free from any dogmatism. " I shall always regret "—he writes in the same letter—" that in order to secure this inner peace and this steady progress, you should not have made use of your dictatorial power to grant Colombia a constitution that would have been backed by the army, which is with us the initiator of tumults against the laws. What the people want is repose and guarantees; for the rest, I do not think they would quarrel over principles or political abstractions from which the right of property and of security have suffered so much."

2

But Bolívar carried on his campaign, refusing with one hand what he demanded with the other. He wrote to Vergara from Buijó (13.vii.29), suggesting a division of the country. This was a tactical move, to frighten the military, whose power rested on the Union. If Congress does not feel strong enough, let the electoral colleges be consulted. (This odd proposal will reappear later.) If all this fails, bring in the Bolivian Constitution with a President for life and an hereditary Senate. Bolívar then lucidly argues against a foreign monarchy to succeed him, mostly owing to the poverty of the country. He writes to Sir Robert Wilson, the London M.P. and father of one of his aides-de-camp, as plain an admission of his monarchical faith as in the circumstances he could make (27.vii.29): " In the capital the question now discussed is how to strengthen and better the nature of the Government, and it is said and can almost be affirmed that the most favoured plan would be that of a government for life under my orders, and a prince to succeed me. It seems to me that the idea, though with advantages of its own, presents peculiar drawbacks. To begin with, I cannot go on ruling the country, for my physique is tired and my endurance almost exhausted. Then come the difficulties arising out of the choice of a successor, for it will not be easy to find one suitable for the needs of the country." He wrote to Urdaneta (30.vii.29) on urgent propaganda matters to defend

" their " position (Urdaneta was the leader of the monarchist group). He remained as thirsty as ever for public recognition and " glory ". The all but universal repulse his despotic ways had won for him in America and in Europe was—he says so himself—the cause of his illness during that summer. " It was due to the simultaneous outcry against me from one pole to the other "—and though he cannot bear the idea of giving up his position, he begins to devise in his own mind some means to compromise. He instructed O'Leary to air a proposal whereby a President would be appointed while he would remain as Generalissimo (21.viii.29). He puts it in an image worthy of his keen sense of humour: " I should be turning round and round the Government like a bull round his herd of cows." His plan, often imitated in later days by Spanish-American " strong men ", was to have the presidential chair kept warm for him by a man he could trust and control. His man was to be Sucre. " He will probably be my successor "—Bolívar wrote to Flores on December 5th, 1829; a plan the key to which may be found in a remark Bolívar once made to Santander (3.viii.22): " All grant him eminent qualities, but not energy." This design has humorously been described in Spanish America with the distich:

> Here's the President. The boss
> Lives over there, right across.

But though Bolívar saw in it both power and liberty (his two chief desires as the super-anarchist he was), he missed his third desire, " glory ". He is moved when Urdaneta writes that the people are coming back to him: " More than with any of your news I am pleased by that which you send me that the nation gives me back my aura as in the first days of my glory. May God grant, my friend, that you do not deceive yourself out of your desire to bring me back to life with the only element which you know could do it. But you say so, I believe you, and I begin to taste the nectar of my health."

The core of his attitude was a fierce personal ambition. But the body of it was his disillusion at the state of America. At this time, he professed to consider leaving America to her fate. His motives were typical of his mixed feelings: "to end his public life in a dignified manner ", and "to inspire confidence not only in Colombia and Peru, but in the other Spanish-American Republics, that he did not seek to remain in power ". He requested the captain of a French frigate, La Vestale, to convey him to Europe. Mosquera claims that it was he who made him give up the plan, painting the state of anarchy which his departure would precipitate; but that Córdova's rebellion so affected Bolívar that he returned to his first idea. If we are to believe Mosquera, Bolívar laid great store on his friendship with Marshal Davout, " a friend of his since 1805, when, as a young man, he had known him in Paris "; through whom he expected to be authorized by Charles X to live in the Little Trianon. The plan overlooked the fact that Davout had died in 1823; but the Napoleonic mania of Bolívar is patent. Mosquera goes on: " There he would occupy himself dictating his Memoirs, and he was to wait for me there in the autumn of 1830 so that I should take on this work, since I had begun it, and he said to me:

' Though I am not confined to exile, as Napoleon was, the desire to preserve my glory makes me leave my Fatherland, and in this voluntary exile you would be my Gourgaud or Montholon '." Mosquera left for Lima convinced that he would meet Bolívar in Europe the following year. But when Bolívar made plans for leaving public life, they never went beyond a kind of day-dreaming, and an enjoyment and contemplation of what public life would look like as his widow. " Dead ", he was alive; " absent " was for him but one of the forms of being present.

3

The chief problem for Bolívar was the anarchy let loose on the continent by the fall of the Spanish régime. Bolívar was led to present to his ministers a plan to put Spanish America under the protection of Great Britain. Though also purely tactical, this proposal reveals that, subconsciously, he was rebuilding the Spanish Empire in his mind: religion, monarchy, re-union to a European Crown—every element had returned except the Spanish name and nation, which his whole past had tabooed. Referring to the " demagogues ", the name he now gave to those who still wanted what he himself had professed to want in 1810, he says to Joaquín Mosquera (3.ix.29): " They want neither monarchies nor presidents for life still less an aristocracy. Why don't they drown themselves once for all in the noisy and merry ocean of anarchy ? That is very popular, and should, therefore, be the best; for, according to my maxim, the *sovereign must be infallible*." These evidently monarchical utterances express his true mind, not the papers he wrote to screen it so as to reinsure his popularity. To such a kind of *ad hoc* paper belongs the long letter he wrote to O'Leary (13.ix.29), arguing with his usual terseness and lucidity against the monarchy, though in favour of a strong presidency for life. This paper is often quoted as proof of Bolívar's republican views. But why should Bolívar have to explain his views in writing to the man who knew them best ? The letter is a piece of propaganda to be used by O'Leary, mostly in Venezuela, where Páez was arousing opinion against Bolívar on the ground that he wanted to have himself crowned. Bolívar himself reveals the game in a letter to Páez (Buga, 27.xii.29) in which, after saying how angry he had been with the placards posted against him in Caracas under the title GUERRA A LOS TIRANOS, he adds: " But I am content to know that the publication of my confidential letter to O'Leary has given the lie to my enemies." Bolívar pursued his plan with a steadiness of mind which his physical mobility concealed. It was the same plan he had put before the world in Angostura. It could be reduced to two words: personal power. So incapable was he of living without personal power that he used it as he breathed. Ignoring the Government in Bogotá, he issued in Guayaquil on his own authority a circular (31.viii.29) inviting the people to express directly their opinions on the Constitution and on the person of the Chief of State, and authorizing the electoral colleges to instruct their elected members of Congress how they were to vote thereon. His intention was to appeal to the people over the heads of their elected representatives. This circular, says Restrepo, was " for Colombia a deadly poison ".

" Monsieur Bresson and the Duke of Montebello arrived here last week " —Henderson reported to London (21.iv.29). " He was received by the President and the Council of Ministers with more distinction than was extended towards General Harrison the American Minister. The latter was received with very little ceremony." Bresson was severely blamed for this by his Foreign Secretary; for he had been sent as a mere agent and not as a regularly accredited envoy, and had ministerial but not royal letters. But apart from Bresson's own desire to shine, the difference was due to the fact that Harrison was a censorious republican, while Bresson was believed to have brought a Crown in his diplomatic bag and would appear to have hinted as much in his first talk with Montilla in Cartagena. Writing to his own Prime Minister (27.iv.29) Bolívar says: " It seems that M. Bresson brings very satisfactory intentions for Colombia and for me. General Urdaneta will have imparted to you what General Montilla reports on the matter." What Bresson's real instructions were, however, is not certain. In writing he was told nothing about the monarchy. " *Nous ne tarderons pas à apprendre que la Colombie s'est constituée, comme le Mexique, en République Fédérale* "—he is told. Ostensibly he is sent to keep his eyes open and to report not merely on Colombia but on every other Spanish-American country as well. But in one of his reports, as it became evident that the monarchist plan would fail, Bresson wrote to his Foreign Secretary: " *V.E. aura remarqué que dans mes communications j'étais resté en deçà de mes instructions verbales.*" There were, therefore, verbal instructions, and precisely on this point; and they were so secret that in two State papers prepared for the internal use of the French Foreign Office, no mention is made of them and the matter is dealt with as if Bresson had acted spontaneously. The most likely (but by no means proved) form the events must have taken is that Bresson had verbal instructions to endeavour to place a French prince on the throne in Bogotá on the understanding that, were he to fail, he would have to take all the blame.

4

This lends a special interest to Bresson's opinion on Bolívar, which he began to form early. From Washington, on his way to Bogotá, he wrote a revealing report to the French Foreign Secretary (24.xi.28), based on documents *d'une authenticité incontestable*, which he consulted there. According to these documents " Bolívar, thirsty for power, works only for himself. Bonaparte is his model; war is his element;* impatient at every contradiction, ardent, impetuous, he has been for so long exclusively at the head of affairs, he has, unaided, accomplished such big things, that his confidence in himself knows no bounds, and such opposition as is natural

* This was in keeping with Bolívar's own opinion. " My element is war," he wrote to Urdaneta.

under a free government appears in his eyes as a kind of military insubordination to be put down forthwith. Everything around him breathes the spirit of despotism. . . . His hypocrisy is as deep as his ambition. He has often resigned only in order to be offered power again, to gain the glory of refusing it and make his authority thrive on the security his simulated moderation had fostered. . . ." Bresson, however, who was a convinced Bolivarist, reserved his own judgment, and even adds that Bolívar's very defects might be turned to good account.

From New Orleans, he wrote again (6.i.29): " This ambition he is credited with would be a powerful spring to use. In my opinion, either we must back him in his scheme, encourage him thereto, enter into it with him, or we must give up the idea of ever seeing America happy and peaceful. . . . After talking with Sr. Santa María and Mr. Wilson, I am practically certain that he harbours designs on Mexico."

On landing in La Guaira, Bresson, struck by the attitude he found in Venezuela, reported to Paris (19.ii.29): " It is no longer a matter of dreaming of a vast Empire, or of fancying himself deciding upon the affairs of Guatimala [sic] or Mexico . . . he will have enough to do to keep his hold on Colombia." Bresson arrived in Bogotá on April 16th and was received on the 19th. He reported that to prevent " another Ocaña ", every measure had been taken " to ensure the election of the candidates previously designated by the Government ". On May 14th he was already able to report on the monarchy. He ascribed to García del Río the initiative of the scheme, on which the Government were at work with the backing of Urdaneta, Montilla, Sucre and Flores; quoting then Bolívar's paragraph about abiding by whatever decision Congress would take, Bresson adds: " Does this mean that he would accept the Crown ? It is certain that he would first refuse, resist for long, write long letters, which would be ostentatiously circulated and published." Pointing out how dependent Bolívar was on the praise and esteem of European and American liberals, " who had been the first to utter and belaud his name ", Bresson adds: " Should he allow his friends' plans to develop (and I find it hard to believe that he did not know them beforehand, though I am told that it is not so), should he not put a stop to them at once . . . he will, in the end, accept the throne which is offered to him. As for the heir, he would be a French Prince; but the English must not be told."

" Show this gentleman the immense pleasure I have at his coming and at the French Government's attitude towards us ", Bolívar wrote to Castillo Rada (19.v.29). Under such a powerful impulse, the monarchical plans went ahead and in Bogotá a meeting of influential civil, military and ecclesiastical personalities resolved to foster the idea in public opinion (30.vi.29). Those who, like Restrepo, endeavour to screen Bolívar from this movement sin both against historical truth and against that Bolívar whom they naïvely endeavour to protect. Restrepo himself contradicts his own statements and reveals the truth when he writes: " There was in Bolívar's mind a hard struggle between his intimate convictions on the system that speculatively he thought best for Colombia and the one he deemed possible to establish following the stream of the republican opinions deeply rooted and widespread among its inhabitants." That is the truth. Bolívar was at that time a monarchist who lacked the courage of his opinions. Had he not been a monarchist he would have been a fool. Harrison, for instance, was a well-meaning, honest republican fool; and Bresson was right, and so were the members of the Government who wanted Bolívar to assume royal powers, and so was Bolívar in thinking he ought to take them; though he was wrong in not daring. For what was the picture ? Páez, in Venezuela; Montilla, on the coast; Flores, in the south; Urdaneta, in Cundinamarca—what were they but four kings, indeed, four Czars ? It is, to say the least, naïve to be horrified at the idea that Bolívar could crown himself king or assume a monarchist position when he was ruling as an uncrowned, unrestrained dictator over and through four despotic satraps. The fact is that, at the time, a constitutional monarchy in Colombia would have meant an immense progress on the actual political life of the country, and every man endowed with both public spirit and common sense was bound to be a monarchist in those days.

5

The Government was unanimously for a constitutional monarchy, and, confronted by Bolívar with a plan for turning Colombia into a British protectorate, they seized their opportunity. Such was, of course, Bolívar's intention in presenting his plan. Throughout his life, Bolívar nearly always acted according to this oblique pattern: he walked straight in one direction so as to provoke a reaction in quite a different one, which was that on which his mind was really set. Why should Bolívar put forward a British protectorate, the absurdity of which was bound to be patent for a mind even much less penetrating than his ? Merely to call forth this reaction: " Rather than that, a monarchy under Bolívar." His ministers were fully aware of this game. They began turning down the scheme (25.v.29); but Bolívar insisted (6.vii.29) and argued that Great Britain should be chosen as the protecting power because Spanish America owed her two hundred million pesos.

By then, Vergara, the Foreign Secretary, had been repeatedly assured by Bresson that France would not recognize Colombia unless a stable régime was set up under Bolívar. Without, by the way, anyone devoting a thought to the Monroe Doctrine, the Council of Ministers took Bresson's hint. Bresson was sceptical when told that Bolívar would not suffer himself to be crowned, and shrewdly suspected a *mot d'ordre*. He soon began to notice Bolívar's duplicity. After explaining the Monarchist plan, he reports (6.vi.29): " The Liberator enters into all these views; he says that the sight of Spanish America must have convinced the whole world that the Republic was but mere anarchy." Later, he reported that, though Bolívar would not answer his Ministers in writing on their proposals, Urdaneta's messenger, sent to put them before Bolívar, came back reporting " all goes well ". And Bresson comments: " What are we to conclude from this silence? . . . At any rate, that Bolívar does not disapprove of what is being prepared." Still, he walks warily, for he mistrusts Bolívar.

At this stage, his mistrust was reinforced from an unexpected quarter. Enters Manuela Sáenz. " She has found here "—Bresson reports (11.vii.29) —" an amiable man she had frequented in Lima. . . . This young man has captivated her and enjoys her confidence." Through this channel, Bresson is able to report to his Government Bolívar's innermost thoughts. " He likes to compare his deeds with those of Alexander, Caesar and Bonaparte; and without hesitation, rates himself above them. . . . He thinks very little of Washington, and his aversion for North Americans comes, in part, from their obstinacy in comparing him with this somewhat pale hero of their revolution. Ambition absorbs every other feeling in him: he wants to command, to govern without fetters, constraint or law; he wants Colombia to be fully his; to be indispensable; and the thought that, when he is gone, all must fall into confusion, does not displease him. Still, he does not throw off the mask of patriotism. . . . He wants but one big figure to be seen in America. He will not give up his ambition to rule over Peru and Bolivia. Immense Colombia is too small for him." Even so, Bresson is in no hurry to condemn the man who is, for him, the only possible ruler of Spanish America.

6

Bresson was not taken in by mere texts. Reporting on two letters received by Castillo and Urdaneta, in the first of which Bolívar insisted on his pessimism and his longing to retire, the shrewd Frenchman writes (18.vii.29): " I must own that when comparing the style of these two letters, sent the same day to two men whose relations with him differ so much, when I bear in mind that, of this deep concern which fills his letter to Sr. Castillo not even a trace appears in his letter to General Urdaneta, into whose faithful heart it should more naturally pour itself, I cannot but suspect some dissimulation. . . . I deeply regret that General Bolívar is not here. . . . Hitherto, he has played his part before an audience of too poor a moral order and too alien to the things of the world. He knows exactly the thoughts and the gestures that will impress them. A European would see through it easily."

Urdaneta told Bresson (27.vii.29) that " he considered himself in possession of the Liberator's assent for his monarchical plans " on the strength of a letter in which Bolívar declared himself ready " to co-operate with them " and " to abide by the decision of the Congress ". " The Liberator "—adds Bresson in his report—" is under the sway of shyness. He is seeking to cloud his thoughts and to ward off others from his secret wishes." Bresson grew impatient, and so did Urdaneta and Castillo, who undertook to " urge Bolívar to conquer what he calls his delicacy and to express himself in positive terms about himself and about the French Prince desired as his successor ".

At last (28.viii.29) Bresson was able to report on an answer, shown to him by Vergara: " He does not believe that, in the present circumstances, a Prince would be flattered by the offer; nor that the country would be ready for a monarchy; but he thinks that a President for life and a hereditary Senate might collect and create the monarchical elements calculated to prepare the future accession of a Prince of the Royal Blood. Furthermore, Generals Flores and Mosquera have just sent an express to General Urdaneta to inform him that General Bolívar, urged to declare his intentions without obscurity, declared to them that he would yield to the wishes of the country and accept the Presidency for life, but that in order to ensure the future it was indispensable to set up a Hereditary Senate and, in agreement with a European Power, to designate a Prince as his successor. Generals Flores, Sucre, Mosquera, put pressure on Urdaneta to proceed with the plan and promise him a devoted army in the south. A similar assurance comes from Venezuela, where General Páez . . . protests that he will co-operate with all his forces. . . . The Administration thinks that General Bolívar's letter and General Flores' and Mosquera's reports empower it to take more decisive steps towards France. . . . So Castillo is drafting a Constitution on the bases of a *President for life*, a *Senate at least for life*, *appointed by the President, etc.* It is to be published as a means for sounding public opinion. General Bolívar having now declared his views, we [i.e. the French Government] must expect an official letter any day." This report is final and puts beyond doubt what any impartial and well-informed student of those days could have realized without it: Bolívar was a monarchist, indeed, the secret promoter of the monarchy in his country.

CHAPTER XXVI

A CROWN WITHOUT A KING

I

BRESSON remains baffled by Bolívar's character, though every day more persuaded by those who see in him a Caesarian type, yet still favourable to him as the only outstanding man in Spanish America. " This extraordinary man appears to me under so many different lights that trust and fear follow each other in my mind. . . . It cannot be doubted that his ambition is extreme. Next to much greatness, one often meets with pettiness. He has a blind confidence in his own powers, and yet his actions are hall-marked by indecision and hesitancy. He will stall before his wisest plans for vain personal considerations, for fear of a newspaper article. He seeks power, accepts it, yet wants to come out at the head of those who protest." Then Bresson reports to Paris the confidences which Heres, Bolívar's right-hand man in Peru, had made to García del Río, and which evidently this other follower of Bolívar had handed on to him. They differ in nothing from the portrait Bresson had penned in Washington after hearing one of Bolívar's enemies. " He will accept no yoke; will never govern within any laws " and so forth.

This documentary background shatters the endeavours of Restrepo and others to screen Bolívar from any responsibility in the monarchical intrigue. Restrepo's own correspondence belies the attempt. He informed Bolívar of the plan (8.iv.29): " There are difficulties in the way of this system, but we do not think them unsurmountable counting with your backing and with the army "; to which Bolívar made answer (Quito, 6.v.29): " I am in full agreement with you in that it is extremely necessary to bring about a change in the constitutional system in the once Spanish America, so that it consolidates itself; and I also believe that, although there are difficulties, they are not unsurmountable." Then Restrepo again (8.vi.29): " I am glad that you agree with the necessity to change constitutional forms. . . . The slightly difficult point is the House which will succeed you, the family of which must perpetuate itself on the throne by succession. . . . It seems that we, your friends, should bring forward the scheme and that you should remain outwardly a stranger to it, though without opposing it "—which is exactly the comedy they all were playing. Bolívar wrote to Castillo (5.viii.29) putting all the arguments that could be adduced against the scheme, yet ending with an assurance that he would by no means oppose it, rather would he be glad to help if he could count on the co-operation of Britain and France. Until he knew about *that*, he declared, he would have to reserve his opinion. By the beginning of September it was plain that the Government would have a comfortable majority in the coming Congress, and that even so striking a departure as the one they were contemplating would meet with approval. So a Note was prepared for the Ministers of

France and Great Britain (3.ix.29), expounding the plan. The Note must be studied in the French files. Bresson forwarded it (6.ix.29) both in its original Spanish and in its French translation. After describing at length the situation of Colombia, the official Note went on to say: " H.E. gathers the suffrages of all; he is the only man capable of safeguarding union and of consolidating a government, and he must of necessity be entrusted with the ruling of Colombia during his lifetime, not with the title of monarch, which neither the Congress would give him nor would he accept, but with that of *Libertador* which is for H.E. a glorious property. His successor might decorate himself with that name, and this successor, should the course of time throw up no circumstance thereagainst, would be sought in one of the royal families of Europe and probably in that of France, with whom for many reasons it is advisable for Colombia to make her relations closer. Such is in all its scope the plan of the Council of Ministers. In order to conceive it, the Council has not counted on the express opinion of the *Libertador*, nor could it be possible for H.E., who has so much dignity in his ways, to give it in these terms; all the Council of Ministers holds from H.E. is a promise that he will uphold every decision of Congress . . . and it most likely that Congress will declare its agreement with such a system of government." The Council of Ministers went on to express fears lest the United States might seek to oppose the plan; and concluded that success required eventual help from Europe, especially " from the Government of France, since it is interested in fostering the propagation of monarchical principles ".

Bresson sent this Note on to Paris with invaluable comments of his own. He emphasized that it was no longer a sudden passage from a republic to a monarchy; but a subtler idea: " The Constitution suggested, which I have seen, is more or less ours without the name of King." Everything will be done, he explains, with and under Bolívar. " To-day the co-operation of Bolívar is certain and we are told in positive terms that Congress will not offer him the Crown and that he would not accept it were it offered. Moreover not a word is said about a loan or any financial help. This would, nevertheless, be a consequence on which we ought to count. The Minister has put forward as a probability that this future monarch would be chosen in the royal family of France. But this is a matter agreed in advance, and it was natural that he should not expressly present a choice which it is in the jurisdiction of Congress to make and which it would make subject to the good pleasure of H.M.'s Government. The Minister could no more tell me without circumlocutions that the Government was acting in full agreement with General Bolívar. The more or less real susceptibility and delicacy of the Liberator on the question of his personal aggrandizement had to be spared and he has never consented to see expressed in writing any assurance about his foreknowledge or his co-operation in this combination which consolidates his power. But I know, beyond all doubt, that *he knows in advance and co-operates*; and I affirm it to Y.E. It is to be presumed, moreover, that his ambition would be satisfied with these proposals and arrangements and that he would work in good faith and in agreement with H.M.'s

Government to the full development of the plan which is proposed to us. So high a connection would restrain him inevitably always within fair limits. It has been agreed between the Minister of Foreign Relations and myself that the English Government would only be informed of that part of this communication which bears on the proposed change in the form of government and for which the Colombian Government also is requesting the approval of H.B.M. . . . the English *Chargé d'Affaires* will therefore be kept in ignorance of the views of the Colombian Government on the successor and on the request for a guarantee and a protection addressed to the Government of H.M."

2

The French Ministry of Foreign Affairs wrote to Bresson in a cool vein (29.viii.29), blaming him for his too ostentatious presentation. As for the monarchical scheme: " The Government of the King is resolved to remain outside it. We are by no means seduced by the overtures which are made to us, and . . . we shall feel no regret were they made to another Government." The French Government disliked the loan of twenty million pesos which Colombia expected. Bresson was instructed to leave Bogotá. How far this was genuine or a screen to cover more secret action under verbal instructions, it is hard to say. At any rate, Bresson decided to stay on when the Government officially presented to him their proposal for a monarchy with French help; and in his covering despatch on this proposal, gave highly suspicious reasons for his decision to stay. " It would mean giving up a work raised with the utmost care and which I should not be able to begin again elsewhere. . . . The events which are taking place here and which will soon transpire in the whole of America, and the part which I shall be made to play in them, make me perhaps less fit to fulfil my mission in other States of this continent." He then reveals a detail which proves how closely he was collaborating with Bolívar's Government in the march of affairs. It is he who underlines: " Congress will assemble on January 2nd. *But it is understood between the Government and myself that the two first months will be wasted in deliberations of pure form and that essential questions will be adjourned until H.M.'s Government has made known its intentions.*"

The British Minister, Campbell, though not very clever, was no fool, and he guessed or suspected that the Frenchman had kept secrets from him. It seems, moreover, that Urdaneta had informed Páez of what was afoot, possibly in too great a detail; and Páez whose game was personal, told the story to Admiral Fleming, who lost no time in sending Campbell a stiff letter. By the frankness with which he showed Bresson all his own papers, Campbell had even reduced his colleague to a state of embarrassment which the Frenchman honestly avows in one of his despatches. Campbell went so far as to mutter something about bringing in " *la maison de Bavière, qui n'éveillerait aucune jalousie* ". His suspicions were heightened when Bresson announced that the Duke of Montebello had suddenly to leave for

Paris " for family reasons ". He did not believe it and asked to call on Bresson, who was embarrassed, for in fact he was sending Montebello with the secret Note, his long despatch above quoted, and verbal reports which have left no trace. The atmosphere in which these movements took place is suggested by a report published in the *Royal Gazette* of Jamaica: " It was whispered at Maracaibo that the mission of the Duke of Montabello [*sic*] from the Court of Versailles to Bogotá was to negotiate a marriage between a French Princess and Bolívar, on condition that he would accept a Crown to place him in a condition to form an alliance with the house of Bourbon. It was reported that Bolívar had yielded to these terms." Whatever the truth or fancy behind these rumours, Urdaneta gave a farewell banquet to Montebello, and, in the presence of Bresson, Urdaneta's son drank the health of Simon I, Emperor of Peru. That was the way they saw Bolívar's future: Field Marshals, dukes and earls; but Bresson saw it in a different light: " I kept silent on the immense advantages of our taking possession of the whole world which gives itself to us."

3

A few weeks go by during which Bresson sends various reports on the scheme. One of the most valuable is, that Sucre favours the plot. The generally accepted view was that Sucre had maintained throughout a strict republican attitude. Bresson, however, reports (29.xi.29) that Sucre, having opened the official despatches passing through his hands for Bolívar, " enters with warmth in all the views of the Government and offers his pressing support ". This can hardly be dismissed as a misreading of Sucre's opinion by Bresson's informant, Vergara. Moreover, Sucre, as will be seen anon, spoke on the matter directly and in unmistakable terms to Bresson. Trouble, however, began to come to the surface soon. Bresson is rightly worried about Páez, and realizes the gravity of Córdova's rising. There were two parties among the generals; those who expected advancement from a monarchy under Bolívar; and those who were either too ambitious, like Páez, or too disgruntled, like Córdova, to hold any hopes from the scheme. Córdova's rebellion was evidently that of an ambitious man. Though he covered it with liberal principles, the impulse was pretorian. Bolívar, who was, of course, as pretorian as any of them, made a bad slip. He sent a cryptically worded letter to a Colonel Jiménez, then under Córdova, urging him to " use his sword " to cut any attempt at insurrection from any man of any grade. Jiménez had risen from the ranks and could not read. The letter was read to him and it reached Córdova's ears. Bolívar wrote to Córdova an involved and not very convincing explanation. Córdova was already busy with his *pronunciamiento*, for he wrote to Santander about it (7.vii.29). Bolívar appointed him Minister of the Navy (13.vii.29). As there was no Navy, Córdova felt insulted. Bolívar made an eleventh-hour attempt (28.ix.29) to win him over by sending him as Minister to Holland. By then, Córdova had already come out or rather been forced into the open. He issued a fiery proclamation in Medellín

(14.ix.29), and a Manifesto (16.ix.29) ending in the usual: " A holy cause unites us: to conquer power in order to put it under the safeguard of the law."

When the news of the *pronunciamiento* reached Bogotá (26.ix.29), General Rafael Urdaneta reacted vigorously and sent 800 seasoned troops under O'Leary, now a general. He was taking no risks. Córdova had but few and untrained men and little following. While O'Leary marched vigorously, Castillo published anonymously a counter-manifesto (25.x.29), indignantly defending Bolívar against Córdova's accusations, most of all against that of having " exiled religion from this world to the next ". This shows the hold religion had on the people twenty years after their liberation. As for their liberators, the force sent by Urdaneta to quell the rebellion of Córdova against the Liberator in Chief was commanded by the Irishman O'Leary, the Piedmontese Carlo Castelli, the Englishman Thomas Murray, the Irishman Richard Crofton, the Irishmen Carr, Hand, etc. With these forces O'Leary left Bogotá (2.x.29) for Honda whence by the Magdalena and Nare rivers, they penetrated into a difficult marshy and malarial land. Córdova was in his element and, though with but few men, could have resisted for long. Confident in his strength, O'Leary invited him to a parley on generous terms; but, fearing a trap, Córdova rejected every compromise unless based on a return to the Cúcuta Constitution—which O'Leary could not accept; let alone the fact that his intention (as revealed by Urdaneta to Bolívar) was merely to buy time for the movements of his troops. But he also succeeded in winning over one of Córdova's seconds, thanks to whom he penetrated into the otherwise strong position Córdova occupied in El Santuario. Córdova was lost from the beginning. He fought desperately but fell badly wounded. Lying on the ground in a field hospital in a hut, he was murdered by the Irishman Rupert Hand by order of O'Leary (17.x.29).

4

There was one man in Bogotá for whom Córdova's rebellion spelt disaster: James Henderson, the British Consul General, and the father of that Fanny who, at thirteen, had conquered the conqueror of Ayacucho. Bresson held a poor opinion of him, and reported to his Government that Great Britain showed her disdain towards the American Republics by the quality of the men she sent there to represent her. Henderson had been aware of Córdova's plans for weeks, for Córdova mentioned them in his letters. Bolívar had been aware of this fact because Urdaneta opened Córdova's letters to Henderson and to Fanny. Henderson wrote an overwhelmed letter to Lord Aberdeen (7.x.29), explaining how, though he knew much and was glad to receive Córdova's confidences so as to inform his Government, he had never meddled in Colombia's internal affairs. He was suspected by the Government, he explained, and the first intelligence of it had come to him through the new American Minister, Thomas Moore. The full flavour of this revelation can only be appreciated in conjunction with another revelation Bresson made to his Government. " Y.E. will doubt no more than I do when I add, *but as a fact which has been entrusted to me under an oath and which I must hold secret*, that the Colombian Government had its first information [of Henderson's alleged meddling] from Mr. Moore himself, to whom the correspondence and the conversations of General Harrison had revealed everything." The trio Henderson, Harrison, Torrens were suspected of sharing in a plot to murder the monarchist leaders, including Bresson; and their agent and spy was supposed to be the Danish Jew Leidersdorf, the representative of the firm of Goldschmidt, who lived in Torrens' house. When Campbell, the British Minister, was summoned by Vergara over this business, he was refused the documents proving Henderson's guilt on the ground that " this latter evidence was of such a nature as to prevent the exhibition of it ". Obviously Vergara could not show the copies of Córdova's letters Urdaneta had been reading, nor give Moore away. O'Leary and his aide-de-camp Carr had been the promoters of the whole intrigue. Henderson, Harrison and Torrens were expelled; but this high-handed action came from the two hotheads of the Ministry, Urdaneta and Vergara; the other Ministers were against such a step, and Castillo had even threatened to resign. Poor Henderson, ill defended by the weak and inept Campbell, had to sell his property and prepare to depart within three days (13.x.29), only to find that the Government tacitly withdrew the expulsion order; and he had the satisfaction of forwarding to Lord Aberdeen an official invitation sent him for a ball in honour of St. Simon (October 28th) signed by the very Urdaneta who had expelled him a fortnight earlier. Urdaneta went so far as to accuse Moore of having instigated the whole intrigue and gave Henderson a letter to that effect. Henderson undoubtedly believed it; but not Bolívar, and in a letter he wrote to Urdaneta much later (6.xi.30), he seems embarrassed, almost inclined to believe that Urdaneta had lied in writing, and still calls Henderson " that Blackguard ".

5

Córdova's insurrection forced Bolívar to alter his residence and possibly also his views. On October 22nd, 1829, he was already in Quito, on his way to Bogotá. This was much against the grain, for his heart was still set on Peru. " I had meant to send Sucre northward to conduct operations " —he wrote to Urdaneta (22.x.29), not having yet heard of Córdova's defeat and death five days earlier—" while I remain here to await the ratification of the peace and to have it carried out according to its terms." The hope of an opportunity to go to Peru is clear. But Sucre, he explains twice in this letter, was reluctant to take command against Córdova and so he decided to go north himself. He received then the visit of Colonel Austria, sent by Páez to find out Bolívar's political views. Páez was preparing to rebel against Bolívar and was angling for a pretext. Bolívar answered in his usual canny way that he would stand by Congress. The secret instructions he had drafted for Congress, revealed by Córdova in a Proclamation, included a President for Life with powers to appoint a successor and to oppose an absolute veto to the Legislative; a Vice-President with powers to be defined by the President; Secretaries of State responsible to the President; a Senate for life and hereditary, to be first appointed by the President; a house of representatives elected among persons with a capital of 6,000 pesos, to meet every second year and examine laws prepared by the President; and a judiciary appointed by the President and with powers defined by him.

Bolívar was therefore thinking of a monocracy with strong personal powers. As for the Crown, a letter he received from Córdova (Medellín, 21.ix.29) must have impressed him deeply. Colonel Austria's mission from Páez frightened him. He had always been ready to panic on this issue, as shown by a curious letter to Urdaneta (13.vii.29): " As for the plan for a monarchy, there is no man; for neither I nor any European Prince wants to ascend a royal scaffold; and were I to forget what I once said in Bolivia, I have beside me Iturbide [the son of the executed Emperor, now his aide-de-camp] to remind me every day. I am telling you because, though you are the most compromised, you still have a way out. If you do not want to go abroad, go to Caracas. . . . If you do want to go abroad, I shall offer you half of what I possess, and count on this as infallible." A final proof that Urdaneta was acting for him as the head of the monarchist faction. Bresson informed his Government that " on the 20th at Popayán, he [Bolívar] found himself surrounded by men who, by conviction or by self-interest, were unfavourable to the administration, and the first news of the attitude of Venezuela reached him ". Fear of Páez and fear of losing his liberal glory drove him then to betray his friends.

6

But he was so secretive and involved that simultaneous and authentic documents bearing on the same matter must be quoted. Don Manuel José Mosquera, father of his aide-de-camp Tomás Cipriano and of his successor as President, Joaquín, wrote from Popayán (22.xi.24): " The *Libertador* arrived yesterday; he is in a very good mood, for, as he has said confidentially, England offers her support for a government as proposed in the *Fourth Meditation*." This was a pamphlet by Bolívar's chief monarchist propaganda agent, García del Río. On the same day, Bolívar wrote to Urdaneta: " With regard to the business engaged with the governments of France and England, I believe we have exposed ourselves too much, and the affair is very dangerous and inevitable. We must therefore advance no further and allow Congress to do its duty as it thinks fit. Everything else means to compromise ourselves too much. I say so to Vergara officially since they have informed me officially." This last idea is more clearly expressed in the letter to Vergara: " I felt compelled to take such a step because you have compromised me officially." On December 13th, 1829, Bresson reported: " A letter from the *Libertador* has thrown the Council into confusion and uneasiness. He says that in so acting he wishes to give the lie to his enemies. The most beautiful lie to his enemies would be to organize his country and not to call down on it all the disasters he is going to do . . . as he is a man who yields to the first promptings, of great inconsequence and mobility, he will think and act in a wholly different way." Meanwhile Bolívar had his secretary write to his Ministers: " H.E. instructs me to protest and I do protest in his name before the Council that he will not recognize as an act of his anything but submission as a citizen to the Government defined by the constitutional Congress. H.E. does recognize and admire the patriotic effort and heroic valour of the Council in attacking for the good of the Republic such a risky venture, entering into the most dangerous negotiations . . . therefore H.E. instructs me to thank the Council for this sacrifice, which, were it to meet with no satisfactory end, might be the cause of the most cruel exposure for the members of the Council."—" When the reading of this note was over "—writes Restrepo, one of the Ministers—" the feeling in the Council was unanimous: indignation."

It is useless to gloss over this betrayal. " His way of acting is a puzzle to everybody "—Bresson reported on the 20th.—" He seems the prey of a thousand feelings and of a thousand contradictory schemes. His ideas, his orders of the morrow, resemble in nothing those of the eve. Everything in him is uncertainty and contradiction. Weakness follows energy, waking up follows sleepiness; one might believe oneself in the presence of the agony of a great soul. A noble, struggling intelligence is becoming extinct; his influence, his popularity, his reputation suffer therefrom. The members of the Government are at a loss what to do next. General Bolívar had encouraged them in their steps towards France and England. He had allowed them to be compromised. His letter to Colonel Campbell proves it; and suddenly, at the first popular outcry, he leaves them in the lurch. This is tantamount not only to mocking them but to mocking also the powers whose help had been requested. Even though he might implore it again, he has lost the right to be listened to." In a later despatch he analysed Bolívar's Note with his usual shrewdness. On January 11th, he reports: " The Foreign Secretary has announced to me that immediately after the *Libertador's* return the present administration would retire, that it would thus yield to the opinion of the moment; but that it remained convinced that the country would only be saved through that scheme which it had meditated and which would bring forth its fruit in the future. General Sucre expressed himself yesterday in the same terms."

CHAPTER XXVII

THE LAST RESIGNATION

I

BOLÍVAR had been forced to disown in public a movement which he was leading in private, partly by the liberal reaction he sensed in Popayán, but mostly by the revolt of Venezuela against his authority. Behind Venezuela was Páez. He had never been Bolívar's friend. He was as ambitious as Bolívar, but lacked the magnanimity and the intellect which justified, qualified, and restrained Bolívar's ambition. In their relationship, Bolívar had always been the more generous, the more reasonable, possibly also the more afraid of a break. But his advances had never conquered the core of enmity hidden under Páez' acceptance of his friendship, due to Páez' determination to get rid of him and to rule Venezuela as an absolute lord. Nor was Bolívar deceived, for though he was always significantly careful not to commit to paper any adverse opinion on his chief adversary, Manuela Sáenz revealed his inner thoughts when, at a time of outward harmony between the two men, she wrote to Bolívar (28.iii.28): " May God grant that all these wicked people such as Paula [Santander], Padilla, Páez may die, and of this last one, one should always expect something." She was right. Páez was a single-minded man, unfettered by any scruple in the pursuit of his aim. He had been the first to suggest to Bolívar to have himself crowned; but now that he saw Bolívar tempted and a definite scheme afoot, he saw his opportunity: he would rally against Bolívar all the republican forces of the country.

Páez was by no means popular, but he was powerful; and he found ready lieutenants in the men Bolívar had left behind, as he rose beyond Venezuela to continental majesty—Mariño, Soublette, Bermúdez and the rest. The collapse of the old régime, in particular of the institutions of local government known as *cabildos*, had left the country at the mercy of the officers of the Executive, military commanders, prefects, chiefs of police, decorative names of practically unlimited army bosses. As military commander in Venezuela, Páez was omnipotent, and the writ of the Colombian Government did not run in his territory. His *Reglamento de Corregidores*, writes Posada Gutiérrez, " reduced to naught the municipal régime respected even under the colonial government "; he ought to have said, created under the Spanish régime. Páez had organized an omnipresent police, " which penetrated "—says Restrepo—" to the most hidden huts of the peasants "; and though it is likely that this police had its good sides, it was bound to arouse resentment, being commanded by the ferocious Arizmendi who exacted passports and " one hundred formalities for anyone to be able to move in any direction, to dispose of his own property, to sow his own fields or raise his own cattle ". A swarm of officials preyed on town and country people; the monopoly of meat organized by Páez secured him a good price for his cattle; and he saw to it that the press was gagged to prevent any criticism.   As, in theory, his powers were delegated from the dictatorial powers conferred on Bolívar, when the Cúcuta Constitution had been abrogated, Páez was able to throw the odium of the situation on Bolívar, while gathering all the political harvest for himself.

Such was the position when Córdova rebelled against Bolívar.   Córdova wrote for help to Páez (18.ix.29), whom he declared capable of having liberated Venezuela by himself, while Bolívar could not have done it without Páez: " And since it is not possible that Y.E. wants to be rewarded for your heroism, your sacrifices and your triumphs with the degrading title of vassal of a monarch, we all trust that Y.E., ignoring General Bolívar's arbitrary government, will put yourself at the head of the free men of those departments, establish relations with me and destroy despotism for ever." Páez would smile at the premises and at the language of this letter, but not at its conclusion.   To have Bolívar's forces busy in distant Popayán afforded him an admirable opportunity which he was quick to seize.   The walls of Caracas were plastered with placards violently attacking Bolívar's despotism and his intention to crown himself a monarch (18.x.28).   Thereupon, Bolívar's friends published his letter to O'Leary, in which he declared himself opposed to a monarchy, and repeated his desire to give up power altogether.   Its effect was not as good as they had hoped.   The letter gave rise to a new crop of posters, many of them ironical and comic.   Páez and his police chief, Arizmendi, looked on and waited.

Their hour came when Bolívar issued his unwise circular (31.viii.29) prescribing that the local communities should freely express their views on the form of government, the constitution and the person to be selected as Chief of State.   The Minister of the Interior forwarded this circular to Páez (16.x.29).   When it reached the Satrap of Venezuela, he was in Valencia, where he had gone, as he wrote to the Government, " to watch over the calm and repose of the Aragua Valleys and of the Western populations, alarmed at the news that there was a plan to organize the republic under a monarchical form ".   Páez at once forwarded the circular to Caracas and to every parish with orders to pass " acts " or resolutions asking the constitutional Congress to decree the separation of Venezuela.   An Assembly of about five hundred citizens of Caracas, convened by Arizmendi at the Convent of San Francisco (25.xi.29), heard a letter written to Páez by Bolívar from Guayaquil (13.ix.29).   It was one of the too many letters he wrote less to express than to hide his opinion.   He thanked Páez for offering him his house and property for the day when he would wish to leave public service, which, he added, was not far distant; and refused to admit that Páez should follow his example as Páez had suggested.   The insincerity of both men in thus professing to retire to private life was patent to each other.   Bolívar went on to explain his circular, and pointed out that the people were now free to choose their way; he declared himself neutral as to the two solutions he saw: the separation of Venezuela from New Granada or a monocracy.   Significantly, he put his trust in Congress, which " was admirable and would therefore decide with wisdom and calm ".   Significantly also he warned Páez against any " turbulent persons who, under cover of *public opinion*, might attempt some crime we must not tolerate "; and, most significantly of all, he added a sentence obviously meant for Páez himself: " I do not want power, but should anyone seek to wrench it from me by force or intrigue, I shall fight to the bitter end."

2

Páez was not the man to be worried by Bolívar's threats. From this letter, as shifty and complex as any Bolívar wrote in those days, he chose to have read out to the Assembly in San Francisco a paragraph in which Bolívar seemed to say: " If you declare for separation, I shall not object." Led by Arizmendi on the spot, and by Páez and Soublette at a discreet distance, the Assembly decided to secede from Colombia and to cease to recognize the authority of General Bolívar; to prepare for a Convention that was to set up a separate Venezuelan Government on a republican basis; and, meanwhile, to grant full military and civil powers to Páez. Two Englishmen took a strange part in these debates: Admiral Fleming, in command of H.M.'s Fleet in the West Indies and General Grant. Fleming, whose wife was Spanish, was believed by everybody to be acting for his Government, and not with much discretion at that. In a secret and confidential despatch to Lord Douglas (20.iv.30), William Turner, the British Minister in Bogotá, complains of the Admiral's open backing of Páez and encloses a copy of the *Royal Gazette of Jamaica* stating that neither he nor Grant remained " idle spectators " of the Assembly. This led to the opinion that Great Britain was splitting Colombia to counteract French intrigues to marry Bolívar to a French princess. The British flavour which the separatist move thus took on added much to its strength.

The decisions of the Assembly were conveyed to Páez, still at Valencia, by three of its secretaries, one of whom was that A. L. Guzmán who had once been Bolívar's commercial traveller to sell a Crown to the Colombians. Páez was canny. He had two good reasons for not coming out too eagerly: one was to hide the fact that the whole intrigue began and ended in him. He sent one of his aides-de-camp to Caracas with orders to erase all inscriptions against Bolívar, " the most illustrious hero of this part of the world, to whom we owe immense services "; and to the delegates from the Assembly he answered that he was bound by his oath to respect the temporary organization set up by Bolívar. He nevertheless intimated that no harm would be done to the promoters of the change and that the Congress to meet in Bogotá would ultimately decide. The other reason for all this reserve was the news then reaching Venezuela that the final peace treaty with Peru had been signed and that Córdova's rebellion had been quelled. This meant that Bolívar's armed forces were now fully available. Páez thought wise, after three weeks of silence, to report to Bogotá the events of Caracas, with protestations of his fidelity to Bolívar (8.xii.29). But as city after city declared for separation (with a spontaneity duly enforced by Arizmendi) some of them, such as Puerto Cabello, heaping insults on Bolívar's name by the way, and when

Bermúdez issued a Proclamation accusing Bolívar of all kinds of crimes, Páez moved to Caracas, openly offered to back the *pronunciamiento* with his army, and wrote to Bolívar advising him not to bar the way to separation, for Venezuela would return to the rule of Spain rather than be governed from Bogotá.

Bolívar can hardly be exonerated from responsibility in these events. His policy, never frank and open, had become opaque after his return from Peru. To O'Leary, his most intimate confidant, he wrote (28.ix.29): " I assume you will not have forgotten all I told you on my opinion and wishes. I am being pressed all round and I do not know what to decide. I should like to insist on what I told you, but without saying it, I mean, in secret." The opacity of his usual Machiavellism became now thicker owing to his hesitations. He was beginning to feel at his wits' end, and his will, still entire, knew hardly where to turn. His now declared policy—if it really *was* his declared policy—to divide Venezuela from New Granada, seems to have been due to a subconscious fear of Páez, and a conviction that the spirit of the fierce cowboy was stronger than his. He would cut off Venezuela and throw it to the wolves of the Apure to save the rest. This would explain his letter to Urdaneta (13.vii.29): " I am writing to Señor Vergara telling him roundly what I think and want. I have stopped at nothing and I advise him to try to divide the country in the next Congress. New Granada may remain intact [he meant without loss of Ecuador] . . . my friends will be able to do whatever they like in New Granada, because they are many and united; but if they do not seize this opportunity, they will later be defeated. The measure is strong but indispensable." Then, forgetting the protestations he has just made and those he will make immediately after about his longing to retire, he adds this revelation of his secret attachment to power: " If Congress will not take it, let it choose another man and not count on me."

His tactics remained the same, a kind of inverted version of that of the German Barons of old, who were willing to have an absolute King provided he did what they wanted:

> Let the people vote quite free,
> So long as it votes for me.

He offered to serve under Páez should Páez be President, and to form " a most sincere and cordial league between Venezuela, you and me ", and he ends: " My ideas can be put in two words: *To back Congress.*" As an apt comment on this cautious letter to his dreaded enemy, here is what he wrote to his most trusted friend Sucre (28.ix.29): " Friend, such is the State of this Continent full of fools led by a few knaves, and now let us trust the opinion of the majority. I will own that I should not do so, were it a mere opinion; but as this opinion gets armed, it cannot be defied unless one is ready to fight. I did so in my youth; but I am tired." This explains his instructions to Urdaneta (27.xii.29) to keep strong troops close to Bogotá. Nevertheless, in all his letters of this period, even when insisting on retiring from the presidency, he suggests that he is to remain as Generalissimo, not merely of Venezuela but of the whole of Colombia. He was advancing towards Bogotá, writing letters at every stage on the way, in particular to Páez, who was uppermost in his mind.   And on January 3rd, at Cartago, he received the news of the Venezuelan rebellion.   Aggrieved at the ingratitude of his countrymen, he wrote to Castillo Rada: " I have lost much with this movement, for I have been deprived of the honour of leaving power spontaneously."   Pressure was put on him to come to Bogotá to inaugurate the new Congress.   He yielded without much resistance and arrived in the capital on January 15th, 1830.

3

" The streets of the capital were more decorated than ever."   Troops lined the streets.   Every man who had a horse rode out to meet him.   " Balconies, windows, towers were black with people; but in such a great crowd, a sad silence conquered animation;   the salvoes and the bells vibrated without joy. The instinct of the masses saw in the ceremony the funeral of the Republic rather than the triumph of its glorious founder.   When Bolívar appeared I saw tears flow.   Pale, exhausted, his eyes once bright and expressive, now lightless; his deep voice, hardly audible; the features of his face, . . . everything foreshadowed the coming disintegration of the body and the imminent beginning of his immortal life."   This description of an eyewitness would not lead one to anticipate the energy and the ambition which still burnt fiercely in that frail body.   He still mastered, by all the superiority of his prestige and magnetism, the mass of the leaders of the country gathered together in Congress, who on January 20th met under his chairmanship. Before the meeting, Bolívar led them from the Palace to the Cathedral, where a mass of the Holy Ghost was heard.   Military honours were rendered to Bolívar (for the last time, as it turned out) as Chief of the State; and from the Cathedral, the procession returned to the Assembly Hall, where he addressed Congress from the Chair and took his oath.   Sucre was elected President of the Congress and the Bishop of Santa Marta, Vice-President. This choice, in which could be guessed Bolívar's masterly hand, was designed to prepare the way for Sucre's election as President of the Executive, and to emphasize Bolívar's own leaning on the Church.   After a short address by Sucre, Bolívar spoke again, to recommend " institutions which should combine the force of the government with the liberty of the people "; and then he uttered words a wiser man would have left unsaid: " I withdraw with the utmost confidence in the success of a Congress presided over by the Grand Marshal of Ayacucho, the worthiest of all Colombian generals." Urdaneta was present.   He had been Bolívar's henchman throughout, his chief of propaganda, judge, and executioner.   " He struck his forehead with his hands and showed the strongest symptoms of agitation and displeasure ", reports Turner to the Foreign Office.   Bolívar realized his blunder; and in the proofs of his speech he wrote " one of the worthiest " instead of " the worthiest ".   It was too late.   Urdaneta was hurt and was soon to give proof of it.

Bolívar addressed to Congress one of his customary messages (24.i.30).

He began by summing up the facts which had led to the convocation of that Assembly, giving himself an opportunity to write his own history in his own way; then came to what, all his life, had been the kernel of this kind of statement: who was to rule? " I fear with some grounds that my sincerity may be doubted when I speak to you about the magistrate who is to preside the Republic. . . . Honour debars me from thinking of myself for this appointment. Will you dare give me your votes without loss of your reputation? Would this not be like appointing myself? Free me from the blame that awaits me, if I remain in office. . . . Believe me: a new magistrate has become indispensable for the Republic. The people wants to know whether I shall ever cease to rule it. . . . The Republic will be happy, if accepting my resignation, you appoint as President a citizen beloved by the nation; it would go under, were you obstinately to insist on making me rule it. Hear my entreaties; save the Republic." His very insistence shows how keenly he felt his lack of political credit in such matters. But how far did he believe in what he said himself? The answer is not simple; and it covers three points: He was tired, depressed and almost repentant about his life work; he wanted to keep out of office for a period, leaving the reins in Sucre's faithful hands; and he had by no means given up his ambition and his thirst for power.

The same message to Congress shows how deeply he had evolved away from the political philosophy of his youth. " You will permit that my last act be to recommend you to protect the holy religion we profess, an abundant spring of heavenly blessings." This came from the same man who had built up his separatist propaganda on the stunning effects of bigotry and superstition. The Bolívar who had once illumined his saturnine ambitions with the abstract skies of Rousseau, who had waved over the battlefields of America the twin flags of republicanism and free thinking, was now advocating monocracy and " our holy religion " as the salvation of Colombia. This has led to the generally accepted view that Bolívar was, at the beginning of his public life, a liberal democratic republican, and only later, and for a time only, a " reactionary " afflicted with ambition and hungry for dictatorship. But the fact is that thirst for personal power is not only a constant feature, not only the axis that unites all his deeds and explains all his words, but the motive power and inspiration of Bolívar's life. Bolívar was as intent, as single-minded in the pursuit of personal power when, in Jamaica or in Cartagena, he wrote his Manifestoes à la Rousseau as when he begged the Congressmen of Bogotá to protect " our holy religion ". The means had changed; the aim was the same. And the change in the means was due in part to experience but in part also to the fact that the republicanism and the irreligion of his first days had not been quite sincere. They had been at first a superimposed rhetoric borrowed by Simón Bolívar from Simón Rodriguez; partly believed in, for Bolívar was young and generous; partly smiled at, for Bolívar was shrewd and witty; partly handled as a tool, for Bolívar was ambitious and cynical. This not altogether sincere radicalism of his early days had been shaken by experience, because he had come to doubt its value as a tool for his aim—the conquest of power. As the abstract skies of his mind grew greyer with the sunset of his life, the ancestral earth drew him closer to the past. His letters (if carefully read, the true history of his mind) show him gradually learning the wisdom that lurked behind many an old institution or tradition of that Spanish régime he had destroyed. The baffling problems that bristled in the land as he removed the Spanish system (evolved in three centuries precisely to meet them) occupied his mind and made him restive; Sucre reported that the Indians preferred to return to the old Spanish head tax, from which the Independents had " liberated them "; Páez begged him to return to the Spanish form of justice; he himself grew more and more convinced of the stabilizing influence of the Church, and of the need for a monocracy or monarchy if Colombia was to be saved. What had he then fought for? " Citizens "—he concluded—" I blush to say it: independence is the only boon we have acquired at the cost of all the others."

Bresson sent his Government a secret report of a conversation he had with Bolívar the day after he had spoken in Congress (25.i.30). Bolívar began in his usual vein by emphasizing the anarchy of Spanish America and foreboding disaster, were Europe not to help. And then added: " that he himself had struggled as long as he could to maintain order, that, had he been backed by Europe and felt free from previous engagements towards liberalism, he would have established in all the countries governments which, under a republican disguise, would have come close to those of royal power; that in the Bolivian constitution he had been unable to go as far as he meant; but that now he felt too weak to struggle and had nothing else to do but to take care of his glory; that moreover anything would be preferable to the present state of things, and that if Europe were not ready at last to make an effort it would be much better that she should help Spain to reconquer them and to put them back in the rank of her colonies. . . ." At Bresson's request he outlined his programme for a European intervention. His first item was an agreement with Spain; then, that the European Powers "declared to the new States that if they wish to be recognized and treated as nations, they must adopt governments that one may recognize, and similar in their form to those of Europe, with more guarantees of duration; that this declaration should be accompanied, if need be, with a demonstration of force; that the Congresses of these States meet, act and freely choose, but that the peoples be compelled to stick to what they will have chosen; that Mexico be erected into a monarchy under a European Prince; a French Prince would be better received there; but one might consider a Spanish Prince or any other, according to the requirements of foreign policy. In the Liberator's opinion, Mexico is the only country presenting to-day enough monarchical factors. There are names, there is nobility, wealth. Everywhere else, even though the clergy, above all, and the army are generally favourable to the monarchy, more solid bases are lacking. Nevertheless they could be given stronger and more durable institutions, hereditary Senates for example." Bresson asked Bolívar whether he would lend a hand for such a programme; and he answered that he would back it and that he still had much following in Peru and in Bolivia. Urged to put his views on paper, he refused; but he assured Bresson that, should the European Powers decide to negotiate with him on that basis, an agreement would be possible. Bresson was so impressed that he sought and obtained a confirmation of all these opinions in two later interviews, on January 28th and 30th.

4

Congress had a difficult task. The traditional view that Bolívar was indispensable was wearing thin. The arbitrary régime he had introduced in 1826 had undermined his popularity everywhere; in his native Venezuela, because Páez and Arizmendi worked against him; in New Granada, because his instruments were mostly Venezuelan, whose unpopularity fell back on him. Nevertheless, though shaky, his authority was the only lynch-pin that kept the rickety machinery together; so that, to gain time, Congress replied to Bolívar's message that his resignation could not be accepted until the new Constitution was ready and new leaders had been sworn in. Congress had to re-think the State while harassed by those who, prejudging its decisions, wanted it split. Páez' attitude grew more defiant. On January 13th, sure of the backing of the local commanders, he officially declared Venezuela an independent and sovereign State, and set up a Cabinet with three Secretaries, of Home, Justice and Police; of Finances; and of Foreign Affairs, War and Navy. He appointed to these posts respectively Peña, Diego Bautista Urbaneja, and Soublette; and called a constitutional Congress to meet on April 30th. Though revolutionary, these decisions were by no means contrary to Bolívar's professed views at the time; but Congress was in no mood for division, though it was not determined to risk a civil war to prevent it. Bolívar suggested to Congress (27.i.30) that he would leave the Executive in Castillo's hands and go to Venezuela to interview Páez; but the plan fell through because Congress did not think the time ripe for Bolívar's departure, while Páez had no intention of meeting Bolívar or of coming to terms. Bolívar, who knew his Páez, prepared as powerful a concentration of forces as he could muster, and characteristically enough, put the Northern Contingent under the Swede Adelcreutz, and the Southern under the Irishman O'Leary, with orders to remain on the defensive, which he had not dreamt of doing in Córdova's case. Part of the troops under Adelcreutz mutinied under the Granadino Colonel Vargas, and deserted to Páez. This made the more precarious the trust the Government could put in the remaining troops. Anxious to avoid a civil war, Congress appointed a Commission composed of its President and Vice-President (Sucre and the Bishop of Santa Marta) to negotiate with Páez, on the basis of no separation, a republican government and no reprisals (i.e. no punishment for Páez). Sucre, who also knew his Páez, forecast a failure. The meetings took place in El Rosario from April 18th, 1830, onward, and Paez' delegates refused to argue on any basis but the recognition of the existing Venezuelan régime. The Conference came to nothing.

Bolívar resigned on grounds of health and asked Congress to appoint a successor, which Congress refused to do. Bolívar then appointed General

Domingo Caicedo, of a wealthy Granadino family, as provisional President, and at the beginning of March withdrew to a country house in Fucha to recover from an acute attack of bile. His ambition burned unabated in his heart; but his bodily energies were ebbing and his spirit was sagging under the heavy experience of frustration within, and anarchy, and what he described as ingratitude, without. Much of this " ingratitude " came from the disappointment he had caused in so many of his political friends, whom he had sacrificed to his tortuous policy. In Fucha he received Congressmen of his way of thinking. One of them, Posada Gutiérrez, has left a sketch of his visit. " He walked slowly and with fatigue, and his voice was so low that he had to strain himself to be heard; he would walk by the banks of a brook that winds its way through the picturesque countryside, and with crossed arms, stopped to watch the stream, an image of life. ' How long '— he said to me—' will this water run before it dissolves into the ocean, as man dissolves in the rot of the grave into the earth from which he came ? Much of it will evaporate and become subtle, like human glory, renown '." And then the great man, whose being bent already towards the earth,

Comme un boeuf ayant soif penche son front vers l'eau,

felt a sudden rebellion of his Caesarian spirit: " My glory! My glory! Why do they wrench it from me ? Why do they slander me ? " As his forces declined to their final setting, he felt the more imperiously that call for greatness which had trumpeted in his youthful heart on that glorious sunny day in Italy when he had seen Napoleon crowned. Was he to go down among the rattling of words and of swords, between the intrigues of verbose lawyers and the betrayals of crooked chieftains ? He, the greatest spirit the American revolution had called from the deep, the Word and the Deed cast in one, the vision and the will of the Spanish-American continent, was he to sink into nothingness between an adverse vote in Bogotá and a dusty gallop of cowboys in the Apure ? Walking on the green meadows of Fucha, Bolívar's brow was darkened by these melancholy thoughts. " I am resolved to leave Colombia "—he wrote from Fucha to Joaquín Mosquera (8.iii.30)—" to die of sadness and poverty in some foreign land. Oh my friend, my grief has no measure, for slander stifles me like Laocoon's serpents! " Couriers came every day. They always brought bad news.

One of these brought news of Vargas' defection. Bolívar called a meeting of the Council of Ministers, of the President of Congress and of Rafael Urdaneta to examine the situation and decide whether he should return to power. Castillo kept away and wrote to Bolívar advising him to keep peace with Venezuela, to accept the separation and not to return to office. This was the line Urdaneta advocated at the meeting. Persuaded that Castillo and Urdaneta were agreed to oust him and to secure the Presidency and the Vice-Presidency for themselves, Bolívar lost his temper and let it loose on Urdaneta. The Conference dispersed without any decisions. Bolívar broke with Castillo and with Urdaneta, his staunchest supporters since the days of Ocaña. His isolation grew more intense.

Bad news kept pouring in. Castillo proposed that Congress should adjourn leaving a President, a Vice-President and the Senate at the head of affairs until better circumstances permitted a constitution to be framed; and though the motion was rejected, it did reflect the trend of opinion. Hardly had Bolívar recovered from the shock of this news, when a petition was presented to Congress by Popayán suggesting the dissolution of the Congress of Colombia and the calling together of a Congress for New Granada only; which of course would have left Bolívar without a land to govern. This petition, so contrary to his interests, was sponsored, and in fact engineered, by Joaquín Mosquera. Hard upon the heels of this news came that of the rebellion of Colonel Macero in Casanare. He was a Granadino, who in a Proclamation rich in heroics, took upon himself to annex the Province of Casanare to Venezuela. There was method beneath his madness. The Jesuits had developed untold wealth in cattle in the valley of the river Meta and this wealth had passed to the Crown upon the expulsion of the Jesuits under Charles III. After providing meat and booty for years to whatever army had occupied them, these estates still counted, in 1829, from 30,000 to 40,000 head of cattle and about 5,000 horses and mares. Bolívar had " farmed " the estates out to Urdaneta; whose agent, Carvajal, unable to cope with cattle thieves, lashed those he caught. Macero's aim was to get rid of Carvajal, whom his men murdered. Twelve years after Macero's rising, the cattle on the estates had been reduced to about 500, " a destruction committed "—says Restrepo—" by those who proclaimed liberty and independence in order to rob with impunity ".

5

All this was bound to depress a man as generous and materially disinterested as Bolívar. But his appetite for power remained intact. While in Fucha, he heard rumours that Mariano Paris, one of his close friends, was plotting to come out with the Militia, of which he was colonel, to declare the separation of New Granada from Venezuela and to proclaim Urdaneta President of New Granada. He immediately returned to Bogotá (21.iii.30). Caicedo had adequately dealt with this conspiracy, the gravity and even the reality of which are still in doubt; but the episode shows how sensitive Bolívar's political skin still was. Caicedo, following the lead of Castillo and of Joaquín Mosquera, sent a message to Congress (15.iv.30) suggesting again the appointment of an Executive and the adjournment of Congress, to be replaced by a Convention for New Granada only. This time, possibly because it emanated from the provisional President, the proposal gave rise to a diplomatic intervention. The Ministers of Brazil and Great Britain presented Notes (19.iv.30) pointing out that, since they were accredited to Colombia and not to New Granada, they would withdraw; and the British Minister added that the treaty with Great Britain would be at an end (" . . . and a good thing too ", comments Posada Gutiérrez, who thought the treaty was ruinous for Colombia). Possibly because of these foreign protests, Caicedo's motion was lost. All these attempts at solving the tangle by separation were due to three causes: the fear of Páez, which made everybody averse to a war; the Granadino desire to get rid of the Venezuelan officers and generals, who lorded it over them and consumed their budget; and the struggle for and against Bolívar's personality. In this light must also be considered Caicedo's decision to free the press from the shackles imposed on it by Bolívar's decree (1828) making printers responsible, with authors and publishers, for any matter that appeared in print; which made it almost impossible to find printers ready to print any but their own lucubrations. Caicedo's counter-measure (6.iv.30) encouraged journalists and pamphleteers and added fire to an already heated situation.

The chief victim of this was Bolívar. His enemies, says Restrepo, " had succeeded in having him hated in Venezuela and in New Granada ". Beyond his real or alleged errors, many, even among his friends, found fault with " his excessive desire to please the military ", by granting them promotions and commands, particularly when his enmity towards Santander forced him to vie with his rival in this ruinous way of wooing the officer class. Bolívar felt public opinion ebbing away; but, despite his protestations, he clung to power and " fathered " a plan to be elected President with Caicedo as Vice-President. So says Restrepo. The plan, however, was not only " fathered " but conceived by Bolívar. This is shown by the very choice of Caicedo, one of the men he had brought out precisely because of his weakness, to use him as a tool. In his description of the Ministry later appointed by Bolívar, William Turner wrote to the British Foreign Secretary: " Of these Ministers the two first [Caicedo and Herrán] may be said to have no characters at all. General Caycedo, as a private individual of large property is extremely benevolent, bestows large sums of money in charity and therefore possesses great influence in the neighbourhood of Bogotá; but such is the feebleness of his mind that he is as easily led by those who have the cunning to dissemble their purpose, to evil as good."

This should suffice to reveal who the true father was of the plan to have Caicedo elected under Bolívar. But there was a typically Bolivarian touch to it, which Restrepo adds. Caicedo was to take charge of the Executive while Bolívar would take command of the Army, " not to make war on Venezuela, but to defend New Granada, were she invaded, and to support the Supreme Government in upholding peace, order and quiet in the Province ". This, though written by Restrepo, is pure Bolívar, " turning in circles round the Government like a bull round his cows ". Bolívar knew full well that the best way to be elected President is to be President already; and so he bethought himself for the second time of taking back the reins of power from Caicedo. For the second time, therefore, he called a meeting with that end in view, of the same persons that had already met in Fucha for the same purpose. The meeting took place in his Bogotá house (21.iv.30). So far, Restrepo. But to judge by what Bolívar wrote to Urdaneta three days earlier, he may have been ready for stronger measures: " Owing to the bad state of affairs due to lack of energy on our part and to excess of it on that of our adversaries, we are resolved to take a decision that may save the fatherland, bringing together all influential men, who, in agreement with the Government, will carry out whatever is decided upon.

To that end I have ventured to count on you to co-operate with us. I beg you therefore to come flying and to try to contribute to the execution of what we decide. I offer you my old friendship and a total and hearty reconciliation." Urdaneta came. The meeting took place. No one would speak out, though privately Urdaneta advised Bolívar to leave the country, at which Bolívar smarted. In the end he was again left alone with his bitter thoughts, his poor health and his incurable ambition.

6

Early on the 22nd, the city was agog with rumours of impending events. Signatures were being collected for Bolívar's re-election; the prelates were to ask him to stay for the sake of religion and the country; a Spanish-born colonel, Demetrio Díaz (who was not altogether sane, as it turned out), went about threatening to lead a squadron of Militia to proclaim Bolívar as President-Dictator. According to Posada Gutiérrez, Caicedo quietly rode about the city and calmed it; but Turner reports that Caicedo's aides-de-camp galloped about the streets raising political fever, while Obando, who had assumed command over the Militia, harangued the passers-by against Bolívar. The news, broadcast no one knew how, that Bolívar was determined to leave the country, threw the foreign colony into a state of despair. The British merchants were afraid of the liberal or " violent " party, which openly expressed its wish to expel them all, " considering their competition hurtful to the interests of native traders ". The Ministers of the United States and of Brazil, Turner reports, " had an official conference with the Liberator for the purpose of persuading him to remain. I thought it unnecessary . . . having been informed on the morning of the 19th inst. [iv.30] that H.E. had expressed his intention to continue here and accept the office of President, if again elected by the Congress, as no doubt is entertained that he will be. During my visit to the Liberator yesterday morning, H.E. expressed to me the same intentions as he had done to my colleagues. I said all I could, to confirm him therein "; for he adds that, without Bolívar, the country would sink into anarchy, endangering " the large interests of British subjects embarked in property and in speculation throughout the country ". This clear statement made by Bolívar to the three foreign ministers of his intention to accept the presidency if elected, contrasted with the uncompromising protestations to refuse it which he made in public, reveals his tactics once again, and must be borne in mind when reading on, in Turner's report, how Bolívar denied " indignantly having ever had the remotest intention of seeking or accepting the Crown ". This report is also notable for a gloomy prophecy which time was soon to fulfil: " The dejection of his mind is evident in his countenance, and has so serious an effect on his health, that unless a beneficial change ensue, Colombia may ere long have to mourn the loss of the only one of her citizens who is capable of preserving her tranquillity or ameliorating her condition."

Bolívar had enough officers in the city to launch a *coup d'état*. Had he been a younger man, he would have done so. But he had come to a point when he lacked the strength either to give up or to reconquer power. In a page of instructions in his own hand (22.iv.30) probably for Briceño Méndez, he suggested that Congress should propose to him to resign, since he " could not suggest it under a threat of dangers and mutinies ". On April 23rd Urdaneta took over the command of the garrison and Province. Congress asked the Government to communicate to it the British, French and Brazilian Notes on the partition of Colombia; but on the 26th the Government refused to hand them on. All this effervescence was due to the fact that Congress was putting the finishing touches to the Constitution, and therefore the elections of President and Vice-President would soon take place. A party led by García del Río favoured the election of Bolívar. Most of the deputies from Venezuela and from the south militated in it. Most of the Granadinos, however, favoured Urdaneta, now backed by the Liberals, in spite of his fierce persecution of all Liberals after the attempt on Bolívar (25.ix.28). It was thought that the first party could count on thirty-two votes, and the second on twenty, so that Bolívar's re-election seemed certain. But for reasons which are not clear, probably a blend of perfidious advice on the part of some of his followers and of his own helplessness at the time, Bolívar for the third time called a meeting of Ministers and other notables to examine, this time in his absence, whether it was advisable to put his name before Congress for President. This meeting unanimously decided that " for the sake of the peace and integrity of Colombia it was advisable that the *Libertador* should *not* be re-elected by Congress, but that, if the electoral Colleges to meet next October gave him their votes, he should accept." Caicedo, Herrán and Baralt, the ex-President of the Senate, were commissioned to report this decision to Bolívar. When Caicedo read it, Bolívar lost his temper and broke in: " How am I left, exposed to the derision of my enemies, cutting the figure of an exile before the world ? Why did not Congress accept my resignation at first and so I should have left the country and my post more elegantly ? " Baralt pointed out that in Colombia he would always be the glory of the fatherland; but Herrán, more precisely, confirmed: " Yes, Sir, in New Granada, wherever you stay, you shall be our Washington." In New Granada . . . for Venezuela had already decreed the proscription of her greatest son. Somewhat calmer, Bolívar apologized to Caicedo to whom he had at first addressed peevish words; and bowed to the inevitable. Caicedo was fearful of an attempt on Bolívar's life, were he re-elected. Bolívar drafted his last message to Congress (27.iv.30), renouncing the presidency " even if honoured by your suffrages ". He also expressed his intention to " separate himself for ever from the country which gave me life ".

The sincerity of this double decision is generally taken for granted. Later events and his letters show that even then he was not sincere. An unpublished document illustrates Bolívar's state of mind then. On Tuesday, April 27th, 1830, Turner called on Bolívar in the company of Colonel Campbell; and, as soon as they left, they wrote a careful account of the conversation, which they sent to London. The visit purported to be to deliver into Bolívar's hands " a packet for him on the subject of his private

Property in Venezuela ", but aimed in fact at testing the rumour current to the effect that he was determined to leave Bogotá and public life altogether, officially confirmed by his message of that very date. " The conversation was carried on in Spanish, and the energy of his Excellency's feelings was vented in that vigorous and copious language, with a strength, I might almost say, violence, which Your Lordship may rest thoroughly assured, is very far from exaggerated in my inclosed report ". Turner explains that Bolívar underestimated his actual strength and popularity with the army, with Congress and with the provinces. He reminded Bolívar of " the assurances given me yesterday week by His Excellency's self that if elected President by Congress he would remain and act as such ", and asked him if it were true that he was leaving, to which Bolívar answered that he was. Turner then repeated his stock arguments against such a course; " to this H.E. replied that he was so thoroughly disgusted by the changeable and capricious character of his countrymen and by the calumnies undeservedly heaped upon him . . . that the restored dominion of Spain, however despotick and tyrannical would be a blessing to South America by ensuring tranquillity, and that he bitterly rued the hour at which he ever thought the Colombians worthy of being freed from it ".

On May 4th, 1830, the President and the Vice-President were elected. The Bolivarist candidate was a prominent citizen of Cartagena, a lawyer, Eusebio María Canabal; the Liberal's, Joaquín Mosquera. The candidacy of Mosquera had been suggested by Bolívar himself, a mystery to be elucidated anon. The first count gave 26 votes for Canabal, 17 for Mosquera and 5 for Caicedo. The British Minister, who was present, held the view that the cabal which ultimately brought about the defeat of Bolívar's party was set in motion by Márquez and Osorio, two Cabinet Ministers, leaders of the liberal faction. A rowdy crowd of 100 or 200 persons, mostly students of the College of San Bartolomé nearby, shouted and protested at the bar of the house while the elections were on with cries of " let's go to the barracks! " They were opposed to Canabal (little knowing that Bolívar backed Mosquera). Yielding to this intimidation, despite the eloquence of García del Río and others, Congress finally elected Mosquera. On the same day, Bolívar wrote to the new President: " I should not wonder if you heard that I was opposed to your election, for I always thought that you would not accept a post so full of worries and hazards. Although I maintain my view, I take pleasure in offering you my congratulations." This is the key to the mystery. Bolívar had suggested Mosquera's name because he was sure he would not accept, and so, in the end, he might himself be brought back to the presidency. The basis for his assurance was the poor opinion he had of Mosquera's courage. On May 31st, 1830, Bolívar was still writing to José Fernández Madrid, the Colombian Minister in London: " I advise union but fear that it may not be achieved. Mosquera will not take the presidency because he will fear to become the victim of the Bogotá students, for, with us, children have the strength of man's age, and ripe men the flabbiness of tottering old people." But on June 9th he heard that Mosquera (who was away) had accepted; and wrote him this Note so singularly at variance with his first :

" I have just learnt, not without surprise, that you have accepted the presidency of the State, at which I rejoice for the country and for myself; but I regret it and shall always regret it for your sake, for I cannot get rid of the idea that Colombia is going the way of Buenos Aires. Will you be hurt because I thought for you what I thought for myself? You may have been told that I did not want you to be elected. Do not believe them, do not; for they do not tell the truth."

A Commission from Congress called on Bolívar to inform him of the election of Mosquera and Caicedo as President and Vice-President, and that, therefore, the Decree (27.viii.28) conferring exceptional powers on him stood abrogated. Bolívar replied that he withdrew to private life and was ready to give Congress any proof it might desire of his blind obedience to the Constitution and the laws. The crowd noisily celebrated the fall of Bolívar and passed under his windows shouting hurrahs for Santander and other liberal exiles. In Bogotá Bolívar was unpopular and the populace was apt to mock him for his thin body and had nicknamed him " *Longaniza* " (sausage). May 4th was a bitter day for the fallen dictator. There were, however, no excesses. " The garrison counted 1,000 veterans, frowning hard and shaking with rage; the majority of the true people was favourable to the proscribed hero; in the upper classes, he counted many personal friends: the slightest threat would have brought about the speedy end of music, rockets, cries and criers." Congress was still sitting and unanimously voted a decree reiterating that of July 23rd, 1823, granting Bolívar 30,000 pesos yearly for life. Bolívar had decided to leave Bogotá on May 8th. He had no cash. He spent freely and gave away the rest. Two months earlier he had sent his silver table service to the Mint, but got no more than 2,500 pesos for it. He sold his jewellery and horses and put together 1,700. He began to prepare for his journey. On May 7th, the grenadiers and the Apure hussars occupied the strategic spots in the city. Their leaders, Portocarrero and General Luque (promoted after his assault on an anti-Bolívar printer's shop in 1828), were behind the *pronunciamiento*. Portocarrero seems to have been both firm and sensible. At the head of Venezuelan troops, he did not cherish the idea of remaining in Bogotá after Bolívar had gone. The evacuation and return to Venezuela of the troops was quietly negotiated, but not without some effervescence on the part of Bolívar's enemies, who accused him of having gone the round of the barracks exciting the soldiers. This was slanderous, even if we do not go as far as Posada Gutiérrez who asserts that Bolívar offered Caicedo to mediate and that his offer was turned down by the Government. Turner, by no means suspect, since he was as strong a Bolivarist as any man, and was throughout very well informed, reports the very reverse. On May 7th, Caicedo asked Bolívar to intervene, and Bolívar refused. " General Caicedo instantly ran to General Bolívar, imploring the exercise of his influence with the troops to tranquillize them, and persuade them to remain. This, however, the *Libertador* positively refused to undertake, assigning as his reason an unwillingness to subject himself to the chance of refusal." The Venezuelan troops left the city in perfect order and discipline; and Turner reports that the " ragged Rabble " recruited as a Militia by the Government committed all kinds of robberies and other excesses. The city became dangerous for Bolívar and for his friends. Caicedo thought it necessary to spend the night of May 7th in Bolívar's house. The next morning, he presented to Bolívar a farewell message, signed by a number of leaders of civil, military and Church life. Bolívar read it and, deeply moved, embraced the Vice-President; " he then took his farewell of all those present, among whom were some ladies, and mounted his horse, with his eyes damp, his body shaking and his heart beating. The Ministers, the diplomatic Corps, many notable military men and civilians, nearly all the foreign residents, particularly the chivalrous English, then numerous in the city, accompanied him more than two leagues out of the city. Some rode on to Facatativá, where he was to spend the night."

Chapter XXVIII

THE LAST REVOLUTION

I

ONE of the curious features of Bolívar's exile is that he left in Bogotá his mistress Manuela Sáenz whom he was not to see again. Though her unconventional ways had been one of the causes of his loss of popularity, their mutual attachment was by no means impaired. Bolívar wrote to her tenderly from Guaduas (11.v.30): " My love; I have pleasure in telling you that I am very well and full of grief at your affliction and mine owing to our parting. My love, I love you very much, but I shall love you even more if you now show much good sense. Be careful what you do; for otherwise you will ruin us, ruining yourself. I am always your most faithful lover—Bolívar." The warning was not heeded. On June 9th, the festivity of Corpus Christi was to be celebrated with a display of fireworks, among other graver and religious ceremonies. Some grotesque figures were to be burnt, including two representing Despotism and Tyranny. It was generally believed that these two figures were to be caricatures of Bolívar and of Manuela. The spirited lady, dressed, as she often did, in masculine attire, rode out with her two negresses, Natán and Jonatás, in similar garb, and two or three soldiers she had kept in her household; and, producing a pistol, threatened to destroy the fireworks-castle with much flourish of anti-governmental eloquence. Caicedo had to intervene and, much to the indignation of the liberal press, called on Manuela to soothe her " instead of having her imprisoned and punished according to the laws ". Nothing daunted, Manuela plastered the city with placards on which she displayed her love for Bolívar and her disregard for spelling. Biba Bolivar, Fundador de la REPca. She was prosecuted and exiled. But even then, though she left Bogotá for a time, she did not join Bolívar. This is a strange circumstance. Why should Bolívar, who had never hidden his relations with her while in office, keep her away precisely when he was retiring into private life ? There are two answers to this question. Bolívar was not really retiring to private life at all; he was merely performing a *reculer pour mieux sauter*. Moreover, his doctors may well have advised him that he was no longer strong enough to live with so exacting a nymph.

While Bolívar wandered slowly towards Cartagena, with an ear on Bogotá, the weak men he had selected to lead the country as his tools were fast becoming the tools of his enemies. On May 22nd the Constitution was read on the steps of the Cathedral in the presence of a group of officials, amidst the indifferent apathy of the citizens who " passed by gazing for a few moments as if they had no concern ". Turner continues: " In the Cathedral, the next day, hardly a respectable person uninvested with an official character attended the service, and not a single cheer was heard from the populace outside as the procession passed from the Cathedral to the

Palace." The coldness of the people was such that Caicedo commented on
it in conversation with the diplomats, recalling the enthusiasm which had
acclaimed the earlier constitution. The authorities tried to stir up the people
by setting up popular gambling tables and running bullfights in the main
square (14.i.30). Turner reports: " On the 25th [of May] information
arrived from the south that Señor Mosquera consented to exercise the
function of President. . . . The news excited general surprise, as scarcely
anyone, and least of all those who extorted his election from the Congress,
had imagined that he would accept the office; abbove [sic] all it overwhelmed with consternation the fiercest ministers who had confidently
calculated on the continuation as head of the Executive, of General Caycedo,
through whom, as their passive tool, they had hoped to preserve their power."
Turner did not think Mosquera would tolerate such a situation. The
liberal press not content with slandering Bolívar, went so far as to regret
the failure of the attempt on his life and asked for another Brutus. The
Government was losing ground through its financial exactions and forced
recruiting in the villages.

Sucre had returned to Bogotá on May 5th, 1830. On arriving at Bolívar's
house the eve of his departure with the intention of accompanying him for
a few miles, he found his leader and friend gone. He wrote a simple and
moving farewell letter in which, though he speaks of the tears he is shedding
as he writes, he sets down this typical sentence: " You know that it is not
your power but your friendship that inspired in me the tenderest affection
to your person." Bolívar's answer is not quite worthy of the situation.
Though he declares himself " full of tenderness " a political current spoils
all, he says, and he even falls into a deplorable: " I shall forget you when
the lovers of glory forget Pichincha and Ayacucho." This difference in
the mood of the two men does not reflect on Bolívar's friendship for Sucre,
which was deep and sincere; it is due to the difference in their attitude towards
the situation: Sucre thought that he would not see Bolívar for long, perhaps
never again, for he realized that Bolívar was a sick man and he thought that
he was truly going into exile; while Bolívar thought he would soon be back
in Bogotá and see Sucre again. In this, he made a twofold mistake: he
never came back to Bogotá and Sucre was murdered within a week.

Three sets of forces converged to push the youthful General to his un-
timely end: the violence of the liberal party; the confidence Caicedo had in
his influence over the south; and his own foolhardy disregard of repeated
warnings. A liberal Junta, composed of anti-Bolivarist hotheads, who used
to meet in the house of Don Pacho Montoya, opposite the Cathedral, resolved
to get rid of Sucre, whom they considered as the main standby of Bolívar.
One of the men present, Don Genaro Santamaría, was the first to leave the
meeting. In later years he told a friend: " I came across Sucre, who was
pacing the forecourt of the Cathedral with crossed arms. I was shocked, as
if I had seen a ghost, having just decreed his death." Hearing that Sucre
was leaving for the south, Caicedo repeatedly urged him to leave soon in order
to preserve the link between Quito and Bogotá, which Flores was endeavouring to break. Caicedo insisted that Sucre should go by sea, fearing his

enemies in Pasto; but Sucre was determined to spend St. Anthony's day in his house and therefore to go by road. On the day he left, the liberal Junta sent a messenger, a blacksmith, to warn Obando. On June 1st, 1830, the liberal newspaper *El Demócrata* carried a violent article against Sucre, ending with the ominous words : " Obando may do to Sucre what we failed to do to Bolívar." Three days later, on June 4th, 1830, as he was riding through a narrow defile in Berruecos, not far from Salto de Mayo, he was shot dead by men posted there by Obando and José Hilario López. Soon after, López was promoted a general.

2

" The new President, who arrived here on the 12th inst."—wrote Turner to the Foreign Office (14.vi.30)—" was greeted with but little enthusiasm." On the 13th Mosquera received the Diplomatic Corps and Turner writes: " The gentlemanly and dignified deportment of Señor Mosquera justified the accounts which we had heard of him and made us certain that the indiscriminate admission of all the Rabble of Bogotá into the Hall of Reception, where they were pushing round us, was not in his act and could not meet his approval." The President issued a Proclamation in which he referred to Bolívar in a gracious and harmless phrase. This drew vehement protests from his Finance Minister, Márquez. Mosquera argued that since Congress had declared Bolívar the best citizen of Colombia, he would have been ashamed to say less. Turner, however, shook his head. Mosquera had no strength of character. The men exiled for their responsibility in the attempt on Bolívar's life (25.ix.28) were returning freely; and two of them, Gómez and Azuero, had been made Counsellors of State; Azuero himself had been appointed Minister of the Interior. Plots of all kinds were simmering. Turner heard of one to murder Urdaneta and Castillo, during the festivities on the inauguration of the President. He provides an interesting, and so far unknown, detail on Sucre's murder: " Señor Areta, a deputy for the south of the late Constitutional Congress, and a friend of Sucre was informed of his assassination by one of the liberal party here *twelve days* before it was publickly known in Bogotá." In this despatch Turner added an illuminating piece of news-cum-views. A variety of reasons he enumerates " are daily increasing the number of the advocates of Bolívar, both in the city and neighbourhood. The *Libertador* is still at Cartagena, and will, it is said, remain there for some little time; and it is thought here by many that in a short time the growing conviction of H.E. being the only man who enjoys the confidence of the country will ensure his almost unanimous recall to power ".

In this, as was often the case, Turner was expressing the views of the Bolivarist party. He knew that Bolívar's absence was, if not a feint, at least a manoeuvre. True, half of Bolívar's mind was bent on going; and in a letter written from Guaduas to his friend and agent Gabriel Camacho, he asked to be assured at least of his personal property, for, though Congress had voted him 30,000 pesos, he feared that political instability might render the gift precarious. The letter is admirable, strong but restrained. The other half of his mind, however, bent on remaining, emerges in these words: " I·shall not leave for Europe until I know the outcome of my law-suit." He gives others, and himself, all kinds of reasons for not leaving. On May 31st, he writes to Fernández Madrid: " I don't know yet whether I shall leave for England, for I am awaiting my passport and I don't know when it will come." And on June 1st, he complains about this to Caicedo, though it was pretty certain that he needed no passport whatever to leave the country. He did not really want to leave. His mental ear was ever on Bogotá. Something was bound to happen. " They " would not be able to do without him.

His friend Posada Gutiérrez has left us a sketch of his stay in Honda which reveals the struggle then going on in his mind between the setting sun of his ambition and the rising moon of his repentance. While *champans* were got ready for his voyage down the Magdalena, he went on a visit to the silver mines of Santa Ana. Resting by the river between two rides, he suddenly rose from a slumber and asked Posada: " Why do you think, dear colonel, that I am here ? " " Fate, general." " ' Fate ! '—he replied vehemently. ' No. I am here because I refused to deliver the Republic to the College of San Bartolomé ',* and he was silent with his head bowed, meditating." As they reached the top of the hill, he stood for long, silently admiring one of those prodigious landscapes of Colombia; and Posada writes: " His first words as he came out of his ecstasies were: ' What greatness, what magnificence! God can be seen, felt, touched. How is it possible for people to deny it ? ' " His ancestral loam was requickening old seeds long left sterile in his being. But later, after he had been received with enthusiasm by the English miners and the native hands, his companion tried to tempt him with a visit to the old aristocratic city of Mariquita, the first built inland by Quesada, the discoverer and conqueror of New Granada, of which he gave Bolívar a glowing description, not forgetting the rills of clear water running through every street and the royal standard of Quesada which, owing to a tradition that it had been embroidered by Queen Isabel, had been held in almost religious veneration until it was burnt in the public square by the patriot governor after Boyacá. " General," concluded Posada Gutiérrez, " forgive me for talking so long about what once was a city now depressed like everything fallen from its old splendour: my mother was born in it." Bolívar would not enter the city. For him, it would have been a city of ghosts.

3

He arrived in Turbaco (25.v.30) very low in health and spirit. He was received with respect and affection, and the city swore the Constitution under the protection, so to speak, of his authority (12.vi.30). On June 24th, he moved on to Cartagena, it would seem to sail on board a British ship. Cartagena received the fallen leader as if he came in triumph—with decorated

---

* A liberal school of turbulent students in Bogotá.

windows, music, troops and illuminations. This reception seems to have been due to a genuine sympathy on the part of the citizens; but, had another man than the Bolivarist Montilla been in actual power there, things would certainly have turned out otherwise. The reception had a political intention; the Bolivarist party were determined not to let him sail. Representations were made to him of the lack of comfort of the British packet-boat. Bolívar had no intention of embarking, either, as shown by his profuse explanations why he did not. On June 24th, he wrote to President Mosquera: " I received my passport by the last mail, and at once came here with a view to embark on a British packet-boat at anchor in this harbour, but I found the cabin already filled by a crowd of ladies. There was, moreover, anguishingly little time to arrange everything, and it did not seem to me decent to sail in the midst of an emigration of women; only if I were escaping would that seem natural." Bolívar does protest too much. He stayed because he never really meant to go; and he did not mean to go because he was conspiring through his friends to bring down Mosquera and Caicedo and return to power.

One evening he was alone with his nephew Ferdinand in one of the newly built *bohíos* at the foot of the Popa hill, when, towards nine o'clock, two carriages approached, and General Montilla, Don Juan de Francisco Martín and a few other friends from Cartagena entered somewhat excited. " What is the matter ? "—asked Bolívar. " General "—answered Montilla —" Sucre has been murdered in the hills of Berruecos." Bolívar struck his forehead with his hand, asked for details and requested his friends to leave him to his thoughts. For long he paced the patio to and fro. He went to bed very late, rose with the dawn and paced the patio again, unable to rest. He caught a chill, and a fever he was to endure until his death. He was depressed because of his personal loss; but also because of the abyss of violence and anarchy the deed revealed in the country. That part of him that hankered after freedom, Europe, a change, was strengthened for a time. His friends realized that and soon came back to persuade him to remain. He needed no persuasion, though he feigned to: " As for me "—he wrote to his cousin Leandro Palacios (24.vii.30)—" I don't know what to do. My friends want me to stay; which I resist seeing no object in it "; but to Fernández Madrid on the same day: " In Venezuela a party in my favour has begun to rise again and if I am not mistaken it is strong." Most revealing of all perhaps, to Manuela Garaycoa (21.vii.30): " I do not know whether circumstances will force me to leave Colombia for ever "—which does not tally with his professed longing to go. Again to Leandro Palacios (14.vii.30): " I am still here not knowing what I shall do, waiting only for a favourable result in Venezuela to put my property in order before sailing for Europe. Public opinion has declared in my favour in the three sections of Colombia. In the south it is universal and without opposition, in Venezuela people fight for me heroically. In New Granada, the immense majority of the people, the whole Church and above all the military are on my side. The September 25th gang are my enemies in Bogotá, and no one else; so that a revolution is expected any day against the Government."

All this shows that he was not sincere in his professed intentions to leave. He knew that Urdaneta, Manuela and the rest were plotting against the Government. And at this stage, a second blow fell to hurt him in his heart as deeply as the death of Sucre. He reports the news in the same letter to his cousin: " Meanwhile those blackguards of the Congress of Venezuela, out of fear, have committed the abomination of proscribing me." The Cuban Yanes or Yáñez had been elected President of the revolutionary Congress of Venezuela, a parliamentary fig leaf covering Páez' dictatorship. Towards the end of May, Yanes sent an official Note (without date) to the President of the Constitutional Congress of Colombia, reporting that, though determined to separate from Cundinamarca and Quito, the Venezuelan Congress had declared itself ready to " enter into relations and transactions with them "; but Venezuela, " taught by a number of evils of all kinds to be prudent, and seeing in General Simón Bolívar the origin of these evils, trembling still at the risk she has run of for ever being his patrimony, protests that such relations cannot be engaged in while he remains on the territory of Colombia ". Vicente Azuero, a sworn enemy of Bolívar, answered in a noncommittal way, emphasizing the importance of negotiations, but ignoring the exorbitant condition; and drafted a letter to Bolívar (14.vii.30) to the effect that the President, embarrassed and not knowing what to do, was passing on the Note to him. Mosquera asked for time to think it over; but Azuero published the Note, his answer and his letter to Bolívar without the President's authority. Mosquera, instead of dismissing his Minister, let the matter take its course. " I assure you "—Bolívar said to a visitor— " that it is the event of my life which has afflicted me most deeply."

4

" I shall not be surprised if a thousand follies are committed, and if they are attributed to me "—Bolívar had written to Caicedo from Turbaco on June 1st. This kind of prophecy nearly always meant that he knew his friends were preparing what he foreshadowed. In Jamaica, two of the men who knew his mind best, Bedford Wilson and O'Leary, were conducting a press campaign against the government of Caicedo and Mosquera. This amounts to a proof that Bolívar was working to bring down the government which he professed to respect. Urdaneta and Manuela Sáenz were busy on the same task. Urdaneta was the usual channel through which Bolívar sent funds to Manuela; and both were so to speak fraternally united in that both had nearly fallen victims to murderous attempts on the part of liberal hotheads.* Things went from bad to worse, and the Finance Minister, having no funds whatever to meet the obligations of the State, endeavoured in vain to extract a loan from the merchants of Bogotá. His plight may be gauged by the fact that a foreign merchant consented to

* On August 12th, 1830, in a despatch on the violence of the liberal press, Turner wrote to London: " Two attempts were made last week to assassinate a woman of Quito, a former mistress of the *Libertador*, her devotion to whom renders her a natural and violent enemy of the liberal party; but they were both of them frustrated by her watchfulness and courage." P.R.O. F.O. Col. No. 77, D. No. 28.

advance a loan of 4,000 pesos. Politics was splitting the army. On July 27th the Regiment of Boyacá, of liberal, i.e. anti-Bolívar sympathies, marched into the city displaying red ribbons with the slogan " *Libertad o Muerte* ". There were banners, rockets, harangues and tears, and shouts of *Death to Urdaneta! Death to the Serviles! Long live Santander and the heroes of September 28th!* Mosquera tried to stem the pernicious tendency, but his timid measures did but stimulate it. " The streets "—Turner reports— " were filled with inhabitants wearing green ribonds, as the colour of Bolívar, yellow as that of Urdaneta, and black as the symbol of liberalism. Frequent quarrels in the street resulted." Urdaneta left for the country, ostensibly to recover from an illness, in fact for fear of being murdered and in order to plot a *coup d'état.* Mosquera fell ill with anxiety and withdrew to Anolaima (1.viii.30).

" On the 9th inst. [August] "—Turner informed his Government—" the Battallion of Callao left the capital by order of the Government for Tunja. As this regiment had declared itself for the Party of Bolívar here, who combine all that is elevated in station and respectable in property, petitions numerously signed by the adherents of that party had been presented to the government requesting the continuance in the Capital of the Regiment of Callao, whose departure would, they say, be the immediate signal for the Liberals, supported by the Regiment of Boyacá, to execute their projects of plunder and assassination against their political opponents. As, of course, the Government was dominated by Márquez and Azuero, two fierce Liberals, the request was refused, and the Regiment marched out. . . . On its arrival at Zipaquirá a numerous body amounting by some accounts to 2,500 men of the opulent landed property of the plain and villages of Bogotá (Orejones as they are here called) and their followers . . . entreated them to join their party offering them pay and provisions if they did, and threatening to prohibit their further progress by withholding the means of transport if they did not." The Regiment accepted the offer; and Turner writes on: " It appeared that the landed proprietors were supported (if not joined) by General Urdaneta ", of whom Turner says that he had prepared everything with Manuela, " who being possessed of great property which she liberally distributes in charity possesses great influence in and around Bogotá, by a body of the clergy and by the heads of the party of Bolívar in the capital and its neighbourhood. The whole force decked themselves with green Ribbonds bearing the inscription: *Por la Religión.*" The Government first made light of it; but later published a fierce proclamation threatening the rebels with the rigour of the decree on conspirators. The ruthlessness of this decree was one of the chief accusations levelled against Bolívar by the Liberals; his friends retorted that the decree had been copied from one issued by Santander earlier. Nothing daunted, the green-beribboned Bolivians advanced on Bogotá; their cavalry was commanded by Colonel Johnson, an Englishman who for such an occasion had neglected the salt mines he had farmed from the State. The Bolivians in the city demanded the dismissal of three Ministers, Márquez, Osorio and Rieux (12.viii.30). Caicedo was ready to drop them; but the liberal faction objected. A proclamation was posted calling all men between fifteen and fifty to arms. Only twenty-seven men answered the call. Indian peasants come to the market to sell their produce were dragged to the barracks and armed.

At dawn (15.viii.30), the rebellious division arrived in the neighbourhood of Bogotá led by Colonel Jiménez. It seems that the Government might have resisted, but it negotiated; and the rebels demanded, along with the redress of a number of complaints, some of them futile, that Urdaneta should be Minister of War. Mosquera returned to Bogotá, losing his escort in a brush with a rebel guerrilla, in circumstances which restored his prestige, for he behaved with coolness and prudence. He endeavoured to bring about a reconciliation between the two parties at war, not without much liberal indignation. He went in person to interview the rebels at Techo, a league out of Bogotá. The Government received a reinforcement of 500 men (23.viii.30), and the amnesty decree was so drafted by Azuero (and weakly signed by Mosquera) as to make a refusal inevitable. Urdaneta sent by Mosquera to negotiate it, advised the rebels to reject it. He was playing not merely a double but a threefold game. He wrote to the Government that he was doing all he could; he was fostering the rebellion with the help of Bolívar's friends; and he was trying to keep Bolívar out of it and seize power for himself. Turner reported: " It is said, and with some probability, that the movement of the Party now menacing the capital, is part of a widely extended Plot of the friends of General Bolívar for restoring his authority throughout the Republick. This is rendered more likely for the fact that a cousin of General Urdaneta, General Luis Urdaneta, left Bogotá for Cartagena a fortnight ago. . . . Little doubt is entertained that the object of his journey was to give notice to General Bolívar and H.E.'s friends there of the rising which has since taken place."

Two features of this small revolution should be brought out: the strong anti-British passion of the so-called Liberals; and the " popular " character of the Bolivarist faction. Both are emphasized by Turner in a despatch (7.ix.30) to be read, however, bearing in mind that, for Turner, " the people " means the opulent landed proprietors, while those the Liberals called " the people " were for Turner " the populace ". Unable to win over the rebels, Mosquera reluctantly allowed a military expedition to be sent from the city against them. It was defeated (27.viii.30), and Mosquera signed a capitulation (28.viii.30), whereby he agreed to exile fourteen " September " Santanderists, including two of his Cabinet Ministers, Azuero and Márquez. At 5 p.m. the rebels occupied the city in perfect order. The Council of State endeavoured to water down the worst clauses of the capitulation and in particular to avoid the exile of the fourteen Liberals; but Mosquera, exposed to the insolence of two English mercenary colonels, Jackson and Johnson, yielded, reluctantly remained in office and appointed a new Cabinet with Urdaneta as Minister of War and Gual as Foreign Secretary. Several provincial cities proclaimed Bolívar President. " An Assembly of fathers of families " met in Bogotá (2.ix.30) and adopted two resolutions: " That the Libertador be recalled to take charge of the destinies of Colombia acting in any way he may think fit to save her; and that meanwhile Supreme Command be invested in General Urdaneta in order that he act in the way he may think best for the happiness of the people." The typically dictatorial character of both decisions will be noted. It was underlined in a third, whereby guarantees offered to the individual citizen by the Constitution would remain in force " pending the *Libertador's* decision ". The Assembly, says Restrepo, " was respectable neither for its numbers nor for the weight of the citizens that sanctioned it ". It was followed by what Restrepo describes as " another ridiculous farce : a crowd of the population led by a few military men walked about the streets carrying the portrait of Bolívar in a procession with music, rockets, Church bells. . . . Nearly all the clergy, secular and regular, of the capital was in favour of Bolívar's rule." They had evidently veered round from the days when they were ready to shelter Santander against Bolívar's bullets. Mosquera asked Urdaneta whether the Government could count on the army to uphold the Constitution; the answer was, that if Bolívar were called at the head of the nation the army leaders would obey, and if not, not. Furthermore, Justo Briceño and Jiménez, both Bolívar's men, presented an ultimatum to the Government on the same lines. On September 4th Mosquera and Caicedo withdrew from the Government and Urdaneta took over (4.ix.30).

BOLÍVAR had expected all this. How far he led it is a matter of opinion. Perhaps not much, for he was far away and in poor health. But though possibly not the actual chief, he certainly was the leading inspiration of the rebellion. From what he himself told Vallarino (11.xi.30), he had expected Mosquera to appoint him Generalissimo, in other words, Mosquera was to take the shadow and Bolívar the substance of power; and seeing that this did not happen, he had taken an attitude which at least allowed and encouraged his friends to do their utmost to oust the Government. There was a British frigate about, H.M.S. *Shannon*, and why not sail to Jamaica? A number of obstacles were suggested, notably that the frigate had orders to sail first as far as La Guaira and back. Bolívar waited, but wrote again for money to Camacho, his agent, for his funds were running out. He was a wealthy man, but was short of cash; partly because of some legal troubles about the sale of his Aroa mines to a British syndicate; partly through Páez' cussedness, partly because of María Antonia's covetous ways. From Cartagena he wrote to Briceño Mendez (1.ix.30), complaining that he had no news from him and adding that " in Venezuela all goes well, for our party is so widespread that it may wipe out all opposition and so we may even spare ourselves the disasters of a civil war ". He also sends a curious summary of the events of Bogotá: " As the Government wished to make the Callao battalion commanded by Jiménez leave the city, the Orejones, who apparently had already combined a plan, seized on this pretext to force the Government to alter the Ministry. . . . The patriots no longer mention me except in one of their representations to the Government, asking that I should be respected; and also when they charged on the enemy shouting Long live the *Libertador*. . . . The post has just come. . . . The odious Ministers have left the Government and our friends ask that they be replaced by Castillo, Urdaneta, Gual and Vergara. But it is believed that they will not stop at that. It is said that they will attempt everything [to bring him back] and that my friends are behind this party. Urdaneta is in command of the troops. Religion and the *Libertador* are everywhere held in triumph. Here there is a kind of *pronunciamiento* brewing and not out yet by a miracle. They want to implicate me and I refuse, which has put a stop to everything."

He wrote to Justo Briceño (4.ix.30) in answer to a report on the *pronunciamiento* of El Socorro. No. He will not meddle in mediations or in anything, while there are two parties; to Vergara (9.ix.30) commenting on Mosquera's capitulation and fearing a long civil war. " Be kind enough to inform General Urdaneta of this letter and persuade him on my behalf to hold me as his friend and ready to serve him in any way I can "; to Briceño Méndez (10.ix.30) protesting he will never be a factious man. " Not content with having destroyed me in public opinion by the advice they gave me in Ocaña and the infamous ' acts ' and the monarchical schemes, they are now trying to rob me of my personal honour, degrading me to the ranks of the enemies of the fatherland." There is no shred of sincerity in this. The " infamous acts " were of his own initiative. The letter is written for propaganda and window-dressing purposes. Five days later he wrote to Justo Briceño approving " that you have gone to the capital to see for yourself the state of things and give your opinion ". A pretty broad hint for a General who had rebelled against the Government. Then: " I intend to leave soon for Ocaña and then Bucaramanga or Cúcuta. I have not yet received the act [he does not say whether it was infamous] of Bogotá. In the anarchy in which we have remained I am bound, as are all citizens and soldiers, to contribute to save the fatherland, and of course I shall offer my services to the Republic for it to use me as a soldier ". He knew full well that he could only serve as a Generalissimo and in fact as a Dictator. He wrote to Santiago Izquierdo (17.ix.30): " You have all behaved like brave soldiers who defend the cause of the fatherland and of religion. . . . You urge me instantly in the name of many good Bogotans and your own, to go soon to take over the government. I cannot refuse to serve the country in such unhappy circumstances; but everything cannot be done in one hour. Within fifteen days I shall be in Ocaña. . . . Believe me that it is a heavy sacrifice for me to return to public life. . . ."

2

On September 18th he received Colonel Vicente Piñeres, sent by Urdaneta, and Colonel Santa María, sent by the Municipal Council of Bogotá, with the act and a message from Urdaneta urging him to come to Bogotá and take power again. Urdaneta wrote: " I entreat you not to forsake us in such a weighty crisis and not to doubt for a moment in taking the decision which befits the good of the nation, its glory and yours." He assured Bolívar of " our faithful friendship and constant adhesion to your person ". Bolívar sent Urdaneta an official and a private answer which taken together show him at his truest. Officially, he assured Urdaneta of all his help: " Of course I shall leave for the capital to reiterate my most solemn protestations to obey the laws and the authorities now constituted until constitutional elections provide us with the benefit of a legislative core . . . until that moment comes I shall serve only as a citizen and as a soldier." This meant that he was going to back Urdaneta with his moral force over the army and the nation, while Urdaneta would take the odium of breaking the Constitution until, he, Bolívar, had been elected a constitutional President. And his private letter dots the i's and crosses the t's of this idea. " What shall I do against a barrier of bronze which separates me from the presidency. That barrier is the law. I shall back the Government with all my influence and all my forces. . . ." Conscious of his selfishness, he adds: " I offer myself to serve in the most difficult and dangerous capacity; in such a way I shall spare myself accusations of selfishness." Note that *secondary* nature of his attitude towards behaviour, one of his chief features: not " I shall not thus be selfish ", but " I shall thus not be accused of being selfish ". He writes also: " The official answer to you must be published so that everybody can see that I am ready to back the administration." And then " I am sending a proclamation which contains utterances calculated to flatter those who long for me most ". Let it be said, he advises, that I am coming with 2,000 men " and that when I arrive it will be known finally whether I accept or not. At this point the entreaties and the urgings will begin and all will be attained."

This letter confirms again a number of other features constant in Bolívar's make up. First his inexorable tendency, his propensity to do things the hard way. He urges Urdaneta to proceed " with all rigidity and firmness, as the cruel circumstances of the day imperiously demand it. Governments must be inexorable when circumstances are horrible." And further, discussing complaints against the new administration: " Criticism is also heard about the tolerance which they forecast the Government will evince towards thieves and murderers [obviously referring to his political enemies, some of whom, it must be owned, deserved the slur]. On this, I shall add nothing, for you know how one should go about in these things and you are the responsible man." Another of the features of Bolívar his letter brings out is his tendency to judge his assistants almost exclusively from the angle of their loyalty to him and to his views. " I think it indispensable to send an excellent Chief to the Cauca Valley "—he writes. " If you promote Jiménez to General, he is the best." Who was Jiménez, the man who had upset the Mosquera-Caicedo régime ? Posada Gutiérrez, a strong Bolivarist, who rallied to this *pronunciamiento*, will tell us: " Colonel Jiménez, a mulatto who forsook the pick and shovel of the peasant while very young enrolled as a soldier with a patriotic army. . . . He knew neither reading nor writing and much later learnt to sign in some kind of hieroglyph which neither he nor anybody could decipher; a simple naïve man of irreproachable private behaviour, religious to the point of devotion, he was totally unable to deliberate in his own mind and easily swayed by outside opinion. . . . He had deserved his promotion owing to his courage. He was a practical chief but quite incapable of anything else." This Jiménez is the officer to whom Bolívar had written requesting him to keep an eye on Córdova and if necessary to use his sword. Bolívar recommended him for promotion to General.*

Finally there is another revelation of Bolívar's character in this letter. " I believe that the notables of Cartagena have not appreciated the new Cabinet. They say that only Vergara is any good. Our friends desire you to give some post to García del Río and he seems to me a man of much weight

---

* The cases of Luque and Luis Urdaneta are even worse. Luque, recommended by Bolívar for promotion to General, is described by Posada Gutiérrez as " a most immoral and corrupt man " in a passage in which he recalls that Luque and Luis Urdaneta were both implicated in the murder of the Peruvian officers put to death after the battle of Tarqui, and that Luque had tried to murder Sucre and was only saved then from being shot because Sucre, with his usual generosity, refused to supply the Court with the proofs of his would-be murderer's guilt. " Luque "—he concludes—" was one of those ignorant and callous young men, frequently found in the Colombian Army, whose terrific aggressiveness, the most esteemed quality in the days of the War to the Death, was the cause of their rise in the army." *P.G.*, Vol. II, p. 321.

for any position and particularly as Minister of Foreign Affairs." García del Río, the author of the *Meditaciones* which Bolívar recommended so much, was his chief monarchist pamphleteer. Now the Minister of Foreign affairs was Borrero; and Bolívar adds this postscript: " In spite of what I say above, I have reflected that Señor Borrero will weigh much on the matter of the Cauca valley joining Cundinamarca; therefore he must not leave his post except of his own free will; and I am writing to him urging him to remain in the Cabinet."

3

One thing is certain. This man's spirit was still far stronger than his broken body warranted. His letter to Justo Briceño (11.ix.30) is concise and authoritative, like that of a Commander-in-Chief, all about moves and forces. That to Diego Ibarra (20.ix.30), equally lively, contains this revealing sentence: " Here we are all very gay, though not so much as you might think, for it is man's misfortune never to be satisfied." To Pedro Briceño Méndez (20.ix.30), he sends also an executive and optimistic message: " At last I have been appointed chief or President; and Urdaneta temporarily in charge of the Executive, pending my arrival." There follows a fresh pro-testation that he will not serve as President until he has been elected by a truly popular vote, and then: " I am old, ill, tired, disillusioned, slandered and ill-paid. I ask no reward but rest and the preservation of my honour "; and then: " Within eight days I leave for Ocaña." And then, speaking of his henchman, Diego Ibarra: " Diego and his brothers, along with others, may do much and even very much if God will perform another miracle there [in Venezuela] as He did with Jiménez and the Callao regiment." A few lines lower he thinks it likely he may soon see his sisters again, i.e. that Páez may soon have fallen. But of all his letters of this period, the most revealing perhaps is the one he wrote to Vergara on September 25th; for, in this letter in which he takes the official line that he cannot accept office from a mutiny, he lets out these words which echo his interview with Turner: " I assure you that I have never looked on insurrections with a good eye; and of late I have deplored even our own against the Spaniards." This recantation can easily be explained. For the first time in his life he had experienced what it meant to be on the losing side in a demagogic scene staged by a few agitators with the backing of the army. He had been ousted from Bogotá, and Mosquera and Caicedo elected, by the same methods which Cortés Madariaga and Martín Tovar Ponte had set in motion to get rid of Emparán. He was now drinking to the dregs the bitter cup of disen-chantment; and, though for the thousandth time, he trots out his repugnance for power, this time he adds: " All my reasons are based on one: *I have no hope of salvation for the fatherland.*" It is he who underlines.

And yet, and yet . . . in the same letter: " Tell General Urdaneta that I have had no letter from him by this post "; and unable to stand it any longer, he wrote straight to Urdaneta from Turbaco (2.x.30): " The post came this time and still no letter from you: this is too much silence in these circumstances." Hear the voice of authority in this man, a physical wreck, an exile, a homeless wanderer, scolding the man in power in Bogotá as if he were his mere private secretary. And so sure was he of his spirit that he at once begins the list of his infirmities—bile, nerves, rheumatism—and the pessimistic conclusion: "The state in which my nature is, is unbelievable. It is almost exhausted and I feel no hope of restoring my health fully." He planned to move to Santa Marta, in the hope of lending a hand to put down a rebellion that had flared up in Río Hacha, in a conference with Montilla and other generals, and also of finding a cooler climate in the Sierra Nevada above the city. The rest of his letter is executive, strategic, policial, ambitious; and so is one he writes to Justo Briceño the same day. That his life was drawing to an end may nevertheless be gathered by the obsequious *post scripta* which his nephew Ferdinand, his amanuensis, adds on his own behalf to his uncle's powerful correspondents.

4

Towards the middle of October, Bolívar was in Soledad, in the neighbourhood of Barranquilla, where he had gone in search of health. On the 16th he reported to Urdaneta: " The ills which I suffer have become complicated in a very painful way." He was planning to sail so as to get rid of his bile by sea-sickness, for he was averse to swallowing medicines. He reveals the source of this repugnance in a later letter: " I hope to be able to sail for a few days to get rid of my bile, for I will take no medicine for anything, least of all when I remember that the emetic I took in Bogotá forced me to leave power at the most critical moment, exposing me to criticism, and possibly to sacrifice." He was afraid of the cold heights for his rheumatism, and of the hot climate for his nerves—" so that, with much pain, I will keep moving and go pacing in the house but am unable to bear a staircase for it makes me suffer too much ". He resolved to devote himself entirely to his health; but gave Urdaneta his advice. He fears the weakness of the Government and the ferocity of the " young demagogues ". Therefore: " Be sure that history has proved that in all civil wars the conqueror has been the most ferocious or the most energetic, according to the meaning of the words." Bolívar had then come to a state of total despair about America. " How could anyone imagine that a whole world could fall into the frenzy of devouring its own kith and kin like cannibals ? "

Though, by October 17th, a Spaniard, Don Joaquín de Mier, at Montilla's suggestion, had already offered him his country house of San Pedro Alejandrino in the neighbourhood of Santa Marta, Bolívar tarried in Soledad. From his bed, he sent the advice he found " on my sad pillow " to Montilla and to Urdaneta; still reporting with evident satisfaction that Cartagena had gone to the polls: " I with 24 votes for President, Urdaneta with 17 for Vice-President." His long letter to Urdaneta (25.x.30) is full of executive energy and generalship. He takes the opportunity to recommend O'Leary and Wilson, " who are useful for everything ", and Luque, " a well-tempered sword "; the same man whom Urdaneta described a few months later as

" the drunkard Luque ".* On October 31st he writes again that he thought his last hour had come, yet goes on to write one of his longest, most executive, indeed imperative letters. His intellect remains unimpaired, his ideas clear, his expression neat and elegant. A third letter to Urdaneta, still from Soledad (4.xi.30), admirably lucid, in which he recommends elections soon in order to regularize the position, contains a notable paragraph: " I must speak to you about a delicate affair. . . . The ill humour and black bile which devour me and my hopelessness about the salvation of the country bring forth in me the blackest thoughts and the least courteous utterances. I shall blurt out the word: I desire you to deliver all my letters of this recent epoch to Colonel Austria, for, in a revolution, they might fall into the hands of my. enemies, who would lend a sinister meaning to them, although I have in all of them one and a thousand times given up supreme power and declared that I had no share whatever in reaction. Austria will send them to me, and if you so desire, I shall return yours or burn them; though yours are edifying for their piety. I also beg you to tear up the letters I write to you, for I am resolved to tell you sometimes what I think, for no one will put out of my head the thought that you are running into a furious hurricane and I do pity you all as good and old companions."

By November 6th he reported some progress to Vergara. He was either diplomatic or premature; for the same day he wrote to Urdaneta that he was worse and so weak that he had suddenly fallen, as if half dead, in a faint. Still, he goes on writing about military affairs and about the incidents between Moore and Henderson, whom he calls " that blackguard ". On the 8th, he writes to Montilla for bread and wine, some beer and some sherry; and in this letter, thirty-nine days before his death, he still says, referring to messages from Flores and from Espinar, both rebellious in their respective satrapies of Ecuador and Panama: " What is absolutely certain is that the populations of both places are among the most devoted to me. . . . It is hoped with good reason that on my answers being received everything will end happily."

5

We catch a glimpse of his life in Soledad through one of his officers, José Vallarino, who arrived (10.xi.30) to report on Panama. " H.E. received me in his bedroom . . . his head covered with a silk cap the colour of an almond shell. After the soup he spoke to me; most deferentially. Lentils were served and he noticed that they had been cooked in oil at which he was annoyed with the cook. . . . And turning again to me, said: ' You will observe that I am somewhat difficult; what would you have, they do not seem able to please me and my state of health makes me intolerant.' The meal was short. Later, coffee was served. It was getting dark and mosquitoes began to be troublesome. H.E. came out with me to the balcony having first covered himself with a hood of embroidered blue cloth lined with crimson velvet, then asked for his boots as the mosquitoes were biting

* See footnote, p. 640.

his feet. We went on talking over the Isthmus and political affairs until nine, when I withdrew. . H.E. kindly came out with me to the stairs. . . . At one o'clock I went to call again . . . he came out to receive me. . . . I asked about his state of health and he answered: I am better. . . . We spoke of the political state of Colombia, ' the peoples ', he said, ' are tired and want nothing but peace and order; for to think that liberal ideas are general is a mistake; many wise people are against the representative system for they think it does not fit these countries.' I argued that a new people could adopt any kind of constitution, so long as it was firmly maintained for long enough for the people to become used to it; ' Do not believe it ', he retorted with liveliness, ' here men are used to the Spanish system, and there is no power strong enough to run contrary to habits rooted in the heart '.'' He spoke with equal liveliness on many other matters present and past. Vallarino reports another meeting: " At sunset I met the *Libertador* who returned from a walk leaning on Major Glen's arm and covered with his embroidered hood. I went with him to his house; as he walked upstairs he had to lean on Glen, for he felt fatigue in breathing, he rested a while on a chair, entered his bedroom, came out again, took some sweets which he offered and I accepted; a little later he invited me to come down to the room below where he was awaited to play cards; he himself went downstairs leaning on his aide-de-camp Captain Iturbide; he went to the table where Señora Molinares, the lady of the house, was waiting, took the cards, called Molinares, begged me to sit as the fourth and we played for two hours, during which I noted that he was ill-humoured when he got a bad deal and that he was frequently fatigued; he took a little sago with yolks of egg and wine, called Iturbide to help him go upstairs and took leave of us."

6

On October 24th, Gasterbond, the doctor, told Bolívar he would not answer for his life if he did not move on to some other climate. Bolívar asked Montilla to send him a boat. On the 26th, he wrote to Urdaneta for a passport, thinking of going to Jamaica. On Wednesday, December 1st, at 7.30 p.m., after a crossing good in itself but painful for him, he arrived in Santa Marta, on board the brig *Manuel*. He had to be conveyed in a sedan chair. That very evening, Montilla brought a Frenchman, Alexandre Prospère Révérend, to take charge of the patient. Some historians have conferred on Révérend the degree of doctor of medicine, which he certainly did not possess. He treated Bolívar with more devotion than science, and from the first diagnosed him as having " his lungs in a bad state " which was safe enough. The next day, Révérend brought in a Dr. M. Night, surgeon of the U.S.A. sloop *Grampus*, who diagnosed chronic lung catarrh. Bolívar took little food, slept but three hours and was often delirious. Night and Révérend went on treating him as best they could. Révérend had tried the open window system; Bolívar had it closed. On December 5th, Night sailed away. Révérend advocated a move to the country. It was decided to take the patient to San Pedro Alejandrino, Mier's country house. Montilla arranged for him to be conveyed in a hammock; but it began to rain, and in the end he went in a carriage. The next day he felt much better; and on December 7th he wrote to Justo Briceño that he was " in hopes of a swift recovery ". He wrote in the same mood to Urdaneta, a businesslike and executive letter.

In these and in others written before and after, he was endeavouring to heal the feud between Urdaneta and Justo Briceño, due mostly to Urdaneta's reluctance to promote Briceño to division general. On the 8th, Bolívar wrote to Vergara explaining that, in view of his turn for the better, he would not go to Jamaica; and that many officers expelled from Venezuela had come to see him and reported that opinion there was " very favourable ". He wrote again to Urdaneta on the 8th, a day on which Révérend notes: " The patient hides his suffering, for when he is alone he groans "; and again: " a perceptible slowing of his intellectual powers." Révérend unfortunately began to prescribe *cantharis*, believing that " the morbid matter, by a metastasic movement of the chest, was going up to the head "—which no doubt must have meant something. Bolívar was worse the next day, and delirious. In the morning of the 10th, he was so ill that Montilla was written to with the weirdest request: " that he send the regimental band to entertain him! " Who was the genius who thought of that is not, unfortunately, recorded. Bolívar's closest circle was then composed of three young men: Bedford Wilson, Iturbide and Fernando Bolívar. The most likely explanation for this tragic-comic incident must be the fact that, while Bolívar was dying, the room next to his was filled with exiled generals, playing cards and noisily arguing about politics. One of them, unable to fathom the drama in the dying man's soul, must have thought that as a cure for melancholy, nothing was so good as a military band. No woman to say " No ". By the bedside of that woman-killer, no woman, mistress, sister, niece, friend, not a single woman was to be seen quietly protecting the dying man from the barrack noises and ill smells which to his last day tormented him. A nemesis perhaps of a life that never sought in women aught but the pleasures they can bring when they surrender.

A second message to Montilla brought the Bishop, with whom Bolívar " conversed while some fifes which had at last been procured to amuse him were played ". The Bishop withdrew for some reflection and came back to recommend Bolívar to put his affairs in order, for he was mortal. Bolívar had a spurt of energy. He called his family (Fernando Bolívar and his brother-in-law Silva were present), and asked them whether the doctor agreed with the Bishop; he was told he did. But Bolívar did not agree with either. He did not feel as bad as all that. He rose from the hammock and began to walk. " For a long while he tried to struggle with nature, saying that he would not allow himself to die of weakness. But his body was unable to bear so violent an effort for long." Montilla called, and they conversed; then, feeling weak, Bolívar lay down on his hammock again, and both the General and the Bishop urged him to consider his spiritual affairs in the little life that remained. He asked to be given time for reflection. He evidently felt no personal, inner inclination to die in the bosom of the

Church; but his two advisers, the General and the Bishop, pointed out to him his uncommon situation, the moral effect of the death of the *Libertador* without the Sacraments of the Church. He asked for time again, rose and began to pace the room. He first gave Montilla instructions as to his property, then " he remained for some time wrapped in thought. Until lunch time he was uneasy, talking sometimes and sometimes evidently in an inner fight with his ideas ". Montilla urged him again to prepare and to put himself right with the Church. He objected that this would " be too solemn while living in the country ". He evidently was reluctant to stage a merely political conversion. " He was assured that this would not be so at all; that he owed it to the moral influence which the act would have." Then, his nephew Fernando who was present writes, " with a greatness of soul which nothing can equal and evincing his great interest in the praise-worthy aims in view without troubling about small obstacles, he agreed immediately to do it ". That very night extreme unction was administered by the priest (an Indian) of the parish of Mamatoco, a village nearby, very simply, in fact humbly, in the presence of a few Indians.

As soon as the priest left, the Notary Public, Catalino Noguera, in a circle of generals and other friends, began to read Bolívar's last address to the Colombians. " You have witnessed my endeavours to sow liberty where tyranny once reigned. I have laboured with distinterestedness, forsaking my fortune and even my peace. I severed myself from power when I became convinced that you mistrusted my selflessness. My enemies abused your credulity and trampled upon what for me is most sacred, my reputation and my love of freedom. I have been the victim of my persecutors, who have led me to the gates of the sepulchre. I forgive them." The reader, too moved to continue, passed the papers to Dr. Manuel Recuero, an army advocate, who went on: " As I vanish from your midst, my love tells me that I must impart to you my last wishes: I seek no other glory than the consolidation of Colombia. You must all work for the invaluable boon of union: the people by obeying the present government to free themselves from tyranny; the ministers of the Sanctuary, by addressing their prayers to Heaven, and the military, by putting their swords in the service of social guarantees. Colombians, my last vows are for the happiness of the father-land. If my death contributes to end all factions and to consolidate the union, I shall go down in peace to the grave."—" Yes, to the grave "—the dying man confirmed.—" That is where my countrymen send me. . . . But I forgive them." The voice coming back from " the gates of the grave ", moved to tears the circle of men, most of them hardened by wars, and they dispersed in silence.

The next day, this man who was to die wrote his last letter. " In the last moments of my life, I write this letter to request you, as the only token that remains for you to give me of your affection and consideration, to reconcile yourself in good faith with General Urdaneta and rally to the Government to support it. My heart tells me, dear General, that you will not deny me this last homage to friendship and duty. Only by suppressing personal feelings can our friends save Colombia from anarchy." The union of Colombia was his last thought. He often spoke in his sleep, and even half awake, a state in which he spent his last days. We may guess what was going on in his delirious head. It had emerged in his letter to Flores from Barranquilla a few weeks earlier (9.xi.30). " You know I have held power for twenty years, and I have drawn but a few sure conclusions. 1.—America is ungovernable for us. 2.—He who serves a revolution ploughs the sea. 3.—The only thing one can do in America is to emigrate. 4.— This country will infallibly fall into the hands of an unbridled crowd of petty tyrants almost too small for notice and of all colours and races. 5.—Devoured by all the crimes and extinguished by ferocity, we shall be disdained by the Europeans, who will not deign to conquer us. 6.—If it were possible for a part of the world to fall back to primitive chaos, America would." The root of this pessimism was Páez, the petty tyrant of all colours and races. Páez had been the chief factor in his life; and now, his head resting on that sad pillow, in the house of one of the few Spaniards he had left alive in Colombia, Bolívar was bound to feel so. For it was in order to turn his back on Páez that he had gone to Bogotá and on to Peru. The union of Colombia, and later the Empire of the Andes were the two grandiose stages he had built for himself in order to leave Páez in control of Venezuela and yet—small. The Empire had proved a chimera. After nearly grasping it in glorious Lima, Bolívar had been bound to let it go and return northwards. Every day northward was one day closer to Páez, one day closer to defeat. But there was still Bogotá. The union of Colombia became sacred because it was the only way whereby he, a Venezuelan, could reign in Nueva Granada and in Quito, and in Venezuela as well—the only way he could reign over Páez. Monocracy was but an aspect of this device, and the way to consolidate it. And his chief collaborators were Venezuelan generals ousted westward by Páez. The dreaded cowboy had neutralized, or reduced to impotence, subservience, or futile rebellion all the Venezuelan generals who had remained in the east—Soublette, Bermúdez, Mariño, Monagas and the rest; those gone west and south had no hope but Colombia. Urdaneta, Montilla, Flores, as Venezuelans, were lost; only as Colombians could they prosper and command. True, Flores carved for himself a kingdom in Quito—but for how long? Union, union, said Bolívar. Union, union, brawled the generals thumping their cards on the table in the pipe-smoke laden room next door. Union was the only way for all who reached power and glory. And since his experience had shown Bolívar that union required a strong government and that Spanish America was too much used to the Spanish system to tolerate other than monocratic institutions, a monocracy as well. Spain was not wrong after all. It was he, Bolívar, who had been wrong. He now saw it—too late. The dying man broke into incoherent phrases. " Let us go . . . let us go . . . this people don't want us in this land! . . . Let's go, boys . . . my baggage . . . take my baggage on board the frigate. . . ." At one o'clock, on December 17th, 1830, exactly the month, the day, the hour, when, in 1819, he had signed the union of Colombia in Angostura, the frigate sailed for eternity.

EPILOGUE

THE POSTHUMOUS RESIGNATION

BOLÍVAR stepped forward before the bar of History and said: I come before you to submit to you the first of my resignations which I present with all my heart. I come to resign my title of Liberator.

You are not astounded. I expected that. At the distance you behold me, all astonishment ceases. But those who were my companions on earth and whose bodily lives were intertwined with my own, would have opened wide their eyes on hearing from me what for them would have been a blasphemy against myself. " Liberator " was ever my most prized title of glory. " Either Liberator or dead," my sister said once. To-day I resign my title of Liberator because I want to live.

I want to live as one wants to live in History—in the light of truth. From these heights, free at last from the clay which clogs the spirit while on the Earth, I realize that the title of Liberator which I carved for myself with my sword on the body of five nations now weighs down my perennial self and prevents it from rising in its true size on the background of things as they are. No, I am not, I never was, your Liberator.

Who could give what he has not ? How could I give you a liberty I did not possess ? And you will ask: why, were you not rich and noble ? Noble and rich, certainly; but not free. For freedom is a gift from Heaven, granted only to the few, and I was not born among those so elected. My cradle was held by the golden chains of privilege; and I was born a slave to the passion for power, less free than my negro slaves, more their slave than they were mine.

I was all my life a slave to my passions. I shall not dwell on the most scandalous—and yet, perhaps the most venial of them, beyond reminding you that from the day I entered Quito, I lived tied to a woman by a chain of roses no less welcome for the thorns it hid. Other passions mastered me more tyrannously. I was cruel. Do not deny it. At this distance, what boots your kindly dissimulation ? I was cruel to the Spaniards, so cruel that I once cried out: " After being Nero to the Spaniards, I have had enough of blood." I was cruel also to the Indians, and as to the men of Pasto, because they stood across my path, I had them exterminated.

I was ambitious; and to pander to my ambition, I did not hesitate to tear the charters I had sworn to respect, when their ink was hardly dry on the paper; nor did my hand tremble when I emptied homes of their youth by forced levies, and when I made cities and countryside desolate with my wars. I crossed the Andes on one hecatomb and took Guayaquil on another.

How could I have liberated you ? All I did was to tear to tatters with my sword a thrice secular tradition which had interwoven your froward

649

freedoms into a social canvas whereon History had embroidered an Indo-Spanish pattern. But the sword neither weaves nor embroiders; and when I tried to recreate in three years what Spain had created in three centuries, the many-coloured tangle of human shreds half torn from that pattern I had destroyed suddenly became a demagogic hydra which ate my heart and threw me into a solitary grave.

One hundred and twenty years have gone by, and what years! Had a malicious spirit revealed them to me when I swore to liberate you on the Monte Sacro, when I declared war on Spain, when I hid my head in my hands at Puerto Cabello, when I conquered in Boyacá and Carabobo, when I saw at last Colombia on her feet and Peru at mine, believe me, had I then seen those hundred years full of Obandos, Gamarras, Páezs, stuffed with paper-constitutions and wind-assemblies, prisons, exiles, dictators—perhaps . . .

But no. I should not have faltered. True, a thousand times true, I did not liberate you. The essence of liberty is precisely that one can only liberate oneself. But true also that when I told you that I was your Liberator, I believed it sincerely. The hour had struck in History when earth, blood, spirit, all clamoured for your separation from Spain. The day needed its man. That man I was. Who chose me for that historical destiny? My ambition. Thus, between you and me a strong chain of mutual service came to be forged: I should emancipate you from Spain; you would emancipate me from my ambition and from that passion for command which commanded me. As nature takes advantage of man's lust to ensure the life of the species, so History took advantage of my ambition to resolve the knot of the Spanish Empire in America.

Behold me now in my real size, shorn by my own hand of the title of Liberator you had granted me. Neither I Liberator, nor Cortés Conqueror nor Colón Discoverer; none of the three protagonists of this trilogy is what he seems to be. The three of us have paced the stage of History with the firm step of those who create their own lineage, eager for fame and glory. The three of us have been mere tools of Something which, even now, we are unable to fathom. Colón knew not that he was discovering America; Cortés saw not that he was creating the Mexican Republic; I dreamt not that the soul of the Tyrant Aguirre, which used to burn as a will-o'-the-wisp over the plains of Venezuela, would again tyrannize over you, pouring itself as a sea of barren oil over your once fertile valleys. *Man proposes and God disposes*, says a proverb which, being Spanish, is ours. Neither Colón discovered himself, nor Cortés conquered himself, nor I liberated myself—nor would he who tried to explain us three be able to explain himself nor to guess the after-effects in History of the triptych of tragedies he has designed with our lives.

ACKNOWLEDGMENTS

A WORK of this scope could not have been attempted without the help of a number of persons and institutions; so that to be strictly fair, this note would have to be lengthened considerably. In the marshalling of all these collaborations as in every other stage in the writing of this book I have benefited by the competence, untiring zeal and good advice of Mrs. Emilia Rauman, who, from the days when I was at work on the Life of Hernán Cortés, has been my right-hand assistant.

Thanks are due to the British Museum, the London Library, the Library of the Oxford Chair of Spanish Studies, and the Library of the Venezuelan Embassy in London; as well as to Miss Sylvia England. The list of keepers of Archives to whom I owe acknowledgments is long. I shall quote, in particular, the National Archives and the Archives of the Ministry of Finance, in Lima; the National Archives and the invaluable private archives of Don Jacinto Jijón Caamaño in Quito; the excellent Provincial Archives of Popayán; the National Archives in Bogotá; the National and the Archiepiscopal Archives in Caracas, as well as the Archives now collected in the house in which Bolívar was born; the National Archives in Havana; the P.R.O. and the Archives of the *Ministère des Affaires Etrangères* in Paris.

I owe thanks to many friends who lent me books; and, in particular, to Don Miguel Angel Cárcano and Don Alfredo González Garaño, of Buenos Aires; Dr. Don Eduardo Santos, who gave me facilities to visit Bucaramanga; General Chiriboga, who, on the spot, explained the battle of Pichincha; Don Manuel Arocha, whose studies in Bolívar's iconography were most valuable; Dr. Perera, a sure guide in Caracas; Don Emeterio Santovenia and Don Joaquín Llaverías, who provided photocopies of the documents I had studied in Habana; Don Enrique Ortega Ricaurte, who provided those needed in Bogotá; and, above all, Don Vicente Lecuna, whose help in Caracas and his advice ever since I was there have been invaluable.

Thanks are also due to my wife (Constance Archibald, M.A.) for her patient and careful reading of the English text.

SOURCES

Only those sources actually quoted are mentioned below. Over and above such sources, obviously many more had to be consulted which, though used, are not quoted. Even of the quoted sources, as enumerated in the Bibliography, the classic ones, such as Baralt, Restrepo, O'Leary, Gil Fortoul . . . have often been left unmentioned in the Notes, particularly when the text itself refers to the origin of the quotation. In any case, specialists are referred to the Spanish edition. All the letters from Bolívar come from *C.L.* unless otherwise stated.

MANUSCRIPTS

1. Archivo del Ministerio de Hacienda, Palacio de Justicia, Lima.
2. Archivo Nacional, Biblioteca Nacional, Lima.
3. Archivo Nacional, Quito.
4. Archivo particular de Don Jacinto Jijón Caamaño, Quito.
5. Archivo Nacional, Bogotá.
6. Archivo Provincial, Popayán.
7. Archivo Nacional, Caracas.
8. Archivo del Arzobispado, Caracas.
9. Archivo de la Casa Natal, Caracas.
10. Archivo Nacional de La Habana.
11. Public Record Office, London.
12. Archives Nationales, Affaires Etrangères, Palais du Quai d'Orsay, Paris.

BIBLIOGRAPHY

A.R. C.H.—Aristides Rojas, *Capítulos de la Historia Colonial de Venezuela.* Madrid, 1919.
A.R. E.H.—Aristides Rojas, *Estudios Históricos.* Caracas, 1926.
A.R. L.H.—Aristides Rojas, *Leyendas Históricas.* Caracas, 1927.
A.S.—*Archivo de Santander.* Bogotá, 1913. 18 vols.
Alamán.—*Historia de Méjico desde los primeros movimientos que prepararon su independencia en el año de 1808 hasta la época presente* por Don Lucas Alamán. Méjico, 1849.
Altamira.—Rafael Altamira, *Historia de España y de la Civilización Española.* Barcelona, 1929. 4 vols.
Amunátegui.—*Los Precursores de la Independencia de Chile* por Miguel Luis Amunátegui. Santiago, 1870. 2 vols.
Arenales.—José J. Arenales, *Segunda Campaña a la Sierra del Peru en 1821.* Buenos Aires, 1920.
Argentina.—*Historia de la Nación Argentina.* Publicada bajo la dirección de Ricardo Levene. Buenos Aires, 1936-39.
Arocha.—Manuel Arocha, *Iconografía Ecuatoriana del Libertador.* Quito-Ecuador, 1943.
B.A.N.H.V.—*Boletín de la Academia Nacional de la Historia.* Caracas-Venezuela.
B.H.—*Extracts from a Journal written on the coasts of Chili, Peru and Mexico in the Years 1820, 1821, 1822 by Captain Basil Hall.* Edinburgh, 1824. 2 vols.
B.M.B.—*Boletín del Museo Bolivariano.* Magdalena Vieja, Lima.
Baralt.—*Resúmen de la Historia de Venezuela desde el descubrimiento de su territorio por los castellanos en el siglo XV hasta el año 1797.* Por Rafael María Baralt. Brujas-Paris, 1939. 3 vols.
Basadre.—Jorge Basadre, *Chile, Peru y Bolivia Independientes.* En Ballesteros: Historia de América, t. XXV. Barcelona-Buenos Aires, 1948.
Beard.—*The Rise of American Civilisation.* By Charles and Mary R. Beard. London, 1944.
Belaunde.—*Bolívar and the Political Thought of the Spanish-American Revolution.* By Victor Andrés Belaunde. Baltimore, 1938.
Bingham.—Hiram Bingham, Ph.D. (Harvard), F.R.G.S. Lectures on Latin-American History, Yale University. *The Journal of an Expedition across Venezuela and Colombia, 1906-1907. An Exploration of the Route of Bolívar's Celebrated March of 1819 and of the Battlefields of Boyacá and Carabobo.* New-Haven, Conn., 1909.
Blanco.—José Felix Blanco. *Documentos para la historia de la vida pública del Libertador de Colombia, Perú y Bolivia.* Caracas, 1875-1878.
Bobes-B.C.—Luis Bermúdez de Castro, *Bobes o El León de los Llanos.* Madrid, 1934.
Botero.—R. Botero Saldarriaga, *El Libertador Presidente.* Bogotá, 1930.
Bourgoing.—*Travels in Spain; containing A New, Accurate, And Comprehensive View Of The Present State Of That Country.* By the Chevalier de Bourgoanne. London, 1789. 3 vols.
Boussingault.—*Mémoires de J. B. Boussingault.* Paris, 1892. 5 vols.
Briceño.—Mariano de Briceño. *Historia de la Isla de Margarita (hoy Nueva España); Biografías del General Juan B. Arismendi y de la Señora Luisa Cáceres de Arismendi.* Caracas, 1885.
Bulnes.—Gonzalo Bulnes, *Bolívar en el Perú.* Madrid, 1919. 2 vols.
C.B.S.—*Bolívar y Santander.* Correspondencia 1819-1820. Estado Mayor General. Ministerio de la Guerra. Bogotá, 1940.
C.C. S.M.—*Vida del Muy Magnífico Señor Don Cristóbal Colón.* Por Salvador de Madariaga. Editorial Sudamericana. Buenos Aires, 1940.
C.H.—Cornelio Hispano, *Historia Secreta de Bolívar.* Bogotá, 1944.
C.L.—*Cartas del Libertador.* Publicadas por Vicente Lecuna. Caracas, 1929. 10 vols. y un vol. adicional (1948).
C.M.A.—Daniel Arías Argáez, *El Canónigo Don José Cortes y Madariaga.* Bogotá, 1938.
C.P.—Carlos Pereyra, *La Juventud Legendaria de Bolívar.* Madrid, 1932.
Camba.—Andrés García Camba, *Memorias del General García Camba.* Madrid. 2 vols.
Carbonell.—Diego Carbonell, *Psicopatología de Bolívar.* Paris, 1916.
Carraffa.—*Enciclopedia Heráldica y Genealógica.* García Carraffa. Madrid.
Cochrane-Journal.—Capt. Charles Stuart Cochrane, *Journal of a Residence and Travels in Colombia During the Years 1823 and 1824.* London, 1825. 2 vols.
Cochrane-Life.—*The Autobiography of a Seaman.* By Thomas, Tenth Earl of Dundonald, G.C.B. London, 1860. 2 vols.
Cordova.—R. Botero Saldarriaga, *General José María Córdova.* Bogotá, 1927.
Crespo.—Alfonso Crespo, *Santa Cruz. El Condor Indio.* Mexico, 1944.
Chesterton.—*Peace, War and Adventure.* An Autobiographical Memoir of George Laval Chesterton. London, 1853. 2 vols.
Chuecos.—Hector García Chuecos, *Don Fernando de Peñalver. Su Vida. Su Obra.* Caracas, 1941.

D.B.—Simón Rodríguez. Maestro del Libertador. *Defensa de Bolívar.* Caracas, 1916.

D.B. C.H.—*Diario de Bucaramanga* por L. Peru de Lacroix. Publicado por primera vez con una introducción y notas por Cornelio Hispano. Bogotá, 1945.

D.B.N.—*Diario de Bucaramanga* por Monseñor Nicolás E. Navarro. Caracas, 1935.

D.B. P.L.—L. Peru de Lacroix, *Diario de Bucaramanga.* Madrid, 1924.

D.L.—*Voyage Aux Iles de Trinidad de Tabago, de la Marguerite, et dans Diverses Parties de Venezuela, dans l'Amerique meridionale.* Par M. Dauxion Lavaysse. Paris, 1812. 2 vols.

D.L. H.M.—Lino Duarte Level, *Cuadros de la Historia Militar y Civil de Venezuela.* Madrid.

Dalencour.—*Alexandre Petion Devant L'Humanité* par le Docteur François Dalencour. Port au Prince.

Depons.—*Travels in South America during the years* 1801, 1802, 1803 *and* 1804, by F. Depons. London, 1807. 2 vols.

Ducoudray.—Gen. H. L. V. Ducoudray Holstein, *Memoirs of Simón Bolívar President Liberator of the Republic of Colombia; and of his Principal Generals; comprising a Secret History of the Revolution and the Events which Preceded it from* 1807 *to the Present Time.* Bentley, 1830.

Duro.—*Armada Española Desde la Unión de los Reinos de Castilla y de León* por Cesareo Fernández Duro. Madrid, 1895. 9 vols.

E.M.C.—*Campaña de Invasión del Teniente General Don Pablo Morillo,* 1815–1816. Contribución del Estado Mayor General a la celebración del Centenario de la batalla de Boyacá. Bogotá, 1919.

Fall.—S. de Madariaga, *The Fall of the Spanish American Empire.* London, 1947.

F.E.—*Examen Imparcial de las Disensiones de la América con la España, de los medios de su reciproco interés, y de la utilidad de los aliados de la España.* Por D. Alvaro Flórez Estrada, Procurador General del Principado de Asturias. Londres, 1811.

G.C.—*Gaceta de Caracas.* Edición Facsímile de la Academia Nacional de la Historia de Venezuela. Paris, 1939.

G.F.—*Historia Constitucional de Venezuela,* por José Gil Fortoul. Caracas, 1930. 3 vols.

G.V.—Eloy G. González, *Historia de Venezuela. Desde el Descubrimiento hasta* 1830. Caracas, 1930. 2 vols.

Grillo.—Max Grillo, *El Hombre de las Leyes.* Bogotá, 1940.

Groot.—José Manuel Groot, *Historia Eclesiástica y Civil de Nueva Granada,* 1889–93.

Guayaquil-C.G.M.V.—Ernesto de la Cruz, J. M. Goenaga, B. Mitre, Carlos A. Villanueva, *La Entrevista de Guayaquil. El. Libertador y San Martín.* Editorial América, Madrid.

Guevara.—Arturo Guevara, *Historia Clínica del Libertador.* Caracas, 1948.

H.C. S.M.—*Hernán Cortés,* por Salvador de Madariaga. Buenos Aires, 1942.

H. P.N.—*Voyage aux régions équinoxiales du Nouveau Continent, fait en* 1799, 1800, *et* 1804 *par Alexandre de Humboldt.* Paris, 1814.

Hamilton.—*Travels through the interior Provinces of Columbia,* by Colonel J. P. Hamilton. London, 1827. 2 vols.

Hasbrouck.—*Foreign Legionaries in the Liberation of Spanish America,* by Alfred Hasbrouck, M.A. New York, 1928.

Heredia.—*Memorias sobre las Revoluciones de Venezuela* por D. José Francisco Heredia Regente que fué de la Real Audiencia de Caracas seguidas de *Documentos Inéditos y Precedidas de un Estudio Biográfico.* Por D. Enrique Piñeiro. Paris, 1895.

Hippisley.—*A Narrative of the Expedition to the Rivers Orinoco and Apure in South America; which sailed From England in November* 1817, *and joined the Patriotic Forces in Venezuela and Caracas,* by G. Hippisley, Esq. London, 1819.

Holland.—*Foreign Reminiscences* by Henry Richard, Lord Holland; edited by his son Henry Edward, Lord Holland. London, 1850.

Humbert.—*Les Origines Venezuliennes. Essai sur la Colonisation Espagnole au Vénézuela* par Jules Humbert. Bordeaux. Paris, 1905.

Humboldt-Lettres.—*Oeuvres d'Alexandre de Humboldt. Correspondance inédite scientifique et littéraire* recueillie et publiée par M. de la Roquete. Paris, 1869.

Humboldt-Life.—*Life of Alexander von Humboldt compiled in commemoration of the centenary of his birth* by J. Löwenberg, Robert Ave-Lallemant and Alfred Dove. Edited by Professor Karl Bruhns, Director of the Observatory at Leipzig. Translated from the German by Jane and Caroline Lassell. London, 1873. 2 vols.

J.D.D.—*Recuerdos sobre la Rebelión de Caracas.* José Domingo Díaz. Madrid, 1829.

J.M.O.—José María Obando, *Apuntamientos para la Historia.* Bogotá, 1945. 2 vols.

J.V.G.—Juan Vicente González, *Biografía de José Felix Ribas* (Epoca de la Guerra a Muerte). Paris, 1913.

Jovellanos.—D. Gaspar de Jovellanos, *A Sus Compatriotas.* MEMORIA en que se rebaten las calumnias divulgadas contra los individuos de la junta central. Coruña. Año de 1811.

L.A.S.—*Historial Genealógico del Libertador* por Luis Alberto Sucre. Caracas, 1930.

L.-Casa.—Vicente Lecuna-Julio Planchart, *Historia de la Casa de Bolívar y Anotaciones sobre su reedificación.* Caracas, 1924.

Laborde.—Voyage Pittoresque de l'Espagne par Alexandre de Laborde. Paris, 1820.

*Larrazábal.—*Felipe Larrazábal, *Vida del Libertador Simón Bolívar.* Edición modernizada con prólogo y notas de R. Blanco Fombona.

*Leturia-B.—*Pedro Leturia, S.J., *Bolívar y León XII.* Caracas, 1931.

Leturia-E.—La Emancipación Hispanoamericana en los Informes Episcopales a Pío VII. Copias y Extractos del Archivo Vaticano por el P. Pedro Leturia, S.I. Buenos Aires. Imprenta de la Universidad, 1935 en Publicaciones del Instituto de Investigaciones Históricas 67–70. Universidad de Buenos Aires, 1935–37.

*Leturia-P.—*P. Pedro Leturia, S.J. *La acción diplomática de Bolívar ante Pío VII.* (1820–1823.) Madrid, 1925.

López.—Recuerdos Históricos del Coronel Manuel Antonio López. Colombia y Perú, 1819–1826. Bogotá, 1878.

*Lozano.—*Fabio Lozano y Lozano, *El Maestró del Libertador.* Paris.

*Mancini.—*Jules Mancini, *Bolívar et l'Emancipation des Colonies Espagnoles des Origines à* 1815. Paris, 1912.

Marion.—Expédition de Bolívar par le Sénateur Marion ainé. Deuxième Edition conforme à l'originale et revue par le Docteur François Dalencour.

Martiñena.—Verdadero Origen, Carácter, Causas, Resortes, Fines y Progresos de la Revolución de Nueva España y Defensa de los europeos en general residentes en ella, y especialmente de los autores de la aprehensión y destitución del Virey D. José de Iturrigaray en la noche del 15 de setiembre de 1808, contra los falsos calumniadores que los infaman y atribuyen el indicado suceso, a opresión, agresión y ofensa de su parte contra los americanos, la desastrosa revolución que ha asolado este reino. Mexico, 1820.

Mier.—Memorias de Fray Servando Teresa da Mier. Prólogo de D. Alfonso Reyes. Madrid. Sin fecha.

*Miller.—*John Miller, *Memorias del General Miller al servicio de la República del Perú.* Traducción por el General Torrijos. Madrid, 1910. 2 vols.

*Miramón.—*Alberto Miramón, *La Vida Ardiente de Manuelita Sánz.* Bogotá, 1944.

Miranda-Archivo.—Archivo del General Miranda, 1750–1810. Caracas-Venezuela, 1929–1938. 15 vols.

*Miranda-Becerra.—*Ricardo Becerra, *Vida de Don Francisco de Miranda.* Madrid. 2 vols.

Miranda-Biggs.—The History of Don Francisco de Miranda's Attempt to effect a Revolution in South America, in a series of letters. Boston, 1810.

Miranda-Life.—The Life of Miranda, by W. S. Robertson. Chapel Hill, 1929. 2 vols.

*Mitre.—*Bartolomé Mitre. *Historia de San Martín y de la Emancipación Sudamericana.* Buenos Aires, 1887. 3 vols.

*Mollien.—*G. Mollien, *Voyage Dans La République de Colombia en 1823.* Paris, 1824. 2 vols.

Morillo.—Manifiesto que hace a la Nación Española el Teniente General Don Pablo Morillo. Madrid, 1821.

*Mosquera.—*General C. de Mosquera, *Memorias sobre la Vida del Libertador Simón Bolívar.* New York, 1853.

*Mulhall.—*Michael George Mulhall, *The English in South America.* London and Buenos Aires, 1878.

*Navarro.—*Monseñor Nicolas E. Navarro, *La Cristiana Muerte del Libertador.* Caracas, 1930.

O.B.—Historia de la Conquista y Población de la Provincia de Venezuela por D. Joseph de Oviedo y Baños. Madrid, 1723.

*O'C.—*F. Burdett O'Connor, *Independencia Americana.* Recuerdos de Francisco Burdett O'Connor. Madrid.

O.C.N.—Recollections of a Service of three Years During the War of Extermination In the Republics of Venezuela and Colombia. By An Officer of the Colombian Navy. London, 1828. 2 vols.

*O'L.—*Daniel F. O'Leary, *Bolívar y la Emancipación de Sur-América.* Memorias del General O'Leary. Traducidas del inglés por su hijo Simón B. O'Leary. 1819–1826. Madrid.

*O'L.-C.—*Daniel F. O'Leary, *Correspondencia de Extranjeros Notables con el Libertador.* Madrid, 1920. 2 vols.

*O'L.-P.—*Daniel Florencio O'Leary, *Historia de la Independencia Americana, La Emancipación del Perú, Según la Correspondencia del General Heres con el Libertador* (1821–1830). Madrid, 1919.

*O'L.-S.—*Daniel O'Leary, *Cartas de Sucre al Libertador* (1820–1826). Madrid, 1919. 2 vols.

*O'L.-U.—*Daniel F. O'Leary, *Ultimos Años de la Vida Pública de Bolívar.* Madrid.

*O'L.-Panamá.—*Daniel Florencio O'Leary, *El Congreso Internacional de Panamá en 1826. Desgobierno y anarquía en la Gran Colombia.* Madrid, 1920.

Orinoco.—Correo del Orinoco, 1818–21. Academia Nacional de la Historia de Venezuela. Paris, 1939. Edición Fotográfica.

P.B.—Simón Bolívar, Papeles de Bolívar. Publicados por Vicente Lecuna. Madrid, 1920. 2 vols.

P.D.L.—Vicente Lecuna, *Proclamas y Discursos del Libertador.* Caracas, 1939.
P.F.—*Outline of the Revolution in Spanish America* by a South American. London, 1817.
P.G.—Joaquín Posada Gutiérrez, *Memorias Histórico-Políticas. Ultimos Días de la Gran Colombia y del Libertador.* Madrid, 1921. 3 vols.
P.L.—Dr. Caracciolo Parra León, *Filosofía Universitaria Venezolana, 1788–1821.* Caracas, 1934.
P.P.—C. Parra Pérez, *El Régimen Español en Venezuela.* Madrid, 1932.
P.P.-H.R.—C. Parra Pérez, *Historia de la Primera República de Venezuela.* Caracas, 1932. 2 vols.
P.P.-M.R.—C. Parra Pérez, *Miranda et la Révolution Française.* Paris, 1925.
P.P.-P.P.—C. Parra Pérez, *Páginas de Historia y de Polémica.* Caracas, 1943.
Páez.—*Autobiografía del General José Antonio Páez.* Nueva York, 1878.
Páez-W.S.—*Wild Scenes in South America or Life in the Llanos of Venezuela,* by Don Ramón Páez. London, 1863.
Paz.—Paz-Soldán, *Historia del Perú Independiente.* Madrid, 1919.
Pérez Soto.—Juan B. Pérez y Soto, *El Crimen de Berruecos.* Roma, 1924.
Pinilla.—Sabino Pinilla, *La Creación de Bolivia.* Madrid.
Ponte.—Andrés F. Ponte, *Bolívar y Otros Ensayos.* Caracas, 1919.
Proceso.—*Proceso del 25 de Setiembre. Documentos sobre la Conspiración.* Publicado por Enrique Ortega Ricaurte. Bogotá, 1942.
Pruvonena.—*Memorias y Documento para la Historia de la Independencia del Perú y Causas del Mal Exito que ha tenido esta.* Obra póstuma de Pruvonena. Paris, 1858. 2 vols.
R.A.B.M.—*Revista de Archivos, Bibliotecas y Museos.* Madrid.
R.D.U.—*Relación Documentada del Origen y Progresos del trastorno de las Provincias de Venezuela.* Escribióla Don Pedro de Urquinaona y Pardo. Madrid, 1820.
R.V.G.B.—Francisco Rivas Vicuña, *Las Guerras de Bolívar, 1812–1814, 1814–1817.* Caracas, 1922. 2 vols.
Restrepo.—José Manuel Restrepo, *Historia de la Revolución de la República de Colombia en la América Meridional.* Besanzon, 1858. 4 vols.
Révérend.—A. P. Révérend, *La Agonía, la Muerte y los Funerales del Libertador.* Bogotá, 1930.
Revista Bolivariana.—Organo de la Sociedad Bolivariana de Colombia. Bogotá.
Rise.—S. de Madariaga, *The Rise of the Spanish American Empire.* London, 1947.
Rojas.—Marqués de Rojas, *Simón Bolívar.* Paris, 1883.
Samper.—Soledad Acosta de Samper, *Biografía del General Nariño.* Pasto, 1910.
Sañudo.—José Rafael Sañudo, *Estudios sobre la Vida de Bolívar.* Pasto, 1931.
Ségur.—M. le Comte de Ségur, *Mémoires ou Souvenirs et Anecdotes.* Paris, 1825.
Sevilla.—Rafael Sevilla. *Memorias de un Militar.* La Guerra de América. Paris.
Sevilla-A.—*Memorias de un oficial del Ejército Español.* Madrid, 1916.
Spell.—Jefferson Rea Spell, *Rousseau in the Spanish World before 1833.* Austin, 1938.
Stanhope.—Philip Henry, 5th Earl Stanhope, *Notes of Conversations with the Duke of Wellington, 1831–1851.* London, 1888.
Temperley.—Harold Temperley, *The Foreign Policy of Canning, 1822–1827, England, the Neo-Holy Alliance and the New World.* London, 1925.
Torata.—*Documentos para la Historia de la Guerra Separatista del Perú,* por el Conde de Torata. Madrid, 1894–8.
Toreno.—*Historia del Levantamiento, Guerra y Revolución de España,* por el Excmo. Sr. Conde de Toreno. Madrid, 1872.
Torrente.—*Historia de la Revolución Hispano Americana* por D. Mariano Torrente, Autor de la Geografía Universal. Madrid, 1829. 3 vols.
Urdaneta.—*Memorias del General Rafael Urdaneta.* Biblioteca Ayacucho, Madrid.
Urrutia.—Francisco José Urrutia, *Los Estados Unidos de América y las Repúblicas Hispano-Americanas de 1810 a 1830.* Madrid, 1918.
Vidocq.—*Mémoires de Vidocq, Chef de la Police de Sureté, Jusqu'en 1827.* Paris, 1823. 3 vols.
Villa.—Antonio Rodríguez Villa, *El Teniente General Don Pablo Morillo.* Madrid, 1908.
Villanueva B. S.M.—*Bolívar y el General San Martín* por Carlos A. Villanueva. Paris, 1913.
Villanueva-I.A.—*El Imperio de los Andes* por Carlos A. Villanueva. Paris, 1913.
Villapaterna.—*Apuntes Histórico-Críticos para Escribir la Historia de la Revolución de España desde el año 1820 hasta 1923* por el Marqués de Miraflores, Conde de Villapaterna. Londres, 1835.
Webster.—C. K. Webster, *Britain and the Independence of Latin America.* Oxford, 1938. 2 vols.
Yanes.—Francisco Javier Yanes, *Relación Documentada de los Principales Sucesos Ocurridos en Venezuela desde que se declaró Estado Independiente hasta el año de 1821.* Caracas, 1943. 3 vols.
Yanes-M.—Francisco Javier Yanes, *Memoria Histórico-Política sobre la Isla Margarita.* Publicada por Don Vicente Lecuna.

NOTES TO THE CHAPTERS

BOOK I

CHAPTER I (pp. 3–9)

1.

H.P.N., Book VI, ch. XII, vol. I, pp. 577 ss.; vol. II, p. 147; see also vol. I, p. 385 and vol. III, p. 29. *Depons*, vol. II, ch. X, pp. 151 ss.; *ibid.*, vol. II, p. 51.

Good summary on the position of slaves in *C.P.*, pp. 92 ss., who gives (from Arcaya) the case of the negro Juan Nicolás (a slave of the priest Dr. Franciso de la Colina) who left to three heirs 90 plough beasts and a considerable number of bulls, calves, mares, asses, mules, goats, a plot of land and a number of credits.

On the *llaneros*, see *Wild Scenes in South America* by Don Ramón Páez, London, 1863.

2.

Ségur, vol. I, p. 423. *O.B.*, quoted by *G.F.*, vol. I, pp. 109–10. *H.P.N.*, *loc. cit.*, p. 581.

3.

Depons, vol. II, pp. 173 ss., 192. *Humbert*, ch. II, p. 171.

4.

Depons, vol. II, pp. 183–4. True he adds: " If we do not also see persons well skilled in political economy, it is because whatever is not in the Canon or civil law is banished from the schools "—but this is one of the many errors on the University of Caracas which have been exposed by *P.L.* and Humboldt, as quoted in the text, proves Depons wrong.—*H.P.N.*, Book IV, ch. XIII, vol. I, p. 591.

A.R.E.H., App. 182. Also *Humbert*, Book II, ch. III, p. 63 and Book III, ch. III, p. 175.

List of Chairs: *Humbert*, *loc. cit.*, p. 178 n.; *P.L.*, notably the footnotes, pp. 69 ss.

I have not even raised the matter of the printing press. There was no printing press in Venezuela till 1808. The article on this subject in *A.R.E.H.*, pp. 1 ss., is typical of this picturesque but often inaccurate writer. Nothing but a deliberate policy on the part of the Council of the Indies to keep Venezuela exceptionally backward and badly governed could explain the facts as he sees them. And of course, he comes to a point where he is bound to admit that he cannot understand what happens. " One cannot understand how the Spanish Government, prodigal in liberal concessions for the other regions of the continent, to which he had known how to send men of initiative who took upon themselves, without referring to the King, the moral and material progress of so many peoples, left Venezuela governed by ignorant authorities growing in the shadows of the most complete obscurantism."—*A.R.E.H.*, p. 2.

The chief points to bear in mind on the lack of a printing press in Caracas till 1808 are: (a) that there were printing presses all over the Indies from the earliest days; (b) that if the leaders of Venezuela had wanted it they would have had it; (c) that it really did not matter so very much since they received heavy consignments of books both from Europe and from the other cities of the Indies. On all these points see *Rise*, ch. III.

Even Humboldt falls into this error typical of his age. But he concludes rather significantly: " *C'est dans les temps modernes, un spectacle assez extraordinaire de voir un établissement de ce genre* [the printing press] *suivre et non précéder une révolution politique.*" Which shows that culture and political development need not depend on a printing press actually on the spot. Indirectly, moreover, he confirms my conclusions when he writes that " *les sciences exactes, le dessein et la peinture*

n'ont point ici [Caracas] *de ces grands établissements que Mexico et Santa Fe doivent
à la munificence du Gouvernement espagnol et au zèle patriotique des nationaux.*" He
might have applied this argument to the lack of a printing press.—*H.P.N.*, Book IV,
ch. XIII, vol. I, p. 594.

As for the anecdote to be found in *A.R.E.H.* on Charles IV having said: " It is
not advisable that the Americans should get educated ", it has been exposed together
with its true origin, by *P.L.*, pp. 171 ss., as well as in *C.P.*, pp. 85 ss. It is to be
regretted that this worthless fable should find uncritical acceptance in *Humbert*, p. 182.

5.

Depons, vol. II, p. 177. Cf. *Frézier* in *Fall*, ch. VIII. *H.P.N.*, Book IV,
ch. XII, vol. I, p. 580; Book IV, ch. XIII, vol. I, p. 593. *Ségur*, vol. I, p. 424.
A.R.L.H., pp. 163–179.

On passivity and Spanish character, see my *Englishmen, Frenchmen, Spaniards*,
Oxford University Press. *Dauxion-Lavaysse*, quoted by *P.P.*, p. 95.

6.

Depons, vol. II, pp. 30, 28. *H.P.N.*, Book IV, ch. XII, vol. I, pp. 566 ss.
Nariño, see *Fall*, ch. XIX. *H.P.N.*, Book IV, ch. XII, vol. I, p. 569.

CHAPTER II (pp. 10–17)

1.

Family tree in *Ponte*, who goes as far back as the Spanish royal family. The useful
part of it is reproduced in *Larrazábal*, vol. I, facing p. 438. Not complete. A few
errors. But useful.

Bolívar only became the paternal line name because Simón de Bolívar the elder took
his mother's name, for his father's name was Ochoa de la Rementería (see *C.P.*,
pp. 45 ss.).

2.

Humbert has the best summary of these events.

3.

For Aguirre and his symbolic value, *Fall*, ch. X.

4.

For Xedler and the Potosí civil wars, *Fall*, ch. X., ch. XIII. On Xedler's family,
Caraffa, vol. 45.

6.

Bolívar's instructions show that he secured powers also from other cabildos, to
wit: Coro, Truxillo, Barquisimeto, Carora, el Tocuyo, Maracaibo, Valencia, San
Sebastián de los Reyes

7.

G.F., vol I, p. 77. Marín's will in *G.F.*, vol I, p. 278. This does not prevent
Ponte, in his genealogy reprinted by *Larrazábal*, vol. I, p. 425, from saying that
Marín married Josefa's mother. The discretion with which the matter is handled
by Bolívar's biographers till the modern, more outspoken school (such as *G.F.*)
take a hand in the matter, is a further proof that Josefa was not white. Moreover:
(1) Marín did not marry her though he could have done so; (2) the family is ever
worried about her when applying for a title of nobility in Madrid. Esteban
Palacios, Simon's uncle, constantly refers to this dark corner of the candidate's
pedigree. See *B.A.N.H.V.*, no. 52, December 1930, pp. 498, 501, 505, 511, 514,
all referring to " the Marín woman ". Now, the difficulty was not merely the lack
of a marriage certificate, for such things were winked at in heraldic matters; but
that in the Indies such a circumstance implied mixed blood.

For an attitude against this conclusion, *B.A.N.H.V.*, no. 106. No argument is
given, except that *Josefa* was christened in the Register for Whites. But it is well

known that money could buy the inscription of any not quite coal-black child on the White Register; and even the transference thereto in later life from the Register of the Not-White.

Documents in monograph on Bolívar's house: Vicente Lecuna—Julio Planchart, *Historia de la Casa de Bolívar*. Caracas, 1924. Hereafter *L.-Casa*.

CHAPTER III (pp. 18–28)

1.

G.F., vol. I, ch. VI

2.

C.P., p. 60; B.A.N.H.V., nos 52, 113.

I have noted no less than 21 references to the title in the family correspondence published in *B.A.N.H.V.*, no. 52: pp. 484–5; 490; 494–5–6; 498; 501; 503; 505; 509; 511; 512; 514; 516; 522; 524; 525; 529; 532–3.

See ceremonies in *Depons*, vol. I, pp. 133 ss.

Loc. cit., pp. 126 ss. and 132. See letters from Esteban Palacios to his father in *B.A.N.H.V.*, no. 52. Quotation from *Depons*, vol. I, p. 132.

Dates of birth: Don Juan Vicente, 15.x.1726; Doña Concepción, 1759; M. Antonia, l.xi. 1777; Juana, 16.v.1779; J.V., 30.v.1781; Simón, 24.vii.1783.

Chapel and church: facts from *Humbert*, p. 156, from Rojas, *Leyendas Históricas*, vol. II, p. 98 and vol. I, pp. 38, 39, 37.

3.

P.B., vol. 2, pp. 181 ss. C.P., p. 62; L.A.S., pp. 140, 141.

The facts bearing on Bolívar's father's behaviour towards his womenfolk are published for the first time. They come from a file I have consulted personally in the Archives of the Archbishopric of Caracas: "*San Matheo. Año de 1765. Autos y Sumarios contra Don Juan Vicente Volíbar sobre su mala amistad con varias mujeres.*" Shelf of Episcopal Visits.

4.

Will in *P.B.*, vol. 2, pp. 194 ss. Good analysis in *C.P.*, pp. 55 ss.

5.

Clause 18 of Bolívar's mother's will says: " Owing to the death of her husband she took upon herself to carry out the will of Doctor Don Juan Felix de Aristeguieta ". —*B.A.N.H.V.*, no. 52, p. 459.

P.B., vol. 2, pp. 146 ss, for letter. B.A.N.H.V., no. 52, p. 454 ss., for will. On treatment of slaves, *Rise, passim. D.B.*, p. 25.

The Early Journey of Charles Wesley. Edited by John Tedford, B.A. London, p. 68. Wesley goes on to say: " Nor is it strange, being thus trained up in cruelty, they should afterwards arrive at so great perfection in it that Mr. Star, a gentleman I often met at Mr. Lasserre's, should, as he himself informed Lasserre, first nail up a negro by the ears, then order him to be whipped in the severest manner, and then to have scalding water thrown over him, so that the poor creature could not move for four months after. One Colonel Lynch is universally known to have cut off a poor negro's legs, and to kill several of them every year by his barbarities. These horrid cruelties are the less to be wondered at, because the Government itself, in effect, countenances and allows them to kill their slaves by the ridiculous penalties appointed for it, of about seven pound sterling, half of which is usually saved by the criminal's informing against himself. This I cannot look upon as no other than a public act to indemnify murder."

M. Antonia's letter, *B.A.N.H.V.*, no. 62, p. 267.

See clause 38 of the will in which Feliciano (junior) is declared to be manager of a number of estates at a salary of 350 pesos, though he is entitled to appoint a steward, presumably to do the work for him (p. 464); and clause 44 in which Esteban gets half of whatever may be saved by his good administration (?) as manager of certain cattle ranches in the Llanos, which of course the elegant and snobbish young man would never look at, and is declared to have collected there a considerable amount of cattle of his own (p. 466). Esteban does not seem very sure about his rights with regard to these animals, to judge by his letter of 24.xi.1792 to his father hoping that the husbands of his two nieces will not " despoil " him of his animals, " since where ten animals feed fifteen can feed equally well ", p. 505.

Esteban's letter in *B.A.N.H.V.*, no. 52, pp. 488–9.

I have done without a number of picturesque stories about this period because they are stories rather than History as shown by *C.P.*

6.

C.P., p. 67. The house was left under María de Jesús, wife of Juan Nepomuceno Ribas; and there were three young girls in it, María Paula, Josefa and María Ignacia, aunts of the young Bolívars, who married respectively three, five and three years after Don Feliciano's death. *B.A.N.H.V.*, no. 113, pp. 62–85.

CHAPTER IV (pp. 29–35)

1.

Portrait in *B.A.N.H.V.*, no. 52. *C.P.*, pp. 65–6; 69.

2.

B.A.N.H.V., no. 113, p. 82; no. 52, pp. 531, 532, 531. *C.P.*, p. 69.

3.

A.R.L.H. C.L., vol. I, p. 60. On Hipólita, A.R. in *La Opinión Nacional*, July 23rd, 1879, reproduced in *P.B.*, vol. I, p. 101, as well as letter to María Antonia.

4.

C.P., pp. 79 ss., is excellent as corrective to errors and fancies of authors such as *Mancini* and even *G.F.* Letter: *C.L.*, vol. IV, pp. 337 ss. On Andújar's classes *B.A.N.H.V.*, no. 107, pp. 260–2. Quotation on Bello: 27.iv.1829 in *C.L.*, vol. VIII, p. 304. On Bello also *C.P.*, *loc. cit.* Quote on Montenegro from *Baralt* through Menéndez Pelayo, *Historia de la Poesía Contemporánea*, vol. I, p. 357. Quito, 27.iv.1829, to José Fernández Madrid, in *C.L.*, vol. VIII, p. 304.

The point about dates and teaching S.B. first letters is well put in *C.P.*, *loc. cit.*; as well as the fact that S.C. was not chosen for his modern ideas. Standard life of S.C. Amunátegui, Santiago de Chile, 1876. Quotation from *C.L.*, vol. IX, p. 426, date 27.vi.25; *C.P.*, p. 84.

On September 3rd, 1792, Don Feliciano Palacios wrote to his son Esteban then in Madrid asking him to buy some books: " They are for the amanuensis who writes for me, i.e., Don Simón, the brother of Cayetanito Carreño. He is a very good man and skilful for all affairs and accounts which is a great rest for me." The books of the " escribiente ", answered Esteban on 26.xii (*B.A.N.H.V.*, no. 52, p. 507) would be ordered, but not all, for they amounted to a good deal of money; and, on 24.i.93 he sent them together with a bill for 2,088 reales, too late for a counter order sent by Don Feliciano not to send the books.

Even Bolívar, as late as 1824 (May 6th) wrote to Santander on S.C.: " He is an amenuensis who can teach much to the man who dictates to him." *C.L.*, vol. IV, p. 151.

CHAPTER V (pp. 36–43)

1.

Fall, ch. VIII, chs. XV–XVIII.

2.

G.F., vol. I, pp. 120 ss. *C.P.*, pp. 92 ss. Pedro M. Arcaya: *Discurso de recepción en la Academia de la Historia*, Caracas 1910.

3

C.P., p. 96.   *P.P.*, p. 55.

4.

Ponte, pp. 30, 33, 68.

On Picton, see *Rise*, ch. XX, with bibliography.   *D.L.*, vol. I, chs. IV, V.   Quote from Wellington in *Stanhope*, p. 69.   The Duke adds: " But he always behaved extremely well."   This was certainly not the case in Trinidad.

Woodford to Bathurst: *P.R.O. C.O.* 295–29, No. 1.   Date: July 1st, 1813.

Of the negroes executed for witchcraft by Picton, one, Thisbe, was a woman; and one, Pierre François, was burnt alive.   *P.R.O. Trinidad Papers, C.O.* 296/4, Fos. 283–98.

Miranda-Archivo, vol. XV, pp. 171, 176.   *C.P.*, p. 111.   Letter of Carlos to Esteban: *B.A.N.H.V.*, no. 52, p. 540.   Miranda on Islands: *Fall*, ch. XX.

5.

Fall, ch. XIX.   *G.F.*, ch. VII.   *C.P.*, pp. 99 ss.

6.

B.A.N.H.V., no. 52.   *C.P.*, pp. 104, 106.   *H.P.N.*, Book IV, ch. XIII, vol. I, pp. 591–2.

CHAPTER VI (pp. 44–50)

1.

B.A.N.H.V., no. 52, p. 526; p. 539.

Military records (*hojas de servicios*): *B.A.N.H.V.*, no. 52, pp. 474–5.   Order signed Carbonell, p. 476.   The military record signed Toro on p. 475 gives S.B.'s seniority as sub-lieutenant October 7th, 1797, but this can only be an error, possibly deliberate to seek some advantage.   Toro was a close friend of the family.

2.

C.P., p. 120.   Borja is the Spanish original name of the family of Borgia.   It evidently gave better fruit in Spain than in Italy.

Miranda-A., vol. VII, p. 332.   *Humboldt-Lettres*, p. 186, a note to Malte-Brun, 17.v.1808.   *Alamán, H.M.*, Book I, ch. III, vol, I, pp. 113–4, 115.

3.

A good discussion on where Bolívar lived and of the story of his bold conversation with the viceroy, on which I waste no time, in *C.P.*, pp. 121 ss.   " Opulent Mexico ": see letter to Governor of Curaçao (20.x.1813) in *C.L.*, vol. I, p. 65.   Mexico metropolis, in *Contestación de un americano meridional a un caballero de esta isla*.   Kingston, 6.ix.1815, *C.L.*, vol. 1, p. 197.   See *Rise*, chs. XI and XIV.   On Guerrero's conspiracy: *Alamán, H.M.*, Book I, ch. III, pp. 128 ss.

4.

C.P., pp. 134, 151.   *B.A.N.H.V.*, no. 52, pp. 552; 554, 562.

5.

B.A.N.H.V., no. 52, pp. 553–4.   *C.P.*, pp. 137 ss.   To the list of authors and quotations on the Mallo story he might have added *Holland*, pp. 94–5.   Letters in *B.A.N.H.V.*, no. 52.

CHAPTER VII (pp. 51–57)

1.

Pedro to Carlos, 22.viii.1799, *B.A.N.H.V.*, no. 52, p. 556.   Accounts, p. 476.   Esteban's biography of S.B., p. 583.   *D.B. P.L.*, p. 94.   *D.B. N.*, p. 220.

2.

Laborde, vol. II, Part II, p. 29.   *Bourgoing*, vol. I, pp. 228, 238 ss.   *B.A.N.H.V.*, no. 52, p. 551.   See S.B.'s tailor's bill in *B.A.N.H.V.*, no. 52, p. 477.   González

Dávila, *Teatro de la Grandeza de Madrid*, p. 5, quoted by B. Sánchez Alonso in *R.B.A.M.*, June 1925, n. 7, p. 326. See Literatura de Cordel, seguidillas, jácaras, gitanas: Meléndez Valdés y la literatura de Cordel: *R.B.A.M.* del Ayuntamiento de Madrid, no. 30, April 1931, p. 117. *El deseo de la Pulpillo* (1787) quoted by Julio Gómez in the same review, October 1925, 8, pp. 540–1.

3.

Accounts, p. 476. Madrid prices in *R.B.A.M.*, October 25th, no, 8, p. 551: *La Fonda de San Sebastián* by Angel González Palencia. Concerts in Madrid: *Loc. cit.*, June 25th, p. 422.

On the influence of the French philosophers, see *Fall*, ch. XIV, on Rousseau's, see *Spell*. Letter P. to C., 22.viii.1799, *B.A.N.H.V.*, no. 52, p. 557.

4.

Miranda-Archivo, vol. I, p. 134. *B.A.N.H.V.*, no. 52, p. 491. *C.L.*, vol. 4, p. 337, 20.v.1825. *C.P.*, pp. 172 ss. Letter S.B. to Pedro, 23.viii.1801, in *C.L.*, vol. I, pp. 6–8. *C.P.*, p. 176.

5.

Data in *C.P. O'L.* provides the detail about the Peace of Amiens festivities, vol. I, p. 77. His developments, admiration of Napoleon, comparisons with Spain, stimulus to S.B.'s republicanism are all possible but they may be later projections of Bolívar himself on to his actual experiences at the time. *B.A.N.H.V.*, no. 52.

CHAPTER VIII (pp. 58–68)

1.

I give no space to O'L.'s fancies about offers of money to his brother and so forth, for they have been, as usual, disposed of by *C.P.*, pp. 183 ss.
D.B.P.L., p. 99. *D.B.N.*, pp. 101, 226.

2.

Mosquera, p. 7. *B.A.N.H.V.*, no. 52, pp. 581–2. *D.B.P.L.*, p. 100; *D.B.N.*, p. 228; *C.P.*, p. 186.

3.

Humboldt's dates: *H.P.N.*, vol. I, ch. II, pp. 263 ss.; ch. IV, p. 290; ch. VIII, pp. 337, 341.
O'L., p. 84; *Mancini*, pp. 147–8.
Humboldt-Life, vol. I, ch. III, p. 277. Letter to his brother William, Cumaná, 7.x.1800; to Friedländer, 16.ii.1805; vol. I, ch. IX, p. 349.
See passages in praise of Spanish Government in *Rise* and *Fall*. Bordeaux: 24 Thermidor, year XII (12.viii.1804). *Humboldt-Lettres*.

4.

Fanny's letters to S.B.: *B.A.N.H.V.*, no. 52, pp. 655 ss.
On Mancini's irresponsible fantasies, *C.P.*, pp. 193 ss., is excellent. Dates of Humboldt's movements in *Humboldt-Life*, ch. IX, pp. 351–2, 3. Letter 10.xi.1821 in *B.A.N.H.V.*, no. 62, p. 219. This letter comes from Boussingault but, unlike other data from this unreliable author, is well authenticated by a letter from Humboldt acknowledging receipt of it. *C.P.*, p. 196. *B.A.N.H.V.*, no. 52, p. 659, 28.iv.1823.

5.

O'L., pp. 80–83; *C.P.*, pp. 190 ss., 187, 204. *D.B.N.*, pp. 228, 324–5; *D.B.P.L.*, p. 100.

6.

O'L., vol. I, pp. 87, 88. *D.B.P.L.*, p. 81. *D.B.N.*, p. 196.
There are three versions of this oath: S.R. in a narrative written long after S.B.'s death: " I swear before you, and I swear by the God of my parents; I

swear by them; I swear by my honour; I swear by my fatherland that I will give neither rest to my arm nor repose to my soul till I have broken the chains which oppress us by the will of the Spanish power." Larrazábal is content to say that Bolívar swore "with an energetic phrase." This very reserve might lend some force to the traditional though seldom printed form: "I swear, Rodríguez, that I will free America from the Spanish domination and that I will not leave there one single of these b . . . s."

An account of the scene is in the opening chapter of *Rise*. It took place on Monte-Sacro and not on Mount Aventine.

CHAPTER IX (pp. 69–83)

1.

D.B.P.L., p. 170. *D.B.N.*, pp. 164, 153, 327, 334. *Hippisley*, ch. XVI, p. 382. *Ponte*, p. 108.

Here is the description of the Gallegos which I give in ch. II of my book *Spain* (p. 17) on the basis of modern research: "The skull is wide, short and somewhat low, yet the face is apt to be narrow; the nose sharp and the eye orbits low but wide; a lively complexion, frequently red or fair hair, clear hazel eyes." It fits Bolívar as to shape and his brother and one of his sisters in every way.

2.

D.B.P.L., p. 104. *D.B.N.*, p. 233. Gabriel Lafond de Lurcy, *Voyages*, Paris, 1840, quoted by *Arocha*, p. 33.

3.

Fall, ch. I. Quotation from Cortés in Letter to the Emperor 15.x.1524 in the collection published by Gayangos, p. 335. Cf. my biography of Cortés, ch. XXVIII. On Sancho's ambition, see my *Don Quixote, An Introductory Essay in Psychology*. At the O.U. Press, no. 135, p. 109. Quotation from Part II, ch. XIII of *Cervantes*. *D.B.P.L.*, p. 144. *D.B.N.*, p. 296.

4.

Fall, chs. IV to VIII.

5.

D.B.P.L., pp. 132, *D.B.N.*, pp. 275, 389, 391. *B.A.N.H.V.*, no. 62, pp. 421–22 *P.P. P.P.*, pp. 163–176. Also *Belaunde*.

6.

D.B.P.L., p. 179. *D.B.N.*, p. 256, 281, 327, 335. Lozano, p. 238. Letter Fanny Villars. *B.A.N.H.V.*, no. 52, p. 660. *O.C.N.*, vol. I, p. 250; vol. II, pp. 6, 33.

It is significant that his nephew, Juan Vicente's son, who resembled him, was mentally deficient.

CHAPTER X (pp. 85–95)

1.

Miranda's doings before 1800: *Fall*, ch. XX. *Miranda-Biggs*, p. 288. *D.L.*, vol. II, p. 119; *Miranda-Archivo*, vol. VI, p. 422; Turnbull to Pownall, 8.x.1801. Clause 11 of Instructions, *loc. cit.*, vol. XV, p. 202. *Miranda-Archivo*, vol. XV, pp. 390–1.

2.

C.P., pp. 232–3. *R.F. passim* and *Miranda-Archivo*, numerous passages. *P.P. H.R.*, vol. I, ch. VII, pp. 87, 92, 99, 105.

3.

Good summaries: *P.P.H.R.*, vol. I, ch. IX; *C.P.*, pp. 238 ss. *Miranda-Archivo*, vol. VII, pp. 331 ss.

4.

Arrival in New York: *Miranda-Becerra*, vol. I, p. 118. *P.P. H.R.*, vol. I, p. 129. *Beard*, p. 412. Casa-Irujo to Government: *Miranda-Becerra*, vol. I, p. 110. *Miranda-Life*, vol. I, p. 294. Miranda to Smith in *Miranda-Becerra*, vol. I, p. 122. Cf. *P.P.H.R.*, ch. X; *C.P.*, pp. 240 ss.

5.

Miranda-Biggs, pp. 2, 4, 25, 26–29, 103. On Madison: *P.P.H.R.*, vol. I, p. 130. On cabildo Caracas: *loc. cit.*, p. 141. On Juan Vicente Bolívar: *C.P.*, p. 246.

6.

American Historical Review, vol. VI, p. 523, quoted by *Miranda-Life*, vol. I, p. 307. Robertson says it was on May 25th but Biggs, p. 92, is clear. The *Leander* saw the *Lily* on the 24th and " the next morning " decided to parley.

MSS. of J. B. Fortescue, vol. VIII, p. 179, quoted by *Miranda-Life*, vol. I, p. 308. *P.P.H.R.*, ch. XI. *Miranda-Biggs*, pp. 95, 102–3, 108, 110, 118. *Miranda-Life*, vol. I, pp. 308, 310.

CHAPTER XI (pp. 96–102)

1.

D.B.N., p. 238. He must have been a member of the R. Mère L. Ecossaise de France sous le Titre Distinctif de St. Alexandre d'Ecosse à l'O.·. de Paris, to judge by a Tableau des F.F. in Rosenthal's catalogue 1948, item 15, p. 3, where he figures as *Bolívar, officier espagnol*.

I waste no time in discussing the spurious letter from S.B. to Fanny swallowed by so many Bolívarists since Aristides Rojas gave it his *exequatur* with a strange lack of both critical sense and sense of responsibility. It will be found in *C.L.*, vol. I, pp. 11–16. Don Vicente Lecuna has rightly nailed it to the counter, p. 17. See also *C.P.*, pp. 209 ss.

Letters Dehollain and Trobriand, pp. 585, 664.

2.

On arrival in Caracas, see note above.
Statement by Dr. Sánz: *B.A.N.H.V.*, no. 52, p. 619.
Robinson, *P.R.O.*, Ad. 1/327. *C.P.*, p. 242. *P.P.H.R.*, vol. I, p. 162. *Miranda-Biggs*, pp. 91, 253.

3.

P.P.H.R., vol. I, p. 158. On events in Buenos Aires, see *Historia de la Nación Argentina* publicada bajo la dirección de Don Ricardo Levene, Buenos Aires, 1936–9.

4.

Documents in *B.A.H.N.V.*, no. 52, pp. 586–615.

5.

There is another letter signed Simón de Bolívar, addressed to Machado: *C.L.*, p. 20. 24.ix.1807. See however below about his letter to Wellesley during his embassy in London.

CHAPTER XII (pp. 103–113)

1.

Miranda-Biggs, pp. 152–3, 260, 217, 218, 230, 248. Wellesley's views: *Miranda-Life*, vol. II, ch. XV; *P.P.H.R.*, vol. I, ch. XIII.

2.

Text of treaties of Fontainebleau, *Toreno*, Book I, p. 6. Treacherous behaviour of d'Armagnac in Pamplona: *Toreno*, p. 15; also of Duhesme in Monjuich, p. 16. *Toreno*, Books II and III. *Stanhope*, p. 69.

3.

Robertson in *Miranda-Life*, vol. I, pp. 81–2, 199–200, is on the whole negative about M. being a freemason. See *R.F.*, ch. XLI, for my reasons for doubting. On the whole I believe he was not a freemason, though he frequently used freemason symbols and methods. See *Argentina*, vol. 5 (1), ch. IX, by Juan Canter, who says he was a Philadelphian (p. 287). On these Philadelphians and their predecessors the Olympians, see *Vidocq*, vol. II, pp. 153 ss. O'H.-Lautaro: Canter. p. 286. *H.P.N.*, Book IV, ch. XII, vol. I, p. 574.

4.

See *Jovellanos'* narrative of French attempts at winning him over in his Memoria, part II, art. I.

5.

P.F., pp. 35 ss. The doctrine rested on the Spanish tradition that the cabildo of the chief city represented the whole province.

6.

F.E. pp. 23 ss. *Toreno*, Book XII, p. 285. *F.E.*, pp. 35 ss.; see *Debates of the Federal Convention of* 1787 *which framed the Constitution of the United States of America, reported by James Madison. NewYork. Oxford University Press*, 1920. The text of the article as passed (art. I, Sec. 2, par. 3) was as follows: " Representatives and direct taxes shall be apportioned among the several States which may be included within this Union, according to their respective numbers, which shall be determined by adding to the whole Number of free Persons, including those bound to service for a Term of Years, and excluding Indians not taxed, three fifths of all other persons " (p. 697). The article lapsed on the adoption of the 13th amendment on 18.ix.1865, when it was ratified by 27 out of 35 States.

Estrada appears to have made an error in his calculation when he thinks that, once Indians and Negroes are left out of account, the proportion of representatives is the same for the New World as for the Old World. On the basis of the peninsular representation, the 24 deputies granted the Indies would correspond only to 1,200.000; while on his own showing, there were 3,000.000.

CHAPTER XIII (pp. 114–122)

1.

R.D.U., pp. 9–10. *P.F.*, pp. 29–33. There is a third version of these events given by the French officer in question, Lamanon: *P.P.H.R.*, vol. I, p. 201.

2.

P.P.H.R., vol. I, p. 200. *R.D.U.*, pp. 8, 11

3.

B.A.N.H.V., no. 52, p. 617. *P.P.H.R.*, vol. I, pp. 211–13 The deplorable style and spelling of José Felix Ribas (who could not even spell his own Christian name properly) contrasts with the correct writing of his brother; the difference came from character and not from family education. José Domingo Díaz describes him as a man full of debts contracted to satisfy his vices. *R.D.U.*, p. 12.

4.

P.P.H.R., vol. I, pp. 214, 224, 226, 227, 231–36. *J.D.D.*.., pp. 11–12. *R.D.U.*, pp. 13–14.

5.

D.L., ch. VIII, vol. II, pp. 196–7. *Sevilla*, ch. XVI, p. 133. *H.P.N.*, Book II, ch. IV, vol. I, p. 292. On Emparán: ch. XVI of the present work. *B.A.N.H.V.*, no. 52, pp. 619, 623. *P.P.H.R.*, vol. I, p. 259.

6.

Bolívar declares war on Spain: *Heredia*, p. 133.

CHAPTER XIV (pp. 123-133)

1.

Narrative based on *F.E.*, Part II, pp. 54 ss. *R.D.U.*, pp. 11 ss.; p. 18. *Martiñena* Document 89, p. 26 of appendix. *R.D.U.*, pp. 15-16. Briceño Méndez Apuntes sobre la vida del General Bolívar, quoted by *P.P.H.R.*, p. 261 note. Level de Goda quoted by *P.P.H.R.*, vol. I, p. 271. *J.D.D.*, pp. 18-19.

2.

For Cortés Madariaga: *C.M.A.*, from which most of this section is drawn, pp. 3 and 7. *P.P.P.P.*, pp. 320 ss., seems to me to have disposed of the revolutionary stories current on C.M.'s early days. The idea that the canonry of Caracas was given him by Mallo through Miranda to foster the independence of Spanish America has no basis either in documents or in common sense. The facts and dates about the canon's trial from *C.M.A.* It is a pity that this treatise blends excellent scholarship with too much faith in Aristides Rojas. Document on Cortés' resignation and passport in *B.A.N.H.V.*, no. 112, pp. 438-441.

3.

R.D.U., p. 18. Urquinaona's seems to me the most likely version. Others claim that Emparán asked the people whether they wanted him or not and that C.M. behind him, led the answer with gestures. Upon the crowd shouting *No lo queremos*, Emparán then cried out *Pues yo tampoco quiero*. See for instance *Larrazábal*, vol. I, pp. 51-52. *G.F.*, vol. I, p. 169 for document. *P.P.H.R.* for details.

4.

See *Rise* and *Fall passim* *C.P.*, p. 282.

5.

Toreno, pp. 244, 282. *P.P.H.R.*, vol. I, pp. 268-9, 284.

6.

P.P.H.R., p. 287. *Toreno*, p. 299.

CHAPTER XV (pp. 134-143)

1.

Heredia, pp. 1-6. *P.R.O. W.O.* 1/104, fols. 231-4 on Miyares. *P.P.H.R.*, pp. 290, 299, 300. *R.D.U.*, pp. 29-31. *Bobes B.C. Heredia*, p. 5n.

2.

P.P.H.R., vol. I, pp. 347-50. *J.V.G.*, pp. 17-20. *Heredia*, pp. 20-1. The posters on Quito will be found in *P.R.O. W.O* 1/106, annexes to a dispatch from Layard, 11.xi.1810. *P.P.H.R.*, vol. I, p. 351; *Baralt*, vol. I, p. 62. *G.F.*, vol. I, p. 178. *Heredia*, p. 9 and appendix, docs. I-XXXI.

3.

Toreno, pp. 287-310. *G.F.*, vol. I, p. 192. *P.P.H.R.*, vol. I, pp. 363 ss. *Heredia*, p. 16.

4.

P.P.H.R., vol. I, pp. 362, 4. *Heredia*, doc. XXIX, p. 263, pp. 10, 11, 19, 20.

5.

G.F., pp. 187-8. *P.P.H.R.*, vol. I, pp. 353 ss. *Heredia*, p. 27.

6.

O'L., vol. I, p. 98. *P.R.O. W.O.* 1/104, fols. 173-4, 139-40, 1 and 2, 190, 192; 315-16. *C.P.*, p. 293. *P.P.H.R.*, vol. I, p. 333.

CHAPTER XVI (pp. 144–156)

1.

Papers relating to this mission collected in *P.R.O. F.O. 72/106*. Contains credentials, correspondence, notes on Caracas by R.W., but no record of interview, which is, however, to be found in an English translation sent from the Governor of Curaçao much later and included in *P.R.O. W.O. 1/106*, fols. 263–270. The F.O. volume contains a letter dated in Portsmouth on 11.vii.1810 in the handwriting of Méndez and signed Simón de Bolívar in which the Commissioners report " our arrival yesterday in this city after thirty one days of a happy crossing in H.B.M. Brig *Whillington* sent from the Island of St. Thomas by General Cochrane to convey our persons to this Kingdom ". There is also a curious note addressed to the F.O. on July 21st which seems in Bolívar's hand, and contains a curious French mistake: " Les Députés du gouvernement de Venezuela ont l'honneur de présenter ses respectueux hommages . . ."

I can settle *C.P.'s* conjectures as to when the British Government received the instructions of the three emissaries from the Government of Curaçao: a copy of these instructions is doc. no. 10 annexed to dispatch no. 21 sent by Layard to Liverpool on October 12th, 1810, to be found fols. 311–317 of *P.R.O. W.O. 1/104*. Documents of interest on this mission in *B.A.N.H.V.*, vols. 72, 82, 83.

See Inst. *P.R.O. W.O. 1/104*, fol. 314. Similar accusations in almost identical words against Emparán for his pro-French leanings will be found in a letter from the Supreme Junta of Caracas to the Regency, 3.v.1810, *P.R.O. W.O. 1/104*, vol. II, fols. 279, 286, particularly fol. 284.

2.

P.R.O. F.O. 72/106. *Miranda-Becerra*, vol. II, pp. 84–6. Cf. *Miranda-Life*. *P.P.H.R.*, vol. II, p. 344. *C.P.*, pp. 312–15. The concluding words of Bolívar's and López Méndez' letter of August 21st, 1810 (W.O. 1/106, fol. 270) are: " The Minister has again sent to acquaint us that the Vessel in which we are to return will be ready in a few days."

3.

Bolívar's and Miranda's movements in *Miranda-Becerra*, vol. II, pp. 86, 87; a good note in *P.P.H.R.*, vol. II, pp. 8–9, where good grounds are given for the view that Bolívar was also at this time in Trinidad. Miranda and British Cabinet, *P.P.H.R.*, vol. II, pp. 8, 12. *P.R.O. W.O. 1/106*, pp. 139, 485–6, 559–60.

4.

P.R.O. W.O. 1/106, fols. 485–6. On Miranda's father's tribulations with the *mantuanos*, *Fall*, ch. XX. *Miranda-Becerra*, opening of Book VIII, ch. I, vol. II, pp 185 ss. *C.P.*, pp. 325, 326. On San Javier: *J.V.G.*, p. 23. On Sánz: *B.A.N.H.V.*, no. 52, p. 624. On oath: *P.P.H.R.*, vol. II, p. 5. On Burke: *Miranda-Becerra*, vol. II, p. 209. *P.P.H.R.*, vol. II, p. 26. *C.P.*, pp. 324 ss., though unfair to Miranda, gives ample documentary proof of his disgruntled state of mind. Foscio to Bello in *C.P.*, p. 332. Roscio wrote to Bello at the time that Miranda called on the archbishop to protest against Burke's articles. Some authors do not believe it (*P.P.H.R.*, vol. II, pp. 26–27), others do (*C.P.*, loc. cit.). The choice is difficult. If true, Miranda's intrigue is despicable; if untrue, Roscio is a liar of the worst kind, for he lived through the incident in a small city and in a position where he could know everything. *Miranda-Becerra*, vol. II, p. 209n.

5.

See *Fall*, ch. XX, for Miranda's mood and opinions with regard to Spanish Government. On Spanish origin of Patriotic Society: *P.P.H.R.*, vol. II, p. 14, who, however, refers to the Spanish model as *Sociedad de Amigos de la Patria*. The real name was *Sociedad Económica de Amigos del País*. *R.D.U.*, p. 189. *P.P.H.R.*, vol. II, pp. 20, 22, 171 ss., 21, caps. I, II. Roscio to Bello, p. 325. *C.M.A.*, pp. 64, 72. *C.P.*, pp. 336, 337.

6.

Bolívar's speech is copied by all authors from *J.V.G.* But no one can say whence J.V.G. took it. The style is as much his as Bolívar's. It reads like the former trying to imitate the latter. I have not transcribed it as a fact but as what tradition considers Bolívar did say; and since in this case tradition is not very old, it may come near enough to the actual fact. But we do not know.

On the Immaculate Conception: *P.P.H.R.*, vol. II, p. 52.

CHAPTER XVII (pp. 157–169)

1.

P.P.H.R., vol. II, pp. 56n, 107–11. *Heredia*, pp. 29, 33, 34, 35. *Miranda-Becerra*, vol. II, pp. 248–9, puts the money wasted and the financial disorder even higher. *C.P.*, pp. 354–55, 359. *R.D.U.*, p. 31. *J.V.G.*, pp. 191, 192.

2.

P.P.H.R., vol. II, pp. 156 ss. I follow *C.P.* for he seems to me on this point more objective than *P.P.H.R.*, vol. II, pp. 64–5, who assumes perfidy in the Valencians; while in my opinion *C.P.* has proved there was none. *J.V.G.*, p. 188n. The text of the *Morning Chronicle* letter is re-translated from the Spanish as I was unable to procure a copy of the newspaper in question.

3.

On all this section, see article by Emiliano Jos in *B.A.N.H.V.*, no. 102.

4.

P.P.H.R., vol. I, p. 330. On Bolívar's entails, see *J.D.D.* In *P.B.*, pp. 201, 208, two legal papers will be found drafted on 17.viii.23 and 9.xii.23 by judges anxious to please Bolívar, and crammed with specious arguments to cover the fact that Bolívar was in fact enjoying the possession of the two incompatible entails. I am unable to accept as genuine the letter of Simón Bolívar to Josefa María Tinoco, his brother's mistress, published in *C.L.*, vol. I, p. 26. It is written, we are told, in Bolívar's hand, on the very paper of the letter he is answering. In this letter of María Josefa, the unhappy unmarried widow writes to Simón that he is " the only help which remained under Heaven ", for her children, but also that " he, Simón, is determined not to see her ". She entreats him to grant her an interview. The answer of Bolívar cannot be genuine because he says: " My first care has been to arrange that the property of Juan Vicente should belong to your children; that you be granted a pension of 50 pesos monthly till this property yields an income, and later everything." He then says he cannot see her " because honour and the fatherland call me to their help ". Bolívar could not write such high-falutin stuff to the poor woman on the eve of his departure for exile in the circumstances told in the coming chapter. But above all, as we shall see in that chapter, Bolívar was determined to secure for himself the property of his brother, a fact which is certainly authentic under his hand. Therefore this letter to Josefa María is spurious.

The letters from María Josefa Tinoco, mother of Juan Vicente's children and of Felicia Bolívar, one of them published by Don Vicente Lecuna in *B.A.N.H.V.*, vol. 62, prove: (1) that María Josefa was grateful for S.B.'s protection of " your adoptive sons "; (2) that this adoption, however, cannot have been official and legal, since it is mentioned in no legal document; (3) that Bolívar paid his nephews a monthly sum out of his own free will only; (4) that Felicia, at any rate, had no protection whatsoever from 1814 till 1821; (5) that Bolívar's sisters were against any such protection and dropped dark hints about its ceasing as soon as S.B. died; (6) that even with S.B.'s protection, in 1824 the nephews had " not one miserable shelter to cover them from the weather if you die "; (7) that S.B. forced Felicia to marry General Silva (a coloured man) with threats to withdraw his pension. All this correspondence confirms my conclusions in the text.

P.B., p. 206. *Mosquera*, p. 12. *P.P.H.R.*, vol. II, p. 66.

5.

Heredia, pp. 38, 41, 44. *P.P.H.R.*, vol. II, pp. 198–9, 210, 258.

6.

Heredia, pp. 26, 45, 46, 47n. *J.D.D.*, pp. 38, 40, 41. *F.O.* 72/139, Curaçao, March 30, 1811, quoted by *P.P.H.R.*, vol. II, pp. 211–12n.

7.

Heredia, pp. 35–6, 41n. *P.P.H.R.*, vol. II, pp. 214–5, 218, 230. *R.D.U.*, pp. 86–7. *C.P.*, pp. 407, 408, 413, 425. *Miranda-Becerra*, vol. II, pp. 219, 220. Letter of Miranda to Martin, also signed by Soublette, in *P.R.O. W.O.* 1/112, fol. 177. *C.P.*, p. 444.

Chapter XVIII (pp. 170–179)

1.

Report complete in *O'L.*, vol. I, p. 127 ss. On the importance of Puerto Cabello, see *P.P.H.R.*, vol. II, p. 294. Poudenx & Meyer quoted by *C.P.*, p. 454.

2.

P.P.H.R., vol. II, p. 298. Most biographers indulge in this game of depicting Miranda and Bolívar estranged precisely during the period leading up to Bolívar's betrayal of Miranda. *Mosquera*, p. 13, goes as far as to say that Miranda made it a condition of his accepting his command against Valencia that Bolívar " was not to command his unit in the campaign because he was a dreadful young man ". As if such a thing was possible for either Miranda to say or Bolívar to tolerate at the time they were exchanging the letters given in the text. *O'L.* (vol. I, ch. III, p. 121) says that Bolívar was anxious to fight but " found no sympathy in Miranda, who, instead of giving him some active service as he desired, sent him to command the Castle of Puerto Cabello, the post which least fitted his enterprising genius. Bolívar realized that he was being set aside from the field of honour and left to occupy his post under the impression of displeasure and of offended dignity ". This of course is sheer nonsense; for Puerto Cabello was as active a service as any in the circumstances, as Bolívar himself recognized in his letters to Miranda on the loss of it. But it shows that Bolívar's entourage wrote in order to justify the fall of Puerto Cabello and Bolívar's behaviour to Miranda.

3.

Heredia, pp. 52, 53. *C.P.*, pp. 463 ss., 469, 477, 483, 485 ss.

4.

P.P.H.R., vol. II, pp. 323, 367, 370, 371. *C.P.*, p. 491.

5.

P.P.H.R., loc. cit., and vol. II, pp. 376–77. *Miranda-Life*, vol. II, p. 180. Monteverde to Hodgson, English version *W.O.* 1/112 (*P.R.O.*), fol. 139, dated Caracas August 19th. Copies of the obligations mentioned: one dated July 20th, fol. 157; the other one July 30th, fol. 161. Endorsed by Casas in Caracas to the Commander in Chief of H.C.M.'s forces in these provinces, being the property of the King our Lord and taken from the Royal Treasury.—August 20th, 1812. *G.F.*, vol. I, p. 267. *Heredia*, p. 124.

6.

It is not certain that Bolívar's property was confiscated at all. *J.D.D.*, p. 92, denies it flatly. *C.P.*, pp. 505, 509, 512, 513–14, 516. Cf. Parra Pérez' opinion (*P.P.H.R.*, vol. II, p. 383) where he rightly points out that since " the patriots were not persuaded of the impossibility of going on boardship till July 31st, i.e., many hours after having arrested Miranda, it follows that it is necessary to take this explanation with caution ". Bolívar to the Cúcuta Congress from *C.P.*, p. 505. *Larrazábal*, vol. I, p. 132. *J.V.G.*, p. 208. Bolívar's Manifesto: *P.D.L.*, vol. I, p. 63.

CHAPTER XIX (pp. 180–190)

1.

On F.L.: *Ducoudray*, vol. I, p. 138. On date and men on board: Cervériz'
report in *Blanco*, doc. 686, vol. III, p. 715. Ribas and nephew in *J.V.G.*, p. 47.
On Díaz Casado: Letter from Salías to Miranda 27.v.1812, in *P.P.H.R.*, vol. II,
p. 247. Personal profit out of confiscations: *Loc. cit.*, p. 323. Miranda to Ribas
through Soublette: 30.vi.12, *P.P.H.R.*, vol. II, p. 315. As for Sosa, he is described
by Salías to Miranda as a selfish scoundrel: 27.v.12, *P.P.H.R.*, vol. II, p. 247.
Miranda to Audiencia: *Rojas*, pp. 767, 769. *Heredia*, p. 53n. Level de Goda,
Nuevas Memorias, quoted by *P.P.H.R.*, vol. II, p. 415n.

2.

C.L., vol. I, pp. 27, 28.
" The plate is claimed by a Don Simón Bolívar but having been landed in a
clandestine manner it has been seized by the collector of His Majesty's Customs
and is now under prosecution; several of the trunks found empty at the seizure,
report says, contained Church plate when they were first landed; however no
satisfactory proof on that point can be adduced." Hodgson to Bathurst.
September 27th, 1812. *P.R.O. W.O.* 1/112, fol. 135.
" Two boxes containing plate have been claimed by Don Simón Bolívar as his
private property; they were seized by the collector of His Majesty's Customs for
a breach of the revenue laws having been landed in a clandestine manner."—Hodgson
to Monteverde, September 25th, 1812. *Loc. cit.*, fols. 154–5.

3.

Rojas, pp. 390–1, 420, 675, 697. *Heredia*, p. 30.

4.

R.D.U., pp. 93, 94, 99, 158–60; on the brothers Gómez also *Heredia* passim.
On Islanders: *R.D.U.*, vol. II, pp. 4 ss. On Oropesa: *Restrepo*, vol. I, p. 99.
This period particularly in Cumaná: *Restrepo*, vol. II, p. 111; admirable criticism
in *Heredia*, p. 60 ss.
See *Heredia*, p. 67n., for refutation of Monteverde's claims that the capitulation
had been violated by the other side. Another argument given to excuse Monteverde
of his breaches of the capitulation, i.e., that Miranda took away public money, is
expressly discussed and destroyed by *R.D.U.*, vol. II, p. 12.
J.D.D. has argued that Miranda and the others were imprisoned because the
capitulation did not extend to territories already conquered; others argue that
Miranda was punished for what he did against Spain while he was still a Spanish
official. All this would appear to be narrow and mean. The broad facts are that
the capitulation was broken by the Spanish authorities.
On prisoners: *Heredia*, p. 65n. On Monteverde: *Heredia*, pp. 79, 87, 160.

5.

Heredia, p. 124. *J.D.D.*, p. 92. *Stanhope*, p. 52.

6.

C.L., vol. I, pp. 31, 33, 34, 35, 36, 37, 41.

CHAPTER XX (pp. 191–203)

2.

Article *Cuartel General en Cúcuta* in *Revista Bolivariana*, Bogotá, May 1930,
vol. II, numbers 20 and 21, pp. 537 ss.

3.

Heredia, pp. 88, 89, 90.

4.

Heredia, pp. 91–4. On Cervériz there is an interesting note in *R.D.U.*, vol. II, p. 34, where he shows how this man who had arrived from Cádiz " naked ", emigrated to Puerto Rico in 1813 " equipped with a silver table service, gold watches, ten to twelve trunks of luggage ", looted from his unhappy victims. *R.D.U.*, vol. II, pp. 35, 36, 50–3. *O.C.N.*, p. 168. Monro to Bathurst, Trinidad 29.i.1813: *P.R.O. C.O.* 295/28, doc. no. 4, doc. no. 13; doc. no. 5. *C.O.* 296/5, fols. 30, 100, 107.

5.

J.V.G., p. 52. The text of the plan of Briceño will be found in *O'L*, vol. I, p. 162 and in *J.D.D.* " There have been some trifling disturbances on the Main among the Spaniards which if not checked in time may bring about great Events. It is certain there is a French party and *Frenchmen are constantly sent there from Spain as sailors* and by that means get into the country. *Our Ministers should keep a good look out otherwise they may repent it.* It is a shame to see the numbers of Frenchmen here and publicly countenanced by the Secretary. If it was not a garrison town I should think it dangerous."—Extract from Curaçao, November 6th, 1809, communicated to Lord Liverpool on January 17th, 1810, by R.B. *P.R.O. W.O.* 1/106, fol. 602 verso.

Mier, p. 236, provides a curious piece of information: " We slept in Añoa, first village of France; this is of the Basques or Biscayans of France, for Biscay is partly of Spain and partly of France, and from both men come to America as Spaniards, just as they do from both French and Spanish Catalonia."

P.P.H.R., vol. II, p. 276. *O'L.*, vol. I, p. 190. *A Short Extract from the Life of General Mina published by Himself*, London, 1825, p. 27. Urdaneta quoted by *O'Leary*, vol. I, p. 191.

6.

Heredia, pp. 126–7. *R.V.G.*, *O'L.*, vol. I, pp. 170–1. *J.V.G.*, p. 77. Text of Decree: *O'L.*, vol. I, p. 192. On the Audiencia, see *Heredia*, numerous places.

CHAPTER XXI (pp. 204–214)

1.

O'L., p. 196, where it will be seen that Bolívar clearly hints at the " timid conduct " of the leaders of New Granada. *Heredia*, pp. 131, 135.

2.

Heredia, pp. 134, 135, 135n and 136., 141, 144.

3.

Heredia, pp. 141, 147, 148, 149, 151, 152. *Larrazábal*, vol. I, pp. 143, 192. *J.V.G.*, p. 85.

4.

Date: 7th in *J.V.G.*, p. 86; 6th in *Larrazábal*, vol. I, p. 194; 4th in *Ducoudray*, vol. I, p. 149. Bolívar hears about Mariño in Barinas: Pedro Briceño Méndez quoted by *O'L.*, vol. I, p. 198.

P.D.L., p. 48. *Heredia*, p. 165. *O'L.*, vol. I, p. 229; *G.F.*, vol. I, p. 305. Restrepo, vol. II, p. 165 and *Larrazábal*, vol. I, p. 199. *J.D.D.*, p. 56. On Mérida: *Heredia*, p. 88. *Ducoudray*, vol. I, pp. 156, 157, 168.

5.

O'L., vol. I, p. 221. " In Taguanes all was destroyed; all officers made prisoner were shot."—*J.D.D.*, p. 54. He says that on the track of Bolívar's troops only four Spaniards remained alive.

On delay in taking Puerto Cabello and how Monteverde used it, as well as on the failure of Bolívar's attempt to take the city, see *J.D.D.* On the true meaning of the exchange of prisoners, *Restrepo*, vol. II, p. 167.

...

J.V.G., p. 86, for dates and text of the letter to La Guaira. *Restrepo*, vol. II, p. 167. For Monteverde's letters on the Jalón-Zuazola incident: *Larrazábal*, vol. I, p. 205. Men shot in *G.F.*, vol. I, pp. 306–7. *Heredia*, pp. 156–7, who does not see the point made by Restrepo, adds that Monteverde " fell into the barbarous quixotry of closing his ears to the negotiations, which cost their lives to over 2,000 men murdered at different times ". It is characteristic that in his first letter to Monteverde Urdaneta says that Zuazola's atrocities were " part of the motives we have had to declare war to the death " (*Larrazábal*, vol. I, p. 204); while we know from *O'L.*, vol. I, p. 198, that " it was in Barinas that Bolívar came to know for certain that in Maturin and in Güiria there was also successful fighting going on for the cause of the fatherland ". Therefore Bolívar cannot have heard about Zuazola's atrocities in Trujillo, where he signed his proclamation. Correspondence (September 3rd, 1813) in *G.C.*, vol. IV, pp. 11–12. Quotation S.B., *G.C.*, vol. IV, p. 121.

6.

Heredia, pp. 163, 164–5, 176. Hostile population: *O'L.*, vol. I, p. 219, where after describing the errors of the republicans and Monteverde's audacity he ends: " Nearly the whole people of Venezuela returned, and not with reluctance, to the old obedience." On negroes: *J.V.G.*, p. 87. Compulsory loans and confiscations: *Restrepo*, vol. II, p. 168. Bolívar to Ribas: *J.V.G.*, pp. 90, 91, 93. *Depons*, vol. I, p. 308. *J.D.D.*, p. 122.

CHAPTER XXII (pp. 215–226)

1.

Bobes-B.C., ch. VIII. *Bobes-B.C.* denies that Boves had ever been under trial. But it seems difficult to dismiss *Heredia*, p. 182: " he was in prison under trial in Puerto Cabello for his dealings in a corsair ship." And this would explain better than does *Bobes-B.C.* why he left the Navy to become a store-keeper in Calabozo. *Bobes-B.C.*'s own story on this is not consistent without the detail added by Heredia. *Ducoudray Holstein*, vol. I, p. 181, seems all too likely: " He obtained the command of a gun boat employed in watching the coast, to prevent fraud upon the customs. Instead of seizing the smugglers, he was gained over and protected them; and being detected and denounced, he was cashiered and punished with some months confinement."

Bobes-B.C., pp. 126–8, endeavours to throw doubt on Heredia for not having taken sides. For precisely this reason I prefer to follow Heredia. On the Llaneros, see *Paez-W.S.*

2.

B.A.N.H.V., no. 86. Memoria Histórico-política sobre la Isla de Margarita by Francisco Javier Yanes. *R.D.U.*, pp. 78–81. *J.V.G.*, p. 107. *J.V.G.* is not quite genuine, nor *Restrepo* either. Arizmendi conspired against the régime; the fact is certain. And since he did so before returning to Margarita his arrest was justified.

3.

Heredia, pp. 171–2, 186. *R.D.U.*, vol. II.

4.

R.V.G.B., pp. 236, 239, 243 ss.

5.

Documents in *P.D.L.*, p. 75, vol. 1811–1830. *R.V.G.B.*, pp. 277–8, 280. *G.C.*, vol. IV, pp. 114 ss.

6.

P.D.L., vol. 1910–1930, pp. 79–81, 89, 92, 100–1.

CHAPTER XXIII (pp. 227–236)

1.

J.V.G., pp. 144, 147, 152. *R.V.G.B.*, p. 332; *Mosquera*, p. 116.

D.B.P.L., p. 225. *G.F.*, vol. I, pp. 317–8; *Mosquera*, pp. 119, etc. The Ricaurte episode has given rise to considerable literature. The most complete study of it is that of Cornelio Hispano in his *Colombia en la Guerra de Independencia*, pp. 94–135. He rejects the version attributed to Bolívar in *D.B.P.L.* It should be pointed out that while in any case Ricaurte died fighting like a brave soldier, the acceptance of Peru de Lacroix's version fits in better with Bolívar's character as well as with Bolívar's policy. See also *D.B.N.*, Ap., pp. 429 ss., where Peru is accused of making up the story. But since the psychological spring is supposed to be anti-Granadine feelings, the argument is weakened by the fact that Peru acknowledges Ricaurte's bravery. *Mosquera*, pp. 122, 130. *J.V.G.*, p. 152.

2.

Mosquera, pp. 134 ss. *P.D.L.*, p. 109. *Heredia*, p. 200. *D.L.H.M.*, pp. 285, 288. Offer to Archbishop: *Archives du Ministére des Affaires Etrangères*. Colombia 1829–30, vol. 6. Letter from Adm. Fleming to Peña. Valencia, 16.iii.30. *Heredia*, pp. 124, 186 ss., 201, 203. *G.F.*, vol. I, pp. 313, 318, 320.

3.

Heredia and *G.F.*

4.

Heredia, Larrazábal, Restrepo.

5.

J.V.G., p. 234. *G.F.*, vol. I, p. 322. *B.A.N.H.V.*, no. 71, pp. 488 ss. *Mosquera*, p. 153. *Larrazábal*, vol. I, p. 327. *Lecuna, loc. cit.* Dr. Lecuna argues that "the Libertador says that Bianchi was more generous than Piar in order to bring out the character of the latter, but there could be no generosity in such a cold-blooded man . . ." Very good, but then, how did Bolívar and Mariño get the silver from him without weapons? *B.D.*, vol. I, p. 284, note by Dr. Lecuna. *B.A.N.H.V.*, no. 71, p. 494. *J.D.D.*, p. 193. *J.V.G.*, p. 226.

CHAPTER XXIV (pp. 237–251)

1.

D.B.C.H., pp. 232–3. *Yanes. J.V.G.*, pp. 222–26—M.S. *P.D.L.*, pp. 111–16.

2.

Date of departure from Carúpano in *Mosquera*, p. 155. *J.V.G.*, p. 226, gives September 8th. See Morán in *B.A.N.H.V.*, no. 71, quoted by Vicente Lecuna. "Calling at Margarita without daring land for fear that the said Bolívar might be killed there."—Statement of two witnesses in Maracaibo on December 7th before Ramón Correa. *Restrepo*, vol. I. *Toreno*, pp. 520, 523.

3.

Restrepo, vol. I. *Ducoudray*, vol. I. *Larrazábal*, vol. I, p. 341

4.

Restrepo, vol. I, p. 295, says: "The capitulation of December 12th was religiously carried out by both sides." No wonder Bolívar said to Peru de Lacroix commenting on his History: "Another defect of Restrepo is the bias which he evinces in many passages. So far as I am concerned, his intention to please me and his fear to criticise

some of my actions openly are evident.   He is determined to flatter me, because I
am alive and I hold power and he needs me and does not want to displease me."
D.B.C.H., p. 190.

5.

Restrepo, vol. I.   *E.M.C.*, pp. 28, 30.

6.

Restrepo.   Baralt.   Ducoudray.   Mosquera.

CHAPTER XXV (pp. 253–262)

1.

On Ferdinand's decree: *Villa*, vol. II, pp. 462 ss., doc. 416.   On mediation:
Webster, vol. I, Introduction pp. 12 ss. doc. *F.O.* 72/131, no. 501 in *Webster*,
vol. II, p. 32.

2.

Villa, vol. I.

3.

Sevilla-A., pp. 22, 23, 24.   *E.M.C.*, p. 43.   *Villa*, vol. I, pp. 121–2.   *Sevilla-A.*,
pp. 24, 26, says Morillo and Morales agreed to take Margarita; but this operation
constitutes point 3 of Morillo's Instructions under the heading Army: *Villa*,
vol. II, p. 440.

4.

Villa, vol. I, pp. 128 ss.   Instructions Morillo to Herraiz: doc. 410, vol. II, p. 452.
On Bermúdez' flight, see letter from Morillo to the Governor of Trinidad, May 2nd
1815, doc. 413, *Villa*, vol. II, p. 459.
Narrative from *Villa*, vol. I, pp. 136 ss.   This passage of Sevilla's Memoirs has
disappeared from the Paris edition.   The harangues of Morales are evidently sub-
edited by Sevilla, whose Andalusian imagination provides a number of wild beasts:
reptile, tiger, crocodile and hyena.   But the scene is undoubtedly historical and is
confirmed time and again by Morillo's constant references to his clemency towards
Arizmendi after Arizmendi's second rebellion.

5.

Ducoudray, vol. I, pp. 242 ss., ch. X.   *P.R.O.* Adm. 1/266, fol. 90, annexes.
Answer from Bathurst to Fuller *P.R.O.* C.O. 138/44, fols. 217–9.   The Spanish
Ambassador Count of Fernán-Núñez sent Castlereagh a letter of protest against
the fact that H.M.S. *Carnation* had conveyed Cavero and Robertson to Jamaica
(22.i.1816).   "These persons remained in Jamaica as did the perverse Bolívar of
whom the undersigned has already made mention to His Excellency on another
occasion and who was reported to be on the point of proceeding thence to this
country."   The protest was reiterated on February 27th.   *E.M.C.*, pp. 92 ss.,
99, 100.

6.

E.M.C., p. 104.   *P.R.O.* Adm. 1/266, fol. 96.   *P.R.O.* C.O. 138/44, fols. 217–19.
P.R.O. Adm. 1/266, fol. 90, from Rear-Admiral Douglas to the Admiralty (16.vi.15)
informing them of the arrival of two commissioners from "the Government of
Carthagena who on June 12th offered 'to place the City of Carthagena and the
fortresses immediately dependent thereon in deposit until they should know the
result of the Mission sent to London, for the purpose of obtaining an acknowledgement of their Independence; and in case it should not be favourable to their wishes,
the possession of Carthagena to remain in the hands of the British Forces, until they
could obtain from the Government of the Peninsula, such conditions as might be
necessary for security of the Persons and property of the Inhabitants of New
Granada ' ".

On August 4th Bathurst wrote to Lieutenant-General Fuller approving his decision to abstain "from taking any part in the existing hostilities in South America, notwithstanding the repeated solicitations of the commissioners from Carthagena". Bathurst added: "However important the political and commercial advantages are which have been held out by the commissioners including even the offer of the occupation of Carthagena by British troops, and however His Royal Highness must deprecate the cruelties which the Commissioners state are to be expected if Carthagena should fall into the hands of the Spaniards, yet His Royal Highness being in Amity with His Catholic Majesty will not be brought to take part in the support of those who have declared against His Catholic Majesty."—*P.R.O.* C.O. 138/44, fols. 217-9.

On Morillo and Boca Chica: *E.C.M.*, p. 120. *Torrente*, vol. I, p. 182. *O'L.*, vol. I, p. 365, says that Morales' soldiers "*eran casi todos de Venezuela*".

Chapter XXVI (pp. 263–276)

1.

Date of arrival: *C.L.*, vol. I, p. 149. Departure: *C.L.*, vol. I, p. 222. Texts: *B-A.*, vol. V, pp. 348-9, doc. 1073. *O'L.*, vol. I, pp. 394-5. *D.B. P.L.*, pp. 66-8; *D.B. N.*, p. 178. *Mosquera*, pp. 174, 5.

Torrente, vol. II, pp. 254-5, uses highly suspicious words: "There and then that scourge of mankind should have perished, but Providence by its unscrutable judgment saved his life in a semi-miraculous way." "That was the night when the sacrifice was to be consummated: the mulatto Luis, Bolívar's slave, had been won to murder his master." It reads almost as if Torrente knew that the Spanish authorities had been behind it all. The details are wrong. The mulatto was a negro and Luis was Pío. He also says that the murderer died without revealing the name of the instigators, which we know from Mosquera to be contrary to the facts.

The worst document for Morillo is the *Antapodosis* of Level de Goda (*B.A.N.H.V.*, nos. 63-4, pp. 608 ss): "This chief [Morillo] had contracted with a Catalan for 5,000 pesos the murder of Bolívar when the latter was in Jamaica, and he agreed with one of Bolívar's servants, who [then follows the story, save that in L.d.G. Amestoy dies of a pistol shot]. The Catalan, who had taken his precautions, was able to run away but Bolívar's servant was hanged in Jamaica. The Catalan came to claim his 5,000 pesos, but Morillo objected that the deed had not been consummated though all had been done thereto, and after much discussion, the Catalan was content with 3,000 pesos which Morillo gave him." This text and even more so the elaborate story L. de G. tells about Morillo's high-handed ways in trying to recover his 3,000 pesos from the civilian authorities, and how he, L. de G., prevented him therefrom with the majesty of the law, make up an impressive testimony against Morillo. But the following objections can be raised: (a) L. de G. is a liar wherever he is personally concerned; (b) the traditional black sheep has always been Moxó until this text was published by Vicente Lecuna; (c) Mosquera's text is a far more reliable authority, since his natural bias would have led him to the very opposite conclusion; (d) next to Mosquera, O'L. is the best authority, and he rejects the Spanish responsibility; (e) after his vague and general accusations in Jamaica, Bolívar himself never accused the Spanish chiefs of this crime which, if true, would have provided good ammunition for his propaganda. He did nevertheless suspect Moxó in conversation with Peru de Lacroix, by the way, mis-naming him La Torre; (f) the events told by L. de G. are supposed to have been public. Yet, after them, on January 26th, 1821, Bolívar wrote a most cordial letter to "his dear friend" Morillo, the terms of which go far beyond diplomatic courtesy, and express cordial friendship.—*C.L.*, vol. II, pp. 305-7.

3.

Hippisley, pp. 233-4. *Ducoudray*, pp. 273-7. *Larrazábal*, vol. II, p. 19.

4.

Arrival: Cf. Letter to Brion (2.i.16). Docs. Pétion in *Larrazábal*, vol. II, pp. 20-1. Payment through Sutherland: *Larrazábal*, vol. II, p. 20. "Il mit donc pour *condition* des secours qu'il allait lui donner en armes, munitions, etc., que Bolívar fit la promesse solennelle de proclamer 'la liberté *générale de tous les esclaves* de la Province de Venezuela et de toutes autres qu'il réussirait à réunir sous le drapeau de l'indépendance'." *Dalencour*, p. 11. The same author, p. 13, tells how Pétion refused Bolívar authority to name him in his proclamations. See also *Marion*, p. 93. *Ducoudray*, pp. 281 ss. *Larrazábal*, vol. II, pp. 22-3. Bolívar wrote to Ducoudray-Holstein on 23.vi.1816 from Carúpano accepting his resignation, that he had refused to accept it twice before because he was convinced that his services were important for the cause of the Republic. *O'L.*, vol. XV. *Ducoudray*, pp. 281 ss. *Marion*, pp. 92 ss. See another version of Aury's episode in *Larrazábal*, vol. II, pp. 22-3 Also article by Vicente Lecuna on Stanley Faye's biography of Aury in *B.A.N.H.V.*, no. 83, p. 313.

5.

Ducoudray, pp. 285-6. The fact that Bolívar and Brion chose Ducoudray as their second proves how wrong are those who to get rid of him as an inconvenient witness endeavour to blacken him as an intriguer against Bolívar. They project backwards later attitudes. Chief among them is *Larrazábal*, for example, vol. II, pp. 22-3.

Ducoudray, p. 287; *Hippisley*, p. 322. On Isabel Soublette: *loc. cit.*, p. 334. All these opinions on Soublette are borne out by Bolívar himself, who in conversation with Peru de Lacroix describes this man who has been his close collaborator since 1813 in terms almost as scathing as those of Hippisley. See, however, criticism by Monseñor Navarro on this passage, *D.B.N.*, p. 355.

Marion, pp. 99-100. *Hippisley*, pp. 249, 461, 465.

6.

O.C.N., p. 54, on Brion. On the date: *Ducoudray*, vol. I, p. 307. *O'L.*, vol. II, p. 425, says March 31st. *Larrazábal*, vol. II, p. 29, says March 20th. *Baralt*, vol. I, p. 324, says March 30th. *Restrepo*, vol. II, p. 337, says it sailed on March 30th. *Mosquera*, p. 185, gives April 16th. See discussion by Lecuna, in *B.A.N.H.V.*, no. 75, p. 332.

Ducoudray, vol. I, pp. 310-11. Naturally, having retired to Haiti, he would be careful to conform to the wishes of Pétion and remain discreet about the negro soldiers Bolívar had received from the Haitian President. *J.D.D.*, p. 200. As this author, a Venezuelan in the pay of Spain, is often accused of inaccuracy, it is well to point out that his data in this case ("one thousand negroes and mulattoes, from Aux Cayes, provided by President Pétion") are confirmed by two first-hand authorities: *Le Président lui permit meme d'y comprendre des haitiens qui voulurent y concourir.*—*Dalencour*, p. 14; *Un grand nombre d'haitiens, militaires, marins et autres, sont reçus à leur bord, pour renforcer ces quelques centaines d'hommes de l'expédition. Les autorités le savaient, mais le mot était donné de n'y faire aucune attention, de fermer les yeux.*—*Marion*, p. 98. Morillo wrote to Madrid on September 9th, 1816: "In March I insisted from Ocaña on this urgency, in view of Bolívar's expedition and since the war had now become a duel of negroes against whites." Doc. 571, *Villa*, vol. III, p. 228.

To all these authorities may be added the following: Salom, the Venezuelan general, in a note to O'Leary on the strange happenings in Ocumare, after Bolívar's flight, says: "As I do not know the name of the French chief who remained in command at Ocumare castle during the operations [his name was Brisel] I agree with that general Soublette gives; nevertheless, I find it strange that general Brion, who was himself head of Staff, could have left such a man in land; for he was a coward who preferred to keep the boat busy from dusk till the time he sailed, transporting a crowd of French negresses with their sons and baggages and other

French subalterns who surrounded him, instead of saving the armament and munitions which remained derelict on the shore." Salom was so indignant that he had to be warned later by Soublette to hold his tongue for " there are around French chiefs and officers"—French meant indifferently, French and Haitians, i.e., blacks. —*O'L.*, vol. I, pp. 437–8.

I do not know why Dr. Lecuna calls Ducoudray's story a calumny, and describes Miss Pepa as Bolívar's fiancée. *B.A.N.H.V.*, no. 75, p. 335. We shall see Ducoudray's version confirmed by Soublette and O'L. in a later chapter. *Ducoudray*, vol. I, pp. 307–9.

CHAPTER XXVII (pp. 277–292)

1.

B.D., vol. I, p. 312. *O.C.N.*, p. 32. " The perjurer and murderer Arismendi seduced you and made you believe that the army had been exterminated, that I was dead and that Carthagena was independent."—24.iv.16, Morillo to the Margaritans. *Villa*, vol. II, p. 36.

B.D., vol. I, p. 313. All Baralt can say against Urreiztieta is that he " tried to arrest the notables " and that Arismendi's wife was the object of uncivil treatment.

Moxó's orders: Doc. 1086, pp. 380 ss. in *Blanco Azpurúa*, vol. V. *J.D.D.*, p. 199. *Torrente*, vol. II, pp. 256, 260. *B.D.*, vol. I, p. 321.

Ducoudray, vol. I, pp. 317, 319, 323. After resigning Ducoudray " *revint aux Cayes à la fin de 1816. Il avait essayé d'y établir une bibliothèque publique, mais comme cela n'alla pas bien il se détermina enfin à donner des leçons de piano qui lui valurent beaucoup* ".—*Marion*, p. 100 n. The author himself was one of Ducoudray's pupils.

2.

Ducoudray, vol. I, pp. 220, 323, 326. Ode in *Blanco Azpurúa*, vol. V, p. 435. *Mosquera*, p. 188. *P.D.L.*, p. 146. Salom (quoted by Lecuna, *B.A.N.H.V.*, no. 75, p. 333) says that in the s.s. *Decatur*, in which he travelled, lieutenants and captains stood on watch as privates. *Yanes*, vol. I, p. 297, says that they were hardly two hundred men, nearly all officers, and so most if not all authors. Yet it is evident that they are aiming at making the negroes disappear. The same Yanes (vol. I, p. 306) says that " the expeditionary force received an increase of four hundred men a few days after Carúpano had been occupied and nine corps were formed under as many lieutenant colonels ". Therefore they had brought enough men to form nine corps, but for the new four hundred. This would not imply less than a force of one thousand soldiers. In the text will be seen more reasons for proving that the expeditionary force had brought over about a thousand negroes.

Lecuna in *B.A.N.H.V. O'L.*, vol. I. *P.D.L.*, vol. I. *Marion. Ducoudray*, vol. I. *Yanes*, vol. I, p. 296.

3.

B.A.N.H.V., no. 77, p. 14. Chamberlain in Revenga, *B.A.N.H.V.*, no. 77, pp. 102–3; Moxó to Morillo, *ibid.*, p. 97. *O'L.*, vol. I, pp. 437–8.

It is typical of Bolívar's so-called history that O'L., after copying the cold indictment of their chief by his subordinate officers, goes on to say (p. 439): " This bulletin was written when Bolívar was far away, and not one complaint, not one word of reproach does it contain against the man who, according to his enemies, had abandoned his companions in a cowardly way." Ducoudray-Holstein must be correct and by no means slanderous when he describes in great detail the panicky scene he witnessed in Carúpano. His picture is too true to the general pattern of Bolívar's life to be dismissed. The story of Soublette as well as Salom's, and later that of O'L. himself confirm D.H. in every way: for instance the abundance of women on board is confirmed by Salom's negresses. Yanes, who knew nothing about Alzuru's story, explains matters differently. According to him (p. 308), the two French corsairs Penó and Declair, disobeying Bolívar, instead of conveying their load of arms to Choroní, where MacGregor had been sent by Bolívar, had sailed to Bonaire, so that Bolívar had to sail after them to recover the arms; "this was the cause of his not having joined his troops and of the loss of one thousand rifles, a great quantity of ammunition, a printing press and other material, private and State jewelry which remained on the shore." This is also Bolívar's own version. But then, why Alzuru?

Marion, p. 110; Ducoudray, vol. II, p. 14; Yanes, p. 309; B.A.N.H.V., no. 77, p. 26; O'L., vol. I, p. 140. O'L. tells a yarn about a Spanish sloop whose captain was so terrified of Bolívar on board a ship run aground that he took upon himself to deliver the ladies in St. Thomas after disengaging Bolívar's ship. Yanes, vol. I, p. 309, says it was a Dutch and not a Spanish sloop, which Lecuna (p. 28) reasonably prefers.

4.

Marion, p. 99; Yanes, vol. 1, pp. 309–10; O'L., vol. I, p. 441. Yanes' story is belied by Bolívar's letter dated Ocumare, July 8th, confirmed by Larrazábal, vol. I, p. 436. The letter to Bermúdez is preserved in the family archives of Don Manuel María Mosquera, at present in the house of Doña Natalia Diez de Iragorri, in Popayán, where I saw it.

Larrazábal, vol. I, p. 436. Bermúdez sailed in the sloop of Antonio Rosales. The scene of Bolívar passing alone, sword in hand, through a double row of his would-be assassins, unscathed, seems to me as theatrical as unbelievable. B.A.N.H.V., no. 77, p. 29. O'L., vol. I, p. 441, where he again represents an all too obvious flight as a free decision of Bolívar to avoid a civil war; Mosquera, pp. 197–8, makes Bermúdez sail in the company of Bolívar, or at least frequent him in Bonaire, which seems to me very unlikely.

5.

Moxó to Governor of Barinas: Caracas, 19.viii.16. B.A.N.H.V., no. 77, p. 105. O'L., vol. I, p. 445, makes Morales' force 3,000. The document above shows they were 2,000. But V.L. in B.A.N.H.V. no. 77, p. 36, proves they were just above 1,000. He says (pp. 35–37) that Piar fled. Mosquera, p. 444. B.A.N.H.V., no. 77, p. 110; Marion. Larrazábal, vol. I, p. 444; Ducoudray, vol. II, p. 20, puts all the initiative on Brion who, according to him, won over Arizmendi through Villaret. P.R.O. C.O. 138/46, fols. 204–5. Goulburn to Hamilton, June 15th, 1816. For the participation of the British Navy in the travels and correspondence of Cortés Madariaga, see letter of C.M. to Bolívar from Pampátar, April 25th, 1817. Archivo Nacional de Colombia. Archivo de la Colonia, Historia, vol. XXII, fols. 149–150 v.

6.

Morillo, p. 19; Sevilla, pp. 68–71; E.M.C., pp. 118–120, 134, 181 ss. Morillo, p. 27, and document annexed, p. 28, Mompox 1.iii.16. True, Sevilla, p. 61, relates how Morillo knew Arizmendi's rebellion through him on December 26, 1815; but the story is too good to be true and Sevilla was a vain man whose witness cannot stand against Morillo's own.

On this section and the next, the cool view is that of Sañudo, pp. 45–7. Competent historians should cease copying Restrepo and others who simply rant on Morillo and on Enrile. It is curious to find Calzada "rebuking" Morillo for his cruel ways in the pages of those who till Morillo appears on the scene had represented Calzada as a prototype of cruelty. Sevilla, p. 94; Morillo, p. 26. The Committee of Purification was created to administer and interpret a so-called amnesty. But the conditions a man had to fulfil to satisfy this amnesty were so stiff that in fact few could have benefited by it and all were at the mercy of the Committee.

See Morillo, Ap. 24, for text.

On the effect of Arizmendi's betrayal on Morillo the documents are too numerous for quotation. For instance, in his letter to Onis, Spanish envoy in Philadelphia,

Santa Fe, June 23rd, 1816, he says: " I must thank Your Excellency for the good opinion you have of my humane character, which I shall never belie, although the outcome of the clemency and pardon granted to the treacherous inhabitants of Margarita should have made me alter my principles."—*Villa*, vol. III, p. 23. See also Proclamation to the Venezuelans, Mompox, 1.iii.16, *Villa*, vol. III, pp 32–3 and many others. Rear-Admiral Fahie of the British Navy writing on board H.M.S. *Salisbury*, August 9th, 1820, Doc. 853, *Villa*, vol. IV, p. 271, pays a handsome homage to Morillo's humane feelings with regard to some English prisoners.

CHAPTER XXVIII (pp. 293–308)

1.

B.A.N.H.V., no. 77, pp. 40 ss. The story of Páez' revolt, as told by him, depicts him as most respectful of the law. *Páez*, pp. 114 ss. He paints himself in colours curiously similar to those in which Mitre paints San Martín, forced to remain as Governor of Cuyo by his own troops in defiance of the orders from Buenos Aires. Yanes, however, who was in the thick of it, positively says that Páez " intimated in writing, in an imperious tone, to President Serrano and other members of the Government, that they were to cease in their functions ", giving among his reasons that Santander "was inept and incapable of carrying out his office ". *Yanes*, vol. I, p. 284.

2.

Doc. 536, Ocaña, 30.iii.1816. *Villa*, vol. III, p. 149.

Doc. 527, Mompox, 7.iii.1816. *Villa*, vol. III, pp. 136–7.

Doc. 539, Ocaña, 5.iv.1816. *Villa*, vol. III, p. 156.

Doc. 549, Santa Fe, 31.v.1816. *Villa*, vol. III, p. 168.

Doc. 557, Santa Fe, 30.viii.1816. *Villa*, vol. III, p. 190.

On Moxó Level de Goda, Antapodosis, p. 564. The data on Moxó, his troops and behaviour come from *Villa*, vol. III: Doc. 685, 22.v.1818, pp. 548–63; Doc. 562, p. 208; Doc. 568, pp. 212–16.

Sevilla, pp. 124–135, 150–152; *O'L.*, vol. I, p. 492. *Villa*, vol. III, p. 265, Doc. 597; p. 268, Doc. 598.

3.

Chuecos, vol. II, pp. 133–4. Officers leaving Páez: *Páez*, p. 147; officers leaving Piar: *O'L.*, vol. I, p. 453.

Mosquera, p. 216. *Ducoudray*, vol. II, p. 23. Of course, about his leaving Barcelona, we hear again, as whenever Bolívar makes a mistake, that he listened to the advice of others, in this case, of Freites, whom he left in command of a paltry seven hundred men, and to the tender mercies of Mariño. On the other hand, *Ducoudray*, p. 27, and *Hippisley*, p. 466, are wrong in saying that Bolívar fled on seeing the Spaniards arrive for he did not leave in the night of April 5–6, as they claim, but on March 25th or 22nd. *Urdaneta*, pp. 109–14.

Memorias del Capitán Lobatón, and Memorias del Sargento Manuel Ostí in *B.A.N.H.V.*, no. 105, pp. 62–65, confirm the usual version about the behaviour of Aldama's troops; although Aldama had been appointed owing to the objections raised by Spanish officers to Morales' cruel ways. *O'L.*, p. 460; *Mosquera*. Anon will be seen that Morillo got rid of Aldama because he proved no better than Morales.

Yanes, pp. 10 ss. *Larrazábal*, vol. I, p. 468. Quotation from *Mosquera*, p. 230. The murder of the friars is a curious and somewhat exceptional case in the historiography of Bolívar. A prominent Venezuelan historian writes on Lara: " In his public life there is an event which stains his brilliant record: the unnecessary execution of the twenty Capuchin civilisers of the Caroní carrying out orders from Bolívar. These orders must have been verbal, for so far there is no document. But that there was such an order is also a historical fact, for otherwise Bolívar would have punished such a crime committed almost in his presence."—Vicente Dávila quoted by *Sañudo*, p. 52. On the other hand the bishop of Popayán, Don Salvador Jiménez de Enciso, a Spaniard and an ardent royalist throughout, having rallied to the Republic in his later years wrote exonerating Bolívar. He, however, expressly says that he had " to get information from persons he was bound to believe," and he wrote on events that had happened eleven years earlier and very far from his see. The most reasonable explanation is that of Mosquera in a way confirmed by *O'L.*, p. 463. *Larrazábal*, vol. I, pp. 466–70, is extravagant; and *Yanes*, vol. II, p. 12, is beautifully simple: the friars were killed by the Indians who, of course, hated them.

Yanes, vol. II, p. 12, says Bolívar recrossed the Orinoco the day after his arrival. *O'L.*, vol. I, p. 464, tries to give Bolívar all the merit for the conception of the battle of San Felix. Mosquera knows of no such intervention of Bolívar. This coming and going of Bolívar's is of course a permanent feature of his character.

Prisoners killed: *O'L.*, vol. I, p. 464. *Larrazábal*, p. 469, says Piar shot 300. The details and the number of 800 in the text come from *López*, p. 22.

O'L., vol. I, p. 471. Better still *Urdaneta*, p. 115. *Páez*, p. 167. Cortés Madariaga's letter MS in *Archivo Nacional de Colombia, Bogotá. Archivo de la Colonia. Historia*, vol. XXII, fols. 149 v. and 150 v. Manifesto in *Yanes*, Doc. 43, vol. II, pp. 208–14. Doc. 44, vol. II, pp. 214–19. Doc. 45, p. 219. Doc. 50, vol. II, p. 223. Doc. 51, p. 223. *Yanes*, vol. II, p. 20.

4.

Sevilla, pp. 163 ss.

5.

Enrile to Minister of War, 19.vi.1817, *Villa*, vol. III, pp. 296–330, 303. Morillo to Moxó, Calabozo, 15.iii.1817: Doc. 605, *Villa*, vol. III, p. 289. Proclamation: Doc. 610, *Villa*, vol. III, pp. 332–4. *O'L.*, vol. I, p. 495. Doc. 610, *Villa*, vol. III, pp. 333–4. Doc. 632, *Villa*, vol. III, p. 399. *O'L.*, vol. I, p. 499. Doc. 638, Morillo to War Minister, 28.viii.1817; Doc. 639, p. 418; Doc. 641, p. 430, Cumaná, 28.viii.1817. *Sañudo. Restrepo. Yanes.*

6.

Villa, vol. I, pp. 303, 310, 311, 313, 332, 333. *O'L.*, vol. I, p. 507; vol. XV. Docs. 337, 341, 348, 352, pp. 337–56, 524, 531, 534. *Boussingault*, vol. II, pp. 67, 70. *Páez*, pp. 169, 172. *O.C.N.*, vol. II, p. 177. Level de Goda in *B.A.N.H.V.*, no. 59, p. 191. *Sañudo*, p. 64.

CHAPTER XXIX (pp. 309–319)

1.

Villa, vol. I, p. 347. *B.A.N.H.V.*, no. 84, p. 387. *Hippisley*, pp 1, 3, 24, 31, 32. *Webster*, vol. I, p. 14.

2.

B.A.N.H.V., no. 88, pp. 664 ss. *Hippisley*, Ap. 12.

3.

Hippisley, pp. 291, 390, 395 ss., 428, 445, 588, 590.

4.

Hippisley, pp. 400 ss.

5.

B.A.N.H.V., no. 88. *Hippisley. Hasbrouck. Urrutia. B.A.N.H.V.*, no. 62.

6.

Orinoco, no. 2.

2.

Hippisley, pp. 289–90. " I can assure Y.E. without the slightest exaggeration that the Spanish army in Venezuela has been defeated in Calabozo, El Sombrero, San Fernando. La Puerta, Ortiz and Cojedes."—Bolívar to the Captain General of Barbados, 1.ix.18.—*O'L.*, vol. XVI, p. 93. There is, of course, not a word of truth in the statement.

Duro, vol. IX, pp. 135–39. The bad quality of the Russian ships was soon known in Caracas through the *Morning Chronicle* of March 24th, reprinted in *Orinoco*, no. 10. On Maipo: *Mitre. Orinoco*, no. 9.

3.

Section based on *Mitre*, as well as the next.

5.

Duro, vol. IX.

6.

Orinoco, no. 19. *D.P.L.*, p. 196.

BOOK II

Chapter I (pp. 333–338)

1.

For all this section *Orinoco*, no. 19, 20.ii.19.

2.

Morillo to War Minister, Valencia, 18.iii.18, Doc. 675, *Villa*, vol. III, p. 522; Valencia, 2.iv.18, Doc. 677, *Villa*, vol. III, p. 525. *Hippisley*, p. 464. *Orinoco*, nos. 19 ss. *P.D.L.*, vol. I, pp. 202 ss. *C.L.*, vol. II, p. 142, 26.iii.20. *P.D.L.*, pp. 214 ss., 222, 229.

Chapter II (pp. 339–348)

1.

Páez, pp. 207 ss., 212. *O'L.*, vol. I, pp. 625 ss., 630–1, 632, 638, 640. *Morillo*, p. 39.

2.

V.L. in *B.A.N.H.V.*, no. 90, p. 275. On Casanare events: *Restrepo*, vol. II, p. 507. *Sañudo*, p. 72. *B.A.N.H.V.*, no. 90, p. 262. *Restrepo*, vol. II, p. 507.

3.

O'L., vol. I, pp. 645, 646, 655. Lecuna in *B.A.N.H.V.*, no. 90, p. 263. *Loc. cit.*, pp. 262 ss.

4.

Lecuna in *B.A.N.H.V.*, no. 90, p. 267. *O'L.*, vol. I, p. 664.

5.

Hasbrouck, p. 197. *Bingham*, pp. 172, 190. *O'L.*, p. 168. Archivo Nacional de Bogotá. Secretaría de Guerra y Marina. T. 325, fols. 374d, 375. *O'L.*, vol. I, p. 670. Lecuna in *B.A.N.H.V.*, pp. 281, 282–3. *Sañudo*, p. 74. On Vargas marshes: Lecuna, *loc. cit.*, *Restrepo*, vol. II, p. 534. *Bingham*, pp. 272 ss.

6.

Lecuna in *B.A.N.H.V.*, no. 90, p. 289. *Loc. cit. D.L. H.M.*, p. 325. *Sañudo*, p. 79. See, for instance, the essay of Sir Alexander Godley: *British Military History in South America* in which he castigates San Martín and Bolívar. Calabozo, 12.v.19, Doc. 771, *Villa*, vol. 4, pp. 25–32; Doc. 781, p. 50; Doc. 787 (Tinaco 24.ix.19), p. 71. *O'L.*, vol. I, p. 688.

CHAPTER III (pp. 349–356)

1.

B.A.N.H.V., no. 90, pp. 296 ss; *Sañudo*, p. 79. *O'L.*, vol. I, p. 688.

O.C.N., Part I, pp. 8, 21, 48. This Blossett is the subject of a certificate of discourtesy Urdaneta gave to Sucre in Maturin 11.xi.19, *B.A.N.H.V.*, no. 90, p. 351. *O'L.*, vol. I, p. 50. The story of *O.C.N.* in Trinidad is rather tall and does not tally with *Chesterton*, vol. II, pp. 44 ss., who say that English left Trinidad in a hurry in view of Woodford's attitude; that when they were approaching Margarita orders were given to clear for action, Woodford having threatened to send a British brig of war *Fly* to prevent the expedition from landing, and English wanting to fight; that Colonel Stopford, however, called a meeting of British officers and drew their attention to the gravity of fighting against H.M.'s forces and that finally it was decided not to fight, though in the end the *Fly* did not turn up at all. *O.C.N.* (p. 51) says they landed on April 19; Chesterton (p. 46) on April 7th. I have searched the P.R.O. in vain for records of dramatic events told by *O.C.N.* There is a report from Woodford to Bathurst (Trinidad 8.iv.19. C.O. 296/48, fol. 325) on the arrival of ss. *Duncombe* and *Francis and Eliza*, the first with ten officers and one hundred and sixty-six men, women and children; the second with fourteen officers and one hundred and forty-six men, women and children, including English and Miller. Chesterton was in the second. Six men deserted and Woodford refused to hand them back.

2.

Lecuna in *B.A.N.H.V.*, no. 90, pp. 304 ss. *Chesterton*, vol. II, p. 66. *O.C.N.*, Part I, pp. 89, 90. *O'L.*, vol. I, p. 647. *O.C.N.* probably by misprint or neglect says September instead of August for the expedition to Cumaná. On the English: *Mosquera*, pp. 341 ss. Lecuna in *B.A.N.H.V.*, no. 90, pp. 302–3. *Orinoco*, no. 41. *P.R.O. C.O.* 295, vol. 48, nos. 333, 335.

3.

Orinoco, no. 31, July 1819. No. 35 for Mariño's responsibilities to Congress. Mosquera's articles accusing Zea of stubbornness in this, p. 344. *Mosquera*, pp. 343–44. *O'L.*, vol. II, pp. 12 ss. Lecuna in *B.A.N.H.V.*, no. 90, pp. 302 ss.

4.

Chesterton, vol. II, pp. 39, 67. *Morillo*, p. 41; also *Villa*, doc. 806, vol. IV, p. 109. Order from War Minister to Morillo, 8.ii.19, Doc. 802, *Villa*, vol. IV, p. 105; Calabozo, 12.v.19, Doc. 771, *Villa*, vol. IV, pp. 25–32.

5.

O.C.N., pp. 175 ss.

CHAPTER IV (pp. 357–364)

1.

Groot, *Historia de Colombia*, vol. IV, pp. 28 ss. Santander to Bolívar, Oct. 17, 1819. Bolívar to Santander, Nov. 8, 1819. *C.L.*, vol. II, p. 117. Soledad Acosta de Samper, *Biografía del General Acosta*, p. 27. Cornelio Hispano: *Historia Secreta de Bolívar*, pp. 134 ss.

2.

Mosquera, p. 349; *O'L.*, vol. I, p. 690; *Restrepo*, vol. II, p. 541; *Baralt*, vol. I, pp. 484–6. He says: " The fierce viceroy would not even receive peaceful envoys "; but Sámano had fled precipitately and was no longer acting; and Baralt himself adds: " but Santander knew nothing of this when, alleging as a pretext that the prisoners were conspiring, and that he had no troops to guard them, and popular commotions and other things, he decreed that horrible execution." *O'L.* is more explicit: it was precisely the execution of Barreiro, what he, O'Leary, describes as the murder of the prisoners, that frustrated Bolívar's plan of exchange. *G.F.*, vol. I, p. 345, concludes commenting on Bolívar's letter to Santander: " A skilful way of combining approval and censure of that vengeance which was a crime." *Boussingault*, vol. III, p. 191. *Hamilton*, vol. I, pp. 139, 218. *Sañudo*, p. 78. Santander to Azuero: Archivo Santander, vol. VI, p. 238. *C.B.S.*, p. 140. *C.L.*, vol. II, p. 152. *C.B.S.*, p. 168.

3.

O.C.N., Part II, pp. 4 ss., 38, 41, 43. *Orinoco*, no. 47. *B.A.N.H.V.*, no. 90.

CHAPTER V (pp. 365–373)

1.

B.A.N.H.V., no. 90, p. 314.

2.

O'L., vol. II, pp. 35 ss. *B.A.N.H.V.*, no. 93, p. 42.

3.

O'C., vol. I, p. 31.

4.

P.D.L., vol. I, p. 248. *Larrazábal*, vol. II, pp. 255–7. *C.B.S.*, pp. 58, 131, 143, 156, 168, 184, 187.

5.

O'C., vol. I, pp. 24 ss. *B.A.N.H.V.*, no. 93, p. 46. *O'C.*, vol. I, p. 27. *O'G.*, vol. I, p. 33. *Larrazábal*, vol. II, p. 260. Lecuna in *B.A.N.H.V.*

CHAPTER VI (pp. 374–382)

2.

Lecuna in *B.A.N.H.V.*, pp. 304 ss.

3.

J.D.D., pp. 238 ss., evidently lends Morillo his own opinion on these circulars. Morillo may have thought it rash to treat with Bolívar at that time (at least at first, and before he realized how well it would suit him); but that he was favourable to the Constitution cannot be doubted in view of his later career. *G.F.*, vol. I, p. 400. *D.L. H.M.*, pp. 349 ss., 357 ss.

4.

Sañudo, p. 88. *C.B.S.*, pp. 208–9. *Urdaneta*, pp. 178 ss.

5.

Villa, vol. IV, pp. 250 ss., Doc. 848. Puerto Cabello, 16.xii.20, pp. 247–50, Doc. 846, Barquisimeto, 31.x.20. *Urdaneta*, p. 184, nota; 185. *Páez*, p. 234. Narrative of the interview: Doc. 881 in *Villa*, vol. IV, pp. 320 ss.

CHAPTER VII (pp. 383–390)

1.

O.C.N., vol. II, p. 110. *G.F.*, vol. I, pp. 402–3, 404. *O'L.*, vol. II, p. 266.

2.

D.B.N., 325/322.

3.

28.viii.20; Doc. 837; *Villa*, vol. IV, p. 223. 30.ix.20, Doc. 842, pp. 234-5. 31.x.20, Doc. 846, p. 249. 16.xii.20, Doc. 848, p. 250. These intrigues are well told in *Duarte*, pp. 378 ss. *Urdaneta*, pp. 189–92.

4.

Lecuna in *B.A.N.H.V.*, p. 431. *O'L.*, vol. XVIII, p. 36. *G.F.*, vol. I, p. 411. *J.D.D.*, pp. 246–7, for the text passed between Urdaneta and La Torre.

5.

Sañudo, p. 93; *G.F.*, vol. I, pp. 408–9; *O'L.*, vol. XVIII, pp. 38–43.

CHAPTER VIII (pp. 391–402)

1.

Urdaneta, p. 185. *O'L.*, vol. II, p. 68. *Villa*, vol. IV, p. 284, Doc. 862. *Fall*, ch. XVI.

2.

Villa, vol. IV, pp. 204 ss., Doc. 832; p. 211, Doc. 834. *D.B.N.*, pp. 327/323.

3.

See letter Bolívar to La Torre, 10.iii.21, *C.L.*, vol. II, p. 327, "attributing the scarcity of cattle to the armistice which has opened to the inhabitants of the Apure the trade in this line". As to whether the armistice was the sole cause to the evil, Bolívar is the best authority. In a letter to Páez, Bogotá, 18.i.21 (*C.L.*, vol. II, p. 301), he says: "I am sending you a commission delegating on you the same powers granted me by the government for distributing national estates (i.e., estates confiscated from monarchists) in the Apure. I shall be glad if it turns out well, but I fear discontent will increase, for everyone cannot receive a share, and thereafter the army will perish, for no one will want to give away his cattle, and everyone will sell his share at any price rather than have it taken away for public service." The armistice was but an added circumstance which increased an evil Bolívar had foreseen, but as usual had felt bound to undergo rather than cross the dreaded Páez. See also V.L. in *B.A.N.H.V.*, no. 96, p. 437. *O'L.*, vol. II, p. 84. On immense resources in men, money and communications brought in by the possession of Maracaibo, *Urdaneta*, p. 190, who considers the Maracaibo operation was essential for the victory of Carabobo. This was confirmed by Bolívar himself in a letter to Santander, 7.iii.21, *C.L.*, vol. II, p. 323: "I have ordered 1,500 rifles to be sent to Maracaibo, towards anything that might happen, and to have an army raised in that part, as the army of the West, under Urdaneta, who has already left for that city." *B.A.N.H.V.*, no. 96. *D.L.H.M. Bingham.*

4.

O.C.N., vol. II, p. 209 *J.D.D.*, p. 257.

5.

O'L., vol. XVIII, pp. 23, 408. *Archivo Nacional de Cuba*, Habana, Asuntos políticos, Nums. 17, 5; 18, 2.

CHAPTER IX (pp. 403–411)

1.

Mitre, vol. II. *Cochrane-Life*, vol. I.

2.

Mitre, vol. II. *Cochrane-Life*, vol. I. *Camba*, vol. I.

3.

Mitre, vol. III. *Camba*, vol. I.

4.

The same and *Alamán*, vol. V.

5.

B.H., vol. I.

CHAPTER X (pp. 412–423)

1.

O.C.N., vol. II, p. 154.

2.

C.L., vol. II, p. 343; *Restrepo*, vol. III, p. 146. *Samper*, p. 178. *O.C.N.*, vol. II, pp. 160 ss. His story is borne out by a number of other documents. Gual condemns Nariño for his "*política tortuosa y pueril*" in a letter to Santander, 23.vi.21, *A.S.*, vol. VI, p. 270. Azuero writes to Santander from Rosario de Cúcuta on 6.vi.21: " He has treated D'Evereux in the most undignified way, putting him in a very bad prison . . . only because he sent him a challenge . . . as Nariño had spoken to the widow of General English in an indecent manner." *A.S.*, vol. VI, p. 234. And again on 20.vi.21: " In order to hide his cowardice or satisfy his coarse vengeance Nariño has treated him in the unworthiest manner, burying him in a room which had just served as a rubbish heap store and had earlier been a kitchen or a forge and where he has kept him incomunicado and deprived of every means of defence. Congress tried to better the fate of this unhappy general and passed a resolution to Nariño instructing him to transfer the prisoner to a better prison and to permit him to provide for his defence and to communicate with Congress. Nariño's answer was a pamphlet of three and a half sheets in which he protests never to obey the resolution of Congress." *A.S.*, vol. VI, pp. 258–60. *Samper*, p. 181. *Restrepo*, vol. III, p. 136. *Baralt*, vol. II, pp. 65, 71. *O.C.N.*, vol. II, p. 209, 218. *J.D.D.*, p. 257.

4.

C.B.S., pp. 51, 126, 128, 129, 131. *López*, pp. 20, 23, 26.

5.

Hamilton, vol. II, pp. 40, 42, 44. *C.B.S.*, p. 118. *C.L.*, vol. II, pp. 167, 207. Lecuna in *B.A.N.H.V.*, no. 100, pp. 366 ss.

6.

C.B.S., p. 241. *Sañudo*, p. 90. *López*, p. 31. *Mitre*, vol. III, p. 559. Lecuna in *B.A.N.H.V.*, no. 100, p. 348. *López*, p. 43, tells how when the prisoners were offered the possibility of returning to the Spanish army owing to an interchange of prisoners negotiated by Sucre, they all shouted *Long live Colombia ! Death to the King of Spain !* They were creoles and declared that they preferred to be prisoners of the Republic rather than serve again under the King of Spain.

CHAPTER XI (pp. 424–435)

1.

Mitre, vol. III, pp. 193, 218, 225.

2.

V.L. in *B.A.N.H.V.*, no. 100, pp. 356, 357. *Archivo P.S.*, 8.ix.21; vol. I. *Archivo Jijón-Caamaño*, vol. I.

3.

V.L., *loc. cit.*, pp. 365 ss. *P.D.*, pp. 270–1.

4.

J.M.O., vol. I, pp. 38 ss. *O'L.*, vol. II, p. 156. *Sañudo*, pp. 110, 121.

5.

B.A.N.H.V., no. 100, p. 383. *J.M.O.*, vol. I, pp 43 ss. *Archivo N.B.,* Guerra y Marina, 1822, Fol. 0324. *Mosquera*, p. 447. *Sañudo*, p. 122.

6.

Mosquera, pp. 447 ss. *Boussingault*, vol. II. *Ricardo Palma*, vol. IV

CHAPTER XII (pp. 436–448)

1.

Mosquera, p. 452. V.L. in *B.A.N.H.V.*, no. 100, pp. 366, 375.

2.

Mitre, vol. III, p. 616. *Sañudo*, p. 126.

3.

V.L. in *B.A.N.H.V.*, no. 101, pp. 14 ss. *Mitre*, vol. III, pp. 119 ss. *Mosquera*, pp. 454 ss.

4.

Mitre, vol. III, app. 31, pp. 818 ss. *Archivo Pérez S.* Casa Bolívar, Caracas, vol. XXI. *Camba*, vol. II, pp. 31 ss.

5.

B.A.N.H.V., no. 101, p. 68. *Mitre*, vol. III, pp. 665 ss. MS. fol. 0403. *Archivo N.B.*, Guerra y Marina.

6.

Sañudo, p. 127. *Urrutia*, pp. 159, 161, 212, 221.

CHAPTER XIII (pp. 449–458)

1.

Paz, vol. I, p. 89; *López*, pp. 92–3.

2.

A Memoir on the political and military situation of the Southern Departments, and in particular of Ecuador, by Paz Castillo, in National Archives of War and the Navy, Bogotá, 1822, Fol. 813.
Archives of the Ministry of the Interior, Bogotá, Fol. 876. Under Murgueitio.
Sucre to Santander, 21.x.22: Archives Pérez Soto in Casa Natal de Bolívar, Caracas, Fol. 430, vol. XXI.
Camba, vol. II, pp. 54 ss. *Paz*, vol. I, p. 102.

3.

Basadre, pp. 52, 59. *Paz*, vol. I, pp. 107, 114. Alamán, vol. V, pp. 444 ss.

4.

Paz, vol. I, pp. 114, 118, 137, 138, 140.

5.

Letter Bolívar to Sucre, Guayaquil, 9.v.23, unpublished, in Sucre Archives (Jijón Caamaño), Fol. 75.

6.

Paz, vol. I, pp. 126–6. Sucre to Santander: Archives Pérez Soto, vol. IV, in Casa Bolívar, Caracas. *Sañudo*, pp. 131, 134, 137.

CHAPTER XIV (pp. 459–470)

1.

Bulnes, vol. I, pp. 185 ss. *O'L.-S.*, vol. I, pp. 37, 47, 63, 88, 98, 105, 108, 121. *Paz*, vol. I, pp. 131–2, 161, 207, 229, 250, 253, 257.

2.

Letter to Sucre unpublished, in Sucre Archives (Jijón Caamaño). *Paz*, vol. I, pp. 257 ss. *Mitre.*

3.

Paz, vol. I, pp. 60, 63, 67, 258. *Sañudo*, p. 143. *Bulnes*, vol. I, p. 324-5.

4.

Bulnes, vol. I, p. 330. *Paz*, vol. I, p. 266.

Wilson's revelation, in the *Diario de Barranquilla*, of José Vallarino Jiménez, in *B.A.N.H.V.*, no. 104, pp. 258 ss. The Bulletin endeavours to reject it, but with no argument whatever, except that Bolívar could not possibly forge papers with political intentions, though this is contrary to well-known facts. That Riva Agüero was actually in touch with the Spaniards has nothing to do with the fact that Bolívar prepared false proofs of it, for lack of documents to convince La Fuente. *P.D.L.*, p. 286.

5.

Temperley, pp. 76, 87, 103. *Villapaterna*, pp. 244, 340.

6.

Temperley, pp. 109, 110, 114 ss., 123-4.

CHAPTER XV (pp. 471-482)

1.

Mosquera, p. 504. *Paz*, vol. I, p. 267. *Miramón*, p. 32.

2.

Camba, vol. II, pp. 122, 128, 132 ss., 137, 145, 200, 205. *Bulnes*, vol. II, pp. 126, 128 ss., 137 ss.

3.

Paz, vol. II, p. 45. *Bulnes*, vol. II, p. 51. *O'L.-P.*, pp. 87, 89.

5.

Paz, vol. II, p. 49. *López*, pp. 107, 108. *Bulnes*, vol. II, pp. 215, 223.

6.

Miller, p. 131. *O'C.*, vol. I, pp. 105 ss. *Bulnes*, vol. II, p. 233. *López*, pp. 109 ss. *Camba*, vol. II, pp. 254 ss.

CHAPTER XVI (pp. 483-491)

1.

O'C., pp. 118, 122. *Bulnes*, vol. II, pp. 255 ss.

2.

Bulnes, vol. II, p. 259. *O'L.-P.*, p. 120. *O'L.-S.*, p. 230.

3.

Sañudo, p. 150. *López*, p. 100. *Bulnes*, vol. II, pp. 277-9.

4.

Bulnes, vol. II, pp. 289, 294. *O'L.-S.*, pp. 211 213, 237, 254. *López*, pp. 137, 138, 143, 144, 148, 150, 151. *O'C.*, ch. IX.

5.

López, pp. 170 ss. He tries to refute that a secret pact existed, on which rumours began to spread immediately after the victory. The public statements made by Valdés, and later by his son, in Spain, only prove their anxiety to cover what actually happened. This was not difficult, for those who accused the Spanish generals did so on grounds of venality, a grotesque accusation easily refuted, which distracted attention from the real issue. If, as I incline to believe, there was a secret pact, it was exclusively due to the political situation, and, of course, easily kept secret since both sides were interested in such a secrecy. See *Documentos para la Historia de la Guerra Separatista del Perú por el Conde de Torata*, Madrid 1894–8.

6.

Bulnes, vol. II, pp. 341 ss.   *O'C.*, p. 156.

Chapter XVII (pp. 493–505)

1.

Temperley, pp. 140 ss.   *Urrutia*, pp. 335 ss.   *Larrazábal*, vol. II, pp. 19, 21 *P.D.L.*, pp. 191, 291, 294.

2.

Sañudo, pp. 105, 161.   *O'C.*, p. 123.   *Mosquera*, p. 545.   *Basadre*, p. 71.

3.

Bulnes, vol. II, pp. 358–9.   *Paz*, vol. I, pp. 131 ss., 241, 261.   *O'L.-S.*, vol. I, pp. 288 ss.

4.

P.D.L., p. 305.

5.

Maling's report was published by Temperley, pp. 555 ss., from a copy at the Foreign Office. The original is in my private files. On Moges: *C.L.*, vol. IV, p. 256.   *Boletin del Museo Bolivariano*, numbers 1, 2, p. 22.

Chapter XVIII (pp. 506–516)

1.

Pinilla, pp 99 ss., 100, 103 ss., 120, 141.   *O'C.*, p. 159.   *O'L.-S.*, vol. I, p. 325.

3.

Unpublished documents in the Archives of the Ministry of Finance, Lima, numbers 5–28.

4.

Pinilla, pp. 138 ss., 150 ss., 164 ss., 183 ss., 200, 212, 231.

5.

Temperley, p. 221.   *Pinilla*, p. 50.   *Hamilton*, vol. I, pp. 223, 252–3.   *Mollien*, vol. II, pp. 207, 208, 230, 314.

6.

B.A.N.H.V., no. 62, p. 273.

Chapter XIX (pp. 517–527)

1.

Camba, vol. II, p. 373.   *Boussingault*, vol. III, pp. 205 ss.   *Pruvonena*, vol. I, p. 196.   *C.H.*, pp. 175 ss.

2.

Mosquera, p. 562.

3.

Sañudo, pp. 171 ss.

4.

Restrepo, vol. III, pp. 138, 200, 202, 234, 253. He says that " the humbler classes were most friendly to the Spaniards "—p. 259; and as for the Calabozo plains, " there was there a party in favour of the Spaniards, who had ruled them for so long. Such was the cause why the government of the Republic was always uneasy, for it did not trust those valiant *llaneros* ".—p. 263. *Páez*, p. 315. Infante's execution in *Hamilton*, pp. 244–5.

5.

G.F., vol. II, pp. 556, 557, 558 ss. *Baralt*, vol. II, p. 171 *G.F.*, vol. II, pp. 559–60. *C.L.*, vol. V, pp. 242, 244. Actitud Bolívar clara en *C.L.*, vol. V, pp. 229 ss., 285, 287, 317, 321, 327, 343.

6.

Archives Nationales Ministère de la Marine, quoted by *Villanueva-I.A.* The detail of the locking up of the deputies, given by Mamyneau for the Assembly of 1826 strengthens Ducoudray's authority, for in his narrative of the meeting in 1816 in Haiti, he says that " Bolívar demanded that no one should come out until all the articles had been drafted and signed "—vol. I, p. 283.

CHAPTER XX (pp. 528–540)

1.

Sañudo, p. 177. *Villanueva-I.A.*, pp. 193 ss. Garabuya letter, found by Morales in the pocket of a Colombian officer after the battle of Garabuya (13.ix.22), in *Villanueva-B.S.M.*, pp. 271 ss.

2.

P.G., vol. I, p. 45, says that these victims were " three famous murderers, royalist guerrilleros who deserved the death penalty. The abuse consisted in not waiting for a regular sentence. Bolívar excused himself alleging that as there was no garrison in Pasto and no safe prison, those murderers would have run away and caused considerable damage." *J.M.O.*, vol. I, p. 87. *P.G.*, vol. I, pp. 49 ss. *P.R.O. F.O.*, Colombia, 1826, no. 34.

3.

Buchet-Martigny to Baron de Damas. Ministère des Affaires Etrangères, 14.ix.26, quoted by *Villanueva-I.A.*, pp. 177 ss. *Grillo*, p. 126. *P.G.*, vol. I, pp. 39, 51. *Hamilton*, vol. I, p. 131.

4.

In a letter to Santander (Arequipa, 30.v.25) Bolívar says on the Federation: " The North Americans and the Haitians, being foreigners, are alien to us. Therefore I shall never agree to have them invited for our American agreements." *C.L.*, vol. iv., p. 348. He does not even mention Brazil. From Potosí (21.x.25) he writes: " I do not think the Americans should participate in the Isthmus Congress "; but this time he argues that it might displease the English. *Villanueva-I.A. Temperley.*

Bolívar's cold objectivity in his pro-English policy is confirmed for instance in his letter to Santander (21.x.25): " I have not yet seen the treaty of Commerce and Navigation with Great Britain, which, you say, is good; but I fear very much that it will not be as good as all that, for the English are terrible in such things." *E.S.*, pp. 62–3, 69, 101. *Temperley*, pp. 171 ss.

5.

María Antonia's letters in *B.A.N.H.V.*, no. 62, unfortunately polished and therefore deprived of their picturesque spelling. *O'L.-U.*, pp. 89. 92, 104. *Sañudo*, p. 186.

6.

P.G., vol. I, pp. 59, 61, 65 ss. *O'L.-U.*, pp. 107, 110, 141.

CHAPTER XXI (pp. 541–553)

1.

Páez, pp. 435 ss. *P.G.*, vol. I, p. 69. Páez's instructions in *O'L.-U.*, p. 143, where " January 2nd " is printed by error.

2.

Páez, p. 449. *Hamilton*, vol. I, p. 262.

45*

3.

P.G., p. 73. *Crespo*, p. 75. *Suplemento a las cartas americanas.* Correspondencia de Vidaurre con los generales Bolívar, Santander y La Mar, vol. I, p. 271.

4

O'L.-U., pp. 149, 160. Unpublished letters Archives Paz Soldán, Lima, vol. V, fols. 76, 78, 79, 80, 82, 83, 91. *Crespo*, p. 77. *P.G.*, vol. I, pp. 83 ss.

5.

P.G., vol. I, pp. 107 ss. *Córdova*, p. 444. *Grillo*, p. 137. *Mosquera*, pp. 594–6.

6.

Mosquera, p. 597. *C.H.*, *Los Cantores de Bolívar*, p. 218. *P.G.*, pp. 127, 131. *Grillo*, pp. 137 ss. *Córdova*, p. 484.

CHAPTER XXII (pp. 554–565)

1.

O'L.-U., pp. 186 ss. *Basadre*, p. 83.

In an unpublished official letter from Larrea to the Secretary General of Bolívar, Lima, 15.ix.25, to be found in the archives of the Ministry of Finance under number 120–98, can be read: " That of the latest loan raised by Robertson there remains available the sum of £324.793/0/48 (*sic*), which, after deducting £300.000 which H.E. has earmarked for paying out the million pesos to reward the conquerors of Ayacucho and half a million for the sums due to the army . . ."

2.

O'L.-U., pp. 196 ss. *Hippisley*, p. 344. *Córdova*, pp. 492–3. *P.G.*, pp. 141 ss.

3.

Sañudo, p. 215. *P.G.*, pp. 135 ss. On Luque and Fergusson, Soublette in *O'L.-U.*, p. 209 Note. *D.B.N.*, p. 235 (224). *Córdova*, p. 494.

4.

O'L.-U., pp. 231 ss.

5.

O'L.-U., pp. 206, 229, 235, 236, 277–9, 321, 322, 333–4, 338, 354. On Philip II, see *Rise*. *D.B.N.*, pp. 223 (210), 305 (300).

6.

O'L.-U., pp. 323–4, 340 ss., 347 ss., 354, 357, 360. *Córdova*, p. 499. *J.M.O.*, p. 104. *P.G.*, p. 176. *Sañudo*, pp. 226–8.

CHAPTER XXIII (pp. 566–577)

1.

P.D.L., p. 485. *J.M.O.*, p. 106. *Córdova*, p. 502. *Boussingault*, vol. III, p. 205 ss.

2.

P.R.O. F.O. 18/56, D. 61, 6.xii.28. Letter *private* 279, 6.viii.28. Events have usually been told on the basis of Bolívar's letter to Córdova without knowing Córdova's letter which it answers. Hence errors such as supposing that Córdova was present (for instance in *Córdova*, pp. 506 ss.) or assuming wrong dates (as in *C.H.*, pp. 218–20 where Lecuna is rapped on the knuckles for assuming it happened in July, which is exactly when it happened). All becomes clear when Córdova's letter is known, as I found it in the P.R.O., the sand on it so that it shone in the sun. Córdova was not present and Bolívar knew the events before Córdova wrote to him. It is likely that the episode occurred precisely on Bolívar's anniversary. *O'L.-U.*, pp. 367, 371. *Proceso*, pp. 95, 270. *P.G.*, p. 187.

3.

Córdova, p. 441. *P.R.O. F.O.* Colombia 18/56 annex to D. 49 *private* to John Bidwell, 7.x.28. *P.G.*, p. 189. *Proceso*, p. 3. *O'L.-U.*, pp. 413, 417 ss.

As Manuela discreetly kept silence, the fact that she was ill-treated is now fully authenticated, thanks to James Henderson's letter which I found in *P.R.O. F.O.* " The Lady who I introduced to your acquaintance in my Note of the 6th of August last, saved the life of the Liberator on the night of the conspiracy . . . she went out to meet the conspirators. She entreated of them to save the life of young Ibarra who was already wounded and promised to lead them to the Council room where she said Bolívar was in Council. This delay allowed the Liberator to escape, but she was so severely beaten for the disappointment she occasioned to the conspirators, that she is still confined to her room." It is also a fact that the weapon she was beaten with was the sabre, as we know from Bresson, Archives des Affaires Etrangères, Colombie, vol. V, D. 27, 21.vii.29: " *Elle fut, par eux, frappée de coups de sabre.*"

4.

Proceso, pp. 13 ss., 72. Henderson to Bidwell, *P.R.O. F.O.* Colombia 18/56, annex to D. 44, 28.ix.58.

The detail about Bolívar being mistaken for a servant comes from Henderson, for, so far, the explanation given was that Carujo had neglected guarding that way out, which is not likely.

P.G., p. 201. Supplement to Gazette in *P.R.O. F.O.* Colombia 18/56, annex 2 to D. 46.

5.

P.G., p. 202. Henderson to Bidwell, P.R.O., as above. Decrees 29, 26.ix.28, in *Proceso*, pp. 27, 39.

Bolívar confirms Henderson's narrative in a letter to Vergara, Quito, 6.v.29. Supplement to Gazette as above. Several dispatches from Henderson on the rest, and in particular D. 44 on the promise of 30,000 pesos to the battalion.

6.

P.R.O. F.O. Colombia 18/56, dispatches 55, 60, 61. *O'L.-S.*, p. 276.

CHAPTER XXIV (pp. 579–595)

1.

O.C., p. 238. Henderson to Bidwell, Ds. 34, 37, *P.R.O. F.O.* 18/56. *Basadre*, pp. 85 ss. *Proceso*, pp. 314, 316. *Sañudo*, p. 245. *O'L.-U.*, pp. 390 ss., 452, 463, 466 ss., 473 ss., 486, 493. *O'L.*, vol. V, p. 625.

2.

O'L.-U., pp. 501, 506, 509, 518, 522, 524, 530, 534. *O'L.-S.*, vol. II, pp. 257, 258, 259, 261, 265, 421. *P.R.O. F.O.* Colombia 18/56 D. 52.

3.

Mosquera, pp. 638 ss. *J.M.O.*, vol. I, pp. 114 ss. *P.G.*, pp. 224, 228–32. *P.R.O F.O.* 18/56 D. 38, 18/68, D. 64. *Córdova*, pp. 144, 148. *O'L.-S.*, vol. II, pp. 282, 426. *O'L.-U.*, pp. 549, 550, 554, 556 ss.

In a letter to Henderson (P.R.O. F.O. 18/68) Córdova explains that the Colombians suggested Britain as the mediator but Gamarra objected that Britain had not yet recognised Perú; thereupon they drew lots and U.S.A. won.—Ds. 19, 18.v.29.

4.

Extracts from Córdova in Ds. X, 7.ii.29, *P.R.O. F.O.* 18/68; also Ds. 14, 17, 20, 24. *Córdova*, pp. 449–554. *J.M.O.*, vol. I, p. 27. *Mosquera*, p. 637.

5.

P.R.O. F.O. 18/68, Ds. 24, 25, and private letter from Henderson.

6.

Basadre, pp. 131 ss. *O'L.-S.*, vol. II, pp. 305, 311, 323.

CHAPTER XXV (pp. 596–604)

1.

O'L.-S., vol. II, pp. 289, 305, 307, 327.

2.

Mosquera, pp. 694–8.

3.

P.R.O. F.O. 18/68.

4.

Archives des Affaires Etrangères, Colombie, vol. V, fol. 108, Ds. 14, 18, 19.

5.

Archivo Santander, vol. XVIII, pp. 131–43. Also *Córdova*, pp. 612–17. *Archives Affaires Etrangères*, D. 27, vol. V, fol. 287.

6.

Archives des Affaires Etrangères, Ds. 29, 33, 34, fols. 293 ss., 335, 15 ss.

CHAPTER XXVI (pp. 605–612)

1.

Archives des Affaires Etrangères, Ds. 38, 40, vol. VI, fols. 26 verso ss., 53 ss., 55, 80 ss. *Sañudo*, pp. 255 ss.

2.

Archives des Affaires Etrangères, Ds. 40, 41, 43, 54, vol. VI, fols. 86 ss, 71, 102 ss. Separate and confidential dispatch from Turner to Lord Douglas (20.iv.30): *P.R.O. F.O.*, vol. 18/68, fol. 75.

3.

Archives des Affaires Etrangères, Ds. 43, 53, 58, vol. VI. *Córdova*, pp. 588 ss., 636, 639–42. *Sañudo*, p. 252. *P.G.*, vol. II, pp. 9 ss. This author tries to white-wash O'L., but the documents adduced by *Córdova*, pp. 648 ss., are final.

4.

Archives Affaires Etrangères, D. 44, fol. 110, 4.x.29. *P.G.*, vol. II, p. 18, tells how Urdaneta opened letters. Bolívar knew all about it. *P.R.O. F.O.* Colombia 18/68. *Archives Affaires Etrangères*, D. 45, vol. VI, fols. 114, 139.

5.

Córdova, p. 677. *Archives des Affaires Etrangères*, Colombie, vol. VI, D. 60, fol. 212.

6.

Archives des Affaires Etrangères, Colombie, vol. VI, D. 61, fol. 221. D. 63, fol. 226; D. 66, fol. 283. *Córdova*, p. 761.

CHAPTER XXVII (pp. 613–628)

1.

C.H., p. 217. *P.G.*, vol. II, pp. 71, 72. *Córdova*, pp. 660 ss.

2.

P.R.O. F.O. Colombia, 18/68, no. 75. Aberdeen answers indignantly denying such intervention.

3.

P.G., vol. II, pp. 61 ss., 65 ss. *B.D.L.*, p. 396. *P.R.O. F.O.* 18/68, no. 75. *Archives des Affaires Etrangères*, vol. VI, fol. 330, D. 73.

4.

P.G., vol. II, pp. 72 ss., 95, 155, 162.

5.

P.G., vol. II, p. 161 (where he denies the existence of the conspiracy), 164.
P.R.O. F.O. Colombia, 18/68, no. 75 D. lo.

6.

P.R.O. F.O. Loc. Cit. Ds. 5, 10, 12. *P.G.*, vol. II, pp, 9, 172, 177, 181, 187 ss., 193, 204, 211.

CHAPTER XXVIII (pp. 629–637)

1.

C.H., p. 245. *P.G.*, vol. II, pp. 277, 285. *P.R.O. F.O.* 18/76, Dispatches 17, 18; vol. 77, Dispatch 29.

2.

P.R.O. F.O. 18/76, Ds. 23, 24. *P.G.*, vol. II, pp. 21, 219.

3.

P.G., vol. II, pp. 326 ss., vol. III, pp. 21, 25–7. *B.A.N.H.V.*, no. 104, p. 261.

4.

Córdova, p. 751. *P.R.O. F.O.* 18/77, Ds. 21, 32, 34. *P.G.*, vol. II, p. 332, vol. III, pp. 42, 59, 68, 76.

CHAPTER XXIX (pp. 638–647)

1.

B.A.N.H.V., no. 104, p. 260. *P.G.*, vol. II, p. 328.

2.

P.G., vol. III, pp. 43 ss., 113. *Córdova*, p. 590.

4.

Córdova, p. 709.

5.

B.A.N.H.V., no. 104, pp. 258 ss.

6.

Révérend, p. 10. *B.A.N.H.V.*, no. 100, pp. 312 ss. *P.D.L.*, p. 407   *Guevara*, p. 205.

A plea has been made by Monsignor Navarro, a member of the Academy of History of Caracas, for the view that Bolívar died a Christian death (*La Cristiana Muerte del Libertador*). In my opinion the combined effect of the narratives of Fernando Bolívar, Révérend and an officer named Centeno finally dispose of even the best arguments in favour of such a view. It is plain from such witnesses that the Bishop, who tried to confess Bolívar on his deathbed, went home disappointed and even disgruntled, so that he was not present either at the extreme unction or at the death or at the burial of Bolívar. A merely formal " confession " was the most that Bolívar would agree to.

INDEX

INDEX

697

DATE DUE

4/3/3			

GAYLORD   PRINTED IN U.S A

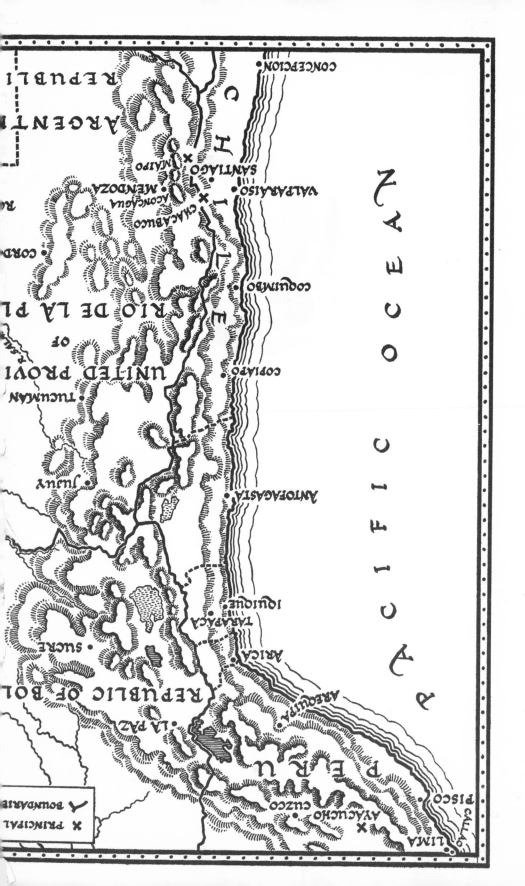